The War of 1812
*A Complete Chronology
with Biographies of 63 General Officers*

ALSO BY BUD HANNINGS
AND FROM McFARLAND

The U.S.–Mexican War: A Complete Chronology (2014)

The French and Indian War: A Complete Chronology (2011)

*Every Day of the Civil War:
A Chronological Encyclopedia* (2010)

*American Revolutionary War Leaders:
A Biographical Dictionary* (2009)

*Chronology of the American Revolution: Military and
Political Actions Day by Day* (2008)

The Korean War: An Exhaustive Chronology (2007)

*Forts of the United States: An Historical Dictionary,
16th through 19th Centuries* (2006; paperback 2020)

The War of 1812

A Complete Chronology with Biographies of 63 General Officers

BUD HANNINGS

McFarland & Company, Inc., Publishers
Jefferson, North Carolina

The present work is a reprint of the illustrated case bound edition of The War of 1812: A Complete Chronology With Biographies of 63 General Officers, *first published in 2012 by McFarland.*

Illustrations are from *Pictorial Field Book of the War of 1812,* Benson J. Lossing, 1869, unless credited otherwise.

LIBRARY OF CONGRESS CATALOGUING-IN-PUBLICATION DATA

Hannings, Bud.
The War of 1812 : a complete chronology with biographies of 63 general officers / Bud Hannings.
p.   cm.
Includes bibliographical references and index.

ISBN 978-1-4766-8366-9
softcover : acid free paper ∞

1. United States — History — War of 1812 — Chronology.
2. United States — History — War of 1812 — Biography.
3. United States — History — War of 1812 — Sources.
4. Generals — United States — Biography.   I. Title.
E355.H36 2020   973.5'2 — dc23   2012015271

BRITISH LIBRARY CATALOGUING DATA ARE AVAILABLE

© 2012 Bud Hannings. All rights reserved

No part of this book may be reproduced or transmitted in any form or by any means, electronic or mechanical, including photocopying or recording, or by any information storage and retrieval system, without permission in writing from the publisher.

Front cover image: Michel Felice Corne, 1752–1845, *In Action,* painting of combat between the USS *Constitution* and HMS *Guerriere.* Oil on canvas. 32" × 48" (courtesy National Archives photo no. 428 K 26254)

McFarland & Company, Inc., Publishers
Box 611, Jefferson, North Carolina 28640
www.mcfarlandpub.com

Contents

Preface 1

Introduction 2

THE CHRONOLOGY 11

BIOGRAPHIES OF GENERAL OFFICERS 305

Appendix A. Generals, U.S. Army and Militia, War of 1812 Era 354

Appendix B. James Madison's War Message to Congress, June 1, 1812 357

Appendix C. Prizes of American Privateers and Vessels Under Letters of Marque, Captured on Unspecified Days, 1812–1815 360

Appendix D. Proclamation Issued by General William Hull to the People of Canada on 12 July 1812 364

Appendix E. General Isaac Brock's Response to General Hull's Proclamation on 22 July 1812 365

Appendix F. Thomas Boyle's Proclamation 366

Bibliography 367

Index 371

Preface

This book focuses on military actions of the War of 1812, known also as the Second War of Independence. When it began the United States was a fledgling republic, following its spectacular victory in 1783 over the British in the American Revolution. The road to complete independence remained clogged, nonetheless, with deadly obstacles. The peace preliminaries had been signed at Versailles on 20 January 1783 and the war officially terminated on 14 February 1783, when the United Kingdom of Great Britain declared that it had ended. However, Britain did not easily accept its former colonies as an independent and sovereign nation, nor did it graciously abide by the terms of the treaty with regard to abandoning British-held bases in United States territory. Britain also continued to incite the Indians and stir other problems, including intimidating and interfering with American vessels on the high seas. During the conflict, the Senecas (Six Nations) aligned themselves with the Americans; however, the Wyandots fought alongside the British. Some of the Wyandots were Roman Catholics, converted by French priests. Chief Walk-in-the-water described them: "Roman Catholic Wyandots pray and fight, with the Bible in one hand, and tomahawk in the other, under the patronage and protection of Protestant Great Britain."

The book depicts the various campaigns, sieges and skirmishes in the United States, its territories and Canada, and provides comprehensive coverage of naval activities, including privateers and vessels issued letters of marque, a principal segment of the war often overlooked. It also tracks hostilities with Indians and focuses on individual units from campaign to campaign; however, it does not focus heavily on the politics behind the conflict. Nonetheless, it does offer in the introduction an overview of the years between the American Revolution and the War of 1812, to present to the reader events in Europe that led up to the war. The chronology proper begins in 1803. The book also gives some coverage to the Napoleonic Wars to provide insight on how incessant foreign conflicts affected both the United States and Britain, the latter remaining unable to concentrate solely on the Americans. During the entire period between the wars, Great Britain, France and Spain continued to endanger the existence of the United States. Once the War of 1812 began, Europe remained engulfed in conflict, while Napoleon maintained his quest to expand his empire. All the while, Britain was compelled to engage Napoleon and the United States simultaneously. The book also includes some highlights, such as the Battle of Waterloo, that occurred in Europe during the War of 1812.

During the course of researching the book, once again, the project's obstacles were overcome thanks in great part to the help of staff members at research libraries and other sources, and to personal visits to various sites where the battles occurred. Other reliable sources included personal memoirs, biographies, government records, and archives that have preserved correspondence, ships' logs and reports maintained for posterity. The book also contains many letters and other correspondence that continually flowed back and forth between officers and commanders and between opposing generals that provide the reader with behind the scenes activity, including contrasting strategies. These letters also provide the reader with some insight into the difficulties facing various commanders. One of the most difficult tasks in completing the manuscript was the search to complete the seemingly never-ending partial names of militia general officers and corresponding information on their service.

The list is not all-inclusive and I am not sure that the list will ever be complete; however, at this time, the names of about 350 general officers of the army (regulars and militia) have been discovered. Another difficult task was the search for personal messages and letters that dealt with the services. Nevertheless, the inclusion of this mostly obscure information regarding letters and or general orders adds a degree of depth and firsthand insight that should give the reader a more personal view of the conflict.

Lastly, the book lists hundreds of prizes captured by American privateers and vessels operating under letters of marque, and the American shipping seized by British privateers, including the date of seizure or recapture; however, some of the captures lack a precise date. Vessels that were not possible to place properly in the chronology are listed in an appendix. Many other captures were not recorded and therefore are not listed in this or any other similar work.

Introduction

Although the American Revolution officially ended in 1783, the United States and Great Britain had not totally mended their differences. Britain, particularly its king, could not accept the former colonies as a united sovereign nation. Nevertheless, during September 1787, the Constitution was born and the United States was independent; however, unlike the major powers of the Old World, it had no large army or navy, nor was it equipped to deal with international threats. Consequently, Britain continued to incite Indians and harass American shipping. Meanwhile, the French and Spanish had not dismissed their respective visions of holding possessions in America. Simultaneously, the Mediterranean became a danger zone due to the Barbary pirates, who intercepted U.S. shipping and held the vessels for tribute.

During January 1787, Congress authorized a negotiated agreement with Morocco by which American vessels could safely pass; however, the U.S. was compelled to pay Morocco the sum of $10,000. The agreement was signed by John Adams and Thomas Jefferson on behalf of the United States. Despite the agreement, the Mediterranean contained other unsavory pirates operating out of Algiers, Tripoli and Tunis.

Out on the frontiers, Americans continued to encounter hostilities with the Indians, and in the Northwest Territory, the British failed to surrender posts that should have been abandoned by the terms of the treaty which terminated the American Revolution. To the south, Spain, finally during 1788 agreed to permit American shipping to use the Mississippi River to receive access to the Gulf of Mexico. Spain, however, which dominated East Florida and West Florida, imposed duties for the passage. Relations between the United States and Spain remained strained. Back in Britain during 1788, King George III was struck by a bout of insanity and a crisis ensued. While plans were in the process for selecting a regent, he regained his health. Russia, which was at war with Turkey, moved to expand the empire under Catherine the Great; however, the plan was interrupted when she was invaded by Sweden. The Swedes pounced upon Russian Finland. A treaty, agreed upon during 1790, ended the hostilities. While Sweden had fought with Russia, the Danes invaded Sweden.

During January 1789, General Arthur St. Clair signed the Treaty of Fort Harmar with the Ohio Indians which renewed the Treaty of Fort McIntosh. Nonetheless, along the frontiers, particularly in Kentucky and Tennessee, hostilities continued unabated.

In April 1789, George Washington was unanimously elected as the first president of the United States, while John Adams became vice president. In August, Congress established the Department of War and appointed Henry Knox as secretary of war. On 29 September, Congress authorized an army to be composed of 1,000 troops. The American regular army, with only 846 men, was formed during September 1789. General Josiah Harman was named commander of infantry. A major was named commander of artillery. The force was known as the First Regiment, United States Army.

On the West Coast, Spain made an attempt in 1789 to establish a colony in present-day Washington at Vancouver; however, the plan was aborted within five years. During that same period, Spanish warships operating off Vancouver Island, British Columbia, seized British vessels. The aggression brought both countries to the brink of war, but it remained only a vicious quarrel. Simultaneously, Britain was engaged with the Hindus in India. Meanwhile, in France, the political situation took a downturn during a financial crisis. King Louis XVI's reign was threatened by rebellion by 1789. In July, the people attacked the Bastille prison in an episode that became the prelude to the Reign of Terror and the French Revolution.

In the United States, the nation was slowly attempting to build up its defenses. Congress established the Revenue Marine Service during April 1790. Later it became the U.S. Coast Guard. Also that month, one of the nation's founders, Benjamin Franklin, succumbed at the age of eighty-four. More than 20,000 people attended his funeral in Philadelphia. Nonetheless, the spirit of the Revolution had not been lost, and the nation's aspirations for greatness against the odds continued. During April of 1790, Congress, in an attempt to combat piracy and treason, passed legislation which defined both, and anyone convicted of either was to be executed. On 29 May 1790, the original thirteen states were completed when Rhode Island entered the Union.

Introduction

During that month, another renowned American leader, General Israel Putnam, died.

Although the United States had remained as a republic longer than the European powers expected, there were still grand expectations that it would fold. Pressures were at times extraordinary and the European powers showed no genuine respect. Spain and Britain continued to incite the Indians. Britain refused to send an ambassador to the United States and even the Barbary pirates continued to constantly threaten United States shipping. While the Old World waited impatiently for the collapse of the fledgling republic, they were unaware of the nation's most powerful armor, a document known as the Constitution, and the man Americans depended upon, President George Washington. The people had confidence that Washington would simultaneously mold the Constitution into an invulnerable weapon to prevent destruction from within, while the cement was being laid to create a permanent foundation to enable the U.S. to withstand any foreign adversary.

During September 1790, General Josiah Harmar led a force into the Ohio Territory to put an end to Indian raids upon the settlers. Following some early success, the Indians trounced Harmar's command near present-day Fort Wayne, Indiana, during October. The battle ignited a conflict that lasted about five years. At about the same time, Spain and England were claiming territory on the West Coat; however, Spain relented and Britain, which had already seized Gibraltar, found itself with sole claim on Vancouver Island. Spain had requested support from France, which was in no position to help due in great part to the French Revolution. Nevertheless, the United States adamantly opposed the English claim on the Pacific Northwest, and yet there was great relief when the Spanish and English avoided war, which would have placed the United States between the two powers and made it extremely difficult for the U.S. to remain neutral during the conflict.

In the meantime, Europe, as usual, was involved in near-perpetual conflict. Prussia was pondering entering the war between the Turks and Russia, which was aligned with Austria. Frederick the Great was preparing to fight alongside the Turks; however, he met with the Holy Roman Emperor Leopold II (1790). The meeting forestalled war between Prussia and Austria.

Although the United States had avoided being drawn into the various battles between the European powers, the situation on the frontiers had continued to deteriorate. During January 1791, settlers at Stockport, Ohio, were massacred (Big Bottom Massacre). American troops afterward constructed Fort Meigs to provide protection for the settlements. The army then constructed a series of forts in the territory. Other problems with the Indians (Cherokee) continued in the south. In Ohio, a force composed of about 1,400 troops commanded by General St. Clair, governor of the Ohio Territory, sustained a devastating defeat by the Miami Indians near Fort Wayne, Indiana. The embarrassing loss opened the territory to even more Indian attacks.

During March 1792, General Anthony Wayne replaced General Arthur St. Clair as commander-in-chief of the Ohio territory. Two officers, each sent separately, were later dispatched to seek peace with the Indians, and both were murdered. Nonetheless, Wayne refused to initiate his offensive until his army was totally trained for the mission. In June, the U.S. Army was reformed as four "Legions of the United States." The army was composed of 4,000 men. Meanwhile, Kentucky, which followed Vemont, entered the Union on 1 June to become the fifteenth state. Congress modified the American flag, changing it to fifteen stripes and fifteen stars. Also that month, another once renowned patriot, John Paul Jones, who was closely aligned with the Stars and Stripes, died in obscurity in France on 18 July. Legend tells us that Jones had stated: "The flag and I are twins born in the same hour from the same womb of destiny. We cannot be parted in life or death." Another former patriot, Lafayette, escaped death during August when he fled from France as a supporter of King Louis XVI. Nevertheless he was captured by the Austrians and imprisoned for seven years. By the latter part of September of 1792, a treaty was forged with the Wabash and Illinois Indian tribes by Brigadier General Rufus Putnam. Despite the problems still plaguing the republic, President George Washington was re-elected, again by unanimous vote. Meanwhile, in Europe, yet another conflict erupted. France declared war upon Austria during April 1792; however, Austria had consummated an alliance with Prussia during the previous February and their combined power proved too great for France to prevail. Nonetheless, the belligerents remained at war until 1797.

Meanwhile, Poland was invaded by Russia during 1792 and was also invaded by the Prussians. By the following year, Poland lost some of its territory. Also that year, the prolonged war between Prussia and the Ottoman Empire terminated. The Russians again entered into hostilities with the Ottoman Empire, while most of Europe was involved in the Napoleonic Wars.

The chaos in Europe continued into 1793. On 27 January 1793, King Louis XVI was executed by decapitation by the Revolutionary government. Shortly thereafter, the French government declared war on Great Britain, the Netherlands (Dutch Republic) and Spain. Amazingly, at the time of the declarations of war, France was already at war against Austria and Prussia, as well as Sardinia. Nevertheless, the French still found time to execute Queen Marie Antoinette. On 16 October 1793, she became a victim of the guillotine.

The United States, up to that point, had been able to remain neutral in the various conflicts in Europe; however, the French, who had proclaimed by decree "A War of All People Against All Kings," and the British each took advantage of the United States by harassing and seizing its vessels on the high seas.

Back in the U.S., war was also raging, but it was a war of words between the Federalists, who supported Great Britain, and the Jeffersonians, who were eager to support France. President

Washington ignored both sides to remain neutral, despite a 1778 treaty with France that committed the United States to supporting the French. Apparently, the French knew the U.S. had no navy or army and did not insist on its support, but the Americans thought the French might ask the U.S. to defend the West Indies (French Antilles) against the British. Later, a French representative, Edmond Genet, arrived in the United States to lobby for France's cause. Washington and his cabinet also ignored his pleas to enter the war. Genet's actions while in the country did bring Britian and the United States close to war, but it was forestalled. All the while, Europe remained at war and the conflicts there (Wars of the French Revolution, 1793–1802, and Napoleonic Wars, 1803–1815) raged for more than twenty years.

For a while, President Washington had contemplated retirement; however, he was urged even by his political opponents to remain at the helm. Even Thomas Jefferson was fearful because of the situation within the country. The greatest fear at the time was that if Washington had been absent, the fragile Constitution might crumble and anarchy might overwhelm the nation. It was essentially unanimous that Washington had to remain until the wobbly Constitution would be firmly set in the land before he resumed his private affairs. To further complicate the ongoing problems within the United States, the French minister, while at Charleston, financed privateers to disrupt English shipping.

On 22 April 1793, President Washington issued his Doctrine of Neutrality, which proclaimed that America would not enter the ongoing conflict between France and Britain; however, the official proclamation omitted the word "neutral." Washington's stance caused him to come under vicious attacks by those Jeffersonians who favored fighting Britain. Nonetheless, the attacks failed to intimidate Washington and they failed to dishonor his name.

Meanwhile, France found itself at war against Austria, Prussia, Sardinia, Spain and the United Netherlands. France also disregarded the nations that professed neutrality. French warships were ordered to confiscate any neutral vessels transporting goods to its enemies. England issued similar orders and the United States, which traded with both France and Great Britain, became victimized by the French and the British. Within one year, beginning in November 1793, the British seized about 100 American vessels.

The summer of 1793 remained a trying time for settlers on the frontiers of the United States. Indians ravaged the settlements in Kentucky and Tennessee. The settlers became impatient with the lack of protection by either federal or state forces. They began to form a force of volunteers to deal with the crisis themselves. All the while, trouble continued to plague the settlers in the Northwest Territory. During December 1793, President Washington, beginning his second term, addressed Congress:

> I humbly implore that Being on whose will the fate of nations depends, to crown with success our natural endeavors for the general happiness.... There is a rank due to the United States among nations, which will be withheld, if not absolutely lost, by the reputation of weakness. If we desire to avoid insult, we must be able to repel it; if we desire to secure peace, one of the most powerful instruments of our prosperity, it must be known that we are, at all times, ready for war.

By about December 1793, hostilities between Portugal and Algiers had ceased, providing the Algerians with ample opportunities to reinitiate the seizure of American seamen, and they held about 100 sailors. Simultaneously, the Americans faced major problems with the Indians, incited by the Spanish, along the southern borders. The U.S. was also compelled to pay tribute to Morocco to ransom American sailors. Meanwhile, in France, Maximilien Robespierre's Reign of Terror was destructing society, destroying the Catholic Church and in general causing the collapse of morals within the country. France had also expanded its quest for territory by invading and seizing Avignon and Venaissin in the Papal States.

During March of 1794, Congress finally moved to correct its dangerous actions following the close of the American Revolution when it disbanded the Continental Navy and the Continental Army. On the 27th, Congress authorized the rebuilding of the U.S. Navy. Nevertheless, the first of these new ships, the USS *Constitution* (Old Ironsides) was not launched until May 1797. However, Congress stipulated that if the hostilities with Algiers terminated, the project would be ended. In 1796, Congress again hindered progress by declaring through legislation that it would build only three ships. In the meantime, the U.S. was nudging closer to opening hostilities against Britain due to its actions against U.S. shipping. At the same time, French instigators had worked to form an American force known as the "French Army of the Mississippi" to attack the Spanish in the south, but the scheme failed.

John Jay was selected in April 1794 as a special representative sent to England to try to negotiate a treaty of commerce and to persuade the British to abandon their posts that remained on U.S. territory. The mission was an attempt to forestall war. Meanwhile, the chaos in France continued. Count d'Estaing, who had fought alongside the Americans during the American Revolution, was executed in April 1794 by guillotine. In spring 1794, Spain began to pressure the U.S. by demanding a form issued by Spain in order to enter a Spanish port. The following June, the British attacked an American convoy that was sailing under the protection of a French squadron. The American vessels were transporting to Brest goods needed to help alleviate the ongoing famine brought about by the French Revolution. Back in the United States, a new threat to the republic emerged in May 1794 when a group under Elijah Clarke became disgruntled by the Treaty of Paris and moved across the across the Oconee River to form a republic (Transoconee Republic) separate from the United States in Creek (Red Stick) Indian territory. However, neither Georgia nor the U.S. government sanctioned the scheme. Nevertheless, it added to President

Introduction

Washington's expanding list of crises. The incident sparked what became known as the Oconee War. The disturbance, which lasted from May through September, ended when federal troops bolstered by militia descended upon Clarke's force. The threat of force ended the conflict. Problems also emerged in Pennsylvania when citizens rebelled due to taxes on whiskey. The Whiskey Rebellion ended without bloodshed when militia arrived to threaten force against the farmers.

In the Ohio Territory, General Anthony Wayne's force departed from Fort Recovery and advanced toward the British-held post on the Maumee River, where a huge Indian force was encamped. Wayne attacked on 20 August 1794, initiating the Battle of Fallen Timbers. The Indians were so swiftly struck that they were unable to form a stiff defense. The British who witnessed the spectacle did not depart from their fort to support the Indians. Following the victory, General Wayne's forces constructed numerous forts for defensive purposes in what was the Indian Territory.

During November 1794, representatives of Great Britain and the United States signed the Jay Treaty (known also as the Hamilton Treaty). One of the terms called for the British to abandon their U.S. posts by 1 June 1796, but an important detail, the American prisoners still held by Britain, was not included in the pact. The controversial treaty, ratified 24 June 1795, did not end the chances of war with Great Britain; rather, the inevitable conflict was only postponed. In the meantime, the French became unnerved by the treaty, which accelerated the tension between them and the Americans. Meanwhile, in Europe, the Poles ignited a rebellion against the Russians, but it failed and Poland was partitioned for a third time. Thaddeus Kosciuszko, former hero of the American Revolution, was seized and imprisoned.

The United States remained threatened during 1795. Indian hostilities continued in Kentucky and Tennessee and neither France nor Britain had changed their positions on expecting the new republic to fail. However, the Spaniards also began to pressure the United States. The Spanish established Fort San Fernando de Las Barrancas at Memphis during March 1795. By 1797, the U.S. compelled the Spanish to abandon the post. In the meantime, the Constitution remained the foundation of the nation, but as time passed the patriots who brought about the victory against the British died one by one. On 23 January 1795, General John Sullivan succumbed.

Congress received some good news during February 1795, when President Washington reported that the recent hostilities with the Cherokees has ceased; however, he cautioned that some small groups of Creeks would "continue their depredations, and it is uncertain where it will lead." He also informed Congress that relations with Portugal were good and that the Portuguese were aiding the U.S. against the Barbary pirates.

During June 1795, France and Spain concluded the Treaty of Basel, which terminated the conflict initiated in 1793. During this period, turbulence was brewing in the West Indies, where the Haitians were preparing to rebel and expel foreigners from Haiti. In September, the U.S. signed a treaty with Algiers; however, the U.S. was still too weak to exclude extortion. The treaty — made under duress — included paying tribute. Subsequently, Tunis demanded tribute. The dey of Algiers had actually compelled the United States to provide him with a ship. The U.S. still had no navy; Congress had disbanded it at the conclusion of the American Revolution. On 8 November, the pirates of Tunis agreed to a truce with the United States, and in June 1796, a new pact was reached, one which was to last six months. The agreement assured the dey of Algiers the sum of $1,000,000 dollars (extortion).

Back in the United States, President Washington, while addressing Congress on 8 December 1795, requested more money for the military. His request was supported by the Federalists, but essentially ignored by the Democratic-Republicans (forerunners of present day Democrats). Meanwhile, until the army and navy were expanded, pirates continued to intimidate the Americans. Washington had also informed Congress that treaties had been consummated with some tribes northwest of the Ohio River. Although the year closed without the United States being drawn into any open warfare with European powers, 1796 signaled more danger on the horizon. During February, France delivered a list of grievances, including displeasure with the Jay Treaty between Britain and the United States. Nonetheless, James Monroe denied the allegations.

Finally, during May 1796, the United States made preparations to take possession of the British posts in the Northwest Territory at Detroit and Michilimackinac. Tennessee entered the Union in June as the 16th state. Another hero of the Revolution was lost when General Nathanael Green died on 15 June. In the meantime, tensions between France and the United States intensified when the French ordered that all ships en route to Great Britain were to be intercepted.

By August 1796, new political problems erupted when James Monroe, adamantly pro–French, was recalled. He was replaced as minister to France by Charles C. Pinckney. Monroe had been closely aligned with Jefferson, who was also pro–France during the ongoing conflict between France and Britain. Pinckney arrived in Paris during December 1796. Also that month, Spain concluded the Treaty of San Ildefonso with France and added its dissent to the Jay Treaty. In conjunction with the treaty, Spain delayed transferring posts along the Mississippi to the United States. In collusion with the French, the Spanish also incited Americans on the Western frontier to establish a separate country.

While the United States continued to withstand internal and external pressures, President Washington was completing his second term as president. His successor, John Adams, was also a Federalist. Washington's farewell address, which was delivered to Congress during December, included thanks: "I find ample reason for a renewed expression of that gratitude to the Ruler of the Universe which a continued series of prosperity has so often and so justly called forth...." During that same period, the United States signed another treaty with Tripoli, which again included tribute and still, the Americans had no navy strong enough to end the extortion. At the same time, France suspended diplomatic relations with the United States, moving the two nations closer to war in a move that was interpreted as French intent to interfere in the nation's election to get a pro–French president, specifically, Thomas Jefferson. Nevertheless, with the election results showing Adams as the victor, the scheme, if it was one, failed.

As the eighteenth century was ending, more severe tests faced the United States. The outside pressures caused the necessity of rebuilding strong armed forces, including a navy that could eliminate the Barbary pirates' interference with American shipping. Before leaving office, Washington warned that neutrality without a naval force had no value and that American seamen would continue to be "exposed to calamity." He also noted: "To secure respect for a neutral flag requires a naval force organized and ready to vindicate it from insult or aggression." General Anthony Wayne, who had recently ended the Indian hostilities in the Ohio Territory, by his victory reminded America of the necessity of a well trained army; however, during December 1796, General Wayne, another of the heroes of the American Revolution, died.

Meanwhile, in Europe, the French invaded southern Germany, and other French forces under Napoleon initiated a campaign in Italy. By mid–May, the French entered Milan.

On 4 March 1797, John Adams was inaugurated as the second president of the United States. Before the month ended, he was compelled to call Congress into session to deal with the escalating problems with France. Adams also informed Congress that he was confident that the United States would meet any threat: "A Naval power, next to the militia, is the natural defense of the United States.... With all the materials our country abounds; in skill our naval architects and navigators are equal to any, and commanders and seamen will not be wanting." Nonetheless, during the following June, the nation was informed that the French had seized 300 ships. President Adams had also inherited the problems with Spain, which continued to stall turning over posts along the Mississippi.

With the U.S. still under the pressure of the Barbary pirates, yet another treaty was signed with Tunis during August 1797 and still, the agreement included tribute payments. The treaty was ratified during January 1800. In the meantime, the U.S. had engaged the French in the conflict known as the Quasi-war with France, which had been fought entirely on the high seas. President Adams sent representatives to France to seek a treaty; however, after their arrival in Paris during October 1797, the French essentially humiliated the party. The scandalous XYZ Affair unfolded when the French attempted to seek bribes. France was also undergoing yet another year of turbulence. Its army under Napoleon had advanced toward Rome during February and compelled Pope Pius VI to cede (through the Treaty of Tolentino) Avignon, Bologna, Ferrara, Romagna and Venaissin. By March, Napoleon was entering Austria where a treaty was consummated at Leoben on 18 April. The treaty was followed by the Treaty of Campo Formio, the latter having nearly terminated the early segments of the French Revolutionary Wars.

The pact (Campo Formio), signed on 17 October 1797 in Venetia, gave France the Ionian Islands, held by Venice since the fourteenth century. In addition, Venetia was divided between Austria and France. France also received territory from Austria. France had invaded the Republic of Venice during May 1797.

Also, during July 1797, Napoleon had established the Cisalpine Republic, which was combined with the Republic of Transpadine, also established by Napoleon. Tearing European nations apart during incessant wars has been occurring for centuries; however, up to that point, the Europeans had still not been able to witness the collapse of the new nation on the opposite side of the Atlantic. Nevertheless, the idea of transforming the United States remained a possibility. In the U.S., slow progress continued as the provisional United States Army was established. Former President Washington was recalled to take command. Nevertheless, the French threat ended without any contact by either army. That conflict was settled by the Treaty of Morfontaine in 1798. Also that year, Fort McHenry was established at Baltimore, along with other forts in various states, including Fort Wolcott in Rhode Island. The U.S. Navy was re-established with the launching of the USS *United States*, commanded by yet another patriot of the American Revolution, Captain John Barry. President Adams, during the latter part of May 1798, ordered the fleet to seize any French vessels interfering with U.S. shipping.

In June, Adams called upon George Washington to assume command of the army: "We must have your name if you will in any case permit us to use it; there will be more efficacy in it than in many an army." Washington was unanimously re-appointed commander-in-chief by the Senate on 3 July 1798. Meanwhile, the conflict with France (Quasi-war) was underway. The French privateer *Croyable* was seized off Egg Harbor, New Jersey, on 7 July by the USS *Delaware*; it was the first French ship to be captured.

Meanwhile, the conflicts in Europe continued to rage. During January 1798, the French invaded Switzerland. The following month, the French seized Rome and captured Pope Pius VI, who refused to submit to Napoleon. Napoleon's thirst for victories continued to increase. During May 1798, he departed from Toulon with 30,000 troops, but rather than invading England he sailed to Egypt from where he intended to strike the British possessions in India. While en route to Egypt, Napoleon seized Malta. Although the French overran Moslem resistance and reached Cairo, unexpectedly, Napoleon was handed a setback. A British fleet under Horatio Nelson arrived during August. Nelson discovered the French fleet moored in the harbor at Abukir (Abu Qir) in the Nile River Delta. Admiral Nelson acted quickly and destroyed the fleet and isolated the French in Egypt, making it impossible for Napoleon to swiftly embark for France if it became necessary.

By November 1798, Naples jumped into the conflict, and its forces moved into Rome, which Napoleon had proclaimed the Republic of Rome. The invasion ignited the "The War of the Second Coalition." Nonetheless, the French regained the city on 15 December. Meanwhile, by about 23 December, the British and the Russians formed an alliance. Shortly thereafter, they were joined by Austria, Naples, Portugal and the Ottoman Empire. Meanwhile, the French bolted from Rome and overwhelmed Naples. King Ferdinand IV (also King Ferdinand III of Sicily) of Naples fled to Sicily. At nearly the same time (December 1798), Charles Emmanuel IV, King of Piedmont (Sardinia) departed for Sardinia.

Back in the United States during 1799, the Spanish were finally compelled to begin to turn over their posts along the Mississippi. The Americans replaced the Spanish colors at Fort Estevan, Alabama, with the Stars and Stripes. The fort was renamed Fort Stephens. The Americans also continued to establish new forts to be prepared for future threats. They included Fort Stoddart in Mount Vernon, Alabama, and Fort Independence on Castle Island in Massachusetts at Boston.

On the high seas, the U.S. Navy continued to cruise to protect the merchant ships. Off Martinique, during February, the USS *United States* seized the French privateer *L'Amour de la Patrie* and later in the month a British ship that had been captured by the French. During that period, the Americans continued to push new ships into the fleet, giving them the strength to neutralize the French warships.

During November 1799, American representatives sailed for Paris to seek an end to the war. Before they arrived, while in Portugal, the men were informed that Napoleon had seized power (Revolution of the 18th Brumaire). Upon their arrival at Paris on 2 March 1800, they discovered that the Directory had been replaced by Napoleon, who had established himself as the ruler of France.

In the United States, the nation sustained a major tragedy when George Washington died on 14 December. Meanwhile, in Europe the conflagration continued. Naples had been transformed into the Parthenopean Republic during January of 1799, but by May, Naples was abandoned. The French forces moved north to engage the Russians. The French also lost the Ionian Islands to a combined Russian-Turkish force during May of 1799. Nonetheless, the French in Egypt succeeded during July by decisively defeating a Turkish force which had landed from British ships.

Genoa, Italy, fell to the Austrians in June 1800, and shortly thereafter, the French regained Milan, where they re-established the Cisalpine Republic. In addition, Napoleon crossed the Alps and struck the Austrians on 4 June in northern Italy (Piedmont) at the village of Marengo. The Austrians were compelled to relinquish their fortresses west of the Mincio River and south of the Po River, giving the French domination of Lombardy up to the Mincio River. By July, the French seized Munich, Germany. In the meantime, other French forces were attacking western Austria. The offensives forced the Holy Roman Emperor to seek peace during February 1801. The French had also concluded a treaty with the Turks during January 1800. France agreed to evacuate Egypt; however, the British did not favor these terms. In addition, Pope Pius VI, still a prisoner of Napoleon, died in captivity at Valence, France. His remains were later returned to Rome. He was succeeded by Pope Pius VII.

By 1800, the Americans had gained respect from France due to the successes of the U.S. Navy; however, during June, Congress, still unable to appreciate the need for a strong defense, again disbanded the United States Army. In the meantime, American representatives had arrived in Paris during March to negotiate an end to the conflict. The talks continued until September, when an agreement was reached to end the war that had never officially begun. Nevertheless, the United States had not yet reached a point that would guarantee its acceptance as a nation. Consequently, while Europe continued to be a battlefield, great dangers still faced the United States when the Treaty of Morfontaine was signed on 30 September 1800. Although peace was achieved by John Adams, memories were short and Adams was defeated in the next election, transferring power from the Federalists to the Jeffersonians.

During 1801, Europe continued to be embroiled in warfare. The French under Napoleon pressed to vanquish their enemies and expand their empire. In Rome, Napoleon succeeded in coercing the Catholic Church to relinquish its claims to regain the land which was confiscated. On 20 January, Spain, in collusion with France, proclaimed that the Spanish would separate Portugal from Britain, which ignited yet another war (War of the Oranges), which raged until the following June. It terminated with the Treaty of Badajoz, by which Portugal was compelled to revoke the treaties between it and Great Britain.

On 3 February 1801, the U.S. Senate, content that the Quasi-war with France had ended, ratified the peace agreement. Congress took additional action the following month that seriously damaged the ability of the United States to defend itself. By Congressional action, the young but proud United States Navy was transformed into a "peace establishment." Congress reduced the navy to a mere fourteen ships with an order that all other vessels be sold. With blatant disregard for the advice of former Presidents George Washington and John Adams, Congress stripped the nation's navy of its potency and once again placed the United States in jeopardy. Peace through strength once again was abandoned, and to validate the wisdom of George Washington, the bashaw of Tripoli declared war against the U.S. on 14 May 1801, about three months after it was determined that John Adams had been defeated for the presidency by Thomas Jefferson.

Despite the orders to reduce the size of the U.S. Navy, President Jefferson, on 1 June 1801, dispatched a four-ship squadron, bolstered by contingents of Marines, to the Mediterranean to put an end to the extortion of the Barbary pirates. The frigates USS *President, Philadelphia*, the schooner *Enterprise* and the war sloop *Enterprise* were under the command of Commodore Dale. Up until that point, Jefferson had been anti-war, and he believed that purchasing frigates was a waste of money; however, since ascending to the presidency, he realized the difference between theory and practice, which compelled him to modify his stances regarding peace and war. While Dale's squadron was en route, Tripoli also declared war on the United States.

By the latter part of June, the USS *Enterprise* schooner, which was out in front of the squadron, was intercepted by the *Tripoli*, which anticipated an easy target and a bonanza of new American prisoners to be held for ransom. The pirates battled the *Enterprise* for about three hours. Their introduction to the U.S. Navy became a humbling experience. Not only did the pirates fail to seize prisoners, but they were unable to inflict any casualties. Lt. Andrew Sterett, following his victory, wrote to Commodore Dale: "Sir, I have the honor to inform you that ... I fell in with a Tripolitan ship of war called the *Tripoli*, as action commenced within pistol shot, which continued three hours incessantly. It then struck its colors, having 30 men killed and 30 wounded ... we have not a man wounded and we have sustained no material damage." The squadron later arrived off Tripoli; however, the navy's guns were unable to penetrate the walls of the fortress. Nevertheless, the squadron remained offshore, out of the range of the fort's guns for more than one year to restrict the activity of the pirates.

During October 1801, France and Britain concluded another agreement, the Preliminary Peace of Amiens, but the pact only suspended hostilities. The treaty caused concern in the United States because it was known that Napoleon was still focused on Louisiana. Napoleon, in an effort to complete his plans for Louisiana, concentrated on not instigating war with the Americans. Meanwhile, Spain had not yet transferred the Louisiana Territory to the French. In the meantime, Napoleon, having eliminated British warships from interfering, moved to Santo Domingo in the West Indies to crush the slave rebellion. From there he intended to jump to Louisiana. All the while, the British continued to hold power on the high seas; however, about 40,000 sailors had deserted during the late war to take advantage of life in the United States.

In other activity, France and Austria concluded a treaty at Luneville on the 9 February 1801. France also concluded a peace treaty with Naples that year. Russia had not been engaged during the war; however, during 1805, when war again erupted, Russia joined the Allies against France. During that time, Russia also annexed Georgia from Iran, which plunged Iran into war against Russia. In March 1802, the French, English and Spanish, concluded a peace treaty (of Amiens). All three of the belligerents had envisioned the downfall of the United States, yet as they continued to enter into conflict after conflict in Europe, they never combined their strength in a pact to join together to conquer the Americans.

During 1802, the United States declared war against Tripoli on 6 February and simultaneously, Congress authorized its merchant ships to carry arms to assist in the struggle. In early June, Morocco declared war on the United States, a conflict which lasted until October 1803. In the meantime, while the U.S. Navy was engaged in fighting pirates while simultaneously protecting shipping from interference on the high seas, the U.S. Army was being strengthened. On 4 July 1802, West Point was officially designated as the U.S. Military Academy, which became the foundation for officers and the beginning of what became known as the "Long Gray Line." Later in the year, the chicanery of the Spanish and French rose again in Louisiana when the Spanish, during October, halted the practice of permitting U.S. citizens to use New Orleans as a depository for their goods, which arrived on flat boats that traveled down the Mississippi. The Mississippi remained open; however, the new crisis for the government placed the U.S. once again on the brink of war with either Spain, France or both simultaneously. President Jefferson, while overseeing that dilemma, also had to concern himself with the latest emerging threats from England.

Napoleon's invasion of Santo Domingo (1802) initially went well, and in conjunction with the operation he had ordered another French army in Holland raised and prepared to land in Louisiana. Nevertheless, unexpectedly, the United States was once again spared from war with France. Napoleon's army was struck by nature when yellow fever broke out and killed about 4,000 French troops during September. The French were compelled to rethink their plans of landing in Louisiana, while they also had to deal with more tenacious resistance from the former slaves on Haiti. French General LeClerc informed Napoleon that thousands of additional troops would be required to succeed in Haiti and of those, many would die from the pestilence. Napoleon was also told that success would mean that the French would have to "destroy all the mountain Negroes, men and women, sparing only children under twelve years of age." LeClerc also stated that about fifty percent of the plains Negroes would have to be liquidated.

While Napoleon pondered his decision, more distressing news arrived. He learned that his brother had been victimized by the fever, and news followed that the severe winter in Europe had caused the French fleets to be caught in harbors that had frozen solid. Consequently, the army in Holland could not depart during January or February 1803. In April, Europe was hit by a series of severe storms that continued to prevent the French from embarking. Napoleon made major changes in his plans during April, about one month after resuming hostilities with England.At the time of the Louisiana Purchase, Napoleon was heavily engaged against the Allies in Europe, and he wanted to eliminate any possibility of Louisiana being acquired by Great Britain. During March 1803, the Union expanded with the entrance of Ohio as the 17th state. The following month, the

Introduction

United States learned that Napoleon would not be holding court in New Orleans. He had aborted the plan and decided to sell Louisiana to the Americans to ensure that the territory was not acquired by Britain. Within about one month, on 18 May, France reinitiated its war with Britain, terminating a truce that lasted about nineteen months. The latest outrage again worked in favor of the United States, which for at least a while did not have to worry about war with either France or Great Britain. The U.S. used the time to continue to build up its defenses.

Although Europe returned to yet another war, U.S. vessels continued to engage in commerce with both sides, but not without difficulties. The British continued to be short of sailors and to increase their numbers, but by 1805 again began to interfere with U.S. ships in search of British subjects. When none were found, the British frequently designated Americans as British and seized them.

In the Mediterranean, the crisis worsened on 31 October 1803, when the USS *Philadelphia* struck a reef while it pursued a pirate vessel and got hung up. The pirates awaited darkness and in great numbers, they surrounded the stranded vessel and captured Captain William Bainbridge and the crew, composed of 22 officers and 315 men. The remaining ships in the squadron sped to the aid of the *Philadelphia*; however, they were unable to reach the ship in time to save the crew. Meanwhile, back in the States, a series of swiftly occurring events changed the fate of the nation. On 30 November, Spain officially transferred Louisiana to the French at New Orleans. France transferred the territory to the United States on 20 December 1803. The sale of Louisiana to the United States doubled the size of the nation.

Spain immediately launched protests; however, it was ignored. President Jefferson wasted no time in using the acquisition to the advantage of the United States by planning to send a contingent on a mission to reach the Pacific Ocean (Lewis and Clark Expedition). In addition, the acquisition gave the United States absolute control of the Mississippi River, which was an important artery, regardless of which adversary would threaten the United States in the future. The Spanish, however, had no intent of entering a war over the loss of Louisiana, and Napoleon also was against war with the United States. Nevertheless, Napoleon worked to incite hostilities between Spain and the United States, while easterners and westerners argued over the purchase. Nonetheless, President Jefferson remained focused on acquiring yet additional territory, specifically, West Florida, which he believed would guarantee the security of the United States.

During 1804, while the government was preparing for the Lewis and Clark Expedition, the navy was still working to eliminate the Barbary pirates in the Mediterranean and to rescue captives. On 16 February, the USS *Intrepid*, commanded by Lt. Stephen Decatur, defied the guns of the fortress and sailed into Tripoli disguised as a blockade runner. The sailors and Marines retook the disabled USS *Philadelphia* and set it afire. Decatur, a daring navy officer, is remembered also for his statement "My country, right or wrong." Although the raid was successful and the Americans sustained no casualties, no genuine damage was done to the fortress at Tripoli. The navy continued to bombard the Tripolitan positions, but it continued to be unaffected.

Later in the year the strategy changed. On 29 November 1804, a small detachment of U.S. Marines, led by Lt. Presley O'Bannon, accompanied by a contingent of mercenaries, departed from Alexandria, Egypt, and traveled overland to strike Tripoli from the rear. The column arrived at Derne in April 1805. On 25 April, in conjunction with a naval bombardment, the Marines and their mercenaries (Greeks and Arabs) launched their attack and scored a devastating victory. The city was captured and the Marines raised the American flag, the first time the American flag was hoisted in the Old World. By early June, a peace treaty was signed with Tripoli, which terminated the Barbary Coast War.

The more Europe continued to be locked in warfare, the easier it became for the United States to continue to build its defenses, while simultaneously working to expand the boundaries of the country without foreign interference; however, on the one hand, to many Americans, Manifest Destiny was on the move, yet, America which so far had been able to maintain peace, it was also inevitable that war with England was just beyond the horizon.

In Czechoslovakia, on 2 December 1805, during the War of the Third Coalition, the French defeated a combined Austrian-Russian force at Moravia. The devastating defeat compelled Holy Roman Emperor Francis II to conclude a truce (Treaty of Pressburg) with the French. The French had caused the Allies to disintegrate. Czar Alexander I initiated a retreat at battle's end. The Austrians ceded to the Kingdom of Italy the Venetian territory that it had been given through a previous treaty (of Campo Formio). In addition, the Austrians relinquished Istria and Dalmatia. Also, according to the terms of the treaty, Bavaria received territory including the Tyrol and the city of Augsburg from the Austrians. Bavaria (Weittelsbach Dynasty) became a kingdom. Baden and Wurttemburg also became kingdoms; they received the remaining western territory of the Hapsburgs.

In England, the news of the defeat caused William Pitt (the Younger) to become gravely ill. Pitt died in late January 1806. He was succeeded as prime minister by Lord William Grenville. The conflict was referred to also as the "Battle of the Three Emperors." France and Russia had also concluded a treaty during 1805, in which Napoleon gave the English province of Hanover to Prussia; however, he later modified his decision. During 1807, Napoleon carved out part of Hanover and gave it to his brother, Joseph, as a portion of the kingdom of Westphalia. During 1810, the remainder of Hanover was divided between France and Westphalia. The Napoleonic Wars continued during the War of 1812, which forced England to divert forces that otherwise would have been committed against the United

States. Although open warfare between Great Britain and the United States did not commence officially until 1812, the conflict, essentially a continuation of the initial war with the British, began to unfold as early as 1806–1807, when Britain renewed its intimidation of American shipping. This reignited hostilities that would determine whether King George III would regain his former colonies. The destiny of the United States depended upon whether the sparks of liberty that originally brought independence could rekindle the Spirit of 1776 into the hearts and minds of the newest line of American patriots who received the overwhelming responsibility of defending the Constitution and preserving the Stars and Stripes. Once again, Britain intended to test the mettle of the United States in its quest to re-hoist the British colors over its former colonies. The conflict that would either solidify or destroy the United States of America had been foreseen by Benjamin Franklin, who stated at the conclusion if the American Revolution during 1783, when he proclaimed that the surrender of Cornwallis "was only the war of the Revolution and that the war of independence was yet to be fought."

THE CHRONOLOGY

1803

September 13 (Tuesday) **In Philadelphia,** Commodore John Barry, a veteran of the American Revolution often referred to as the father of the U.S. Navy, dies of natural causes.

1804

Spring Colonel Samuel Hammond, a veteran of the American Revolution, having recently been named the military and civil commander of the District of St. Louis, departs from Georgia to assume his new office. Hammond is accompanied by his wife, Amelia O'Keefe, and a party that includes about 200 servants. Louisiana had been divided into the Territory of Orleans and the District of Louisiana. The District of St. Louis was composed of the entire region west of the Mississippi north of the 33rd degree latitude. Hammond, in addition to speaking English, also spoke French and Spanish, which became of great value upon reaching St. Louis, which at the time was only a small French town. During 1824, Hammond returned to South Carolina and settled on property near Horse Creek several miles below Augusta, Georgia, on the South Carolina side of the creek. Hammond died there at age 83 on 11 September 1842.

December 5 (Wednesday) President Thomas Jefferson is reelected. George Clinton, governor of New York and former Revolutionary War general, is elected vice president.

1805

April 25 (Thursday) **In Tripoli,** a 7-man contingent of Marines and Midshipman George Mann, commanded by Lt. Presley O'Bannon, U.S. Marine Corps, bolstered by Greek and Arab mercenaries, arrives at Derne, Tripoli, from Alexandria, Egypt. The contingent had traveled 500 miles since they departed Alexandria the previous November. O'Bannon launches the attack in synchronization with a bombardment from U.S. naval vessels. The forces of the dey, which have prevented the U.S. from penetrating their fortress from the sea, are caught by total surprise. By midday, the Marines control the city. Lt. O'Bannon hoists the Stars and Stripes, which becomes the first American flag to fly over a captured fort in the Old World. The Marines reinstall the rightful ruler, Pasha Yusuf's brother. O'Bannon is presented with a Mameluk sword. To this day, United States Marines continue to carry this symbolic sword. The capture of Derne, Tripoli, terminates the war with Tripoli that lasted about four years and simultaneously, it ends Tripoli's practice of extorting tribute from the United States. For America, it is a great victory; however, for the Barbary pirates it was an end to an era. The Barbary Coast pirates from this point forward begin to fear the power of the United States.

June 4 (Tuesday) The United States and Tripoli sign a peace treaty ending the Barbary Coast War. The U.S. pays approximately $60,000 for the release of the crew from the captured vessel *Philadelphia*. The treaty is ratified by Congress on April 12, 1806. The Marines depart from Tripoli on 12 June; however, the squadron does not return to the U.S. due to problems with other Barbary pirates. The Americans move against the Bey of Tunis, who continues to be defiant. The navy arrives off Tunis on 1 August.

June 11 (Tuesday) The Territory of Michigan is formed by land carved from Indiana.

July 23 (Tuesday) **Great Britain,** using its Rule of 1756, forbids neutral vessels from trading with any nation that it hasn't been trading with during peacetime. The use of this rule causes many problems with American merchant vessels and provides the British with an excuse to seize U.S. merchant ships.

August 1 (Thursday) **In Africa** at Tunis, Commodore Rodgers' squadron of thirteen ships anchors within sight of the bey's capital. The bey of Tunis, despite the plight of Tripoli, which was vanquished, remained arrogant. However, Rodgers' squadron prompts a quick change of attitude. The bey hurriedly sends an ambassador to the United States. The capture of Tripoli and the submission of the bey of Tunis signals the end of threats from the Barbary pirates to North America in the Mediterranean. Pope Pius VII afterward proclaims that the "Americans had done more for Christendom against the North African pirates than all of the European powers united."

Commodore Rodgers had assumed command of the squadron when Commodore Barron became ill. Barron had served under his father, James Barron, Sr. (Commodore of Virginia Navy), during the Revolution. The American squadron instills fear into the remainder of the Barbary Coast pirates, and while the Europeans continue to batter each other, the Mediterranean again is opened. The ongoing animosity between Britain and France had intensified since Napoleon had been proclaimed emperor during May of 1804, and during May of 1805, Napoleon had been anointed king of Milan. The United States, so far, has not been directly drawn into the wars of the European powers; however, the Americans are aware of their precarious position.

September 27 (Friday) General William Moultrie, a veteran of the American Revolution, dies.

1806

January 2 (Thursday) The expeditionary force under Lt. Zebulon M. Pike, which had departed St. Louis during 1805, comes in contact with a British trading post (North West Company) at Lower Red Cedar Lake in the vicinity of present day Aitkin, Minnesota. Pike's primary mission is to discover the source of the Mississippi and acquire treaties with Indians, but his orders also direct him to gather intelligence on British operations in the region. The encounter is friendly and Pike pauses the operation to spend some time at the post.

January 6 (Monday) James Madison, the secretary of state, informs Congress of Britain's escalating efforts to harass U.S. vessels by intercepting them on the high seas. Congress takes the matter under consideration and in mid–February issues a resolution that condemns the British aggression, which the British ignore.

January 8 (Wednesday) **In Minnesota,** a small contingent of Lt. Zebulon Pike's command that had moved ahead from Little Falls reaches Sandy Lake. From here the party continues north toward Leech Lake, where the men arrive on 1 February. The original unit under Pike consisted of twenty-one men, but only Pike and one other actually reaches Leech Lake and both are in poor health. The others lag behind. While at Leech Lake, Pike encounters the British Northwest Company and reminds the party there that the area is under the U.S. government and the American flag. He also demands that all British influence with the Indians is to cease and desist, essentially informing them that their interference to incite the Indians must halt. Pike's threat is mostly rhetoric because the U.S. Army is not yet prepared to dominate the area. Nonetheless, the British accommodate the Americans and concur, but only for the moment. After the Americans leave, the British ensign is re-hoisted and the Indians, already friendly with the British, remain on good terms. The party heads back for the St. Anthony Falls near Minneapolis, where Fort St. Anthony (later Fort Snelling) will be established on 11 April. Pike's command returns to St. Louis, arriving there on 30 April, completing a journey which had begun the previous year.

April 10 (Thursday) **In New York,** General Horatio Gates, a veteran of the French and Indian War and the American Revolution, dies. He is survived by his wife (2nd), Mary Valance Gates. General Gates' son, Robert, had predeceased him. Robert was killed during the Battle of Camden.

Zebulon Pike.

April 12 (Saturday) The U.S. ratifies the treaty with Tripoli, which had been consummated during June of 1805.

April 18 (Friday) **In Washington, D.C.,** Congress passes the Nicholson Act, which prohibits the importation of particular British goods into the United States if the goods can be acquired from any other place. The bill remains controversial after its effective date of November 15 and is postponed on December 19 by President Jefferson. The targeted items, including woolen textiles, brass, hemp and tin, again become prohibited during 1808 as the tension between Great Britain and the U.S. accelerates.

April 26 (Saturday) **In naval activity,** the HMS *Leander*, a frigate, without provocation, fires upon an unarmed American vessel off Sandy Hook. One American is killed. Tempers flare throughout the country; however, the Americans do not retaliate. Nevertheless, British harassment of American shipping continues. During June of the following year another tension raising incident occurs when the USS *Chesapeake* is encountered by the HMS *Leopard*, a double-decker warship.

May 16 (Friday) **In England,** Parliament declares a blockade of European ports in the area that stretches from Brest, France, to Germany extending to the mouth of the Elbe River. The action is taken to block shipping to territory held by Napoleon. In response, Napoleon retaliates about six months later by issuing the Berlin Decree.

In other activity, President Jefferson dispatches William Pinckney to England to join the U.S. minister, James Monroe, in an effort to convince Great Britain to cease and desist the practice of impressing American seamen. Jefferson also directs his ministers to negotiate a treaty which would open trade in the West Indies.

May 30 (Friday) **In Tennessee,** Major General (militia) Andrew Jackson engages Charles Dickenson, a lawyer, in a duel. Dickenson, a marksman who had bragged that he would kill Jackson, is slain. Jackson is wounded. The shell broke some ribs but did not penetrate. Jackson believed he would die but survived and later became president.

July 15 (Tuesday) An expedition led by Lt. Zebulon Pike departs from Bellefontaine, Ohio, to explore the Southwest. During the previous year, Lt. Pike had unsuccessfully led an expedition to discover the mouth of the Mississippi.

July 20 (Sunday) **In Ohio,** Aaron Burr, former vice president (March 1801–March 1805) under President Jefferson, confers with Harman Blennerhassett on an island named after the latter. The two apparently had laid plans to seize territory in the west or southwest, but the exact location remains unknown. The small force of about eighty men sail down the Mississippi, but the mission is suddenly aborted. On November 27, President Jefferson is informed of the plot by General Wilkinson, the commander of U.S. forces in the Mississippi Valley region. Jefferson, once alerted to the plan, issues a heavy warning to any Americans who might consider participating in a hostile act toward the Spanish, with which the U.S. is at peace, but he doesn't inform Congress until January of 1807.

When Burr learns of the warning, his small flotilla of about ten boats is about twenty-five miles outside of Natchez, Mississippi. Burr abandons the plan and heads for Florida, but he is intercepted on February 19, 1807, and captured while moving through Alabama. He is arrested for the crime of conspiracy to form and command an expedition against Spanish territory.

September 23 (Tuesday) The team of explorers led by Lewis and Clark arrives back in St. Louis from their journey, which began during May of 1804 when they departed in search of a route to the Pacific Ocean. It gathered scientific information about the areas visited and provided much documentation on the terrain itself. The mission also further expanded the fur trade in the United States, pushing it west of the Mississippi River. The success of the mission, in addition to the sacrifices of the party, was due in great part to the actions of Sacajawea, a Shoshone Indian who had acted as an interpreter and who persuaded her brother to provide supplies and horses to the expeditionary force. Sacajawea, born sometime between 1784 and 1787, was earlier kidnapped by another tribe, thought to have been either the Hidatsa or the Minnetares, and married off to a French trapper, Touissant Charbonneau, during 1804. During February 1805, she became the mother of a boy named Jean Baptiste. Little is known about her life after the expedition; however, it is known that she was one of two wives of Charbonneau.

John Colter, a scout who accompanied the expedition in its entirety, had received authorization to leave the party. He returned to the Yellowstone area, leading another team on a mission to trap beaver. However, during 1808, Colter is captured by Blackfeet Indians. He manages to escape by outrunning his captors. In 1809, he departs the mountains and returns to Missouri, where he succumbs during 1813.

November 21 (Friday) Napoleon issues the Berlin Decree in response to England's recent action ordering the blockade of European ports from the Elbe River in Germany to Brest in France. Napoleon's order mandates a naval blockade of England. American merchantmen are caught in the middle and subject to interference by both England and France.

December 2 (Tuesday) President Jefferson delivers a message to Congress requesting that the importation of slaves to the United States be forbidden. He urges that the law should become effective on January 1, 1808.

December 31 (Wednesday) In England at London, on behalf of the United States, James Monroe and William Pinckney consummate a treaty with the British, as directed by President Jefferson; however, the agreement is not highly received in the United States, as the British concede no primary points, essentially snubbing the U.S. request to halt the impressment of U.S. seamen, and they refuse to commit to reinitiating genuine trade in the West Indies, instead offering a meaningless proposal. So one-sided is the pact that Jefferson, upon receiving it during March of 1807, chooses not to send it to Congress. Jefferson dispatches new orders to the U.S. ministers, instructing them to utilize the treaty as a tool to reopen negotiations.

1807

January 7 (Wednesday) Great Britain forbids all commercial shipping in French waters; it also prohibits shipping within the territories and with allies of the French. The action is taken in response to Napoleon's Berlin Decree of November 1806.

January 17 (Saturday) Aaron Burr, the man who had lost the election for the presidency to Thomas Jefferson in 1801 (the electoral votes ended in a tie, giving the decision to the House of Representatives, which elected Jefferson and gave the vice residency to Burr) is apprehended in the Mississippi Territory (Alabama) on charges of treason. He is held for a while at Fort Stoddart. The case comes to trial during June with acquittal in September. Burr, although acquitted, is to be tried on other charges, including the murder of Alexander Hamilton in a July 1804 duel. To avoid the upcoming trial Burr flees to Europe.

February PIKE EXPEDITION Lt. Lt. Zebulon Pike and his party, while on an expedition in the territory along the Arkansas and Red Rivers, are seized by Spanish troops. When the encounter occurs, according to Pike's journal of the mission, he is informed by the Spanish that he is at the River Del Norte rather than the Red River and in Mexican territory. The Spanish inform Pike that they are under orders to escort his party out of Spanish territory. The Spaniards inflict no harm. The Americans are then taken through Santa Fe and deeper into Spanish territory to Durango (Mexico). Later the party is escorted back through Spanish Texas to Louisiana.

June 22 (Monday) The USS *Chesapeake*, a nine-gun frigate, commanded by Captain James Barron, is harassed by the double-decker British man-o-war *Leopard* off Norfolk, Virginia. The incident occurs soon after the *Chesapeake* embarks from Hampton Roads on a cruise. Unfortunately, none of its nine guns are prepared for action and the crew had been ordered to take their battle stations. Nonetheless, Captain Barron declines the British demand to board to search for British deserters. The British retaliate by opening fire when the Chesapeake struck its colors. The broadsides kill three of the crew of the *Chesapeake* and wounds 18 others. The British select four men and brand them deserters, but the British had actually discovered only one Englishman. Later, the three Americans are released; the fourth is tried at Halifax and convicted. He is afterward executed by hanging.

The British depart and the *Chesapeake* limps back to Norfolk. The Americans become outraged to the point of revenge. Nonetheless, instead, a ship is dispatched to England to deliver orders to the American minister to demand an apology and to press for reparations. The English acquiesce; however, the apology is essentially hollow, as the Royal Navy continues its illegal practice of seizing seamen from U.S. vessels. The British government makes no move to halt the seizures. President Jefferson, who intends to avoid war at any cost, does take some action by ordering all British warships to immediately depart from the United States. Captain Barron is punished with 5 years' suspension due to his lackadaisical leadership and unpreparedness for battle against a foe. At the time the *Chesapeake* arrived back at Norfolk, the anger became so high that the British sailors in the city on liberty were compelled to quickly depart and return to their vessels.

The seizure was like a flashback to earlier times when the British sparked the patriots to band together and proclaim independence. The unprovoked attack by the British instilled an instantaneous bond between the various political factions that created a sense of national pride and a unanimous desire to seek reprisals. The Americans become galvanized in an effort to avenge the attack and to defend the country's honor. Nonetheless, the anger did not persuade Jefferson to declare war. The president, after ordering the British to depart American waters, continues to cling to his posture of peace. He believes that he can solve the nation's problems peacefully. Meanwhile, the British press prints derogatory remarks about the *Chesapeake*'s crew, dubbing them cowardly. The same article, which praises the bravery of the Royal Navy, only further infuriates the Americans. While incessantly badgering the Americans as inferior, the British also taunt the Americans for not joining with them against France. Captain Barron, later a commodore, engages Commodore Stephen Decatur in a duel during 1820, in which Decatur sustains a fatal wound.

June 25 (Thursday) France and Russia sign the Tilsit Agreement. This pact between Napoleon and Czar Alexander I bolsters Napoleon's posture in Europe, but the agreement also guarantees a continuation of the Napoleonic Wars, which pit the British, who rule the sea, against the French, who dominate the land. Napoleon seizes all the Prussian terrain lying west of the Elbe River, and in addition, he confiscates Hanover,

Hesse-Darmstadt, Hessee-Kassel and the Grand Duchy of Brunswick. The Russians up to this point have been fighting on the side of England. This deal between Czar Alexander and Napoleon bestows dividends to the Russians also, as Napoleon agrees to permit Russia to take action against Sweden and Turkey. At this time, Russia is engaged with Turkey and it goes to war against Sweden during 1808. As a term of the Tilsit Agreement, the Ionian Islands (Greece), taken from France by Russia during 1799, are returned to France. Queen Louise of Prussia tries in vain to persuade Napoleon to lessen the severity of the terms against Prussia, but he ignores her pleas.

Summer In Missouri, a band of Indians (Sacs and Pottawatomies) raid Loutre Island to steal horses, but no settlers are harmed. Nonetheless, a group of five seasoned frontiersmen initiate pursuit. During the evening of the second day of the chase, the frontiersmen establish night positions on the Salt River Prairie near Spencer Creek, but apparently they post no guard, thinking the place safe, despite being aware the Indians are nearby. Afterwards, the Indians spring a night-attack. Of the five men, three, including William T. Cole, are immediately struck down before they can bolt from their prone positions. Another is able to find some temporary safety by the creek's bank; however, the lone frontiersman, Stephen Cole, is left with no escape. Despite multiple wounds, he is able to break away and make it back to Fort Clemson. The other survivor, Murdock, straggles back to Lutre Island in a few days.

Shortly thereafter, a relief party heads back to Spencer Creek to retrieve the dead and discover a typical gruesome scene—the bodies are horribly mutilated, and all have been decapitated. When the missing heads have been found years later, the scene becomes known as Skull Lick.

July 2 (Thursday) In Washington, D.C., President Jefferson orders all British warships to leave American waters, in response to the badgering of the USS *Chesapeake* by the HMS *Leopold*. Jefferson attempts to negotiate the incident to avoid confrontation, but he includes the termination of "impressment" of U.S. seamen in the negotiations, which the British ignore, thereby setting the stage for both parties to prepare for war. As the war clouds begin to slowly drift across the Atlantic, the British accelerate their attempts to gather Indians as allies in the event of an American invasion of Canada. The French become convinced that the U.S. is fainthearted and willing to continue to sustain as much punishment as the British choose to dole out.

August 3 (Monday) In Virginia, Aaron Burr, initially arrested on a misdemeanor charge, is now being tried for treason. The trial, which is being held in Richmond, continues until 1 September.

August 25 (Tuesday) Commodore Edward Preble (a naval hero of the Barbary Wars) dies. Preble was admired by many for his extraordinary leadership. The men under him were known as

Aaron Burr.

"Preble's Boys" and many followed his example to become great navy leaders.

September 1 (Tuesday) In Virginia at Richmond, the trial of Aaron Burr concludes; he is acquitted of charges of treason. However, his ordeal does not end. He still must stand trial on other charges, including the murder of Alexander Hamilton, with whom he fought in a duel. Burr, rather than face another trial, bolts from the country by jumping bail and absconding to Europe. Once there, he unsuccessfully attempts to plot against Jefferson and the United States by inciting France and England to combine their forces against the U.S.

October 17 (Saturday) In England, in reaction to the declaration of President Jefferson ordering all British ships out of American waters, the British proclaim their indignation by calling for a more concentrated policy of halting U.S. merchant ships to give the British more opportunities to impress American seamen for the Royal Navy.

In the United States, President Jefferson, aware that the U.S. is still not prepared for hostilities, remains hopeful that the crisis can end without war. He concludes that if he forbids the shipment of goods to Europe, both the French and the British will surely seek ways to end the boycott and thereby agree to end the practice of harassing U.S. merchant vessels. The plan is put into effect during December of this year when he issues the first Embargo Act.

October 27 (Tuesday) In France, Napoleon and King Charles IV of Spain consummate the Treaty of Fontainbleau. King Charles, obviously dealing from a weakened position, agrees to the division of Portugal, a sector going to Charles, but the other part is to be given to Manuel de Godoy, the latter being the actual leader of France. The spoils are to be divided subsequent to an upcoming invasion and the anticipation of a victorious campaign. Napoleon dispatches a French Army under General Junot to bolster the Spaniards, who launch the attack during October. Godoy has been losing support in Spain due to the perception of the people that dishonesty permeates his government, and this treaty basically reinforces the theory. Ferdinand (later Ferdinand VII), the son of King Charles, initiates solid opposition to his father and Godoy.

November A Spanish Army bolstered by a French Army, led by General Junot, invades Portugal. They advance and capture Lisbon. The regent, John, and his mother, Queen Maria I, escape capture and flee to Brazil. John VI (later King John VI) had been governing since 1792; however, he has officially been acting as regent since 1799; he attempts to reign from South America in Rio de Janeiro, Brazil.

December 17 (Thursday) In France Napoleon issues the Milan Decree which denationalizes all vessels that are submitted to the British Order in Council. Subsequently, this French decree instigates the seizure of American vessels. This French insolence brings France and the United States to the brink of war.

December 22 (Tuesday) Congress passes the Embargo Act, which places an embargo on all U.S. shipping to Britain and France because of their adversarial acts. The United States had chosen to pass this act rather than declare war; however, it only inflicts great financial pain on American seamen when it is obeyed. The act becomes increasingly unpopular and the government finally repeals it during 1809. Although it is looked upon with disfavor by most, the Embargo Act is particularly unpopular in the seafaring states, especially in New England. Nonetheless, the Federalists having lost the White House and Congress, are unable to stop the act from passing.

The Essex Junta, a strong wing of the Federalists, continues to murmur about secession from the Union. Upon knowledge of the new law, those ships already out of U.S. ports for the most part remain away to avoid compliance, and many of those vessels engage in smuggling to make up for their losses. The Jefferson-inspired law mainly harms U.S. commerce while rarely disrupting that of England or France. However, France increases its seizures of U.S. ships that are captured in foreign ports. The British take the law as a bonus and breathe a sigh of relief, believing that it eliminates some of their competition. Congress passes a second Embargo Act during early January 1808, followed by yet a third during mid–March 1808.

The additional laws, combined, remain ineffective. Nevertheless, the U.S. vessels remain paralyzed. Consequently, the U.S. government's actions caused little immediate harm to France or Great Britain, but it prevents American seamen from being able to make a living. Businesses near the ports slip into bankruptcy and the ships in port begin to enter a state of dilapidation. The impoverished conditions, actually unintended consequences, breed crime and instigate smuggling, particularly in ports across the Canadian border and on Lake Champlain. The acts, intended to halt the impressment of U.S. seamen, propels many men to join the British Navy to forestall starvation. In time, without knowledge in the U.S., the law does inflict harm on Britain, but for now, it sustains no great loss because Europe's farms produces a huge crop during 1808. Initially, the loss of imported U.S. cotton creates some major problems for English textile manufacturers. Later, Jefferson's embargo also harms other British industry; however, Parliament ignores the pleas of the British businessmen.

1808

In Iowa, at about this time Fort Madison, named in honor of President James Madison, is established along the upper Mississippi River in the vicinity of present-day Fort Madison. It is in territory inhabited by the Fox and Sauk Indians as well as the Winnebago tribe. The fort is garrisoned by the U.S. 1st Regiment, commanded by Lt. Alpha Kingsley. The fort remains active until 1813.

In Maine, Fort Sullivan is established by the Americans in the vicinity of Eastport (Moose Island). The fort is surrendered without a fight to the British during 1814. It reverts back to the U.S. in 1818. During the Civil War it is fortified with nearby batteries. Fort George is established at present-day St. George. During 1814, it is seized by the British and put out of action. Also, Fort Edgecomb, a blockhouse, is established at present-day Edgecomb. It remains active, but not in action until about the close of the War of 1812. In 1814, Fort Macdonough will be established on Westpoint Island opposite Fort Edgecomb as an additional defense against the British on the Great Lakes. In addition, Fort Preble and Fort Scammel will be established as part of the defense of Portland during the War of 1812. Fort Preble, formerly Spring Point Battery (1776), and Fort Hancock (1778), will stand at Spring Point (South Portland), and Fort Scammel is constructed at House Island in Portland Harbor. Also, Fort William (formerly Fort Pepperell) at Kittery, Maine, had been abandoned during 1779. At this time a new fort is established there and named Fort McClary in honor of a New Hampshire hero, Major Andrew McClary, who was killed at the Battle of Bunker Hill in June 1775 in Massachusetts. Fort McClary is deactivated during the late 1840s, but at the outbreak of the Civil War, it again is reactivated.

In Maryland, Fort Severn is established at Annapolis. During the War of 1812, the fort receives a garrison, but the town does not come under attack. Later, during 1845, the U.S. Naval Academy is officially established here when the fort is transferred to the U.S. Navy.

In Massachusetts, Fort Andrew is established in Plymouth at Duxbury Beach (Gurnet Point). Subsequently, during 1863, the fort is reconstructed and seven coastal guns are deployed to protect the harbor.

In Missouri, Fort Osage, also known as Fort Clark (separate from Fort Clark established at Troy) is established at present-day Sibley. It remains active until the termination of the War of 1812 and then it is relocated at Arrow Rock, where it remains in service until 1827.

In South Carolina, Fort Marion, named in honor of Francis Marion (the Swamp Fox), is established at Beaufort. It replaces Fort Lyttelton, named in honor of royal governor William Henry Lyttelton when it was established during 1758.

January 1 (Friday) The Congressional Act abolishing the importation of slaves is enacted.

January 9 (Saturday) Congress, in an attempt to strengthen its ban on trade with foreign nations by U.S. vessels, passes a second Embargo Act. It has the uintended effect of encouraging U.S. merchant vessels to sail to Canada and use it as a base of operations for shipping or smuggling. Those who choose to obey the rule continue to slide into a deep financial freefall, which has a devastating effect on the U.S. economy.

March 12 (Saturday) Congress passes the third Embargo Act in the past four months, and like its predecessors, it too forbids U.S. vessels from engaging in commerce with foreign countries. Instead of punishing Britain and France, the act delivers harsh blows to the U.S. shipping industry and the economy. Many Americans continue to call for an end to the embargo and the situation begins to seriously threaten the Union. In New England, the calls to repeal the act remain at high pitch and include some, like George Logan, known for their pacifism. Logan, who had sailed to France as a private citizen in an attempt to convince France to end the undeclared war, now clamors for an end to the embargo and the beginning of raising armed-resistance against the British. It had been Logan's trip to France that prompted Congress to forbid private American citizens from negotiating with all foreign governments; the legislation passed during 1799 and, still active, is named the Logan Act.

April 17 (Sunday) In France, Napoleon issues the Bayonne Decree ordering the capture of all American ships entering French and Italian ports. (America loses about $10 million worth of cargo and ships over the two year period that the order is enforced.) Napoleon uses the recently passed U.S. Embargo Acts to gain advantage. Based on the supposition that any U.S. vessels found in European ports are violating their country's law, he seizes them.

July 16 (Saturday) In St. Louis, the Missouri Fur Company is founded by several partners, including William Clark, who co-led the Lewis and Clark expedition to the Pacific Ocean. Others included Manuel Lisa, William Morrison, Pierre Chouteau, Sr., and Andwer Henry. A fort (trading post) named Fort Raymond had been recently built at the mouth of the Big Horn River.

October 7 (Friday) John Parker Boyd returns to military service of the United States as colonel of the 4th Infantry Regiment. He joined the service in 1786, traveled to India and served there for the Mahratta. Boyd arrived in Madras during July 1789 and shortly thereafter became the commander of 10,000 troops. After his service in the East Indies, he traveled to Paris before returning to the U.S. earlier this year. He was later a brigadier general.

December 7 (Wednesday) James Madison is elected president and George Clinton is elected vice president. Madison had been supported by Jefferson, who chose not to run for a third term. Clinton had served as vice president under Jefferson, and failing to gain enough votes to win over Madison, he is re-elected to the post of vice president. Although the Federalists are unable to gain the majority in either House, they do make some progress in the New England states, due in great part to the dubious Embargo Acts. Madison will begin serving in March 1809.

Late Year America's expansionism is creating problems for the Indians. In one instance, the Osage Tribe signs a treaty with the Americans which cedes their lands lying north of the Arkansas River (present day Arkansas and Missouri). The U.S. Congress will ratify the Osage Treaty during April of 1810.

In other activity, the U.S. at this time has its eyes on Cuba. The Adams administration makes it clear that it will not tolerate the island coming under either English or French domination, particularly because of its strategic location, which could give them the ability to control the entrance to the Gulf of Mexico ports. It is thought that Cuba will eventually fall away from Spanish control and become part of the United States.

1809

In Idaho, Thompson's Trading Post is established during September in northern Idaho on Lake Pend Oreille between East Hope and Clark Fork to the north and south respectively. The post initiated by a Canadian David Thompson is also known as the Kullyspell House, named for local Indians. The exact length of time it operates in not known, but it is thought to have had a short span. Thompson's Post is the initial trading post constructed in the future state of Idaho.

In Montana, John Coulter a Mountain Man and trader and his partner are captured by Blackfeet Indians. Coulter is able to escape, barely, literally as the Indians give him a head-start before giving chase. Coulter has had all his clothing and footwear taken from him. Luckily he is not caught. During the following year, Coulter returns to the region and establishes Fort Three Forks (St. Louis Missouri Fur Company) at the forks of the Missouri River. In New Spain (New Mexico region), a force of Comanches, Cuampes and Kiowas attack a group of Utes and Jicarilla Apaches (allies of the Spanish) along the Arkansas River. Several of the Ute leaders including Chief Delgadito.

January 9 (Monday) In Washington, D.C., the Enforcement Act, designed to toughen the Embargo Acts by implementing harsh penalties for violations, is passed by Congress. The legislation authorizes the confiscation of goods thought to be bound for foreign ports. New Englanders become more incited, as the initial acts have them in dire straits and they believe this will make matters worse. Sentiments expressed by opponents of the bill provoke a string of town meetings that raise loud outcries of the governments' purposeful anti–British posture and pro–French legislating. By the beginning of February, Massachusetts Senator Timothy Pickering, still holding views of his former association as a member of the Essex Junta, proclaims the need for a convention of New Englanders to end the embargo.

February 3 (Friday) The Territory of Illinois is organized. It is carved out of the Indiana Territory and will include the present states of Illinois and Wisconsin and the eastern part of Minnesota.

March 1 (Wednesday) Congress repeals the unpopular Embargo Act of December 22, 1807. This act and two succeeding acts had never won acceptance, and the unrelenting pressure to repeal the legislation finally forces President Jefferson to sign into law the Non-intercourse Act; it becomes effective March 15, but it is only for a duration of about one year. In its place, Congress during May 1810 will enact yet another bill, Macon's Bill Number 2. In England, the people who fared the worst because of the embargo had not been able to vent their frustration, as they were not eligible to vote. And in Europe, the crops had been in abundance, lessening the need for American goods in Britain. The Non-intercourse Act holds an exception that if Great Britain and France revoke their decrees against neutral nations, trade with the U.S. would resume. The act does achieve progress. Later France revokes the Milan and Berlin decrees, effective 1 November 1810. The British, however, balk and inform the U.S. through some ambiguity that Britain's "Orders in Council" would be repealed after France's action takes effect. Nonetheless, Britain procrastinates, insisting that France must make its repeal to include all neutral nations. Subsequently, during 1812, two days before President Madison declares war against England, the British finally repeal the act, too late to prevent hostilities.

March 4 (Saturday) James Madison is inaugurated as the 4th president of the U.S.

March 15 (Wednesday) The Non-intercourse Act becomes effective; it re-establishes the ability of U.S. vessels to engage in commerce with European nations, but France and England, because of their actions against U.S. vessels, are not included. U.S. vessels still are not permitted to deal with the two countries excluded until they halt the practice of interfering with U.S. shipping. In April, President Madison, informed that Britain will halt the practice of interference effective June 10, decides to reinitiate commerce with Britain; however, the agreement between the British minister to the U.S. is disapproved by the British foreign secretary. Madison's action proves to be premature. The treaty never is consummated, compelling Madison, during August, to revert back to the rules of the Non-intercourse Act.

Spring An expedition that moves up the Missouri River is initiated by the Missouri Fur Company. The party includes Pierre Chouteau, military commander, and Andrew Henry, field commander. The expedition also has the task of returning Mandan Chief Shahaka to his land in Dakota in the vicinity of present day Bismarck. Shahaka had come to St. Louis with the Lewis and Clark expedition when it returned from the Pacific.

The expedition force is composed of Americans and Frenchmen, a combustible combination. Fort Lisa, a trading post, is constructed, but it is the French who hold it with the Americans nearby. At one point the Americans lose their arms and ammunition to the French, but before the episode erupts into extended hostilities, the situation is calmed. The expeditioners eventually make it to the mouth of the Big Horn River and establish themselves at Fort Raymond on the Yellowstone River for the winter of 1809–1810.

April 19 (Wednesday) In the United States, a pact is signed on behalf of Great Britain by the minister to the U.S., George Erskine, and by Secretary of State Robert Smith. Erskine, married to an American woman, is pleased to have concluded the pact which mandates that England halt the interception and harassment of U.S. merchant vessels; however, back in England, the treaty will be dismissed as not being in the favor of Great Britain, and it will not be ratified. Nevertheless, in the interim, President Madison will reinstate trade with the British.

May 30 (Tuesday) Britain turns down the agreement consummated on April 19 between British Minister David M. Erskine and the United States. Erskine is recalled and will be replaced during September by Francis J. Jackson, a man who holds a huge ego and a condescending attitude that causes only more tension between the two countries. The U.S. has to again modify its tactics; President Madison reinstates the Non-intercourse Act in retaliation for the British refusal to reinstate civil relations.

June 8 (Thursday) Thomas Paine succumbs in New Rochelle, New York, on a farm which he had received from the government following the American Revolution. Paine's passing is uncelebrated, as many of his writings turned his friends against him, and since his return to the United States from France during 1802, his health was poor and he lived in relative obscurity. Paine's remains are later returned to England; however, his final resting place remains a mystery.

Paine had become friendly with Benjamin Franklin while the latter had been in England and subsequently, during 1774, Paine immigrated to the United States to work with Franklin. Paine had been a true patriot to the American cause, but in the end, his explosive writings had overshadowed his many contributions to the American Revolution. He had not, during the struggle for independence, been a "Sunshine Patriot" who had shrunken from his service to his country.

July 4 (Tuesday) In New Hampshire, an accidental explosion occurs at Fort Constitution in Portsmouth, killing several people and causing some damage at a celebration for Independence Day.

August 9 (Wednesday) President Madison is informed that a proposed treaty between Great Britain and the U.S. was not ratified. The president suspends all trade with Britain.

September Francis James Jackson arrives in the U.S. to become the British foreign minister to the U.S. His initial contacts, defamatory remarks and general demeanor create instant friction Consequently, the talks remain insincere. Following statements that imply the U.S. was aware that the previous minister, Erskine, had overreached his authority, Robert Smith, the secretary of state, ignores him completely. Jackson will be terminated from his post, and it remains vacant for about two years until Britain finally sends a replacement. The new minister, Augustus Foster, arrives in the U.S. in June 1811, just a few weeks following another naval clash.

September 30 (Saturday) The Treaty of Fort Wayne is signed. The agreement, signed by Governor William Henry Harrison of Indiana and the Indians in the southern part of Indiana, cedes more terrain along the Wabash River to the United States.

1810

In Sweden, pressure applied by France compels the Swedes, ruled by King Charles XIII, to sign a treaty (of Paris), essentially guaranteeing a pro–French position. At this time the French are at war with Britain and its allies. One of the French generals, Marshal Jean Baptiste Jules Bernadotte is selected in May by the Swedish Riksdag to succeed Charles XIII as king; however, this move, in an effort to appease Napoleon Bonaparte, never comes to fruition regarding allegiance to France, as Bernadotte will choose during 1813 to join with the allies against the French.

In the meantime, Napoleon pressures Sweden to declare war against Britain. Having little choice, the declaration is reluctantly made, but the Swedes and the British do not actually enter into hostilities during the period lasting until 1812. Nonetheless, Jean-Baptiste Bernadotte is adopted by Charles XIII, and he is selected as Charles' heir. Bernadotte becomes Lutheran and assumes a new name, Charles John (also Carl or Karl Johan). King Charles XIII essentially transfers power to him as regent at this time. Prince Christian of Denmark (Holstein-Augustine) had been selected during January of this year to succeed King Charles; however, he succumbs prematurely during May.

In Mexico, an insurrection against Spanish rule erupts in the province of Guanajuato. The rebellion is led by a Mexican Catholic priest, Miguel Hidalgo y Costilla, with the support of many, including local Indians. Hidalgo's battle flag boasts a picture of the "Blessed Mother" as "Our Lady of Guadalupe." The rebels inflict some defeats upon the Spanish; however, following a victory at Monte de los Cruces during October, the rebels reverse their progress. Rather than advancing toward the original objective, Mexico City, they retire. The Spanish intercept them at Aculco and deliver a punishing defeat. The Spanish again pummel the rebels in January of the following year.

The picture of Our Lady of Guadalupe originated during the Sixteenth Century when the Blessed Mother is said to have appeared to Juan Diego and left an imprint of her image on his cloak. The cloak, made of poor cactus material and unable to last for more than fifty years, still remains in the cathedral in Mexico City. Art experts and other professionals cannot explain the mystery. Scientists also maintain that the colors are not paint.

In Georgia, Fort Jackson, in use for more than one year, receives its name. The fort, built of brick in the vicinity of Savannah, stands where other fortifications had previously stood (one built during 1772 and another during 1792). Fort Jackson, known as Old Fort Jackson is protected by a moat and a drawbridge.

In Idaho, the Missouri Fur Company establishes Fort Henry in the vicinity of St. Anthony. Operations last only about one year.

In Ohio, settlers establish forts in Ohio, including Norftsinger's Blockhouse in present-day Darke County, Carey's Blockhouse in Hardin and Manary's Blockhouse in Bellefontaine. Also, the army establishes Fort Ferree where a former French trading post had stood along the upper Sandusky River.

In Montana, John Coulter, a mountain man and trader who had during the previous year been captured by the Blackfeet and later escaped, establishes Fort Three Forks (St. Louis Missouri Fur Company) this year at the forks of the Missouri River at present-day Three Forks, Montana.

In New York, an arsenal is established at Plattsburgh. It is destroyed by the British during the summer of 1812.

In Washington, the Northwest Company, a fur trading establishment, is built in the vicinity of Nine Mile Falls and named the Spokane House. It remains operational and engages in trading with the Indians until 1823. Within about a year, a competing trading post, Fort Spokane, is established by the Pacific Fur Company at Spokane. Fort Spokane is taken over by the Northwest Company by 1813. By 1821 the two remaining trading companies in the region, Northwest and Hudson Bay Company, merge their operations, and later during 1826, the post is moved to Fort Colville. This Fort Spokane is separate from Fort Spokane established during 1880 at Miles.

March 23 (Friday) **In France,** Napoleon issues what is known as the Rambouillet Decree, empowering the French to confiscate U.S. vessels in French ports. The U.S. roars like a lion, but actually remains timid, limiting its indignation to toothless rhetoric. Then during May, while still being mauled by both Britain and France, President James Madison offers an act which ostensibly is for appeasement, designed to keep the U.S. out of a war.

April The Missouri Fur Company expedition arrives at the Three Forks of the Missouri River from their winter quarters at Fort Raymond on the Yellowstone River. The party intends to trade with the Blackfeet, but also intends to initiate trapping on their own. The party comes under frequent attack by the Blackfeet. The Indians inflict many casualties on the trappers and one, George Drouillard, is decapitated and his body sliced into pieces. The area is soon after abandoned. One group under Pierre Menard moves back to Fort Raymond and another under Andrew Henry moves to the territory near the Columbia River headwaters, where a fort is established (near present day St. Anthony, Idaho). Henry's fort is unsuitable and the combination of Indians and lack of food and supplies nearly costs the loss of all men during the winter of 1810–1811.

April 12 (Thursday) **In Virginia,** Colonel Robert Gamble, a veteran of the American Revolution who survived the war without being injured, is killed when he falls from his horse while riding on a street in Richmond. Colonel Gamble, reading a newspaper while in the saddle, is suddenly thrown when some buffalo hides are tossed from the upper floor of a warehouse into the path of his horse. He lands on his head and goes into a coma from which he never recovers. He is survived by his wife, Catherine, the daughter of Major John Gratton. Catherine was known for her beauty, but also for her pioneer courage. Catherine is known to have ridden through her town (Augusta) in the darkness of night to forewarn her neighbors of a pending Indian raid. The Gambles had relocated in Richmond about 1792 and established their residence on what became known as "Gamble's Hill." During the construction of their home, being built by Colonel John Harvie (Congressman 1778–1779), Colonel Harvie fell from a ladder in 1791 during an inspection of the construction when the ladder broke.

At the time of his death, Gamble had been operating a successful business at 14th and Main Streets with his two sons, John Gratton and Robert. Subsequent to his death, the sons continued running the business; however, the outbreak of war changed circumstances and both followed their father's military career to become officers during the War of 1812. Later during 1827, both brothers moved to Florida. John Gratton married (Miss Duncan) and later he took a daughter of Governor Christopher Greenup of Kentucky as his second wife. Robert married a daughter of General James Breckinridge of Virginia. Agnes, a daughter of Colonel Gamble, married Governor William H. Cabell, who also became a judge on the Supreme Court of Appeals of Virginia. Daughter Elizabeth married William Wirt (attorney general of the U.S.) to become his second wife. Colonel Gamble is interred in the church yard of St. John's in Richmond. His grave site is marked by an "altar-shaped tomb."

April 28 (Saturday) Congress ratifies the Osage Treaty, which had been signed on November 10, 1808. The Osage tribe had agreed to sell their lands (present day Arkansas and Missouri) and move to an Indian reservation at the Arkansas River in what would be the State of Oklahoma.

May 1 (Tuesday) **In the United States,** Congress remains perplexed by the actions of Britain and France against U.S. shipping. The latest pact to fall through between the U.S. and the British has done little to ease the dilemma. The president is preparing to reactivate the Non-intercourse Act, but this day, Congress attempts to forestall this by passing a bill known as Macon's Bill Number Two; the law forbids British and French naval vessels from entering U.S. waters, and it authorizes reinstatement of commerce with Britain and France, but it also gives Madison the option of moving back to the Non-intercourse Act with either country if it interferes with U.S. commerce prior to March 3 of the following year. It is a naive plan, but not to some foreign observers. And there remains great disagreement in the U.S. The Federalists mount opposition to the bill, but they can't prevent it from being passed. Napoleon is informed of the new law during August, and immediately he exploits the situation and pulls an effective ruse on the United States.

August *In naval activity,* Captain John Shaw, a veteran of the Quasi-War with France and now the commander at Norfolk, is transferred to New Orleans. His new orders direct him to prepare the city for an attack by the British in the event war erupts. Shaw remains in the post and participates in General James Wilkinson's campaign of 1813 to seize Mobile, Alabama. In spring 1814, Shaw is transferred to command of a naval squadron in Connecticut. The squadron is on the Thames River between Norwich and New London; however, the vessels are blocked by a British squadron, which prevents Shaw from departing. After the war, Shaw sails in September 1815 for the Mediterranean. He is aboard the USS *United States*, and afterward, when Commodore Bainbridge returns to the U.S., Shaw receives command of the squadron.

August 5 (Sunday) France, having learned of the recently passed U.S. law that reinitiates commerce with France and Great Britain and of the attached conditions, initiates a Napoleonic shell game. Napoleon issues the Trianon Decree which instructs the French Navy to seize all U.S. vessels that have moored in French harbors between May 30, 1809, and May 1 of this year. This decree follows closely on the heels of his Rambouillet Decree, issued on March 23 and publicized on May 14, 1810, that directs his forces to capture and subsequently sell any U.S. vessels in French ports.

Meanwhile, this day, Napoleon also directs his foreign minister to dispatch a letter to the U.S. stating that effective November 1, France will discontinue both the Milan and Berlin Decrees, contingent upon the U.S. implementing a non-intercourse policy toward Britain. The French minister's letter gives the impression that the practice of harassing U.S. vessels has been halted. President Madison takes the bait. During November he reacts by severing trade with Britain.

September 26 (Wednesday) Americans residing at the Spanish port of Florida rebel, capture the Garrison at Baton Rouge, and seek annexation to the United States. The area remains a republic (Republic of West Florida) for a short time until October 27, 1810, then President Madison annexes the land for the United States, joining it with the Territory of Orleans (State of Louisiana in 1812). The United States will also annex East Florida from the Spanish on February 22, 1819.

October 27 (Saturday) President James Madison issues a proclamation authorizing the occupation of West Florida.

November 2 (Friday) President Madison, recently disappointed by the British due to a failed treaty agreement, is now misled by the French. Based on a letter inscribed on August 5 referred to as the "Cardone Letter," Madison, believing France has finally stopped intercepting U.S. vessels in accordance with Macon's Law Number 2 of May 1, 1810, authorizes reinitiation of commerce with France. And in accordance with the terms of Macon's Law Number 2, he informs the British that, effective February 2, 1811, trade with Britain will again cease. Napoleon, using Britain and the United States as stringless marionettes, continues to confiscate U.S. vessels without detection while the British and the Americans slash and parry at each other as they move closer to hostilities.

Meanwhile, King George III, having aged much since the American Revolution, becomes totally insane during November, causing the British-American talks to be tossed on the back burner while the Crown's affairs are being put in order; these unexpected circumstances permit the possibility of a prompt, amicable settlement of differences to dissipate. Nevertheless, no matter which way the U.S. turns, it doesn't seem to be able to find Napoleon under any of the rapidly moving political nutshells. Napoleon's ruse remains undetected until September 1811, when Joseph Barlow, minister to France, arrives in Paris.

1811

In Indiana, Fort Harrison is established at Terre Haute by forces under General William H. Harrison (later president). Another future President, Zachary Taylor of Mexican War fame, is stationed at this fort, and during 1812, his forces repulse an Indian attack. Zachary Taylor's brother died in 1808 while serving in the army. President Thomas Jefferson appointed Zachary as a lieutenant to "fill the vacancy." Zachary, a young man from the backwoods of Kentucky since his parents left Virginia to relocate there, decided to go directly to the White House to thank the president. After arriving there (pre–Secret Service days), Zachary actually began to bang on the door of the White House until a servant finally answered the door and rebuked him for not ringing the bell. Zachary, however, had never encountered a doorbell in Kentucky. Nevertheless, he did get to meet President Jefferson.

His entrance into the army began what became forty years of service; however, at the time he first entered the White House he had no idea that during 1849, he would be living there as the 12th president of the United States.

Other forts, including Fort Vallonia at Vallonia and Fort Turman at Sullivan, are established this year to bolster the efforts against Indian raids. In addition, a fort is established at present-day Fort Branch, Indiana.

In Maine, the Americans establish Fort Madison (later Fort Porter) in honor of President James Madison at Castine in the vicinity of Fort George (separate from Fort George at Brunswick) which had been seized by the British during the American Revolution and later abandoned during 1784. Fort Pentagoet, established by the French during the 1630s, had been in this vicinity until 1688.

In Ohio, settlers construct Sprague's Blockhouse at Florence. Also, Lewis Fort (Old Lewis Fort) is established at Lucerne, a short distance from Fredericktown.

In Oregon, at about this time, the Pacific Fur Company establishes a trading post in the vicinity of present-day Donald, Oregon. By 1813, the American-held firm sells to the Northwest Fur Company, which later merges with the Hudson Bay Company. The trading post had initially been known as Fort Wallace and later as Fort Champooick. When the fur trade begins to fall off and settlers move in the region to establish farms and homes, the town of Champoeg rises. One of the more famous mountain men, Joe Meeks, becomes sheriff subsequent to a town meeting held during 1843 to determine whether Oregon should become affiliated with the U.S. or Canada. Canadians and Americans are at the meeting, but the Americans win out.

In Washington, Fort Okanogan, a trading post, is established by David Stuart for the American Pacific Fur Company, the initial American post in what becomes the state of Washington. The post, however, is acquired by the British-held Hudson Bay Company during 1821. The trading post receives furs from many parts of western Canada via the Okanogan River and then transports them to Vancouver. By about 1838, the post is relocated at a site near the Columbia River. Later, during 1857, gold is discovered in British Columbia, Canada, and Fort Okanogan receives an influx of prospectors speeding to what they hope is their ticket to riches in the Cariboo gold fields. By 1860, the post is abandoned.

In France and Italy, Napoleon II, the son of Napoleon and Empress Marie Louise, becomes king of Rome. He retains the title until 1814, when he becomes the prince of Parma.

January In Louisiana at New Orleans, a contingent of U.S. Marines, commanded by Major Daniel Carmick, moves out from their barracks in search of "Negro insurgents" operating in the county of German Coast slightly outside of New Orleans. The encounter is short-lived. The insurgents flee at the first of approach of the Marines and afterward, when they decide to launch an attack, the insurgents fire momentarily, then again they vanish.

February 2 (Saturday) Russian immigrants land on the West Coast in an area north of San Francisco and establish a trading post to engage in the fur trade; the post is named Fort Ross. Later during 1841 Fort Ross is bought from the Russians by John A. Sutter.

February 11 (Monday) In London, William Pinckney, the U.S. minister to Britain, resigns his post and returns to the United States. Pinckney, an astute attorney from Maryland, has exhausted his patience while attempting to negotiate with the British.

February 20 (Wednesday) Congress fails to renew the charter of the Central Bank (First Bank of the United States). The ongoing friction between the Federalists and Democratic-Republicans continues with the former strongly opposed to the bank because of its ties to England; the majority of stockholders are British. Following heavy debate, the vote for renewal of the charter ends in a tie, tossing it into the hands of the president of the Senate, Vice President Clinton, who casts a no vote. The charter terminates on March 4.

Spring A rescue force departs St. Louis to extricate Andrew Henry's party in the mountains of Idaho at present day St. Anthony. By the latter part of June, the keelboat relief force arrives at the fort in the Mandan villages. Henry arrives there about September. By January of the following year, the Missouri Fur Company reorganizes; however, the investing partners lose some of their enthusiasm due to learning of the hostile Indians and the apparent imminent outbreak of war with Great Britain.

April 2 (Tuesday) James Monroe is appointed secretary of state.

April 12 (Friday) The first permanent settlement on the West Coast, Fort Astor (Astoria Post), named after John J. Astor, is founded at the mouth of the Columbia River in the vicinity of where Lewis and Clark had reached the Pacific Ocean. Astor had founded the Pacific Fur Company. The colonists had relocated from New York and had sailed from there to what is present day Washington State aboard the *Tonquin*, commanded by Captain Jonathan Thorn. He navigated around Cape Horn and the settlers debarked at Cape Disappointment to begin their new lives. The *Tonquin* then departed Astoria to trade with Indians at Vancouver Island, but while there at Nootka Sound, it is attacked by Indians. Apparently, one of the ship's crew, while mortally wounded and the last one alive, detonated the ship's powder magazine, terminating the attack by killing off the Indians and sinking the ship.

After the outbreak of the War of 1812, the British from the Northwest Company, a competitor of Astor, arrive at Fort Astor during 1813 to proclaim news of the war. Shortly thereafter, the British dispatch a naval force to seize Fort Astor. However, the American company sells the fort to the Northwest Company, which later merges with the Hudson Bay Company. Consequently, the fort changes hands and becomes Fort George.

May 1–16 The American vessel *Spitfire* is boarded by the British off Maine. The British forcibly take an American sailor on board the HMS *Guerriere*, causing the infuriated Americans to dispatch the USS *President* to search for and destroy the *Guerriere*. American Captain John Rodgers, commanding the 44-gun *President*, encounters a British warship while cruising off Sandy Hook. The vessel detected, thought to be the *Guerriere*, is another ship. Nevertheless, the *President* prepares for battle. Suddenly the guns are rapidly firing following an opening shot of unknown origin. At one point, the more powerful *President* is ordered to cease fire; however, the British resume their fire. Consequently, Commodore Rodgers reactivates his guns and the *Little Belt* receives more thunderous fire that rakes the British ship and renders it out of action. Dusk arrives and the *President* remains dormant until the following morning. At dawn, a party boards the ship, which turns out to be the *Little Belt*. Both the Americans and the English claim the opposing side fired first. It is a long, drawn out diplomatic battle over who shot first and who will pay reparations, but one thing is clear, war between the United States and Great Britain is imminent. The British sustain 31 casualties killed or wounded; the British reject help offered by the Americans. In contrast, the *President* sustains one casualty, a young boy is wounded. After the encounter in which the British refuse any assistance, both ships sail off for their respective friendly ports. Subsequently, the opposing commanders testify to widely different versions of what transpired; however, the respective nations each accept the version delivered by their commander. War is not declared by either the British or the United States; however, it becomes apparent that the conflict is imminent.

June 4 (Tuesday) In Canada, Colonel Isaac Brock is promoted to the rank of major general. Another British officer, Sheaffe, is also promoted to major general. In October, Lt. Governor Francis Gore (Upper Canada) departs for England. General Brock becomes president of Upper Canada and administrator in Gore's absence. His new responsibilities will make him the military commander as well as head of the civil government.

July At Vincennes, Indiana, settlers wary of being attacked by the Shawnee Indians lay plans to attack their encampment along the Tippecanoe River. There has long been speculation that the ongoing hostilities, including scalping, have been instigated by the British military command in Canada. It is understood by the settlers that the British have been paying the Indians $5 to $6 per scalp with no exceptions, placing even women and children at risk. The allegation has never been substantiated, but at this time it is accepted as fact. Other factors are also included as the settlers widen their perimeters and encroach upon the Canadian fur trading with the Indians. These incidents parallel the ongoing crisis among the U.S., France and Britain; these frontier problems only add to the concerns of President James Madison, who is moving ever so carefully to avoid war.

August 5 (Monday) In Indiana, Tecumseh, along with twenty Indians, including two Creeks, departs from Vincennes en route to visit the Creeks and Choctaws to convince them to join with the British against the United States. After he completes his mission about August–September 1812, he returns by way of the Missouri River. During his return, Tecumseh also visits with the Osage Indians.

August 24 (Saturday) In Louisiana at New Orleans, Major Daniel Carmick, a U.S. Marine, in a letter to the commandant, Lieutenant Colonel Franklin Wharton, mentions that the plague is taking the lives of five people a day in the city of New Orleans; however, he notes that his Marine contingent has "been more fortunate." Nevertheless, the next month, the Marines lose two officers, 1st Lt. Francis Thornton, and 2nd Lt.

William Pinckney.

Robert B. Ridle, and 16 enlisted men. In October, 16 additional men are killed by the disease. On 18 October, the commander of the Marines in New Orleans states in a letter: "The fever still rages here. It is almost certain death for a stranger to enter the city."

September 18 (Wednesday) The U.S. minister to France, Joel Barlow, arrives in France with instructions to determine the status of the Berlin and Milan Decrees, thought by President Madison to have been rescinded by Napoleon Bonaparte. To his dismay, Barlow learns through the French foreign minister, Duc de Bassano, that the Decree of St. Cloud, which had rescinded the two decrees, had been issued and approved by Napoleon on April 28, 1811; it had been retroactive, becoming effective on November 1, 1810. Nevertheless, the document had not been made public, nor forwarded to the American government. The Decree of St. Cloud had been drawn as one more part of the Napoleonic ruse to sting the United States and Britain simultaneously. The severing of mutual commerce by the United States enrages the British and the recent incident between the British Royal Navy and the USS *Spitfire* fuels the fires of war in the United States. The collision course is set. And with the federal bank having been dissolved during March by Congress, the U.S. will face huge financial problems as it attempts to get on a war footing to engage the British.

Autumn Captain William Bainbridge of the U.S. Navy embarks on a second journey to St. Petersburg, Russia. Bainbridge is on a mission including mercantile negotiations, and he intends to remain in Russia until the following spring. While there, he receives information regarding the engagement between the USS *United States* and the HMS *Little Belt* of May 1811. Bainbridge, anticipating war, decides to return home as soon as possible; however, the Baltic Sea is frozen, leaving him with the option of remaining in Russia or initiating his journey by an overland route to Sweden, where he will be able to embark on an American merchant ship.

Bainbridge, before departing on a journey of about 1,100 miles, meets with John Q. Adams at the court of St. Petersburg. Adams provides Bainbridge with authorization as a courier of document for the minister at the court of St. James. During his time in Russia, Bainbridge had acquired a close friendship with Doctor Jacques Wylie, the personal physician of Emperor Alexander, and through the relationship, Bainbridge is provided with Russian protection by Count Romanskoff. A Russian officer accompanies Bainbridge until they reach the frontier of Sweden. Bainbridge is inundated with letters that include those for various leaders which he received from the Russian premier, Romanskoff, to Baron Nicholn, the Russian minister at Sweden, and yet other correspondence for General Steingal, the governor and Captain General of Finland.

The trip is dangerous, dreary and dreadful. No public houses are along the route. Bainbridge's carriage travels all day and through the nights. After arriving at Abo on the Gulf of Bothnia, the weather continues to hinder his progress. Ice prevents him from moving to Stockholm by water. After a hazardous trip by ferry — the carriage disassembled and carried by several boats — to Alands, the carriage is reassembled.

He finally makes it to Stockholm; however, the obstacles continue to mount. While en route to Gotheburg, the driver of the carriage becomes careless and the carriage goes over a cliff of about 30 feet. The driver is killed, along with one of the horses, and the carriage is demolished. Bainbridge sustains some serious bruises. Undaunted, Bainbridge ignores his injuries and the intolerable weather as he resumes his trek. Finally, he arrives at Gotheburg on 20 December 1811. Later on 31 December, he embarks aboard a British warship that is sailing as part of a squadron.

Despite having overcome the elements and the other pitfalls, Bainbridge finds little comfort at sea. A terrible storm strikes the squadron on its second day at sea while the ships are off the coast of Jutland. One British three decker and a frigate are consumed by the wicked seas. Bainbridge's vessel escapes for the moment, but it too becomes endangered until Bainbridge manages to persuade the British captain to change course and sail toward Normandy. The ship escapes disaster, but new perils soon emerge. While the vessel moves through the channel separating the Orneys and Shetland Islands, again it is nearly lost. However, Bainbridge, despite being an American on the British warship, "countermands" an order of the captain while huge breakers appear. Bainbridge's actions save the ship and it finally arrives at Liverpool. Those aboard the endangered ship thank Bainbridge profusely for saving their lives. Bainbridge delivers his correspondence, then he embarks for Boston, where he arrives during February 1812.

Bainbridge, who literally risked his life to get back to America to participate in the imminent conflict, discovers after arriving in Washington that there is great trepidation and a decision has been made to keep all naval vessels in port once the war begins. Captain Bainbridge receives orders to assume command of the Boston Navy Yard; however, the distressing news regarding the navy prompts him in June 1812 to align with Captain Charles Stewart to take on the secretary of the Navy, the president and his cabinet to persuade them of the value of the navy against the British Royal Navy.

November 4 (Monday) Congress convenes. This 12th Congress faces a deluge of problems. Still the French and English are harassing U.S. vessels, with no end in sight. In the West, the Indians are involved with hostilities against the settlers and Congress itself has again been transformed, the election having swept out many representatives. In their place now stand some who become known as "Warhawks," who defiantly push for a stand against Britain and for the annexation of Florida. The Warhawks are separated into two groups, those from Southern states who desire the remainder of Florida, not yet under the Stars and Stripes, and those from the Northwest, intent on invading and seizing Canada.

The Democratic-Republicans still control both Houses. However, the newest Congressmen are not inclined to continue being slammed around by the British. Henry Clay will be selected as speaker of the House due to the efforts of the Warhawks, and he immediately begins to establish committees controlled by Congressmen of similar ideas; this maneuver lays the foundation for the steps to war which they believe is imminent. And they realize the country lacks the ability to engage in war against the ruler of the seas, Great Britain, because of the critical shortage of troops and ships.

November 5 (Tuesday) American ships are being further harassed by both British and French vessels, causing President Madison to emphasize in his speech to Congress the necessity of being prepared in the event of war. At this time the American Army is ill-prepared and the American Navy quite small.

November 6 (Wednesday) In Indiana, General William Henry Harrison's forces advance to a point about five miles from Prophet's Town. Once the objective is discovered, Harrison places his troops on alert and some are deployed to ensure the Indians do not launch a surprise attack. Meanwhile, Captain Dubois is dispatched under a white flag after interpreters were turned back. The Indians attempt to cut off Dubois' party. The Indians fail to trap Dubois; however, they succeed in infuriating General Harrison, who considers the Indians' action as hostile. Harrison immediately after the incident plans an attack. Before the Americans launch the assault, several chiefs approach Harrison's positions ostensibly to keep peace. An agreement is reached whereby hostilities would be delayed until the following day. Harrison, keenly aware of Indian treachery, redeploys his force above Prophet's Town; however, he selects an advantageous position in the event the Indians break their word. His instincts prove true. After dusk, the chiefs gather in council and decide to strike the American camp while the troops are asleep.

November 7 (Thursday) BATTLE OF TIPPECANOE In Indiana, during the predawn hours, the Indians disregard a truce they requested on the previous day and close against General Harrison's camp. The early morning sky is heavily overcast and a sporadic pesky rain is falling as the Indians creep close to the sleeping troops. However, the guards are awake and alert. Private Stephen Mars, a Kentuckian, spots the approaching Indians and fires a warning shot. The timely warning permits the troops to quickly rise to meet the threat which is upon them. The Indian war whoops are heard just after Mars' shot is fired. During the first moments of the surprise attack, Harrison, already awake, flies to the first horse he spots and speeds to the point being struck. Indian pressure pushes back the guards; however, the regulars under Colonel John Parker Boyd hold steady against the onslaught. Meanwhile, General Harrison arrives, and he rallies all of his troops. Afterward, the Indians are met by muskets and bayonets.

The Indians lose some of their impetuousness when they meet the bayonets in close quarters and the Americans drive them back after some ferocious combat. The Indians repeatedly press forward, but each time, they are repulsed. Major Davis and Colonel Isaac White both sustain mortal wounds during the melee. General Harrison crashes into the left wing of the Indians and strikes their right with two companies. The Indians by that time are overwhelmed. They take flight and Harrison has his victory in hand by dawn.

The Americans lose 39 dead and 151 wounded. The attack is led by Tecumseh's brother, Prophet (Elskwatawa). After repelling the attack, General Harrison destroys Prophet's Town the following day.

During the battle of Tippecanoe, General Harrison is checking the battle lines. As he approaches a young soldier about to fire his weapon, Harrison inquires: "Where's your captain?" "Dead, sir." "Your lieutenant?" "Dead, sir." "Your ensign?" "Here, sir." Inspired by this action, Harrison remains, rallying his men to victory.

Following the battle at the Wabash River, Harrison's troops discover weapons conspicuously marked with fresh British insignia, which amplifies the American cries for war. The frontiersmen seek revenge for the loss of their families to the tomahawk and for the British-inflicted indignities on the high seas. The victory at Tippecanoe terminates the hostilities, and later, Tecumseh, renounced by various tribes, is compelled to sue for peace.

November 8 (Friday) Americans under General William Henry Harrison (later president of the United States) burns Prophet's Town, which had been established by Tecumseh and his

The Prophet.

brother, the Prophet, during 1808. Prophet's Town was the capital of Tecumseh and his brother's pan–Indian Confederacy. Various Indian representatives of the midwestern tribes either spent time there or trained there to resist American encroachment. Nonetheless, Harrison's victory, along with the destruction of the Indians' capital, terminates the once formidable confederacy.

November 12 (Tuesday) Following years of on-again, off-again negotiations, the British and U.S. agree to settle the matter regarding the British attack on the USS *Chesapeake*, which had occurred June 22, 1807. The U.S. had agreed to settle during November, but Britain declined the proposal to rescind the order in council. Secretary of State James Monroe accepts the British counterproposal on behalf of the United States, but it seems to be too little too late.

December In Maryland at Fredericksburg, the court-martial of General James Wilkinson, which began the previous September, continues. Wilkinson had been charged with the conspiracy of Aaron Burr with regard to land deals in the western territory. The court adjourns on Christmas Day. Wilkinson is acquitted. General Peter Gansevoort, who had been the presider, departs for home; however, he becomes ill en route. Gansevoort arrives back at his home, but he never completely regains his health. He dies on 2 July 1812.

December 26 (Thursday) In Virginia, Governor George William Smith dies in a fire at the Richmond Theater. Peyton Randolph, senior member of the Council of State, becomes acting executive of Virginia; however, shortly thereafter, the Virginia Assembly, which is in session, elects James Barbour as governor on 3 January 1812. Peyton Randolph was the son of Governor Edmund Randolph.

1812

Although there is much dissent in New England regarding support for the war, the British express little empathy for those who might not want to participate. British warships frequently bombard New England. One such place is Rockport, Massachusetts. A harbor fort there (Old Stone Fort) on far edge of Bearskin Neck (Sandy Bay) becomes a frequent target of the British Navy.

In Washington, Gouverneur Morris and DeWitt Clinton, the president and vice president of the board of internal navigation, respectively, appoint Le Ray de Chaumont representative for a mission to Europe to try to secure a loan of $6 million to build the Erie Canal. After arriving in Switzerland, word of the declaration of war against Great Britain causes the investors to decline making the loan. Subsequently, Le Ray journeys to negotiate the loan with Belgian bankers, but there, too, the bankers believe that peace is out of range because of the re-election of President James Madison. The Belgians also decline making the loan.

In Georgia, the U.S. Navy acquires a brigantine, the 16-gun USS *Troup*, at Savannah. The navy assigns it to duty as a guard and receiving ship. The *Troup* sees no action. It remains in Savannah for the duration of the war. In 1815 it is sold.

In other activity at about this time, the Americans establish Fort Pickering near Coleraine (Charlton County), and it is apparently con-

Gouverneur Morris.

structed at the site where a Revolutionary post, Fort Tonyn, stood.

In Maryland, General Perry Benson, a veteran of the American Revolution, will be appointed commander of the militia in several counties (Talbot, Caroline and Dorchester).

In Massachusetts, Fort Lee, on the western end of a causeway that leads toward Winter Island, is established near Salem. It is designed to guard Beverly Harbor and a section of Salem Harbor. Salem is a major home base for many privateers during the war. Some document precise times of capturing British shipping, but others leave lesser documentation regarding specifics. The privateer *Nancy*, under Captain R. Smart, captures the brigantine *Resolution*, which is transporting a cargo of flour, and sails it into Portland. Another, the *Thomas Pickering*, is known to have seized the vessel *Eliza Ann*, which is sailed into Eastport. Not long after the *Eliza Ann* had been taken into port, a British warship, the HMS *Martin*, arrived to demand its return, and the townspeople were informed that if it was not returned, the town would be reduced. Nevertheless, the Americans essentially dare the British to strike and they do, however, not nearly as forcibly as the Americans, who return fire and cause the British to retire. The *Pickering* is also credited with the seizure of the brigantine *Dart*.

In Ohio, the practice of establishing settlers' forts and Army forts continues in the territory as the U.S. braces for another conflict with Britain, as well as the ongoing conflict between the settlers and the Indians. The forts and blockhouses established this year are Fort McArthur at Kenton, Fort Findlay at Findlay, Fort Portage at Grand Rapids, Fort Stephenson at Fremont, Fort Murray at Jeromesville, and Fort Necessity at Williamstown, only several miles from Fort McArthur. Also, Fort Defiance, established during 1794 and later abandoned, is discovered to be dilapidated; however, the army decides to reconstruct it at a site less than 100 yards away. It is renamed Fort Winchester. Others include Beall's Camp at Canton, Green Camp at Green Camp, Grand Prairie Blockhouse at Prospect, Fort Morrow at Waldo, Bellville Post at Bellville, Berlin Blockhouse at Cheshire (settlers fort), Clinton's Blockhouse at Clinton, Coulter's Blockhouse (vicinity of Perrysville), Fredericktown Blockhouse at Fredericktown, Miller's Blockhouse at Chesterville (settlers fort), Mount Vernon Blockhouse at Mount Vernon, Starks Corner Blockhouse at Kingston in Delaware County north of Columbus, Simon's Blockhouse (settlers fort) at Huron, Hudson's Blockhouse at Hudson (settlers fort), Lake Fork Blockhouse (vicinity of Mohickanville), Levering Blockhouse at Waterford, Lewis' Blockhouse (vicinity of Butler), Beam's Blockhouse, Mansfield's Blockhouse and Shaffer's Blockhouse (all three at Mansfield), New Dover Blockhouse at New Dover, Wayne Blockhouse at Green Valley in the vicinity of Mount Vernon Blockhouse, Wooster's Blockhouse at Wooster, New Haven Camp at New Haven, Trucksville Post at Ganges, Camp Council (vicinity of Shenandoah), Camp Whetstone (vicinity of Olivesburg) and Workman's Blockhouse at Danville.

During the War of 1812, the Americans continue to fortify their positions in Ohio and in some cases, the exact dates for the establishment of forts and blockhouses are uncertain. Some of these include Fort Jennings at Fort Jennings, Fort Brown in the vicinity of Melrose that supports a series of forts including Amanda (at Wapakoneta), Winchester (formerly Defiance at Defiance) and Fort Meigs (built during 1813) at Perrysburg.

In Oregon, in November, a party from Astoria, Washington, composed of about fifteen men and affiliated with the American Pacific Fur Company establishes Williamette Post in the Williamette Valley (Marion County). The following year, while the War of 1812 is ongoing, the company sells its interests to the British-held Northwest Company. At that time it becomes known as the Henry House.

In Virginia, John Floyd, a native of Kentucky, born during April 1783 in Jefferson County and the son of Colonel John Floyd (Revolutionary War era), is appointed as brigadier general of militia.

January 11 (Saturday) **In Washington, D.C.,** Congress, in anticipation of imminent conflict with Great Britain, passes an act "to raise an additional military force." Congress authorizes the "immediate establishment of ten regiments of infantry, two of artillery, and one of light dragoons for the period of five years." The legislation places the infantry regiments' numbers at 1,800 privates per regiment, while the artillery regiments are to contain 1,440 privates and the dragoon regiments are to contain 960 privates. Each of the regiments will contain a full complement of non-commissioned officers and musicians. In addition, the legislation provides for two major generals and five brigadier generals, along with an adjutant general and an inspector general, with both positions being accompanied with the rank of brigadier general. The legislation establishes a judge-advocate for each army division with the rank of major.

January 27 (Monday) **In Washington,** President James Madison, convinced that war with the British is imminent, appoints Henry Dearborn as first major general. He receives command of the Northern Department. General Dearborn, a veteran of the American Revolution, had studied medicine and opened his practice in Nottingham Square. After the war, Dearborn moved to Maine and later rose to the rank of major general of militia. He also served in Congress (Democratic-Republican, present-day Democrat, 1793–1797). During the Jefferson administration, Dearborn served as secretary of war (1801–1808).

At about this time, General James Wilkinson, a Revolutionary War veteran, known for his close association with Aaron Burr and his involvement in the Conway Cabal, an attempt to oust General Washington, is dispatched to New Orleans to replace General Wade Hampton (grandfather of Confederate General Wade Hampton) at New Orleans. Other promotions that follow include Joseph Bloomfield (New Jersey), John Armstrong (Pennsylvania), James Winchester (Tennessee), William Hull (governor of Michigan Territory), Thomas Flournoy (Georgia), John Chandler (Maine), Morgan Lewis (New York) and Alexander Smyth (Virginia), all promoted to the rank of brigadier general. Thomas Humphrey Cushing is named adjutant general and Alexander Macomb is promoted to colonel. Other officers promoted to lieutenant colonel are Edmund P. Gaines, Eleazar Wheelock Ripley and Winfield Scott.

January 30 (Thursday) **In North Carolina,** Brigadier General John Scott dies.

In naval activity, the HMS *Surveillante*, sailing with the HMS *Sybille* (Captain C. Upton) and the HMS *Spitfire*, intercepts and seizes the American vessel *Zone*.

February **In Canada,** Major General Isaac Brock, the minister of Upper Canada, senses that war is approaching and makes a statement at the opening of a session of the legislature at York that includes his "hope that cool reflection and the dictates of justice may yet avert the calamities of war." He urges the importance of early adopting such measures as will "best secure the internal peace of the country, and defeat every hostile aggression."

General Brock, a seasoned veteran with service in the 19th Regiment in Europe and in the West Indies, had wanted to transfer back to Europe; however, during this year when the opportunity is presented to him by Sir George Prevost (governor general), he declines going to England due to the high probability of imminent war. He chooses to remain in Canada.

February 6 (Thursday) **In Washington, D.C.,** Congress passes the third act since the previous December that provides land grants for those who serve in the military. The previous acts passed on December 24, 1811, and January 11, 1812. The act passed this day authorizes the president to call up 50,000 men as volunteers for the regular army to serve for one year. In the event of death in combat or while on active duty, the deceased soldier's (non-commissioned officers and enlisted men) heirs are to receive tracts of 160 acres.

On 6 May, Congress authorizes 6,000,000 acres of land to be surveyed for the purpose of fulfilling the obligations established by the acts. The selected territory includes two million acres in the Michigan Territory and identical amounts in Illinois and Louisiana; however, after the war, Congress modifies its action on 29 April 1816 when the land bounties in Michigan are repealed and "that in lieu thereof 1,500,000 acres should be laid off in the Illinois Territory, and 500,000 acres in the Missouri Territory, north of the river Missouri."

One of the new units is the Michigan Legion, composed primarily of Frenchmen. The outfit contains three infantry companies commanded by Captains Antoine Deqolodre, Hubert la Croll, Stephen Mack, and Richard Smythe. The legion also contains one company of dragoons, commanded by Captain Richard Smythe.

Command changes also take effect. At about this time, Captain George Izard is promoted to the rank of colonel with command of the 2nd Artillery. Winfield Scott is appointed lieutenant colonel of the regiment. Later, Izard is promoted to brigadier general and Lt. Colonel Scott assumes command of the regiment. General Izard receives command of the 3rd Military District in April 1813.

February 21 (Friday) **In Louisiana,** the *Louisiana Gazette* publishes the 21 articles of association of the Missouri Fur Company, established by Manuel Lisa. During this year in Nebraska, Manuel Lisa, who had earlier established Fort Lisa (Fort Manuel) in Montana, establishes Fort Lisa in Nebraska near Omaha. Lisa, a fur trader, operates the Missouri Fur Company based in St. Louis. Unlike some of the traders, Lisa is known to have treated the Indians especially well, and he often acted as intermediary between the Indians and the U.S. He succumbs during 1820 at the age of 48.

March 8 (Sunday) David E. Twiggs receives a commission through the intervention of his father as captain in the U.S. 8th Infantry. Captain Twiggs served for the duration and later served under General Andrew Jackson in the Indian wars that followed.

March 12 (Thursday) **In Washington, D.C.,** Congress establishes a quartermaster's department for the United States Army. It will consist of a quartermaster general, supplemented by four deputy quartermaster generals. The act also authorizes the creation of as many assistant deputy quartermasters as the president believes necessary, and the legislation provides the president the authority to appoint up to four additional deputy quartermasters if he believes it to be necessary. The act stipulates "that in addition to their duties in the field, it shall be the duty of the quartermaster-general, his deputies and assistant deputies, when thereto directed by the Sec'retary of War, to purchase military stores, camp equipage, and other articles requisite for the troops, and generally to procure and provide means of transport for the army, its stores, artillery, and camp equipage."

In other activity, Eleazar Wheelock Ripley, a practicing lawyer in Portland, Maine, and a member of the Massachusetts legislature (1810–1812), relinquishes his public life to join the army as lieutenant colonel of the 21st U.S. Infantry Regiment. On 12 March of the following year, he is promoted to colonel. Stephen Kearny (later a general in the Mexican War) is appointed lieutenant of the U.S. 13th Infantry Regiment. He serves for the duration.

In Georgia, U.S. troops take control of Amelia Island off the Georgia coast. This Spanish island remains under American control until U.S. troops withdraw during May 1813. John Clarke, a veteran (lieutenant) of the American Revolution and the son of Colonel Elijah Clarke, will be elevated from brigadier general to major general (Georgia militia) by the outbreak of the conflict. John, who participated at the siege of Augusta and later during 1787 at the Battle of Jack's Creek, receives responsibility for protecting the Georgia seacoast.

March 16 (Monday) **In Pennsylvania,** volunteer units across the country are beginning to form. On this day, a contingent of volunteers named the Benevolent Blues inform Governor Simon Snyder that the unit is volunteering to serve. The unit is commanded by Captain Henry Read.

March 17 (Tuesday) **In Florida,** a contingent of troops from Georgia known as the Patriots ford the St. Mary's River and push into Spanish East Florida. The little band composed of slightly under 200 men occupies Rose's Bluff across from St. Mary's, Georgia. The force can see Amelia Island from the bluff, which they enter and seize from a sparse Spanish garrison deployed there. Once the Patriots take control of Amelia Island, they plan to hand it over to the United States on the following day, which essentially begins to place Florida under American control. At present, East Florida remains a Spanish possession and West Florida is controlled by the British.

March 18 (Wednesday) **In Florida,** the Georgians (Patriots) who entered Florida on the previous day and seized Amelia Island hold a formal ceremony regarding the captured island. The leader of the Patriot Army, composed of fewer than 200 men, John H. McIntosh, acting on his authority as the leader of the new government, delivers a thunderous speech in which he proposes to cede the island to the United States government. Brigadier General George Matthews of Georgia, the U.S. commissioner, also delivers a rousing speech, and he accepts the island on behalf of the United States. Afterward, Lt. Colonel Thomas A. Smith, U.S. Army, assumes command of the troops in Florida.

In related activity, U.S. troops, including Army and Marine Corps contingents, move into Florida via the St. Mary River. This venture is known as the "Patriot's War." An unsuccessful attack will be launched against the Spanish at St. Augustine, but the Americans will seize Fort San Nicholas (1812) along the St. Johns River during the attack against St. Augustine. The Americans remain in Florida until 6 May 1813. As the U.S. is being intimidated by the British, who have been imprisoning American seamen, the Americans are also pressured by the Spanish in Florida, who are inciting Indians. There is serious concern about Spanish intentions of seizing Georgia while the United States is facing still another threat from Britain. At this time, Spain remains an ally of the British.

The Americans hold a base (Battery at Point Peter) at Kings Bay about sixty miles north of Savannah. It had been constructed during the 1790s, but now it could be jeopardized by either the Spanish or the British.

In other activity, Colonel Thomas A. Smith, writes to Secretary of War William Eustis that he had dispatched a contingent of 50 troops to Amelia Island and to Fernandina due to General Matthews' belief that a British contingent is being prepared to "occupy the military posts within East Florida." Smith, concerned about the "propriety of exceeding my instructions," said he would not attack any post until further ordered,

Governor Joseph Bloomfield (*History of Middlesex County, New Jersey*, Lewis Historical Publishing Company, Inc., 1921).

"as I consider the order imperative as to occupying & defending places peaceably surrendered, I shall do it to the last extremity." Nevertheless, Smith also informs the secretary of the condition, stating: "If Amelia Island or the Town of San. Ferdinandina is not defended by suitable works provided with necessary artillery, it may be destroyed at any time a Naval Force superior to the Gun Boats at present on this station may think proper to attack it." Colonel Smith also requests that arms and ammunition be forwarded as soon as possible. Smith makes it clear that the available rifles are unable to fire. There are also shortages of bayonets and clothing.

March 19 (Thursday) **In Florida,** General Mathews, with a contingent of Marines led by Captain Williams and army regulars under Lt. Colonel Thomas A. Smith, take control of Amelia Island and Fernandina. Afterward, Lt. Colonel Smith departs from the island and moves toward St. Augustine. Meanwhile, the Marine contingent remains in place to hold the ground.

March 27 (Friday) **In Washington,** President Madison appoints Thomas Pinckney of South Carolina as second major general. He receives

Major General Thomas Pinckney.

command of the Southern Department (North Carolina, South Carolina and Georgia). General Pinckney, a veteran of the Revolutionary War, had afterward served as governor of South Carolina, minister to England and as a special envoy to Spain. At the time of his appointment, President Madison, for his own purposes, favored Pinckney in great part because he was a conspicuous Federalist. General Pinckney remains active throughout the conflict, but his primary contribution is providing support to General Jackson during the Creek War.

In New Jersey, Governor (brigadier general of militia) Joseph Bloomfield is appointed brigadier general in the U.S. Army. He remains in active service until discharged on 15 June 1815.

April The Indians initiate another series of attacks on settlers in the Northwest Territory. General William Hull assumes command of the Army of the Northwest, in preparation for war with Great Britain. There is still much thought of an American invasion of Canada, thought to be an easy prey for the frontiersmen who are convinced they must eradicate British presence to terminate the continuing hostilities of the Indians. General Hull is a veteran of the American Revolution who as a young officer had exhibited courage and gallantry at the battles of Saratoga and Stony Point.

He had requested that his command be composed of 3,000 troops for the expedition; however, Washington informs him that 2,000 are all that can be spared. The force of his army stands at about 2,000 troops (including Ohio troops that join him in May) at this time and is composed of three companies of the U.S. 3rd Artillery Regiment, three regiments of Ohio volunteers, one company of rangers and the Michigan militia. Hull later arrives at Dayton, Ohio, where the 1,200 volunteers join him; however, they lack sufficient arms, equipment and even clothing.

Early April In Washington, D.C., Governor William Hull of the Michigan Territory, while in the capital and acutely aware that war was imminent, requested strongly for President Madison to dispatch a large number of troops into the Northwest. He also had repeatedly urged the president to consider as a priority the establishment of a fleet on Lake Erie. At about this time, the president, having pondered Hull's suggestions, directs Ohio Governor Return J. Meigs to provide 1,200 troops for immediate service at Detroit, which would become a primary objective of the British once hostilities open. The president takes other steps. He appoints Commander Stewart as agent on Lake Erie and he delegates Stewart with the construction of ships to be used in defense of American territory. On 8 April, Governor Hull is commissioned as brigadier general and given command of the Ohio troops.

April 4 (Saturday) Congress places an embargo on all vessels in U.S. posts in anticipation of the outbreak of hostilities between the U.S. and Great Britain.

General William Hull.

In other activity, Brigadier General George Mathews, the U.S. commissioner who accepted Amelia Island from the Georgia Patriots on behalf of the United States the previous month, is succeeded by Georgia Governor David B. Mitchell.

In naval activity, the HMS *Emulous* intercepts and captures the *Cossac* (John Upton, master), a schooner which had sailed from Salem, Massachusetts.

April 6 (Monday) **In Georgia,** at the Creek Agency, Colonel Hawkins reports that on 26 March, Thomas Meredith, while en route to the Mississippi Territory with his family, was killed along the Kittomea Creek. He is buried on the property of Sam Macnac, who claims it was an accident. Nonetheless, the Indian responsible for the murder is caught and put to death on 19 July of this year.

April 6 to August 22 *In naval activity,* it is noted in one of the New York City newspapers that 266 American merchant ships arrived safely in New York. They include 84 brigantines, 40 schooners and 142 ships, all of which evaded British ships.

April 7 (Tuesday) **In Florida,** Lt. Colonel Smith, having recently departed Amelia Island, arrives at Picolata on the St. Johns River. The town surrenders to Smith on the 12th.

April 8 (Wednesday) **In Florida,** Brigadier General George Mathews (former governor of Georgia) at Picolata, located along the St. Johns River west of St. Augustine, writes to Lt. Colonel Thomas A. Smith, U.S Army:

> Dear Sir: By virtue of the powers vested in me as U. States Commissioner, with which you are furnished a copy, I have to request you to march tomorrow, or as soon thereafter as possible, to Moosa Old Fort, a military station in the vicinity of St. Augustine, with the troops under your command to hold & defend the same & the country adjacent it being ceded to the U. States by the local constituted authorities (Georgia Patriots) of E. Florida, & accepted by me as U. States Commissioner. You will please to have such Detachment at this station as you deem adequate to hold and defend for the U. States.

April 10 (Friday) President Madison, on authorization of Congress, calls up a 100,000 man militia for six months' service.

April 12 (Sunday) **In Washington, D.C.,** Congress, which had authorized increasing the size of the army during the previous January, authorizes five more infantry regiments — one regiment composed of riflemen, one of dragoons and one artillery regiment.

In Canada, General Sir George Prevost establishes a regiment, the Voltigeurs, a light infantry unit, composed of all Canadians. Lt. Colonel Charles de Salaberry receives command. Headquarters is established at Fort Chamby. The regiment contains ten companies. Although the companies contain French and British troops, all orders are issued in English.

In Florida, Lt. Colonel Thomas A. Smith, following a harrowing journey, debarks at Moosa Old Fort. While en route, Colonel Smith paused along Six Mile Creek to drop off supplies under a sergeant's guard. Shortly after debarking at the old fort, the Georgia Patriots holding the place transfer it to Smith's command at 1600. At the same time, the troops hoist the American flag.

April 13 (Monday) **In Florida** at Fort Mose (Moosa Old Fort), a Spanish gunboat fires at Lt. Colonel Thomas A. Smith's positions during the morning; however, once the U.S. flag is hoisted, the gunboat withdraws.

April 14 (Tuesday) **In Florida,** Lt. Colonel Thomas A. Smith, at Moosa Old Fort, in a letter dated this day to the Secretary of War William Eustis, informs the secretary of his journey from Picolata and of the recent activity after arriving at the post on the 12th. Thomas also informs the secretary about the location of the post, stating that it is less than three miles from St. Augustine.

Also, General Mathews dispatches a flag to the Spanish lines, which was sent back. The Spanish have requested reinforcements from Bermuda and from Cuba. Colonel Smith also tells the secretary that once the fresh troops arrive, he will have to retire, but he assures Secretary Eustis that he will oppose the enemy until the Georgia volunteers arrive to bolster his force.

April 15 (Wednesday) **In Washington, D.C.,** William Eustis, secretary of war, distributes a circular letter to the various states regarding their quotas of militia. Some of the New England states are reluctant to cooperate with the federal government.

April 20 (Monday) **In Washington, D.C.,** Vice President George Clinton, 73, dies while in his office at about 0900. The office of vice president remains vacant for the remainder of President James Madison's first term. Vice President Clinton is interred at the Congressional Cemetery in the capital on 21 April. In 1908, his remains are reinterred next to his wife, Cornelia, in Kingston, New York, at the cemetery of the First Dutch Reformed Church. Clinton had been a general during the American Revolution, and he also served as governor of New York and as a member of Congress.

April 21 (Tuesday) **In Washington, D.C.,** the War Department issues a general order that divides the New York detached militia into two divisions, composed of four brigades each. General Stephen Van Rensselaer is appointed overall commander. Van Rensselaer, lacking military experience, accepts the position with the condition that his cousin, Colonel Solomon Van Rensselaer, adjutant general of New York, be appointed his "aide and counselor." Colonel Solomon Van Rensselaer had participated in the campaign of General Anthony Wayne in the northwest during 1794.

Stephen Van Rensselaer is commissioned major general. He commands the 1st Division. Command of the 2nd Division goes to Benjamin Mooers, and he too is commissioned as a major general. The commanders of the eight brigades are Gerard Steddiford (New York City); Reuben Hopkins (Orange County); Micajah Pettis

Colonel Solomon Van Rensselaer.

William C.C. Claiborne.

(Washington County); Richard Dodge (Montgomery County); Jacob Brown (Jefferson County; later, general-in-chief of the U.S. Army); Daniel Miller (Cortland County); William Wadsworth (Ontario County); and George McClure (Steuben County).

In other activity, Secretary of the Navy Paul Hamilton, displeased with the ongoing activity in East Florida, orders Captain Williams to abandon Amelia Island and lead his Marine contingent back to Cumberland Island. However, contrasting orders, issued by Governor Mitchell on 16 May, are received by Williams and they direct him to hold Amelia Island. Williams holds his Marines in place.

April 29 (Wednesday) *In naval activity,* the USS *Essex,* commanded by Captain David Porter, seizes two British vessels while cruising in the Pacific Ocean.

In other activity, a flotilla of merchant ships departs from Ogdensburg en route to Lake Ontario, and a contingent of Canadian provincial militia gives chase. Two of the vessels, the *Sophia* and the *Island Packet,* are caught and burned, but the other vessels make it back to Ogdensburg.

April 30 (Thursday) *Louisiana* enters the Union as the 18th state. William C.C. Claiborne becomes its first elected governor. After Louisiana becomes a state, the remainder of the territory purchased from France is called the Missouri Territory, incorporating all of the Louisiana Purchase except Louisiana. This occurs during June 1812.

May 4 (Monday) In Florida, Governor David B. Mitchell of Georgia writes to Lt. Colonel Thomas A. Smith and countermands Smith's previous orders: "Sir: I have received a dispatch from the Secretary of State [James Monroe] of the United States in which is enclosed the duplicate of an order from the Secretary of War addressed to yourself, revoking the order which required you to obey the orders or requisitions of General Mathews, and, transferring that authority to myself as Governor of Georgia." Governor Mitchell orders Smith to remain in place unless he is forced to retire because of a superior enemy force.

May 5 (Tuesday) In Florida, at Fort Mose (Moosa Old Fort), Lt. Colonel Thomas A. Smith, in a letter to the to U.S. Adjutant and Inspector Brigadier General Thomas H. Cushing, informs the adjutant of the situation at his post just west of St. Augustine; he also informs General Cushing that he believes the Spanish will not launch an attack and that the Patriot force increases every day as reinforcements arrive. In addition, Smith reports that he is of the opinion that the Patriots will hold the territory if the United States remains out of the operation.

May 12 (Tuesday) In Pennsylvania, Governor Simon Snyder directs the adjutant general to raise the state's quota of militia:

> There shall forthwith be drafted, in the manner prescribed by law, 14,000 militia, officers and privates, to be formed into two divisions, four brigades, and twenty-two regiments.... The quotas of the several divisions of the state shall be formed into two divisions for the present service. The quotas of the first, second third, fourth, fifth, sixth and seventh divisions of the state, shall form the first division for service under the command of Major General Isaac Worrell, a Brigadier from the first division, and a Brigadier General from the third division of the state. The quotas of the eighth, ninth, tenth, eleventh, twelfth, thirteenth, fourteenth, fifteenth and sixteenth divisions of the state, shall form the second division for service, under the command of Major General Adamson Tannehill, with a Brigadier General from the second division, and a Brigadier General from the fourth division of the state.

May 14 (Thursday) The U.S. annexes Western Florida, a Spanish territory which has recently declared independence to become the Republic of West Florida. It is incorporated into the Mississippi Territory. Spanish troops remain in Mobile, but during April 1813, a force led by General James Wilkinson moves in and secures it without bloodshed. The Spanish, clandestinely allied to Britain, protest the annexation, but they are unable to prevent it.

In Pennsylvania, the Harrisburg volunteers, commanded by Captain Samuel Agnew, informs Governor Samuel Strong by letter that the contingent is prepared to serve "when ordered, on any tour of duty, which the honor and safety of their country may require."

May 16 (Saturday) In Florida, despite recent statements by the Spanish governor of East Florida that the American flag will be respected, an advance guard under Lt. Colonel Thomas A. Smith encamped outside of St. Augustine comes under attack. Smith had recently pulled most of his force out of Fort Mose; however, a guard was left inside the post to maintain the position.

One Spanish armed schooner supported by four launches arrives within striking distance. Reinforcements move up to bolster the pickets to intercept any landing party that might attempt to debark. Smith's order stipulates that if the balls of the naval bombardment penetrate the walls of the fort, the defenders, except for 15 men, are instructed to abandon the post. More than twenty shells are catapulted beginning at about 1100, and the 22nd ball, a 24-pounder, penetrates two walls. As ordered, part of the detachment withdraws from the fort. The remaining troops are under orders to hold their fire until the Spanish approach a point about 60 yards from shore; however, the sergeant in charge orders the troops to fire while the vessels are more than 300 yards distant. The unexpected fire causes the Spaniards to halt and reinitiate the bombardment. Meanwhile, the sergeant displays cowardice and takes flight. The fort is effortlessly seized and in a flash, the Spaniards burn it. The landing force also spots the main encampment; however, no attack is launched. Nonetheless, the Spaniards return to their vessels and continue to bombard the American positions until about 1600. The only damage inflicted in addition to the fort is a few tents that are struck by 24-pounders. No casualties are sustained. The troops remain in the camp until the Spanish depart for St. Augustine.

May 18 (Monday) In New York, two companies of militia, pursuant to orders of Governor Daniel D. Tompkins, raised in Ontario and Seneca Counties, depart from Canandaigua for Fort Niagara. The companies, commanded by Captains Elias Hall and Samuel Jennings, are quickly introduced to traveling via a route that is inundated with mud. The trek takes about eleven days, according to Archer Galloway, who participated in the grueling march. Once there, the troops, who have enlisted for a period of one year, are delegated to erect batteries at various points, including Lewiston. Subsequently, a contingent of regulars arrives at Fort Niagara and the militia departs from the post. Afterward they redeploy at Black Rock. Galloway, an officer at the time, relates a story about how both sides faced each other, but neither the British-Canadians at Waterloo nor the Americans fired against the other. The firing of the guns was confined to blank cartridges. Despite being ordered to not fire, Galloway's crew secretly loaded one gun with a live round and fired a shot that intentionally came close, but fell short. The British were covered in dust and surrounded by smoke. The Americans raised three cheers. Officers arrived to inquire how the gun was loaded with a shell, but no one claimed to have any knowledge. The officers inquired no further. Many years later, when Galloway related the story, he took pleasure in taking credit for firing the first shot on the frontier.

May 20 (Wednesday)   In Philadelphia, a large public meeting is held on the State House (Independence Hall) yard to encourage the government to declare war against the British due to their impressment of American seamen and other acts of oppression. The man who presides at the meeting, William Jones, is shortly afterward appointed secretary of the U.S. Navy. Most of the New Englanders are against war; however, Pennsylvania favors ending the British intimidation. Another attendee is John Binns, the editor of the most prominent newspaper in the state, the *Democratic Press*. Binns is also a close friend and a trusted confidante of the governor, Simon Snyder. One of the onlookers is Major Zebulon Pike, who within the year is promoted to brigadier general.

May 24 to June 1   *In naval activity,* a squadron under Commodore Decatur sets sail aboard the USS *United States* and moves into Long Island Sound. As it arrives off Hunt's Point during an ongoing storm, a powerful bolt of lightning strikes the main mast. The ship's colors plummets with it: "It entered a port-hole — went down the after hatchway, through the wardroom, into the surgeon's room — tore up his bed and put out his candle: then passed between the skin and ceiling of the ship, and tore up about twenty nails of her copper at the water's edge." For a short while, it is thought that the magazine might be struck. Nevertheless, the *Macedonian* and the *Hornet*, both of which are nearby, escape damage, and the squadron is able to resume its cruise.

On 1 June, the American squadron spots a British raze ("74 gun-ships, with a little portion of their decks cut down, and the exclusion of their smaller guns which are of but little value except in close engagements") and a frigate that are close behind off Montauk Point. The American squadron retires and moves into the harbor at New London, Connecticut.

May 25 (Monday)   In Georgia, at the Creek Agency, Colonel Hawkins is informed by Mr. Cornells that on the 25th, a Mr. Lott had been killed near his residence by four Indians. Hawkins also states that a report had been received detailing the murders of two families by Indians in Tennessee.

In Pennsylvania, the various units offering to serve the governor continue to rise. On this day, a unit in Lancaster informs the governor that the members are offering their services. The letter reads: "The Lancaster Phalanx, commanded by Captain James Humes, under the impulse that led their ancestors of glorious memory into an arduous and then almost hopeless contest, have this day unanimously resolved on a voluntary tender of their service to their country."

In Ohio, Governor Hull, recently appointed brigadier general in the United States Army, while at Dayton, Ohio, pursuant to instructions from President Madison, assumes command of the Ohio troops (three regiments) that have been provided by Governor (Colonel) Return Meigs. Colonel Duncan McArthur and Majors James Denny and William A. Trimble command the 1st Regiment; Colonel James Findlay and Majors Thomas Moore and Thomas Van Horn command the 2nd Regiment. The 3rd Regiment is commanded by Colonel Lewis Cass and Majors Robert Morrison and J.R. Munson.

The column, after departing from Dayton, advances to Detroit. While en route the 4th U.S. Regiment joins with the column at Urbana on the 10 June. During the journey, four blockhouses are constructed as posts to leave the invalids and as a series of blockhouses, each with small detachments to protect and escort convoys.

In naval activity, the HMS *Surveillante* intercepts and seizes the *Young Connecticut*, an American schooner.

May 28 (Thursday)   In Pennsylvania, the Independent Blues, commanded by Captain William Mitchell, offers to serve the governor. The unit, based in Philadelphia, says in a letter to the governor: "Sir: I have the honor of tendering the services of the Independent Blues to you, the Governor of the State of Pennsylvania, as part of the first quota of the militia of the city of Philadelphia, agreeable to general orders and are ready to march at a moment's warning."

May 29 (Friday)   In New Hampshire, pursuant to President Madison's requisition upon New Hampshire for its quota of troops under the Act of Congress of 10 April 1812, Governor John Langdon orders the militia to "detach three thousand five hundred men from the militia of this State, and organizing them into companies, battalions, and regiments, the same to be armed and equipped for actual service, and in readiness to march at the shortest notice."

Governor Langdon's term is nearly over, prompting him to leave the details of completing the organization of the units to his successor, Governor William Plumer, who assumes office on 5 June. Plumer is succeeded by John Taylor Gilman during 1813; however, Plumer is re-elected during 1816, 1817 and 1818. He declines running during 1819.

May 30 (Saturday)   In Florida, outside of St. Augustine, Lt. Colonel Thomas A. Smith writes a letter to Georgia Governor David B. Mitchell to update the governor on the situation of his troops. He says his troops are positioned from where they can clearly observe the harbor and the town of Spanish-held St. Augustine. Smith also reports that although the Spanish have observed the Americans building defensive positions, he does not anticipate any Spanish offensive action. The report also states that the gunboat armed with 6-pounders is en route to Six Mile Creek.

June   The actual strength of the U.S. Army is approximately 11,700 officers and men, including 5,000 recent recruits authorized by Congress. The U.S. Navy consists of 16 vessels — seven frigates ranging from 32 to 44 guns and nine others ranging from 12 to 28. Of these, only one squadron consisting of six ships, commanded by Commodore John Rodgers, is prepared for war. The puny U.S. Navy faces larger problems than the Royal Navy.

The government had decided that the navy could not compete with the British naval forces and that the ships would remain in port to guard harbors rather than venture out on the high seas and be destroyed. Captain William Bainbridge and Captain Charles Stewart possess neither an inferiority complex nor fear of the British naval forces. They believe that the government's plan assures failure. Both officers meet with Secretary of the Navy Paul Hamilton (formerly a U.S. senator and governor of South Carolina) to make their case that the U.S. seamen should not be harbor guards.

After listening to the officers, Hamilton remains adamantly opposed to their proposal. Hamilton states that the matter has been settled in a cabinet meeting. He also informs both officers that the frigates would be moored in the New York harbor and afterward, the guns on one side of the ship would be relocated to the opposite side. Afterward the vessels would be utilized as water batteries. Hamilton then delivers them yet another demoralizing statement. He informs the officers that the landlocked warships would be manned by their regular crews and command would remain with the respective officers. Captains Bainbridge and Stewart respectfully refuse to acquiesce. They inform Hamilton that the U.S. sailors are more qualified than their British counterparts and their gunners' skills greatly overshadow those of the British gunners. Pressing further, they tell Hamilton that the U.S. Navy in an equally fought battle would prevail eight out of ten times. Hamilton is unimpressed; however, he does inform them that there will be another meeting at the White House.

Following that meeting, Hamilton speaks with Stewart and Bainbridge, who are at the White House and anxiously waiting to receive the results. Both are dismayed when they are told that he ships would not sail and they would be used only to guard the harbors. The news is devastating. Bainbridge and Stewart emphasized the Americans' ability to sight their cannons, which gives the U.S. an advantage because the Royal Navy had not yet progressed to that stage, but still, their advice and requests fell on deaf ears. Albert Gallatin, secretary of the treasury, is the most determined opponent of permitting the squadrons to sail.

As soon as the officers depart from their talk with Hamilton, they combine their ideas and pen a joint letter to President Madison. When shown to Hamilton, he is startled and informs both officers that the letter is too strongly worded to be given to the president. Nevertheless, having seen their careers sink in front of their eyes along with the entire navy, they refuse to change even a comma. Hamilton blinks and agrees to present the letter to the president.

Shortly thereafter, to the jubilation of Bainbridge and Stewart, they had resurrected the navy. President Madison overrules his cabinet and suddenly the harbors lose their water batteries and the U.S. Navy goes to sea to challenge the Royal Navy.

The British naval forces are overconfident. The Royal Navy is recognized by the French, and Spanish, along with the Dutch and the Danes as the dominant force, and they expect to quickly clear the seas of the diminutive United States Navy. London had been forewarned that despite its size, the American naval force has been modernized, and the newly constructed vessels are capable of traveling at high speed and that the ships carry heavy weaponry. Nevertheless, the British Admiralty essentially laughs off the threat and disregards reports of the newfound power of the American navy and the skill of its officers.

Back in Washington, similarly to London, the government is skeptical of its navy's ability to challenge the Royal Navy. Unexpected surprises will stun both governments once the British attempt to immobilize the American naval forces. Despite only about 6,000 enemy troops being captured by U.S. land forces during the conflict, the naval forces, including privateers, seize about 30,000 prisoners.

At the opening of the conflict, British merchants anticipate great success without competition from the U.S., and there are no thoughts of American naval forces threatening British commerce and no thoughts of Britain itself being under threats by the U.S.

The sixteen ships of the U.S. Navy are:
1. USS *Adams*, 28 guns (built in 1799).
2. USS *Argus*, 16 guns (1803).
3. USS *Chesapeake*, 38 guns (1799).
4. USS *Congress*, 38 guns (1799).
5. USS *Constellation*, 38 guns (1797). English blockaders prevent the *Constellation* from leaving Norfolk. It is confined to port for the duration of the conflict.
6. USS *Constitution*, 44 guns (1797).
7. USS *Enterprise*, 12 guns (1799).
8. USS *Essex*, 32 guns (1799).
9. USS *Hornet*, 18 guns (1805).
10. USS *Nautilus*, 14 guns (1803).
11. USS *President*, 44 guns (1800).
12. USS *Syren*, 16 guns (1803).
13. USS *United States*, 44 guns (1797).
14. USS *Viper*, 12 guns (1810).
15. USS *Vixen*, 14 guns (1803).
16. USS *Wasp*, 18 guns (1806).

In Western New York, An American force led by Captain Hubbard seizes British-held Fort Haldimand on the St. Lawrence River (Buck Island). The British had not transferred the fort to the U.S. after the American Revolution. The Americans demolish the fort.

June 1 (Monday) **In Washington, D.C.,** President Madison urges Congress to declare war on Great Britain. In the House, John C. Calhoun of South Carolina and Henry Clay of Kentucky, Speaker of the House, conspicuously back the president to ensure the yea vote. There is much opposition to the war in New England. With re-

John C. Calhoun.

gard to the president's recommendation, the Committee on Foreign relations made these remarks:

> Your committee, believing that the freeborn sons of America are worthy to enjoy the liberty which their fathers purchased at the price of much blood and treasure, and seeing, by the measures adopted by Great Britain, a course commenced and persisted in, which might lead to a loss of national character and independence, feel no hesitation in advising resistance by force, in which the Americans of the present day will prove to the enemy and the world, that we have not only inherited that liberty which our fathers gave us, but also the will and power to maintain it. Relying on the patriotism of the nation, and confidently trusting that the Lord of Hosts will go with us to battle in a righteous cause, and crown our efforts with success, your committee recommend an immediate appeal to arms.

In Ohio, General William Hull (governor, Michigan Territory) departs from Dayton en route to Urbana. He is joined there by the U.S. 4th Regiment, which arrives from Vincennes. The 4th Regiment had departed Newport during the previous August under the command of Major James Miller due to the absence of the commander, Colonel John P. Boyd, who had been ordered by General Harrison to arrive early. The regulars, whose reputation preceded their arrival due to their heroic performance at the Battle of Tippecanoe with General Anthony Wayne, are welcomed enthusiastically by Hull's Ohio troops upon their arrival in September.

The 1st Regiment under Colonel Duncan McArthur is the first to depart from Urbana. McArthur's command is tasked with carving a road through the wilderness from Urbana to the Scioto River. After reaching the river, near present-day Kenton, the troops construct two blockhouses, which are linked together by palisades. The post is later named Fort McArthur.

June 2 (Tuesday) **In Pennsylvania,** Captain Henry Jarrett, commander of a cavalry troop in Lower Nazareth Township, writes to the governor that his unit is prepared to serve "as part of the quota of the Seventy-first regiment required by General Orders lately issued." The letter continues:

> When our country is insulted by foreign nations, when our citizens are murdered in our own waters by the British, when our fellow-citizens are taken captive on the high seas, and compelled to bear arms against their country, to become the executioners of their friends and brethren, or to fall themselves by their hands, and when internal enemies threaten a dissolution or our happy Union, it is time for those who care [for] their country and who are ready to die in its defense to be up and doing. Under this conviction, sir, the troop I have the honor to command, alive to the interest and honor of their country, and convinced of the wrongs, the injustice, and the accumulated insults heaped upon us by the British government, have determined to offer to their country their services and their lives, if required, in defense of its violated rights. I have in charge from them to state to you, sir, that we will be ready, at a moment's warning, to go on any service our country may call us, to defend and preserve those rights and liberties which were secured to us by the heroes of '76.

June 4 (Thursday) In Washington, Missouri is organized into a U.S. territory. It comprises the entire area originally acquired as the Louisiana Territory, the exception of what is now the state of Louisiana (formerly Orleans Territory). William Clark (co-leader of the Lewis and Clark Expedition) becomes governor of the territory. After the war begins, Missouri raises additional regiments, bringing the total to seven. Andrew Henry, formerly of the Missouri Fur Company, will assume command of the 1st Battalion, Sixth Regiment, under Lt. Colonel William H. Ashley.

June 4–18 **In Washington, D.C.,** the House of Representatives, by a vote of 79 to 49, passes the bill to declare war against Great Britain. The U.S. Senate debates the bill until the 17th, when it passes by a vote of 19 to 13. President Madison signs it on the18th.

June 5 (Friday) *In naval activity,* the USS *Oneida* seizes the HMS *Lord Nelson*. The prize is taken to Sackets Harbor. Later, it becomes the USS *Scourge*.

June 10 (Wednesday) **In England,** although many politicians and high ranking British officers express little if any respect for the American military and disregard any possibility of serious resistance to British forces if war erupts, the sentiments are not unanimous. On this day, the *London Statesman* publishes the following:

> It has been stated, that in a war with this country, America has nothing to gain. In opposition to this assertion it may be said, with equal truth, that in a war with America, England has nothing to gain, but much to lose. Let us examine the relative situation of the two countries. America cannot certainly pretend to wage a maritime war with us. She has no navy to do it with. But America has nearly 100,000

as good seamen as any in the world, all of whom would be actively employed against our trade on every part of the ocean in their fast sailing ships-of-war, many of which will be able to cope with our small cruizers; and they will be found to be sweeping the West India seas, and even carrying desolation into the chops of the channel. Every one must recollect what they did in the latter part of the American war. The books at Lloyd's will recount it; and the rate of assurances at that time will clearly prove what their diminutive strength was able to effect in the face of our navy, and that, when nearly one hundred pendants were flying on their coast. Were we then able to prevent their going in and out, or stop them from taking our trade and our storeships, even in sight of our garrisons? Besides, were they not in the English and Irish channels, picking up our homeward bound trade, sending their prizes into French and Spanish ports, to the great terror and annoyance of our merchants and ship owners?

These are facts which can be traced to a period when America was in her infancy, without ships, without seamen, without money, and at a time when our navy was not much less in strength than at present. The Americans will be found to be a different sort of enemy by sea than the French. They possess nautical knowledge, with equal enterprise to ourselves. They will be found attempting deeds which a Frenchman would never think of; and they will have all the ports of our enemy open, in which they can make good their retreat with their booty. In a predatory war on commerce, Great Britain would have more to lose than to gain, because the Americans would retire within themselves, having everything they want for supplies, and what foreign commerce they might have, would be carried on in fast-sailing armed ships, which, as heretofore, would be able to fight or run away, as best suited their force or inclination. Much is also to be apprehended from the desertion of our seamen, who will meet with every encouragement in the United States, by protecting laws made in their favor, perhaps large douceurs offered for their disaffection, and it is well known the predilection which our sailors have for the American shores. These are considerations which by far outweigh any advantages that ought partially to arise to individuals from a few scattering prizes that might be taken by our cruizers. Their harvest seems much more abundant under those wretched and impolitic regulations, called the Orders in Council, the existence of which gives rise to the present differences between the two countries, has drained our treasury, and is starving thousands of our manufacturing brethren. America could sustain no possible injury, but internal taxation, from a war with this country, which would not bear any proportion to what we might feel from the circumstances already mentioned, and from which we would most seriously have to apprehend; for our ships, without a large military force, durst not enter the ports of the United States, and that military force, in our present situation, is nowhere to be found. The probable consequence would be the starvation of our West India colonies, and the loss of Upper, if not of Lower Canada; while the total want of specie (which latterly has been wholly drawn from the United States) to pay our troops at Halifax and Quebec, could not fail to accelerate the mischief.

In Florida, Colonel Ralph Isaacs, aide to Governor Mitchell of Georgia and U.S. commissioner, writes to Lt. Colonel Thomas A. Smith that the U.S. government intends to protect the Patriots and heir property in East Florida. Smith is also informed that reinforcements from Savannah, Georgia, should arrive shortly. Smith is also authorized to take any action necessary if the Spanish again show any offensive action.

In Pennsylvania, the Shippensburg Troop of Light Horse, commanded by Captain David Duncan, in a letter to the governor, offers to serve as part of the quota of Pennsylvania troops required for the militia. The offer stipulates for service in the United States. The influx of militia units offering to serve continues to grow throughout the commonwealth. On the 12th, the Lehigh Rifle Company (attached to 94th Regiment, Pennsylvania militia), commanded by Captain Abraham Rinker of Allentown, writes to the governor to volunteer for service.

June 11 (Thursday) **In Florida,** Spanish governor Sebastian Kindelan, in a letter to Lt. Colonel Thomas A. Smith, makes it known that he had just arrived at St. Augustine and that it distressed him to see American troops encamped near the town. He requests a conference with Colonel Smith. On the following day, Smith informs Kindelan that he had received his letter, which was delivered by Sergeant Major Don Francisco Rivera, and that two American officers — Captain Joseph Woodruff of the 3rd U.S. Infantry and Lt. George Haig of the U.S. Dragoons, representing Smith — will arrive for the meeting.

June 12 (Friday) **In Washington, D.C.,** Secretary of War William Eustis writes to Governor Caleb Strong of Massachusetts regarding the state's quota of militia: "Sir: I am directed by the President to request your Excellency to order into the service of the United States, on the requisition of Major-General Dearborn, such-part of the quota of the militia from the State of Massachusetts, detached conformably to the act of April 10, 1812, as he may deem necessary for the defense of the sea-coast." On the 22nd, Dearborn submits his request for the troops. The governor does not respond. On the 26th, he sends another letter to the governor. Meanwhile, on the 22nd, the governor responds, but the letter evades the intent of the request. The lack of cooperation continues into the following month when Dearborn dispatches yet another letter that closes with explicit language that underscores the peril: "The danger of invasion, which existed at the time of issuing the order of the President, increases, and I am specially directed by the President to urge the consideration to your Excellency as requiring the necessary order to be given for the immediate march of the several detachments, specified by General Dearborn, to their respective posts."

Governor Strong continues to flaunt his indifference, but on 5 August, he does communicate with the secretary with the following: "The people of this State appear to be under no apprehension of an invasion; several towns, indeed, on the seacoast, soon after the declaration of war, applied to the Governor and Council for arms and ammunition, similar to the articles of that kind which had been delivered to them by the State in the course of the last war; and, in some instances, they were supplied accordingly. But they expressed no desire that any part of the militia should be called out for their defense, and in some cases we were assured such a measure would be disagreeable to them." The governor includes opinions of the "Justices of the Supreme Judicial Court of the Commonwealth, Theophilus Parsons, Samuel Sewall, and Isaac Parker," who concur with the governor's stance that the right "is vested in the commanders-in-chief of the militia of the several States." Strong adds: "I am fully disposed to afford all the aid to the measures of the national government which the Constitution requires of me; but I presume it will not be expected or desired that I shall fail in the duty which I owe to the people of this State, who have confided their interests to my care."

During this same period, the secretary is also rebuffed by Governor Roger Griswold of Connecticut, who also refuses to place the militia under federal jurisdiction. Connecticut establishes a state corps (authorized by the General Assembly) under the command of Brigadier General Nathaniel Terry. The corps is composed of two regiments, commanded by Colonel Timothy Shepard and Colonel Elihu Sanford, augmented by a cavalry regiment commanded by Major Deming and four artillery companies under Major William Stanley. In addition to Governor Griswold's two independent companies, known as the Foot Guards, Connecticut's militia force is composed four divisions as follows: the 1st Division (1st and 7th Brigades), commanded by Major General Solomon Cowles. Cowles' 1st Brigade is composed of the 1st, 18th, 19th and 22nd Connecticut Infantry Regiments, along with the Connecticut 1st Cavalry Regiment under the command of Brigadier General Moses Tryon, Jr. The 7th Brigade, composed of the 6th, 16th, 23rd and 24th Connecticut Infantry Regiments, along with the Connecticut 7th Cavalry Regiment, is commanded by Brigadier General Levi Lusk. The 2nd Division, commanded by Major General John Hubbard, is composed of the 2nd Brigade, comprising the 2nd, 7th, 10th, 27th and 32nd Connecticut Infantry Regiments, along with the 2nd Connecticut Cavalry Regiment and the 1st Artillery Battalion, under Brigadier General James Merriman, until he is succeeded by Brigadier General Hezekia Howe.

The 4th Brigade, composed of the 4th, 9th and 28th Connecticut Infantry Regiments, bolstered by the Connecticut 4th Cavalry Regiment, is commanded by Brigadier General Matthias Nicoll, who upon his retirement is succeeded by Brigadier General Enoch Foote. The 3rd Division, commanded by Brigadier General William Williams, is composed of the 3rd and 5th Brigades. The 3rd Brigade, commanded by Brigadier General Jirah Isham, is composed of the 3rd, 8th, 20th, 30th and 33rd Connecticut Infantry Regiments, along with the Connecticut 3rd Cavalry

Regiment. The 5th Brigade, commanded by Brigadier General David Holmes, is composed of the 5th, 11th, 12th and 21st Connecticut Infantry Regiments and the Connecticut Cavalry Regiment. The 4th Division, composed of the 6th and 8th Brigades, is commanded by Major General Augustine Taylor. The 6th Brigade, composed of the 14th, 17th, 25th and 35th Connecticut Infantry Regiments and the 6th Connecticut Cavalry Regiment, is commanded by Brigadier General David Thompson.

The 8th Brigade, composed of the 8th, 13th, 16th, 26th and 29th Connecticut Infantry Regiments and the 8th Connecticut Cavalry Regiment, is commanded by Brigadier General Ephraim Hinman, who is later succeeded by Brigadier General Gerrit Smith. The total number of Connecticut's military force is about 15,000 men, a figure the governor determines is capable of defending the state if attacked.

In Florida, Spanish Governor Kindelan, at St. Augustine, advises Lt. Colonel Thomas A. Smith in a letter to pull his troops back to the opposite bank of the St. Johns River and warns Smith not to provide any support for the Revolters (Georgia Patriots). Smith responds on the following day (13th). He informs the Spanish commanders that his present orders require him to hold his force where it stands and not to pull back under any circumstances. Smith also warns the Spanish that if any of their troops venture out of St. Augustine and move toward the American camp, they will forcefully defend their positions, which are out of the range of the Spanish guns.

June 13 (Saturday) **In Florida** at St. Augustine, the governor, in response to a letter of the previous day from Lt. Colonel Thomas A. Smith, writes to inform Smith not to send any additional communication to the town, because "it will be discharged without hearing."

In New Hampshire, Governor William Plumer appoints Lt. Colonel John Montgomery brigadier general of the New Hampshire 6th Brigade. On 23 July, Montgomery is named brigadier general of the "Western Brigade of the detached militia." After the war, Montgomery is appointed major general (18 October 1818), a post he holds until 1821.

In naval activity, a grand reunion occurs when the Americans captured by the British, who were attached to the HMS *Leopard* when they boarded the USS *Chesapeake* on 22 June 1807, return to the *Chesapeake* in Boston Harbor. The former prisoners are escorted aboard by a British officer, Lieutenant Simpson, and met by Lieutenant Wilkinson of the *Chesapeake.* Initially four men had been seized; however, one identified as British and accused of treason had been hanged and one other had died.

June 14 (Sunday) *In naval activity,* a small group of American vessels owned by Archibald Gracie and Sons of New York depart from Portugal unaware that war with Great Britain had begun, and initiate their voyages back to the United States. Nevertheless, there is great anxiety that the war could erupt, prompting the vessels to get underway before they could become prizes of the Royal Navy. The *America, Eliza Gracie* and *Oronoko* leave port together, along with a large number of other vessels that are moving out of the Tagus River.

After a while, the *America* breaks away from the pack to return by itself. For about one week, the winds are less than fair, hindering progress of the *America* under Captain George Coggeshall, while the *Eliza Gracie* under Captain James Brown and the *Oronoko* under Captain John Richards continue on a more northerly course under favorable winds. The crew of the *America* does not appreciate the calm conditions until they learn the lack of a breeze actually prevents them from being captured. While the *America* is stalled, the *Eliza Gracie* and the *Oronoko* run into a strong British squadron, composed of the 64-gun *Africa* (Captain Bastard); 38-gun *Shannon* (Captain Broke, the senior officer of the squadron); 38-gun *Guerriere* (Captain Dacres); 36-gun *Belvidera* (Captain Byron) and the 32-gun *Aeolus* (Captain Lord James Townsend). The British inform the Americans that the war had begun and that they are prisoners. The officers and crewmen are transferred to British vessels and afterward, the *Oronoko* is taken into port at Halifax. The *Eliza Gracie,* a recently built ship, is destroyed.

The British had actually been in search of an American squadron under Commodore John Rodgers, which had departed New York on 21 June. About one week after the capture of the two American merchant ships, on 17 July the squadron encounters the USS *Constitution.*

Mid-June **In Florida,** by this date, Captain Williams, U.S. Marine Corps, and his 60-man contingent continue to hold Fernandina (Amelia Island). Colonel Thomas A. Smith is operating from the old Spanish post, Fort Mose (Moosa), that was garrisoned by Negroes during the early 1700s. The fort is just outside St. Augustine. A Spanish schooner approaches the fort and launches an attack, which compels Smith to withdraw to Pass Navarro (Four Mile Creek), where Smith's regulars remain. Meanwhile, the Patriots withdraw to the St. Johns River and establish Camp New Hope. Seminole Indians led by Chief Bowlegs offer to support the Americans, but the offer is declined. Chief Bowlegs, insulted by the refusal of his help, decides to fight alongside the Spanish. All the while, the Marines at Fernandina are assigned responsibility to maintain communications with the army at Four Mile Creek and the Patriots at Camp New Hope. The Marines move to Camp New Hope and take responsibility for guarding supply trains and convoys that move between the two camps.

June 16 (Tuesday) **In England,** the will of the people finally convinces Parliament to take action to break the deadlock with the United States regarding the importation of British goods to the U.S. The ongoing practice of British ships intercepting U.S. vessels and pressing American seamen into the Royal Navy had previously caused America to implement Embargo Acts, followed by a Non-intercourse Act, each intended to force Great Britain to halt its harassment policies, without committing the U.S. to war. In addition to the normal delays in reaching a mutual pact, two other unexpected incidents had caused complications, the recent disclosure of the insanity of King George and the assassination of Prime Minister Percival.

In the House of Commons this day, Lord Castlereagh, the foreign secretary, proclaims the end of the Orders in Council, which stops the British practice of interfering with U.S. commercial vessels and opens the path to avoid outright war with the United States. The repeal officially becomes effective on June 23. The embargo imposed by the U.S. had inflicted pain on the British, but until now, it had been hidden behind the stiff British upper lip. It had been the financially hurt merchantmen and manufacturing industry that prevailed up on Parliament to repeal the orders. Similarly to what happened in the States, bankruptcies had occurred, and British goods were wasting in storehouses. In addition, the crops in Europe had not duplicated the previous seasons of abundance.

News of the repeal raises expectations in Great Britain and the merchants exhibit exuberance at the thought of soon flooding the American market with British stores. However, in America, Congress, unaware of this repeal of the Orders in Council, prepares to proclaim war, which it does two days later.

In related activity, while Britain and the United States engage in hostilities, the English this month conclude peace agreements with Russia and Sweden.

June 17 (Wednesday) **In Florida,** Lt. Colonel Thomas A. Smith at his camp outside St. Augustine writes to Governor David B. Mitchell of Georgia, the U.S. commissioner, to inform him that he expects the Spanish to initiate offensive action against his command. Smith reports that Captain Massias, whom he sent to deliver a message to the Spanish governor, had been permitted to enter St. Augustine. While there he was able to listen to the Spanish discussing the troop strength of the Americans along the St. Johns River, and he also heard a discussion of how to best get their naval vessels there from St. Augustine. Most of the gained intelligence came from

General John Montgomery.

the naval officer who transported Governor Kindelan from Havana, Cuba, to the town.

June 18 (Thursday) The United States declares war on Great Britain. After a two-week debate, the House vote was in the affirmative 79–49 on 4 June and the Senate vote was 19–13 on the 17th. The act reads:

> Declaring War between the United Kingdom of Great Britain and Ireland, and the dependencies thereof, and the United States of America, and her *Territories*.
>
> *Be it enacted by the Senate and House of Representatives of the United States of America, in Congress assembled,* That WAR be, and the same is hereby declared to exist between the United Kingdom of Great Britain and Ireland, and the dependencies thereof, and the United States of America and their territories; and that the President of the United States be, and he is hereby authorized to use the whole land and naval force of the United States, to carry the same into effect, and to issue to private-armed vessels of the United States commissions, or letters-of-marque, and general reprisals, in such form as he shall think proper, and under the seal of the United States, against the vessels, goods and effects of the government of the same United Kingdom of Great Britain and Ireland, and of the subjects thereof. Approved, June 18th, 1812.
> JAMES MADISON.

A vote to declare war on France fails in the Senate by two votes. Secretary of War William Eustis writes two letters to General Hull, the commander of the Michigan Territory; however, only one mentions that war has been declared. They are sent separately and he does not receive the news that war had begun until 2 July. Meanwhile, the Federalists persist with their claims that the Democratic-Republicans and Madison ignore the nastiness of the French and show great favoritism to them, while they hastily seek war with the British. At this time it is well known that the French use barbaric methods against American captives, subjecting them to cruel punishment while being held in French dungeons. The French seemingly find joy in capturing the Americans in port and then forcing them to march well inland to their rat-infested prisons. These Yanks must endure the lash and constant anguish as they walk, sometimes lacking even shoes and frequently without proper clothing, along harsh roads through nasty weather. Nevertheless, war is fought only against the British, primarily because President Madison and others are convinced that to simultaneously declare war against both nations would surely spell doom for the United States. The British are forced to endure additional problems because of the war. Up to this point, the British armed forces fighting the French in Spain have been depending on supplies being delivered to them from the United States. The British, in an attempt to circumvent the new situation, begin to issue licenses to American ships that are willing to continue to carry provisions to the British despite the war. The licenses give the vessels willing to run the risk free passage without threat of capture by either British warships or British privateers.

The U.S. Navy is insufficient in number to engage the British Navy, let alone the British and French navies combined. Also, it is still thought that Canada would be the key to victory, and once secured, it would be the trump card that would compel the British to forfeit their hold in North America. And the reality of distance between the U.S. and France make it improbable that U.S. warships could venture into French waters and successfully gain control of the seas. The U.S. had been attempting to avert war, but its repeated efforts to convince Britain to repeal the Orders in Council had all failed; now war had been declared before the lifting of the orders, but Congress is unaware that Parliament had finally acquiesced on the 23rd.

War might have been averted if there had been any way to quickly dispatch the news across the mighty ocean (*see also*, **June 16, In England**). For better or worse, the inevitable has arrived. The diplomatic pouches are shelved, the quills and ink are abruptly laid aside and the negotiating tables are left barren. Negotiations soon resume, but neither country relents. Instead, the exchange of dispatches will be propelled by cannon, rifles and clashing steel, which guarantees yet another violent confrontation to determine the fate of the nation, which is at this time deeply divided. The sword is unsheathed, the flag unfurled, and the ships are underway.

The ships that soon embark had nearly been landlocked due to fear in the president's cabinet of letting the navy venture out in the open sea to be devoured by the Royal Navy, which has about 1,000 ships and is considered to be the most superior force on the high seas. On this day, Secretary of the Navy Paul Hamilton, in a letter to Captain Isaac Hull, expresses his anxiety by instructing Hull not to engage unless attacked.

> SIR: This day war has been declared between the United Empire of Great Britain, Ireland, and their dependencies, and the United States of America and their territories, and you are, with the force under your command, entitled to every belligerent right to attack and capture, and to defend. You will use the utmost dispatch to reach New York, after you have made up your complement of men, &c., at Annapolis. In your way from thence you will not fail to notice the British flag, should it present itself. I am informed that the *Belvidera* is on our coast, but you are not to understand me as impelling you to battle previously to your having confidence in your crew, unless attacked, or with a reasonable prospect of success, of which you are to be, at your discretion, the judge. You are to reply to this, and inform me of your progress.

In another letter from Hamilton on 3 July, Captain Isaac Hull is ordered to New York, where the plan is to have the vessel used as a floating battery; however, the British prevent the *Constitution* from reaching New York. It moves to Boston. Had the *Constitution* entered New York, the explosive encounter with the HMS *Guerriere* would not occur. Two determined naval officers, Captain William Bainbridge and Captain Charles Stewart, overcome insurmountable odds to persuade the president to override his cabinet and let the ships sail (*see* **June**).

Also, the declaration of war is not favored by all and the animosity between states below New England and the states of Connecticut, Massachusetts and New Hampshire actually declines, committing any troops to the federal government. Some other states offer only tepid support. In Pennsylvania, the legislature makes the state's position clear by sharply criticizing the New Englanders. The Ohio legislature, another strong supporter of the declaration, takes similar action by stating: "The man who would desert a just cause is unworthy to defend it."

The most recent addition to the Union, Louisiana, also takes a stand; Governor William Claiborne states: "If ever war was justifiable, the one which our country has declared is that war. If ever a people had cause to repose in the confidence of their Government, we are the people." Vermont, nestled in New England, supports the war, as does New York; however, the New York congressional delegation did not vote in favor of the declaration.

In New York has had concerns about the war for a long time. Governor Tompkins, during 1808, directed that 500 stand of arms be stored at Champion (present-day Jefferson County) during a period of uncertainty with regard to revenue laws on the Canadian frontier. One year later, Tompkins authorizes the construction of an arsenal at Watertown, slightly more than ten miles from Sackets Harbor.

In other activity, Secretary of War William Eustis sends a message to General William Hull, governor Michigan Territory, who is en route to Detroit from Ohio with a force of regulars and Ohio volunteers. The message directs Hull to speed up his march; however, it fails to mention that war has been declared. The government's failure to inform the outposts that war had been declared causes problems. Fort Michilimackinac (formerly Fort de Buade) in Michigan is seized by the British on 17 July, and it is the British who inform the commander that the war had begun.

The Southern ports contribute 36 privateers

President James Madison.

during the war and these exclude those that sail out of Baltimore. They operate out of Charleston, New Orleans, Norfolk, Savannah and Wilmington. Six of the privateers, including the *Dash* and the *Roger*, operate out of Norfolk, and of those, the 1-gun *Chance*, the 1-gun schooner *Four Friends*, the *Franklin* and the 3-gun schooner *George Washington* leave no records of any distinctive service.

The arsenal at Watertown, New York.

Six privateers operate out of New Orleans. The 4-gun lugger *Cora* (Captain J. George), the 3-gun schooner *Hornet* (Captain F. Thomas), the *John* (Captain J. Coates), and the 1-gun schooner *Victory* (Captain J. Degres) are among those; however, these four leave no record of accomplishment. The other two are the 4-gun schooner *Spy* and the 3-gun schooner *Two Friends*. Also out of Savannah, five privateers operate, and of those, the 3-gun schooner *Atlas* (Captain T.M. Newell, the 3-gun schooner *Elizabeth* (Captain R. Cleary), the 1-gun Felucca *Bee* (Captain P. Massabeau) and the 4-gun schooner *Maria*, combined, are unable to succeed in seizing any enemy vessel of value.

Charleston commits more than thirteen privateers to the war, and these include the 1-gun schooner *Advocate* (Captain A. Dougle), the 2-gun sloop *Blockade* (Captain J. Graves), the schooner *Eagle*, the schooner *Firefly* (Captain W. Clewley), the 3-gun schooner *Hazard* (Captain P. Le Chartrier) and the 4-gun schooner *Revenge*. None of the aforementioned privateers out of Charleston achieve great success. Other privateers out of Charleston are the *Lady Madison* (Captain A. Garrison), the *Lovely Cornelia* (Captain P. Sicard), the 1-gun schooner *Mary Ann*, the 1-gun *Poor Sailor* and the *Saucy Jack* (Captain J.P. Chazel). The *Poor Sailor* succeeds in seizing a ship carrying a cargo of rum; however, later during 1813 it is lost at sea. The *Rapid* seizes one ship (*Experience*) with a high value cargo estimated at about $250,000 and captures one brigantine and two schooners.

The privateer *Teazer*, out of New York, is one of the ships that gets to sea early. The *Teazer*, commanded by Captain F. Johnson, makes several early seizures, including the packet *Ann*, and a schooner, the *Greyhound*. The Americans, after taking possession of the *Greyhound*, send it into an American port with a prize crew, but while en route, it is intercepted by a British warship, the *La Hogue*, which is carrying 74 guns. Once halted, the Americans, still possessing the ship's original papers, resort to their ingenuity. When the boarding party begins its examination, the crew announces that the vessel is British and also the crew. The officer examining the papers accepts the explanation and believes all the papers are in order. Shortly thereafter, as the 74-gun *La Hogue* pulls away, there is a huge sigh of relief aboard the *Greyhound*. The ruse worked perfectly. The prize crew afterward arrives at an American port without further incident.

The *Teazer* in the meantime continues its cruise, and one of its prizes later this year is the *Orient*, which is captured while en route to England from Quebec. Later, during December of this year, it encounters a squadron of the Royal Navy.

Also, some of the privateers out of Baltimore include the *Delila* (letter of marque), the *Fairy*, the *Patapsco* and the *Tuckahoe*. Their captures are not well documented regarding the specific dates. The *Delila* is credited with some captures, and in one instance it seizes a vessel carrying a cargo of dry goods while sailing from France to New Orleans. It is not able to take the prize because of a shortage of crewmen already sent out as prize crews. The intercepted ship is released. The *Fairy* is credited with capturing two prizes, including the sloop *Active* (destroyed at sea) and a schooner carrying dry goods that is sent into a friendly port. The *Patapsco* seizes three vessels during its time at sea. The Tuckahoe captures the schooner *Hazard* (1814) and seizes the schooner *Sea Flower* (1814), while heading into France and destroys it at sea. During March 1814, the *Tuckahoe* barely escapes capture off Long Island and afterward safely reaches Boston.

June 19 (Friday) **In Canada,** the number of British troops at the outbreak of war is nominal. The total number in the country stands at about 4,500, and of those, fewer than 2,000 are posted above Montreal. The units include the 8th 41st, 49th and 100th Regiments, along with a small contingent of artillery. The other units are the 10th Royal Veterans Regiment, the Newfoundland Fencibles and the Glengarry Fencibles. The troops stationed above Montreal are the 41st Regiment, 10th Veterans, the Newfoundland Regiment and some Royal Artillery. About 50 provincial seamen are also deployed above Montreal, bringing the troop total there to about 1,500 men.

In Ohio, General William Hull (governor of Michigan Territory) arrives at the Scioto River, where his vanguard, the U.S. 1st Regiment, has been constructing blockhouses. Hull is en route to Detroit. He sends the 2nd Regiment under Colonel James Findlay ahead to carve out a road. Meanwhile, after leaving those troops who have become sick under the care of Captain Dill's company, which will garrison the post (Fort McArthur), the column departs on the 22nd.

In naval activity, Commodore Rodgers, at Sandy Hook, embarks with his squadron—the frigate USS *Congress*, frigate USS *President* and the sloop of war USS *Hornet*—on a mission to intercept a British squadron which is escorting a West Indies merchant ship convoy. The Americans engage in a minor encounter with the British; however, by about midnight (19th–20th), the squadron returns to port.

June 20 (Saturday) **In Maryland** at Baltimore, an unruly pro-war mob attacks a newspaper, the *Federal Republican*, due to the anti-war stance of the paper's owners, editor in chief Jacob Wagner and assistant editor Alexander Hanson. The office is demolished and the equipment is wrecked, but neither Hanson nor Wagner is in the building. On the same night, the thugs also attack the homes of several well known Federalists, and they cause other damages. The mob also gathers on the following night and inflicts more damage, including burning down a house and setting two vessels on fire.

Wagner is out of town during the time of the attack but is quickly notified of the outrageous activity. Friends, including John Howard Payne (author of "Home Sweet Home!"), encourage him to restart the paper and to prepare to defend it, along with the foundation of "liberty of the press." After repeated discussions, Wagner and Hanson decide to heed the advice. Within about one month, the paper is back on the presses, printed at Georgetown and distributed from Wagner's home in Baltimore. About twenty of Wagner's friends participate in preparing the home in case of a new attack. Two of the leaders are Revolutionary War veterans, General James M. Lingan and General Henry "Lighthorse Harry" Lee. As anticipated, the pro-war mob will strike again on 26 July.

In Virginia, at Augusta, the citizens begin to prepare for the war. They establish a Military Association at Staunton for the purpose of opening military schools where recruits can receive training. A committee of correspondence is also formed with the following members, William Boys, General John Brown, Thomas Jackson, John H. Peyton and James McNutt. Also, Francis Preston of Augusta County serves in the war as a brigadier general (volunteers). His wife, Sarah Buchanan Campbell, was the daughter of Colonel William Campbell of King's Mountain fame and Elizabeth Henry Campbell, sister of Patrick Henry.

June 21 (Sunday) **In New York,** the USS *United States* (Captain Decatur), USS *Congress* (Captain Smith) and the USS *Argus* (Captain Sinclair) arrive to join Captain Rodgers' squadron. With the USS *President* (Captain Rodgers), USS *Hornet* (Captain Lawrence) and the USS

Essex (Captain David Porter) already in port, the squadron sails southeast en route to intercept a British convoy of merchant ships. The USS *Nautilus*, commanded by Lt. Crane, arrives later; however, it departs alone and soon is captured by the British.

Meanwhile, within about one hour after receiving the proclamation of war against Britain, Commodore John Rodgers sails. Rodgers has intelligence that a huge convoy is en route from Jamaica to England. By 1700, the squadron passes the Sandy Hook bar. During the chase, an American merchant ship informs Rodgers on the 23rd that a British frigate was close by. Rodgers modifies his course to search for the vessel, the HMS *Belvidera*. Contact is made and fire is exchanged; however, the British frigate escapes from the squadron. After the encounter, Rodgers reinitiates his pursuit of the convoy. Later the Americans come close when they spot coconuts and orange peels in the water off the Banks of Newfoundland. Nonetheless, the convoy safely makes it to the destination.

On 18 July, Rodgers' squadron stands at the entrance of the English Channel when he aborts the chase. Afterward, the Americans change course and sail to Madeira and from there to the Azores. After departing from the Azores, Rodgers heads back toward the Banks of Newfoundland as it sails to Boston. The squadron, having failed to intercept the convoy, arrives at Boston on 31 August. During the cruise, which kept the men at sea for more than 70 days, the squadron captured 6 vessels and recaptured one American ship that had earlier been seized by the British. Until Decatur's orders to join Rodgers arrived, he had been in command (winter of 1811–1812) of a squadron designated as the protecting naval force of the southern coasts and the entrance to Chesapeake Bay.

June 22 (Monday) **In Ohio,** General William Hull departs from Fort McArthur to complete his journey to Detroit; however, the column is pelted with incessant rain that impedes progress and forces the troops to struggle with the mud that develops. The troops reach the headwaters of the Blanchard River. It has become so swollen that General Hull is forced to halt after having advanced only slightly more than 15 miles from Fort McArthur. The troops find themselves among armies of black flies and mosquitoes. While stalled, General Hull orders another post to be constructed. The troops erect a stockade that contains houses and the post is named Fort Necessity. It is near Williamstown in Hancock County. From this point, the journey becomes more difficult. The provisions for man and beast are rapidly depleting. The entire plan is by necessity modified. Rations are cut for the horses and for the oxen. In addition, Hull orders that the loads in the wagons get lightened by transferring some of the supplies onto packs to be carried by the horses. In the meantime, two men sent ahead to Detroit to deliver dispatches to Acting Governor Atwater return with distressing news. The men inform Hull that Indians have joined with the British. Nevertheless, the weather begins to clear and the column resumes the march. Several days later, the column arrives at the Blanchard River, where an advance contingent under Colonel Findlay had begun to construct another post (Fort Findlay).

June 23 (Tuesday) **In England,** Parliament repeals the Orders in Council, with the confidence that the issue that had caused enormous problems with the United States would, after repeal, improve relations with the Americans. Nevertheless, by this time, war had been declared by the United States, but the news had not yet reached London.

In New York, Commodore Rodgers' squadron, including the USS *President*, had departed New York on the 21st in pursuit of a convoy that sailed for England from Jamaica. The *President* encounters the HMS *Belvidera* in the Gulf Stream this day. The *President* closes upon the British warship, which is escorting the merchant convoy. By about 1600, the *President* moves into firing range and begins to fire. The initial shot strikes the *Belvidera*'s rudder-coat, then passes through and penetrates the gun-room. At nearly the same time more punishing fire from the *President* whacks the *Belvidera* with two additional effective shots that inflict more damage and cause casualties; however, when the fourth shot is fired, the gun explodes and destroys the forecastle deck. At the time of explosion, sixteen members of the crew are either killed or wounded, including Commodore Rodgers, who is propelled into the air by the powerful explosion. Rodgers survives the blast but sustains a broken leg. The exchange of fire ceases momentarily, but within a short while, the *Belvidera* reinitiates the action and subjects the *President* to some effective fire. After regaining momentum following the explosion, the President's guns return to action. Nonetheless, the British begin to toss their boats and other items overboard to lighten the weight, then the *Belvidera*, armed with fifteen carronades and two long guns, sails to Halifax. The Americans sustain a total of 22 casualties during the battle and the British aboard the *Belvidera* sustain 10 or 11 casualties. The *President* remains at sea for several uneventful weeks before returning to port at Boston.

In other activity, Governor Tompkins, in a letter to Brigadier General Jacob Brown, announces the declaration of war. He directs Brown to be prepared to bolster the Mohawk Valley militia of Colonel Christopher P. Bellinger with militia from Lewis, Jefferson and St. Lawrence Counties in the event that a British threat emerges. Colonel Bellinger's forces are deployed at Sackets Harbor and Cape Vincent. Brown is also instructed to acquire arms at the state arsenals in Russell and Watertown. Also, Colonel Thomas B. Benedict of St. Lawrence County is ordered to place troops on the frontier stretching between Ogdensburg and St. Regis. Meanwhile, General Jacob Brown takes steps to deploy troops at Cape Vincent and Ogdensburg.

Brown, originally a Pennsylvanian, until he relocated near the Black River less than five miles from Watertown, had been appointed as brigadier general during 1811. At the outbreak of war, General Brown is responsible for defending a 200 to 300 mile frontier that stretches from Oswego to Lake St. Francis. Also, soon after the declaration of war reaches the frontier, a small attack against the British occurs. A Revolutionary War veteran, Abner Hubbard, acting on his own and accompanied by one friend and a boy, raids and captures Fort Carleton. The post was initially built by General Guy Carleton on Carleton Island slightly below Cape Vincent. It was abandoned as a British post during 1808; however, it remained in the hands of the British. The adventuresome trio takes the fort without firing a shot and the garrison, composed of three men, each an invalid, and two women offer no resistance. On the day following the seizure, a boat moves to the island and the stores are confiscated. Afterward, the buildings are burned.

June 24 (Wednesday) **In Ohio,** General Hull, while en route to Detroit from Ohio, is intercepted at Fort Findlay by Colonel Dunlap, who arrives from Washington to deliver orders to Hull. The general is to accelerate his advance to Detroit, but the order does not mention that war has been declared. Also this day, Colonel McFarland receives a dispatch from Chillicothe which states that "war would be proclaimed before this writing could be delivered to him." The letter is shared with General Hull.

Upon receipt of his orders, Hull prepares to move out. He orders most of the heavy baggage to be stored at the post. The 3rd Regiment under Colonel Lewis Cass jumps off in advance to carve a road, and later the column follows. Hull arrives

Fort Findlay (*The History of the Maumee River*, Charles Elihu Slocum, 1914).

at the Maumee (Miami) River following a 3-day march, and he establishes camp opposite where the army under General Wayne had defeated the Indians at the Battle of Fallen Timbers. Afterward, the army crosses the river at the Rapids and advances to the foot of the lower rapids near the former site of Fort Miami. General Hull, at that place, charters a vessel, the *Cuyahoga*, to transport much of the baggage, luggage and heavy supplies to Detroit. The vessel departs on 1 July.

In naval activity, the HMS *Belvidera* intercepts the 197-ton brigantine *Malcolm*, which is transporting a cargo that includes wine from Madeira, Portugal, to Portland, Maine. The *Belvidera* captures the *Malcolm* before it reaches its destination.

Late June Although Congress has declared war against the Great Britain, still ruled by King George III, the colonists' nemesis during the American Revolution, the country remains divided by regions. The Southern and Western states hold to supporting President Madison, but in New England, there is little support, much opposition, and in some instances, treason. The land known as the home of the famed Minutemen, who boldly refused to kneel to the pressure of the Redcoats, now lies prone with self-inflicted paralysis. New England sends no militia out of the respective states to aid the cause. Some New Englanders, who are steadfastly against Napoleon and conspicuously pro–British, concentrate on supporting the enemy by supplying goods and arms to the British. North of Massachusetts beyond the Penobscot River in Maine, some Americans disavow their country and swear allegiance to the British Crown, a most unsettling occurrence to the president and all those who sacrificed so much to attain independence. Nevertheless, lacking the support of the New England Yankees, the remainder of the country rallies to the colors. The Federalists and the Democratic-Republicans (present-day Democrats) continue to argue and at times, such as the Baltimore riots (June–July 1812), violence erupts.

In Europe, Napoleon, backed by an Army of more than 600,000 men, storms into Russia. The ranks include soldiers who had been enlisted from other conquered countries. Russia had been an ally of France; however, Napoleon has become suspicious of Russian friendliness since it had chosen to trade with Great Britain, despite the Continental System, imposed by Napoleon during 1805, which forbids all of France's allies from trading with Britain. Rather than risk Russia linking with Britain as an ally, Napoleon had decided to invade and conquer the Russians. Czar Alexander I, keenly aware that his forces are mismatched against the French, orders his people to make disciplined withdrawals and to destroy the food supply and farms to prevent future use by the invaders. Seemingly, the Russians know full well that their most powerful ally is the horrid Russian winter, and as they pull back, the French will become entrenched in untenable positions.

The Grand Army plows over the ground, and by September, it stands at the vestibule of Moscow, but the shrewd czar has assured that Napoleon has overstretched his supply lines. With Britain engaged with France and the United States, the British can spare no troops for intervention along the Russian Front. The stage seems set for another Napoleonic victory. The czar hopes for an early end to the hostilities between the British and the Americans in order to get support from the British in his struggle against France. English troops would greatly help in the campaign to push Napoleon's hordes out of Russia. The czar suggests during September 1812 that he is available to become the intermediary between Britain and the United States in hopes that a quick settlement could be achieved.

June 25 (Thursday) **In Florida,** outside St. Augustine, Lt. Colonel Thomas A. Smith responds to a letter from Captain John Tate. He mentions an incident regarding the Spanish: "The party that left St. Augustine have not yet returned & I think never will without getting a severe drubbing, as 160 men are in pursuit of them." Meanwhile, several U.S. gunboats and one revenue cutter arrive at Cowford (Jacksonville). Smith notes in his response to Captain Tate that reinforcements (infantry and dragoons) are en route from several places, including Augusta, Georgia, and from North Carolina. Colonel Smith is awaiting new orders which will authorize him to seize St. Augustine.

In Tennessee, Major General Andrew Jackson commits his Tennessee volunteers to service for the United States.

In naval activity, the 317-ton ship *Fortune*, while traveling from Cape de Verdes to Newbury Port, crosses paths with the HMS *Belvidera*, which terminates the voyage by seizing the ship and its cargo. The *Fortune* is separate from the schooner *Fortune* seized on 28 August 1812 and the schooner *Fortune* seized on 31 August 1813.

June 26 (Friday) **In Washington, D.C.,** Congress passes legislation (Act of June 26) directing that the army "shall consist of twenty-five regiments, of ten companies each."

In England, at London, the American charge d'affaires is directed to propose an armistice to the British government in conjunction with the repeal of the Orders in Council and an end to the impressment of American seamen during the truce. The British reject three proposals, making it clear they are not concerned about settling the differences.

In Pennsylvania, James Steel is commissioned major general of the 3rd Pennsylvania Division, composed of the militia of Chester and Delaware Counties. Steel succeeds General Pearce.

July **In New Hampshire,** Lt. Colonel Timothy Upton (militia) is commissioned as a major in the U.S. 11th Infantry Regiment. Later, with the rank of lieutenant colonel, Upton participates with the 21st Regiment in Canada at Chrysler's Farm. Afterward, he participates at Fort Erie, and that duty is followed by recruiting duty. He resigns from the service after the war. Subsequently, on 15 May 1819, he is appointed brigadier general of the 1st Brigade, 1st Division, New Hampshire militia, and the following year, he is raised to the rank of major general. He dies at Charlestown on 2 November 1855.

Also, the state military organization at the outbreak of war was as follows: Major General Henry Butler, 1st Division; Major General Samuel Hale, 2nd Division; Major General Philemon Whitcomb, 3rd Division; Brigadier General Moody Bedel, 6th Brigade; Brigadier General Samuel Dinsmore, Quartermaster General; Brigadier General Richard Furber, 2nd Brigade; Brigadier General Elisha Huntley, 5th Brigade; Brigadier General Michael McClary, Adjutant General; Brigadier General Asa Robinson, 3rd Brigade; Brigadier General John Steele, 4th Brigade; and Brigadier General Clement Storer, 1st Brigade.

General Bedel, the son of General Timothy Bedel of the Revolutionary War, had been appointed brigade general of his brigade on 10 June 1806; however, he relinquished it on 6 April of this year. Also in 1812, he is commissioned lieutenant colonel of the U.S. 11th Regiment, ranking from 6 July. On 8 May, he was assigned command of the District of New Hampshire for recruiting. By 16 September, Lt. Colonel Bedel recruits just under 400 men, whom he takes to Burlington. On 26 September, the 11th Regiment under the command of Colonel Isaac Clark departs from Burlington. Lt. Colonel Bedel remains in command of the regiment until 22 August 1813. From then until mid–September 1814, he remains on special duty, unable to rejoin his regiment until General Brown takes possession of Fort Erie (Canada).

In naval activity, the schooner USS *Wasp* (third), constructed in Maryland at Baltimore during 1810, departs for the West Indies as a privateer (authorized by the U.S. government). The cruise is somewhat prosperous; however, the HMS *Garland* nearly ends its brief career. Three British merchant ships are intercepted and of those one is permitted to resume its voyage. The *Wasp* is intercepted by the HMS *Garland* during the time a boarding crew is preparing to sail with the final prize, the vessel *Dawson*. The British give chase to the *Wasp*, permitting the *Dawson's* prize crew to make it safely to Savannah, while the *Wasp* outpaces the *Garland* only to encounter a hurricane. The storm inflicts heavy damage to the *Wasp*; however it arrives at its home port, Baltimore, on 28 November.

The privateer *Lion*, operating out of Salem, completes its initial cruise, during which it captures several British shallops out of Nova Scotia. Captain J. Hitch directs the three prizes to be taken into Salem; however, the *Lion* also operates with the *Snowchild* (Captain S. Stacy) and together, they seize five additional British vessels, each a brigantine caught while sailing from Liverpool to St. John's. On its own, the *Lion*, also receives credit for seizing one brigantine, two schooners and three sloops during the war.

In early July, the American privateer *Atlas* comes within range of the American vessel *Tulip* (Captain Monk). The *Atlas* suspects that the *Tulip* is transporting cargo intended for the British in Spain. The *Atlas* acts slowly and flies an English ensign. Once the *Tulip* is halted and

Captain Monk becomes convinced he has been halted by a British privateer rather than by an American, he produces his English license and requests that he be permitted to continue his voyage. Captain Maffit of the *Atlas* agrees with Captain Monk that his papers are "quite satisfactory," but before Monk can breathe a sigh of relief, he also hears Captain Maffitt proclaim that his voyage is terminated. Maffitt states: "Now, instead of sending you into a British port, I will send you into port at Philadelphia."

Also, the American 16-gun privateer *John* (Captain J. Crowninshield) completes a three-week cruise during which it captures eleven vessels, including one that is recaptured. Of the eleven prizes, three are destroyed. The prizes taken into port include *Ceres*, a brigantine; the brigantine *Elizabeth*; the *Union*, a schooner carrying a cargo of rum; the ship *Apollo*; and another schooner carrying a cargo of rum. Subsequently, the *John* captures the brigantine *Henry* out of Liverpool, the ship *Jane* out of Port Glasgow, the brigantine *Neptune* out of Gibraltar, the schooner *Blonde* from the Dominican Republic and an unnamed schooner carrying a cargo of rum. The *Neptune* is taken into port at Boston, while the others are sailed into Salem. Despite its successes, the *John* is captured during the early part of the war.

The American privateer *Paul Jones*, operating out of New York, intercepts and seizes a British brigantine, the *Ulysses*, which is en route to Halifax from the West Indies. The prize is taken into port at Norfolk.

In yet other naval activity, a British warship intercepts the letter-of-marque *Gypsey*, which is en route from New York to France; however, before it can be taken into a British port, the Americans regain it. The *Gypsey* arrives safely at its destination. Also, a 6-gun British brigantine, en route to St. John's from Liverpool, is seized during a joint effort by the American privateers *Lion* and *Snow Bird*. After being seized, the vessel arrives at Marblehead, Massachusetts. The prize is captured without incident.

Early July *In naval activity,* the American privateer *Black Joke* returns to port. The sloop carrying five guns, commanded by Captain B. Brenow with a crew of 60 men, is one of the first pilot-boat privateers to take to the sea. During its cruise, the *Black Joke* had seized two small British vessels. During the same time period, another privateer, *Jack's Favorite*, commanded by Captain Johnson, also returns to New York. During the cruise, *Jack's Favorite* had seized the schooner *Rebecca*, carrying a cargo of molasses from Trinidad to Halifax. The prize is taken into port at New London, Connecticut. *Jack's Favorite* also seizes the brigantine *Betsey*, which is en route to St. Petersburg from Malaga with a cargo of raisins and wine, valued at about $75,000. The prize is taken into port at Plymouth, Massachusetts. *Jack's Favorite* captured three other sloops that were destroyed at sea.

In other activity, other American privateers are also becoming active. The *Dolphin*, *Fair Trader*, *Jefferson*, *Lion* and the *Snowbird*, operating out of Salem, Massachusetts, along with the *Rapid* out of Boston are on the hunt for vulnerable British vessels. The *Rapid* intercepts and seizes three vessels, including the brigantine *St. Andrews* and the ship *Enterprise*. The remaining brigantine is ransomed. The *Rapid*, with its crew of 84 men and carrying 14 guns, also engages the British privateer *Searcher*, a 1-gun schooner, with a crew of 20 men. The overmatched *Searcher* falls easily. After it is seized, the Americans destroy it. Also, the *Jefferson*, during its initial cruise, seizes one brigantine, one sloop and four schooners, while the *Dolphin* captures one brigantine, four schooners and one shallop, all of which are taken into Salem.

One of the very successful privateers to sail from Salem is the privateer *Frolic*, commanded by Captain Odiorne. During its sea cruises the *Frolic* seizes eleven vessels; most are destroyed at sea. Its prizes include the *Reprisal*, a ship out of Scotland, captured while en route to the Bay of Chaleur (Canada); the brigantine *Friends* out of Bristol, England; the brigantine *Betsey*; a galliot, the *Guttle Hoffnung*, out of Portsmouth, England; the brigantine *Jane Gordon*, out of London; and the *Encouragement*. The crews and cargoes are all transferred to the *Frolic* before the vessels are destroyed. Some are exceptions to destruction. The *Hunter* is transformed into a cartel and used to transport some of Captain Odiorne's large number of prisoners to England. The prizes *Susan* and *Vigilant* also become cartels. The schooner *Traveller*, along with the schooner *Grotius*, both of which contain valuable cargoes, are taken into American ports by prize crews.

Another privateer operating out of Salem is the 2-gun *General Stark*, manned by only 12 crewmen. During its service at sea during the conflict, the *General Stark*'s seizures include a heavy schooner taken into Machias, Maine, and the brigantine *Cossack* intercepted between Martinique and Bermuda and taken into port at Georgetown, South Carolina.

July 1 (Wednesday) **In Florida,** at St. Mary's, Governor Mitchell of Georgia, the U.S. commissioner, writes to Lt. Colonel Thomas A. Smith in camp outside of St. Augustine to inform him that he (Mitchell) received a dispatch from Major General Thomas Pinckney that war had been declared against Britain on 18 June. Mitchell is anticipating some decisive action. He states: "I confess my patience is nearly exhausted by the dilatory manner in which we have been proceeding for some time past. I hope the Savannah Volunteers have reached you in safety." Mitchell tells Smith that additional reinforcements, about 180 men, would soon be arriving from the Oconee. The message is delivered to Smith by Mr. Gleason, one of the Patriots, because Colonel Isaacs became ill and is not well enough to return to Smith's camp.

In naval activity, on or about this day, a U.S. cutter captures a British merchant ship en route to London. The vessel, thought to have been seized off Cape Hatteras, is taken into port at Norfolk to become the first British merchant ship seized during the war.

July 1–3 **In Ohio,** General Hull is at the Maume River close to the site of Fort Miamis in the vicinity of Maume on the outskirts of Toledo. A 25-man contingent under Lt. Davidson is assigned the task of erecting a blockhouse at the ruins of Fort Miamis. The post was initially established by the British on the property of Benjamin Starbird during the early 1790s. On this day, the vessel *Cuyahoga* under Captain Chapin, transporting Hull's supplies and luggage, sails for Detroit. It is accompanied by a sloop that is transporting soldiers who had become sick during the journey. An armed guard of about 30 troops is assigned to protect the vessels during the voyage. Prior to its departure, Captain Mc-Pherson warns Hull of the danger involved because he is certain that the war had begun, and he feared that the vessel would surely be captured by the British; however, Hull is not swayed. Nonetheless, the ship which is also transporting several wives of officers and soldiers who had become sick is intercepted on the following day off Malden in Canada.

When the British seize the vessel, they discover a bonanza. General Hull's commission, personal papers, complete muster rolls of the army and even his orders from the secretary of war are aboard the ship. The sloop transporting the sick troops is sailing well behind the *Cuyahoga* and moving up a separate and shallow channel west of Bois Blanc Island. The British fail to intercept it, and it arrives at Detroit on 3 July.

July 2 (Thursday) **In Michigan,** American General William Hull's troops arrive at Frenchtown (Monroe), Michigan, a three-day march from Detroit. Hull receives the official news on this day when a messenger arrives that war has been declared. Another letter had been sent to him by the secretary of war on the same day, 18 June, and he received it on the 24 June; however, it omitted the news regarding the war.

During the advance to Michigan, the U.S. 4th Regiment, commanded by Colonel Miller (formerly Colonel Boyd's regiment), had joined Hull's army on 10 June. Meanwhile, the Canadian army commanders had been informed of the opening of hostilities several days before Hull.

In other activity, a British-Indian contingent crosses into Michigan from Canada and arrives at the Wyandotte village at Monguagon, about 15 miles below Detroit. The Wyandotte tribe had not participated in the war. Nevertheless, the British take them as "willing prisoners" to Malden and the British expect them to fight with the Indians already aligned with the British.

In New York, General Peter Gansevoort, a veteran of the American Revolution, dies. Shortly thereafter, on the 6th, John Armstrong, a veteran of the American Revolution and the son of General John Armstrong (Pennsylvania), is appointed brigadier general by President Madison to replace the vacancy caused by Gansevoort's death. General Armstrong had also been a veteran of the Revolutionary War. He had been the minister to France during the previous year.

Also around this time, Morgan Lewis is appointed quartermaster general, Thomas H. Cushing (Massachusetts), adjutant-general, and Alexander Smyth (Virginia), inspector general. Alexander Macomb is named colonel of artillery.

Winfield Scott and Edmund P. Gaines, both from Virginia, are appointed lieutenant colonels and Eleazar W. Ripley (speaker of the Massachusetts Legislature) becomes a lieutenant colonel. The Macomb family owns a large amount of land in New York. Alexander's father, also named Alexander, purchased three and one-half million acres along Lake Erie and the St. Lawrence River during 1792. The elder Alexander had been a member of the New York legislature during the period when the U.S. Constitution was adopted.

July 2–30 During the early days of the conflict between England and the United States, there is much activity on the high seas off the coast of the United States as both nations attempt to gain the advantage. The USS *President*, operating in the North Atlantic, engages and captures the HMS *Traveller*, *Duchess of Portland* and *John of Lancaster*. The frigate *Essex* encounters the HMS *Samuel* and *Sarah* on the 11th and makes a successful capture. Afterward, about two days later, the *Essex* captures the British brigantine *Lamprey*. Toward the latter part of the month, it seizes the HMS *Leander*, and that encounter is followed by the capture of a British brigantine off Newfoundland. The sloop *Hornet* engages and captures the HMS *Dolphin* on the 9th. Also, the American privateer *Yankee*, while operating off Newfoundland, captures two British brigantines, the *Alfred* and the *Mary*.

Supremacy of the seas is to be of primary importance during the war, and the British ships far outnumber those of the United States; however, the British are simultaneously engaged in other parts of the globe, which restricts the number of warships that the British can commit against the United States. American privateers play a large role in bolstering the power of the U.S. Navy during this conflict. It is not until after the War of 1812 that privateering is terminated and the United States Navy operates as a single unit, without benefit of taking prizes.

July 3 (Friday) **In Canada,** a French Canadian, Lieutenant Rolette (Provincial Marine) pulls off a major upset this day when his 8-man contingent pulls alongside an American schooner and successfully boards it. The vessel, in addition to the crew, is transporting General William Hull's baggage and personal papers. Rolette directs that the vessel, already close to the Canadian shore, be moved in closer under the guns of a British battery. Shortly thereafter, a small contingent led by an officer arrives in a batteaux to ensure the prize is kept. Meanwhile, after the astonishing discovery of having gained Hull's papers, the British find themselves with a treasure trove of intelligence, including Hull's plans and strategy.

July 4 (Saturday) **In Canada,** Captain Charles Roberts, commander at Fort St. Joseph, receives word from General Brock that war with the United States had erupted during the previous month. Roberts is ordered to mount a force and lead a mission to seize American-held Fort Michilimackinac on Lake Huron. The mission gets underway on 17 July. Roberts takes Toussaint Pothier (agent of the Hudson's Bay Company) into his confidence regarding his plan for the attack. Toussaint becomes enthusiastic and participates in the mission.

In Maryland, where privateers are converging to initiate cruises to support the diminutive U.S. Navy, an article in a local newspaper states: "Several small, swift privateers will sail from the United States in a few days. Some have already been sent to sea, and many others of a larger class, better fitted and better equipped, will soon follow."

July 5 (Sunday) **In Michigan,** Brigadier General William Hull, governor of the Michigan Territory, arrives at Fort Detroit on Lake Ontario. General Hull's army as reported in *Defense of General Dearborn* was listed as "Fourth regiment of infantry 483; Colonel Findlay's regiment of volunteers and militia 509; Colonel [Lewis] Cass' regiment of volunteers and militia 483; Colonel McArthur's regiment of volunteers and militia 552; and Captain Sloan's troop of Cincinnati light dragoons 48, for a total of 2,075." Soon after General Hull surrendered Detroit, he reported that "but fifteen hundred men passed with him into Canada, and that none of the Michigan militia, and only a portion of the Ohio militia, would cross the river."

Hull's army immediately prepares to cross into Canada. Nonetheless, Hull does not know that the British have become aware of his strategy. On July 3, the British had captured an American packet, the USS *Cuyahoga*, which was transporting baggage as well as hospital stores and a small contingent (one officer and 30 troops) of General Hull's force. The ship was seized as it entered the Detroit River and the British had seized Hull's papers, which included his battle plan and strategy.

In naval activity, the HMS *Emulous* intercepts a brigantine, the 119-ton *Bellisle* (William Brown, master) while it is en route from Savannah, Georgia, to Salem, Massachusetts. The *Emulous* captures its prey along with a cargo that includes coffee, sugar, molasses and wood.

July 6 (Monday) **In Washington, D.C.,** Congress passes legislation (Act of July 6th) that specifies:

> To any army of the United States, other than that in which the Adjutant-General shall serve, the President may appoint one Deputy Adjutant General who shall be taken from the line, and in addition to his pay, be entitled to fifty dollars per month, which shall be in full compensation for his extra service, and there shall be to each Deputy Adjutant-General such number of assistant deputies (not exceeding three to each department) as the public service may require, who shall each be entitled to thirty dollars per month in addition to his pay and other emoluments, which shall be in full compensation for his extra services.

Also, Hugh Brady is commissioned as colonel of the U.S. 22nd Infantry Regiment. He had been discharged from the army on 15 June 1800 and joined the Pennsylvania militia in 1808.

In New York, at Albany, Governor Tompkins, in a letter to General William Wadsworth, informs the general that he is sending his secretary to assist him:

> SIR: In consequence of your suggestion that a Gentleman intimately acquainted with the details of camp duty would be of great service to you, I have requested Mr. [Nicholas] Gray who is well acquainted with those subjects to repair to Niagara and to confer and advise with you and the other officers, in establishing the necessary regulations upon that subject and in planning any other operations which may be deemed necessary in the service upon which you have entered. Mr. Gray will not assume any authority or command, but proceeds to Niagara at my request and for the purpose of being useful to you in relation to the subjects upon which you desired assistance by your letter of the 28th ulto. Mr. Gray has seen service in Ireland in the capacity of General of Brigade and has made Military science his study. He is possessed of a manuscript treatise upon the duties of Staff officers & upon the details of Garrison, Camp & field duty, which will be very useful.

In naval activity, the 256-ton brigantine *Minerva*, en route from Liverpool to Boston with a cargo of coal and salt, encounters a strong British squadron composed of the HMS *Aeolus*, HMS *Africa*, HMS *Belvidera* and the HMS *Shannon*. The *Minerva* is seized. This *Minerva* is separate from other vessels of the same name: a ship seized on 8 September 1812, the brigantine captured on 30 June 1813, the sloop seized on 5 August 1813, the schooner seized on 30 August 1813, a brigantine seized 21 April, 1814, the schooner captured on 11 August 1814, and a schooner captured 26 September 1814.

In other naval activity, some of the citizens at Gloucester, Massachusetts, while peering out in the harbor, spot a vessel approaching. The ship is flying two flags, the Stars and Stripes and the British ensign, and both are at half-mast. Afterward, it is identified as the *Pickering*, an American merchant ship which had recently been seized by the HMS *Belvidera*. A party in the boats explains how the *Pickering* was retaken from the prize crew by the Americans and some passengers before it reached a British port. The *Belvidera*, after a narrow escape from Commodore John Rodgers' squadron, encountered and seized the *Pickering*.

July 7 (Tuesday) **In Canada,** due to an unexplained delay by the British minister in Washington, D.C., official word that the United States had declared war on Great Britain on the 18 June finally reaches Sir George Prevost. Meanwhile, General Brock in Upper Canada receives no official word that war had been declared; however, due to his own instincts and information from unofficial sources, Brock had been prepared. Brock had recently designated Major General Shaw responsibility for the Eastern frontier, which includes Kingston, while Brock himself assumes responsibility for Niagara and Detroit.

Once he is informed, Brock takes steps to meet the threat. He calls for the legislature to convene on the 17th, and he chooses Fort George as his headquarters. With fewer than 2,000 troops in Upper Canada, General Brock urgently requests reinforcements from Lower Canada; however, none will be available until fresh troops arrive from Britain. In addition to preparing militarily, Brock calls for a day of fasting and prayer. Meanwhile, his military force is not well equipped, and in some cases there is even a shortage of clothing and shoes. Nevertheless, he initiates training and drilling of the troops, while he also directs that the militia be organized.

In naval activity, the privateer *Mary,* a schooner, is commissioned in Maine this day. Joseph Sturdivant receives command. In other activity, the 198-ton brigantine *Enterprise* (F. Bourne, master), while en route from St. Ubes with a cargo of salt, is intercepted and seized by the HMS *Ringdove* before it arrives at New York. The *Enterprise* is separate from the schooner of the same name seized on 21 May 1813, a schooner captured on 8 December 1813, another seized 16 December 1813 and yet another seized on 30 August 1814.

July 8 (Wednesday) *In naval activity,* the HMS *Guerriere* while on patrol intercepts and seizes the 149-ton brigantine *George* (J. Robertson, master), which is en route to New York from Rochelle with a cargo that includes brandy and other items. This *George* is separate from the 21-ton brigantine *George* seized on 17 July 1812, the brigantine *George* seized on 22 July 1812, and the 172-ton brigantine *George* seized on 22 February 1815.

In other naval activity, the HMS *Indian* intercepts and seizes the 167-ton brigantine *Mary Elizabeth* (C. Crandall, master) while it is en route from St. Ubes to Portland with a cargo of ballast and some cash. The *Mary Elizabeth* is separate from the brigantine *Mary* seized on 17 July 1812, the schooner *Mary Ann* captured 23 July 1812, the 97-ton schooner *Mary* seized on 23 March 1813, the schooner *Mary* captured 23 March 1813, the schooner *Mary* taken over on 27 March 1813, the sloop *Mary* seized on 4 July 1813, the sloop *Mary* seized on 27 July 1813, the schooner *Mary* captured 7 August 1813, the schooner *Mary* seized on 10 September 1813, the schooner *Mary* taken over on 13 September 1813, the sloop *Mary Ann* captured on 22 December 1813, the sloop *Mary* seized on 6 January 1814, the ship *Mary* captured on 1 June 1814 and the 92-ton schooner *Mary* captured on 6 October 1814.

Also, the HMS *Indian* recaptures the bark *William.* Other ships of that name captured are a brigantine, 16 August 1812; a schooner, 12 March 1813; a brigantine, 31 May 1813; a sloop, 7 August 1813; a schooner, 27 October 1813; another schooner, 19 June 1814; a brigantine, 11 October 1814; and a schooner seized at an unspecific time during 1814.

July 9 (Thursday) *In naval activity,* the HMS *Collector,* operating out of Halifax, intercepts the 270-ton *Benjamin Franklin* (James Whelan, master), which is en route to Philadelphia from Liverpool. The privateer *Fame* returns to port at Salem, Massachusetts, along with a British ship of about 300 tons carrying lumber, along with a second prize, a brigantine transporting tar. In other naval activity, the American privateer *Fame* (Captain Webb) arrives back at Salem after having seized a brigantine, carrying a cargo of tar and a ship transporting a cargo of lumber. Also, at about this time, or possibly earlier, Governor Mitchell of Georgia, once informed of the outbreak of war, orders the capture of 17 British vessels, each carrying lumber intended for use by the Royal Navy. The seized vessels are at Amelia Island and St. Mary's.

July 10 (Friday) **In Florida,** Lt. Colonel Thomas A. Smith, at his camp outside St. Augustine, writes to Governor David B. Mitchell to inform him that the commanders of the Georgia Patriots have proposed that they urge their volunteers to enter federal service. Smith requests authorization to accept their services and he stipulates that he will accept only "the most active, hardy, and those disposed to submit to discipline." However, Smith makes it clear that his force has no cartridge boxes that can be spared for the Georgians who lack proper arms. He suggests that if the authorization is forthcoming, the required arms should be forwarded to him from Amelia Island.

In naval activity, Captain Isaac Hull, commanding the USS *Constitution,* is preparing to take his ship from Annapolis to remove it from British threat by sailing for New York. Captain Hull sets sail on the 12th. However, on the 17th, a British squadron under Captain Broke intercepts him off the coast of New Jersey.

In other naval activity, the 859-ton ship *Marquis De Somerlous* (T. Moriarity, master) — while transporting a mixed cargo including brandy, dry goods, silks and wine — is captured by the HMS *Atalanta.* The 4-gun British schooner *Whiting,* commanded by Lieutenant Maxcey, is captured in Hampton Roads by the privateer *Dash,* commanded by Captain Carroway. At the time of capture, the crew was not aware that the war had begun. The *Whiting* is taken while at anchor making preparations for a party to land. Lieutenant Maxcey is taken prisoner while in a boat heading for shore at Hampton. Nevertheless, the U.S. government orders that the *Whiting* be released. On board the *Whiting,* the British attempt to destroy documents by tossing them into the water; however, some survive. Later on 12 August, the USS *Gallatin* (Captain Edward Herbert), a revenue cutter, guides the *Whiting* back to Hampton Roads and the British are directed to immediately depart from American waters.

At nearly the same time the *Whiting* had been seized, another American privateer, the *Cora,* operating out of Baltimore, had captured a British dispatch boat, the *Bloodhound,* and taken it into port at Annapolis. The U.S. government also orders this craft released; however, complications develop because many of the crew prefer to remain in America and they refuse to return to their vessel. Some crew members of the *Whiting* also refuse to return to the Royal Navy and join either the U.S. Navy or the American privateers.

Also, while the crew of the *Bloodhound* is at Annapolis, it is determined that one captive is an American who had been impressed by the British three years earlier. The *Cora,* following this incident, is not known to have had any eventful service. It is captured in February 1813 in Chesapeake Bay by a British squadron. Four of the crew escape and make it to shore. The *Dash* is also not known for any additional captures of British vessels.

Another privateer operating out of Baltimore is the *Mammoth,* commanded by Captain Rowland. During its initial cruise, the *Mammoth* intercepts its first prize, the brigantine *Camelion,* which is carrying a cargo of molasses and rum. That successful seizure is followed by the interception of the sloop *Farmer.* The privateer removes the cargo from the *Farmer* before destroying it at sea; however, the *Camelion* is taken into an American port by a prize crew. During this cruise, several brigantines are seized and destroyed at sea, and the *Caroline* also captures the brigantine *Britannia,* also destroyed at sea. Nonetheless, the *Caroline* also encounters a British transport while off Newfoundland and the British vessel raises tenacious resistance. The *Caroline,* after determining that the transport is carrying a large force of British troops, disengages and resumes its search for a less lethal target.

Subsequently, during other cruises, the *Caroline*'s prizes continue to increase, to a final total of 21 ships. Also, an American privateer out of Newport intercepts the schooner *Sally* out of Cape Ann and seizes it along with a cargo of molasses. The prize is taken into port at Newport.

July 11 (Saturday) *In naval activity,* the USS *Essex,* commanded by Captain David D. Porter, while operating in the West Indies spots a convoy of seven British vessels off Bermuda. After dusk the *Essex* closes on the convoy and snatches one of the transports. The *Essex,* acquired by the Navy during 1799, had participated in the Quasi-war with France and the Barbary Coast War. It had been at Tripoli during 1805 when U.S. Marines captured the pirate stronghold. Afterward, when it returned to the United States during 1806, it laid in reserve until February 1809, when it was re-commissioned. The *Essex* continues its cruise after seizing the transport, and on 13 August, it encounters the HMS *Alert.*

In other naval activity, the HMS *Emulous* intercepts and captures the 254-ton brigantine *Illuminator* (Robert Patterson, master), which is transporting a cargo of hides, molasses, sugar and other items en route from Havana, Cuba, to Boston. Also, the 427-ton ship *Oronoke,* carrying a cargo of ballast, is cornered and captured by a British squadron, composed of the HMS *Aeolus, Africa, Belvidera, Guerriere* and *Shannon.*

July 12 (Sunday) **In Canada,** American General William Hull's command crosses from Detroit into Sandwich, Canada, unopposed. He informs the Canadians there that he intends no harm to non-violent Canadians and that he is not seeking their support, but he makes it clear in his proclamation that volunteers would be accepted. Hull also informs the Canadians that any who adopt the Indian warfare or fight alongside the Indians would receive no quarter: "No white man found fighting by the side of an Indian will be taken prisoner — instant death will be his lot. The United States offer you peace, liberty and security. Your choice lies between these and war, slavery and destruction" (see Appendix D for complete proclamation).

Barracks at Sandwich, Canada.

A number of Canadians desert to join the Americans; however, optimistic thoughts for the American cause soon fade away. A copy of Hull's proclamation had been dispatched to the secretary of war and it was approved by him. General Hull immediately begins to strengthen his encampment, and he sends out reconnaissance detachments to gather intelligence on Fort Malden in Ontario. All the while, Hull awaits the arrival of artillery. He refuses to move against Fort Malden without artillery. The delays keep the army at Sandwich for several weeks. Nonetheless, Hull dispatches a 280-man contingent under Colonels Cass and Miller, which reconnoiters the route to Fort Malden. The force clashes with British pickets and Indians at a bridge near the fort.

By August, General Hull's command is in full retreat for Detroit. The Canadian deserters make no significant difference in the campaign. In reaction to Hull's invasion, General Brock dispatches Colonel Henry Proctor to Amherstburg with the 41st Regiment. In another strategic move, Brock had sent Captain Roberts to deploy at Fort St. Joseph (Lake Huron), and with Hull in Canada, Brock orders Roberts to make a bold strike against American-held Michilimackinac.

In New York, at Albany, Governor Tompkins, in a letter to Colonel R. Macomb, informs the latter that some Canadian militia are unwilling to fight against the U.S:

> The Militia at Lacheane near Montreal, have already refused unanimously to bear arms against us and have been fired on by the Regulars. Eleven of the Militia were killed. A second insurrection I am informed by General [Benjamin] Mooers of Plattsburgh, is rumored to have taken place and that Indians were employed with the Regulars to quell it. I am satisfied that if we appeared on the lines with a Commanding force adequate to their protection, and extended the hand of fellowship, one half the Militia of both provinces would join our standard. Delays are dangerous—& the truth of that proverb was never manifested with greater force than it will be if we suffer the present golden opportunity to pass unimproved.

In naval activity, the USS *Constitution* leaves Annapolis en route to New York. During the journey, it encounters a British naval squadron off the coast of New Jersey on the 17th. Also, John T. Shubrick is appointed fifth lieutenant aboard the *Constitution*. The HMS *Emulous* intercepts and seizes the 78-ton schooner *Lively*, which is en route from St. Bartholomews to Boston with a cargo of molasses, rum and sugar. The *Lively* is separate from the schooner *Lively* seized on 20 July 1813, the schooner *Lively* seized on 24 July 1813, the sloop *Lively* captured on 7 June 1814 and the sloop *Lively* seized on 26 October 1814. The *Emulous* on this day also seizes the 108-ton schooner *Traveller* and its cargo of timber. It is taken into the service of the British Navy. The *Traveller* is separate from the sloop *Traveller* seized on 4 April 1813.

In other naval activity, the *Rossie*, an American privateer under Joshua Barney, sets out on its first cruise. The ship was expected to depart just after war was declared; however, due to a private debt incurred by Barney, he was detained by the authorities at Baltimore. Barney, an excellent seaman and a veteran of the American Revolution, seemed to frequently get himself in financial trouble due to inattention. Nonetheless, a friend of Barney's, Isaac McKim, learned of the problem and settled the debt. Also, the American privateer *Nonpareil*, operating out of Savannah, which recently seized a schooner on its first cruise, is on this day seized by the HMS *Decouverte*.

July 13 (Monday) **In New York,** General Stephen Van Rensselaer III, having recently been named commander of militia in the northern and western frontiers of the state by Governor Tompkins, assumes the position this day.

Stephen's father (Stephen II) died while Stephen was young. After his father's death, Stephen was educated through the efforts of his grandfather, Philip Livingston (signer of the Declaration of Independence). Stephen III married Margaret Schuyler, the daughter of General Philip Schuyler. Subsequent to Margaret's death, he married Cornelia, the daughter of Judge William Patterson. He also served in the U.S. Congress from 1822 to 1829; his was the deciding vote that elected John Quincy Adams to the presidency.

Governor Tompkins said in a letter dated this day to General Van Rensselaer:

> SIR: As Commandant of the First Division of the Detached Militia of this State you are required to assume the Command upon our Northwesterly and Westerly Frontier. The District which is more immediately under your care, extends from St. Regis along the St. Lawrence to Lake Ontario, along Lake Ontario to Niagara River, along Niagara River to Lake Erie, and along the shore of Lake Erie to Pennsylvania. All the militia heretofore ordered out upon that Frontier, as well detached as others, are under your command, and the enclosed General Orders place at your disposal likewise, all the residue of the Detached Division to the Command of which you were assigned by a General Order dated the day of [18th June] last.

General Van Rensselaer departs from Albany on this day en route to the frontier.

Governor Tompkins also writes to General Abraham Rose:

> DEAR SIR: Upon the declaration of War, I had directed Mr. McLean to enquire of the United States officers as to the supply of ordnance arms, ammunition which the General Government had or intended to have at Sag Harbour and if a sufficient supply were not provided from that quarter, to forward a quantity from the State Arsenal. I have just received a letter from McLean dated the 9th Instant, in which he says "I am now packing up 500 muskets, 500 setts of accoutrements, 1000 Flints, 10,000 rounds of fixed ammunition one Iron nine pound Cannon on Field Carriage with all needful apparatus, 100 nine pound balls, 100 three pound balls, 6 quarter casks of powder and one coil of slowmatch." Finding that there was nothing prepared by the United States for Sag Harbour, I thought it my duty agreeable to your instructions to transmit the above Warlike stores to the care of Genl. Rose and Mr. Dering the Collector of the Port of Sag Harbour.

In naval activity, the HMS *Emulous* intercepts and seizes the 344-ton ship *Maria*, which is en route from Cadiz, Spain, with a cargo of ballast, some cloth and about $31,000. The *Maria* is separate from a ketch named *Maria* also captured this year at an undetermined time, the *Maria Windsor*, seized on 29 March 1813, the brigantine Maria seized on 24 June 1813, the *Maria Francisca* seized on 14 May 1813, the brigantine *Maria* seized on 24 June 1813, the brigantine *Maria Francisca* captured on 4 May 1814, the brigantine *Maria Frederica* seized on 14 July 1814, and the schooner *Maria* captured 4 September 1814.

July 14 (Tuesday) *In naval activity,* two American privateers, the *Madison* (Captain T. Hardy) and the *Polly* (Captain D. Ewell) with a combined power of five guns spot two sail and give chase; however, the vessels are not what they expected. One of the ships is the brigantine HMS *Indian*. Suddenly the pursuers are being chased by the *Indian*. The *Madison* and the *Polly* split up to improve their chances of not being forced to engage the more powerful ship. The British remain focused on the *Polly*, and after a chase the *Indian* closes. About 40 men climb into longboats and begin to row toward the *Polly*. Once the boat arrives within musket range, a loud cheer erupts on the boat as British muskets open fire along with a 4-pounder. Nonetheless, the crew aboard the *Polly* opens fire in return, and suddenly the longboats are caught in a cauldron. One of the boats quickly surrenders and the other hurriedly returns to the *Indian*. Captain Hardy concludes he has no extra time to bring in the launch. Instead, he makes his escape.

During this same period, the *Madison* (possibly the *Polly*) snatches the *Eliza*, a schooner moving from Halifax to Jamaica. After completing the capture, the *Eliza* is taken into port at Salem. Meanwhile, before it returns to Salem, the *Polly* captures the sloop *Endeavor* out of Bermuda while it is sailing from Newfoundland to St. Andrews. Meanwhile, the *Madison*, left on its own by the *Indian*, pounces upon the other vessel (British government transport No. 50, a 200-ton brigantine) that had been under escort. The *Madison* seizes the vessel, which is manned by only twelve men. The Americans also find pleasure in the cargo, including 880 uniforms destined for the British 104th Light Infantry. The vessel also contains gunpowder, wine, musical instruments and other items.

July 15 (Wednesday) *In naval activity,* two British warships, the HMS *Juniper* and the HMS *Spartan,* while cruising together, intercept and seize the 71-ton brigantine *Start* (P. Hazelton, master), which is transporting a cargo of salt. In other naval activity, on or about this day, American privateers out of Rhode Island begin to head out to sea in search of British shipping. The first vessel to sail is the brigantine *Yankee,* commanded by Captain Oliver Wilson, who sets a course for Nova Scotia. The American privateer *Matilda,* an 11-gun schooner commanded by Captain H. Rantin, departs from Philadelphia and within several days intercepts a brigantine transporting a cargo from San Domingo to London. A prize crew is sent aboard and the vessel is taken into Philadelphia, where it arrives on 10 August. After sending the prize off to Philadelphia, the *Matilda* resumes its hunt and several days later the British brigantine *Ranger* is encountered. It has no desire to surrender. The two ships exchange heavy blows and during the confrontation, American fire inflicts a mortal wound upon the English commander, Captain John Heard. At battle's end, the Americans prevail and the *Ranger* is sailed into Philadelphia. After the *Ranger* arrives in the city, preparations are made to give Captain Heard an honorable burial, which is held, according to a Philadelphia newspaper, on 22 August. American officers representing the U.S. Army and the U.S. Navy attend the service. Funeral honors are provided by the Philadelphia Blues.

Also, on or about this day, a British schooner out of New Providence (Bahamas) arrives at Amelia Island. The vessel, reported to be carrying $20,000 in specie, is detained by a U.S. revenue cutter. The American vessel *Margaret* at about this time (July), while en route to the United States from Liverpool, is intercepted and captured by a British vessel. Nonetheless, its cargo of "salt, earthenware and ironmongery" does not arrive at a British port. It is intercepted by the American privateer *Teazer* out of New York; afterward, the *Margaret* arrives safely at Portsmouth.

July 16 (Thursday) *In Canada,* a contingent of the British 41st Regiment — about 60 militia troops and some Indians posted near a bridge near British-held Fort Malden — detect an American reconnaissance force commanded by Colonels Cass and Miller. The British send a party of Indians over the bridge to draw the Americans out; however, once the Indians cross they are struck by fire from Americans holding concealed positions. Two sustain wounds and one is killed. The officers send word to General Hull that if the army advances, the British fort can be taken. They also inform Hull that if he authorizes it, they will take and hold the post until reinforcements arrive. Hull adamantly refuses to advance and refuses to permit his reconnaissance force to act unless they take responsibility. He also states that neither reinforcements nor supplies will be forthcoming. Cass and Miller refuse his peculiar offer. The column returns to Sandwich. Some Canadian sources claim that other than the Indians that skirmished, the two sides did not engage.

In New York, General Stephen Van Rensselaer, en route to the frontier, arrives at the village of Herkimer and he receives a grand welcome from the citizens, many of whom meet him outside the village. A dinner is held in his honor. Afterward, Van Rensselaer resumes his journey. John Lovett, a skilled attorney, joins with Van Rensselaer to become his secretary. He is known for his mastery of the English language and for his writing skills; however, he is also known for his intense dislike for the "dry study of law." General Van Rensselaer asks Lovett if he would consider becoming his military aid and his secretary. Lovett quickly and unhesitatingly responds: "I am not a soldier," and Van Rensselaer retorts: "It is not your sword, but your pen that I want." At that point, Lovett agrees. Lovett, in a letter to Joseph Alexander, provides an example of his sardonic wit: "If flying through air, water, mud, brush, over hills, dales, meadows, swamps: on wheels or horseback, and getting a man's ears gnawed off with musquitoes and gallinippers make a *Soldier,* then have I seen service for — one week."

After the war, Lovett relocates in Ohio on a tract that he purchased. He founds a settlement and names it in honor of Commodore Perry, the hero of Lake Erie, by calling it Perrysburg. Lovett later dies of fever at Fort Meigs during 1818.

In naval activity, the HMS *Emulous* intercepts and seizes the 197-ton brigantine *Cordelia* (Joshua Kilby, master) while it is en route from Figuera, Mallorca (Spain), to Boston. On the following day, the brigantine USS *Nautilus,* commanded by Lt. W. Crane, is caught by a British squadron composed of the HMS *Africa, Aeolus, Belvidera, Guerriere* and *Shannon.* After capturing the *Nautilus,* the cargo of ammunition and guns is confiscated for use by British forces.

In other activity, the HMS *Indian* (British Captain Jane) encounters and seizes a privateer, the 29-ton schooner *Fairtrader* (John Morgan, master), in the Bay of Fundy after it had sailed from Salem, Massachusetts, with a cargo of ammunition, guns and provisions. The prize is taken into port at New Brunswick. Prior to its capture, the *Fairtrader* had succeeded in seizing three schooners, carrying cargoes of beef, flour, fish, gin and tobacco, and the final prize with its cargo of lumber. After seizing the schooners, the *Fairtrader* takes the British ship *Jarrett* (Captain Richard Jacobs), manned by 18 men and carrying two guns. Four men on the *Jarrett* are Americans. Once they realize the privateer is American they refuse to fight. The *Fairtrader* is separate from the 29-ton schooner *Fairtrader* seized on 6 December 1814.

Also, the 2-gun American privateer *Active* (Captain Patterson) is intercepted and captured by the 36-gun frigate Spartan, commanded by Captain Brenton at a point off Cape Sable, Nova Scotia.

July 17 (Friday) *In Canada,* a British force composed of about 40 regulars, 150 Canadians and several hundred Indians under Capt. Charles Roberts (Colonel McDonel's command) departs Fort St. Joseph (St. Joseph's Island, Canada) and effortlessly captures the garrison of 57 troops under Lt. Porter Hanks at Fort Michilimackinac (formerly Fort de Buade), Michigan. Lt. Hanks, until being captured, had not known the war had begun.

Fort Mackinac (Fort Michilimackinac).

The British garrison the fort and abandon Fort St. Joseph in Canada. Subsequently, during 1814, Americans destroy the unoccupied fort, which had been renamed Fort George by the British. Meanwhile, the captured fort, located in the Indian country, provides the opportunity for the various northern tribes to join with the British. The tribes include the Chippewas, Crees, Saultes and Winnebagoes.

In other activity, General Brock convenes a special session of the legislature (Upper Canada) to deal with the crisis caused by General Hull's invasion.

In naval activity, the USS *Nautilus,* built during 1799 and acquired by the Navy in 1803, is captured by a British squadron, composed of the 32-gun *Aeolus,* 64-gun *Africa,* 38-gun *Shannon* and other vessels. The *Nautilus* is the first ship to be captured by either side. The British take the *Nautilus* into service of the Royal Navy.

British warships HMS *Plumper* and HMS *Indian* intercept the privateer *Argus* (W. Heath, master), a schooner. The prize and its cargo, including ammunition and guns, are taken into port at New Brunswick. The HMS *Emulous* catches the 211-ton brigantine *George*, which had sailed from Messina with a cargo including brandy, wine, juniper berries, lemons, oil and nuts. The *George* is seized before it arrives at its destination. The *George* is separate from the 211-ton brigantine *George* seized on 8 July 1812, the brigantine *George* captured 22 July 1812, and the 172-ton brigantine *George* seized on 16 February 1815.

In other naval activity, the 200-ton brigantine *Mary*—transporting a cargo of currants, juniper berries, wines and wool from Gibraltar to Boston—is cut off and captured by the HMS *Spartan*. This *Mary* is separate from other captured ships similiarly named: *Mary Elizabeth*, 8 July 1812; schooner *Mary Ann*, 23 July 1812; 97-ton schooner *Mary*, 23 March 1813. Other seizures include schooner *Mary*, 27 March 1813; sloop *Mary*, 4 July 1813; sloop *Mary*, 23 July 1813; schooner *Mary*, 7 August 1813; schooner *Mary*, 10 September 1813; schooner *Mary*, 13 September 1813; sloop *Mary Ann*, 22 December 1813; sloop *Mary*, 6 January 1814; ship *Mary*, 1 June 1814; and the 92-ton schooner *Mary*, 6 October 1814.

Also, the HMS *Paz* recaptures the schooner *Nimrod*. The American privateer *Rossie* (Commodore Joshua Barney) encounters the ship *Electra* out of Philadelphia. During the brief pause, the crew of the *Electra* is informed that war with England had begun.

July 17–19 *In naval activity,* the USS *Constitution*, a frigate, while en route from Annapolis to New York, discovers a five-ship convoy on the 17th. No close contact is made until the following day, when the commander of the *Constitution*, Commodore Isaac Hull, faces a colossal threat when he discovers that the ships spotted off the coast of New Jersey are British warships, part of the 11-ship squadron commanded by Captain Philip Bowes Vere Broke. By the 18th, the winds have subsided. The *Constitution*, despite being surrounded, outmaneuvers the hunters by sending one of its boats out front "with a kedge anchor and lines." The crew of the boat drops the kedge anchor and the lines are taken back to the *Constitution*, allowing the crew in the boat to essentially drag the ship up to the anchor. The process is successively repeated as the boat advances to drop one kedge anchor after the other. The British eventually figure out Hull's strategy and duplicate the process. Nevertheless, Hull maintains his lead. In addition, Hull orders holes to be cut in the walls of his cabin, then places two 24-pounders from where men can fire upon the British, and he also deploys a long gun on the spar deck.

Despite the enormous pressure, Hull remains confident that his ship will outrun the British, and for nearly the entire ordeal, eleven enemy warships are within sight of the deck of the *Constitution*. While the British concentrate on seizing the *Constitution*, a merchant ship comes into view. The British choose not to chase it and instead continue the chase to overcome the American warship. The British attempt to lure the merchant ship into coming to them. They hoist an American flag as a ruse. However, the Americans aboard the *Constitution* observe their flag being raised on the British warship, and they counter the action by raising a British flag to warn the merchant vessel of the lurking danger. Meanwhile the peculiar contest that so far has not prompted any fire from either side continues into the night of the 18th. By then, a brewing storm viciously sweeps into the area. The *Constitution* receives a heavy blow from the initial squalls, but the crew adjusts the sails and, despite the thrashing, survives.

The British squadron is soon struck shortly afterward, but as the winds cause some concern, the situation changes when the trailing rain storm pounds the ships and inadvertently inserts a shield that prevents the crews from making eye contact. While the British fight the elements and simultaneously toil to prevent their ships from crashing into one another, Commodore Hull orders the fore and main topgallant sails hoisted at about 2100. The breeze swiftly carries the ship far in advance. In a flash, while the British squadron is still held captive by the storm, Hull's *Constitution* rides the winds to safety. After the storm, the British again spot the *Constitution*, but to their dismay, it had cunningly escaped the trap and was only barely in sight. The British resume the chase throughout the night into the third day (19th), but to no avail. The bloodless engagement had, at no cost, presented the British with a preview of the ability of the U.S. Navy and the excellent naval skills of its officers. It would become evident that the Royal Navy was facing more than a ragtag fleet and a naval force up to the task of challenging the most dominant naval force on the high seas.

After evading the Royal Navy, Hull sails for the port at Boston, rather than New York, where he pauses for a short while until he re-embarks on 2 August. Captain James Brown, a prisoner aboard the HMS *Shannon* at the time the squadron is chasing the *Constitution*, relates to Captain Coggeshall, his personal friend, that he had been able to watch the *Constitution* while it was "kedging," but he kept it to himself. About one hour later, a British officer discovered what was happening aboard the *Constitution* and how the prey kept gaining distance despite having fewer towing boats than the British.

July 17–20 *In naval activity,* the USS *Allegany* (*Alleghany*), commanded by Master Ebenezer Eveleth, arrives off Algiers on the 17th to deliver military and naval stores; however, the cargo being delivered in accordance with a treaty is rejected on the 20th when the items are being unloaded. The dey of Algiers orders the American consul, Tobias Lear, to leave with the ship. Efforts to work out the problem fail. The consul, his family and all Americans in Algiers board the *Allegany* and return to the United States. In a letter dated the 20th, Lear writes: "On the 13th inst. a squadron of cruisers sailed from Algiers to the eastward, consisting of 5 frigates, 3 corvettes, 2 brigs, 1 Xebec, 1 schooner, 1 row galley, and 5 gunboats; and there is reason to apprehend that they had orders to capture American vessels."

July 18 (Saturday) *In naval activity,* the letter-of-marque *Falcon* (Captain George Wilson), operating out of Baltimore, while en route from Baltimore to Bordeaux, France encounters the 5-gun HMS *Hero*, a cutter, off the French coast. The *Falcon*, armed with four guns and a 16-man crew, engages the *Hero*, which is manned by a crew of fifty. The two ships pound each other for more than two hours, but the Americans remain equal to the task. Despite the superior number of Englishmen, the crew of the *Hero* repels three separate attempts to board and finally the British relent. On the following day, another British vessel, carrying 40 men and six guns, strikes the *Falcon*, which has not recovered from the damages sustained the previous day. Nevertheless, the Americans, having also sustained wounded the day before, fire incessantly against the more powerful enemy vessel for about one and one-half hours. Nonetheless, the English finally board the *Falcon*, seize it and take it into Guernsey.

Also at about this time, a British warship seizes the privateer *Gypsey* after it sails from New York for Bordeaux, France. The prize crew sails for a British port, but en route, the Americans devise a successful plan to regain their ship. After overpowering the British prize crew, the *Gypsey* makes it to a French port. The HMS *Spartan* seizes a 4-gun sloop, the privateer *Actress*, commanded by George Lumsden and operating out of New Haven with a 53-man crew. It is carrying a cargo of ammunition, guns and provisions. The prize, commissioned one week earlier, is taken into port at New Brunswick.

Two British warships, the HMS *Emulous* and the HMS *Spartan* intercept and seize the 182-ton schooner *Hiram* (Josiah Onne, master), which is en route to Salem, Massachusetts, from Lisbon, Portugal, with a cargo of fruit and about $13,000 in cash. The *Hiram* is separate from the schooner *Hiram* seized on 12 September 1812. In other naval activity, the HMS *Ringdove* seizes the 172-ton ship *Magnet* (T. Drew, master), which is en route from Belfast, Ireland, to New York. The *Magnet* is pressed into service of the British. Also, the HMS *Paz* intercepts and seizes the schooner *Martha*.

July 19 (Sunday) **In Canada,** an American contingent under Colonel McArthur on a reconnaissance mission approaches the bridge near Fort Malden. McArthur's force of about 150 Ohio infantry troops is later joined by a contingent under Colonel Cass. The bridge is under the control of the British. Two artillery pieces at the bridge compel the Americans to withdraw. Two British troops are captured after they cross the bridge, and the British take out one of the American guns.

In New York, a British squadron moves against Sacket's Harbor to attempt the capture of the USS *Oneida* and another vessel, the former HMS *Lord Nelson*, a prize of the *Oneida*. The *Oneida*, captained by Commander (Lieutenant) Melancton Woolsey, had been at anchor when the British arrive. Upon the approach of the British squadron, which includes the *Earl of Moira, Duke of Gloucester, Prince Regent, Royal George, Seneca* and the *Simcoe*, Woolsey rejects an ultimatum to surrender and tries to break out of the harbor. The escape attempt fails; however, Woolsey still refuses to surrender.

He sails back into the harbor and drops anchor close to the bluff from where his guns can still dominate the entrance to the harbor. He also redeploys some of his guns by taking the ones that face land and redeploys them on shore to meet the threat from the sea. Afterward, he departs from the *Oneida* and hurries to a small fort (battery) at the tip of the peninsula, which contains only one gun, an old iron 32-pounder named the Old Sow. It had been lying in the mud before being activated by Woolsey. Woolsey also has two 9-pounders and two 6-pounders in a battery.

The Old Sow strikes first; however, it results only in giving the British on the flagship a hearty laugh. Two more shots are fired without effect, while the British guns open up with a bombardment, which is also ineffective. Most of the shells fall short and crash into the rocks under the fort. One of the British shells, fired by a 32-pounder, soars overhead and crashes into the dirt beyond the bluff. A sergeant extricates it and delivers it to Captain William Vaughn, who is the commander of the Old Sow. While handing it to the officers, the sergeant says, "I've been playing ball with the redcoats, and have caught 'em out. See if the British can catch back again." At about the same time, the *Royal George* is moving closer to shore, and to the delight of the Americans, the shell fits the Old Sow perfectly. Before the *Royal George* can fire its broadside, the shot fired by the Old Sow strikes violently. Fourteen men are killed and about 18 are wounded. The shot changes the tone of the struggle. The *Royal George*, already damaged, sustains more punishment, and two other British ships had been severely damaged. The British disengage as the signal to retire is hoisted. An American band serenades the squadron as it sails out of the harbor listening to "Yankee Doodle."

The British, under Commodore Earle, a Canadian, depart without their prize, the *Oneida*. Neither the *Oneida* nor the Americans sustain any harm and the American fire had prevented the British from achieving their goal.

Pursuant to orders, Woolsey next begins to acquire vessels for a fleet by transforming merchant ships into warships. Also, Colonel Christopher P. Bellinger's militia regiment had been at Sackets Harbor during the attack.

In naval activity, the *Commodore Barry*, a sloop, is encountered by two British warships, the HMS *Maidstone* and the *Spartan*. The *Commodore Barry* is seized and taken into port at St. John's, New Brunswick. In other naval activity, the HMS *Indian* intercepts and seizes the schooner *Friendship* (A. Richard, master), a privateer operating out of Boston and carrying a cargo of ammunition, guns and provisions.

This *Friendship* is separate from other vessels of the same name: a schooner seized 11 September 1812; another schooner captured 5 March 1813; a sloop seized 6 July 1813; a sloop seized 11 July 1813; a schooner captured on 13 July 1813; and yet another schooner taken over on 28 July 1813. Elsewhere, the HMS *Ringdove* seizes the *Rover* (William Chapman, master), a 98-ton vessel transporting a cargo of coal and other items. The *Rover* is separate from the schooner *Rover* seized on 6 November 1813.

July 20 (Monday) In New York at Albany, Governor Tompkins writes to James Watson that, pursuant to the declaration of war of 12 June, Tompkins intends to construct an arsenal at Malone or "other suitable place in Franklin County." The governor suggests several names for commissioners to oversee construction; however, he authorizes Watson to appoint whomever he believes is best suited for the position.

In naval activity, the HMS *Ringdove* while on patrol intercepts and seizes the 264-ton brigantine *Hesper*, which is en route from Liverpool to Norfolk, Virginia, with a cargo of ballast.

July 21 (Tuesday) *In naval activity,* the American privateer *Highflyer*, a 5-gun schooner out of Baltimore, intercepts a British merchant ship, the *Jamaica*, carrying seven guns and a crew of 21 men under Captain Wells. After a fight of about forty minutes in which two Americans sustain wounds, Americans board the *Jamaica* and force its surrender.

In other activity, the American privateer *Rossie* (Commodore Joshua Barney) encounters the brigantine *Triton* off the New England coast. During the brief pause, the crew of the *Trition* is informed that war with Britain had begun. On the same day, the *Rossie* also encounters the *Rising Sun* out of Baltimore, and that crew also learns that the United States is at war.

July 22 (Wednesday) In Canada, in response to General Hull's recent proclamation, British General Brock reacts, stating that the "crown of England would defend and avenge all its subjects, whether red or white."

In naval activity, the HMS *Maidstone* intercepts and recaptures the brigantine *George* (T. Gossard, master) while it is en route from Poole to Nova Scotia. The *George* is seized before it arrives at its destination. The *George* is separate from brigantine *George* seized on 8 July 1812, the brigantine *George* seized on 17 July 1812, and the 172-ton brigantine *George* captured 16 February 1815.

In other naval activity, the HMS *Colibri* recaptures the ship *Mariner*, which is en route from Glasgow to St. Andrews. The *Mariner* is separate from a brigantine of the same name seized 29 August 1813. Also, the American privateer *Highflyer* intercepts and seizes the British ship *Mary Ann* without a prolonged fight. Once the *Highflyer* moves alongside of the 12-gun *Mary Ann*, it surrenders. The American privateer *Rossie* (Commodore Joshua Barney) intercepts and seizes an American vessel, the *Nymph*, after discovering that it is not carrying goods for the British.

July 23 (Thursday) *In naval activity,* the privateer *Gleaner* (J. Robinson, master), a 56-ton sloop operating out of Kennebec, is intercepted and captured by the HMS *Colibri*. At the time of its capture, the *Gleaner*, on its initial cruise, is carrying a cargo that includes ammunition and guns. The British press the *Gleaner* into provincial service. This *Gleaner* is separate from the 70-ton schooner *Gleaner* that is seized on 3 December 1814.

In other activity, the HMS *Emulous* encounters and captures the *Gossamer* (letter of marque; Charles Goodrich, master), which had sailed from Boston with a cargo of ammunition, guns and other items. Also, the 402-ton ship *Melantho* (William Davidson, master), en route from Chile to Baltimore, gets trapped by a full British squadron composed of the *Acasta, Aeolus, Emulous, Maidstone, Nymphe, Orpheus, Spartan* and *Statira*. The *Melantho*, at the time of its capture, is transporting a cargo of copper, furs and just under $150,000 in cash.

The privateer *Dolphin* (Captain Endicott) returns to port at Salem following a harrowing cruise that included several cases of eluding capture by pursuing warships. In between running from superior British warships, the *Dolphin* seized six prizes during its 20 days at sea. Captain Endicott earned great respect from his prisoners. At one point during a chase that lasted about 24 hours, the British on board literally helped the *Dolphin* avoid capture by operating boats and towing the *Dolphin* out of range of the British guns. These prisoners made it clear that they preferred going to the United States to returning to a British warship. The *Dolphin*'s prizes included the brigantine *Antelope*, the ship *Waibisch*, the schooner *Ann Kelly* out of Halifax, the brigantine *St. Andrews*, the ship *Mary* out of Bristol, the ship *Empress*, and the ship *Venus* (American vessel recaptured), and a schooner, *Jane*, en route to Halifax.

The *Dolphin* soon sails on another mission. It is encountered by a British vessel on 12 August. On or about the 26th, a British schooner carrying a cargo of sugar, seized by the *Dolphin*, arrives in Baltimore to become the first British vessel to be brought into the harbor.

In other activity, a British warship encounters the American privateer *Rossie* (Commodore Joshua Barney) and gives chase. Nevertheless, the British frigate is unable to catch its prey. During the pursuit, about 25 shots are fired by the British, but without effect.

July 24 (Friday) *In naval activity,* the privateer *Curlew* (William Wyer, master), operating out of Boston, is intercepted and captured by the HMS *Acasta*. The British confiscate the cargo, which includes ammunition, guns and provisions. The *Curlew* is taken into service of the Royal Navy. The privateer *Madison* arrives in port at Savannah with two prizes, a 6-gun British snow and the brigantine *Shamrock*.

The American privateer *Globe*, commanded by Captain J. Grant (possibly Gavet), sails from Baltimore, passes the Chesapeake Capes and begins a search for British shipping. The *Globe* leaves port with another Baltimore privateer, the *Cora*. The *Globe*'s cruise remains uneventful until the 31st, when it spots what appears to be an enemy vessel. The *Globe* had only recently arrived at Hampton Roads, bringing with it a 22-gun British ship that it seized while the prize was en route to Glasgow from Jamaica.

The *Benjamin Franklin*, one of 55 privateers that head to sea out of New York during this conflict, sails on its maiden mission. During its time at sea, the *Benjamin Franklin* succeeds in seizing 28 prisoners and seven prizes before it returns to port on 24 August. With its eight guns and crew of 120 men, commanded by Captain J. Ingersoll, the *Benjamin Franklin* aggressively seeks out British shipping. During its early days on the hunt, it seizes the brigantine *Friends and Mary* and the sloop *Louisa Ann*. Its first prize is sailed to Boston by a prize crew. The *Louisa Ann* does not capitulate as easily as the *Friends and Mary*, although the prize is captured without firing a shot.

While the *Louisa Ann* is anchored in Martinique in Trinity harbor, safely secured by the protection of a strong battery mounting twelve 18-pounders, Captain Ingersoll and his crew conclude that the ship can be seized despite its heavy guard. A small party of seven crewmen, using one of the privateer's boats, creeps into the harbor without being discovered and catches the crew of the *Louisa Ann* by total surprise. Once the Americans gain control, they casually run the sloop out of the harbor without disturbing the guns of the battery, and by so doing, they relieve the British of a valuable cargo of molasses. Afterward, the *Benjamin Franklin* adds more prizes to its list: the 10-gun brigantine *John*, en route to Gibraltar with a cargo of cocoa and coffee from La Guayra, Venezuela; the brigantine *Two Brothers*; and the schooner *Success*. Following its adventurous cruise, the *Benjamin Franklin* returns to port on 24 August.

Other privateers out of New York include the *Divided We Fall* and the *United We Stand*, two vessels that often sail as a pair. They do not run up a large score of successes; however, one enemy 10 gun brigantine falls to them and is taken into Savannah. The *Divided We Fall* is also credited with capturing and ransoming two vessels, along with destroying some others after confiscating their cargoes. Their prizes were primarily West India trading ships. Also, the privateers *Flirt*, *Galloway*, *Henry Guilder*, *Hero*, *Morgiana* and *Mars* are known to have operated out of New York; however, very scant information on many of the vessels has been recorded for posterity. The *Galloway* is known to have captured the brigantine *Commerce* while it was en route to Halifax from Martinique, and in spring 1814, it achieves additional success. The *Hero* later seizes a schooner, the *Victoria*, which is sailed to the United States as a prize. While en route, it is recaptured by a British warship. Afterward a British prize crew takes possession of the vessel and all but one of the prisoners are transferred to the British ship. The British prize crew is persuaded by the sole American to divert the ship and into an American port. Once contact is lost with the warship, the British change course and take it to Charleston, South Carolina.

Also another of the lesser known privateers out of New York, the *Hero*, manages to seize the schooner *Robert Hartwell* during 1814 while it is en route to Bermuda with a cargo worth about $20,000. Once the Americans take possession, it is taken into port at New Bern. Another vessel, a cutter also named *Hero* operating out of Stonington, Connecticut, and manned by volunteers, is known to have seized the British schooner *Fox*, which had been a tender to a British ship of the line. Also, the *Henry Guilder* is known to have captured a schooner the *Young Farmer* during 1814, which is afterward sailed into New York. In the early part of the war, the privateer *Young American* engages two enemy vessels simultaneously, the 11-gun *Grenada* and a schooner, the *Shadock*. Despite having only one gun, the *Young American*, carrying a 42-man crew, prevails and captures both ships. The *Shadock*, which is transporting molasses, loses its captain during the engagement and it is taken into port at Charleston. The *Grenada*, carrying a crew of 30 men and eleven guns, is also taken to Charleston. At the time it is captured, the *Grenada* has a cargo including coffee, cotton and sugar that had been en route to London. The victorious *Young American* had seized both vessels within about one and one-half hours of fighting. No casualties are sustained by the *Young American*.

July 25 (Saturday) **In Michigan**, a contingent of the U.S. troops skirmishes with a British force on the outskirts of Detroit.

July 26 (Sunday) **In Canada**, Colonel Henry Proctor, with a force of about 300 regulars, arrives at Malden. Meanwhile, at Detroit, General Hull remains unaware that the British have captured Mackinac (Fort Michilimackinac). General Hull has also refrained from attacking his main objective, Malden, except for a reconnaissance force that approached it on the 19th.

In Florida, the hostile Indians launch a raid to the rear of Lt. Colonel Thomas A. Smith's positions outside St. Augustine. The strike kills one white and five Negroes. The Indians also seize 32 captives at a place on the north side of the St. Johns River.

In Maryland at Baltimore, the *Federal Republican*, which recently went back into operation after being attacked by a pro-war mob the month before, again becomes a target on or about this day. The editor, Alexander Hanson, had anticipated the return of the thugs and is prepared. When the mob begins to gather during the night, they soon discover that Hanson is not alone. Friends, including General James M. Lingan and General Henry Lee, are there to help defend the newspaper. The mob crashes through the barred door but the men are not expecting the welcoming party. They are met with fire that kills one and wounds another three. The authorities delay taking action, but eventually militia arrives.

While the defenders inside the improvised fort express relief at the appearance of the militia, they become dismayed when they are asked to surrender. Instead of quelling the rioters, Mayor Edward Johnson and Brigadier General John Stricker inform the defenders — including editor in chief Jacob Wagner and assistant editor Alexander Hanson — that if they surrender, no additional violence will take place.

The men in the house-fort capitulate. They are arrested and escorted to jail. On the following night, the thugs gather again and strike the jail. The attackers murder General Lingan. General Henry Lee survives but is so badly beaten that the attack leaves him permanently crippled. During the attack, about eight of the men held at the jail manage to fade into the unruly mob and escape without notice. The others that had been arrested are also beaten, and one man is tarred and feathered, while some others are tortured.

Jacob Wagner, the chief editor of the paper, had been a Federalist "of the black cockade school" who worked in the state department under Pickering and James Madison and a vehement opponent of the war. Consequently, it had been decided by pro-war Republicans that if the opposition continued after war was declared, the paper would be eliminated. Nonetheless, the infamous attack further inflamed the animosity between the anti-war (pro–Britain) Federalists and the pro-war (pro–France) Republicans. The city of Baltimore receives the nickname "Mobcity" by Federalist newspapers, and in Philadelphia leaflets depict the rioters as "Madison's Mob."

General Lingan was born in Maryland about 1762. He was also a veteran of the American Revolution. During the fighting in Long Island, as a member of the Maryland Line, he was captured at Fort Washington and afterward held on a prison ship. General Lingan's family was left destitute due to his death. Also, news of the riots reach New England and create a furor. Frequently, the attack is compared to the actions of the French during the Reign of Terror. Many people in Boston who gather at Faneuil Hall express enormous anger and blame the origin of the riots on France.

In naval activity, the HMS *Colibri* recaptures the letter of marque *Catherine* (F.A. Burnham, master), with a cargo that includes ammunition and guns. The Americans hold off the British for more than one hour; however, after the boatswain is killed and the first officer and others become wounded, Burnham surrenders. The *Catherine* is separate from the *Catherine* (brigantine) seized on 2 May 1813 and the *Catherine* (schooner) captured 4 December 1813. Elsewhere, the 14-gun American privateer *Tom*, commanded by Captain T. Wilson, encounters a British brigantine armed with twelve guns and carrying a cargo of coffee weighing 400,000 pounds. The British raise some tenacious resistance and the contest rages for more than one hour before the British finally surrender. The vessel *Braganza* had been en route to London from Port au Prince, but the Americans send it to Baltimore. After reaching port with the prize, the *Tom* is refitted before sailing on its second cruise on 2 August.

In other naval activity, the American privateer *Highflyer* encounters and captures the British schooner *Harriet* near the Shot Keys at about 1900. After being informed by the captain that specie had been concealed aboard the prize, Captain Gavet of the *Highflyer* orders an inspection. On the following day, the specie is discovered.

July 27 (Monday) **In Florida,** the Indians again launch a strike, following their raid of the previous day. Four men are killed within four miles of Lt. Colonel Thomas A. Smith's command outside St. Augustine at Point Peter. Colonel Smith will shortly receive orders from Governor Mitchell to "chastize the Indians."

July 28 (Tuesday) **In Canada,** a contingent of Colonel Cass' command encounters and attacks a band of Indians near a bridge at the Riviere aux Canards, which is called the Tar-on-tee by the Indians. The Indians are driven back, but one of their party is killed. The troops remove his scalp and the British report that the Indian's body had been mutilated. Afterward, the Americans retire rather than seek out the main body, and the troops fail to destroy the bridge. By the following day, British troops, bolstered by some artillery, arrive to protect the bridge.

In naval activity, Secretary of the Navy Paul Hamilton dispatches a letter to Captain Isaac Hull instructing him that upon his arrival in New York he is to transfer command of the *Constitution* to Captain Bainbridge and afterward repair to headquarters to assume command of the frigate *Constellation.* In other naval activity, the HMS *Maidstone* intercepts and seizes the 118-ton brigantine *Rayo,* which is en route to Puerto Rico from Baltimore with a cargo of flour.

July 29 (Wednesday) **In Canada,** a force under Colonel Cass, bolstered by Colonel Duncan McArthur's wing, attacks to secure the bridge it failed to destroy the previous day. Despite a short artillery duel, the British retire. Two troops of the 41st Regiment, Privates Dean and Hancock, attempt to hold their ground; however, Hancock is slain and Dean is seized after being wounded.

July 30 (Thursday) In Florida, Lt. Colonel Thomas A. Smith, in a letter to the U.S. Adjutant and Inspector (Brigadier General) Thomas H. Cushing, dated this day at Point Peter, informs the adjutant that he had ordered the companies at Fort Hawkins (Macon, Bibb County, Georgia) to repair to his camp; however, he also informs the adjutant that he did not believe an order from him to summon a contingent in South Carolina would be accepted as proper. Also, Smith informs the adjutant of the recent Indian depredations and of his orders from Governor Mitchell to take action. After mentioning that the governor (Mitchell of Georgia) has directed about 200 volunteers to join his command, Smith closes his letter: "I am making arrangements for that purpose & expect by the end of August to have destroyed all their towns in East Florida."

Also this day, Colonel Smith writes to Major General Thomas Pinckney to bring him up to date. Smith informs Pinckney of his orders to deal with the recent Indian raids and his orders to hold his positions unless "compelled to retire by a superior force." The letter also mentions his intent to dispatch Colonel Daniel (Neil) Newman and his force of Marines and volunteers to attack the Indian strong points within about 100 miles of the St. Johns River. Smith's concern is that the villages contain a few hundred fugitive slaves and if the problem is not immediately eliminated, new arrivals from Georgia and Florida will greatly increase their numbers and make the task too difficult for his small force. Although Colonel Newman's contingent is a disciplined unit, they had recently arrived in Florida "lacking shoes, canteens, or camp equippage of any kind."

In New York, General Brown writes to Governor Tompkins with details of an upcoming expedition:

> The expedition for Ogdensburgh is fitted out. The *Julia* [schooner], with the long thirty-two pounder, two long sixes, and about sixty volunteers under the command of Lieutenant Wells, from the *Oneida,* seconded by Captains Vaughn and Dixon, now lies off the harbor ready to sail with the first favorable wind. We count upon her being underway in the course of this day, and we pray God, she may do something toward saving the honor of the country.... Our means are humble, but with the blessing of Heaven, this republican gunboat may give a good account of the Duke and the Earl; and a successful termination of this enterprise will give us an equal chance for the command of the lake.

In naval activity, HMS *Emulous* seizes the 14-gun American privateer, the *Gossamer* (Captain C. Goodrich) off Sable Island. Prior to its capture, the *Gossamer,* operating out of Boston, had seized only one vessel, the *Ann Green,* which had been intercepted while en route to Quebec from Jamaica with a cargo of rum. Within a few days, the *Emulous* is lost on Ragged Island. The crew, however, is not marooned for long. Another British ship, the HMS *Acasta,* which had recently captured another American privateer, the *Curlew,* is able to assist. The *Acasta,* while swamped by a dense fog, suddenly receives a surprise when the fog lifts and the *Curlew,* which had drifted during the fog, winds up alongside the *Acasta.* The *Curlew,* carrying a crew of 172 men and 16 guns, having no options, had surrendered. Meanwhile, the crew of the ill-fated *Emulous* takes possession of the privateer and resumes their cruise.

In other naval activity, the American privateer *Rossie* (Commodore Joshua Barney) is spotted by a British warship, which initiates pursuit, but to no avail. The privateer is too fast and easily loses the frigate.

July 31 (Friday) *In naval activity,* the HMS *Emulous* intercepts and recaptures the schooner *Prevoyante.* Also, the American privateer *Globe* intercepts a vessel thought to be a British merchant ship and pursuit is initiated. After several hours, the *Globe* arrives within range of the ship and uses its long tom to try to bring the target to a halt. In response, the *Globe* comes under fire from the guns on the ship's stern. The exchange becomes a major confrontation that ensues for about 40 minutes, the *Globe* holding the edge with sailing skills. Meanwhile, as both vessels come to closer range, each receives two strong broadsides. And as they reach positions not much farther than arm's length, the opposing crews bludgeon each other with musket fire and even pistols. Neither side exhibits any signs of relenting. The antagonists pound each other for more than one hour until finally, the British are unable to continue their resistance and they capitulate. The prize proves to be the *Boyd,* which had sailed from New Providence in the Bahamas. Its cargo of coffee, cotton and dyewoods is diverted to an American port rather than the original destination, Liverpool. A prize crew from the *Globe* sails the *Boyd* into Philadelphia.

In other naval activity, the American privateer *Rossie* (Commodore Joshua Barney), which has been spending time outrunning British warships, including an encounter on the previous day, spots a British merchant ship and again becomes the hunter rather than the hunted. The *Rossie* intercepts the ship *Princess Royal,* seizes it and burns it at sea.

Late July *In naval activity,* a British squadron commanded by Captain Sir Home Popham (74-gun HMS *Venerable*) launches an attack against the Castle of Ano and the town of Santander in an effort to support Spanish guerrillas who are fighting the French. A contingent of Royal Marines debarks and capture the castle. Meanwhile, French reinforcements from Santander arrive, forcing the British and the guerrillas to withdraw to the castle. During the fighting, two British officers, Captain Sir George Collier, leading the landing force, and Captain Lake (HMS *Magnificent*) sustain wounds. The HMS *Surveillante* participates in this action.

July–November *In naval activity,* the American privateer *Comet,* commanded by Captain Boyle, embarks on a cruise that intersects with a British vessel, the 400-ton ship *Hopewell,* carrying a crew of 25 men en route to London from Surinam. The *Hopewell* had been attached to a 5-vessel convoy until it got separated. The engagement ignites when the two antagonists come into close range. The British raise resistance; however, after one of the crew is killed and six others are wounded, the *Hopewell* capitulates. At the time of its capture, the *Hopewell* is carrying a valuable cargo of cocoa, coffee, cotton, molasses and sugar, with an estimated value of $150,000. The *Comet* also intercepts and seizes the 10-gun ship *Henry,* carrying a cargo of Madeira wine and sugar (valued at $100,000) from St. Croix to London. Afterward, the British ship *John* falls prey to the *Comet,* a 400-ton ship with 14 guns and a crew of 35 men. The *Henry*'s cargo, composed of coffee, copper cotton, rum, sugar and dyewood, is valued at about $150,000. Captain Boyle is able to seize a British document from one of his prizes that clearly reveals American naval forces are inflicting great damage to English shipping. The document, named "Recommendations by their Lordships of the Admiralty," states:

> The Lords Commissioners of the Admiralty recommend that all masters of merchant vessels do supply themselves with a quantity of false fires, to give the alarm on the approach of an enemy's cruiser in the night, or in the day to make the usual signals for an enemy being chased by or discovering a suspicious vessel; and, in the event of their capture being inevitable, either by night or by day, the masters do cause their gears, trusses, and halyards to be

cut and unrove, and their vessel to be otherwise so disabled as to prevent their being immediately capable of making sail.

August *In naval activity,* the American privateer *Saucy Jack,* commanded by Captain J.P. Chazel, is set to sail on its first cruise; however, it is delayed because an unknown person or party disables its six guns. After finally getting to sea, the *Saucy Jack* captures 6 brigantines, 6 ships, 9 schooners and two sloops. Other British vessels seized during August include the *Wabisch* (cargo of timber) by the privateer *Dolphin,* taken into port at Salem; the schooner *Ann* by the privateer *Nonpareil,* taken into Charleston; the 2-gun *Jarrett,* en route from Bristol to St. Andrews, by the 1-gun *Fair Trader* without incident, taken into Salem; and the schooner *Ann Kelly,* which is also taken into port by the *Dolphin,* along with a brigantine that is captured between St. Andrews and England.

The privateer *Lion* captures a schooner which enters port at Marblehead, Massachusetts. Another American privateer, the *Argus,* out of Boston, seizes a merchant ship carrying a cargo of indigo and sugar, which is taken into port at Portland. And yet other prizes include the schooner *Fanny,* captured by the American privateer *Dolphin* and taken into port at Baltimore; the 14-gun ship *Mary* en route to St. John's from Bristol, England (cargo of arms and ammunition) by the *Dolphin,* sent into Salem; a schooner seized by the American privateer *Fair Trader,* taken into port at Wiscasset; the schooner *Diligent* (cargo of brandy) by the American privateer *Polly* and taken into port at Salem; two schooners (carrying a cargo of corn, pork and other items) by the privateer *Snowbird* and taken into port at Salem;

Also the schooner *Jane,* en route to Halifax to the West Indies by the *Dolphin* and sent into port at Marblehead; the 10-gun *Ann Green* (cargo of rum and other items) by the privateer *Gossamer* and taken into port at Boston; the 8-gun barque *St. Andrews* by the privateer *Rapid* and taken into port at Portland; the schooner *Nelson* (cargo of fish, furs, oil and other items) by the privateer *Buckskin* and sent into port at Salem; a schooner seized by the privateer *Fame* and taken into port at Machias, Maine;

Also, the schooner *Three Brothers* captured by the *Wiley Renard* and taken into port at Boston; a barque seized by the American privateer *Catherine* and taken into port at Portland; a brigantine seized by the American privateer *Polly,* which is afterward ransomed, and the schooner *Elizabeth,* seized between Jamaica and Halifax and taken into Salem; the 4-gun brigantine *Lady Sherbrook* (cargo of fish and lumber) by the American privateer *Marengo* out of New York and sent into port at New York; the brigantine *Elizabeth and Esther* (cargo of dry goods, fish and pork) seized between St. Johns and Bermuda by the American privateer *Governor McKean* out of Philadelphia and sent into port there;

Also, the 6-gun brigantine *Ranger* (cargo of coffee and logwood) en route to London from St. Domingo by the privateer *Matilda* out of Philadelphia and sent to port there; the schooner *Polly* captured by the privateer *Wiley Reynard* and sent into port at Boston along with two brigantines and a ship; the sloop *Mary Ann* (cargo of salt) seized by the *Paul Jones* and sent into port at Philadelphia; the 14-gun ship *Hassan* (carrying a cargo including dry goods, wine and other items, valued at $200,000) seized between Gibraltar and Havana, Cuba, by the 3-gun *Paul Jones* (the guns on the *Hassan* are transferred to the *Paul Jones*) and sent into port at Savannah, Georgia;

Also, the 4-gun brigantine *Harmony* (cargo of dry goods) captured by the American privateer *Yankee* out of Bristol, Rhode Island, and sent into port at New York; a brigantine seized by the *Yankee* and afterward used by the *Yankee* to parole its prisoners; the 12-gun ship *Braganza* (cargo of coffee and logwood) by the American privateer *Tom* out of Baltimore following a running battle of slightly under one hour and sent into port at Baltimore; the brigantine *Peter Waldo* en route from Newcastle, England, to Halifax by the American privateer *Teazer* and sent into port at Portland; the 8-gun ship *Prince Adolphus* en route from Martinique to Falmouth, England, by the privateer *Governor McKean* and sent into port at Philadelphia along with passengers including the governor of Demara;

Also, the brigantine *Ceres* by the American privateer *John* out of Salem; a brigantine initially taken by a privateer, recaptured by the British before being regained by the American privateer *Lynn* and taken into port at Gloucester, Massachusetts; the brigantine *William* while en route to St. John's from Bristol, England, by the American privateer *Rossie* out of Baltimore and taken into port at Boston; the brigantine *Mary* en route from Scotland to Newfoundland by the American privateer *Yankee* and afterward, released to 70 prisoners;

Also, the schooner *Venus* (cargo of fruit, sugar and other items) by the American privateer *Teazer* and sent into port at Portland; the 10-gun *Osborne* en route to St. Andrews from Gibraltar by the *Teazer* and sent into port at Portland; the brigantine *Eliza* en route to Halifax from Jamaica with a cargo of rum, by the American privateer Marengo and sent into port at New York; the brigantine *Richard,* carrying a cargo of timber, by the American privateer *Industry* of Lynn; the brigantine *Nancy* (cargo of provisions) by the privateer *Free Trader* and sent into port at Salem; a brigantine captured while sailing from Quebec by the American privateer *Bunker Hill* and sent into port at New York;

Also, a schooner captured by the American privateer *Leander* and sent into port at Providence, Rhode Island; the 14-gun brigantine *Leonidas* (cargo of coffee, rum, sugar and other items) en route to Belfast, Ireland, from Jamaica by the American privateer *Mars* and sent into port at Savannah, Georgia; the schooner *Skylark,* en route to Martinique from Quebec by the American privateer *Bunker Hill* and taken into port at New York; the brigantine *Lady-Provost,* en route to Jamaica from Halifax by the privateer *Marengo* and sent into port at New York; the brigantine *Friends* by the privateer *Benjamin Franklin* and sent into port at Boston; the brigantine *Mary* en route to England from Pictou, also seized by the *Benjamin Franklin* and sent into Boston; the 12-gun ship *Jenny* en route to St. John's from Liverpool by the American privateer *Rossie* and sent into port at Salem; and a 170-ton schooner carrying rum and sugar, captured by the American privateer *Teazer* and sent into port at Portland. The *Benjamin Franklin,* following its cruise, returns to New York with 28 prisoners.

August 1 (Saturday) **In Maine,** the privateer *Rapid,* a brigantine, is commissioned. The 246-ton brigantine *Hare* (Charles Bertoddy, master), while en route from Naples to Boston, is intercepted and seized, along with its cargo including brandy, silks and soaps by the HMS *Belvidera.*

In Michigan, news arrives that the British had captured Fort Michilimackinac.

In naval activity, the American privateer *Yankee,* out of Rhode Island, encounters a ship that is later identified as the 10-gun British privateer *Royal Bounty,* commanded by Captain Henry Gambles. As the *Yankee* moves in close to the vessel, its crew unfurls the British ensign. Within minutes, both vessels are trading broadsides and maneuvering to gain the advantage. The Americans follow with another broadside, by a whirlwind of musket fire that decides the encounter. The British, having sustained severe damage, are forced to capitulate. The Americans sustain three men wounded. The British sustain two men killed and seven wounded. An American surgeon provides medical aid to the British wounded. In addition, the prisoners are transferred to the *Yankee* and a prize crew takes the *Royal Bounty* into an American port. The *Yankee* seizes a few additional vessels, including the *Eliza Ann,* before returning to port. Later, during October, the *Yankee* sails on its second cruise.

In other naval activity, the American privateer *Globe,* one day after seizing a prize, resumes its cruise in search of other vulnerable shipping. A schooner is spotted and the *Globe* gives chase without success. Later the same day, another unidentified sail is spotted and another chase begins; however, the latter target also escapes capture. In other naval activity, the American privateer *Rossie* intercepts and seizes the *Kitty.*

August 1–29 The United States is employing its navy as well as can be expected against the armadas of the British Royal Navy, which are closing against the U.S. waters from various parts of the globe. The privateer *Yankee,* still off Newfoundland, encounters and engages the HMS *Royal Bounty* and the brigantine *New Liverpool.* The USS *Essex,* stalking the waters of the Atlantic, sends its guns into action and seizes the British vessel *Brothers,* then victimizes the HMS *King George* after a heated battle on the 8th. The following day, the *Essex* takes the HMS *Mary.* Another American vessel, the frigate *Constitution,* which sailed from Boston on 2 August, sees vicious action as it encounters the brigantine HMS *Lady Warren* off Cape Race (Newfoundland). Sailors and Marines on board the *Constitution* successfully capture the *Lady Warren.* The *Constitution* afterward, on the 11th, seizes the HMS *Adeona* in the Gulf of St. Lawrence. HMS *Harriet* also falls prey to the *Constitution.*

On the 19th, Commodore Isaac Hull's *Constitution* encounters and engages the British frigate *Guerriere* in a memorable battle not soon forgotten by the British. Also, the Americans on the USS *President* recapture the Sloop *Betsey* after encountering it under the British flag in the North Sea on the 25th.

In other activity, in late August, the United States focuses on the British naval forces operating on the Great Lakes. Captain Isaac Chauncey, in command of the Brooklyn navy yard, is selected as commander-in-chief on the Great Lakes. He arrives at Sackets Harbor during October. Chauncey selects the *Oneida*, already at Sackets Harbor, as his flagship. Commodore Chauncey, a veteran of the Barbary Coast War, had commanded the USS *John Adams* during that conflict.

Commodore Isaac Chauncey.

August 2 (Sunday) *In naval activity,* the American privateer *Globe*, while cruising off Cuba, flies the English colors. At about dusk, the lookouts spot a sail in the distance, and having failed on some previous opportunities to seize the prey, the crew becomes optimistic. Nonetheless, after moving closer, the ship is identified as a British warship, which prompts the *Globe* to change course and run. Nonetheless, the British intend to seize it. The British pursue, but thanks to its superior speed, the *Globe* easily escapes capture after darkness falls.

In other naval activity, the American privateer *Tom* embarks on another cruise. Shortly after sailing, the *Tom* encounters the 9-gun British packet *Townsend*, which is en route to Barbados from Falmouth, England. A tenacious contest erupts. The *Tom* sustains some minor damage to its rigging and hull; however, only two men are wounded. The British vessel sustains damage and casualties and the men surrender. In an act of desperation, the British toss all of the mail overboard. Later, the mail bags, which do not sink, are discovered by another American privateer, the *Bona*, commanded by Captain J. Dameron out of Baltimore.

In other naval activity, the USS *Constitution* departs Boston to initiate a new cruise. Also, the American privateer *Rossie* (Commodore Joshua Barney) intercepts and seizes a British vessel, the *Fame*, along with the brigantine *Devonshire*, the schooner *Squid* and the brigantine *Brothers*. The *Brothers* is utilized by Commodore Barney to transport 60 prisoners to St. John's, Canada, to be exchanged for an equal number of American prisoners being held by the English. The other vessels seized this day are burned at sea.

August 3 (Monday) *In naval activity,* the American privateer *Globe* under Captain Grant once again spots a merchant ship and gives chase, but fails when the prey slips away. The American privateer *Rossie* (Commodore Joshua Barney) intercepts several vessels. The brigantine *Henry* and a schooner *Race Horse* are both sunk. Another vessel, the schooner *Halifax*, is burned at sea, and yet another vessel, *Two Brothers*, is seized and utilized as a cartel to take 40 prisoners to St. John's, Canada, on parole. One other vessel, the *William*, is taken and a prize crew assigned to it.

August 3–4 *In naval activity,* the 32-gun HMS *Maidstone* and the 38-gun HMS *Spartan* encounter the American privateer *Madison*, along with another privateer as they are arriving at Eastport, Maine. Captain Elwell of the *Madison* changes course in an effort to keep his prizes and both privateers from being captured. He lands about six miles below the port and hurriedly establishes a battery, which almost immediately comes under attack. The Americans inflict about 20 to 30 casualties and the British withdraw; however, the Americans, who sustain no casualties, are not able to compel the British to retire. On the following day, the British reinitiate their attack, and they greatly increase the number of men committed. The Americans are forced to retreat, leaving the vessels to the British. The *Madison*, prior to being taken by the British, had seized three brigantines and one schooner. During the fighting on the 4th, the Americans sustain some casualties.

The American privateer *Shadow*, commanded by Captain J. Taylor, spots an unidentified sail in the distance and immediately initiates pursuit. Nonetheless, the Americans discover that they have come upon a warship, not a merchant ship. Suddenly, the predator becomes the prey as the *Shadow* attempts to escape. By dusk, the *Shadow* outruns its nemesis. On the following day (4th), slightly after noon, the lookouts on the *Shadow* spot an unidentified ship east of their position. The Americans move to seize it, but during pursuit, the *Shadow* suffers damage when at about 1730, its square-sail boom is severed. After making some modified repairs, the chase is resumed and the *Shadow* is able to eventually catch up to its prey by about 1800. At that time, the *Shadow* comes under fire from the guns on the enemy ship's stern. Captain Taylor directs his crew to disregard the incoming fire and to withhold their own until Taylor is convinced that he is in a better position. By about 1700, Captain Taylor orders his gunners to commence fire to ignite a battle in the dark, but there is a delay. A lantern is hoisted by the enemy vessel and the signal is received. The *Shadow* hoists a similar light and afterward, the Americans are informed that it is the *May*, a letter of marque vessel out of Liverpool. A boat from the British ship comes alongside of the *Shadow*, but without the ship's papers that had been requested by Captain Taylor. The British inform the Americans that no papers will be forthcoming. In addition, the British commander, Captain Affleck, informs Captain Taylor that his vessel is the letter of marque *May* (or *Nancy*) out of Liverpool and en route to St. Lucia. He also informs Taylor that the English had repealed the Orders in Council. Nevertheless, Taylor decides the vessel is going to become a prize. By about 2030 the contest renews and continues for about one hour without a victor, and the *Shadow* requires repairs.

The battle resumes on the following day (5th). By 0730, the *Shadow* has sustained several damaging hits, including one shot that kills six men and wounds three others. Nonetheless, the *Shadow*'s crew maintains its fire. About one hour later, Captain Taylor sustains a mortal hit in the temple. Shortly thereafter, the British inflict another deadly hit that causes the ship to take on water. The remaining officers decide to disengage and escape before being captured. The *Shadow* is able to break away and make it back to Philadelphia. After being refitted, the *Shadow* returns to the sea. However, it is captured by the British, renamed the *Fanny* and mounted with nine guns. Later, during 1815, the British privateer *Fanny* is again captured when the American privateer *Lawrence* seizes it. The *Fanny*'s rescue from the British is short-lived. During the voyage back to America it is wrecked in Cuba. After receiving repairs, the *Fanny* sails again, only to be lost at sea with all of the crew going down with ship.

August 4 (Tuesday) **In Louisiana,** a council of war convenes in New Orleans. General James Wilkinson had assumed command of the forces in Orleans and the Mississippi Territory, and he arrived in New Orleans on 9 July. It is decided "to embody the troops of the line at Pass Christian and hold them in readiness for prompt and active service." Command of the troops at Pass Christian is given to Colonel Leonard Covington.

In New York, General Jacob Brown writes to Governor Daniel D. Tompkins that the schooner *Julia* had engaged the vessels *Duke* and *Earl* on the St. Lawrence about 12 miles above Ogdensburg in a contest that lasted for three hours. Brown states that no American casualties had occurred and the *Julia* suffered only minor damage. Brown also tells the governor that "without ordnance to a much greater extent than has yet to been supplied, we are completely at the mercy of the enemy, whenever they may deem it an object to unite their forces and make a serious attack upon us; for, though we have as gallant a people as the Lord ever created, we must not expect them to resist heavy ordnance with small arms."

In naval activity, a British squadron encounters and seizes the *Concordia* (A. Adams, master) after it sails from Liverpool. Also, the *Nerina*, recently captured by the *Belvidera*, arrives at New London, Connecticut. After seizing the *Nerina*, the British transfer the crew except for Captain Stewart to the British vessel and a prize crew is assigned to take the *Nerina* into a British port. Unknown to the prize crew, about 50 American passengers remain undiscovered in the hull. Once the *Nerina* moves out of the sight of the *Belvidera*, Captain Stewart innocently urges the British to open the hatch to air out the hull. The British agree and shortly thereafter the concealed Americans burst from the hull and overpower the prize crew, giving Stewart the opportunity to sail into the American port.

August 5 (Wednesday) **In Canada,** British General Brock, accompanied by a contingent of the 41st Regiment and militia, departs York for Fort George and Long Point. Later on the 8th, Brock departs Long Point and moves to Amherstburg where he arrives on the 12th. At the latter, reinforcements join the column and Brock then advances to Sandwich, which had been evacuated by the Americans.

In Michigan, at Detroit, word arrives at about this time that a supply train convoy, commanded by about 200 Ohio Volunteers under Captain Brush, is at the Raisin River en route to Detroit. General William Hull, not yet out of Canada, had dispatched a column to intercept the train and escort it to the post. The contingent, composed of about 200 men under Major Thomas B. Van Horne, arrives at Brownstown and is struck by a British-Indian force. The column is caught by total surprise. Van Horne, alarmed due to believing his command is about to be encircled, orders a retreat; however, the troops, having already been stunned, lose their discipline and Van Horne is unable to restore order. He orders yet another retreat, which merely compounds the debacle. The contingent, ordered to halt and reform at a cluster of trees, ignores the order and flees beyond the trees. All organization collapses and suddenly the troops scatter haphazardly.

The command loses 18 killed, 12 wounded and about 70 troops missing. Nevertheless, the British are able to seize mail, and its contents include Hull's complete plans. The engagement is known as the Battle of Brownstown. Van Horne makes it back to Detroit later in the day and most of his scattered command arrives still later. In the meantime, the supply train had remained unmolested. Hull dispatches a much stronger force under Colonel James Miller to make contact with the train and get the supplies into Detroit.

In naval activity, the schooner *Wiley Renard*, a one gun privateer initially commissioned the *Wiley Renard*, arrives back in Boston Harbor after a successful cruise in which it seized two brigantines and four schooners. Also, the American privateer *Atlas* (Captain Maffitt) comes upon two vessels at about 0830. The *Atlas* moves to close on both vessels with its American colors flying. Later in the morning, one of the vessels fires upon the *Atlas*, but it intentionally does not retaliate. Shortly thereafter the other vessel opens fire, but no return fire is forthcoming. Afterward, the *Atlas* moves into close range and maneuvers into position between both ships, which by now have hoisted their British flags.

The *Atlas* pounds both vessels with broadsides and musket fire. After about one hour, the smaller vessel (12-gun *Planter*, Captain Frith of Bristol, England) hauls down its colors. Meanwhile, the *Atlas*, aware that the one opponent is finished, focuses all of its attention on the larger and more formidable opponent, the 16-gun *Pursuit* (Captain Chivers of London). The remaining British vessel maintains tenacious resistance, but the *Atlas* pours relentless fire upon it and inflicts severe damage. Suddenly, the Americans again come under fire from the *Planter*, which had capitulated. Maffitt's crew responds immediately with a raking fire that clears the decks within minutes, without withholding fire upon the other vessel. After about 1220, the British cease fire and haul down their colors to finally end the engagement.

Both of the captured vessels had been en route to London from Surinam with each carrying a cargo of cocoa, coffee, cotton and sugar. During the engagement, Captain Maffitt's crew sustains two killed and five wounded. Captain Maffitt, after a quick examination of his ship, realizes that significant damages had been sustained. He decides to immediately head for an American port.

As a precaution, he transfers the prisoners from the *Pursuit* and the *Planter* to his *Atlas*, where more security is available, and he sends a prize crew to both of the British ships; however, they sail together on what turns into a harrowing voyage. While still at sea for slightly less than one month, on 2 September, lookouts spot a large vessel, which is soon identified as a frigate, and it is giving chase. Captain Maffitt orders the *Pursuit* to sail southward and enter the first available port. At about the same time he nudges near the *Planter* and directs its prize crew to take a northward course in hopes that both prizes would escape, while the *Atlas* intends to engage the frigate. Nonetheless, the *Atlas* is spared and Captain Maffitt is unable to assist the *Planter*, which had been targeted by the unidentified frigate, flying an English flag. Meanwhile, the *Pursuit* moved beyond the horizon and vanished. The *Atlas* safely arrives at an American port; however, in addition to the surprises that had already occurred, Captain Maffitt afterward receives yet another. The potent frigate that chased the *Atlas* and its prizes and halted the *Planter* had actually been an American warship, the USS *Essex*, commanded by Captain David Porter. Captain Maffitt later learns that the *Planter* had safely arrived in a friendly port.

August 6 (Thursday) **In New York** at Albany, Governor Tompkins writes to the mayor of New York, DeWitt Clinton, and others reiterating some of the subjects discussed when he had recently been in New York, including a mutual agreement that an arsenal must be constructed at the Narrows "along the channel side of the Curtain or rear Wall of Fort Richmond and be so constructed as to answer for Barracks when not used for an Arsenal."

In naval activity, the USS *Gallatin*, initially acquired by the Treasury Department during 1807, is acting under orders of the U.S. Navy during the War of 1812. On this day, the *Gallatin* intercepts a British letter of marque vessel that is en route from Jamaica to England. A fierce battle erupts. After about six hours of intense combat, the *Gallatin* prevails. Afterward the *Gallatin* seizes a few merchant ships; however, its service ends unexpectedly on 1 April 1813 when a fire breaks out at Charleston, South Carolina. Efforts to save it fail. A devastating explosion occurs and the *Gallatin* sinks.

August 7 (Friday) **In Canada,** Lieutenant Rolette, aboard the HMS *Hunter*, intercepts and captures a flotilla of bateaux moving from Maguaga to Detroit.

In New York, at Albany, Governor Tompkins, concerned about New Jersey troops and New York troops being posted together, writes to Secretary of War John Armstrong:

> I think a requisition of Jersey Militia to occupy the heights at the Narrows, whilst New York troops occupy the works below, will lead to difficulties & misunderstandings. There must be one Lt. Col. to command the whole. If he be from Jersey, the New York troops will be dissatisfied; if he be from New York the Jersey troops will not be pleased. If troops be taken from Jersey for the defence of New York, Bedlows and Ellis Island would be more eligible positions for the Jersey troops as they are more accessible to them on an emergency and will be independent.... Will you advise me in relation to the above matters as early as possible.

In naval activity, the brigantine *Grace*, en route from St. Mary's to England, is intercepted and recaptured by the HMS *Chub*.

August 7–14 **In Canada,** General William Hull begins his retreat from Canada by the 7th. His visions of a swift and grand victorious cam-

Major Thomas B. Van Horne.

paign begin to crumble. Hull's anticipated swarms of Canadian volunteers failed to materialize. Equally devastating to his cause, the Indians whom he expected to become allies joined with the British. General Hull writes to Secretary of War Eustis to report on why he retired from Canada. He said his action was necessary because of the defection of the Wyandotte Indians, the fall of Mackinac, the advance of British reinforcements from Niagara and the resultant interruption of communication with Ohio.

The column returns to Detroit; however, a small contingent remains at Sandwich (Fort Hope). The campaign had been disappointing and the initial objective, Fort Malden, had not been attacked. Hull had called a war council to decide whether to attack the post despite the lack of artillery officers, and it was determined that the regulars were prepared; however, the commanding officers of the militia units made it clear that their troops were incapable of assaulting Fort Malden without the support of artillery. Meanwhile, British General Brock had arrived to reinforce Fort Malden. The British seize the advantage. Proctor dispatches a contingent across the river to cut off Hull's supplies. The British force includes Indians under Tecumseh.

At Detroit, General Hull sends out a larger contingent following the failure on the 5th of Major Thomas Van Horne to reach the isolated convoy under Captain Brush at the Raisin River and escort it to Detroit. The 600-man column, commanded by Lt. Colonel James Miller, departs from Detroit at 1700 on the 8th. Miller's force is composed of the greater part of the U.S. 4th Infantry (one company left back at Sandwich), a detachment of the 1st Infantry, and a few artillerists (Captain Tyson's company), bolstered by the Michigan Legion, composed of about 60 native Frenchmen under Captain De Cant, along with a contingent of forty mounted spies led by Captain Sloan attached to the volunteer corps of cavalry. The contingent is rounded off with about 200 infantrymen (Ohio volunteers), commanded by Major Robertson Morrison, which places the total number of men at about 600, augmented by two pieces of artillery. The 6-pounder is commanded by Lt. Jonathan Eastman of Dyson's artillery company and the other piece, a 5.5 inch howitzer, is commanded by a detachment of the 1st U.S. Regiment commanded by Lt. James Dalliba, master of ordnance in General Hull's army.

Just before departing, Colonel Miller speaks to his troops, saying:

Soldiers, we are going to meet the enemy, and to beat them! The reverses of the 5th [Van Horne's defeat] must be repaired! The blood of your brethren, spilled by savage hands, on that day, must be avenged by their chastisement and by the chastisement of the enemy who employs them, more savage than they! I shall lead you—I trust that no man will disgrace himself or me—every man who is seen to leave the ranks, to give way or fall back, without orders, shall instantly be put to death. The officers are hereby charged with the execution of this order. My brave soldiers! you have once faced the enemy in a hard conflict, and beaten them, and gained glory to yourselves and honor to your country! Let this opportunity be improved to add another victory to that of Tippecanoe and new glory to that which you gained on the *Wabash*. Soldiers, if there are any now in the ranks of this detachment, who are afraid to meet the enemy, they are now permitted to fall out and stay behind—

Before Colonel Miller finishes his thoughts, the cry "I'll not stay" begins to ring out from within the ranks.

The column advances to the Rogue River about six miles below the city; however, the river is not easily crossed until about 2200 due to its depth. The troops are ferried aboard scows. Afterward, due to a pesky rain and the darkness, the troops are ordered to establish camp for the night. On the following morning, the march is resumed. The column passes through a cornfield in which the corn stalks had grown to a height of about 7 to 8 feet, and then into and through a clearing without incident; however, soon after, at about 0900, a band of about ten Indians who are lurking behind the house of Chief Walk-in-the-water commences firing. The Indians kill one man, a civilian from Detroit, and take his scalp before help arrives. The Indians, all of whom are on horses, easily escape and make it back to the British fort at Brownstown, commanded by Major Adam Muir. His force is composed of about 750 regulars, 100 militia and about 400 Indians.

The American spies fall back, while the advance guard under Captain Josiah Snelling advances. By about 1200, the Americans begin to close upon their objective and to this point they have encountered only some Indians who are shadowing the advance. Snelling's command, still at the point as vanguard, passes through an empty Indian village and the ground upon which Van Horne had been defeated. Miller's troops pause there to bury the dead, including Captain McCullock, whose remains are discovered lying underneath an Indian bark.

Afterward, the column resumes the advance. Shortly thereafter, Snelling's force encounters the enemy and the skirmishing erupts. Nonetheless, Snelling's command is able to hold its ground while waiting for the main body to arrive. Meanwhile, Miller had heard the firing and is rushing troops forward to bolster Snelling. Despite his force's small size and being under an avalanche of blistering fire, Snelling's line holds firmly. Reinforcements arrive just as the British and their allies begin to let out ringing yells. They rush from the fort to deploy in a line, in which the British 41st Regiment is stretched out two deep. The right part of the line is manned by Canadian militia and some Indians under Chief Walk-in-the-water and Marpot; however, the militia, peculiarly, are adorned in Indian clothes and wearing war paint. Muir's left flank is composed entirely of Indians, led by Tecumseh.

Miller, unaware of the strength of the British, immediately forms his troops, including two companies of the 1st Regiment, commanded by Lieutenant D. Stansbury and Ensign R.A. McCabe. During the ferocious encounter Colonel Miller determines that he is outflanked. Miller signals the men to launch a bayonet attack to dislodge the British, commanded by Major Muir. The Americans hit tenacious resistance; however, Miller's troops react by firing their artillery piece, a 6-pounder that instills instant terror into the Indians. Nonetheless, an unintended but not unexpected consequence occurs when Colonel James Miller's horse becomes as frightened as the Indians. As it rears and tumbles, Miller is thrown from his saddle, which places him in imminent peril. Indians race to catch him on the ground to take his scalp, but they are repelled. By that time, Miller is able to remount his horse and urge his troops on to victory.

At nearly the same time as Miller gets back upon his horse, the artillery unleashes another shot that succeeds in collapsing the British line. DeCamp's command (Michigan Legion and a contingent of Ohio riflemen) at about the same time crashes into the right flank held by the Canadian militia and Indians, and compels them to retreat. Nonetheless, the Indians under Tecumseh on the left flank had been so overconfident of the victory that they are caught in front of the British line. They continue to raise heavy resistance, but the American bayonets drive them back. Tecumseh spots the British in full retreat as they retire down the river and likewise disengages. His force moves westwardly and vanishes into the woods. Miller's force becomes divided as one contingent pursues the Indians while the rest give chase to the British.

Miller's troops relentlessly continue the attack in what becomes two running battles. Meanwhile, the British, after moving about two miles to the rear, reach the spot on Lake Erie where they had concealed their boats. Miller's command inflicts heavy casualties before the British re-cross to reach Malden. For a while, Miller remains greatly concerned because his force had been divided, but once he hears from Van Horne in command of the right flank that Tecumseh's force had retreated, he orders his forces to reunite. The British sustain 15 killed and about 40 wounded. Major Muir is among the wounded. In addition, almost 100 Indians had been killed and left on the field. Miller's command sustains 15 killed and 60 wounded. British reports give "two wounded and nine disabled."

One American news source, the *National Intelligencer*, reports that militia, many of whom are trappers, return to Detroit from the battle in Brownstown with 30 to 40 "fresh scalps" hanging from the points of bayonets. Colonel Miller's path to the supply train had been cleared; however, he halts the advance after being ordered to return to Detroit by Hull. He arrives there without making any contact with the supply train. On 14 August, General Hull dispatches yet another column to reach the supply train and escort it into Detroit. The column, commanded by Colonel Lewis Cass and Colonel Duncan McArthur, is directed to return by a separate route to avoid being spotted by British gunboats on the river.

Once the two forces are reunited, Colonel Miller addresses them:

My brave fellows! you have done well! Every man has done his duty. I give you my hearty thanks for your conduct on this day; you have gained my highest esteem; you have gained fresh honor to yourselves, and to the American arms: your fellow soldiers in arms will love you, and your country will reward you. You will return to the field of battle to collect those who have gloriously fallen; your friendly attentions to your wounded companions is required.

In his official after-battle report, he singles out various officers for their actions, but makes it clear that all of the men who deserved praise could not be mentioned. Those mentioned included Captain Daniel Baker (1st U.S. Infantry Regiment); Captain Return B. Brown (Ohio volunteers); Lt. Eastman (Dyston's artillery company); Captain Hrenvort; Captain Hull; Lt. Johnson; Michigan dragoons Major Morrison (Ohio volunteers); Major Van Horne and Ensign Whistler.

Later that day, Captain Maxwell returns from a reconnaissance mission and reports that Brownstown had been abandoned by the British. On the following day (10th), fresh patrols are dispatched to locate a missing soldier. He is located; however, he had been killed. During the operation one man is killed. The troops advance to the suspected position from where the shot originated and discover a wounded Indian who had chosen to fight to the end. He is accommodated. Meanwhile one of the officers has a close encounter with death when several shots barely miss him. A search is initiated but no signs of an Indian are immediately discovered. However, after glancing up toward the tip of a tree, an officer spots a partially concealed Indian who is reloading his weapon. A shot rings out and the Indian plummets to the ground. Meanwhile, by about 1000, all of the American dead are collected and interred beneath a house of an Indian and afterward, the structure is torched to conceal the grave site.

During the battle, the Americans sustain 18 killed and 63 wounded. None are captured. The British-Indian force sustains 102 Indians killed, and more than one-half (about 58) of those had been left on the field. The British loss is estimated at 58 killed. An artillerist at the battle who is later captured claims that after being taken to Malden, he had determined that the estimate of British casualties had been too low because he witnessed higher numbers at the British hospital there. He also learned while held there that "Major Muir, Tecumseh, Blue Jacket, and other commanders were wounded."

Miller's mud-soaked column re-enters Detroit at about noon on 12 August. They are heartily greeted by troops and civilians alike, and are given a musical reception beginning with "the tune of the soldier's return, and closed with yankee doodle." After reaching their camp, they finally get an opportunity to rid themselves of the soaked clothes they had been wearing for two and one-half days.

August 8 (Saturday) *In naval activity,* the privateer *Buckskin* (Isaac Bray, master) a 1-gun, 89-ton schooner transporting a cargo that includes ammunition, guns and provisions is captured by two British warships, the HMS *Statira* and the *Colibri*. Before its capture, the *Buckskin* had seized four schooners and recaptured the American brigantine *Hesper*, seized earlier by the HMS *Maidstone*. It had also regained a brigantine that sailed originally from Kennebec, Maine.

Forty privateers out of Salem by themselves seized about one-half of the total number of prizes captured by privateers during the war. During this conflict, most of the Salem privateers carry only 1 to 5 guns. Some of the "little privateers are the *Fly, General Putnam, Leech, Scorpion* and the *Viper*." The *Fly*, commanded by Captain H. De Koven, during its cruises seizes the schooner *George*, carrying a cargo of dry goods, and the *Experiment*, a sloop which is also transporting dry goods (and lumber and hardware) when seized. The *Viper* counts the following among its prizes: a schooner with a cargo of rum and sugar, another schooner with dry goods and yet another attempting unsuccessfully to fool the privateer by flying a Spanish flag while carrying a British license.

The list of activity by the Salem privateers seems never ending. The privateer *Scorpion* under Captain J. Osborn seizes a schooner that is destroyed at sea and captures a sloop that is sailed into Salem. The *General Putnam* and the *Leech* are also able to capture prizes. The *Leech* is credited with the seizure of two vessels, both schooners. The *General Putnam*'s sailing career as a privateer is short lived; however, before being captured by the British it seizes the 380-ton ship *Ocean* and has it taken into Salem before the British capture it.

One other privateer out of Salem, the *Cadet*, also plays a part in dismantling British shipping late in the war. It is credited with the capture of the schooner *Betsey and Jane* en route to the British stronghold at Castine, Maine, before entering port with a dry goods cargo valued at $150,000. It also captures the schooner *Mary*, also en route to Castine with dry goods.

The British vessel *Mary* had been under escort by a warship identified as a schooner when it first departed from St. John's. Shortly thereafter, the American privateer *Charles Stewart*, commanded by Captain H. Purcell, intercepts them and begins to engage the warship. During the duel the *Charles Stewart* spots another vessel heading toward it, prompting Captain Purcell, who is convinced it is another warship, to disengage and get out of the area, leaving the *Mary* and its escort alone. Nonetheless, the advancing vessel is actually another American privateer, the *Cumberland*, operating out of Portland. Although the *Charles Stewart* had departed, the *Cumberland* decides to battle the schooner. During this period of combat and confusion, the *Mary* becomes separated from its escort, which is focused on destroying or capturing the *Cumberland*. The *Cumberland*, shortly after engaging the schooner, realizes that it is up against a superior vessel. It disengages and sails off to evade capture by the British.

Although neither the *Charles Stewart* nor the *Cumberland* had been unable to capture the *Mary*, by diverting the attention of the British schooner, they had inadvertently set the stage for the *Mary* to be caught by the *Cadet*.

August 9 (Sunday) **In Canada,** Colonel Henry Proctor, having been informed that the American force under General Hull had retreated, decides to strike Hull's supply column. He dispatches a contingent under Major Muir to cross the Detroit River and attack a supply train that is en route to Detroit (*see also*, **August 7–14**, 1812).

In Florida, Lt. Colonel Thomas A. Smith, at his camp near St. Augustine, in a letter to Lt. Elias Stallings, directs him to maintain the project to finish the construction of the blockhouse at Davis Creek (Julianton Creek) that has become an urgent task due to the recent Indian raids. Colonel Smith includes a sketch to lay out the blueprint for inhabitants who choose to build cabins nearby. Cabins must include port holes. Colonel Smith also takes precautions by directing Stallings to inform him in detail all approaches to his position that can be used by reinforcements if the Indians gather in the swamp. On the following day, Colonel Smith informs Lt. Stallings that the Georgia Patriots had abandoned the camp and that he (Stallings) should acquire it by force if necessary. He should also take steps once the mules are secured to prevent them from being stolen. In addition, Colonel Smith orders that no weapons are to be fired and no fires are to be lit. He adds that the position is to be defended "to the last extremity."

In Louisiana, a violent hurricane rips through New Orleans. The U.S. Navy vessels in port suffer greatly. The USS *Enterprise* is literally blown ashore and the "Shear Hulk *Etna*" is sunk, costing the lives of the sailors and Marines aboard. Another vessel, the brigantine *Viper*, sustains damage but survives. On 31 August, Major Carmick, U.S. Marine, in a letter to Commandant (Lt. Colonel) Franklin Wharton, states that "one gunboat had been lost and two were 'up in the weeds,' that the brig Siren was safe-chased into Pass Christian by a British Frigate. She had lost two men, however, one of them a corporal of Marines." During the storm with its ongoing confusion, some Negroes along with Indians, incited by whites, threaten rebellion.

In Michigan, near the Indian village of Monguagon, an American force of about 600 troops, composed of regulars and militia, encounters a British-Indian contingent en route to Frenchtown to acquire supplies that are desperately needed at Detroit. Advance scouts under Captain Josiah Snelling first spot the British under Captain Adam Muir and the Indians under Tecumseh. Snelling's contingent is also the first to come under fire; however, the Americans hold their ground until the main body under Lt. Colonel James Miller arrives. The British are then compelled to retire through present-day Trenton, Michigan, and cross back into Canada.

This running skirmish, referred to as the Battle of Monguagon, is the only victory gained by the Americans in Michigan during the entire conflict. Nevertheless, the Americans pay a high price. They sustain 20 killed and 60 wounded, a much higher number than the British casualties. Within about one week, General Hull surrenders Detroit without a fight (*see also*, **August 7–14**, 1812).

In naval activity, the HMS *Bream* seizes the sloop *Pythagoras* (Cyrus Libby, master), a privateer, which is carrying a cargo of ammunition, guns and some provisions. Also, the American privateer *Rossie* under Joshua Barney (U.S. Navy, retired) encounters and engages the British privateer *Jeannie.* After some heavy exchanges of fire, the British surrender.

August 10 (Monday) *In naval activity,* the HMS *Morgiana* encounters and captures the 260-ton *Bolina* (John Fairfield, master) while it is en route from Gibraltar to Salem, Massachusetts. The *Bolina* is transporting a cargo that includes wine, salt and other items. The *Morgiana* on this day also seizes the brigantine *Sally.* The *Sally* is separate from the *Sally Ann* seized on 16 September 1812, the ship *Sally* seized on 16 April 1813, the brigantine *Sally* captured on 24 April 1813, the schooner *Sally* seized on 13 May 1813, the schooner *Sally* seized on 12 July 1813, the schooner *Sally* seized 15 September 1813, the schooner *Sally* captured 16 October 1813, and the sloop *Sally* seized 19 May 1814.

In other naval activity, the USS *Gallatin* (Captain Edward Herbert), a revenue cutter, intercepts the British brigantine *General Blake*, which is attempting to deceive the Americans by flying a Spanish flag. The ruse fails and the prize is taken into port at Charleston, South Carolina. The USS *Constitution* encounters and seizes a British brigantine off Cape Race, Newfoundland, while it is en route to Halifax. The prize is deemed of no value. After transferring the crew to the *Constitution*, the vessel is burned. Also, the American *Betsey*, a 127-ton brigantine commanded by Captain William B. Orne and en route from Naples to Boston with a cargo of brandy, is seized by the HMS *Guerriere* off the Bank of Newfoundland. Captain Orne and a boy are transferred to the *Guerriere* while the remainder of the crew is taken to Halifax aboard the *Betsey*. Captain Orne is aboard the *Guerriere* when it encounters the USS *Constitution* on 19 August.

In other naval activity, the American privateer *Rossie* (Commodore Joshua Barney) intercepts an outlaw brigantine, the *Rebecca*, out of Saco, Maine. The *Rebecca* is en route to London in violation of the U.S. laws regarding carrying goods for the British. A prize crew is assigned and it is taken into an American port.

August 11 (Tuesday) **In Florida,** a contingent of 125 Georgia volunteers under Captain Tomlinson Fort, dispatched earlier by Governor David B. Mitchell, arrives at about this time near the Zephaniah Kingsley Plantation, known as Laurel Grove, along the St. Johns River. Lt. Colonel Smith, at his camp outside St. Augustine, writes to Captain Fort and directs him to repair to Picolata, designated by Smith as the point where all volunteers from Georgia are to assemble. In the same letter, Captain Fort is instructed to send a detachment from his position at Picolata to apprehend a Mr. Wanton, who resides near the town. He is also ordered to send out a larger contingent to Bona Vista to seize a boat there, which is being used by the hostile Indians to ferry Indians and Negroes across the St. Johns River.

In New York, General Stephen Van Rensselaer arrives at Buffalo following his journey from Albany.

In naval activity, the HMS *Emulous* encounters and recaptures the ship *Henry*. The *Henry* is separate from the 181-ton *Henry* seized on 28 April 1813, the 89-ton schooner *Henry*, seized 19 June 1813, and the 194-ton brigantine *Henry Gilder* captured 12 July 1814.

In other naval activity, the British warships HMS *Acasta* and the HMS *Colibrie* intercept and seize an American privateer, the schooner *Polly*. The *Polly* is separate from other so-named vessels: the schooner seized 14 October 1812, the 92-ton sloop captured 28 July 1813, the schooner seized on 13 August 1813, the 88-ton schooner overtaken on 10 December 1813, and the 45-ton sloop captured on 10 August 1814.

Also, the HMS *Morgiana* intercepts and seizes the 157-ton brigantine *Prudence* (John Anderson, master), which is en route from Dublin to New York. This *Prudence* is separate from the schooner *Prudence* seized on 10 July 1814. The HMS *Colibrie* intercepts and captures the 40-ton schooner *Regulator*, a privateer operating out of Salem, Massachusetts. At the time of its capture, the *Regulator* (J. Mansfield, master) is carrying a cargo of ammunition, guns and some provisions. Also, the USS *Constitution*, while continuing its cruise near Cape Race, Newfoundland, intercepts and seizes another English brigantine, the *Adiona*, en route to England from Nova Scotia with a cargo of lumber.

August 12 (Wednesday) **In Florida,** a rider dispatched by Captain Tomlinson Fort at the blockhouse on Davis Creek is intercepted by a band of Indians and Negroes before he reaches Lt. Colonel Thomas Smith at his camp near St. Augustine. Colonel Smith believes the rider was murdered by the band. His body is discovered about three miles from the blockhouse. According to a letter written by Colonel Smith on the 21st, he was "flogged, his nose, one ear, & ____ cut off. He had three shot wounds in his body & his scalp was taken."

In Michigan, Colonel Miller's column arrives back at Detroit following his victory at Brownstown on the 9th (*see also,* **August 7–14,** 1812).

In naval activity, the 26-ton schooner *Dolphin*, while operating out of Portsmouth, Maine, and carrying a cargo of ammunition and guns, is seized by the HMS *Earl of Moira*. This vessel is separate from others so named: a schooner taken 13 August 1812, a vessel captured 3 April 1813, a schooner overtaken 29 July 1813, a vessel captured 16 August 1813 and the 28-ton *Dolphin* seized on 22 October 1814.

In other naval activity, the privateer *Science* (Captain W. Fernald), a sloop, sails from Portsmouth, New Hampshire, along with the privateer *Thomas* (Captain T. Shaw). The *Science* is seized by the HMS *Emulous* on its 13th day at sea; however, before its capture, the *Thomas* succeeds in seizing one brigantine, three ships and one sloop.

August 13 (Thursday) **In Canada,** General Isaac Brock arrives at Amherstburg with a contingent of several hundred regulars. Once there, he assumes command of all the British forces. His presence seems to immediately build the confidence of the British and Canadian troops, especially the militia, which until his arrival had not displayed any type of positive attitude or enthusiasm. At about the same time Brock arrives on the scene, the American contingent at Sandwich hurriedly re-crosses the river to get back in the United States. The British, having entered Sandwich after the Americans withdrew, begins without interference to construct batteries with which to shell Detroit. The batteries are completed and ready to fire within two days.

In Illinois, a contingent under Captain William Wells arrives at Fort Dearborn (Chicago) from Fort Wayne with about 30 Miamies who are to escort the garrison to Detroit as ordered by General Hull.

In naval activity, the USS *Essex*— attached to Commodore Rodgers' squadron and under the command of Captain David Porter — which left later than the other ships in the squadron, is sailing under the guise of a merchant ship. The HMS *Alert*, a 20 gun sloop, formerly a coal carrier until acquired by the Royal Navy during May 1804, spots the *Essex*. The *Alert* is cruising in the North Atlantic west of the Azores about one-third of the distance between the Azores and the Delaware Capes.

British Captain Thomas L.P. Laugharne is informed by lookouts that the vessel in the distance resembles an "English Indiaman, earlier captured by the U.S. Navy," but he is also informed that it is flying English colors. Nonetheless, the British also detect that the vessel is attempting to run.

The *Essex* captures the British ship *Alert* (*Valor and Victory [The Age of Vindication], Volume X,* Edwin Markham, 1912).

Laugharne becomes anxious to close on the vessel and if it is sailing under false colors, seize it as a prize. As the *Alert* moves in closer, the guns of the *Essex* remain camouflaged because they had not been designed for long distance firing.

Meanwhile, the *Alert* prepares to hail the vessel and board it. Just as the *Alert* moves into range, Captain Porter orders the British colors lowered and replaced by the Stars and Stripes, while simultaneously opening the gun ports. The British, annoyed by the ruse, take immediate action and fire a broadside at the *Essex*. The *Essex* absorbs the broadside, which has little effect; however, the guns on the *Essex* return fire and the British crew is stunned after discovering they have encountered a formidable warship rather than a vulnerable merchant ship. The captain of the *Alert* orders its colors struck. It becomes the prize of Captain Porter and the first British warship to be captured by the U.S. Navy in the War of 1812.

During the same cruise, the *Essex* also seizes a British transport that is carrying troops. Captain Porter, after capturing the *Alert*, has a problem on his hands with a large number of prisoners seized earlier on merchant ships. He takes an unusual step of transferring all of the seamen onto the *Alert* and sends the vessel to Canada to exchange them for American captives. When it arrives at St. John's in Newfoundland, the British commander, Admiral Sir John T. Duckworth, is annoyed and claims that the *Alert*, not having sailed from an American port, cannot be considered a cartel and such endeavors would render future prizes immunity from being recaptured. Nonetheless, he relents and the *Alert* sails with 200 American prisoners. The *Alert* arrives in New York during autumn, and during its cruise, seizes ten prizes. After its arrival, the *Alert* is condemned by the New York Admiralty Court and later purchased by the U.S. Navy. Nonetheless, the navy concludes the ship is unsuited for cruising and instead uses it as a storeship. It remains in service in New York harbor until 1818, when it is transformed into a receiving ship. During 1829, the ship is dismantled at Norfolk.

In other activity, the HMS *Statira* recaptures the *Apollo* and the brigantine *Prince of Austria*. The privateer *Lewis*, an 86-ton schooner out of New London, is seized by the British. The *Lewis* is carrying a cargo of ammunition, guns and some provisions. Before being captured, the *Lewis* had seized a valuable 8-gun British ship before it could arrive at Quebec. Also, the British privateer *General Smyth* intercepts and recaptures the brigantine *Penelope*, along with its cargo of coffee and rum. The records of the Vice Admiralty Court at Halifax, Nova Scotia, which lists the recapture of the *Penelope* on 13 August 1812 also lists the capture of the brigantine *Penelope* and its cargo of coffee on 15 July 1813 by the privateer *General Smyth*.

August 14 (Friday) **In Canada,** the British under General Isaac Brock establish batteries across from Detroit. On the following day, the artillery begins to pound General William Hull's positions. Meanwhile Brock's ground forces, having been spared meeting any ground attack prepares to cross into Michigan. On the 16th, Brock launches his invasion force expecting to meet fierce resistance.

In naval activity, the HMS *Morgiana* intercepts the brigantine *Union*, which is en route to Newfoundland from Liverpool, and recaptures it. The *Union* is separate from the ship *Union* seized on 16 August 1812, the schooner *Union* seized on 14 October 1812, the schooner *Union* captured on 19 October 1812, the schooner *Union* seized on 3 April 1813, the ship *Union* seized on 26 June 1813, and the schooner *Union* captured on 30 July 1814.

In other naval activity, the American privateer *Globe*, after having lost several prizes that evaded capture, comes upon another potential prize and seizes it without incident. The prize, the schooner *Ann* en route to Guernsey, is taken into Baltimore with the *Globe*. Captain Grant's crew had been desperately short of water and the crisis actually caused crew members to trade with each other, a quart of liquor for a quart of water. Once the *Ann* is secured, the *Globe* departs and sails into Baltimore.

The *Globe* afterward returns to the sea and completes several cruises. During that time, it seizes a number of vessels, including the *Sir Simon Clark*, which is carrying a cargo of coffee, rum and sugar. The enemy raises tenacious resistance before finally falling to the Americans. During the struggle, on the decks of the prize, the British commander and three crewmen sustain severe wounds and four men are killed. The Americans sustain two killed — the 2nd officer and a drummer — and one man is wounded. A prize crew takes the vessel and cargo into port at Norfolk, Virginia.

Subsequently, while cruising off Portugal, the *Globe* comes under attack by an Algerian warship. The *Globe*'s commander is Captain John Murphy. The two vessels pound each other from close range but more or less sporadically for no less than three hours. The Algerians apparently sustain too much damage to continue. Suddenly, the sloop of war disengages and retires. Meanwhile, the *Globe*, having sustained at least 82 shots that rivet its sails, sustains only two men wounded.

The *Globe*, in addition to capturing the prizes mentioned previously, also has three other prizes to its credit. They are the *Kingston Packet*, carrying a cargo of rum, which is taken into Ocracoke Inlet, North Carolina, the ship *Seaton*, and the 14-gun ship *Venus*, transporting a cargo of salt. The *Seaton* had been captured earlier by the privateer *Paul Jones*, which operates out of New York. However, while en route to the States, it had encountered the *Globe*, and by the time of the encounter the prize crew had determined the ship unsafe. At the request of the prize crew, Captain Murphy orders the vessel destroyed. Also, the American privateer *Rossie* (Commodore Joshua Barney) encounters a sail; however the encounter is with a friendly vessel, the brigantine *Hazard*, which had sailed from Cadiz, Spain. The crew of the *Hazard* is informed that the war with the British had begun. Several days later, on the 17th, the *Rossie* encounters another friendly vessel, the brigantine *Favorite*, which is en route to Boston.

August 14–15 FORT DEARBORN MASSACRE Captain Nathan Heald, under orders of General Hull, abandons Fort Dearborn (Chicago). The fort, garrisoned by about 50 troops, also contains several families including children. Captain Heald, responsible for the safety of the troops as well as the civilians, during a trek of 200 miles standing between him and Detroit, holds a conference with the Indians to try to prevent them from turning hostile. Heald informs the chiefs that he had been ordered to Detroit and that as a token of good will, he would leave items he cannot transport in the fort for their use. Nonetheless, Heald remains concerned. Before departing, he orders the destruction of all arms, powder and liquor that cannot be taken.

On the following morning (15th), the column departs from the post at 0900. A party of Miamies holds the point and the remainder of the Indians that arrived earlier under Captain Wells holds the rear of the column. After they leave, the Indians discover to their surprise and dismay neither ammunition nor liquor was left behind. The enraged Indians decide to take immediate revenge.

While the column is cautiously moving through the wilderness, the Indians speed to the front of the column and establish an ambush along the shore of the lake. Holding concealed positions, the Indians await the approach of Heald's column. As it approaches the summit of a range of sandhills, the troops are struck by a volley. Heald's command fires one round and then a charge is initiated. The Indians to the front

The Fort Dearborn Massacre (*Valor and Victory [The Age of Vindication], Volume X*, Edwin Markham, 1912).

fall back and join those on the flanks. In the meantime, the wagons are formed into a defensive position, while the skirmish continues. The women and children are gathered together in and about the wagons to provide some protection; however, the friendly Indians under Captain Wells had not offered any aid to the besieged command. Nonetheless, the Indians greatly outnumber the diminutive force of soldiers.

As the incessant fire begins to cut the ranks, women begin to move to the firing line where they retrieve weapons of the fallen troops and participate in the fight. But still, the pressure remains overwhelming. Within about 15 minutes, the Indians seize all of the horses, along with the provisions and baggage.

Heald and his remnant force move to a small hill lying on the prairie, but he is not immediately pursued. Afterward, the Indians, numbering between 400 and 500, holding at the top of the bank, motion for Heald to approach them. He advances alone and encounters one of the chiefs, Black-bird, who is accompanied by an interpreter. Heald is told that if he surrenders his command, none will suffer harm.

Finally, aware of his great losses and the inability to continue the fight, Heald reluctantly capitulates. During the desperate defense, one of the Indians makes his way to a wagon in which twelve children had been concealed from the fire. In a merciless act, the Indian bludgeons each child with his tomahawk. After the surrender, the wounded receive no mercy. The survivors are taken back to Fort Dearborn. Captain Heald, in letter dated 23 October at Pittsburgh, stated:

> Our strength was 54 regulars, and 12 militia—out of which, 26 regulars, and all of the militia, were killed in the action, with two women and twelve children. Ensign Ronan, and Doctor Voorhis, of my company, with Captain William Wells, of Fort Wayne, to my great sorrow, numbered among the dead. Lieut. Helm, with 25 non-commissioned officers and privates, and 11 women and children, were prisoners when we were separated. Mrs. Heald and myself, were taken to the mouth of the river St. Joseph, and, both being badly wounded, were permitted to reside with Mr. Burnett, an Indian trader.

After Heald's surrender, the Indians had also scalped the wounded and proclaimed that they were not part of the surrender agreement. Within a few days after the massacre, the Indians depart for Fort Wayne. At that time, Heald persuades a Frenchman to transport him and his small party to Mackinac. He receives parole along with a sergeant that accompanied him. From there he travels to Detroit, where Colonel Proctor arranges for him to return to Buffalo. He arrives there on 22 October.

August 15 (Saturday) **In Florida,** a force of Georgia volunteers and a contingent of U.S. Marines under Colonel Daniel (Neil) Newman arrive at the St. Johns River en route to strike the Lotchway (Seminole) and Alligator Indian strongholds in East Florida.

In Illinois, a small garrison of Americans at Fort Dearborn (Chicago) abandons the fort on orders of General Hull. Indians attack these men and accompanying civilians while they travel toward Fort Detroit. The Indians also burn down the fort. There is a small marker near the Wrigley Building in Chicago that indicates where the fort stood (*see also*, **August 14–15,** 1812). During the war, Illinois establishes forts across the territory. One of these, Fort Russell at Edwardsville in Madison County, is used as a supply base and frequent headquarters for governor Ninian Edwards.

Other War of 1812 era forts in Illinois include Fort Chilton at St. Jacob, John Hill's Fort at Carlyle, and two forts at Warsaw known as the Warsaw Forts. In addition, a civilian fort known as Fort La Motte is constructed at Palestine during 1812, and within two years more than twenty-five families reside within its stockade, supported by rangers.

In Kentucky, several regiments raised by the governor during the previous May assemble at Georgetown in Scott County. The regiments, under the overall command of Brigadier General John Payne, are commanded by Colonels John Allen, William Lewis, and John M. Scott. Also, Thomas P. Metcalfe, the son of Revolutionary war veteran Captain John Metcalfe, is among the first Kentuckians to volunteer at the outbreak of war. He serves at various places, including Fort Meigs under General Harrison, and later acquires the rank of brigadier general. Later, he is elected governor of Kentucky as successor to General (Governor) Joseph Desha.

In Michigan, British General Sir Isaac Brock issues an ultimatum to General William Hull. Two British officers, Lieutenant Colonel McDonald and Captain Glegg, carrying a white flag, arrive at the American positions to deliver the ultimatum. Both men are blindfolded and taken to a house near the fort. After meeting there with General Hull, the officers return to their lines to inform General Brock that General Hull refused to surrender. Shortly thereafter, the British batteries commence fire. The Americans' three batteries respond with equal tenacity. The dueling batteries remain active well after dusk. The American batteries, two on the river bank and another in what was known as "Judge Woodward's garden," succeed in silencing only one of the British batteries.

The ultimatum offered General Hull two options, capitulate or face annihilation by massacre. Brock's letter includes: "It is far from my intention to join in a war of extermination; but you must be aware that the numerous bodies of Indians who have attached themselves to my troops will be beyond my control the moment the contest commences." Brock's demands are adamantly declined.

General Hull, within about two hours after receiving the ultimatum, responds, stating that "the town and fort would be defended to the last extremity." The Americans, possessing seven 14-pounders, return fire.

Subsequent to dusk, General Brock sends a large contingent of about 600 Indians across the river; however, his main body awaits dawn on the 16th to launch the main attack. Brock had chosen the landing place, Springwell, less than five miles from Detroit because of its strategic location. Once secured, the British will control the sole path of retreat from the fort. The Indians under Tecumseh deploy along the roads and in the woods. The British force, according to Brock, is bolstered by two warships, including the HMS *Royal Charlotte*, and numbers more than 1,300 troops and about 600 Indians. The British movement is spotted. Before dawn on the 16th, General Hull directs Major Thomas S. Jesup to send riders to intercept Colonel Duncan McArthur and Colonel Lewis Cass, both of whom had earlier been dispatched to locate a supply train. McArthur and Cass are directed to speed back to support the defense of the post. Meanwhile, the British, across the river at Sandwich, commence an artillery bombardment at about 1600, and it continues until midnight (15th–16th).

In naval activity, the 164-ton brigantine *John* (John Alden, master) is intercepted and seized by the HMS *Maidstone* while it is en route from Liverpool to Portland, Maine, with a cargo of salt and earthenware. The *John* is separate from the 130-ton brigantine *John* seized on 5 April 1813 and the sloop *John* seized on 18 May 1814.

In other naval activity, lookouts aboard the USS *Constitution* at about dawn spot a small convoy to their front. After a short chase, the *Constitution* moves up closer and discovers that one of the ships is a warship that is towing a brigantine. By about 0600, the British warship cuts the brigantine loose and sets it on fire. At about the same time, the British direct another brigantine to maneuver into place between the warship and the *Constitution* to permit the British warship to get away. The *Constitution* moves against another vessel and discovers it is a prize of the American privateer *Dolphin* out of Salem.

Meanwhile, as the boarding party is going aboard, the warship increases its distance from the Constitution. After deciding that the *Constitution* might not be able to catch the prey, it moves to pounce upon the convoy beginning with a brigantine. By 1400, the brigantine is halted and identified as the American *Adeline*, which had sailed from Liverpool with a cargo of dry goods. The prize master and the crew are removed and replaced by Midshipman Madison and a crew. Madison is afterward ordered to take the *Adeline* to the closest U.S. port. Captain Hull is also informed by the prize master taken off the ship that the merchant ship that was burned was out of New York and carried a cargo of hemp and other items.

In other naval activity, the 16-gun American privateer *Alfred*, manned by a crew of 130 men, prepares to sail from Salem, Massachusetts.

August 16 (Sunday) THE SURRENDER OF DETROIT **In Michigan** at Fort Detroit, General Hull's force is separated. The militia is deployed in the town, while the regulars hold the fort. Nevertheless, it is later revealed at General Hull's trial that the men and civilians "were so crowded inside the fort as to render it impossible for them to act offensively—that is, just before the articles of capitulation were agreed upon." The militia has two 24-pounders that command the approach road and the artillery is poised to fire. At daybreak, the British artillery, which had halted at midnight, resumes firing. Meanwhile, General Brock—leading a force composed of a 30-man contingent of artillerymen, a 50-man contingent of the Newfoundland Regiment and about 250 men of the 41st Regiment—crosses from Canada and lands at Springwell, several miles outside Detroit. About 600 Indians, led by Tecumseh, had earlier landed about two miles below Brock's force and they are deployed in the woods to the left of the main body. At about dawn, General Hull gives his son, Captain Abraham Hull, a letter to deliver to General Brock: "I propose a cessation of hostilities for one hour

General Isaac Brock (*Canada, An Encyclopedia of the Country, Volume I*, 1898).

to open negotiations for the surrender of Detroit." Captain Hull, traveling under a white flag, reaches the opposite bank, but too late to deliver it to Brock, who had already moved out. Actually, Hull does not deliver the letter to any British officer; rather, he remains on the Canadian bank of the river and holds the message until after the Americans surrender.

Later, at about 1000, the Redcoats are spotted as they advance. To the surprise of the British, the militia retreats to the main fort, leaving the approach to the post undefended. Nevertheless, the British, marching in tight formation, anticipate heavy resistance. Nonetheless, before the thunderclap is unleashed, both sides become startled when unexpectedly a white flag is swung over the front wall of the fort. Even the British commander is puzzled by the scene. A British party is sent ahead in an attempt to receive an explanation for the exposure of the flag. At that point, Brock receives a bigger shock. The flag is not a ruse.

Left: Map of the Michigan Territory.

General Hull, despite the counsel of his officers, all of whom wanted to defend the fort, had decided to capitulate without a fight. The British, according to their reports, also gain "two thousand and four hundred stand of arms besides those in the arsenal; also of cannon as follows: of iron, nine 24-pounders; five 9, three 6, four 2, and two 1-pounders: and of howitzers, one 8 inch and one 5-inch."

During the final hours of the ordeal, a court-martial was convening in the fort regarding the conduct of Lt. Hanks when he surrendered Fort Michilimackinac. One of the British shells struck the building in which the court-martial was being held. The explosion killed Lt. Hanks and five others, including two officers, two enlisted men and a surgeon. Also, the troops under Colonel Findlay, including some of his regiment as well as contingents of Colonel Lewis Cass and Duncan McArthur, are deployed slightly west of the post, prepared to fire against the British advance, but Hull denies permission and orders Findlay to withdraw to the fort.

During the column's retreat, the troops spot the white flag at the fort. Colonel Findlay becomes infuriated with Hull. Findlay yells: "What in the hell am I ordered here for?" Hull tries to persuade Findlay that he was recalled to get better terms from the British, only to increase Findlay's anger. He shouts back: "Terms! Damnation! We can beat them on the plain. I did not come here to capitulate; I came here to fight." Findlay's troops, despite their immense anger, obey the order by stacking arms. Another officer, Colonel Lewis Cass, upon learning of Hull's refusal to fight for possession of Detroit, becomes so angry

Hull's surrender to Brock at Detroit (*Valor and Victory [The Age of Vindication], Volume X*, Edwin Markham, 1912).

that he breaks his sword. Later, after his regiment is paroled, Colonel Cass repairs to Washington to defend the honor of his regiment and the others who opposed capitulation. Cass gives testimony against General Hull at his court-martial.

The American representatives at the surrender are General Hull, Colonel E. Brush, Colonel James Miller and Captain Charles Fuller. The British representatives are Colonel McDonald and Major Glegg. The articles of surrender state:

Camp Detroit, August 16th, 1812.
   Capitulation of surrendering Fort Detroit, entered into between Maj. Gen. Brock, commanding his Britannic Majesty's forces of the one part, and Brig. General Hull, commanding the Northwest army of the United States of the other part.
   Article First. Fort Detroit, with all the troops, regulars as well as militia, will be immediately surrendered to the British forces under the command of Maj. Gen. Brock and will be considered prisoners of war, with the exception of such of the militia of the Michigan Territory, as have not joined the army.
   Article 2nd. All public stores, arms and public documents including everything also of public nature, will be immediately given up.
   Article 3d. Private property and private persons of every description will be respected.
   Article 4th. His excellency, Brig. Gen. Hull, having expressed a desire that a detachment from the state of Ohio on its way to join his army, as well as one sent from Fort Detroit, under the command of Col. McArthur, should be included in the above capitulation, it is accordingly agreed to. It is, however, to be understood, that such parts of the Ohio militia as have not joined the army, will be permitted to return home on condition that they will not serve during the war; their arms, however, will be delivered up if belonging to the public.
   Article 5th. The garrison will march out at the hour of 12 o'clock this day and the British forces take immediate possession of the fort.
   J. McDonald, Lieut. Col. Militia, P. A. D.C.
   J.B. Glegg, Major, A. D.C.
   James Miller, Lieut. Col. 5th U.S. Inft.
   E. Brush, Col. 1st. Reg. Mich. Militia.
   Approved,
   Com. Hull, Brig. Gen. Isaac Brock, Maj. Gen.
   Comm'g. N. W. Army. A true Copy:
   Robt. Nichol, Lieut. Col. & Qr. M. Gen. Militia.

The British also capture the USS *Adams*, a 6-gun brigantine, which actually belongs to the American army. At this time, the U.S. Navy has no armed warships on the Great Lakes. The frigate is renamed the HMS *Detroit*. General Brock, cautioned by Prevost to avoid any attacks and to remain on the defensive, was unconvinced. He believed only a bold and daring move could preserve Upper Canada. His instincts proved correct and his victory produced accolades that continued incessantly. Victory over Hull caused the Canadians to explode with enthusiasm and catapulted Brock to hero status that never diminished.

Soon after taking possession of Fort Detroit, the British enjoyed dinner, but Brock had a particular soldier on his mind and he wanted to thank him before dinner. Private Dean of the 41st British Regiment, captured recently at the bridge, was immediately released and taken to General Brock, who paid him great thanks for his actions.

Hull's officers had adamantly opposed the surrender. General James Taylor, Major Thomas Jesup and other officers worked to replace Hull with General Duncan McArthur; however, capitulation occurred before McArthur arrived back at the fort. To add further embarrassment to Hull's failed Canadian campaign, he also agrees, as governor of the Michigan Territory, to surrender the entire territory. Hull's debacle creates a huge crisis that hands Michigan Territory to the British without a fight. After the debacle at Detroit, Brigadier General Simon Perkins of the Ohio militia receives the responsibility of defending the northwestern frontier.

At the time of the surrender of Detroit, a force of Kentucky troops, commanded by General William Henry Harrison, is preparing to move to Fort Detroit to bolster it. Once news of the surrender is known, General Harrison is sent instead to Fort Wayne, Indiana, which is also under threat from the British and Indians. Harrison, while advancing to Fort Wayne, sends word to Governor Shelby requesting that he raise troops to protect Indiana and Illinois against incursions by the Indians. Meanwhile, Harrison is also considering his strategy to move against the British at Detroit. Governor Shelby responds immediately to Harrison's request. In less than three weeks, a large force of mounted Kentuckians under Major General Hopkins converges on Vincennes.

General Hull receives a court-martial that convicts him of being a coward in the face of the enemy. The court sentences him to death. However, President Madison intervenes and grants General Hull a pardon. His name is stripped from the rolls of the U.S. Army. The president based his decision on General Hull's meritorious service during the American Revolution and also because of his age. During the trial, General Hull presented a defense in which he claimed that had he defended the fort, his supplies would not have lasted and that the entire territory would have been ravaged by Indians once the fort fell. He also placed the blame on the Madison administration, which was the cause of his inferior numbered force. General Hull accepted no blame for himself.

Also, following the surrender, the militia troops are released on parole; however, the regulars, including General Hull, are taken to Montreal and afterward to Quebec. General Hull is later exchanged for thirty British soldiers. The Ohio volunteers are taken across Lake Erie and from there they march back to their homes. They are exchanged during spring of 1813.

Captain (later general) George Sanderson of the Ohio militia, at Detroit when it was surrendered, had no kind words for Hull. He later stated:

Hull was an imbecile, not a traitor or a coward, but an imbecile caused by drunkenness. He was an ardent drinker. On the day before his surrender, his son, Captain Abraham F. Hull, came among my men in a beastly state of intoxication. On the day of the surrender I saw Hull frequently. His face about the mouth and chin was covered with tobacco juice and I thought in common with other officers that the general was under the influence of liquor. He was surrounded by a military family, the members of which were fond of high times, wines and liquors. After his surrender and before the enemy had entered, many of the officers begged Colonel James Findlay to take command of the American forces and resist the enemy, but he declined to take command. Colonel James Miller was also urged to take command, but he refused to assume the responsibility, saying matters had gone too far, but had Hull signified to me his intention of surrendering, I would have assumed command and defended the fort to the last.

Another Ohio contingent, the 230 men under Captain Henry Brush, who remain near the Raisin River with the supply train, including cattle and other provisions that never reached Detroit, had been included in the surrender. News of the surrender reaches Brush, but he is in disbelief and is not anxious to believe Detroit quit without a fight. Another officer with Brush, Captain Thomas Rowland, proclaims: "It is treason!" After a hurried council, Brush and the others decide that their command is not included in the surrender.

Soon a British contingent under Captain Elliott (son of Indian agent Mathew Elliott) arrives at the river to take command of the Americans, but to his surprise, his return to Detroit is succinctly diverted. Captain Elliott is taken prisoner. Captain Brush leads his column back to Ohio and afterward, the British are released.

Meanwhile, back at Detroit, the British place the American officers aboard British vessels that carry them to Montreal. General Hull is kept isolated from the other officers. Hull and his daughter who is with him are taken aboard the *Queen Charlotte*, which sails from Detroit on the 17th. Captain Dyson and his regulars are kept at Amherstburg, while the other regulars are taken to Montreal. The Ohio volunteers are taken to Buffalo, New York, and once there, the British permit them to return to their homes in Ohio.

Later on a plaque is placed on a building "at the northwest corner of McGill and Notre Dame streets in Montreal." It reads: "General Hull, United States Army, 25 officers, 350 men, entered prisoners of war 10th September 1812." Several days after the fall of Detroit, according to Lieutenant Eastman (a prisoner), about 250 Indians arrived from Saginaw, Michigan, and these were followed by about 1,100 to 1,200 additional Indians from Mackinac around 10 September. Nonetheless, their services were not required because the siege never had to be extended. Their presence in Detroit, however, causes concern for the American prisoners and for the British.

Back in Ohio, once Governor Meigs is informed of the surrender of Detroit, he speeds up the process of committing the remainder of the Ohio quota of volunteers. He prepares to send

1,200 troops to Urbana to join with General Edward Tupper, and he authorizes a large operation in which the frontiersmen initiate construction projects to quickly build blockhouses to protect the settlers on the frontier.

Captain Isaac Hull of the U.S. Navy is the nephew of General William Hull, and Hull's grandson is Joseph Wheeler (West Point, 1859), who later left the army to join the Confederacy, where he became a major general. Afterward, he rejoined the United States Army and served as major general of volunteers during the Spanish American War (1898).

General Brock issues a proclamation for the people of the Michigan Territory assuring them they will be able to retain their property and continue the "free exercise of their civil and religious rights," even though Britain has taken control. He prepares to depart Detroit for York. He designates Colonel Henry Proctor as commander at Detroit.

While Brock is en route to York to further his plan to totally control the Niagara frontier, his ship, the HMS *Chippewa*, is intercepted by the HMS *Lady Prevost* and news is given to him regarding an armistice that had recently been agreed upon by Sir George Prevost and General Henry Dearborn. Brock becomes alarmed because of the agreement. After reaching Kingston, Brock writes to Prevost urging an immediate attack upon Sackets Harbor on Lake Ontario. Brock is convinced that once Sackets Harbor falls, Canada will be spared an attack from the Lake. His letter states: "With our present naval superiority it [Sackets Harbor] must fall. The troops at Niagara will be recalled for its protection. While they march, we sail, and before they can return, the whole Niagara frontier will be ours." Brock is not alone in his disappointment with the armistice. His opinion is shared by President Madison.

On 27 August, Colonel James Miller, one of the capitulants, writes in a letter:

> When I last wrote you my feelings were very different from what they are now. I thought things appeared prosperous and flattering; I considered we had a sufficient force to break down all opposition, and I still think had we done as we ought, we could have carried conquest to a very considerable extent. But, alas! times are now altered. We are now all prisoners of war.... Only one week since I, with six hundred men, completely conquered almost the whole force which they then had, but now they came and took Fort Detroit and made nearly two thousand prisoners, on Sunday the 16th inst. There being no operations going on against them below us, gave them an opportunity to reenforce. The number they brought against us is unknown, but my humble opinion is we could have defeated them without a doubt, had we attempted it, but Gen. Hull thought differently and surrendered.

Also, British General Brock writes Lt. General Sir George Prevost: "Sir, I hasten to appraise your Excellency of the capture of this very important post; 2500 troops have this day surrendered prisoners of war, and about 25 pieces of ordnance have been taken without the sacrifice of a drop of British blood. I had not more than 700 troops including militia, and about 600 Indians, to accomplish this service. When I detail my good fortune, your Excellency will be astonished."

The loss of Detroit caused shock throughout the civilian population as well as the military; however, it did spark more patriotism. Recruits began to rush to join the services and one of them was William O. Butler (later a major general during the Mexican war). Butler joins soon after the surrender as a private in Captain Hart's company. He was the second son of Percival Butler, one of the five Butler brothers who served admirably during the American Revolution. The outbreak of the war sidelined his law studies, but it added one more of the Kentuckians to the American force. Shortly thereafter he was raised to corporal and then to ensign, attached to the U.S. 17th Infantry. William Butler later displays great courage at the Raisin River (January 1814), where he is captured. While held captive, he survived the depredations and after exchange joined with General Jackson at the Battle of New Orleans.

Also, at about this same time, Robert Patterson of Pennsylvania is appointed as lieutenant. On 19 April 1814, he is promoted to the rank of captain. Patterson later becomes a general during the Mexican war and serves for a short while during the Civil War. His son, Francis Engle Patterson, born during 1821, also serves in the Civil War with the rank of brigadier general.

In naval activity, the HMS *Emulous* seizes the ship *Union*. The *Union* is separate from the brigantine *Union* seized on 14 August 1812, the schooner *Union* seized on 14 October 1812, the schooner *Union* captured on 19 October 1812, the schooner *Union* seized on 3 April 1813, the ship *Union* taken over on 26 June 1813 and the schooner *Union* captured 30 July 1814.

In other naval activity, the HMS *Statira* intercepts the brigantine *William* and recaptures it. This *William* is separate from other captured vessels of the same name: a bark, 8 July 1812; a schooner, 12 March 1813; a brigantine, 31 May 1813; a sloop, 7 August 1813; a schooner, 27 October 1813; a schooner, 19 June 1814; a brigantine, on 11 October 1814; and a schooner, sometime in 1814.

Also, the American privateer *Alfred* (Captain Williams), mounting 16 guns, departs from Salem carrying 16 guns and a complement of 130 men. It intercepts the 12-gun brigantine *Diamond*, which is transporting a cargo of cotton, logwood and slightly more that two thousand dollars in gold, making it the first prize. Afterward, it captures the brigantine *George* as its second prize and the second vessel out of Brazil. The combined value of both prizes is listed as $120,000. The *Alfred* continues cruising until 1814, and its other prizes include the brigantine *Tercilla* and another vessel, the *Curfew*.

August 17 (Monday) *In naval activity,* Captain David D. Porter writes this day to the Navy Department: "Sir, I have the honor to inform you that upon the 13th, his B.M. sloop of war *Alert*, Captain T.L.P. Laugharne, ran down on our weather quarter, gave three cheers and commenced an action (if so trifling a skirmish deserves the name) and after eight minutes firing, struck her colors with 7 feet water in her hold, much cut to pieces, and 3 men wounded.... The *Essex* has not received the slightest injury. The *Alert* was out for the purpose of taking the *Hornet*."

In other activity, the HMS *Africa* intercepts and seizes the *Eastern Star* (Samuel Medcalf, master), a 217-ton ship en route from Corunna, Spain, to New York with a cargo of ballast and more than $21,000 in cash. Also, the ship *Nancy* is recaptured by the HMS *Statira*. The *Nancy* is separate from the schooner *Nancy* seized on 28 May 1813, the schooner *Nancy* seized on 28 June 1813, the sloop *Nancy* captured on 28 July 1814, the brigantine *Nancy* seized about 1–18 September 1814, and the brigantine *Nancy* captured on 13 September 1814.

Also, the American privateer *Saucy Jack* out of Charleston intercepts and seizes the 10-gun vessel *Three Brothers*, and it also captures the 10-gun *Laura*. The American prize crew aboard the *Laura* is intercepted by the HMS *Peruvian*, which initiates pursuit. The Americans refuse to halt and after it becomes apparent that the *Laura* will be caught, the crew sets it on fire and abandons it. After getting into a boat, the crew manages to escape capture and eventually makes it back to the United States. The *Peruvian*, which fails to seize its prey, later is lost when it gets wrecked on the Silver Keys (West Indies).

August 17–18 *In naval activity,* on the 17th, the American privateer *Decatur* under Captain Nichols encounters the HMS *Guerriere*. The *Decatur* is able to outdistance the *Guerriere* and avoid capture, but on the following day, it is chased by another warship. During its escape on the 17th, to gain speed, nearly all of its guns are thrown overboard. On the 18th, the privateer is spotted and pursued by another warship. After about two hours, the chase ends when it is unable to outrun its pursuer, but luckily no harm comes.

The USS *Constitution*, on the prowl for the *Guerriere*, spots the privateer and believes it to be an enemy vessel. After halting the *Decatur*, it becomes clear that it is American. The *Decatur* resumes its cruise and the *Constitution* continues its search for the *Guerriere*, which is discovered on the following day (19th). The Decatur, having only two of its original 14 guns, had decided to continue its cruise toward Cape Race and seize prizes off the cape by boarding them. The *Decatur* is separate from the privateer *Decatur* out of Charleston under Captain Dominique Diron and the privateer *Decatur* out of Maine under Captain S.N. Lane.

August 18 (Tuesday) **In Pennsylvania,** the secretary of the commonwealth, Lt. Colonel Nathan Brittan Boileau, writes to General William Reed regarding brigadier generals in the Commonwealth:

> If I am to designate the Brigadier Generals that are to serve under the Major Generals [Isaac] Worrall and [Adamson] Tannehill, the rule that obtains generally must prevail in this case. I, therefore, designate the oldest brigadiers in each of the two divisions mentioned in general orders of May last. It appeared on

examining our military book, when you were here, that William Duncan was the oldest Brigadier in the First division, and William Harris, of the Third division; Samuel Smith, of the Second division, and Jacob Hilghman of the Fourth division. Those, therefore, I suppose, are to be the Generals. You will report them accordingly, and perhaps it would be proper for you to give them notice.

Colonel Boileau, concerned about the critical situation in the militia that lacks a sufficient amount of blankets, uses his personal finances to aid the cause. He actually mortgages his property in Hatboro to acquire blankets for the troops. Nevertheless, the commonwealth never reimburses him.

In naval activity, the HMS *Statira* intercepts and recaptures the brigantine *Russell*. Also, at about eight weeks since the outbreak of the war, the British have seized one American warship, the *Nautilus*, and they have captured 53 other vessels, including 14 brigantines, 10 schooners, 15 ships, one sloop and 13 privateers. During this same period, including only those American privateers sailing out of Gloucester, Marblehead and Salem, 37 British prizes have been seized.

August 19 (Wednesday) ***In naval activity,*** the 56-gun USS *Constitution*, which sailed from Boston on 2 August, while cruising off Nova Scotia, spots a ship in the distance at about 1400. Captain Isaac Hull issues the order to pursue, and in about one and one-half hours, the distance closes sufficiently to discover that the target is a British frigate. The British, with their usual confidence, adjust their sails to permit the *Constitution* to come into range, while they prepare to engage and dispose of the pursuer. The British, in general, have neither fear nor respect for the young navy of the United States. The *Guerriere* is flying an extra flag, intended to imply its superiority. The words on the flag: "Not the Little Belt." The *Little Belt* had been in a contest with the USS *President* during July 1811.

Earlier, the *Constitution* was described in an English journal as "a bunch of pine boards, under a bit of striped bunting." The *London Courier* had proclaimed the invincibility of the 44-gun *Guerriere* (some reports list 48 guns), the target of the *Constitution*, stating: "There is not a frigate in the American navy able to cope with the *Guerriere*." At this time, neither commander is aware of the identity of his foe; however, British Captain James Richard Dacres is convinced that his opponent is either an American or a French warship. Captain Dacres hands American Captain William Orne, his prisoner, his spyglass and requests his opinion. Orne replies that the ship which is closing fast is an American frigate, which prompts Dacres to state that he thought it came down too boldly for an American, but soon after added: "The better he behaves, the more honor we shall gain by taking him."

The crewmen on the *Guerriere* prepare for action. To increase the confidence of his men, Captain Dacres has a flag planted on each masthead. Meanwhile, Dacres remains intent to wait for the closing frigate to commence firing before the British guns go into action. At about 1700, while

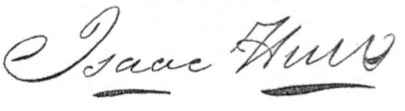

Captain Isaac Hull.

British Captain James Richard Dacres.

the *Constitution* remains several miles out, Captain Dacres, while speaking to American captain Orne, states: "Captain Orne, as I suppose you do not wish to fight against your own countrymen, you are at liberty to go below the waterline." At that time, Captain Orne leaves the quarter deck and repairs to the cock-pit, unaware of any first-hand knowledge of the battle until after the guns fall silent.

The *Constitution* closes to a distance of about fifty yards before it commences fire. The broadside plows into the *Guerriere* and inflicts devastating damage, including the loss of its mizzen mast. Meanwhile, the British had delivered successive broadsides, but the *Constitution* absorbs the fire without sustaining any damage that prevents the crew from returning fire. Nevertheless, it does not immediately return fire. The British apparently believe the silence is weakness. Their guns continue to catapult broadside after broadside without receiving return fire. Meanwhile, the gunners on the *Constitution* are anxious to get the order to return fire. During this crucial period, one officer informs Captain Hull twice that two men had been killed at their positions while waiting to return fire, but Hull continues to wait for the right moment. It comes shortly after 1700. Suddenly, the guns roar and broadside after broadside is propelled toward the *Guerriere*.

The *Constitution*, carrying a crew of 476 men, including U.S. Marines, while maneuvering to gain a position from where the British could be pummeled with a raking fire, misses the mark and British gunners score a huge hit that ignites a fire in the cabin. Nevertheless, panic is avoided by the actions of Lieutenant B.V. Hoffman. Maintaining a calm demeanor, Hoffman gets the fire extinguished before it spreads. At about the same time, American fire takes out the gun that inflicted the damage. All the while, U.S. Marines who are posted high in the ship's rigging continue to take out British crewmen with their effective musket fire. Within about fifteen minutes, the *Guerriere*, commanded by Captain Dacres, becomes unmanageable after its mizzen mast is severed and the decks riveted with destructive fire. Still, as the two ships become nearly joined and each crew attempts to board the opponent's ship, the Marines maintain incessant fire to pick off potential intruders. During the attempt to board the *Guerriere*, Lt. Bush, a Marine, sustains a mortal wound.

After determining that boarding the *Guerriere* is not possible, Hull orders the *Constitution* to bolt forward. During this maneuver, the *Guerriere*, already badly damaged, is struck by more devastation when its foremast is severed. As it plunges toward the deck, it crashes into the main mast and severs it. Suddenly, British Captain James R. Dacres is the commander of a crippled frigate. The incessant fighting succinctly terminates because the *Guerriere* is totally uncontrollable. The *Guerriere*, the pride of the Royal Navy, lies paralyzed, while the crew of the *Constitution* is able to repair its damages without coming under fire. The scene aboard the *Guerriere* is described by American Captain Orne:

> At about six o'clock, when I heard a tremendous explosion from the opposing frigate, the effect of her shot seemed to make the Guerriere reel, and tremble as though she had received the shock of an earthquake. Immediately after this, I heard a tremendous crash on deck, and was told the mizzen-mast was shot away. In a few moments afterward, the cock-pit was filled with wounded men. At about half-past six o'clock in the evening, after the firing had ceased, I went on deck, and there beheld, a scene which it would be difficult to describe: all the Guerriere's masts were shot away, and as she had no sails to steady her, she lay rolling like a log in the trough of the sea. Many of the men were employed in throwing the dead overboard. The decks were covered with blood, and had the appearance of a butcher's slaughterhouse; the gun tackles were not made fast, and several of the guns got loose, and were surging to and fro from one side to the other. Some of the petty

USS *Constitution* and the HMS *Guerriere* (*Battles of America by Sea and Land, Volume II*, Robert Tomes, 1878).

officers and seamen, after the action, got liquor, and were intoxicated; and what with the groans of the wounded, the noise and confusion of the enraged survivors on board of the ill-fated ship, rendered the whole scene a perfect hell.

Nevertheless, the English colors are still hoisted. Captain Hull, at about 1900, moves back into a position from which he intends to resume firing. However, before the guns return to action, Captain Dacres orders the English colors, which are affixed to the remaining part of the severed mizzenmast, to be lowered. Captain Hull later remarks: "In thirty minutes after we got fairly alongside of the enemy, she surrendered, and had not a spar standing, and her hull, above and below water, so shattered, that a few more broadsides must have carried her down."

Captain Isaac Hull sends a boarding party aboard the *Guerriere* but awaits daylight before taking any further action. The *Guerriere*, however, is not out of danger. Rough seas increase the level of jeopardy, as the ship's hull is taking on water. By the following morning, the *Guerriere*'s hull contains about four feet of water and the ship is close to plummeting to the bottom. Captain Hull orders all of his prisoners to be transferred to the *Constitution*. After all of the British crewmen are aboard, the U.S. prize crew departs from the imperiled *Guerriere* and reboards the *Constitution*. When the operation is complete, the *Guerriere* is set afire. Within fifteen minutes, the flames spread to the ship's magazine and in a flash, the explosion blows the *Guerriere* into oblivion, while those aboard the *Constitution* watch its demise.

British Captain Dacres offers his sword to Captain Hull, who declines. However, Hull quickly states: "But I'll trouble you, Sir, for that hat!" Captain Dacres had earlier boasted that he "could beat any American warship in fifteen minutes of fighting."

The U.S. sustains seven men killed and seven wounded. The deceased are Lt. William S. Bush, a Marine, and six seamen: James Ashford, Robert Brice, John Brown, James Read, Jacob Sago and Caleb Smith. The British aboard the *Guerriere*, with a crew of about 300, according to a report by Captain Dacres, sustains 15 killed and 63 wounded, including Dacres, who was struck in his back. In addition, 24 men are reported missing.

Following the victory, the *Constitution* sails back to Boston and the crew is received with jubilance. Captain Hull and his crew become the guests of Boston at a banquet in their honor. Praise is also showered upon the victors by Congress, which presents Captain Isaac Hull with a gold medal. His officers receive silver medals and in addition, Congress awards $50,000 in prize money to each member of the crew.

Back in England, when word arrives regarding the defeat of the *Guerriere*, it is received in disbelief. The British initially find it incomprehensible that the *Guerriere* could have been defeated. For Captain Dacres, the son of Vice Admiral James Richard Dacres, there are no parades in his honor; rather he receives a court-martial. The military trial is held on 2 October of this year aboard the HMS *Africa* at Halifax. Vice Admiral Herbert Sawyer presides. At the conclusion of the trial, Captain Dacres is acquitted.

In the meantime, the superlative action of the crew aboard the *Constitution* injects a boost in the morale of the Americans, while in England, the British begin to wonder about their belief that the Yankee navy is inferior.

In his official after-action report, Captain Isaac Hull states: "It gives me great pleasure to say that, from the smallest boy in the ship to the oldest seaman, not a look of fear was seen. They all went into action giving three cheers, and requesting to be laid close alongside the enemy."

The *London Times* reports: "It is not merely that an English frigate has been taken, after what we are free to confess may be called a brave resistance, but that it has been taken by a new enemy, an enemy unaccustomed to such triumphs, and likely to be rendered insolent and confident by them. He must be a weak politician who does not see how important the first triumph is, in giving a tone and character to the war. Never before in the history of the world did an English frigate strike to an American and though we cannot say that Captain Dacres, under all circumstances, is punishable for this act, yet we do say there are commanders in the English navy who would a thousand times have rather gone down with their colors flying than have set their brother officers so fatal an example."

The *Guerriere*, thought to be unconquerable, had been destroyed by the *Constitution*, the "bunch of pine boards." It becomes the undefeated pride of the U.S. Navy, and although it no longer engages any adversaries, the USS *Constitution* becomes better known by the nickname this battle earned it in the U.S., *Old Ironsides*. It is still afloat and on active duty in Boston harbor and still carries a crew, which out of respect for *Old Ironsides* and pride in its service wears uniforms from the War of 1812 era.

In other naval activity, the HMS *Belvidera* seizes the ship *Bainbridge* (R. Gray, master) en route from Liverpool to Philadelphia, Pennsylvania. Also, the HMS *Emulous* recaptures the ship *Osbourne*.

In yet other naval activity, the American privateer *Highflyer* spots a British squadron at about 0600. Cautiously, the privateer begins to shadow the British from a safe distance. By the following day (20th), a British frigate begins to pursue the *Highflyer* at about 1330. Later, by about 1700, the *Highflyer* loses the frigate and resumes a course to catch the squadron. Within about one hour, contact is reinitiated, and by the following day (21st), the *Highflyer* intercepts and boards the vessel *Diana*, a ship attached to the Jamaica fleet. The *Diana*, commanded by Captain Harvey, is transporting a cargo of coffee, rum, sugar, and other items intended for consignees in Bristol, England. Nevertheless, the captain assigns a prize crew and orders it to be sent into a United States port. On the 22nd, the *Highflyer* engages two vessels simultaneously; however, Captain Gavet's instincts prompt him to decide not to board either. He disengages at about 1600.

The next day at about 1600, the *Highflyer* attacks the 7-gun vessel *Jamaica* (Captain Neil), which is sailing close to another vessel in the fleet, the 12-gun *Mary and Ann* out of London under Captain Miller. The *Highflyer* launches its strike once it arrives within musket range. The British immediately return fire, igniting a tenacious exchange that continues unabated for about 20 minutes. Nonetheless, a boarding party bolts from the *Highflyer*, overwhelms the crew and seizer the vessel. The Americans discover that the

Mary and Ann does not have to be beaten. The crew lowers the colors at about the same time as the *Jamaica* falls. Captain Gavet and one crewman are wounded. Prize crews are assigned to both vessels and they are ordered to be taken into an American port. Several British crewmen are wounded during the operation, but no fatalities are sustained.

August 20 (Thursday) *In naval activity,* the American privateer *Shadow,* commanded by Captain Taylor, having survived an engagement with a British letter of marque vessel, arrives in Philadelphia. The *Shadow,* however, had sustained two killed and 12 wounded along with heavy damages that caused it to limp into port.

In other naval activity, the American privateer *Rossie* encounters the brigantine *John Adams* (separate from the USS *John Adams*) which had recently been seized by the HMS *Guerriere,* and after having removed its valuables, the British permit the *John Adams* to resume its voyage.

August 21 (Friday) **In Florida,** near St. Augustine, Colonel Thomas A. Smith of the U.S. Army issues orders to Colonel Daniel (Niel) Newman, U.S. Marine Corps, to launch an attack against the hostile Indians in East Florida. At this time, about one-half of his force (250 men including Georgia volunteers and a contingent of U.S. Marines) have become ill. The sickness, which has also struck Newman, delays the push-off.

While making final preparations to launch an attack against the hostile Indians, Newman receives an urgent message from Smith explaining that his (Smith's) wagons and the escort had been attacked and that he has only 70 troops which are "fit for duty." Smith orders Newman to move immediately with 90 troops and every available horse and carriage to assist Smith's command by removing the baggage and artillery, as well as the sick troops. Colonel Newman assembles a contingent, composed of 130 men and 25 horses. Newman speeds to the aid of Colonel Smith and supports him in a move to a blockhouse at David's Creek. Nonetheless, Newman's scheduled attack jump-off is again postponed for several days. However, the string of delays has also caused other complications. The term of enlistment for Newman's force is nearing expiration, which is endangering the expedition of Newman against the Lotchaway (Seminole) and Alligator Indians. Colonel Smith, aware that Newman's force has only six or seven days remaining, sends another message to Newman, who had returned to his camp with a request to speak with his command in an effort to persuade the men to extend their service for an additional fifteen to twenty days to prevent the expedition from being aborted.

Colonel Newman, after receiving the request, calls his contingent together and asks that they extend their service by three weeks. The men respond. Eighty-four troops, including officers, step forward to re-enlist and Newman also receives 23 volunteers from Smith's command, along with nine Patriots under Captain Cone. The expedition resumes on 24 September.

In naval activity, the HMS *Belvedera* intercepts and seizes the privateer *Bunker Hill* (Jacob Lewis, master), a 175-ton schooner that operates out of New York. At the time of its capture, the *Bunker Hill* is carrying a cargo that includes ammunition and guns, along with provisions.

August 22 (Saturday) **In Canada,** General Isaac Brock arrives at Fort Erie (Toronto) from Detroit. The captives seized at Detroit have accompanied his force. Brock, having seized Detroit and essentially the entire Michigan Territory upon the surrender of General William Hull, is anxious to add to his successes. He intends to invade New York and seize the U.S. fort at Niagara and also Buffalo; however, to his dismay, he is informed that an armistice had been agreed upon about one week before he arrived. During the pause in hostilities, the Americans continue to funnel troops into the region.

By about mid–September, the American commander, General Stephen Van Rensselaer, has about 8,000 regular and militia troops deployed between Fort Niagara and Buffalo. In addition, Van Rensselaer acquires about 400 bateaux that contain supplies and arms, which had arrived from various locations including Sackets Harbor.

In Ohio, General Elijah Wadsworth at Canfield receives the distressing news of the surrender of Detroit. He reacts instantaneously and without any authorization by calling up his entire militia force with instructions to converge on Cleveland. His call to arms becomes overwhelming when it is answered by men of all ages and from all walks of life, including many who are exempt from military service. General Wadsworth is compelled to send about half of the troops home with directions that they would form a secondary force to guard the homeland if needed.

General Wadsworth writes to the secretary of war to inform the secretary of his action: "I immediately ordered out all the militia under my command, consisting of the first brigade, commanded by Brigadier-general Reasin Beall; the second brigade, commanded by Brigadier-general Miller; the third brigade, commanded by Brigadier general [Simon] Perkins, to repair immediately to Cleveland." Some early works list General J. Miller as having commanded the 1st Brigade (Jefferson County) and General R. Beall (initial Columbiana County) as commander of the 2nd Brigade; however, there is general agreement that General S. Perkins commanded the 3rd Brigade (Trombu and Ashtabula). In addition, the 4th Brigade (Portage, Geauga, Cuyahoga) was commanded by Brigadier General Joel Paine. Also, General Miller of the Ohio militia is separate from Colonel James Miller, U.S. Army, of New Hampshire.

During this same period, a report circulates that a British force, including Indians, was spotted off Avon Point in Cleveland. The alarm causes women and children residing near the Cuyahoga to abandon their homes and seek safety in the interior.

In naval activity, the HMS *Emulous* intercepts and seizes the ship *Monsoon.*

August 23 (Sunday) *In naval activity,* the HMS *Statira* seizes the brigantine *Adeline.* The HMS *Plumper* intercepts the 258-ton brigantine *Hector* (P. Newford, master) while it is en route to Quebec from Dublin and recaptures it. The *Hector* is taken into port at New Brunswick. The *Hector* is separate from the 156-ton brigantine *Hector* seized on 30 April 1813.

In other naval activity, the HMS *Colibri* intercepts and seizes the 253-ton ship *Monk,* which is en route from Rio de Janeiro to Salem, Massachusetts, with a cargo of hides, horns and sugar. Also, the American privateer *Dolphin,* following a 20-day cruise, returns to Salem. During its cruise, it captures six prizes without sustaining any casualties.

August 24 (Monday) **In New York,** during an ongoing armistice agreed upon by General Dearborn and British General Sir George Prevost, a small detachment of Americans cross over to Buckhorn Island. The troops return with six prisoners, including one sergeant. On the following morning, Van Rensselaer releases the captives and they return to Canada by a boat that the Americans confiscated while on the raid.

In naval activity, the HMS *Nymphe* intercepts and captures the 300-ton ship *Honestus* (J. Stevens, master), which is transporting a cargo of salt from St. Ubes to New Bedford.

August 25 (Tuesday) **In Kentucky,** William Henry Harrison, upon an invitation from Governor Charles Scott, is in Frankfort. He reviews the troops and is honored with a grand reception arranged by prominent citizens, including Henry Clay. On this day, Governor Scott commissions Harrison as brevet major general of the Kentucky militia, making him the commander-in-chief of Kentucky's militia. However, neither Harrison, nor the governor is aware that President Madison had commissioned General Harrison as a brigadier general in the United States Army several days earlier on 22 August.

Harrison had married Anna Symmes, the daughter of Judge Symmes, during 1795, however, on the day of their wedding, Judge Symmes missed the ceremony; he departed for Cincinnati before the ceremony began and did not meet his son-in-law until about two weeks later.

In Pennsylvania, general orders are given: "The President of the United states having, through the Secretary at War, and General Dearborn, under date, respectively, of the 18th inst., required a detachment of 2,000 militia to be marched, with the least possible delay, from the northwestern parts of Pennsylvania to Buffalo, in the State of New York."

In naval activity, the HMS *Emulous* intercepts and seizes the ship *Henrietta.* The HMS *Emulous* also intercepts and seizes the schooner *Science,* a privateer that is carrying ammunition, guns and some provisions.

August 26 (Wednesday) Colonel John Parker Boyd is promoted to the rank of brigadier general.

In naval activity, the American privateer *Highflyer,* having seized the 4-gun schooner *Harriot* while it is en route to Havana from New Providence in the Bahamas, diverts and sends the schooner into Baltimore. At the time of capture, the vessel is transporting specie.

August 27 (Thursday) **In Ohio,** General Henry Harrison writes from Cincinnati to Governor Meigs that he is traveling with three regiments, two infantry and one mounted infantry and that the regiments had been ordered to Urbana. Harrison also informs he governor that he is awaiting the arrival of three more infantry regiments, one mounted regiment and a dragoon regiment, which will increase his force to more than 4,000 troops. At this time, Harrison is unsure whether General Hull had surrendered Detroit. He intends to intercept the Kentucky contingent at Urbana; however, after he hooks up with the Kentuckians, he is intercepted on 2 September by a dispatch rider who arrives to deliver his commission in the U.S. Army.

In naval activity, the HMS *Colibri* seizes the ship *Jane* (N. Thomas, master). The *Jane* is separate from the sloop *Jane*, seized on 6 December 1813, the schooner *Jane* captured on 10 December 1813, the sloop Jane seized on 2 August 1814, the brigantine *Jane* captured on 9 November 1814 and the sloop *Jane* seized on 12 November 1814.

August 28 (Friday) *In naval activity,* the 202-ton ship *Doris* (S. Chamberlain, master) is intercepted and seized by the HMS *Nymphe* while it is en route from Londonderry to Philadelphia with a cargo of ballast. The *General Smyth,* a British privateer, seizes the 114-ton schooner *Fortune* (J. Crocker, master) and takes it, along with its cargo of rum and lumber, into New Brunswick. The *Fortune* is separate from the 317-ton ship *Fortune*, seized on 25 June 1812, and the schooner *Fortune* seized on 31 August 1813.

In other activity, the HMS *Nymphe* seizes the ship *Georgiana* (E. Chamberlain, master) while it is en route from Liverpool to Norfolk. Also, the HMS *Colibri* intercepts and seizes the ship *Merchant* (T. Noyes, master) which is en route from Liverpool to New York. The *Merchant* is separate from the ship Merchant seized on the following day. Also, the HMS *Alpha* intercepts and seizes the 309-ton ship *Zodiac* (J. Hague, master) while it is en route to Lisbon, Portugal, from Norfolk, Virginia. The privateer *Orlando,* identified as both a ship and a schooner, arrives back at port in Gloucester, Massachusetts, after successfully seizing four vessels, two brigantines, one schooner and one sloop.

Master Commandant Christopher Gadsden, Jr. (son of Revolutionary War general Christopher Gadsden), the commander of the USS *Vixen,* dies. Lt. George Washington Reed, the son of General Joseph Reed, assumes command of the ship. Also, the American privateer *Rossie* (Commodore Joshua Barney) intercepts and captures another American outlaw ship, the *Euphrates* out of New Bedford, Massachusetts. A prize crew is assigned and it is taken back to an American port.

August 29 (Saturday) *In naval activity,* the 270-ton ship *Merchant* (C. Hopkins, master), while en route from Gottenburg to Portsmouth, Maine, with a cargo of iron, is intercepted and seized by the HMS *Statira.* This *Merchant* is separate from the ship *Merchant* seized on the previous day.

August 30 (Sunday) **In Florida,** Lt. Colonel Thomas A. Smith writes to Colonel Newman that he has nearly 100 troops in his command on the sick list, which is preventing sending reinforcements to bolster Newman's force for the expedition against the Indian strong points. Smith also states that he is disabled from illness, but if he recovers within a few days, he will travel to confer with Newman. Smith, however, does tell Newman that a 40-man contingent of the Georgia Patriots under Captain Peter Cone will be joining with him.

In Georgia, Brigadier General George Mathews dies in Augusta, where he was born on this same date in 1739. General Mathews was on active duty during the invasion of the Patriot Army into Spanish East Florida in March 1812. He served as an officer during the French and Indian War. During the Revolutionary War era, he participated in the pre-war Battle of Point Pleasant in 1774 and later as colonel of the 9th Virginia Regiment. He was captured during the conflict and exchanged in December 1781. Afterward he was appointed colonel of the 3rd Virginia Regiment in the army under General Nathaniel Greene. After the war, General Mathews became a farmer in Oglethorpe County in Georgia; however, his life as a farmer was interrupted when he was elected governor of Georgia during 1787 and again from 1793 to 1796. General Mathews afterward was elected to the First U.S. Congress and served from 4 March 1789 until 4 March 1791. He was appointed brigadier general during 1811.

In other activity, a contingent under Lt. George Rockingham Gilmer (later governor of Georgia, 1829–1831 and 1837–1839) establishes Fort Peachtree to defend Atlanta at about this time; however, it could have been as late as 1814. Other forts constructed for the same purpose include Fort Daniel. Fort Peachtree is located at the terminus of the Creeks' Peachtree trail and on the line which separates the Creeks from the Cherokee.

In naval activity, the British capture the 66-ton sloop *Sophia* while it is en route to New Bedford. The prize is taken into port at New Brunswick. Also, the American privateer *Rossie* (Captain Joshua Barney) arrives at Newport, Rhode Island. After a stay of about ten days, Commodore Barney departs again in search of British prizes. During his last cruise, Barney's *Rossie* had seized 15 vessels while cruising off the U.S. coastline for 45 days. Of the 15 prizes, nine were destroyed at sea, and the combined value of the prizes amounted to just under $130,000. During his pause in Newport, Commodore Barney was joined at dinner by Captain Coggeshall, who was in Newport and staying in the same hotel.

August 31 (Monday) **In Florida,** Colonel Daniel Newman, U.S. Marine Corps, at New Switzerland Plantation in western St. Johns County, responds to recent letters from Lt. Colonel Thomas A. Smith. He informs Smith that his force is also suffering from illness, leaving him short of 37 able-bodied troops, and he has also become ill with fever. Colonel Newman ells of their shortage of rations and of his disdain for the contractor, stating: "Had it not been for our own endeavors, we would have been left without anything to eat — in fact, ever since we left the block house the Contractor has been useless to us."

Newman also informs Smith that he did not go to Picolata after learning that all the cattle in the area had been driven away by Captain Cone's contingent. Newman remains concerned because many of the men will be heading home in about four weeks due to the expiration of their enlistments. Meanwhile, Newman still intends to strike the Indians; however, he needs pack horses, and large numbers of troops remain sick, but yet another problem is that no cavalry reinforcements are going to arrive.

In New York, Captain Isaac Chauncey, commander of the New York Navy Yard, is appointed as commander of the Great Lakes. His orders direct him to establish a fleet. Chauncey is a veteran of the Barbary Coast Wars, and he has also commanded commercial vessels of John Jacob Astor that operated between the United States and the East Indies. Soon after his appointment, Chauncey dispatches a shipbuilder, Henry Eckford, and a party of carpenters to Lake Ontario. Chauncey also directs Commander Woolsey to acquire merchant ships that are to be transformed into warships at Sackets Harbor.

In naval activity, the *Ceres* (S. Webber, master), while en route from Liverpool to Boston, is intercepted and captured by the HMS *Spy,* a store ship.

September **In Idaho,** MacKenzie's Post is established about five miles outside of present-day Lewiston as a trading post. Built by Donald Mackenzie, it is affiliated with the Pacific Fur Company (John's Astor's company). It is near the Clearwater River at its convergence with the Snake River and remains active only until the following year.

In Kentucky, Governor Isaac Shelby dispatches Major General Samuel Hopkins and a large force of mounted Kentucky Volunteers to attack the Kickapoo and Peoria Indian camps in Indiana. The American troops return in October, without success. During his first expedition, he is plagued by mutiny and the mission fails. Hopkins is compelled to return when his troops, all volunteers, become disgruntled due to a lack of supplies and too many hardships. They decide to abort the mission. On a later mission, Hopkins gains some minor success when a village is destroyed, but the Indians afterward inflict high casualties and the contingent retires in disarray.

Shelby, earlier this year, succeeded General Charles Scott as governor of Kentucky.

In Iowa, Fort Madison comes under attack by Indians incited by the British in Canada. The attack is repelled, but an outside building known as the "factory" is destroyed by fire by the army. One trooper is killed when he is out of the fort.

In Europe, the French Legions penetrate deeper into Russia facing little opposition. Nevertheless, the supplies continue to diminish, as the Russian landscape in their path is barren from the Russian torch. Still the Russians evade massive direct confrontation. The French maintain the forced march, finally engaging and defeating a Russian force at Borodino, about seventy miles west of Moscow. Soon after, the French triumphantly enter Moscow, but there is no prize, as the city had been gutted and its inhabitants gone. Napoleon's troops control the charred ruins of the Russian city, but Moscow lacks even buildings to house the troops, assuring a stay of short duration; by October 19, Napoleon is compelled to retire.

Meanwhile, on 12 September, the czar proposes that he mediate the crisis between the U.S. and Britain. It is a curious situation. Russia needs Britain's help to subdue Napoleon; however, it is Napoleon who prevents Britain from striking with its full fury against the United States. President James Madison is informed of the Russian proposal during March 1813.

Also, Britain, because of its war with France, has only 11 ships of the line, 34 frigates, and about 34 smaller vessels in the Western Atlantic to oppose the United States.

In naval activity, the American privateer *Saucy Jack*, out of Charleston, arrives at St. Mary's after having seized two prizes, the *Three Sisters* and the 10-gun *Eliza*. At this time other privateers are preparing to go to sea, including the 20-gun *Captain Bulkely*, which had also served as a privateer during the American Revolution. It is being refitted at New London, Connecticut. Another is the 22-gun *Volunteer*, which is being prepared at New York. Others include the privateer *Chinese* carrying 18 guns, the *Isaac Hull*, a schooner carrying 17 guns, and the 6-gun schooner *Swallow*. Meanwhile, the British continue to capture some of the privateers, including the *James Madison* by the HMS *Jason*, a frigate. Despite the ongoing seizure of privateers by the British, American privateers continue to increase in numbers, and to the dismay of the British, these newer privateers are primarily bigger, faster and more powerful, making the task of seizing them much more difficult.

September 2 (Wednesday) **In Ohio,** at about this time, a dispatch rider out of Washington, D.C., intercepts General Harrison outside of Dayton. The rider delivers General Harrison's commission as brigadier general in the U.S. Army and gives the general fresh orders out of the capital. Harrison's thoughts of heading for Detroit are cancelled. His orders direct him to take command of the troops in Illinois and Indiana. On the following day, upon arriving at Piqua, he is informed that Fort Wayne is under siege, and he also learns of the British force en route from Malden, Canada, to seize control of the Maumee and Wabash valleys.

Harrison confers with Colonel John Johnston, the Indian agent at Piqua, and afterward a part

Colonel John Johnston, Indian agent.

of Shawnee scouts remove to the site of Fort Defiance (Fort Winchester) to gather intelligence on whether any British had passed the fort, while moving on the Maumee en route to Fort Wayne. In addition, General Harrison dispatches Captain John Logan, a half-breed, to Fort Wayne to see how critical the situation is there. Meanwhile, Harrison is to cooperate with General Hull (orders cut before Hull's surrender) and Brigadier General Benjamin Howard, governor of the Missouri Territory.

Meanwhile, General James Winchester has been appointed commander of the Northwestern Army. Nonetheless, Harrison is convinced that he must move out, even without orders due to the situation at Fort Wayne. General Harrison sends a contingent (Lt. Colonel John Allen's regiment, one company of Colonel Scot's regiment and two companies of regulars) as a vanguard toward Fort Wayne.

In naval activity, the American prize *Planter* is chased by an unidentified frigate and another American ship; the privateer *Atlas* observes the pursuit. The *Planter* had apparently been chased by an American vessel. It later arrives in an American port. The *Planter* is separate from the 48-ton sloop *Planter* seized on 2 September 1814. Also, the HMS *Aeolus* and the HMS *Maidstone*, operating together, intercept and capture the 145-ton schooner *Stockholm* (L. Chaplin, master), which is transporting a cargo of coffee, rum and sugar from St. Bartholomews to Boston.

September 3 (Thursday) **In Indiana,** near Fort Harrison, two young settlers who are gathering hay are attacked, scalped and killed by Indians. Although four shots are heard, Major Zachary Taylor chooses not to send out a patrol until the following morning because he had been warned by intelligence that Indians in force were preparing to strike the fort. On the same day, a small band of Indians pounces upon a settlement at Pigeon's Roost (Scott County). Many of the settlers are massacred. The Indians destroy most of the houses; however, at the home of William Collings, the raiders encounter resistance which buys time for survivors to race toward the protection of nearby blockhouses. Nevertheless, more than twenty people, most of whom are women and children, are killed. The dreadful news spreads rapidly and by the afternoon of the following day, a large number of volunteers arrive at the ghastly scene. Mutilated bodies are scattered about and all but one home had been burned down. The contingent of men initiates pursuit, but in vain. The Indians also take two children, Ginsey McCoy and Peter Huffman. Ginsey is known to have later married a chief and Peter also takes on the life of the Indians. During 1904, a monument is erected at the location of the massacre.

September 4 (Friday) **In Indiana** at Terre Haute, Captain Zachary Taylor sends out a patrol to search for two young settlers that were thought to have been killed on the previous night. Both men are discovered about 400 yards from Fort Harrison. Taylor, once informed, sends out a party to retrieve their remains and later notes in his report: "I sent the cart and oxen, and had them brought in and buried they had been each shot with two balls, scalped and cut in the most shocking manner...."

Later that night, a band of Indians, estimated at 30 to 40 in number (including about ten women) approach Fort Harrison. The group appears friendly and they are carrying a white flag; however, the commander, Captain Zachary Taylor is not fooled by the ruse. The Indians' request to enter the fort is denied. Taylor had been forewarned about his post coming under attack. Nevertheless, the garrison, which is small, has been drastically reduced due to sickness, and Taylor himself had just recovered from fever. He has only about fifteen men fit for duty. However, he instructs the guards to keep on constant alert, and he directs one non-commissioned officer to walk around the perimeter of the post for the entire night to ensure the Indians are not able to seize an advantage. By about 2300, Taylor is awakened by small arms fire of the sentinels. At

Colonel (later, 12th president of the U.S.) Zachary Taylor.

about the same time, a sergeant tells him that the lower blockhouse had been set afire.

As the situation becomes more ominous, the garrison begins to commence fire, while some take quick action to try to douse the fire. Taylor's diminutive force is facing about 300 Pottawatomies and Winnebagoes. Nonetheless, Taylor remains calm and focused on the immediate task of preserving the post. To eliminate the threat of the quick-spreading fire, Taylor orders the troops to dismantle part of the barracks' roof which is closest to the fire and simultaneously, he directs the men to pour water upon the barracks to ensure it remains soaked. During the operation, sick and wounded personnel hold positions in the two bastions.

Meanwhile, the troops, initially overwhelmed by confusion, finally get the doors of the blockhouse open, but by then the fire spread to a supply of whiskey that ignites and sends the flames up to the roof. All the while, the available troops are maintaining a steady fire upon the Indians to provide an umbrella of protection over the men working the roof. Despite the size of the garrison, Taylor's troops prevent the fire from spreading. They also build a breastwork to control the gap that opened when the blockhouse was destroyed, and they succeed in thwarting the Indians' plan to funnel through the gap to annihilate the garrison. The attack continues for about eight hours before the Indians abort the attempt to reduce the fort.

Captain Taylor afterward receives praise for his actions and is promoted to the rank of major. Taylor rises to the rank of general and later becomes the 12th president of the United States.

During the battle, two of the troops are killed and two others are wounded. Indian casualties are unavailable. Also, Captain Taylor, in his official after-battle report, states:

> One man lost his life by being too anxious; he got into one of the galleys in the bastions, and fired over the pickets, and called out to his comrades that he had killed an Indian, and, neglecting to stoop down, in an instant he was shot dead. One of the two men that jumped the pickets returned an hour before day, and, running up toward the gate, begged for God's sake for it to be opened. I suspected it to be a stratagem of the Indians to get in, as I did not recollect the voice; I directed the men in the bastion, where I happened to be, to shoot him, let him be who he would; and one of them fired at him, but fortunately he ran up to the other bastion, where they knew his voice, and Dr. Clark directed him to lie down close to the pickets, behind an empty barrel that happened to be there, and at daylight I had him let in. His arm was broke in a most shocking manner, which he says was done by the Indians — which I suppose was the cause of his returning. The other they caught about one hundred and thirty yards from the garrison, and cut him all to pieces.

The siege ends by the 5th when the Indians pull back beyond the range of the garrison. Captain Zachary reports to General Harrison:

> A party of them [Indians] drove up the horses that belonged to the citizens here, and as they could not catch them very readily, shot the whole of them, in our sight, as well as a number of their hogs; they drove off the whole of the cattle, which amounted to 65 head, with the public oxen.... We lost the whole of our provisions, but must make out to live upon green corn until we can get a supply, which I hope will not be long. I believe the whole of the Miamies or Waes were with the prophet's party, as one chief gave his orders in that language, which resembled Stone-eater's voice, and I believe Negro-legs was there likewise; a Frenchman here understands their different languages, and several of the Waes that have been frequently here, were recognized by the soldiers next morning; the Indians suffered smartly, but were so numerous as to take off all that were shot; they continued with us until the next morning, but made no further attempt on the fort, nor have we seen any thing more of them since.

In New York, at Lewiston, General Stephen Van Rensselaer receives supplies and ordnance when Lt. Colonel John R. Fenwick arrives at Van Rensselaer's camp at Lewiston. The American force under Van Rensselaer, prior to the arrival of Fenwick, stood at 691 able-bodied troops.

In naval activity, the HMS *Junon* intercepts and recaptures the ship *Britannia*. Also, the American privateer *Providence* (Captain Hopkins), on its initial cruise, is seized by the British vessel HMS *Dominica*.

September 5 (Saturday) **In Kentucky,** Governor Shelby writes to Secretary of War William Eustis to request a board of war for the western region of the country, and he includes an urgent recommendation that General Winchester, who recently was appointed commander of the Northwestern Army as successor to General Harrison, be replaced by the latter. The governor provides details on why Harrison should resume his position as commander-in-chief, and he listed some "evils" that would occur if the command change does not occur.

The letter is not placed on a back burner. The secretary responds to Governor Shelby in a letter dated 17 September that General Harrison would at once be given chief command. Shortly thereafter, on 24 September, a dispatch arrives at Piqua and is delivered to Harrison. He is officially informed that President Madison "is pleased to assign to you the command of the Northwestern Army which in addition to the regular troops and rangers in that quarter, will consist of the volunteers and militia of Kentucky, Ohio, and three thousand from Virginia and Pennsylvania, making your whole force ten thousand men." General Harrison has full authority to conduct Shelby's proposal to convene a board of war.

In Missouri, Fort Madison (sometimes referred to as Fort Mat- son), in the vicinity of Sublette, comes under attack by a force of about 200 Winnebago Indians. The garrison, composed of about 40 troops of the U.S. 1st Infantry Regiment, is commanded by Captain Horatio Stark and Lieutenant Thomas Hamilton. When the Indians strike, they seize one man from the garrison who is outside the gates. Soon after, within sight of the garrison, the captive is scalped. Nevertheless, the troops meet the attack with return fire. On the 7th, the garrison remains in control of the fort and the two days of exchanging fire has brought no progress for the Indians. In a show of contempt, the Indians place the decapitated head of their former captive on a pole to display for the garrison, and in another grotesque action, they place his severed heart on another pole. The despicable actions do not intimidate the troops; however, shortly thereafter when flaming arrows set some roofs on fire, that does cause some panic. Nevertheless, Lt. Hamilton remains confident. He improvises by using "eight old gun-barrels." The gun barrels are pushed through small holes that are cut into the roof, and water is forced onto the roof to soak it to prevent the fires from spreading. The experiment works. Undaunted, the Indians seize a stable near the fort and from there, the fort again comes under fire. Hamilton redirects the fort's artillery and after a short time, the shells rain upon the Indians' positions. They hurriedly abandon the stable and abort the attack.

In naval activity, the 162-ton brigantine *Howe* (J. Askew, master) en route from Penzance, England, to Pictou, Nova Scotia, is intercepted and recaptured by the HMS *Plumper*. The *Howe* is taken into port at New Brunswick.

September 6 (Sunday) In Ohio, General Harrison and his main body depart from Piqua at dawn en route to Fort Wayne (Indiana), which is under siege by Indians. The column is leaving two days after the vanguard under Lt. Colonel John Allen had departed; however, they rejoin on the 8th at St. Mary's (Girty's Town), where James Girty operates a trading post. A runner sent out earlier by Harrison instructed Allen to halt to there, and he also orders a post to be constructed there (Fort Barbee) with palisades to protect the provisions and soldiers who become ill or wounded during the relief expedition. The post is actually erected by Colonel Joshua Barbee's regiment.

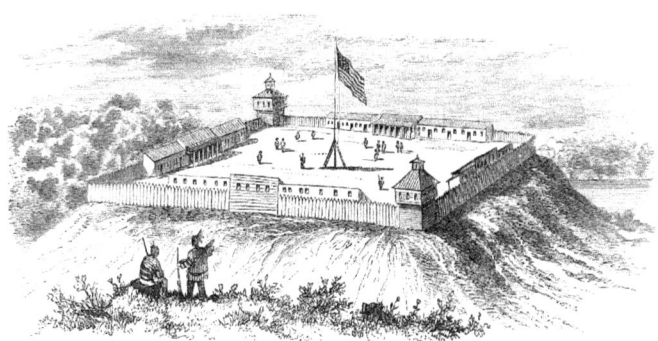

Fort Wayne during 1812.

While there, a contingent of mounted Kentuckians under Major Richard M. Johnson arrives to bolster Harrison's force. Harrison establishes his camp and it is kept under surveillance during the night (6th-7th) by Indians; however, they take no aggressive action. While at his camp, Captain Logan returns from his reconnaissance mission at Fort Wayne and reports to Harrison informing him that the situation is critical. Meanwhile, the Indians maintaining surveillance on the camp return to their positions outside the fort and report that the Kentuckians are "becoming as numerous as the trees."

In other activity, by this day, General Perkins arrives at the Huron River with his brigade, composed of about 400 men. The region is overwhelmed by "a poisonous malaria [that] filled the valleys of the rivers." The epidemic strikes Perkins' command heavily. At some point between this day and 15 September, a patrol, led by Major Austin and Lt. Colonel John Allen, while returning to camp from Kelley's Island, discover the scalped body of one of the soldiers, Michael Guy, attached to Colonel Rayen's regiment; however, no enemy Indians are encountered.

In naval activity, the HMS *Emulous* intercepts and captures a ship, the *Charles Fawcett*. This vessel is separate from the 95-ton sloop *Charles* captured on 4 October 1813, the 75-ton sloop *Charles* seized on 10 December 1813, the schooner *Charles* captured 26 June 1814, and the brigantine *Charles* overtaken on 5 November 1814. In other activity, the British privateer *Shannon*, operating off the East Coast, intercepts and seizes a ship, the 460-ton *Fabius*, which is en route from Amelia Island to Portsmouth, Maine.

September 7 (Monday) **In New York,** Commodore Chauncey, at the navy yard, orders Lt. Jesse Elliott to report to Lake Erie:

> SIR,— You will immediately proceed with all possible expedition to the head-quarters of General Van Rensselaer, which is, I believe, at or near Buffalo, at the bottom of Lake Erie. You will consult General Van Rensselaer as to the best position to build, repair, and fit for service, such vessels or boats as may be required to retain the command of Lake Erie, bearing in mind to select such a place as can be defended from the attacks of the enemy, as well as to keep them from a knowledge of our operations. After you have selected a proper place, you will, with the advice of General Van Rensselaer, purchase any merchant vessels or boats that can be converted into vessels of war or gun boats, and commence their equipment immediately. You will also cause to be sawed by the mills in the neighborhood, a sufficient quantity of plank for the decks and bottoms of two vessels of three hundred tons each, consulting with the master carpenter as to quantity and thickness. You will also procure and get ready a sufficient quantity of boards to build six boats of 40 feet long, and 10 feet wide. You will have quarters prepared for three hundred men, and a temporary magazine built for our powder. Thirty carpenters will leave here on Thursday next for Buffalo; you will lose no time in setting them upon the work of preparation, as every day is of importance to US, the season being far advanced. You will ascertain as near as practicable, the force of the enemy on Lake Erie, also their general rendezvous; and also you will inform yourself upon the following points, to wit; the number and kind of vessels and boats that can be procured upon Lake Erie, that will answer our purpose.... I should advise you to travel in plain clothes: and by no means communicate the object of your visit to any person except General Van Rensselaer.

In naval activity, the British privateer *Liverpool Packet* seizes the 291-ton ship *Factor*; however, earlier, on 20 August, another British warship, the HMS *Hero*, had seized about $130,000 and a supply of wine from the vessel. The *Factor* is taken into port at Liverpool and its cargo is afterward returned to its owners, who are Portuguese.

In other naval activity, the HMS *Acasta* intercepts and seizes the 140-ton schooner *Patriot* (W. Reardon, master) which is transporting a cargo of beans and flour from Norfolk, Virginia, to Lisbon, Portugal. The *Patriot* is separate from the sloop *Patriot* seized on 19 December 1813. The privateer *America*, commanded by Captain Joseph Ropes, sails from Salem, Massachusetts, as one of 40 privateers sent out by Salem. It departs the harbor at 1130 and by about 1200, it reaches Baker's Island. Also, the American privateer *Rossie* (Commodore Joshua Barney) encounters an American vessel which had sailed from Providence, Rhode Island, and encountered trouble. A revenue cutter out of Newport arrives to provide assistance and the *Rossie* resumes its cruise.

September 8 (Tuesday) *In naval activity,* the HMS *Plumper* seizes a brigantine, the *Argo* (W. Middleton, master), a recapture, and takes the vessel into port at New Brunswick. The British privateer *Liverpool Packet* intercepts and seizes the ships *Middlesex* and the ship *Minerva* (M. Pollard, master). Both are taken into port at Liverpool. This *Minerva* is separate from likewise named vessels: a brigantine seized 6 July 1812, a brigantine captured 30 June 1813, a sloop seized 5 August 1813, a schooner captured 30 August 1813, a brigantine seized 21 April 1814, a schooner overtaken on 11 August 1814, and a schooner captured on 26 September 1814.

Also, the 10-gun American privateer *Diligent*, commanded by Captain Grassin, intercepts a British vessel, the 12-gun *Laura*, which is close to seizing its fourth prize. Once the *Diligent* is detected, the British commander, Lt. Charles Newton Hunter, recalls his party which had boarded the merchant ship to enable him to take on the *Diligent*. Just before 1600, both ships are within pistol range of each other. The British fire first, but not without a response. American fire is immediately returned. Both ships continue to maneuver for position, which decreases the effectiveness of each other's fire. After a while, American small arms fire slims down the British crew, and at 1655, the Americans board the *Laura*.

During the engagement, the English sustain 15 killed or wounded. The Americans sustain 9 killed and 10 wounded. The prize and its crew, including Lt. Hunter, are taken into port at Philadelphia, where Hunter is taken to a hospital for medical aid. The *Laura* is transformed into a 12-gun privateer and renamed the *Hebe*.

September 9 (Wednesday) **In Ohio,** General Harrison's army advances to Shane's Crossing and establishes camp there near the banks of the St. Mary River in the vicinity of present-day Rockford. A strong contingent of Ohio cavalry under Colonel George Adams arrives to further bolster the force. From here, the column begins to move more cautiously by traveling through the woods during the daytime with scouts out to prevent the Indians from establishing an ambush. At night, the camp is heavily guarded to prevent a surprise attack. The army is guided by Captain Logan and another Shawnee. When the column approaches a narrow crossing of the St. Mary River slightly southeast of Fort Wayne, unknown to the Indians who are waiting in ambush, the Americans had advance intelligence of the location. Harrison sends out cavalry in two columns. Major Johnson's detachment swings out to the right, while the other column under Major Adams circles to the left to demolish the obstacle; however, after one of the Indians is spotted, the Indians choose to bolt from their concealed positions and retire. Harrison's relief force arrives at the fort on the 12th; however, by then the siege had ended.

In other activity, General Winchester arrives at Cincinnati en route to Fort Wayne. While in the city, he writes to Governor Meigs requesting reinforcements to support his forces on his mission.

In New York, General Tompkins becomes irritated with General Dodge. He writes to Dodge in a letter dated this day: "DEAR SIR: I was astonished to find on my return from New York as late as the 8 inst, that a party of your Brigade had been at Schenectady from the 25 of Augt. to that day. The news from the frontiers renders it necessary that the utmost expedition should take place in the movements of the troops. That part of the Brigade which proceeds by land must be hurried on as fast as possible, and the whole must be expedited by every Exertion in your power."

In naval activity, the American privateer *Rossie*, while continuing its cruise, suddenly spots several

Lt. Jesse Duncan Elliott, U.S. Navy.

British warships that are eager to trap and seize it. Nonetheless, the *Rossie*, becoming accustomed to outrunning one pursuer, is tasked with displaying its sailing skills by attempting to lose all three. The British pursuit is in vain; the *Rossie* easily outsails the trio.

September 10 (Thursday) **In Ohio,** a contingent of Indians, allied with the British, attack two settler families in Mifflin (Ashland County). Frederick Zimmer and his family along with a neighbor, Martin Ruffner, are killed.

In naval activity, the American privateer *Rossie* (Commodore Joshua Barney), after losing three pursuers of the Royal Navy, spots another sail. It is not a British warship; it is American, the *Joseph.* During the brief encounter, the crew of the ship *Joseph* is informed that the war with Britain had begun.

September 11 (Friday) **In Florida,** a contingent of 20 Marines and Georgia militiamen under Captain John Williams and Captain Fort, respectively, are escorting supply wagons from the Patriots Army camp at St. Augustine to the blockhouse at Davis Creek, a distance of about 22 miles. The armed escort (Captain Williams, Captain Fort, four officers and 19 privates) is caught off guard at Twelve Mile Swamp and a heavy skirmish develops when Indians and Negroes under a free black man, Prince, spring their attack during the darkness of night. The convoy is moving without lanterns to avoid being spotted and the drivers are familiar with the routes; however, the incessant fire kills some of the horses, which leads to the path being blocked. Captain Williams becomes wounded at the first burst of fire but refuses to relinquish command. The enemy outnumbers the Americans by about four to one. Nonetheless, neither the Marines nor the militia flee the murderous fire. The attackers move in close with their tomahawks, and the Marines initiate a charge that expeditiously drives the enemy back and opens an opportunity for the Americans to extricate themselves. However, in the meantime, the indomitable Captain Williams has been hit seven more times, forcing him to turn command over to Captain Fort of the Milledgeville militia.

Captain Williams, after the ambush, remains with the wounded and a small guard while he dispatches the remainder of the force to Davis Creek to get reinforcements. On the following day, a contingent arrives. They discover Captain Williams in critical condition but still alive. His "right leg broken, his right hand shot through with three balls, his left arm broken, his left leg shot through, a ball in his left thigh near the groin, and another through the bottom of his belly." In a letter to his commandant, Captain Williams wrote: "You may expect that I am in a dreadful situation, though I yet hope I shall recover in a few months."

The Marines are part of the American force dispatched to East Florida in an attempt to annex the Spanish Territory to prevent Britain from using it as a stepping stone for an invasion. The ambush ends with one Marine being stripped and scalped and six others wounded. This was the first Marine killed in action since the Marines captured Tripoli in the early 1800s. This action soon prompts the end of America's attempt to annex East Florida with armed troops. The Marines learn from the experience and they become more adapted to the tactics of the Indians.

Captain John Williams, the commanding officer, having been mortally wounded, dies on 29 September. Captain Williams becomes the first Marine Corps officer killed in action since the American Revolution.

Marines will hook up with Army troops during February of 1813 to destroy two Indian villages. Captain Williams is initially interred at Christ Church; later his remains are re-interred at Arlington National Cemetery. Also, there is some confusion with the date of the ambush. The Marine Corps Historical Division lists it as 11 September and other sources give the date as 12 September.

In naval activity, the HMS *Belvidera,* operating off the East Coast, intercepts the 98-ton schooner *Friendship,* which is en route from Charleston to New York with a cargo of cotton. This *Friendship* is separate from like-named vessels also captured: a schooner, 19 July 1812; a schooner, 5 March 1813; a sloop, 6 July 1813; a sloop, 11 July 1813; a schooner, 13 July 1813; and a schooner, 28 July 1813.

In other naval activity, the privateer *America* encounters heavy seas and devastating winds. The ship's main topmast is severed the five men on the mast are thrown into the sea. Desperate attempts are undertaken. Other crew members board boats to fight the sea and attempt to rescue the endangered men. The rescue operation succeeds without any additional casualties.

In other naval activity, the American privateer *Rossie* (Commodore Joshua Barney) encounters a sail, and once the ship is caught, it is discovered that it is a prize seized by the American privateer *Saratoga,* which is en route to an American port.

September 12 (Saturday) **In Indiana,** General William Henry Harrison's force arrives at Fort Wayne, which has been under siege. Upon the appearance of Harrison's column, the Indians lift the siege and depart from the area. The siege had been initiated about two weeks before Harrison's arrival; however, the garrison commander, Captain Rhea, was not fooled by the Indians' ruse when they arrived as friendly. Rhea's command, composed of only about 70 men, had sufficient arms and provisions to defend the post. Nonetheless, Harrison's arrival was cause for some jubilation. After the siege, the troops retaliate by moving into the Indian villages. The villages are destroyed and the troops wipe out their corn crops. Fort Wayne is located where the Indians had inflicted a decisive defeat upon General Josiah Harmar during September 1790.

In New York, General Joseph Bloomfield arrives at Plattsburgh with his brigade. His brigade soon comes under the direct command of General Dearborn. Afterward, upon Bloomfield being transferred to Philadelphia, General Wade Hampton assumes command at Lake Champlain. By summer of 1813, Hampton, with headquarters at Burlington, Vermont, has about 4,000 troops under his command.

In naval activity, the brigantine *Ambition* (Benjamin Shaw, master), while en route from Baltimore to Boston, is spotted by two British blockade ships and intercepted. The HMS *Orpheus* and the *Maidstone* seize it and the cargo of flour. Also, the HMS *Belvidera* seizes the 195-ton schooner *Hiram* (John Hays, master) while it is en route from Palermo, Italy, to Philadelphia with a cargo including medicine, oil and soap. The *Hiram* is separate from the schooner *Hiram* seized on 18 July 1812.

In other naval activity, the American privateer *Rossie* yet again comes into the sights of a British warship which initiates pursuit. The British frigate chases relentlessly, intent on capturing the elusive privateer. Nonetheless, the *Rossie* leads the frigate on a fruitless chase for about six hours before it outdistances its pursuer and once again evades the clutches of the Royal Navy.

September 13 (Sunday) **In Indiana** at Fort Wayne, a contingent under Colonel Payne departs from the fort and moves down Little River to the Wabash River. The troops discover no Indians; however, they come upon several villages which are destroyed, along with the corn crops. On the 13th, a contingent of infantry and cavalry commanded by Colonel Samuel Wells moves out from the fort and arrives at the Elk Heart River about 60 miles distant. Again there is no resistance, but the troops destroy the village and crops of Chief Onoxse (Five Medals) of the Pottawotamis tribe. The return march takes a toll on the men in the infantry and some collapse from exhaustion. Nevertheless, the cavalry, moving with the main body, is able to give aid and help get those afflicted back to the fort.

September 14 (Monday) **In New York** at Albany, Governor Tompkins informs General Mooers of a change in command by letter, dated this day:

> Dear Sir: The number of Militia of the State of New York in Service at Plattsburgh not amounting to a Major Genl's. Command and Brigadier Genl. Bloomfield having arrived with a Brigade of Regular troops, I am apprehensive your continuance in service at that Post will not be acceptable to the Commanding officer of the Regular Army, or may be misconstrued into a disposition on my part to retain in the hands of a Major Genl. of Militia the Command of the Frontiers notwithstanding the principal officer may be regulars; and the whole be short of a Major General's Command. You will, therefore, consider your Command at that place suspended from the time of your arrival at Plattsburgh and according to directions of Genl. Dearborn, Brigadier Genl. Bloomfield of the Army, will take the Command of the troops in the service of the United States at that Post in its vicinity.

September 15 (Tuesday) **In Washington, D.C.,** Captain Daniel Dobbins, a skilled navigator, is on or about this day appointed sailing master and directed to begin constructing gunboats at Erie (Presque Isle). Dobbins had suggested Erie as the place for such a facility due to

Captain Daniel Dobbins.

its harbor, too shallow for large ships to navigate but perfectly suited for gunboats.

In Ohio, a band of Indians attacks the Copus family. Reverend Copus and three militia troops are killed while defending the home. This raid follows an attack on the 5th in which other settlers are killed. The three militia troops who lose their lives are George Shipley, John Tedrick and Robert Warnock. By tradition, it is thought that Johnny Appleseed had sped through the area to warn settlers of the danger. During the 1880s, when a monument is erected to the families and the troops at Mifflin (Ashland County), Johnny Appleseed's name is included.

September 16 (Wednesday) **In Canada,** the HMS *Royal George* arrives at Fort George to debark an artillery contingent of about 100 men. As reported by General Van Rensselaer, about 100 boats have passed up the St. Lawrence en route to deliver supplies to the British troops in Upper Canada. In addition, two British regiments are en route to bolster the region. Van Rensselaer believes the artillery contingent that arrived at the fort is also going to advance to further bolster their force.

In New York, a contingent of about 100 sailors, including officers, departs the navy yard en route to Sackets Harbor to participate as part of Commodore Chauncey's fleet on the lakes. Chauncey departs later and arrives at Sackets Harbor during early October.

In Florida at Davis Creek, Lt. Colonel Thomas A. Smith writes to Georgia Governor Mitchell of the serious situation due to sickness, which is close to paralyzing his efforts. He explains that about 125 of his troops are too ill to take to the field, which will permit him to have about 120 men fit for any movement. He also informs the governor of the death of Captain Samuel Neeley of the Georgia Volunteers on the 20th and of the great spirit if his men, despite having neither clothes or shoes. Colonel Smith essentially pleads for the governor to devise a way to get the necessary supplies to the men, because the federal government will not supply the items to volunteers. Colonel Smith also states that the journey from his camp outside St. Augustine to the creek culminated without incident; however, he mentions that the Indians launched an unsuccessful raid against Picolata, but some success occurred when they burned the trading posts there. The governor is also says that a strike against St. Mary's was being planned.

In naval activity, the 124-ton schooner *Sally Ann* (J. Day, master) is intercepted and seized while en route to St. Bartholomews from London. The *Sally* is separate from the brigantine *Sally* seized on 10 August 1812, the ship *Sally* seized 16 April 1813, the brigantine *Sally* captured on 24 April 1813, the schooner *Sally* seized 13 May 1813, the schooner *Sally* seized on 12 July 1813, the schooner *Sally* overtaken 15 September 1813, the schooner *Sally* captured on 16 October 1813, and the sloop *Sally* seized on 19 May 1814.

In other naval activity, the American privateer *Rossie*, commanded by Joshua Barney, encounters the packet HMS *Princess Amelia*, commanded by Captain Moorsom. The engagement erupts during darkness and the vessels are at close quarters, which permits the Americans with the aid of the moonlight to battle it out using short guns. The fighting continues for about one hour with no clear victory when suddenly, despite their initial advantage, including sharpshooters, the *Princess Amelia* signals surrender. By that time, the commanding officer and two others had been killed and about 7 or 10 wounded. The Americans sustain one fatality when 1st Officer Long receives a mortal wound and six others are wounded. Barney completes the successful cruise and arrives back in Baltimore on 10 November 1812.

In other naval activity, *Rossie* encounters four ships, one an armed brigantine. An exchange of fire erupts; the *Rossie* sustains some damage and one man is wounded. Nevertheless, the convoy continues and the *Rossie* shadows it for four days without results.

September 17 (Thursday) **In Washington, D.C.,** President Madison appoints William Henry Harrison to the position of brigadier general to command the Northwest Army. Harrison is given responsibility to expel the British Army from Detroit, which has surrendered to British General Isaac Brock during August 1812 without a fight.

In New York, General Stephen Van Rensselaer, in a letter, informs General Henry Dearborn that the British are improving their strength in Canada across from Fort Niagara. He also informs Dearborn that "his little army" is becoming "critical," while explaining the British defenses are improving with each day and reinforcements are pouring into their positions. Reinforcements are also en route from Fort Malden to Fort Erie. Also, Van Rensselaer informs Dearborn that he expects an attack at any time, but he will defend Niagara:

> I have reason to believe we shall be very severely pressed, but so serious will be the consequences of any retrograde movement, or a total abandonment of Fort Niagara, that, upon mature consideration of all circumstances, I have determined to hold, if possible, my present position, and dispute every inch of ground. My force bears no proportion to the duties required; besides, the discipline of the troops is not such as to warrant perfect reliance, and many of our arms are not fit for action.... I hope I shall be able to justify myself to my country. My greatest fear is, that the troops destined to reinforce me, will not join me in season.

Colonel Henry Bloom's regiment had arrived to bolster Van Rensselaer; however, it is composed of only about 400 troops rather than the 700 that were expected. Also, the cavalry with Van Rensselaer is poorly equipped and the supply of grain for the horses is extremely low.

Also, General Jacob Brown states in a letter to Governor Tompkins, dated this day:

> I must say to your Excellency that, unless more vigor and energy is infused into the national council, it is not in human nature that

The privateer *Rossie* battles the *Princess Amelia* (*History of American Privateers [and letters of marque]*, George Coggeshall, 1856).

this war can be brought to a conclusion worthy of the American people. Excuse me, sir. Of vessels we have on this lake ten, besides the *Oneida*, and vessels they are of the first class for their burthen; six of them are here, viz: the *Genesee Packet, Experiment, Collector, Lord Nelson, Niagara* and the *Julia*. At Oswego, *Charles and Ann, Diana, Fair American*, and *Ontario*. These vessels are from 70 to 100 tons burthen and, if armed with long 32 pounders, and manned with such men as this nation could furnish, would at once command the lake and the St. Lawrence to the rapids; and may I ask your Excellency, in the name of all that is holy, why this has not been done? ... Let this be done, and we will soon see these waters ours, and then Upper Canada will not be of so difficult acquirement.

In naval activity, the *Federal*, a 115-ton brigantine commanded by Samuel Swan, en route from Africa with a cargo of coffee, old copper, ivory and other items, fails to reach Boston. It is seized by the British before arriving at its destination.

September 17–18 In New York at Albany, at a convention of delegates of several counties, a few resolutions are passed which indicate alignment with the New England states that oppose the war. The resolutions include:

Resolved, That we shall be constrained to consider the determination on the part of our rulers to continue the present war, after official notice of the revocation of the British Orders in Council — as affording conclusive evidence that the war has been undertaken from motives entirely distinct from those which have been hitherto avowed, and for the promotion of objects wholly unconnected with the interest and honour of the American nation.

Also:

Resolved, That we contemplate with abhorrence, even the possibility of an alliance with the present Emperor of France [Napoleon], every action of whose life has demonstrated that the attainment, by any means, of universal empire, and the consequent extinction of every vestige of freedom, are the sole objects of his incessant, unbounded, and remorseless ambition. His arms, with the spirit of free men, we might openly and fearlessly encounter, but of his secret arts, his corrupting influence, we entertain a dread we can neither conquer nor conceal. It is therefore with the utmost distrust and alarm that we regard his late professions of attachment and love to the American people, fully recollecting that his invariable course has been by perfidious offers of protection, by deceitful professions of friendship, to lull his intended victims into the fatal sleep of confidence and security, during which the chains of despotism are silently wound round and rivetted on them.

September 18 (Friday) In Indiana at Fort Wayne, Colonel James Simrall, who trailed Harrison's army to Fort Wayne with his command of 320 dragoons and one company of mounted infantry, arrived at the post on the previous night. On this day, during the evening, General Harrison dispatches the contingent on a mission to destroy Little Turtle's town, northwest of the post at the Eel River. The troops reduce the town; however, they leave one house standing, that which was earlier built by the U.S. government "in recognition of his adherence to the Treaty of Greenville."

September 19 (Saturday) In Indiana, General James Winchester arrives at Fort Wayne and assumes command of the army. Winchester, a native of Maryland, is a veteran of the American Revolution. After the revolution, General Winchester relocated in Tennessee. His appointment had occurred before Governor Shelby proposed that General Harrison, recently succeeded, be returned to the position (*see also,* **September 5,** 1812).

In naval activity, the HMS *Aeolus* intercepts and seizes the 200-ton brigantine *Phebe*, which is carrying a cargo of brandy, juniper berries and some paving stones for delivery in Boston.

September 20 (Sunday) In New York, a contingent of about 95 to 100 men (regulars and militia), led by Captain Benjamin Forsyth, embark from Cape Vincent during the night on a mission to capture ammunition. On the following morning, the troops land in the vicinity of Gananoqui, Canada, about twenty miles below Kingston. Militia officers who participate in the mission include Captain McNitt, Lt. Brown, Ensign Hawkins and Ensign Johnson. Gananoqui is a small village that contains one public building and a sawmill, along with a residence, described as a hut, belonging to Captain Stone of the militia.

The Americans encounter a British force of about 110 men, including Canadian militia, and a skirmish erupts. Forsyth orders a charge; however, his force does not open fire until the troops are about 100 yards from the enemy position. The Americans prevail against an equally sized contingent of militia, and after the British retire, the Americans count ten killed. In addition, they seize some wounded and some other troops. Before returning to New York, Forsyth's troops move to their initial objective, a military storehouse, and destroy it. The captured Canadian militia are paroled; however, the British regulars, along with captured ammunition and arms, are taken back to the United States. Forsyth's command loses one man killed. Some Canadian sources claim only one Canadian killed and that no English regulars participated in the skirmish. The supplies maintained in the village had been noted as two kegs of "fixed ammunition and about 30 muskets."

Also, an English author, William James (*Military Occurrences of the Late War*, 1816) claims that one of the troops fired into a window and wounded Captain Stone's wife. He states that the militia force numbered only about 30 to 40 men and that when they arrived, fewer than ten of them were carrying arms.

General Jacob Brown, in a letter to Governor Tompkins regarding the raid, states: "Twelve prisoners were taken, 3000 ball carttridges and 41 muskets. There were in the King's store about 150 barrels of provisions, and as there were no boats to bring it away, it was consumed by fire, together with the store. Private property was held sacred."

In naval activity, the HMS *Epervier* intercepts and captures an American ship, the *Active* (E. Altberg, master), which is transporting a cargo of iron from Gottenburg to Boston. In other activity, the ship *Diana* (A. Wilson, master) is intercepted and recaptured by the HMS *San Domingo* while it is en route to Jamaica from Glasgow. The *Diana* is separate from a sloop of the same name seized 19 July 1814.

September 21 (Monday) In Canada, an American contingent raids Gananoque to destroy a sawmill at about midnight. During the attack, a woman, Mrs. Stone, while in her bed at home, is wounded.

In New York, Brigadier General Richard Dodge, accompanied by a contingent of militia from the Mohawk country, arrives at Watertown. He directs General Jacob Brown to repair to Ogdensburg with his militia force and assume command of the post at Fort Presentation. At this time, the roads are extremely poor and nearly impassable. Brown travels by water and arrives at Ogdensburg on 1 October. Some of Captain Forsyth's regulars accompany Brown, while the rest stay with General Dodge.

In Ohio, General William Henry Harrison orders Colonel William Jennings to direct his regiment to begin cutting a road from Fort Barbee, located at St. Mary's, the midpoint between it and Defiance. Once the section of road is completed, Jennings' orders include instructions for him to construct a fort. The post the regiment erects is completed the following October and named in honor of Colonel Jenkins. Subsequently, the road is extended to Fort Winchester (formerly Fort Defiance) in Defiance by troops under Colonel John Poague.

Colonel Poague, during 1813, constructs Fort Amanda along the west bank of the Au Glaize (Auglaize) River near Wapakoneta. The road becomes a primary supply route for Harrison's army. Other posts established in Ohio include Fort Ball (Tiffin), Fort Huntington (Cleveland), Fort Meigs (Perrysburg) and Fort Seneca in the vicinity of Old Fort. Fort Meigs, another post, becomes the anchor post for Forts Amanda, Brown, Jennings, and Winchester.

In naval activity, the vessel *Abigail* (G. Johnson, master) is intercepted and seized by the HMS *Poictiers*.

September 22 (Tuesday) In Indiana, at Fort Wayne, General Winchester writes to Governor Meigs of Ohio to request reinforcements for his campaign against British-held Detroit: "I rejoice at the prospect of regaining lost territory and with hope to winter in Detroit or its vicinity. You will please furnish two regiments of soldiers to join me at the foot of the lowest Maumee Rapids about the 10th or 15th of October well clothed for a fall campaign.... It is extremely desirous to me that no time be lost in supplying this requisition. The cold season is fast approaching, and the stain on the American character by the surrender of Detroit not yet wiped away."

September 23 (Wednesday) *In naval activity,* the privateer *America* intercepts and seizes a brigantine, the *James and Charlotte.* The prize is taken into Salem.

September 24 (Thursday) **In Florida,** Colonel Daniel Newman, U.S. Marine Corps, departs from his camp along the St. Johns River to strike the hostile Lotchawy, Seminole and Alligator Indians in Spanish East Florida. However, due to the expiration of the force's terms of enlistment, his manpower is reduced from 250 troops to only 117. Newman later states in his report: "I was determined to proceed to the nation and give those merciless savages, at least, one battle; and I was emboldened in this determination, by the strong expectation of being succored by a body of cavalry, from St. Mary's [Florida]; and which, it has since appeared, did assemble at Colerain, but proceeded no further." The column advances from Colerain on this day, the 24th. Captain Humphrey's company of riflemen is at the front of the column, but it trails a small vanguard, followed by Lt. Fanuir's company and Captain Coleman's company. The rear of the column is held by a contingent under Lt. Broadnax and similarly to the front of the column, a small guard trails it. On the fourth day out, the 27th, contact is made with the enemy.

In Ohio, at Piqua, a dispatch rider arrives and delivers General Harrison's appointment as successor to General Winchester as commander-in-chief of the Northwestern Army. On the 30th, Harrison receives a message from Governor Meigs that informs him of a British force that is closing on Winchester's army. At the time, about 3,000 troops, including cavalry (companies of Captain Bacon, Captain Clark and Captain Roper) and the volunteers under Major Richard M. Johnson, are at Fort Barbee. Johnson is appointed colonel and commander of these combined units.

The Ohio cavalry troops under Colonel James Findlay are also at the post. The cavalry units are formed into a brigade under the overall command of Brigadier General Edward Tupper. General Harrison dispatches the entire force toward Defiance. Meanwhile, word arrives that the British under Major Muir had retreated. General Harrison, relieved that the British had not launched an attack, orders Colonel Joshua Barbee to return to Fort Barbee. In addition, he orders Colonel Poague to cut a road to Defiance. Poague's orders also direct him to build a new fort near the Ottawa town, near the Auglaise River slightly more than ten miles north of Fort Barbee. The fort is constructed and named Fort Amanda in honor of Colonel Poague's wife. The fort, on the left bank of the Auglaize River in Auglaize County (previously Allen County), was built either on or close to the fort at the head of the Auglaize built by General Wayne during the 1790s. The next year, the post becomes an important depot for passing troops to get some rest and for storing supplies. During the latter part of March 1813, Colonel Miller arrives at Fort Loramie from Chillicothe with about 150 men to begin building boats to transport supplies along the river.

September 25 (Friday) **In Ohio,** a detachment of spies, out in advance of General Winchester's main body, is operating on a reconnaissance mission. The detachment is led by Captain Bland Ballard and Lt. Harrison Mundy of the 17th U.S. Regiment. Ensign Leggett requests permission to lead a four-man detachment to the ruins of Fort Defiance. Permission is granted. Nonetheless, the mission concludes prematurely. That evening, while the men (attached to the Woodford Kentucky company) are preparing their meal, a band of eight Indians, along with one Frenchman, creep up and strike by surprise. Leggett and the other four men are killed. Their bodies are discovered on the following day when Captain Ballard's company arrives. Indians that remain nearby try to draw the Americans into an ambush, but it fails. The troops safely return to their regiment.

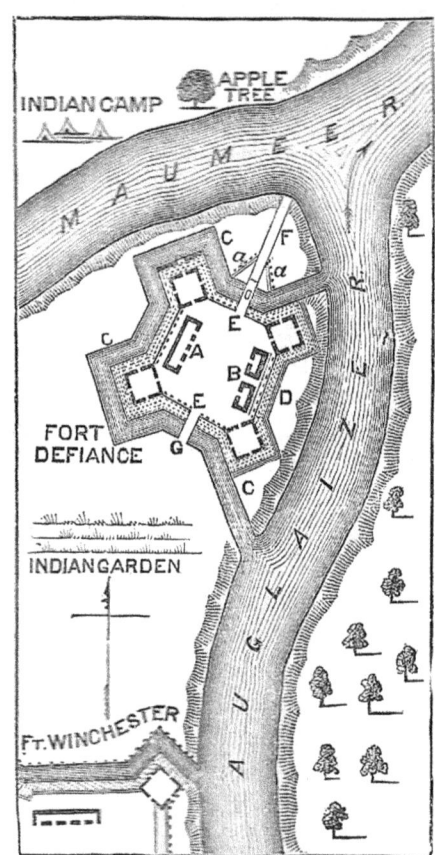

Fort Defiance (Fort Winchester).

September 26 (Saturday) **In New York** at Fort Niagara, General Stephen Van Rensselaer receives word from headquarters at Greenbush that the reinforcements he expects might not arrive in time to ensure that the post can be held if a strong attack is launched. Nonetheless, in the same correspondence, Van Rensselaer is informed that he is expected to meet the enemy, and "to carry the war into Canada before the winter sets in." In the meantime, reinforcements do arrive and as they build, morale also rises. Suddenly, the thoughts of scoring a victory over the British in Canada replace the melancholy that has overtaken the Americans since Detroit was surrendered without a fight. General Van Rensselaer makes the decision to initiate his offensive.

In Ohio, two advance scouts, attached to Captain Ballard's company, ford the Maumee River to the south bank and afterward they move to the Auglaise River, cross it, then make their way to a point slightly below Defiance, where they re-cross the Maumee to the north bank. The mission fails to discover any enemy presence.

September 27 (Sunday) **In Florida,** an American contingent composed of volunteers and a detachment of Marines under Colonel Niel Newman are en route to attack the towns of the Lotchway (Seminole) and Alligator Indians. At about 1200, the force fords the St. Johns River at Picolata and advances toward Payne's Town. Less than ten miles from the objective at a point near the Great Allachua Savannah (later Lake Levy) and Lake Pithlachocoo (later Newman's Lake), the column comes under attack by about 150 Indians led by Chief Payne and Chief Bowlegs when the two sides are about 130 yards apart. The Americans push the Indians back more than one mile to the beginning of a swamp. The skirmish continues for about two hours, and during the opening of the contest, Payne and a few other Indians are slain, while the Americans lose one man killed. During the tenacious skirmish, the Indians attempt to turn the flanks of Newman's lines, but without success.

The Americans, despite being hit by surprise, hold formidable positions. Their left is protected by a swamp and their right is protected by a pond. Meanwhile, the center of the line contains fallen pine trees that provide excellent protection. After about two hours, the Americans appear to be retreating; however, it is ruse. Suddenly the Indians, having been reinforced, reinitiate the battle about one-half hour before dusk. The Indians and their Negro allies seemingly in unison begin to yell as a number of chiefs lead the attack under the howls that imitate the various noises of the animals that inhabit the woods. At a point about 200 yards from the column, the charge comes to a halt and the column comes under a hurricane of fire.

The Americans, as ordered, retain their discipline and remain perfectly silent and prepared to fire from their positions behind fallen logs and standing trees. The enemy suspects the silence to have been inflicted by fear, which encourages them to advance. The advance encounters a wall of effective fire created by the silent riflemen. The powerful barrage instantly causes the Indians to retreat back to their original positions by the swamp. Newman holds off ordering a charge because he had, by this time, sent about half of his force back to the camp to protect it. The Indians, despite their superior numbers, fail to dislodge Newman's command, which maintains its positions and repels repeated assaults until 2000, when the Indians and Negroes are totally repulsed.

By daylight on the following day, Newman's lines are intact. The force had sustained two killed and one wounded. During the following two days (28th–29th), the Indians remain concealed; however, Newman had in the meantime built breastworks with port holes added. By the night of the 30th, the fortification comes under fire; however, the enemy remains far from close range. Nonetheless, the incoming fire inflicts neither harm nor injuries. Newman's command, however, still faces perilous times. The surgeon accompanied a party that returned to the camp and the provisions had reached critical levels while waiting for a relief force.

Meanwhile, Newman refuses to move out of the breastworks due to the high probability that the Indians had received reinforcements from St. Augustine or from the Makasukie tribe. The original force was accompanied by twelve horses, and rather than risk tragedy by leaving their fortification, one of the horses is slain for food. During the siege, Newman is informed that one of his companies is losing its spirit and is preparing to depart from the breastworks, and the officers also inform him that some of the men have given up hope that a relief party will arrive. Those troops are ready to begin deserting Newman to avoid death or capture by the Indians and Negroes.

All the while, Newman is also burdened by an increasing number of sick troops, which is adding to the mounting peril. Newman concludes that he must break out and make it back to the camp at the St. Johns River.

At about 2100 under the cover of darkness, Newman begins to abandon the breastworks. Five of his men are carried on litters and another few require help to make the march. After traveling about eight miles, the entire contingent has reached the point of complete exhaustion, making it impossible to continue to carry the wounded. To further complicate matters, a 25-man mounted relief force arrived with provisions and ammunition; however, they traveled on a separate road. Rather than attempt to catch up with Newman's beleaguered contingent, the relief force turns back and returns to St. Johns.

Colonel Newman dispatches Sergeant Major Reese to Picolata to discover what occurred to keep the supplies from reaching his command, while he remains in place; however, the mood of his forlorn troops compels him to resume the march at 1500. By this time, Newman has become one of the sick and his fever makes walking extremely difficult. After struggling to advance about five miles, the vanguard discovers Indians to the front. At nearly the same time, four men are shot. One man dies instantly and two others are fatally wounded. Colonel Newman, not intending to offer his troops as sacrifice to the enemy, orders a detachment to charge at the first sounds of the guns. The Indians are reluctant to stand and fight, giving Newman's fatigued troops an unexpected advantage. After about fifteen minutes, the Indians are soundly defeated. Many of the attacking force drop their weapons before they scatter. The victory does little to rejuvenate the troops; however, the flight of the Indians does permit the troops to get some rest. Camp is established and once again, breastworks are built to provide protection if the enemy returns. On the following day, the column moves out at 1000 and advances about five more miles without incident. A new camp is established and in the meantime, the situation remains critical. Colonel Newman, in his report, says his men were "living upon gophers, alligators and Palmetto stocks."

The Indians do not reappear, but morale improves when Sergeant Major Reese arrives with the provisions and fourteen horses. Afterward, Colonel Newman's force completes its journey to the St. Johns River, where a gunboat is awaiting the arrival of the beleaguered column. The troops are transported to Colonel Thomas Smith's encampment, where they receive excellent care.

In Colonel Newman's report to Georgia's governor, David B. Mitchell, he estimates the enemy's losses: "The number of Indians, in the first engagement, from every circumstance that appeared, must have been from 75 to 100. In the second engagement, their number must have been double our's; and, in the third engagement, there appeared to be 50, which was nearly equal to our force, deducting sick and wounded. I believe the loss of the enemy was fifty."

In New York, at Lewiston, General Van Rensselaer, in a letter to General Dearborn, informs him that three regiments under Colonel William Henry Winder are due to arrive shortly; however, Van Rensselaer also informs Dearborn that he is "mortified" because the total number of troops will only amount to 900 men and that the troops lack "cloth clothing."

In Ohio, scouts under Captain Ballard and about 40 dragoons under Captain Garrard (General Winchester's force) spot an Indian ambush site before they get snarled just to the front of the Tiffin River. The Indians had remained close to where a skirmish had occurred the day before. Nevertheless, they fail to remain any longer. The Americans initiate a charge and the Indians flee. A chase begins, but the Indians vanish. They are part of an advance British force that originated at Malden (Canada), composed of about 200 troops under Major Muir and at least 1,000 Indians commanded by a villainous officer, Colonel Matthew Elliott. Reports of this force moving against Fort Wayne have been picked up by the Americans at Piqua. A British detachment seizes Sergeant Mccoy (a scout attached to General Winchester's force) and during his interrogation, he misleads the British by inflating the numbers of the American army, and he informs them that a large force is moving down the Auglaize River to reinforce the army and trap the British.

September 28 (Monday)   In Ohio, the British under Major Muir intend to set up an ambush against General Winchester's force; however, Muir finds that most of his Indians had abandoned him. In other activity, while General Simon Perkins is away from Camp Avery at the Huron River, conferring with General Wadsworth at Cleveland, Colonel Hayes, the temporary commander, dispatches a 64-man contingent on a mission to attack a band of Indians. The detachment under Captain Joshua A. Cotton and Lts. Bartholomew and Ramsey departs from the camp during the evening. On the following day, the Indians are discovered and a skirmish erupts. Six men in the command are killed and ten others are wounded. One of the wounded, Joseph McMahon, escapes, but he is intercepted later and killed en route to his home.

In naval activity, the privateer *Nonsuch,* operating out of Baltimore, encounters two vessels, a ship and a schooner, flying British colors off Martinique. The *Nonsuch,* commanded by Captain Levely, which is carrying twelve 12-pound carronades and a crew of about 80 to 90 men, comes under fire once it raises the American flag; however, it immediately returns fire, sending ten broadsides. The Americans, despite being outmanned and out-gunned, trade fire for nearly three and one-half hours. Late in the duel, the American guns had become inoperable, but they continue to fire their small arms. The British disengage and sail toward Martinique, but the *Nonsuch,* its sails and rigging devastated, is unable to give pursuit. The Americans lose one officer (Wilkinson) killed and three sailors killed (Samuel Christian, David McCarthy and Lewis Riley). Six other seamen are wounded. The British sustain 23 casualties, including 7 killed.

September 29 (Tuesday)   In Washington, D.C., by this date, the Union Light Infantry Company, commanded by Captain Davidson, and the Washington Troop of Horse, commanded by Captain Elias B. Caldwell, had been formed and a full company of 160 men is at Alexandria prepared to serve at the president's pleasure. On this day, the president accepts their service and the unit becomes the First Legion of the District of Columbia. Lt. Colonel William Smith is elected as commanding officer.

In Indiana, General Hopkins, in a letter to Isaac Shelby, the governor of Kentucky, dated this day, informs the governor of his immediate plan of action: "My present intention is to attack every Indian settlement on the Wabash, and to destroy their property, then fall back upon the Illinois [river]; and I trust, in all the next month, to perform much service. Serious opposition I hardly apprehend, although I intend to be prepared for it." Hopkins does not depart from Fort Harrison until 11 November.

In Ohio at Marble Head peninsula, a band of about 130 Indians, allied with the British, ambush a contingent of militia (General Elijah Wadsworth's command). Twenty of the militia troops position themselves in a cabin and they engage the raiders, while the remaining forty men board boats and escape to Cedar Point. Meanwhile, the 20 defenders hold off the Indians until reinforcements arrive to rescue them two days later. During the attack, the Indians sustain about 40 killed, including a few of their chiefs. The Americans lose 78 killed. Also, the British, having advanced to about ten miles from Defiance, after considering the erroneous intelligence gained from Sergeant McCoy, which was similar to that gained by the British spies, Muir retires to Defiance where the boats are waiting and the force moves down the Maumee. Meanwhile, American mounted detachments begin a search for the enemy, while another detachment is sent to inform General Harrison that provisions have become dangerously low.

September 30 (Wednesday) The British float an offer of peace to the Americans and in return receive an option to negotiate if the British will consent to stop imprisoning American seamen. They had imprisoned over 8,000 prior to the outbreak of hostilities.

In Ohio, General Winchester strengthens Encampment Number 1 on the south bank of the Maumee across from the mouth of the Tiffin River. Meanwhile, as the troops toil to clear the ground of high growth from there to the Auglaize River and beyond to Fort Defiance Point, the dragoons under Garrard return with provisions acquired from Colonel Jennings.

September–October   In Alabama Tecumseh arrives at Autauga after crossing the Alabama River. He had headed south after meeting with the British earlier in the year at Detroit after they took possession. Tecumseh and about thirty others had traveled on horses and while en route, his mission was to enlist the Indians of the south to rise up against the Americans. The party scored no success while passing through the lands of the Chickasaw and Choctaws; however, in Florida the Seminoles had been receptive. After arriving in Alabama, Tecumseh discovers that his reputation had preceded him, which eases his task of turning the Creeks against the Americans. By the time he departs from Autauga for Coosawda, his followers increase dramatically. Later, he arrives at Tookabatcha on a day when Colonel Benjamin Hawkins, Indian agent, is meeting in council with the Indians.

The contingent under Tecumseh moves into the square just as Hawkins concludes the parley: "They were entirely naked, except their flaps and ornaments. Their faces were painted black, and their heads adorned with eagle plumes, while buffalo tails dragged from behind, suspended by bands which went around their waists. Buffalo tails were also attached to their arms, and made to stand out, by means of bands." After the pompous entrance, they are greeted and the customary exchange of tobacco follows; however, Tecumseh encounters one antagonist, Chief Isaacs, who refuses to exchange tobacco.

The chief is unimpressed and describes Tecumseh as a "bad man." Meanwhile, Hawkins returns to his agency on the Flint River. Tecumseh ignores Chief Isaacs and focuses on his speeches that will turn the Creeks against the Americans. Tecumseh explains that the king of England is prepared to provide large rewards for all who join the cause to expel the Americans from Georgia. He also tells the Creeks to discard their clothes and arms, and dress in the "skins of beasts." He also tells them to pick up their war clubs, their bows and their scalping knives. Nevertheless, many of the Creeks have long been friendly to the Americans, and they are unwilling to pick up the hatchet.

Tecumseh, not to be rebuffed, turns to some trickery and even a bit of concocted divine providence. One of the party, a prophet, proclaims that he had spoken with the Great Spirit and he guarantees them that all who fight will suffer no harm and none will be killed while engaging the Americans. Tecumseh also uses the prophet to further impress the Creeks. One Indian, Josiah Francis, the son of a trader and a Creek woman, is selected as a blind man and the ruse works. The Creeks are told that he will regain his sight. About ten days later, Josiah suddenly regains his sight. By that point, a large number of Creeks had decided to go to war, but still many chiefs oppose fighting the Americans.

Tecumseh, in an attempt to get a particular chief, Big Warrior, to pick up the hatchet, returns to visit Big Warrior at his house in Tookabatcha, but his attempts fall on deaf ears. Big Warrior declines the proposal to the dismay of Tecumseh, who proclaims that he is going back to Detroit and once there, to prove he had been sent by the Great Spirit, he will "stamp his foot," which will knock over every house in the town. Big Warrior remains indifferent, fails to reply to the boast and continues to smoke his pipe. Subsequently, during December 1812, a minor earthquake strikes the region and the Indians declare that Tecumseh had arrived in Detroit, saying, "We feel the shake of his foot." Settlers in the area had been aware of the earthquake; however, the superstitious Indians remain convinced that Tecumseh had caused the earth to shake.

Meanwhile, Tecumseh and his party, including Little Warrior, a Creek, and some of his band arrive at Detroit. The British, encouraged by the mission's success, dispatch directions to their contacts in Florida, which authorize the agents to arm the Creeks. During the return to their territory, on 13 February 1813, the Creeks attack some settlers' families near the mouth of the Ohio River.

October   In naval activity, the American privateer *Sarah Ann* (Captain Richard Moon) is seized by the British and taken into port at New Providence in the Bahamas. Before its capture, the *Sarah Ann* had engaged and captured a British merchant ship, the 10-gun *Elizabeth*, while it was en route to England from Jamaica with a cargo including coffee, ginger, 323 hogsheads (one hogshead equals 64 U.S. gallons) and sugar. Nonetheless, the capture had not been effortless. The British resistance continued until four of the crew sustained wounds. Two Americans were wounded.

In other naval activity, at about this time (autumn 1812) the American privateer *Siro*, commanded by Captain D. Gray, while en route to the United States from France, intercepts a British vessel, the 10-gun ship *Loyal Sam*. After seizing the vessel, the Americans discover that the Loyal Sam is carrying $23,500 in specie. The prize is taken into port at Portland.

October 1 (Thursday)   In New York, General Jacob Brown, pursuant to orders, arrives at Ogdensburg from Watertown.

October 2 (Friday)   In Canada, the British, in retaliation for a recent American attack against the Canadian town of Gananoqui, embark on a mission to strike Ogdensburg, New York. The force of about 750 men travels along the St. Lawrence in forty boats. The operation is bolstered by British land batteries opposite Ogdensburg at Preston, Canada. The British commence fire which is immediately met by return fire from the American positions at Ogdensburg. No offensive is launched on the 3rd; rather the British continue to finalize preparations. On the following day (4th), 25 additional boats embark from Preston and they are shadowed by two gunboats that have been acting as escorts during the operation. The flotilla of 25 boats moves past Ogdensburg as a ruse, but afterward, the boats reverse direction and close upon the town, in synchronization with the British artillery at Preston, which begins to bombard the American positions.

All the while, the American commander, General Jacob Brown, waits patiently for the appropriate time to order his riflemen and his battery to open fire. Time seemingly moves slowly as the Redcoats approach, and still the Americans refrain from opening fire. The boats begin to approach the debarkation point, still without resistance. Then suddenly, just as the British reach

Defense of Ogdensburg (*Life of General Jacob Brown*, New York: Nafish and Cornish, 1847).

point-blank range, they are struck with a thunderous avalanche of devastating fire. They retain their discipline and return fire. The shore-to-sea exchange continues for about one hour; however, two of the British boats are destroyed and the occupants are forced to abandon them. Another of the boats is seized by the Americans. Finally, General Brown is able to order a cease fire. The British abort the attack and begin their return to Canada. During the attack, the only British troops to land on shore are those captured.

Brown's victory receives accolades, and despite his total lack of military experience, he is offered the rank of brigadier general in the regular army. His natural military instincts continue to be a huge asset. Following this action, General Brown's service ends. He remains in the militia, although he returns to his home at Brownsville. In May, Brown's abilities will again be tested when a British fleet attacks Sackets Harbor.

Also, General Van Rensselaer, at Ogdensburg during this action, departs from there on the 3rd and moves to Oswego.

In Ohio, General Harrison, accompanied by cavalry, arrives at Three Mile Creek. Camp is established; however, Harrison continues moving and arrives at General Winchester's camp at the Maumee during the evening. Harrison becomes alarmed when he discovers the situation at the camp. The troops lack proper clothing and many have become sick. He also learns that provisions are dangerously low. Morale had reached a dangerous level and one of the regiments had been considering abandoning General Winchester and returning home; however, Colonel Allen and Major Hardin succeeded in persuading the men to remain. However, on the following morning, morale begins to rapidly improve.

October 3 (Saturday) **In Canada,** British Colonel Lethbridge, commanding at Preston, dispatches a force of militia and elements of the Glengarry Regiment across the river to raid Ogdensburg, New York. American batteries spot the flotilla and once it crosses the midpoint of the river, the British are greeted by grape and shot. The artillery fire compels the British to abort the crossing and reverse course. Subsequent to this incident, Colonel Lethbridge is succeeded by Lt. Colonel Thomas Pearson. Meanwhile, work begins to strengthen the town's defenses and the project is completed by end of the year. Preston, located about half-way between Montreal and Lake Erie, is a strategic point, particularly for receiving shipping for Upper Canada from England. All items en route to Upper Canada are off loaded at Preston and transferred to bateaux or boats, which then transport the goods up the St. Lawrence River. Fort Wellington is erected at Preston during 1813.

In Ohio, while the left wing of General Harrison's army under General Winchester is handling the transportation of supplies to Fort Winchester, under construction at this time, the right wing, composed of brigades from Pennsylvania and Virginia, along with one Ohio brigade, is advancing down the Sandusky River. By the end of this year, the force completes the construction of a fort, composed of four blockhouses, at the Upper Sandusky in the vicinity of the present-day Wyandot County Courthouse. It was built where the French had established a trading post about 1745. The fort is named Fort Feree. The location of the post is out of the way and the area is reached only by difficult travel. The army contracts ox-wagon teams to carry supplies and the route is so primitive that often the oxen are worn out. Nonetheless, General Harrison is compelled to continue establishing posts to maintain a supply line for his campaign to retake Detroit.

Among posts under construction by the right wing during this period is Fort Ball (not fully completed until July 1813), named in honor of Colonel James V. Ball of the 2nd Light Dragoons. It is composed of three blockhouses and capable of housing a garrison of 500 troops. The troops also construct Fort Stephenson at Lower Sandusky (later Fremont).

While the left and right wings of the army are engaged in their respective responsibilities, the center of the army commanded by General Edward Tupper advances by way of Hull's Road, upon which are located Forts McArthur, Necessity and Findlay. Tupper's task is to lead his 960 cavalry troops down the Maumee to the lowest rapids and beyond to clear the area of any enemy forces discovered. Once the mission is accomplished, the cavalry is to return to Fort Barbee; however, Tupper is unable to execute the mission due to unforeseen reasons, including much of the force's powder being ruined, along with a lack of provisions to sustain the force for seven to ten days. Other complications include a constant threat against Fort Winchester by the Indians and last but not least, the unexpected relationship that has developed between General Tupper and General Winchester, with the latter apparently holding a condescending opinion of Tupper. Kentucky troops begin to question being led by an Ohio militia general. The situation deteriorates rapidly and endangers the entire campaign after the withdrawal of the Kentucky troops and Simrall's dragoons from Tupper's command.

General Winchester also replaces General Tupper as commander of the expedition with Colonel Allen, U.S. Army, which infuriates the Ohio troops, who move back across the Auglaize River and proclaim that they will not serve under Allen or anyone else except a leader chosen by themselves. This private war between the militia and the regulars causes the expedition of the left wing of the army to be aborted. General Tupper, following the departure of about 350 Kentucky mounted riflemen, whose enlistments had expired, fails to move down the Maumee and instead moves past the Ottawa towns and goes directly to Fort McArthur. General Winchester becomes infuriated and lodges charges of insubordination, which is followed by General Harrison issuing an order to have General Tupper placed under arrest. The incident does not end there.

In the meantime, General Winchester's army sustains a devastating defeat at the Raisin River, and when Tupper's court-martial convenes, all of the witnesses, including Winchester, are absent due to being captives of the British. Consequently, General Tupper is acquitted of all charges.

In Ohio at General Winchester's camp, the cavalry that had accompanied General Harrison and encamped at Three Mile Creek arrives at the camp, halts and comes to a parade dress. Soon after, all of General Winchester's able-bodied troops are called to assemble. Once the formation is in line, they hear the following order, read by General Winchester:

> General Order: CAMP AT DEFIANCE, October 3, 1812. I have the honor of announcing to this army the arrival of General Harrison, who is duly authorized by the executive of the Federal Government to take command of the Northwestern Army. This officer is enjoying the implicit confidence of the States from whose citizens this army is and will be collected and, possessing himself great military skill and reputation, the General is confident in the belief that his presence in the army in the character of its chief, will be hailed with unusual approbation.

The troops instantaneously snap back into shape and their spirits are lifted further by the appearance of the disciplined cavalry. Harrison speaks informally with the troops, which inspires them, and they are treated with a substantial breakfast, compliments of the cavalry, which arrived with provisions. Also, General Winchester, subsequent to being relieved, remains with Harrison and receives command of the left wing of the army, which is composed of regulars and six regiments of Kentucky and Ohio militia.

It is determined that Fort Defiance, earlier constructed by General Wayne, is too deteriorated to maintain. Harrison selects a new site for a fort to be built. About 250 troops under Major Joseph Robb are assigned to the project of building Fort Winchester. The post named in honor of General James Winchester, in addition to its four blockhouses, one at each corner, also contains a cellar at its northeast corner. From the cellar, the troops build a tunnel that allows the troops to remain concealed, while moving to the river to acquire water, if the fort is under siege. Also, a new encampment, designated Number Two, is established on the left bank of the Auglaise River at a point less than two miles above the mouth of the river.

Meanwhile, General Harrison, escorted by Colonel Richard M. Johnson's battalion, departs from Defiance en route to Fort Barbee, where the column arrives on 7 October.

October 4 (Sunday) **In New York** at Ogdensburg, General Brown's force (regulars and militia) repulses a British raid (*see also*, **October 2**, 1812).

In naval activity, on or about this date, the *Wiley Renard*, a privateer schooner operating out of Boston, is seized by the HMS *Shannon*, commanded by Captain Philip Bowes Vere Broke.

October 5 (Monday) *In naval activity,* the HMS *Nymphe* intercepts and recaptures the brigantine *Pitt*. Also, the privateer *America* passes by St. Michael Island (West Indies) on what is becoming an uneventful cruise. It does not encounter any British shipping until early November.

October 6 (Tuesday) **In New York,** Captain Isaac Chauncey arrives at Sackets Harbor. He is acting under orders to form a fleet. The USS *Oneida* under Commander Woolsey and the schooner *Julia* are there at the time of his arrival. Chauncey's fleet, built around the *Oneida*, includes other schooners—*Conquest, Fair American, Growler, Pert, Scourge, Governor Tompkins,* and *Hamilton*—which are armed with swivel guns at Sackets Harbor. Chauncey's party also includes about 100 sailors, including officers and about 40 ships' carpenters.

The fleet will carry 40 guns and about 430 men, including U.S. Marines. After he completes the task of readying his fleet, Captain Chauncey prepares to attack the batteries at Kingston (Canada), along with the HMS *Royal George* and other British vessels that operate on the lakes. The *Governor Tompkins,* until its purchase this month at Oswego, had been the merchant ship, *Charles and Ann.* It is named in honor of Daniel D. Tompkins, governor of New York (1807, 1810, 1813 and 1816) and later 6th vice president of the United States (1817–1825, under President James Monroe).

Also, the *Fair American* is purchased this month. Command is given to Lt. Wolcott Chauncey. The 3-gun schooner USS *Pert,* initially named *Collector* until acquired by the U.S. Navy for service on the Great Lakes, is commanded by Sailing Master Robert Arundel. The *Pert* remains with Chauncey's fleet until the conclusion of the war. It is sold during May 1815.

In other naval activity, Captain Stephen Decatur receives orders from Commodore William Bainbridge to prepare for a prolonged cruise on the *Essex.*

October 7 (Wednesday) *In naval activity,* the HMS *Surveillante,* as part of a large British squadron, which includes the *Briton, Constant* and *Latona,* intercepts and seizes the American schooner *Baltimore.*

October 8 (Thursday) **In Ohio** at Fort Winchester, Indians continue to mount harassing raids and ambushes. In one recent incident, five troops divert from their duties to pick some wild plums, but the few moments of leisure turn tragic. Indians lurking nearby spring upon the men, then kill and scalp each one. The Indians have also been lurking close to Encampment Number 2, where they fire upon the camp from the opposite bank. On this day, a sentinel at the encampment literally falls asleep while on guard duty. Unfortunately for him, he is discovered and given a court-martial. The soldier, Frederick Jacoby, receives a severe punishment, execution by firing squad. The lackadaisical attitudes of the garrison that had emerged from the dullness of camp life is seemingly eradicated by the sentence. The platoon designated to carry out the sentence moves into position, and just as they are about to receive the order to fire, almost as in a Hollywood script, a dispatch rider arrives with orders from General Winchester to cancel the execution. Jacoby, obviously, is jubilant at having his life spared. Nonetheless, the sentence in itself served to bring about more sober thought about responsibility among the men of the garrison.

Fort Winchester is completed by 15 October and afterward the Indians begin to wander away from the area. Nevertheless, other problems emerge. General Harrison around this time is moving from Defiance to Fort Barbee and is intercepted by a dispatch rider who informs him that Fort Wayne is again under serious threat by Indians. After arriving at Fort Barbee, he confers with Colonel Allen Trimble (Ohio cavalry) regarding Fort Wayne, and soon after, Trimble and 500 troops depart from the post en route to terminate the threat. The threat ends upon the arrival of the cavalry, as the Indians immediately flee.

Trimble's command was at Fort Barbee preparing to join with General Tupper's force, which was advancing against Detroit; however, General Harrison's orders superceded his previous orders. Colonel Trimble, after lifting the siege, has difficulty with his men. Harrison's orders directed Trimble also to attack the village of Chief White Pigeon, a Pottawatomie, but about half of the troops refuse to penetrate any farther to the north. Colonel Trimble continues with those who obey orders. While moving against the town, one of the Indian guides betrays the column by sounding the alarm. Nonetheless, although the Indians are able to evade the thunderclap of the galloping horses, the cavalry does destroy two villages.

In naval activity, Commodore Rodgers's squadron embarks on a cruise. The USS *Argus,* initially known as the *Merrimac,* was launched during August 1803. On this day, it begins a cruise which lasts until 3 January 1813. During its time at sea, it seizes six prizes, and when intercepted by a British squadron, it evades capture after outrunning the squadron during a three-day chase. After losing the British, the *Argus* succeeds in making it back to New York. One of the prizes is also brought back to New York.

The *Argus* is accompanied by the USS *President* and the USS *Congress.* The *Congress,* which had laid in ordinary in Washington since November 1804 until re-commissioned during autumn 1811, remains at sea until late December. During the cruise, nine prizes are captured. By the 13th, the *Constitution* breaks off and sails alone.

Also, the American privateers *Rossie* and *Globe* intercept the schooner *Jubilee.* A prize crew takes it into an American port.

October 8–9 An American force, including seamen and soldiers under the command of Lieutenant Jesse D. Elliott, U.S. Navy, assisted by Captain Nathan Towson (U.S. Army), prepares to move against two British warships. Initially, Elliott is informed that the two vessels are the HMS *Detroit* (formerly the brigantine USS *John Adams*) and the brigantine HMS *Hunter;* however, the latter is actually the brigantine HMS *Caledonia.* Elliott had only recently arrived in Buffalo, with orders to acquire merchant ships to be used as gunboats. Elliott is informed that a contingent of about 50 men is close by; however, when he requests their help for the attack, he discovers they have hardly any ammunition or arms. Elliott notes that they arrived at noon and that they "had only 20 pistols, and neither cutlasses nor battle-axes."

Elliott requests help from General Alexander Smyth. Lt. Colonel Winfield Scott, with the artillery at Black Rock, borrows weapons including swords, pistols and some sabers. Through the actions of Smyth and Scott, Elliott's force is supplied with the arms and ammunition required for the mission, along with additional men. Smyth orders Captain Nathan Towson and Lt. Isaac Roach to augment Elliott's contingent with 50 regulars, which increases Elliott's force to slightly more than 100 men; however, only 100 embark.

Once Elliott has everything in order, by about midnight (8th-9th), the contingent embarks in two boats from the Black Rock Navy Yard (Buffalo) in an effort to seize the targets, which had sailed down Lake Erie and anchored close to Fort Erie. Elliott commands one boat and is aided by Lt. Roach (engineers) and Lt. Presstman, who command the infantry. The other boat under Sailing Master Watts is carrying 20 sailors and 28 artillerists under Captain Towson.

One of the targeted vessels, the HMS *Detroit,* is actually the USS *Adams,* which was captured when Detroit fell the previous August. And the other, the HMS *Caledonia,* had recently participated in the seizure of Michilimackinac. While the boats cross the river, the one carrying Towson gets out in front and contact with Elliott's boat is lost. Lt. Watts is soon under fire from the *Detroit.* He decides that his pilot miscalculated and discerns that the *Caledonia* must be passed because a successful attack cannot be made; how-

General Nathan Towson (*The American Generals,* **John Frost, 1850).**

ever, Captain Towson overrules Watts and assumes command of the boat, then directs the pilot to close upon the *Caledonia* to permit the troops to board it. In a flash, the grapplings are tossed, but only one takes hold. Meanwhile, the boat becomes imperiled as it slips astern and is exposed to fire. Nonetheless, the one grappling is sufficient to pull the boat alongside, and in less than two minutes, the ship is boarded and seized.

Meanwhile, the crew on the *Detroit* becomes distracted by the commotion and while the crew is transfixed on the attack against the *Caledonia*, Elliott's party remains undetected. Elliott's men bolt from their boat and board the *Detroit*. With little effort it is seized.

Both ships immediately head for the American shore; however, due to the conditions on the *Niagara*, both vessels are temporarily grounded in the river, but by about dawn they are again in motion. The soft winds do not push them upstream, which causes the Americans to come within range of British shore guns. British guns begin to catapult grape and canister. The flying artillery joins in with the heavier guns and at its first shot, Elliott hails the British onshore and informs a British officer: "If another gun is fired, I would bring the prisoners on deck and expose them to the same fate we would all share. The British continue to fire, but Elliott does not move the prisoners for fear of later being charged with the "imputation of barbarity."

By this time, the *Caledonia* has been beached within the range of the American guns at Black Rock and Elliott begins rearranging the guns of the *Detroit* by placing all of them on one side of the vessel to provide him with double fire power. At the same time, he attempts to get the *Detroit* to the American bank of the river, but all efforts fail due to the absence of wind and an unwieldy current. Elliott, unable to accomplish his goal, cuts the cable to permit the vessel to drift down river to prevent the British guns from sinking it. Elliott's intent to exchange shots with the Flying Artillery fails due to treachery. The pilot abandons Elliott and in about 15 minutes, the *Detroit* runs ashore at Squaw Island.

Elliott sends a boat that carries the British prisoners ashore where they are transferred to troops there. The officer in charge of the prisoners is directed to return to the ship to pick up Elliott and for whatever items that can be carried to shore. However, again, the stiff current interferes and prohibits him from getting back to the vessel. Meanwhile, Elliott discovers a skiff and heads for shore to retrieve the boat. After landing he asks Lt. Colonel Scott to protect the ship.

At about the same time, from shore, Elliott spots an enemy boat, carrying about 40 troops, closing on the *Detroit*. The boarding party does gain possession; however, only for awhile. An American battery opens fire and inflicts heavy casualties. The few survivors are compelled to return to the boat. For the remainder of the morning, artillery on both sides of the river continues to maintain its fire. Elliott has concluded that the *Detroit* cannot be refloated due to the severe damage, including the total devastation of its rigging.

Later that evening (9th), the British send another detachment to secure the vessel, but in the meantime, an American contingent is dispatched to prevent the *Detroit* from again flying the British colors. The *Detroit* is boarded by Americans who destroy the vessel by fire. The British *Caledonia* and its cargo of furs remain under American control.

During the operation, Elliott received information that General Brock was advancing against Black Rock. He sends a messenger to Towson to deliver the intelligence and some combustibles with instructions to set the *Caledonia* on fire; however, Towson is reluctant to destroy the ship. He believes his command can resist an attack. In the meantime, Towson orders the cargo to be removed. Three men remain on the *Caledonia* with orders to set it afire if the British compel the Americans to retreat to Flint Hill. Nonetheless, the information regarding an attack by Brock had been erroneous. Consequently, Towson's decision not to burn the *Caledonia* provides Captain Perry with a new addition to his fleet.

Of Elliott's force, six are killed during the operation. Congress, when informed of the exploit, gives a vote of thanks to Elliott, and he is awarded a sword for his actions.

In Lieutenant Elliott's report to the Secretary of the Navy Paul Hamilton, he states that the crew of the *Detroit* included a lieutenant of Royal Marines, a boatswain, one gunner and 56 men, along with 36 Americans who had been held aboard the ship. His report also states the vessel carried six 6-pounders. The Americans lose one man killed during the operation to seize the *Detroit* and one officer. Acting midshipman John C. Cummings sustained a bayonet wound in his leg.

Elliott's report also mentions the other vessel as follows: "The Caledonia mounted two small guns, blunderbusses, pistols, muskets, cutlasses, and boarding pikes, 12 men including officers — 10 prisoners (American) on board. The boat boarding her was commanded by sailing-master George Watts, who performed his duty in a masterly style. But one man killed, and four wounded badly, I am afraid mortally. I enclose you a list of the officers and men engaged in the enterprise, and also a view of the lake and river in the different situations of the attack. In a day or two I shall forward the names of the prisoners. The *Caledonia* belongs to the N.W. Company, loaded with furs, worth, I understand, $200,000."

In July 1813, Lt. Elliott is jumped ahead of thirty other lieutenants by President Madison and the secretary of the Navy to the rank of master commandant, and with the promotion, he receives command of the flagship of Commodore Chauncey, the USS *Madison*. Also, Captain (later brigadier general) Nathan Towson is breveted as a major for his actions during this operation.

October 9 (Friday) **In Maine**, the privateer *Partridge*, a schooner, is commissioned.

October 10 (Saturday) **In New York** at Sackets Harbor, General Richard Dodge is directed by Governor Tompkins to detach the remainder of Captain Forsyth's rifle company and dispatch the contingent to Ogdensburg to bolster General Jacob Brown's force. Other units ordered detached and sent to Ogdensburg by the governor include the artillery companies of Captain Brown, Captain Foot and Captain King. The governor, concerned about the safety of the troops during the journey, requests that Dodge maintain secrecy. He also suggests that the two brass 9-pounders at Sackets Harbor also get transferred to Ogdensburg, along with "their carriages, harness and implements, and 250 twelve pound balls, 300 nine pound and; 200 six pound balls." The governor's list also includes the following which he wants sent to Brown: "about 10,000 Musket cartridges; or powder, lead and cartridge paper sufficient to make that number. Should a supply of blankets, Watch coats for sentinels, and other articles for winter accommodation arrive at this station, you will please to forward to Genl. Brown for the troops under his command, such proportion thereof, as may in your opinion be equitable." Brigadier General Richard Dodge commands the 4th Brigade, 1st New York Division from 18 June 1812 to 9 February 1813.

In naval activity, the 182-ton brigantine *Reward*, while en route to Lisbon, Portugal, from Salem, Massachusetts, with a cargo of beef and flour, is intercepted and seized by the British privateer *General Smyth*. Also, the American privateer *Fame*, commanded by Captain Green, arrives at Boston after being at sea for fifteen days. The *Fame*, which also served during the American Revolution as a privateer, captures two prizes during this recent cruise. One of the schooners is transporting a cargo of oil and salmon, and the other, a new vessel, carries sugar as ballast to keep it stable.

In other naval activity, the American privateer *Rossie* (Commodore Joshua Barney) spots a flag and initiates pursuit. At close range it discovers the vessel is the American privateer *Rapid*, a schooner out of Charleston.

October 10–11 **In New York,** following a period of procrastination by General Stephen Van Rensselaer, whom some believe has caused a delay in an attack because of his strong ties to the Federalists, finally prepares to launch an attack upon Queenston, Canada, from his positions at Niagara. The blueprint for the cross-river assault is to be sprung from Lewiston. Van Rensselaer' troops, who number about 6,000, by this day had become extremely disgruntled due to the inaction of their commander. That ever-rising pressure had essentially sparked the operation to get underway. Although the troops' morale builds with the knowledge that the offensive is ready to begin, new complications quickly develop when it is learned that command of the operation had been given to Lt. Colonel Solomon Van Rensselaer, a New York militia officer, who is also General Stephen Van Rensselaer's cousin. The decision ignites anger among the regulars, some of whom held rank in the U.S. Army regulars, giving them superior rank. Nonetheless, the decision stands.

Embarkation is set for 0300 the next morning. However, when the troops arrive during the night, they are greeted with a pelting rain. The heavy rain and cold temperatures causes the troops great discomfort during the 28-hour storm. To make the situation worse, the thirteen boats scheduled to transport the force across the river fail to arrive, leaving soaked troops stranded along the river bank when dawn arrives. The attack is postponed. Later it is discovered that Lt. Sims intentionally diverted the boats to prevent the crossing. Although it was never officially determined why Sims sabotaged the operation, one of the theories was that as a regular, he became incensed with the decision to place a militia officer in command of the operation. The attack is rescheduled for 13 October.

October 11 (Sunday) *In naval activity,* the privateer *Fame* (Captain Green), which had also operated as a privateer during the American Revolution, returns to port at Boston following a short but productive cruise of only fifteen days in which it captures five schooners. The prizes are *Four Sons,* carrying a cargo of fish and furs; *Four Brothers, Three Sisters; Betsey Ann;* and the *Delight.* All of the *Fame*'s prizes arrive at American ports.

October 12 (Monday) **In New York,** General Van Rensselaer makes final preparations to prepare to relaunch the attack against Queenston, Canada. During the night, Lt. Colonel Winfield Scott arrives at Lewiston from Buffalo; however, his request to join in the offensive is declined. After his arrival, Colonel Scott establishes a battery on some high ground above the Lewiston Ferry close to the Barton residence. The battery is to provide cover fire for the scheduled attack on the following morning. Also on or about this day, General Richard Dodge, pursuant to a request of Governor Tompkins, releases the elements of Captain Forsyth's company that he had retained when he dispatched General Brown to Ogdensburg. The contingent, accompanied by artillery companies of Captains Brown, Foot and King, repairs to Ogdensburg to join Brown's force.

In Washington, D.C., President James Madison requests 1,500 volunteers from the State of Tennessee for a campaign against the Creeks in Florida. The force, commanded by Major General Andrew Jackson, departs Nashville on December 10, 1812. Jackson's force comprises 2,000 men.

October 13 (Tuesday) BATTLE OF QUEENSTON, CANADA **In New York,** General Van Rensselaer, having failed to get his attack against Queenston, Canada, launched on schedule on the 11th, resumes the offensive on this day. Artillery at Fort Niagara propels red hot shot toward the town, inflicting damage and igniting fires. One officer, Captain Fry, a former ranger, is struck and killed by a ball. The incoming fire is returned by guns under Brigade Major Thomas Evans (8th Regiment) at Fort George.

Meanwhile, the American force, divided into two groups under Lt. Colonel John Chrystie commanding regulars and Lt. Colonel Solomon Van Rensselaer leading the militia, cross the river at Lewiston in thirteen boats. Three of the boats miss the landing spot. The other ten boats debark the troops, then return to the New York side of

General Stephen Van Rensselaer.

the river to pick up the remainder of the troops. The total force, composed of about 300 regulars and 300 militia troops, embark during yet another rain storm. However, British forces under Captain Dennis oppose the landing and the Americans sustain casualties even before they hit shore. In addition to the opposition by Dennis' troops, the Americans also come under fire from the one-gun battery at Brooman's Point; however, the artillery, due to the darkness, is not particularly effective. Colonel Chrystie had been in one of the boats that missed the landing spot, leaving command to Captain John Ellis Wool. The Americans under Wool reach positions at Queenston Heights, but British reinforcements from Fort George, about seven miles distant, arrive there nearly simultaneously.

The British strike first. Their infantry fire is bolstered by artillery. The Americans take a pounding after being struck heavily on their right flank and to their front. Meanwhile, on the left flank, defended by militia, the pressure is less severe. Nonetheless, the Americans lack artillery, which provides the British with a huge advantage. Wool continues to return fire and for a while, the Americans hold steadfastly. Of the ten officers at the scene, two are killed and four others, including Captain Wool, are wounded. Lt. Colonel Rensselaer is hit multiple times while fighting alongside the militia. During the heated contest, the Americans succeed in forcing the left wing of the British line to retreat back into town; however, the right wing holds steadfastly on the heights. Punishing fire from that quarter forbids progress. Wool's force withdraws back to the riverbank in an attempt to regroup for another advance. While regrouping, a contingent of regulars arrives to bolster Wool. By this time, Colonel Rensselaer's wounds have crippled him. He is evacuated and taken back to Lewiston.

Captain Wool, after ordering the reinforcing company of regulars to deploy to the right of his line, orders the attack to resume. Simultaneously, Lt. Lush is positioned in the tail end of the column under orders to open fire on any of the troops who might balk during the trek. Initially, while Wool's column is moving in a southward direction, it is shielded from sight of the British by the river bank. Later, as the column moves away from the river's edge, still the British are unable to detect the Americans as they ascend the heights where their initial objective, a British battery, is in place. The ascent becomes nearly too difficult due to the degree of the incline. The troops find themselves needing help from one another to advance. Finally, when they encroach the top, Captain Wool encounters what turns out to be an obscure path, thought to be impassable by the British, who post no sentries. The Americans take the route which leads directly to the plateau near the British battery.

The British, who dominate the high ground, fail to detect Wool's contingent in time to block their passage. By this time, General Brock had arrived at the battery after rushing from Fort George, Canada. He becomes aware of the approaching Americans when from their positions to the right-rear of the battery, an unexpected burst of gunfire signals the presence of the intruders. Brock had expected the light of dawn, not the flash of gunfire during the predawn hours. While Wool's contingent initiates its charge, the British react immediately. Brock is among the first to retire. He begins his descent without bothering to bring his horse. He is followed by the others, including the infantrymen and the artillerymen, leaving the abandoned battery to the Americans who seize the ground just before dawn and immediately hoist the American flag on the summit.

Queenston in 1812.

In the meantime, General Sheaffe at Fort George is directed to get reinforcements to the area. He is to commence a bombardment of the American positions across the river at Niagara. Although surprised by the attack, General Brock remains convinced that the primary objective of the assault would be at the mouth of the Niagara River near Fort George rather than Queenston. After recovering from initial loss of the battery, General Brock moves to evict the Americans from the summit.

In anticipation of the counterattack, Captain Wool prepares to defend his newly won ground with his sparse force. A contingent is deployed to meet an attack against his left flank; however, Brock leads not only the troops that had manned and protected the battery, but also other troops from the town of Queenston. After ascending the slope, it becomes apparent that Wool lacks the numbers to repulse the assault. The British storm the diminutive American line on the flank, which compels Wool's entire force to pull back. The British pressure imperils the entire contingent. Within a short time, Wool finds himself trapped. The more powerful British force corrals the Americans between it and a sheer drop to their rear.

Despite his ominous positioning, Wool displays no signs of fearfulness. However, the confidence is not unanimous. One of Wool's officers immediately falters and without orders begins to wave his musket in the air with a white handkerchief attached to its bayonet. Captain Wool, infuriated by the captain's conduct, instinctively reacts and rips the white cloth from the musket. Before others begin to show signs of quitting, Wool utters some words to bolster their confidence and at about the same time, he issues an urgent request to regroup and continue the fight. Suddenly the shattered line is again galvanized against a sea of Redcoats.

The rejuvenated Yanks regain their confidence and reinitiate the battle for control of the battery. Nevertheless, more British reinforcements begin to arrive, while the Yanks' ammunition is nearly depleted. Once again, Captain Wool refuses to consider capitulation. He orders a stunning and unexpected bayonet attack to drive the British back down the slope—the assault succeeds. Meanwhile, British General Brock remains equally determined to regain the summit. He regroups for yet another ascent. Brock, at the head of a contingent of the 49th Regiment (grenadiers), pauses at a stone wall to permit his force to gain a second breath.

Afterward, Brock becomes totally animated as he bolts over the wall to lead the attack. Brock's sword is swinging back and forth as he rallies his troops and those to the rear, the York militia under Colonel McDonnell. Nevertheless, the treacherous climb begins to overwhelm the British, who struggle step-by-step. Brock becomes impatient and proclaims his disappointment in the grenadiers: "This is the first time I have ever seen the 49th turn their backs." Nonetheless, his apparent rage erroneously impugned the courage of the troops. They had not turned; rather, the terrain had caused them to stumble and fall. Nevertheless, General Brock does not receive an opportunity to make amends with his troops. Shortly after his outburst, at about the same time he is pressing McDonnell to advance his militia, Brock sustains a wound to his wrist. He ignores that as he plunges ahead, but then an American musket takes him out with a shot to his chest. After receiving the fatal wound, he urges that his death "not be noticed, or prevent the advance of his troops." General Brock makes it known that he wants a message sent to his sister, then dies.

At nearly the same time, British Colonel McDonell is struck. He falls close to where Brock is lying. McDonel's wound is also fatal, but he lives until the following day.

By the time the new attack commences at about 1000, American reinforcements arrive to bolster Wool's command on the summit, providing Wool with some fresh troops and additional ammunition. The British, who rallied to the words "Revenge the general," once again encounter an avalanche of fire that devastates the Redcoats. Lt. Colonel McDonel sustains a mortal wound. Two other officers receive debilitating wounds. The attack falters and Wool continues to hold his captured ground. The British had been bolstered by their Indian allies, and during the frantic melee, one of the chiefs is captured, along with ten troops.

Despite their heavy losses during the latest attempt to regain the ground, the British retain their persistence and refuse to allow the Americans to retain the battery. By this time, Captain Wool, who had been wounded, is compelled to leave the field. By that time, several other officers had arrived with the reinforcements, General William Wadsworth and two lieutenant colonels, Winfield Scott and John Chrystie, the latter having been with the boats that landed well beyond the original landing site. General Wadsworth declines command and passes it to Colonel Scott.

At about the same time, Colonel Scott forms his defensive line to meet the next counterattack. His force is composed of about 600 troops and of these about 250 are militia. The militia, still across the river, are ordered to join with Scott. As the afternoon passes, the British receive additional forces when General Sheaffe arrives from Fort George with reinforcements of 390 regulars, two companies of militia and a contingent of Indians to once again place the Americans in jeopardy.

The British forces by the time of Sheaffe's arrival swells. The units include four companies of the 41st British Regiment; the remaining able-bodied men of the 49th Regiment; two companies of the 1st Lincoln militia, commanded by Captain James Crooke and Captain McEwen; two companies of the 4th Lincoln militia under Captain William Crooke and Captain Nelles; three companies of the 5th Lincoln militia, commanded by Captain Applegarth, Captain Hatt and Captain Durand; and several companies of the York militia. The ground forces are bolstered by artillery contingents (Royal Artillery and Provincial Artillery) and a small detachment of dragoons (Merritt's). The British-Canadian force is also bolstered by the Indians under John Norton and John Brant.

Sheaffe's arrival underscores another strategic mistake of the Americans, who have failed to secure an escape route if necessary, and they also had failed to deploy troops that could have severed communications between Queenston and the other British outposts. The miscalculation is detected by the British, who deploy Indians in positions in the woods from where they dominate the route to Chippewa.

Across the river, the troops are able to observe the arrival of the British reinforcements, and the sight does little to instill courage in the militia, who refuse General Van Rensselaer's direct order to cross the river to bolster Scott's command. The militia clings to a technicality that they, according to the laws of New York, do not have to obey an order to move out of the state. The refusal of the militia to advance causes a calamity. Another problem is that Rensselaer had also requested reinforcements from General Smyth; however, none arrive. Meanwhile, Colonel Scott, similarly to Captain Wool, remains calm, while the British send a contingent of Indians into his left flank. Scott counters and launches a deadly bayonet attack, which drives back the Indians and preserves his left flank. However, the British under Major General Roger Hale Sheaffe launch a full scale assault, which includes additional reinforcements that arrived from nearby posts, by about 1600.

The British strike the opposite flank, compelling the Americans to shift their positions to meet the threat. The overwhelming thrust against the left and the rear forces the line to burst. The retreat becomes haphazard. A number of troops break for the cliff and succeed in descending the rugged slope, but when they reach the river, to their dismay, none of their boats are there. Troops under General Wadsworth and Colonel Chrystie surrender at the cliff. The rest of the retreating force, under Colonel Scott, tries to reach the falls, but it is impossible. Surrender is the only option.

The Americans dispatch a messenger under a white flag to the British positions, but Indians are posted between the U.S. troops and the British. The Indians ignore the flag and fire. Two other attempts are made to carry the message that the body will surrender, but each time the Indians open fire. Finally, on a fourth try, the flag is carried by Lt. Colonel Scott, and he reaches the British to end the battle for Queenston.

The blame for the defeat is elusive. The commanding general, Van Rensselaer, who remained in New York, noted in his official reports that the cause was directly linked to the refusal of the militia to cross the river; however, his reports omit the fact that by the time the order to cross was given, the boats had already drifted away, which would have forced the troops to cross in small numbers. Nevertheless, the militia is tagged with cowardice. Following the victory, General Sheaffe fails to take the advantage; rather, he consummates another armistice that is to last three days, to the dismay of even Sir George Prevost.

Van Rensselaer's reports also totally omit the names of Captain John Wool and Lt. Colonel Scott, both of whom had led so courageously while under fire from superior forces. The gains of both officers had suddenly been cast into obscurity. Meanwhile, the British had turned a thrashing into a victory that adds to the laurels of Canada. Different sources report varying numbers of Americans killed and wounded, as well as the number of men who drowned while attempting to reach the New York side of the river, but it is accurate that nearly 1,000 men were captured. Of the captives, about two-thirds had not participated in the fighting. They were seized while trying to conceal themselves among the rocks and the woods below the embankments.

Later on the day of the surrender, while Colonel Winfield Scott is having dinner with British General Roger Hale Sheaffe, a party of Indians (Jacob Norton and Brant the Younger) arrives at Sheaffe's quarters in search of Scott, whom they describe as "the tall one." Unknown to Scott, the Indians had specifically targeted him during the battle, leaving them frustrated because he seemed invincible. Unexpectedly, Jacob Norton grabs Scott by the arms to spin him around and scrutinize his uniform, "to see his wounds, balls through his uniform." Scott takes offense and pushes the Indian away, proclaiming: "You shoot like a squaw." The Indians instinctively draw their weapons to threaten Scott with their knives and tomahawks. Undaunted, despite the odds, Scott draws his sword to defend himself at a spot in a small passageway.

At that instant, Colonel Nathaniel Coffin, aide-de-camp to General Sheaffe, appears, senses the danger and places his pistol on Norton's head, while calling for assistance. Suddenly, the situation defuses when Coffin's pistol nudges Norton's head and other Redcoats rush from a nearby room. The Indians lose their enthusiasm and once again, they fail to inflict a wound on the "tall one." The Indians instead depart from Sheaffe's quarters. Colonel Coffin, who most probably saved Scott from injury or even death, is later, during January 1813, named deputy adjutant general of the Upper Canada militia, a post he retains for about 25 years.

In Canada, the British and the American wounded are taken by boats to Niagara for medical help. Various places — including Government House, the Indian council house and St. Mark's Church — are transformed into temporary hospitals. During that time, on the 16th, while General Brock is being mourned and interred in the northeast bastion of Fort George, the American batteries at Lewiston fire a salute to the fallen general. The British, after securing their prisoners, grant parole to the militia; however, the regulars including officers, are transported to Quebec. It is also determined that 23 Irishmen are among the prisoners.

Once in Quebec, the British decide to treat the Irish troops as traitors and put them on trial for treason for lifting arms against Great Britain. The decision raises the ire of the U.S. government, which accumulates an identical number of English captives, and each is informed that their fate will hang upon the fate of the Irish-American prisoners seized at Queenston. The threat of instant vengeance is effective. The British relent; however, before the Irish captives are freed; rather than being executed, two of them die in captivity. The remaining 21 men are returned to the United States.

Captain John Wool and Lt. Colonel Winfield Scott later become general officers who participate in the Mexican War. The late British General Brock becomes the legendary hero of Queenston. A monument in his memory is later erected there.

After the battle at Queenston, Colonel Solomon Van Rensselaer states that General Henry Dearborn had informed him that Dearborn was "pleased with my conduct." Colonel Van Rensselaer, while recuperating at Buffalo, also states that Generals Lewis and Van Rensselaer, at headquarters at Greenbush, told him that a separate corps would be established and placed under his command. At about the same time, he states that "as a man of honor," he must defend General Stephen Rensselaer against severe attacks due to his political status as an opponent of Daniel D. Tompkins, incumbent, in the governorship race.

Colonel Van Rensselaer claims that Secretary of War Eustis, prior to resigning his office, had added his (Van Rensselaer's) name on the list for promotion to brigadier general and that Eustis expressed "astonishment" that he did not get promoted by the succeeding secretary of war, John Armstrong. Van Rensselaer later also claims that General Wilkinson, who arrives to assume command of the northern army (1813), requests the promotion for Van Rensselaer, and that too is declined. However, Colonel Van Rensselaer does later receive the rank of brevet major general of militia by Governor DeWitt Clinton.

The day after the battle, Major General Van Rensselaer relinquishes command of the Niagara frontier to General Smyth. For a while earlier, Major General Amos Hall had commanded the militia along the frontier. Also, on the 15th, the British release the captured militia and the wounded regulars, all of whom are sent back across the river. The officers, after being paroled, except for a few, including Major Mullany (pointed out as a British subject), are also returned. Meanwhile, the non-commissioned officers and enlisted men are taken to Montreal, where they are detained until exchanged. The officers who stormed the fort included John Ellis Wool, Henry B. Armstrong (son of General John Armstrong), Richard Malcolm, Peter Ogilvie, and Stephen Watts Kearny (later hero of the Mexican War and governor of California). Among the officers killed are Ensign Robert Morris, Lieutenant Rathbone, and Lieutenant Valleau. Also, General Nathaniel Watson participates at this battle.

October 14 (Wednesday) *In naval activity,* the British privateer *Liverpool Packet* intercepts and seizes the 85-ton schooner *Polly* (H. Snow, master), which is transporting a cargo of rice and leather to Boston. The *Polly* is separate from the 84-ton schooner *Polly* seized on 11 August 1812, the 92-ton sloop *Polly* captured 28 July 1813, the schooner *Polly* seized on 13 August 1813, the 88-ton schooner *Polly* overtaken 10 December 1813, and the 45-ton sloop *Polly* captured on 10 August 1814.

The *Liverpool Packet* also seizes the schooner *Union,* transporting a cargo of corn and flour from Philadelphia to Kennebec, Maine. The *Union* is separate from the brigantine *Union* seized on 14 August 1812, the ship *Union* seized on 16 August 1812, the schooner *Union* captured on 19 October 1812, the schooner *Union* seized on 3 April 1813, the ship *Union* seized on 26 June 1813 and the schooner *Union* captured 30 July 1814.

October 15 (Thursday) **In Ohio,** the construction of Fort Winchester is completed. Once a garrison force is chosen, the army advances to the north bank of the Maumee River (Richland Township) less than two miles below the mouth of the Auglaise River. The command at Camp H is suffering due to the changing weather and the shortage of winter clothing. The number of sick troops rises rapidly. Before long, the camp becomes too wet and damp, forcing another move. The new camp, designated Camp J, is also unsuitable, and the army moves yet again.

The next camp, still in Defiance County, is designated Camp Number Three. The conditions are much more tolerable; however, the army has sustained not only high casualties from sickness, but serious problems emerging from hunger and the lack of discipline that accompanies it.

General Harrison, at his headquarters in Franklinton (later Columbus), is continuing to press the government to get supplies to his forces. On this day, he writes to Secretary of War William Eustis that if autumn remains dry, he will recapture Detroit before winter arrives, but if the season brings a large amount of rain, his force would be compelled "to remain at the Rapids until the Miami of the Lake [Maumee] is sufficiently frozen over to bear the army and its baggage."

October 15 1812 to March 1813 *In naval activity,* the American privateer *Yankee* on or about this day embarks on its second cruise. Captain Oliver Wilson sets a course for Africa's west coast. During the cruise, it encounters and engages the 4-gun *Mary Ann,* a coppered sloop manned by only eleven men, commanded by Captain Sutherland. Captain Wilson orders the cargo (camwood, gold dust and ivory) transferred along with the crew, then the prize is burned. Later, the *Yankee* encounters and engages the 6-gun schooner *Alder,* manned by 21 men under Captain Crowley. The two ships bash each other, but the Americans destroy the *Alder's* quarter-deck with fire that kills seven men, including Captain Crowley. At that point, the British capitulate. The *Alder* had been carrying a cargo including musket flints, lead, iron and dry goods.

Captain Wilson observes a British vessel at anchor under the protection of Fort Appollonia with fifty mounted guns. A party from the *Yankee* boards and seizes the vessel, which is identified as the *Fly,* carrying a cargo including gold dust, gunpowder, ivory, iron and dry goods. The Americans sail out of the harbor with a 6-gun prize, manned by 14 men under Captain Tydeman. Captain Wilson orders a prize crew to take the *Fly* into an American port. Following the seizure of the *Fly,* the *Yankee* captures a brigantine out of Liverpool, the *Thames* carrying 8 guns and a crew of 14 under Captain Toole. The prize (separate from the *Thames* seized on 20 May 1813) is taken into port at Boston.

The *Yankee* afterward continues its successful cruise by intercepting the brigantine *Harriet and Matilda* carrying 8 guns and 14 men under Captain Inman. After it is captured, the Americans discover the *Harriet and Matilda* had initially been a Portuguese warship until seized by the British during 1808. The *Yankee* also seizes the brigantine *Shannon*, sometimes referred to as the *Andalusia* under Captain Kendall. The *Shannon*'s crew of 100 men included 81 free black men. It is taken into port at Savannah, Georgia.

The *Yankee* culminates its cruise and returns to port in March 1813 after being at sea for about 150 days. During the cruise, just under 200 prisoners were seized, along with eight British ships. The estimated value of the prizes was nearly $300,000.

October 16 (Friday) **In Washington, D.C.,** the commandant of the Marine Corps, unaware of the recent death of Captain John Williams at Twelve Mile Swamp, Florida, directs Lt. Alexander Sevier, who is on leave from Williams' command, to repair to St. Mary's, Georgia, and from there he is to report to Captain Williams at the camp of Colonel Smith, U.S. Army, or in his absence to report to Colonel Smith. Sevier is to take command of the Marines during the absence of Williams. Nevertheless, after word of the death of Williams reaches Washington, Sevier's orders are changed. On 19 October, new orders are cut. The commandant's letter states: "The official report of the death of Williams was received. You must now consider yourself as the officer detailed under the orders of the Department to receive the Command, late Williams, of the Marines, and will so proceed to the Camp near St. Augustine and report to Colonel Smith."

In Canada at Niagara during the last day of the armistice, the town is in mourning due to the death of General Brock. A huge funeral procession forms near Government House when the units, including regulars and militia, assemble for the procession which will escort his remains and those of Colonel McDonell to Fort George. Cannon fire greets the procession as it arrives at the fort, and the Americans at Fort Niagara fire a respectful salute to display their admiration of the fallen leader. The people also turn out in the thousands to pay their last respects. The procession, which begins at 1300 at Government House, stretches from the town nearly to the gates of the fort. Orders for the day include: "The officers will wear crape on their left arm and on their sword knots, and all officers throughout the Province will wear crape on their left arm for the space of one month. Capt. Holcroft will be pleased to direct that minute guns will be fired from the period of the body leaving Government House until its arrival at the place of interment, and also after the funeral service shall have been performed three rounds of seven guns from the artillery."

Upon arrival at Fort George, the remains of General Brock and Colonel McDonell are interred in the northeast bastion (Cavalier bastion). General Sheaffe succeeds General Brock. Later, during 1815, an act is passed by the Canadian Upper Parliament which authorizes the construction of a monument in honor of General Brock and his aide, Colonel McDonel. On 13 October 1824, a public funeral service is held in Queenston Heights where the remains of both General Brock and Colonel McDonel are re-interred in the monument. The funeral procession stretches about five miles long.

The following inscription was placed on the monument:

> The Legislature of Upper Canada has dedicated this monument to the very eminent civil and military services of the late Sir Isaac Brock, Knight of the Most Honorable Order of the Bath, Provincial Lieutenant-Governor and Major-General commanding the forces in this Province, whose remains are deposited in the vault beneath.
>
> Having expelled the North Western army of the United States, achieved its capture, received the surrender of Fort Detroit and the territory of Michigan, under circumstances which have rendered his name illustrious, he returned to the protection of this frontier, and advancing with his small forces to resist a second invasion of the enemy, then in possession of these Heights, he fell in action on the 13th of October 1812, in the forty-third year of his age, honored and beloved by the people whom he governed, and deplored by his Sovereign, to whose service his life had been devoted.

The casket of Colonel McDonel is laid to rest next to General Brock.

In naval activity, the British privateer *Liverpool Packet*, while on patrol for targets, spots the 134-ton schooner *Four Brothers* (J. Coombs, master), which is transporting some lumber from Machias, Maine, to New York. The *Liverpool Packet* seizes the schooner and its cargo. The *Four Brothers* is separate from the schooner *Four Brothers* captured 4 August 1813.

October 17 (Saturday) *In naval activity,* the HMS *Acasta* intercepts and recaptures the schooner *Blonde* (G.H. Gilbert, master). Also, the British privateer *Liverpool Packet* seizes the schooner *Little Joe*, which is transporting a cargo of pepper, sugar and other items from Boston to New York. The HMS *Maidstone* and the HMS *Spartan* encounter and engage the American privateer *Rapid* out of Portland, Maine. Despite having only fourteen guns, the crew refuses to capitulate. The privateer, unable to match the British firepower, makes a run to escape. The British initiate pursuit, but the *Rapid* continues to try to outrun its pursuers. During the prolonged chase, the crew of the *Rapid* tosses equipment overboard to gain speed. About eleven hours later, having discarded all of their guns and even the boats, the British finally seize it.

October 17–18 *In naval activity,* an engagement develops off the coast of Virginia between the 18-gun USS *Wasp*, commanded by Lieutenant Jacob Jones, when it encounters a convoy of 6 ships, some of which are armed, being escorted by the 22-gun HMS *Frolic*, commanded by Captain Winyates. The encounter occurs during the darkened hours of the 17th about 500 miles off Cape Hatteras; however, close contact is not made until the following morning. The sloop *Wasp* had recently returned from Europe

Captain Jacob Jones, U.S. Navy (*The History of the United States Navy [Biographical Sketches of American Naval Heroes]*, Charles J. Peterson, 1860).

following the declaration of war and after being refitted, embarked on this cruise. The battle begins at about 1130 on the 18th when the pesky *Wasp*, an agile, fast-sailing sloop, moves in close to the convoy and is hit by a British volley. The *Frolic* and the *Wasp* exchange broadsides from a distance of about 65 yards. British guns, within about five minutes, cause massive damage, taking out the *Wasp*'s main topmast. When it topples, it crashes upon braces which disable the headyards. Meanwhile, the British unleash more shots but the damage is not fatal. At nearly the same time, the *Frolic* loses its gaff along with the mizzen-topgallant mast. By this time, the *Wasp* also loses nearly all of its rigging.

Nevertheless, during the short burst of incessant fire, the *Wasp*, thought lost by the British, is actually still in operation. The *Wasp* unexpectedly appears at close range and delivers a broadside while the *Frolic* is on a down wave. The pounding penetrates the *Frolic*'s water line. At nearly the same time, the *Wasp* comes within touching range, from where the Americans snap off yet another blistering broadside, while two of the *Wasp*'s gun muzzles are literally within the bow ports of the *Frolic*.

Despite the punishing fire, the Americans sense that the British intend to continue the fight. Lieutenant Jones prepares to order yet another broadside at point-blank range; however, without orders, two of his crew, John Lang and Lt. Biddle, followed by others impulsively begin to board the *Frolic*. With swords drawn and pistols in hand, the Americans suddenly find only a few injured British officers and the seamen at the wheel on deck. Those men not injured had gone below to fight the water in the hull, leaving the deck free of organized resistance. The American boarding party immediately accepts the swords of the British officers. However, the scene remains ghastly due to the dead and wounded who are scattered about the deck. Casualties aboard the *Frolic* are estimated between 75 and 93.

Captain Winyates states in his report that "not twenty of his men escaped injury." His crew had been composed of about 107 men. Casualties under Lieutenant Jones, aboard the *Wasp*, totals five killed and five others wounded. The violent, close-quartered battle lasted just over forty minutes. The *Wasp* prepares to have a prize crew take the *Frolic* into port at Charleston, while the crew of the *Wasp* makes repairs before resuming. Nonetheless, before the plan can be carried out, the two damaged ships are spotted by another vessel, the 74-gun HMS *Poictiers*. The *Frolic* is recovered and the *Wasp* is captured. Both vessels are taken into a British port in Bermuda.

The *Wasp* was commissioned at an unknown time during 1807. Its record remains unknown until 1809, when it patrols along the U.S. coastline. In 1811, the *Wasp* arrives in Hampton Roads where it and the brigantine *Nautilus* are attached to the squadron being formed by Captain Stephen Decatur. The *Wasp*, however, is lost during this, its only hostile action. For a short while, the *Wasp* operates as the *Peacock* under the British ensign. It is lost off the Virginia Capes during 1813. The *Nautilus* had been captured the previous July.

Lieutenant Jones (brother of the secretary of the Navy William Jones), subsequent to his exchange, is promoted to the rank of captain, and Congress gives him a gold medal for his actions during the engagement with the *Frolic*. Captain Jones receives command of the *Macedonian*, a frigate; however, the British blockade has it locked into New York harbor. Jones is subsequently ordered to repair to the Lake Erie region. There he receives command of the USS *Mohawk* for the final year of the conflict.

October 18 (Sunday) *In naval activity,* the frigate USS *United States*, commanded by Captain Stephen Decatur, encounters and seizes the HMS *Swallow* and its cargo of coins. On the same cruise, the *United States* encounters the HMS *Macedonia* on 25 October. Also, the HMS *Maidstone* and the HMS *Spartan*, cruising together, intercept and seize the privateer *Rapid*, a brigantine operating out of Portland. At the time of its capture, the *Rapid* is carrying a cargo of ammunition, guns and some provisions.

October 19 (Monday) *In Europe,* the French pull out of Moscow and initiate a return trip to Prussia, but the withdrawal becomes a wild retreat. The relentless Russian winter pounces on the French, turning the westward march into a journey through hell. The French troops, lacking proper clothing and sufficient food and supplies, become easy prey for the Russians. Even the peasants seek vengeance. French stragglers are eliminated by both the Russians and the severe cold. Frozen corpses permeate the line of retreat. The French are also boldly attacked by Russian Horse Soldiers, who strike terror into the hearts of the French troops who at times are unable to even hold their weapons, which have become frozen. The retreat moves quickly from disorder to total disarray as the Grand Army is shattered. Only the fittest shall survive as the combination of Russian attacks and death-biting cold reduces Napoleon's finest to a rag-tag, tattered mob. As the desperate retreat continues toward Prussia, the ability and will to fight vanishes and the French look only toward survival from the deadly elements. The over-clothed Russian forces maintain the bludgeoning of the troops who do evade death by freezing or starvation. The French remnants, still led by Napoleon, that make it back to Prussia number only about 40,000, giving this French Grand Army the dubious honor of sustaining one of the most severe military defeats in the annals of history.

Napoleon finds no solace upon his return because in Prussia, which is a German state, forces have been working against him in his absence. High feelings of nationalism, incited by anti-French Prussians, set the stage for more violence as Prussia declares war against France during 1813. The ongoing conflict in Europe essentially works for the benefit of the U.S.; British troops in battle against Napoleon could be transferred to America, once Napoleon is stopped.

Many years later, during March 1941, another powerful Army, the German National Socialists dispatched by Adolf Hitler, will invade Russia and repeat the mistake; it too is poorly dressed and will incur the merciless wrath of a Russian winter. Similarly to this instance of Russia being an ally of France, when Russia is invaded by Germany, the two nations are allies.

In naval activity, the British privateer *Liverpool Packet* encounters and seizes the schooner *Anson* (John Smith, master) while it is transporting a cargo of china, salt and vinegar from Boston to Baltimore. Also, the HMS *Maidstone* and the HMS *Spartan*, while cruising together, intercept and seize the 83-ton schooner *Union*, which is carrying a cargo of fish. The *Union* is separate from like-named vessels also captured: a brigantine, 14 August 1812; a ship, 16 August 1812; a schooner, 14 October 1812; a schooner, 3 April 1813; a ship, 26 June 1813; and a schooner, 30 July 1814.

October 20 (Tuesday) *In Canada,* the village of Odelltown in Lower Canada near the Richelieu River is raided by an American contingent.

October 21 (Wednesday) *In Canada,* an American contingent surprises a group of Canadian voyagers under Captain McDonnell. Four are killed and four wounded, and the remainder (about 40) except one man who escapes, are captured, along with the British baggage.

In naval activity, the American privateer *Governor Gerry*, fitted for 18 guns, is launched at Fair Haven, Connecticut.

October 22 (Thursday) *In Canada,* Commodore Chauncey at French Mills sends out a small party which he describes as "confidential friends" to reconnoiter the Indian village of St. Regis. The party returns and informs Chauncey that British troops had arrived in the village and their number totals more than 100, with some estimates taking the total to several hundred. The intelligence also suggests that the British are preparing to mount an attack against headquarters at French Mills. Chauncey moves to take the place before more British troops arrive. A force is assembled and provided with two days' rations; however, Chauncey increases the whiskey rations by doubling them. At 2300, the column departs from camp and marches along a circuitous route to attempt to gain surprise. At 0330 on the 23rd, the column reaches Gray's Mills, where Chauncey is informed that "two cribs of boards" had been discovered, along with one boat and one canoe. The column crosses the river and arrives just outside the village by 0500. Chauncey suspends the march to allow time to eat some food, send out a reconnaissance patrol and plan the final step of the assault.

Afterward, he detaches Captain Lyon's company with orders to maintain silence while advancing down the road that runs along the bank of the river until he reaches the rear of the home of British Captain Montaigny and one other house (Donally's) from where he can sever the escape route. While Chauncey advances directly toward Montaigny's house, he detaches Captain Tilden, who moves to the St. Lawrence to secure the boats of the British and positions his command within view of Donally's property.

In the meantime, Lyon's force arrives near the house, and by the time Chauncey reaches a point about 150 yards from Montaigny's front property, the sounds of gunfire make it clear that Captain Lyon's command is in action. The skirmish is short and Chauncey's force seizes 40 prisoners. The British also lose four killed and one fatally wounded. The Americans seize one stand of colors, two bateaux and 28 guns.

Afterward, the troops re-cross the river and return to their camp. During the operation at St. Regis, located along the border between Canada and the United States, Lt. William Marcy (later 11th governor of New York) captures a British flag.

The British report that twenty men had been at the outpost, and of those, six men, including Lieutenant Rotette and Sergeant McGillivray, were among the fatalities. The others, according to the British, were taken as captives. Also, the British reject the American claim that a stand of colors was seized, claiming that the British flag which was confiscated was taken from "the cupboard of the wigwam of the Indian interpreter." The British mock the seizure: "This windfall was announced to the world as the 'capture of a stand of colors,' the first colors taken during the war. Dozens of them might have been obtained at far less cost, in any American shipyard."

In Ohio, General Harrison, at Franklin (later Columbus), remains unsure of when the advance against Detroit can begin. He writes to William Eustis, the secretary of war, of the situation: "I am not able to fix any period for the advance of troops to Detroit. It is pretty evident that it cannot be done upon proper principles until the frost shall become so severe as to enable us to use the rivers and the margin of the lake for transportation of the baggage and artillery upon the ice." Harrison also informs the secretary that it would be "absolutely impossible" to try to move his force 200 miles through the swamps and wilderness, using wagons or packhorses. Harrison intends to reach Upper Sandusky and remain there while supplies and provisions are acquired, and from there he will use sleds to move the items to the Raisin River.

Later, this month, General Harrison orders General Reasin Beall, encamped at Mansfield, to depart from there with his force (about 500 men) and repair to the mouth of the Huron River to join General Elijah Wadsworth, who holds there with about 800 men. Brigadier General Simon Perkins will assume command of these and other forces in that area, which will form the right wing of Harrison's Northwestern Army. This force is directed by Harrison to carve a road leading from Fort Stephenson to the foot of the lowest rapids.

In naval activity, the American privateer *Rossie* (Commodore Joshua Barney) intercepts an American vessel, the ship *Merrimack*, and discovers it is an outlaw.

October 23 (Friday) **In Canada,** an American contingent attacks the Indian post at St. Regis.

In New York, General Stephen Van Rensselaer writes to Governor Tompkins that he has permission from General Dearborn to resign his command and that he is leaving immediately for Albany. Van Rensselaer had essentially resigned due to the failure at Queenston. General Alexander Smyth, who did not participate at the battle and had not been an ally of Van Rensselaer, succeeds General Van Rensselaer.

October 24 (Saturday) *In naval activity,* the British privateer *General Smyth* seizes the 89-ton schooner *Lydia*. The *Lydia* is separate from the schooner *Lydia* seized on 4 April 1813 and the schooner *Lydia* captured on 7 August 1813. In other naval activity, the HMS *Peruvian* intercepts and seizes the American privateer *Yankee American*, a 7-gun schooner with a crew of 40 men, commanded by Captain T. Pillsbury (successor to Captain Stanwood, who commanded the privateer on its initial voyage). The *Yankee American* is among a group of privateers out of Rhode Island or manned primarily by Rhode Islanders with the name "Yankee." These include the *Yankee*, the *True Blooded Yankee*, the *Yankee Lass* and the *Yankee Porter*. The *Yankee* and the *True Blooded Yankee* are the most prominent. Rhode Island, the smallest of the states, also commits some other privateers, but they do not score significant recognition. These are the *Waterwitch*, *Hiram*, *Hunter*, *Juno* and the *Swift*. One other privateer from Rhode Island is the *Governor Gerry*. It carries 18 guns and is launched but it gets to sea too late to capture any prizes.

October 25 (Sunday) *In naval activity,* Captain Stephen Decatur, commander of the frigate USS *United States*, sends his squadron toward the Mediterranean while he cruises alone near the Canary Islands off the coast of Africa. At a point between the Azores and the Cape Verdi Islands, the *United States* spots a frigate, the 38-gun *Macedonian*. The British spot the *United States* at about the same time but are not sure of its country of origin. Just after breakfast, the British lookout's voice bellows: "Sail ahoy." The captain inquires and after some back and forth the lookout informs the captain that the ship is a large frigate. The crew is ordered to maintain silence, but still the origin remains unknown. The British, according to a crew member, stare ahead in hopes that it is a French ship rather than American. Nevertheless, it is soon identified as an American vessel.

Instantly, the fife and drums signal all hands to report to their battle stations. The British, except for the band, to a man prepare to engage. Only one Englishman is on the sick list, but once the call to battle stations is heard, he bolts from his cot to participate. The British warship also has Americans aboard and one, John Card, reports to the captain and states that he will not fight an American vessel. The captain orders him to his quarters and threatens Card, stating that if he mentions it again, he will be shot. Card is later killed by the American fire.

The *Macedonian* for awhile is able to remain in the distance. Nevertheless, the *United States* finally closes the gap sufficiently to engage with its long guns. Suddenly, the two antagonists begin to exchange fire, and once again the British discover that the effectiveness of the American guns surpasses that of the British. A member of the British crew describes the action:

> Thus we all stood, awaiting orders, in motionless suspense. At last we fired three guns from the larboard [port] side of the main-deck; this was followed by the command, Cease firing; you are throwing away your shot! Then came the order to wear ship, and prepare to attack the enemy with our starboard guns. Soon after this, I heard a firing from some other quarter ... a strange noise, such as I had never heard before, next arrested my attention; it sounded like the tearing of sails, just over our heads. This I soon ascertained to be the wind of the enemy's shot. The firing, after a few minutes cessation, recommenced. The roaring of cannon could now be heard from all parts of our trembling ship, and, mingling as it did with that of our foes, it made a most hideous noise. By-and-by I heard the shot strike the sides of our ship; the whole scene grew indescribably confused and horrible; it was like some awfully tremendous thunder-storm, whose deafening roar is attended by incessant streaks of lightning, carrying death in every flash, and strewing the ground with the victims of its wrath: only, in our case, the scene was rendered more horrible than that, by the presence of torrents of blood which dyed our deck.

USS *United States* captures the *Macedonian* (*Life and Character of Stephen Decatur,* S. Putnam Waldo, 1822).

Captain John Surman Carden of the *Macedonian* is dismayed after being unable to destroy the *United States* from long range, and to his further distress, the American ship scores devastating damage and inflicts casualties by its rapid incessant fire. As the two ships move into closer range following about 30 minutes of exchanging blows, both sides resort to their respective carronades (short guns), but yet again, the British, who anticipate victory, sustain more severe damage that cripples the *Macedonian* and knocks it out of action. The same witness, a young boy at gun No. 5, further describes the action: "Grape and canister-shot were pouring through our port-holes like leaden rain, carrying death in their trail. The large shot came against the ship's side like iron hail, shaking her to the very keel, or passing through her timbers, and scattering terrific splinters, which did more appalling work than even their own death giving blows."

By this time, the *United States*' guns had destroyed the *Macedonian*'s main mast, along with its fore topmast and mizzen mast. In addition, its main yard had been severed. During the relentless bombardment, the British colors had vanished. The battered *Macedonian* had sustained heavy casualties and fatal damage, including about 100 hits in its hull. After being hailed by the *United States*, a response was received that its colors had been struck. Captain Decatur, after taking possession of the *Macedonian*, takes it into New York. The *United States* sustains some damage to its rigging, but otherwise it remains mostly unharmed and quite seaworthy.

Aboard the USS *United States*, according to the report of Decatur, five privates were killed. One lieutenant (Lt. John Musser Funk) and six privates were wounded. The British sustain 36 killed and 68 wounded. The *Macedonian* had seven Americans aboard who had been impressed into the Royal Navy and of those, two were killed. Upon his arrival in New York, on 1 January 1813, Captain Decatur and his crew receive a hero's welcome. Congress, once informed of Decatur's victory, duplicates its show of thanks to Captain Hull for his victory over the *Guerriere* the previous August.

Captain Decatur is given a gold medal and each of his officers receives a silver medal; the crew gets $50,000 in prize money. One British sailor notes after the battle: "Our part of the ship [*Macedonian*] was called slaughter house ... Nelson's red paint could not conceal blood spilled here." The *Macedonian* is the only captured British warship to arrive in an American harbor in sailing condition during the entire war. The *United States* and the *Macedonian* arrive at New London on 4 December.

Nonetheless, the magnitude of the blockade established by the Royal Navy neutralizes the vessel's capture. The USS *United States* and its popular prize, the 49-gun *Macedonian*, are both isolated in New London, Connecticut, unable to penetrate the blockade.

Back in England, when word of the defeat of the *Macedonian* arrives, the news is totally rejected as false. By the following day, the defeat is confirmed. Gloom begins to permeate London while the British continue to ponder the loss of the *Guerriere* and now face another grievous loss to the fleet at the hands of the insolent Yankees. The London *Times* had initially proclaimed: "There is a report that another English frigate, the *Macedonia*, has been captured by an American. We shall certainly be very backward in believing a second recurrence of such a national disgrace.... Certainly there was a time when it would not have been believed that the American navy could have appeared upon the high seas after a six months' war with England; much less that it could, within that period, have been twice victorious."

On the following day, the *Times* prints: "In the name of God, what was done with this immense superiority of force!" The *Times* follows on the third day with another less than optimistic statement: "Oh, what a charm is hereby dissolved! What hopes will be excited in the breasts of our enemies! The land spell of the French is broken [alluding to Napoleon's disastrous retreat from Moscow], and so is our sea spell."

Another London publication, the *Chronicle*, expresses its sentiments by inquiring: "Is it not sickening to see that no experience has been sufficient to rouse our Admiralty to take such measures that may protect the British flag from such disgrace."

British Captain Carden receives a court-martial, which convenes on 27 May 1813. After several days of testimony, the court, held aboard the HMS *San Domingo* at Bermuda, acquits Captain Carden: "The Court is of opinion, that Captain John Surman Carden, his officers and ships' company, in every instance throughout the action, behaved with the firmest and most determined courage, resolution and coolness; and that the colours of the *Macedonian* were not struck until it was unable to make further resistance. The Court does therefore most honorably acquit Captain John Surman Carden, the officers and company, of H. M. late ship *Macedonian*; and Captain Carden, his officers, and company, are hereby most honorably acquitted accordingly."

As 1812 comes to a close and word of the disasters inflicted upon the Royal Navy arrive back in England, it becomes apparent to the Admiralty that the U.S. Navy would not easily be humbled; still, the Admiralty rejects any idea that the pygmy-sized American navy presents a challenge to Britain's domination of the high seas.

October 27 (Tuesday) *In naval activity,* Captain David Porter, U.S. Navy, aboard the USS *Essex*, embarks to rendezvous with Commodore Bainbridge to participate in a cruise with the USS *Constitution* and the USS *Hornet*. Porter, according to a later letter to the secretary of the Navy, departs from the Delaware this day and sails to "Port Praya, Fernandode Noronho and Camp Frio." While en route, the *Essex* seizes the packet HMS *Nocton*. Porter removes about eleven pounds sterling from the *Nocton* before assigning Lt. Finch to sail it back to the United States.

While cruising off Rio de Janeiro and Cape Frio in January 1813, he seizes a schooner and has it taken into port at Rio. The *Essex* sails around Cape Horn during early February 1813 in search of British vessels. Porter, after surviving a horrific storm on 3 February, arrives in Chile during March 1813, where he harasses the British whaling industry throughout the year. The British do not catch up with Porter and the USS *Essex* until February 1814.

October 28 (Wednesday) *In naval activity,* according to the U.S. Naval Historical Division, Captain Bainbridge (previously captain of the *Philadelphia*, captured at Tripoli) departs Boston Harbor on this day, sailing the USS *Constitution* toward Central America. An encounter with a British vessel occurs at the end of the year when the *Constitution* locates the distant sails of the HMS *Java*. The 18-gun brigantine USS *Hornet* accompanies the *Constitution*; however, during the journey, the *Hornet*, commanded by Captain James Lawrence, halts at either San Salvador or Bahia, Brazil, to wait out a British brigantine which is carrying a large amount of specie. Nonetheless, the British frigate remains in port after declining repeated challenges from Captain Lawrence to engage.

October 31 (Saturday) **In Illinois** at Camp Russell (Fort Russell), Colonel William Russell, commander of a contingent of U.S. Rangers, writes to Acting Secretary of War James Monroe of his arrival at the camp from Vincennes and of the fact that he had been joined by Territorial Governor Ninian Edwards and his contingent of mounted riflemen, which had increased the strength to about 300 men. The combined force had moved deep into Indian territory with expectations of linking with the force of General Hopkins, which had departed from Vincennes for Fort Harrison (Indiana). The appointed place for the two forces to join had been at the Peoria towns located along the Illinois River. Colonel Russell informs the secretary that the 13-day expedition inflicted punishment on the Indians, but the failure of making contact with Hopkins impeded the mission and prevented Russell and Governor Edwards from accomplishing further success. Nonetheless, the American force struck Pimartam's town, about 20 miles from Peoria, and others were forced to cross the Illinois River. The Indians flee with such haste that their plunder is left in the village. The precise number of Indian casualties remains unknown; however, Governor Edwards places their losses at about twenty killed. The Indians also leave about 80 horses behind and abandon a large amount of corn. American casualties amount to four men wounded. Colonel Russell, in closing his letter, states: "This tour was performed, from this camp, and back to this place, in 13 days."

Fort Russell was established just outside of Edwardsville in Madison County. It is used as a primarily post in the Illinois Territory (carved from the Indiana Territory) as a base of operations for the troops in the region and as a supply depot.

In naval activity, a British squadron — composed of the HMS *Curlew*, HMS *Nymphe*, HMS *Shannon* and the HMS *Tenedos* — intercepts and seizes the brigantine *Thorn*, a 291-ton privateer manned by 124 men out of Marblehead and carrying 18 guns. The *Thorn* is separate from the schooner *Thorn* captured on 8 November 1813 and the schooner *Thorn* seized on 11 July 1814.

November **In Ohio,** General Edward Tupper at Fort McArthur moves out of the fort with about 700 Ohio militia troops on a mission to the rapids of the Maumee River near the place where General Wayne had defeated the Indians at the Battle of Fallen Timbers during 1794; however, the operation fails. He is compelled to return to the fort. Tupper's force is part of General Harrison's army and is scheduled to participate in Harrison's expedition to regain Detroit.

In naval activity, the U.S. Navy acquires the schooner *Ferret* at Charleston, South Carolina. It is assigned patrol duty in the South Carolina region, particularly in the inlets and sounds, to protect shipping.

Also, at about this time (autumn 1812), the American privateer *Highflyer* (Captain J. Grant), a 5-gun schooner operating out of Baltimore, intercepts and captures the British packet *Burchall*, while the latter is sailing from Barbados to Demara (South America).

November 1 (Sunday) **In Ohio,** General James Winchester, in an effort to encourage the troops at Fort Winchester who have been disheartened by the conditions there, issues the following general orders: "With great pleasure, the general announces to the army the prospect of an early supply of winter clothing, amongst which are the following articles shipped from Philadelphia on the 9th of September last: 10,000 pairs of shoes, 5,000 blankets, 5,000 round jackets, 5,000 pairs pantaloons, woolen cloth to be made up, besides the underclothing for Colonel Well's regiment 100 watch coats, and 1,000 yards of flannel, 10,000 pairs of wool socks, 10,000 wool hose."

Nonetheless, these supplies do not arrive at Fort Winchester. By now, the fort and nearby camps have been overwhelmed with sickness and hard hit by a typhoid fever epidemic. More than 300 troops are sick and three or four soldiers die daily. Some of the troops who departed from Kentucky the previous August still wear the clothes they wore when they left Kentucky, and the clothes have turned to rags. Others who had earlier rushed to relieve Fort Wayne had left many of their belongings at Piqua. Essentially, the troops are paralyzed by the weather and the sickness, unable to march any distance even if necessary. Because a large number of men lack shoes, they are compelled to remain close to the camp fires or face being frozen to death.

November 6 (Friday) *In naval activity,* the privateer *America,* commanded by Captain Ropes, after sailing for about one month with no contact with British shipping, encounters an unidentified sail and initiates pursuit. After closing on the brigantine *Benjamin* (Captain James Collins), the Americans board it and take possession. A prize crew takes it into an American port.

November 8 (Sunday) **In New York,** Captain Isaac Chauncey, having recently put his squadron together at Sackets Harbor, departs from there to cruise on Lake Ontario in search of the British squadron, including the HMS *Royal George*. The *Royal George* (260-man crew) is en route from Fort George to Kingston, Canada. It is accompanied by the 18-gun *Earl of Moira* (200-man crew), and the schooners 18-gun *Prince Regent* (150-man crew), 14-gun *Duke of Gloucester* (80-man crew), 12-gun *Simcoe* (76-man crew) and the 4-gun *Seneca* (40-man crew).

Commodore Chauncey's squadron includes the *Oneida* (Lt. Woolsey), *Conquest* (Lt. Elliot), *Hamilton* (Lt. McPherson), *Governor Tompkins* (Lt. Brown), *Pert* (sailing master Arundel), *Julia Tompkins* (sailing master Trant), and *Growler* (sailing master Mix). Commodore Chauncey's squadron carries a total of forty guns and the combined crews total 430 men, including Marine contingents.

The British warship is detected off False Duck Island during the afternoon. A chase ensues; however, the *Royal George* manages to enter the Bay of Quinte and under cover of darkness it evades the American squadron. Nonetheless, contact is again made on the following day.

November 9 (Monday) **In Ohio,** General Tupper's detachment that was sent to the Maumee Rapids returns with a British officer as a prisoner and intelligence that leads him to decide to initiate an operation against the British who remain there. He writes to Governor Meigs that he intends to "capture these British or drive them from the Rapids to save the corn." The intelligence gained by Captain Hinkston's patrol and from their prisoner places the force at about 75 British troops and between 300 and 400 Indians. The captured officer also provides details on the English headquarters at Malden (later Amherstberg) and at Detroit. With regard to Detroit, the officer offered that the post had been aware of General Winchester, but the British had been of the belief that his force would remain at Defiance until the following spring.

In naval activity, the USS *Constitution,* which sailed from Boston late in the last month en route to South America, encounters and captures the brigantine *South Carolina.*

November 9–10 *In naval activity,* Captain Isaac Chauncey's squadron spots the HMS *Royal George* on Lake Ontario on the 9th. A chase continues until daylight is lost and the *Oneida* enters the Bay of Quinte. The *Royal George,* commanded by Commodore Hugh Earle, remains concealed in the darkness throughout the night; however, on the morning of the 10th, although contact is not immediately made, the squadron does encounter and destroy a British schooner. Just afterward, contact with the *Royal George* is regained. It is spotted as it sails toward Kingston. Captain Chauncey, with the greater part of his squadron, renews the pursuit and trails the British warship directly into port at Kingston.

The *Conquest* and the *Julia* hold the point and come under fire from the *Royal George* and the land batteries. The land batteries and the Americans exchange blows for about one hour, before Chauncey retires at about dusk to reposition his ships in deeper water. While exchanging fire with the batteries, the Americans sustain eight wounded and one man is killed. Five of the casualties result from an accident when one of the naval guns explodes.

At the time Chauncey withdraws, the winds become stronger, and by the following morning (10th), the winds increase further and remain in the area for about 48 hours. Nevertheless, the *Royal George* remains aloof. The Americans, however, spot the HMS *Simcoe,* while they conclude that the weather is too nasty to resume their attack from within the harbor. The *Simcoe* comes under fire by the *Hamilton* and the *Julia* and sustains damage; however, it makes it across a reef and reaches safety. Another British vessel, the cruiser HMS *Seneca,* is attacked and afterward sunk.

The weather continues to deteriorate as a strong snow storm moves in behind the heavy gales. The elements fail to convince Chauncey to abort the cruise. Anticipating support from the approaching harsh winter, he deploys four ships of his squadron to keep the harbor at Kingston blocked until it ices over. In the meantime, Captain Chauncey sails toward the head of Lake George in search of another British warship, the HMS *Prince Regent,* known to be operating near York (Toronto). The ongoing search for the *Prince Regent* fails. Chauncey returns with his squadron, and by the beginning of December, Lake Erie receives a new dominant force, the Canadian winter, which closes the lake for navigation.

Also during this mission, the *Growler* captures a sloop, the *Elizabeth,* which had been escorted by the HMS *Earl of Moira.* The *Elizabeth* is carrying a relative of the late General Brock, and the relative is carrying the personal effects and correspondence of General Brock. The relative is paroled and the Americans return his property.

During the winter, Captain Chauncey continues to concentrate on building projects to provide more sea power when spring arrives. He writes to the governor following the mission:

> On the 14th we got sight of the *Earl of Moira,* entering Kingston harbor, but it blowing a gale of wind, we concluded not to follow, and after beating about almost all that day, I made the signal for all the squadron to bear for this place, where we arrived on the same evening. During these two short cruises we captured three vessels, two have arrived, one we burnt, a fourth was so injured that she sunk, and we learn from one who came in the flags yesterday, that the *Royal George* was so much injured that she had to haul on shore to keep from sinking, having received several shots between wind and water, several guns disabled, and a number of persons killed or wounded, besides considerable injury (though not intentional) to the town. Amongst the prisoners is Capt. Brock of the 29th regiment, and a relative of the late Gen. Brock, who was returning from York with part of the baggage of his deceased friend. Our loss was trifling; one man killed and four wounded, two of the latter by the bursting of a gun on board of the *Pert,* the commander of which vessel, Mr. Arundell, was knocked overboard and drowned. The damage done to the rigging and sails not much, and a few shot in the hulls of one of the vessels, but the injury from which was soon repaired. The *Governor Tompkins, Hamilton, Conquest,* and *Growler,* are now blockading the vessels in Kingston. I am taking on board guns and stores for Niagara, for which place I shall sail the first wind, in company with the *Julia, Pert, Fair American, Ontario* and *Scourge,* and I am in great hopes that I shall fall in with the *Prince Regent,* or some of the royal family which are cruising about York. Had we been one month sooner we could have taken every town on this lake in three weeks, but the season is now so tempestuous that I am apprehensive we can not do much more this winter. I am, however, ready to cooperate with the army, and our officers and men are anxious to be engaged.

November 10 (Tuesday) **In Maryland,** Commodore Joshua Barney arrives back in Baltimore following a successful cruise aboard the privateer *Rossie.* It seizes 8 brigantines, 3 schooners, 4 ships and 3 sloops with a total estimated value of more than $1.5 million. Barney's crew had captured, in all, about 3,600 tons of shipping and about 217 prisoners. Of the prizes, seven were burned at sea. Barney delegates one of the brigantines as a cartel which transports most of the prisoners to Newfoundland. This cruise is the final service of Barney as a privateer during the war. He returns to the U.S. Navy.

In Ohio, General Tupper advances toward the Maumee Rapids in search of a British force that had arrived with a large band of Indians to confiscate corn that was planted earlier by the Americans. Tupper's force is bolstered by one light 6-pounder. The column, composed of 650 troops, travels along a road carved out earlier by General Hull's army. Despite having the road to follow, the journey is arduous and the mud hinders progress. The artillery piece becomes so cumbersome that General Tupper leaves it behind at one of the forts they pass. The Americans finally encroach the suspected British positions and scouts report that the encampment is active.

General Tupper plans his attack for the following morning; however, he orders a crossing to be made at once. The water is frigid and about waist-high. The first section makes it across the river without difficulty; however, the second section gets caught by the current, which carries some of the troops downstream. Thanks to the horses with the column, the men are rescued and only their weapons are lost. The unexpected mishap prompts General Tupper to recall those who reached the north bank to consolidate the column.

The next morning, Tupper sends out a few scouts who are to draw out the British and convince them to pursue. The British do not take the bait. Undaunted, General Tupper advances briskly to a spot which displays his entire contingent. The Indians and British are startled. Squaws break for the woods while the British flee to nearby boats, leaving only Indians to raise resistance. The Americans come under fire, including artillery fire from the north bank, but very few mounted Indians are seen crossing the river when Tupper feints a withdrawal to tempt the Indians to give chase.

Afterward, when it seems clear that the Indians had decided not to fight, overconfidence causes some troops to disregard their orders by wandering away to gather corn and some others decide to attempt to catch some hogs that are near the lines. All the while, the troops are under observance and those who strayed come under a swift and unexpected attack that kills four of the men. Acting as quickly as possible, the rest return fire and repel the mounted Indians.

Chief Split-log, who crossed over to the south bank above the American positions, arrives with his main body. By that time, Bentley's battalion is in place to engage the enemy. A fierce skirmish develops; however, Bentley's troops prevail by forcing the Indians to withdraw. With provisions nearly exhausted, General Tupper returns to Fort McArthur rather than remain and try to subsist on the corn that settlers had planted before being forced by the Indians to abandon their homes. When the force began its return to the post, they discover that one soldier, who became ill, had been accidentally left behind. He was discovered by the Indians and victimized by the tomahawk and also scalped. General Tupper, during this mission, had twice sent word to General Winchester to send reinforcements; however he fails to send word that he is retreating.

On the 15th, the relief column heads down the Maumee, advancing along the north bank, and this day, Tupper's second message is delivered at Fort Winchester. The message is relayed to the column under Colonel William S. Lewis, who upon receiving it, accelerates the speed of the advance only to cause the force to become exhausted on the 2nd night out. Lewis sends a small detachment under Ensign (later colonel) Charles S. Todd to move ahead and reconnoiter. The party is accompanied by five guides. The men discover no signs of life after they cross the river, but there are obvious signs that the force had made a hurried retreat. Once they enter the deserted camp, they discover the mutilated corpse of the one man left behind. Without delay, the detachment returns to Lewis' position to inform him of the empty camp.

Once informed that Tupper had retreated, Colonel Lewis departs from the area and marches toward Encampment Number 3. The column, because of exhaustion and the imminent possibility of being attacked, moves cautiously. Camp fires are prohibited during darkness to prevent the Indians from spotting their position. The column receives food from a detachment of scouts, including Captain John Logan and some other Shawnees, that had been dispatched by General Harrison on a reconnaissance mission to the river. After the troops make it back to Encampment Number 3, General Winchester is informed of the hazardous return march and the large Indian force that gave chase; however, the general is unconvinced of the veracity of the statements. Captain John Logan takes personal offense at General Winchester's doubts about his loyalty to the United States. He decides to take the trip again to remove all doubts. He departs on the 22nd.

In naval activity, the British privateer *Liverpool Packet*, operating off the New England coast, intercepts and seizes the 108-ton schooner *Edward and Hiram*, which is en route from Nantucket to Kennebec with a cargo that includes cheese and leather.

November 11 (Wednesday) In Indiana, General Samuel Hopkins' force departs from Fort Harrison en route to Prophet's Town. While the column, composed of about 1,200 troops, advances toward the Upper Wabash, a flotilla of seven boats under Lt. Colonel William Butler is moving upriver with the force's provisions and supplies. Hopkins moves cautiously in case the Indians have established any ambush sites. The journey remains slow moving and the march is also impeded by high waters and some heavy rain.

In naval activity, the British privateer *Liverpool Packet*, while on patrol, intercepts and captures the 97-ton sloop *Lucretia*, which is en route from Boston to Savannah, Georgia, with a cargo of beef, butter and candles. The *Liverpool Packet* also seizes the 47-ton schooner *New Forge*, which is en route from New York to Boston with a cargo of sugar, wheat and other items.

November 12 (Thursday) In Massachusetts at Salem, the townspeople, infuriated at a British privateer known as the *Liverpool Packet* that has been disrupting shipping, decide to capture it. A group of 69 men under Captain John Upton borrow a vessel, the *Helen*. At the docks, following a parade, the crew loads some cannon and ammunition aboard. By the following morning the *Helen* gets underway, only to discover that the privateer had departed for Halifax on the previous day. The pursuers believe sympathizers had forewarned the British crew. Despite missing their target, they do capture the American Samuel Yorke, who served aboard the privateer while it was operating off Massachusetts. He is seized shortly after arriving back on shore and he shows no remorse. In addition, he implies that the *Liverpool Packet* and the *Sir John Sherbrooke*, another British privateer, are both owned by Americans.

This *Liverpool Packet* is separate from another privateer also named *Liverpool Packet*, which remains active throughout the war and captures more than fifty prizes. Meanwhile, the *Liverpool Packet* that has eluded capture is shortly thereafter seized by the Americans and turned into an American privateer named the *Young Teazer's Ghost*. (See also, **July 13** [1813], *In naval activity.*)

November 13 (Friday) *In naval activity,* the British privateer *Liverpool Packet* intercepts and seizes the 80-ton schooner *Julian*, which is en route from Boston to New York with a cargo of fish, oil and salt. The *Julian* is separate from the *Julian* seized on 8 December 1813, the *Julian* seized on 6 August 1814 and the *Julian* captured on 17 November 1814.

November 14 (Saturday) In Indiana, General Hopkins' column, which had departed from Fort Harrison on the 11th, arrives at Sugar Creek, but the force remains several days from the objective. Hopkins avoids advancing on the west bank of the Wabash and pushes forward on the east bank, which he believes is less likely to contain an ambush site. Nevertheless, the column arrives at Prophet's Town on the 19th.

November 15 (Sunday) In Ohio, General Harrison writes to Secretary of War William Eustis that he now believes it is too late in the season to advance his army beyond the Maumee Rapids because the task of transporting the supplies would be "insurmountable." General Harrison also writes to Governor Shelby of Kentucky on this day to share his disappointment: "I know it will be mortifying to Kentucky for this army to return without doing anything; but it is better to do that than to attempt impossibilities.... In my opinion, we should in this quarter disband all but those sufficient for a strong frontier guard, convoys, etc., and prepare for the next season."

The entire region around Fort Winchester is hit by incessant rain storms toward the latter part of this month that totally devastate logistics. Moving supplies and provisions through the "Black Swamp" regions becomes a perpetual nightmare as the drivers attempt to push through mud that reaches at least 20 inches deep. Consequently, the troops are always short of food. By the first of December it becomes necessary for orders to be issued to construct huts because their worn tents are no longer a match for the incoming frigid weather and pouring rain. The animals also endure much pain from a variety of reasons, primarily from lack of food, but many other horses are lost due to the carelessness of drivers who fail to properly assess the conditions of the deplorable roads. If the conditions could be condensed into one word, abominable would suffice.

November 17 (Tuesday) In Canada, the British at St. Philips receive intelligence that an American army under General Henry Dearborn is on the march and closing toward Odelltown. A contingent including several companies and about 300 Indians moves out toward the Lacole River. Afterward, additional troops trail the lead units.

November 18 (Wednesday) American General Alexander Smyth, who had recently assumed command of the troops at Buffalo following the resignation of General Van Rensselaer, now has 4,000 men under him when an additional 2,000 men arrive from Pennsylvania. This influx of additional soldiers causes Smyth to consider another invasion of Canada. Recently, Smyth had boasted in a proclamation to his troops on 10 November: "In a few days, the troops under my command will plant the American standard in Canada to conquer or to die. Men of New York, you deserve your share of fame. Then seize the present moment. If you do not, you will regret it; say the valiant bled in vain, the friends of my country fell and I was not there."

In naval activity, the British privateer *Liverpool Packet* intercepts and captures the 80-ton brigantine Economy (R. Homes, master), which is en route from Alexandria, Virginia, to Boston with a cargo of corn, flour and cigars.

November 18–19 *In naval activity,* the privateer *America* spots an unidentified sail and initiates pursuit. The stranger is able to complicate the chase and the *America* at times loses sight. It persists, and on the 19th, permanent contact is established. The American finally get its prey, the 8-gun *Ralph Nickerson,* en route to England from Quebec with a cargo of lumber. The prize is diverted to Salem, Massachusetts.

November 19 (Thursday) **In Canada,** American General Henry Dearborn reluctantly calls off his attack on Montreal when his militia refuses to cross the Canadian border based on what they consider to be their constitutional right. This action dispels any future thoughts of Dearborn's army invading Canada. By 23 November, Dearborn's command withdraws; regulars are returning to bases within the United States and militia are heading home.

In other activity, General Alexander Smyth informs the British at Fort Erie that the armistice agreed up earlier by General Van Rensselaer and British General Sheaffe will terminate in 36 hours. The notice is in accordance with the pact that either side will give 36 hours' notice before reopening hostilities.

In Indiana, General Samuel Hopkins' column arrives without incident near Prophet's Town. Hopkins sends a 300-man contingent to attack a Winnebago town at Ponce Passu Creek about 4 miles from Prophet's Town; however, the Indians had abandoned it. On the following day (20th), the troops begin to reduce Prophet's Town, but they don't completely destroy it until the 22nd. During the operation, they also destroy a nearby large Kickapoo village. The Indians, however, strike part of Hopkins' command on the 21st and 22nd. Hopkins terminates the mission on the 25th and returns to Fort Harrison.

November 20 (Friday) **In Canada,** an officer detects an American force (part of General Henry Dearborn's army) under Colonel Zebulon Pike moving into Canada from Champlain Town. The British raise resistance, but the darkness hinders the action. Neither side seems intent on a serious clash. One American unit misidentifies a friendly contingent as British and friendly fire inflicts about 10 casualties. Afterward, the Americans retire and move back to their camp. General Dearborn is not with the force, nor is either General John Chandler or General Joseph Bloomfield. Following this clash the Americans move into winter quarters with Chandler at Burlington and Bloomfield at Plattsburgh. Dearborn had not even once led his army into battle. At the time of Dearborn's advance into Canada only a few British regulars were in the area.

November 21 (Saturday) **In Canada and New York,** the Americans at Fort Niagara and the British at Fort George engage in an artillery battle throughout the day. At 0600, the British at Fort George (Canada) and their other nearby batteries commence a bombardment of Fort Niagara. According to Lt. Colonel McFeeley, commander at Niagara, the bombardment continues "without intermission, until after sun-down. They had 5 detached batteries; 2 mounting 24 pounders, 1 mounting a 9 pounder, and 2 mortar batteries; one ten and a half, and the other five and a half inch-the batteries firing hot shot." The American artillery responds to the incoming fire and shells are zooming back and forth across the river nearly without pause. Fires are ignited during the day in the fort and the city of Newark (New York); however, heroic efforts manage to extinguish them. Meanwhile, the British at Fort George also sustain major fires that erupt from the American artillery. During the cross-river artillery duel, one American 4-pounder under Lt. Harris sinks a British schooner.

Colonel McFeeley reports that 4 troops were killed during the day's fighting and 7 were wounded. Of those killed, two deaths were caused by the burst of a shell in southeast battery.

In Indiana, a band of Indians strikes a detachment under General Hopkins. The main body is at Prophet's Town destroying it. One soldier is killed.

November 22 (Sunday) *In naval activity,* the HMS *Southampton,* operating in the West Indies, intercepts and captures the USS *Vixen.* Neither vessel survives for long. Both get wrecked at Conception Island in the Bahamas. Despite the loss of both vessels, the crews are saved. The commander of the *Vixen,* Lieutenant Joseph Reed, the son of Revolutionary War General Joseph Reed, is taken to Jamaica. Reed dies there of yellow fever before an exchange can be carried out.

November 22–24 **In Indiana,** a contingent of about 60 mounted troops, under Lt. Colonel Miller and Lt. Colonel Wilcox, who are in the process of burying one of their fellow troops (named Dunn and attached to Captain Duval's company), comes under attack by a band of Indians. The column gets caught by an ambush as it encroaches an Indian camp. Eighteen troops are killed, wounded or missing. The 8th Regiment sustains four of the casualties and the rest are rangers.

The column afterward returns to General Hopkins' camp near Prophet's Town and informs the general of the large gathering of Indians. Hopkins prepares to launch an attack. Nonetheless, his plan gets foiled when a tremendous blizzard strikes the region and continues to rage until the night of the 23rd. On the 24th, Hopkins moves out to destroy the camp, but once again the elusive Indians abandoned their positions before the snow arrived and moved beyond the Ponce Passu. Hopkins, unable to discover their new positions, returns to his camp. The column begins its return to Fort Harrison on the following day.

In Ohio at Encampment Number 3, near Fort Winchester, Captain John Logan and a few others, including Lightfoot (Bright Horn), depart from the camp en route to the Maumee, where General Tupper's force had encountered the British; however, a British officer, Captain Elliott, and a small party of Indians intercept the party and captures it. Afterward, while Elliott is becoming more jubilant over seizing Captain John, the captives exchange signs that are codes and at the first opportunity, they spring a vicious attack on their captors. One of the men in the British party, Chief Win-e-mac, a Pottawatomie chief, is killed by Captain John Logan, while the others take out Elliott and an Ottawa chief. During the bloody exchange of fire, Logan and Bright Horn both sustain wounds.

Despite their wounds, both men mount the horses of the slain enemy and complete a ride of about 20 miles to reach the post. Logan's wound is fatal. Despite the untiring efforts of the surgeon, he dies two days later. Bright Horn, whose wound is in his thigh, recovers. The remains of Chief John Logan are taken to Wapakoneta (Auglaise County) under escort of a detachment led by Major Hardin. He is interred with a combination of Indian rites and military honors.

November 23 (Monday) **In Philadelphia,** the Aurora newspaper runs an editorial (from information thought to have come from General Joseph Bloomfield), stating that 6,000 men under Brigadier-General Bloomfield had moved from their position at Plattsburgh, destined for Canada. The army must have entered the enemy's country about the 20th, and three days will have brought the troops to conflict, unless the British make war like the Russians. The gallantry and fidelity of the militia Green Mountain boys and brave Yorkers will save them from the reproach cast upon the hitherto boasted bulwark of the republic by the brutality and cowardice displayed by idle spectators at Queenstown [Queenston], and put to shame the faithlessness and treachery of neighbours in Massachusetts.

The newspaper's editor is Colonel Duane, appointed to the army by President Madison. Nonetheless, similar to the earlier attempts at victory in Canada, this one under General Dearborn's overall command also fails due in great part to the British intercepting intelligence on the 17th.

November 24 (Tuesday) **In New York,** a British contingent composed of units of the 49th Regiment, Glengarry Light Infantry, and troops drawn from the Cornwall and Glengarry militia raid an American post on the Salmon River across the St. Lawrence River from St. Regis. The invading force is spotted by the Americans; however, after taking positions in the blockhouse, they find themselves surrounded by a superior force that is bolstered by a contingent of Royal Artillery. They surrender to the British without a fight. The British capture one captain, two subalterns and forty-one enlisted men, along with a small number of bateaux and fifty-seven stand of arms.

In naval activity, the privateer *America,* operating out of Charleston, intercepts a 12-gun ship, the *Hope,* which is transporting a cargo of cotton, rum and sugar from St. Thomas to Glasgow. After seizing the vessel, a prize crew takes it into an American port. Captain Ropes of the *America* is informed by the prisoners that the *Hope* had been part of a huge 45-ship convoy moving under the escort of the HMS *Ringdove* and the HMS *Scorpion* until it became separated several days earlier. The news hits Ropes as if he is receiving a bonanza, and his privateer is not concerned about the two war sloops. He intends if possible to begin to snag the merchant men. The *America* modifies its course and sails toward the convoy. Contact is made on the following day.

November 25 (Wednesday) In New York, General Smyth issues orders instructing his entire army to prepare to "be ready to march on a moment's notice."

In Ohio, General Harrison dispatches a detachment of men under Lt. Col. John B. Campbell from Franklinton (Columbus), Ohio, to initiate an attack on the Miami and Delaware Indian camps situated on the Mississiniwa River.

In naval activity, the privateer *America,* in late afternoon, spots a vessel from the convoy it had been chasing. Shortly afterward, the vessel *Dart,* a British brigantine, is halted and boarded. The Americans inspect the cargo and find that the *Dart* is carrying cotton, rum and other items. During the operation, while five British prisoners are being transferred to the *America,* the boat encounters difficulty and gets tangled with the privateer. The two Americans in the boat and three of the prisoners are rescued, but the other prisoners perish. After capturing its prize, the *America* continues to search for additional stragglers from the convoy, without success.

The next day, Captain Ropes orders the prize party to sail the *Dart* into an American port. All of the crew except for its captain and two others, including one passenger, are transferred to the *America.* The *Dart* is taken into port at Salem, Massachusetts. The crew of the *America* gets struck with some type of eye infection which appears to be contagious and by this time, the water supply has been rapidly diminishing, prompting Captain Ropes to cut the cruise short and return to port.

November 26 (Thursday) In New York at Sackets Harbor, the USS *Madison,* constructed in forty-five days, is launched this day. Later this month, its fleet attempts to sail to the head of the lake; however, powerful gales impede the mission. The *Growler* loses its mast, and in addition to the strong winds, ice imperils the fleet. The mission is cancelled.

November 27 (Friday) *In naval activity,* the USS *Essex* arrives at a spot between the isles of Mayo and St. Jago, the first rendezvous point designated by Commodore Bainbridge. Neither of the islands is attractive to the Yanks with regard to acquiring provisions. On the mountainsides at St. Jago, some scattered villages can be seen and some goats; however, no abundance of vegetation or trees is visible. Only some well scattered coconut trees come into view. The squadron under Commodore Biddle is also absent.

November 28 (Saturday) In New York, an American contingent—composed of elements of the 12th, 13th, 14th and 15th U.S. Regiments, led by Colonel William Henry Winder and accompanied by a small naval contingent—sails from Buffalo on a mission to seize the British batteries on the opposite shore in advance of a major assault against Fort Erie to be launched by General Smyth. The force is carried across the river during the predawn hours in ten boats. At Fort Erie, the garrison is composed of only an 80-man contingent of the 49th British Regiment, commanded by Major Ormsby, and a 50-man contingent of the Newfoundland Regiment under Captain Whelan. Another nearby force, two companies of militia, is posted at the ferry, which is directly across the river from Black Rock. The troops at the ferry are commanded by Captain Bostwick. And yet the British hold another position, the Red House, located on Chippewa Road, less than three miles from Fort Erie. Lt. Lamont (49th Regiment) is posted at the Red House with about 35 troops, bolstered by some artillerymen under Lt. King. Other units in the area include a contingent of the 41st under Lt. McIntyre and the 49th under Lt. Bartley.

The British positions reach French Creek, less than five miles from Fort Erie. The headquarters of Lt. Colonel Bishopp, commander of the line, is at Chippewa with a battalion-company of the 41st Regiment, bolstered by artillerymen and militia, the latter under Major Hatt.

Despite the darkness, the British detect the boats, and when they reach the middle of the river, the troops at the ferry open fire, prompting the raiders to abort landing near the ferry. They move downstream and debark near the Red House. The British also greet them with fire; however, the darkness complicates the defenders with regard to use of their guns. Nonetheless, elements of the 14th and 15th Regiments under Lt. Colonel Boerstler and Captain King, along with about 60 seamen under Lieutenant-commandant Angus, manage to advance against the Red House. The British repel three successive attempts to take the Red House and force the Americans to move back to their boats. Meanwhile, Lt. Lamont is awaiting a contingent of militia to bolster his small force; however, the American Captain King had remained determined to take the objective. He mounts a new attack. While moving forward, Lt. Lamont mistakes the column as his reinforcements. The misidentity is deadly. The Americans open fire and seven defenders fall. Eight others are wounded, including Lamont, who had been hit five times. Those able escape and three prisoners in addition to the wounded are seized. Lamont is among the wounded that are being taken back to New York, but the Americans, believing he had died, leave him behind and he survives. British Lt. King of the artillery had received a serious wound, but he is carried to New York, where he later dies.

Meanwhile, the other American contingent, which had landed about one or two miles below the Red House, is intercepted by the contingent of the 49th under Lt. Bartley. The British raise tenacious resistance; however, superior numbers compel Bartley to retire. At about the same time, Lt. Bostwick's contingent of militia arrives, but the Americans also force the militia to retire. By daylight, British reinforcements arrive to stem the tide. The aggressiveness of the Americans subsides as more reinforcements give Lt. Colonel Cecil Bishopp a force of about 300 regulars plus militia. His officers include Colonel Kirby and Colonel Powell. By that time, the Americans, having spiked the guns at the Red House, begin to retire across the river. Nonetheless, as the force returns to New York, some of the boats are not in place. A contingent under Captain King is left behind and captured. Also at about dawn, a flotilla moves to cross the river with a force under Colonel Winder, but British artillery forces the boats back to shore.

At about 1300, General Smyth demands the surrender of Fort Erie. The British defenders, although having suffered casualties, staunchly decline the ultimatum. The following day, Smyth initiates orders for his Army to cross into Canada; however, indecision causes him to countermand his own order, postponing his attack until December 1. A force of about 2,000 troops under General Peter B. Porter is actually about halfway across the river when General Smyth cancels the expedition and essentially prevents any reinforcements from reaching the vanguard. Subsequently, General Porter publicly accuses General Smyth of cowardice. In turn, Smyth responds to Porter's newspaper article by accusing Porter of fraud. He also states that Porter's "courage and patriotism were solely actuated by gain or loss, as he was contractor to supply the troops."

The exchanges between Smyth and Porter escalate. Smyth challenges Porter to a duel. The contest is covered in a newspaper, the *Buffalo Gazette,* in its publication of 18 December of this year. The paper publishes a "communication from Colonel Wm. H. Winder, and Lieutenant Samuel H. Angus, the seconds, by which it appeared that the two generals repaired that day to Grand Island and exchanged a shot." Neither has the aim of an expert and both emerge unscathed. Afterwards, the two men each retract their sharp words and they depart after having reconciled their differences.

George Mercer Brooke, who joined the army during 1808, participates in the attack against the fort. He is breveted lieutenant colonel during 1814. He is promoted to brigadier general in 1824. During the Mexican War, General Mercer is breveted major general.

In naval activity, the privateer *Wasp* (third), having escaped capture by the HMS *Garland* and surviving a hurricane, limps into port at Baltimore. The *Wasp* is sold to some businessmen who have the ship rearmed, and afterward, the *Wasp* is chartered by the U.S. Navy. During the summer of 1813, the *Wasp* is utilized as a dispatch vessel. By autumn 1813, the *Wasp* reverts back to its owners.

In other naval activity, the privateer *Rover*, a schooner, is commissioned in Maine this day. The vessel is commanded by John Webster.

November 30 (Monday) *In naval activity,* the American privateer *Holkar* intercepts a transport, the *Emu*, carrying women convicts. The crew of the *Emu* pays no attention to orders issued by its commander and in fact declines fighting the Americans. Nonetheless, the vessel is well armed and referred to as a king's ship, mounting 12 guns. The prize is taken into port at New York. The crew, including Lieutenant Alexander Bissett, and the women are put ashore at Porto Grande at St. Vincent in the Cape Verde Islands during mid–January 1813, where they are essentially marooned until finally rescued by a British ship and returned to England. For the women, however, their saga does not end. The British refuse to allow the women convicts to enter England. After being compelled to remain on board a ship off Portsmouth for about one month, the convicts are transferred to another vessel which sails for New South Wales, Australia, in late February 1813 and arrives at its destination the following July.

December *In naval activity,* at about this time (late 1812), the War Department acquires the 12-gun sloop USS *President* (second) for service on Lake Champlain. It misses the pivotal battle on Lake Champlain in September; it had been captured by the British and taken into service as the HMS *Icicle*. The American privateer *Teazer* is intercepted and captured by the HMS San Domingo. The crew is paroled on the condition that they agree not serve against the British until they are exchanged. Nonetheless, Captain F. Johnson, anxious to resume his commitment to serve, ignores his conditions of parole. After he arrives back in the United States, Captain Johnson wastes no time before heading back out to sea as first officer aboard another privateer, the *Young Teazer*.

December 1 (Tuesday) **In New Hampshire,** the fear of an attack against Portsmouth has passed due to the winter weather having arrived in New England. At Fort McClary and at Fort Constitution, the detached troops under Major Bassett are discharged. During the previous June, Major Timothy Upham, U.S. Army (later major general), had led a detachment of New Hampshire troops to garrison the post.

In naval activity, the American privateer *Jack's Favorite*, a schooner out of New York commanded by Captain Miller, having recently arrived at St. Bart's to acquire fresh water and some provisions, is soon joined within a few days by the HMS *Subtle*, which intends to capture the privateer once it departs from the neutral port. After remaining in port for a few days, to avoid engaging a British warship, *Jack's Favorite* embarks only to discover that it is being chased. The privateer runs, and terrific winds arrive threatening both vessels and causing both to struggle to beat the storm. After the squall ends, *Jack's Favorite* is not able to spot the warship. Despite the good fortune of losing his pursuer, Captain Miller, believing the British ship might have been victimized by the elements, searches for it. The results are grim. After sailing toward the last known position of the *Subtle*, the Americans find only debris and some items including "hats, caps and hammock-cloths." The *Subtle* had gone to the bottom with all hands aboard, leaving no survivors.

December 1–22 **In New York,** American General Alexander Smyth, contemplating a move on Canada from his base in Buffalo since November, when the Pennsylvania reinforcements reached him, meets with his officers. At the conclusion of the conference, the decision is made not to invade Canada. This decision ends Smythe's military career. The troops under his command react with great animosity, which leads to Smyth nearly being tarred and feathered. He departs from his post before any violence occurs. General Smyth is stripped from the rolls of the U.S. Army without a trial. He appeals to the U.S. Congress, which in turn hands his complaint to the secretary of war. He is not reinstated. Later, he is elected to Congress, where he serves from 1817 to 1825.

In Ohio, on or about the third day, Major Bodley, quartermaster of the Kentucky troops, aware of the difficulties in trying to get supplies to Fort Wayne by overland route, attempts to ship about 200 barrels of desperately needed flour to the left wing of General Harrison's Northwestern Army. The provisions are loaded upon about 20 pirogues in a flotilla commanded by Captain Jordan and Lt. Cardwell, which move down the St. Mary River; however, once the flotilla arrives at Shane's Crossing about 100 miles distant, the problems begin to mount. The waterway becomes too narrow to properly maneuver and passage is impeded by obstacles, including logs and overhanging trees. The craft struggle during the final leg of the journey, which is about 20 miles.

Shortly thereafter, the flotilla encounters a particularly frigid night and the pirogues become ice-bound. The predicament prompts Lt. Cardwell to make his way to land and move to Fort Barbee to seek help to extricate the party. Meanwhile, the men on the mission are offered more money to break through the ice and try to get to the destination. The project gets underway and after two days of struggling with the ice, they advance about one mile. The operation is then aborted. Unexpectedly, the paralyzed flotilla receives some aid from nature. Several days before Christmas, the weather breaks and a thaw occurs. The troops undertake an exhausting task and gnaw their way forward, but still the flotilla fails to reach the post. The flotilla again becomes immobilized by the ice about one mile from the fort. The troops become exasperated, but they remain determined to deliver the flour. The troops improvise by building sleighs, loading cargo and then delivering the flour overland to Fort Wayne a few days before Christmas.

December 2 (Wednesday) **In Maine,** the privateer *Parrot*, a schooner, is commissioned this day. John Webster receives command.

December 3 (Thursday) **In Washington, D.C.,** Secretary of War William Eustis resigns. James Monroe, the secretary of state, temporarily replaces him until John Armstrong is named to the post on February 5, 1813.

December 4 (Friday) *In naval activity,* the HMS *Paz* intercepts and seizes the 69-ton sloop *Revenge*, a privateer operating out of Salem, Massachusetts, which is carrying ammunition, guns and some provisions.

December 6 (Sunday) *In naval activity,* the 12-gun American privateer *Montgomery*, commanded by Captain Upton of Boston, encounters the 20-gun HMS *Surinam* off the port of Surinam in South America. The Montgomery runs, but within about one-half hour, the British warship closes. The Americans, once the British come into range, commence fire and inflict serious damage to the Surinam's fore mast. The British abort the chase.

December 9 (Wednesday) **In Georgia,** Major David Blackshear is appointed as brigadier general of militia by Governor David B. Mitchell. Also, at an undetermined time, Daniel Stewart, a veteran of the Revolutionary War, is named brigadier general. General Stewart is the great-grandfather of President Theodore Roosevelt. General Stewart's daughter, Martha, married John Elliott, a U.S. senator and later an officer in the army, Major James S. Bullock. From her second marriage, James and Martha's daughter was the mother of Theodore Roosevelt.

In naval activity, the 98-ton schooner *Chase* (S. York, master), transporting a cargo of lumber from Portland, Maine, to Norfolk, Virginia, is intercepted and seized by the British privateer *Liverpool Packet*.

December 9–13 *In naval activity,* aboard the American privateer *Saratoga*, Captain Charles W. Wooster, while off La Guayra, Venezuela, dispatches his 1st officer to confer with the American consul. The officer informs the consul that the *Saratoga* had been at sea 24 days without encountering other sail. On the 10th the *Saratoga* drops anchor in the roads and almost immediately the consul sends word to the ship instructing Captain Wooster to take precautions, while forewarning him that the commandant intends to sink it if it enters within range of the batteries. Captain Wooster, not anxious to lose his vessel, pulls back to a safer position.

Before long a lookout aboard the *Saratoga* detects a schooner cruising along the coast. Pursuit is initiated. The *Saratoga* after a short chase seizes the schooner and its cargo, which is valued at about $20,000. The *Saratoga* spots another sail on the following day slightly after a heavy fog lifts. Although the Americans are unable to immediately identify the vessel, some of the people on shore realize it is a British ship, the letter of marque *Rachel* out of Greenock, which is carrying 6-pounders and 9-pounders. Even on shore it becomes obvious that a sea battle is about to erupt.

While the ships are closing against one another, they engage about five miles off land. The

Saratoga initiates the offensive action by commencing fire with its starboard bow gun. The British privateer responds with its port quarter guns to ignite a ferocious confrontation. The opposing guns fire incessantly; however, the extreme intensity does not become a prolonged engagement. The *Saratoga*'s guns succeed in silencing the British vessel within a few minutes. The *Rachel* sustains devastating blows that nearly annihilate the crew. Only one officer escapes the brief but deadly thunderclap unscathed, the *Rachel*'s 2nd officer. The Americans take possession of the badly battered privateer. On the 13th, 25 prisoners are taken to shore in a longboat with all of their personal property.

Also at about this time, the American privateer *Rapid* out of Charleston intercepts and captures a small, unidentified British privateer. Another American privateer, the *Liberty*, operating out of Baltimore, seizes another British privateer. After disabling its guns and confiscating the valuable articles aboard the vessel, the ship is left in possession of the prisoners.

In yet other action on the sea, the American privateer *Midas* finally disposes of the British privateer *Dash* in a decisive action fought off Tybee lighthouse (Georgia). The *Dash* had been causing problems in the region, including having captured several coastal vessels operating out of Savannah. Captain Thompson of the *Midas*, once informed of a possible location of the *Dash*, immediately set sail to remove it from interrupting American shipping.

December 10 (Thursday) **In Tennessee,** General Andrew Jackson departs Nashville with his expeditionary force of approximately 2,000 men to find and destroy the Creek Indian strongholds in East Florida.

December 12 (Saturday) **In Jamaica,** an American prisoner relates the condition of the prison in a letter dated this day:

> I wrote you on the 8th inst. informing you of my being captured by the sloop of war *Fawn*, Captain Fellows, about twenty miles to northeast of Cape Tiberon, and carried to Jamaica, where we were all immediately sent to prison, and we were treated more like brutes than human beings. Our allowance is half a pound of horse meat, a pound and a half of bread that had been condemned, being more of worms than bread, and one gill of beans. That is all our allowance for twenty-four hours! When I was taken I had all my charts, quadrant, and clothes taken from me, and was not allowed even to ask for them. There are now in this prison ship four hundred and fifty-two prisoners and more arriving daily. It is reported today that we are all to be sent to England by the fleet which is to sail in six days.

From other similar correspondence, it becomes known that the British prison ships at Jamaica are "infested with rats, centipedes, snakes, roaches and lizards." Most of the American seamen taken prisoner by the British are privateers. The British, throughout the conflict, capture only a small number of U.S. Navy ships, and of those that are captured, the sailors are usually exchanged expeditiously.

In naval activity, the HMS *Atalanta* intercepts and seizes the 150-ton brigantine *Tulip* (James McCullough, master), which is transporting a cargo of codfish, cotton and rice. In other naval activity, the USS *Essex*, at about 1400, spots an unidentified sail thought to be a British brigantine. At about dusk, British colors are hoisted on the *Essex*. By about 2100 the *Essex* closes to about musket range and hails the vessel. Nevertheless, the ship is reluctant to halt. The Americans resort to using muskets to cut down on casualties. The vessel, the *Norton Packet*, is seized and during the operation one man aboard the prize is killed. Captain Porter transfers the crew to the *Essex* and confiscates about $50,000 (specie) which was being carried.

December 12–15 *In naval activity,* the American privateer *Rolla*, in search of British merchant ships off Madeira, Portugal, is nearly destroyed by a horrific gale after recently sailing from Baltimore. Captain E.W. Dewley (or J. Dooley) and the crew fight the elements to forestall foundering, and the heroic effort includes tossing four of the five guns overboard. The privateer survives, but Captain Dewley decides that the pragmatic choice is to return to port due to the loss of nearly all of the armaments. Nonetheless, the crew remains enthusiastic and members persuade the captain to continue.

Within a few days, the *Rolla* arrives off Madeira, where it begins to attack enemy shipping on the 12th. The *Rolla* encounters ships that had initially been attached to a very large escorted convoy that had sailed from Cork, Ireland. Without its warship escort, the *Rolla* is given the opportunity of an extremely lucrative cruise if it can succeed with only one gun. By the 15th, the *Rolla* captures seven vessels, all of which are more heavily armed than the American privateer. Nonetheless, the prizes are seized and they are carrying a total of 58 guns and 150 crewmen. The *Rolla* seizes its seven prizes without losing a single man.

The Americans, at the time of the seizures, are unaware that they had within the short span of four days provided the *Rolla* with the distinction of becoming one of the most successful privateers during the war. The combined value of the captured cargoes is more than two million dollars. The *Rolla* had, during this same period, seized a less valuable vessel, the brigantine *General Prevost*, which was en route to Halifax until diverted as a prize to New Orleans. One other vessel, the schooner *Swift*, en route to Plymouth, England, is captured and burned at sea. The *Rolla* is subsequently captured in December 1813.

December 13, 1812, to January 24, 1813 **In Ohio,** General Harrison writes to Secretary of War William Eustis; however, Eustis had resigned. The letter will be received by his successor, John Armstrong. It addresses preparations to retake Detroit: "Obstacles are almost insuperable; but they are opposed [by his army] with unabated firmness and zeal.... I fear that the expenses of this army will greatly exceed the calculation of the government. The prodigious destruction of horses can only be conceived by those who have been accustomed to military operations in the wilderness during the winter season.... I did not make sufficient allowance for the imbecility and inexperience of the public agents, and the villainy of the contractors."

Later in the same letter, Harrison discusses alternate plans for his manpower if the navy gains possession of the lakes, and he complains about a delivery of arms, saying: "I am disappointed in the artillery which has been sent me. There are in all twenty-eight pieces of which ten are sixes and ten twelve-pounders. The former are nearly useless. I had five before and if I had a hundred I should only take three or four with me. You will perceive by the return of Captain Gratiot, which is enclosed, that all carriages for the howitzers, and eight out of ten for the twelve-pounders, are unfit for use."

In naval activity, the USS *Constitution* and the USS *Hornet* arrive off Sao Salvador (Bahia), Brazil. The *Constitution* departs the area for a few days to permit the *Hornet* on its own to take the British warship that is in the port. The *Hornet* remains in the area to prevent a British sloop, the HMS *Bonne Citoyenne*, commanded by Captain Green, from sailing. The *Hornet*'s commander, Captain James Lawrence, tries to get the British ship to engage. Captain Lawrence's message to U.S. Consul Hill states: "When I last saw you I stated my wishes to meet the *Bonne Citoyenne*, and authorized you to make them known to Captain Green. I now request you to state to him, and pledge my honour, that neither the Constitution, nor any other American vessel shall interfere." The challenge is declined. The *Bonne Citoyenne* is transporting a large amount of money and Captain Green is apparently unwilling to risk losing the currency.

After the *Hornet* departs from Brazil in late January, it sails toward British Guiana (northern South America), where it encounters the HMS *Peacock* on 24 February.

December 16 (Wednesday) *In naval activity,* the *Fenelon*, a 109-ton schooner cruising from Baltimore to Boston with a cargo of corn and flour, is intercepted by the British privateer *Liverpool Packet* and seized. Also, the privateer *America*, en route to its home port at Salem, Massachusetts, spots an unidentified sail off the Western Isles (Outer Hebrides, Scotland). By about 0800, the target is identified as a brigantine, and it is determined to be speeding eastward to escape capture. Nonetheless, by about 1100, the *America* intercepts the vessel — the *Euphemia* carrying a full cargo of 400,000 pounds of coffee. The prize is taken into Portland, Maine.

In other naval activity, the American privateer *Swordfish*, a schooner carrying 12 guns and a crew of 82, including some boys, sails from Gloucester, Massachusetts; however, its cruising days are short-lived. After being at sea for about 12 days, it is spotted by the HMS *Elephant*, a frigate. The privateer runs to escape the warship, and in an effort to gain speed, the crew resorts to tossing guns overboard. Nonetheless, after an 11-hour chase, the *Swordfish* is captured. Only two of its guns remain on board.

December 17 (Thursday) *In naval activity,* the 77-ton schooner *Dove* (William Rodgers, master) is caught and captured by the British privateer *Liverpool Packet*. The *Dove* is separate from the *Dove* seized 27 November 1813, the *Dove* seized on 28 August 1814, and the *Dove* captured on 21 September 1814.

In other naval activity, the British privateer *Liverpool Packet* intercepts and seizes the 39-ton sloop *Susan*, which has a cargo of flour going to Boston. The *Liverpool Packet* also seizes the 38-ton schooner *Two Friends* (S. Clarke, master), which is transporting a cargo of flour from Baltimore to Boston. The *Two Friends* is separate from the schooner *Two Friends* seized on 11 June 1814.

December 18 (Friday) In Indiana, an American contingent of about 600 Kentucky and Pennsylvania cavalry, commanded by Colonel John B. Campbell of the 19th U.S. Infantry, having recently arrived from Ohio, had begun an operation to seek out hostile Miamis and Delaware Indians. The contingent up to this day had destroyed four villages; however, only a small number of braves had been killed. The troops had captured 8, along with 32 women and children.

On this day, the force engages and defeats a band of Indians at what becomes known as the Battle of Mississinewa. Seven or eight soldiers are killed and 42 are wounded during the skirmish, which occurs near present-day Jalapa, close to Marion. The force also loses 107 horses killed. The Delawares, who arrived from the White River in Indiana, had joined with the Miamis. At the time of the battle, Campbell is preparing to return to Dayton, Ohio, to avoid being intercepted by Tecumseh's force, which is far superior and less than twenty miles distant.

The skirmish was fought during extremely cold weather and the ground had been covered with knee-deep snow. The return march to Ohio is slow and arduous. Seventeen of the troops that had been wounded have to be carried in litters. The weather becomes so terrible that for a while, about 300 of the troops are unable to perform their duties. The next year, other American units return to Indiana to raid Indian positions in various places across the state. The small-scale raids are led by Colonel Joseph Bartholomew, Colonel William Russell and Colonel John Tipton.

Colonel Tipton, a Tennessean, had relocated in Indiana about 1807. He served in the military during the Tippecanoe campaign. After the war, he is promoted to the rank of brigadier general in the militia. Also, he becomes sheriff in Harrison County during 1816 and holds the position until 1819. He serves in the state legislature (1819) before he is appointed Indian agent (Miami and Pottawatomie tribes) during 1823. Later, during 1828, General Tipton is elected to the U.S. Senate as a Jacksonian to complete the term of James Noble, who died. Later, he becomes a Democrat. Tipton remains in the senate until 1839, when he is compelled to retire due to failing health. General Tipton dies on 5 April 1839.

In naval activity, the *Liverpool Packet*, an aggressive British privateer, intercepts and captures the 87-ton schooner *Columbia* (S.T. Wheldon, master), while it is transporting a cargo of flour and tobacco from Richmond, Virginia, to Boston, Massachusetts. The *Columbia* is separate from the schooner *Columbia* captured on 10 May 1813 and the brigantine *Columbia* captured on 15 May 1813. Also, the *Liverpool Packet* intercepts the 79-ton schooner *Three Friends* and captures it and its cargo of corn and flour. The *Three Friends* is separate from the *Three Friends* seized on 30 July 1814 and the schooner *Three Friends* captured 12 November 1814.

December 20 (Sunday) American General Harrison's Army, although divided into three parts, totals over 6,000 men. Harrison moves toward Frenchtown (Monroe), Michigan. American General Winchester departs Fort Defiance (Fort Winchester), Ohio, on or about the 25th, with his force of over 1,000 to join Harrison. Winchester's troops reach the rapids of the Maumee River, where they strike on January 10, 1813. Harrison will not be within striking distance, as he will be about 35 miles from Frenchtown.

Harrison's force is bolstered by elements of the 17th U.S. Regiment, 19th U.S. Regiment, 17th Kentucky, 19th Ohio, and about 200 dragoons. His force — including the troops from Kentucky, Ohio, Pennsylvania and Virginia — totals about 10,000 men. The Ohio troops are commanded by General Edward Tupper.

In naval activity, the HMS *Java*, commanded by Captain Lambert, departs Spithead en route to the East Indies. Lambert, having some knowledge of the Americans due to service in North America during 1808, is reluctant to sail with his motley, inexperienced crew. It is composed of "poachers and smugglers, desperadoes, devoid of discipline." Nonetheless, the men are also anxious to fight, though most have never fired a cartridge. Lambert is assured that after his cruise to Bombay, the crew would be proficient. Late that month the *Java* encounters the USS *Constitution* before it reaches its destination.

In other naval activity, the *Surveillante* intercepts and seizes the American brigantine *Ocean*, which is en route to New York from Lisbon, Portugal, with a cargo of flour.

December 22 (Tuesday) In New Hampshire, the legislature passes an act which establishes the pay scale of men detached or scheduled to be detached, "including the pay from the General Government at the following rates: Sergeant Major, $13 per month; Quartermaster Sergeant, $18 per month; Principal Musician, $12 per month; Sergeant, $12 per month; Corporal, $11 per month; Private, $10 per month." An act also passes authorizing a "Volunteer Corps of Infantry." The corps is to be composed of men who otherwise are not required by law to serve in the military. It is essentially raised for an emergency such as an invasion by the British, and only the captain general is authorized to activate the corps. Although companies are formed in various towns, the corps is not called into service.

December 23 (Wednesday) *In naval activity,* the American privateer *Comet*, commanded by Captain Thomas Boyle, is penned in port by a British squadron that is blockading the Chesapeake Bay. On this day, Captain Boyle decides to break out. Using the cover of darkness, the *Comet* creeps out of the harbor and heads for the open seas. Initially, the path remains clear, raising morale aboard ship. But just before dawn on the 24th, the *Comet* unexpectedly comes under fire from a warship that had been concealed by the morning fog. The broadside causes little damage and fails to derail Boyle's plan. The *Comet* does not halt to surrender or engage. It makes it out of the bay and sails southward toward Cape St. Roque, Brazil. The privateer arrives off Pernambuco on 9 January 1813.

In other activity, the American privateer *Hunter* (Captain Jeduthan Upton) is intercepted and captured by the British frigate *Phoebe*, commanded by Captain James Hillyar. Although U.S. Navy seamen are usually exchanged, seamen, including officers and men aboard, are rarely paroled, and they remain unseparated during their incarceration. One exception is that parole might be granted if the privateer is carrying more than fourteen guns. Unfortunately for Upton, during the chase, the crew had thrown twelve of their fourteen guns overboard, leaving Upton without chance of parole.

December 25 (Friday) *In naval activity,* the privateer *Governor Tompkins* (Captain Nathaniel Shaler) spots three vessels in the distance at about daybreak and immediately initiates pursuit. When the *Governor Tompkins* closes the distance, Shaler is able to identify the vessels as one brigantine and two ships. He becomes concerned when he notices that one of the ships seems much more than a merchant transport. Soon a sudden squall moves in and drives the *Governor Tompkins* forward within about one-quarter of a mile from the ship that caught Shaler's attention. The unidentified merchant transport is actually a full-scale British frigate. The *Governor Tompkins* receives a deadly broadside that kills two men and wounds six others, one of whom dies from his wound.

During this initial exchange, the English ensign aboard the *Tompkins* is taken down while the Stars and Stripes is unfurled.

The *Tompkins* returns fire against its more powerful opponent, while it unsuccessfully tries to maneuver into an advantageous position. The *Tompkins* attempts to run, but the British frigate is right behind during what becomes a running battle. One of the crew, a black sailor, John Davis, having been fatally wounded, requests that he be thrown overboard so that he would not impede the action of the guns. After about one-half hour, the *Governor Tompkins* is able to place some distance between it and the pursuer, but by about 1630, the stiff winds subside and once again the frigate's guns are back in range.

Captain Shaler takes additional drastic action to evade capture or destruction. The crew begins to toss all the lumber on the deck into the sea and the crew also throws about 2,000 pounds of shot overboard. The discarded items give Shaler the additional speed he requires to escape. Just before 1730, the British frigate, thought to be the HMS *Laurel*, aborts the chase and returns to the other vessels. After returning to port, Captain

Shaler takes command of the privateer *Anaconda* at New York. The *Governor Tompkins* remains in service under various commanders. The privateer *Governor Tompkins* is separate from the USS *Governor Tompkins*, which is attached to Commodore Chauncey's squadron.

During the first year of hostilities with Great Britain, American warships and privateers have scored great success against the much larger Royal Navy, seizing nearly 300 British vessels.

December 26 (Saturday) Great Britain announces a naval blockade of the Chesapeake and Delaware Bays. It then initiates attacks along the Chesapeake. Also, the schooner *Amelia* is acquired by the U.S. Navy. After the vessel is inspected, it is determined that it is unsuitable to begin active service. In May 1815, it is sold at Erie, Pennsylvania.

December 29 (Tuesday) **In Lower Canada,** the legislature renews and extends the Army Bill Act, which authorizes the distribution of £500,000, including £15,000 for the militia.

In Washington, Secretary of the Navy Paul Hamilton resigns. William Jones, a veteran of the Revolutionary War from Philadelphia, replaces Hamilton.

December 29–30 *In naval activity,* the USS *Constitution*, commanded by Captain William Bainbridge, while operating off the coast of Brazil, encounters two unidentified vessels. Bainbridge notes in his journal:

> At nine, A.M. [29th], discovered two strange sails on the weather bow. At ten, discovered the strange sails to be ships; one of them stood in for the land — the other stood off shore, in a direction toward us. At forty-five minutes past ten, A.M., we tacked ship to the northward and westward, and stood for the sail standing toward us. At eleven, A.M., tacked to the southward and eastward — hauled up the mainsail, and took in the royals. At thirty minutes past eleven, made the private signal for the day, which was not answered, and then set the mainsail and royals, to draw the strange sail off from the neutral coast, and separate her from the sail in company.

Bainbridge doesn't know it yet, but the unidentified vessel is a British warship, the 38-gun HMS *Java*, which is transporting General Thomas Hislop and some other officers, including his staff, to the East Indies.

On the 30th, Bainbridge discovers the ship's origin. He notes in his journal:

> At twenty-six minutes past one, P.M., being sufficiently from the land, and finding the ship to be an English frigate, took in the mainsail and royals, tacked ship, and stood for the enemy. At fifty minutes past one, P.M., the enemy bore down with an intention of raking us, which we avoided by wearing. At two, P.M., the enemy being within half a mile of us, and to windward, and having hauled down his colours, except the union Jack, at the mizenmast head, induced me to give orders to the officer of the third division, to fire a gun ahead of the enemy, to make him show his colours, which being done, brought on a fire from us of the whole broadside, on which the enemy hoisted his colours, and immediately returned our fire. A general action, with round and grape then commenced.

The British warship under Captain Henry Lambert initially is bolstered by the winds; however, at about 1350, when the encounter turns violent, the two vessels exchange heavy fire. The *Java* maneuvers to gain a position from which to pound the bow of the *Constitution*; however, the *Constitution*'s movements foil the maneuver. Nonetheless, the *Java* persists and continues to gain an advantage to rake the Americans. After about thirty minutes of vicious fighting the wheel of the *Constitution* is destroyed, which severely affects the ship's steering; still the *Constitution* prevents the *Java* from properly positioning itself. By this time the *Java* loses the advantage, as the *Constitution* rakes it with a hurricane of fire.

During the fighting at close-quarters, at 1450, the jibboom of the *Java* becomes entangled with the *Constitution*'s mizzen rigging, making it impossible to break away. It also prevents the British from their attempt to board. Within ten minutes the gunners aboard the *Constitution* sever the *Java*'s bowsprit and jibboom; however, the fire does not slacken, and by 1505, the *Java*, which is undergoing a devastating pounding, loses its foremast. All the while during this violent combat, Marine sharpshooters positioned in the *Constitution*'s main topmast pick off some in the boarding party, including Captain Lambert, who sustains a mortal wound. Lieutenant Chadds assumes command of the battered vessel; however, the *Java* receives no reprieve. It remains under incessant fire from the guns of the *Constitution* and the punishment continues unabated.

Afterward, for a short period, the two antagonists become separated, but only momentarily. As they come back alongside of one another broadsides are catapulted by both vessels at about 1540. When the smoke clears, it becomes evident that the *Java* sustains the heaviest of the damage, having had its mizzen mast blasted away, leaving it with only its main mast. By 1555, the British guns fall silent and Bainbridge, still in command despite a severe wound to his thigh, sees no colors flying. He pulls back to make repairs.

After the *Constitution* completes repairs, it bolts forward and prepares to pound the bow of the *Java* at 1725. Nevertheless, before Bainbridge can complete the total destruction, the British lower the colors. After the tenacious duel which had lasted just under two hours, the *Java* becomes the prize of the Americans, delivering yet another unexpected blow to the Royal Navy. Captain Bainbridge soon discovers that the prize is unsalvageable. For a while, he ponders whether to tow the *Java* to port at Bahia in Brazil, but aware that the Brazilians are pro–English, he orders it to be sunk. Within a couple of days, the Americans, after transferring their prisoners to the *Constitution*, destroy the *Java*.

Subsequent to the striking of the colors, Captain Bainbridge sends Lt. Parker in one of only two remaining boats to claim the prize, which the Americans discover is the HMS *Java*, commanded by Captain Lambert, who had been mortally wounded. After boarding the *Java*, Parker is unable to get an accurate account of the ship's complement due to the reluctance of the officers to provide true numbers. Nonetheless, at 1900, Parker's party returns to the *Constitution* and brings British officers, including 1st Lt. Chads, Lt. General Hislop (governor of Bombay), Major Walker, and Captain Wood. Captain Lambert's wound had been too severe, preventing any attempt to transfer him to the *Constitution*. Later, the Americans return to the *Java* to transfer the prisoners, including Captain Marshall of the Royal Navy, who had been en route to the East Indies. General Hislop and his staff had been en route to Bombay.

Captain Bainbridge, despite two wounds — a musket ball in his hip and a fragment of langrange in the thigh — refuses to leave the deck even after the victory. He does not retire from the deck until 2300. The langrange remains in Bainbridge's thigh for some days and symptoms of tetanus emerge; however, the ship's surgeon, Doctor Evans, brings him back to excellent health.

Through the good fortune of the capture, Captain Bainbridge seizes dispatches that are addressed to officials at St. Helena, the Cape of Good Hope, as well as every post or station in India and the China Seas. Captain Bainbridge notes in his journal some other items gained: "There was copper for a seventy-four, and two brigs, building at Bombay, and a great many other valuables, but every thing was blown up in her, except the officers' baggage."

Also during the ordeal, after British Captain Lambert had been transferred to the *Constitution*, Captain Bainbridge, himself wounded and assisted by two of his officers, stopped by Lambert's cot on the quarterdeck. Bainbridge returned Lambert's sidearms and said: "I return your

Commodore William Bainbridge.

sword, my dear sir, with my sincerest wish that you will recover, and wear it as you have hitherto done, with honour to yourself and country."

Exact numbers of British casualties are never determined. Estimates vary from 22 killed and 101 wounded (about 25 percent of the men on board, including those with General Hislop) and from there the numbers rise. Captain Bainbridge reports that 60 of the British had been killed. In addition, about 100 British are wounded. The Americans sustain 9 killed and 21 wounded, including Captain Bainbridge. Also, on the 29th Lieutenant Aylwin dies of his wounds. John Cheever, a sailor from Marblehead, who himself is wounded, is lying next to a dead seaman. He hears that the British had struck their colors and finds the strength to raise himself up by his left hand, gives three rousing cheers and then expires.

Before departing from the area, Captain Bainbridge sails into the harbor at Bahia, Brazil, and releases his prisoners on parole. The *Hornet* is there to greet the crew of the *Constitution*, and it remains in place to blockade the HMS *Bonne Citoyenne*.

On 3 January 1813 at St. (San) Salvador, Bainbridge writes to Secretary of the Navy Paul Hamilton regarding casualties: "The action lasted 1 hour and 55 minutes, in which time the enemy was completely dismasted, not having a spar of any kind standing. The loss on board the *Constitution*, was 9 killed and 25 wounded, as per enclosed list. The enemy had 60 killed, and 101 wounded, certainly; (among the latter, Capt. Lambert, mortally,) but, by the enclosed letter, written on board this ship, (by one of the officers of the *Java*,) and accidentally found, it is evident that the enemy's wounded must have been much greater than as above stated, and who must have died of their wounds, previously to their being removed-the letter states, 60 killed, and 170 wounded."

While at San Salvador, Captain Bainbridge releases all of the crew and others (about 100 supernumerary officers and sailors en route to the East Indies) aboard the *Java*. They are paroled and transported back to England, where they are to remain until exchanged.

Back in London, once the news of a third major naval loss arrives, the *Times* reacts with the following:

The public will learn, with sentiments which we shall not presume to anticipate, that a third British frigate has struck to an American.... This is an occurrence that calls for serious refection — this and the fact stated in our paper of yesterday, that Lloyd's list contains notices of upward of five hundred British vessels captured in seven months by the Americans. Five hundred merchantmen and three frigates! Can these statements be true? And can the English people hear them unmoved? Any one who had predicted such a result of an American war this time last year would have been treated as a madman or a traitor. He would have been told, if his opponents had condescended to argue with him, that long ere seven months had elapsed the American flag would have been swept from the seas, the contemptible navy of the United States annihilated, and their marine arsenals rendered a heap of ruins. Yet down to this moment not a single American frigate has struck her flag.

The USS *Constitution* arrives at Boston during February 1813. The Bostonians greet Captain Bainbridge and the crew in similar fashion as Captains Hull and Stephen Decatur had earlier received from other cheering Americans. Congress later presents Captain Bainbridge and his officers similar medals, and it authorizes $50,000 in prize money for the crew.

Back in England, the successive defeats have still not convinced the British to give credit to the naval skills of the Americans. The British, including later historians, seem to lean toward discovering new reasons and theories to rationalize the embarrassing defeats rather than recognize that the U.S. Navy had gained their successes through skilled seamanship and the high quality of the American gunners.

The most often used defense for the British losses are accusations that the Americans would list a vessel as a frigate, although it is actually carrying 74 guns, along with a claim that the British crews had been undermanned and primarily unseasoned. General Winfield Scott, while attending dinner in London, encounters a young British naval officer who inquires of Scott whether the Americans have "continued to build a line-of-battle ships, and to call them frigates." General Scott retorts: "We have borrowed a great many excellent things from the mother country, and some that discredit both parties. Among the latter is the practice in question. Thus when you took from France the *Guerriere*, she mounted forty-nine guns, and you instantly rated her on your list a thirty-six-gun frigate, but when we captured her from you, we found on board the same number, forty-nine guns."

Some prominent Englishmen had not discounted the validity of the U.S. Navy, and among them is Admiral Lord Nelson. While observing a U.S. squadron under Captain Richard Dale in the bay of Gibraltar, it was reported that while in conversation with an American who was aboard his flagship, Nelson made an observation that "there was in those transatlantic ships a nucleus of trouble for the maritime power of Great Britain. We have nothing to fear from anything on this side of the Atlantic; but the manner in which those ships [American] are handled makes me think that there may be a time when we shall have trouble from the other (side of the Atlantic)."

As the year closes out, the U.S. Navy and the American privateers have carved a remarkable record against the British. Since the war began the previous June, the Americans defeated more than 50 armed vessels and captured about 250 merchant ships. During that same period, several thousand British subjects were captured. The British, unaccustomed to defeat on the high seas, have difficulty accepting that the U.S. Navy has in six months proven to be a formidable force that eagerly challenges the British for superiority.

In other naval activity, the USS *Essex*, off Rio de Janeiro, Brazil, encounters the British schooner *Elizabeth* and successfully engages and captures it.

December 30 (Wednesday) *In naval activity,* the British privateer *Liverpool Packet* intercepts and seizes the 90-ton schooner *Eliza* (P. Joy, master), which is en route from Philadelphia to Boston. Another vessel, the schooner *Eliza*, had been captured by another British ship earlier in the year. This *Eliza* is separate from liked named vessels also seized: a brigantine, 31 March 1813; a schooner, 1 July 1814; a schooner , 1 July 1814; a schooner, 3 July 1814; and a sloop, *Eliza Ann*, captured 31 October 1814.

December 31 (Thursday) **In Washington, D.C.,** by this time, the president has been authorized by Congress to raise twenty infantry regiments (regulars) to make up for the deficiencies caused by the ineffectiveness of the volunteer system. The troops that enlist sign for a period of one year and each enlistee receives a bonus of $16. Congress also authorizes six additional major generals and eight brigadier generals, along with an increase in the number of lower ranking officers. These new major generals will be William Henry Harrison, James Wilkinson, Wade Hampton, Morgan Lewis, William R. Davie and Aaron Ogden. Nonetheless, Ogden, an officer during the American Revolution, a former U.S. senator and the governor of New Jersey during 1812, never serves. He was to serve on the Canadian frontier. Ogden, the brother of Brigadier General Mathias Ogden, later becomes the collector of customs at Jersey City, a position he holds at the time of his death during 1839.

The additional brigadier generals will be George Izard, Zebulon Pike, William Henry Winder, Duncan McArthur, Lewis Cass (secretary of state under President James Buchanan) and Benjamin Howard. Robert Swarthout succeeds Morgan Lewis as quartermaster. With his new position, he also receives the rank of brigadier general. Also, General Harrison maintains his army on the Canadian frontier in three divisions. General Edward Tupper (Ohio militia) holds at Fort McArthur (near Kenton, Ohio), while General Winchester is headquartered at Fort Defiance, while he personally commands a division at Sandusky. Fort Defiance was originally built at the convergence of the Auglaize and Maumee Rivers by General Anthony Wayne during August 1794. General Harrison rebuilds it about 100 yards from its original position and it is renamed Fort Winchester.

1812–1813 During the winter of 1812–1813, a party departs Fort Astor en route for St. Louis. The small group of six men led by Robert Stuart travels across what becomes the Oregon trail via the South Pass that crosses the Continental Divide. Stuart arrives in St. Louis in late April 1813.

1812–1815 In Western New York, Fort Tompkins, named in honor of Governor Daniel D. Tompkins, is established in Jefferson County as a defensive line to prevent a ground attack against Sackets Harbor. Other forts established in conjunction with the land defense include Fort Chauncey (named in honor of Commodore Isaac Chauncey), Fort Kentucky, Fort Stark and Fort

Virginia. This series of fortifications will be linked to a primary installation, Fort Pike (later Madison Barracks) built along the bay.

Also, Fort Volunteer is established at Sackets Harbor. Its purpose is to defend the approaches leading to the northeast entrance route. By the following year, a bigger and more formidable fort named Fort Pike rises in its place. Fort Pike will be bolstered by four other smaller forts to defend the line. In addition, another Fort Tompkins is established. This Fort Tompkins, also known as Fort Adams, is constructed along the Niagara River in Buffalo (Erie County); it is attacked by the British during July of the following year. In addition, Flint Hill Camp is established in Buffalo. The installation is utilized as a camp as well as a hospital. Several hundred soldiers who served during the War of 1812 were interred here. The camp is in present-day Parkside (Buffalo).

In related activity, the Tonawanda Blockhouse is established at Niagara Village in Tonawanda (Erie County) near Buffalo. The small installation is constructed along the south side of Tonawanda Creek. The fort is threatened with attack later this year, but it is thwarted; however, during December of 1813, the fortification comes under assault.

Fort Gray (named for Nicholas Gray) is established at Niagara Falls (Niagara County) across from Queenston (Toronto). Gray constructs the fort near the location of a former French installation and of a previous English supply depot. The fort comes under attack during December 1813. In addition, Fort Hickory, a blockhouse, is established in the vicinity of present-day Larkville at the village of Chateugay (Franklin County).

1813

In Alabama, Fort Mitchell is established near Holy Trinity, close to the site former of an old Spanish fort, Apalachicola. General John Floyd names the fort in honor of Georgia Governor David B. Mitchell. The fort is deactivated prior to Civil War and its site remains within the boundaries of Fort Benning (Georgia-Alabama). Also, Fort Armstrong is established about two miles south of Cedar Bluff on present-day Williamson Island. The fort is utilized as a supply depot and trading post.

In Connecticut, Fort Saybrook, initially established during 1635–1636, is re-fortified due to the hostilities with Britain. The fort will be renamed Fort Fenwick in honor of George Fenwick, the second governor of the Saybrook colony. Fort Wooster is also built during the War of 1812 near New Haven.

In Georgia, General John Floyd establishes Fort Perry along the old Alabama Road near Buena Vista. The post is named in honor of Commodore Oliver Perry.

In Illinois, Fort Clark is established at Peoria in a spot where the French had opened a post during 1730. It remains active until 1819. After its abandonment, it is destroyed by Indians. In addition, settlers construct Fort Foot near Fort LaMotte, built the previous year in the vicinity of present-day Palestine.

In Maine, Fort Burrows, named in honor of Commander William Burrows, is established at Portland by militia. It remains active for several years after the War of 1812.

In Maryland, in an effort to further bolster the city of Baltimore, Fort Babcock, Fort Covington and Fort Lookout (Camp Lookout), later Fort Wood, are established as harbor defenses along with Fort McHenry, which had been built in 1798. Also, several batteries are built as added strength against possible provocation by the British. In addition to the harbor defenses, the city of Baltimore will contain many more forts, camps and batteries during the war; many are designated by numbers rather than names. Fort Defiance and Fort Hollingsworth are established near Elkton.

In New York, the U.S. Army establishes an arsenal along the Hudson River just outside of Albany. It is named Watervliet Arsenal during 1817. The U.S. Army post remains active and is the oldest continuing arsenal in the U.S. Also, the U.S. Army establishes an arsenal at Rome (Oneida County). It remains on active duty until 1873.

In Ohio, the U.S. continues to increase its strength as more forts are established. They include Fort Amanda at Wapakoneta, Fort Ball at Tiffin, Fort Barbee at St. Mary's, Fort Huntington at Cleveland, Fort Meigs at Perrysburg and Fort Seneca in the vicinity of Old Fort. Fort Meigs becomes an anchor for Forts Amanda, Brown, Jennings, and Winchester (formerly Defiance). Also, settlers establish Adler's Post, a fortified blockhouse in the vicinity of Marysville.

In Vermont, Fort Cassin, named for a Lt. Cassin, a U.S. naval officer, is established in the vicinity of Vergennes for the purpose of defending the town and its shipbuilding activities from the British on Lake Champlain.

In naval activity, the American privateer *Expedition* intercepts and seizes a British schooner, the 202-ton *Louisa*, carrying only one gun and a crew of 26 men. At the time of its capture, the *Louisa* is en route to St. John's from St. Vincent with a cargo of rum and sugar. In 1814, the American schooner *Adeline* departs Bordeaux with important U.S. government documents and about 4,000 letters, but after being at sea for four days, a British warship intercepts it. The Americans discard the documents and correspondence before their captors can gain them. While the British are sailing the prize to an English port, the American privateer *Expedition* cuts it off on its sixth day of the voyage and recaptures it. Afterward, the *Adeline* arrives safely at New York, but without the correspondence which had been thrown into the sea.

The American letter of marque *Sabine*, en route to France from Baltimore, intercepts an unidentified brigantine after it departs from Lisbon with a cargo of cotton. The *Sabine*, commanded by Captain J. Barnes, captures it before it arrives at its destination, London. The cargo and the prisoners are transferred before the vessel is destroyed at sea. Another lesser known American privateer, the *Baltimore*, commanded by Captain E. Veasey, operating out of Baltimore, captures two prizes, the brigantine *Point Shares* and a schooner. Little information regarding the *Baltimore* has been handed down to posterity.

Also, the privateer *Liberty* out of Baltimore captures the schooner *Huzzar*, which is carrying treats intended for British Admiral John Borlaise Warren on the American station. Nonetheless, the turtles are instead consumed by the crew of the *Liberty*, which also seizes the two-gun schooner *Dorcas* and its cargo of dry goods valued at $60,000. After seizing its cargo, the *Dorcas* is released. During its time at sea, the *Liberty* is credited with the capture of six vessels.

January   In Oregon, news about the outbreak of war between the Americans and Britain reaches Astoria, causing some trepidation, due to the proximity to Canada and the possibility of the arrival of British warships. By summer of 1813, the Americans sell out to the British-held Northwest Company. An agreement is consummated and the new owners take control by autumn.

In naval activity, the American privateer *Orders in Council* is intercepted by several British privateers. Captain Howard attempts to escape, but without success. He is forced to surrender. Before being captured, the *Orders in Council*, which carried 16 guns and a crew of 120 men, had captured four prizes during its time at sea. The prizes include the brigantine *Lady Harriot*, transporting a cargo of wine, another brigantine (unnamed) carrying a cargo of salt, and the king's cutter *Wellington*, carrying 12 guns and a crew of 57 men.

Early January   In Washington, D.C., President James Madison, in his previous year as president, experienced few successes against the British on the battlefield. Generals Dearborn, Hull and Van Rensselaer, along with General Smyth had failed to check the British. Madison also had lost his secretary of war, William Eustis, who resigned the month before. Madison, following the dismal activities of his generals and displeased with his secretary of the navy, Paul

Hamilton, requests the resignation of Hamilton. Afterward, Madison nominates John Armstrong as successor to Eustis, and he nominates William Jones as successor to Hamilton.

By the early next month, both men are confirmed by the U.S. Senate. Shortly after his appointment, Armstrong conceives of a plan to invade Canada and conquer Montreal; however, no action is taken to initiate the campaign until the following October. Secretary Armstrong reorganizes the army by dividing it into nine districts before the arrival of spring.

In Connecticut, the war up to this point had not affected the state; however, by a recent act of the General Assembly, a state corps is established. Nathaniel Terry receives command with the rank of brigadier general. The corps is composed of two regiments, commanded by Colonels Timothy Shepard and Elihu Sanford. The corps also contains a cavalry regiment commanded by Major David Deming and a four-company contingent of artillery, commanded by Major William Stanley.

Also, the militia is composed of four divisions and two independent companies (Governor's Foot-guards). The 1st Division, commanded by Major-General Solomon Cowles, has two brigades (1st and 7th). The 1st Brigade (1st, 18th, 19th and 22nd Connecticut Infantry Regiments and 1st Cavalry Regiment) is commanded by Brigadier General Moses Tyron Jr. The 7th Brigade (6th, 16th, 23rd and 24th Infantry Regiments and the 7th Cavalry Regiment) is commanded by Brigadier General Levi Lusk.

The Second Division, commanded by Major General John Hubbard, is composed of the 2nd and 4th Brigades. The 2nd Brigade (2nd, 7th, 10th, 27th and 32nd Infantry Regiments and the 2nd Cavalry Regiment and the 1st Battalion of Artillery) is commanded by Brigadier General James Merriman (and later, Brigadier General Hezekiah Howe). The 4th Brigade (4th, 9th, and 28th Infantry Regiments and the 4th Cavalry Regiment) is commanded by Brigadier General Matthias Nicoll (later, Brigadier General Enoch Foote).

The Third Division, commanded by Major General William Williams, has the 3rd and 5th Brigades. The 3rd Brigade (3rd, 8th, 20th and 33rd Infantry Regiments and the 3rd Cavalry Regiment) is commanded by Brigadier General Jirah Isham. The 5th Brigade (5th, 11th, 12th and 21st Infantry Regiments and the 5th Cavalry Regiment) is commanded by Brigadier General David Holmes.

The Fourth Division, commanded by Major General Augustine Taylor, comprises the 6th and 8th Brigades. The 6th Brigade (14th, 17th, 25th and 35th Infantry Regiments and the 6th Cavalry Regiment) is commanded by Brigadier General David Thompson. The 8th Brigade (13th 16th, 26th and 29th Infantry Regiments and the 8th Cavalry Regiment) is commanded by Brigadier General Ephraim Hinman (later General Gerrit Smith).

Connecticut, one of the states that refuses to turn its militia over to the federal government, has a force of about 15,000 troops. During the spring of 1813, a British fleet appears offshore and causes concern that an invasion is imminent.

In Ohio, a contingent of troops, primarily Kentuckians, under General James Winchester, is advancing through the state en route to join with General William Henry Harrison and participate in the assault against British-held Detroit and another British post at Malden. The column advances to the rapids of the Maumee (Miami) River. After arriving there, two French settlers inform General Winchester that the British and Indians are in the process of attacking the settlements along the Raisin River. The urgent message to Winchester: "Our women and children are in danger. Without it, we have no hope. With it, we may be able."

General Winchester dispatches a force of about 650–670 troops under General Eleazar Payne, along with Colonels Lewis and Allen to ensure the route is cleared of obstacles. The column—which has to overcome knee-deep snow and at times, drifts taller than the men—reaches Frenchtown (present-day Monroe) on the Raisin River on 18 January. Earlier, General Winchester had also dispatched one of the Kentuckians, Leslie Combs, along with a guide, A. Ruddle, on a mission to inform General Harrison on the progress of his advance, and that by 30 December, the left wing had arrived at the rapids of the Maumee. The journey was hazardous and the route was primitive, causing even ill health for Combs.

In naval activity, at about this time, the American privateer *Grand Turk* embarks on a cruise that takes it down to South America off Brazil and from there to the West Indies before arriving back in Maine during May. During the cruise, it seizes four vessels; each prize is taken into a French port.

January 1 (Friday) *In naval activity,* the British list of ships on station, according to the "Navy List of the Royal Navy on Station," is as follows:

Bermuda Station: 32-gun *Minerva* (R. Hawkins), 18-gun *Frolic* (first name unknown Whinyates), 18-gun *Sylph* (William Evans), and 14-gun *Muros* (Lt. C. Hobart).

Off Western Islands: 74-gun *Elephant* (C.J. Austin), 36-gun *Inconstant* (E.W.C.R. Owens), 20-gun *Hermes* (Philip Brown), and 10-gun *Rolla* (William Hall).

Halifax Station: 74-gun *San Domingo* (Admiral Sir J. B. Warren and Captain Charles Gill), 74-gun *Cumberland* (Thomas Baker), 74-gun *Marlborough* (Rear Admiral Cockburn and Captain B.H. Ross), 74-gun *Poictiers* (Sir J.P. Beresford), 74-gun *Ramiles* (Sir Thomas Hardy), 50-gun *Grampus* (Robert Barrie), 40-gun *Acasta* (A.R. Kerr), 38-gun *Junon* (James Saunders), 38-gun *Nymphe* (E.P. Epworth), 38-gun *Sea Horse* (J.A. Gordon), 38-gun *Spartan* (E.P. Brenton), 38-gun *Statira* (Hassard Stackpole), 38-gun *Tenedos* (Hyde Parker), 36-gun *Belvidera* (Richard Byron), 36-gun *Maidstone* (George Burdett), 36-gun *Orpheus* (Hugh Pigott), 32-gun *Aeolus* (Lord J. Townsend), 24-gun *Laurestinus* (Thomas Graham), 20-gun *Fawn* (Thomas Fellows), 20-gun *Tartarus* (John Pasco), 20-gun *Wanderer* (F. Newcomb), 18-gun *Arachine* (C.H. Watson), 18-gun *Arab* (John Wilson), 18-gun *Atalanta* (Frederick Hickey), 18-gun *Colibri* (J. Thompson), 18-gun *Curlew* (Michael Head), 18-gun *Goree* (H.D. Byng), 18-gun *Heron* (William M'Culloch), 18-gun *Martin* (John Evans), 18-gun *Morgiana* (David Scott), 18-gun *Moselle* (first name unknown Mowbray), 18-gun *Recruit* (H.F. Banhouse), 18-gun *Sophia* (N. Luckyer), 16-gun *Magnet* (D.M. Maurice), 16-gun *Rattler* (A. Gordon), 12-gun *Plumper*, lost of Eastport, Maine (Lt. J. Bray), 12-gun *Variable* (R.R.B. Yates), 8-gun *Holly* (Lt. S.S. Treacher), 4-gun *Bream* (Lt. C.D. Browne), 4-gun *Cuttle* (Lt. W.L. Patterson), 4-gun *Fierce*, 4-gun *Herring* (Lt. John Murray), and *Mackerel* (Lt. T.H. Hutchinson).

Jamaica and Leeward Islands Stations and en route to the West Indies: 74-gun *Dragon* (Rear Admiral Sir F. Laforey and Captain F.A. Collier), 38-gun *Arethusa*, 38-gun *Sybelle* (C. Upton), 32-gun *Southampton*, lost on the Bahama Keys (Sir James Yeo), 32-gun *Jason* (William King), 32-gun *Narcissus* (J.R. Lumley), 28-gun *Mercury* (C. Milward), 22-gun *Garland* (first name unknown Davies), 20-gun *Coquette* (John Simpson), 20-gun *Cyane*, lost on Bahama Keys (Thomas Forrest), 20-gun *Lightning* (B.C. Boyle), 18-gun *Brazen*, 18-gun *Bold* (John Skekel), 18-gun *Crane* (James Stuart), 18-gun *Dauntless* (D. Barber), 18-gun *Demerara* (W.H. Smith), 18-gun *Peruvian* (A.F. Westropp), 18-gun *Indian* (Henry Jane), 18-gun *Sappho* (H. O'Grady), 16-gun *Maria* (Lt. Bligh), 16-gun *Swaggerer* (G.J. Evelyn), 14-gun *Protection* (Lt. G. Mitchener), 14-gun *Liberty* (G.M. Guise), 14-gun *Morne Fortunee* (J. Steele), 14-gun *Netley* (G. Green), 14-gun *Spider* (F. G. Willich), 12-gun *Elizabeth* (Lt. Edward F. Droyer), 12-gun *Rapide* (N. W. Pere), 10-gun *Algerine* (D. Carpenter), 10-gun *Dominico*, lost on Bahamas Keys (Robert Hockings), 10-gun *Opossum* (Thomas Woolridge), 8-gun *Ballahon* (Norfolk King), 6-gun *Green Linnet*, and 8-gun *Subtle*, sinks while pursuing *Jack's Favourite*, an American privateer (Lt. Charles Brown).

Newfoundland Station: 50-gun *Antelope* (Admiral Sir E. Nagle and Captain Edward Hawkes), 32-gun *Hyperion* (W.P. Cumby), 18-gun *Electra* (William Gregory), 18-gun *Hazard* (John Cooksley), 16-gun *Alert*, captured by the USS *Essex* (Lt. William Smith).

January 3 (Sunday) *In naval activity,* British Lt. General Hislop, in response to Captain Bainbridge's decision to parole him and his staff (seized when the HMS *Java* was taken), states in a letter to Bainbridge:

> Your acquiescence with my request in granting my parole with the officers of my staff, added to the obligations I had previously experienced, claim from me this additional tribute of my thanks. May I now finally flatter myself that in the further extension of your generous and humane feelings, in the alleviation of the misfortunes of war, that you will have the goodness to fulfil the only wish I am now anxious to see completed, by enlarging on their parole, (on the same conditions you acceded to with respect to myself,) all the officers of the Java still on board your ship; a favour I shall

never cease duly to appreciate by your acquiescence thereto.

Bainbridge replies on this day and agrees to parole all of the officers taken on the *Java*. Also around this time, General Hislop presents Captain Bainbridge with a "splendid gold mounted sword" in gratitude for the treatment he and the other British officers received from the Americans during their captivity aboard the *Constitution*.

January 4 (Monday) **In England,** it is becoming apparent to the British that American sea power has made an indelible impression because of the depth and speed of ships such as the USS *Constitution*, USS *President* and the USS *United States*. The *London Courier* of this day states that "some of the most famous British line of battle ships — some of them having been under Nelson's orders — including the *Culloden, Monarch, Thunderer,* and *Resolution,* were selected to be cut down as frigates."

In naval activity, Captain Bainbridge is informed by British Lt. Chadds that Captain Lambert of the *Java* had expired.

January 6 (Wednesday) *In naval activity,* the *Constitution*, commanded by Captain William Bainbridge, departs from its position off the coast of Brazil and returns to the United States, arriving in February. Meanwhile, the USS *Hornet* under Captain James Lawrence remains off the coast of St. Salvador, where it continues to prevent the HMS *Bonne Citoyenne* from leaving port.

January 7 (Thursday) *In naval activity,* the privateer *Paul Jones*, a schooner which had recently embarked on its second cruise, seizes the 12-gun *Seaton*, which is transporting a cargo of flour from San Salvador to Lisbon, Portugal. Also, the privateer *America*, having completed its cruise, which lasts 120 days, arrives in port at Salem, Massachusetts. During its time at sea, six prizes had been seized with a combined value of about $158,000. Later this month, the *America* embarks on another cruise which keeps it on the prowl until the following July, when it arrives back at Bath, Maine.

January 9 (Saturday) *In naval activity,* the American privateer *Comet*, shortly after arriving off Pernambuco, Brazil, this day, receives information that British vessels in the harbor are preparing to sail. On the 11th, Captain Boyle communicates with a Portuguese brigantine, the *Wasa*, which is entering the port. Captain Boyle decides to lurk in the area to intercept the British merchant ships he expects to leave port.

January 10 (Sunday) **In Ohio,** General Winchester arrives at the rapids near the site of the Battle of Fallen Timbers (1794) with the remainder of his force to link up with General Payne. Earlier, General Harrison, after being informed that General Winchester was en route to join him for an attack against Detroit, sent word back to Winchester urging him to abort the advance due to word that a large gathering of Indians under Tecumtha (Tecumseh) had been on the Wabash and his (Winchester) supply trains in the rear would be jeopardized. Winchester ignores Harrison. A force of more than 650 men under General Payne arrives ahead of Harrison. While Payne's column advances, it is to search for Indians thought to be at an old fortification near Swan Creek. The column passes near Fort Miami, but no evidence Indians is revealed; however, an abandoned Indian camp is discovered. A contingent led by Captain Williams moves out in pursuit of the Indians. Later, the troops encounter a band of the Indians. A fight develops and the Indians are vanquished; they disengage and move toward Malden in Canada.

Meanwhile, at General Winchester's encampment, the troops begin to relax due to having completed this leg of the march without opposition. The camp is near the encampment held by General Hull the previous summer (1812). After General Harrison had learns of the threat of the Indians he departs from his headquarters to confer with Governor Meigs (Ohio). Also, while General Winchester remains in his camp, his troops construct a storehouse to hold the supplies and baggage. It is built within his fortified camp and referred to as Fort Deposit, the same name given to a fort built at the same place during 1794 by General Anthony Wayne.

January 11 (Monday) **In Canada,** British Colonel Henry Proctor is informed that an American force had arrived at Frenchtown along the Raisin River from where the intelligence pointed to an attack against Brownstown. Proctor, also aware of the imminent arrival of General William Henry Harrison, makes preparations to attack Winchester's lines before the two American forces can join together. He initiates the assault on 22 January.

January 13 (Wednesday) *In naval activity,* the American privateer *Siro*, while cruising off the coast of Ireland, is intercepted by the HMS *Pelican* and captured. The British take it into port at Plymouth, England. After being refitted, the *Siro* heads back out to sea with its new name, the *Atlanta*.

January 14 (Thursday) *In naval activity,* the American privateer *Comet* is waiting patiently outside the harbor at Pernambuco, Brazil. The crew's patience is paying off. Three British merchant ships are departing; however, Captain Boyle, having been in the area since the 9th, had been informed that no British warships were in the harbor, causing him some apprehension when a brigantine warship is escorting the vessels, two brigantines and one ship. By 1500, the convoy reaches a point about 35 miles from port. The *Comet* initiates the chase at full sail which brings it in close proximity by about 1800. Captain Boyle, who believes the fourth vessel is another merchant ship, is able to identify it as a brigantine warship.

Through earlier intelligence, the captain is aware that the merchant ships are heavily armed, and he begins to ponder his chances of success now that they are bolstered by the brigantine man of war. After a minute or two he makes his decision and orders the decks cleared for action. Boyle's decision to fight comes as no surprise to the crew; their captain has a reputation as someone who is fearless against an enemy. The guns are loaded as the *Comet* closes on the warship. By 1900, the *Comet* is within firing range of the brigantine and at the same time, the American flag is hoisted.

Once the American colors begin to flutter in the wind, the brigantine hoists its colors, and to the surprise of Boyle and his crew, no British ensign is spotted; rather the Portuguese ensign is raised, leaving Boyle with some doubt as to the origin of the ship. The mystery soon ends.

A boat pulls alongside the *Comet* and an officer attired in a Portuguese uniform moves aboard the *Comet* to inform Captain Boyle that his ship is a Portuguese warship designated as the protector of the British convoy. He also stresses that his crew numbers 165 men and his vessel has 32 guns mounted. The Portuguese officer then instructs Boyle that the convoy, while under his protection, must not be harmed. This grave news, intended to intimidate Boyle, once again causes him to ponder his decision whether to engage the quartet. After a few seconds of silent deliberation, Boyle informs the officer that his vessel is authorized to capture British vessels on the open seas and he questions why the Portuguese would inject themselves into the matter. The discussion continues for a while. The officer tells Boyle that the merchant ships will assist if a battle ignites. Boyle, unimpressed, retorts that he holds little confidence in their combined strength, but he will provide them the opportunity to use it.

The officer returns to his ship and reports the results of his conversation with Captain Boyle to his commanding officer. Before departing, the officer informs Captain Boyle that he will return. Boyle's patience comes to an end after he inquires whether the officer is going to return and receives a response that the Portuguese intend to speak with the British aboard the merchant ships. The Portuguese ask Boyle send over a boat in the meantime. Boyle, suspicious of the Portuguese stall tactic, unambiguously replies that no boat would be sent, and to cement his intentions to the Portuguese, he informs them that the merchant ships will be attacked.

Shortly thereafter, the *Comet* goes into motion. It moves close to the ship and orders the crew to "back their main topsail." Meanwhile, the *Comet* moves ahead of the ship only to observe that his order was not carried out, prompting him to send them a new message. In a yelling voice, he informs the British on the ship that within a short time the *Comet* would again be alongside, and if his directive was not followed by then, the ship would be broadsided. The *Comet* moves in close with the Portuguese brigantine just behind. At about the same time, with the warship closing, one of the brigantines moves up next to the ship and to their surprise, both come under fire. Boyle's seamen are skilled, which enables him to maintain the *Comet* at close quarters. The Portuguese enter the fight and fire upon the *Comet*, only to receive return fire from a long tom and other guns that deliver broadsides. By this time, the ships are closely intermingled, and because of the high amount of smoke, the vessels become indistinguishable, a disadvantage for the Portuguese and the other ships which might inadvertently fire upon a friendly ship. However, the American gunners are not impeded. They are able to fire at any of the other vessels with the certainty that their target is the enemy.

Captain Boyle, using the smoke and the darkness to his advantage, remains close to the merchant ships. The British separate to provide the Portuguese with a more conspicuous target, however, thanks to the skills of the Portuguese gunners, the *Comet* sustains only some minor damage. Just after midnight (14th-15th), the crew of the *Comet* hears voices from a ship that proclaims its surrender. After only a short while, one of the brigantines, which had been severely damaged, joins the chorus and it too informs the *Comet* that it has capitulated.

Captain Boyle prepares to send a boarding party to take possession of the ship, but before it reaches the vessel, the Portuguese gunners fire at the boat carrying the party, compelling the men to abort and return to the *Comet*. The shots that nearly destroyed Boyle's boat cause him to focus all of his attention on the Portuguese. Effective fire forces the warship to move back, giving Boyle time to seize the third vessel, which had also sustained devastating damage. All the while, Boyle is also concentrating on preventing the Portuguese brigantine from getting in close. While moving to seize the remaining vessel, the crew of the *Comet*, while passing the ship again, hears British voices, but the sounds are much more intense. They are screaming that their vessel is about to sink.

By about 0130 on the 15th, the Americans finally take possession of the merchant brigantine. The Portuguese, however, attempt to prevent the other two vessels from falling to the *Comet*. The night fighting has been grueling, but the crew of the *Comet* seems to disregard their exhaustion. The gunners maintain fire to keep the Portuguese vessel at a distance. The Portuguese also fire upon the captured brigantine but don't intimidate the prize crew, which refuses to surrender. Nevertheless, the engagement does not conclude. By 0200, the weather changes and the light of the moon vanishes, causing the *Comet* to lose sight of its prizes. At nearly the same time, the Portuguese warship can no longer be seen, but it has positioned itself close to the other two prizes.

Back on the *Comet*, Captain Boyle remains next to the vessel with the prize crew for the remainder of the night. At daybreak, the Portuguese warship begins to move toward the *Comet*, and the latter's crew prepares to resume the engagement. Nonetheless, the Portuguese stop short, and from the *Comet*, the crew is able to see signals directing the two British ships to head for port. Both vessels, having been badly damaged, move slowly, prompting Captain Boyle to discern that it would not be pragmatic to try to seize the cripples. The warship then joins the two other vessels, and it becomes evident that it, too, had been bludgeoned. All three of the vessels limp toward the harbor.

Afterward, it is determined that the ship was the *George*, commanded by Captain Wilson, and the brigantine was the *Gambia*. It is also learned that the Portuguese had sustained five killed and some others wounded. Meanwhile, the *Comet* remains seaworthy and soon after the engagement resumes the hunt. The *Comet* seizes a ship out of Scotland, the *Adelphi*, which is transporting a cargo of dry goods and salt from Liverpool to Bahia, Brazil. Later, the *Comet* has a harrowing encounter when it is pursued by the frigate HMS *Surprise*. Thanks to the skill of his crew and the speed of the *Comet*, the *Surprise* is unable to catch its prey, leaving Captain Boyle to continue his cruise in the West Indies.

January 15 (Friday) Major Timothy Upham, 13th U.S. Regiment, is ordered to Portland, Maine, to become the superintendent of recruiting in the District of Maine. Later, during spring of this year, he rejoins his regiment to participate in the upcoming campaign of Major General Wade Hampton, which is to attack and seize Montreal.

January 16 (Saturday) In Ohio, a dispatch rider arrives at General Harrison's headquarters at Upper Sandusky with news that General Winchester had advanced to the Rapids and was preparing to take offensive action. The information is not kindly received. Harrison is aware of the conditions of Winchester's troops, who have suffered from the weather and shortages of rations and winter clothing since they arrived at Fort Winchester. Harrison immediately orders his artillery to expeditiously advance to bolster Winchester. An escort of about 300 troops under Major Orr escorts the artillery.

Meanwhile, Harrison speeds to Lower Sandusky where General Perkins is encamped with a force of one battalion and one regiment. Once there, he orders the battalion, under Major Cotgrove, to initiate its advance as soon as possible. Harrison intends to spend the night and resumes his journey to catch up with the troops on the following day. The next day, another dispatch rider arrives to deliver another update on Winchester's progress, which General Harrison receives just after rising. The news only causes Harrison more concern. Colonel Lewis is moving to attack Frenchtown. Without even waiting for an escort, Harrison finishes his breakfast, and after directing General Perkins to order his remaining troops to move expeditiously to the Rapids, both Harrison and Perkins depart from the camp in a sled. While en route, yet another express rider intercepts the sled and informs General Harrison that Colonel Lewis had struck the British at the Raisin River and his force was victorious. The news exasperates Harrison. General Winchester has not consulted with General Harrison before taking action.

He mounts a horse and without any escort, he rides through the snow-filled swamps until he finally arrives at the Rapids during the morning hours on the 20th. Nonetheless, Harrison had departed the fort en route to the Raisin River on the night of the 19th, leaving Harrison only one option, to await the arrival of the forces under General Perkins, along with the contingent under Cotgrove and the artillery. Meanwhile, the troops under Colonel Payne, who are still at the Rapids, are directed to advance toward the river. Captain Hart is dispatched to catch Winchester and inform him that Harrison's force is advancing to augment his wing of the army. Nevertheless, Winchester's advance continues without any artillery support. Meanwhile, as the reinforcements are struggling to reach the rapids, General Winchester arrives at Frenchtown on the 19th.

In naval activity, the American privateer *Anaconda* (Captain David Maffitt), while operating off Cape Cod, encounters a schooner. The crew prepares for action; however, after the *Anaconda* fires, it becomes evident that a devastating misidentification had occurred. The schooner that is struck is the USS *Commodore Hull* and its commanding officer, Lieutenant H. S. Newcomb, receives a grievous wound. The blame for the tragic mistake falls upon First Officer Burbank of the *Anaconda*. Nonetheless, at a court-martial the crew of the Anaconda "is relieved from responsibility in the matter."

In other naval activity, the privateer *Decatur* under Captain Nichols is intercepted and captured by the HMS *Surprise*. After Captain Nichols is transported to Barbados, his past comes back to haunt him after he is recognized by a British officer who commands the HMS *Vestal*. Prior to the war, the *Decatur* had the name *Alert* and Captain Nichols was in command when the HMS *Vestal* captured it. Afterward, Nichols was able to devise a plan by which he recaptured his ship, relieving the British commander of his prize. After being recognized, Captain Nichols receives cruel punishment. The British also confine him to a room not much larger than a closet until they transfer him to England. The *Decatur* is separate from the privateer out of Charleston under Captain Dominique Diron and the privateer out of Maine under Captain S.L. Lane.

January 17 (Sunday) *In naval activity,* the USS *Viper*, originally the USS *Ferret* until 1809, is captured off Belize, British Honduras, by the 32-gun frigate HMS *Narcissus*. The British take the *Viper* to New Providence in the Bahamas. The U.S. Navy has no details on the *Viper* after its capture. Also, the HMS *Magicienne* spots the American privateer *Thrasher* and initiates pursuit. The privateer runs and for awhile escape remains possible, but after about nine hours the chase ends and the *Thrasher* is captured off St. Mary's. During its time at sea, the *Thrasher*'s prizes include the brigantine *Tor Abbey* and the 350-ton ship *Britannia*.

Also, the American privateer *Terrible*, also out of Salem, despite its diminutive size and description of being "scarcely more than an open boat," during its time at sea seizes several prizes, including the schooner *Harmony* out of Nova Scotia.

January 17–18 BATTLE OF FRENCHTOWN In Michigan, a detachment of General Winchester's Army led by Colonels William Lewis and John Allen is moving toward at Frenchtown (present-day Monroe) along the Raisin River, where a combined British-Indian force had arrived a few days earlier. The Americans had been sent to protect inhabitants that are threatened by the British.

At this time, General Harrison is at Upper Sandusky more than 60 miles distant, and General Winchester had initiated the action without consulting with his commander-in-chief. Colonel Lewis, commanding about 550 troops, arrives first and is trailed by a 110-man contingent under Colonel John Allen. On the morning of the 18th, Colonels William Lewis and John Allen move out for the Raisin River, and they advance undiscovered until the column reaches a point less than five miles from Frenchtown.

Colonel Lewis, after being informed that the British are prepared, appears no less confident. The column presses forward, oblivious to the cold until it reaches the south bank of the frozen river, less than one-half mile from the objective just across the river. At Frenchtown — held by the British since shortly after the surrender of Detroit — is defended by about 200 men of the Essex militia (Canadians) under Major Reynolds and about 200 to 300 Indians led by Roundhead and Walk-in-the-water. The British observe Lewis' force while it prepares to ford the river, and an artillery piece pounds the south bank of the river, without much effect.

Meanwhile, Lewis signals the attack and the line crosses the river and the troops for a while struggle to get up the slippery embankment. Despite heavy fire, the Americans continue to advance. Troops under Major Benjamin Graves and Major George Madison desperately attempt to capture the howitzer, but the British preserve it as they continue to defiantly defend, while simultaneously being driven back toward the woods to the rear of the village.

After regrouping in the woods, the British continue to resist. Majors Graves and George Madison pound against the British right. At the same time, the British left is focused on preventing Colonel Allen's contingent from penetrating. The fighting intensifies and the British are slowly compelled to give ground, while the Americans gain the ground yard-by-yard.

Finally, the skirmish that began at about 1500 concludes at just about dusk. The Americans retire and occupy the village. During the day's fighting, the U.S. sustains 12 killed and 55 wounded, including Captain Bland W. Ballard, who was wounded while leading the vanguard. British-Indian casualties are not calculated; however, 15 dead had been discovered on the field.

Meanwhile, a report is sent to General Winchester. After receiving it, Winchester dispatches reinforcements to augment the force at Frenchtown in the event British Colonel Proctor arrives from Malden, which is less than 20 miles distant. Nonetheless, although the British had been vanquished, the Indians had not completely departed from Frenchtown. After dark, the Indians retrieve their dead and wounded and before they head for Malden, they pause at some settlers' houses, where they pillage. Some of the settlers in the area are killed and scalped.

Word of the seizure of Frenchtown is relayed to General Harrison, who becomes alarmed that the British might well attack Winchester before the main body can arrive to reinforce him. Nonetheless, Winchester, who disobeyed Harrison's orders, is not recalled. However, he does dispatch Captain Nathaniel Hart to Frenchtown. Upon his arrival, he advises Winchester that his force in totally unprepared to defend against a British attack. General Winchester, however, is confident that he has sufficient time before the British can prepare to attack.

January 19 (Tuesday) **In Michigan** at Frenchtown, Colonel Lewis confers with the other officers and they decide to hold Frenchtown. Lewis is aware that a major British force under General Proctor is at Malden, but he and the other officers are confident they can hold until the reinforcements arrive. On the following day (20th), General Winchester and Colonel Samuel Wells arrive from Fort Deposit with about 250 to 300 troops during midday. Curiously, General Winchester places Colonel Wells in command of the reinforcements, while he and his staff move back to the south side of the river. He establishes his headquarters at the house of Colonel Francis Navarre, which is outside of the American lines. Meanwhile, the reinforcements under Wells encamp in some open ground to the right of Lewis' command. A small detachment acting as rear guard under Captain Morris stays with the baggage from the rapids of the Maumee River.

Despite the high probability of an attack by the British, General Winchester fails to order the distribution of ammunition. In addition, no reconnaissance patrols are dispatched, nor does he send out any spies. His force is already exhausted by the sufferings at camp during the horrible weather, lack of proper clothing and rations; however, they are surprised on the following day because of Winchester's failure to have his troops prepared to defend.

In naval activity, the USS *Essex* arrives at St. Catherine's. A party is sent ashore to inform the authorities that the ship is American and that they are in need of water and provisions. On the 21st, a party goes ashore for supplies. After a long delay, concern builds on the *Essex* when the party does not return, and for a while, it is thought that the torrential rains had been the cause. Nonetheless, at about 0200 on the 22nd, two officers, Lieutenants Gambit and Wilmer, appear at Captain David Porter's cabin to report. Both men had lost nearly all of their uniforms. The boat had overturned, but the good news was that all hands had been spared. Following a long time clinging to the craft, the men reached an island lying in the middle of the bay where they were able to right the boat. The bad news, overshadowed by the news that no one was lost, is that the men had not only lost all of their clothes, but also all of the provisions they were attempting to bring back to the ship. Nonetheless, the provisions and supplies are all recovered. The beef had gone bad and it is thrown overboard to the delight of some sea creatures that had arrived.

On the previous night, some of the crew had been swimming near the ship for relaxation unaware of what was swimming nearby. Soon after the meat is discarded, from their safe positions on the deck, the crew spots a monstrous shark described by Captain Porter as being "25 feet long in length ... with a quarter of a bullock in his mouth." The shark was initially identified by some as a "young whale." Captain Porter remarks about the officers and men who were swimming on the previous night, "A man would scarcely have been a mouthful for him."

In the meantime, Captain Porter meets with the fort's commanding officer, an elderly man named Don Alexandre Jose de Azedido. The commander is cordial, and as Captain Porter describes: "He received me with great civility, and, as has been generally the case with the Portuguese, expressed a great desire that our cruise might be successful." The fort, also described by Porter,

has been erected about seventy years; there are mounted on it fifteen or twenty honey-combed guns of different calibres. Vegetation has been so rapid, that the walls of the fortress are nearly hid by the trees that have shot up in every part. The gun-carriages are in a very rotten state, and the garrison consists of about twenty half naked soldiers.

There is a church within the fortress; here, as a substitute for a bell, is suspended at the door, part of a broken crow-bar; and at the entrance of the commandant's apartments is the stocks, (for the punishment of the soldiers,) which, from their greasy, polished appearance, I have reason to believe are kept in constant use. There are three forts for the protection of the bay, of which this is the principal: one on a high point on the island of St. Catharines, and another on the island where our boat landed after upsetting, called Great Rat Island. About one league and a half below the chief fortress, on the starboard hand going into the bay, behind a rocky point, are the houses for the accommodation of those employed in the whale fishery, as well as the stores, boilers, and tanks to contain the oil.

The crown has the exclusive privilege of fishing here. About five hundred men are employed in it. Nearly the same number of whales are taken annually in the bay, where they come to calve, and are then perfectly helpless.... The people of this place appear to be the most happy of those who live under the Portuguese government, probably because the more they are distant from it, the less they are subject to its impositions and oppressions; still, however, they complain. There are two regiments of troops at St. Catharines: if provisions are wanted for them, an officer goes to the houses of the peasantry, seizes on their cattle or grain, and gives them a bill on the government, for which they never receive payment. The peasantry are well clad, and comfortable and cheerful in their appearance; the women are handsome and graceful in their manners; the men have the character of being extremely jealous of them, and I believe they have some reason to be so.

January 21–23 BATTLE OF RAISIN RIVER (RAISIN RIVER MASSACRE) At Frenchtown, less than 20 miles from British Ft. Maiden (Canada), on the western section of Lake Erie, the Americans under General James Winchester have taken no steps to defend against an attack. On the 21st, following a tranquil night, General Winchester sends a small party (Peter Navarre and his brothers) on a scouting mission to the Detroit River. They encounter a man, Joseph Bordeau, who had escaped from Malden. Bordeau relates that the British are en route to the river and will arrive sometime during the night. Nonetheless, when Winchester is informed of the intelligence, he disregards the threat. However, some of his officers, including Colonel Samuel Wells, who arrived with General Winchester, remain convinced that the British are en route. Wells, accompanied by Captain Langham, departs from camp and speeds to the rapids on the Maumee in an attempt to get reinforcements. In the meantime, no additional guards are posted, nor are any other precautions taken to ensure the camp is not hit by surprise. The units encamped include Colonel Wells' regiment, Colonel Allen's regiment and the 1st and 5th Kentucky Regiments. Colonel William Lewis advises General Winchester to deploy Colonel Wells' force near Lewis' positions in a spot with some concealment; however, Wells, who is in the regulars, outranks Lewis, and he insists upon deploying his several hundred troops to the right of Lewis upon naked ground in a field.

General Winchester, totally unconcerned about an attack, remains at his headquarters outside of the American lines. All the while, Colonel Henry Proctor continues to approach without detection. His force is composed of about 140 troops of the 41st Regiment and of the Royal Newfoundland Regiment, a detachment of the 10th Veteran Battalion, along with militia and a contingent of Canadian seamen. The force is bolstered an artillery contingent and more than 400 Indians. The Americans estimate the force at about 1,100.

Nonetheless, due to the indifference of General Winchester, the Americans are not anticipating the threat, leaving the British to advance without detection during the predawn hours. The American camp is totally quiet. At about the time reveille is sounded there is a crack in the silence when a sentry who spots the British fires to alert the camp. Despite the warning shot, which is followed by the fire of other sentinels, the reaction is slow. Meanwhile, the British guns also announce the presence of the Redcoats. The Americans find themselves the recipients of a thunderous bombardment. The unprepared Americans are under severe attack by the ground troops and the Indians.

The British charge through the snow and crash into the flanks as well as the front; however, the Americans, defending at the fences around the houses in the village, earlier used by the British during Winchester's attack, hold the line along the front. Simultaneously, British pressure collapses the right flank. Meanwhile, troops under General Winchester and Colonel John Allen arrive to support the faltering line; however, the reinforcements are too little and too late. The Americans on the flank by this time fail to regroup, while the British pour more pressure into the charge, and suddenly pandemonium emerges.

Colonel Wells' force on the right is ordered (after its ammunition is nearly depleted) to withdraw to Lewis's positions, which have some protection, but orders get confused and it is apparently thought that the order was to retreat. Nonetheless, suddenly there is a stampede. Efforts to halt the runaways fail. General Winchester's aloofness has transformed the recent victory at Frenchtown into a debacle. While the Americans on the right flank are haphazardly fleeing across the river to the opposite bank, an identical scenario is unfolding on the left flank, which also gives way to the thrust of the British. The Americans lose all discipline as they retreat while under punishing fire. Wells' force, holding untenable positions from the beginning, is nearly annihilated. Of the several hundred in his command, the survivors include 28 men and another forty that are captured by the British.

All the while, the wild yells of the Indians inflict additional panic as troops bolt from their lines on the left flank to escape the shot and shell, as well as the tomahawk. However, as the troops flee from their defensive fences, they find themselves coming under incessant fire from Indian warriors deployed near the fences. The panic reaches epidemic proportions as the Americans pivot to avoid the deadly fire along the road and make it to the woods on the west side of the village. But the path to possible safety only leads the retreating troops into yet another cauldron. Other Indians posted in the woods block passage and many troops that reach the woods are liquidated by the tomahawk. In one instance, a group of about 20 troops including one officer, Lieutenant Ashton Garrett, conclude that escape is impossible. They surrender and their plight only becomes worse. The Indians accept the surrender, then swoop down upon them, murdering every one except the lieutenant.

The British continue their rout of the Americans at Frenchtown; however, despite their successes, they are unable to dislodge the Kentuckians who continue to steadfastly hold the center of the line. Repeatedly, the British attempt to penetrate, but each thrust is repelled. The fences at that point, defended by Kentucky marksmen, remind the British that they are not immortal. Nevertheless, while Colonel Proctor becomes frustrated at the inability of his regulars to crush the center, he also begins to weigh the high cost paid in the unsuccessful attempts to complete his victory. Consequently, he turns to General Winchester, who had been captured, along with Colonel Lewis, shortly after arriving on the field by an Indian, Brandy Jack. Brandy Jack, attached to Roundhead's band, had also stripped Winchester of his uniform before handing him over to Proctor, while he himself dons the general's coat and cocked hat. General Winchester is threatened by Colonel Proctor, who informs Winchester that the entire command will be annihilated if his remaining troops do not capitulate immediately. General Winchester, half frozen since losing his uniform and aware that his force has been thrashed, acquiesces to Proctor's ultimatum.

However, Winchester's bargaining power is extremely weak. At the time when Proctor approached him, Winchester was near a camp fire and being held by Chief Roundhead (Wyandotte), who was boasting of his new coat.

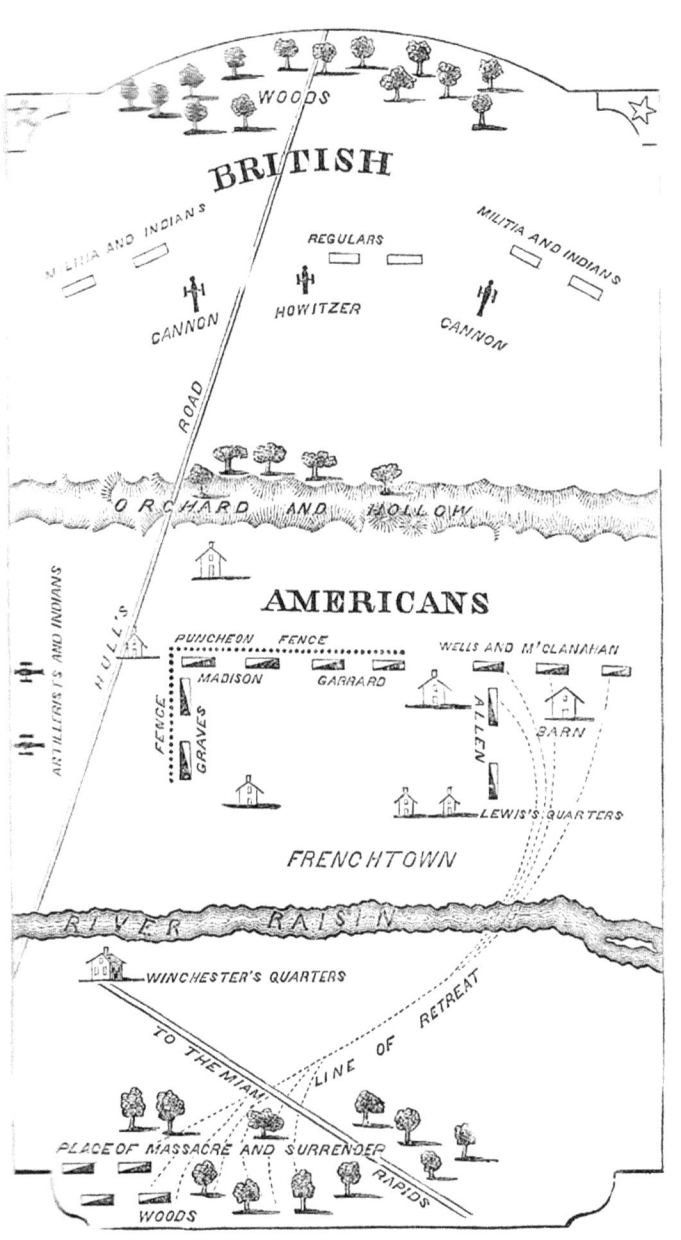

Movements at Frenchtown.

Nonetheless, General Winchester sends word to Lieutenant Madison by a messenger (Colonel Walter H. Overton, Winchester's aide) who approaches Madison's positions with Colonel Proctor under a white flag. Madison and his Kentuckians reject Winchester's order to surrender after concluding that General Winchester, as a prisoner, has lost his authority to issue such an order. Madison sets his own conditions in a proposal to Proctor: "It has been customary for the Indians to massacre the wounded and prisoners after a surrender; I shall therefore not agree to any capitulation which General Winchester may direct, unless the safety and protection of all the prisoners shall be stipulated."

The situation for the Americans remains grim. Colonel John Allen, who had been able to retreat after his lines were overrun, had evaded capture, but afterward, he was intercepted by several Indians. Although suffering from a wound, Colonel Allen takes out one of them by his sword; however, he is then shot by another. With Winchester and Lewis being held captive and Colonel Allen having been killed, the sole resistance remains with Madison's command. Proctor, after initially receiving Madison's response, displays his disbelief and bellows: "Sir, do you mean to dictate to me?" Madison retorts: "I mean to dictate to myself. We prefer selling our lives as dearly as possible rather than be massacred in cold blood." Essentially, Major Madison has caused a stalemate. The British, unable to vanquish Madison's Kentuckians unless they are willing to accept high casualties, are eventually compelled to accept Madison's offer to surrender.

The Kentuckians, after receiving the guarantees from Proctor, surrender; however, Proctor's word is worthless. While Proctor takes no action to protect the prisoners, the Indians begin to attack the Kentuckians in full view of the British who promised protection. Nonetheless, the Kentuckians refuse to be mauled. They retrieve their arms and shortly thereafter, the Indians discover that there is no time to begin scalping the prisoners, due to a sudden turn in the tide. The Kentuckians, with fixed bayonets, mount a ferocious charge. The Indians, always fearful of close contact with the bayonet, are scattered. Meanwhile, Colonel Proctor, having been informed of the approach of American reinforcements under General Harrison, focuses on self-preservation. He departs from Frenchtown for Malden about one hour after the surrender of Madison. He leaves without taking either his wounded or dead, including Colonel St. George, who had been wounded three separate times. Only the prisoners who can walk are taken with the column. Those more seriously wounded are left behind at Frenchtown, and Proctor has deceivingly left word that sleds would be arriving from Malden to transport them to the post. The troops in his command remain puzzled about why Proctor absconded so prematurely, with Harrison about 8 or 10 miles out. Many place the blame on him for the atrocities of the Indians.

Colonel Proctor does, however, suffer some disappointment. Following his victory over General Winchester, he had tried to convince the Indians to destroy the French settlers' homes because it was his belief that they were strongly aligned with the Americans; however, the Pottawatomie Indians had retained a strong relationship with the French who inhabited the area on the Raisin, and they totally reject the idea.

During the following morning (23rd), while the British are paused at Stoney Creek, about 200 of the Indians depart from the column and return to Frenchtown, where the American wounded are guarded only by a British officer, Major Reynolds. Once there they decide to murder all prisoners that cannot be marched back to their villages. The defenseless Americans — under the care of two surgeons, Doctor Todd and Doctor Bowers — are pounced upon. The houses are set on fire and the entire village is pillaged. During the rampage, the Indians, most of whom are inebriated, discover more whiskey in the cellar of one of the houses. The yells of the Indians afterward become more frequent and much louder, increasing the fears of the inhabitants and the wounded prisoners. Some of the disabled troops attempt to escape the flames. After succeeding in getting out of the burning buildings, they are confronted by more brutality. Indians remove their scalps and the mutilated troops are thrown back into the fires. Survivors are dragged toward Amherstburg, and while en route, the sick and exhausted troops begin to falter. The Indians react by killing them with blows from the tomahawk, and once they are killed, the Indians scalp them.

Following the victory over the Americans, Colonel Proctor arrives at Amherstburg on the 23rd, and from there he proceeds to Sandwich, where some of the prisoners are sent to Detroit and others to Fort George. Others, including General James Winchester, Colonel William Lewis and Major George Madison, are sent to Quebec until being transferred to Beauport just outside of Quebec, where they are confined until they are exchanged in spring 1814.

Colonel Madison is elected governor of Kentucky during 1816 and his term is to last until 1820; however, Madison dies on 14 October 1816 before he is inaugurated. Colonel Gabriel Slaughter, the lieutenant governor, is inaugurated instead. Also, one of General Winchester's officers, Captain Hickman was killed after being wounded in Frenchtown. Captain Nathaniel Hart, wounded in the knee, had been taken out of the village by one of the doctors and a half-breed Indian and British officer, William Elliott (previously an acquaintance of Hart when Hart stayed at the family home in Lexington). Elliott promises Hart he will have him carried to Malden where he will get medical attention. During the journey, Hart is mounted until he is shot by a band of Indians, then tomahawked and afterward scalped. Captain Hart (Lexington light infantry), a Virginian who relocated to Kentucky, is left lying on the road where he dies. There is no word on Major Graves following the battle at the village.

The Creek warriors who participate in the Raisin River Massacre, had traveled from Creek country, and upon their return, they are punished by the peaceable Creeks in the area who fear retaliation by the white settlers. Chief Little Warrior and his followers are killed, which causes a civil war between the Upper and Lower Creeks. The upper Creeks, supporting Chief Little Warrior, attack both lower Creeks and white settlers in the area. Other Kentuckians (officers) killed during the massacre include Captains Edwards, Hickman, Mead, McCracken and Price. Also, Lt. Colonel John Allen, a native Virginian who moved to Kentucky with his family about 1779 when he was only about eight years old, is killed during the retreat. Colonel Allen had unsuccessfully run for governor of Kentucky during 1808; however, he was elected to the U.S. Congress. Another officer, U.S. Congressman-elect Captain Simpson, is also killed. He was first shot at the edge of the woods and afterward tomahawked. Simpson, who was quite tall at about 6 feet, 6 inches, became a grotesque curiosity for the Indians, who gathered about his corpse to gaze in wonderment about his build.

While the loss at the Raisin River is burdensome for the Americans, particularly the Kentuckians, Colonel Proctor rides a wave of joy in Upper Canada, and he is promoted to brigadier general. His reports omit the ghastly atrocities of the Indians and instead rings of praise for their support during the fight at the Raisin River. Meanwhile, as the facts make their way back to Kentucky, the words "Raisin River" ignite different sentiments, and the Kentuckians adopt a new slogan, "Remember the River Raisin." The initial American success at Frenchtown on the 17th-18th soon was reversed by the devastating defeat that costs the Americans more than nine hundred casualties, including just under 400 killed or missing and the remainder captured. Only about 33 troops escape. The British under Proctor, according to his report, sustain 24 killed and 158 wounded. No casualty figures for the Indians are available. Also, one American officer, Captain John Woolfolk, initially escapes harm; however, Indians discover him hiding in a house. He attempts to gain his freedom by offering $1,000 to permit him passage to Detroit. His offer is rejected and he is shot, then left on the road to die. The French settlers who are unable to save Woolfolk do manage to save some other Americans.

The grievous loss at the river also causes totally unintended consequences. Although the Raisin River Massacre greatly inspires the Northwestern Army and brings about the rallying cry, "Remember the River Raisin," revenge is postponed. General Harrison is compelled to suspend his winter campaign to seize Detroit. Meanwhile, Harrison orders the establishment of Fort Meigs (Perryville, Ohio) near the rapids of the Maumee River. Colonel John Wood supervises the construction of the post. Harrison bolsters the fort's defenses with artillery and some block houses that are enclosed within the eight-acre site, located on high ground on the right bank of the river.

At the time of the defeat, Charles Scott, a general during the American Revolution, is governor of Kentucky. He is succeeded by Governor Isaac Shelby, another prominent leader of the Revolution before the British move against the fort. Also, Colonel John Anderson (owner of Anderson's trading post) is seized at the battle. His wife, while alone at the trading post, is accosted by Indians. She had emptied all the barrels of whiskey before the Indians arrived. Nevertheless, the Indians begin to consume the whiskey on the floor. Meanwhile, Mrs. Anderson remains seated atop the family's chest which contains money. She is threatened, but defies the Indians saying: "Shame, so many Indians fight one squaw." Her words apparently embarrass the Indians. They depart without causing her any harm.

After the devastating defeat of General Winchester at the Raisin River, John Armstrong, the secretary of war, takes the opportunity to chastise General Harrison for not immediately launching an attack. Harrison, a competent and not impetuous commander, had chosen not to immediately attack to ensure that the British could not score yet another devastating defeat upon the American force in the region. Harrison, if defeated, would have cleared the way for the British and Indians to terrorize the entire frontiers of Ohio and Pennsylvania.

January 22 (Friday) **In Ohio,** General William Henry Harrison—while at the Rapids awaiting the forces of General Simon Perkins (Ohio militia), en route to bolster General Winchester who has moved to Frenchtown—receives word that General Winchester's left wing of the Northwestern Army had been devastated at the Raisin River. Harrison orders a contingent of General Perkins' force to speed to the river. Harrison also moves there, but en route he is met by some of the few who had escaped. Soon a few more stragglers are spotted racing toward Harrison, who is informed that the defeat had been complete and that no number of troops could save the command. Harrison confers with the available officers and they conclude that to continue the advance would be folly. A detachment, however, is sent ahead to try to extricate whatever troops they could discover.

Meanwhile, General Harrison and the vanguard of the relief force returns to the Rapids. After arriving, Harrison again holds council with the officers. It is decided to withdraw to the Portage, less than twenty miles from the rapids, and establish a strong defensive camp, while they await the arrival of the artillery and the remainder of Perkins' force. When the other troops arrive to bolster his present force of about 900 men, he intends to return to the Rapids.

Once General Harrison receives reinforcements to replace Perkins' force, Perkins' command is dismissed. General Perkins departs from the army on 28 February 1813. General Harrison, aware of Perkin's value and ability, contacts President Madison, and in turn, the president sends a colonel's commission in the regulars to Perkins to entice him to remain in the service; however, personal matters compel him to decline the commission. (*See also,* **January 21–23 BATTLE OF RAISIN RIVER.**)

January 23 (Saturday) **In Canada,** at Malden, General James Winchester, a prisoner of the British, writes to the Secretary of War explaining the circumstances of the defeat on the previous day: "However unfortunate may seem the affair of yesterday, I am flattered by a belief, that no material error is chargeable upon myself, and that still less censure is deserved by the troops I had the honor of commanding. With the exception of that portion of our force which was thrown into disorder, no troops have ever behaved with a more determined intrepidity." (*See also,* **January 21–23 BATTLE OF RAISIN RIVER.**)

January 24 (Sunday) *In naval activity,* the USS *Hornet* under Captain James Lawrence, while blockading the HMS *Bonne Citoyenne* and a British packet at St. Salvador, becomes imperiled when the 74-gun HMS *Montague* arrives. Once the Montague is spotted, the *Hornet* heads for the harbor, but later that day, after dusk, the *Hornet* sails out of the harbor undiscovered and makes its escape.

January 25 (Monday) *In naval activity,* the *Dolphin,* an American privateer commanded by Captain W.S. Stafford, encounters two British vessels, the Hebe and an unidentified brigantine, while it is operating off the coasts of Portugal and Spain. The *Dolphin,* carrying ten guns, engages both vessels simultaneously. Following a hard-fought contest, both ships become prizes. Captain Stafford places prize crews aboard both vessels and they are sailed to Baltimore. The Americans sustain four fatal casualties.

In other naval activity, the privateer *Paul Jones* intercepts and seizes a brigantine, which is identified as the American vessel *Little James.* The *Paul Jones,* during this cruise, seizes 15 vessels, including the *St. Martin's Planter* and the transport *Canada,* which unexpectedly presents the *Paul Jones* 100 British troops and more than 40 horses. After the Americans remove the troops' weapons, the *Canada* is ransomed for £3000. The *Paul Jones* also seizes the *Quebec,* transporting a cargo of dry goods, the sloop *Pearl* carrying a cargo of fruit, the brigantines *Return, John and Isabella,* and the *London Packet.* The *John and Isabella* is released as a cartel for British prisoners.

January 27 (Wednesday) **In Washington, D.C.,** President Madison sends a private and confidential message to the U.S. Senate which includes a report of the secretary of war regarding the British and Spanish inciting the Creek Indians. The president had been responding to a resolution of 7 January. After receiving the communication, Congress authorizes the president to seize territory south of the Mississippi Territory and west of the Perdido. The confidential proceedings are made public in October. Meanwhile, during February, Congress gives Madison authority to evict the Spanish from the tip of Louisiana, referred to as Spanish Florida. During April, the Americans seize Mobile (Alabama), held by the British.

January 30 (Saturday) **In Ohio,** reinforcements (a Virginia brigade and a Pennsylvania regiment) under Colonel Leftwich arrive at General Harrison's camp at the Portage River. The column is accompanied by artillery.

February **In Washington, D.C.,** Congress passes legislation authorizing the occupation of Florida, west of the Perdido River; however, no invasion occurs. The secretary of war orders Generals Jackson and Pinckney to dismiss their soldiers on the spot, with neither pay nor food. General Jackson ignores the order to disperse, and during the latter part of March, he marches back to Tennessee as a unit.

In Tennessee, outside of Nashville near the Duck River, the Creeks under Little Warrior, who are returning to their lands from Detroit, attack and massacre seven settler families. One survivor, Mrs. Crawley, is taken prisoner while she is close to the bodies of her children. She is taken to Tuscaloosa Falls. The incident is remembered as the Duck River Massacre. Afterward, General James Robertson is told of the massacre and he informs Colonel Benjamin Hawkins, the agent for the Chickasaws. On 18 April, a council is held on how to deal with the atrocities.

In naval activity, Captain David Porter, U.S. Navy, who failed to hook up with Commodore Bainbridge, alters his plans and sails toward Chile in the Pacific in search of British whalers. The ship experiences inclement weather and tumultuous seas as it rounds Cape Horn. On his day Porter's ship nearly sinks from heavy damage and high seas. He notes in his report: "But the wind freshened up to a gale, and by noon had reduced us to our storm stay-sail and close-reefed main-top-sail. In the afternoon it hauled around to the westward, and blew with a fury far exceeding anything we had yet experienced, bringing with it such a tremendous sea as to threaten us every moment with destruction." Porter also notes "our pumps had become choked by the shingle ballast, which, from the violent rolling of the ship, had got into them, and the sea had increased to such a height as to threaten to swallow us at every instant. The whole ocean was one continual foam of breakers, and the heaviest squall that I ever experienced had not equaled in violence the most moderate intervals of this tremendous hurricane." Porter falls three times and is injured during the harrowing fight against the sea.

On 3 February, the *Essex* continues to encounter horrific weather. Porter states:

> We had shipped several heavy seas, that would have proved destructive to almost any other ship. About three o'clock of the morning of the 3d, the watch only being on deck, an enormous sea broke over the ship, and for an instant destroyed every hope. Our gun-deck ports were burst in, both boats on the quarter stove, our spare spars washed from the chains, our head-rails washed away, and hammock stanchions burst in,—and the ship perfectly deluged and water-logged. Immediately after this tremendous shock, which threw the crew into consternation, the gale began to abate, and in the morning we were enabled to set our reefed foresail.

During the struggle to remain afloat, Lewis Price, a U.S. Marine, dies. He is buried at sea; however, the crew is not permitted to be on deck due to fears that the weight of the men would cause the ship to overturn. The seas finally relent and the *Essex* arrives at Valparaiso during March. Commodore Bainbridge, who was operating off Brazil, returns to Boston this month due to the severe damage sustained while defeating the USS *Java.*

Also, the HMS *Poictiers* intercepts the American privateer *Highflyer* and seizes it. Before being captured, the *Highflyer* had seized eight British vessels. The British transform the *Highflyer* into a ship's tender, which will be manned by 72 men, commanded by a British lieutenant.

February 1 (Monday) In New Hampshire, the 1st New Hampshire Infantry Regiment of Volunteers, organized in November 1812, is ordered into camp and remains there until spring, when it marches to Burlington, Vermont, under the command of Colonel Aquila Davis. On 29 January 1813, Congress had repealed the "Volunteer Act," which causes the regiment to be dissolved. The other volunteer regiments, including one from Maine, are also disbanded. Many of the men from both regiments choose to enter the federal service. Those troops are combined to form the U.S. 45th Regiment, and Colonel Denny McCobb of the Maine regiment is commissioned as its colonel. Colonel (later brigadier general) Aquila Davis of the 1st New Hampshire is commissioned as the lieutenant colonel of the 45th Regiment.

In Ohio, General Harrison, with a force of about 1,700 to 2,000 troops, arrives back at the Rapids (Maumee River). Camp is established on the eastern bank of the river where Fort Meigs, named in honor of the governor of Ohio, is built. Except for some minor skirmishes with Indians, the area remains tranquil until the latter part of April.

In the meantime, work on the construction of the fort had been way behind schedule during the absence of General Harrison and his chief engineer, Captain Elenzer Wood. Upon Wood's return to the post from Sandusky during April, he discovers that the temporary commander, Colonel Leftwich, had totally disregarded his responsibilities. Leftwich, in addition to abandoning the project, had used lumber that was assigned for pickets as firewood. Shortly afterward, the enlistments of Leftwich's Virginians expire and the men begin to return to their home state. Pennsylvania troops deployed at the post also begin returning to their homes for the same reason. Nevertheless, about 200 of the Pennsylvanians dismiss the expiration dates and agree to remain, but the garrison is down to only about 500 troops.

In the meantime, the British have continued to monitor the activity of the Americans. They are aware of the departure of troops. Plans are laid to launch an assault before General Harrison can receive reinforcements. General Harrison, acutely aware of the precarious situation at Fort Meigs, leads about 300 men from various nearby forts whom he gathered at Fort Amanda and speeds back to Fort Meigs. At the same time, Harrison, against orders, dispatches a runner who rides from Fort Amanda to Kentucky to deliver an urgent request to Governor Shelby to expeditiously send reinforcements (Kentucky militia) to Fort Meigs. Harrison anticipates a British attack soon after the winter ice on Lake Erie is completely gone.

The Americans have also established a chain of forts in Ohio. They include Fort Amanda along the Auglaize River near Wapakoneta; Fort Ball (Tiffin); Fort Barbee (St. Mary's), Fort Huntington (Cleveland), and Fort Seneca in the vicinity of Old Fort. Fort Meigs becomes the anchor post for Fort Amanda, Fort Brown (Paulding County), Fort Jennings and Fort Winchester (formerly Fort Defiance).

February 1–23 *In naval activity,* the American privateer *Hazard* (Captain Le Chantier) seizes the ship *Albion*. On the 23rd, while on the Savannah bar, a British privateer out of New Providence recaptures it. Nonetheless, the *Hazard* afterward (probably a few days later) spots the British privateer *Caledonia* and a prolonged engagement ensues. After about seven and one-half hours, the Americans prevail and regain the ship; however, due to the approach of dawn, the Americans let the privateer, despite having struck its colors, slip away rather than run the risk of again losing their prize. During the encounter, five men are wounded, two of them seriously.

February 4 (Thursday) *In naval activity,* a British fleet composed of four ships of the line and twelve frigates, commanded by Admiral Sir John Borlase Warren with Admiral Cockburn (second in command), arrives at Chesapeake Bay. The fleet is transporting an invasion force commanded by General Sir Sydney Beckwith and a naval force commanded by Admiral Warren. The Americans at Norfolk and at Hampton maintain a close watch on the intruders. Militia from various Virginia counties are called upon and other militia from North Carolina are dispatched to Norfolk to assist in meeting the threat. A large number of militia that arrive from the upper counties of Virginia do not adapt well when the summer heat arrives and causes outbreaks of malaria. Many troops become seriously ill and some die. Also, General Robert Barraud Taylor holds command of the military district and the naval commander is Commodore John Cassin, U.S. Navy. The British move against Norfolk on 20 June. In the meantime, additional ships continue to arrive. By late March, the British establish naval blockades along the east coast; however, Massachusetts, New Hampshire and Rhode Island, considered to be opposed to the war, are not targeted.

In other naval activity, the USS *Hornet* encounters and captures a British brigantine, the 10-gun *Resolution*, while it is en route from Rio De Janeiro to Maranham. Captain Lawrence, unable to spare a prize crew, seizes the currency, about $23,000 and orders the ship to be burned. Following the capture, the *Hornet* cruises off the coast of Brazil and Surinam. On 24 February, it encounters the HMS *Peacock*.

February 6 (Saturday) In New York, a contingent of about 200 men under Captain Forsyth, supported by Colonel Benedict (New York militia) at Ogdensburg, launches a night-raid across the river at Elizabethtown (later Brockville), which lies about 10 miles from Fort Wellington (Canada). About 62 men are captured, but none are regulars. The report claims that several officers — including two majors, three captains and two lieutenants — had been seized; however, it was not mentioned that the captives were militia. During the raid, Forsyth also frees prisoners held at the jail. The Americans sustain no casualties and return to Ogdensburg before dawn on the 7th.

In naval activity, a merchant ship, the schooner *Mary,* is purchased by the U.S. Navy. The vessel is renamed the USS *Raven*.

February 6–17 to March *In naval activity,* the American privateer *Comet*, 12 miles off St. John, spots two brigantines. Captain Thomas

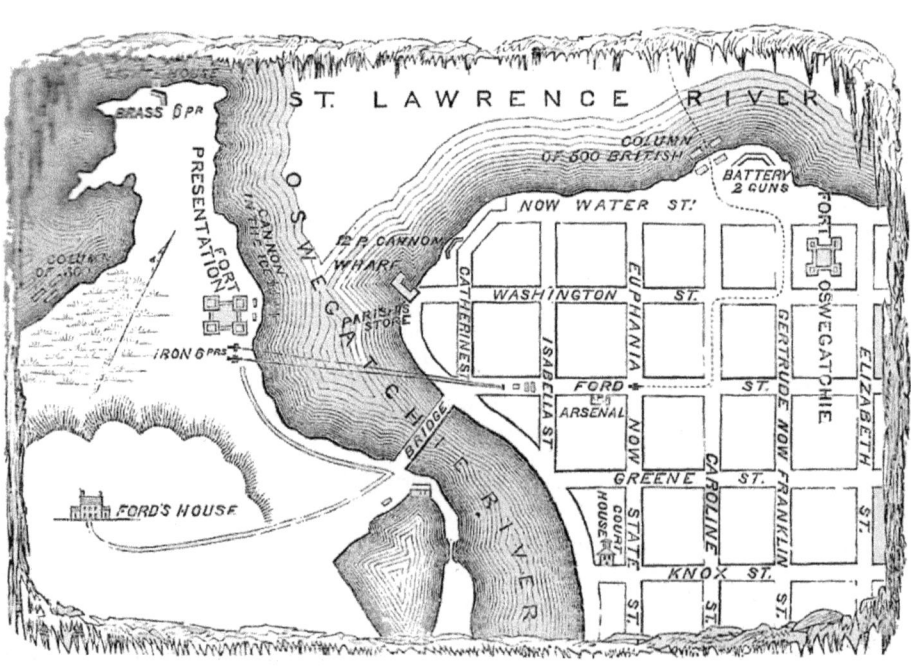

Map of operations at Ogdensburg, February 1813.

Boyle moves quickly to intercept them and by 0600, it is determined that at least one is armed. The crew of the *Comet* prepares to engage. At about the same time, the nearest vessel hoists its colors and Captain Boyle discerns that a new prize is at hand. The British vessel fires a shot, but at nearly the same time, the British apparently realize the *Comet* holds superior firepower, prompting the vessel, identified as the brigantine *Alexis*, to surrender. At the time of its capture the *Alexis* is transporting a rich cargo of coffee, cotton, rum and sugar. Boyle dispatches a prize crew which takes possession and prepares to take the *Alexis* into an American port. Meanwhile, most of the crew is transferred to the *Comet*.

Afterward, the *Comet* advances to seize the second vessel and in the process, by about 0800, the Americans spot yet a third vessel, which is not a merchant ship; rather a British warship. Captain Boyle questions his captives and learns that he has encountered three ships which had initially been part of a 9-ship convoy that had sailed from Demerara (South America) en route to St. Thomas. The two brigantines and the warship had lagged behind, but the other ships reached port on the previous day. The new intelligence identifies the warship in the distance as the HMS *Swaggerer*. Boyle moves to overpower the other merchant ship before the *Swaggerer* can reach it. Boyle orders the colors to be hoisted at 0900 and the British respond by opening fire. Nonetheless, return fire from the *Comet* convinces the vessel to capitulate.

Complications begin to develop when the British, heeding earlier instructions from the Admiralty, begin to disable their ship to prevent the Americans from getting it underway before the warship arrives on scene. Boyle senses the plot and rushes a prize party to take possession, while the *Swaggerer* is rushing forward to support the merchant ship. The prize crew transfers most of the British crew to the *Comet* and instantaneously, they begin to make repairs to enable the vessel to run. Time begins to run out on the operation, as the *Swaggerer* is getting too close for comfort. Boyle can easily see that the *Swaggerer* is poised to engage and its decks are crowded with men. Boyle rushes additional men to the prize to quicken the repair effort and to get the prize out of harm's way. Meanwhile, Captain Boyle concludes that he can divert the attention of the *Swaggerer*, and he is convinced he can outrun it. The prize ship is ordered to speed through a passage running between St. John and St. Thomas, while the *Comet* deals with the *Swaggerer*.

Boyle's quick thinking succeeds in getting the brigantine, identified as the packet *Dominica*, underway to assure that the prize and its valuable cargo (coffee, cotton, rum and sugar) is taken to the States. At about the same time, the *Comet* advances directly toward the superior *Swaggerer* in what to the British appears to be a suicide mission; however, the *Comet* is only feinting its intent to engage. The *Swagerer* reaches firing range as Boyle anticipated, and he initiates a series of movements that proves to him that the British are incapable of matching the speed of his *Comet*. He has bought the time for the brigantine to escape. Boyle's confidence builds to the point where he maneuvers the *Comet* skillfully to harass the *Swaggerer*, which is not able to intercept its prey. The *Comet* darts back and forth and essentially runs circles around the *Swaggerer*, which maintains its chase in vain.

By about 1200, Boyle is certain that the brigantine has made its escape, prompting him to halt his antics and sail northward. Within two hours, the *Comet* has greatly opened the distance and its pursuer has no chance of closing. At nearly the same time, the crew of the *Comet* spots another vessel. Boyle modifies his course, closes on the vessel, and introduces it to the Stars and Stripes. The Americans withhold firing their guns, but they do open fire with muskets, and it is sufficient to cause the schooner identified as the *Jane* to surrender. Suddenly, the *Comet* adds another cargo of coffee, cotton, rum and sugar to its treasure chest.

Meanwhile, the *Swaggerer* continues its pursuit without any opportunity to trap its prey. Boyle sends a prize party aboard the *Jane*, and the schooner is taken into a friendly port. Afterward, the *Comet* resumes its course, amused by the *Swaggerer*, which remains well behind. Soon the *Swaggerer* vanishes from view and the *Comet* heads for the United States. It arrives on 17 March.

February 8 (Monday) **In Washington, D.C.,** Secretary of War John Armstrong delivers a plan for a second invasion of Canada to President Madison. Armstrong's calculations indicate about 12,000 troops, including militia in and about Montreal. The plan calls for the attacking force to be on Lake Erie by 1 April and at the St. Lawrence by 15 May. President Madison approves the plan on 10 May. Armstrong also estimates British strength (regulars) in Upper Canada at about 2,000, with 300 at Preston, 600 at Kingston and another 1,200 split between Fort George at the mouth of the Niagara and Fort Erie. Also, the secretary of war prefers, as part of his proposed plan, that General James Wilkinson command the expedition in place of General Henry Dearborn. Nevertheless, Dearborn commands the expedition until later, when President Madison replaces Dearborn with Wilkinson.

In naval activity, the American privateer *Lottery*, having recently sailed from Baltimore en route to Bordeaux, France, gets spotted by a British squadron at about 0900 as it tries to get out of the Chesapeake Bay into the open seas. An idle squadron at Lynnhaven Bay reacts quickly. The ships at anchor include the *Belvidera* (Captain Richard Byron); the *Junon* (Captain James Sanders); the *Maidstone* (Captain George Burdett) and the *Statira* (Captain Hassard Stackpole). A contingent of 200 troops is carried by boats to seize the privateer. The Americans attempt to escape; however, as the boats come within range at about 1300, Captain Southcomb orders the crew to commence fire. The vanguard is forced to halt and await the trailing boats. The British again move to board, and despite the heavy, effective fire, the British succeed in boarding and finally overpowering the survivors. During the ferocious attack, the Americans resist tenaciously, but in vain. Captain Southcomb is mortally wounded during the brawl and only eight of the 28 crewmen are spared from either death or being wounded when the vessel is finally surrounded. The British send the body of Captain Southcomb back to them, and afterward, they receive a letter of thanks from Captain Charles Stewart of the USS *Constellation* who is presently at anchor in the James River outside of Norfolk. The British take the *Lottery* into service and rename it *Canso*.

February 9 (Tuesday) **In Florida,** American troops, including men from the army and a Marine Corps contingent (led by Lt. Sevier), commanded by Colonel Newman, are engaged in destroying the Indian strongholds of East Florida. The Indian village of Payne is struck and ruined on this day. The next day, the column moves to Bowlegs, and it too is reduced.

In Ohio, General Harrison, having been informed by scouts operating near the Portage River that a large number of Indians is gathered along the northern shore of Maumee Bay, personally departs from his camp with a force of 600 troops and one piece of artillery to engage; however, the Indians scatter upon the approach of the vanguard. Harrison orders pursuit. As the troops advance along the ice close to shore, the horses pulling the artillery piece fall through the ice close to the lowest part of the bay.

In the meantime, Harrison's main body arrives and continues the chase while the vanguard struggles to save the cannon. Later, scouts operating in front of the column return and inform Harrison that the Indians had made it to Malden. The column returns to camp. The submerged cannon is finally saved, but the troops do not complete the salvage operation until the following day.

In naval activity, the privateer *Saratoga* encounters and captures the British merchant ship *Lord Nelson*, considered to be among the top vessels in British service. The Americans sail the *Lord Nelson* to New Orleans. In other activity around this time, the *Saratoga*, after evading capture by a British warship, intercepts a British packet, the 18-gun *Morgiana*. During the harrowing chase by the British warship, the *Saratoga* had been compelled to dump 12 of the ship's guns into the sea to permit the *Saratoga* to increase its speed during its escape. The loss of the guns provides the *Saratoga* the opportunity to outrun the frigate; however, it leaves the *Saratoga* with only four guns with which to engage the *Morgiana*. Nonetheless, the superior fire power of the *Morgiana* is still insufficient. The *Saratoga* captures the *Morgiana* and the Americans transfer some of the British guns to the *Saratoga* to bring it back to full strength. Meanwhile, the *Morgiana* is taken to Newport, Rhode Island. During the engagement, the British toss the mail overboard to prevent it from falling into the hands of the Americans. The Americans sustain 3 killed and 7 wounded. The British sustain 2 killed and 5 wounded.

In other naval activity, the *Saratoga*, during this month, seizes a brigantine off Caracas. Captain Wooster assigns a prize crew to sail it back to the United States. The prize master, in desperate need of fresh water for the journey, sails into Santa Marta, Colombia, to acquire the water and instead discovers a belligerent Spanish government that seizes the vessel and sells it for profit. The Spanish arrest the Americans and transport them as prisoners to Havana, where they are forced to work on the construction of a Spanish arsenal. During their incarceration, the Americans are treated inhumanely, fed insufficient food and barely clothed.

February 10 (Wednesday) **In Florida,** an American force under Lt. Sevier and Colonel Newman destroys Bowlegs, the second Indian town to be reduced in two days. Afterward, the Americans return to the demolished Payne's Town, where they establish camp. The Indians launch an attack with a force of about 200 braves. The Americans instantly respond and launch a charge, and the Indians scatter. The Americans inflict severe casualties but their own losses are low, one man killed and seven wounded.

February 11 (Thursday) **In Ohio,** General Harrison, at his headquarters (Foot of the Maumee Rapids) writes to Secretary of War John Armstrong that a force under Colonel Joel Leftwich (Virginia militia) joined him on 30 January. He states that on 2 February he arrived at his camp with a force of 1,600 troops, but afterward fresh reinforcements, a contingent of Ohio troops attached to General Tupper's brigade and a regiment of Kentuckians, arrived to increase his command to 2,000:

> I have ordered the whole of the troops of the Left Wing (excepting one company for each of the six forts in that quarter) the balance of the Pennsylvania brigade and the Ohio brigade under General Tupper and a detachment of regular troops of twelve-months volunteers under command of Colonel Campbell to march to this place as soon as possible. The disposition of the troops for the remainder of the winter will be as follows: A battalion of militia lately called out from this State with a company of regular troops now at Fort Winchester [Defiance] will garrison the posts upon the waters of the Auglaise and St. Mary. The small block-houses upon Hull's trace [M'Arthur, Necessity, and Findlay] will have a subaltern's command in each. A company will be placed at Upper Sandusky, and another at Lower Sandusky. All the rest of the troops will be brought to this place, amounting to from fifteen to eighteen hundred men. I am erecting here a pretty strong fort [Meigs] capable of resisting field artillery at least. The troops will be placed in a fortified camp, covered on one flank by the fort. This is the best position that can be taken to cover the frontier, and the small posts in the rear of it, and those above it on the Miami [Maumee] and its tributaries. The force placed here ought, however, to be strong enough to encounter any that the enemy may detach against the forts above.

February 12 (Friday) **In Maine,** the privateer *Thistle*, a schooner, is commissioned. Zadoc Crowel receives command.

February 13 (Saturday) *In naval activity,* the USS *Essex*, under Captain David Porter, arrives about 35 miles from Cape St. John's, the eastern section of Staten Island; however, visibility is limited to about one mile. The weather worsens as the day passes and for a while, it is feared that the ship might be lost. Nevertheless, Captain Porter takes every precaution and by 1830, realizes that safety is not yet assured. He is very close to the breakers but knows "with the hope of weathering them, that we had not room to wear; there was a tremendous sea running, the ship driving forecastle under; no chance of weathering the land, which could now be seen." He relates that the "only hope of safety was in getting the ship in stays; the mainsail was set with the utmost expedition, and we were so fortunate as to succeed: after getting the ship about, the jib and spauker were set, and the top-gallant yards sent down; but, in a few moments, the jib was blown to pieces." Nonetheless, the current changes, the seas calm and suddenly whales begin to come alongside the *Essex*. Shortly thereafter land is sighted about one mile ahead.

By the 14th, the weather clears sufficiently to enable the crew to see the horizon, but great dangers continue to lurk. At Cape Horn, the weather again worsens, but despite the heavy seas and horrific winds that nearly destroy the ship, again it escapes disaster. On the 18th, with no land in sight, torrential rains and high winds strike. Day after day, the ship remains imperiled, then on 1 March even worse weather descends on the area. For three days, the ship is pummeled by the sea and the winds without mercy. Captain Porter is among those who sustain injuries during the nightmarish encounter. He is tossed several times as if he were a rag doll and the falls incapacitate him, making it impossible for him to go up to the deck.

During the early morning of the 3rd, shock strikes the *Essex* when a monstrous wave or possibly waves breaks over it, bringing instant thoughts of disaster upon the crew. Initially, hope for survival is lost, but only temporarily; the *Essex*, seemingly having a protective shield over it, remains afloat despite the powerful blow. Captain Porter describes the harrowing moments: "Our gun-deck ports were burst in; both boats on the quarters stove; our spars washed from the chains; our head-rails washed away, hammock-staunchions burst in, and the ship perfectly deluged and water-logged, immediately after this tremendous shock." The force of the wave had also created additional panic when one of the British prisoners from the vessel *Nocton* proclaimed that "the broadside was stove in, and that she was sinking."

During the night, a Marine, Lewis Price, having been long on the sick list due to a problem with his lungs, expires. He is given a burial at sea. The crew is not allowed to attend the ceremony due to the violent seas and the fear that their weight on the deck during the precarious circumstances could cause the ship to overturn. Once the *Essex* regains its stability, Captain Porter rewards the sailors at the wheel for their courage, particularly while the prisoner's false rumor had inflicted much fear in some of those unaware of the true situation. The individuals are promoted up one rank, however, others who failed to uphold the standards of Porter during the crisis are, as Porter related, "rebuked."

February 15 (Monday) **In Mississippi,** General Jackson arrives at Natchez with his force of Tennessee volunteers to complete a journey of about 1,000 miles. General Jackson discovers that the mounted troops under General Coffee had been in camp close to where he landed. The Tennesseans remain in the town until late March.

February 17 (Wednesday) **In Rhode Island,** Oliver Hazard Perry, in command of a gun flotilla, receives orders to report to Sackets Harbor, New York. Lt. Perry had been commander of the USS *Revenge* until it was destroyed after hitting a reef in 1811. Perry had earlier sent a request to the secretary of the navy for a more active post; however, no action was taken. Nevertheless, a separate request sent to Commodore Chauncey received immediate attention. Chauncey contacted Washington requesting that Perry be ordered to the Great Lakes. Perry, shortly after receiving his orders prepares to depart for Sackets Harbor. Before the end of this day, about 50 men are sent in advance, followed within less than five days by another detachment of slightly more than 100 additional troops. Perry follows shortly thereafter. Within twenty-four hours of receiving his orders, Perry and his younger brother, Alexander, only thirteen, board a sleigh and both repair to New York. From New York, he travels to Sackets Harbor and arrives in early March.

In naval activity, the *Adeline* is acquired by the navy at Alexandria, Virginia, and outfitted as a warship. It becomes the 3-gun *Asp* and sails on its first cruise on 14 July.

February 19 (Friday) *In naval activity,* the HMS *Tenedos* intercepts the 255-ton brigantine *Sarah* (R. Pendergast, master), which is en route to Amsterdam from New York with a cargo of cotton and other items. The *Sarah* is separate from the schooner *Sarah* seized on 18 April 1814 and the *Sarah* captured on 28 September 1814.

February 20 (Saturday) **In Ohio,** Captain Wood returns to Fort Meigs following a trip to Sandusky. He immediately discovers that Colonel Leftwich, in command during his absence, has totally neglected to continue the construction of the post. Wood resumes his responsibility and the work is also resumed. Wood later describes Leftwich as "an old phlegmatic Dutchman who was not even fit for a packhorse master much less to be entrusted with such an important command."

In naval activity, the American privateer *Hazard*, operating out of Charleston, captures the 12-gun British merchant ship *Albion*, mounting 12 guns and carrying a crew of 25 men. The prize has a cargo including coffee, cotton, rum and sugar and is sent to an American port.

February 22 (Monday) *In naval activity,* the American privateer *Hazard* encounters the British privateer *Caledonia*. At the same time, its captain, P. Le Chartrier, observes that the prize *Albion* he just sent into port had been recaptured by the *Caledonia*. The *Hazard* and the *Caledonia* engage; however, as dusk begins to arrive, the *Caledonia* disengages and retires, leaving the Albion to fall back into American hands. During the engagement, the *Hazard* sustains 7 killed and 7 wounded.

February 23 (Tuesday) **In New York,** with the permission of General Sir George Prevost, Major McDonnell moves across the iced-up river toward Ogdensburg from Canada. Prevost's orders stipulate a demonstration only—an attack is prohibited. Nevertheless, McDonnell believes that the garrison might have been abandoned, while the troops there move to capture Prevost. McDonnell, with a force of about 250 regulars, 300 militia and a small contingent of artillery, advance across the ice on the St. Lawrence at 0730 on a march of about one and one-half miles. The force crosses in two columns, commanded by Captain John Jenkins (right) and Lt. Colonel McDonnell (left).

Meanwhile, the garrison had not departed and the Americans are in place to meet the threat with artillery and muskets. British captain Jenkins sustains a wound to his left arm from grape shot, but he continues to advance with his column struggling with his wound and the deep snow. Shortly thereafter, he gets hit again, in his other arm. Nevertheless, he continues to advance. Later he collapses into unconsciousness due to loss of blood. Captain Jenkins survives but loses his left arm.

Meanwhile, the defenders under Captain Forsyth receive reinforcements when a militia regiment under Colonel Benedict arrives. However, McDonnell's force maintains the pressure and the Americans are compelled to abandon their positions. The British take the town and they seize eleven guns, including two 19-pounders, which had been captured from General Burgoyne at Saratoga during October 1777. The British, after taking the town, burn two barracks, two schooners (armed), both of which are frozen in place on the river, and two gunboats. In addition, they capture supplies and prisoners, 70 troops and four officers.

Some sources place this incident on 22 February; however, a letter of the 23rd written to General Sir George Prevost indicates that the British attack occurred on the 23rd:

> Sir,—I have the honour to acquaint you, for the information of his excellency the commander of the forces, that, inconsequence of the commands of his excellency to retaliate, under favorable circumstances, upon the enemy, for his late wanton aggressions on this frontier, I this morning, about 7 o'clock, crossed the river St. Lawrence upon the ice, and attacked and carried, after a little more than an hoar's action, his position in and near the opposite town of Ogdensburg, taking eleven pieces of cannon, and all his ordnance, marine, commissariat, and quarter-master-general's stores, four officers and 70 prisoners, and burning two armed schooners, and two large gunboats, and both his barracks.

February 24 (Wednesday) ***In naval activity,*** the USS *Hornet,* commanded by Lieutenant James Lawrence, while cruising off British Guyana (Guiana) in northern South America, encounters the HMS *Peacock,* commanded by Captain Peake. The *Hornet,* which had been on a cruise with the *Constitution* for several months, has been operating independently since the previous month when the *Constitution* returned home for repairs. During the morning, the *Hornet* spots a brigantine and initiates pursuit; however, Captain Lawrence, lacking a pilot, halts the chase near the entrance to the Demarara River where a fort dominates the approach.

During this time, Lawrence observes a vessel (HMS *Espiegle*), thought to be a brigantine of war, flying the British ensign at anchor in the harbor. At about 1500, Lawrence discovers yet another British craft that is closing upon the *Hornet.* Suddenly, the approaching ship (HMS *Peacock*) hoists its colors, the British ensign. The British, soon after hoisting their colors, observe the Americans raising their flag and at about the same time, both vessels form for battle. At just before 1730, the two antagonists are well within pistol shot of each other when broadsides are traded. The *Peacock* maneuvers to position itself from where it can rake the *Hornet;* however, the Americans are simultaneously maneuvering to check the *Peacock.*

The *Hornet* succeeds in gaining the advantage, and at about the same time, the *Hornet*'s guns deliver a thunderclap of devastating fire that continues relentlessly for about fifteen minutes. The British are unable to match the firepower, which has pummeled the *Peacock.* The British colors are hauled down and at the same time, the British signal great distress by re-hoisting the flag upside down. Within minutes, the *Peacock*'s main mast crashes down.

The Americans take possession of the *Peacock,* when Lt. Shubrick boards it and returns to the *Hornet* with its first lieutenant and a report that Captain Peake had been killed during the latter part of the battle and the crew had sustained heavy casualties, but Lawrence is also informed that the ship is about to sink. About six feet of water has already entered the hold. The victory is suddenly transformed into a desperate race against time to rescue the British survivors.

Captain Lawrence dispatches boats and both of the ships are brought to anchor to rescue the

The surrender of the *Peacock* (*A History of the War of 1812 Between the United States and Great Britain*, Rossiter Johnson, 1882).

The USS *Hornet* vanquishes the HMS *Peacock* (*The History of the United States Navy [Biographical Sketches of American Naval Heroes]*, Charles J. Peterson, 1860).

wounded, who are expeditiously transferred to the *Hornet.* Simultaneously, desperate efforts are underway to plug the holes and lessen the *Peacock*'s weight to try to keep it afloat.

The guns are thrown overboard; however, the sea prevails. Nine of the crewmen are lost when it sinks, along with three men (John Hart, Joseph Williams and Hannibal Boyd) from the *Hornet.* Four of those remaining on the vessel during those final minutes manage to board a damaged stern boat and they reach shore. Four others climb the rigging and reach the rigging of the fore-top. The latter are also rescued because the rigging there is above the water, which is only 33 feet deep.

During the battle, the British sustain five killed, including Captain Peake, and two others sustain mortal wounds. Thirty-three are wounded, including those with mortal wounds. The Americans, excluding those that went down with the *Peacock,* sustain one man killed (John Place) and two (Samuel Coulson and Joseph Dalrymple) wounded. Another British vessel, the HMS *Espiegle,* is nearby during the contest between the

Hornet and the *Peacock*, but it does not attempt to engage the *Hornet*.

Following the victory, the crew repairs the *Hornet*, and within four hours, the *Hornet* sails for Martha's Vineyard, where it arrives on 19 March. According to Captain Lawrence's report, the muster on the following morning accounted 277 men. The count included the crew and the British prisoners; however, with the capture of the *Peacock*, Captain Lawrence had inadvertently freed the crew of the USS *Hunter*, which had been seized earlier by the Phoebe.

Afterward, the *Hornet* sails to New York.

Lieutenant (later captain) Lawrence receives a gold medal from Congress and each of his officers is given a silver medal. Lt. Lawrence is promoted to the rank of captain and receives command of the USS *Chesapeake*, which is at Boston. Also, on 19 March, in a letter from Captain Lawrence to Secretary of the Navy William Jones, Lawrence states: "The cool and determined conduct of my officers and crew, during the action, and their almost unexampled exertions afterwards, entitle them to my warmest acknowledgments; and I beg leave, most earnestly, to recommend them to the notice of the government."

In other naval activity, the American privateer *Viper*, commanded by Captain D. Dithurbide, sails from Charleston, South Carolina, in search of British shipping. While out at sea during this cruise, the *Viper* encounters several merchant ships that are carrying high value cargoes with a total value of about $150,000. At the close of its cruise, the *Viper* arrives back at New Bedford on 4 August.

February 25 (Thursday) *In naval activity,* the American privateer *Dolphin*, commanded by Captain W.S. Stafford, while preparing to depart from Cape St. Vincent following an uneventful period, spots a sail in the distance and then another. The *Dolphin* chases after both and the strangers appear to be well armed. A spirited engagement erupts and the *Dolphin* prevails, taking both as prizes. One of the prizes, the 16-gun *Hebe* (some sources list it as the *John Hamilton*) had previously been the American privateer *Laura* before being captured by the British the previous September. The other is the 10-gun *Three Brothers*. Both prizes are sent back to the United States; however, only the *Three Brothers* reaches port at New York. The *Hebe* is recaptured by the British. Nonetheless, the British crew from the *Hebe* had been transferred to the *Dolphin*. Its captain had received severe burns during the struggle, but he receives excellent care from Doctor Chidester while with the Americans and he makes a complete recovery. The *Dolphin* later arrives in Baltimore.

February 26 (Friday) **In Ohio**, General Harrison, acting on intelligence he received from scouts, orders a contingent composed of 68 regulars and about 120 militia troops (Pennsylvania and Virginia), along with another special unit of 32 soldiers and 22 friendly Indians, to destroy a number of British war vessels that have become trapped in the ice off Malden. The contingent is commanded by Captain Augustus L. Langham (Ohio) and a Frenchman, M. Madis, an artillerist. The party departs on twenty-two sleds on 2 March.

February 27 (Saturday) *In naval activity,* the USS *Constitution* arrives back at Boston. Captain Bainbridge remains aboard the ship until the following day. Upon his arrival on shore Captain Bainbridge receives the red carpet treatment. A contingent of light infantry escorts him to the Exchange Coffee House, following his initial greeting from a party of officers and some prominent people of the town. Captain Bainbridge is also greeted by a banner that stretches across the street with the names Hull, Jones and Decatur as in Isaac, Jacob and Stephen, three naval heroes; however, the big surprise was that a fourth name had been inscribed: William Bainbridge.

He is later informed that Congress had recently authorized the construction of three battle ships of the line, one of which is to be built at the Boston Navy Yard. It is requested that Bainbridge oversee the construction of the ship and he accepts. He relinquishes command of the USS *Constitution* during March to accept the appointment of command at the navy yard in Charlestown and other eastern naval stations in Maine, New Hampshire and Rhode Island. This would become the first line-of-battleships to be constructed in the United States; however, the navy yard is not properly equipped for the task.

March *In naval activity,* as part of the Royal Navy's operation to blockade American ports, a British squadron under Commodore John P. Beresford patrols off Lewes, Delaware, and the Delaware Capes to intercept vessels and to interrupt shipping. The British succeed in seizing American vessels, and during the course of the blockade there is a lot of minor action, including a two-day bombardment early the next month. Meanwhile, the Americans in Delaware build a series of forts and blockhouses to protect the state. Lewes Battery is constructed this year soon after the attack that is launched in April.

March 1 (Monday) **In Mississippi** at Natchez, General Andrew Jackson, obviously upset by the embarrassing defeats in Canada, writes to Secretary of War John Armstrong. Jackson offers to take his command to Canada: "Should the safety of the lower country admit it, and government so order, I would with pleasure march to the lines of Canada and there offer my feeble aid to the army of our country, and endeavor to wipe off the stain on our military character occasioned by the recent disasters."

Meanwhile, his army continues to train at Natchez, while awaiting orders to proceed to Florida; however, the heat is taking its toll on the troops. Later, Jackson writes a second letter to Armstrong indicating that once he returns to Tennessee, if the secretary would designate Canada as the destination, he would lead 3,000 Tennesseans, each with a one-year enlistment. By that time, the month of March was beginning to fade away; however, before the month ended, an express arrived from the secretary: "Sir: The causes of embodying and marching to New Orleans the corps under your command having ceased to exist, you will, on receipt of this letter, consider it as dismissed from public service and take measures to have delivered over to Major-General Wilkinson all the articles of public property which may have been put into its possession. You will accept for yourself and the corps the thanks of the President of the United States."

There is no need to attempt to describe Jackson's thought while he read the letter, which instructed him to dismantle his 2,000-man force and let them return to Tennessee, a 500-mile trek on their own. The letter also omitted the fact that most of the route would be through hostile Indian territory. Jackson's mind was made up before he finished the astonishing letter. His troops would not be dismissed. Many of them had already worn out their shoes and he had no intentions of betraying his personal honor by losing the trust of the parents and wives who entrusted their loved ones to him. General Jackson responded to the letter and it did not mince words. General Jackson pledges his entire estate to the merchants as well as to the farmers and teamsters to acquire the necessary items to ensure that his force could return as a body to Nashville, and he signs his name to each draft. Later a new message arrives from the government that states that the troops should be paid.

At nearly the same time, General Jackson receives a letter from General James Wilkinson which attempts to press Jackson to persuade his troops to enlist as regulars. Jackson again becomes infuriated. He does not trust Wilkinson and the timing of the letter, just after having been ordered to dismiss his force, does not sit well with him. The crafty Wilkinson had somehow arranged for a recruiting officer to arrive at Natchez. Jackson makes it clear that if the officer attempts to enlist even one of his troops, he would be "drummed out of the camp in the presence of the whole corps."

Jackson leads his command back to Nashville, including 56 men who had to be transported. General Jackson himself, who brought three of his horses, gave them up to wounded troops and made the entire march on foot.

In New York, General Henry Dearborn arrives at Sackets Harbor on or about this day. Upon his arrival he is informed that General Sir George Prevost is at Kingston and finalizing plans for an offensive. The intelligence gathered estimates British strength at 6,000 to 8,000 troops. Dearborn shows no signs of being fearful of an attack against Sackets Harbor; however, an immediate call for reinforcements is sent out to all corners. At this time, there are only about 3,000 troops in place and they include the regulars under Captain Forsyth that had been pushed out of Ogdensburg the previous month.

In Ohio, on or about this day, some residents who live in Detroit arrive at Fort Meigs with intelligence. They report that British Colonel Henry Proctor is planning to attack the post. According to their information, his force is to converge on Sandwich (Canada) on 7 April. The British intend to establish batteries on the opposite side of the river from where the British will initiate a bombardment, while their allied Indians assault the fort. They also report that British Major Muir claimed that the artillery would succeed in driving the garrison from the fort with about three hours of bombardment, and that the troops would be met by the Indians.

In naval activity, the American privateer *True Blooded Yankee* departs France after being fitted out there by a Mr. Preble of Rhode Island. The *True Blooded Yankee* became an American privateer by circuitous route. It was originally a French brigantine that was seized by the British during the days just preceding the War of 1812 and later recaptured by the French, who sold the ship to Preble. On this its first cruise as a privateer, it heads straight to the Irish Channel in search of British shipping.

Due to the *True Blooded Yankee* initiating its service at France, American seamen were difficult to find; however, the French government permitted the Americans to enter various French prisons to solicit crew members. One of the prisoners, an Englishman, John Wiltshire, proclaims that he is an American and his story is believed by the French, who release him for service on the privateer. Nonetheless, his career is cut short. The *True Blooded Yankee* seizes the *Margaret* as its first prize and Captain Hailer delegates Wiltshire as one of the six men assigned as a prize crew. While sailing to Morlaix, France, the British cutter Nimrod intercepts it and upon inspection, Wiltshire is identified as an Englishman. The British immediately hang him.

Meanwhile, the *True Blooded Yankee*, as if following the course of the *Yankee* another privateer that finds great success, concentrates on waters along the Irish coast. A series of British vessels are captured and at one point, Hailey's crew actually seizes an island where the *True Blooded Yankee* remains for nearly one week while undergoing repairs.

Following its cruise of 37 days, during which the *True Blooded Yankee* takes 270 prisoners in addition to its prizes, it arrives at Brest. Also, the crew of the *True Blooded Yankee* had selected a large amount of goods from the ships they captured and transferred them to the hold. These items include Turkish carpets, raw silk and beaver skins.

Following this cruise, Captain Hailey departs again from France and returns to the waters off Ireland and Scotland. The *True Blooded Yankee* exhibits audacity as it bolts from place to place, frequently landing a force to seize a town and demand ransom. At one port town in Ireland, the crew of the privateer sets fire to seven vessels. In May, Captain Hailey initiates a bold intrusion. He sails directly into the harbor at Dublin, Ireland, to destroy a schooner that had escaped from him on the previous day. Daringly, the *True Blooded Yankee* enters the harbor, destroys the schooner and retires unscathed.

March 2 (Tuesday) *In U.S. Army activity,* Brigadier General James Wilkinson is promoted to the rank of major general. Afterward, he leads a force, transported by Commodore Shaw, from New Orleans to Mobile, which is captured during mid–April. After the expedition to Mobile, Wilkinson is ordered to the Northern Department. First he serves under General Dearborn, but then succeeds Dearborn as commander of the 9th Military District. General Wilkinson afterward leads an invasion force into Canada with the objective being Montreal. The force in support of Wilkinson is led by General Wade Hampton, the grandfather of Confederate General Wade Hampton. Serious complications develop due to the intense animosity between Wilkinson and Hampton.

In Ohio, a contingent of troops (regulars and militia) under Captain Augustus L. Langham departs from General Harrison's encampment en route to the area near Malden, Canada, to destroy some immobilized vessels. Once the troops, traveling by sleds, reach the Portage River, the full intent of the mission is explained and they receive the option of returning to camp if they are fearful of continuing. Six of the Indians and 20 militia troops choose to return due to the danger involved. The remainder continues and moves to Lower Sandusky and onto ice-covered Lake Erie. The troops are to proceed to Middle Bass Island, where they are to leave the sleds before advancing on foot to set fire to the vessels. The contingent loses some members to desertion, but they also begin to encounter dangerously thin ice. The mission is aborted and the troops return to camp. (*See also,* **February 26.**)

March 3 to mid–May **In New York,** Oliver H. Perry arrives at Sackets Harbor. He remains in the village for about two weeks before Commodore Chauncey directs him to move to Erie (Presque Isle), Pennsylvania. Upon his arrival at Erie, work is underway on two gunboats through the efforts of Sailing Master Dobbins and Ebenezer Crosby. In addition, a third gunboat is being prepared for its planking, and progress is made on two 20-gun brigantines. Nonetheless, the government has not provided any guns for the vessels. Additional complications for Perry include the fact that there are no small arms available in Erie and no bullets to be found. The place is defenseless, and Perry also discovers that his force has no access to canvas and there is also an absence even of rope.

However, Perry takes his obstacles in stride and immediately begins to rectify the situation. He dispatches parties to raise about 50 seamen at Buffalo, and while there the men are ordered to acquire cartridges and muskets. All the while, Perry remains concerned about the safety of his emerging squadron, which has no protection. Perry improvises by contracting civilians from Erie to guard the ships that are under construction to prevent sabotage. Perry himself also moves into action by traveling to Pittsburgh to arrange for other supplies required to build his ships. The pace accelerates under Perry's guidance. More craftsmen arrive later from Philadelphia and a contingent of local militia undertakes the task of guarding the town of Erie, which is being transformed into a navy yard.

By the beginning of May, Perry receives the satisfaction of seeing three gunboats that carry arms during their launchings. In two more weeks, the workmen remove two sloops from the stocks. By about that time, Perry departs from Erie to join with Commodore Chauncey, who is supporting General Henry Dearborn in the campaign to seize Fort George in Canada at the mouth of the Niagara River.

March 3 (Wednesday) **In Washington, D.C.,** Congress passes the Act of March 3rd which calls for the organization of the general staff of the U.S. Army and the establishment of the adjutant general's department. The legislation also authorized the president, when he should deem it expedient, to assign one of the brigadier generals to the principal Army of the United States, who should, in such case, act as adjutant and inspector general, and as chief of the staff of the Army. This was the first mention of the "adjutant general's department," by that name. On March 12, Brigadier General Cushing relinquished his junior and now superseded commission of adjutant general, and was assigned to the command of Military District No. 1, comprising the states of New Hampshire and Massachusetts.

March 5 (Friday) **In Maryland,** the governor, greatly concerned about the British presence in the Chesapeake Bay, writes an urgent letter to Secretary of War John Armstrong to inform him that Annapolis is vulnerable to attack because the number of defenders at Fort Severn, and the other forts are too few in number to mount a defense. The governor receives no response. On 20 March, he again writes to the secretary and notes that the secretary failed to respond. The governor

Fort Severn at Annapolis.

in his second letter informs the secretary that Annapolis is not isolated and that other sections of Maryland are also defenseless. The governor also states: "In this situation we must repeat our anxiety to be informed what protection on any emergency may be expected from the general government; what regular forces can be furnished; and in the event of the militia of the State being called out for its defence, whether the expenses will be defrayed by the United States."

The secretary gets around to responding in a letter dated 27 March: "One battalion of the drafted militia is ordered for the particular defence of the City of Annapolis — that a strong body of militia had been organized by the orders of the Executive of the United States, for the protection of Baltimore; and should there be any *new* evidence of annoyance from the enemy additional measures will be taken."

In naval activity, the British privateer *Liverpool Packet* continues its spree of capturing American vessels. The 114-ton schooner *Friendship* (P. Gibbs, master) is intercepted and captured by the *Liverpool Packet*, while en route from Oporto to Boston with a cargo of ballast. The *Friendship* is separate from the schooner *Friendship* seized on 19 July 1812, the schooner *Friendship* seized on 11 September 1812, the sloop *Friendship* seized 6 July 1813, the sloop *Friendship* overtaken 11 July 1813, the schooner *Friendship* captured 13 July 1813, and the schooner *Friendship* seized on 28 July 1813.

March 8 (Monday) President Madison is informed that Czar Alexander of Russia has offered his services as a mediator between the United States and Great Britain in an effort to end the conflict. Word of the offer is delivered by the Russian minister in Washington, Mr. Daschkoff. Since the day of the proposal, the French threat against Russia has vanished, as Napoleon has sustained a horrendous defeat since his occupation of Moscow the previous September.

Madison, aware that a total defeat of Napoleon by Britain would seriously imperil the U.S., decides to jump at the chance to find a quick diplomatic solution to end the war. He dispatches James Bayard and Albert Gallatin to St. Petersburg, Russia, with instructions to meet with John Quincy Adams, the minister to Russia, and to assist him with the proposed negotiations. Both men sail for Russia during May aboard the USS *Neptune*, which is commanded by Captain Jones, the brother of the Secretary of the Navy William Jones, who succeeded Paul Hamilton.

The *Neptune* sails from Norfolk on 8 May and rendezvous with a British squadron in the Chesapeake Bay, where it is provided with a British warship assigned to protect it on the voyage. However, the British have not agreed to the czar's plan and they reject it outright, having no desire to negotiate with the U.S. through a Russian mediator. Britain informs Russia of its decision, but the U.S. diplomats are en route before word reaches them. By November, negotiations will begin, but without Russian intervention. The *London Courier* publishes an article about the proposed intervention by the Russians, which states:

We hope the Russian mediation will be refused. Indeed, we are sure it will. We have a love for our naval preeminence that cannot bear to have it even touched by a foreign hand. Russia can be hardly supposed to be adverse to the principle of armed neutrality, and that idea alone would be sufficient to make us decline the offer. We must take our stand, never to commit our naval rights to the mediation of any power. This is the flag we must nail to the national mast, and go down rather than strike it. The hour of concession and compromise is past. Peace must be the consequence of punishment to America; and retraction of her insolent demands must precede negotiation. The thunder of our cannon must first strike terror into the American shores, and Great Britain must be seen and felt in all the majesty of her might, from Boston to Savannah, from the lakes of Canada to the mouths of the Mississippi.

During the course of the conflict Russia on three separate occasions offers to intervene; however, England rejects all of them.

In other activity, General Ferdinand L. Claiborne at about this time is promoted to the rank of brigadier general and assigned command at Baton Rouge, Louisiana. In late June, he is ordered by General Thomas Flournoy to move from Baton Rouge to Fort Stoddert to focus on the defense of Mobile. General Claiborne had initially joined the service during 1793 when he was commissioned an ensign.

In naval activity, the 83-ton sloop *General Green* (J.P. Hand, master) which had sailed from Boston with a cargo of fish, iron, rum and other items, is intercepted and seized by the British privateer *Liverpool Packet* before it reaches Boston.

March 9 (Tuesday) In New York at Sackets Harbor, General Dearborn writes to the secretary of war: "Sir, I have not yet had the honor of a visit from Sir G. Prevost. His whole force is concentrated at Kingston, probably amounting to six or seven thousand, about three thousand of whom are regular troops. The ice is good and we expect him every day, and every measure for preventing a surprise is in constant activity.... I begin to entertain some doubts whether Sir George will venture to attack us; but shall not relax in being prepared to give him a decent reception."

On the 14th, Dearborn again writes to the secretary: "From the most recent and probable information I have obtained, I am induced to believe that Sir George Prevost thinks it is too late to attack this place. He undoubtedly meditated a coup-de-main against the shipping here.... From various sources I am perfectly satisfied, that they are not in sufficient force to attack this place, knowing, as they do, that we have collected a fine body of troops from Greenbush and Plattsburgh." Dearborn proclaims that they are strong enough to defend Sackets Harbor, but not strong enough to "hazard an offensive movement." Dearborn orders General John Chandler to repair to Sackets Harbor with the 9th, 21st and 25th Regiments to bolster his forces.

In Ohio, a small detachment of troops, while on a reconnaissance mission, are also permitted to hunt for game. At a point close to dilapidated Fort Miami near the Maumee River, the party is fired up by Indians. The unexpected barrage kills Lt. Walker. Another soldier that is hit survives without injury. The shell strikes his left pocket, but lodges in his Bible (or his hymn book). On the following day, Lt. Walker's body is recovered. His remains are taken back to Fort Meigs, where he is interred.

In naval activity, the British privateer *Liverpool Packet* intercepts and seizes the 104-ton schooner *Lawry*, which is en route from Boston to New York with a cargo of chinaware, sugar and other items.

March 10 (Wednesday) *In naval activity,* the *Liverpool Packet*, a British privateer, seizes the 29-ton schooner Bunker Hill (B. Boddely, master) which is en route to New York from New England with a cargo that includes food and liquor, along with clothes and other items. On this day, the *Liverpool Packet* seizes the 56-ton sloop *Reliance* (S. Crowel, master), which is carrying a cargo including iron, molasses and tea.

March 11 (Thursday) *In naval activity,* an American privateer, the *General Armstrong*, falls for a ruse perpetrated by a British frigate. The *General Armstrong*, operating out of New York, spots the British vessel at about 0700 off Surinam in South America. The vessel appears to be a British privateer. The Americans close the distance, and at about 0800, the British spot the *General Armstrong*, which has not yet hoisted its colors. Shortly thereafter at about 0830, the British weigh anchor and sail toward the *General Armstrong*. The British colors are soon hoisted and three cannon shots are propelled toward the American vessel. At about 0910, the Stars and Stripes is hoisted, and as the British vessel comes into range, the Americans fire their long tom. The targeted vessel appears vulnerable. Captain Guy R. Champlin orders his boarding crew to prepare to seize the prize; however, unexpectedly, the British privateer turns out to be a formidable 24-gun British warship. The order to board is lost in the fury as the *General Armstrong* becomes heavily engaged.

The British uncover their guns while the two vessels are within musket range. Suddenly the *General Armstrong* is struck by an avalanche of fire. Despite the carnage, the Americans continue to return fire and the British warship sustains devastating damage due to the accuracy of the American gunners. The guns of the privateer sever the fore topsail tie and the blasts also sever the mizzen gaff halyards. The British colors plummet and for a moment, it seems as if victory was at hand. Nonetheless, return fire smashes into the *General Armstrong* and at the same time the fallen British colors are re-hoisted.

The violence intensifies as the two antagonists remain locked in a torturous close-range struggle. The British vessel for a while is unmanageable; however, the situation is brought under control. Nevertheless, the British are perplexed by the severe punishment being delivered upon them. In contrast, the Americans seemingly remain undaunted, despite being outgunned. The tenacity of the Armstrong's crew and their persistence keeps them in the fight, which has both vessels spaced at only pistol shot. The British, tiring of the unexpected menacing fire, maneuver to a point from where they can finally dispose of the Yankee privateer.

Captain Champlin personally handles the long tom, which is his key to being able to forestall disaster, but the two ships are so close that he also uses his pistol, and it too delivers an effective shot; however, before he fires a second round, a British musket round fired from the enemy's main-top strikes his left shoulder. The wound is severe, but Champlin disregards it and continues to engage. Shortly thereafter, however, the surgeon convinces him to retire to his cabin.

Following about 45 minutes of unharnessed savage combat, while Captain Champlin remains in his cot, he overhears enough of a conversation to realize his ship's colors are about to be struck. Champlin — adamantly opposed to capitulation — holds a trump card. The thought of his ship being surrendered overrides his pain and rejuvenates him. Champlin's cabin is just above the ship's magazine and despite his condition, he continues to hold his loaded pistol. He directs the ship's surgeon to confront the crew: "Tell those fellows that if any one of them dares to strike the colors I will immediately fire into the magazine and blow them all to hell." The surgeon gives the message to the faltering crew and he does not have to repeat it or give any clarification. Champlin's character is well known and the crew knows he is not bluffing.

The colors continue to fly and the bewildered British lose their prize. The *General Armstrong* outruns the British warship, which had also sustained severe damage.

The *General Armstrong* arrives at Charleston on 4 April. Captain Champlin notes in his log book: "In this action we had six men killed and sixteen wounded, and all the halyards of the headsails shot away; the fore-mast and bowsprit one quarter cut through, and all the fore and main shrouds but one shot away; both mainstays and running rigging cut to pieces; a great number of shot through our sails, and several between wind and water, which caused our vessel to leak. There were also a number of shot in our hull."

In the early part of the war, the *General Armstrong* had engaged another strong British vessel, manning 22 guns, and following a hard-fought engagement lasting slightly more than one-half hour, the British ship was driven to shore near the mouth of the Demerara River. It had also prevailed against a 16-gun ship, the *Queen* out of Liverpool, which carried a cargo valued at £90,000. The *Queen*, manned by a prize crew, is wrecked off Nantucket. Some of its other prizes include the *Lucy and Alida* (*see also*, **September 7**). Nonetheless, the *General Armstrong* is remembered more for an engagement in September 1814 when a strong British force en route to Louisiana to destroy General Andrew Jackson's forces at New Orleans delays the voyage to liquidate the *General Armstrong* in the Azores.

In other naval activity, the British privateer *Retaliation* intercepts and captures the 33-ton sloop *Hunter* while it is en route from Edgartown, Massachusetts, to Boston, transporting a cargo including corn and staves.

March 12 (Friday) *In U.S. Army activity,* Colonel Lewis Cass is appointed brigadier general. At this time, he is the commander at Detroit. In October 1813, he is appointed as governor of the Michigan Territory, a post which runs concurrently with his military position as brigadier general until the following year, when he resigns from the army.

In naval activity, the British privateer *Retaliation* captures the 102-ton schooner *William* (John Williams, master), which is en route to Lisbon, Portugal from Charles Town with a cargo of corn. This *William* is separate like named vessels also captured: a bark, 8 July 1812; a brigantine, 16 August 1812; a brigantine, 31 May 1813; a sloop, 7 August 1813; a schooner, 27 October 1813; a schooner, 19 June 1814; a brigantine, 11 October 1814; and a schooner, sometime during 1814.

March 13 (Saturday) *In Washington, D.C.,* Congress authorizes the construction of the sloop of war USS *Peacock*. It is launched the following September.

March 14 (Sunday) *In naval activity,* the USS *Essex*, following a harrowing journey in which it was nearly lost in a storm in early February, arrives at Valparaiso, Chile. The crew had been on short rations, due in part to an acute shortage of food in Argentina that prevented Porter from acquiring provisions at Buenos Aires. Porter was also received unkindly by the government at Montevideo, Chile. The *Essex* by this time had captured two vessels and would seize 13 more, including the *Essex Jr.*, in the next five months. The others are *Montezuma, Policy, Georgiana, Greenwich, Atlantic, Rose, Hector, Catherine, Seringapatam, Charlton, New-Zealander* and the *Sir A. Hammond*. Captain Porter, in a report following his return to port, also notes that the *Rose* and *Charlton* "were given up to the prisoners"; 302 men were captured during the cruise.

The Americans receive excellent treatment at Valparaiso. Initially, when they purchase items, the prices are outrageous, but within a short while, the deck of the *Essex* resembles a farmer's market and prices drop rapidly. Captain Porter becomes concerned because of the high number of hogs purchased by the crew and the officers. He issues orders stipulating how many hogs can be retained and the number is higher than 100. Also, the governor invites the Americans to a party and Captain Porter accepts. He mentions that about 200 women are in attendance. He states: "We found a much larger and more brilliant assembly of ladies than we could have expected in Valparaiso. We found much fancy and considerable taste displayed in their dress, and many of them, with the exception of teeth, very handsome, both in person and in face; their complexion remarkably fine, and their manners modest and attractive." Captain Porter also describes more of the details of the party:

With their grace, their beauty of person and complexion, and with their modesty, we were delighted and could almost fancy we had gotten amongst our own fair country, women; but in one moment the illusion vanished. The ballas de tierra, as they are called, commenced: they consisted at the most graceless, and at the same time fatiguing movements of the body and limbs, accompanied by the most delicate and lascivious motion gradually increasing in energy and violence, until the fair one, apparently overcome with passion and evidently exhausted with fatigue, was compelled to retire to her seat. They disfigure themselves most lavishly with paint; but their features are agreeable and their large dark eyes are remarkably brilliant and expressive. Were it not for their bad teeth occasioned by the too liberal use of the matti (herb), they would, notwithstanding the Chilian tinge, be thought handsome, particularly by those who had been so long as we out of the way of seeing any women.

In other naval activity, the British privateer *Liverpool Packet* captures the 48-ton schooner *Nymphe*. The *Nymphe* is separate from the schooner *Nymphe* seized on 11 June 1813. The *Liverpool Packet* also intercepts and seizes the 107-ton brigantine *Swift* (B. Cook, master), which is en route to Providence, Rhode Island, from Savannah, Georgia, with a cargo of cotton and leather. The *Swift* is separate from the schooner *Swift* captured 7 July 1813.

March 16 (Tuesday) *In naval activity,* two British warships, the HMS *Belvidera* and the HMS *Maidstone*, while cruising together, intercept and recapture the schooner *Margaret*. The *Margaret* is separate from the sloop *Margaret* seized 10 October 1813 and the brigantine *Margaret* captured on 28 February 1815.

March 17 (Wednesday) In Ohio at Chillicothe, General Harrison writes to John Armstrong, the secretary of war, stating his opposition to using Cleveland as the jump-off point for the expedition to regain Detroit:

There are already accumulated at the Rapids of the Miami [Maumee] or in situation to be easily sent thither, to an amount equal to the consumption of a protracted campaign. I am well aware of the intolerable expense Upon the whole it is my decided opinion that the [foot of the] Rapids of the Miami [Maumee] should be the point of rendezvous for the troops, as well as the principal depot. The artillery and a considerable supply of ammunition are already there. Boats and pirogues have been built in considerable numbers on the Auglaise and St. Mary Rivers and every exertion is now making for the double purpose of taking down the provisions to the Rapids, and for coasting the Lake with the baggage of the army in its advance. I had calculated on being able partially to use this mode of transportation, even if the enemy should continue his naval superiority on the lake. Amongst the reasons which make it necessary to employ a large force, I am sorry to mention the dismay and disinclination to the service, which appears to prevail in the western country.

Also at about this time, the secretary writes to General Harrison with a strong request to "to dispense with militia as much as possible, to fill up the 17th, 19th and 24th Regiments of United States troops, to garrison the forts built, and to make feints toward the enemy, but no actual attack, until the contemplated vessels were ready to advance by the lake." The letter receives a prompt response from Harrison, who rejects the secretary's proposals by defining specific reasons that show why his plans should be scrapped. In turn, Armstrong, after receiving Harrison's response terminates his interference with the operations of the Northwest Army.

In naval activity, the American privateer *Comet,* commanded by Captain Thomas Boyle, following a successful cruise, evades the British blockading squadron on the Chesapeake and arrives at Baltimore. In addition to prizes seized that were mentioned earlier, others included the schooner *Messenger* with its cargo of molasses and rum and the tender *Vigilant.* Both prizes are taken into port at Wilmington, North Carolina.

Captain Boyle hurries his return to port in great part because the *Comet* is holding a large number of prisoners. During the cruise, Captain Boyle, after removing the cargo from nine of his prizes, orders the vessels destroyed due to his concern they present too much of a risk in getting them into port. The *Comet* during this cruise seizes a total of 27 prizes.

Later, during 1814, the *Comet* engages the more powerful 22-gun ship *Hibernia* for about eight hours, but it is unable to seize the British vessel, which manages to escape. During the duel, the British sustain 8 killed and 13 wounded. The Americans sustain 3 killed and 16 wounded. Afterward, the *Comet* arrives at Puerto Rico for repairs. While there, Captain Boyle learns that one of his prizes that arrived there was returned to the British.

After his service aboard the *Comet,* he receives command of the privateer *Chasseur,* described by some as one of the finest privateers in action during the conflict and known as the "Pride of Baltimore." During its first cruise, the *Chasseur* seizes nineteen British vessels, including the brigantine *Alert,* the brigantine *Antelope,* the brigantine *Amicus,* the brigantine *Atlantic,* the brigantine *Eclipse,* the ship *Carlbury,* the sloop *Christiana,* the brigantine *Commerce,* the schooner *Favorite,* the schooner *Fox,* the brigantine *Harmony,* the ship *James,* the brigantine *Marquis of Cornwallis,* the brigantine *Reindeer* and the ship *Theodore.* Captain Boyle returns to the United States in October 1814 and arrives in Baltimore in April.

In addition to ravaging British shipping, Captain Boyle takes personal offense at the British admirals who had been proclaiming naval blockades on the United States ports. He issues his own proclamation that declares a blockade of Great Britain to further tantalize the British by mocking the admirals. Boyle actually dispatches a cartel to London to deliver his proclamation with a request that it be displayed in Lloyd's Coffee House.

March 19 (Friday) **In New York,** William Jenkins Worth is commissioned as first lieutenant of the U.S. 21st Infantry. The previous year, Governor Tompkins recommended Worth for appointment as midshipman. Worth serves as an aid to General Winfield Scott and rises to the rank of major during July 1814. In March 1842, he is breveted major general during the conflict in Florida with the Seminole Indians and later, during the Mexican War, he is again breveted major general. General Worth succumbs from cholera while in command of the Department of Texas on 17 May 1849. He is initially interred at Green Wood Cemetery in Brooklyn; he is re-interred on 26 November 1867 in Manhattan in a monument at Fifth Avenue and Broadway, near Madison Square Garden.

General Worth's son, William S. Worth, serves during the Civil War as an officer in his father's old regiment, the U.S. 8th Infantry, and he too later rises to the rank of brigadier general and serves in the Spanish American War during 1898.

In naval activity, the British privateer *Retaliation* intercepts and seizes the 40-ton schooner *Three Brothers* (J. Cairns, master), which is transporting a cargo of corn and flour from Baltimore to Boston. The *Three Brothers* is separate from the schooner *Three Brothers* captured on 7 August 1813. Also, the brigantine *Victory* (E. Bradley, master), while en route to Boston from Lisbon, Portugal, is intercepted and seized by the British privateer *Retaliation.* The *Victory* is separate from the schooner *Victory* seized on 6 January 1814, the schooner *Victory* captured 7 August 1814 and the ship *Victory* seized during September 1814.

March 20 (Saturday) *In naval activity,* the 54-ton sloop *Apollo* (J. Smith, master), which is transporting a cargo of corn from North Carolina to Boston, is intercepted and captured by the British privateer *Sir John Sherbrooke.*

March 21 (Sunday) **In Ohio** at Chillicothe, General Harrison writes Governor Shelby of Kentucky explaining his dissatisfaction with a letter he received from the secretary of war on the 20th regarding regular troops:

> Last night's mail brought me a letter from the Secretary of War in-which I am restricted to the employment of the regular troops raised in this State to reinforce the post at the Rapids. There are scattered through this State about one hundred and forty recruits of the 10th Regiment and with these I am to supply the place of the brigades from Pennsylvania and Virginia whose time of service will now be daily expiring. By a letter from Governor Meigs I am informed that the Secretary of War disapproved the call for militia which I had made on this State and Kentucky and was on the point of countermanding the orders. I will just mention one fact which will show the consequences of such a countermand. There are upon the [banks of the] AuGlaise and St. Mary Rivers eight forts [Forts Winchester, Brown, Jennings, Amanda, Barbee, Adams, Decatur and Wayne] which contain within their walls property to the amount of half a million of dollars from actual cost and worth now to the United States four times that sum. The whole force which would have had charge of all these forts and property would have amounted to less than twenty invalid soldiers.

In naval activity, the British privateer *Sir John Brooke* intercepts and seizes the *Rising Sun,* a 64-ton schooner (L. Hallet, master) transporting a cargo of beans and tar from North Carolina to Barnstable, Massachusetts. The *Rising Sun* is separate from the schooner *Rising Sun* seized on 31 March 1813 and the sloop *Rising Sun* seized on 1 December 1813.

March 23 (Tuesday) **In Maryland,** a group of citizens presents a memorial regarding Easton, which remains defenseless, to the governor (General Levin) and council. The memorial requests troops to protect the town and is forwarded to the secretary of war with an accompanying letter that states:

> By the laws of Maryland, in case of invasion or threatened invasion the brigadier-general or the commanding officer of the place invaded or threatened to be invaded has power to call out the militia; and it was the opinion of this Executive, that no step within its power to take could give to the inhabitants of that place further security. We thought it due, however, to the memorialists, to represent their situation to the general government; and would beg leave to observe that the town of Easton, being a place in which many of the public records are lodged, and in which too, there is an armory of the State, it is or importance that every protection and security which can be afforded to it by either government, should promptly be given.

A negative reply that soon arrives from the secretary ignites anger. The secretary informs the governor that it is "impossible to place troops at all points threatened." He suggests that the armory be relocated. Marylanders are disappointed and disgruntled at the refusal of the federal government to supply the needed help, particularly because they believe that Virginia receives everything that is requested.

In Virginia, Lt. Colonel Thomas Mann Randolph (1st Light Corps) is promoted to colonel commandant of the U.S. 20th Regiment. Colonel Randolph, who married Martha Jefferson, is the son-in-law of Thomas Jefferson. After the war, Colonel Randolph is elected governor of Virginia in December 1819.

In naval activity, the British privateer *Sir John Brooke* intercepts and seizes the 97-ton schooner *Mary* (J. Matthews, master), which is en route from New Haven to Baltimore with a cargo that includes apples, cheese, corn and sugar. This *Mary* is separate from like named vessels also seized: the *Mary Elizabeth,* 8 July 1812; brigantine *Mary,* 17 July 1812; schooner *Mary Ann,* 23 July 1812; 97-ton schooner *Mary,* 23 March 1813; sloop *Mary,* 4 July 1813; sloop *Mary,* 27 July 1813; schooner *Mary,* 7 August 1813; schooner *Mary,* 10 September 1813; schooner *Mary,* 13 September 1813; sloop *Mary Ann,* 22 December 1813; sloop *Mary,* 6 January 1814; ship *Mary,* 1 June 1814; and 92-ton schooner *Mary,* 6 October 1814.

March 25 (Thursday) **In New York,** the USS *Hornet,* following its victory over the HMS *Peacock* the previous month, arrives in port at New York City. Its captain, James Lawrence, had attained the victory with minimal casualties, only one man killed and two wounded during the battle. New Yorkers are jubilant upon the arrival of the ship. A grand celebration in honor of Lawrence is held on 4 May at Washington Hall.

March 26 (Friday) *In naval activity,* the British privateer *Sir John Sherbrooke* intercepts and seizes the 45-ton sloop *Betsy* (J.T. Barney, master) while it is en route to Havana with a cargo including provisions, leather, lumber and tobacco. In other naval activity, the 457-ton ship *Volant* is overtaken by a British squadron and captured. The squadron includes the HMS *Curlew*, HMS *La Hogue* and the HMS *Valiant*.

March 27 (Saturday) *In naval activity,* a British contingent under Lt. Sweeney (commanding officer at St. John) seizes the schooner *Mary*, which is carrying a cargo of brandy, butter, candles, fish, tea, tobacco and rum. Also, the HMS *Bream* and the HMS *Rattler*, cruising together, intercept and seize the 131-ton schooner *Two Brothers*. The *Two Brothers* is separate from the schooner Two Brothers seized on 6 July 1813, the schooner *Two Brothers* captured on 7 July 1813, the bark *Two Brothers* seized 25 May 1814 and the schooner *Two Brothers* overtaken on 4 September 1814.

March 28 (Sunday) *In naval activity,* the 113-ton schooner *Holstein* (M. Bates, master) gets captured by the HMS *Belvidera* while it is en route from Matanza Island, Cuba, to Rhode Island with a cargo of molasses.

March 29 (Monday) **In Louisiana,** General James Wilkinson departs New Orleans aboard the armed schooner USS *Alligator*. His force, composed of about 600 troops, drawn from the 3rd and 6th Divisions, is being transported by Commodore John Shaw's squadron, which is en route to Mobile. Wilkinson's force is protected by Shaw's gunboats and bolstered by U.S. Marines attached to Shaw's squadron.

In naval activity, the HMS *Belvidera* intercepts the 70-ton schooner *Esperanzo* (J. Massa, master), which is en route to New London, Connecticut, from Puerto Rico. The *Belvidera* seizes the schooner and its cargo of cocoa, coffee, hides and other items. In other naval activity, the British privateer Sir John Sherbrooke intercepts and seizes the Maria Windson, a 181-ton schooner en route from North Carolina to Eastport, Maine. The *Maria* is separate from a ketch named *Maria* also captured during 1812 and the ship *Maria* seized on 13 July 1812, the brigantine *Maria* seized 24 June 1813, the brigantine *Maria Francisca* captured 4 May 1814, the brigantine *Maria Frederica* seized 14 July 1814 and the schooner *Maria* captured on 4 September 1814.

March 30 (Tuesday) **In Ohio,** General Harrison, en route to Kentucky to raise additional troops, is informed by a messenger from Fort Meigs who intercepts him at Cincinnati, where he is visiting with his family, some of whom have become ill, that the militia is preparing to return to their homes and that due to the weather change, rain had been destroying the ice on the lake, making it probable that a British attack is imminent. Although the reinforcements acquired up to this point are not ready to march, Harrison decides to speed back to the post. While en route, he encounters some regulars and some militia, and they join with the general to form a relief force.

In naval activity, the schooner *Lucy* is intercepted and seized by the HMS *Rattler*. The *Lucy* is separate from the brigantine *Lucy* seized 25 May 1813 and the schooner *Lucy* captured 15 September 1814.

March 31 (Wednesday) *In naval activity,* the British privateer *Sir John Sherbrooke*, which had seized on 26 March a 45-ton sloop, the *Betsy*, intercepts another sloop named *Betsy* (L. Forsyth, master) while it is en route from Providence, Rhode Island, to New London, Connecticut, with a cargo including hemp and cotton yarn. Also, the 118-ton schooner *Defiance* (T. Altham, master) is intercepted and seized by the HMS *Bream* on its way from Castine, Maine, to Boston with a cargo of wood. The prize is taken into port at New Brunswick. Other vessels named *Defiance* are: the 104-ton sloop seized 4 April 1813, the 62-ton sloop taken on 3 June 1814, the schooner seized 19 May 1814, and the 46-ton sloop taken on 3 August 1814. One other sloop named *Defiance* is seized by the HMS *Superb* and the HMS *Sylph* at an undetermined time in 1814.

The 105-ton brigantine *Eliza* is intercepted and recaptured by the British privateer, the *Liverpool Packet* while it is en route from St. Kitts to London. The *Eliza* is separate from the two *Elizas* captured during 1812, the schooner *Eliza* seized on 1 July 1814, the schooner *Eliza* overtaken on 3 July 1814 and the sloop *Eliza Ann* captured on 31 October 1814.

In other naval activity, the HMS *Bream* intercepts and seizes the 98-ton schooner *Neptune*, which has a cargo of wood. A British squadron composed of the HMS *Endymion*, HMS *Loire* and the HMS *Ramillies* intercepts and seizes the sloop *Rising Sun*. This vessel is separate from the schooner *Rising Sun* seized on 21 March 1813 and the sloop *Rising Sun* captured 1 December 1813.

April **In Washington, D.C.,** the United States is divided into military districts. Nine are established at this time and a tenth is added in July. The districts are:

No. 1) Massachusetts and New Hampshire, commanded by Brigadier General Thomas H. Cushing.

No. 2.) Rhode Island and Connecticut, commanded by Brigadier General Henry Burbeck.

No. 3) New York, extending from the sea as far as the Highlands and a portion of New Jersey, commanded by Brigadier General George Izard.

No. 4) The part of New Jersey excluded from District No. 3 and Pennsylvania and Delaware, commanded by Brigadier General Joseph Bloomfield.

No. 5) Virginia stretching south from the Rappahannock, commanded by Major General Wade Hampton and Brigadier General Thomas Parker.

No. 6) Georgia, North Carolina and South Carolina, commanded by Major General Thomas Pinckney.

No. 7) Louisiana, Mississippi and Tennessee, commanded by Brigadier General Thomas Flournoy.

No. 8) Illinois, Indiana, Kentucky, Michigan, Missouri and Ohio, commanded by Major General William H. Harrison, assisted by Brigadier General Lewis Cass and Brigadier General Duncan McArthur.

No. 9) New York extending north from the Highlands and Vermont, commanded by Major General Henry Dearborn, assisted by Major General James Wilkinson, Major General Morgan Lewis, Brigadier General John P. Boyd, Brigadier General John Chandler, Brigadier General Zebulon M. Pike, Lt. Colonel Winfield Scott (Adjutant General) and Brigadier General William H. Winder.

No. 10) Maryland, Virginia (between the Potomac and the Rappahannock) and the District of Columbia, established July 1813.

In other activity, Lt. John Brooks, U.S. Marine Corps, departs from Washington with a small party composed of "a sergeant, two corporals, two privates, a fifer, and a drummer." Brooks is en route to Erie, Pennsylvania, to enlist Marines to bolster Commodore Perry's force on Lake Erie. While en route, some Marines are enlisted, and after reaching Pittsburgh, Lt. Brooks remains there for a while, but he sends Sergeant James McClure, also a Marine, to continue to Erie to report to Commodore Perry. On 18 May, Brooks arrives with his detachment of only 18 Marines. Later more men are recruited and the Marines also receive some Kentucky volunteers who are dubbed "Horse Marines" by the sailors.

In North Carolina, Major William S. Hamilton, U.S. Army, is assigned recruiting duty in the state. He is promoted to the rank of colonel in conjunction with his new duty. He uses the incentive of informing recruits that he will ensure they receive their favorite weapon. The monthly pay is not overly attractive. It ranges from $8.00 to $12.00 per month, but as incentive, recruits are to receive a bonus of $124.00 once they enlist, and they receive a promise of a grant of 160 acres of land after the war. Men from North Carolina serve in various units, but the 10th U.S. Regiment is heavily composed of North Carolinians.

Major General James Welborn, who resigns his commission in the militia, receives command of the 10th Regiment with the rank of colonel. During the winter of 1813–1814, Welborn leads his regiment northward to New York, where it participates along the frontier.

In naval activity, the British vessel *Poictiers*, commanded by Captain John Bersford, arrives at Lewes, Delaware, and immediately issues demands from the citizens for both food and supplies. The people refuse and the British begin a naval bombardment. The guns cause little damage and the British sail away without their much needed supplies.

In other activity, an American naval squadron raids York (Toronto). The British, garrisoned at York, later burn their own vessel, the uncompleted *Sir Isaac Brock*, to ensure it would not be captured and used by the U.S. Navy. Other forts, including Fort Mitchell in Mobile County on the Tombigbee River, will be established this year.

April 1 (Thursday) **In Ohio** at Fort Meigs, on or about this day, about twelve French volunteers on a reconnaissance mission are attacked by Indians while their boat is off Ewing Island. The Frenchmen are surprised by Indians in two boats. The encounter is fought at close quarters and it becomes vicious; however, the Frenchman prevail. The Indians, except for one who escapes, are wiped out. The volunteers sustain several killed and about six wounded.

In naval activity, the schooner *Centurion* (C. Blanchard, master) is intercepted and captured by the HMS *Atalanta* while it is en route from Charleston, South Carolina, to Providence, Rhode Island, with a cargo of cotton. Also, the British privateer *Sir John Sherbrooke* intercepts and captures the sloop *Fame* (G. Walden, master) on its way with various items from Newport, Rhode Island, to New York. The *Fame* is separate from the sloop *Fame* seized on 14 May 1814, the 85-ton sloop *Fame* overtaken 31 May 1814, and the 48-ton sloop *Fame* captured 23 July 1814.

In other naval activity, the USS *Gallatin*, commanded by Captain John H. Silliman, sustains devastating damage and loss of life when its magazine explodes one day after it arrived in port at Charleston. The fire spreads quickly and the *Gallitin* sinks. The wounds of the survivors were so horrific, some said they might have been better off if they had not survived. Captain Herbert had gone ashore just before the explosion. The cause of the accident was never discovered. Also, the American privateer *Hebe* (formerly the HMS *Laura*), commanded by Captain J. Picarrere, is intercepted by a British squadron and captured.

April 3 (Saturday) ***In naval activity,*** a British squadron arrives at the mouth of the Rappahannock River. It includes the 74-gun *San Domingo* (Captain Charles Gill, with Admiral Sir John Warren's flag aboard), the *Marlborough* (Captain Charles Bayne Hodgson Ross, with Admiral Cockburn's flag aboard) two brigantines (*Fantome* and *Mohawk*), several frigates, including *Maidstone* and *Statira*, and a pair of pilot boat tenders.

After dropping anchors, a contingent of about 600 troops carried by 17 launches moves against a group of four American vessels still anchored in the river. The *Dolphin*, a privateer operating out of Baltimore and three vessels operating under letters of marque, two heading for France and the other to Savannah, are besieged. The British quickly take two of the ships and a third runs ashore; however, the *Dolphin* is unprepared for surrender. The crew raises fierce resistance and the British discover that they will not seize it without a stiff price. The *Dolphin* trades blows for about two hours. For the last part of the duel, the fighting is close quartered and ferocious, after the British finally get a boarding party aboard. Nevertheless, the greatly outnumbered Americans are compelled to surrender.

The British claim their losses at two killed and 11 wounded, including Lt. Polkinghorne among the latter. The Americans, according to a report of Captain Stafford, list British casualties at 50 either killed or wounded. Captain Stafford lists his casualties at 6 killed and 10 wounded. The *Dolphin*, *Lynx* and the *Racer* are taken into British service. The *Dolphin* remains the *Dolphin* and the *Racer* and *Lynx* become the *Shelbourne* and *Musquetobite*, respectively. The *Dolphin* is separate from the schooner *Dolphin* seized on 12 August 1812, the *Dolphin* captured 13 August 1812, the schooner *Dolphin* seized 29 July 1813, the *Dolphin* seized on 16 August 1813 and the 28-ton *Dolphin* overtaken 22 October 1814.

During this same action, the British overwhelm and capture the schooner *Arab*, which operates out of Baltimore. Also, the squadron seizes the *Lynx*, a 225-ton schooner (E. Taylor, master), which is carrying a cargo coffee, cotton and sugar destined for France. The British also seize the privateer *Racer*.

In other naval activity, HMS *Bream* intercepts the 85-ton sloop *Semerimes*, which is en route to Boston with timber and wood. The prize is taken into port at New Brunswick. Also, the British privateer *Sir John Sherbrooke* seizes the 95-ton schooner *Union*. This *Union* is separate from like named vessels captured: a brigantine, 14 August 1812; a ship, 16 August 1812; a schooner, 14 October 1812; a schooner, 19 October 1812; a ship, 26 June 1813; and a schooner, 30 July 1814.

April 4 (Sunday) **In South Carolina,** the privateer *General Armstrong*, having survived a blistering battle against a British warship of the coast of Surinam, South America, arrives at Charleston. Two weeks later, the stockholders of the privateer during a meeting in Tammany Hall in New York officially thank the crew for their performance against the superior warship. Also, Captain Champlin, the commander of the *General Armstrong*, is presented with a sword (*see also*, **March 11**).

In naval activity, the British privateer *Liverpool Packet* intercepts and seizes the 104-ton sloop *Defiance* (T.J. Farrow, master) while it is en route from Wicasset to New York with a cargo of wood. The *Defiance* is separate from the 118-ton sloop *Defiance* seized on 31 March 1813, the schooner *Defiance* captured 19 May 1814, the 62-ton sloop *Defiance* taken on 3 June 1814, and the 46-ton sloop *Defiance* taken on 3 August 1814. One other sloop named *Defiance* is seized by the HMS *Superb* and the HMS *Sylph* at an undetermined time during 1814.

In other naval activity, the HMS *Valiant* intercepts and seizes the 67-ton sloop *Favourite* (George West, master) while it is traveling from Plymouth, Massachusetts, to East Port, with a cargo that includes corn, hams, hogs and tar. The *Favourite* is separate from the 158-ton brigantine *Favourite* seized on 2 September 1814. Also, the British privateer *Liverpool Packet* intercepts and captures the 130-ton brigantine *John* (C. Woodward, master) which is transporting a cargo of flour from New York to Portland, Maine. The *John* is separate from the 164-ton brigantine *John* on 5 April 1813 and the sloop *John* seized 18 May 1814. The *Liverpool Packet* also intercepts the 118-ton schooner *Lydia*. The *Lydia* is separate from the *Lydia* seized on 24 October 1812 and the *Lydia* captured on 7 August 1813.

The HMS *Rattler* intercepts and seizes the 94-ton sloop *Traveller*, with its cargo of cord wood. The prize is taken into port at New Brunswick. The *Traveller* is separate from the 108-ton schooner seized 12 July 1812.

April 6 (Tuesday) ***In naval activity,*** the USS *Lady of the Lake* is launched at Sackets Harbor. It is attached to Commodore Chauncey's squadron and assigned to duty as a dispatch boat on Lake Erie. Sailing Master Flinn receives command. It departs with the squadron within two weeks, and once its service is activated, it seldom serves as a dispatch boat; rather, the *Lady of the Lake* becomes a participant in many of the actions against the British.

April 6–7 **In Delaware,** a British squadron commences a bombardment of the town of Lewes after their demand for supplies is rejected. Colonel Samuel Boyer defiantly refused to comply with the ultimatum. The naval bombardment continues into the 6th, but only minor damage is sustained. The Rodney store sustains a hit in its door. (The door becomes a souvenir that remains on display in Lewes at the Zwaanendael Museum.) Ships that participate in the bombardment include the HMS *Poictiers* and the HMS *Belvidera*.

Other fortifications in the area include Fort Delaware, located on Pea Patch Island on the Delaware River between Delaware and New Jersey. Fort Delaware remains unscathed during the war. During the Civil War, the post is used to hold Confederate prisoners. On the opposite side of the river in New Jersey at Finns Point, an obscure cemetery contains the remains of Confederates who died at the fort. During 1875, it becomes a national cemetery. It also contains the remains of some Union troops and even a few German prisoners of war. Yet another fortification Fort Union at Wilmington, built due to the British naval threat, but it apparently ceases to be active after 1813.

April 7 **(Wednesday) In Canada,** as earlier ordered by General Proctor, the Canadian militia arrives at Sandwich. Intelligence gathered by American scouts had also determined that Tecumseh and about 1,500 Indians had been at Malden. Proctor is preparing a large offensive to reduce Fort Meigs. The army embarks on 23 April.

In Louisiana, the government at New Orleans takes legal action to attempt to halt the smuggling operation of Jean Lafitte and his older brother Pierre. The legal action is initiated in the U.S. District Court of Louisiana. Although the two brothers are charged with breaking the revenue and neutrality laws of the United States, neither is charged with piracy. Both men and others in their band are seized by a contingent led by Captain Andrew Holmes, but afterward they are released and the case never goes to trial.

Also, the USS *Etna*, recently purchased at New Orleans, remains on duty in the region, but details on its service are scarce because few records survive. However, under command of Sailing Master J.D. Ferris, it seizes the Spanish schooner *Terrible* for attempting to violate an embargo. Nevertheless, it does not participate in the defense of New Orleans in late 1814. The *Etna* is rendered unfit for service during November 1814. It is dismantled in 1817.

In New York, at Sackets Harbor, the brigantine *Jefferson* is launched.

In naval activity, the British privateer *Retaliation* intercepts and seizes the *Belfast* (P. Pendleton).

April 8 (Thursday) *In naval activity,* the HMS *Nymphe* intercepts and seizes the 98-ton schooner *Specie*, which is en route to Boston with a cargo of flour.

April 9 (Friday) *In naval activity,* the frigate USS *Chesapeake* arrives back at Boston after a cruise in which it sought out British shipping. While in port, it receives repairs and a new captain, James Lawrence. Most of the crew is also new and time is required to prepare them for action against the British. By 1 June, the *Chesapeake* departs and encounters the HMS *Shannon*.

In other activity, the British privateer *Sir John Sherbrooke* intercepts and captures the 328-ton ship *Frederick Augustus* while it is en route from Cadiz, Spain, to Newport with salt and Spanish clothes. Also, the HMS *Curlew* intercepts and recaptures the 182-ton ship *Plutus*.

April 10 (Saturday) **In Alabama,** Commodore Shaw's flotilla, transporting General Wilkinson's force, arrives in Heron Bay. A contingent under Captain Atkinson lands on Dauphin Island and seizes the Spanish guard (a corporal and six troops) and pilot. The captives are taken to Pensacola. Meanwhile, a contingent under Colonel Bowyer moves down the Tensaw River. Upon arriving at Mobile, Bowyer deploys six brass artillery pieces while awaiting Shaw's squadron.

In New York, the brigantine *Jones* is launched.

In naval activity, the HMS *Valiant* seizes the 57-ton *Packet*, which is on its way from Providence, Rhode Island, to Savannah with a cargo of hides and cotton along with some other items. The *Packet* is separate from the sloop *Packet* seized 19 June 1813 and another *Packet* (ship) seized sometime in 1812.

April 11 (Sunday) *In naval activity,* the HMS *La Hogue* captures the *Caroline* (John Homer, master), a 195-ton brigantine with a cargo that includes pitch, tar and turpentine going from Wilmington to Boston. The *La Hogue* also seizes the 320-ton ship *Montezuma* sometime this year, while it is en route from Boston to Cadiz. Also, the HMS *Emulous* and the HMS *Rattler*, while on patrol, intercept and capture the 125-ton schooner *Expedition*. Its cargo includes flour, gin, tobacco, wine and other items. The prize is taken into port at St. John, New Brunswick.

April 12 (Monday) *In naval activity,* the privateer Alexander (B. Crowninshield, master), manning 20 guns and a crew of 180 men and operating out of Salem, is intercepted by the HMS *Bream* and the *Rattler*. The British seize the ship and take it into port at New Brunswick. Also, the *Bream* and the *Rattler* capture the schooner *Cranberry* sometime during the year; the exact date is unknown. The cargo is transferred from the *Cranberry* but the British determine that their prize is unfit for service. Also, the American schooner *Flight*—en route from Bordeaux, France, to Baltimore with a cargo of brandy, wine and other items—is intercepted by two British warships, the HMS *Spartan* and the HMS *Victorious*.

In other naval activity, the brigantine *Jennett* (J. Pritchard, master) en route from Eastport, Maine, to the Chesapeake Bay with a cargo including bread, beef butter, candles and soap, is seized by the HMS *Junon*.

April 15 (Thursday) **In Alabama,** Spanish Fort Carlotta (formerly Fort Charlotte under the British) at Mobile is attacked by about 600 troops under General James Wilkinson. The force had been transported by Commodore Shaw's squadron, which sailed from New Orleans on 29 March. The U.S. Army is bolstered by U.S. Navy gunboats with Marine units aboard. After landing, apparently during the night of the 14th–15th, the Americans prepare to seize the post. At about noon on the 15th, while the Americans are deployed in the woods to the immediate front of the fort, General Wilkinson dispatches his aide-de-camp, Major Pierre, to issue the ultimatum to surrender. The Spanish had known the Americans were close by because they were able to hear their drums while Mobile was seized.

The Spanish governor, Don Gayetano (Coyeltano) Perez, agrees to capitulate and the fort is gained without a fight. The Americans quickly hoist the American flag and soon discard the French name Carlotta in favor of Fort Charlotte, the previous name when the British received it from the Spanish during 1763. The Spanish post had been armed with 62 artillery pieces. The governor and the garrison are transported to Pensacola by U.S. transports. Militia under Colonel John Bowyer participate.

Also, Wilkinson dispatches a contingent with nine pieces of artillery to Mobile Point, where a battery is established. Meanwhile, Wilkinson moves to the west bank of the Perdido River to instill fear into the Indians who have been incited by the Spanish to initiate hostilities against Americans. At a point along the road to Pensacola, Bowyer is ordered to construct a stockade on the west bank of the river; however, it is later abandoned. Two days later, on the 17th, the Americans seize a minor Spanish post on the Perdido River. The detachment there, one sergeant and seven troops, repair to Pensacola. Nevertheless, Wilkinson moves back to Mobile. Captain Chamberlain is dispatched to Mobile Point with instructions to erect a fort, which is completed in about two years. The post is named Fort Bowyer. General Jackson's force was in Natchez and was unable to participate in the victory.

Fort Charlotte is subsequently named Fort Mobile. It remains active until 1819. The French had initially established Fort Conde here during 1711, when Mobile was the capital of French Louisiana. At this time, there is no Spanish minister to the United States who is recognized and there is no American minister in Spain. Meanwhile in Spain there is a contest for power between Ferdinand VII and Joseph Bonaparte. Ferdinand VII, the son of Charles IV (renounced his throne to Napoleon) and Queen Maria Louisa, had been imprisoned in France by Napoleon, who raised his brother Joseph to the throne of Spain during the Peninsular War.

U.S. gunboats.

In naval activity, the British privateer *Liverpool Packet*, while prowling off the coast, intercepts and captures the sloop *Consolation* (David Joy, master) and its cargo of various items including tobacco, flour and salt.

April 16 (Friday) **In Georgia,** General Pinckney issues orders, in conjunction with President James Madison's decision to evacuate East Florida, which directs the U.S. Forces to withdraw from Camp New Hope and repair to Point Peter on the St. Mary's River in Georgia. The orders direct that the move should be executed on 29 April. Also, a deactivated fort, Fort Morris, at Sunbury, built during 1777, had been reactivated after the eruption of war and renamed Fort Defiance.

In Maryland, Baltimore becomes threatened by the British fleet. Word of the threat spreads. A Philadelphia newspaper, after hearing that Baltimore's port is under blockade, publishes an article that mentions the riots of the previous year: "Who would pity such a city and its ill-fated inhabitants? Baltimore has brought the curse of Heaven upon itself, and has last summer prevented the law from giving protection to the best of citizens. Leave Baltimore to itself and let it make the best of its own situation."

Meanwhile, the army under General Samuel Smith begins to fortify Baltimore. Work to build furnaces for heating shot is undertaken and General Smith orders that a water battery be constructed for 32-pounders. Meanwhile, artillery, infantry and cavalry units deploy along the Patapsco River and the bay. They use a uniform set of signals to communicate. Lookout boats also move way down the river to maintain a vigil. Back in the city, heavy artillery is deployed at Fort McHenry, while regulars (engineers) under Colonel Wadsworth begin constructing other fortifications. During this tedious period some old hulks are placed strategically in the river where they can be sunk to create obstacles if the British try to approach the channel.

In naval activity, the 168-ton brigantine *Dispatch* (H. Bancroft, master) is intercepted and seized by the HMS *La Hogue* while it is en route from Boston to Cadiz, Spain. The *Dispatch* is separate from the brigantine *Dispatch* seized on 25 October 1813. Also, the British privateer *Retaliation* intercepts and seizes the 63-ton schooner *Portland Packet*, which is en route to Boston from New Bern, North Carolina, with a cargo of tar and turpentine. The *Portland Packet* is separate from the schooner *Portland Packet* seized on 5 October 1813.

In other naval activity, the 194-ton ship *Sally* (A. Baker, master) is intercepted and seized by a British squadron, composed of the HMS *Curlew*, HMS *La Hogue* and the HMS *Nymphe*. The *Sally* is separate from other seized vessels of the same name: a brigantine, 10 August 1812; *Sally Ann*, 16 September 1812; a brigantine, 24 April 1813; a schooner, 13 May 1813; a schooner, 12 July 1813; a schooner, 15 September 1813; another schooner, 16 October 1813; and a sloop, 19 May 1814.

April 17 (Saturday) *In naval activity,* the privateer *Reaper*, a schooner, is commissioned this day in Maine.

April 18 (Sunday) **In Alabama** at Tookabatcha, Colonel Benjamin Hawkins holds council with the Indians to deal with the Duck River Massacre inflicted by Little Warrior. It is decided to secretly dispatch a force to Hickory Ground. The contingent is led by McIntosh. Once they arrive at the objective, McIntosh divides his force into two bands. One column advances to the Tallapoosa River at Red Warrior's Bluff. Five of Little Warrior's braves are intercepted there. A fierce contest erupts at the house where the five braves are held up. All five are killed. Another contingent, under Captain Isaacs, intercepts Little Warrior, who tries to evade his pursuers by moving into a swamp near Wetumpka; however, he is caught and killed.

In naval activity, the HMS *Emulous* encounters and captures the 80-ton schooner *Bird* (J. Hammond, master), which is en route from Frenchman's Bay to the Spanish Main with a cargo of barrel staves and shingles. The prize is taken into port at New Brunswick. The 18-ton schooner *Caroline* (A. Burgess, master) is intercepted and captured by a British privateer, the *Sir John Sherbrooke*, while it is en route from North Carolina to Massachusetts Bay with a cargo of beans and corn. The prize is taken into port at Liverpool. Also, the British privateer *Retaliation* seizes the 75-ton schooner *Patty* (E. Hamblen, master), which is on its way to Rhode Island from Portland.

April 18–21 *In naval activity,* the American privateer *Ned*, while sailing to New York from France, is intercepted on the 18th by two British warships, a frigate and a menacing 74-gun ship of the line, near the Virginia Capes while trying to enter Chesapeake Bay. The privateer evades capture by heading north where it can enter the Delaware Bay, but on the following day, the British blockading squadron there again prevents passage. Nonetheless, the *Ned* escapes capture and sails farther north only to again be chased on the 20th, by British blockading ships patrolling off Sandy Hook. Captain Dawson, determined to not become a British prize, outmaneuvers the ships pressing him at Sandy Hook and proceeds toward New London, Connecticut.

On the 21st, while the crew observes a string of about five blockading vessels, the Americans react with insolent determination. Captain Dawson refuses to be intimidated by the insurmountable odds. He issues the order and on command the privateer plows through the floating barricade established by the Royal Navy. The *Ned* evades every vessel, about four or five giving chase, and defiantly enters the harbor at New London to the dismay of the British. Once safely in port, the *Ned* acquires a skilled pilot to guide it through Long Island Sound. Shortly afterward it skirts through the blockade unscathed and safely enters the harbor at New York. During the summer of 1813, the *Ned* embarks on another cruise under the command of Captain Hackett.

April 19 (Monday) *In naval activity,* the HMS *Bream* intercepts and seizes the 70-ton sloop *Lark* (J. Dodge, master) off of Maine. The *Lark* is separate from the *Lark* captured on 15 June 1813. In other naval activity, the British privateer *Retaliation* intercepts and seizes the 150-ton brigantine *Richmond*, which is transporting a cargo of flour from Cuba to Rhode Island. The prize is taken into port at Liverpool. The *Richmond* is separate from the schooner Richmond seized on 25 April 1813.

April 20 (Tuesday) **In Maine,** the privateer *Reaper* is commissioned this day. Ephraim Sturdivant receives command of the schooner. Another privateer, the *Razor*, is also commissioned. Joseph Sturdivant receives command.

In New Hampshire, trepidation rises rapidly at Portsmouth when the inhabitants suspect that the British will be launching an attack. Governor Plumer dispatches a reinforcing company (Sea Fencibles) under Captain William Marshall of the 35th Regiment at Little Harbor to repair to the town to bolster the defenses.

In naval activity, the British privateer *Sir John Sherbrooke* intercepts and seizes the 109-ton schooner *Paulina* (W. Hathway, master) on its way to New York from Norfolk with a cargo of coal, flour and tobacco. The HMS *Bream* seizes the 89-ton sloop *Susannah*, which is transporting a cargo of wood, and takes it into port at New Brunswick. The *Susannah* is separate from the schooner *Susannah and Lucy* seized 5 May 1813. Also, the HMS *Orpheus* intercepts and seizes the 156-ton brigantine *Ulysses*, which is en route from Cuba to Newport, Rhode Island, carrying molasses and sugar. The *Ulysses* is separate from the brigantine *Ulysses* seized on 30 June 1813. Also, the 180-ton brigantine *Vivid* is intercepted and seized by the HMS *Nymphe* while transporting cargo from Boston to St. Domingo.

April 21 (Wednesday) *In naval activity,* the HMS *Belvidera* recaptures the ship *New Zealander*.

April 23 (Friday) **In Canada,** the British under Brigadier General Proctor sail from Malden. His force, composed of about 522 regulars and 461 militia troops are transported to Fort Meigs by a brigantine and a few other vessels. Some of the Indians traveling in small boats accompany the flotilla. The craft are escorted by two gunboats. Tecumseh and the main body of the Indians take a separate route.

In naval activity, two British privateers, the *Atalante* and the *Crown Solomon*, intercept and seize the 115-ton brigantine *Sibae*, which is carrying a cargo of cotton.

April 24 (Saturday) *In naval activity,* the HMS *Curlew* intercepts and seizes the 148-ton brigantine *Sally* (T. Patch, master). This vessel is separate from the brigantine *Sally* seized 10 August 1812, the *Sally Ann* seized on 16 September 1812, the ship *Sally* captured 16 April 1813, the schooner *Sally* seized on 13 May 1813, the schooner *Sally* overtaken 12 July 1813, the schooner *Sally* seized on 15 September 1813, the schooner *Sally* captured on 16 October 1813, and the sloop *Sally* captured 19 May 1814.

In other naval activity, the American privateer *Ned*, commanded by Captain J. Dawson out of Baltimore, arrives at New York from La Teste, France. Captain Dawson reports that during the return voyage, his ship encountered a British privateer, the 19-gun *Malvina*, in latitude 44° 54 north, longitude 15° west, while the latter was en route to London from the Mediterranean. As reported by Dawson, a battle ensued. After about one hour of close-range combat, the *Malvina* was seized. The prize, carrying a cargo of wine, was assigned a prize crew which sailed it into a port in North Carolina.

In New York, General Zebulon Pike writes his father:

> I embark tomorrow in the fleet at Sackets Harbor, at the head of 1,500 choice troops, on a secret expedition. If success attends my steps, honour and glory await my name; if defeat, still shall it be said that we died like brave men, and conferred honour, even in death, on the American namer. Should I be the happy mortal destined to turn the scale of war, will you not rejoice, O my father? May heaven be propitious, and smile on the cause of my country! But if we are destined to fall, may my fall be like Wolfe's — to sleep in the arms of victory.

April 25–27 BATTLE OF YORK Captain Isaac Chauncey continues his project of adding more ships to his fleet. By this time, the number has risen to fourteen. In cooperation with General Henry Dearborn, the Americans sail from Sackets Harbor on the 25th en route to seize York, Toronto, Canada. Chauncey is aboard the *Madison*, his flagship. Dearborn's force has about 1,700 troops. One of the objectives is the HMS *Royal Regent*, a warship that Chauncey failed to intercept the previous fall. The Americans also hold intelligence that at York, commanded by General Roger H. Sheaffe, the British are in the

Major General Henry Dearborn.

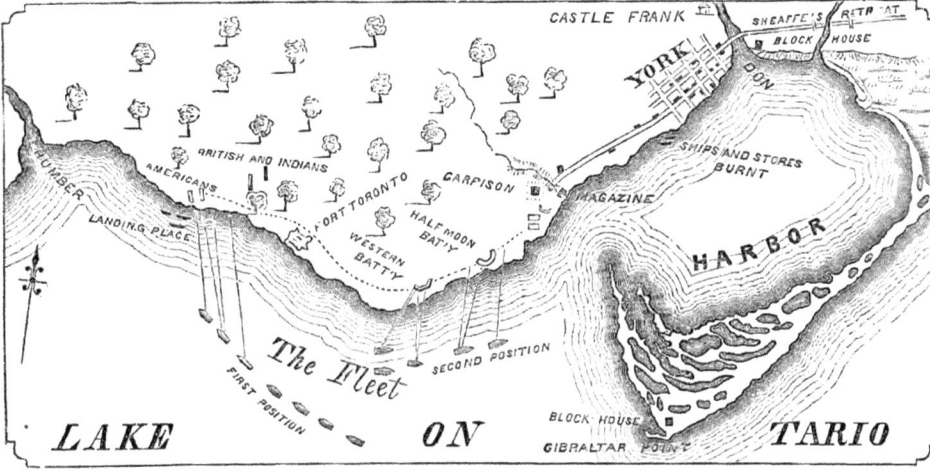

Attack to seize York.

process of constructing another vessel, the HMS *Brock*.

Captain Chauncey has not lost his zeal to eliminate the two vessels to ensure he is able to dominate on the Lake. The fleet departs on the 25th; however, the contained enthusiasm becomes sedated when the winds become unfavorable. The objective, York, which is located along a landlocked bay, is reached on the 27th. York at the time the Americans begin to land is defended by two companies of the 8th (King's) Regiment, one company of the Glengarry fencibles, a contingent of the Royal Newfoundland Regiment and a detachment of artillery, totaling, according to British sources, only about 600 men and 40 to 60 Indians. The Americans are under the immediate command of General Zebulon Pike.

Orders issued just before departure include the following: "No man will load until ordered, except the light troops in front, until within a short distance of the enemy, and then charge bayonets; thus letting the enemy see that we can meet them with their own weapons. Any man firing or quitting his post without orders must be put to instant death, as an example may be necessary."

The mission hits a snag after the force arrives at about 0700 due to unruly seas and the depth of the water. Initially the fleet encounters problems because the water is too shallow for the USS *Madison* to move in closer. Nonetheless, Lt. Elliott, commander of the *Madison*, volunteers to take command of one of the schooners and lead them. The boats are pushed too far, placing them out of the close range support of he fleet, which stands about 600 yards from the enemy shore; however, they are able to bombard the forts. The troops begin to debark at Humber Bay about 0800, but the landing is not uneventful. British troops had been summoned; however, they are late.

Meanwhile, about 50 Indians hold concealed positions, and as the boats encroach the shore line, the enemy commences fire, catching the landing force by total surprise. Despite being in open boats and unable to receive any effective protective naval fire, the riflemen in the boats under Captain Benjamin Forsyth disregard their personal safety. As they are being raked, they stand up in the swaying boats to return fire. The hurricane of fire is insufficient to halt the landing. Infantry in another wave of boats arrives on shore, and just behind them the main body arrives, preventing a debacle. General Pike is finally able get his main body ashore, but the British have received reinforcements — guaranteeing even more tenacious fighting between Pike's command and the defenders of York.

The difficulties begin to mount quickly as the terrain itself becomes an obstacle. Pike leads the first platoon, and just after climbing the embankment, he initiates a charge that forces the British to retire. At about the same time, Major Forsyth's riflemen signal that they had succeeded at another point. The Indians panic and break for the woods.

Nevertheless, Pike's artillery becomes valueless because the men cannot carry it forward. The advance itself is punishing for the troops who slowly trod forward while several British artillery pieces pound away at their flanks. The Americans, however, remain undaunted, and they slug their way forward engaging at close quarters with a sudden burst that gains ground only to be met with counter attacks that lose the ground.

By this time the Indians, apparently unwilling to face the American bayonets during the struggle, have faded away, leaving the British to fend for themselves. All the while, the American persistence intensifies. After both sides badger each other in mortal combat, finally the British are compelled to give more ground, destroying bridges behind them as they retire and regroup on the outskirts of the town. By this point, the British sustain just under 100 killed, wounded or missing. The defending force of about 300 reg-

Powder magazine at York.

The fort at York.

ulars and militia had been finally compelled to give ground or be overrun.

The Americans continue their sluggish progress to positions near a British battery that is unattended. From there General Pike becomes suspicious when he spots a barracks that appears inactive; however, his instincts call for extreme caution. Rather than charge ahead into a possible ambush, Pike sends a detachment forward to reconnoiter the barracks. The small party under Lt. Riddle moves up close and discovers the barracks is not occupied; however, while Riddle begins his return to American lines, just as the men cross a ravine, a powder magazine blows to ignite a massive explosion of about 500 barrels. The debris flies in all directions in conjunction with a huge cloak of choking smoke that blankets the area. Riddle's detachment receives unexpected protection from the bank of the ravine and all are spared from harm. Nonetheless, the detonation makes the immediate area look like a wicked tornado had just passed through.

Back at the American lines at the battery, General Pike becomes one of the casualties when sections of a stone wall descend and crash upon Pike, two members of his staff, including his aide, Captain Benjamin Nicholson (14th U.S. Infantry), and a wounded British sergeant that General Pike is giving some aid to. All in the group are fatally injured. The massive explosion causes huge casualties to both sides. At the time of the explosion, British troops are also near the magazine and about 40 of them are also killed. The scene becomes chaotic and apparently the British resistance dissipates. British General Roger Hale Sheaffe is not around when the Americans rebound from the tragedy and move toward the town. The column is led by Colonel Cromwell Pearce, who assumed command after General Pike became disabled.

When Colonel Pearce arrives in York, he discovers that it is held only by militia. General Sheaffe had taken the opportunity to depart from the town with all of the regulars. Before leaving, he had drawn up terms for the surrender of York and handed the document to a militia officer. The Americans had expected more resistance from within the city; however, upon their approach, they are met by the militia officer, Colonel Chewitt, who hands over the surrender offer from Sheaffe. The document of surrender includes possession of the city and the military stores; however, before departing, Sheaffe begins to destroy the stores and the ship which is under construction. The Americans also fail to seize the HMS *Royal Regent*. It had left port before the Americans arrived. In the meantime, General Sheaffe advances toward Kingston. General Dearborn remains offshore aboard Commodore Chauncey's flagship, the *Madison*.

Although the British regulars had escaped from York, just under 300 men (including Royal Navy and militia) surrender with the town. The militia troops are paroled. Nonetheless, the victory is subdued due to the losses sustained and the fatal injury sustained by General Zebulon Pike. He is taken out to the fleet while he remains alive. After the British flag is lowered in York, it is taken to General Pike, and in response to his request, it is placed on the bed under his head. Shortly thereafter, General Pike succumbs. He is embalmed at York and his remains are taken to Sackets Harbor and interred at Fort Tompkins. Pike's aide, Captain Nicholson, who was alongside of Pike when the explosion occurred, is interred beside General Pike.

According to a report sent to the secretary of war, the Americans sustain "a loss of 44 killed in battle, and 38 by the explosion — 32 wounded in battle [including Colonel Ripley, who sustains a minor wound], and 222 by the explosion; total, killed and wounded, 306." Commodore Chauncey reports that his squadron had sustained 4 killed and 8 wounded. Also, in a report written on 3 May, General Dearborn states: "As nearly as I have been able to ascertain, the loss of the enemy, in the late affair of York, amounted to 100 killed, 200 prisoners, and 300 wounded. I have not been able to ascertain, precisely the amount of militia put on their parole; I presume it could not be less than 500." General Dearborn also notes in his report that the Americans discovered a scalp hanging by the speaker's chair.

The Americans also acquire the *Duke of Gloucester*, which is in port undergoing repairs, along with a few gunboats. A large amount of stores and provisions are also gained; however, due to a shortage of transports to carry the prisoners, about 500 are paroled. General Dearborn receives a bonus. General Sheaffe's papers and baggage are also captured.

After the campaign against York, the American fleet sails southward toward the mouth of the Niagara River where British-held Fort George is located. The fleet arrives there on 10 May. Also, subsequent to the loss of York, Governor Prevost, due to serious complaints regarding Sheaffe's conduct, relieves Sheaffe. General John Vincent succeeds him. General Sheaffe is transferred to Montreal, where he receives command of the forces there.

It is never conclusively determined whether the explosion was intentional or accidental. British General Sheaffe calls the explosion as "an unfortunate accident," yet some British historians portray the explosion as a "regularly laid plan." Some American authors also portray the explosion as intentional. Nevertheless, one of the American participants, Captain Isaac Chauncey, writes: "I am much inclined to believe that General Sheaffe was correct when he stated that it was accidental. Nor could I condemn the enemy, even if a train had been laid. It is a perfectly legitimate mode of defence, as every student of history knows; and why should we censure the garrison for thus employing an acknowledged means of defence, to check the progress of an invader?"

The USS *Governor Tompkins*, the *Lady of the Lake* and the schooner *Madison* participate in this action. The *Madison* remains in service for the duration, but despite its speed, it is not considered to be a safe vessel. After the war it remains at Sackets Harbor until 1825, when it is sold.

In naval activity, the British privateer *Retaliation*, which had recently seized the brigantine *Richmond*, intercepts a 94-ton schooner, also named *Richmond*, which is transporting a cargo

General Green Clay.

of molasses. The prize is taken into port at Liverpool.

April 26 (Monday) In Ohio, the flotilla transporting the army under General Proctor arrives at the mouth of the Maumee and begins to ascend the river to launch the attack against Fort Meigs. The vessels are spotted and word is delivered to General Harrison at Fort Meigs. The intelligence also includes the fact that a large number of Indians accompany the British, but that they are advancing by foot on both sides of the river. The alarm places the post on high alert. General Harrison sends out an officer, Captain William Oliver (the fort's commissary), to intercept the expected Kentuckians under General Green Clay to get them to expedite their march. Oliver, one other soldier and a friendly Indian depart from the fort, escorted part of the way by a contingent of dragoons under Captain Garrard. The party makes it to Fort Winchester soon after Clay's force arrives there.

By the time Captain Oliver arrives, General Clay had already been informed of the situation at Fort Meigs. General Clay had already dispatched Captain Leslie Combs and a small party, including two troops and two Shawnee brothers, Black Fish Jr. and Walker, to inform Harrison that they are closing on the post. Nevertheless, unknown to General Clay, the detachment is attacked by Pottawatomie Indians just as they reach a point from where they spot the colors over the post. The two soldiers, Johnson and Paxton, are wounded, and both are captured. Johnson succumbs from his wounds, but Paxton later is rejoined with the army. Lt. Combs and Black Fish escape injury and they are able to make it back to Fort Winchester at nearly the same time as General Clay and the detachment under Captain Oliver.

In naval activity, the HMS *Bream* encounters and captures the 78-ton schooner *Branch* (H. Luskin, master) while it is transporting a cargo of ballast from Boston to Deer Island. The prize is taken into port at New Brunswick.

April 27 (Tuesday) **In Canada,** Commodore Isaac Chauncey's fleet arrives at York. The American vessels bombard the forts that protect the town in support of the landing of about 1,700 troops under General Henry Dearborn and General Zebulon Pike. The schooner *Fair American,* commanded by Lt. Chauncey, and the USS *Ontario* participate in this action. The town is captured and the squadron seizes a British schooner. The *Fair American* continues to cruise on Lake Ontario until December, when the fleet is compelled to halt activity on the lake until spring 1814. The *Fair American* at that time is modified to be used as a transport. Subsequently, on 15 May 1815, the *Fair American* is sold.

During the operation, the fleet comes under fire from Indians and British ground forces who are positioned along the shore line, but the naval guns catapult grape toward the British positions to drive the attackers back. The Americans also gain a large amount of supplies and capture the British brigantine *Duke of Gloucester.* Another vessel, still under construction, is burned. Nonetheless, the Americans determine that the town is of no military value and lacks natural defenses. The Americans decide to abandon it (*see also,* **April 25–27 In New York**).

In Ohio, near Fort Meigs, British General Proctor's forces debark on the left bank of the Maumee River close to the dilapidated Fort Miamis less than three miles below Fort Meigs. Proctor intends to establish batteries opposite Fort Meigs. However, the British encounter nasty weather that hinders the operation. Heavy rains continue to pound the area, and it becomes extremely difficult to move up their artillery. Initially they toil only under darkness using two oxen and about 200 troops to move each of the 24-pounders. The British have been under observance since the arrival of the flotilla at the mouth of the river on the previous day, when it was spotted by a detachment under Captain Hamilton, during a patrol along Maumee Bay.

General Harrison at about this time delegates Peter Navarre to perform an urgent mission, to rush letters from Harrison to each of the garrisons extending from the Lower Sandusky to the Upper Sandusky to inform them of the massive British force that is preparing to attack. Meanwhile, the British carry the Indians on the left bank over to the opposite side of the river, where they are positioned to harass the Americans by initiating a siege.

In naval activity, the HMS *Bream* intercepts and seizes the *Pilgrim* (boat), which is carrying a cargo of flour, gin, tobacco and other items. The *Pilgrim* is separate from the brigantine *Pilgrim* seized on 18 May 1813 and the schooner *Pilgrim* seized 8 July 1813.

April 27 to May 20 **In Ohio,** British General Henry Proctor, leading a massive force of more than 2,000, including about 1,200 to 1,500 In-

Peter Navarre.

dians, the latter led by Tecumseh, arrives at a point less than three miles below Fort Meigs on the 27th. Proctor's expeditionary force is accompanied by two gunboats. A British battery is erected near the point of debarkation, and by the 30th, two British batteries are in place within the village of Maumee. One battery has two 24-pounders and the other contains one 8-inch howitzer and two 5-inch howitzers. American fire had inflicted some casualties while the cannon were being brought up from the landing place. While the British are mounting the guns at the batteries, American fire inflicts additional casualties.

In the meantime, Proctor is consumed with confidence since he defeated General Winchester at the Raisin River the previous January, and he anticipates a short siege and a quick kill. Nonetheless, General William Henry Harrison, commander at Fort Meigs, is preparing to retaliate for what the Americans called the "Raisin River Massacre." As an added potent defense, Harrison has overseen the construction of a massive wall along the high ground within the camp that stretches for about 300 yards in length and stands 12 feet in height, atop a 20-foot foundation. The protective wall is near a line of tents. Once they are removed, the British spot the huge wall, and it becomes apparent that the U.S. post will not easily be conquered.

Proctor's recent prophecy that he would "smoke out the Yankees" is quickly debunked. In conjunction with the construction of the giant wall, the British are unable to see even the Yankees. Nonetheless, General Proctor makes preparations to launch an assault, which unfolds on 1 May. The attack is bolstered by artillery which fires about at least 250 to 300 rounds into the American positions without causing any substantial damage or large numbers of injuries; however, two men are killed and Major Amos Stoddard is struck by a shell fragment. Initially Stoddard's wound is not thought to be fatal; however, tetanus takes his life ten days later. Most of the troops are protected by remaining in deeply dug holes covered by logs and dirt. Al-

though the troops remain relatively safe in their bunkers, the incessant rain saturates the holes that lack a tent to cover the top.

Despite the ineffective fire, the British continue their bombardment to terrorize the garrison, and they continue to receive return fire from the fort's guns. By the night of 1 May, the British complete a third battery, and it is deployed between the other two. A fourth battery (mortars) is activated by the 3rd, and on the same night, the British move some small cannon and mortars to the opposite bank, with some being deployed as close as 250 yards from the rear of the post. The additional fire power does not intimidate the garrison, but it does help galvanize the defenders. Having failed to force a surrender by the 4th, General Proctor replays his strategy used against General Winchester at Frenchtown; however, General Harrison is not yet his captive and he lacks the apprehension and anxiety of Winchester. General Proctor issues an ultimatum to surrender. Shortly thereafter, the messenger, British Major Chambers, receives Harrison's succinct response: "Tell General Proctor, that if he shall take the fort, it will be under circumstances that will do him more honor than a thousand surrenders."

On the same day, a 17-man detachment, including Captain Oliver and Major David Trimble, penetrate the British positions and reach the fort to inform General Harrison that Clay's reinforcements of about 1,100 troops, transported by eighteen flatboats equipped with "high sides to protect the soldiers from the bullets of the savages they meet," had arrived at the head of the Grand Rapids, less than 20 miles from the fort.

Harrison, also informed that the pilot was reluctant to pass the rapids due to the blackness of the night, dispatches Captain Hamilton and one other man to deliver instructions to General Clay. Upon receiving the orders, Clay dispatches 800 troops under Colonel Dudley in twelve boats to eliminate the guns before crossing the river. His command includes his regiment of 761 troops, bolstered by 60 men attached to Colonel William E. Boswell's regiment and 45 regulars. In the meantime, the rest of the troops proceed directly to the post.

As ordered, the Kentuckians strike the British positions on the 5th. A brisk and deadly contest erupts. From the fort, General Harrison observes the British colors being lowered on the opposite (left) bank, a sign of success; however, the commander of the attacking force, Lt. Colonel W. Dudley, becomes overconfident and dismisses Harrison's order by signal to immediately cross the river after taking out the batteries. At about the same time, the remainder of the force under General Clay debarks on the right bank, and he encounters resistance by Tecumseh's Indians. Clay's column sustains some casualties; however, he overcomes the resistance and reaches the post. At the same time, the column encounters the contingent sent out of the fort by Harrison. Clay hooks up with Colonel John Miller's 350 men and they seize the battery on the right bank. After disabling the guns and collecting 43 prisoners, the combined force returns toward the post.

Indians under Tecumseh and some British troops attempt to sever the route by attacking the flank, but due to General Harrison's comprehensive knowledge of Indian tactics, the Americans foil the scheme. Consequently, neither the rear nor the left flank is penetrated. The troops, with fixed bayonets, initiate a charge which drives the Indians scattering into the woods.

In the meantime, on the opposite bank, the British, stunned by the attack and the loss of the batteries, launch a stiff counterattack. Dudley's command, composed of some fresh troops, had taken their objective without casualties; however, the troops afterward endanger the mission by giving chase in an attempt to intercept a group of Indians that seem to be in flight. Due to a lack of experience in fighting Indians, they are unaware that those they pursue are leading them into a deadly trap. Once the column enters the woods, the British spring their ambush. Dudley's command holds its ground and holds off the enemy in heated combat for several hours; the troops fail to break out.

The engagement is remembered as "Dudley's Massacre" or "Dudley's Defeat." Many in the command are killed and the large number of wounded are stripped naked and scalped. The rest, except for 170 troops who break away and make it to the fort, are taken to the British camp near Fort Miamis, where those who aren't killed by Indians during the march are subjected to torture, including running the gauntlet.

Lt. Colonel Dudley, a native of Virginia (Spotsylvania County), relocated in Kentucky at an early age. He was last spotted in the swamp suffering from multiple wounds, trying to defend himself until encircled by a large number of Indians. Another officer, Captain Combs (earlier served with General Winchester at the Raisin River) is among the captured. He is taken to British-held Fort Miamis.

General Harrison absorbs the setback caused by Lt. Colonel Dudley's (General Green Clay's command) impetuous action; however, the unnecessary losses in Dudley's command do not change his strategy. He holds his belief that the main body of the British force is still in the area near Fort Miamis and that the Indians involved with the siege had been encamped on the east (right) side of the river. His instincts prove to be accurate, which permits the reinforcements to safely enter the fort on the west bank of the river. General Harrison, bolstered by the reinforcements, also sends a 350-man contingent on the 5th to attack the British batteries. The unexpected attacking force strikes boldly and swiftly. The batteries are taken, and with the loss, General Proctor's vision of another victory dissipates.

After the failure to defeat the reinforcements and the rout in the woods, the Indians begin to lose their enthusiasm. They begin to abandon Proctor. Combined with the lack of solid Indian support and his failure to reduce the post, Proctor lifts the siege and retires. However, on 20 July, the British under Proctor launch yet another assault to reduce Fort Meigs. General Harrison's report of 9 May states: "In the siege, and the several sorties of the 5th instant, there were 81 killed, and 189 wounded — total, killed and wounded, 270. Other reports indicate 467 men captured.

The British-Indian casualties are not available; however, it is believed that their losses had been fewer than those of the Americans. Estimates amount to 14 killed, slightly under 50 wounded and about 40 missing.

Proctor's misfortune is responsible for Fort Meigs gaining the nickname the "Gibraltar of the Northwest." Proctor's prisoners come under severe brutality. While held at Fort Miamis, Proctor takes no action to intervene when the Indians without cause murder about twenty men. Captain Wood, who observes the atrocities, later states: "The Indians were permitted to garnish the surrounding rampart, and to amuse themselves by loading and firing at the crowd, or at any particular individual. Those who preferred to inflict a still more cruel and savage death selected their victims, led them to the gateway, and there, under the eye of General Proctor, and in the presence of the whole British army, tomahawked and scalped them." It is said that the horrible work was stopped by Tecumseh, who, coming up when it was at its height, buried his hatchet in the head of a chief engaged in the massacre, crying... For shame! It is a disgrace to kill a defenceless prisoner!" Wood also states: "Tecumseh displayed more humanity, magnanimity, and civilization than Proctor, with all his British associates in command, displayed through the whole war on the northwestern frontiers."

April 28 (Wednesday) **In Ohio,** General Harrison dispatches Captain William Oliver to intercept General Green Clay and tell him of the situation at Fort Meigs. General Clay had departed Cincinnati in early April with a force of Kentuckians. Meanwhile, Captain Leslie Combs joins with General Clay at Dayton. General Clay utilizes Combs by commissioning him as captain of a company of riflemen, which acts as scouts and spies. The riflemen are drawn from Lt. Colonel William Dudley's corps.

While at St. Mary's blockhouse, General Clay splits his force, sending Dudley to the Auglaize River, while Colonel Boswell's corps descends the St. Mary's River, accompanied by General Green Clay. During the operation, Dudley receives intelligence regarding the precarious situation of General Harrison at Fort Meigs.

In naval activity, the *Aeolus* (F. Hocquard, master) is recaptured by the HMS *La Hogue*. The *Aeolus* is carrying a cargo of dry goods and tea when intercepted. The *La Hogue* also seizes the 181-ton ship *Henry* (B. Gardiner, master) on its way from Liverpool to Boston with earthenware

Tecumseh stopping a massacre (*Battles of America by Sea and Land, Volume II*, Robert Tomes, 1878).

and salt. The *Henry* is separate from the ship *Henry* seized 11 August 1812, the 89-ton schooner *Henry*, captured 19 June 1813, and the 194-ton brigantine *Henry Gilder* seized on 12 July 1814.

April 29 (Thursday) **In Maryland,** following the recent attacks against Poole's Island, Poplar's Island, Sharp's Island and Tilghman's Island, the British on this day set out to plunder another target. British troops commanded by Cockburn arrive at Frenchtown. The force, about 400 strong, under Lt. Westphall, debarks from the 13-barge flotilla attached to the HMS *Marlborough* and proceeds to destroy the town and confiscate supplies. Frenchtown is unable to raise much resistance. It is defended by only a few men, including some militia, a few wagoners and several stage drivers. Nonetheless, the Spartan force repels two attacks against their redoubt before they are compelled to withdraw.

Afterward, the British destroy the wharf and fishery, along with the warehouses; however, they spare private homes. Once they complete their destruction, the British move to White Hall and advance to Elk Landing, where an American battery is deployed. A brief skirmish erupts, and after only a few volleys, the British return to their barges and re-embark. Consequently the defenses near Elkton, nearly opposite Frenchtown, Fort Defiance and Fort Hollingsworth hold and Elkton (Cecil County) is not torched. Cockburn then moves on toward Havre de Grace (Harford County) on the west bank of the Susquehanna River.

In naval activity, the USS *Essex,* in the Pacific off South America, dispatches a contingent of sailors and Marines in assault boats to capture the HMS *Montezuma*. The vessel is boarded and captured. Also this day, the *Essex* seizes the British vessel *Essex Junior* (formerly a whaler, the *Atlantic*) off the Galapagos Islands. The *Essex Jr.* is afterward transformed into a U.S. cruiser under the command of Commander John Downes.

April 30 (Friday) *In naval activity,* the USS *Congress* embarks on a cruise in the Atlantic. It operates off the Verde Islands several hundred miles off the west coast of Africa and cruises off the coast of Brazil before returning to Portsmouth on 14 December. The *Congress* seizes four vessels during its final cruise of the war. At Portsmouth it undergoes repairs but does not return to sea. Subsequently, during 1822 and into 1823, it participates against the pirates in the Caribbean. It sees additional service until 1824, when it is placed in ordinary art Norfolk. In December of that year, it is taken to Washington for repairs, but upon its return to Norfolk, it serves as a receiving ship for a few years. Finally, during 1834, it is rendered unfit for service and dismantled at Norfolk.

In other activity, the 156-ton brigantine *Hector*, en route to New York from Havana, Cuba, with a cargo of coffee and sugar, is intercepted and seized by the HMS *Spartan*. The *Hector* is separate from the brigantine *Hector* seized 23 August 1812.

May In Alabama, the Indians who have decided to pick up the hatchet and join with Tecumseh and the British are starting to increase their hostility, even against Indians who had chosen to remain aligned with the United States. The pro–Tecumseh leaders, including a half-breed, Peter McQueen, and Hobothe Micco continue to urge warfare. The situation deteriorates into near–civil war. The pro–American chiefs, including Big Warrior, call for a council, but many chiefs decline attending. Big Warrior sends a messenger to the Alabamas, requesting proof that the Great Spirit had appeared to them. No response is forthcoming. The messenger is killed and scalped. In the meantime, the Indians also begin to openly attack Americans.

In Ohio, the forces under William Henry Harrison repulse an attack on Fort Meigs in northwestern Ohio. The British have erected two batteries, and the fort survives a pounding that included a day-long bombardment that catapulted about 500 shells on the post.

In other activity elsewhere, by late May, the British have extended the blockade of American ports, this time southward from New York to Charleston and Savannah. Governor Shelby of Kentucky, who previously received a request for reinforcements by General Harrison, dispatches General Green Clay and a force of 1,200 to reinforce the defenders at Fort Meigs. American troops stationed at Amelia Island off the coast of Georgia since March 1812 withdraw.

Also, the Americans react to the British who had seized 23 privates at Queenston (October 1812) and had taken them to England without notifying American authorities. As British subjects, they are to be tried for treason for fighting against their king. The troops had been attached to the 1st, 6th and 13th Regiments, commanded by Colonels Kingsbury, Simonds and Schuyler, respectively. President James Madison, having received the news from the American commissary of prisoners in London, directs General Henry Dearborn to select 23 British troops to be held. England is informed that if they proceed with the trials, the English prisoners being held will meet an identical fate.

In naval activity, the British vessel *Cossack*, seized earlier by the American privateer *General Stark* out of Salem, Massachusetts, after being transformed into an 8-gun privateer under Captain Nash, is commissioned this month. Salem comes under close scrutiny by the British because of the effective privateer activity that is ravaging British shipping. Late in the year, the British realize that sparing the New England port towns from naval blockades due to the impression New England is pro–British is in error. Salem comes under heavy blockade. By November, the privateers out of Salem that fall into British hands include the *Active, Cossack, Enterprise* and a privateer boat, the *Owl*. The results only prompt the Americans to build better and speedier privateers to replace those lost. Essentially, the blockade is ignored. One of the notable privateers that defies the blockading squadron late in the conflict is the defiant *Diomede* under Captain Crowninshield, which scores some success until its career comes to an end on 25 June 1814.

May 1 (Saturday) In Canada, the Americans initiate the abandonment of York. British troops that are captured are paroled rather than being taken to Niagara. A schooner departs for Niagara to deliver a report on the operations against York to the commanding officer there, Major General Morgan Lewis. He is also brought up to date on the intended advance by the Americans toward Four-mile Creek. Meanwhile, unfavorable winds prevent Commodore Chauncey's naval force from sailing. Finally, on 8 May, the fleet moves out and arrives at the creek later the same day.

In Ohio, American-held Fort Meigs comes under siege by British General Henry Proctor. British artillery pummels the fort, but Harrison holds. General Harrison, as the first British shells begin too fall, directs Colonel William Christy, acting quartermaster, to affix an American flag: "Sir, Go and nail a banner on every battery, where they shall wave so long as an enemy is in view." The Stars and Stripes remains atop the fort. Reinforcements under General Green Clay, dispatched by Governor Shelby of Kentucky, arrive during the dark hours of the 4th, into the morning of the 5th. Heavy fighting occurs on the 5th, when Kentucky volunteers attack the British batteries, stalking the fort. A British counter-attack causes severe casualties to one part of General Clay's command, which is led by Lt. Colonel William Dudley. The other American column captures several British guns, making it safely to the fort. Major Amos Stoddard is wounded. He dies of tetanus on the 11th. The British siege on Fort Meigs continues until May 9th. Captain Combs, at Fort Defiance, volunteers to carry messages to General Harrison at Fort Meigs. His party arrives at the post the following day. Also, the British arrive back at Amherstburg on 13 May.

Colonel William Christy.

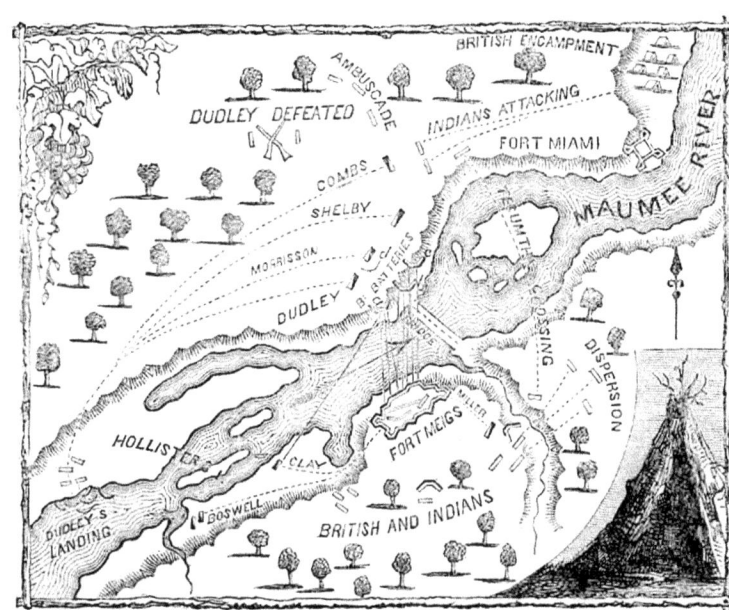

Siege of Fort Meigs.

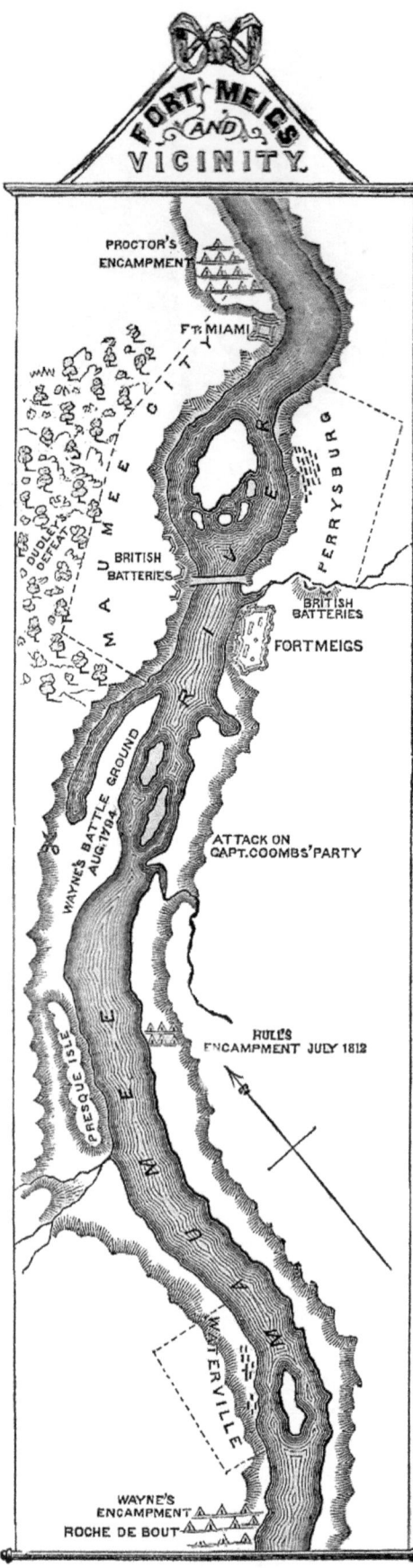

Fort Meigs and vicinity.

In naval activity, the British privateer *Retaliation,* cruising on the sea path from Bermuda, intercepts and seizes the 105-ton schooner *George Washington* and its cargo of ballast before it arrives at New Haven, Connecticut. Also, the sloop *Juana*— en route from Havana, Cuba, to Newport, Rhode Island, with a cargo of coffee, wood and raisins — is seized by the HMS *Spartan.*

In other naval activity, the American privateer *Grand Turk* (Captain Holten J. Breed) embarks on its second cruise. Once out in the open seas, it sails directly to European waters, where it ravages British shipping before returning to port at Salem during November. Its prizes include the schooner *Rebecca* out of Halifax, carrying a cargo of livestock and provisions destined for Bermuda and diverted to Portsmouth; the schooner *Agnes* with a cargo of fish (taken to France); the 10-gun ship *William,* carrying a cargo including wine and dry goods from Cork, Ireland, going to Buenos Aires (taken into Salem); the *Indian Lass,* a brigantine en route to St. Michael from Liverpool (sent into Salem, with 30 crewmen); the *Catharine,* a brigantine en route to London from Lisbon, Portugal (soon after recaptured by the British); the *Britannia,* en route to the West Indies (taken into Portland); again the *Catharine* (recaptured by the HMS *Bacchus,* only to be lost again to the *Grand Turk* before it reaches a British port and soon after burned by the Americans); the sloop *Caroline,* transporting a cargo of dry goods from London to St. Michael's (cargo removed and prisoners aboard the *Grand Turk* transferred to it with orders to land); the *Cossack,* with a cargo of wine (recaptured by the HMS *Bulwark,* but only temporarily; it is recaptured by the American privateer *Surprise*); the schooner *Pink* (destroyed at sea); the brigantine *Brothers* while en route to Liverpool from S. John's; the *Robert Stewart,* a brigantine carrying a cargo of lumber; and the *Commerce,* a schooner transporting a cargo of fish. The final prize, the brigantine *Belgrade,* is intercepted. The Americans confiscate some of its guns and then permit it to resume its voyage to Falmouth, England. The *Grand Turk* then sails for home.

The privateer, having drained its crew by assigning prize crews, arrives in Salem in November, following a successful cruise of 103 days with only 44 men out of the original number of 150. One of the prize crews had been responsible for safely getting the vessel to port to preserve its cargo, thirty thousand pounds sterling.

May 2 (Sunday) **In Ohio,** Captain Leslie Combs and his party arrive near Fort Meigs following an arduous journey from Fort Defiance. Combs is immediately faced with a crucial decision once he determines that the British siege had been initiated. To delay his journey would be too dangerous, but to return would be equally dangerous. He tells those in his party: "We must go on boys and if you expect the honor of taking coffee with General Harrison this morning, you must work hard for it. The party moves around Turkey Point bend and the fort, its Stars and Stripes still flying, comes into view."

About this time, the Americans detect a solitary Indian, and then suddenly, a large band is moving to cut off Combs' canoe. The Indians commence fire and injure Johnson and Paxton. Paxton survives, but Johnson suffers a mortal wound. The survivors, including an Indian, Black Fish, are forced to retreat; Paxton and Johnson are left behind. On 4 May, Captain Combs and Black Fish reach Fort Defiance just after General Clay had arrived there. The remaining members of Combs' party, two Walker brothers, had arrived before Comb.

In naval activity, the brigantine *Catherine,* transporting a cargo of rum and other items from St. Bartholomews to London, is intercepted by the HMS *La Hogue* and recaptured. The *Catherine* is separate from the letter of marque *Catherine* seized during July 1812 and the schooner *Catherine,* captured 4 December 1813. Also, the HMS *Curlew* (formerly the American privateer *Curlew*) encounters the USS *President* but is able to escape. Also, the American privateer *Gallinipper,* out of Salem, is intercepted by the HMS *Rattler,* driven to shore and wrecked. Another American privateer, the *Dart,* had been shipwrecked during the early days of the war after being run ashore; however, before being destroyed, the *Dart* had succeeded in seizing some British vessels, including the brigantines *Concord, Diana* and *Hope,* another brigantine with a cargo of rum, and the snow *Friends.*

May 3 (Monday) **In Maryland,** the British attack and burn Havre de Grace, a town with about fifty homes. The residents had erected Potato Battery with one 9-pounder and two 6-pounders on some elevated ground just below the town in anticipation of the arrival of the British. The residents had also constructed a small battery at Concord Point (also known as Lower Point). The British arrive on nineteen barges and the ships commence a bombardment that sounds a fearful reveille for the citizens, most of whom are still asleep. The guns at Potato Bat-

Captain Leslie Combs.

tery return fire, but shortly thereafter, they abandon the position, except for Lt. John O'Neil, who singlehandedly tries to forestall the British, but he is wounded while manning the gun. Apparently, the recoil of the artillery piece injured O'Neil's thigh. Other militia had been assigned to the battery at Concord Point, but only a small number appeared and not for long. It vanished once the bombardment began.

It is reported that O'Neil's daughter seeks and gains his freedom from the British, who had been impressed with her boldness. O'Neil, held aboard the HMS *Maidstone*, is released three days later. Only one of the houses at Havre de Grace escapes destruction. Some women, including the wife of Commodore John Rodgers, Mrs. William Pinckney and Mrs. Goldsborough, sought safety in the home of Mark Pringle. A British detachment arrives with orders to burn it; however, Mrs. Goldsborough pleads with the men, telling them that her aged mother is inside. The officer listens and explains that he cannot disobey his orders. After taking the women to his commanding officer, they spare the home, but when they return the house is on fire. Nevertheless, two Royal Marines, along with Mr. Pinckney are able to save it. In addition to plundering and destroying homes, the British wreck a church on the fringes of the town before moving down the road toward Baltimore, burning farms as they advance. Any civilians encountered are relieved of their money.

John O'Neil was born in Ireland on 23 November 1768 and arrived in America when he was eighteen years old. He also served in the Army under General Henry "Lighthouse Harry" Lee in 1794, and later, during 1798, he served in the U.S. Navy against the French. The British attack had destroyed his business; however, in 1829, when a lighthouse was built at Concord Point, he was appointed its keeper. In the meantime, the city of Philadelphia awarded John O'Neil a sword for his actions at the Potato Battery. He died in Baltimore on 26 January 1838.

In Ohio, Captain Oliver reaches Fort Winchester (Fort Defiance) and discovers that General Clay had arrived there. At the time, the sounds of the guns that are plastering Fort Meigs can be heard at Defiance. General Clay accelerates his movement to relieve the siege. He sends 18 "large scow boats" modified with protective shields to protect the troops from enemy fire from the banks of the river. By nightfall, the flotilla reaches a point within about 18–20 miles from the besieged garrison at Fort Meigs. Captain Oliver and 15 troops volunteer to push on to the post to inform General Harrison that help is near.

May 4 (Tuesday) In Ohio, Captain Oliver, Major David Trimble and the remainder of the party, 15 troops, succeed in reaching Fort Meigs by penetrating the British siege lines. General Harrison becomes jubilant. He gives a message for General Clay to Captain Hamilton and a subaltern with instructions to deliver it to General Clay. Hamilton reports to General Clay:

> You must detach about eight hundred men from your brigade, and land them at a point I will show you, about a mile or a mile and a half above Camp Meigs. I will them conduct the detachment to the British batteries on the left bank of the river. The batteries must be taken, the cannon spiked, and carriages cut down, and the troops must then return to the boats and cross over to the fort. The balance of your men must land on the fort side of the river, opposite the first landing, and fight their way into the fort through the Indians.

In naval activity, the American privateer *Lovely Lass* (Captain J. Smith, U.S. Navy), out of Wilmington, North Carolina, on its first cruise and 40th day at sea, is intercepted by the HMS *Circee*. The British give chase and the *Lovely Lass*' race to evade capture is terminated about 19 hours after it is discovered. During the chase, the crew of the privateer tosses four of its five guns overboard to lessen the weight and gain speed, but the effort is in vain.

May 5 (Wednesday) In Maryland, the forces of British Admiral Cockburn, which have recently plundered various towns, including most recently Havre de Grace, arrive at the eastern shore of Maryland. The Redcoats are met at the landing site by a contingent of militia, which holds its ground at a battery for about one-half hour until British pressure compels the troops to withdraw. Admiral Cockburn personally leads this destructive contingent, which destroys the towns of Georgetown and Fredericktown. Similar to the British raid upon Havre de Grace, both towns are looted and the homes are destroyed. The British continue to conduct raids throughout spring and summer, including frequent incursions in St. Mary's County near Point Lookout; however, they encounter resistance at nearly every turn.

During July, the Redcoats land at Mattoax Creek, but they are disappointed after being confronted by infantry under Captain Hungerford. The militia holds steadfast and British abort their landing. Nevertheless, following the setback, they move against Blackstone and St. George Island and seize both. Later, about 2,000 troops land less than three miles from Point Lookout and begin to plunder the region in a series of raids along the Patuxent and Potomac Rivers. The British destroy many small craft and high numbers of private residences.

In Ohio, at Fort Meigs, the British strike General Harrison's left flank, defended by a company of the 19th Regiment under Captain Waring, Major Alexander's contingent of 12-month volunteers and Kentuckians (militia) under Colonel Boswell. The British force, about twice that of the Americans, is repulsed. Meanwhile, on the right flank, the Americans seize the British batteries, defended by the British 41st Regiment, along with militia and Indians. The troops that participate, according to a letter from General Harrison, include "all the men off duty, belonging to the companies of Croghan and Bradford, of the 17th regiment, Langham, Elliott's and Waring's, of the 19th, about 80 of Major Alexander's volunteers, and a single company of Kentucky militia, under Captain Sebry, amounting in the whole, to not more than 340."

Captain Hamilton, dispatched by General Harrison, intercepts General Green Clay, who is en route to Fort Meigs at a point along the Miami Rapids. Harrison's orders direct Clay to land at a point from where they are to attack the British siege batteries (*see also,* **April 27 to May 20 In Ohio**).

In naval activity, Admiral John Warren arrives in the Chesapeake Bay to bolster Admiral George Cockburn's naval forces. Although Warren had been in Bermuda, he proclaimed "New York, Charleston, Port Royal, Savannah, and the whole of the Mississippi River under blockade." Nonetheless, the Americans did not take the proclamation seriously.

In other naval activity, the *Ann*, a 142-ton schooner (J.B. Allison, master), carrying a cargo including cotton and lead, is trapped and captured after sailing from New Orleans by four British warships, the HMS *Emulous, Nymphe, Shannon* and *Tenedos.* Also, the brigantine *Montgomery* (J. Strout, master) operating out of Salem is snagged by the same British squadron. The *Montgomery* is carrying a crew of 90 men and 12 guns. Before its capture, the *Montgomery* had seized six ships. Also, the British privateer *Liverpool Packet* seizes the 117-ton schooner *Susannah and Lucy* and takes it into port at Liverpool. The *Susannah and Lucy* is separate from the sloop *Susannah* seized on 20 April 1813. Also, the 1-gun *Mary Ann,* an American privateer operating out of Charleston, is intercepted and seized by the HMS *Sapphire,* following a chase. The *Mary Ann* had captured two brigantines, two schooners and one ship before it was seized.

May 6 (Thursday) In Florida, this day marks the conclusion of the "Patriots War," which had commenced on March 18, 1812, when Americans crossed into Florida and raised the American Flag. The last of the American troops depart Florida today. The Spanish continue efforts to assist the Indians and tensions will continue to rise.

In Maryland, a group of patriotic women from St. Michael's delivers an American flag to General Perry Benson. The flag is for Captain Will Dodson's artillery company. General Benson accepts the flag and tells them "the women of St. Michaels were not behind those of Carthage or Rome, or of any other nation in patriotic devotion."

May 8 (Saturday) In Washington, D.C., on or about this day, the militia is reorganized. The commanding officers are Major General John P. Van Ness and Brigadier Generals Walter Smith and Robert Young.

In Maryland, Brigadier General Henry Miller writes to British Admiral John Warren reacting to the seizure of Lt. John O'Neil on 3 May:

> [O'Neil] has been recently taken in arms, and in defence of his property and family at that place, by a detachment from his B. M. fleet, serving under your command; and that the said O'Neale [O'Neil] has been menaced with immediate and capital punishment, as a traitor to the government of his B. M. on the ground of his being, by birth, an Irishman. Nothing, in the course of public duty, would

be more painful to me, than the obligation of resorting to the law of retaliation on this, or any other occasion; but, Sir, in the event of O'Neale's execution, painful as may be the duty, it becomes, unavoidable: and I am authorized and commanded to state to your excellency, that two British subjects shall be selected, by lot or otherwise, and immediately executed. It is for your excellency to choose, whether a character of such barbarism be, or be not given to the war, waged under your immediate direction."

Admiral J. B. Warren responds by letter on 10 May.

In naval activity, Commodore Chauncey takes advantage of the weather, which clears on this day. The squadron, impeded by bad weather at York, is able to sail. Chauncey's naval force arrives at Four-mile Creek later this day and after debarking the troops, Chauncey sails for Sackets Harbor to acquire reinforcements. Afterward, he initiates a mission to funnel supplies from New York to General Dearborn's army in Canada.

May 9 (Sunday) British General Proctor lifts his siege of Fort Meigs. Jubilant Americans are relieved, having held on against heavy odds. The British under Proctor re-group, attacking Fort Meigs again in July. After the British depart, General Harrison sends out a detachment to search for and retrieve the bodies of the fallen troops of Dudley's command. The British had professed that they buried the dead Americans, along with the British; however, the troops discover mutilated remains of 45 men. The remains are taken back to the post and buried near the fort with the other bodies. General Harrison and other officers inspect the post for damages. Harrison then leaves General Clay in command of the post, while he departs with an escort for Lower Sandusky.

In naval activity, the HMS *Orpheus* intercepts and recaptures the ship *Young Phoenix.*

May 10 (Monday) **In Canada,** the U.S. fleet under Captain Isaac Chauncey arrives at the mouth of the Niagara River from York. The force of ground troops under General Henry Dearborn are debarked less than five miles east of the river's mouth, where British-held Fort George stands. The *Lady of the Lake* participates in this action. A detachment led by Lt. Petti, U.S. Navy, is carried to the head of Lake Ontario by two schooners. Once there, the Americans overcome the guards, who are compelled to take flight. After capturing the supplies, the troops burn the buildings, then re-embark and return.

In the meantime, Captain Chauncey returns to Sackets Harbor to get the wounded ashore to receive medical treatment. While in port, he acquires supplies, provisions and fresh troops. Afterward he returns to where he had debarked General Dearborn's force, arriving there on 25 May. During the absence of the fleet, General Dearborn had been making plans to capture Fort George.

In Maryland, British admiral J.B. Warren, aboard the HMS *San Domingo,* in response to a recent letter from Brigadier General Henry Miller, states: "SIR— I have to acknowledge the receipt of your letter, of the 8th inst. respecting a man named O'Neale [John O'Neil], taken by a detachment from the squadron, under the orders of Rear Admiral Cockburn. This man has been released, upon the application of the magistrates of Havre de-Grace, on parole. I was not informed of this man being an Irishman, or he would certainly have been detained, to account to his sovereign and country, for being in arms against the British colors" (*see also,* **May 3** and **May 8**).

In naval activity, the 39-ton schooner *Columbia* (D. Carleton, master), while en route from Penobscot, Maine, to Martinique is intercepted and captured by the HMS *Rattler.* The *Columbia* is separate from the schooner *Columbia* captured on 18 December 1812 and the brigantine *Columbia* captured on 15 May of this year. The prize, carrying lumber and potatoes, is taken into port at New Brunswick. Also, the 238-ton brigantine *Diomede* (J. Bruce, master)— on its way from Salem, Massachusetts, to Manila (Philippines) with a cargo that includes indigo, sugar, tea and redwood— is intercepted and seized by the HMS *Nymphe* and the HMS *La Hogue.* The *Diomede* is separate from the privateer *Diomede,* captured on 28 May 1814.

In yet other activity, two British warships, the HMS *Orpheus* and the HMS *Ramillies,* intercept and seize an American schooner, the *Emperor,* which is en route from North Carolina to Boston with a cargo of Indian corn. Also, the HMS *Paz* intercepts and captures the 92-ton schooner *Juliet* (C. Southworth, master), which is en route from Cuba to Newport, Rhode Island, with a cargo of molasses.

May 11 (Tuesday) *In naval activity,* the HMS *Nymphe* intercepts and captures the 37-ton schooner *Juliana Smith* (H. Cooper, master), which had sailed from Boston with a crew of 31 men and three guns.

May 12 (Wednesday) **In Ohio,** General Harrison arrives at Lower Sandusky from Fort Meigs. He confers with Governor Meigs, who is there with a force of Ohio volunteers which are en route to reinforce Fort Meigs. Nevertheless, the army is not prepared to advance against the enemy. The troops are diverted and instead ordered to the south "to conserve food."

In Pennsylvania, Governor Simon Snyder writes Major General Steele: "SIR: I have much pleasure in the perusal of the communication you made me, under date of the 9th inst., that a portion of the militia of your division have volunteered on an expedition to Maryland, there to assist their fellow-citizens of the Union in repelling the wanton aggression of a cruel and vindictive foe."

In naval activity, at about 1600, the lookouts on the *Essex* spot land. By the following morning the island in the Galapagos stands at a distance of about four leagues, but it cannot be identified. Afterward, the *Essex* sails to Charles Island and arrives there about 1600.

May 13 (Thursday) **In Florida,** on or about this day, the remaining American troops at Fernandina evacuate the post. The Marines under

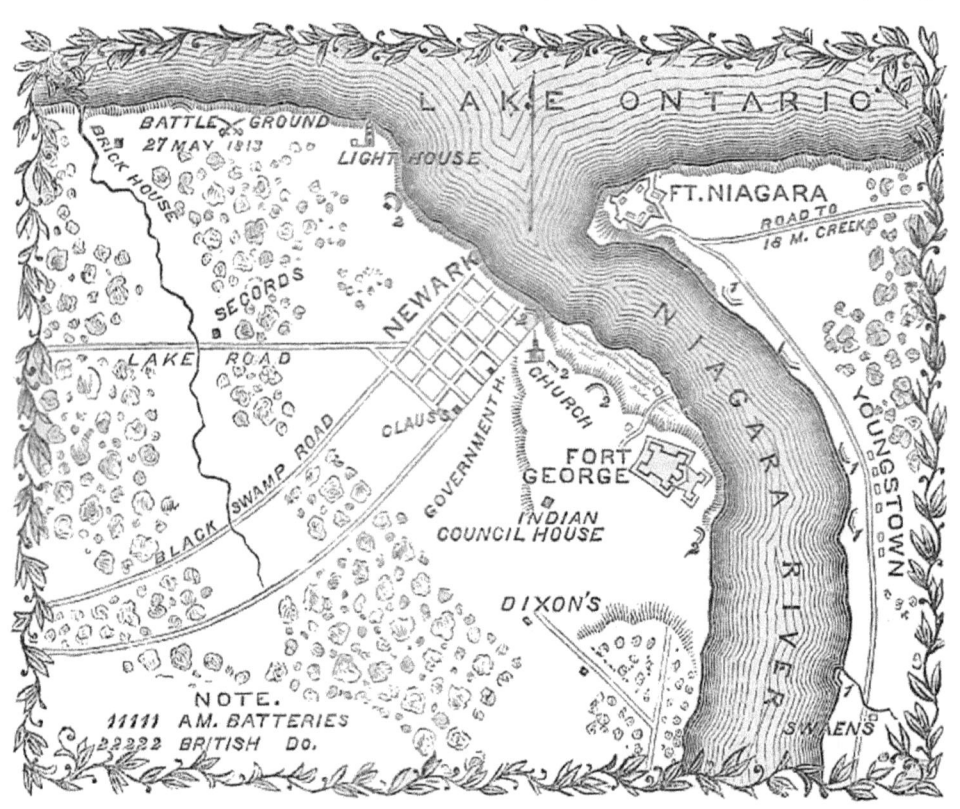

Plan of operations at the mouth of the Niagara River.

Lt. Sevier number only 49 men. The Marines accompany the army during the move to Point Peter, Georgia. Upon his arrival, General Pinckney had become so impressed with Sevier's handling of the artillery (two guns), he orders him to remain with the southern army. Nonetheless, Pinckney is soon disappointed when Sevier receives orders from Secretary of the Navy Jones to move with his entire detachment to Beaufort, South Carolina, and from there to Norfolk.

In Louisiana, in conjunction with recent orders directing General Wilkinson to proceed to New York State near the Canadian border, Colonel Covington departs by horseback from New Orleans en route to Washington, D.C. From there, he departs for New York State.

In naval activity, the HMS *Bream* seizes the 74-ton schooner *Sally* (J. Cousins, master), which is en route to Boston from East Port, Maine, with a cargo of fish, plaster of Paris and salt. The prize is taken into port at New Brunswick. This *Sally* is separate from like named vessels seized: a brigantine, 10 August 1812; a ship, 16 April 1813; a brigantine, 24 April 1813; a schooner, 12 July 1813; a schooner, 15 September 1813; a schooner, 16 October 1813; and a sloop, 19 May 1814.

May 14 (Friday) *In naval activity,* the American privateer *Anaconda* (Captain Nathaniel Shaler) intercepts the 11-gun *Express,* a British packet ship on its way to England from Rio de Janeiro. The encounter erupts into a tenacious engagement that lasts over a half hour. The *Express,* despite raising resistance, sustains heavy damage, and it begins to take on water which rises in the hold to about five feet. After capturing the *Express,* the Americans discover that the vessel is carrying about $80,000 in cash and 230 stands of muskets. The Americans transfer the weapons and confiscate the cash before ransoming the *Express* for $8,000.

May 15 (Saturday) British Commodore James Yeo arrives at Kingston, where he prepares to attack American-held Sackets Harbor on May 26. Two American ships, the *Fair American* and the USS *Pert,* both schooners, will be dispatched by Commodore Chauncey to maintain a vigil at Kingston; however, the British fleet is unable to depart until seamen arrive from Quebec.

In naval activity, the British privateer *Sir John Sherbrooke* intercepts and seizes the 98-ton brigantine *Columbia.* At the time of capture, the *Columbia* is en route from Savannah, Georgia, to Boston with a cargo of cotton and other items. The *Columbia* is separate from the schooner *Columbia* captured earlier this month and the schooner *Columbia* seized 18 December 1812.

May 16 (Sunday) *In naval activity,* the HMS *La Hogue* intercepts and seizes the 191-ton *Orion* (J.M. Jubon, master), which is transporting a cargo of flour and Indian meal from New York to Lisbon, Portugal. Also, the *Invincible Napoleon,* a French privateer originally captured by the British and later seized by the American privateer *Alexander* and taken into Cape Ann, Massachusetts, is on this day recaptured by the British while it is anchored. While the British are sailing it to a friendly port, another American privateer, the *Young Teazer,* intercepts the vessel and gets it to port at Portland on or about 1 June.

May 18 (Tuesday) **In New Hampshire,** after the March election in which John Taylor Gilman is elected governor, Adjutant General Daniel McClary resigns his commission on this day. He is succeeded by Colonel Benjamin Butler, who is also raised to brigadier general. On 5 June, Governor Gilman, a veteran of the Revolutionary War, is inaugurated.

In naval activity, the HMS *Bold* intercepts and seizes the ship *Duck* (T. Selly, master), which is en route from Waterford to Newfoundland with a cargo of provisions. Also, the 269-ton brigantine *Pilgrim* is trapped and seized by a British squadron composed of the HMS *Fantome,* HMS *La Hogue,* HMS *Maidstone,* HMS *Marlborough,* HMS *San Domingo* and the HMS *Statira.* The *Pilgrim* is separate from the *Pilgrim* (boat) seized on 27 April 1813 and the schooner *Pilgrim* captured 8 July 1813.

In other naval activity, the British privateer *Sir John Sherbrooke* captures the 55-ton sloop *Red Bird* and its cargo of corn and tar. Also, at New London, Connecticut, American prisoners taken aboard the privateer *Fox* (Captain Jack) arrive under a flag. Before its recent capture, the Fox had tried to outrun the British in a chase that lasted for about 100 miles. The port inspector takes responsibility for the returned prisoners the next day. It is reported that Captain Jack had been treated extremely well by Commodore Hardy, who makes it known that he disapproved of the actions of some earlier British troops who were bombarding coastal towns. British Commodore Hardy makes it clear no such action will occur under his command. Hardy also makes certain his intent to soon visit New London as a friend, not an enemy.

May 19 (Wednesday) *In naval activity,* the brigantine *Delphin* (A.C. De Selvia, master) on its way from New York to Oporto, Portugal, with a cargo of candles and various foods, is intercepted and captured by the HMS *La Hogue.* In other activity, the *Fidella* (A. Gardner, master), a 243-ton ship, is intercepted and seized while en route to Cadiz, Spain, from New York by the HMS *Orpheus* and the HMS *Ramilles.* The 61-ton sloop *General Hodgson* is intercepted by the British privateer *Sir John Sherbrooke* while it is transporting a cargo that includes fish and lumber from Halifax to Martinique. The British privateer *Sir John Sherbrooke* intercepts and seizes the brigantine *Paragon.* The *Paragon* is separate from the schooner *Paragon* captured 13 August 1813. Also, the British privateer *Sir John Sherbrooke* overtakes the brigantine *San Gabriel* (A. Drummond, master), while it is en route to New York from Savannah, Georgia.

May 20 (Thursday) **In New Hampshire,** British warships continue to cruise off the coast, which continues to keep the residents of Portsmouth in a state of fear. A town meeting is held on this day to try to get government help. The meeting concludes with a decision to pressure the legislators to place the problem regarding the defenselessness of Portsmouth in the hands of the legislature. Governor William Plumer, however, is taking steps to improve the situation.

With the cooperation of the legislature and the governor, Adjutant General McClary acquires cannon which are distributed to each of the artillery units in the 15th, 31st, 34th and 35th New Hampshire Regiments. Ammunition at Exeter is transported to Portsmouth for use by the troops. Also during the meeting, Daniel Webster delivers a speech stating that the citizens want action, not words, and he calls for volunteers to arrive at the morning's the parade with the tools to begin repairing the forts and bolstering the defenses along the coast. He is not disappointed. Hundreds of volunteers arrive to begin the task. They complete the forts' repairs within several days.

In naval activity, a British squadron composed of the HMS *Barrossa,* HMS *Junon,* HMS *Narcissus* and the HMS *Marlboro* intercept the *Finland* (William Chapman, master), a 245-ton ship, while it is en route from Alexandria, Virginia, to Halifax with a cargo of flour. The *Finland,* unable to escape, is captured. A British squadron composed of the HMS *Martin, Spartan* and *Statira* seizes a brigantine, which is en route to Havana, Cuba, from Philadelphia.

The American privateer *Yankee,* commanded by Captain Elisha Snow, who succeeded Captain Wilson, departs Newport, Rhode Island, on another cruise. Captain Snow, aware that a British squadron is lying off Block Island to capture his vessel, slips past them and safely reaches the open sea. On the 23rd, the *Yankee* intercepts and seizes the British brigantine *William.* The prize is taken into an American port; however, one of the blocking ships that failed to intercept the *Yankee* succeeds in recapturing the *William.* Two British warships, the HMS *Bream* and the HMS *Rattler,* operating together, encounter the American privateer *Alexander,* commanded by Captain Benjamin Crowninshield. The British drive the *Alexander* to shore at Well's Bay in the Caribbean. The British had remained so close to their target that there was insufficient time for the entire crew to escape capture. Nevertheless, the British fail to seize the entire crew. Many had departed earlier as prize crews on seven previously captured vessels, including the brigantine *Edward* and the 16-gun brigantine *Alexander.* One other capture was originally a French privateer, the *Invincible Napoleon,* that had been captured by the English. The Americans, after seizing it, took the vessel into port at Cape Ann (see also, May 16). Twenty of the remaining crew members aboard the privateer *Alexander* are able to escape to shore. Luckily for the Americans the British were unable to capture more of them because of the original crew, had earlier been transferred to the seven prizes and they all avoided capture. Nonetheless, the British refloat the *Alexander* and as a bonus, they repatriate more than 100 Englishmen that had been aboard the privateer *Alexander* as prisoners. Also, later during August of this year, Captain Crowninshield embarks from Salem aboard the USS *Henry* to retrieve the remains of Captain James Lawrence (killed on 1 June).

May 21 (Friday) *In naval activity,* the 225-ton schooner *Enterprise* (T.A. Morgan, master), on a cruise after sailing from Salem, is intercepted and seized by the HMS *Tenedos* and the HMS *Curlew*. The *Enterprise* at the time of its capture is manned by 100 men and has 4 guns. The *Enterprise* is separate from the schooner *Enterprise* seized on 7 July 1812, the schooner *Enterprise* captured on 8 December 1813, the schooner *Enterprise* seized on 16 December 1813 and the schooner *Enterprise* overtaken 30 August 1814.

In other naval activity, on or about this day, the HMS *Highflyer* (formerly the American privateer *Highflyer*), operating near Hampton Roads, captures an American lookout boat, the *Betsey*, commanded by Captain Smith. The crew of the *Betsey* is taken aboard the *Highflyer*, but the British destroy the boat.

May 22 (Saturday) **In Tennessee,** General Andrew Jackson, having refused to dismiss his force at Natchez as ordered by Secretary of War John Armstrong, arrives back in Nashville with his entire command, including the 56 invalids. They are greeted with a heroes' welcome. A problem soon follows when the drafts he signed in Natchez were refused by the government and described as unauthorized expenditures by Jackson, which threaten to ruin him financially.

Colonel Thomas H. Benton of Jackson's staff, while preparing to repair to the capital, offers to intervene. Colonel Benton convinces the government to cover the costs. During the talks, he makes it clear that the people throughout Tennessee support Jackson and it does not seem wise for the administration to lose the support of the entire state. Nevertheless, afterward, things turn downward between Jackson and the colonel when General Jackson acts as second for a friend at a duel between his friend and Colonel Benton's brother Jesse. A bitter feud develops, and finally a raucous brawl erupts in Nashville. General Jackson is severely wounded and nearly dies.

He recovers, however, and Colonel Benton (later U.S. senator) joins the regulars, where he serves for the duration. Years later Benton and Jackson reconcile and the former becomes Jackson's confidant. Benton, in his book *Thirty Years in the Senate*, Volume I, states: "His [Jackson's] temper was placable, as well as irascible, and his reconciliations were cordial and sincere. Of that, my own case was a signal instance. After a deadly feud, I became his confidential adviser; was offered the highest marks of his favor, and received from his dying bed a message of friendship, dictated when life was departing, and when he would have to pause for breath."

In naval activity, a newspaper (unnamed) publishes an article regarding a British practice of issuing licenses to American vessels to carry provisions to the British despite the ongoing war: "The ship *Action*, of and for Boston from Cadiz, though protected by a real genuine Prince Regent's license, was captured off our coast by the 74-gun ship of the line *La Hogue*. Its captain the honorable Thomas Blanden Capel, plundered the brig *Charles*, also with a license, and would have burnt her, but thought it best to give it up to get rid of his prisoners, and it has arrived at Boston." Some British officers justify seizing money from the vessels before letting them continue their voyages by stating that some British seamen have not received pay "for nine years."

May 23 (Sunday) *In naval activity,* the *Paul Jones*, which had earlier seized the British brigantine *Ulysses* and sent it into Norfolk, on this day engages and captures the British vessel *Leonidas*. Also, the American privateer *Yankee*, while cruising off the coast of Ireland, chases down a vessel and after seizing it, identifies it as the American brigantine *William*, which had been captured by the British.

May 24 (Monday) *In naval activity,* a British squadron, composed of the HMS *Rattler*, *Shannon* and the *Tenedos*, seizes the schooner *Post Boy*. The prize and its cargo of brandy, candles, fish, soap and other items are taken into port at New Brunswick. The 14-gun American privateer *Roger*, commanded by Captain R. Quarles, evades the British blockading squadron at Hampton Roads and gets to sea. On this day at about 2100, the *Roger* encounters the HMS *Highflyer*, formerly an American privateer. The British hail the *Roger* and their call is ignored. The British repeat the process and demand an answer. If none is forthcoming, they intend to sink the *Roger*. The threatening warning compels the American ship to respond. Captain Quarles orders his gunners to answer by delivering a broadside. Suddenly, a ferocious exchange at close-range erupts and the opposing vessels pound each other for about two hours. At about 2330, the *Roger* breaks away. During the engagement, two of the American captives, aboard the *Highflyer* since their recent capture with the *Betsey*, take advantage during the donnybrook by seizing a boat and using it to reach safety on shore.

On the following day, the British release the other Americans seized on the *Betsey*. The Americans board one of the ship's boats and row to shore at Norfolk. Unknown to the Americans aboard the *Roger*, the *Highflyer* sustained some heavy damage. American fire had inflicted six fatalities, including the commander. Ten others, including one midshipman and nine sailors, had been wounded, leaving the vessel vulnerable to capture, but the *Roger* broke off prematurely. The *Roger*, operating out of Norfolk during its cruises, captures seven prizes, including the 10-gun *Windsor Castle*, a British government packet.

May 25 (Tuesday) *In naval activity,* the USS *Madison*, Commodore Chauncey's flagship, arrives at Sackets Harbor with a 350-man contingent of artillerymen and some heavy artillery pieces. The British, having sustained the loss of York, are preparing to avenge the loss by striking Sackets Harbor, which at this time is not well-prepared to repel a strong attack. Fort Tompkins is garrisoned by about 200 dragoons led by Colonel Backus, along with a contingent of artillerists led by Lt. Ketchum and some other partial units. The post also holds about 70 to 80 invalids. Fort Volunteer, built during the previous year, is just east of the town and dominates the northeastern approaches. Fort Pike (later Madison Barracks), a blockhouse and a barracks, also constructed the year before, stands close to Fort Volunteer at the bay. Fort Pike is actually the anchor post for a series of forts built at Sackets Harbor, including Fort Chauncey, Fort Kentucky, Fort Stark and Fort Virginia.

In other naval activity, the HMS *Shannon* intercepts and recaptures the brigantine *Lucy*. The *Lucy* is separate from the *Lucy* seized on 30 March 1813 and the schooner *Lucy* captured on 15 September 1814.

May 26 (Wednesday) *In naval activity,* in preparation for an attack to seize British-held Fort George, near the mouth of the Niagara River, Commodore Chauncey initiates a reconnaissance mission to examine the landing place. At this time Canadian sources list the number of defenders on the Niagara Line as 500 along with 1,800 regulars. The regulars include the 49th Regiment and contingents of the 8th and the 41st, along with detachments of the Glengarry and Royal Newfoundland Regiments. The British, commanded by General John Vincent (successor of General Sheaffe) are also bolstered by royal artillery contingents.

Within Fort George, five companies of the 8th Regiment and eight companies of the 49th Regiment garrison the post. They are bolstered by several companies of the Glengarry Regiment and two companies of the Royal Newfoundland Regiment, placing slightly less than 1,000 men (including the artillery contingent) in the fort, which also contains several hundred militia and about 40–50 Indians. Also, the fort has also received five 24-pounders, which had been confiscated when Detroit was taken without a shot being fired. The British have mounted four of the American guns on three bastions, and they have deployed the remaining 24-pounder on a battery less than one mile below Newark.

In related activity, British artillery commences fire upon some American boats which are departing the Five Mile Meadows to rendezvous with the fleet. The American artillery at Fort Niagara retaliates and pounds Fort George, inflicting damage to the blockhouses standing near the fort; however, Fort George sustains no damage.

May 26–27 **In Canada,** General Henry Dearborn's plan to seize Fort George at the mouth of the Niagara River begins to unfold. However, similarly to the attack against Kingston, General Dearborn does not lead the force. He remains offshore aboard ship during the attack. While the Americans are moving to make more gains in Canada, the British at this time are in the process of launching a raid across the river to seize Sackets Harbor. Boats recently built on shore are launched at their positions on the 26th. They will carry the troops to the landing place from where the British-held fort will be attacked by land rather than by an amphibious landing from the fleet. However, the fleet will participate in the assault.

At this time, Captain Chauncey has returned from Sackets Harbor with his fleet and reinforcements. The force is also augmented by Commodore Oliver Hazard Perry's naval force, which has arrived from Lake Erie to participate. Meanwhile, the British are immediately aware of the

General John Parker Boyd (*Harper's Cyclopaedia of United States History, Volume I*, Benson Lossing, 1905).

threat. Their land batteries commence firing upon the boats as they are launched. Nevertheless, the operation continues.

During the predawn hours on the 27th, the fleet departs from its positions and redeploys near the objective. Five of the warships drop anchor at a point from which their respective guns can deliver bombardments upon the British batteries near where the troops are scheduled to land, while the rest of the fleet maneuvers into positions from where they can support the troops and bombard the fort. The artillery across the river at Fort Niagara also opens fire upon Fort George.

The tranquil morning suddenly is transformed into a boisterous artillery exchange. The British, alerted to the attack by deserters, are prepared for the landing. The guns of Fort Niagara open fire to begin the bombardment of Fort George; however, soon the shelling subsides due to a lingering fog that obscures the target. Regardless, two American schooners maneuver into positions from which they plaster the battery near Newark and another near the lighthouse. During these first crucial moments of the attack, other schooners and the *Lady of the Lake*, *Madison* and *Oneida* join in the bombardment, providing the landing force with the firepower of eleven vessels and their 51 guns. Meanwhile, the ground attack takes hold. General John Parker Boyd, successor to the late General Pike, commands the operation on the ground. He is assisted by Lt. Colonel Winfield Scott, Captain Forsyth, who commands riflemen, and Colonel McComb, who commands the artillery.

As the first wave of boats approaches shore, the fog is lifting and the troops are met by a hurricane of riveting fire originating in a ravine where about 200 troops are deployed to intercept the landing force. Despite the heavy fire, the boats do not abort the landing. Riflemen aboard the landing craft return fire while the craft move onto shore. Meanwhile, the ferocity of the British fire seemingly has a reverse effect. Rather than intimidate the landing force, it apparently increases their enthusiasm. An artillery officer, Major Jacob Hindman, is the first man to touch the beach, and many in his command, still offshore, bolt from their boats into the water to speed their arrival. Shortly thereafter, the first column is ashore and prepared to eliminate the resistance in the ravine. The British, however, are reluctant to give ground. A fierce contest begins as troops of the Glengarry and Newfoundland Corps battle ferociously; however, despite their steadfastness, the superior numbered American force compels them to pull back. The withdrawal is sluggish as the British continue to raise tenacious opposition with each backward step.

While the American advance continues, the retreating British receive support when another force, posted at a second ravine, rushes forward to provide protective fire for the vanguard as it continues its running fight to the rear. All the while, the sky is consumed with streaking artillery shells as both sides maintain a consistent inferno that nearly overshadows the bloody contest on the ground. While the British and the Americans bash each other on the ground, the former eventually form a combined line atop a sheer bank, while Lt. Colonel Scott's contingent converges upon the defensive position. The Americans struggle to ascend the bank. British muskets deliver horrific volleys that descend with vicious effectiveness that repeatedly prevents the Yanks from completing the ascent. A fourth ascent seems to present folly until reinforcements, including artillery, arrive to support the beleaguered troops under Scott.

Once in position, Colonel Moses Porter's light artillery opens fire, supported by other troops attached to General John Parker Boyd's brigade. The arrival of the reinforcements and the artillery rejuvenates Scott's command, and once again, the troops begin their perilous ascent. The fourth assault succeeds. After Scott finally conquers the heights, he advances without pause in pursuit of the British, who have been compelled to retire toward the town of Newark.

At Newark, Scotts' troops continue to ignore their exhaustion. A detachment is dispatched to sever an escape route to Burlington, which lies west of Newark, while he leads his main body directly against Fort George, which by the time he begins his advance has already been partially destroyed by incessant bombardments from the fleet and from Fort Niagara. Shortly thereafter, Colonel Scott barely escapes the fate of the late General Zebulon Pike. The besieged British garrison, reduced to a diminutive size, intentionally detonates one of its magazines. The explosion propels debris in all directions and Colonel Scott becomes the recipient of some catapulted lumber. The flying wood knocks Scott off his horse; however, unlike General Pike, Colonel Scott survives and retains command. The British had set two other magazines for detonation; however, American troops discover them before they are detonated, thereby preventing any additional explosions.

Colonel Scott, having remounted his horse, is at the front of the column when it arrives at Fort George. Once the Americans push through the gates, Scott remains at the point. He is the first to enter, and rather than delegate someone to lower the British Union Jack, he tends to the matter himself. Scott's arrival had caused a small rivalry with Colonel Porter, who arrives just after Scott, approaches him, and as if coming in second in a race, bellows: "Confound your long legs, Scott, you have got in before me!"

The Americans easily take possession of the fort and only a few prisoners are seized. Nonetheless, Colonel Scott, having been frustrated at the high bank and also being earlier knocked from his horse, remains adamant about continuing the fight, although the victory is complete. After a short period of pause, he jumps back in the saddle to pursue the British. He departs without the cavalry under Colonel Burn, who is to await troops who had not yet arrived before joining in the pursuit. During the chase, he is twice handed orders from General Boyd to halt the pursuit and return to the captured post. He ignores the messengers and informs a lieutenant who delivered one of the orders: "Your General does not know that I have the enemy within my power; in seventy minutes I shall capture his whole force."

British General John Vincent's attempt to defend rather than abandon the fort is valiant, but in vain. His escape before total encirclement permits him to retreat and his column arrives later in the day at Beaver Dam about twenty miles west of Fort George. Once there, General Vincent summons other units, including Colonel Cecil Bisshopp at Fort Erie and Major Ormsby at Chippewa. Upon their arrival and support from Captain Barclay's naval force, Vincent moves to Burlington Heights and establishes a strong defensive position where the city of Hamilton later stands. General Vincent remains in place awaiting new orders from Quebec.

The Americans also seize the British post at Queenston on the Niagara River, about seven miles above Fort George. Also, General Vincent's shattered command is reinforced when a British contingent from Fort Erie (Canada), under Colonel Bisshopp, joins Vincent at Beaver Dam at about midnight (27th-28th), along with other troops from separate posts along the Niagara River. Including Captain Barclay of the Royal Navy and 19 sailors, troops on the way to Fort Erie a total about 1,600. On the 28th, the British move from Beaver Dam and arrive at Burlington Heights near Dundern Castle. From there, General Vincent, holding positions with earthworks, is able to communicate with the British forces under General Proctor, who is operating on the Detroit frontier, about fifty miles from Fort George.

Despite Colonel Scott's determination to intercept the retreating British column, his plan comes to a halt shortly afterward when General John P. Boyd arrives on horseback to personally order Scott to abort the pursuit. It is a peculiar part of the operation that has led to unanswered questions regarding the motives of General Boyd. The primary lingering questions surrounded whether General Scott might cause victory to be turned into defeat, or did he halt the pursuit to prevent Scott from achieving more glory?

Nonetheless, by about noon, the battle for Fort

George is terminated. American casualties are 153 men either killed or wounded. The British estimated casualties total about 271 killed or wounded. In addition, the Americans parole more than 600 able bodied troops, most of whom belong to the militia. The militia, composed of about 500 of the prisoners, receive parole. British sources claim that after seizing the fort, the Americans move from house to house locating the males and that is how they reach the number 500 that are paroled. General Dearborn comes ashore after the fort is seized.

While General Dearborn, Captain Chauncey and Lieutenant Oliver Hazard Perry were vanquishing the British force of about 1,000 troops (including militia and Indians) under General Vincent at Fort George, other British forces were not dormant. At nearly the same time, a British force attacks Sackets Harbor, from where Captain Chauncey has his fleet based, the opposite (eastern) end of Lake Ontario. Commodore Perry gets some additional strength as the British pull back from the Niagara. Perry's fleet above Niagara Falls is able to reach Lake Erie after the fall of Fort George. Despite the absence of the British guns, the task remains difficult. General Dearborn supplies Perry with a contingent of about 200 men who support the operation to move the vessels up the rapids. The troops also use ox teams during the tedious project. Nevertheless, the vessels make it to Buffalo, and from there they depart for Erie during mid–June.

The USS *Governor Tompkins* participates in the capture of Fort George. The *Governor Tompkins* remains active for the duration, and at the end of the conflict it is moored at Sackets Harbor until it is sold in May 1815. Also, the USS *Ontario* participates in this action.

May 27 (Thursday)   In Canada, Commodore Isaac Chauncey, aboard the USS *Madison* off Fort George, writes to the secretary of the Navy to inform him of the operation at the British post: "Sir, I am happy to have it in my power to say, that the American Flag is flying upon fort George. We were in quiet possession of all the forts at 12 o'clock." Also this day, General Morgan Lewis, in a letter to General Dearborn, states: "Fort George and its dependencies are ours; the enemy, beaten at all points, has blown up his magazines, and retired. It is impossible, at this time, to say any thing of individual gallantry; there was no man who did not perform his duty in a manner, which did honor to himself and country. Scott's and Forsyth's commands, supported by Boyd's and Winder's brigades, sustained the brunt of the action. Our loss is trifling; not more than 20 killed, and twice that number wounded. The enemy has left in the hospital 124, and I sent several on board of the fleet. We have also made about 100 prisoners of the regular forces." (*See also*, **May 26–27.**)

In New York, at Sackets Harbor, Lt. Colonel Electus Backus, left in command of the Spartan contingent of regulars during the absence of General Dearborn, sends a message by Major Swan to General Jacob Brown, commander of the militia, to move to the post and assume command, as requested by General Dearborn, in the event of a threat. General Brown assembles about 500 troops and his men are deployed by the time a British fleet comes into view on the following day. General Brown had received personal notice from General Dearborn on the 25th.

In naval activity, Chauncey's squadron, led by the *Julia* and the *Growler*, move into the Niagara River to bombard Fort George and debark a landing force. At 0400, when all the boats are in the water and preparing to cross the river, General Dearborn and General Morgan Lewis board the USS *Madison*. Lieutenant Oliver Hazard Perry orders the ground force to land. Within about three hours, the British are compelled to retire. Consequently, the Americans gain the fort and domination of the river.

In other naval activity, the British privateer *Sir John Sherbrooke* captures the schooner *Governor Plumer* (J. Mudge, master), operating out of New Hampshire and carrying 50 men and 6 guns.

May 28 (Friday)   In Canada, during the night, General Vincent receives information that a large American force is closing fast. The British, once notified, destroy more of their ammunition and accelerate the pace of their retreat to Burlington. The loss of the ammunition depletes their supply to a dangerous level, leaving only about 90 pounds per gun. Nonetheless, the British evade their pursuers. Meanwhile, the Americans, unable to intercept General Vincent, take possession of Fort Erie, which had been abandoned. General Morgan Lewis leaves a contingent under Lt. Colonel Preston of the 12th U.S. Regiment to garrison the post. Afterward, General Lewis aborts pursuit and retires to Fort George.

In naval activity, the HMS *Victorious* and other warships of the Chesapeake blockading squadron seize the schooner *Nancy*. Other vessels of the same name captured are: a ship, 17 August 1812; a schooner, 28 June 1813; a sloop, 28 July 1814; a brigantine, about 1–18 September 1814; and a brigantine, 13 September 1814.

In other naval activity, lookouts on the *Essex* spot a hostile sail. At the time of detection, the *Essex* is towing the *Montezuma*, a prize. Nevertheless, Captain Porter leaves the *Montezuma* and gives chase. By about dusk, the prey remains in the lead and Captain David Porter concentrates on not losing it. He dispatches a contingent under Lieutenant Wilmer to head back to the Montezuma in three fast-moving boats. Once there, Wilmer is to take the command of three of the *Montezuma*'s boats and proceed to a point astern of the unidentified vessel from where he can dispatch a message to the *Montezuma*, which will be forwarded to the *Essex*. Porter, intent on taking the vessel by surprise, orders Wilmer not to attack unless "it is perfectly calm." He also instructs Wilmer that the boarding party carries "no other arms than a pistol, cutlass, and boarding-axe, each." Soon after, the *Essex*, flying English colors, pulls alongside of the vessel (letter of marque *Atlantic*) and the captain is ordered to come aboard the *Essex*. At the same time, the *Essex* spots yet another unidentified sail.

Meanwhile, the *Montezuma* moves up to the *Essex* and a contingent under Lieutenant McKnight is placed on the *Atlantic*, with Captain Porter aboard. The *Atlantic* loses sight of the vessel after dark, but only temporarily. Porter has "night-glasses," which permits him to relocate the vessel, which is convinced it is safe in the darkness. The ship is seized and identified as the 10-gun letter of marque *Greenwich*.

Obadiah Wier, the captain of the *Atlantic*, is an American out of Nantucket, and upon his entrance onto the *Essex*, he is pleased to state that he is happy to meet a British frigate, unaware that the British ensign is a ruse. Captain Porter remains extraordinarily congenial, while Captain Wier proclaims his ability to evade American privateers. Captain Porter also listens with attentively as Wier tells him that he had no second thoughts on his activity, because "although he was born in America, he was an Englishman at heart." Meanwhile, Captain Porter, while outwardly expressing great interest in Wier's tales and pretending to have great empathy, permits Wier to continue talking freely. Captain Wier's confidence eventually deflates in conjunction with the disappearance of his British security blanket after Captain Porter caps the informative discussion by having Wier introduced to two other reluctant guests aboard the *Essex*, British captains of the *Montezuma* and the *Georgiana*.

Captain Porter begins to assess his circumstances regarding the increase of prisoners as well as additional vessels. One of his more pleasant surprises occurs when he is informed that the *Atlantic* is carrying the item most needed by the Americans, fresh water. The *Atlantic* is carrying 100,000 tons of water. The *Essex* also, thanks to its prizes, accumulates a bonanza of provisions capable of serving each of the crews of Porter's flotilla for one month. At this time the following vessels are with Porter and the prizes are manned by volunteers: the 46-gun *Essex*, the 16-gun *Georgiana*, the 6-gun *Atlantic*, the 10-gun *Greenwich*, the 2-gun *Montezuma*, and the *Policy*, which carries no guns.

The prisoners, numbering 80, are spit into small groups and distributed among the flotilla's vessels. The Americans, excluding one midshipman and six men aboard another vessel, the *Barclay*, number 333 men. Captain Porter places a U.S. Marine officer, Lt. Gamble, in command of the *Greenwich*. Porter, however, aware of Lt. Gamble's inexperience, appoints two skilled seamen as mates. Also, the British prisoners are given freedom of movement, as long as they contribute to the work. They do, and even when they go ashore at Charles Island, none desert.

May 28–29   Battle of Sackets Harbor   In New York, a British fleet arrives off Sackets Harbor from Kingston, Canada, from where it sailed on the 27th, coincidentally, the day that the Americans seized York. It includes the 24-gun HMS *Wolf*, 24-gun HMS *Royal George*, 18-gun HMS *Earl of Moria*, HMS *Prince Regent*, a brigantine, two schooners and two flat-bottomed gunboats, commanded by Sir James Lucas Yeo.

The American post there has been a consistent threat, particularly since it has become a station

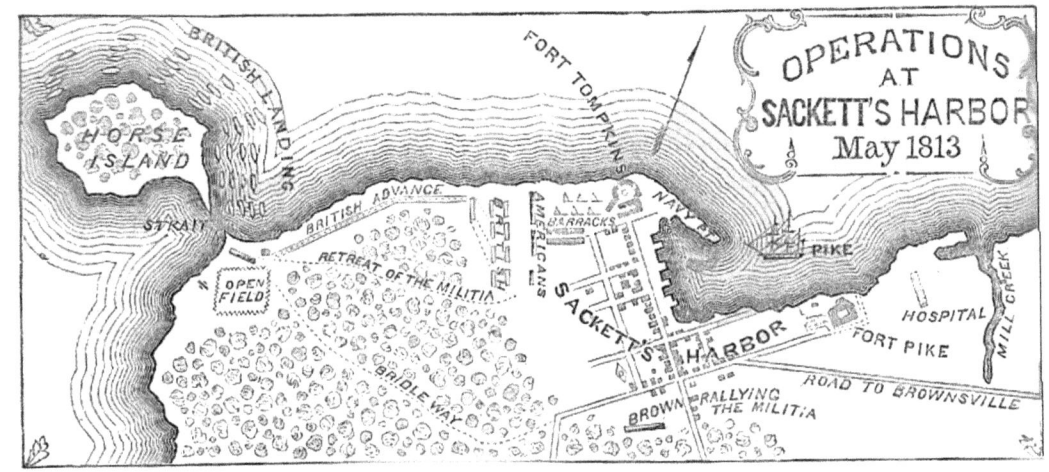

Operations at Sackets Harbor, New York, May 1813.

General Jacob Jennings Brown (*A History of Jefferson County New York*, Frank B. Hough, 1854).

for Captain Chauncey's fleet and a large naval supply depot. The fleet is transporting an expeditionary force estimated by the Americans at about 1,300 men, including Indians under General George Prevost. British sources place the number at about 750 men and the units they name are a grenadier company of the 100th regiment, a contingent of the Royal Scots, two companies of the 8th Regiment, four companies of the 104th Regiment, one company of the Glendarry Regiment, two companies of the Canadian Voltigeurs and a contingent of the Royal Newfoundland Regiment.

The launching of the assault is timed to the absence of Captain Chauncey's fleet, which has transported General Dearborn's force to the west end of Lake Erie to attack British-held Fort George at the mouth of the Niagara River in Canada. The fleet is sighted by about noon on the 28th by the *Lady of the Lake*. Lt. Wolcott Chauncey, the brother of Captain Isaac Chauncey, returns to the harbor and fires the pre-approved signal to sound he alarm. Meanwhile, the Americans on shore begin preparation for raising a stiff defense. Shortly thereafter it becomes evident that the landing craft are about to move to shore, and then suddenly all the troops aboard the boats are recalled to the surprise of the men, particularly the Indians, who become frustrated with the aborted landing. The fleet then begins to retire. No explanation for the recall ever emerges.

While the British initiate their retirement, nearly twenty boats transporting American reinforcements are observed as they approach the south shore. The sight of the reinforcements gives the Indians a reason to ignore the order to reboard the ships. Instead, they begin to row toward the boats to strike the reinforcements. The action complicates the fleet's withdrawal. An order is given to reverse course to provide support for the impetuous Indians. Nonetheless, while the ships maneuver to get back in proper positioning, the Indians reach shore and barely miss a struggle. They seize twelve of the boats but none of the troops, who safely make into some woods. Nevertheless, some English historians claim the Indians capture about 70 dragoons who surrender under a white flag. The remaining seven boats arrive in the harbor uninterrupted. The boldness on the part of the Indians affects the thinking of General George Prevost, who countermands his previous order to abort the attack and decides to resume the operation and land his force.

By the time the second phase begins, the Americans remain poised to meet the invaders. In addition to the volunteers from Oswego, General Brown had arrived on scene during the early morning with about 500 militia, bolstering the diminutive command of Lt. Colonel Electus Backus' regulars. Brown confers with Colonel Backus and Lt. Chauncey on how to best defend the town. The slim number of artillerymen is deployed at Fort Tomkins and Fort Volunteer, while Lt. Chauncey concentrates of supporting and fortifying Navy Point, where he is in command of the guns. General Brown deploys the militia where he expects the British to land, Horse Island, just west of the village of Sackets Harbor. The regulars are deployed near their encampment and other volunteers, augmented by one artillery piece, are posted to the right of the militia. Nonetheless, the remainder of the day passes without a major landing.

During the night (28th-29th), however, a detachment of about 40 Indians under British Lt. Anderson debark on the mainland at Henderson Bay with orders to strike the militia from the rear. Before dawn, the militia is ordered to withdraw from the island and redeploy on the opposite shore. The militia, about 400 strong under Colonel Mills (Albany volunteers), redeploy on shore opposite the island and their orders mandate that fire must be held until the British are within pistol shot. Meanwhile, other militia deploy in the woods, and nearby, the dragoons under Colonel Backus hold at the woods that adjoin the town. Backus' orders direct him to await the landing of the British, and at that instant rush toward Horse Island. Another force under Colonel Aspinwall holds the ground to the left of Backus' dragoons. Brown's one artillery piece is anchored at Fort Tompkins.

On the following morning (29th), General Prevost signals the attack; however, due to the calmness of the wind, the ships are prevented from moving in close to shore. The 33 boats move toward shore and their selected landing spot is precisely where General Brown expected it. The men in the boats are greeted while still in the water by volleys from militia and from the volunteers to their right, but the landing on the island is unopposed. In turn, the two British gunboats assigned to protect the landing force commence fire to try to break up the defensive line. The gunboats are unable to quiet the militia. During this period, the boats, unwilling to brave additional close-range fire, are rerouted by the crews who move instead to Horse Island, where the troops debark and initiate their advance upon the village. The route takes the soldiers across a small causeway that terminates at the mainland near the mouth of the harbor.

The British column, after reaching the mainland, advances toward a ridge, and as they encroach it, they are struck with yet another volley from the militia, which then abandons the position, leaving a gun on the field while they begin to scatter into the woods. One of the officers, Colonel Mills of the Albany Volunteers, is killed while trying to stop the stampede. Afterward, General Brown persuades fewer than 100 of them to regroup and stand against the attackers. He deploys them on the fringes of an open field where they use a fallen tree for cover. All the while, the British press forward, seemingly unconcerned about the militia. As they march into range, the militia resumes its fire, then it delivers several more volleys, but still, the troops are unwilling to enter into hand-to-hand combat. The militia again retreats, permitting the British to continue its advance; however, the volunteers on the right do not falter so quickly. They raise tenacious and effective opposition until compelled to withdraw and even then, while under fire from the gunboats, the troops continue to fight, and they pull back in disciplined fashion until they finally arrive near the position of Backus' regulars. During their retreat they received some detachments of regulars who bolstered the confidence of the volunteers, while their sharpshooters increased the number of British casualties.

At the next line of defense, essentially the remaining complete line of defense, Backus' regulars hold the center, with a contingent of light dragoons (dismounted) on the right and the volunteers on the left. The British maintain their advance with high morale. After unceremoniously disposing of the militia, they sense a quick kill. Unexpectedly, a minor work, referred to as Fort Tompkins, is introduced to the British when it fires upon the formation to instill some shock into the column and display the audacity of the defenders. At about the same time, the British plunge against the right flank, and again, they are met by fire, not a collapsed flank. The British launch successive assaults to crush the line with each attempt being violently repelled as the dragoons remain calm and refuse to surrender their ground. The line holds for about one hour until the Americans are compelled, due to facing far superior numbers, to withdraw.

Further to the rear, while the British continue to advance, part of the command regroups at a barracks built from logs to draw yet another formidable line of defense. This third defensive position is threatened by a confident contingent led by Colonel Gray (quartermaster general). Gray is at the front when the British encroach the barracks and his quest to quickly vanquish his remaining foe does not come to fruition. Gray is at the point walking backwards as he encourages his troops, shouting: "Come on, boys; the day is ours! Remember York!" At that exact time, one of the defenders, a young drummer boy, drops his drum, grabs a rifle and then, acting as a seasoned veteran, he fires and strikes Colonel Gray and the colonel is instantly killed. A recuperating American officer, Lieutenant Fanning, ignores his wounds and takes command of an artillery piece. Fanning propels three shots into the British formation and his accuracy bursts the enthusiasm of the Redcoats. Rather then initiate a charge to dislodge the defenders, the British, minus their usual swagger, lose their momentum. The British begin to fall back; however, the Americans are far from victory.

General Prevost still holds a far superior force and the Americans, in addition to being squeezed into a confined area, had sustained a grievous loss when Colonel Backus was fatally wounded during Gray's assault. His loss helps to drain the stamina of the defenders; however, beyond that, the officer in command, Lt. Chauncey, thinking that Fort Tompkins is lost, orders the stores to be burned. The defenders at the Marine barracks unexpectedly observe the smoke, which is billowing from the burning supplies (those captured at York) at Navy Point. The situation becomes more grim and while the troops are still anticipating a major assault. In the meantime, General Brown, who initially believes the fire was started by the British, rushes to it. He is told of why the fire began and is relieved to know that it was not done by the British. Aware that the British are still only on one side, he encourages Lieutenant Ketchum at Fort Tomkins to continue firing at the British fleet. He receives the response: "General, I cannot discharge this gun again, the flame from the Marine barracks is so hot that my men cannot exist here." After listening to Ketchum, Brown encourages Ketchum to do the best he can, then he departs from the fort.

In the meantime, pursuant to previous instructions from General Brown, Lt. Chauncey is to move his men from Navy point to join with Brown at Fort Volunteer on the high ground. General Brown at about this time learns that Lt. Chauncey had not ordered the ship to be burned and those under him who did had told Chauncey that "all was lost on the right of our line of battle." General Brown sends Major Brown with a message to Chauncey that "all was safe on the right & that Victory was ours." Slightly afterward, General Brown spots about 100 militia troops far from the fighting near the intersection of the "Brownville, Midale & Adams roads." At the same time Major Swan rides up to the general to inform him that "the fixed ammunition was expended." Brown does not buy the story and says to the major: "It may be so. I do not believe it — but if it is so, tell no man." Brown, having been with the militia when the British landed, realizes that many of them never fired a shot. He is acutely aware of the minimum abilities of his militia against British regulars, and of General Prevost's strengths and liabilities. Brown focuses on one of Prevost's liabilities, which he describes as "timidity." He orders the gathered militia to advance toward the British right flank in a maneuver to get them positioned in the woods if Prevost would order an advance. Meanwhile, he directs Major Luckett to advance with his dragoons to positions between the British and the ship, and afterward, Brown joins with the regulars who continue to hold their line.

Meanwhile, General Prevost realizes that he might get encircled and be unable to reach the boats. General Prevost, while on the brink of victory, orders a retreat, which surprises the beleaguered Americans, who are bracing for what they expect to be their final defense. Cunningly, General Brown's instincts regarding General Prevost's timidity proves true. Prevost, greatly alarmed by the maneuvering of the militia, which he believes are regulars under Colonel Tuttle and the dragoons, cause the British to retire hurriedly, so quickly that they leave their wounded behind.

After the departure of the British, the Americans receive some additional surprises. Although the fires have caused major losses, without interference from the British troops the fires are extinguished in time to preserve some of the supplies and provisions. Nature also lends a hand. The U.S. ship *Pike*, which had recently been constructed, did not burn quickly due to the wood being green. Lt. Talman, aware of the dangers, boards the *Duke of Gloucester* and extinguishes the fires before the powder explodes. He moves the ship away from the nearby burning buildings. Two other vessels, the schooners *Fair American* and *Pert*, are able to cut their cables and move farther up the river.

In the meantime, the battle that ended embarrassingly for General Prevost causes him to try to redeem himself. While back aboard ship, he decides to make another return to the village. Prevost dispatches a party under a white flag to issue an ultimatum to General Brown to surrender the post and the entire village to the British. Upon receipt of the ultimatum, General Brown wastes no time in returning a response. He immediately declines. The response is taken back to the fleet, while the Americans wait for Prevost's next move and ponder whether he might launch yet another assault. The reaction of the general is soon known when another party arrives under a white flag. There is no second ultimatum offered, nor is there an attack. The second message from General Prevost is a request that the Americans provide care for his wounded and provide the British dead with proper burials. Prevost is assured that his troops will be cared for properly. The response officially terminates the battle for Sackets Harbor.

Once General Prevost receives his answer, Commodore Yeo departs with the fleet. The Americans sustain about 156 casualties, including killed, wounded or missing. The fatalities include Colonel Mills, who had been slain in the opening part of the battle. Colonel Backus (1st Light Dragoons) survives for eight days. The British sustain an estimated 260 casualties. British reports place 29 killed in the field and 22 wounded, but these numbers exclude casualties in the boats. British fatalities include Colonel Gray (adjutant general), Colonel Moody, Major Edwards and one captain. Also, three captains, one ensign and 32 men are captured. The British make no further attempts to seize Sackets Harbor; however, their naval forces on Lake Ontario continue to interfere with American vessels.

General Prevost, upon his return to Canada, issues his report on the engagement at Sackets Harbor which is distributed to the Canadian people. Copies are forwarded to the government in England. Prevost's account of the battle portrays a "brilliant and unparalleled victory." He also claims that he had driven the Americans back for three hours and left them defeated, but reluctantly ordered retreat because of the coordination between his force and the fleet had not been well synchronized. Despite his attempts to embellish his failure, Prevost's reputation never recovers. One Canadian source referred to Prevost as "the evil genius of the campaign."

Following General Brown's victory, he states in a report to Governor Tompkins that Lt. Colonel Tuttle (regulars) had attempted to reach the battlefield in time, but although he arrived late, Brown assured the governor that Tuttle's troops were prepared to fight. His remarks on the militia are less kind: "The noble men both officers and soldiers of the Regular Army & some few, precious few Citizen Soldiers who nobly resisted the Shock of the Foe of Basswood Cantonment are the men who merit the honor of this Victory. &

Sir they must have it. Of the precious few Citizen Soldiers who distinguished themselves Mr. Channing stands conspicuous." Also, subsequent to the battle, Captain Benjamin Forsyth is promoted to major.

May 29 (Saturday) In Washington, D.C., a grand dinner is held in the capital to celebrate the U.S. Navy's recent victories over the Royal Navy. Both political parties and many other prominent citizens attend to praise the navy and give toasts to the valor of the troops. George Clinton (vice president), Henry Clay (speaker of the House) and General Robert Bowie (governor of Maryland) are among the attendees. One of the memorable toasts of the night: "The Flag of Decatur. To the lightning of heaven it bows, to British thunder, never."

In naval activity, the uncompleted USS *General Pike* is set afire during a British attack on Sackets Harbor. However, it is saved from total destruction, repaired and launched on 13 June.

May 30 (Sunday) *In naval activity,* the 185-ton brigantine *Commerce* (James Ives, master), while en route from Philadelphia to Gottenburg, Germany, with a cargo including cotton and staves, is intercepted by a British squadron and captured. The British vessels include the HMS *Martin, Spartan* and the *Statira*. The *Commerce* is separate from a vessel of the same name captured 2 May 1814. The HMS *Martin,* HMS *Spartan* and the HMS *Statira* intercept and seize the sloop *Plough Boy* (R. Ogden, master).

In other naval activity, the American privateer *Yankee* encounters a British vessel, and the incident erupts into an engagement that continues for about one hour before the *Yankee* finally prevails. The ship is identified as the *Thames,* the same name as one of the earlier prizes of the *Yankee*. The prize and is taken into port (Portland, New Hampshire or Maine), along with its cargo of about 2,000 bales of cotton which are later sold for $110,000.

May 31 (Monday) *In naval activity,* the HMS *Shannon* intercepts and recaptures the brigantine *William.* Other vessels named *William* captured are a bark, 8 July 1812; a brigantine, 16 August 1812; a schooner, 12 March 1813; a sloop, 7 August 1813; a schooner, 27 October 1813; a schooner, 19 June 1814; a brigantine, 11 October 1814; and a schooner seized at an unspecific time in 1814.

June In Alabama, a band of Creeks ambush a mail-rider named Greggs. Although he is not killed, they steal the mail and beat him, leaving Greggs along the Federal Road (Old Horse Path) between Burnt Corn and the Escambia River. The mail is forwarded to Pensacola. After wandering in the woods for about ten days, Greggs makes it to safety at Montgomery Hill. By this time a civil war is erupting among the Creeks. A young prophet, Letecau, uses a ruse to gather pro–American chiefs to assassinate them. Letecau and eight other prophets move from Abaucooche to old Coosa Town, and then he sends messengers to the nearby chiefs to come and witness their supernatural powers. Upon their arrival, along with a large number of other Indians, Letecau and his band begin to dance within a circle that he had drawn in the sand. The dance is intense, but there are no signs of magical powers. During the exhibition, the "dance of the lakes," Letecau yells his war cry, which is the signal to strike. Without warning, three of the unsuspecting chiefs are murdered. The others bolt for the river and escape harm. Soon a force is raised by the friendly chiefs and they return to retaliate. Letecau and his eight prophets are each killed. Afterward, the chiefs move to Little Ocfuske where followers of Tecumseh are discovered, and they too are killed. In the meantime, Tecumseh's allies strike the friendly chiefs' villages, including Hillibee towns and Kialigee. Big Warrior becomes concerned. He sends a request to Colonel Benjamin Hawkins for federal troops to provide him with safety. Hawkins responds by sending about two hundred Indians to rescue the chief at Tookabatcha. The rescuers arrive, fend off some resistance from the hostile Indians and escort Big Warrior and his followers to a place near the Chattahoochee River.

In naval activity, the *Anaconda* intercepts and captures another British vessel, the *Mary,* an 8-gun brigantine carrying a cargo of silks and wine from Gibraltar to Brazil. The prize is taken into port at New Haven, Connecticut. Also, the *Anaconda* captures the brigantine *Harriet,* which is en route from Buenos Aires to London. The *Harriet* is taken into port at New Bedford. By early July the *Anaconda* arrives at Ocracoke Inlet, where it encounters the privateer *Atlas*.

In other naval activity, The American privateer *Young Teazer,* commanded by Captain W.B. Dobson, while cruising off Halifax, Nova Scotia, is intercepted by the *Sir John Sherbroke.* Dobson has few options because his vessel is caught between the British vessel and the harbor; however, rather than surrender, Dobson attempts to pass off the *Young Teazer* as his prize and his crew as a British prize crew. The ruse works, although the *Sir John Sherbroke* does follow it into the harbor. With the British colors flying, the privateer is not fired upon by the shore guns.

Later, the *Young Teazer* manages to slip out of the harbor using darkness to provide safety so it can resume its cruise. Two days later, Captain Dobson, totally unconcerned about the strength of the British naval forces at Halifax, dispatches a proclamation to the British that declares Halifax to be under an American naval blockade. To further infuriate the British, the *Young Teazer* dares the captain of the HMS *La Hogue* to move out to engage. Captain Capel enthusiastically accepts the challenge, which erupts on 13 July.

June 1 (Tuesday) *In naval activity,* the USS *Chesapeake,* commanded by Captain James Law-

The USS *Chesapeake*, disabled by the HMS *Shannon*.

British Captain Philip Bowes Vere Broke.

rence, is being prepared to embark on a cruise to confront the British whaling vessels operating off Greenland. On this day, the HMS *Shannon* is spotted offshore as part of the blockading force. Captain Lawrence sails from Boston harbor to engage, but many in his crew are not thoroughly trained, and there are some seasoned but disgruntled crew members, upset over not yet having received their shares of prize money that is due them. And yet others had been in Boston drinking just before the ship departs. Lawrence is also concerned because some of his officers are on shore due to sickness and unable to sail.

The *Shannon*'s commander, Captain Philip Bowes Vere Broke, has sent a challenge daring the *Chesapeake* to come out and fight; however, the *Chesapeake* sails before Broke's message arrives. The challenge reads: "I doubt not that you, equally confident of success, will feel convinced that it is only by repeated triumphs in even combats that your little navy can now hope to console your country for the loss of that trade it can no longer protect."

Captain James Lawrence, U.S. Navy.

By about 1700, both ships are within range of the other's guns and the fireworks begin with the *Shannon* firing the first shot. The *Chesapeake* does not immediately respond; rather it remains sheepish while maneuvering into position from which it can deliver a broadside. Shortly thereafter, the *Chesapeake* begins to unleash a broadside and suddenly, the cannon roar and ignite a savage duel. The British fire damages the rigging of the *Chesapeake*, and due to the closeness of the antagonists, the fore-chains of the *Shannon* get tangled with the *Chesapeake*'s mizzen rigging. While the crew of the *Chesapeake* struggles to regain control of their ship, British guns pour riveting fire into the upper deck.

By this time, the *Chesapeake* has sustained severe casualties, including fatalities. The sailing master, Mr. White, falls from the first shot. Some others—including the ship's first lieutenant, fourth lieutenant (Mr. Ballard), the boatswain and the Marine commander—sustain mortal wounds. Captain Lawrence also becomes wounded after being hit in his leg. Nonetheless, Captain Lawrence continues to hold command. He orders his bugler to signal for the boarding party to board the *Shannon*. The bugler, however, apparently terrified by the gruesome scenes on the decks, had hidden under a launch, creating additional problems. After a quick search, the bugler is located and brought out of his hiding place. He remains frozen with fear; unable to give the signal. The bugler had been aboard in place of a drummer. Consequently, the order to board is passed on man-to-man, but due to the ongoing confusion of the battle, there is no clarity and the order to board fails to get executed.

The plight of the Americans becomes graver. As Captain Lawrence issues his verbal boarding party orders, a British shell inflicts a fatal wound. All the while the gunners are exchanging blows. By this time, British fire has killed the man at the helm and successively two others, leaving the ship's steering unsteady. Consequently, the anchor gets snared in one of the ship's afterports, placing the *Chesapeake* at an even greater disadvantage. The crew is unable to maneuver the ship into a position from which it can pound the *Shannon*. All the while, the *Shannon* continues to pour riveting fire upon the *Chesapeake*. The men on the upper deck are bludgeoned, and to add more grief to the situation, the quarterdeck is struck by a grenade. It ignites several musket cartridges, but the damage was not severe.

About 20 of Lawrence's crew, anxious to attain victory and end the horrendous shelling that is wrecking the *Chesapeake* and killing large numbers, boards the *Shannon* without orders. Lawrence displays his courage and his will to continue the fight, but it comes too late to rally the crew. While he is issuing the order to board, a musket ball lodges in his intestines. This wound is mortal. At nearly the same time, the British swarm aboard the *Chesapeake*.

Meanwhile, Lieutenant Cox responds to Lawrence's call to board, but as he rushes forward he arrives next to the captain just as he is hit. While moving to carry Lawrence below deck, British captain Broke, leading the British boarding party, crashes onto the *Chesapeake*. Resistance is raised during a wild clash that lasts only a short time. Samuel Livermore, the ship's chaplain, seeks revenge for the mortal wounding of Lawrence. He takes a shot at Captain Broke, but misses the mark, then becomes a target of Broke. Captain Broke swings his sword at Livermore's head. Livermore escapes harm, but only momentarily. While he protects his head by diverting the sword, he sustains a deep cut in his arm. By this time, Lawrence's officers on the upper deck, except one, Lt. Ludlow, have been knocked out of action. Ludlow is also wounded, multiple times, and too severely to resist, leaving the men without an officer to lead them. Nevertheless, the savage fighting continues. Meanwhile the British are finally able to gain control. Troops under Lt. Budd attempt to ascend to the upper deck, but the British easily overwhelm them before they reach the deck.

Confusion abounds as the fighting becomes more desperate. One officer, Lt. Cox, inadvertently finds himself among what he believes to be part of the crew; however, he is in the middle of a British group. The mistake is costly. He is quickly slashed by their swords. Meanwhile, Captain Lawrence, although below deck and dying, remains conscious. He directs the ship's surgeon to go on deck to deliver an order: "Fight on to the last, and never to strike the colours. They shall wave, while I live." Nonetheless, by that time, the British have prevailed. The crew resisted tenaciously; however, further fighting was in vain. Lt. Ludlow had surrendered the ship. Astonishingly, after Ludlow surrenders, an Englishman strikes him in the head with a sword and fractures his skull. Lt. Ludlow dies from the wound.

Due to the death of nearly every officer early in the fight, the British encounter bitter resistance; however, it is disorganized. The British boarding party completes the seizure by firing at anyone spotted, and they fire down the hatches to increase the number of casualties. The battle, which had lasted only about fifteen minutes, leaves large numbers of wounded men on both vessels. The Americans sustain about 47 or 48 killed and 97 or 98 wounded (the Naval Historical Center gives the number killed as more than 60, which might include those who were mortally wounded).

Captain Lawrence, having sustained a fatal wound, remains aboard the *Chesapeake*. He succumbs, according to the U.S. Navy Historical Center, on 4 June and is later buried at Halifax, Nova Scotia, on the 7th. The British sustain about 23 or 24 killed and 56 or 58 wounded. Captain Broke receives a serious wound while he is aboard the *Chesapeake*, but he survives.

After the battle both vessels are in wretched condition. The wounded are tended, the American captives are secured and the deceased are buried at sea. The *Shannon* and the captured *Chesapeake* sail to Halifax, and when the ships enter the harbor, it becomes evident that the *Shannon* had prevailed. The *Chesapeake* is flying the British colors, with the Stars and Stripes directly underneath. Captain Lawrence dies during the journey, but his remains are taken to Halifax. The ships arrive within sight of the harbor on 6 June at about 1530. Word of the victory spreads rapidly and within minutes many who had gathered at church begin to stream out of the pews before the ships are actually at anchor.

At Halifax, excitement fills the air and some of the people still have no idea what has caused the jubilance. Citizens rush for a spot from where they can witness the spectacle. Suddenly the rooftops are overcrowding at just about the time both vessels are in sight as they reach Georges Island. The crowds at the docks increase, and shortly thereafter, the people raise cheer after cheer. In turn the band aboard the *Shannon* begins to play "Rule Britannia," and one of their favorites from the American Revolution, "Yankee Doodle." Until this victory at sea, the more experienced Royal Navy had not fared well against the American warships in either seamanship or gunnery. The defeat of the *Chesapeake* propels British and Canadian morale sky high.

When word of the victory over the Chesapeake arrives in London, Parliament is in session. The British revel over the news, which temporarily removes the shadow of gloom which had been hovering due to the Royal Navy's inability to quash the American naval forces. Captain Broke is given a rare honor, the "freedom of the city" solely because he had been victorious "over an American [ship] of equal force."

Captain Lawrence's words "don't give up the ship" become immortal as the rallying cry of the United States Navy. Captain Lawrence is interred by the British at Halifax, and he is given the full honors of war. Also, one American, Lt. W.S. Cox, later receives a court-martial for deserting his post under fire during the battle. However, during 1952, the United States Navy reinstates Cox's good name, when they agree with his descendants' claims that he had been under orders to carry Captain Lawrence below deck.

Along with the loss of the *Chesapeake*, the United States also sustains a devastating loss with regard to intelligence. The British receive a bonanza, the code book for America's naval signals. Secretary of the Navy William Jones delegates Commodores William Bainbridge, Stephen Decatur and Isaac Hull as the board to write a new code book. At this time, Decatur and Hull are involved with other duties. Bainbridge designs the new signals by himself and forwards the completed project to the Navy Department. The new naval signals are afterward considered foolproof, "except for treachery." The "numerical, private, day, night and fog signals were highly approved of, and were immediately introduced into the navy." Also, the U.S. officers killed include Peter Adams, Edward J. Ballard, James Broome and William Augustus White. Wounded officers include Lieutenants Budd, Cox and Samuel Livermore.

In other naval activity, a British squadron operating off Connecticut encounters a squadron, composed of the *Hornet* (Captain James Biddle), *Macedonian* (Captain Jacob Jones) and the *United States*, under Commodore Stephen Decatur. The Americans had been attempting to get out of New York and onto the open seas by running the blockade between Montauk Point and Block Island. Initially, Decatur anticipated only the *Ramillies*; but suddenly, just before entering into an engagement, the battleship *Valiant* and two frigates, the *Acasta* and the *Orpheus*, move out from beyond Montauk Point. The British maneuver to block the Americans from entering the mouth of the harbor. Nonetheless, the British force, too powerful to engage, fails to intercept Decatur's squadron, which makes it back to the harbor at New London.

The British blockading force off New London is particularly effective, due in great part to shore signals from an unidentified source. Each time Decatur attempts to sail, unidentified persons signal the British by using "blue lights." Meanwhile, the British, once alerted, take preventive action that keeps Decatur's naval force tied up in New London. Decatur's force is corralled at New London.

However, soon after arriving there, Decatur authorizes a raid upon British positions on Gardiner's Island. A contingent moving in one boat avoids detection and safely lands on the island. The troops set a trap by lurking in the woods along the path to the manor house, and the plan appears to be auspicious. A short while later a party of British, including some officers from one of the warships, comes ashore. While they leisurely walk toward the home, the Americans burst from the woods and corral the entire group without causing a stir. The British, stunned by the unexpected appearance of the Yankees, get no opportunity to escape or resist. They are prodded into the boat and carried to Connecticut.

Meanwhile, the British who control the island become infuriated by the incident. They take immediate action to prevent any further incursions by sending out barges to patrol around the island. In addition, the British, convinced that the lord of the manor (6th), John Lyon Gardiner, had conspired with Decatur's contingent, dispatch a detachment to arrest him. However, the British underestimate his wife, Sarah Griswold Gardiner, who outwits the British with a bold and daring plan. John retires to the green room under the pretense of being extremely ill, and the color scheme of the room aids in the ruse. The bedroom's color scheme including green curtains reflect a ghostly green coloring on his skin that creates an illusion that totally fools the troops who had barged into the residence. Sarah enhanced the scheme by placing bottles of medicine, some glasses and even spoons on a small bedside table.

After gaining entrance, the troops demand to confront her husband. With crocodile tears flowing down her cheeks, Sarah pleads with the officers to tread lightly and remain as quiet as possible so her ill husband will not be unduly disturbed. The British are escorted into the room and their belligerent demeanor crumbles as they peer at the bed at what appears to be a fragile man at death's door. His skin has a ghastly green tint. Suddenly, the British officers are transformed. They decide that it would not be advisable to take Gardiner aboard their ship. Instead, they decide to take his oldest son hostage. Nonetheless, David, only ten years old, is away at school, leaving the British empty handed.

Commodore Hardy was convinced that Gardiner had not been involved with the raid. Sarah learns that her ruse worked when a letter from Commodore Hardy to John Gardiner, dated 31 July, arrives at the residence:

> As it is probable that the government of the United States may call you to account for permitting refreshments to be taken by the British squadron from your place, I think it necessary for your satisfaction, and to prevent your experiencing the censure of your government, for me to assure you, that had you not complied with my wishes as you have done, I should certainly have made use of force, and the consequences would have been the destruction of your property, yourself a prisoner-of-war, and whatever was in the possession of your dependents taken without payment. But it is not my wish to distress individuals on the coast of the United States who may be in the power of the British squadron.

During April 1814, Decatur and his men depart New London and move by land to New York. The frigates are afterward dismantled and the rest of the ships make it to sea in November 1814. Some people blame the Federalist Party for the treachery; however, the militia in Connecticut is primarily composed of Federalists, and it is the militia that bars the British ships from entering the harbor to capture or destroy Decatur's squadron. Commodore Decatur holds the opinion that the treachery is undertaken by traitors. Another theory is that the British had landed spies to maintain communication.

While Connecticut and other states to the south remain under steady blockading by the British, the Massachusetts coastline is not blockaded. Nonetheless, pressure is rapidly mounting because British fleets are receiving provisions and supplies from vessels departing from Massachusetts' ports. Also, it is reported that a brigantine, the *Active*, chartered by the Revenue Service, had operated as part of a flotilla off New London, but it became trapped by the blockade. The Navy has no records that it ever served as an official U.S. Navy vessel and no documentation regarding details on its service has ever been discovered.

In other naval activity, a fresh British squadron under Admiral Warren arrives in the Chesapeake to bolster Admirals Cockburn and Beresford. The squadron is transporting a force of British soldiers and Royal Marines under the command of Sir Sidney Beckwith. With the arrival of Warren's squadron, the British naval force, excluding smaller vessels, includes eight ships of the line and twelve frigates.

In Maryland at Baltimore, the government believes the city is the paramount objective of the British expeditionary force. The work to fortify the city intensifies. Brigadier General Robert Miller commands a force of about 2,000 troops. Militia from other counties, including Prince George's, are dispatched by the governor's order to Baltimore to relieve the Baltimore citizens from garrison duty. At this same time, militia units on the Eastern Shore are deploying at various strategic points to meet any attempted landing by the English ground troops.

In other naval activity, the *Hetty* (H. Skinner, master), a 151-ton brigantine which had departed from Madeira, Portugal, with a cargo of ballast, is intercepted and captured by a British squadron, composed of the HMS *Martin*, HMS *Spartan* and the HMS *Statira*, terminating the voyage before the *Hetty* arrives at Philadelphia. Also, the British privateer *Dart* intercepts the 48-ton schooner *Joanna* while it is en route from Eastport, Maine, to Boston with a cargo of corn. The *Joanna* is seized and taken into port at New Brunswick. Also, the American privateer *Yankee*, carrying a crew of 200 men, sails from Newport, Rhode Island, to begin a new cruise. The 15-gun privateer *Blockade* departs with the *Yankee* and they cruise as a pair.

June 2 (Wednesday) *In naval activity*, a British squadron comprising the HMS *Martin*, *Sparta* and *Statira* encounters the brigantine *Flor de Lisboa* (F.D. Viena, master) while it is transporting a cargo of rice and sugar from Puerto Rico to Philadelphia. The brigantine and its cargo are seized before it reaches its destination.

June 3 (Thursday) *In naval activity*, the gunboat USS *Eagle*, formerly a merchant ship until acquired by the Navy in 1812 and attached to Commodore Macdonough's squadron, is captured on Lake Champlain on the Canadian side of the lake. The British also capture the gunboat USS *Growler*. The British rename the *Eagle* the HMS *Finch*. Subsequently, the *Finch* is recaptured during September 1814 at the Battle of Lake Champlain and re-entered into the U.S. Service until it is sold during July 1815. The sloop USS *Eagle* is separate from the brigantine USS *Eagle* and the HMS *Eagle* (separate from the *Finch*). Also, later in the year, the sloop *Wasp* (fourth) is chartered on Lake Champlain for duty as a tender to the fleet of Macdonough. The *Wasp* sees no action during its service. During 1814, it is returned to its original owners. The battery aboard the *Wasp* is transferred to the recently launched USS *Ticonderoga*. Also, the American privateer Yankee encounters a Portuguese vessel, and after releasing the prisoners recently seized (30 May) on the Thames on parole, Captain Oliver Wilson transfers the British crew to the Portuguese brigantine.

June 5 (Saturday) **In Canada,** the pursuit of the British who abandoned Fort George had been delayed about five days after the fort was seized (27 May); however on this day, the forward elements of the American contingent in pursuit of the British arrive at Stoney Creek. The two brigades, bolstered by about 250 cavalry troops under Colonel Burns, are commanded by Generals John Chandler and William Henry Winder. Earlier, after advancing less than 25 miles, General William H. Winder requested reinforcements. General Chandler also arrives this day with his contingent. In the meantime, the British under General Vincent had halted their retreat at Burlington Heights. Although holding inferior numbers, the British decide to stand and fight. At the time, American forces essentially control the entire Niagara district, stretching from Stoney Creek back to Fort George. Another option for the British is to evacuate if the fleet under Admiral James Yeo can arrive at Brandt House, about four miles from their positions, in time to evacuate Vincent's force. An overland retreat would force General Vincent to move about 200 miles by way of York and beyond to Kingston. The route would be treacherous due to the presence of a U.S. fleet at York.

Nonetheless, General John Vincent, after conferring with Colonel John Harvey (later Sir John Harvey, lieutenant governor of Nova Scotia) is persuaded by Harvey's suggestion of reversing their dilemma by launching a surprise attack against the American encampment at Stoney Creek. Strategy is discussed and the plan unfolds at about midnight (5th-6th) when Colonel Harvey leads slightly more than 700 men toward the American lines.

In naval activity, the British privateer *Dart* intercepts and seizes the 65-ton schooner *Washington,* which is transporting a cargo including shingles from Portland, Maine, to Boston. The prize is taken into port at New Brunswick.

June 6 (Sunday) BATTLE OF STONEY CREEK **In Canada,** a British contingent of about 700 troops departs from Burlington Heights en route to Stoney Creek. No Indians accompany the column, which departs in absolute darkness at about midnight (5th-6th) and cautiously advances through the wilderness under strict orders to remain silent. The British also take precautions. The troops advance without having flints in their muskets to prevent any accidental premature firing, which would sound an alarm and alert the American camp and cause the British to lose the element of surprise, the advantage which can overcome the far superior numbered American force.

The confidence of the Americans, following their recent successes in the Niagara district, remains high. There are no suspicions that the retreating British would consider something as brash as launching an attack against so great a force. Nevertheless, the British, renowned for

General William H. Winder.

their bravado as they march into battle, approach the encampment without the sounds of a single drum or bagpipe, nor any signs of the British colors.

At the camp no extra precautions have been made to prevent any intrusions. Before dawn at about 0200, a forward detachment encroaches several sentries and without warning, the first and second sentinels are silently liquidated; however, a third breaks for safety and fires his weapon to sound the alarm, but too late to permit the U.S. to form for a strong defense. The bayonets of the troops in the vanguard strike violently against the sleeping or groggy troops even before the British had inserted the flints and loaded their cartridges. Nevertheless, during the confusion in the darkness, the Americans form for battle, and some of the British become easy targets before the illumination of camp fires. A sudden effective volley inflicts casualties into the ranks of the British.

The American force under General Dearborn is in pursuit of the British under General Vincent. The British, numbering about 750, mount a surprise attack during the early morning hours against about 3,000 Americans (or more, according to some estimates). Two American generals, John Chandler and William H. Winder, are both captured. The British attack brings a halt to Dearborn's advance. The Americans retire back to Fort George at the mouth of the Niagara River. By this time, the British complete the complicated process of getting their muskets in shape to return fire; however, the piercing steel of the bayonet had caused confusion, and by this time, Colonel Harvey incites more pandemonium when he directs two contingents of the 49th Regiment to strike the center and left of the U.S. line.

At the center of the line, three guns are deployed along the main road; however, the British thrust succeeds in seizing the artillery and killing or capturing nearly all of the artillerymen. The 12-man detachment of the 49th Regiment, responsible knocking out the guns, is under the command of Sergeant (later colonel) Frazer from Perth, Ontario. Frazer's troops had crept up too the positions without detection. Sergeant Frazer, himself, eliminates about seven of the gunners with his bayonet. The enormous tenacity displayed by the British causes the Americans to believe the British are in much greater numbers and the situation for the Americans quickly deteriorates. Luckily for the Americans, the British force lacks artillerymen, which prevents them from turning the guns on the camp.

Apparently, after Generals Chandler and William H. Winder both become captives of the British, command had fallen directly upon Colonel James Burn (2nd Light Dragoons), who assumes command during the chaotic fighting in the darkness; however, the troops had not galvanized; rather the ranks dissipate as soldiers break out of formation and hurriedly sprint to some nearby high ground on their left. In the meantime, Colonel Burn and his cavalry contingent, unable to maneuver in the darkness, make no attempt to intercept the British. They gallop off toward Fort George. Harvey's incursion had inflicted irreversible harm to the cohesion of the Americans. Before the sun rises, the British, despite being greatly outnumbered, secure not only the victory, but they also preserve Canada from being overrun by General Dearborn's army. Sergeant Frazer, responsible for the capture of the two U.S. generals, afterward receives a commission in the field for his actions and bravery under fire. The British initiate their return to their positions at Burlington Heights without fear of pursuit by the Americans, who are in the process of retreating back to Fort George. Nonetheless, the bold action by Colonel Harvey did not come without an expensive price. His Spartan force sustains about 150 casualties, including killed, wounded and missing.

By about dawn, the British return to their camp; however, later a contingent returns to the field. Afterward, the Americans return; however, after destroying their ammunition, blankets, and other equipment, the pursuit is aborted. The Americans abandon the field and retire to positions at Forty Mile Creek, slightly more than ten miles to the rear. In the meantime, the British return to the battlefield at about 1100. There are no signs of the Americans, except for those lying dead on the field. To their great surprise, the British discover that two of their officers, Major Clerk and Captain Manners, thought dead, had survived, along with some other British troops.

During the return march to General Vincent's encampment at Burlington Heights, just over 100 American prisoners and the three captured guns also accompany the column. Meanwhile, during the American trek back to Fort George, the column again comes under attack at Forty Mile Creek by British land troops and naval vessels. The column retreats about ten miles, but the troops afterward make it back to the captured fort. U.S. units that participate include the 5th, 13th, 14th, 16th, 22d, and 23rd Regiments, which had been divided into two brigades. British losses amount to about 23 killed, 136 wounded and 65 missing. American losses are reported as 17 killed, 88 wounded and more than 100 captured.

An official letter from General Dearborn does

little to bring clarity to the circumstances surrounding the attack; however, Dearborn had not been present. His letter indicates that the attacking force was composed of British and Indians, but no Indians participated. The letter also states that the British were "completely routed and driven from the field." In addition, it states that Generals Chandler and Winder had been captured after advancing to an artillery position when the assault commenced. Inexplicably, the letter states that British General Vincent had been killed during the assault; however, he was not present, and in fact, on the following day, Generals Chandler and Winder were guests of General Vincent at his camp. Other inconsistencies in the letter include a statement that the British "sent in a flag with a request to bury their dead." It was the British who buried the American dead.

In naval activity, the British privateer *Retrieve* seizes the 98-ton *Betsy* (N. Walton, master), a sloop, after it leaves Boston with a cargo of corn and ballast. A British privateer, the *Dart,* intercepts and seizes the *Cuba* (Geo. Thomas, master), a 107-ton ship with a cargo of flour. The prize is taken into port at New Brunswick. In other naval activity, the USS *Essex* arrives at Narborough Island (Galapagos). During the afternoon, the crew observes that the sky is permeated with a rising column of thick smoke that is sending off white curling spirals of smoke. Initially, the origin of the smoke is undiscovered. Some believe it is on Narborough and others think it is on another island east of Narborough. By the following day, it is confirmed that a volcano on Albemarle Island, east of Narborough Island, had erupted.

Summer **In England,** the British are feeling heavy pressure at home due to the effectiveness of American naval forces that have seriously impeded British shipping. The prices of products and cost of insurance have risen sharply. Flour is about $58 a barrel and beef is $38. Lumber is about $72 per 1,000 feet. Newspapers report that very few vessels are able to acquire any insurance at Halifax, and the few that succeed are compelled to pay heavily. Insurance rates also soar for voyages between Ireland and Scotland due to the losses inflicted by American privateers.

In Maryland, Major Armistead writes to Sam Smith, "We sir, are ready at Fort McHenry to defend Baltimore against invading by the enemy, and it is my desire to have a flag so large that the British will have no difficulty in seeing it from a distance."

June 7 (Monday) British Commodore James Yeo's fleet arrives near Forty Mile Creek, where American cavalry had arrived after retreating from Stoney Creek on the 5th. The British naval guns commence fire on the American positions. The arrival of Admiral James Yeo, combined with the devastating defeat of the U.S. at Stoney Creek, ensures that the column aborts its pursuit of the British under General Vincent. Yeo's appearance causes additional problems for General Dearborn, who is already unsteady. Dearborn orders Lewis back to Fort George, and shortly after his return, Lewis is placed in temporary command of Dearborn's Ninth District.

The following day, Admiral Yeo bombards the Americans and sends troops ashore in small boats. The British seize more than ten bateaux and destroy some others; the Americans also lose other items, including their tents. Meanwhile, circumstances for the British under General Vincent have drastically changed since Colonel John Harvey's stunning victory at Stoney Creek on the 5th. The British, while under pursuit, had anticipated being extricated by the fleet; however, with the threat having ended, General Vincent moves to Chippewa above Niagara Falls. By early July, the British again dominate the Niagara district except the American-held post at Fort George at the mouth of the Niagara River.

In related activity, Generals Morgan Lewis and John P. Boyd join the battered American force at Forty Mile Creek. General Lewis assumes command. The force, including a contingent of troops attached to the 6th and 15th Regiments and an artillery contingent that joined the force after the previous day's battle, brings the strength up to about 4,000 troops. Also, before returning to Kingston on 29 June, Commodore Yeo's squadron seizes two schooners and some supplies across Lake Ontario, and afterward seizes a supply depot on the Genesee River. From there the British move to Sodus Point (Great Sodus).

June 8 (Tuesday) **In Canada** at Halifax, American Captain James Lawrence, commander of the USS *Chesapeake,* is interred. The British and Canadians afford the naval officer the honors of war. His remains are taken from the *Chesapeake,* accompanied by 300 men of the British 64th Regiment and a party of officers. Captain Lawrence's coffin is draped with the Stars and Stripes and his personal sword is placed atop the flag. Another group, composed of six naval captains, act as pall bearers. They are followed by the surviving officers of the *Chesapeake.* Other officers and prominent citizens of Halifax also join in the funeral procession. The funeral service is conducted by the rector of St. Paul's Church. Captain Lawrence is re-interred in New York.

In naval activity, the *Belle* (F.R. Steinhaven), a 107-ton schooner en route from Madeira, Portugal, to Egg Harbor, New Jersey, is seized by several British warships, the HMS *Martin, Spartan* and the *Statira.* Also, elements of the British blockading squadron and the HMS *Victorious* seize the brigantine *Harriet.* The *Harriet* is separate from the schooner *Harriet* seized on 28 June 1813 and the sloop *Harriet* captured 13 July 1813.

In other activity, an American naval prisoner, held in England aboard the *Samson,* a prison ship moored at Chatham, writes: "I have been now a prisoner, during which time I have been on board eleven of their floating hells. In this ship, besides Americans, are five hundred Frenchmen, some of whom have been prisoners ten years. Lice, hunger, and nakedness are no strangers here. There are one thousand two hundred Americans and five thousand French prisoners in this harbor. Of the Americans about seven hundred have been heretofore impressed, and have been sent here from on board English men of war. Would to God I were at home again!"

Although the conditions on the prison ships are horrific and inhumane, land prisons are considerably worse. Dartmoor prison, one of the infamous installations in England, is about 15 miles northeast of Plymouth, and descriptions of conditions there vary in degrees, but each describes intolerable. The compound, sometimes referred to as Dartmoor Depot, was constructed at an elevation of about 1,000 feet above sea level, guaranteeing that the prisoners would be suffering from the cold during most of the year. The facility is surrounded for miles by ground that is nearly completely devoid of plant life, leaving the impression that nature passed without a pause. Other than a few well scattered near-primitive cottages, the panorama exhibits gloom and doom. The prison is guarded at times by about 2,000 troops bolstered by a contingent of artillery. By the end of the conflict, about 5,600 Americans remain in the prison and of those about one-half had been pressed into the Royal Navy prior to the outbreak of the war.

June 11 (Friday) *In naval activity,* British privateer *Matilda* intercepts and seizes the 20-ton schooner *Nymphe* (W. Ryan, master) which is en route to Machias, Maine, from Boston. The *Nymphe* is separate from the schooner *Nymphe* seized on 14 March 1813.

June 12 (Saturday) *In naval activity,* two American supply ships en route to Sackets Harbor, New York, are intercepted and seized by British warships. Also, the USS *Surveyor,* a revenue cutter commanded by Captain Samuel Travis, comes under a severe attack on the York River by a British force being carried by barges. The *Surveyor* is at anchor on the river; however, Travis' crew had been on alert. The barges from the HMS *Narcissus* are unable to gain surprise, as they are spotted when they reach a point about 50 yards from the ship. Nonetheless, the guns of the *Surveyor* are not able to be placed into action. Travis improvises and distributes two muskets to each man in the crew, along with orders to withhold their fire until the British reach pistol range. Shortly thereafter, the crew commences fire, but the British are not halted. They press forward and board. The British lose three men killed and reportedly a high number of wounded. Travis and his entire crew, composed of fifteen, including men and boys, are captured and transferred to the HMS *Junon.*

Captain Travis surrenders his sword; however, the British commander is so impressed with the bravery of him and his crew that the sword is returned to him the next day. The British officer, John Crevie, also attaches a letter:

> Sir: Your gallant and desperate attempt to defend your vessel against more than double your number, on the night of the 12th inst., excited such admiration, on the part of your opponents, as I have seldom witnessed, and induced me to return you the sword you have so ably used, in testimony of mine. Our poor fellows have severely suffered, occasioned chiefly, if not solely, by the precaution you had taken to prevent surprise; in short, I am at a loss which to admire most, the previous arrangement on board the *Surveyor* or the determined manner by which her deck was disputed, inch by inch.

You have my most sincere wishes for the immediate parole and speedy exchange of yourself and brave crew; and I cannot but regret that I myself have no influence that way, otherwise it should be forthcoming.

In other activity, a three-ship British squadron (HMS *Martin*, *Spartan* and *Statira*) intercepts and recaptures the 165-ton brigantine *Hero* while it is en route to Lisbon, Portugal, from Limerick, Ireland, with a cargo of beef, pork and provisions. The *Hero* is separate from the schooner *Hero* seized 29 August 1813, the schooner *Hero* captured 14 November 1813, the sloop *Hero* taken 13 January 1814, the schooner *Hero* captured on 3 July 1814, and the sloop *Hero* seized during early November 1814.

June 13 (Sunday) **In Vermont,** a British squadron appears off Burlington and commences a bombardment of the town. The Americans, deployed at a 13-gun battery (Burlington Battery) built during 1812 by a contingent under Lt. Sylvester, are up to the task of defending the harbor. Return fire from the battery causes the British to abort the attack and withdraw.

In naval activity, a British squadron, composed of the HMS *Maidstone*, *Nimrod* and *Poictiers*, seizes the 125-ton brigantine *Anna*, which is transporting beef, butter, flour, soap and about 80 barrels of gin. Also, the sloop *Morning Star* is intercepted and captured by a British squadron composed of the HMS *Martin*, *Spartan* and *Statira*. The *Morning Star* is separate from the schooner *Morning Star* seized on 18 August 1813 and the sloop *Morning Starr* captured 11 June 1814.

In other naval activity, Captain Oliver H. Perry's flotilla departs from Buffalo en route to Erie, where it arrives on the 19th. Captain Perry, aboard the *Caledonia*, is ill from fever and the trip is arduous. Doctor Usher Parsons, Perry's surgeon, noted in his diary: "We made twenty-five miles in twenty-four hours."

Doctor Usher Parsons.

June 14 (Monday) **In New York** at Buffalo, the five vessels which had been trapped in a creek at Black Rock had recently arrived at Buffalo. During the night, they embark for Erie to bolster Perry's naval force. The journey is risky due to British warships; however, all five vessels arrive and pass the bar at Erie on the 18th. British warships arrive but not until the final vessel moves beyond the bar.

In naval activity, the USS *Carolina* is commissioned this day. The ship, built in South Carolina, was launched on 10 November of the previous year. Command is given to Lt. J.D. Henley. The *Carolina* proceeds to New Orleans and while en route, it captures a British schooner, the *Shark*. In a separate incident, two British warships, the HMS *Statira* and the *Martin*, intercept the 874-ton ship Carl Gustaff (G.B. Baker, master) while it is en route from New York to Beaufort, North Carolina.

In other activity, the schooner *Del Carmen* (J. Ivinada, master) is captured by the HMS *Martin*, HMS *Spartan* and HMS *Statira*, on its way with a cargo of soap from New York to Savannah. The ship *Starr*, a 409-ton vessel, carrying a cargo of flour, is encountered and captured by a strong British squadron, composed of the HMS *Barossa*, HMS *Junon*, HMS *Mohawk*, HMS *Marlborough*, HMS *Narcissus* and the HMS *Victorious*.

June 15 (Tuesday) **BATTLE OF SODUS POINT In New York,** intelligence arrives at Sodus Point (Wayne County) that a British force had landed along the Genesee River and that the objective was Sodus Point. The militia in the region had been experiencing British raids since the previous spring. Elements of Colonel Philetus Swift's regiment and a contingent of Major Williams' battalion are directed to expeditiously move to Sodus Point. The troops remain posted at the Point; however they depart, except for a guard, on the morning of the 19th. The troops that remain are to safeguard the military.

The British, who failed to arrive while the main body had stood ready, move into view in the afternoon. Riders are directed to gallop toward the column to attempt to get them to speed back to the village, while other troops spread the alarm in and around the village. By evening about 60 militia troops arrive back at the Point. Only a few of these have had any genuine military experience. Later, under cover of darkness, the British move against the village; but there is no surprise. The column is heard easily because of the noise, and troops carrying lanterns become conspicuous targets that draw fire from the defenders. One of the Americans takes a bead on one of the lanterns and hits the mark.

At the first sound of gunfire, the British receive their command to commence firing. Although the one lantern had been abruptly extinguished, the British fire creates a massive display of gun flashes that illuminate their positions, providing the Americans with the ability to take accurate aim. The British fire does inflict some casualties; however, American return fire is right on target. Some British are killed and others are wounded. Nevertheless, total darkness still dominates. The British are unable to determine the strength of the American defenders and they retire rather than advance through the darkness.

Meanwhile, the Americans are acutely aware that the Redcoats greatly outnumber them and they too retire, but they do not draw a new line. The militia takes flight. Some vanish into the woods while others head for their homes. The British await daylight on the 20th before debarking. Once they arrive on shore the advance begins; however, to their surprise they encounter only nominal resistance. Once they move into the village, the British seize the stores and afterward, they burn the buildings, except for one structure in which a wounded militiaman (Asher Warner) was placed on the previous day after he received a mortal wound. Following the raid, the British return to Commodore Yeo's squadron, which departs for Kingston.

In naval activity, the schooner *Lark* is recaptured by the HMS *Borer*. The *Lark* is separate from the sloop *Lark* seized 19 April 1813.

June 16 (Wednesday) *In naval activity,* the USS *Lady of the Lake*, commanded by Lt. Wolcott Chauncey, while operating on Lake Ontario off Presque Isle (later, Erie, Pennsylvania), encounters and captures the British schooner *Lady Murray* during the morning and confiscates its cargo, which is ammunition and provision. The vessel was en route from Kingston to York. The Americans also capture one ensign and fifteen privates attached to the 41st and 104th British Regiments. The prize is taken into Sackets Harbor and soon after, the *Lady Murray* becomes a supply boat and a dispatch boat.

In other activity, the brigantine *Christiana* (C. Finley, master) is intercepted by two British warships, the HMS *Borer* and the HMS *Wasp*. At the time of its capture, the *Christiana* had with it a captured privateer, the *Teazer*. The *Teazer* had earlier recaptured the copper-bottomed *Margaret* seized by the HMS *Plumper* (Captain Bray) after it had sailed for England without its crew knowing that the war had begun. Also, before its capture, the *Teazer* had overtaken fourteen vessels, including six brigantines, six schooners and two ships. Of the prizes, only one failed to make it to an American port. British records at Halifax list this capture of the *Teazer*, which makes it a separate privateer than the *Teazer* seized in December 1812 by the HMS *San Domingo* and the *Young Teazer* that engages the HMS *La Hogue* during July 1813.

In other naval activity, the ship *Loyal Sam* is intercepted and recaptured by two British privateers, the *Matilda* and the *Sir John Sherbrooke*. Also on or about this day, the USS *Essex*, commanded by Captain David Porter, arrives at La Plata. It has landed at numerous places but found no fresh water. Captain Porter later relates some of his thoughts on La Plata:

> The only birds we found here were boobies, and man-of-war hawks. We saw no seals on or about the island, and only two turtles at some distance from the shore. No animals or their traces were discovered on the shore; and the aspect of the whole island was the most desolate imaginable. It is about eight miles in circumference, and offers no advantages whatever, that

I could discover, to induce navigators to touch there. Although it is represented to have been a favourite resort for the buccaneers, who stopped there for the purpose of watching the Spanish fleets, I am induced to believe that the want of anchorage would have prevented their using it for that purpose.

June 17 (Thursday) **In Ohio,** at Fort Meigs, by this time, the fort's damage caused by Proctor's unsuccessful attack has been repaired and the garrison had increased the clearing to the front of the post. However, during this entire month and the following month, the garrison is struck by a more powerful enemy — sickness. Through July, the troops suffer from fevers, dysentery and other illnesses that kill several men per day. Within about six weeks, more than 100 troops die. In the meantime, a Frenchman attached to Colonel Dudley's command who was captured and escaped from Amherstburg informs General Green Clay that the British are gathering a large force to spring another attack against Fort Meigs. Word is passed to General Harrison and reinforcements begin to move to the post.

In naval activity, three British warships, the HMS *Acasta,* HMS *Valiant* and the HMS *Wasp* intercept and seize the 330-ton brigantine *Porcupine,* which is transporting a cargo of brandy, dry goods, wine and other items from Bayonne, New Jersey, to Boston.

June 18 (Friday) **In Pennsylvania,** late in the day, five vessels arrive at Erie from Buffalo to bolster Oliver H. Perry's naval force. With the new arrivals, Perry's force is composed of the 20-gun *Lawrence* and the 20-gun *Niagara,* along with eight other smaller vessels which carry from one to four guns for a total of 55 guns.

In naval activity, the USS *Argus* embarks on a special mission. It is assigned to transport the minister to France, William H. Crawford, to France. The vessel completes the journey without incident and arrives off L'Orient on 11 July. Several days later, on the 14th, the *Argus* cruises in and near the English Channel. On 14 August it encounters the HMS *Pelican.*

In other activity, the 189-ton schooner *Eunice* (A.R. Riggs, master), transporting a cargo of salt from St. Ubes to Boston, is caught and captured by the HMS *Wasp.* The brigantine *Manchester* sails into trouble when it is recaptured by a British squadron comprising the HMS *Maidstone,* HMS *Nimrod* and the HMS *Poictiers.* Also, the British privateer *Matilda* seizes the sloop *Packet.* This *Packet* is separate from the sloop *Packet* seized on 10 April 1813 and another *Packet* (ship) seized at an undetermined time during 1812.

Also, a British squadron — the HMS *Barrossa,* HMS *Junon,* HMS *Mohawk,* HMS *Marlborough,* HMS *Narcissus* and the HMS *Victorious* — seizes the 292-ton ship *Protectress* (W. Jeffrey, master), which on its way to Lisbon, Portugal, from Norfolk with a cargo of flour.

June 19 (Saturday) *In naval activity,* the USS *Essex* and the other ships, former prizes, arrive at St. Close, known also as Deadman's Island in the mouth of the Gulf (or Bay) of Guayaquil. Its topography resembles "a corpse with its head lying to the westward." Captain David Porter notes: "It is equally desolate in its appearance with the island of La Plata." Porter's flotilla moves to the Tumbez River at the southern side of the gulf and anchors in about five and one-half fathoms of water. Shortly after dropping anchor, Captain Porter requests that Captain Randall go into Tumbez, carrying an expensive present for the governor, to inquire about the reception he would be willing to give, and with a personal invitation from Captain Porter to come aboard the *Essex.*

In other activity, Captain Oliver H. Perry's flotilla arrives safely at Erie from Buffalo by evading a British squadron under Captain Finnie. The British arrive, but too late. Perry's vessels had crossed the bar just before Finnie's squadron appeared.

June 20 (Sunday) **In New York,** the Americans repulse a British attack against their positions near Oswego.

In Ohio, British General Henry Proctor, bolstered by Indians under Tecumseh, launches yet another attack to reduce Fort Meigs, commanded by General William Henry Harrison. Proctor's strategy, following his failed attack of April–May 1813, is to draw the Americans outside the fort. However, Harrison does not take the bait and yet again Proctor fails. His force, including Indians, totals about 5,000, but his superior strength is insufficient to outsmart Harrison. Proctor, after being rebuffed at Fort Meigs, turns his attention toward another American post, Fort Stephenson along the Sandusky River at present-day Fremont.

General Harrison, before departing Fort Meigs, places General Green Clay in command. Afterward, Harrison concentrates on trying to regain the territory relinquished by General William Hull, who earlier surrendered Detroit and the entire Michigan Territory without a fight.

In naval activity, the 89-ton schooner *Henry* (J. Merryman, master) en route from Passamaquaddy, Maine, to Boston with a cargo of boards, is intercepted and recaptured by the British privateer *Matilda.* The *Henry* is separate from the ship *Henry* seized 11 August 1812.

June 20–21 **In Virginia,** the HMS *Junon,* attached to Admiral Cockburn's fleet, approaches Norfolk; however, U.S. vessels turn it back. On the following day, the British move toward Newport News. The American commanders believe that the main objective of the British fleet is Craney Island at the mouth of the Elizabeth River. The British are aware that Craney Island is strategically located; it dominates the sea route from Hampton Roads to Norfolk.

June 22 (Tuesday) **In Virginia,** a British fleet encroaches Craney Island, a defensive position of the Americans for the protection of Norfolk. American defenders on the island, including those who arrived on the 21st, include 400 infantry of the line, a contingent of riflemen led by Captain Roberts of Winchester, and two companies of artillery, commanded by Captain Arthur Emerson and Captain Richardson. Lt. Colonel H. Beatty retains overall command, supported by Major Wagner, an infantry officer and Major Falkner, an artillery officer. Other units that arrive on the 21st include a 30-man contingent of regulars from Fort Norfolk and a 30-man contingent of militia from Isle of Wight County under Lt. Atkinson of Culpeper Country. Other reinforcements include a contingent of about 150 sailors and U.S. Marines attached to the U.S. *Constellation,* which is blockaded; however, its guns continue to protect Craney Island.

In naval activity, the American privateer *Yankee* intercepts the British sloop *Earl Camden* just off the coast of Ireland. The vessel is captured and taken into a French port. Within about one week, the *Yankee* intercepts another vessel, the brigantine *Elizabeth,* which is also caught just off the coast. The prize and its cargo of cotton are taken into a French port, and on the same day, the *Yankee* captures yet another vessel, the brigantine *Watson,* also transporting a cargo of cotton. The combined value of the two cotton cargoes is about $140,000.

About 100 seamen under Lt. Neale and about one-half that number of Marines under Lt. Breckenridge, deployed on the island, open fire on the barges, which are transporting about 2,500 troops, including sailors and Royal Marines. The American fire is bolstered by the guns of the USS *Constellation* and creates havoc on the sea. Effective fire rips into the closing flotilla and casualties begin to rapidly rise. Admiral Warren is aboard one of the larger barges, the *Centipede.* American fire becomes so horrific that the vessel is essentially shredded, leaving only a short time for the troops aboard and the admiral to abandon it. Finally, the British realize that the American fire is too intense. The boats abort the landing and row back to the ships.

In the meantime, another British contingent of about 800 troops is debarked at a point from which they can advance against Norfolk from the ground. However, here, too, the British encounter unexpected stiff resistance. Virginians patiently observe the landing, and before the entire contingent touches Virginia soil, they are struck by an avalanche of effective fire from six separate guns deployed as a battery. The thunderclap prompts the Redcoats to retreat; however, some deploy in a nearby house. By then an American gunboat arrives to augment the battery. Incoming 24-pounders descend on the targeted house and it is immediately abandoned. The British head for their boats. In a flash they are also returning to the ships. The British boats had been commanded by Captain John M. Hanchett (natural son of King George III) of the HMS *Diadem.* Hanchett receives a serious wound to his thigh.

The failure to take Norfolk infuriates the British, who quickly select a new objective, Hampton, less than 20 miles distant. The British intend to redeem their honor by seizing Hampton, thereby severing communications between Hampton and the upper region of Virginia. At the time, Georgia militia are stationed at Norfolk and they observe the action but do not participate. Brigadier General Joseph F. Dickinson of Hertford County holds responsibility for the levies at Norfolk. Also, General Robert Williams of Surry County, as adjutant-general of the state, holds responsibilities of Norfolk's defenses.

After the British leave Chesapeake, the Georgians return to their home state. British casualties are estimated at about 200, excluding prisoners taken and a number of deserters. The Americans sustain no casualties.

In other naval activity, the HMS *Martin*, accompanied by two other warships, the *Spartan* and the *Statira*, intercept and seize the brigantine *Carlotta* (J. DeLonza Carvatho Souza, master), which is en route from Puerto Rico to Philadelphia with a cargo of coffee and rice; however, the vessel is also carrying money. In a separate incident, the *Gustava* (C. Swenburg, master) — a 128-ton brigantine en route from Boston to Madeira, Portugal, with a cargo of beef, pork, gin, butter, tar and other items — is intercepted and seized by the HMS *Sylph*. The *Gustava* is separate from the *Gustava* seized on 22 January 1814. Also, the HMS *Wasp* seizes the brigantine *Thomas*. The *Thomas* is separate from the *Thomas and Sally* seized on 26 May 1813 and the schooner *Thomas* captured 30 June 1813. The American privateer *Yankee* continues to cruise off the Irish coast.

In yet other naval activity, the USS *Essex* remains in port at St. Close (Deadman's Island) in the mouth of the Gulf of Guayaquil. Captain Randall, who went ashore on the 19th, can be seen from the decks during his return to report to Captain Porter aboard the *Essex*. Nevertheless, some other people are seen with Randall when his boat crosses the bar of the river. One of the unidentified people is wearing a uniform. The visitors turn out to be the governor of Tumbez, the collector of customs and one other, an elderly man who represented himself as the godfather of the governor and of the governor's son. Captain Porter later describes the party as it approaches the *Essex*: "Although the appearance of the whole was as wretched as can well be imagined, policy induced me to show them every attention; and, to impress them with a belief of my friendly disposition and respect, I gave them a salute of nine guns on their coming aboard." The party remains on the *Essex* until the following day and receives Porter's constant attention, while the visitors also manage to keep themselves under the eyes of the crew; however, with the latter, there is unabated quiet laughter due to their appearance. On the 23rd, Captain Porter visits the village of Tumbez.

June 23 (Wednesday) **In Canada,** General John Boyd at Fort George dispatches a contingent of about 400 men, which is later reinforced with about 150 additional troops. Boyd had taken command there after General Morgan Lewis (temporary successor to General Henry Dearborn) had departed for Sackets Harbor. The force, led by Lt. Colonel Charles G. Boerstler (14th U.S. Infantry), advances to seize a British supply depot at Beaver Dam, about 15 miles from the fort and less than ten miles southwest of Queenston. The column departs after dusk with the intent to strike by surprise the following morning. Nevertheless, the British are informed of the column's advance. Boerstler's voice, particularly loud, is heard across the river and suddenly the secret is out.

A Canadian militia captain, James Secord, after hearing of Beaver Dam as a target, insists on getting word to the commander there, Lieutenant (later captain) James Fitzgibbon; however, he is not well enough to make the trek due to a wound sustained at Queenston. His wife, Laura, volunteers to deliver the message. She is intercepted in the woods by Indians, but after conveying the purpose of her trip, she is guided to Fitzgibbon and forewarns him of the imminent attack. After thanking her profusely and urging her to get some rest, the British immediately prepare to intercept the Americans. Just as the column arrives at the town of Thorold, it hits an ambush established by more than 400 Indians led by John Brant (son of Chief Joseph Brant), who is accompanied by Captain Kerr. The Indians include Caughnawaga under Lorimer and Decharme.

The column absorbs the shock without losing

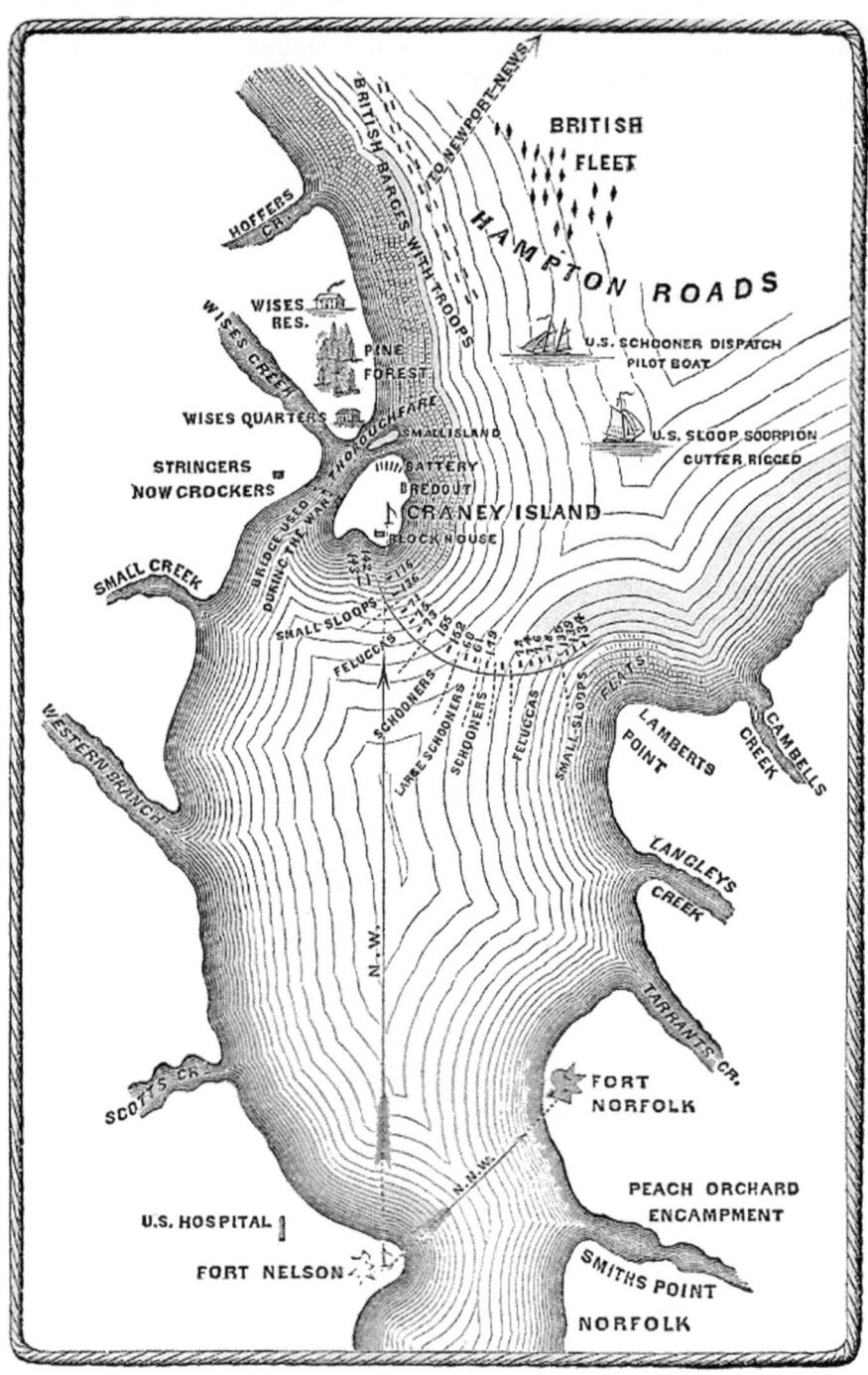

Craney Island operations.

its discipline and it reacts by dashing into the woods from where the fire had originated. Nonetheless, the cunning Indians, always prepared to evade the bayonet, take flight, not to retreat; rather to reposition themselves from where they can spring another unexpected attack. Suddenly, Boerstler's command faces a new assault with the Indians using the brush for concealment. Boerstler's troops return fire and they are able to forestall capitulation, but after several hours, the attackers finally compel the Americans to pull back. Boerstler moves toward an open field where he can regroup while awaiting for reinforcements to arrive and extricate his force; however, before he reaches the field, Canadian militia arrives. Undaunted, the Americans do reach the field, when at about the same time, a British 47-man contingent of regulars led by Lt. Fitzgibbon arrives. By this time, Boerstler's troops are beginning to believe their new positions are untenable unless the relief force arrives.

In the meantime, Lieutenant Fitzgibbon scatters his small force to create the illusion that he has arrived with a large detachment. He dispatches a messenger to issue an ultimatum for surrender. Fitzgibbon's message implies that his force is only the vanguard of a massive 1,500 man contingent that is close behind, and Boerstler is also informed that about 700 Indians are accompanying the main body.

After considering his options and concluding that it would be impossible to break through such a large enemy force, Boerstler agrees to capitulate with the condition that his troops receive parole and be allowed to return to the United States. The British agree. Shortly thereafter, British Major P.W. DeHaren arrives with about 200 troops. Five hundred and forty-two men are taken prisoner, along with two artillery pieces and the flag of the 14th Regiment. Before the ink on the surrender papers dries, the document becomes meaningless. One of the officers present, Major Chapin, describes the scene: "The articles of capitulation were no sooner signed than they were violated. The Indians immediately commenced their depredations, and plundered the officers of their side arms. The soldiers, too, were stripped of every article of clothing to which the savages took a fancy, such as hats, coats, shoes, etc." The British permit the Indians to run rampant and they also ignore the surrender document. The militia becomes enraged. The British guards do not anticipate violence from their prisoners, but they are attacked by the militia and overwhelmed. Many of the militia break for freedom and they take some guards along with them.

The British actions against their captives cause enormous consternation in the United States and inadvertently become the last straw with regard to the president's patience with General Dearborn. President Madison replaces Dearborn with General James Wilkinson.

In naval activity, Captain David Porter, who received the governor of Tumbez as a guest (22nd–23rd) on the USS *Essex*, goes ashore to visit Tumbez. The governor has been friendly; however, Porter leans heavily on the side of caution due to his knowledge of their past practices of "treachery." During the trip from the *Essex* to shore, Captain Porter takes notice of the terrain and of the crops as well as the houses. He notices that the houses are "formed of reeds, covered with rushes, open at all sides, and having the floor elevated about four feet from the earth, to protect them from the alligators, which are here numerous and of an enormous size." He arrives at the village at 1100, expecting a casual day, but in the event something unexpected occurs, his boat crew is heavily armed and plans are in place to provide protection if a retreat becomes necessary.

Captain Porter is received like royalty as he moves about in the village, and the possibility of the governor becoming treacherous fades away; however, Captain Porter does come under intense pressure. While acquiescing to the request to come into the houses, he is in the company of the respective families, but he is also under attack. The people share their huts with, as Porter describes, "hogs, dogs, fowls, jackasses, men, women and children." Consequently, Captain Porter is attacked by fleas at every stop. He also mentions that the governor's house "was no more exempt from this plague than those of the plebeians [lower class]." Nonetheless, Porter gets back to the ship and apparently without bringing back an invasion of fleas. On the following day (24th), the lookouts spot three vessels moving into the bay.

June 24 (Thursday) *In naval activity,* the British privateer *Dart* intercepts and seizes a sloop, the *Experiment* (J. Boardman, master), which is transporting a cargo of coffee and other articles from Machias, Maine, to Portsmouth, Maine. The prize is taken into port at New Brunswick. The *Experiment* is separate from the *Experiment* seized 13 May 1814 or the sloop *Experiment* captured 21 January 1815. Also, the 413-ton ship *Herman*, sailing from Baltimore, Maryland, to Lisbon, Portugal, with a cargo of flour, is encountered by a large British squadron that includes the HMS *Atalante, Diadem, Diomede, Emulous, Laurestinus, Mohawk, Moselle, Narcissus, Success* and *Victorius*, leaving little chance of continuing its voyage. The *Herman* and its cargo are seized.

In other naval activity, the HMS *Bold* intercepts and seizes the 110-ton brigantine *Maria* (G. Wierman, master) which is en route from Stockholm to Boston. The prize is taken into port at New Brunswick. The *Maria* is separate from a ketch named *Maria* captured during 1812, the ship *Maria* seized 3 July 1812, the *Maria Windsor*, seized on 29 March 1813, the brigantine *Maria Francisca* captured 4 May 1814, the brigantine *Maria Frederica* seized on 14 July 1814, and the schooner *Maria* captured on 4 September 1814. Also, the HMS *Tenedos* intercepts and captures the 177-ton brigantine *North Star*, which is en route from St. Salvadore to Boston with a cargo including brandy, sugar, tea and other items.

June 24–30 *In naval activity,* the lookouts aboard the USS *Essex* spot three vessels moving into the bay at St. Close. Tension eases when the vessels reach a point less than six miles apart. One of the vessels hoists a "private signal" which informs Captain Porter that it is the *Georgiana*. Shortly thereafter, Porter is greeting Lt. Downes when he is welcomed aboard the *Essex*. Downes arrives with good news. The *Georgiana*, while off James Island, had captured several British vessels, the 11-gun *Hector* (crew of 25 men), the 8-gun *Catherine* (crew of 29 men) and the 8-gun *Rose* (crew of 21 men). The new prizes are added to Porter's squadron, bringing it up to nine ships. Captain Porter makes some rather quick adjustments to the squadron. The *Atlantic*, far superior to the *Georgiana*, receives a face-lift. Captain Porter directs that it be mounted with 20 guns. Porter also transfers Lt. Downes and his crew from the *Georgiana* to the *Atlantic*. Meanwhile, Mr. Adams assumes command of the *Georgiana*. The *Atlantic* also receives a new name. Captain Porter gives it the name *Essex Jr.*, and according to himself, he also "appoints Midshipman Dashiel sailing master." Captain Porter directs that the *Essex Jr.* be mounted with 20 guns. Thanks to his extra manpower (volunteers from his prizes) a crew of 60 men is assigned to it.

Nonetheless, the *Essex Jr.* remains an important concern of Captain Porter due to its unreadiness for a tedious cruise, and he is also faced with some difficulty due to the large number of prisoners that have accumulated. With regard to the latter, including the various captains, Captain Porter, at their successive requests, provides them with several boats, along with provisions sufficient to last for three months, and permits them to go ashore at Tumbez. All items taken earlier from the captains, including Wier, the South Carolinian, are returned. Captain Porter, having relieved himself of the prisoners, weighs anchor on 30 June. The *Essex* remains close to the *Essex Jr.* until Captain Porter is convinced that its modifications and repairs are complete.

June 25 (Friday) **In Alabama,** General Wilkinson arrives at the residence of Sam Nac, the brother-in-law of the prophet Josiah Francis. Wilkinson, aware of the dangers of passing through Creek territory, remains determined to reach Georgia.

In Virginia, a British fleet, recently repelled at Norfolk, arrives off Hampton, across the Chesapeake Bay about 16 miles from Norfolk. At dawn, a force of about 2,500 men, commanded by General Sir Sydney Beckwith, is taken to shore by boats and landed slightly below Hampton. While the troops are in the process of landing, a number of British boats, one of which is transporting Admiral Cockburn, moves in close to shore along with the HMS *Mohawk*, which shepherds the boats to initiate a bombardment. Meanwhile, the U.S. garrison at Hampton, composed of fewer than 600 troops under Major Crutchfield, prepares to defend. A pair of Crutchfield's artillery pieces begins to pound the boats as they move into range. The fire is effective and the British pull back and maneuver to a position to the rear of some land from where they can reinitiate the bombardment from concealed positions. The tactic keeps the British from being fired upon; however, the British fire becomes erratic and ineffective. Nonetheless, the British guns continue to fire for about one hour. In the meantime, the ground troops had begun to ad-

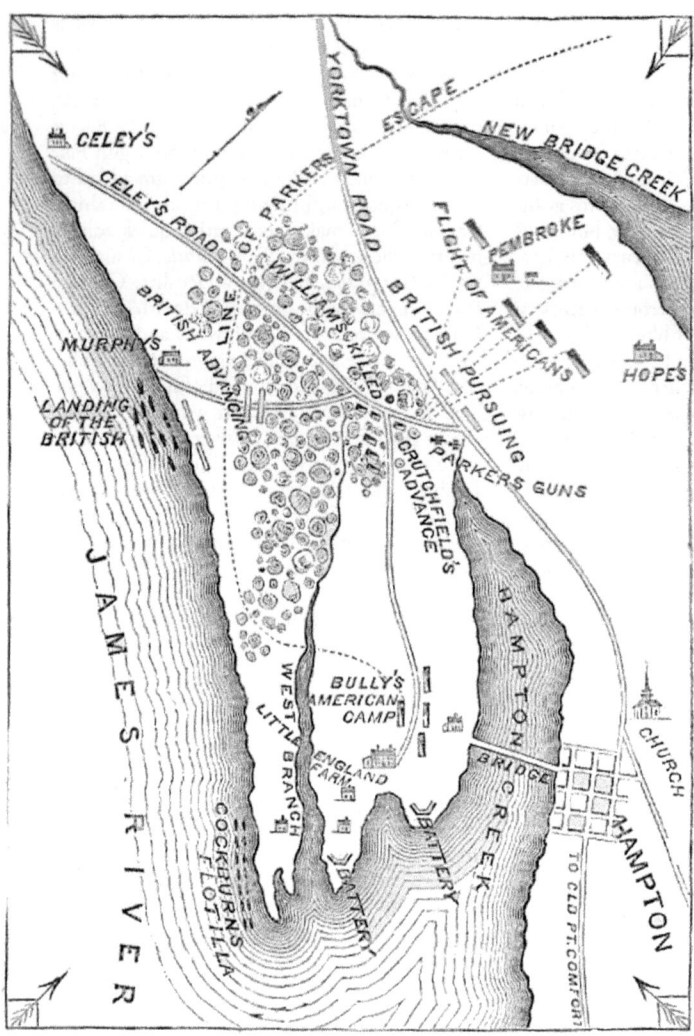

Plan of operations at Hampton.

vance against the town, unaware that Major Crutchfield had dispatched a detachment of riflemen to establish a blocking point along the road leading to Hampton.

As the British march toward Hampton, they approach the spot where Captain Servant's riflemen are holding formidable concealed positions and the woods spring to life as small arms fire strikes unexpectedly. The British, once again, after attempting to land in Virginia, find themselves facing a disciplined foe that does not easily collapse. While the riflemen are impeding the progress of the column, Major Crutchfield concludes that the British barges will not resume their approach until the ground troops secure Hampton. Consequently, Crutchfield leaves only a small contingent to hold the post while he leads the remainder of the garrison to join with the riflemen. During the trek, the British surprise his column when they fire from concealed positions. Undaunted, Crutchfield orders a charge to clear the woods, only to be again surprised when British artillery commences fire. Crutchfield's column collapses under the withering fire and the British succeed in driving some of the Americans from the field, while the remainder brave the fire and fight their way to hook up with Servant's riflemen.

British pressure continues to increase; however, still Major Crutchfield continues to rally his troops. He receives some help from a small detachment of cavalry under Captain Cooper, who maintains pressure on the left flank of the British. Nonetheless, the superior numbers of the Redcoats eventually compel the Americans to surrender ground. Meanwhile, at the American battery, held by Captain Pryor, the British barges continue to be stymied by his six artillery pieces, but here too, pressure mounts. By the time the Redcoats reach a point about 60 yards from the rear of the battery, Pryor, aware that his position is becoming untenable, directs his troops to disable the guns and prepare to abandon the battery. The situation quickly becomes more dangerous for the men at the battery.

British Marines are closing fast and expect a quick surrender. However, Pryor, having silenced his guns, bellows his order, which directs his troops to abandon the battery, but not by retiring his order instructs the men to advance and crash through the approaching Marines. The troops require no second order. They bolt from their positions as if propelled by a cannon, to the amazement of the British Marines. In a flash, the American gunners pass straight through the Marines' formation, so quickly that the British fail to capture any of Pryor's command, nor are they able to even wound a single American. To further exasperate the British, Pryor completes his embarrassment of the British by jumping into a creek. Every man in his command follows and those carrying rifles or pistols manage to also get them to the opposite bank. The Redcoats initiate pursuit, but without success.

The British also fail to seize Crutchfield's column during its retreat. The column pauses at various spots to fire upon the pursuers. After chasing Crutchfield for about two miles, the pursuit is terminated. During the fighting, the British, who secure Hampton, sustain 90 men killed and 120 wounded. The Americans sustain 7 killed, 12 wounded and 12 missing.

After occupying Hampton, the British repeat their cruel actions. The town is ransacked and pillaged during a rampage that continues unabated for two days. The townspeople are all victimized. Women, children and even the aged are not spared from the depredations that have been reported as inhuman as any acts by the Indians on the frontiers. Nonetheless, none of the houses are burned and only two homes had been preserved without harm, those chosen as quarters for the officers. The scene in Hampton as described by Rossiter Johnson, a nineteenth century historian: "In one case an old and infirm citizen was murdered in the presence of his aged wife; and when it remonstrated, a soldier presented a pistol at her breast and shot her dead. Women with infants in their arms were pursued till they threw themselves into the river to escape, children were wantonly killed, and such shameful scenes were enacted as cannot even be mentioned in a history written for youth."

Some of the other obscenities committed by the invading force including leaving dead bodies where they fell, and violating women and instigating the slaves to violate their mistresses. The British are also accused of murdering some sick people who had been confined to their beds. and they even pillage the Episcopalian (Anglican or Church of England) church at Hampton. They confiscate and carry off the church's communion table and pulpit. Before the British depart Hampton, they destroy all of the town's medical supplies, which places the sick and the wounded in danger. When they do depart, a number of slaves are taken aboard the ships to be sold in the West Indies. The devastation inflicted upon the town and the depredations sustained by the citizens ignites fury among the Americans.

General Robert R. Taylor, the commander of the district, sends a terse message to British Admiral Warren asking whether the British officers had condoned the atrocities of the troops who had occupied Hampton. Taylor also inquired whether the British command intended to punish the violators. The letter sparks additional correspondence after it is forwarded by Warren to General Beckwith. Taylor receives an answer: the British claim the ill treatment was retaliation for Americans having shot British troops who were in the water after their boats were shot up at Craney Island off Norfolk. The allegation is investigated and proven false. Some Americans had actually gone into the water to help save British troops and none were fired upon, except one soldier who attempted to join up with the troops who landed. The findings also indicate that the man in question had not been killed. The results of Taylor's investigation are forwarded to the British. Taylor's message is forwarded to General Beckwith, where it dies. No response is sent back to General Taylor.

In Connecticut, General Jirah Isham directs the lieutenant colonels of each of the regiments in his brigade (3rd Connecticut) to release about one-half of the men and officers of the respective regiments. The order instructs the men to return to their homes. However, the rest of his militia brigade remains on active service.

In naval activity, a schooner encroaches the British blockading squadron that is holding the line off New London and it explodes, causing the destruction of some British boats and some fatalities. Captain Hardy, the commander of the squadron, places the blame on Commodore Decatur's squadron, which is hemmed in at New London.

June 26 (Saturday) **In Ohio,** General Harrison, while moving northward, encounters Colonel William P. Anderson, who is moving from Upper Sandusky to reinforce Fort Meigs with his U.S. 24th Regiment, along with a contingent of the U.S. 17th Regiment under Major George Croghan and a detachment of cavalry led by Colonel Ball. After conferring with Anderson, 300 troops are detached and ordered to initiate a forced march due to gained intelligence that a large mass of hostile Indians had arrived near the post. In the meantime, a force under Colonel Richard Johnson is en route from Fort Winchester to Fort Meigs. The horses in Johnson's command had been exhausted from the constant patrols, which force the colonel to leave many at the fort.

In naval activity, in reaction to an incident the day before in which a schooner exploded near a British squadron, a proclamation is issued and sent ashore: "The inhabitants of Stonington, New-London, and the vicinity, are hereby informed, that after this date, no boat of any description shall be suffered to approach or pass his Britannic majesty's squadron, lying off New-London, flags of truce excepted. Given, on board his Majesty's ship *Ramllies*, the 16th June 1813. T.M. HARDY, Capt."

In other naval activity, the HMS *Woolwick* intercepts and seizes the 267-ton brigantine *Santiago* while it is en route from Salem, Massachusetts, to Malaga, Spain, with a cargo of bacon, beef, tobacco and other items. Also, the British privateer *Dart* intercepts and captures the 231-ton ship *Union*, which is en route to Cadiz, Spain, from Boston. The prize is taken into port at New Brunswick. The *Union* is separate from the brigantine *Union* seized on 14 August 1812, the ship *Union* captured 16 August 1812, the schooner *Union* seized 14 October 1812, the schooner *Union* captured on 19 October 1812, the schooner *Union* seized 3 April 1813, and the schooner *Union* captured 30 July 1814.

June 27 (Sunday) **In Virginia,** the British fleet under Admiral Cockburn departs from Hampton after pillaging the town. The naval force sails from the Chesapeake toward North Carolina. In other naval activity, the HMS *Loup Cervier* intercepts and seizes the schooner *Little Bill*, which is en route from St. Bartholemew's to North Carolina. Also, the HMS *Boxer* seizes the 86-ton schooner *Rebecca* (G. Vaughan, master), which had left New York with a cargo of flour. The prize is taken into port at New Brunswick. The *Rebecca* is separate from the *Rebecca* seized on 27 July 1813 and the *Rebecca* overtaken 3 August 1813.

June 28 (Monday) **In Louisiana** at Baton Rouge, General Ferdinand Claiborne is ordered by General Flournoy to repair to Fort Stoddert, Alabama. Claiborne's command numbers about 550 troops; however, the federal government supplies no financial help.

In Ohio, General William Henry Harrison arrives at Fort Meigs and discovers that Colonel Johnson, sent by General Clay, had already arrived with a contingent of about 150 cavalry troops. Harrison instructs Johnson to initiate a reconnaissance mission to the Raisin River. The cavalry during the mission encounters no enemy presence; however, it does inadvertently succeed in delaying a band of Indians that had departed Amherstburg en route to disrupt American forces wherever they can be found.

In naval activity, the HMS *Dover* seizes the schooner *Harriet* (A. Winnerholt, master) as it carries a cargo of oil and sealskins from Newfoundland to London. The *Harriet* is separate from the brigantine *Harriet* seized on 8 June 1813 and the sloop *Harriet* seized on 13 July 1813. The HMS *Dover* is also known to have seized a brigantine, the *Roscio*; however, the exact date during 1813 is unknown.

In other naval activity, the HMS *Boxer* captures the schooner *Nancy* while it is at anchor in Little River harbor. The *Nancy* is separate from the ship *Nancy* seized on 17 August 1812, the schooner *Nancy* seized on 28 May 1813, the sloop *Nancy* captured on 28 July 1814, the brigantine *Nancy* seized sometime 1–18 September 1814 and the brigantine *Nancy* captured on 13 September 1814.

June 29 (Tuesday) **In New York** at Albany, Governor Tompkins directs General Rose to bolster the troops at Sag Harbor: "Dear Sir: If it has not already been done, will you please to order into the service of the United States forthwith, a Company of 100 men, including officers, for the defence of Sag Harbour or other parts of Suffolk County."

In naval activity, the HMS *Persian*, while involved in an encounter with the American privateer *Saucy Jack*, succinctly and unexpectedly terminates its chase. It is wrecked on the Silver Keys, ending its service, while extending the sealife of the *Saucy Jack*.

June 30 (Wednesday) *In naval activity,* a terrific storm moves into the region. The schooner USS *Alligator*, while operating in Port Royal Sound, is overwhelmed and 23 men drown. This *Alligator* is separate from the schooner USS *Alligator* which is commissioned during March 1821 and the *Alligator* also dubbed Gunboat No. 166. The HMS *Dover* intercepts and seizes the ship *Liverpool Packet* (S. Nichols, master). The *Liverpool Packet* is separate from the British privateer *Liverpool Packet*.

The HMS *La Hogue* intercepts and seizes the 184-ton brigantine Minerva (T. Patterson, master) on its way from Boston to Lisbon, Portugal, with a cargo of beef, pork and staves. The *Minerva* is separate from the brigantine *Minerva* seized on 6 July 1812, the ship *Minerva* captured 8 September 1812, the sloop *Minerva* seized on 5 August 1813, the schooner *Minerva* overtaken 30 August 1813, the brigantine *Minerva* seized 21 April 1814, the schooner *Minerva* captured on 11 August 1814, and the schooner *Minerva* captured on 26 September 1814.

In other naval activity, the HMS *Nymphe* intercepts and captures the schooner *Thomas*. This vessel is separate from the brigantine *Thomas* seized 22 June 1813 and the brigantine *Thomas and Sally* seized 26 May 1813. Also, the HMS *Majestic* encounters the 248-ton brigantine *Ulysses* and terminates its voyage. The *Ulysses* and its cargo of cotton en route to Bordeaux, France, from Savannah, Georgia, are seized. The *Ulysses* is separate from the brigantine *Ulysses* overtaken 20 April 1813. Also, the American privateer *Yankee* captures two brigantines, the 2-gun *Elizabeth* and the *Watson*, both of which are carrying cargoes of cotton with a combined value of more that $100,000. Both prizes are taken into port at France.

Late June **In Connecticut,** Brigadier General Henry Burbeck arrives in New London to assume command of that district on behalf of the United States federal government. At the time of his arrival, about 800 men are on duty in the militia. The militia in Connecticut is under the orders of only the governor, John Cotton Smith (Federalist, former lieutenant governor), who assumed the office in October upon the death of Governor Roger Griswold. The government in Connecticut at this time does not release its militia to the federal government to ensure it remains in Connecticut to defend the state. Burbeck, pursuant to orders from Secretary of State James Monroe, dismisses the entire militia force on 12 July. However, Burbeck retains the guard under Lt. Horatio G. Lewis at Stonington. Nevertheless, two primary posts, Fort Griswold and Fort Trumbull, are left totally undefended.

Summer to Autumn With the increasing hostilities by the creeks, stockades are being constructed in the Mississippi Valley. These include some which had been built before 1813. These forts include Fort St. Stephens on the west bank of the Tombigbee River (established during early 1700s by the French and afterward held by the Spanish and Americans); Fort Stoddert, built by Americans during 1799 less than five miles from Mount Vernon; Fort Charlotte, built at Mobile; Fort Mims; Fort Pierce, about two miles southeast of Fort Mims; Fort Glass, built across the Alabama River in Clark County on the property of Zacharia Glass; Fort Madison at the eastern boundary of Clarke County near Fort Glass; Fort Sinquefield, on the western side of Bassett's Creek about 10 miles north of Fort Madison; Fort White, just outside of present-day Grove Hill; Landrum's Fort, slightly west of Fort Sinquefield; Mott's Fort, near Landrum's Fort; Fort Easley, built near Wood's Bluff; Turner's Fort, near the home of Abner Turner on the west bend of the Tombigbee, near the Choctaw town of Turkey Town (Fakit Chipunta); Cato's Fort, built about five miles below Coffeeville; Rankin's Fort in Washington County; McGrew's Fort, about 3 miles north of Fort St. Stephen's; Fort Carney; Powell's Fort, built near Oven Bluff several miles south of Fort Carney; Lavier's Fort (sometimes erroneously referred to as Rivier's Fort), which

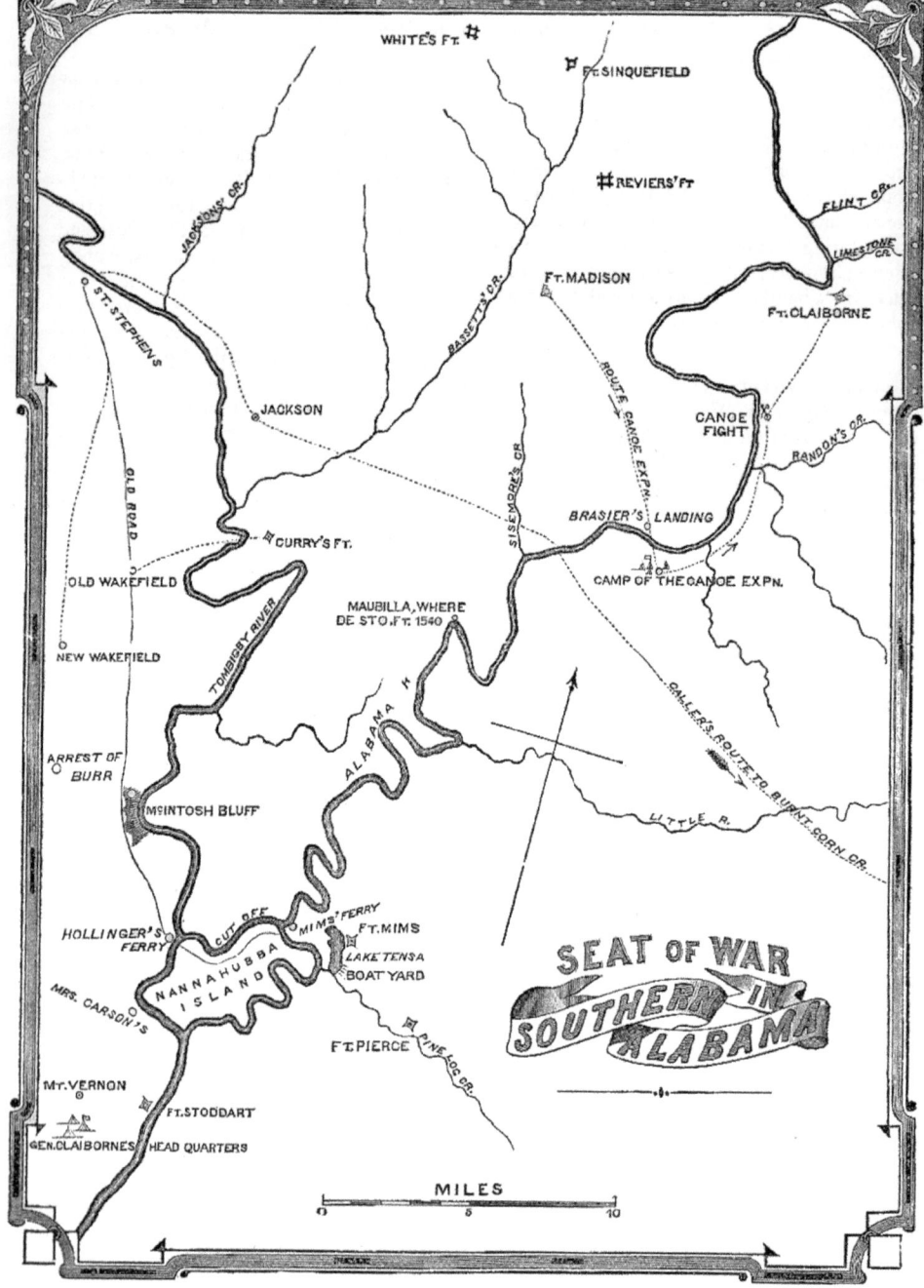

Seat of war in Southern Alabama.

them in motion, to protect their rights and liberties, which our brethren, the Americans, are now defending." The declaration is signed by the Grand Councillors.

In Ohio, a contingent of troops under Major James V. Ball establishes Camp Ball along the Sandusky River at Tiffin. It is one of a series of supply posts established by General Harrison. The camp is not permanent. Following the close of hostilities, a house and a tavern is established on the site by Erastus Bowe.

In naval activity, the privateer *America* returns to Bath, Maine, following its cruise that began the previous January. During its time at sea, the *America* captures ten separate vessels. The prizes include an American vessel, the St. Lawrence, seized after it arrived at Portsmouth, New Hampshire, with a cargo of British goods. Three of the captured vessels are transformed into cartels to handle the large amount of prisoners. The *America* had captured 160 prisoners, and of those only 30 had been taken to the United States, the others (130) were released on parole and departed on the cartels. Two of the prizes had been recaptured before arriving at a friendly port and three others had been taken into French ports. The rest arrive at American ports.

In other naval activity, the American privateer *Matilda* spots a sail, and believing it to be a merchant ship, initiates pursuit, only to discover it is a British privateer, the *Lion*, equipped for 28 guns and carrying a crew of 120 men. The strength of the vessel remains unknown to the Americans, who catch up with it. Captain Rantin and nearly all of his officers bolt from the *Matilda* and board the *Lion*. Initially, many of the men aboard the *Lion* head for the lower deck; however, as the American officers look to their rear, none of the remainder of the crew had followed them, leaving their captain and the officers trapped.

Just after the boarding party arrives aboard what they expect to be their prize, the rough seas push the two vessels apart. The British quickly sense the hopelessness of the Americans that have no means of escape and no possibility of receiving any additional boarders. The British, suddenly rejuvenated, spring back into action and seize the officers. Immediately thereafter, the *Lion* moves alongside of the *Matilda* and the British compel the crew to surrender. During the engagement, the Americans lose between 20 and 30 killed, including Captain Rantin. The British transport the prisoners to Bahia, and from there, the Americans return to New York aboard the ship *William* (Captain Davis).

The Americans aboard the *Matilda*, having seized defeat from near-victory, do fare well. The Royal Navy shows little mercy to privateers, and unlike U.S. Navy sailors, privateers are rarely exchanged or set free. Luckily, they had been captured by a privateer, which probably had saved them from being sent to Dartmoor prison or some British prison ship. Although in war there is often uncertainty, and nearly all plans change once a mission is undertaken; on the sea, there is usually more uncertainty. In the case of the *Matilda*, the Americans lost the prize they were

was erected at an unknown location in Clarke County; and two forts are built at Mount Vernon where General Claiborne maintains his headquarters. Also, two other forts are built during this period in Mississippi (Wayne County), Patton's Fort at Winchester and Roger's Fort slightly more than five miles above the former.

July **In Iowa,** a work party of troops attached to Fort Madison is attacked by Indians. It is self-destroyed. About one week later the Indians again ambush a contingent of Rangers who are stationed at the construction of a nearby blockhouse. The raids intensify and by September, the decision is made by the commander, Lt. Thomas Hamilton, that the position had become untenable. The fort is set afire to distract the Indians and to cover the escape. After dusk, the garrison makes it to the boats and heads own the Mississippi.

In New York, the Six Nations declare war: "WE, the Chiefs and Councillors of the Six Nations of Indians, residing in the state of New-York, do hereby proclaim, to all the War-Chiefs, and Warriors of the Six Nations, that war is declared, on our part, against the provinces of Upper and Lower Canada. Therefore we do hereby command, and advise all the War-Chiefs to call forth, immediately, the Warriors under them, and put certain would be gained. After it is taken by the British, they immediately refit it and send it into England, however, while still in the Channel, the British lose their prize to the USS *Argus,* which returns to American control, only to be lost again to a 74-gun British ship-of-the-line. After its latest capture, again the *Matilda* is sent into England. Nonetheless, the voyage is cut short when the *Matilda* is intercepted by the American privateer *General Armstrong* and brought back into American control. The *General Armstrong,* having been the fourth vessel to seize the *Matilda,* succeeds in getting it to a friendly port to end its saga. The USS *Argus,* which initially recaptured the *Matilda,* is seized by the HMS *Pelican* the next month.

Early July **In Canada,** Major General De Rottenburg (former president of Lower Canada) succeeds Major General Sheaffe as lieutenant governor of the Upper Provinces. De Rottenburg assumes command of all troops under Major General John Vincent.

In naval activity, the American privateer Anaconda arrives at Ocracoke Inlet, North Carolina, where the privateer *Atlas* had arrived earlier.

July 1 (Thursday) **In Ohio,** General Harrison departs from Fort Meigs and heads eastward to check the forts along the lake as far as the Cuyahoga River. He also at about this time instructs Colonel Johnson to deploy his cavalry along the Huron River. The intelligence regarding an imminent attack against Fort Meigs has kept the entire frontier on the alert; however, no indication of a British or Indian force has yet been discovered.

In naval activity, the American privateer *Yankee* continues to operate near the Irish coast and snags yet another vessel, the schooner *Ceres.* Captain Elisha Snow determines that its cargo of fruit is of no value and permits the schooner to continue its voyage. Nonetheless, before the *Ceres* is allowed to move, the Americans confiscate some items. By this time, the British have become well aware of the ongoing threat of the *Yankee* against the Irish coast, prompting Captain Snow to prepare to depart and head back to the United States.

July 2 (Friday) **In Canada,** the British execute a small operation designed to destroy the stores at Sackets Harbor, and while there, the contingent is to set the vessel *Pike* on fire. During the operation, the contingent lands at the isthmus of Point Peninsula and conceals the boats in the brush. The plan goes awry when one man in the party deserts and sneaks off to the town. The Americans, once informed of the scheme, send out a force to intercept the raiders; however, they depart and make it back to Canada.

In New York, Major General Morgan Lewis arrives at Sackets Harbor to assume command. On the 6th, General Wilkinson will be appointed successor to General Dearborn.

July 3 (Saturday) *In naval activity,* the British privateer *Weazel* intercepts and seizes the schooner *Franklin* (H. Nickerson, master). The *Franklin* is separate from the sloop *Franklin* seized 23 November 1813.

July 4 (Sunday) **In Maryland,** Joshua Barney proposes constructing a small fleet of gunboats that could be flexible enough to take on the Royal Navy's blockade of Chesapeake Bay. His blueprint includes gunboats that can also be rowed to provide additional means of navigating the rivers and outmaneuvering the large warships of the British Navy. His plans are deemed bold, but at the time of crisis also pragmatic, and they are approved by William Jones, the secretary of the Navy, making Barney's fleet a temporary part of the U.S. Navy. Consequently, Barney, who had retired after the American Revolution, is reactivated. He will receive the rank of commodore.

A naval battery — a fort at St. Leonard's Creek — is established to provide protection of the gunboats on the Patuxent River. The fleet is constructed and will set sail from Baltimore in May of the following year. Also, the blockade has an effect on the privateers by preventing them from getting out on the open sea. One privateer, the *Patapsco,* is contracted at an unknown time by the U.S. Navy to patrol the lower sector of the bay and warn of any approach by British raiders. The *Patapsco* is also tasked with providing some protection for commercial shipping in the bay. Another privateer, the *Revenge* (fourth), is also confined by the blockade, and it is purchased by the navy to patrol in the lower bay with responsibilities similar to those of the *Patapsco.*

In Ohio, Colonel Johnson, while en route to the Huron River, halts at Fort Stephenson. His arrival coincidentally occurs while the garrison is celebrating the Fourth of July. He takes the opportunity to accept an invitation to speak and delivers an enthusiastic, heart-lifting speech that invigorates the garrison. Other posts along the frontier are also enjoying the celebration in honor of Independence Day. At Fort Meigs, the general order sets the tone: "The General commanding announces to the troops under his command the return of this day, which gave liberty and independence to the United States of America; and orders that a national salute be fired under the superintendence of Captains Gratiot and Cushing. All the troops reported fit for duty shall receive an extra gill of whisky. And those in confinement and those under sentence attached to the corps be forthwith released and ordered to join their respective corps."

In naval activity, the British privateer *Retaliation,* while cruising off the New England coast, intercepts and seizes the 43-ton sloop *Mary,* which is en route to Boston from Kennebec, Maine, with a cargo of glass, molasses, rice and other items. The prize is taken into port at Liverpool. This *Mary* is separate from likewise named vessels also captured: the 167-ton *Mary Elizabeth,* 8 July 1812; a brigantine, 17 July 1812; a schooner, 23 July 1812; a 97-ton schooner, 23 March 1813; a schooner, 23 March 1813; another schooner, on 27 March 1813; a sloop, 27 July 1813; a schooner, 7 August 1813; a schooner, 10 September 1813; a schooner, 13 September 1813; a sloop, 22 December 1813; another sloop, 6 January 1814; a ship, on 1 June 1814; and a 92-ton schooner, 6 October 1814.

July 4–9 *In naval activity,* Captain David Porter's squadron, while en route to Valparaiso, gets an opportunity to enjoy the Fourth of July celebration. Three of the ships, the *Essex, Essex Jr.* and the *Greenwich* fire a seventeen-gun salute to underscore the celebration of independence from Great Britain. In a sense, the British contribute to the celebration. Spirits taken from the prizes permit the ration of grog to be doubled for each crew member. The celebration goes well, but everyday business also continues. On the 9th, Captain Porter, convinced the *Essex Jr.* is ready to fly on its own, orders Lt. Downes to take it into Valparaiso, along with the American ship *Barclay* and the prizes *Catherine, Hector, Montezuma* and the *Policy.* Downes is ordered, once he arrives at Valparaiso, to leave the *Barclay* in port and sell the others. The USS *Essex* sails for the Galapagos after the *Essex Jr.* and the others move out of sight. The *Essex* sails in company with the *Georgiana* and the *Greenwich.*

Captain Porter is anxious to reach his destination due to recent intelligence informing him that several British warships had left Tumbez a short while before the Americans arrived there. The intelligence pinpoints that the destination of the British squadron had been the Galapagos. Part of Porter's strategy is to send the *Georgiana* back to the States after he reaches the destination in hope of having it arrive during the winter months to increase its chances of making port while the British, affected by the elements, would not be able to maintain their blockade with any great success.

July 5 (Monday) **In Canada,** a contingent of the British 49th Regiment, bolstered by about 35 militia troops, cross the Niagara River at dawn. After landing on the New York shore, they attack Fort Schlosser (present-day Niagara Falls) at the southern terminus of the Lewiston Portage. The British force, commanded by Lt. Colonel Thomas Clark (2nd Regiment, Lincoln Militia), springs the attack and catches the garrison by complete surprise, which permits the British to gain the post with little effort. The British seize some prisoners, a brass cannon as well as a huge supply of ammunition, small arms and other military supplies. In addition, the British seize one gunboat and two bateaux. Word of the attack spreads and militia flock to the post to intercept the intruders; however, the fire from the militia inflicts no harm. The British re-cross the river and return to Canada without sustaining any casualties.

In naval activity, a fishing boat, the *Yankee* (Master Percival), in New York Harbor becomes a temporary ship of war. The boat is used to fool a British warship, the sloop HMS *Eagle,* which hails the vessel as it moves down the bay. The British spot several men along with a goose, one sheep and one calf on the deck; however, after halting the *Yankee* near Sandy Hook, the British direct the vessel to report to the British commodore. Unknown to the British, the *Yankee* is also carrying 40 armed volunteers who bolt from their positions below deck when the signal

"Lawrence" is given. Before the British can react, they are stung by a volley that cuts down three of the crew, while the rest of the men on deck seek safety without returning fire. In what becomes a stunning accomplishment, the crew of the *Yankee* observes one of the British seamen aboard the *Eagle* entering the deck from the hold and strikes the colors without firing a single shot. Shortly thereafter, the British warship is approaching the battery when cheers begin to ring out from people there who are still celebrating the Fourth of July.

On the following day, J. Lewis, commander of the flotilla, sends a report to the secretary of the Navy:

> SIR, I have the pleasure to inform you of the capture of the British sloop tender [*Eagle*], which, for some time, had been employed by Com. Beresford, for the purpose of burning the coasters, &c. Her force was 2 officers, and 11 seamen, with a-32 brass howitzer. This service was performed, in a most gallant and officer like manner, by sailing-master Percival, who, with volunteers from the flotilla, which I have the honor to command, jumped on board a fishing-smack, ran the enemy along side, and carried him by a coup-de-main. I am sorry to add, that, in this little affair, the-enemy lost its commanding officer, one Midshipman, mortally wounded, and two seamen badly. I am happy to say we suffered no injuries, which is to be attributed to the superior management of sailing-master Percival, and the coolness with which his men fired; for which they all deserve well of their country.

British Master's Mate H. Morris attached to the HMS *Poictiers* is killed. Midshipman W. Price receives a mortal wound and one other man is also killed.

July 6 (Tuesday) American General James Wilkinson replaces General Henry Dearborn as commander of the Northwestern American Army. The disastrous defeat launched by the British at Beaver Dam against the Americans at Stoney Creek the previous month contributed greatly to Dearborn's relief by Wilkinson. General Dearborn at this time is at Fort George. On the 13th, he takes leave of the army in accordance with orders from the secretary of war. According to the orders, General Dearborn is to relinquish his command until he returns to good health.

Meanwhile, at Fort George, General John Parker Boyd with a force of about 4,000 men is under orders not to fight. British General Vincent and his force of fewer than 2,000 troops continue to maintain pressure on the post. Boyd, similarly to General Harrison, is not highly thought of by Secretary of War John Armstrong. The secretary believes that General Boyd should not command more than a brigade, and furthermore, Armstrong refuses to permit Boyd to initiate any offensive action as commander-in-chief. The restrictions placed upon General Boyd, who is also a veteran who fought at Tippecanoe as colonel of the 4th U.S. Infantry, tie his hands and essentially, except for some minor actions, closes the American offensive action on land for the year.

In naval activity, a British squadron, composed of the 36-gun HMS *Phoebe,* HMS *Cherub* and HMS *Racoon,* along with a 20-gun store-ship commanded by Commodore James Hillyar, departs from the vicinity of Brazil to search for Captain Porter's squadron operating in the Pacific. Also, the schooner *Calson* (J. Alson, master) is seized by the British privateer *Weazel*. In other naval activity, the HMS *Boxer* seizes the sloop *Friendship* after it departs from Black Rock, New York, with a cargo of flour and tar scheduled for delivery at Eastport, Maine. The prize is taken into port at New Brunswick. The *Friendship* is separate from the schooner *Friendship* seized 19 July 1812, the schooner *Friendship* captured 11 September 1812, the sloop *Friendship* seized on 5 March 1813, the sloop *Friendship* taken 11 July 1813, the schooner *Friendship* seized on 13 July 1813, and the schooner *Friendship* seized on 28 July 1813. Also, the British privateer *Retrieve* seizes the 96-ton sloop *Valaria,* which is transporting a cargo of lumber and oars.

July 7 (Wednesday) *In naval activity,* the HMS *La Hogue* spots an American brigantine, the *Ellen* (J. Asken, master). The *Ellen* and its cargo of molasses are captured while it is en route from St. Bartholomews to Portland, Maine. In other naval activity, the British privateer *Weazel* intercepts and seizes the sloop *Leonidas* (E. Cummings, master). Also, the HMS *Rattler* intercepts and seizes the ship *Prudentia* (Domingo Pagia, master), which is transporting flour, tar and tobacco from Ocracroke, North Carolina, to Cadiz, Spain. The prize and its cargo are taken into port at New Brunswick.

The British privateer *Retaliation* intercepts and seizes the 58-ton sloop *Rose in Bloom* (J. Colbroth, master) while it is transporting a cargo of lumber from Saco, Maine, to Rhode Island. The prize is taken into port at Liverpool. Also, the HMS *Curlew* intercepts and seizes the 63-ton schooner *Swift* off the coast of Massachusetts with a cargo of salt. The *Swift* is separate from the brigantine *Swift* seized on 14 March 1813. Also, the HMS *Curlew* intercepts and seizes the 53-ton schooner *Two Brothers,* which is transporting a cargo of wood and other items. The *Two Brothers* is separate from the schooner *Two Brothers* overtaken 27 March 1813, the schooner *Two Brothers* seized on 6 July 1813, the bark *Two Brothers* captured 25 May 1814 and the schooner *Two Brothers* seized 4 September 1814. In yet other activity, the HMS *Curlew* seizes the sloop *Unice*. Also, the American privateer *Growler* is intercepted by the HMS *Electra*. The privateer runs, but after a chase that lasts about six hours, it is captured.

July 8 (Thursday) **In Canada,** a small British detachment under a young officer named Merritt arrives near the residence of John and Peter Ball, located near Fort George. Merritt had been tasked with retrieving a stash of medicine that the British had hidden during the American attack against the fort in May. The detachment is under the protection of a large body of Indians led by the notorious Chief Blackbird. During the mission, while the detachment is at the Ball residence (Ball's farm), an American picket detachment arrives in the area and a skirmish erupts. American reinforcements under Lt. Eldridge move out to support the pickets; however, he speeds to the place way in front of another contingent under Major Malcolm. Unknown to Eldridge, the Indians had been waiting in ambush. Once the contingent comes into sight, the Indians have them trapped. Of the 40 men, including Eldridge, only five escape. The troops that had been wounded while encircled and the others are savagely killed and afterward scalped. No British troops participate in the massacre.

In Louisiana, General Claiborne, while at Bueller's Plains, slightly more than 20 miles from Baton Rouge, writes to General Flournoy that 250 men attached to Colonel Joseph Carson's regiment had already arrived. He also informs Flournoy that the $200 he received from the quartermaster at Baton Rouge had already been expended. General Flournoy receives lots of other unfavorable news, including that the roads are horrible and that it has been raining every day for about six weeks.

In Ohio, at Fort Meigs, in conjunction with the expiration of some enlistments, General Green Clay decides to enlighten the day as the troops prepare to depart from the fort by issuing the following general order: "The commanding General directs that the Old Guard, on being released, will march out of camp and discharge their guns at a target placed in some secure position; and as a reward for those who may excel in shooting, eight gills of whiskey will be given to the nearest shot, and four gills to the second. The officer of the guard will cause a return, signed for that purpose, signifying the names of the men entitled to the reward." Despite the good spirited sendoff, the situation in the region remains quite serious. The Indians continue to converge upon the Maumee River. During this intense period, one group of fourteen troops that depart from the fort en route to their homes by moving overland are ambushed several miles from the post while they are moving toward Fort Winchester. Of the fourteen men, all but two are killed. Meanwhile, General Harrison continues to oversee the situation, and he continues to check on the various forts with regard to the defenses. Colonel Johnson, earlier ordered to the Huron River by General Harrison, while continuing the journey, receives new orders from John Armstrong, the secretary of war, who again interferes with the operations of the army by directing Johnson to abort the mission to the Huron and instead move to the Illinois and Missouri Territories to deal with Indian hostilities there by Indians who had departed from Detroit.

General Harrison, once informed of the meddling by Armstrong, acts to get the order countermanded and succeeds. Johnson's column is intercepted and recalled; however, the troops had covered a large distance, and much valuable time had been squandered. Harrison is also concerned with the relations with the friendly Indians. He holds a council with several tribes, including the Senecas, Delaware, Shawnees, and Wyandottes, primarily due to reports that some are considering going over to the British. The council is held at Franklinton (later Columbus). Also this month, Harrison orders the construction of Fort Seneca to enable the Americans to maintain vigil on the region. He establishes his headquarters at Seneca town. The post is established along the Sandusky River less than ten miles below Fort Ball and about the same distance above Lower Sandusky.

In naval activity, the USS *Erie*, commanded by Sailing Master Daniel Dobbins, arrives at Presque Isle (later, Erie, Pennsylvania) to join with Commodore Oliver Hazard Perry's squadron. It had for a while been at Black Rock, unable to get to Lake Erie due to a British blockading force on the Niagara River.

In other naval activity, the British privateer *Matilda* seizes the 22-ton schooner *Pilgrim*, which is transporting a cargo of ballast. The *Pilgrim* is separate from the *Pilgrim* (boat) seized on 27 April 1813 and the brigantine *Pilgrim* seized on 18 May 1813. In other naval activity, the HMS *Fantome* recaptures the brigantine *Sea Flower*.

July 9 (Friday) **In Maine,** the privateer *Pilot*, a schooner, is commissioned this day. Joseph Sturdivant receives command.

In naval activity, the HMS *Curlew* intercepts and seizes the 61-ton schooner *Priscilla*, which is transporting a cargo of fish. In other naval activity, the British privateer *Retaliation* seizes the 99-ton schooner *Wasp* (J. Springer, master), which is en route to Falmouth, Massachusetts, from Kennebec, Maine. The prize is taken into port at Liverpool. The *Wasp* is separate from the sloop *Wasp* seized on 8 August 1813.

Also today, David Rodgerson Williams is commissioned brigadier general in the United States Army. Initially, he serves in the South, but afterward, he repairs to western New York. He becomes ill just before the Battle of Lundy's Lane and resigns from the service on 6 April 1814. That year, he is elected governor of South Carolina.

July 10 (Saturday) **In Alabama,** more than 300 Indians, including Autaugas under High Head Jim, Alabamas led by Josiah Francis, and Tallase under Peter McQueen are headed toward Pensacola, Florida, to receive weapons from British agents at the Spanish port. Friendly Indians reject the pressure to join in the fight and suffer some repercussions. The village of Hatchechubba is burned to the ground this day. Other villages threatened include Tombigby. Requests pour into the governor's office to send federal troops to protect them against the Creeks, but General Flournoy (General Wilkinson's successor) declines to dispatch any federal troops or volunteers.

Meanwhile, the Americans, having learned of the mission, begin to plan to attack them upon their return. This recent trouble has the settlers in Florida hurrying to construct forts. Of these, Patton's Fort (known also as Roger's Fort) will be established at Winchester. The master plan of the British in conjunction with the Indians is to entirely expel the Americans from Alabama. British warships and transports are off the coast of Pensacola and other Florida ports with arms for the Creeks.

In naval activity, the British privateer *Retrieve* intercepts and seizes the 71-ton schooner *Hannah* while it is en route to Nantucket from Frenchman's Bay with a cargo of lumber. The *Hannah* is separate from the brigantine *Hannah* seized on 30 April 1813 and the schooner *Hannah* captured on 3 August 1813. In other naval activity, the HMS *La Hogue* intercepts and seizes the ship *Roxana*. In yet other naval activity, work on Captain Perry's fleet at Erie is completed this day.

July 11 (Sunday) In Canada, a contingent of about 240 men under Lt. Colonel Cecil Bisshopp sailed in the predawn hours to raid Black Rock, a supply center and navy yard near Buffalo. The raid surprises the troops under Major Adams at their camp. Meanwhile, General Peter B. Porter escapes by climbing out of a window at his house and heading straight to Buffalo, where he gathers a relief force. Before returning to Canada on the opposite bank of the Niagara River, the troops set fires at the buildings in the navy yard. They also burn the barracks and blockhouses. A burned schooner is discovered at the dock.

The rampage, not yet complete, gets interrupted when a contingent of Americans, including regulars, militia and volunteers, arrive to drive out the British. The small force under General Peter B. Porter is also bolstered by Indians who support the Americans. Porter's command attacks the British to attempt to end the rampage. After skirmishing for just under one-half hour, the British disengage and retreat to their boats; however, the Americans capture nine and the British sustain nine dead. After the boats depart, the British continue to receive fire from the troops. During this period, Colonel Cecil Bisshopp and Captain Saunders are among the 9 or 10 killed. About 15 others are wounded. Also, while on the raid, the British enter some private houses; however, no damage occurs and no civilians are harmed. The Americans sustain three killed and three to five wounded.

General Peter B. Porter.

General Isaac Shelby (*The Battle of the Thames*, Colonel Bennett H. Young, 1903).

In Kentucky, Governor Isaac Shelby, after the massacre at the Raisin River, calls for 2,000 volunteers. The Kentuckians, eager to seek revenge against the Indians, rush to the call and Shelby's expectations are exceeded. About 4,000 men volunteer. At the time, Fort Meigs had suffered two separate sieges and enlistments had been expiring. The army under General Harrison continues to dwindle and it is possible that Ohio and Michigan would have to be abandoned. Nevertheless, Shelby is greatly interested in bolstering Harrison. Efforts to persuade the troops to extend their enlistments are unsuccessful, even though they are offered an additional seven dollars a month. Shelby also dispatches Colonel Anthony Crockett, a well respected officer, but his pleas are also rejected.

Nonetheless, Shelby's proclamation saves the army. Ten regiments are formed. The final place of assembly is Urbana, and from that place, Shelby's column moves out to join General Harrison on 13 September. General Richard Hickman, the lieutenant governor of Kentucky, becomes acting governor during the absence of Governor Shelby.

In naval activity, a British squadron under the Rear Admiral Cockburn arrives off Ocracoke bar, North Carolina. The British are en route to attack New Bern. The squadron is detected when it enters the sounds. The USS *Mercury* takes Thomas Singleton, a U.S. customs officer, aboard, and the ship moves to New Bern to warn of the attack. Singleton had brought the money and bonds with him; however, the British do not attack. Once the *Mercury* sounds the alarm, the British lose the element of surprise. Admiral Cockburn aborts the mission and retires. The *Mercury* remains in service for the duration. After the war, it is returned to the Treasury Department, where it remains active until 1820.

In yet other activity, the HMS *La Hogue*, while on patrol, intercepts and seizes the sloop *Friend-*

ship. The *La Hogue* on this day seizes the sloop *Jerusha* (W. Freeman, master) and the 56-ton sloop *Mentor* (J. Perry, master) while it is en route to New Bedford, Massachusetts, from Provincetown, Massachusetts. The *Mentor* is separate from the 227-ton *Mentor* seized on 27 October 1814.

Also, the British privateer *Retrieve* and the HMS *Rattler*, while cruising together, encounter the 228-ton brigantine *John Adams* while it is en route from Portland, Maine, to St. Bartholomews. The *John Adams*, along with its cargo of lumber, shingles and staves, is seized and taken into port at New Brunswick. In yet other naval activity, the HMS *Nimrod* intercepts and seizes the ship *Republican* (A. Baupen, master) and its cargo of dry goods, fruit, lumber and tobacco from New York to Port au Prince.

July 12 (Monday) *In naval activity,* the HMS *Bream* intercepts and seizes the 99-ton schooner *Jefferson* (J. Colcord) after it had sailed from Boston. The prize is taken into port at New Brunswick. In other naval activity, the HMS *Manly* intercepts and seizes the brigantine *Ohio*. The British privateer *Retaliation* intercepts and captures the 33-ton schooner *Sally*. The prize and its cargo of lumber are taken into port at Liverpool. The *Sally* is separate from the brigantine *Sally* seized on 10 August 1812, the *Sally Ann* seized on 16 September 1812, the ship *Sally* seized on 16 April 1813, the brigantine *Sally* captured on 24 April 1813, the schooner *Sally* seized on 13 May 1813, the schooner *Sally* taken 15 September 1813, the schooner *Sally* captured 16 October 1813, and the sloop *Sally* seized 19 May 1814.

July 12–13 *In naval activity,* a British squadron, composed of the 74-gun HMS *Sceptre* and six other warships under Rear Admiral Cockburn, aware of the location of two highly successful American privateers, the *Anaconda* (Captain Nathaniel Shaler) and the *Atlas* (Captain David Maffitt), arrives off Ocracoke Inlet, North Carolina, to destroy or capture both to eliminate them from marauding British shipping. Cockburn's squadron is bolstered by about 500 troops of the British 103rd Regiment. After arriving on scene during the night of the 12th, the British immediately prepare to launch their attack, which commences at 0200 on the 13th. The weather is uncooperative, making it impossible for the heavy vessels to move close to shore, which impedes the operation. Nevertheless, the boats, divided into three divisions, row to shore. Some do not reach shore until after daybreak, costing the British the luxury of a night attack.

Captain Shaler of the *Anaconda* quickly realizes his crew has no chance of defending against the massive force in the boats. He orders the cables cut and the entire crew is able to reach shore. The British easily take possession of the *Anaconda* and turn its guns against the *Atlas*, which seals the fate of the remaining privateer. Captain Maffitt is compelled to surrender. The British confidence quickly reaches a pinnacle after effortlessly seizing the privateers. To add to their laurels, the British immediately march inland toward nearby Portsmouth and that too falls to the British. However, after deciding to advance farther to seize New Bern, intelligence is received that New Bern is preparing to defend, and it will not be an easy target. The attack is cancelled.

The British remain in and around Portsmouth for two days before the entire force returns to the ships. Afterward, the squadron retires with its prizes. The British incorporate both vessels into British service. The *Atlas* is renamed the *St. Lawrence*; however, the *Anaconda* retains its name. Also, the other British warships that participate are the frigate HMS *Fox*, frigate *Nemesis*, frigate *Romulus*, brigantine *Conflict*, tender *Cockchafer* and the tender *Highflyer*. Captain Shaler's service as commander of a privateer ends; however, Captain Maffitt returns to sea in another privateer, the 16-gun brigantine *Rattler*, which cruises in company with the privateer *Scourge*, the latter having embarked on a cruise into British waters the previous April.

In other naval activity, the USS *Essex*, along with the *Greenwich* and the *Georgiana*, arrive off Charles Island. On the following morning, a boat goes ashore, and when the party arrives at the post office, it is discovered the all correspondence had been removed from the box. Afterward, the *Essex* and accompanying ships move to Banks' Bay at midnight (13th–14th).

July 13 (Tuesday) **In Alabama,** General Claiborne, en route from Baton Rouge, arrives near Fort Stoddert. He writes to General Flournoy to inform him that sick troops had been left at Liberty, Mississippi. Claiborne also requests that they receive medical help and that he would bear responsibility for the cost.

In Canada, Captain Cyrenus Chapin and his party of 28 men, having escaped after their capture on 23 June, arrive back at Fort George. Chapin writes to General Dearborn this day detailing how his men overwhelmed their captors to take possession of two boats in which they completed their escape.

In naval activity, the British privateer *Matilda* seizes the 97-ton schooner *Friendship* (J. Smith, master) after it leaves Union River with a cargo that includes cord wood and shingles. Other vessels named *Friendship* seized during the war are a schooner, 19 July 1812; a schooner, 11 September 1812; a sloop, 5 March 1813; a sloop, 6 July 1813; a schooner, 11 July 1813; and a schooner, 28 July 1813. Also, the *Matilda* captures the sloop *Harriet* (J. Collins), which is en route from Penobscot, Maine to Portland, Maine. The *Harriet* is separate from the brigantine *Harriet* seized on 8 June 1813 and the schooner *Harriet* taken 13 July 1813. In other naval activity, the British privateer *Matilda* captures the 72-ton schooner *Venus*, which is transporting a cargo of ballast and corn. The *Venus* is separate from the ship *Venus* captured 24 September 1813 and the schooner *Venus* seized on 24 November 1813.

In other naval activity, the HMS *La Hogue*, having recently been challenged by the American privateer *Young Teazer*, moves out of Halifax to engage and destroy the American privateer. Upon the approach of the *La Hogue*, which is carrying 74 guns, the *Young Teazer* is caught by surprise. It moves into the harbor, knowing the British guns would be trying to take it out. Nonetheless, Captain Dobson manages to remain out of the range of the guns while it seeks cover in a nearby bay, aware that the *La Hogue* cannot follow. The British, however, remain intent on taking the privateer. A force of 130 men is sent by boat into the shallow bay to seize the American vessel.

Dobson evades capture and manages to get back to sea, but the *La Hogue* is running close behind. Pursuit lasts for about eighteen hours before the Americans realize they will not be able to escape. Captain Dobson summons his officers to discuss the situation. During the council, British fire continues to target the prey. Meanwhile, Lieutenant F. Johnson of the privateer *Teazer*, captured during December 1812, quietly leaves the council. Johnson, having failed to honor his parole, is aware that if recognized by the British he will be hanged. Carrying a hot coal, he ignites the magazine and blows it to oblivion. Of the 37 crew members, only seven — on the forecastle at the time of the explosion — survive the blast. Johnson's act of selfishness unnecessarily costs the lives of the other crewmen. One of the seven afterward dies of his injuries.

Captain Dobson is among the survivors and gets command of another privateer within about two months after the tragedy. It becomes *Young Teazer's Ghost* and flies under the Stars and Stripes; however, it had formerly been the a British privateer, the *Liverpool Packet*. This *Liverpool Packet*, captured in late 1812 or early 1813, is separate from the like named British privateer that ravages American shipping during the war and captures more than fifty prizes. Also, Captain Dobson seeks a new command after a while because of the failures of the *Ghost*. (See also, **November 12,** 1812.)

July 14 (Wednesday) *In naval activity,* the sloop USS *Asp*, accompanied by the USS *Scorpion*, enters Chesapeake Bay from the Yeocomico River. Within a short time the British warships HMS *Contest* and the HMS *Mohawk* spot the sail and begin to chase both ships. The *Scorpion* has the speed to outrun its pursuers; however, while the *Scorpion* vanishes in the Chesapeake, the *Asp* is forced to try to make it back into the river because of its inferior sailing abilities. Meanwhile, the British anchor at the bar and dispatch boats to intercept the *Asp*. Upon the approach of the boats, the *Asp* severs its cables and tries to advance farther up the river. Nonetheless, the boats initiate their attack, but it fails. Immediately, two more boats join with the initial three and a second attack is launched. The British finally gain the ship. Its commander, Midshipman Sigourney, and ten of his crew (one-half) are killed. Although the British seize the *Asp*, the ten surviving crew members escape by making it to shore. The British choose to destroy the vessel and then return to the ships.

Meanwhile, the surviving crew members lurk nearby on shore. After the British set the *Asp* on fire, they depart, confident that it was destroyed. The crew, now commanded by Midshipman H. McClintock, re-boards the burning *Asp* and extinguishes the fires to give the vessel some added sea life. Although prepared to renew the fight, inexplicably, the British fail to launch their third attack. The *Asp* afterward becomes a tender to the USS *Java*, which is not yet completed at Baltimore. It is transformed into a receiving ship at Baltimore for the remainder of its service, which terminates during 1826 when it is sold.

In other activity, the *Betsy* (Moses Hall, master), a 117-ton schooner, is captured while en route from Tortola (British Virgin Islands) to Portland, Maine. The prize and its cargo of rum are taken into port at New Brunswick. Also, the *Malaren*, a 139-ton brigantine, is intercepted and seized by the HMS *La Hogue* sailing from Portsmouth to St. Bartholomews with lumber, staves and other items. Also, the HMS *Bream* intercepts the 122-ton schooner *Triton*, which is transporting molasses and rum from St. Thomas to Kennebec, Maine. The vessel is seized and taken into port at New Brunswick.

July 14–19 **In naval activity,** the USS *Essex*, *Georgiana* and *Greenwich* (storeship), off the island of Albemarle, spot three ships off Banks' Bay at about 1100. The *Essex* initiates pursuit of the ship sailing in the center. Meanwhile, the remaining two ships appear to be in the process of trying to evade capture. The *Greenwich* heaves to, permitting the *Georgiana* to speed up. Shortly thereafter, the prize is seized. It is the a 10-gun British ship *Charlton*. Captain Porter is informed by its captain that one of the other two vessels is the *Seringapatam*, manned by 40 men and carrying 14 guns. Porter also learns that the remaining ship is the 8-gun New Zealander. The *Seringapatam*, a whaling ship operating as a privateer without a commission, is intercepted by the *Greenwich* (a prize of the *Essex*) commanded by U.S. Marine Corps Lieutenant Gamble off Tumbez, Peru. The prize adds yet another vessel to Porter's flotilla. Master's Mate James Terry is appointed prize master of the *Seringapatam* and it continues on the cruise with the *Essex* and the other vessels.

Later, during the following September, Captain Porter will set a course for Nuka Hiva (Marquesas Islands) to receive repairs. Four of his prizes, including the prize captured this day, will accompany him on the voyage of about 3,000 miles.

The *Greenwich* and the *Seringapatam* exchange broadsides. The latter sustains devastating damage. It lowers its colors; however, despite being crippled, it attempts to run. The *Greenwich* gives further chase and after a while, the British crew realizes escape is impossible, particularly after they see the USS *Essex* closing fast. After taking possession of the *Seringapatam*, crew members of the *Greenwich* take control of it, while the *Essex* moves to seize the remaining vessel, the *New Zealander*, and succeeds in about one hour. Captain Porter later professes that "the capture of this ship gave me more pleasure than that of any other which fell into my hands; for, besides being the finest British ship in those seas, her commander had the character of being a man of great enterprise, and had already captured the American whale-ship *Edward*, of Nantucket, and might have done great injury to the American commerce in those seas."

Captain Porter requests that Captain Stavers present his commission, but he has none. Captain Porter identifies him as clearly a pirate and decides that the entire crew will be kept in irons; however, after speaking to American prisoners held aboard the *Seringapatam*, he discovers that they had received fine treatment by the crew. Porter countermands his own order and gives the crew of the *Seringapatam* the same privileges as the other prisoners. Nonetheless, Captain Stavers remains in irons. Following the operation, Captain Porter sets a course for James Island. While en route, the winds change drastically and the squadron is being pushed northwest, hindering progress and ensuring that it will not be a short voyage. Captain Porter returns the *Charlton* to its captain on the condition that he takes it into Rio De Janeiro to land all of the prisoners. All its guns and other military items are transferred to the *Seringapatam*. On the 19th, the *Charlton* sails off with 48 prisoners, but not without incident. According to Captain Porter, "the mates and sailors, however, expressed their determination not to go to Rio de Janeiro with the ship, for fear of being pressed on board a British man of war. They were very solicitous that I would allow them whale-boats, and let them take their chances in them, declaring that any fate, however dreadful, would be preferable to a servitude in his Majesty's navy." Porter refuses to give his consent and for a while he is leaning toward using force. Nevertheless, after explaining their own misconduct to them, he relents. As the *Charlton* sails off the crew cries out loudly with three cheers and good wishes that the Americans get safely back to the States.

Meanwhile, Captain Porter directs the crew on the *Seringapatam* to expedite their work to complete the modifications. Within several days, 20 guns are mounted and ready for action if necessary. Porter places Mr. Terry (master's mate) in command, and he gives command of the *New Zealander* to the purser, Mr. Shaw. All the while, the ships are struggling against the winds to reach the southeast. During the voyage, they come upon Wenam's Island and Culpepper's Island.

July 14–27 **In New York,** at Sackets Harbor, a contingent of 24 volunteers and 21 men of the U.S. 21st Regiment, led by Lts. Burbank and Perry, prepare for a cruise on the St. Lawrence in two vessels, the *Fox* and the *Neptune*. The *Fox* is a public armed boat under Captain Dimock and the *Neptune* is commanded by Captain Samuel Dixon. Both vessels embark with letters of marque, issued by the deputy collector of the district. The troops attached to the 21st Regiment board the *Fox*. The flotilla intends to intercept enemy craft carrying stores and provisions. On the 17th, they enter a creek at Thousand Islands, pick a secluded place to pause and debark to examine their ammunition and to spend time getting their boats in proper order. During the pause, while the boats are being cleaned, each vessel sends out a reconnaissance boat to gather intelligence; however, neither scouting detachment discovers any intelligence. The mission remains uneventful until the pre-dawn hours of the 18th, when they spot a large number of British bateau under escort by the gunboat HMS *Spitfire*. The convoy is at Simmond's Landing, preparing to move to Kingston.

The *Fox* and the *Neptune* quickly move in close to shore where Lt. Perry (9th Regiment) and Sergeant James (Captain Forsyth's company) with 27 volunteers debark and establish positions to sever any means of escape, while the others strike with total surprise, leaving no time for the British to react. Fifteen bateaux and the gunboat are seized without anyone firing a shot. Later that day at 0900, the flotilla arrives at Cranberry Creek at Alexandria, and at about 1100, 69 prisoners are taken to shore under escort by Lt. Burbank and a 15-man guard. The *Spitfire* is armed with a 12-pound carronade and carries a crew of 15 men.

On the 21st, at dawn, four British gunboats, escorting transports carrying about 250 troops, are spotted in the creek. A flotilla of gunboats under British Lieutenant Scott (Royal Navy) and a contingent of the 100th Regiment, under Captain Martin, had arrived from Kingston to intercept the Americans during the night of the 20th; however, they had awaited the predawn hours of the 20th to launch the attack. The flotilla had been joined by another gunboat carrying elements of the 41st Regiment led by Major Frend. After joining with Scott, Frend assumes command of the operation. At 0300 on the 21st, the gunboats close upon the American positions; however, the channel is too slim for the gunboats to properly navigate. The British cannot maneuver nor turn; their oars become useless. Meanwhile, the Americans had cut trees to further block the channel.

While the British expect to debark effortlessly, the Americans are not surprised. Thirty of the men meet the landing force, while about 20 others are deployed in scattered positions to prevent the British from trapping the force. American fire is heavy and effective, causing severe damage to two of the boats. The crews are compelled to abandon them. Nevertheless, by 0600, the British, who retire to their boats, send a boat to shore to demand surrender. The Americans decline the invitation to become guests of the British and instead resume their fire, including a resumption of cannon fire. Apparently, the British ultimatum had been a bluff. Rather then resuming their fire, the British retire.

The Americans sustain three dead and wounded. British casualties are unknown, but the Americans, based on the amount of blood discovered at the landing place, estimate losses were high. Precautions are taken in the event of a return of the British; however, the remainder of the day remains tranquil. On the following day, American reinforcements arrive, but still the British fail to return. The Americans work on repairing their boats until they sail back to Sackets Harbor on the 23rd.

On the return journey, the HMS *Earl of Moira* encounters the boats. A chase is initiated off Tibbet's Point. The British gunboat fails to seize or destroy them and the flotilla arrives at Sackets Harbor on the 27th. During the final leg of the journey, the captured gunboat and a few of the bateaux are sunk. Consequently, the owners of the vessels lose much of what the mission had gained.

July 15 (Thursday) **In Virginia** at Norfolk, a party attached to the HMS *Plantagenet*, which is lurking off Norfolk, is preparing to land near the lighthouse, something they have been doing on a frequent basis. On this day, a company of militia from Princess Anne County is lying in wait. The troops had been "watering their boats" and digging wells there. At about 1730, a British boat is spotted as it is being rowed toward shore, but no action is initiated. At about 1600, the British party, composed of sailors and Royal Marines, lands and proceeds toward the wells; however, unexpectedly, a benign sand hill, behind which the militia had concealed themselves, becomes the origin point of a furious burst of fire that stuns the intruders and compels the entire force to surrender. The British contingent was composed of "two lieutenants, 16 sailors and 8 Marines," Commodore J. Cassin writes to the secretary of the Navy. The casualties: three killed (Marines) along with one of the lieutenants; two sailors and three Marines wounded. The militia also destroys the boat. The Americans sustain no casualties.

July 15–26 **In Washington, D.C.,** word spreads that a British squadron is approaching the capital. A large force of regulars, along with militia troops, encamp at Warburton Heights (Fort Warburton) along the Potomac. Other troops deploy within a short distance this day. The secretary of the Navy arrives at the fort to make plans to erect a 9-gun battery. The threat causes the government to urge all men, even if exempted from service, to volunteer. Nevertheless, the British squadron under Admiral Sir John Borlase Warren by the 25th cancels its advance. The militia at that time is dismissed.

July 16 (Friday) **In Virginia,** former Governor James Wood dies this day at Olney, Virginia. He was a veteran of the American Revolution. During 1774 he was appointed captain. The following year, he ventured into Indian Territory with only one other man and displayed extraordinary courage that gained him the respect of the western Indians. During November 1776 he was promoted to the rank of colonel. In 1777 he received command of the guard holding prisoners from General John Burgoyne's surrender at Saratoga. He was governor from 1796 to 1799.

July 17 (Saturday) **In New York,** the Americans remove a large number of bateaux and about five gunboats out of Sackets Harbor and redeploy them at Goose Creek.

In naval activity, a British squadron, composed of the HMS *Maidstone*, HMS *Nimrod* and the HMS *Poictiers* intercepts and seizes the ship *York Town*. The British take it into port at Halifax. Before being captured, the *York Town* had seized eleven prizes. Also, the American privateer *Saucy Jack* intercepts and seizes the ship *Louisa* and the brigantine *Three Brothers*, both of which carry 10 guns. During this cruise, the *Saucy Jack* also seizes some smaller vessels.

July 18 (Sunday) *In naval activity,* the American shallop *Hope for Peace* (E.W. Crowel, master), sailing from Massachusetts Bay to Halifax, is seized by Captain McPherson and a contingent of militia. In other naval activity, the HMS *Recruit* intercepts and recaptures the ship *Lavina*.

July 18–29 *In naval activity,* the USS *President* encounters the HMS Brigantine *Daphne* off the coast of Ireland and a sea duel erupts with an American victory. The *President* engages and captures the HMS *Eliza Swan* after another confrontation in the Irish Channel within the week. The British and Americans are deadlocked again the following day when the victorious crew of the *President* continues its streak and successfully fights the British Brigantine *Alert*, capturing it on the 29th.

July 19 (Monday) **In New York,** Brigadier General Jacob J. Brown of the New York militia is named brigadier general in the regular army. Brown had been offered the rank of colonel with command of a regiment in the United States Army the previous year, but he declined.

In naval activity, the HMS *Picton* intercepts and seizes the 128-ton brigantine *Isabella* (P. Slaygur, master) traveling from Algesiras, Spain, to Boston. The *Isabella* is carrying a cargo of oil, silk, wine and other items when captured. Also, the American privateer *Scourge* (Captain Nicholl) encounters the USS *President* (Commodore John Rodgers) off Cape North and joins with the frigate. During the *Scourge* and *President's* time at sea, a string of British vessels are captured while moving to and from Archangel, Russia. The prizes are usually sent into Norwegian ports. After separating from the *President*, the *Scourge* joins with the American privateer *Rattlesnake*, commanded by Captain David Maffitt, formerly the commander of the privateer *Atlas*. After the *Scourge* and the *Atlas* link, both vessels move into port at Drontheim, Norway.

July 20 (Tuesday) **In Canada,** a large convoy of bateaux taking supplies from Montreal to Kingston is intercepted by an American contingent, which had been lying in wait along the St. Lawrence at Goose Creek below Gananoque. The entire convoy is seized and the Americans afterward return to Sackets Harbor. A British force, including three gunboats under British Lieutenant Scott, is dispatched from Kingston to intercept the Americans. Scott is transporting a contingent of the 100th Regiment under Captain Martin. The British reach Sackets Harbor after dark. Their attack is postponed until daylight. A fourth gunboat arrives with some reinforcements under Major Frend (4th Regiment).

While en route, Captain Milnes, aide-de-camp to Sir George Prevost, joins the contingent. At about 0300 on the 21st, the British, confident they will gain the element of surprise, advance; however, once they overcome some obstacles, including rocky and precarious embankments felled trees that hinder passage, the gunboats finally arrive near a log fort. However, rather than launch an attack against a slumbering garrison, the British encounter well fortified riflemen who control the woods. Nevertheless, the British seamen and soldiers bolt from their craft and succeed in forcing the defenders to retire into the fort. They realize they have encountered an insurmountable objective. Major Frend orders his force to retire and the troops are able to fight their way back to the gunboats, but at a cost. The Americans inflict about 21 casualties, including Captain Milnes, whose wound is fatal.

In New Hampshire, Major General Henry Butler of Nottingham dies. General Butler, a veteran officer (captain) of the American Revolution, was appointed brigadier general during 1803. In 1812 he was named major general and commander of the Division of Detached Militia.

In Ohio, a British army, accompanied by a massive Indian force that had departed from Amherstville, Canada, earlier in the month, arrives at the mouth of the Maumee River. The force totals about 5,000 men and is under British Colonel Henry Proctor, who again attacks Fort Meigs, only to be repulsed again.

In naval activity, the HMS *Epervier* intercepts and recaptures the schooner *Lively*. The *Lively* is separate from the schooner *Lively* seized on 12 July 1812, the schooner *Lively* seized 24 July 1813, the sloop *Lively* captured 7 June 1814, and the sloop *Lively* overtaken 26 October 1814.

July 21 (Wednesday) **In Ohio,** a band of Indians attached to General Proctor's army surprises a detachment of pickets (twelve men) about 300 yards from Fort Meigs. The entire party is either captured or killed. By this time, it is estimated from various sources that many more than 2,000 Indians have joined General Proctor for his second assault against Fort Meigs. The warriors are also accompanied by women and children, and estimates of their numbers take the figure up to about 7,000, with the British responsible for feeding all of them. Nevertheless, the Indians succeed in only minor incidents, including the capture of the small detachment and the seizure of some horses and oxen. The fire inflicts no damage to the post.

In related activity, after midnight (21st–22nd), twenty regulars, along with Lt. Montjoy, penetrate the enemy lines and enter the fort. The detachment had engaged Indians at the Portage River blockhouse and was able to escape capture; however, one man was lost. Once the troops report to General Clay, he dispatches Captain McCune (Ohio militia) to inform General Harrison of the situation. Harrison in turn sends McCune back with word that reinforcements are en route. Although Harrison is concerned with the threat against Fort Meigs, his instincts have him believing that Proctor will tire of failing at Fort Meigs and cause him to swing toward the right wing of the army where huge stockpiles of supplies were stored and the forts were more weakly defended. The reinforcements moving to the relief of Fort Meigs include

U.S. Infantry units under Lt. Colonel George Paul and the cavalry under Colonel Ball, which totals about 450 men. Others include the Ohio troops under General Duncan McArthur and General Cass, along with about 500 troops approaching from Fort Massac.

In naval activity, the USS *General Pike*, launched the previous June, is attached to Commodore Isaac Chauncey's squadron. It arrives off Niagara on the 27th, and afterward on 10 August the *General Pike* encounters a contingent of British Commodore Yeo's squadron on Lake Ontario.

July 23 (Friday) **In Washington, D.C.**, Secretary of War John Armstrong resubmits his original plan for the invasion of Canada and the capture of Montreal. President Madison once again approves of the expedition. Armstrong's plan for success calls for Kingston to fall first by attacking it from Sackets Harbor. The secretary also has an alternative plan which calls for Malden to be seized, followed by domination of Lake St. Francis, which would then permit General Wilkinson in coordination with General Wade Hampton to take Montreal. Nonetheless, Wilkinson, presently on duty in the South, does not arrive until the following August.

In Ohio at Fort Meigs, General Green Clay, having observed the nearby Indian activity, dispatches Captain McCune to report to General Harrison that it appears the Indians spotted moving up the opposite bank at Fort Meigs are en route to attack Fort Winchester (Fort Defiance). Harrison receives the intelligence; however, he remains convinced that Proctor's real goal is to strike the right wing where the defenses are not very strong. He sends McCune back to Fort Meigs, and he is accompanied by another man, James Doolan, a French-Irish Canadian. The pair gets confused in the darkness and they fail to reach the fort until about daybreak. Before they can reach the gates, they are spotted by Indians and are forced to gallop away. They press ahead until they reach a ravine and after descending it they pass through onto some lowland and continue their escape. They hit the river, which forces them to reverse their course and retrace the path. Nevertheless, while the Indians are in the ravine, both riders vanish in the woods just as the pursuers are beginning to close upon them. Shortly thereafter, to their jubilation, the Indians abort the chase as the riders come into the range and protection of the fort's guns. They report to General Clay that General Harrison is unable to spare any troops, but once the reinforcements arrive, he would advance to relieve the fort if it becomes necessary.

In naval activity, the British privateer *Fly* intercepts and seizes the 32-ton sloop *Randolph* (J. Webster, master), which had sailed from Boston en route to Eastport, Maine, with a cargo of beef, flour and other items. The *Randolph* is separate from the schooner *Randolph* seized on 14 October 1813. Also, the American privateer *Yankee*, while still operating near Ireland, spots a vessel flying a Spanish flag. Captain Elisha Snow closes on the vessel, believing it to be British, and fires a warning shot and then another without a response. At that point, the Stars and Stripes is hoisted and the *Yankee* fires for effect. After a series of broadsides, the Spanish colors come down. After a boarding party is sent to the ship, Snow discovers he had been mistaken and the target is a Spanish vessel. Apologies are presented and the Spaniards are authorized to proceed. The vessel is identified as the 8-gun privateer *Nuera Constitucion*.

July 24 (Saturday) **In Ohio** at Fort Meigs, a strong reconnaissance force of about 200 troops under Colonel Edmund Pendleton Gaines moves around the fringes of the woods near the fort to see if the British are constructing batteries. General Proctor sends out a force in an attempt to cut off Gaines' return; however, the British are tardy and the Americans return safely without having to engage.

In naval activity, the 22-ton schooner *Lively*, while en route from Boston to Penobscot, Maine, with coffee, rum and gin, is seized by the British privateer *Fly*. The *Lively* is separate from the schooner *Lively* seized on 12 July 1812, the schooner *Lively* seized on 20 July 1813, the sloop *Lively* captured 7 June 1814, and the sloop *Lively* seized 26 October 1814. In other naval activity, Captain David Porter, aboard the Essex, makes a decision to dispatch the prize *Georgiana*. It departs from the squadron on the following day en route to the United States.

July 25 (Sunday) **In Alabama**, an American force arrives at Sisemore's Ferry on the Alabama River. It is en route to intercept the Creeks who are returning from Pensacola, where they had received arms from the British. The number of Americans under Colonel James Caller has increased in size due to other units that have joined during the march, and he will receive additional troops upon the arrival of a company of volunteers under a half-breed Creek, Dixon Bailey. The volunteers under Bailey are drawn from Tensaw Lake and Little River. Bailey's reinforcements bring Colonel Caller's force up to 180 men. Meanwhile, Callers establishes night positions on the west bank of the river.

In naval activity, the HMS *Boxer* comes upon the sloop *Fairplay*, seizes it and takes it into New Brunswick. The HMS *Nymphe* intercepts and recaptures the schooner *Providence*.

An American seaman, Thomas King, captured earlier while serving aboard the USS *Vixen* when it was overtaken on 22 November 1812, breaks for freedom this day. King had been released on parole from Jamaica; however, while nearing Philadelphia on the cartel *Rebecca Sims*, the vessel was intercepted by the 74-gun ship HMS *Poictiers* just as the cartel was entering the Delaware Bay. King is seized after being falsely accused of being an Englishman. The British impress him into the Royal Navy aboard the HMS *Ruby*.

King immediately started to plan his escape. On this day, he seizes an opportunity while one of the ship's boats, having all its sails up, notices that the officers had left it unattended after returning from a leisure trip. Just after dark, with only a compass and some bread and water, King sneaks into the boat and sails away without being discovered, leaving Bermuda in hopes of reaching the United States. Amazingly, King continues his precarious voyage for nine days, at which point he goes ashore on 3 August, at a point about 10 miles south of Cape Henry, Virginia.

July 25–27 **In Ohio** at Fort Meigs, British General Proctor directs his main force to cross to the right bank of the river; however, the troops remain out of the range of the fort's guns, while Proctor and Tecumseh concoct a scheme to seize the fort during the night by a ruse. The British deploy in a ravine where they are essentially concealed but poised to strike once General Green Clay's force moves out of the garrison to engage the Indians who ignite a battle close to the fort along the road that reaches the fort from Lower Sandusky. The Indians begin their fire, and there is a huge commotion in an attempt to convince the garrison that a relief column is under severe attack. Meanwhile, the Redcoats await the arrival of the garrison to rush out to save the beleaguered phantom column. While the Indians are annihilating the column that does not exist, the British in the ravine are pounded with rain waiting to rush into the fort.

Instead, they discover that General Clay has ruined their night. The gates remain closed and the garrison sacrifices the invisible column. Nevertheless, some men get hooked by the ruse and insist on getting permission to rush out to save them, but General Clay, convinced of the trickery, refuses permission. However, his refusal to charge toward the scene does not prevent his artillery from entering the fray. His guns begin to rivet the scene of the action and the fighting soon terminates. General Proctor, having again failed to seize Fort Meigs, continues to linger, but he takes no further action. On the 27th, the British retire. Part of the command departs for Fort Stephenson. The flotilla moves through Lake Erie to Sandusky Bay, and from there it moves up the Sandusky River to the objective that is expected to fall with little effort.

Meanwhile, General Harrison, convinced that Proctor would move against Fort Stephenson, has been preparing the garrison for the assault.

Malden, a British strong-point and shipbuilding facility.

July 26 (Monday) **In Washington, D.C.,** Congress establishes the Sea Fencibles (Sandy Bay Militia) by passing an act "to authorize the raising [of] a Corps of Sea Fencibles, not to exceed one year [service], and not to exceed ten companies who may employed for the defense of the ports and harbors of the United States."

In Alabama, Colonel Caller's force begins to cross the Alabama River. The troops are carried across the river by canoes; their horses swim alongside them. After reaching the east embankment, the troops advance southeastwardly. The advance continues until the column arrives at the wolf-trail, which is close to the primary route into Pensacola. Colonel James Caller halts the march and establishes night positions. Caller's companies include two from St. Stephens, commanded by Captain Bailey Heard and Captain Benjamin Smoot. Smoot's second in command is Lieutenant Patrick May. The others include a company from Washington County, commanded by Captain David Cartwright; a company out of Clarke County under Captain Samuel Dale and Lieutenant Girard W. Creagh; and yet other contingents under William McGrew, Robert Caller and William Bradberry.

In naval activity, the American privateer *Yankee* spots a brigantine and initiates pursuit, but soon Captain Elisha Snow decides the vessel is a British warship disguised by flying the Stars and Stripes. The *Yankee* declines acting impulsively and risking capture or destruction. It distances itself from the ship and heads for home port, which it reaches safely on 20 August. The *Yankee*, during its three cruises, has seized 22 British vessels and had not lost a single man. It begins its fourth cruise on 13 September 1813.

July 27 (Tuesday) **BATTLE OF BURNT CORN** **In Alabama,** during the morning, Colonel James Caller's force undergoes some reorganization changes. Captains Jourdan, McFarlin, Zacharia Phillips and Wood are promoted to the rank of major. Major William McGrew is promoted to lieutenant colonel. Afterward, the march resumes. At about 1100, scouts return and report to Colonel Caller that the Creeks under McQueen have been discovered at a point only several miles distant on a peninsula at Burnt Corn Creek. The Creeks, not anticipating encountering any American forces, are relaxed while cooking and enjoying breakfast. Caller and the other officers hold a council and decide to launch a surprise attack. The command is divided into three divisions under Smoot (right), Bailey (center) and Dale (left).

The columns advance cautiously without detection, then without warning the troops spring upon the Creeks' encampment. The Creeks raise resistance but the power of the unexpected thrust compels them to break for the creek. They are pursued; however, some of the troops become diverted by the Indians' pack horses. Those who seek loot from the pack-horses create a disaster. Colonel Caller, having lost a large part of his command, is unable to continue pursuit. He calls for retreat to enable him to regroup on high ground to establish a defensive line. Meanwhile, his vanguard withdraws from the swamp, and when they are spotted by the troops with the pack-horses, a stampede begins. The men who did not continue the chase begin to flee in total disarray, but they are reluctant to abandon the horses. Colonel Caller and other officers attempt but fail to restore order.

At about the same time, the Creeks re-emerge from the swamp and their war cries become louder as they approach about eighty of the Americans who are at the base of the hill. The Creeks move to annihilate the contingent, commanded at the time by Captains Dale, Bailey Heard and Smoot. Nonetheless, the officers do not intend to capitulate. Ferocious fighting erupts and the Americans hold open ground. The Creeks' marksmanship is poor, but Captain Dale sustains a severe hit that strikes him in the chest and passes out of his back. Undaunted, Dale remains in the fight. Nevertheless, having lost about two-thirds of his command, Caller is compelled to retreat. A few troops remain separated from the main body. The retreat is haphazard and most men have lost their horses. The troops launched the assault dismounted and many of the horses scattered.

While the retreat continues, three of the Americans—Lt. Patrick May, Lt. Girard W. Creagh and Private Ambrose Miles—who were isolated continue to hold their ground near some reeds where the Creeks are concealed. One Indian and May exchange shots and May prevails. The Indian is killed. At nearly the same time, the brave threesome decide it is time to break away. While they race toward their horses, Lt. Creigh is struck in the hip. May manages to get Creigh onto his feet and then carries him piggy-back. They safely reach the horses and May places the wounded lieutenant in his saddle while Private Ambrose holds the horse's reins. In a flash, they dash to the top of the hill where they discover Lt. Bradberry's detachment. Bradberry is bleeding profusely, but he refuses to surrender. The Indians reach Bradberry's body and they scalp him.

Following their witnessing of the gruesome scene of Bradberry's last moments, they too join the general retreat that continues into the following day. Stragglers are strung all along the path of retreat. Those wounded move slowly. It is later determined that despite the bedlam, the Americans had sustained only two dead and 15 wounded. For a while, it was though the losses included Colonel Caller and Major Wood; however, they were not killed or captured; rather, both men get lost in the woods and wander aimlessly for about ten days. Both are rescued and apparently just in time, as they are nearly lost to starvation.

Meanwhile, the Creeks under Peter McQueen had lost their newly acquired British arms and ammunition. They return to Pensacola to seek more. The Indian casualties are never determined. The Indians, instigated by the British and Spanish, have been terrorizing the settlers. The British are paying $5 per scalp and those of women and children are included. The settlers receive no protection from the army because no armies are in the territories. Nonetheless, militia drawn from Alabama, Georgia and Tennessee take responsibility for eliminating the ongoing threats of the Creeks. In the meantime, the victory at Burnt Creek instills confidence in the Creeks. They plan to attack Fort Mims on Lake Tensas, less the 50 miles from Mobile.

In New York at Albany, Governor Tompkins, in a letter to Brigadier General T. S. Hopkins, dated this day, informs Hopkins that as a brigadier general, he has the authority to call up militia; however, the governor explains, "But in order to entitle them to receive pay from the United States, it is indispensible that there be made a requisition of the officer of the United States commanding on that frontier by authority from the President."

In naval activity, a British naval force advancing toward Washington encounters difficulty at Kettle-bottoms. In other naval activity, the HMS *Nimrod* intercepts and recaptures the sloop *Mary*. Also, the British privateer *Fly* intercepts and seizes the 64-ton schooner *Rebecca*, which is transporting a cargo of wood from Penobscot, Maine, to Marblehead, Massachusetts. The *Rebecca* is separate from the *Rebecca* seized 27 June 1813 and the *Rebecca* taken 3 August 1813. Also, the HMS *Ring Dove* intercepts and recaptures the brigantine *Stamper*.

July 28 (Wednesday) *In naval activity,* the British privateer *Fly* intercepts and seizes the 74-ton sloop *Friendship* (D. Rider, master) while it is en route from Providencetown (Maine or Massachusetts) to Penobscot, Maine, with a cargo of ballast. Other like named vessels seized are a schooner, 19 July 1812; a schooner, 11 September 1812; a sloop, 5 March 1813; a sloop, 6 July 1813; a schooner, 11 July 1813; and a schooner, 13 July 1813.

In other naval activity, the British privateer *Fly* intercepts and seizes the 92-ton sloop *Polly*. The *Polly* is separate from the 84-ton schooner *Polly* seized 11 August 1812; the 85-ton schooner *Polly*, 14 October 1812; the schooner *Polly*, 13 August 1813; the 88-ton schooner *Polly*, 10 December 1813; and the 45-ton sloop *Polly*, 10 August 1814.

July 29 (Thursday) **In Washington, D.C.,** President Madison issues orders to all U.S. naval officers directing them "to exercise the greatest vigilance in capturing American vessels engaged or suspected of being engaged in carrying provisions to the enemy."

In New York, the British under Colonel Proctor prepare an attack on Fort Stephenson. American General Harrison, quartered at Senecatown, learns of the imminent attack and orders the Fort evacuated. The commanding officer, Major George Croghan, a bold Kentuckian, decides that by the time he received the orders it was too late to abandon the post. He remains confident that he can hold the fort. The British launch their attack on 2 August.

In naval activity, the HMS *Martin*, a sloop-of-war, runs aground while operating in Delaware Bay. A flotilla of 2 sloops and 8 gunboats under the command of Captain Angus, move in to attack the stranded vessel. In the meantime, another British ship, the *Junon*, arrives to support the *Martin*. Shortly thereafter, the British send

Major George Croghan.

out some barges and cutters to seize U.S. gunboats that are lingering at the tail-end of the flotilla. One of the gunboats, commanded by Sailing Master Shead, becomes the primary target. Ten of the barges maneuver to circle Shead's vessel. He tries to fight them off by dropping his anchor and preparing to keep the British from boarding it. Nevertheless, despite the heroic stand, the gunboat is finally overwhelmed after Shead's guns stops operating. The British eventually seize the gunboat at a cost of seven killed and 12 wounded. Shead's crew sustains seven wounded. I

The 67-ton schooner *Dolphin* (R.O. Bean, master) is intercepted and by the HMS *Dart*, while transporting a cargo of wood from Portland, Maine, to Boston. The prize is seized and taken into port at New Brunswick. Also, the British privateer *Dart* takes possession of the 76-ton sloop *Maquatt* with its cargo of fish, corn and rye going from Bath, Maine, to Portland, Maine. The course is changed. The prize is taken into port at New Brunswick.

July 29 to August **In New York,** a British force of about 1,400, composed of infantry, seamen and Royal Marines under Colonel John Murray, take advantage of the small American militia force at Plattsburgh. A British squadron under Commander Thomas Everard departs Isle aux Nois this day. It carries Murray's contingent — elements of the 13th, 100th, and 103rd regiments, commanded by Lt. Colonels Williams, Taylor, and Smith and a contingent of artillery under Captain Gordon — up Lake Champlain to the objectives, including Plattsburgh, New York, and Swanton, Vermont.

On the 30th, the British anchor off Chazy Landing and a contingent debarks. The town suffers some plundering. On the 31st, the British launch their raid against Plattsburgh without any resistance from regulars. The town is plundered and the nearest regulars are on the other side of the lake at Burlington, Vermont, under General Wade Hampton. Inexplicably, Hampton had advance notice of the intent of the British from a local official who spotted the squadron cruising off Alburg, Vermont. The official was seized, but not before sending word to Hampton at Burlington.

Before raiding Plattsburgh, the British destroy several warehouses and private dwellings. Inside the town, they destroy many buildings, including an arsenal and a blockhouse, and pillage some private homes. Other contingents of the force plunder some private residences at Cumberland Head.

The British apparently make a hurried departure from Plattsburgh on 1 August, and in the process, they leave twenty of their troops behind. The Americans eagerly seize them and have them taken to Burlington. After sailing, the British squadron splits; one section with Murray aboard sails northward carrying most of the troops, while another contingent, under Commander Everard, sails south toward Burlington, Vermont.

Troops under Murray raid Swanton on Missisquoi Bay and destroy military facilities; however, no active troops are in the area. The British also destroy military supplies and facilities at Champlain Town. In the meantime, Everard's force arrives off Burlington on 2 August. Lieutenant Macdonough's naval force is there but not battle ready. Nonetheless, Everard easily discerns that the defenses are too strong to attack with only the HMS *Broke* (formerly USS *Growler*) and his one gunboat. He also detects two inviting sloops along with another, the latter sloop under the protection of a 10-gun battery deployed on a steep bank and two floating batteries, along with field artillery on shore. Despite the heavy armaments, the British succeed in seizing four vessels before they depart.

After failing to bait Macdonough into coming out for battle, the British terminate their bombardment and sail to Shelburne Bay. Lacking heavy resistance, the British effortlessly seize several commercial vessels. By 3 August, the entire squadron reunites at Cumberland Head. Before returning to their camp, the British pause at Cumberland Head, which is defenseless. They take time to pillage two private homes, those of Judge Treadwell and Jeremiah Stowe. After another quick raid on Chazy, the squadron sails back to Isle aux Noix.

July 30 (Friday) **In Alabama,** General Ferdinand Claiborne, recently ordered by General Flournoy to depart Baton Rouge, Louisiana, with his entire command for Fort Stoddart, arrives at the post this day with the rear guard of his command. Fort Stoddert is located at Mount Vernon Landing along the Mobile River near present-day Mount Vernon. Claiborne's orders instruct him to focus primarily on the defense of Mobile. General Claiborne had received only two hundred dollars from the quartermaster at Baton Rouge; he used mortgages tied to his own estate to cover nearly all of the cost of moving his force. Claiborne is informed of the recent debacle at Burnt Corn. Settlers and friendly Indians in large numbers are converging upon the post due to the threats of attack by the Creeks. Claiborne, after arriving, dispatches 175 troops under Major Daniel Beasley to the post. With the arrival of Beasley's command, the fort's complement rises to about 245 men. The fort is under the command of officers Dunn and Plummer; however, neither has experience. An election is held on 6 August. Dixon Bailey is chosen as the post captain and a man named Crawford is elected ensign.

General Claiborne reaches Fort Mims on 7 August. He writes to Colonel Hawkins to inform him of his arrival with the volunteers. He also mentions that he expects the 39th U.S. Infantry to join him shortly. Claiborne tells Hawkins that he is waiting to hear from General Thomas Flournoy to receive permission "to strike for the heart of the Creek nation." However, Flournoy believes the Creeks are only going to enter hostilities between themselves, based on information supplied to him by Hawkins. Nevertheless, when Flournoy's response arrives, Claiborne is disappointed. The response: "Your wish to penetrate into the Indian country, with a view of commencing the war, does not meet my approbation; and I again repeat, our operations must be confined to defensive operations."

Claiborne also receives another response to his request that Flournoy call out the militia to protect the settlements — his request is denied. Flournoy responds: "I am not authorized to make the call." General Claiborne decides on his own to dispatch troops to provide protection. In addition to the contingent being sent to Fort Mims, he sends 150 troops under Colonel Joseph Carson to Fort Madison. Captain Abram M. Scott repairs with one company to St. Stephens. He also dispatches a small contingent led by Captain Benjamin Dent to Oke-a-tapa along the Choctaw line to place eyes upon them in case they decide to join with the Creeks.

In Canada, Commodore Chauncey arrives near Burlington Heights from Niagara during the morning. A force of several hundred troops, including sailors and U.S. Marines, under Lt. Colonel Scott, debarks. About 150 British under Major Maule raise stiff resistance. The Americans seize some prisoners (civilians, possibly militia in the town) and return to the ships.

In Ohio, a squadron of the 2nd Light Dragoons, commanded by Major Ball, is caught by an ambush of Indians aligned with the British at Fremont. The detachment is escorting the 17th U.S. Infantry Regiment from Fort Seneca to Fort Stephenson. Colonel Wells of the 17th Infantry is heading to Fort Meigs to relieve Major Croghan, the latter having failed to abandon Fort Meigs as ordered by General Harrison. The Indians delay the column, but only for a short time. Major Ball initiates a charge and the Indians, who despise facing a bayonet, are equally fearful of the cavalry's sabers. The squadron charges and

17 of the Indians suddenly die by the sabers. Afterward the column resumes the march. (*See also,* August 1–4.)

Late July to October *In naval activity,* the British increase their presence in the area, including the eastern approach to Long Island Sound and at the Thames River in an effort to tackle the growing problem of American privateers ravaging British merchant shipping. The constant British pressure causes anxiety to the citizens of Connecticut. General Henry Burbeck, commander of the U.S. troops in New London, approves the citizens' request to petition Governor John C. Smith for the protection. On 29 October, at New Haven, Governor Smith issues the following order: "Col. William Randall, 30th Regiment of Militia: SIR— Pursuant to a request of certain Inhabitants of the Town of Stonington and of Brigadier Gen. Burbeck, commanding the United States troops at New London, I do hereby, In conformity to advice of the Council, direct you to detach from your Regiment one subaltern, two sergeants, two corporals, and twenty-six privates, for a guard at Stonington Point, to serve from the first day of November next to the 30th of the same month, Inclusive, unless sooner dis-charged." The order is signed "JOHN COTTON SMITH, Capt. General." The troops are placed under the command of Lt. Horatio G. Lewis.

In other naval activity, Commodore Rodgers, aboard the USS *President,* is operating in the North Atlantic and continues to do so throughout the summer. The *President*'s incursion into British waters causes the Royal Navy to initiate a massive search. While the *President* sails completely around Ireland, more than 20 British warships are diverted to intercept it, but in vain. Rodgers evades the British navy, while his crew captures 11 merchant ships and one armed schooner, the HMS *Highflyer.* Rodgers releases most of the captives on parole; they return to England aboard captured ships. After successfully concluding its cruise in hostile waters, the *President* sets sail for the United States and arrives at Newport in late autumn. The cruise, which began at Boston during the latter part of April, lasts 148 days. After a short stay in the States, Rodgers again departs in early December.

For nearly all of 1813, the United States has only two frigates in addition to the *President* operating against the British. The other two are the *Congress* and the *Essex.* The British have the *Constellation* locked in at Norfolk and the British have been able to prevent the *Macedonia* and the *United States* from getting through the blockade off New London. The other frigates include the *Constitution,* which is out of service for repairs until the latter part of the year, and the *John Adams* has been deemed unfit for service. The remaining two frigates, the *Boston* and the *New York,* had been condemned. To cause more disadvantages, the only brigantine remaining in service is the USS *Enterprise.*

July 31 (Saturday) *In naval activity,* the 2-gun privateer *Wasp* engages the 10-gun HMS *Bream,* an 18-gun schooner. Despite the superior firepower of the Bream, the *Wasp* exchanges blows for about nine hours. The two ships spend the final 45 minutes badgering each other from close range. The *Wasp,* by this time, is incapable of further resistance, which compels it to capitulate.

In other activity, Commodore Chauncey arrives off York with the General Pike, the *Madison* and the *Oneida.* The ships are escorting nine schooners carrying a force under Lt. Colonel Scott, which is augmented by the U.S. Marines of the fleet. Based on information recently gathered during a raid on Burlington Heights, the troops land as expected; the town is undefended. The Americans free some prisoners held in the jail and they also enter the hospital, where they parole some patients. Before departing the town at about 2300, the troops also confiscate a few hundred barrels of flour, which are placed aboard vessels and are taken back to New York.

The Americans return to York on the following day. Two boats carry a landing party which moves about in search of stores and arms. The raiders destroy some artillery and boats and confiscate supplies and ammunition before returning to New York.

In other activity, the brigantine *Flor De Tejo* (P.J. Mezado, master), carrying a cargo that includes camphor, coffee and "dragon's blood wine" from Batavia to Providence, is intercepted by the HMS *Manly.* The cargo is later restored, but the inventory is short fourteen casks of wine. Also, the British privateer *Matilda* spots a sail, which is the sloop *May Flower* (A. Barnes, master), en route from New York to Boston with a cargo of corn, flour and rye. The *Matilda* closes and seizes the sloop. The HMS *Rattler* intercepts and seizes the 32-ton schooner *Porpois.* The prize and its cargo are taken into port at New Brunswick. Also, the HMS *Nimrod* intercepts and recaptures the 77-ton sloop *William and Ann.*

August 1–2 *In Ohio,* the British fleet under Captain Barclay, which is transporting the expeditionary force under General Proctor, moves up the Sandusky River en route to attack Fort Stephenson.

August 1–4 *In Ohio,* British General Henry Proctor, leading a force of about 5,000, including Indians under Tecumseh, moves against Fort Stephenson, named in honor of Colonel Mills Stephenson. Proctor, intent on reducing an American fort, following successive recent failed attempts to reduce Fort Meigs, moves to strike Fort Stephenson along the Sandusky River at present-day Fremont, Ohio. General Harrison, aware of Proctor's mission, had sent word to the commander, Major George Croghan (17th U.S. Infantry), that his positions would be untenable and that the stores should be burned and the fort abandoned once the enemy approaches. Nonetheless, the messenger from Harrison gets lost. By the time the orders reach Croghan, it is too late to evacuate because the Indians under Tecumseh had arrived before Proctor and their presence prohibits an attempt to safely evacuate.

Croghan, however, does not share General Harrison's concerns. Despite having only one piece of artillery and a Spartan force of about 160 men, he remains convinced that his troops will prevail. The British, accompanied by gunboats after sailing into Sandusky Bay, moved up the river while their Indian allies under Tecumseh had been closing upon the post by an overland route. Fort Stephenson, the British objective, is protected by pickets and further bolstered by a sizable ditch. Within the fort, a blockhouse stands at each corner. However, it lacks an abundance of artillery.

On the 1st, General Proctor, with his usual condescension, sends an ultimatum to the gar-

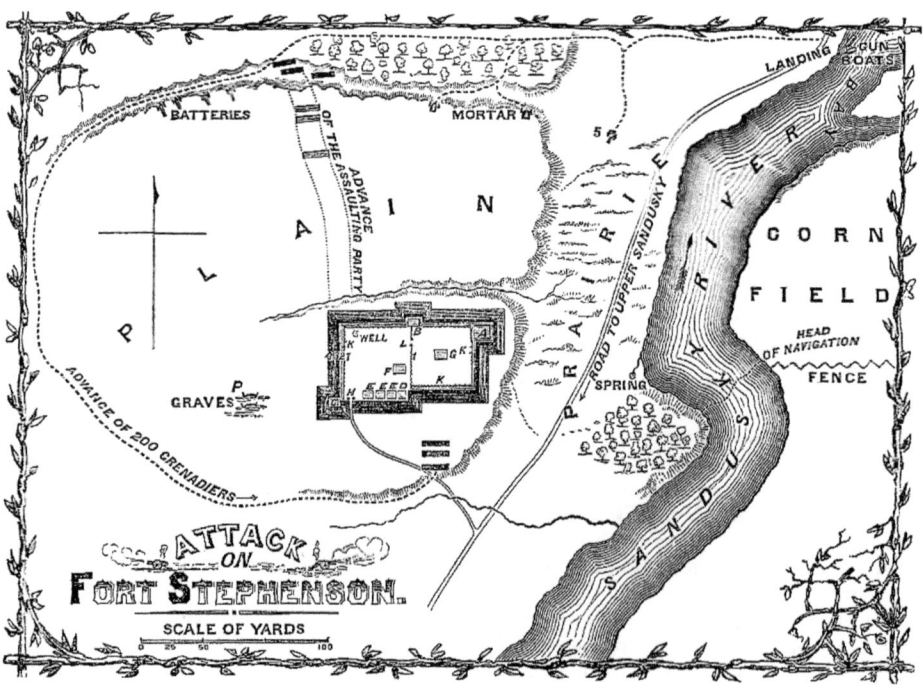

Attack on Fort Stephenson.

rison under the proposal that he is "anxious to spare the effusion of blood." The party, moving under a white flag, including British Colonel William Elliott and Major Chambers, approaches the post under the flag. Major Croghan is given two options, capitulate at once or face total annihilation by the Indians after the fort is taken. The half-breed officer, William Elliott, also reminds Croghan that the Indians are "excellent surgeons."

Elliott receives a response from an officer, 2nd Lt. Shipp, who informs the British that the post commander (Croghan) and his entire garrison has decided "to defend the post to the last extremity, and bury themselves in its ruins, rather than surrender it to any force whatsoever." Nevertheless, the British persist in convincing the garrison to surrender. One of the British officers, named Dixon, tries to intimidate Lt. Shipp: "Look at our immense body of Indians. They can not be restrained from massacring the whole garrison, in the event of our undoubted success."

Chambers, another officer in the British party, interjects: "Our success is certain." Dixon re-enters the conversation: "It is a great pity that so fine a young man as you [Shipp], and as your commander is represented to be, should fall into the hands of the savages. Sir, for God's sake, surrender, and prevent the dreadful massacre that will be caused by your resistance." Nonetheless, Lt. Shipp remains unimpressed by the rhetoric and retorts: "When the fort shall be taken, there will be none to massacre. It will not be given up while a man is able to resist."

After the British conclude that further negotiations would be fruitless, Lt. Shipp moves to return to the fort. All the while, Major Croghan had remained in earshot of the conversation. Suddenly, an Indian attempts to grab Shipp's sword and the lieutenant moves to liquidate the thief; however, a British officer intervenes and saves the Indian's life. Meanwhile Croghan, infuriated by the incident, yells to Shipp: "Come in, and we will blow them all to hell!"

Croghan's confidence remains high but the fort has only one piece of artillery. However, Groghan had discovered a huge cache of arms inside the fort which was for the militia. Croghan improvises and distributes four to five rifles to every man in the garrison and all are loaded and ready to fire, which greatly increases his firepower.

Proctor, once again unable to frighten an American garrison into surrendering, reacts to the rejection by ordering his battery and his four gunboats to commence a thunderous bombardment soon after Croghan's response reaches him. The fire continues incessantly for two days; however, Proctor's guns concentrate primarily on the fort's northwest angle.

Croghan detects Proctor's strategy at about 1600 on the 1st and immediately moves to strengthen the part of the post that he expects to become the object of the main thrust. Croghan instructs the garrison to fortify that point with sand bags and bags of flour. Based on his instincts, Croghan also redeploys his solitary gun there. In addition, the troops reinforce the walls with bags of flour and sand while they await the assault. On the 2nd, Croghan's defensive moves had proved correct when the British advance to the precise point Croghan had fortified.

Just after dusk, unaware that the garrison is totally prepared, the Redcoats advance in three columns. One approaches the northwest angle while the other two pass near the western side of the post to feign an attack there. The British column under Lt. Colonel Short receives no fire from the fort as it encroaches the ditch and the concealed 6-pounder. As their confidence builds, they begin to close under clouds of smoke from a distance of about 20 yards when they are spotted. At that same time, the British are greeted by a terrific volley from Kentucky riflemen. British troops begin to fall but the advance continues.

Lt. Colonel Short bellows encouraging words as his troops climb the pickets and descend into the ditch, saying: "Now, then, scale the pickets, and show the d—d Yankee rascals no quarter!" However, the attacking force lacks ladders. At nearly the same time that Colonel Short bellows his orders, the American gunners unmask their artillery piece and from near point-blank range, the British force is mauled. The guns rake the intruders and its deadly fire is bolstered by the riflemen who complete the destruction of the column.

Lt. Colonel Short, having just ordered his men to give no quarter, is mortally wounded. He is able to wave a white handkerchief atop the tip of his sword in an attempt to request quarter. While Short's decimated column is knocked out of action, the British send another column to complete the task and break through. Nevertheless, the second column receives identical resistance. The combined fire of the solitary gun and the Kentucky riflemen eliminate yet another British column.

The British troops near the south side of the fort encounter more ferocious fire from the riflemen, who force those troops into a hurried retreat after only a single volley. General Proctor's force is so thoroughly decimated that he is unable to continue. Meanwhile, the Indians posted at the rear of the fort to cut off any advancing reinforcements encounter none; however, more importantly, Croghan's men did not require any. His riflemen and their one gun, which is shortly after the victory nicknamed "Ole Betsy," had added one more embarrassing defeat to Proctor's record.

A British soldier, Squire Reynolds, the brother of Major Reynolds, later described the scene:

> Fire was opened on the work from the six-pounders, and on the evening of the 2nd August, Colonel Short, of the 41st, led on the storming party. They rushed through the smoke, down into the ditch, up against the palisades, but neither ladders, nor facines had been provided; the tools they had were bad, some of the axes had no handles. The attempt to tear down the palisades failed. The men then tried, desperately, to clamber over, and while doing so, the enemy opened from a concealed gun, which flanked the ditch, and which charged with grape, did deadly execution. Lieutenant Gordon and Colonel Short were both killed; about 100 men were killed and wounded, and the recall was sounded.

The British await darkness before retrieving their dead and wounded; however, some are left behind. They depart on the following morning (4th) to Malden but they fail to take many of their military stores and some of their deceased troops. The bodies of Lt. Colonel Short, Lt. Gordon, and 25 troops attached to the British 41st Regiment are discovered by the Americans when they inspect the ditch.

The Americans, who chose to fight a major force rather than surrender, sustain only one man killed and seven with minor wounds. The British, who came under menacing effective fire during the failed attack, claim their losses at 27 killed and 70 wounded, the same number recovered by the Americans. Major Croghan states in his report: "My whole loss, during the siege, was one killed, and seven slightly wounded. The loss of the enemy, in killed and wounded, and prisoners, must exceed 150. One Lieut. Colonel, a Lieutenant, and 50 rank and file, were found in and about the ditch, dead or wounded; those of the remainder, who were not able to escape, were taken off during the night by the Indians."

In a subsequent letter from Croghan to General Harrison, Croghan states: "I was determined to defend the place to the last extremity; and that no force, however large, should induce me to surrender it." Major Croghan and his officers had decided that to defend the fort would be less dangerous than to surrender. Major Croghan is later awarded a gold medal by the U.S. Congress, which gives a sword to each of the officers who participated in the defense of the post. The British also leave a small vessel containing clothing and supplies behind when they depart.

Lt. Shipp, a Kentuckian, following the success at Fort Stephenson, is promoted to become General Duncan McArthur's brigade major. In March 1814, he is promoted to 1st lieutenant and then to captain in May 1814. He remains in the service following the close of hostilities until his death at Bellefontaine, Ohio, on 22 April 1817.

August 2 (Monday) **In Washington, D.C.,** Congress assesses the states $3,000,000 to continue the war with England. The U.S. had previously borrowed $16,000,000 during February for the identical purpose.

In Alabama, General Claiborne again writes to General Flournoy to inform him that the inhabitants in the region have sought safety in stockades; however, he also states that very few of them are capable of defending themselves. Claiborne makes it known that he had divided his force to provide protection to the vulnerable settlers who have a high probability of being victimized by the tomahawk. Claiborne's decision to defend settlers has decreased the force at his headquarters to about 80 men. He urgently requests that reinforcements (7th U.S. Regiment) be sent to enable his force to move into the Creek nation, if authorized, stating: "I will do so in ten days, and give to the frontiers peace, and to the government as much of the Creek country as it desires. A strong force should enter the nation before they are every where in arms. With a thousand men, and your authority to march, I pledge myself to burn the principal towns. Three months hence it may be difficult to effect with three thousand men what may now be done with a third of that number." Nonetheless, Flournoy's response is negative due to fear of a Spanish attack against Mobile.

In naval activity, the 164-ton ship *Hope* (J. Jordan), transporting a cargo of fruit, wine and whalebone from Lisbon, is seized by the HMS *Manly* before it arrives at Boston. The *Hope* is separate from the ship *Hope,* seized on 28 August 1813, the brigantine *Hope* seized on 29 June 1814, the schooner *Hope* captured 16 August 1814, the sloop *Hope* seized on 4 December 1814, and the shallop *Hope for Peace,* overtaken 18 July 1813.

August 3 (Tuesday) **In Massachusetts,** a Boston newspaper publishes the following: "The ship Fair American, Captain Weathers, which arrived here Monday from Lisbon, was boarded on the 26th of July in latitude 42 degrees, longitude 64 degrees from his Britannic Majesty's frigate Maidstone, Captain Burdett, after a chase of seventeen hours and the following particulars respecting the infamous treatment received from Captain Burdett." The article continues by inserting exchanges between Burdett and Captain Weathers in which Weathers is repeatedly called a liar, as well as Burdett's accusation that the United States is a nation of liars. Burdett also demands that the Americans pay him a large amount of money before they are permitted to continue. Burdett had also refused to accept that the *Fair American* was carrying British licenses to pass all British warships.

In New York, Commodore Chauncey orders Commandant Jesse Elliott to select 100 men, including officers, from the USS *General Pike,* which is on Lake Ontario, and afterward repair to Lake Erie to assume command of the Niagara.

In Ohio, the British under General Henry A. Proctor are repulsed at Fort Stephenson (*see also,* **August 1–4**).

In naval activity, the HMS *Boxer* intercepts and seizes the 47-ton schooner *Hannah* on its way from Boston to Thomas Town with a cargo of corn. The prize is taken to New Brunswick. The *Hannah* is separate from the brigantine *Hannah* seized on 30 April 1813 and the sloop *Hannah* captured 10 July 1813. The HMS *Martin* intercepts and seizes the sloop *Louisa* before it arrives at Providence, Rhode Island, with a cargo of hides and indigo. The *Louisa* is separate from the brigantine *Louisa* seized on 26 March 1815. The HMS *Boxer,* which had recently seized the 86-ton schooner *Rebecca,* encounters a 117-ton schooner also named *Rebecca,* and it too is seized.

August 4 (Wednesday) **In Georgia,** Governor David B. Mitchell directs General Blackshear to provide protection to the civilians in the area from ongoing Indian hostilities.

In naval activity, the HMS *Emulous* intercepts and recaptures the schooner *Four Brothers* (R. Sinclair, master). The *Four Brothers* is separate from the schooner *Four Brothers* seized 16 October 1812. The British privateer *Broke* encounters and captures the sloop *Freeport* (A. Dyer, master). Also, Captain David Porter's squadron arrives at a point between James Island and Albemarle Island. After some minor difficulty, the ships enter the harbor at James Island during the afternoon. The crew paints the ships and makes other repairs that could not be accomplished at sea. In the meantime, every day, boats are dispatched to catch tortoises, a common task undertaken by all ships arriving in the Galapagos Islands. Captain Porter notes that within four days, the total weight of the turtles was fourteen tons. Porter also states: "They require no provisions or water for a year, nor is any farther attention to them necessary, than that their shells should be preserved unbroken."

August 4–5 **In Pennsylvania** at Presque Isle (Erie) by this day (4th), commodore Oliver H. Perry has his entire squadron moored in one harbor. He has placed his flag on a new brigantine, which had been named USS *Lawrence.* Up to now, the bar had been a protective barrier against an approaching British fleet; however, that same bar becomes a huge obstacle for Perry. His squadron, standing at ten ships, cannot get the heavier vessels over the bar except when the weather is extremely calm and then, all of the armament must first be removed before the excruciating task of passing the bar. Even greater dangers threaten Perry. A British fleet is lurking. If the British strike while the Americans are engaged in getting their larger vessels over the bar, it could be catastrophic for Perry's squadron and the United States in general. Perry has the Herculean responsibility of halting the British on Lake Erie or leaving a clear path open for the British to push through Pennsylvania to New York.

Perry receives some luck when British Commodore Barclay accepts an invitation to dinner from a man who lives on the opposite side of the lake. Barclay sails there with his entire squadron. The Americans make their move this day while Barclay is absent. The smaller vessels easily pass the bar; however, the passage of the *Lawrence* becomes a complicated endeavor that is not completed until the following morning. The *Lawrence* is provided with a large scow on each side, and on her arrival at the bar these scows were nearly filled with water, and sunk very low. Great beams were then passed through her port-holes, the ends projecting over the scows. Piles of blocks were provided for these ends to rest upon, and then the holes in the scows were plugged up, and the water pumped out. As the scows rose, they lifted the brig with them. But though her guns had been taken out and left on the beach, as well as all other heavy articles that could be removed, it still drew too much water to pass the bar. Another lift was made, which occupied the night, and finally she floated across.

Meanwhile, the Niagara, also a large ship, is taken over the bar with a considerably less effort.

On the 5th, at about 0800, the British reappear. The *Lawrence* by this time is beyond the bar and all of its guns have been brought back aboard. The British are greeted with a bombardment from long range. No damage is inflicted, but the fire is sufficient to cause Commodore Barclay to delay his attack. With Perry's squadron at or over the bar, the British, having lost the advantage, retire. Nonetheless, Perry is out and able to navigate. The two antagonists will not encounter each other until the following month.

August 5 (Thursday) **In Washington, D.C.,** the secretary of war, in conjunction with President Madison's recent orders to U.S. Naval officers, mandates that "all officers of the army of the United States commanding districts, forts or fortresses are commanded to turn back, and in case of any attempt to evade this order, to detain all vessels, or river or bay craft, which may be suspected of proceeding to or communicating with, any station, vessel, squadron, or fleet of the enemy within the waters of the United States."

In naval activity, the 7-gun privateer *Decatur,* out of Charleston and commanded by Captain Dominique Diron, spots two vessels in the distance while patrolling the trade route traveled by British merchant ships en route from the West Indies to England. The *Decatur,* carrying a crew of 103, including officers, immediately after detecting the sails at about 1030, begins to close upon the target by moving southward to get the weather-gage. Within about one-half hour, the *Decatur,* armed with one long 18-pounder and six 12-pound carronades, comes close enough to know that it has intercepted a schooner and a ship. Captain Diron is unable to determine the origin of the vessels; however, they are the *Princess Charlotte,* a packet and the HMS *Dominica.* British colors are hoisted at about noon to set the stage for the engagement.

The *Decatur* eventually comes abreast of the *Dominica,* commanded by British Lieutenant Barrette. The *Dominica* carries a crew of 88 men (about 8 or 10 of them are young boys), slightly less than the *Decatur*'s 103; however, it is more heavily armed, carrying twelve 12-pound carronades, one 32-pound carronade, two long 6-pounders and one brass 4-pounder. For nearly

The schooner *Decatur* battles the schooner *Dominica* (*History of American Privateers [and letters of marque],* George Coggeshall, 1856).

three hours, the *Dominica* and the *Decatur* maneuver for advantage and at about 1330, the *Dominica* fires a shot, but it inflicts no harm. At the sound of the British gun, Diron orders his boarding party to prepare to board. Meanwhile, the British are being informed of the *Decatur*'s origin just as the American flag is hoisted.

Meanwhile, all men aboard the *Decatur* are at their battle stations and their guns are poised to fire upon orders. The *Decatur* closes and Captain Diron moves to position the *Decatur* at a point which will permit its guns to blaze in unison, then use the cover of the blinding smoke to permit the boarding party to spring upon the *Dominica* and strike with surprise. Before the *Decatur*'s guns begin to fire, the *Dominica* is able to deliver a broadside, but most of the shot is propelled beyond the *Decatur*. At about 1415, the *Decatur*'s long gun goes into action. Nonetheless, the British guns do not remain dormant. The guns on the *Dominica*'s main deck return fire. The close-range fire from the *Decatur* apparently inflicts heavy damage to the *Dominica*, and Captain Diron suspects it is about to run.

To prevent flight, the *Decatur*'s bowsprit swings over the stern of the *Dominica*; however, the British move to negate the action by delivering another broadside, but yet again, the *Decatur* escapes serious damage. The *Decatur* resumes firing with its long gun. All the while, Diron's boarding party awaits the order to move into action. As the *Decatur* nudges closer to the *Dominica*, again it is met by a broadside at about 1445, and at the same time, by the boisterous cheers of the British crew who sense the imminent demise of the Yankee privateer. Nevertheless, the *Decatur*, which sustains some damage and the loss of two men, continues to drive forward. While it advances, riflemen on its deck begin to pick off British crewmen, while its guns maintain their fire.

The British continue to maneuver to keep some distance from the *Decatur* to prevent being boarded. The *Decatur* does come up close, but the British repel the attempt to board. At about 1530, the *Decatur*'s bowsprit is shoved over the *Dominica*'s stern, while simultaneously, the jibstern penetrates the *Dominica*'s main sail. Musket fire becomes incessant while the boarding party bolts from the bowsprit onto the *Dominica* to ignite a feverish close-quartered battle.

As the Americans crash aboard the *Dominica*, the brutal close-quartered fighting quickly begins to shred the British crew. The decks of the *Dominica* display the gruesome results of the slashing swords and the shots fired from pistols at point-blank range. The deck becomes coated with blood and crowded with dead and wounded from the ferociousness of both sides as they bludgeon each other with no quarter given. The British wounded and dead, including nearly all of the officers, makes the path to victory insurmountable. Nonetheless, the British refuse to capitulate, and twice, they have repelled the boarding party. However, on the third attempt at 1530, the Americans succeed in boarding the *Dominica* and the British become more determined to cast them off. A donnybrook ensues. The attackers and the defenders become intertwined and bash each other at close-quarters. Nearly 200 men are slugging it out with fists, swords and even pistols. All the while musket fire from the Decatur adds to the terror. During this uncontrollable melee, the British commander, Lieutenant G.W. Barrette, is killed. His demise, combined with the high casualty toll, finally compels the British to surrender. After seizing control of the *Dominica*, the Americans remove the British ensign. Captain Diron oversees the operation to provide medical attention to the wounded, American and British, and the burial at sea of the dead before proceeding back to port.

Meanwhile, the *Princess Charlotte* had made no attempt to aid the *Dominica*; rather it remained aloof, satisfied to merely observe the hour-long duel. Once the *Princess* senses an American victory, it moves southward and vanishes by about dusk. When it arrives in England, its commander turns in a report that when he separated from the escort, the *Dominica* had been "in hot pursuit of a Yankee privateer."

The American casualties vary from five killed and 15 wounded to 13 killed and 47 wounded. The British lose 60 either killed or wounded. Only two British officers, the ship's surgeon and one midshipman, escape unscathed. One officer, the *Dominica*'s first lieutenant, had not been aboard due to sickness. After completing repairs, the *Decatur* and its prize sail for Charleston. On the following day, the *Decatur* encounters a merchant ship, the *London Trader*, transporting a valuable cargo (coffee, cotton, molasses, rum and sugar), from Surinam to London. The *London Trader* had been under convoy with the *Dominica* on the previous day. Its journey is terminated. The *Decatur* seizes it and afterward, it is sailed into Savannah. The *Decatur* and *Dominica* sail to Charleston. The *Decatur* evades two British warships on blockade duty and slips safely into port on 20 August. Captain Barrette, wounded twice in the arm before being killed, had vowed "not to survive the loss of his vessel."

The *Decatur* is separate from the privateer *Decatur* under Captain S.N. Lane out of Maine and the privateer *Decatur* out of Newburyport under Captain Nichols. Also, the *Decatur* subsequently seizes other vessels, including the ship *Nelson* (a three decker) while it is transporting a valuable cargo to Jamaica. The *Decatur* also captures the 2-gun brigantine *Thomas*. In other naval activity, the sloop *Amelia* (J. Skidmore, master), traveling from New Haven to New Brunswick, is intercepted and seized, along with a cargo of corn and flour, by the British privateer *Retrieve*. The British privateer *Matilda* intercepts and seizes the 43-ton sloop *Minerva* on its way to Newport, Rhode Island, from New York with a cargo of flour and other items. The *Minerva* is separate from the brigantine *Minerva* seized on 6 July 1812, the ship *Minerva* taken 8 September 1812, the brigantine *Minerva* captured 30 June 1813, the schooner *Minerva* seized on 30 August 1813, the brigantine *Minerva* seized on 21 April 1814, the schooner *Minerva* captured on 11 August 1814, and the schooner *Minerva* captured on 26 September 1814.

August 6 (Friday) In Alabama, General Claiborne arrives at Fort Mims from Mount Vernon. He directs Captain Dixon Bailey (elected post captain the day before) to strengthen the post by building two more blockhouses. Bailey is directed to increase the picketing. However, Bailey begins to receive requests for protection from other locations, which causes him to drain his own strength by sending detachments to Fort Easley, Fort Madison and Fort Pierce. Bailey also sends a detachment to Joshua Kennedy's sawmill. The sawmill had become a gathering place for settlers, and it also is responsible for supplying lumber for Fort Charlotte at Mobile and a new post at Mobile Point. Bailey believes the sawmill must be defended to ensure that it is not destroyed by the Creeks.

In naval activity, the sloop USS *Preble* (also known as *Commodore Preble*), acquired by the navy earlier this year, is commissioned. Lt. Charles Budd receives command. The *Preble* participates at the Battle of Lake Champlain the following September.

In Maryland, a British naval force seizes Kent Island. Several thousand troops land but the island is essentially deserted because most of the residents had already evacuated. Nonetheless, the ships remain there and marauding expeditions are launched from the island to terrorize the region.

August 7 (Saturday) In Maryland, 45 barges leave Kent Island to attack militia under Major Nicholson at Queenston, a tiny town along the Chester River that has just over ten dwellings. Nicholson's force includes some infantry and cavalry bolstered by artillery; however, the total strength amounts to only about 280 troops. The British force, composed of about 1,500 men, advances against the front of the town, while a contingent is carried by barges to a point from which the Redcoats can plow into the rear to prevent the defenders from escaping the net. Nonetheless, the scheme is foiled when a British contingent is detected by a patrol led by Captain Massey as the column arrives at a point about two miles from the town. Massey deploys his 18 men behind a fence and patiently waits for the column to reach near point-blank range before giving the order to fire. Soon after delivering the volley, Massey retreats on a ragged route. After a while, they pause behind another fence to wait to spring yet another ambush. The British pursuers advance and are again hit with some blistering fire before the patrol hurriedly takes off for the village.

The main body in the town has been alerted by the firing in the distance which gives them time to assemble. Captain Massey requires little time to discern that his command is imperiled and that his force is insufficient to defend its positions. He orders a retreat and inadvertently gets some assistance from the British landing force that hits the ground at Blakeford Shore, where they encounter a creek that separates them from the town. Massey, with the help of the mistake in landing, leads his force to Centerville. His column is pursued, but after a short time, the chase is terminated. The patrol led by Nicholson sustains no casualties and the main body also escapes unscathed. The British sustain a few men killed or wounded.

In naval activity, the British privateer *Matilda* intercepts and seizes the *Alligator*, carrying a cargo of codfish and other items. Also this day, the *Matilda* captures the 39-ton sloop William. The *William* is separate from the bark *William* seized on 8 July 1812, the brigantine *William* captured 16 August 1812, the schooner *William* seized 12 March 1813, the brigantine *William* seized on 31 May 1813, the schooner *William* overtaken 27 October 1813, the schooner *William* seized 19 June 1814, the brigantine *William* captured 11 October 1814, and the schooner *William* seized at an unspecific time during 1814.

In yet other naval activity, the British privateer *Matilda* intercepts and captures the 74-ton schooner *Lydia* and its cargo of codfish and oil. The *Lydia* is separate from the *Lydia* seized on 24 October 1812 and the *Lydia* captured on 4 April 1813. The brigantine *Caravan* (J. Snow, master), transporting a cargo of molasses and rum, is intercepted and captured by the British privateer *Retrieve* while it is en route from Antigua to Portland, Maine. The British privateer *Broke* takes possession of the schooner *Mary* (Pyam Prince, master). Also, the British privateer *Dart* captures the 94-ton schooner *Three Brothers*. The prize and its cargo of ballast are taken to New Brunswick. The *Three Brothers* is separate from the schooner *Three Brothers* seized on 19 March 1813.

August 7–8 ***In naval activity,*** the schooners USS *Scourge* and the USS *Hamilton* are struck by heavy gales while operating on Lake Ontario. Both vessels capsize and sink. More than 80 men are lost. The *Julia* and other nearby vessels are able to rescue 16 men and both vessels. The *Scourge* was earlier the HMS *Lord Nelson*, captured on the lake by the USS *Oneida* during May 1812 and renamed the *Scourge*. Sailing Master Joseph Osgood receives command.

August 7–13 ***In naval activity,*** the American squadron under Commodore Chauncey engages a British squadron on the 7th; the contest is a running battle. Later a similar engagement occurs on the 11th, as both sides fight for supremacy on Lake Ontario. Chauncey had set sail on the 7th to draw the British into an engagement, but the operation suffers tragedy with the sinking of the *Hamilton* and the *Scourge* (8th). On the 9th, the *Growler* and the *Julia* are taken by the British, which causes Chauncey to return to Sackets Harbor on the 13th with the *Conquest, Governor Tompkins, Lady of the Lake, Madison, Oneida, Ontario* and *Pert*. The *Asp* and the *Fair American* remain at Niagara.

August 7–23 In Massachusetts, the brigantine USS *Henry*, commanded by Captain George Crowninshield, acting upon authorization from President Madison and flying a flag of truce, departs from Salem en route to Halifax to request the remains of Captain James Lawrence and Lt. Augustus C. Ludlow, both of whom died as a result of the recent sea battle between the USS *Chesapeake* and the HMS *Shannon* on 1 June. The *Henry* arrives at Halifax on the 10th. By the 13th, the quest is successful. The *Henry* returns to Salem on the 18th with the remains of both officers. They are interred on 23 August at Salem. "The coffins were covered with black velvet, with the monograms of the heroes inclosed in wreaths, swords crossed, and a marginal border all embroidered in silver. The interior of the church was hung in black and decorated with cypress and evergreen; and in front of the sacred desk the names of LAWRENCE and LUDLOW appeared in letters of gold." The remains of Lawrence and Lt. Ludlow are taken to New York City, where they are re-interred in August in the Trinity churchyard. The grave sites are "marked by a mausoleum of brown freestone, around which are placed eight trophy cannon, with chains attached, forming an appropriate enclosure." At the time of his death, Captain James Lawrence was 32 years old.

August 8 (Sunday) Secretary of War John Armstrong strongly urges General James Wilkinson to make Kingston the first objective of the campaign to deprive the British of one of their primary depots. Wilkinson becomes disgruntled because of the claims that he lacks seasoned troops. General Wade Hampton, selected to coordinate with Wilkinson, despises him. The sentiments are mutual and the animosity creates problems before the offensive is even launched. The hostile feelings between Wilkinson and Hampton filter down through the respective forces, which only increases the chances of the failure of the expedition.

In Maryland, a British naval force — three ships of the line, five frigates, three brigantines and two schooners, supported by a number of smaller craft — is spotted off Baltimore. The defenders quickly move into action. Colonel Jamison's regiment (attached to the Baltimore County Brigade) deploys in some high ground about seven miles outside the city from where they can dominate a narrow pass near North Point, while another contingent, including the Marine Artillery Company, moves to high ground east of the city and deploys about 40 artillery pieces.

Meanwhile, Captain Stiles takes command of the Marine Battery on the waterfront at Fort McHenry. The British linger offshore, but no attack is launched. Afterward, the squadron moves toward Annapolis, but the defense is prepared here as well. A force composed of 220 sailors and about 100 Marines are deployed to meet a landing force if it debarks. The British, after evaluating the situation, depart from Annapolis to seek weaker targets.

In naval activity, the schooner *Dart* (W. Glover, master), transporting a cargo of coffee, flour and corn, is intercepted and seized by the British privateer *Broke*.

August 9–10 **In Maryland,** during the night of the 9th, a British force moves up the St. Michael's River to launch a raid on St. Michael's, a shipbuilding town in Talbot County. The British bombard the town; however, due to the darkness and because of preparations taken by the residents who were informed of the approach of the British, the British fail to inflict heavy damage. Meanwhile, after being informed by scouts of the imminent arrival of the British, General Perry Benson calls out the militia to be in position to meet the attack. The units that rush to the town include the companies of Captain Henry, Captain Kerr and the artillery company (Eastern Point Artillery) under Lt. Vickers and Captain William Dodson's artillery company. While the militia is deploying a British deserter arrives and he too informs Perry that the attack is imminent.

The militia is on full alert at 0200 on the 10th when the British barges arrive off Parrott's Point, where a small battery is deployed and manned by 15 men, led by Dodson. As the barges move close to shore during a rainstorm, they remain undetected until they reach the point where they begin to debark. The landing party quickly assembles and launches their assault oblivious to the fact that their movement is under observation. To the surprise of the British, they fail to see the militia take flight; rather, they are greeted by Dodson's two 9-pounders which stand less than thirty yards from the attacking line. Stunned by the unexpected barrage, the British regroup. The small American detachment finds that the position is not tenable and about to be encircled. Dodson orders both guns to be spiked and afterward, the men retreat.

The British seize the position and their confidence begins to build as they anticipate the quick seizure of St. Michael's. Nevertheless, the victors at the battery had not anticipated General Benson's strategy. Shortly after raising cheers in celebration of taking the battery, the bombardment of the lost battery continues until dawn, leaving no time for the intruders to get any rest. Shortly after dawn, the British determine the position is untenable. They too abandon the battery and returned to the barges, those that survived the artillery bombardment.

It is reported that the ill-fated raid had cost the British 29 killed and wounded, including two officers. General Benson's militia sustains no casualties. One of the original artillery pieces used to repel the British remains in the town square. The British launch another attack to seize St. Michael's on 27 August.

August 10 (Tuesday) **In Alabama,** General Ferdinand Claiborne dispatches a contingent of troops led by Colonel Carson to Fort Glass in Clarke County. Once there, he is to also establish Fort Madison. Another contingent under Captain Scott is dispatched to St. Stephens to secure and garrison an old Spanish Blockhouse there. Other missions are initiated to prepare for any Indian incursions, including mounted reconnaissance patrols. Later in the month, yet another force is sent to Oaktupa to fortify blockhouses there.

In naval activity, American Naval Captain Jesse D. Elliott arrives at Presque Isle with a force of approximately 100 men to reinforce Perry. Commodore Perry places him in command of the USS *Niagara,* sister ship of the *Lawrence*. Perry earlier requested badly needed reinforcements to meet the British challenge on the Great Lakes. In other activity, two American vessels, *Julia* and the *Growler*, lose contact with the remainder of Commodore Chauncey's squadron. The British capture both vessels; they are renamed the *Confiance* and *Hamilton* respectively. The two prizes are used as transports; however, their service under the British ensign is short-lived. Both are recaptured in early October.

August 10–11 *In naval activity,* the USS *General Pike,* recently attached to Commodore Chauncey's squadron, encounters a contingent of British Commodore Yeo's fleet. An engagement erupts, but the battle is inconclusive. On the following day, they resume the engagement, but again it ends without a victor. The *General Pike* returns to Sackets Harbor on the 13th to acquire supplies and afterward resumes its patrol on the Lake Ontario.

August 10–22 *In naval activity,* the American privateer *Rattlesnake* is especially active during this period. It seizes five brigantines, the *Betsey, Diligent, Friends Adventure, Paz* and *Thetis,* along with two sloops, the *Fame* and the *Perseverance.* During the cruise, the *Rattlesnake,* under Captain David Maffitt, captures a total of 18 vessels.

August 11 (Wednesday) *In naval activity,* the HMS *Borer* intercepts the brigantine *Ocean* and recaptures it.

August 12 (Thursday) There is concern for Annapolis, Maryland. U.S. Marines are rushed there from Washington to fortify it against an anticipated British assault.

In naval activity, the British privateer *Weazel* intercepts and captures the schooner *Don Carlos* (P. Miguel, master) while it is en route from Boston, Massachusetts, to Halifax with a cargo of flour and other items. The 35-ton schooner *Gannett* (J. Marble, master), sailing from Hingham, Massachusetts, on a fishing trip, is spotted and seized by the British warships HMS *Curlew* and HMS *Nymphe.*

August 13 (Friday) **In Maryland,** an American contingent under Major William H. Nicholson (Queen Anne's County militia) skirmishes with a British force of about 300 troops under Sir Thomas Sidney Beckwith. The British sustain two killed and General Beckwith has a close call. He is uninjured, but his horse is shot from under him. The incident known as the Battle of Slippery Hill occurs along the route leading to Queenston.

In naval activity, the 20-gun USS *Argus,* commanded by Captain William Henry Allen, captures a vessel transporting a cargo of wine (or liquor). The crew over consumes the wine during the night while it transfers the cargo to the *Argus.* The *Argus* had also recaptured the American privateer *Matilda.* During the predawn hours of the 14th the captured vessel is set afire. Shortly thereafter, the HMS *Pelican,* commanded by Captain Maples, is drawn to the area by the flames. A battle erupts; however, the gunners on the *Argus,* having celebrated too much, cannot fire effectively. The two ships exchange blows and during

Captain William Henry Allen, U.S. Navy.

the first few minutes, Captain William Henry Allen receives a mortal wound and 1st Lieutenant Watson sustains a severe wound. Nonetheless, the duel ensues for about one hour with command having passed to Captain Allen's younger brother. The Americans resist tenaciously until the *Argus* is no longer controllable. The steering has been badly damaged and the rigging is shredded. At that time, it surrenders.

Before its capture, the *Argus* had seized more than 25 British merchant vessels. The Americans sustain six killed and 17 wounded. The British sustain three killed and five wounded. In other activity, the brigantine *Chance* (W. Rodgerson, master), transporting a cargo of ballast, is intercepted and seized by the HMS *La Hogue* and the HMS *Tededos.* Also, the HMS *Curlew* and the HMS *Nymphe,* cruising together, intercept and seize the 157-ton schooner *Paragon.* The *Paragon* is separate from the brigantine *Paragon* seized 19 May 1813. Also, the HMS *Statira* recaptures the sloop *Polly.* The *Polly* is separate from the 84-ton schooner *Polly* seized 11 August 1812, the 85-ton schooner *Polly* captured 14 October 1812, the 92-ton sloop *Polly* seized on 28 July 1813, the 88-ton schooner *Polly* overtaken 10 December 1813, and the 45-ton sloop *Polly* captured on 10 August 1814.

August 14 (Saturday) **In Alabama,** Fort Mims is becoming overcrowded, despite the fact that Captain Bailey had sent part of his force to other locations to bolster other posts and a strategic sawmill. The post contains about 530 people, including the troops, settlers, Indians and Negroes. However, due to overcrowding and the intense summer conditions, many of the people, including the troops, become ill. Also, by this time, Ensign Crawford had been discovered as a deserter from the regular army. He is dismissed from his position as ensign. Peter Randon, a half-breed, is appointed to replace him. The Creeks, who had returned to Pensacola to receive arms and ammunition they had lost at Burnt Corn, have been re-supplied. The Creeks are moving back from Florida to the Tallapoosa River, while other Creeks are moving southward from various points including Cooloome, Ecunhutke, Fooshatche, Wewocoe and Woccocoie. Meanwhile, Creeks from Ottose, Tallase and other villages are acting as scouts to ensure the movement is not discovered.

In naval activity, the USS *Argus* is encountered by the HMS *Pelican* near St. George's Channel. The *Pelican* begins pursuit and closes on the *Argus* from the rear. The *Pelican* is the first to fire; however, the *Argus* returns fire. Nevertheless, the incoming fire strikes Captain William H. Allen. His right leg gets severed by the shot. Despite the agonizing pain from what is a mortal wound, Allen remains in command until he falls unconscious due to loss of blood. As the battle continues, the *Argus* sustains more damage that causes the vessel to be uncontrollable. Before the British board it, the crew strikes its colors. After a contest of about 45 minutes, the defeated *Argus* had sustained 10 killed, including Captain Allen, and 13 wounded.

The following year a new *Argus* is laid down at the navy yard in Washington, but it never gets to sea. When the British initiate their Maryland Campaign in the summer of 1814, the *Argus* is destroyed to prevent the British from capturing it when they advance toward the capital. It is destroyed on 24 August 1814.

In other activity, the British privateer *Dart* arrives off Newport, Rhode Island, with two prizes and in search of its next prey. By this time, the *Dart* has captured at least 20 vessels and possibly as many as 30. The USS *Vigilant* at port in Newport moves out to engage. Before embarking, Captain Cahoone of the *Vigilant* gathers an additional 20 men to bolster his crew. Once prepared, the *Vigilant* moves out and advances directly toward the privateer. Despite moving directly into the range of the *Dart's* guns, the privateer does not fire. Neither does the *Vigilant*; however, it closes and when it comes alongside, the crew of the privateer is stunned. A boarding party bolts onto the *Dart* and seizes it. Two Americans are killed during the operation. Both fall into the water while the troops board the vessel and both drown. The *Vigilant* remains in service beyond the war until at least 1835. It is sold at Boston in 1842.

August 15 (Sunday) **In Alabama,** General Claiborne continues to fret about whether the Choctaws will join with the Creeks. He dispatches Major Ballenger of the 24th Infantry Regiment to meet with Pushamataha of the Choctaws this day, but Major Ballenger dies in several days. Nevertheless, through the efforts of Colonel George S. Gaines, United States factor, John Pitchlyn, and Colonel John McKee, Chickasaw agent, Chief Pushmataha is persuaded to visit Mount Vernon. He is given the uniform of a brigadier general, which plays a large part in his decision to commit some of his warriors to side with the Americans and have the rest of his nation remain neutral. Chief Colbert, the principal Chickasaw chief, also visits with General Claiborne, who succeeds in keeping Colbert from siding with the Creeks.

August 16 (Monday) In New York at Albany, General Wilkinson dispatches orders to General Wade Hampton regarding the campaign to seize Canada. However, the friction between the two men immediately reignites when Hampton receives the communication. By the 23rd Hampton communicates with Secretary of War John Armstrong, and in the letter, Hampton insists that his command is separate and must not be taken from him before his campaign ends. He also stipulates that he should not be "encroached upon" by a superior officer. Wilkinson's letter struck a raw nerve with Hampton, who displays no signs of serving as a subordinate obliged to follow orders from Wilkinson, who will be several hundred miles distant. Hampton submits his resignation and requests a discharge. On the 25th, Armstrong writes to Hampton in an attempt to end the friction that could cause the campaign to fail. Armstrong's letter attempts to "reconcile him [Hampton] to a distinction between separate and independent commands."

In naval activity, the HMS *Fly* takes possession of the 229-ton brigantine *Diamond* (A. McLelland, master), which is transporting molasses from Antigua, Portugal, to Portland, Maine. In other activity, the sloop *Dolphin* (E. Johnston, master) is intercepted and seized by the British privateer *Fly*. The HMS *La Hogue*, while on patrol, intercepts and captures the 311-ton ship *Flor De Mar*, which is en route from Fayal (a Portuguese colony in the Azores) to Boston with a cargo that includes wine and wood.

August 17 (Tuesday) *In naval activity,* Commodore Oliver Hazard Perry arrives at Sandusky, Ohio, after spending some time searching for a British squadron. The USS *Erie*, which joined the squadron at Presque Isle the month before, is sent back to Presque Isle to acquire supplies. It returns to the squadron on 3 September. Upon its return, again it is sent back to Presque Isle. While on its special duty, the *Erie* is away from the squadron during the engagement with the British on 10 September on Put-in-Bay.

In other activity, the HMS *Curlew* and the HMS *Nymphe*, while patrolling off the New England coast, encounter and capture an American sloop, the 104-ton *Endeavor* (N. Stover, master) going from Castine, Maine, to Boston.

August 18 (Wednesday) *In naval activity,* the 204-ton brigantine *King George* (J. Thompson, master), which had left Liverpool with a cargo of salt, is recaptured by the HMS *Recruit*. In other naval activity, he HMS *Curlew* and the HMS *Nymphe*, take possession of the schooner *Morning Star*. The *Morning Star* is separate from the sloop *Morning Star* seized 13 June 1813 and the *Morning Starr* captured 11 June 1814.

August 20 (Friday) *In naval activity,* the British privateer *Broke* encounters and seizes the schooner *Industry* (T. Rice, master). The *Industry* is separate from the schooner *Industry* seized on 3 November 1813, the schooner *Industry* seized on 10 September 1814, and the sloop *Industry* captured on 16 January 1815. Also, the British privateer *Broke* intercepts and seizes the schooner *John and Miriam* (S. Rhodes, master). The British privateer *Broke* takes possession of the schooner *Samuel* (T. Snow, master). The privateer *Decatur* and its prize HMS *Dominica* arrive off Charleston. The British blockading ships go off in pursuit of a vessel, leaving the *Decatur* an opportunity to slip into port without incident. After going ashore, the prisoners relate how their captors had treated them kindly. The *Dominica* is transformed into a 4-gun privateer.

August 21 (Saturday) *In naval activity,* the USS *Sylph*, carrying 20 guns, built in just over 30 days, joins Commodore Chauncey's fleet and embarks this day on its first cruise.

August 23 (Monday) In Alabama, a Choctaw Indian comes to Fort Madison at St. Stephens with intelligence. He reveals that Fort Easley is to be attacked and afterward the Creeks plan to move against Fort Madison. The Indian states to Colonel Carson at Fort Madison that about 400 Indians would launch the strikes. Meanwhile, General Claiborne, assured by Major Daniel Beasley that Fort Mims was prepared to withstand any attack, decides to aid Fort Easley, which is defended by only about ten to fifteen men.

Claiborne places Captain Kennedy in charge of Mount Vernon, and he moves out toward Fort Easley with about 80 troops: 20 mounted dragoons, 30 troops from Captain Scott's company and 30 from Captain Dent's company. Claiborne also dispatches a message to Major Beasley directing him to keep the post on alert. Beasley receives the message on the 29th, the day before Fort Mims is attacked. Meanwhile, General Claiborne's movement to Fort Easley succeeds in convincing the Indians to abort their attack. They also believe that Fort Madison is too strong to assault.

In naval activity, the USS *Carolina* arrives at New Orleans from Charleston. Initially it patrols in search of British vessels and against pirates of the Caribbean. In September 1814 the *Carolina* participates in an attack against the stronghold of Jean Lafitte at Barataria; afterward, with Lafitte as an ally of General Andrew Jackson, the *Carolina* remains active against the British outside of New Orleans.

August 24 to October 6 *In naval activity,* the USS *Essex* arrives at the passage running between Albemarle and Narborough (Galapagos). Captain Porter is amused watching the seals and turtles that run alongside the *Essex*, and he gets the opportunity to watch the seals when they go after their prey, something he said had "been a mystery to him." The *Essex* remains in the area for a while. On 3 September, it departs from Chatham Island and moves to Hood's Island, where it drops anchor in a bay on the northern side of the island. Porter names the bay Rodgers' Bay in honor of Commodore John Rodgers, and the small land mass to the east of Chatham, he names Rodgers' Island.

On the 15th, after a chase, the *Essex* seizes the letter of marque ship *Sir Andrew Hammond*, which is carrying 12 guns. By 6 October, Captain Porter departs from the Galapagos for the Washington Islands. During this period, war erupts between Chile and Peru.

August 25 (Wednesday) *In naval activity,* the British privateer *Star* moves to the rear of Moose Island, then boards and effortlessly captures the sloop *Elizabeth*, which has no crew members on board.

August 26 (Thursday) In Maryland at St. Michaels, American militia about 600 strong under General Perry Benson engages and halts the advance of a British column. The British had landed on about 60 barges at Colonel Auld's farm in a new attempt to seize St. Michaels. That force, commanded by Sir Sidney Beckwith, is estimated at 1,600 to 1,800 troops. By evening the British column retires to the barges that carry the troops back to the ships. The participants, primarily from Talbot County, include the 4th and 26th Infantry, deployed in the woods, bolstered by the 9th Cavalry.

In New York at Sackets Harbor, a council of war is held. Participants include Generals Wilkinson, Lewis, Brown and Swarthout, along with Commodore Chauncey. The primary topic is an attack against Kingston and the seizure of Upper Canada. American intelligence that has been gathered estimates British strength standing between the head of Lake Ontario, Kingston and Prescott at about 9,000 men, including militia and Indian allies, and of those, it is thought that the British will be able to field about 4,000. However, according to American intelligence, Kingston would be an exception, and about 6,000 men would be prepared to defend against the attack.

In contrast, the American force which is to launch the offensive is estimated at about 9,000, excluding militia and naval forces. When the militia comes under discussion, there is little confidence that a sufficient force can be available by 20 September. It is determined that the American army is too widely scattered and that the fierce Canadian winter is fast approaching, leaving little time to act.

In naval activity, the brigantine *Elizabeth* is recaptured by the HMS *Shelbourne*. In other activity, the HMS *Statira* intercepts and seizes the schooner *Eposy Mina* (J.D. Olaguebel, master) while it is en route from La Guira, Cuba, to New York with a cargo of hides and indigo.

August 27 (Friday) In Maine, the privateer, *Mary* (a schooner separate from the privateer *Mary* commissioned July 1812) is commissioned this day. John Prichard receives command.

In Maryland, the British abandon Point Lookout, from where they had been conducting ravaging raids in St. Mary's County since the previous spring. In that region, the citizens had been compelled to resist on their own with no outside help. The region had also suffered from sickness. Furthermore, the British, who launched a failed attack against St. Michaels (Talbot County) on the 9th, launch a stronger force in a new attempt to seize the town. A flotilla, composed of more than fifty barges, arrives at a point about two miles below the town. Nonetheless, for an unspecified reason, thought to be that the American defenders had been stronger in number than expected, the attack is aborted.

In naval activity, the HMS *Majestic* seizes the 90-ton schooner *Euphemia* (J.D. Maria, master) which is transporting a cargo of copper and wood from Havana, Cuba, to Boston. Also, the HMS *Manly* intercepts and seizes the schooner *Raven*.

August 28 (Saturday) *In naval activity,* Commodore Chauncey's fleet again engages the British fleet under Commodore Yeo off York in Canada. During the engagement, two British ships sustain damage and the British retire into Burlington Bay. The USS *Ontario* participates. Following the contest, the *Ontario* continues to operate on Lake Ontario. After the cessation of hostilities, the *Ontario* is placed in ordinary until May 1815, when it is sold. In other activity, the 416-ton *Hope* (J. Emery, master) en route from Lisbon, Portugal, to Newport, Rhode Island, is seized by the HMS *Loup Cervier*. The *Hope* is separate from the ship *Hope*, seized on 2 August 1813, the brigantine *Hope* captured 29 June 1814, the schooner *Hope* seized 16 August 1814, the sloop *Hope* overtaken 4 December 1814, and the shallop *Hope for Peace* seized on 18 July 1813.

August 29 (Sunday) In Alabama, a large band of Indians led by Chief Red Eagle (William Weatherford), fresh from their victory at Burnt Creek, arrive at the vicinity of Fort Mims. Their presence goes undetected by the garrison; however, two slaves report seeing a party of Indians, all wearing war paint. The commander of the post, Major Daniel Beasley, had recently arrived due to the incessant raids by the Creeks. After being informed of the possible presence of hostile Indians, Beasley dispatches a detachment under Captain Middleton to investigate. The column moves out on a reconnaissance mission, but it returns and reports that there is no indication that Indians are in the area. One of the slaves responsible for reporting the presence of the Creeks, owned by John Randon, gets a flogging for lying; however, Fletcher, the owner of the other slave, forbids it because he believes the story. Beasley becomes infuriated with Fletcher and orders him to leave the fort with his family by the following morning. After the return of the column to the post, the alarm is disregarded. In the meantime, the Indians had concealed themselves in a ravine just outside of the fort, where they remained undiscovered until the following morning.

Fort Mims, initially built by a Mr. Mims to provide protection for the settlers, by this time has become overcrowded due to the influx of terrified settlers and the recent arrival of Beasley's command. Mr. Mims had enclosed about one acre for his stockade fort, which also contains a blockhouse still under construction. Since the arrival of the militia, the fort was enlarged by a new enclosure on the eastern side.

In naval activity, the schooner *Hero* (E. Langdon, master) is caught and captured by the British privateer *Dart* while it is en route from Kennebeck to Boston with a cargo of ballast. The prize is taken into port at New Brunswick. The *Hero* is separate from the schooner *Hero* seized on 12 June 1813, the schooner *Hero* captured on 14 November 1813, the sloop *Hero* taken on 13 January 1814, the schooner *Hero* captured on 3 July 1814, and the sloop *Hero* seized in early November 1814. Also, the HMS *Poictiers* recaptures the brigantine *Mariner*. The *Mariner* is separate from the ship *Mariner* seized 22 July 1812.

August 30 (Monday) MASSACRE AT FORT MIMS **In Alabama,** the militia at Fort Mims, about 40 miles north of Mobile, having disregarded a warning on the previous day about Creek Indians being nearby, takes no precautionary action. A scouting detachment dispatched the day before detected no intrusions. Due to the high tension in the region, many false alarms have been reported. Consequently, Major Beasley, the militia commander, dismisses the warning as just one more incident without merit. Operations remain casual and no additional guards are posted.

In response to a letter that Beasley received on the previous day from General Claiborne, he responds: "SIR,—I send inclosed the morning report [30th from Mim's Blockhouse] of my command. I have improved the fort at this place, and made it much stronger than when you were here. Pierce's Stockade is not very strong, but he has erected three substantial block-houses." The confidence within the fort is so high that the gates are open. John Randon's slave, who received a flogging on the previous day, moves out of the fort to take care of the cattle. Again he spots the Indians; however, he is afraid to report the sighting and face another flogging. He takes off for Fort Pierce. Nevertheless, about 1,000 Creeks under Chief Red Eagle are lurking in the shadows, concealed in a ravine about one-quarter of a mile from the fort. At the appointed time, 1200, a drum beat signals dinner. The troops converge on the mess hall and they leave their weapons behind. The drum beat apparently also sends a signal to Chief Red Eagle. At about the same time, the Indians, fully armed by the British at Pensacola, bolt from the ravine and without any resistance they charge though the gates.

Pandemonium erupts as officers rush to seal the gates and war cries permeate the air. Major Beasley rushes toward the outer gate, but in vain. The horde literally crashes through and Beasley is struck by tomahawks and clubs and then is trampled. He crawls behind the gate and dies. Every white person encountered is instantly murdered. Meanwhile, the Indians finally encounter stiff resistance when they plow against the inner enclosure and receive riveting fire from men who have reached the loop-holes. By this time, command has fallen to Captain Bailey. His marksmen stall the attackers, particularly after five of their chiefs are killed by the first volley when they penetrate the eastern part of the picketing. The deaths temporarily stun the Creeks. All five of the deceased chiefs had proclaimed that they were invulnerable to the bullets fired by the Americans. Once the shock wears off, the Indians renew the attack. Despite the overwhelming numbers of Indians and the tragic mistake of not being prepared, Captain Bailey maintains order and his militia show no outward signs of fatigue. Captain Middleton is at the eastern sector, while Captain Jack defends the south

REFERENCES.

1 Block House.
2 Pickets cut away by the Indians.
3 Guard's Station.
4 Guard House.
5 Western Gate, but not up.
6 This Gate was shut, but a hole was cut through by the Indians.
7 Captain Bailey's Station.
8 Steadham's House.
9 Mrs. Dyer's House.
10 Kitchen.
11 Mims' House.
12 Randon's House.
13 Old Gate-way—open.
14 Ensign Chambliss' Tent.
15 Ensign Gibbs'.
16 Randon's.
17 Captain Middleton's.
18 Captain Jack's Station.
19 Port-holes taken by Indians.
20 21 Port-holes taken by Indians.
22 Major Beasley's Cabin.
23 Captain Jack's Company.
24 Captain Middleton's Company.
25 Where Major Beasley fell.
26 Eastern Gate, where the Indians entered.

Fort Mims (*History of Alabama and Dictionary of Alabama Biography, Volume III*, Thomas McAdory Owen, 1921).

The Massacre at Fort Mims (*Valor and Victory [The Age of Vindication], Volume X*, Edwin Markham, 1912).

wing and Lieutenant Randon holds at the guard house. All the while, Captain Bailey defends the northern line of pickets.

The men at the loop-holes continue to pour fire into the attackers and the fighting continues without pause for a few hours. Even the civilians move to support the defenders. The troops at the loop-holes receive help from some of the women and boys. Some elderly men also choose to participate. The older civilians form a group that deploys inside the fort's tallest structure and once holes are cut through the roof, they add their firepower to the struggle. The Americans continue to inflict casualties upon the Indians and the fort is being held.

In the meantime, the garrison is essentially surrounded, and the yelling and screaming of the Indians does little else but annoy the foe. The sounds fail to intimidate the defenders. Captain Bailey urges everyone in the fort to join the fight, based on his belief that the Indians would soon tire if they can hold longer. After failing to get volunteers to break through the enemy lines to get reinforcements at Fort Pierce less than three miles distant, Bailey decides to go himself, but others fearful that he would be killed pull him back from the pickets.

At about 1500, as Bailey contended, the Indians begin to lose their focus. They turn their attention to pillaging. They loot the home of Mrs. O'Neil along the road to the ferry; however, William Weatherford (Red Eagle) intercepts the party and turns them around to have them rejoin the fight. Meanwhile, the women and children in the fort aid the defense by loading weapons for the men and by carrying water from the well. The surgeon, Doctor Osborne, sustains a mortal wound. One of the women, the wife of Captain Bailey, is conspicuous during the desperate battle; she encounters Sergeant Mathews cowering against a wall. She becomes incensed and stabs him with a bayonet because of his cowardice under fire.

Chief Red Eagle becomes frustrated at the failure of his force to reduce the resistance, while his casualties continue to mount. Red Eagle instructs his Indians to prepare burning arrows and deluge the post with the flying flames. Shortly thereafter, waves of fiery arrows descend upon the buildings within the fort. The effort is successful, and as the flames spread from building to building and the smoke overwhelms the garrison, the defenders have been driven by the choking smoke to a corner of the post.

A small group of defenders, including Captain Bailey's two brothers, James and Daniel, regroup on the roof of Mr. Mims' home, but here too the fires and smoke cause more problems. The defenders fire effectively; however, the faster the Indians fall, the more quickly more arrive. All the while, the painful cries of the women and children can be heard above the firing. Bailey and other survivors make it to Patrick's loom-house, where the surgeon, Doctor Osborne, had been taken after he sustained a mortal wound. From their final line of defense, Captain Bailey's survivors continue to raise ferocious resistance. During this tumultuous period, some other survivors are trying to reach the loom-house. Many do not complete the trek. David Mims runs the gauntlet, but he is struck in the neck with a mortal wound. He is able to speak only a few words: "Oh my God, I am a dead man." They were his final words before he fell to the ground and expired. A nearby Creek quickly takes his scalp and begins to swing it back and forth to further intimidate the remaining survivors.

Others, including some Spanish who had deserted from the Spanish post at Pensacola, Florida, are caught at the well where they are kneeling in prayer and making the sign of the cross. They are quickly liquidated by Creeks who swing their tomahawks. In the meantime, Bailey's last position at the loom-house is so crowded that there is literally no room for the men to defend the position. The Mims house had been reduced and its defenders dead. The fires by now are rapidly moving toward the last bastion and there is no chance of holding off the Creeks. Bailey urges the survivors to attempt an escape. Captain Bailey's 13-year-old son is carried to safety by Bailey's "negro man, Tom"; however, after reaching safety, the boy Ralph is brought back and handed to the Creeks, who "dashed out his brains with war-clubs." Those remaining alive try to break through to safety; however, the Creeks had warriors spread out to cover the escape routes. Captain Bailey, seriously wounded, along with the assistant surgeon at the post, Doctor Holmes, and one Negro woman named Hester are the first to break out. They make it as far as the swamp, but Bailey soon dies of his wounds. Doctor Holmes had been hit several times by balls that passed through his clothing but inflicted no wounds. Hester, however, despite being wounded in the chest, is able to reach a canoe, with which she arrives at Fort Stoddert with the first news of the massacre.

By this time, the defenses had crumbled and the Indians are completing their rampage. They show no mercy even to the women and children. Some of the smaller children are grabbed by their ankles, then swung into the walls where their heads are smashed and their "brains dashed out." In the same description, given by a noted historian, Rossiter Johnson; he says the "women were butchered in a manner unknown since the wars of the ancient Jews; a few Negroes were kept for slaves, but not one white person was left alive, excepting twelve, who had secretly cut an opening through the stockade." The subjects not covered in detail by Johnson included: "The women were scalped, and those who were pregnant were opened, while they were alive, and the embryo infants let out of the womb." Other settlers in the region that escape the wrath of the Indians are resettled at Fort Madison and nearby Fort Glass.

William Weatherford had attempted to stop the slaughter of the women and children, but to no avail. The Creek perpetrators threatened Weatherford with the same fate. The Creeks had extra incentive for their barbarous actions offered by the British agents at Pensacola, who placed a reward of five dollars for each scalp taken from an American. After five hours of furious fighting, the defenders had nearly been annihilated. Only about fifteen white people escape the massacre. Some Negroes are spared death; however the Creeks keep them as slaves. Also, some of the half-breeds are kept as prisoners. The following are the known survivors: Dr. Thomas H. Holmes (assistant surgeon); Socca (friendly Indian); Peter Randon; Josiah Fletcher; Sergeant Mathews (survives the attack and a stabbing by Mrs. Bailey); Hester (Negro woman who carried news of the attack to General Claiborne); Martin Rigdon; Samuel Smith (half-breed), Mourice (first name unknown); Joseph Perry (Mississippi volunteers); Edward Steadman; Jesse Steadman; John Hoven; Jones (first name unknown) and Lt. W.R. Chambliss (Mississippi volunteers).

On the day following the massacre, the Indians bury their dead in a potato field. They place some of their wounded in canoes and evacuate them, but some other wounded Indians begin their trek on foot and die along their journey at Burnt Corn. Nonetheless, some of the able-bodied Creeks remain in the region to continue their terror raids, while others move to Pensacola with the scalps of the dead on the tips of poles.

Prior to the massacre, Captain Beasley maintained steady contact with General Claiborne, and in each correspondence, Claiborne is informed that there had been no Indian presence. In the last communication, Beasley expressed confidence that the fort could hold regardless of the number of Creeks that might attack. Meanwhile, General Claiborne had led a force to Easely's Station in response that it was threatened; however, the station was not in danger. Following a 70 mile one-day journey, Claiborne arrives back at Fort Stoddert where he learns of the massacre at Fort Mims. Also, the few people at nearby Fort Pierce do not come under attack. They flee from the fort and reach the Alabama River, but they are unable to cross. Peggy Bailey, a sister of Captain Dixon Bailey, volunteers to swim the alligator infested river to get a flat-boat, and she succeeds. Once she brings it back to the opposite bank, the settlers cross and make it to Mount Vernon. The United States government later rewards Bailey for her heroic action by giving her a tract of land.

At the first sounds of the battle, at about noon, 553 people, including civilians and militia, were within the walls of the fort. The Indians had paid a high price to gain entrance; however, except for 12 people who cut their way out of the fort, nearly all of those still confined die before midnight (30th-31st). The gruesome story of the barbaric massacre spreads throughout the country and at every point, cries of vengeance are heard.

The first state to take action is Tennessee. At the time of the tragedy, about 1,500 Tennessean volunteers had already committed to service. The legislature immediately calls for an additional 3,500 volunteers. The sum of $300,000 is appropriated to cover the cost. Command of the force is given to General Andrew Jackson. General John Cocke is assigned responsibility for raising the force from East Tennessee. While it is being assembled, another officer, Colonel John Coffee, moves out in advance en route for Huntsville, Alabama. Coffee's contingent is composed of about 500 cavalrymen when it departs;

however, the strength rapidly grows while the column is en route. When Coffee arrives at Huntsville, his force stands at about 1,300. In the meantime, the volunteers continue to converge at the rendezvous point, Fayetteville, Tennessee, which lies at the border with Alabama. At the time of Jackson's appointment, he is laid up in a hospital in Nashville due to injuries sustained during an altercation with two brothers, Thomas H. and Jesse Benton.

Although Andrew Jackson is not yet a prominent name in the military annals, he does have experience with conflict in both the military and in his private life. As a young boy, he served as a spy during the American Revolution. Later, in his private life Jackson engaged in a duel with Colonel Waightstill during 1788, followed by a duel with Charles Dickenson in 1806. Jackson, also a lawyer and a former member of the U.S. Senate, had been elected as major general of Tennessee militia during 1801. Shortly after the massacre, a British warship arrives at Pensacola from the Bahamas. It is transporting arms, ammunition, clothing and blankets for distribution among the Creeks.

In naval activity, the British fleet threatening Baltimore and Washington, D.C., begins moving up the Chesapeake. Also, the British privateer *Weazel* seizes the 136-ton schooner *Minerva* (J.E. Scott, master) which is en route from Barbados to Wicassset, Maine, with a cargo of ballast. Separate vessels named *Minerva* also seized are a brigantine, 6 July 1812; a ship, 8 September 1812; a brigantine, 30 June 1813; a sloop, 5 August 1813; a brigantine, 21 April 1814; a schooner, 11 August 1814; and a schooner, 26 September 1814.

August 31 (Tuesday) In Alabama, some survivors of the massacre at Fort Mims reach Fort Stoddart, about 15 miles distant. The first survivor to arrive, a Negro woman named Hester, delivers the tragic news to General Claiborne. Due to concerns that Fort Stoddert would be in the path of the Creeks, the people there decide to vacate the post. Amid confusion and fear, the women and children are evacuated, and the garrison moves to Mobile. Most of the people at Fort Stoddert had friends and relatives at Fort Mims, which contributes to the anxiety. The evacuees travel by overland routes and by water to reach Mobile. The entire area is in great peril and there is no possibility of receiving help from the federal government, leaving the responsibility of preventing annihilation of the settlers to volunteers from Georgia, Mississippi and Tennessee. Until help arrives, the settlers seek safety at the forts. It was fortunate General Wilkinson had seized Mobile, or the entire southern frontier would be facing annihilation.

In Kentucky, Marquis Calmes, a veteran of the American Revolution, is promoted to the rank of brigadier general.

In New York, General Hampton writes to Secretary of War John Armstrong that he will be prepared to advance with a force of about 3,000 men by 20 September. Hampton notes that the force numbers 4,000, but he has allowed for about one-quarter of them being on the sick list. Earlier, on 2 August, the number of troops in the 9th district by Washington's count stood at 14,856 men (regulars) located at Sackets Harbor (3,668), Fort George (6,636) and at Burlington (4,053).

In naval activity, the *Camden* (B. Dowers, master), a 105-ton schooner, is encountered by a British privateer, the *Dart*, while it is en route to Penobscot from Boston. The *Camden* is seized and taken into port at New Brunswick. The schooner *Fortune*, while on a fishing expedition, is intercepted and seized by the HMS *Boxer*. The *Boxer* also confiscates the catch of codfish and mackerel. This *Fortune* is separate from the ship *Fortune* captured 25 June 1812 and the schooner *Fortune* seized 28 August 1812.

August 1813 to April 1814 *In naval activity,* during August and September, the American privateer *Snap Dragon*, a 6-gun schooner, while cruising for British vessels, intercepts and seizes the brigantine *Good Intent*, the brigantine *Happy* and the Brigantine *Venus*, along with the bark *Reprisal* and the schooner *Elizabeth*. The Americans find no value from the prizes which, except for one, are burned, however, the Americans confiscate most of the cargoes' expensive items. Nonetheless, the vessel that is spared destruction is turned over to the prisoners. The *Snap Dragon* is also credited with the capture of the bark *Henrietta* at an unspecified time. The *Snap Dragon*, out of Wilmington, North Carolina, in the following September seizes the brigantine *Ann* with its cargo estimated to be about $500,000 with some estimates as high as $1,000,000. The *Henrietta* and the *Ann* are taken into port at New Bern, North Carolina. The *Snap Dragon* continues its cruise into April 1814. During that time, it captures the vessel *Linnet* with a cargo of fish and a schooner carrying mahogany.

September The federal government requests more than 3,000 troops from the state of Georgia. The troops are to be commanded by General Daniel Stewart, but he declines the command. Instead, Major General John Floyd receives command.

September 1 (Wednesday) KIMBELL-JAMES MASSACRE **In Alabama,** settlers in Bassett's Creek Valley had gathered at Fort Sinquefield in anticipation of an imminent attack by Red Sticks (Creeks). Due to the large number of people in the fort, including friendly Creeks, some inexplicably believe that it safe enough to leave. The Kimbell and James families pay the ultimate price for this choice. While at the Kimbell home, only about two miles from the fort, the Indians under Prophet Francis strike. It is a devastating attack that shows no mercy even for women and children. One man visiting the place and Abner James are nearby but not in the house and Ransom Kimbell is off the plantation, giving the renegades an effortless entry. Soon blood spills profusely. In addition to the British-supplied weapons, the Red Sticks have their clubs and tomahawks, and they use them to bludgeon the women and children. Although it is nearly incomprehensible and borders on being indescribable in horror, the Red Sticks pound the innocents with their tomahawks, separating body parts and crushing skulls. These women and children also have their scalps removed, some while they are still alive. Nevertheless, Abner James, his son Thomas, about 14 years old, and his daughter Mary are able to escape and arrive safely at Fort Sinquefield. Isam Kimbell, about 16 years old, also escapes.

Sarah Merrill, a married daughter of James Abner, thought by the Indians to be dead, had only been unconscious. When she awakes, minus her scalp, she glances around at the mangled bodies of the dead and spots her baby, who also had survived the massacre. The surviving men previously mentioned and several of the children (not in the house) make it to the fort, as does Sarah Merrill and her child. Twelve people die in this massacre by Creeks in Clarke County.

In naval activity, the British privateer *Dart* intercepts and seizes the schooner *Deborah* (H. Snow, master), which is carrying a cargo that includes salt and corn. The prize is taken into port at New Brunswick. In other activity, the 885-ton ship *Divina Pastora* (J.G. Colado, master), which is transporting a cargo that includes coffee, molasses and sugar from Havana, Cuba, to New York, is intercepted and captured by the HMS *Statira*.

Also, the British and the Americans are both attempting to gain superiority on Lake Ontario. At this time, the American naval force includes the 34-gun *General Pike* (Captain Sinclair); 24-gun *Madison* (Captain Crane); 20-gun *Sylph* (Captain Woolsey); 18-gun *Oneida* (Lt. Brown); 10-gun *Duke of Gloucester*; 6-gun *Governor Tompkins*; 3-gun *Conquest*; 2-gun *Ontario*; 2-gun *Asp*; 2-gun *Fair American*; 2-gun *Lady of the Lake*; and the 2-gun *Raven*, all of which give Commodore Chauncey 126 guns.

The British fleet has the 32-gun *General Wolfe*; 22-gun *Royal George*; 16-gun *Earl of Moira*; 14-gun *Prince Regent*; 12-gun *Simcoe*; 4-gun *Seneca*; 5-gun *Hamilton* (formerly USS *Growler*), and the 3-gun *Confiance* (formerly USS *Julia*). The British force also includes some gunboats; however, they are also constructing two sloops of war and one 40-gun frigate at Kingston.

September 2 (Thursday) In Alabama, the settlers at Fort Sinquefield retrieve the remains of 12 victims of an Indian massacre that occurred the day before at the Kimbell plantation and bring them back to the fort for a Christian burial. During the ceremony, the settlers spot more Indians. Suddenly, about 100 Red Sticks (Creeks) under Prophet Francis descend upon them. The burial site is about 50 feet from the gate; however, nearly the entire garrison is participating in the funeral service, making it easy for the men to pick up all of the children and race for the gates. All of the people, except ten women who are washing clothes, make it back into the fort. The Creeks spot the defenseless women and move to attack them. At the same time, one of the settlers, Isaac Heaton (Hayden), alone on horseback, leads the fort's dogs against the Indians. Suddenly Heaton cracks his whip and Prophet's force becomes distracted by the charging canine corps, which quickly neutralizes their tomahawks. Most dogs of the settlers are trained to hate the scent of the Indians. The Indians see their prey sprinting to the gates of the fort while they are embattled with Heaton's dogs. Heaton singlehandedly covers their retreat and then he and his dogs head for the fort. An Indian's shot takes out Heaton's horse; the animal gets back up and it too passes through the gates just after Heaton. The rider himself had been hit with several rifle balls, but they only pass through his coat.

One of the women, Minnie Odom, collapses from exhaustion and fear before she reaches the gates; however, one of the men defies the attacking Indians, bolts out of the post and drags her to safety. One pregnant woman, Sarah Phillips, is unable to move swiftly enough to reach the gates. She is caught and slaughtered. Following an attack against the fort itself, which lasts for a couple of hours, the Indians abandon the assault. They sustain eleven killed. At that time, Mrs. Phillips' mutilated and scalped body is retrieved. The fort also sustains one man killed.

The Prophet, who fails to capture the women and fails to reduce the fort, does succeed in gaining some horses remaining outside the fort before his force departs. The settlers at Fort Sinquefield, including reinforcements that arrive this day, decide to move to Fort Madison for additional security. The terror strike of this day, combined with the memory of Fort Mims, compels the relocation.

One report of this massacre, handed down by family members and recorded in an early history of the period by Halbert and Ball, describes the beginning of the attack. When the Indians were first spotted before they attacked the settlers at the burial, one guard at the fort's gate thought he saw "turkeys" rushing forward due to the amount of feathers the Red Sticks were wearing. The abandonment of the fort was haphazard, as individuals and small groups departed throughout the night. In one instance, a man abandoned his wife and children to flee by himself. His wife struggled all through the night, but she finally arrived at Fort Madison on the following morning.

September 3 (Friday) In Alabama, the settlers and militia from Fort Sinquefield are arriving at Fort Madison, which is more secure; however, the post is becoming overwhelmed by settlers and militia forces, including the garrisons of Fort Glass and Fort Lavier. By about 8 September, more than 1,000 people will be inside the fort. The troops there also include about 220 men under Colonel Joseph Carson. It is a common practice for settlers to venture out from the post to tend to their crops or gather food, despite the lurking danger. One incident involves the Fisher family. Mr. Fisher, along with three of his sons, comes under attack while they are on the farm. One of the sons is shot and Mr. Fisher, who comes to his aid, is also hit. The other two boys race back to the fort and report that their brother and father had been killed. However, Mr. Fisher and his son had vanished into the woods, and despite their wounds, they make it back to the post the next day.

The attack on the Fishers and similar incidents raise the fear level, prompting the settlers in the eastern part of the Mississippi Territory to increase the number of forts in the region. The new strongholds include Fort Hawn built at Gullet's Bluff, which contains a garrison force of sixty men under Captain James Powell, and at Mount Vernon, where Fort Stoddert stands, two additional settlers' forts, including Rankin's Fort. Rankin's Fort contains about 530 people; however, due to sickness, only about 83 men are fit for defending the post.

In naval activity, the HMS *Majestic* encounters and captures the 760-ton ship *Jerusalem* while it is en route from Havana, Cuba, to Boston with a cargo of coffee, sugar hides and other items. Also, the HMS *Poictiers* recaptures the brigantine *Watson.*

September 5 (Sunday) In New York, Secretary of War John Armstrong arrives at Sackets Harbor. Armstrong is of the belief that he can better manage the upcoming offensive by being on scene than by remaining in Washington. General Wilkinson arrives at American-held Fort George in Canada.

In naval activity, the HMS *Boxer* encounters and engages the brigantine USS *Enterprise* off the shores of Pemaquid Point, Maine. The *Enterprise* is searching for Canadian privateers. The *Boxer* and the *Enterprise* clash at about 1500 at close range. Broadsides are exchanged and the effective fire from the *Enterprise* inflicts devastating damage. The *Enterprise* then maneuvers to a point from where the *Boxer* receives raking fire. After about 40 minutes of intense combat, the *Boxer* is hailed, but problems develop because the British ensign cannot strike its colors, which had been nailed to the mast as a sign that it would fight until the last man. From the decks of the *Enterprise*, the scene prompts some laughter as they observe a British ship with its colors nailed to the mast attempting to capitulate. Nevertheless, the guns of the *Enterprise* are silenced. A boarding party takes possession of the prize.

The opposing commanders, Lt. William Burrows of the *Enterprise* and Captain Samuel Blythe of the *Boxer*, are killed during the engagement at nearly the same time. Captain Blythe is hit by an 18-pound ball that cuts him in half, while Burrows is mortally wounded by a canister shot. The Americans sustain one man killed and 13 others are wounded; of the latter, three men succumb to their wounds. The precise number of British fatalities are never ascertained; however,

HMS *Boxer* and USS *Enterprise* (*The History of the United States Navy [Biographical Sketches of American Naval Heroes]*, Charles J. Peterson, 1860).

it is known that 14 crew members of the *Boxer* are wounded.

In a letter from Lt. Edward R. McCall of the *Enterprise* to Captain Isaac Hull, McCall states: "As no muster-roll that can be fully relied on, has come into my possession, I cannot exactly state the number killed, on board the *Boxer*; but, from information received from the officers of that vessel, it appears that there were between 20 and 25 killed, and 14 wounded. On board the *Enterprize*, there was 1 killed, and 13 wounded, among whom was Lieut. Burrows, (since dead,) and Midshipman Warters, mortally.— Sixty-six prisoners."

After the *Enterprise* and its prize return to Portland, funeral arrangements are made for both commanders. They are interred alongside each other in Portland, Maine. The militia establishes a fort at Portland named it Fort Burrows.

In New York, Secretary of War John Armstrong arrives at Sackets Harbor. He sends a message to General James Wilkinson informing him that General Wade Hampton, who has turned in his resignation, will participate in the campaign "cordially and vigorously," and after it concludes, he will resign his commission. Besides the enormous animosity between Wilkinson and Wade Hampton, Wilkinson is not a fan of Armstrong and is jealous of Armstrong's authority. On 24 August, Wilkinson had penned a letter to Armstrong saying: "I trust you will not interfere with my arrangements, or give orders within the district of my command, but to myself, because it would impair my authority and distract the public service."

Armstrong, Wilkinson and Hampton make a peculiar trio and the campaign is not invigorated by the interaction. Nevertheless, Armstrong manages to maintain a cordial relationship with both commanders; however, that is subject to immediate change if the campaign, Armstrong's plan, fails.

September 6 (Monday) *In naval activity,* the American privateer *Ned*, during the fourth day of pursuit by the HMS *Royalist*, is caught and compelled to surrender. The *Ned* is commanded by Captain Hackett, successor to Captain Dawson.

September 7 (Tuesday) **In Maine,** the privateer *Revenge*, a sloop, is commissioned this day. Robert Stover receives command. Another privateer named *Revenge* is a schooner that operates out of Salem, Massachusetts, and yet another is the 14-gun schooner *Revenge* commanded by Captain R. Miller out of Baltimore. The schooner *Revenge* out of Salem is known to have seized several prizes, including the schooner *Neptune*, the schooner *Robin* and a brigantine, the *Bacchus*, before it is captured by the British. The privateer *Revenge* out of Baltimore is credited with recapturing the brigantine *Lucy and Alida* and its cargo of dry goods after it had been seized by the privateer *General Armstrong* and then recaptured by the British letter of marque *Brenton* out of Liverpool the previous year. After it was taken, the *Lucy and Alida* was sailed into Norfolk, Virginia. The *Revenge* is sometimes said to operate out of Norfolk.

In naval activity, Commodore Chauncey's fleet encounters the British fleet under Commodore Yeo, and for the next several days, the two antagonists engage in a running battle. Chauncey's fleet sustains no casualties; however the British sustain some casualties and some vessels are damaged.

September 8 (Wednesday) **In Alabama,** Colonel Carson, pursuant to orders from General Claiborne, departs from his quarters to reinforce Fort Madison against an expected attack. The settlers are fearful because of continuing attacks in which Indians are killing mercilessly, stealing cattle and burning homes they pass. When Carson's column departs, about 500 settlers follow the troops to Fort Madison. The evacuation leaves Clarke County defenseless and General Claiborne gets the blame; however, there was a miscommunication. Carson believed he had to immediately depart, but the order did not specify immediate movement. Nonetheless, the fort, thought to be threatened, is not attacked.

Meanwhile, at the time of the evacuation, about 80 men join up as volunteers under Captain Evan Austill and Captain Sam Dale, who is still recuperating from his wound sustained at Burnt Corn. Austill and Dale remain at Fort Madison to defend it, while the regulars depart. Captain Dale takes extraordinary precautions to prevent a surprise attack, and he uses women to inflate his numbers. In his own description, he stated:

> At night I illuminated the approaches, for a circuit of one hundred yards, by a device of my own. Two poles, fifty feet long, were firmly planted on each side of the fort; a long lever, upon the plan of a well-sweep, worked upon each of these poles; to each lever was attached a bar of iron about ten feet long, and to these bars we fastened, with trace-chains, huge fagots of light-wood. The illumination from such an elevation was brilliant, and no covert attack could be made upon my position. As a precaution against the Indian torch, I had my blockhouses and their roofs well plastered with clay. We displayed ourselves in arms frequently, the women wearing hats and the garments of their husbands, to impress upon the spies that we knew were lurking around an exaggerated notion of our strength. For provisions we shot such cattle and hogs as fed within the range of our guns, but I carefully noted the marks and brands, and afterward indemnified their owners.

September 9 (Thursday) President Madison has proclaimed this a day of "fasting, humiliation and prayer" for the nation.

In Kentucky, Governor Isaac Shelby and his army of volunteers depart Urbana en route to join General Harrison in Ohio on the Portage River. The 1st Division, composed of the 1st, 3rd and 4th Brigades, is commanded by Major General William Henry. The 2nd Division, composed of the 2nd and 5th Brigades and the 11th Regiment, is commanded by Major General Joseph Deesha. The 1st Brigade, commanded by Brigadier General Marquis Calmes (later, Colonel George Trotter), comprises the 1st and 2nd Regiments. The 2nd Brigade, General David Chiles, commander, includes the 3rd and 4th Regiments. The 3rd Brigade, commanded by General George Edward King, is composed of the 5th and 7th Regiments. The 4th Brigade, commanded by General James Allen, comprises the 6th and 8th Regiments. The 5th Brigade, commanded by General Samuel Caldwell, is composed of the 9th and 10th Regiments.

The 1st Regiment is commanded by Colonel George Trotter. It is composed of the companies commanded by Captains David Todd, Matthews Flournoy and Stewart W. Megowan (Fayette County) and from Jessamine County, the companies of Captains Gustavus W. Bowers and

General David Chiles (*The Battle of the Thames*, Colonel Bennett H. Young, 1903).

General William Henry (*The Battle of the Thames*, Colonel Bennett H. Young, 1903).

Mason Singleton. The other companies (Woodford County) are those commanded by Captains John Christopher and Joseph Reading. The 2nd Regiment, commanded by Colonel John Donaldson, comprises the companies under Captain Isaac Cunningham (Clark County), Captain Richard Menifee (Bath County), Captain George Matthews (Fleming County), Captain James Mason (Montgomery County), Captain James Simpson (Clark County) and Captain George W. Botts (Fleming County). The 3rd Regiment, commanded by Colonel John Poague, includes the companies of Captain Aris Throckmorton (Nicholas County); Captain William Reed, Captain Moses Demmitt and Captain Jeremiah Martin of Mason County, and Captain Francis A. Gaines (Greenup County) and Captain Aaron Stratton (Lewis County).

The 4th Regiment, Colonel William Mountjoy, commander, comprises the companies of Captain Conrad Overturf (Bracken County), Captain John H. Morris (Gallatin County), Captain Thomas Childers (Pendleton County), Captain Squire Grant (Campbell County), Captain Thomas Ravenscroft (Harrison County), and Captain William Hutchison, Jr. (Bourbon County). The 5th Regiment, Colonel Henry Renick, commander, is composed of the companies of Captain Martin H. Wickliffe (Nelson County), Captain John Hornbeck (Bullitt County), Captain Thomas S.T. Moss (Green County), Captain Thomas W. Atkinson (Adair County), and Captain Samuel Robertson (Washington County).

Later, another company under Captain William R. McGary joins the force at the Portage River, and it is assigned to the 5th Regiment. The 6th Regiment, commanded by Colonel Richard Davenport, is composed of the companies of 1st Lieutenant Archibald Bilbo (Boyle County), Captain Abram Miller (Lincoln County), Captain John Faulkner (Garrard County), Captain Jesse Coffee (Casey County), and later, Captain Michael Davidson's company is attached. The 7th Regiment, Colonel Micah

Taul, commander, comprises the companies of Captain Samuel Wilson and Captain William Wood (Cumberland County), Captain William Stephens (Wayne County), Captain Thomas Laughlin (Knox County), and Captain Samuel Tate (Pulaski County). The 8th Regiment, commanded by Colonel John Calloway, is composed of the companies of 1st Lieutenant Edward George (Henry County), Captain Eleazor Hedden (Henry County), Captain James Hite and Captain Philip Shiveley (Jefferson County), Captain Robinson Graham (Franklin County), and Captain Samuel Kelley (Jefferson County). The 9th Regiment, commanded by Colonel James Simrall, includes the companies of Captain John Hall, Captain James S. Whittaker, and Samuel Harbison (Shelby County), Captain Warner Elmore (Green County), Captain Richard Bennett (Franklin County), and Presley C. Smith (Washington County).

Colonel Philip Barbour is commander of the 10th Regiment, comprising the companies of Captain William Whitsett (Logan County), Captain Robert E. Yates (Grayson County), Captain William Ewing (Butler County), Captain James Gorin (Barren County), Captain Joseph McCloskey (Nelson County), Captain William R. Payne (Warren County), and Captain Daniel Wilson (Henderson County). The 11th Regiment, commanded by Colonel William Williams, is composed of the companies of (Colonel George R.C. Floyd), Captain Sylvanus Massie, Captain Richard C. Holder and Captain John C. McWilliams (Madison County), Captain Thomas McGilton (Clay County), Captain Johnston Dysart (Rockcastle County), Captain John Haydon (Harrison County) and later the companies of Captain William Berryman and Captain Henry R. Lewis.

In naval activity, The British fleet commanded by Barclay sails out on Lake Erie to challenge the American fleet under Captain Oliver Hazard Perry. The British fleet consists of 6 vessels, the *Chippeway, Little Belt, Lady Prevost, Detroit, Queen Charlotte* and *Hunter.* The British fleet finds its objective the following day when the battle for Lake Erie begins.

Captain Perry, of Rhode Island, is the son of Captain Christopher Perry, the commanding officer of the frigate *General Greene* that participated in the American Revolution.

In Ohio, Colonel Richard Johnson's regiment, which had been recalled from the Northwest, arrives at Fort Winchester with a train of "thirty wagons and a brigade of packhorses."

September 10 (Friday) BATTLE OF LAKE ERIE
At this time, American successes on land have been few. Now the crisis is becoming more grave. The British, who have already bottled up most of the harbors and taken U.S. territory along the Great Lakes, are poised to storm Lake Erie to devastate General William Henry Harrison's positions. The British realize that once they finish with the rag-tag navy under Captain Oliver Hazard Perry and chase the meek defenders into the woods, they can roll through the land. The British already occupy Illinois, Michigan and Minnesota. From there it will be easy to seize Wisconsin and Ohio, then break through Pennsylvania to New Jersey and New York. Only one ingredient is missing: they must crush what they perceive as the cardboard fleet of Oliver Hazard Perry, whose ships are held together only by the sailors manning the guns.

At about 0800, while Perry's squadron is at Put-in-Bay, a lookout on the top-mast spots the British fleet, which had remained evasive since the previous month. The fleet is approaching from the northwest and battle appears inevitable. While the British continue to bear down on the American squadron, there is no confusion or indecision. Perry had already issued his instructions and his commanders are prepared to engage. Perry's force weighs anchor near an island in the western part of the lake and sails toward the oncoming British warships. By about 0900, the American squadron is moving out of the bay en route to meet its foe.

The winds are from the southwest, presenting a challenge for the Americans; however, Captain Perry, having little time to spare, advances without having gotten the weather gage. Within a short while, the disadvantage suddenly vanishes when the winds unexpectedly change to the southeast. While Perry has acquired the weather gage, Commodore Barclay's fleet has been unable to receive it despite his repeated maneuvers. By about 1000, the two forces are shaving the distance separating them to less than ten miles. When Perry's squadron closes confront the British, he assesses Barclay's battle formation, then issues orders to his commanders. Perry directs two of his schooners take the point as vanguard, followed by the *Lawrence, Caledonia* and the *Niagara*, with his remaining ships to the rear.

The British line, being prepared for battle with the respective crews at their stations, receives the signal to attack just before noon. The booming sound of the bugle call ignites rousing cheers from deck to deck throughout the fleet. And just after the ringing ovations, there comes another boisterous sound when British Captain Barclay's flagship fires at the approaching USS *Lawrence* to ignite the battle. The shot is ineffective. Nonetheless, it is answered by the USS *Scorpion,* commanded by Captain Stephen Champlin (Perry's first cousin).

The confident British armada, with the Union Jack fluttering from the top masts like peacocks on parade and the band playing "Rule, Britannia! Britannia, rule the waves!" focuses primarily on Perry's flagship. The Americans are equally determined to halt the British juggernaut. Perry's seagoing Kentuckians are anxious to match their rifles against the king's heavy cannon. The HMS

Captain Oliver H. Perry in a boat (*Battles of America by Sea and Land, Volume II,* Robert Tomes, 1878).

Battle of Lake Erie (*The American Generals,* John Frost, 1850).

Detroit, commanded by Captain Barclay, is trailed by the formidable *Queen Charlotte* (Lieutenant Robert Finnis), the *Lady Prevost* and the *Hunter* with a combined total of more than sixty guns. Other ships in the fleet include the HMS *Chippeway* and the HMS *Little Belt.* A few reserve vessels trail close behind the main body.

The British expect to destroy the *Lawrence* and then dispose of the remaining resistance by compelling the Americans to strike their colors. Nonetheless, the *Lawrence,* lacking long-range guns, presses ahead with its challenge. As the battle intensifies, the British gain even more confidence as they observe the *Lawrence* being pum-

Captain Oliver H. Perry at the Battle of Lake Erie (*Battles of America by Sea and Land, Volume II*, Robert Tomes, 1878).

Battle of Lake Erie (*The History of the United States Navy [Biographical Sketches of American Naval Heroes]*, Charles J. Peterson, 1860).

meled. During this tenacious exchange that has lasted nearly two hours, the *Lawrence* is still afloat, but barely. Many of its guns are out of action and most of its crew have been killed or wounded. The British firepower has inflicted devastating damage, and among the *Lawrence*'s crew of about 100 men, fewer than 20 have escaped injury or death. Nonetheless, while the *Lawrence* is being shredded, Commodore Perry gives no indication he is willing to capitulate.

Meanwhile, the USS *Caledonia* drops back and the *Niagara* moves up behind the *Lawrence*. Finally, the British sense victory as the *Lawrence* is compelled to fall out of the battle formation. They are jubilant when they see Perry's flag being lowered, giving them the satisfaction of victory. However, back on the *Lawrence*, which is also flying a flag which carries the words, "Don't Give Up the Ship," there are no thoughts of capitulation.

While the British await a quick termination, Commodore Perry is transferring his flag to the *Niagara*, commanded by Captain Elliott. Through the gloom of battle smoke and silent guns covered with fallen heroes and sails crimson with American blood, the colors are lowered in a disciplined fashion. The few remaining men, following the orders of Perry, board the rowboat, and as the British await surrender, Perry races across the lake as if powered by machine instead of ten exhausted men. The *Lawrence* had been lost in glory to the sea, but its spirit lives on through Perry, who takes command of the *Niagara*.

Shortly thereafter, to the astonishment of the British, who had ceased fire in preparation for accepting surrender; instead, discover that their thought on the demise of Perry's squadron had been premature. Perry's flag reappears on the mast of the *Niagara*, which effectively subdues the British cheers that had been ringing out from Barclay's fleet, while simultaneously the fluttering flag reinvigorates the beleaguered but undaunted American crews.

Once aboard the *Niagara*, Captain Perry resumes command. Captain Elliott delivers orders from Perry to each of the respective captains: "Close up and attack the enemy at half pistol-shot with grape and canister." The entire American squadron begins to close to engage. British countermaneuvers to be positioned to deliver potent broadsides fail to unfold properly, which causes Barclay's formation to become disorderly. While the British struggle to untangle the confusion, the *Niagara* moves into the gap and finds itself at near point-blank range with British vessels on either side.

The *Niagara* plunges through the middle of the British formation with all of its guns blazing. The gunners receive an opportunity to propel powerful broadsides that pummel the ships on either side, while the Kentucky sharpshooters (about 150 troops, drawn primarily from the regiments of Colonel William E. Boswell and Colonel R.M. Johnson) deliver ferocious fire upon the British on the decks as well as those in the rigging.

The *Niagara* maintains its swift pace as it passes by the respective bows to deliver more punishing fire. In the meantime, the remaining ships in the squadron, all having reached close-range positions, join in the thunderous bombardment. The overwhelming menacing fire jolts the British, who are unable to recover from the incessant blows. Within about one-half hour, it is the Americans who sense victory, first signaled by the HMS *Queen Charlotte*. At nearly the same time a white flag is hoisted on the *Queen Charlotte*, the Americans spot the colors being lowered on several other British ships. The remaining two vessels, the *Chippeway* and the *Little Belt*, break for safety; however Perry orders pursuit.

The USS *Scorpion* and the USS *Trippe* give chase and both British vessels are intercepted and seized, giving Perry's squadron total victory.

Following this action, the *Scorpion* participates in the support of General Harrison's force along the Thames. After remaining in Presques Isle for the winter, the *Scorpion* cruises on Lake Erie and Lake Huron from May through September 1814, and during that duty, it cooperates with the American troops in the region; however, it also blockades the British at Lake Simcoe and at the Nottawasaga River. This is the only action in which the *Trippe* is a participant. The *Trippe* was initially a merchant sloop named *Contractor* that was converted to a warship during 1812 and renamed.

The mighty *Detroit* had succumbed to the United States Navy. Its commander, Captain Barclay, who had lost the use of his left arm during an earlier engagement, survives the battle; however, injuries during this ferocious engagement cost him the use of his other arm. The commander of the HMS *Hunter* is killed during the battle. As the smoke begins to clear and the cannon fire terminates, the Stars and Stripes remains the only flag above sea level. The British threat ends in a victory for Perry and his men. General William Henry Harrison can now continue the fight against the remainder of the British army without fear of the Royal Navy controlling the Great Lakes.

Perry, who achieves this momentous victory at the age of 27, sends the following message to General William Harrison: "We have met the enemy and they are ours: two ships, two brigs, one schooner, and one sloop." General Harrison, through the efforts of Governor Isaac Shelby of Kentucky and Governor Return Meigs of Ohio, had been able during the summer to build his army to about 7,000 troops. Perry also sends a similar letter to the secretary of the Navy: "It has pleased the ALMIGHTY, to give to the ARMS OF THE U. STATES a signal victory over their enemies, on this lake.... The British Squadron, consisting of TWO SHIPS, TWO BRIGS, ONE SLOOP, and ONE SCHOONER, have, this moment, surrendered to the Force under my command after a sharp conflict."

The Americans sustain 27 killed and 96 wounded. The squadron surgeon, Doctor Horsely, having become ill, caused the responsibility of tending the wounded to fall upon the youthful Doctor Usher Parsons. Doctor Parsons had to amputate six legs from the wounded; of the 96 wounded, three men died. Perry's force has just over 100 who were not actively engaged due to cholera and dysentery.

Lt. John Brooks, U.S. Marine Corps, is among the fatalities. Brooks was the son of General John Brooks (Revolutionary War general and governor of Massachusetts). The British sustain 41 killed and 94 wounded. Officer casualties amount to 12 sustained by each side. In addition to the captured troops, the Americans discover a most unusual prisoner, a bear that had been kept as a pet by one of the crews, and they also capture several Indians who are discovered in hiding places down in the hold. Initially, the Indians were posted in the rigging from where they could pick off U.S. officers; however, by the time the American fleet had come into close range, the incoming artillery had prompted them to seek shelter.

The brigantine *Hunter* was originally built during 1806 for the Canadian Provincial Marine and named *General Hunter*. It is taken into service by the Navy. It remains in service on Lake Erie for the duration, and after the war it is sold. Also, more than 300 British seamen and Marines are captured. They are transported to Ohio where General Harrison directs that they be marched to Chillicothe to be confined in an encampment along the Scioto River which becomes known as Camp Bull, a play on the name John Bull, a personification of the British much like Uncle Sam in the U.S. The prisoners remain there until 16 July 1814. While there, the prisoners witness the execution of six American troops whom were sentenced to death for desertion.

In naval activity elsewhere, the privateer *Orange*, a schooner, is commissioned this day in Maine. Also, the British privateer *Wolverine* intercepts and seizes the 36-ton schooner *Mary*, which is carrying a cargo of bread, flour and tobacco.

September 11 (Saturday) In Ohio, Governor Shelby's force arrives at Fort McArthur close to Kenton. The fort is along the supply route among a series of forts.

In naval activity, Commodore Chauncey's squadron encounters a British squadron, and the two antagonists engage in a long-range battle near the mouth of the Genesee River. Later, on the 28th, Chauncey again encounters a British squadron and a major confrontation occurs. The USS *General Pike* and the *Lady of the Lake* participate in this action. In other naval activity, the HMS *Canso* intercepts and seizes the 286-ton ship *Massachusetts* (B. Weeks, master) which is en route from Lisbon, Portugal, to New York. Also, the British privateer *Star* intercepts and seizes the sloop *Resolution* (W. Gibbs, master). The *Resolution* is separate from the ship *Resolution* seized on 25 September 1813. The HMS *Plantagenet* seizes the schooner *Topedo*, however, by the time the vessel is boarded, the American crew has had time to gather all the documents on board and safely escape.

September 12 (Sunday) In Ohio, General William Henry Harrison, at Seneca on the Sandusky River, receives a message from Commodore Oliver H. Perry of the stunning victory over the British fleet on Lake Erie on the 10th. The news ignites Harrison to begin to initiate his offensive against British General Proctor to gain Malden in Canada and also regain Detroit. In other activity, Governor Isaac Shelby's force, which is en route to join with General Harrison, reaches the Upper Sandusky in Wyandot County, slightly more than 60 miles north of Columbus.

In naval activity, the schooner USS *Scorpion* and another ship seize the 3-gun sloop HMS *Little Belt*, named after an earlier vessel the 22-gun sloop of war that exchanged broadsides with the USS *President* off the mouth of Cape Henry on 16 May 1811. The *Little Belt* is acquired by the U.S. Navy during October and participates as part of Commodore Perry's squadron.

September 13 (Monday) In Ohio, Governor Shelby's force, en route to join with General Harrison, arrives at Fort Ball, recently established at Tiffin by the U.S. Army. The post is between Fort Stephenson at Sandusky Bay and Fort Feree at the Upper Sandusky. Fort Ball is also near Fort Seneca, another post established as a supply depot. Fort Ball, constructed by the 2nd Dragoons, is commanded by Colonel James V. Ball.

In naval activity, the HMS Sylph seizes the 61-ton schooner *Mary*, along with its cargo of coffee and sugar. The 115-ton schooner *Richard D. Staley* is intercepted and seized by the HMS *Paz*. The American privateer *Yankee* out of Rhode Island embarks on its fourth cruise with its third captain, Thomas Jones, who succeeded Captain Elisha Snow. Following the success of its previous cruises, the *Yankee* seizes a string of prizes, beginning with the brigantine *Ann*, carrying a cargo of salt, run and dry goods, the brigantine *Mary*, carrying a cargo including coal, crockery and salt. Both prizes are taken into port at Chatham, Massachusetts (Barnstable County). After capturing the two brigantines, the *Yankee* intercepts and seizes two additional brigantines, the *Dispatch* and the *Telemachus*, with the latter being recaptured. And still other British vessels are encountered and seized by the privateer. They include a schooner, the *Katy*, and a 10-gun bark, the *Paris*. The Americans transfer the cargo from the *Paris* to the *Yankee* and send it into an American port, but before it arrives, the British recapture it.

The *Yankee* had received some assistance from mother nature. All of the prizes had sailed from Cork, Ireland, under escort of British warships. Those captured had been among the vessels that got separated during a violent storm, which left them on their own and vulnerable to the prowling *Yankee*. It seizes two additional vessels, the brigantine *Howe* and the brigantine *John and Mary*, both stragglers from the convoy. The *Howe*, deemed of no value, is set free, but the other prize is carrying a cargo of shot and provisions and claimed as a prize. Afterward, the *Yankee* sets its course for home and arrives in November following a 49-day voyage. Once in home port, the *Yankee* remains there until spring.

September 14 (Tuesday) In Ohio, Governor Shelby's force arrives at Lower Sandusky (present-day Fremont) in Seneca County. The column is one day out from joining with General Harrison at his encampment along the Portage River.

In naval activity, the New Englanders are not too enthusiastic about the conflict with the British since it has stifled their commerce. New England goes so far as raise the possibility of withdrawal from the Union. Meanwhile, the U.S. is holding well against the British on the high seas. After the American victory on Lake Erie, the Navy is still patrolling the waters in search of British vessels. The *Essex*, in the South Pacific, encounters the HMS *Sir Andrew Hammond*, under a letter of marque in the vicinity of the Marquesas, and successfully engages and captures the British warship.

The *Essex*, under Porter, remains in the locality for some time, and during the stay natives manage to raid and steal property. Lieutenant Gamble, U.S. Marine Corps, under Porter's command, leads a force of men late in December, landing on Nookaheevah Island, Marquesas Islands, taking retaliatory measures against the natives and reclaiming the stolen property. The *Essex* after departure will encounter two British warships during March 1814, when the valiant ship is defeated.

In other activity, the 26-ton schooner *Flower* (A. Burgess, master), while traveling from Rochester to Manchester, New Hampshire, encounters the British privateer *Star*, which terminates the voyage. The privateer takes possession of the *Flower* and its cargo of fish. Also, the HMS *Wasp* intercepts and seizes the ship *St. Cecilia* while it is en route from Lisbon, Portugal, to New Bedford, Massachusetts, with dry goods and salt.

September 15 (Wednesday) In Ohio, Governor Isaac Shelby arrives at the camp on the Portage River with his force of Kentuckians to bolster General Harrison's dwindling army. Shortly after his arrival, Governor Shelby meets with General Harrison. Governor Shelby declines accepting command and defers to General William Henry Harrison. General John Adair is

General John Adair (U.S. Congress).

appointed first aide-de-camp to Governor Shelby, who selects Major John J. Crittenden as his second aide. Major William T. Barry is appointed as secretary to General Harrison. Also, Major Thomas Barr is appointed judge advocate-general and Major Joseph McDowell is appointed adjutant-general. Colonel George Walker is commissioned inspector-general. Some sources allege there was friction between Shelby and Harrison; however, there is no foundation to the allegations and the relationship between the two men is cordial, with both having the same objectives: evicting the British, avenging the Raisin River Massacre and recapturing Detroit. In addition, Shelby enthusiastically supplied the troops needed by Harrison, and it was by his own initiative that he declined command to permit Harrison to be the commander-in-chief.

In naval activity, the *Gleaner* a British provincial schooner, intercepts and recaptures the schooner *Sally*. The *Sally* is separate from the brigantine *Sally* seized on 10 August 1812, the *Sally Ann* captured 16 September 1812, the ship *Sally* seized 16 April 1813, the brigantine *Sally* captured 24 April 1813, the schooner *Sally* seized 13 May 1813, the schooner *Sally* seized 12 July 1813, the schooner *Sally* overtaken 16 October 1813, and the sloop *Sally* seized 19 May 1814.

September 16 (Thursday) **In New York,** Governor Daniel D. Tompkins orders Brigadier General Reuben Hopkins to repair with his command to Plattsburgh. Hopkins is instructed to report to General Wade Hampton, commander of the Northern Army, or any other officer who is in that command. Hopkins is also informed that Major Tunis Riker of the 42nd Regiment is en route to join his command as assistant adjutant general for whatever time the service continues.

In naval activity, American gunboat No. 164 gets caught in a strong squall at St. Mary's, Georgia. The gunboat sinks and 20 members of the crew drown. In other activity, the HMS *Shannon* intercepts and captures the ship *Alianza* (J.E. Estella, master). The *Shannon* also seizes the ship *Catalina Patriota* (J. Riva, master).

September 17 (Friday) *In naval activity,* Captain Jesse Elliott, aboard the USS *Niagara* at Put-in-Bay, writes to Commodore Perry, who is also at Put-in-Bay aboard the schooner *Ariel*: "I am informed a report has been circulated by some malicious persons, prejudicial to my vessel when engaged with the enemy's fleet. I will thank you if you will, with candor, state to me the conduct of myself, officers and crew." This is the beginning of a prolonged period of back and forth accusations between Elliott and Oliver H. Perry, the latter being joined by others, including Perry's brother, who keeps the controversy active after Oliver's death.

Commodore Perry responds to Elliott's letter the next day:

> My dear sir,— I received your note last evening, after I had turned in or should have answered it immediately. I am indignant that any report should be circulated prejudicial to your character as respects the action of the 10th inst. It affords me just pleasure that I have it in my power to assure you, that the conduct of yourself, officers and crew, was such as to merit my warmest approbation; and I consider the circumstance of your volunteering to bring the small vessels to close action, as contributing *largely* to our victory. I shall ever believe it a premeditated plan to destroy our commanding vessel. I have no doubt, had not the Queen Charlotte have ran away from the Niagara, from the superior order I observed her in, you would have taken her in twenty minutes. With sentiments of esteem, I am, dear sir, Your friend and ob't servant.

September 18 (Saturday) The British begin to evacuate Fort Detroit in Michigan. The British also withdraw from Fort Malden in Ontario, Canada, to avoid the pursuing troops of U.S. General Harrison.

In other activity, the sick list for the Americans at Sackets Harbor and the region is growing. Six hundred and eighty-one men are listed. Officers who have become ill include Secretary of War General Armstrong, General Henry Dearborn, General James Wilkinson, General Wade Hampton, General Morgan Lewis, General George Izard and Commodore Isaac Chauncey.

In naval activity, the privateer *Superb*, a schooner, is commissioned this day in Maine. In other naval activity, the HMS *Belvidera* and the HMS *Statira* intercept and seize the schooner *Little Sisters*.

September 19 (Sunday) *In naval activity,* the USS *Peacock* is launched. It embarks on its initial mission on 12 March 1814. The HMS *Orpheus* seizes the American sloop *Elvira*. Also, the HMS *Highflyer*, a tender to the HMS *San Domingo*, intercepts and seizes the 162-ton brigantine *Gamala La Delso* (C.C. Berg, master), which is en route from Gothenburg, Sweden, to Rhode Island with a mixed cargo including iron, steel and glass.

September 20 (Monday) **In Canada,** at Fort George, General James Wilkinson, who arrived at the post during early September, holds a council with General John Parker Boyd and other officers, including eleven colonels and lieutenant colonels along with ten majors. They decide to abandon Fort George before moving to Kingston, where the force will link with General Lewis' force from Sackets Harbor.

In naval activity, the privateer *Mary* is commissioned in Maine this day.

September 21 (Tuesday) **In Ohio,** the army under General William Henry Harrison and Governor Isaac Shelby departs from camp on the Portage River and moves to Put-in-Bay. The operation is completed on the following day when the entire force is at Bass Island.

In New York, Governor Tompkins responds to a letter from Brigadier General Pierre W. Courtlandt, Jr., regarding calling out the militia. He informs Courtlandt: "I have, therefore, no doubt of the legality and propriety of the course you have pursued upon the advance of the enemy into that part of the East River opposite the County of Westchester and as far as depends on me approve and confirm the same."

In naval activity, the American privateer *True Blooded Yankee*, after being refitted and acquiring a larger crew which now amounts to 222 men, departs from Brest. The privateer succeeds in seizing six ships and 21 smaller vessels. Nonetheless, after losing many of its crew to sailing prizes into safe ports, it is caught and captured by the HMS *Nimrod*. At the time of its capture, *True Blooded Yankee* has crew of only 32 men, all of whom are taken to Gibraltar, where they stay until the close of hostilities.

September 23 (Thursday) **In Canada,** General William Henry Harrison lands just below Amherstburg about 1500 without incident. By 1600, the Americans take possession of the town without opposition. Harrison states in a letter to the War Department this day:

> General Proctor has retreated to Sandwich with his regular troops and his Indians, having previously burned the fort, navy-yard, barracks and public stores; the two latter were very extensive, covering several acres of ground. I'll pursue the enemy to-morrow, although there is no probability of overtaking him, as he has upwards of 1000 horses, and we have not one in the army; I shall think myself fortunate to be able to collect a sufficiency to mount the general officers. It is supposed; here, that General Proctor intends to establish himself upon the river French, 40 miles from Malden.

In Michigan, the British abandon Detroit and the remainder of Michigan.

In naval activity, the American privateer *Thomas* is intercepted by the HMS *Nymphe*, which initiates pursuit. The *Thomas* is able to run; however, the *Nymphe* refuses to abort the chase. The *Thomas*, in an attempt to pick up speed, begins to toss equipment and guns overboard, but in vain. After running for 34 hours, the *Nymphe* finally nabs its prey.

In other naval activity, the HMS *Highflier* (formerly the American privateer *Highflier*), a tender which participated in the capture of the American privateers *Atlas* and *Anaconda* the previous July, is captured by the USS *President*, a 44-gun frigate commanded by Commodore John Rodgers.

September 24 (Friday) **In Alabama,** Colonel John Coffee, while serving with General Andrew Jackson, is promoted to the rank of brigadier general.

In Ohio, Canada, the army under General Harrison and Governor Shelby remains on Bass Island while supplies continue to arrive. On the following day, the army moves to Middle Island, the final stepping stone before the force is transported to the Canadian shore. Both Harrison and Shelby, while rallying the troops, state "Remember the Raisin," Referring to the Raisin River Massacre of January 21–23.

In naval activity, the HMS *Borer* intercepts and seizes the 208-ton ship *Venus*, which is en route from Cuba to Salem, Massachusetts, with a cargo of coffee, molasses and sugar. The *Venus* is separate from the schooner *Venus* seized on 13 July 1813 and the schooner *Venus* captured 24 November 1813.

September 25 (Saturday) **In Michigan** at Fort Meigs, Colonel R.M. Johnson receives orders from General Harrison to depart from the post and repair to the Raisin River. Johnson's cavalry regiment (minus one company) had been at Fort Meigs for a couple of weeks with the task of impressing the Indians with the strength of the Americans, and he had been directed to monitor the area west of the post and keep Harrison updated. General Harrison had earlier also changed commanders at Fort Meigs. General McArthur succeeded General Green Clay, who had been ordered to lead his command and the regulars to the mouth of the Portage River to join with the Kentuckians arriving there.

In naval activity, the HMS *Majestic* seizes the ship *Resolution* (C. Olson, master) that is en route to New Bedford, Massachusetts, from Gottenburg, Germany. The *Resolution* is separate from the sloop *Resolution* seized 11 September 1813.

September 26 (Sunday) **In Michigan**, Colonel Richard M. Johnson, pursuant to orders on the previous day, departs Fort Meigs with his cavalry regiment (Kentuckians) and moves toward the Raisin River. While en route, Johnson's command passes through Frenchtown. The troops encounter a shocking scene. The remains of the Kentuckian troops killed at the Raisin River Massacre in January are still scattered about the ground. Johnson's troops bury the remains before resuming the march.

In naval activity, the privateer *Saratoga* captures the British brigantine packet ship *Morgiana* while it is en route to Surinam from Falmouth. The two ships engage in a severe duel following a day-long chase at about 1500. It continues until nearly 1625, when the Americans board the *Morgiana* to complete the victory with close-quartered combat. The British casualties, reported by the commander of the *Saratoga*, Thomas Aderton, are two killed and eight wounded, with six of the eight, including Captain James Cunningham, receiving fatal wounds. The Americans sustain two killed, including 1st Lieutenant Sebring. One sailor is mortally wounded and several others sustain minor wounds.

Prior to this action, the *Saratoga* had several narrow escapes while being pursued by British warships, and during that period, some of its guns had been thrown overboard to lessen its weight to gain speed. At the time of this encounter, it carries only four guns and a crew of 116 men. The *Morgiana* had reportedly in its past been a Spanish sloop, a French sloop of war and an English packet. As Aderton states in his report, it is "now a Yankee prize."

September 27 (Monday) **In Ohio**, General Harrison's army, bolstered recently by the arrival of about 3,500 mounted Kentuckians under General Isaac Shelby, stands at about 5,000 men, including several hundred Indians. Harrison had been preparing an invasion of Canada, but the British fleet under Commodore Barclay had prevented the initiation of the campaign. Nonetheless, the spectacular victory of Commodore Perry over Barclay earlier this month had cleared the sea of the threatening naval forces of the king. The army on Middle Island, poised for advance along the peninsula close to Sandusky, is transported to the Canadian shore at a point just a few miles below Amherstburg, Canada. Commodore Perry, responsible for eliminating the Royal Navy from the Great Lakes, had taken on the task of transporting General Harrison and nearly his entire force up the Detroit River.

The troops, crammed aboard Perry's battle tested fleet, where the aura of heroism and victory continues to permeate the air, debark. By 1500, the entire force is on Canadian soil. Within about two hours, the vanguard — regiments of Colonel Ball and Colonel James Simrall — arrive at Amherstburg where they discover Fort Malden, which had been abandoned and burned. Harrison had written in a letter during the night: "I will pursue the enemy to-morrow, although there is no probability of overtaking him, as he has upward of one thousand horses and we have not one in the army." Fort Malden was formerly known as Fort Amherstburg.

While Harrison's main body is encroaching, Colonel Richard M. Johnson is leading his cavalry regiment along an overland route toward Detroit. At Fort Malden, the British under General Proctor had destroyed the barracks and supply buildings by fire and had evacuated the post before the Americans arrived. Proctor, rather than defend his position, chooses instead to flee and head for Niagara. Meanwhile, General Harrison assigns contingents to hold Sandwich and Detroit, which had also been seized without a struggle. Meanwhile, Harrison leads the main body, composed of about 3,500 troops, in pursuit of the retreating British. Harrison initiates pursuit on 2 October.

He arrives at Detroit aboard the USS *Ariel* this day. Within two days, a flotilla including the *Niagara, Porcupine, Scorpion,* and *Tigress* under Captain Elliott moves into Lake St. Clair to attempt to intercept the baggage of the British. Also, General Harrison, in a letter dated this day to Secretary of War John Armstrong, states that he will initiate pursuit on the following day (28th); however, Harrison explains that he does not believe his force will catch the retreating British. Nonetheless, the Kentuckians, consumed with rage due to the recent massacre at Fort Mims, are determined to close the gap and destroy the retreating columns. They are on the advance without their horses, which had been left at a point about fifty miles to the rear. Only one Kentuckian, Governor Shelby, is mounted. A pony had been acquired for the governor.

In naval activity, the HMS *Manly* intercepts and recaptures the brigantine *Shannon*.

September 28 (Tuesday) *In naval activity,* Commodore Chauncey, having received intelligence on the previous day that British commodore Yeo's fleet had been at York (Toronto), moved out of the river and onto the lake. On this day, he moves toward the objective with the *General Madison, Pike* and the *Sylph,* along with three schooners which are being towed. The squadron encounters Yeo's squadron on Lake Ontario (York Bay) just as it is weighing anchor. Yeo has remained elusive throughout the summer; however Chauncey maneuvers to engage. The encounter turns into a running battle. The *General Pike* sustains damage and the loss of 22 men when one of its guns bursts. Meanwhile, the *Madison* sustains several hits but no casualties, while the *Governor Tompkins* is hit and its foremast is severed. Another vessel, the *Oneida,* sustains heavy damage to its main topmast. Meanwhile, Commodore Yeo's flagship sustains heavy damage, which compels him to retire. The remainder of his fleet follows suit. The duel essentially ends as the British outdistance the Americans and avoid further battle.

Chauncey maintains the blockade of Kingston and sends Lt. Jesse D. Elliott to Lake Erie with instructions to establish a naval base there. The project continues until winter when Lt. Elliott is compelled to suspend the project; however, the toil contributes to the success of Commodore Oliver Perry in the spring. The *General Pike*, heavily engaged with the HMS *Royal George*, returns to Sackets Harbor in early October. Subsequently, it moves to the Niagara peninsula to support troop movements from Fort Niagara to Sackets Harbor. It spends the winter at the latter in the spring resumes service with Chauncey's squadron. After the war, the *General Pike* remains at Sackets Harbor until it is sold in 1825. Also, the *Lady of the Lake* participates in this action.

September 29 (Wednesday) **In Canada**, General Harrison's Army occupies Sandwich, just across from Detroit. The Americans anticipate resistance but are surprised that the British under Proctor had not drawn a defensive line.

In Florida, Spanish Governor Manrique of Pensacola writes to William Weatherford and the Creek chiefs with his congratulations for their victory over the Americans at Fort Mims. The letter encourages them by informing the Indians that they will continue to receive arms and ammunition; however, the message also discourages them from burning Mobile because it is the property of the king of Spain and the Spanish intend to imminently take it back.

In naval activity, the British privateer *George* intercepts and seizes the ship *San Domingo* (B. Bogman, master), while it is en route to New Haven, Connecticut, from St. Bartholomews with coffee, sugar and other items.

September 30 (Thursday) **In Michigan**, the Americans occupy Detroit. Colonel Johnson's regiment, which had been moving overland, is spotted by Harrison, who is on the opposite shore. Harrison dispatches Major Charles S. Todd to direct Johnson to cross the river as soon as possible to join him. Todd delivers the order before the Kentuckians even dismount. Johnson's command crosses after dusk. General Duncan McArthur at about this time crosses over the Detroit River from Detroit to assume responsibility for Sandwich, Canada, occupied on the previous day by forces under General Harrison. Also, some of the American troops cause damages to prop-

Colonel Charles S. Todd.

erty. Once word of the incidents reaches General Harrison, he issues the following order:

> The Commander-in-Chief of the Kentucky Volunteers has heard with extreme regret that depredations have been committed upon the property of the inhabitants of this town, by some of the troops under his command. He did not expect that it would ever be necessary for him to admonish citizens who are proud in the enjoyment of property at home of the impropriety of wantonly injuring that of others. Violations of this kind, while they disgrace the individuals who are guilty of them, will tend to injure the character of the army and detract from the merit which the success of the present campaign would entitle them to claim. While the army remains in this country it is expected that the inhabitants will be treated with justice and humanity, and their property secured from unnecessary and wanton injury. The Commander-in-Chief of the Kentucky Volunteers enjoins it upon the officers of every corps to use their exertions to prevent injury being done to the private property of the inhabitants. He is determined to punish with the utmost rigor of martial law anyone who shall be guilty of such violation.

Also, Captain Charles S. Todd is promoted to the rank of colonel during May 1815; however, he resigned from the service during June 1815. Todd returned to Kentucky and resumed his law practice. He married Leticia, a daughter of Governor Isaac Shelby, and later became secretary of state (Kentucky). In 1841, Charles was appointed as minister to Russia.

In naval activity, Commodore Perry sends orders to Captain Jesse Duncan Elliott by letter: "With the Niagara, accompanied by the Scorpion and Tigress, [go] to Lake St. Clair, and endeavor to intercept the enemy's vessels that have probably gone to the River Thames. I shall follow with an additional force. Great caution must be observed when you arrive at the mouth of the Thames, as the enemy is well protected with artillery. I rely entirely on your discretion and judgment."

The letter makes it clear that he has confidence in Elliott; however, during June 1818, when Perry is questioning Elliott's courage and accusing him of cowardice and treachery, particularly at the Battle of Lake Erie, he makes several accusations that clash with this letter and others. A letter of 18 June, written aboard the USS *Ariel*, states:

> How imprudent as well as base is it in you, by such misrepresentations, to reduce me to the necessity of reminding you of the abject condition in which I had previously found you, and by which I was moved to afford you all the countenance in my power; sick (or pretending to be sick) in bed in consequence of distress of mind, declaring that you had missed the fairest opportunity of distinguishing yourself that ever man had, and lamenting so piteously the loss of your reputation, that I was prompted to make almost any effort to relieve you from the shame which seemed to overwhelm you. This you very well know, was the origin of the certificate I then granted you.

October In Canada at Kingston, the Canadian commander-in-chief, General George Prevost, is faced with multiple threats. A plan devised by General John Armstrong, the secretary of war, during the early part of this year to invade Canada and conquer Montreal is underway but way behind the initial schedule for jump-off in February. Armstrong's plan had been immediately accepted by President Madison, but it lies dormant even beyond the summer before it begins to be executed. Weather is a factor in initiating a campaign against Montreal during late October, but Armstrong's plan also begins with a fatal flaw.

A cardinal rule for any military campaign through the ages mandates that a force have one commander-in-chief. This campaign, which is to be overseen by Armstrong, with headquarters at Buffalo, is to be led by two separate commanders, Generals James Wilkinson and General Wade Hampton. The great animosity between Hampton and Wilkinson makes it nearly impossible for the two forces to act in concert. Despite holding lower rank than Wilkinson, General Hampton insists that his force — the left wing of the expeditionary force at Plattsburgh — will be responsible only to the secretary of war rather than under the command of General Wilkinson, who is at Sackets Harbor, New York. General Wilkinson's force of about 8,000 men rendezvous at Grenadier Island, slightly less than 20 miles below Sackets Harbor. Wilkinson is scheduled to move down the St. Lawrence, while Hampton's force advances northward to hook up with Wilkinson near the mouth of the Chateaugua River.

In other naval activity, Commodore Porter lands at Nukahiva, in the Pacific, founding the first American overseas naval base (Madisonville). He then sails for Valparaiso, leaving Lieutenant John Gamble, U.S. Marine Corps, and a detachment of U.S. sailors with four captured ships to hold the base. Also, the American privateer *Polly* intercepts and seizes the British brigantine *President*, which is carrying a cargo of molasses, and takes it into port at Savannah. The American privateer *Lovely Cornelia* operating out of Charleston, while cruising off Jamaica, intercepts and captures sixteen prizes by the end of the month. Only one is sent to the United States. The other prizes are destroyed at sea. The prize sent to America does not reach port. It is wrecked off the coast of Florida.

October 1 (Friday) In Michigan, the Kentuckian cavalry regiment under Colonel Richard M. Johnson, which had passed through Springwells on the previous day to the cheers of the citizens, enters Sandwich, Canada. Johnson's force is bolstered by four artillery pieces that had been at Fort Meigs. Each of the guns is assigned to a captain and 10 men.

In naval activity, the privateer *Wasp* (third), a sloop, is again sold to new owners. The ship is acquired at auction in Baltimore. Its new owners, Joseph Lane and Thomas White, arrange to have it refitted and rearmed for service as a privateer. The *Wasp* does not achieve a record of success. It may have been sold in conjunction with a meeting held by the owners in August 1814.

In other activity, Commodore Chauncey informs General Wilkinson at Fort George that his fleet is prepared to transport the army down the St. Lawrence. Within a short time, Wilkinson leaves the post; however Colonel Winfield Scott remains at the fort with his regiment to ensure the British do not regain it. General George McClure, with his New York militia, bolsters Scott's force.

In naval activity, the HMS *Statira* seizes the *Alicia* (George Meirers, master). The brigantine had been en route from Kennebec, Maine, to St. Bartholomews with a cargo of fish, lumber, sheep and soap.

October 2 (Saturday) In Canada, General William Henry Harrison initiates pursuit of the British under General Proctor who are in retreat. The march is not expected to be effortless. The land along the line of advance has already been stripped of provisions. One brigade, that of General Lewis Cass, had left its blankets and knapsacks back at Middle Island, which prevents the brigade from joining the advance. The Kentuckians under Shelby move out; however, they march as infantry because their horses had been left about fifty miles in the rear. At about 1600, mounted scouts encounter a small party of British deserters who inform the Americans that Proctor is leading a force of about 700 troops and more than one thousand Indians. Except for a short pause at about noon, the column, which set out at sunrise, advances about 25 miles by dusk.

On this day, Colonel Richard Mentor Johnson's mounted force joins with Harrison. Commodore Perry provides the vessels which carry the baggage and Harrison's artillery. The Americans trace the route of the British by moving along the southern bank of Lake St. Clair to the Thames River. After the boats continue up the river for some distance, Commodore Perry joins with Harrison's force and serves with Harrison as a member of his staff. Meanwhile, the chase continues until both sides clash on the 5th. During the retreat, British General Proctor does not issue orders to destroy a bridge to his rear, leaving

Colonel Lewis Cass (*Battles of America by Sea and Land, Volume II*, Robert Tomes, 1878).

the Americans free passage. Later, the British attempt to demolish a second bridge; however, the American vanguard easily overwhelms the contingent and preserves the bridge. Two other bridges are crossed by Proctor; however, there too, the Indians left behind to stall Harrison are incapable of cutting off the advance. Both bridges, partially destroyed, are repaired by Harrison. At the final bridge, the Indians succeed in burning a house, and they set fire to a distillery. Nonetheless, once the bridge is secured, the Kentuckians also manage to extinguish the burning house. Once the fire is extinguished, an inspection of the house uncovers 2,000 stand of arms.

October 3 (Sunday) **In Canada,** General Harrison's force continues its advance in pursuit of General Proctor. The column reaches a point about ten miles above the mouth of the Thames River. Harrison establishes camp there for the night, and at dawn on the following day, the march resumes.

Earlier in the day at about dawn, a detachment of spies under Major James Suggett, chaplain, intercepts a party of British dragoons comprising one lieutenant and 11 privates. They had been on a mission to demolish a bridge that spans a small creek near the mouth of the Thames River. Captain Berry, an officer of Johnson's spies, coerces five of the dragoons who try to cross the river in a boat to return to shore. During the confrontation, the British comply with Berry's demand; however, one of the dragoons' horses breaks away and returns to Proctor's lines. As the riderless horse approaches the lines, he discerns that American troops are closing on him. Meanwhile, the army repairs the bridge and afterward establishes camp at Drake's farm.

October 4 (Monday) **In Alabama,** a 25-man contingent of mounted militia under Colonel William McGrew, while in pursuit of a band of Creeks, intercepts them at Tallahatta (Barshi Creek). The encounter quickly becomes deadly. McGrew and several others are killed. The rest of the company retreats.

In Tennessee, volunteers heed the alarm sounded earlier by General Jackson and meet at Fayetteville, Tennessee, to retaliate against the Creeks for the massacre at Fort Mims on August 30. Lt. John Coffee and Davy Crockett are among the volunteers.

In Canada, General Harrison's force reaches the fork of the Thames during the afternoon. A contingent of British and Indians block passage at the right fork by pulling up the planks of the bridge. Cavalry under Colonel Richard Johnson drives against the upper bridge and propels the Indians into retreat. The Kentucky cavalry prevails. Two troops are killed and seven others, including Captain Elijah Craig, sustain wounds. Craig's wound is mortal. The Indians sustain 13 killed; an unspecified number, thought to be high, are wounded.

After the blockage is cleared the advance resumes, but the column, with each man carrying his ammunition, blankets and weapons, begins to bog down. After gaining six more miles, the column is ordered to halt and Harrison establishes night quarters. At about the same time, the Americans seize two 24-pounders and a large supply of ammunition including bullets. The night remains tranquil; however, the troops, aware that Proctor's force is nearby, sleep with their weapons at their sides. Also, General Hampton's division departs from Chateauguay; however, the force expected to coordinate with General Wilkinson for the campaign to seize Montreal is en route to a destination known only to Hampton. The column moves out, but without taking any baggage and carrying provisions for only five days.

In naval activity, the *Charles* (J. Cook, master), a 95-ton sloop with a cargo of flour, is intercepted and captured by the HMS *Paz* after it sails from St. John's, New Brunswick. The *Charles* is separate from the *Charles Fawcett* captured on 6 September 1812, and the 75-ton sloop *Charles* seized on 10 December 1813, the schooner *Charles* captured 26 June 1814, and the brigantine *Charles* captured on 5 November 1814.

October 5 (Tuesday) THE BATTLE OF THE THAMES At the crack of dawn the American camp in Moraviantown, Ontario, begins to come alive. The troops are roused from their sleep and within a short time, the units are formed and prepared to resume the chase and intercept the British under General Henry Proctor. Meanwhile, during the predawn hours, an American contingent had crossed the river and surprised a small British detachment, including one officer, along with several boats and a group of fully loaded barges carrying stores and ammunition. The British there (at the mill on the north side of the river) also held some prisoners. Intelligence gained from the British captives informs the

Tecumseh (Tecumtha).

Americans that Proctor's force is nearby and that the British had established a defensive line and were prepared to defend it. The main body of Harrison's army arrives at the mill about 0900. Colonel Richard M. Johnson's cavalry regiment, accompanied by Harrison and his staff, holds the point, trailed by Governor Isaac Shelby and the infantry. Major General William Henry is with the Kentuckians, and he is second in command.

The cavalry is able to ford the river at Arnold's Mills, and each rider that crosses has one infantry troop with him. The maneuver places about 1,200 infantry on the north bank. The remaining infantry are carried across the river by canoes. Signs of the British are soon discovered as the column advances. Various enemy items including provisions, military stores and even clothing are

General William Henry Harrison (*Battles of America by Sea and Land, Volume II*, Robert Tomes, 1878).

strewn along the route, indicating that the British had been in a fast-paced retreat. Harrison calls a halt at the camp that the British, under Colonel Augustus Warburton, had established on the night of the 4th-5th less than ten miles from the river. While the column is halted, General Harrison is informed that Johnson's spies had captured a British wagon. Its driver had provided information on the location where Proctor's force had established its defensive line.

General Harrison dispatches Johnson's cavalry to race forward to confirm the intelligence. Once verified, Johnson is to provoke Proctor to initiate the battle. The cavalry locates the British lines about three miles outside of Moraviantown, north of Fort Erie and less than five miles from Harrison's positions. In the meantime, some of the Indians accompanying the British become more disgruntled. More than fifty of Tecumseh's warriors under Walk-in-the-water approach Harrison's position and volunteer to fight alongside the Americans. Harrison declines the offer. Harrison, acutely aware of Indian tactics, is not persuaded and remains convinced that his new allies could just as quickly decide to switch back to the British, depending on the situation on the battlefield.

Colonel Johnson's cavalry and Major Suggett's spies advance to positions from which they observe the British defensive line. Johnson is able ascertain that the earlier intelligence gained from prisoners had been accurate. He notes that the British had selected an excellent location from which to defend.

General Proctor, anticipating a direct attack on the path about 100 to 200 feet from the river, had deployed artillery at a strategic point from where his force could effectively rivet the road with fire. The British line, manned by artillery and his regulars of the 41st Regiment, extends from the Thames River to an open marsh. The artillery is deployed to dominate a road that stretches from the marsh to the river. Proctor deploys his Indians between the small marsh and a separate and larger marsh, from where they are able to strike at Harrison's left flank. Proctor also bolsters his line by deploying his reserves to the rear of the regulars.

General Harrison, finally within striking range of a stationary target, prepares his attack. Harrison's strategy calls for forming two columns of mounted troops, with each being followed by the greater part of his infantry until close contact is established. At that point his cavalry will converge into one column to increase the strength of the spearhead when it crashes into the enemy's line.

Harrison positions Acting General George Trotter's crack 1st Brigade (1st and 2nd Regiments) behind Colonel Johnson's cavalry in position from where the 2nd Battalion, 1st Regiment, will strike against the 41st and the artillery. Trotter's brigade is trailed by General George E. King's 3rd Brigade (5th and 7th Regiments), and it is trailed by the reserves, the 2nd Brigade (3rd and 4th Regiments), commanded by General David Chiles. The 5th Brigade (9th and 10th Regiments) under General Samuel Caldwell, is positioned to the front of the Indians' position

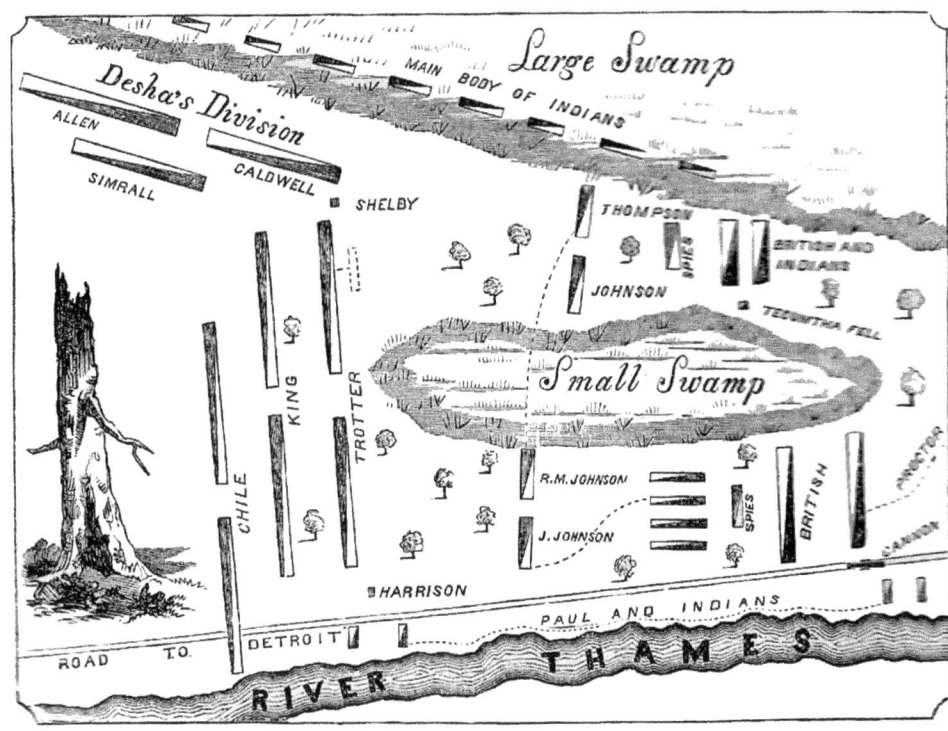

Battle of the Thames.

in the swamp, and Caldwell is bolstered on his left by General James Allen's 4th Brigade (4th and 8th Regiments).

The Americans take about two and one-half hours to form to storm the British lines, and during this time the British are becoming more confident due to their advantageous positions. However, Colonel Johnson, General Harrison and Governor Shelby remain ever observant and spot a flaw in the formation. Proctor's artillery is posted at the northern tip of the swamp on an elevation slightly west of Longwood Road. The regulars are deployed about to the front of the guns in two parallel lines, with the second formation separated from the first line by 100 feet; however, a three-foot gap stands between each man in the respective lines. Johnson's troops had been well trained for such an occasion, and even the horses had the necessary training to ignore the fire of both the artillery and the muskets.

General Proctor, along with his staff, remain behind the artillery to oversee the unfolding battle. Proctor also has his Indian allies stretched along the eastern sector of the swamp, which provides Proctor with dominating fire that can be unleashed on the ridge that extends between the two swamps. The regulars remain confident that with the support of the artillery, they will prevent the Americans from passing the ground lying between the road and the smaller swamp. Nevertheless, up until this confrontation, Johnson's regiment had primarily been in scouting operations.

The only remaining question is whether the regiment's training will provide it with success under fire. General Harrison, having great confidence in Johnson's ability, orders the cavalry charge. Colonel John Calloway of the 8th Regiment provides his troops with succinct instructions: "Boys, we must either whip these British and Indians, or they will kill and scalp every one of us. We can not escape if we lose. Let us all die on the field or conquer." The other commanders give similar advice to their units.

Colonel Johnson discerns that the available room in front of the British positions is too small to accommodate more than one battalion; however he also has spotted some maneuverability at the swamp to the right of the British positions. He directs the 2nd Battalion under Major David Thompson to break off from the 1st Battalion under Major DeVall and redeploy in front of the lines of Generals Allen and Caldwell, commanding the 4th and 5th Brigades respectively. The flank of the two brigades is covered by the 9th Regiment under Colonel James Simrall, posted on the far left.

Meanwhile, the 1st Battalion is formed in four divisions (columns) under Colonel James Johnson and Major Payne. In a flash, the long awaited order is called out: "Forward charge." The Kentuckians move out as if powered by the spirits of their fallen brothers and suddenly without prompting and nearly in unison, the battle cry "Remember the Raisin!" rings out in a thunderous yell. It had been eight months and eleven days since the barbarous massacre, but the memories of the ghastly scene had left an indelible mark on every Kentuckian in the columns. The columns, led by Colonel Richard M. Johnson and his brother Lt. Colonel James Johnson advance at a rather slow and cautious pace, permitting the infantry to keep up with the mounted troops. As the columns close toward the British positions, the rest of Harrison's infantry remains on the left, poised to strike the Indians under Tecumseh who hold the marsh.

The cry had been clearly heard by the British, and they too effortlessly recall the massacre because they were there and they sense that vengeance had increased the intensity of the attacking force. In each successive yell it becomes evident to the British that they are facing much more than a usual charge. The British remain steadfast and they are seasoned fighters; however, the Kentuckians' anger has raised them beyond what any foe might expect, and the more they hear the cry, the more determined they become. There are no thoughts of defeat as the horses move like lightning, with the ground trembling as they advance.

The British strike first and Lt. Colonel Johnson's right column sustains casualties just as it arrives within range of the British muskets. At nearly the same time, both columns of mounted troops converge to form a powerful line of galloping horses that bulldozes straight through the British defensive line. Suddenly the Redcoats are swarmed by a sea of horsemen, with each rider slashing his way through the British positions with lightning speed and devastating results. The Americans pass through with the speed and devastation of a hurricane. The troops, after reaching the far end of the British position, regroup, then, still badgering their enemy, they gallop back through the lines inflicting more grievous harm. Although the Kentuckians do not carry swords or pistols, they each carry hatchets, hunting knives and tomahawks along with their rifles.

The British are mauled by the deadly stings of the Kentuckians. The entire left wing of the British line disintegrates into mass chaos, and it occurs so swiftly that the British are overwhelmed before they are able to fix their bayonets. While the British (just under 475 men) are capitulating to Lt. Colonel James Johnson, the other British wing is undergoing similar punishment. Colonel Richard Johnson's horsemen approach the marsh, and just as they strike the Indians, a burst of fire from point-blank range inflicts heavy casualties upon the vanguard (Forlorn Hope).

Of the 20 men designated to draw the fire of Tecumseh's Indians, only one survives. Colonel Johnson at the front of the charge is among the wounded. Despite his wound, Johnson is able to assess the situation and remains in command. After quickly concluding the terrain standing between the two marshes is unsuitable for his horses, he changes strategy. Johnson directs his men to dismount and charge the positions. A donnybrook ensues when close-quartered fighting erupts. The savage exchange is underway for only about ten minutes when the Indians begin to falter. The reserves under Governor Isaac Shelby arrive to bolster the dismounted forces of Johnson and apply more pressure to the Indians. Before Governor's Shelby's reserves pounce, the Indians begin to disengage. Once the Indians to the front are vanquished and their leader, Tecumseh, is killed, the rest vanish in the wilderness.

There is no evidence confirming who fired the shot that killed Tecumseh, but one contemporary historian, named Thomson, credits Colonel Johnson with killing the Indian warrior after he had been repeatedly wounded himself. "At the instant when he [Johnson] discovered Tecumseh, his horse received a second wound. Tecumseh, having discharged his rifle, sprang forward with his tomahawk, and had it already raised to throw, when Colonel Johnson's horse staggered back, and immediately the colonel drew forth a pistol, shot the Indian through the head, and both fell to the ground together."

Tecumseh's body was identified by James Knaggs, a resident of the Raisin region who ran a ferry at the Huron River until he joined army at the start of the war. Knaggs was not present at the Battle of the Raisin because he was in Ohio on parole. Four of his brothers also served during the war, acting as spies under Captain William Wells, who was killed at Chicago. Colonel R.M. Johnson, a conspicuous target while riding his white horse, had been wounded five times during the engagement.

Colonel Johnson, due to his wounds, is unable to resume his position in Congress for a long time; however, later with the aid of crutches, which he requires for several years, he does retake his seat. His service spans the administrations of Presidents Thomas Jefferson, James Madison, James Monroe, John Q. Adams and Andrew Jackson. Also, the Indians who believed Tecumseh to be invulnerable lost heart after his death. He is buried but his grave site is never discovered. The Indians, abandoned by the British, begin to vanish into the woods and uncharacteristically, they leave their dead on the field.

By the time of Tecumseh's death and the arrival of Shelby's reserves, British General Proctor finds his defensive lines shattered and his Indian allies, now commanded by the Chippewa chief, Oshawahnail, in fast retreat. By this time, the British infantry, overwhelmed by the American thrust, requests quarter and the Kentuckians, their hearts consumed with vengeance, still grant quarter. Nonetheless, Proctor seeks no quarter, nor does he intend to remain with his troops. With an escort of dragoons and some Indians, Proctor vanishes from sight so quickly that he gets a head start that prevents his pursuers from intercepting him.

During Proctor's inglorious flight, he even abandons his carriage, along with a substantial amount of booty and papers. By this time, the pursuers lose all contact. After bolting from his carriage with the belief he is close to being captured, he mounts a horse and gallops off through the woods toward Burlington Heights. Using his familiarity with the terrain to his advantage, he loses his pursuers in the woods. Once again, General Proctor evades capture and in his mind, escapes what might have been intolerable consequences if captured by the Americans. Proctor had no knowledge that General Harrison had issued strict orders that if captured, no harm was to come to him. Proctor had escaped but neglected to take his private papers and his sword, which are seized by the pursuing Americans. He reaches the town but no laurels or cheers greet him upon his arrival; rather, he is renounced by the governor general of Canada and accused of "cowardice and avarice."

Back at the scene of the battle, nearly all of Proctor's force had been captured. In addition, the British had sustained about 180 casualties, ei-

Chief Oshawahnail.

General Joseph Desha (*The Battle of the Thames*, Colonel Bennett H. Young, 1903).

ther killed or wounded. Although the Indians had left 33 of their dead warriors on the field, their total killed are estimated at about 120. The Americans also discover that they have regained some well known cannon. The three brass cannon, acquired from the British during the American Revolution at the time of General John Burgoyne's surrender at Saratoga, had been deployed at Detroit. Upon the surrender of General Hull, they were recovered by the British.

When the Americans return to Detroit, the captured artillery is taken back and redeployed at the post. A large amount of captured British supplies and provisions are also carried back to Detroit. General Harrison's force loses seven

General Richard M. Johnson (*The Battle of the Thames*, Colonel Bennett H. Young, 1903).

killed and 25 wounded, with five of the latter receiving mortal wounds, according to a report from Harrison to the secretary of war. The same report estimates British losses at 12 killed and 22 wounded, along with 601 prisoners. General Harrison, unaware of total Indian casualties, reports that 33 Indian dead had been counted on the field. One of the slain Americans, Private Whitley, was a veteran of the American Revolution who served during that conflict with the rank of colonel. He had rejoined the army during this war and served with the rank of private.

General Harrison orders his troops to destroy Moraviantown by fire before he returns to Detroit. Meanwhile, General Proctor, upon his return to British territory, receives a court-martial, which concludes with a ruling that suspends him for six months.

General Harrison's decisive victory is not hailed in U.S. history books on a scale with other crowning achievements; however, Harrison's victory includes several profound accomplishments, not the least of which is the recapture of Detroit and the restoration of the entire Michigan Territory (except Mackinaw, which the British retain) to the United States. The flawless campaign also greatly erodes the dominance of the British in that sector of Canada, while simultaneously defanging the Indians with the demise of their prominent leader Tecumseh.

Tecumseh's death drains the tribes in the West of their will to continue to fight alongside the British, and the victory causes some tribes to acquiesce and accept peace on the terms presented by Harrison. It was reported that when the Kentuckians returned to the field following the battle, they discovered Tecumseh's body alongside about thirty other Indians, and the sight of him brought instant thoughts of the Massacre at the Raisin River. The Kentuckians are known to have "cut long strips of skin from the thighs for razor straps to be kept in memory of the massacre."

Before departing from the area, General Harrison appoints General Lewis Cass as provisional governor of the Michigan Territory. The Kentuckians under Governor Shelby return to Kentucky. General Harrison establishes a garrison of two brigades of regulars (about 1,000 men) to maintain the fort and guard the frontier while he prepares to embark with Commodore Perry for Buffalo with the remainder of his army.

General Marquis Calmes of Kentucky, a veteran of the American Revolution who participated at the Battle of Monmouth (1778), participates at this action, but only as a spectator due to illness. General Simon Kenton, a native Virginian born during 1755 and a veteran of the Revolution, participates; it is his final battle. Afterward he retires to private life at his home in the mountains. In April 1836, at the age of 83, the hunter and warrior dies in the same place where Indians had threatened to torture him to death during the Revolution. Also, Major General Joseph Desha participates in this action. His division is composed of the brigades of Generals Chiles and Caldwell, along with the Kentucky 11th Regiment, commanded by Colonel (later major general) William Williams. Major General Desha serves in Congress in 1816–1819, and in 1824, he is elected governor of Kentucky.

In his report to the secretary of war General Harrison emphasizes the services of the following general officers: Major General Henry, Major General Desha, Brigadier General Allen, Brigadier General Caldwell, Brigadier General Chiles, and Brigadier General Trotter, along with all of the Kentucky volunteers. Also, General James Allen, a native of Virginia who relocated in Kentucky, participated in the Battle of the Thames. Before the war, Allen organized a company of mounted riflemen who engaged against hostile Indians.

Later, during 1811, Allen commanded the Kentucky 10th Brigade (militia). Allen was requested by Isaac Shelby to join in the campaign that culminated with the Battle of the Thames. He was commissioned as brigadier general of militia on 8 September 1813. Also, Brigadier General Simon Kenton participates at this battle; however, he joined with General Shelby's Kentuckians and served as a private. Brigadier General John King and Brigadier General Robert McAfee, both of Kentucky, also participated during this campaign.

In Canada, General Prevost orders that Burlington Heights be abandoned; however, the order is not carried out. Also, a British contingent under Colonel Bostwick seizes 18 traitors in the vicinity of Port Dover.

In naval activity, Captain Chauncey's fleet spots some British sail on Lake Ontario. He initiates pursuit. Although it is not Commodore Yeo's fleet, the Americans intercept seven British gunboats that are in use as transports. Captain Chauncey's ships capture five of the gunboats and they destroy one other. The remaining vessel escapes. About 260 British soldiers are on the ships when they are seized. Two of the captured vessels had earlier been captured from Captain Chauncey in the vicinity of the Niagara River. During the previous month, while Chauncey was attempting to engage Commodore Yeo, two of his officers, captains of schooners, disregarded orders and were both captured along with their vessels. Both the USS *Julia* and the USS *Growler* are regained by Chauncey and their recent names, the HMS *Confiance* and HMS *Hamilton*, are quickly discarded. Nonetheless, the *Julia* and the *Growler* are unable to operate safely in heavy seas. Consequently, soon after they are regained, both are removed from service.

Chauncey's squadron also seizes the vessels *Drummond, Lady Gore* and the *Mary Ann*. The British abandon another vessel and set it on fire. Nonetheless, one schooner, the *Enterprise*, escapes capture. The captured craft are taken into port at Sackets Harbor, along with several hundred troops attached to De Waterville's German regiment, which was being transported from York to Kingston.

In other naval activity, the HMS *Conflict* encounters and captures the 70-ton brigantine *Medil Padria*, which is en route to Halifax with a cargo of flour. Also, the HMS *Fantome* seizes the schooner *Portland Packet*, which is separate from the schooner *Portland Packet* seized on 16 April 1813.

October 6 (Wednesday) **In Canada,** at Sandwich, General Duncan McArthur's force arrives and dispatches a contingent across the river to scatter a band of Indians that had been plundering the town. General McArthur writes to the secretary of war this day about Indians seeking peace: "Since General Harrison's departure, five nations, of Indians, viz.— Ottowas, Chippewas, Pottawatamies, Miamies, and Kickapoos, who were but a few miles back have come in for peace; and I have agreed that hostilities should cease, for the present, on the following conditions: they have agreed to take hold of the same tomahawk with us, and to strike any who are, or may be enemies to the U. States, whether British or Indians; they are to bring in a number of their women and children and leave them as hostages, whilst they accompany us to war. Some of them have already brought in their women; and are drawing rations."

In naval activity, Captain Porter orders the *Essex Jr.* (Lieutenant Downes) to depart for the Marquesas, where Porter expects that Lieutenant Downes will intercept the British vessel *Mary Ann* on its way to India. Downes is also directed to later rendezvous with the *Essex* at Port Anna Maria at Nooaheevah (Nuka Hiva) in the Washington Islands.

October 7 (Thursday) **In Tennessee,** General Andrew Jackson arrives at Fayetteville and assumes command of his army of volunteers. The force begins its training in drill; however, within a week, word arrives from Colonel Coffee at Huntsville, Alabama, that the Indians have been located. Without spending any time pondering his next move, General Jackson assembles his force on the day he receives the intelligence (11th) and the column sets out for Huntsville, about 32 miles distant. Jackson's troops are primarily seasoned Indian fighters and familiar with the tactics of their wily foe. The column arrives at Huntsville following a tedious five-hour march.

In Canada, the American Army under General William Henry Harrison begins its return to Detroit. General Isaac Shelby is in command because General Harrison had departed earlier. The troops arrive at Sandwich on the 10th during a snow storm. General Lewis Cass will be appointed as the civil and military governor of Michigan, with instructions to maintain his force of about 1,000 troops to ensure the British are unable to launch a new invasion and to impress the Indians with the strength of the American army. Cass' appointment is afterward confirmed by the United States Senate. Also, Fort Lernoult at Detroit undergoes repairs and it is renamed Fort Shelby in honor of Governor Shelby.

October 10 (Sunday) In Canada, a British force supported by gunboats lands at Hamilton, a port city along the St. Lawrence River in Ontario.

In naval activity, the HMS *Martin* recaptures the 128-ton sloop *Margaret* and takes it into port at New Brunswick. The *Margaret* is separate from the schooner *Margaret* seized on 16 March 1813 and the brigantine *Margaret* captured 28 February 1815.

October 11 (Monday) In Alabama, General Andrew Jackson's army arrives at Huntsville from Fayetteville, Tennessee, to link up with his vanguard, Colonel Coffee's Tennessee cavalry. Two of the volunteers are men who later become heroic legendary figures in American history, Davy Crockett and Sam Houston. While at his encampment, Jackson sends out cavalry to forage, while he prepares to deal with the hostile Creeks. He also dispatches Colonel Coffee with about 600 men to Black Warrior's town; however, the column finds the village abandoned. Coffee's troops, after collecting about 300 bushels of corn, burn the village before returning to join the main body at Thompson's Creek.

No Indians were encountered during the entire mission. Meanwhile, word arrives from a group of friendly Creeks that they are besieged at their positions at the Ten Islands of the Coosa. Jackson breaks camp and descends upon the place to rescue the beleaguered allies. While en route, the army destroys several villages. By 2 November, the Americans arrive within striking distance of the Creeks who are at Talluschatches (now Jacksonville), Alabama. Also, during this period, there has been concern about the Choctaw Indians; however, one of the prominent chiefs, Pushmataha, had traveled to St. Stephens to meet with George S. Gaines to enlist a force of his warriors to fight against the Creeks. Afterward, both men moved to Mobile to meet with General Flournoy at Fort Charlotte to present him with the proposal.

Chief Pushmataha becomes disillusioned when Flournoy declines accepting Choctaws as soldiers in the U.S. Army. Flournoy later has a change of heart. Gaines is dispatched to inform the chief that his offer has been accepted. The Choctaws are elated by the news, and as word spreads around the settlements, there is also a sense of great relief. It had been thought that the Choctaws were going to join the Creeks.

The Choctaws at this time are essentially ruled by three separate governments: Pushmataha governs in the east, Puckshenubbe in the west and Mushelatubba in the north. Pushmataha gives a long but effective speech that mentions Tecumseh "is bad." The Chickasaw agree and slap their breasts as the chief is drawing his sword and saying "You can all do as you please. You are all freemen. I dictate to none of you. But I shall join the St. Stephens people. If you have a mind to follow me, I will lead you to glory and to victory!" In the meantime, Colonel McKee, greatly assisted by John Peachland, persuades the Chickasaws to align themselves with the Americans.

In naval activity, the brigantine *Atlantic* is intercepted and recaptured by the HMS *Maidstone* and *Poictiers*. In other activity, the HMS *Comet* encounters and seizes the 208-ton ship *Charlotta* (B. Ellstrom, master), which is transporting a cargo of glass, iron, steel and other items from Landscrona, Sweden, to Rhode Island.

October 12 (Tuesday) In Alabama, General Flournoy orders General Ferdinand Claiborne to initiate offensive action to protect the settlers who are threatened by Indians allied with the British. Before this, Flournoy's orders had confined Claiborne to defensive activity. Flournoy's new order, by his own description, is "contrary to that of civilized nations, but the conduct of Great Britain and the acts of her Indian allies fully justify it." The order, which instructs Claiborne to protect the citizens while they tend to the harvest and clear the area of the hostile Indians, also instructs: "Follow them up to their contiguous towns, and to kill, burn and destroy all their Negroes, horses, cattle, and other property, that cannot conveniently be brought to the depots."

Claiborne immediately moves out on the mission. He is at the point with Major Hinds' dragoons, followed by militia. The column departs St. Stephens en route to Fort Easley. During the journey, on the 16th, the column comes upon the bodies of Colonel McGrew and three other men who had been killed in a skirmish at Tallahatta (Barshi Creek) on 4 October. The column pauses to permit the deceased troops to receive a proper burial. Afterward, the advance is resumed. Some contact is made with the Indians, but only small bands, and they avoid combat with the column; however, at one point along the route, the Indians spring an ambush on an infantry picket detachment. Several troops are wounded, but they suffer no fatalities. Major Hind's dragoons arrive and the Indians bolt for a nearby cliff and rapidly descend it to escape from the dragoons.

Afterward, Claiborne remains at Fort Easley for two days. During that time, contingents are dispatched in various directions in search of the enemy. Claiborne is convinced that the Indians are present and in great numbers, but they remain elusive. During the missions, five of the troops sustain serious wounds. After failing to entice the Indians to engage his column, General Claiborne departs for Pine Levels, where farms are plentiful and his depleted provisions can be replaced. Captain William Bradberry, one of the wounded, has to be carried back to St. Stephens; however, after his arrival he dies of his wounds.

After arriving at Pine Levels near the Tombigbee River, Claiborne dispatches scouts to the Alabama River. He also sends a messenger to General Flournoy to deliver a request that he dispatch all available troops that can be spared to Creek country.

In other activity, at this same time, General Andrew Jackson's army of Tennesseans has arrived at Huntsville. During this period, the Americans construct forts, including Fort Strother, built by General Jackson's forces in St. Clair County about 75 miles southwest of Fort Payne. Jackson will maintain his headquarters there and later, during February 1814, the 39th U.S. Infantry Regiment arrives to augment his Tennesseans. Another post, Fort Deposit, is established by General Claiborne. During December, General Claiborne is moving from Fort Claiborne toward the Creeks' "Holy Ground" (Econachaca), which the Indians believe to be invulnerable to attack by the Americans. Claiborne uses the post primarily for troops who become ill.

In Vermont, Colonel Isaac Clark leads a contingent against the village of Missisquoi, where the British are anticipating an American force attacking from Lake Champlain; however, Colonel Clark approaches by land and the British are caught off guard. The British fire against Clark's left flank, but the effort is in vain. Within about ten minutes, the enemy drop their arms and capitulate. Although the victory occurred in lightning-quick time, Colonel Clark is aware that another British force of about 200 troops is en route to intercept his command. Clark dispatches a contingent under Captain Finch to observe the progress of the advancing column. Fortuitously, Finch's troops capture the advance cavalry guard, except for one man who makes it back to the main body. Clark's luck continues. The relief force, once informed of the capture of the advance troops, aborts the advance. Afterward, the prisoners, including the commander, Major Powell, are placed aboard boats and taken to Burlington. Colonel Clark reports that his force that engaged the enemy numbered 102 men. He also reports no American casualties, and he gives the British losses at 9 killed and 14 wounded.

October 13 (Wednesday) In Canada, pursuant to orders from General Wilkinson, Colonel Winfield Scott departs from Fort George with the fort's complement of regulars and the invalids en route to Fort Niagara. Once there, he is to take the remaining regulars and the convalescents and move to the mouth of the Genesee River, where the force is to be met by vessels. However, his orders include that the two companies of the 1st Artillery Regiment at Fort Niagara are to remain there. Meanwhile, Brigadier General McClure assumes command of the post. The garrison is composed of his New York militia.

October 14 (Thursday) *In naval activity,* the HMS *Paz* intercepts and seizes the schooner *Randolph*. The *Randolph* is separate from the schooner *Randolph* seized on 23 July 1813.

October 16 (Saturday) *In naval activity,* the 262-ton ship *Baltic* (J. Jameson, master), transporting a cargo of salt from St. Ubes (St. Elbes Setubal), Portugal, to Boston is intercepted and captured by the HMS *La Hogue*. In other naval activity, the HMS *Loire* intercepts and captures the 89-ton schooner *Sally*.

October 17 (Sunday) **In New York** at Sackets Harbor, General James Wilkinson sails with a force en route to seize Montreal. His brigade commanders include Generals John Parker Boyd, Leonard Covington, Robert Swarthout and Jacob J. Brown, bolstered by a reserve brigade under General Alexander Macomb. The flotilla moves toward Preston; however, the movement had not been unnoticed by the British. At Kingston, a naval force — eight gunboats augmented by some artillery — begins to shadow the American invasion force that lands close to Preston. The British gunboats are also transporting troops commanded by Colonel Joseph W. Morrison and Colonel John Harvey (adjutant general). Morrison debarks at Point Iroquois. Counting some reinforcements that joined with Morrison at Preston, his force numbers about 800 troops.

October 18 (Monday) *In naval activity,* the privateer *Saratoga* arrives at Newport, Rhode Island, and it has brought a prize, the British packet HMS *Morgiana*, carrying 18 guns.

October 19 (Tuesday) *In naval activity,* Commodore Perry orders Captain Jesse Elliott to take command of the squadron and move to Erie, Pennsylvania. Perry mentions that if he is not there, instructions will be left for Elliott. Elliott is to direct the USS *Somers* to pick up as many men of the Pennsylvania militia and the Petersburg volunteers as will fit on board and transport them to Cleveland, Ohio. After debarking the troops, Elliott is to take on supplies and provisions and sail for Put-in-Bay, where he will bring aboard General Cass' brigade and drop off supplies, then advance to Detroit. Elliott's squadron will be busy. Perry also directs Elliott to dispatch the *Porcupine* after it returns from Portage to sail to Middle Sister Island to retrieve the army's baggage. After returning, it is to take on as many men attached to General McArthur's brigade as can be crammed aboard. Meanwhile, the *Tigress* is ordered to take the wounded British prisoners to Erie, while the *Scorpion* debarks militia and volunteers at Cleveland and, after acquiring supplies, move down the lake to join the squadron.

In other activity, the *Alert* (A. Child), a sloop transporting molasses and pitch, is seized by the HMS *Boxer*.

October 20 (Wednesday) **In Maryland,** at Easton, a British squadron appears at the mouth of Choptank. The militia at Easton under General Perry Benson is prepared to defend but is not tested. After the threat ends, the militia is dismissed on 2 November.

In naval activity, the British privateer *Retrieve* seizes the 120-ton brigantine *Ann* commanded by J.H. Winter, master, while it is en route from Cape Ann to St. Bartholomews. The *Ann* is transporting a cargo of food. Also, another brigantine named *Ann* had been recaptured during the previous year at an undetermined time by the HMS *Chubb*. Yet another vessel named *Ann* (W. Bartlett, master), also a brigantine, is captured by the HMS *Jaseur* on 4 November.

In other naval activity, the American privateer *David Porter*, named in honor of Captain David Porter, is in port at Newport, Rhode Island, gathering a cargo for delivery in Charleston, South Carolina. Once the loading is completed, the privateer sails without incident into Newport to await an opportune time to run the blockade to get to the open seas. George Coggeshall, its commander, takes the risk on 14 November.

October 20–25 **In Canada** at Kingston, the Canadian commander-in-chief, General George Prevost, is faced with multiple threats. An American force of about 10,000 troops under General James Wilkinson is near Kingston and preparing to move against Montreal. And yet another U.S. force, also composed of about 10,000 men led by General Wade Hampton, is advancing by way of Chateauguay against Montreal. The strategy calls for the forces to combine near Lake St. Louis in southwestern Quebec. A small British force under Lt. Colonel Charles de Salaberry is shadowing Hampton; however, his command is overmatched by Hampton's army.

Before departing from Kingston for lower Canada, General Prevost calls upon Lt. Colonel McDonnell with an urgent question about whether he could accomplish the impossible and how soon could he begin. Provost asks if McDonnell, known more commonly as Red George, could muster his battalion, which at this time is training at Kingston, and speed to Chateauguay. Provost asks how soon McDonnell could move out. General Provost instantly receives the response from Red George that his battalion, the French Canadian Fencibles, would depart once they finish their dinner.

McDonnell suddenly faces a remarkable challenge which would involve traveling about 170 miles by water, including some deadly rapids and passing by American outposts and sharpshooters. McDonnell has one major obstacle to overcome before his battalion of about 600 men can depart. No boats are available and he has no pilots to get him over the rapids on the St. Lawrence River. McDonnell begins gathering bateaux from around Kingston and securing other vessels. By the next morning, McDonnell's battalion embarks, then passes no fewer than four separate sections of treacherous rapids without the loss of any vessels or men. The flotilla arrives at Beauharnois, Quebec, during the night of 24 October, but the journey is not ended. Without pause, McDonnell's troops debark and begin their 20-mile overland march that lasts throughout the night which pushes their stamina to the limits. The force arrives during the morning of the 25th in time to join with Charles de Salaberry at Chateauguay.

The fact that the reinforcements had completed the entire journey is remarkable; however, at the time of their arrival it is hardly noticed by De Salaberry. Nonetheless, the troops are jubilant when the McDonnell's force arrives. Suddenly and unexpectedly, De Salaberry's command of about 400 swells to about 1,000 troops, and they are in time to engage the Americans (*see also,* **October 25–26**).

October 21 (Thursday) **In Maine,** the privateer *Washington*, a schooner, is commissioned his day. Also, the HMS *Majestic* encounters and captures the schooner *Betsy and Jane* (S. Brown, master).

October 23 (Saturday) *In naval activity,* Commodore Perry's squadron takes General Harrison and his force to Buffalo. Once there, Harrison moves to Newark. Afterward, Harrison receives orders to send his brigade to Sackets Harbor. General Harrison is also informed by the War Department that he "has permission to return to his family." Harrison complies; however, the success of Harrison's service and the recovery of Michigan makes the move by the War Department undefendable. Harrison goes back to Cincinnati and maintains headquarters there until he resigns his commission on 11 May 1814, with the resignation effective 31 May. In other naval activity, Captain David Porter, aboard the USS *Essex*, arrives at Teebooa, Marquesas.

October 24 (Sunday) **In New York,** after his victory over General Proctor at the Battle of the Thames, General Harrison arrives back at Buffalo with Captain Oliver H. Perry's squadron. General Duncan McArthur's brigade also arrives with Harrison. Harrison remains in the area until fall before departing to visit a series of cities (New York, Philadelphia, Baltimore and Washington) prior to returning to his home in Ohio, where he resigns his commission on 31 May 1814. Harrison's resignation arrives at Washington when President Madison is absent from the capital. Nevertheless, Secretary of War John Armstrong, a long-time detractor of Harrison, is authorized by the president to act upon orders. Shortly after the package is opened, Armstrong accepts Harrison's resignation and soon proposes Andrew Jackson as his successor.

Subsequent to the conclusion of William Henry Harrison's military career, he becomes a Congressman and a U.S. Senator, followed by his election to the U.S. presidency. He is inaugurated on 4 March 1841 as the 9th president and dies one month later from pneumonia on 4 April. On the same day, Vice President John Tyler, a Virginian, is sworn in as the 10th president of the United States. President Tyler is remembered for his support, against Congress' resistance, of admitting Texas as a state. Tyler is able to cap his presidency by signing the legislation just days before his presidency ends.

In naval activity, the USS *Essex* and its accompanying vessels spot the island of Roahooga (Washington Islands), a name given to it by the natives; however, Porter's men refer to it as Adams Island. On the following day, Porter arrives at his destination, Nooaheevah, and shortly thereafter, the Americans refer to it as Madison's Island.

October 25 (Monday) *In naval activity,* Commodore Perry transfers command of the upper lakes to Captain Elliot. Also, the brigantine

Dispatch (J. Thompson, master) is recaptured by the HMS *Albion*. The *Dispatch* is separate from the 168-ton *Dispatch* seized 16 April 1813. Having left Gottenburg, Germany, with glass, iron, aluminum and other items, the 150-ton brigantine *Hoppet* never makes it to Boston. It is overtaken by the HMS *Romulus*. In other naval activity, the HMS *Narcissus* intercepts and recaptures the brigantine *Telemachus*.

Also, the American squadron under Captain David Porter, having arrived at Nooaheevah (called Madison's Island by the Americans) on the previous day, observes a boat approaching. Porter notes that the occupants are three white men: "One of them is perfectly naked, with the exception of a cloth about his loins; and as his body was all over tattooed, I could not doubt his having been a long time on this or some other island." The boat is turned back by Porter, and afterward, with a contingent of Marines, Porter lands. During the trip to shore, the natives abscond. One of the three white men approaches and to Porter's surprise, he is a midshipman, John M. Maury of the U.S. Navy. He had been stranded before the war erupted. Until the arrival of Porter's squadron, he remained unaware that war had begun. The man who approached the ship without wearing any clothes is named Wilson, an Englishman. He had been there for years and now speaks the native language. Despite Captain Porter's initial feelings to dislike and distrust him, he later finds Wilson "indispensably necessary to us, and without his aid I should have succeeded badly on the island." Porter again changes his opinion of Wilson and describes him as "a consummate hypocrite and villain."

Meanwhile, after Porter reaches shore, he inquires about various groups of natives in the mountainsides that encircle the village. He is informed that they are hostile and have come to the opposite side of the mountain and for a few weeks have been raiding the friendly villages in the valley.

A raid was expected on the day Porter's squadron arrived but did not materialize because of the appearance of the ships. Once informed of the belligerents, Captain Porter moves to quash the turmoil. Porter, aware that his ships are quite visible to those on the mountain, sends one of the natives to inform the hostile people of his intent, which he later recounts as to "tell them that I had come with a force sufficiently strong to drive them from the island, and if they presume to enter the valley while I remained there, I should send a body of men to chastise them; to warn them to cease all hostilities so long as I remained among them; and say that if they had hogs or fruit to dispose of, they might come and trade freely with us, as I should not permit the natives of the valley to injure or molest them."

Also, during the morning, the Americans discover the island of Roahooga, which they name Adams' Island (Washington Group).

October 25–26 **In Canada,** General Wade Hampton's army is on the advance to link with the army under General Wilkinson; however, the British are rushing to interrupt Hampton's march. By the 25th, reinforcements under Lt. Colonel McDonnell (Red George) have arrived to bolster Lt. Colonel Charles de Salaberry's diminutive command. With the reinforcements, the British force totals about 400 to 500 men, including Indians. The British down trees to create obstacles along the road through the wilderness. General Hampton dispatches a regiment to clear the woods by maneuvering into positions to the rear in an open space, while other troops construct a separate road. The strategy succeeds and the column proceeds without difficulty; however, the British have erected yet another and more formidable obstacle less than ten miles away. Hampton's columns arrive at a new forest and find heavier blockages, including breastworks, along with fallen trees with pointed tips. General Hampton assesses the situation and with his officers devises a plan by which he would send a contingent to cross the river and maneuver to positions below the British roadblock, from where they would bolt back across the river to strike the British rear and their flank to clear passage in coordination with the main body, which is to plow directly into the front.

The plan has a flaw. The men delegated to get the troops to the jump-off inform General Hampton that they lack familiarity with the terrain. The operation is executed anyway. One man in Hampton's force is familiar with the land, but he does not move out with Purdy. Initially all goes well. As expected, the river crossing is fordable. Nevertheless, once the column is across, the situation begins to rapidly deteriorate. The force becomes disoriented in the darkness and gets ensnared in a swamp. The troops move blindly and inadvertently in a circle without ever reaching the point where the column is to re-cross the river. The entire night is lost, and on the following day, Purdy's column is still out of contact with the main body and still on the opposite bank. Nonetheless, despite having no communications with Colonel Purdy, Hampton's main body launches an attack against the front line of the British during the afternoon of the 26th.

The British holding the blockade are prepared for the onslaught and bitter fighting ensues. The main thrust pounds against the British and the defenders return equally tenacious fire. The assault troops are led by General George Izard. The support troops under Colonel Purdy have yet to find the crossing spot. Nevertheless, Purdy's force is able to hear the constant roar of small arms fire. In the meantime, British troops on the opposite bank discover the American column and they pounce upon Purdy's vanguard. While the point troops are pulling back, yet another British contingent, composed of militia, springs from its concealed positions and delivers volleys that thoroughly disrupt the cohesion of Purdy's command. Chaos emerges and the British seize the advantage. Purdy's command suddenly collapses and a hurried, haphazard retreat occurs.

Back on the opposite bank, the British continue to hold against the American pressure. During this intense skirmish, De Salaberry plucks an ancient ruse out of his bag of tricks. Off in the distance, well placed buglers begin to signal a charge, creating an illusion that the Americans are about to be attacked from several different positions. The failure of his attack, combined with the sounds of the buglers in the woods, convinces Hampton to disengage. He orders a general retreat and his army returns to Plattsburgh. Consequently, Hampton's army does not link with General Wilkinson's army, which causes Montreal to be spared from the attack.

During this battle at the Chateauguay River, the Americans sustain about 40 killed or wounded. The British sustain about 25 casualties. De Salaberry's defenders hold the line and prevent General Hampton's army from completing the advance to link up with General Wilkinson.

October 26 (Tuesday) *In naval activity* at Buffalo, Commodore Perry writes to Captain Jesse D. Elliott to transfer command:

SIR,— The Honorable Secretary of the Navy having granted me permission to leave the lake service, the command of course devolves on you, which I now resign to you. I enclose you attested copies of Commodore Chauncey's letters to me which are so full, and having communicated with you fully before I left Erie, that it will be unnecessary for me to say any thing more as to the distribution of the squadron; I beg you will comply with Commodore Chauncey's directions respecting the muster rolls. Those of the Lawrence and Flotilla were signed before I left Erie. Every assistance in your power must be rendered to the army. The Ariel is directed to remain here, and assist the Chippeway and Little Belt, that have unfortunately grounded. I enclose you an extract of a letter from the Honorable the Secretary of the Navy, for your government.

October 27 (Wednesday) *In naval activity,* the HMS *Paz* seizes the schooner *William* (S. Nevis, master), which is en route to Charlestown from New York with a cargo of provisions.

October 28 (Thursday) In Alabama, on or about this day, General Jackson has paused at Will's Creek. Jackson's supplies and provisions had become dangerously low. He dispatches a cavalry contingent under Colonel Dyer with instructions to destroy the Creek village of Littefutchee along Canoe Creek. The cavalry arrives at the village at 0400 on the 29th. The village is destroyed by fire, and 29 prisoners, including men, women and children, are seized and returned to Jackson's camp. Other contingents on separate missions bring in a few other prisoners. Old Chinnobe, an ally of the Americans, with the aid of his son, brings in two prisoners. All of the captured are taken to Huntsville.

In naval activity, the HMS *Ring Dove* intercepts and recaptures the bark *Paris*. Also, Captain David Porter's squadron, while still at Nooaheevah (Madison's Island), inadvertently gets tangled in some native warfare. Porter had demanded that the Happahs from the opposite side of the mountain cease their raids or face attack by the Americans. In the meantime, the people in the valley had pleaded without success to convince Porter to attack the intruders. He did promise to protect the villagers, but only if their enemy came into the valley. The Happahs have come to believe the Americans, out of fear, would not attack and the valley people are coming to the same conclusion. The warriors' primary weapon is the spear (two types), and they are also skilled with deadly slingshots, described by Captain Porter as being "as effective as musketry." The Happahs have remained overconfident during the absence of any offensive activity by the Americans, and they have informed Captain Porter that they would make peace only if his force could defeat them.

October 29 (Friday) *In naval activity,* the HMS *Loup Cervier* intercepts and seizes the brigantine *John and Mary* (T. Collins, master).

October 29 to December 9 *In naval activity* at Nooaheevah, Captain David Porter's force selected to drive the belligerents from the mountains is composed of his detachment of Marines and the crewmen from the *Essex Jr.* The troops advance from the valley to drive the Happahs from the mountains that surround the town. About 40 men total, with natives carrying their weapons and provisions to the heights of the mountains, bolt from one height to another to clear the ridges of the hostile warriors. During the operation, one of the valley people is carrying the Stars and Stripes. The advance, which begins at 1100, runs out of opposition about one hour after the Americans reach the top. At about 1600 the hostile tribe reappears descending the mountain with five corpses hanging from poles. The American contingent arrives at the base of the mountain with each man thoroughly exhausted.

The commander, Lieutenant Downes, reports that they were initially successful in driving the Happahs from one place to another in the heights until they converged on one fortress with somewhere between three thousand and four thousand warriors. From there they taunted the Americans, daring them to attack. Downes, infuriated by the actions, defiantly ordered a charge. During the ascent, a stone from one warrior's slingshot struck Downes in his stomach and laid him out breathless for a while. At nearly the same time, a thrown spear strikes another in the neck to essentially force a pause in the assault. The Happahs were jubilant as the attacking contingent began to falter. Retreat was the next step, and by now, the valley natives were convinced that the Americans had plenty of bluster but nothing to back up their words.

The Happahs, according to Downes' report to Captain Porter, began "exposing their posteriors to us." By this time, Downes realized that the Happahs must be dislodged particularly because of the people in the valley were losing their respect. Downes, having regained his breath and his composure, had no thoughts of retreating. He ordered another assault and in a flash, the sailors and Marines bolted forward, dodging a hail of spears and stones descending upon them. Their agility paid dividends, and they reached the fort, then burst inside. Five of the defenders died suddenly and another refused to yield until he was struck by the muzzle of a musket which "was presented to his forehead, when the top of his head was entirely blown off." Suddenly, the greatly outnumbered Americans controlled the

The Mighty Gattanewa.

fortress and the enemy had vanished, leaving no one to further taunt Porter's troops.

Meanwhile, the villagers in the valley are terrified that they would be the next victims. Captain Porter moves to visit the leader, Gattanewa, king of the Taeehs, to inform him that his enemies had retreated; however, when he arrives, he hears a horrific type of shouting that mystifies him before he can deliver the pleasant news. He inquires of Gattanewa's wife as to the reason for the alarm. She responds that the villagers are expecting to be Porter's next victims, and she continues speaking to Captain Porter. He said she grasped his hand, "which she kissed, and moistened with her tears: then placing it on her head, [she] knelt to kiss my feet." She also informs Captain Porter that the villagers "were willing to be our slaves, to serve us, that their houses, their lands, their hogs, and everything belonging to them were ours." During this unnecessary plea, she "begged that I [Porter] would have mercy on her, her children, and her family, and not put them to death." Moving quickly to end the fear that had overtaken the villagers, Captain Porter eases the woman up from her submissive position and explains that the Americans are their friends and that no one will be harmed in any way, paving the way for the terror-filled villagers to become overjoyed.

Porter's squadron, while on the island, works with the villagers to construct a fort beginning on 3 November. About 4,000 natives from nearly every tribe arrives at the camp to assist. By nightfall of the 4th, a house for Captain Porter and another house for the officers are completed. The various tribes have no chiefs and no government; however, they are diligent and anxious to do fine work. Gattanewa, obviously a leader, according to Captain Porter is more like a father with his children. Nevertheless, he does hold privilege, and it is considered a sacrilege by the natives "to touch the top of his head, or any thing that touched his head." He has servants, but they come and go as they please. It is forbidden to have a closed gateway or a house with a door, to ensure that Gattanewa or his family members never pass a closed gate or a closed door. The mat on which Gattanewa sleeps cannot "be touched by a female, not even his wife."

By the time the fort is completed, the crews had removed everything from the frigate and transferred all of the provisions and powder to Captain Porter's prizes. Afterward, according to Captain Porter's subsequent description, "the ship had been thoroughly smoked with charcoal, to destroy the rats, which on opening the hatches, were found in great numbers dead about the large pots in which the fires were made. Several tubs full of them were collected and thrown overboard and it was supposed that, exclusive of the young, which were killed in the nests, and could not be found, we had not destroyed a less number than from twelve to fifteen hundred."

Meanwhile, one tribe, the Typees, are lagging behind in their commitments and making false accusations about the Happahs, claiming they could not gain passage through the Happahs' valley. Nevertheless, Porter discerns the truth and he threatens war. Suddenly, Porter's force numbers about 5,000 men. The force advances against the Typees and hits solid resistance. The Americans rapidly run out of most of their ammunition and the Typees remain behind a seven-foot-high barrier with their flanks protected by thicket too dense to penetrate.

Meanwhile, Porter's makeshift army has dwindled to less than a platoon, excluding one tribe, the Mouina. The others had retreated. Of the nineteen Americans, three had been injured by stones from slingshots. Suddenly, while the Americans are pulling back, the Typees charge. The Indians, yelling wildly as they charge, are struck by effective fire, and those close behind who attempt to carry them away are also hit and wounded. Nonetheless, Porter continues to head to the opposite bank of the river before his command is overrun. They do make it across, but those Typees, using their slingshots, continue to catapult stones across the river. Captain Porter is once again faced with an insurmountable task. He realizes he must regroup and plan a new attack to forestall disaster, which would occur once the friendly Indians believe the Americans had been defeated. It is a normal practice for the Indians to switch sides and join the winning force.

On the following day, Captain Porter renews his attack, but he relies on his squadron, 200 men from the *Essex* and the recently arrived *Essex Jr.*, along with men from the prizes. Porter awaits darkness and the operation is unfolded quietly to avoid alerting the Indians. Nevertheless, problems arise when it is determined that the boats leak badly and will not carry the men. Undaunted and determined to undo the previous day's failure, Porter advances on land. The march continues without incident and the guides prove to be useful. The Typees remain unaware of the presence of the sailors and Marines until they receive a volley just before dawn. Unexpectedly, Porter finds that some Indians had joined with him to increase his numbers. From the top of a ridge, the troops initiate a quick descent into the valley and the accompanying Indians begin to shout loudly while the beating of their drums creates wild noises that are enjoined by squealing hogs and women and children who begin to scream and cry. The force moves into the village and remains there; however, the Happahs retire. The Typees remain throughout the night with the Americans and strong guards keep a vigil until dawn.

At daybreak, Captain Porter moves out. Shortly thereafter, the Typees, on the opposite bank of the river, dare the Americans and their allies to descend and attack. Suddenly, the troops descend the slope; it is difficult terrain which causes some exhaustion. Acting pragmatically, Porter calls a halt at the foot of the slope to permit the rear to join the main body and to grab some rest before crossing the river. All the while, slingshots continue to be used to propel stones upon the attackers. Having become accustomed to the incoming stones, the Americans more easily figure out how to avoid becoming a casualty.

Once the rear catches up, Porter orders the advance. By the time, the rear gets across the river, the vanguard had already seized the fortified village. Afterward, a contingent engages defenders at another fort and seizes it, but the Typees launch a strong assault and regain it within about one-half hour, compelling the American contingent to return to the main body. In the meantime, the Typees strike the fort that had been captured by pushing past a contingent under Lieutenant McKnight. At the time, large numbers of Typees and Happahs are in and around the fort, but they all vanish. Although the Typees threaten, the first volley compels them to hurriedly retreat. The Americans continue to fire, but no Typees are killed during their withdrawal.

Afterward, the Americans proceed deeper into the valley, aware that their foes are formidable. They reach and destroy three villages before the main bastion is reached; the advance is gained nearly yard by yard. The Typees tenaciously defend their capital; however, American firepower prevails and the capital falls. Captain Porter is impressed with the Typee fortifications as well as their valor, which causes him to reluctantly out of necessity burn the capital. Captain Porter later states: "The beauty and regularity of this place was such, as to strike every spectator with astonishment, and to their grand site, or public square, was far superior to any other we had met with." During the destruction of the capital, many of their goods are destroyed, along with large numbers of war canoes that had not yet been used. Meanwhile, the Indians accompanying Porter fail to run away. They are too focused on plunder. Meanwhile, the valley recently described as beautiful resembles a continuing line of burning debris.

Despite having been driven from their valley, the Typees are happy when word reaches them that Captain Porter continues to desire peace with them. They eagerly accept the proposal and the terms which include making peace with all the tribes allied with the Americans, and they agree to provide four hundred hogs in exchange for presents. With peace having returned, Captain Porter returns to readying his ships. By 9 December, he sails, leaving a small contingent behind.

October 30 (Saturday) *In naval activity,* the British privateer *Shannon* intercepts and seizes the schooner *Swallow* (S. Frisbec, master).

November **In Washington, D.C.,** President James Madison gets a letter from the British prime minister offering to negotiate an end to the conflict. President Madison names John Quincy Adams and others to a peace committee, after agreeing to British Prime Minister Castlereagh's offer. During May, Albert Gallatin and James Bayard had gone to Russia to join with John Quincy Adams for negotiations, but these never began. Now Madison dispatches two additional men, Henry Clay and Jonathan Russell, who will join with the other three to begin the peace talks in Ghent, a small Flemish town. Although Czar Alexander's offer to mediate the problem was declined by the British, his initiative is certainly the reason these talks are to begin. Of the five men, only Russell lacks diplomatic experience. However, the five personalities also vary widely, and although Adams is the head of the team, he doesn't dominate, primarily because the others also have strong personalities, which leads to much tension among the group. The American diplomats converge at Ghent during late June.

In Alabama, General Claiborne dispatches a contingent of troops to Fort Warren, known also as Fort Burnt Corn. The troops are needed to fortify some blockhouses in the area near the Federal Road to provide protection for settlers and those who travel the road during the ongoing hostilities with the Creeks. Fort Warren was established in the vicinity of Burnt Corn near Pine Orchard by Colonel Richard Warren, who had served in the Revolutionary War and subsequently moved from Georgia to Alabama. The fort is used to protect settlers along the Federal Road during the hostilities with the Indians.

November 1–2 **In New York–Canada,** the British, who have maintained surveillance of General Wilkinson's movements, initiate an attack by sending a naval squadron against Wilkinson's vanguard under General Jacob Brown, which is thought by the British to be moving against Kingston (Canada). Brown's positions are farther up French Creek and Brown has fortified it with three 19-pounders, commanded by Captain McPherson on elevated ground at Bartlet's Point. The British are stymied by the artillery fire. The British return on the following day to renew the attack, but again they are repelled. One of their brigantines sustains heavy damage and must be towed out of harm's way. Brown's force sustains two killed and four wounded. Meanwhile, Wilkinson establishes French Creek as his second rendezvous point to enhance the illusion that the Americans are preparing to attack Kingston rather than the real objective, Montreal. General Wilkinson, in the meantime, makes preparations to depart from Grenadier Island on 5 November.

November 2–3 BATTLE OF TALLASEHATCHE (TALLUSEHATCHIE) **In Alabama,** Brigadier General John Coffee departs from General Jackson's camp after dusk on November 2. Coffee's column has about 900 cavalry and mounted troops, accompanied by a small band of friendly Creeks and Cherokees, all adorned with white feathers and deer tails, led by Richard Brown. Coffee's orders call for him to divide his force, with one-half moving to the area around Ten Islands to protect the operation, while the other half strikes the Creek camp. The column fords the Coosa at Fish Dam, less than five miles from Ten Islands. On the morning of the 3rd, the column stands about one and one-half miles from the town. It moves straight to Tallusehatche (later Jacksonville). The cavalry in the right column is commanded by Colonel Allcorn and the mounted rifles on the left are led by Colonel Cannon. Allcorn's cavalry maneuvers to encircle one-half of the town, while the mounted infantry forms a semi-circle on the left side of the objective.

Pursuant to Coffee's orders, the units form a link that places the head of both columns at the front of the town. At about an hour after the crack of dawn on the 3rd, while the enemy drums are beginning to beat in cadence with the uproarious yells of the Indians signaling their preparations to launch an attack, Colonel Coffee signals the spearhead of his force to charge. Two companies, led by Captain Hammond and Lieutenant James Patterson, drive forward toward the buildings to prompt the enemy to move out from their protected positions. The horsemen gallop to the fringes of the town and conspicuously hold positions in open ground while they pour fire toward the defenders. As General Coffee had anticipated, the Indians, seeing only a small mounted force, mount a charge. The troops quickly pivot and move out of the line of fire of the right column under Colonel Allcorn. Suddenly the Indians are struck by menacing fire which brings a succinct halt to their charge at about the same time as the cavalry begins its charge, while the Indians hurriedly retreat to the buildings. Despite the initial overpowering shock inflicted by the right column, the Indians, from within the protection of the buildings, raise tenacious resistance. Coffee's command increases the pressure by charging the doors of the buildings. Shortly thereafter, the entire defending force is annihilated. The Indians, still consumed with overconfidence since their massacre of the people at Fort Mims, suddenly finds themselves in an inescapable cauldron. Nevertheless, they all die with honor.

The Tennesseans, according to a report by General Coffee, lose five killed and 41 wounded. The Creeks sustain about 200 killed and of those, the Americans count 186 Creeks left dead on the field. Others had died in the woods. No warriors escape death and some women and children are killed, although that was not the intent of the troops. The deaths of family members occurred after the Indians had retreated to the buildings. In his report, General Coffee mentions the deaths of the innocents: "Our men, in killing the males, without intention killed and wounded a few of the squaws and children, which was regretted by every officer and soldier of the detachment, but which could not be avoided." After the lopsided victory, Coffee's command also seizes 84 women and children, who are taken to Huntsville. In his after-battle report, Colonel Coffee states: "Our men rushed up to the doors of the houses, and in a few minutes killed the last warrior of them. The enemy fought with savage fury, and met death with all its horrors, without shrinking or complaining. Not one asked to be spared, but fought as long as they could stand or sit."

By about this time, General Jackson's force increases with the arrival of the volunteers from East Tennessee under General John Cocke. After the victory, General Andrew Jackson writes to Governor Willie Blount: "We have retaliated for the destruction of Fort Mimms." Later, during the evening, General Coffee moves back across the Coosa and returns to camp at Ten Islands. Afterward, General Jackson pushes across Coosa Mountain and arrives at Ten Islands, where he orders the construction of a new supply depot (Fort Strother).

In naval activity, the American privateer *Globe* engages two British vessels in a ferocious duel off Madeira, Portugal just two days after barely escaping from a brigantine, a more powerful British man of war. The ships trade broadsides from extremely close range. Despite having damage, the *Globe* engages both vessels simultaneously in a tenacious fight on the morning of the 3rd. While engaged in a running fight with one of the ships, the *Globe* slips back just after two officers and three seamen board the British vessel, preventing the full number from boarding. Those who do board are killed by the British. At about the same time, the other British brigantine eases up close and pours fire upon the *Globe* that kills and wounds a few men and damages it's rigging and sails. The fire also increases the number of casualties aboard the *Globe*. The guns of the *Globe* remain operational and return fire is maintained; however, the vessel is crippled. Repairs begin in order to permit the *Globe* to rebound and resume the clash.

Meanwhile, the *Globe* moves against the first brigantine, and following some heavy fire from the ship's guns and muskets, the brigantine surrenders at about 1530. While the crew of the *Globe* is focused on the first brigantine, the second brigantine moves into closer range to intensify its fire. Captain Richard Moon, having seized the first vessel, is able to refocus his efforts on the second British vessel. By about 1630, while there is not yet a victor, the *Globe* becomes imperiled due to successive hits at the water line. Captain Moon quickly orders his vessel to move back toward the first brigantine, which had earlier surrendered. The *Globe* nudges alongside one of the brigantines, and when the boarding party moves to seize the ship, the British stun the Americans by re-hoisting the colors and simultaneously launching a broadside. Both British warships sail off. The final and unexpected broadside prevents the *Globe* from giving chase. The *Globe* sustains the loss of 23 men.

The *Globe*, again engaging two British vessels, becomes imperiled, which compels her to disengage or face the possibility of sinking, or being captured. The British fail to gain the advantage by initiating pursuit, providing the *Globe* with the opportunity to live to fight another day. While the British sail off in a different direction, the *Globe* still faces the possibility of sinking. While the crew toils with making temporary repairs to save the ship, she sets a course that takes her into port in the Canary Islands. The all-out effort to save the ship succeeds and the ship reaches port safely.

Once in port in the Canary Islands, the Americans discover that two British vessels had recently arrived, and the crews mention they had engaged an American vessel in a tenacious sea battle and that in the process, the British claimed that they had lost 27 killed or wounded. Five men in the *Globe*'s boarding party were killed: John Harrison and John Smith, both officers; Joshua Brown; Richard Blair; and James Thelis. Others killed were Seaman Oliver, Samuel D. Smith and Sandy Forbes, bringing the total killed to eight. The *Globe* also sustains about 15 wounded, including Captain Richard Moon. Subsequently, the *Globe* arrives at Wilmington, North Carolina.

In other naval activity, the HMS *Arab* captures the schooner *Industry* (T. Rice, master). The *Industry* is separate from the schooner *Industry* seized on 20 August 1813, the schooner *Industry* captured 10 September 1814 and the sloop *Industry* overtaken on 16 January 1815. Also, two British warships, the HMS *Epervier* and the HMS *Fantome*, cruising together, intercept the 91-ton sloop *Peggy* (W.O. Fuller, master) which is en route to Boston with a cargo of wood and timber.

November 3 (Wednesday) **In Alabama,** American General John Coffee and his Tennessee cavalry (militia) attack and destroy the Indians at Tallusehatche in the Mississippi Valley (*see also,* **November 2–3 BATTLE OF TALLASEHATCHE**). Davy Crockett takes part in this battle. Crockett remains in the militia for several months until his enlistment expires. During the evening, the vanguard of General James White's force — composed of about 400 Cherokees and a small detachment of white troops under Colonel Gideon Morgan and John Lowery — arrives at Tallasehatche, which was in ruins. The contingent gathers about 20 wounded Indians and takes them to Turkey Town.

In Ohio, Major General Nathaniel Massie dies.

November 4 (Thursday) **In Canada,** British Major General De Rottenburg arrives at Kingston with the British 49th Regiment. He dispatches two companies to Fort Wellington. Meanwhile, at Kingston, eight companies of the 49th and nine companies of the 2nd Battalion, 89th Regiment, are under Lt. Colonel Morrison. Later, on the 7th, Morrison leads his command and some artillery to Fort Wellington.

November 5 (Friday) **In Alabama,** three men who had recently departed Fort Madison on a mission as spies ford the Alabama River and creep up on an Indian camp at Burnt Corn without being detected. This group, "Tandy Walker, Benjamin Foster, and Evans, a colored man," without warning opens fire from concealed positions. The Indians offer no resistance. They flee, leaving horses behind. The settlers destroy the camp and depart with the horses, then move to Sisemore's Ferry. While resting there, Indians sneak up and fire upon them. Evans is instantly killed. Foster escapes and makes it back to Fort Madison, where he reports the deaths of Evans and Walker. However, unknown to Foster, the announcement of Walker's death is premature. Walker had been wounded in the side and suffered a broken arm, but he survives and makes it back to the fort the next day.

In New York–Canada, General Wilkinson's force departs from Grenadier Island. The troops, transported by more than 300 boats, descends the St. Lawrence. Wilkinson, aware of British batteries along the river at Preston in Canada, halts his boats at a place just above the battery. The troops land and take an overland route to Red Mill that bypasses the British obstacle. After dusk, the boats resume the journey. The British bring the boats under fire as they pass the battery; however, the boats safely pass. Nevertheless, more danger lurks. The British, aware of the movements of the Americans, had also established other batteries in an attempt to disrupt the giant flotilla. To counter the more recent batteries, Colonel Alexander McComb is directed to cross to the Canadian side of the river and advance in coordination with the boats to eliminate the obstructing batteries. McComb's force, composed of about 1,200 regulars, is bolstered by riflemen under Major Benjamin Forsyth. During this period, a British force of about 1,500 men led by General De Rottenburg had recently departed from Kingston. The British, supported by seven gunboats and two schooners, are charged with harassing General Wilkinson's rear. Wilkinson had not been anticipating any interference from Kingston due to the presence of Commodore Chauncey's fleet, which is tasked with keeping the British warships corralled in the harbor. Nonetheless, Chauncey's fleet fails in its mission.

November 6 (Saturday) *In naval activity,* the British privateer *Shannon* intercepts and seizes the schooner *Rover* (J. Atkins, master). The *Rover* is separate from the *Rover* seized on 19 July 1812.

November 7 (Sunday) **In Canada,** Lt. Colonel Morrison's command boards the HMS *Beresford* and the HMS *Sir Sidney Smith* at Kingston to go to Fort Wellington at Preston to bolster the post against the advancing army of General Wilkinson. The flotilla is escorted by seven gunboats, and a number of bateaux also make the journey.

November 7–9 **In Canada,** General Wilkinson's force continues moving down the St. Lawrence, still anticipating linking up with General Wade Hampton for the offensive to seize Montreal. All the while, the British harass the fleet. During the journey, troops are sent ashore to clear the enemy from their positions.

November 8 (Monday) *In naval activity,* the British privateer *Shannon* intercepts and seizes the schooner *Thorn* (P. Shirley, master). The *Thorn* is separate from the *Thorn* seized on 31 October 1812 and the schooner *Thorn* captured on 11 July 1814.

November 9 (Tuesday) BATTLE OF TALLADEGA In Alabama, Major General Andrew Jackson at Fort Strother had been informed that Fort Leslie, a fortified house established by part–Indian Alexander Leslie, was under attack and encircled by about 1,000 Indians. The friendly Indians were surrounded, unable to get free; however, one man executed a peculiar escape attempt by covering himself with the skin of a hog, including the head and legs. The man literally passed through the enemy lines in the darkness on the night of the 8th by pretending to be a hog. He moved out of the range of the arrows of the Creeks, discarded his hog's skin and made it to General Jackson's lines to seek help. Jackson responds immediately. He leaves a small contingent to defend the camp and speeds to the besieged fort and arrives there this day.

Back at the fort, the situation remains desperate. The fort has become crowded as settlers aware of the Indian trouble there seek safety in the stockade. The defending settlers in the garrison are short of supplies and in desperate need of help, but they are unaware that Jackson's force is just shy of the fort at Talladega, more than twenty-five miles from Fort Mims. Jackson's force is somewhat reduced because on the previous day, he was informed by a runner that the troops under General White were not moving down to support the attack, nor to reinforce Fort Strother during Jackson's absence.

Nevertheless, White is not missed during the assault. One contingent under Colonel Carroll acting as vanguard deploys where they can lay fire upon the camp. Other forces form a semicircle to provide only the creek for an escape route. In quick time, the vanguard commences its fire and the Red Sticks react by advancing against the line defended by Colonel Roberts. Here the line falters, giving the Creeks some added confidence at the expense of the militia. Colonel Bradley is ordered to fill in the gap; however, he fails to carry out the order. Shortly thereafter the hole is filled by dismounted cavalry under Colonel Dwyer, but again the line is not solid. Taking advantage of the break, more Creeks break out; however, the line under Colonel Dwyer is firmly held and great walls of fire descend upon the Red Sticks.

The militia, which had retreated, is inspired by the actions of those who hold firmly and returns to the line to perform admirably. The regalvanized lines of Jackson prove superior to the Creeks, who take heavy losses once they abandon their discipline. Nevertheless, Bradley's failure to carry out his orders and the cavalry under Alcorn swinging around too far out create an opportunity for some to attempt an escape. A full-scale charge devastates the Creeks. Two hundred and ninety-nine dead Indians scattered about the woods are counted. Those who escape are driven into the mountains. General Jackson's force loses 15 killed. Two others sustain fatal wounds and 86 more are wounded. Those wounded who are unable to return on their own are placed in "litters made of raw hides" and carried back to Fort Strother. Colonel William Pillow, Colonel Lauderdale, Major Boyd and Lieutenant Barton are among the wounded. Barton's wound is mortal.

At Fort Leslie, there is great jubilation when the relief force arrives to rescue the 160 warriors, their wives and children. The Creeks had planned to liquidate all the inhabitants later this day. When Jackson gets back to Fort Strother he is upset because no provisions had arrived in his absence, as expected. The lack of provisions is becoming more of a problem than the hostile Creeks. Famine and mutiny are real threats that force Jackson to suspend his operation until provisions can be attained. At one point, Jackson and the volunteers physically block passage of militia troops who have decided to return home.

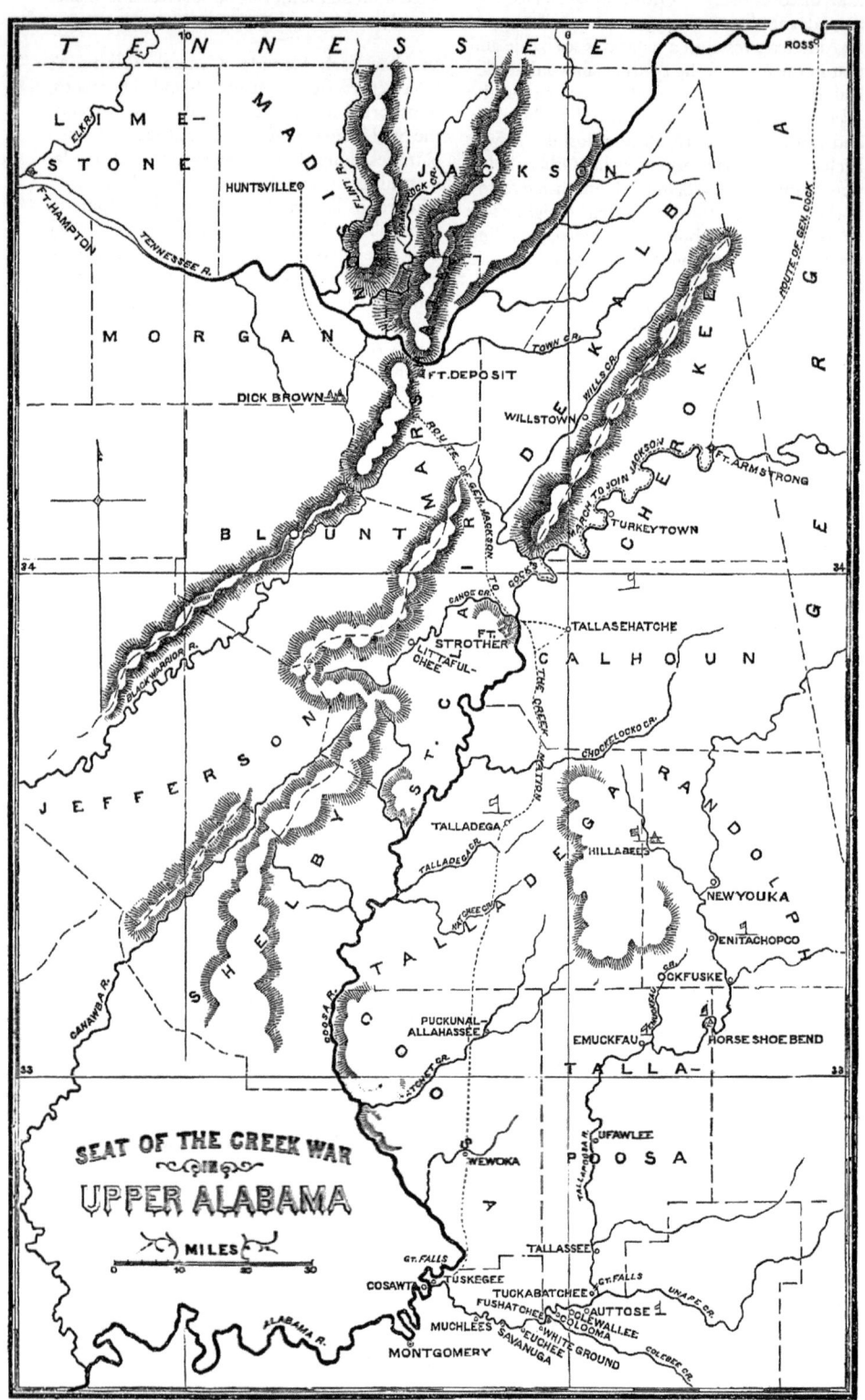

Seat of war, Upper Alabama.

Even after provisions are acquired, their desire to return to Tennessee remains. On one occasion, Jackson threatens to shoot the first man to advance. Not a man decides to test Jackson's will. Once again, his presence, more so than the musket, prevents disaster. Unknown to the troops, Jackson's weapon cannot be fired due to its condition.

In the meantime, the Indians from the Hillibee towns (present-day Cherokee County) begin to sue for peace. General Jackson responds by informing the Indians that for them to achieve peace, they must release all of their captives. The Indians are also told that they must turn over all warriors who had participated in the massacres perpetrated at Fort Mims and other places and all stolen property must be returned. While the Indians are pondering their options, another American force under General John Cocke is moving down the Coosa River, where Indian villages are located. Cocke dispatches a force under General James White, which descends upon a primary Indian village on 18 November.

In Canada, Major Forsyth's riflemen who are supporting Colonel McComb's force, which is providing some extra protection for General Wilkinson during his advance toward Montreal, encounters a force of Canadians and Indians. A skirmish erupts on the north bank of the Niagara; however, the British are unable to disrupt the Americans. The riflemen drive the attackers off, then resume the march. Also on or about this day, Colonel Macomb's main body skirmishes with a British contingent below the town of Hamilton. Nonetheless, the British holding formidable positions in a blockhouse are evicted and driven away.

In naval activity, the British privateer *Shannon* encounters and seizes the schooner Financier (A. Webber, master).

November 10 (Wednesday) **In Canada,** General James Wilkinson's force arrives at the Long Rapids. Unwilling to risk running the rapids with boats packed with troops, he orders most of his men to debark. In the meantime, British gunboats arrive and come under fire. The Americans react rapidly and place two 18-pounders on shore to neutralize the British guns. Consequently, the boats are spared harm and the gunboats are compelled to retire. By this time, Wilkinson concludes that British progress had placed a formidable force to his rear and that further advancement without confronting the looming threat would merely put his entire force in jeopardy. Wilkinson at this time is paused at the farm of a British officer, Captain John Chrysler, just below the village of Williamsburg. On the following morning, the clash occurs. General Wilkinson is ill and unable to command.

In related activity, at about noon, a contingent of General Brown's force arrives at Hoople's

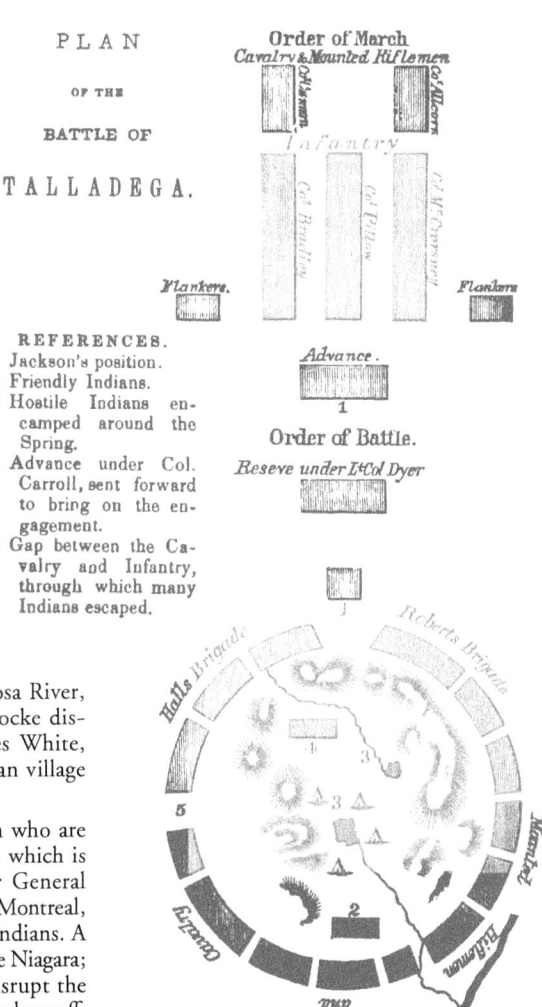

Battle of Talladega (*History of Alabama and Dictionary of Alabama Biography, Volume III*, Thomas McAdory Owen, 1921).

Creek, less than ten miles from Cornwall and about twelve miles from General Wilkinson at Chrysler Farm. Word of the American presence is sped to Captain Dennis at Cornwall. He leads a militia about 300 strong to fight a delaying action. Captain Dennis is attached to the British 49th Regiment; however, only one sergeant and one enlisted man from the regiment is with him. They arrive at the creek on the opposite bank and Captain Dennis orders a detachment to destroy the bridge. He succeeds in delaying General Brown's advance. Back at Cornwall, he is able to get about twelve bateaux to safety, and his force removes the stores from the town.

On the following day at 1100, Brown informs Wilkinson that he had advanced beyond Cornwall on the St. Lawrence River and that he had taken the post at the foot of the rapids. Brown also informs Wilkinson that Major Forsyth and one other man had been wounded. Also, General Brown urges Wilkinson to get the boats and supplies to his command due to their needs, particularly because of the rain and their lack of any cover.

November 11 (Thursday) BATTLE OF CHRYSLER'S FARM (BATTLE OF WILLIAMSBURG) **In Canada,** during General James Wilkinson's advance toward Montreal, the British who have been trailing his force have caught up and are deployed to launch the attack against the American camp at a point midway between Aultsville and Morrisburg, known as Chrysler's Farm. It is owned by John Chrysler and located outside of Williamsburg.

The British positions to Wilkinson's rear are spotted at about dawn. The line extends left to right from a swamp to the river. British gunboats are nearby and the British also have deployed several artillery pieces. The British force, which has been shadowing Wilkinson's progress since his army departed from Sackets Harbor, is commanded by Lt. Colonel Joseph W. Morrison. The units under his command include elements of the 39th and 49th Regiments, the Canadian Fencibles and a contingent of the Royal Artillery. Morrison's force is also bolstered by a small contingent of Indians and militia from Dundas County.

General John Parker Boyd assumes command of the Americans due to the illness of General Wilkinson and General Morgan Lewis. General Boyd takes immediate action to beat back the British from their fixed positions; however, when he orders General Robert Swarthout to evict the British from the woods, the Americans had not anticipated several ravines that impede progress. Nonetheless, a full scale battle erupts under less than favorable weather. The British are fending off Swarthout, who is pressing against the left wing in coordination with another brigade, while General Leonard Covington is supporting Swarthout by crashing against the right wing of the British line.

Meanwhile, the British match the ferocity of the Americans and the woods are transformed into a cauldron. Neither side is able to steadily hold the ground as the close-quartered fighting continues in a see-saw struggle. The elements provide even more obstacles as the antagonists are bashing each other amid sporadic sleet and snow, which compels both sides to also fight their way through deep, sloppy mud. Subsequent to repeated attacks and counterattacks, the superior numbered Americans finally drive the British back toward their main body. Nevertheless, the Americans, despite intense efforts, are unable to advance their artillery though the mud and across the ravines. The British guns remain active throughout the contest. By this time, both sides have nearly exhausted themselves and neither side has been able to claim victory.

The Americans continue to press forward and appear close to victory; however, the incessant combat has caused an unanticipated crisis. The American right wing suddenly becomes imperiled when the ammunition supply is totally expended. At nearly the same time, the left wing begins to falter when General Leonard Covington sustains a severe wound while leading a charge against the British right, while Colonel Eleazar Ripley crashes against the British left. British sharpshooters deployed in Chrysler's house spot Covington and he is targeted while

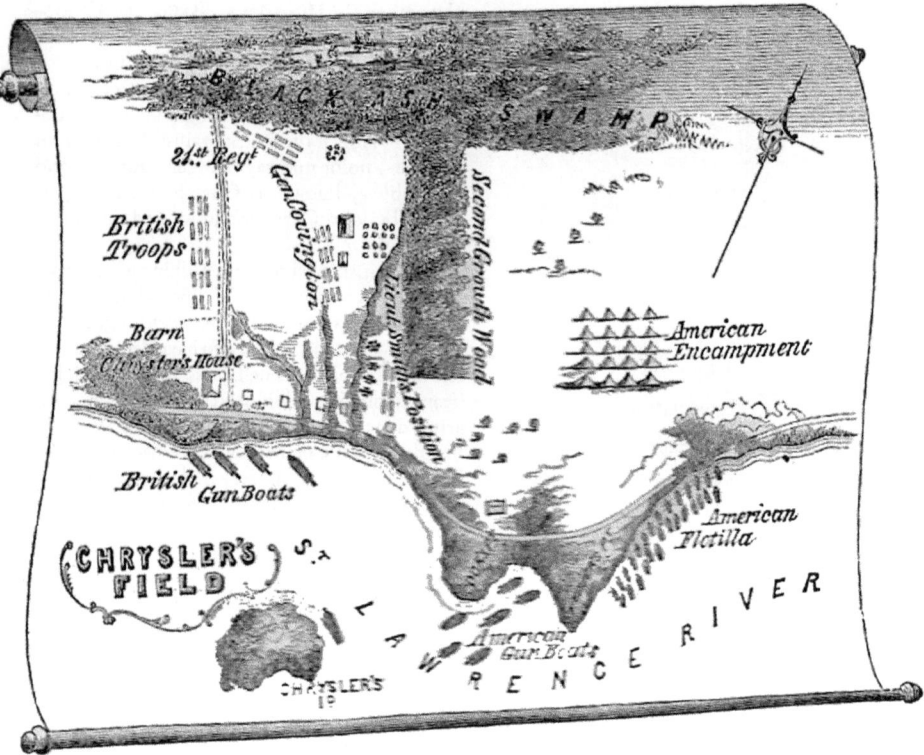

Map of Chrysler's Field.

General Leonard Covington (*The American Generals*, John Frost, 1850).

he is beyond the first line and attacking the second. A bullet strikes him in the lower portion of his vest and he falls from his horse. He is safely carried from the field but his wound is mortal; he dies on the 13th.

Temporary chaos reigns in Covington's brigade and the British have time to regroup. They then strike a powerful blow which adds to the confusion and disorientation of the American line. The British plunge forward and seize one of the American guns and nearly secure the others. However, the holes are plugged by the arrival of cavalry under Adjutant General Walbach and some heroic action by Captain Armstrong Irvine. A rout is eliminated and the Americans are able to reform and stabilize their position.

Nonetheless, the British have not become discouraged; the also become rejuvenated, which reignites the donnybrook. Both sides relentlessly struggle to vanquish the other and the vicious and gruesome battle ensues up and down and around the muddy ground unabated for about two more hours. And still, no victor emerges.

Finally, yet another American force arrives to bolster the two exhausted brigades. Lt. Colonel Upsham arrives with about 600 fresh troops. They quickly anchor the line, providing some time to prepare and await the next British onslaught. By this time, preservation becomes more of a priority than victory. Nonetheless, the line is not prepared to retire; rather to hold. The waiting begins to wear on the troops who have had to fight the staggering cold as well as the enemy. Nevertheless, the British have been equally punished by the bitter cold and the soggy mud. No further counterattack occurs. The Americans await darkness and then retire to the landing place and re-board the boats without further interference from the British, who nearly disrupt the entire operation.

Both the Americans and the British claim victory. The Americans, according to General Wilkinson's report, sustain 102 killed and 237 wounded. The British report their casualties at 22 killed, 147 wounded, and 12 missing. However, the Americans place the number of British casualties higher than those they claim. British prisoners are reported as 2,170; however, Wilkinson lists the number at 2,500. General Boyd's command had secured 1,600.

Colonel Cromwell Pearce, 16th Infantry, and Colonel Isaac Coles, 12th Infantry, sustain severe wounds. Colonel James Patton Preston, 23rd Infantry, has a debilitating wound to his thigh that causes him to be crippled; however, he remains in the service until discharged in August 1815. After the war, he is elected governor of Virginia on 16 December 1816 as successor to Governor Wilson Cary Nicholas. Lt. William J. Worth (subsequently major general) participates at this action. Colonel (later brigadier general) Edmund Pendleton Gaines also participates, as does Lt. Colonel Timothy Upham (recently promoted), 21st U.S. Regiment, formerly of the 11th U.S. Regiment.

The next year, General Morgan Lewis assumes command of the defenses of New York City, expected to be a priority objective of the British; however, the British decide to seize New Orleans, leaving New York unscathed.

November 11 (Thursday) **In Alabama,** a force under General James White, dispatched on the 11th by General John Cocke, has been on a fast-paced advance that is wreaking havoc on the Hillibee Towns. White's contingents are composed of infantry under Colonel Burch and cavalry under Major Porter, bolstered by a small contingent of Cherokees under Colonel Morgan. At Little Ocfuske, five Creeks are seized and the town's 30 houses are reduced by fire. From there, the column arrives at Genalga and its 93 houses are burned to the ground. The column then arrives at a town called Nitty Chaptoa; however, General White, who decides that it might be of later use to the Americans, spares the town's 25 houses. On the 17th, White's column arrives near a primary Hillibee Town that contains about 20 houses. It is near Grayson's farm, according to intelligence, and is a stronghold of the Creeks. At about five miles from the town, General White directs part of his force to proceed on foot under the command of Colonel Burch, supported by the Cherokees under Colonel Morgan. The vanguard is ordered to encircle the town before dawn on the 18th in order to be poised to launch the attack at first light. The troops finally complete the encirclement, but not until after daybreak. The Indians, however, retain the element of surprise. The troops pounce upon the village and cut a path of total destruction that includes the deaths of about 60 warriors, slain by the bayonet during the initial charge. The warriors who hold up a white flag indicating surrender are spared the blade. The women and children are also spared and seized by the troops. The victory is total and General White does not commit the remainder of his force. According to General White, about 256 Indians, including women and children, are captured.

General White reports to Major General Cocke on 4 December: "We lost not one drop of blood in accomplishing this enterprize.... In justice to this gallant band, I am proud to state, that the whole of the officers and men, under the command of Col. Burch, performed their duty cheerfully, and without complaint — that from the cool, orderly and prompt manner in which Major Porter, and the cavalry under his command, formed and conducted themselves in every case of alarm, I had the highest confidence in them."

No Americans sustain wounds. The incident causes unintended consequences. General White is under the command of General Cocke, not General Jackson; however, the Indians believe that all of the troops are under Jackson. Consequently, the Indians in the process of seeking peace become convinced that Jackson has betrayed them. Meanwhile, General White comes under intense scrutiny for the attack, which brings about his court-martial. He is acquitted of any wrongdoing.

In naval activity, two British warships, the HMS *Borer* and the HMS *Valiant*, working together, intercept and seize the *Huntress* (J. Currie, master).

November 11–12 In Alabama at Fort Madison, Captain Samuel Dale receives permission from Colonel Carson to execute a mission to clear the area of the roaming bands of Creeks. By this time Dale has fully recuperated from his wounds sustained at Burnt Corn. Captain Dale is assisted by Lt. Creigh with 40 militia troops from Clarke County and Captain Jones' Mississippi volunteers, numbering about 30 led by Lt. Montgomery. The column moves out of the post and advances northward through several uninhabited plantations. Signs of the Indians are detected but no contact is made. The column returns to the fort until the following day (12th), when Dale again departs. The column moves southwestwardly until it arrives at Brazier's Landing (later French's Landing). Part of the column crosses the Alabama River in two canoes which had been hidden there by Caesar, an "Indian-Negro" who is with Dale. After crossing the river, Dale establishes night positions on the east bank. The troops experience an uncomfortable night due to cold weather and lack of proper clothing.

November 12 (Friday) In Canada, the advance of General James Wilkinson's force, following the engagement at Chrysler's Farm on the previous day, resumes. The main body gets beyond the Long Rapids and rejoins the vanguard under General Jacob Brown. Although General Wilkinson has reinitiated his advance, he has failed to eliminate the British, who continue their pursuit, leaving a large enemy force in his rear. In addition, General Wilkinson receives distressing news when a rider arrives to deliver a message from General Wade Hampton. It states that his force will not link with Wilkinson as his original orders had dictated, and Hampton will not lead his army any deeper into Canada. However, Hampton's message completely omits his ordeal at the Chateauguay River, where the British halted his advance on October 25–26. Once informed that Hampton's army had dropped out of the advance on Montreal, General Wilkinson convenes a war council. It is determined that the scheduled advance against Montreal cannot be maintained. Lower Canada, once again, is preserved and the ill-timed invasion is aborted. Wilkinson's army prepares to move up the Salmon River to establish winter quarters. The entire operation ends as a dismal failure.

November 13 (Saturday) BATTLE OF THE CANOES In Alabama, an operation out of Fort Madison is initiated to attack a band of Indians near Randon's Plantation. A contingent of about 70 men under Captain Samuel Dale prepares to strike. The night before about thirty troops had crossed the Alabama River to its east bank, while Dale and the others remained on the west bank.

The alarm is raised at about 1030 on the western bank signaling the approach of Indians. The small group takes cover near the embankment as the Indians approach. At about the same time, other Indians in a flat-bottom canoe carrying eleven over-painted warriors comes into view. Inexplicably, the Indians on land withdraw, giving the troops an opportunity to take to the water and board the canoe.

Dale, followed by some of his men, engage the Indians just as they begin to land. The incident remembered as the Battle of the Canoes, which lasted only a short while, is described by Captain Dale: "Observing that they [the Indians] were about to land at a cane-brake just above us, I called to my men to follow, and dashed for the cane-brake with all my might. Only seven of my men kept up with me. As the Indians were in the act of landing, we fired. Two leaped into the water. Jim Smith shot one as he rose, and I shot the other."

The canoe approaches the Americans, unaware of their presence until shots ring out. The Indians attempt to find cover by firing while lying low in the canoe. Captain Dale directs his troops on the opposite bank to move against the flat-bottom boat, but after a feeble attempt, the men retire to the west bank. In the meantime some of the Indians had made it to the left shore with troops in pursuit. Still the Indians control the canoe. Dale, apparently perplexed but undaunted, bolts down the bank and jumps into a canoe followed by two others. In a trailing canoe, Cesar, a Negro who had been at the crossing with two concealed canoes, moves up and manages to keep the two opposing canoes together as the brawl continues. Samuel Dale and James Smith swing their rifles as clubs and shortly thereafter, a chief rolls to the bottom. Simultaneously, Jeremiah Austill (son of Captain Evan Austill) engages two other Indians, both of whom are eliminated from the fight. However, yet another brave pounds Austill with a heavy blow that sprawls him across both canoes. Caesar continues to use his strength to keep the boats together while not sustaining any harm to himself. As an Indian moves to finish off Austill, a precision blow of a rifle butt from Dale saves Austill's life and alters the skull of the Indian. Dale states later: "I broke my rifle over his head. It parted in two places."

Meanwhile, Jeremiah Austill, a little groggy but full of fight, rejoins Smith and Dale. Meanwhile, Dale becomes disarmed; however, Caesar gives his bayonet and rifle to Dale. At this time, Dale has one foot in each of the two canoes, but he is unable to keep the two together, so he bolts into the Indians' boat. While Dale's craft, carrying Austill, Smith and Caesar begins to drift away, Smith fires and wounds one of the Indians. The remaining four Indians continue the struggle, but one of them is shot by Austill and another is bayoneted by Dale. Two remain in the fight. Dale finishes off another with his bayonet. The remaining Indian, Tarchachee, leaps over the dead to strike Dale and succeeds in dislocating Dale's shoulder. Dale plunges his bayonet into Tarchachee's heart.

The fight, however, is not yet completely ended. The lone Indian, still alive but wounded, tries to fire his weapon at Dale. As Dale moves to end the ordeal, the Indian begins to cry out with his war-whoop: "I am a warrior. I am not afraid to die." At about the same time he completes his words, as described by Dale, "I pinned him down with my bayonet, and he followed his eleven comrades to the land of spirits." The Indians' bodies are conspicuously tossed into the river to the cheers of the men on both banks.

Following the bloody eviction, which had ensued for only about ten minutes of savage

Captain Samuel Dale (*Life and Times of Gen. Sam Dale, the Mississippi Partisan*, J.F.H. Claiborne, 1860).

combat, the current of the river remains a problem. The craft carrying Austill, Smith and Caesar are struggling to reach Dale, but their sole paddle had broken and their weapons had become inoperable. Nonetheless, another danger emerges as Dale's troops begin to shout warnings that "Weathersford [Red Eagle] was coming." The linkage is made and Dale gets his canoes across the river. The contingent, finding no Indians at Curnell's Ferry, returns this day to Fort Madison.

November 14 (Sunday) *In naval activity,* the schooner *Hero* is seized by the HMS *Belvidera*. The *Hero* is separate from the schooner *Hero* seized 12 June 1813, the schooner *Hero* captured 29 August 1813, the sloop *Hero* taken on 13 January 1814, the schooner *Hero* captured 3 July 1814 and the sloop *Hero* seized during early November 1814. Also, the *Husaren* (P.T. Isnardon, master), a brigantine, encounters the HMS *Jaseur* while it is en route from St. Bartholomews to New Haven, Connecticut. The *Jaseur* seizes the *Husaren*.

November 14 to December 20 *In naval activity,* the American privateer *David Porter*, commanded by Captain George Coggeshall, decides to run the blockade leaving Newport. As nightfall arrives on November 14 amid a typical New England blizzard, Coggeshall correctly assumes that the British will relax their guard. To increase his anticipation of success, the night is moonless, while according to his deductions, the British would be concentrating on keeping warm rather than maintaining a keen vigil on deck. The privateer heads out, and despite the stark darkness, Coggeshall's knowledge of the coastline permits him to avoid the deadly obstacles; however, once at sea, the voyage is on several occasions endangered when British warships attempt to intercept the privateer. On each occasion, the *David Porter* is able to outsail its pursuers.

On one such chase, the British come close to ending the voyage. On 26 November, one brigantine is closing as Coggeshall approaches Charleston and two others are ahead of him, stationed to the front of the Charleston bar. The brigantine presses hard to force the privateer directly into the waiting warships. Nonetheless, Coggeshall senses the trap and declines the bait. The captain drives his ship toward the bar and once there he positions the *David Porter* from where his long tom can fire upon the brigantine at the point. The shot falls close to the brigantine and splashes water on the its port quarter. The encounter is observed from Charleston. The brigantine is carrying only short guns, preventing it from retaliating unless it moves closer and surely into harm's way.

Disregarding the potential danger, the brigantine advances and to its crew's surprise, at about the same time, they spot vessels speeding to support Coggeshall. The privateer *Decatur* and the privateer *Adeline*, commanded by Captains Diron and R. Craycroft respectively, are a short jump from the *David Porter* and prepared to engage the British intruders. The arrival of the additional American ships convinces the British to abandon the effort. They retire, leaving the *David Porter* to move into port without harm. While the *David Porter* is maneuvering to pull into the dock, the *Decatur* and the *Adeline* depart Charleston to embark on their cruises. On 20 December, the *David Porter* departs from Charleston.

November 16 (Tuesday) Britain extends the naval blockade to Long Island, attempting to cut off supplies.

November 17 (Wednesday) In Alabama, General Claiborne, leading about 300 men—dragoons, militia, and contingents under Captain Kennedy, Captain Bates and Lt. Osborne and Choctaw Indians—crosses the Alabama River in rafts from the east to the west bank at about noon on this day, after having arrived the night before. Afterward, Colonel Gilbert C. Russell arrives with the 3rd U.S. Regiment to join with Claiborne's force. Claiborne completes the construction of a fort afterward known as Fort Claiborne. The post in Wilcox County (later Monroe County; present-day Claiborne) forms a half-moon and is bolstered by three blockhouses. It is completed in less than two weeks and the post dominates the Alabama River.

November 19 (Friday) In Georgia, Brigadier General Blackshear receives orders from Major General David Adams to recruit fresh troops and to construct blockhouses along the frontier.

November 20 (Saturday) *In naval activity,* the American sloop *Osiris* encounters and makes contact with the American privateer *Caroline* (Captain Almeda) operating out of Baltimore; however, its captain believes the *Caroline* to be a British vessel. Captain Oliver of the *Osiris* boards the *Caroline* and explains how he had just provided another British vessel with provisions. Captain Almeda listens sheepishly as he is informed by Oliver of the great danger involved and the threat of being hanged if caught. Captain Oliver at the same time presents his British license, bringing an abrupt end to his cruise. His vessel is immediately seized and a prize crew takes it into an American port. The *Caroline* subsequently bags another of the ships designated as being a "traitor ship," the *Criterion*, which is carried into Stonington, Connecticut. Also during this cruise, the *Caroline* seizes the brigantine *Able* and diverts it to Charleston, and it captures a schooner that had sailed from Martinique; it is taken into port at Elizabeth City, North Carolina. One other captured vessel, a brigantine, its first prize, fails to reach port. Just before it moves into the harbor at Charleston, the British recapture it.

The *Caroline* intercepts at least ten additional vessels, and after transferring the respective crews and the cargoes, the ships are destroyed at sea. The schooner *Joseph* is taken to Georgetown, South Carolina, along with its cargo of coffee, sugar and rum. During subsequent cruises, the *Caroline* seizes a string of vessels, including the brigantine *Elizabeth*, which is sailed into port at Charleston, and the schooner *Jason*, destroyed at sea. Another brigantine, the *Experience*, is intercepted and captured, but afterward it is lost when the British force it to run ashore at Cuba. The *Caroline* seizes two additional vessels, and after transferring the cargoes, both are destroyed. The *Caroline* returns to port at Charleston before it embarks on its final cruise, during which it captures the schooner *Mariner*, the sloop *Eliza* and the brigantine *Stephen*. Both the *Mariner* and the *Stephen* are transformed into cartels, but the *Eliza* is destroyed at sea. After completing a successful cruise, the *Caroline* returns to port at Wilmington, North Carolina.

November 23 (Tuesday) *In naval activity,* the HMS *Belvidera* intercepts the 80-ton sloop *Franklin* (S.B. Vail, master) while it is en route to New York. The *Franklin* and its cargo, including cotton and rice, are seized. The *Franklin* is separate from the schooner *Franklin* seized on 3 July 1813.

November 24 (Wednesday) *In naval activity,* the *Venus* (N.D. Blyden), a 100-ton schooner en route to St. Bartholomews from Boston, is intercepted and seized by the HMS *Rifleman*. The *Venus* is separate from the schooner *Venus* captured on 13 July 1813 and the ship *Venus* seized on 24 September 1813.

November 25 (Thursday) *In naval activity,* Oliver Hazard Perry receives his commission as a captain. The Navy Department has a letter in its records in which Perry, having held the rank of commander for about one year, is reluctant to accept his promotion because it propels him over more senior officers. Perry also receives command of a new frigate, the USS *Java*.

November 27 (Saturday) *In naval activity,* the schooner *Dove* (Benjamin Barker, master) is captured by the HMS *Martin*. The prize is taken into port at New Brunswick. This *Dove* is separate from like named vessels seized 17 December 1812, 28 August 1814, and 21 September 1814. In other naval activity off Charleston, the American privateer *Dolphin* comes under attack while it is anchored just outside the harbor. A British warship sends a contingent aboard five boats to seize the *Dolphin*. While still approaching the privateer, its commander, Captain Stafford, orders his gunners to commence fire. One of the five boats is immediately blown apart and the remaining boats scramble to permit the crews to rescue survivors. Afterward, the crews return to their ship and the attack is aborted. Before leaving, the British fire an ineffective broadside at the *Dolphin*.

November 29 (Monday) In Alabama, a large force of Georgians and the 39th U.S. Infantry, along with several hundred friendly Indians, commanded by Brigadier General John Floyd, complete a 120-mile march to attack a Creek stronghold that contains about 400 houses at Auttose along the east bank of the Tallapoosa at the mouth of Calebee (Chalibbee) Creek. The town is less than twenty miles from Hickory Ground, the main bastion of Creek Territory. The column arrived about nine miles from the objective on the previous night and after a pause resumes the march at 0100 on this day.

During the predawn hours Floyd approaches the objective. Major Booth's column advances on the right, while Major Watson's holds the left.

Floyd's flanks are covered by two rifle companies, those of Captain Adams and the other by Captain Merriweather (under the command of Lt. Hendon). Floyd's artillery, commanded by Captain Thomas, is out in front of the right column and moving down the road. The darkness combined with the frigid weather apparently aids the Americans, who begin to encroach the town without being discovered. Nevertheless, as the sun begins to peek over the horizon, the Americans are surprised, not by ambush; rather, while they begin to encircle the town, a second town is discovered about 500 yards below their initial objective.

The sight of the second town forces General Floyd to drastically modify his strategy to include it in his plan of attack. Floyd detaches Merriweather's rifle company, several infantry companies and two contingents of light infantry, the latter commanded by Captain Irwin and Captain Steele, and sends those units against the second town, while the main body attacks the initial objective. The Creeks initially advance with great enthusiasm, but shortly thereafter, Floyd's artillery deflates their ferociousness. The Americans charge with fixed bayonets to the dismay of the Creeks, who hurriedly scatter to evade contact with the piercing steel. Some of the Creeks break for the river to seek concealment in caves, while others converge upon buildings and the woods. Nonetheless, Floyd's allied Indians fail to ford the Tallapoosa River to block the escape routes on the opposite bank. Instead most retire to positions to the rear of Floyd's force. Meanwhile, the Cowetas Indians under McIntosh and the Tookabatchas led by the son of Mad Dragon remain in the thick of the fight and join with the troops to perform with tremendous courage.

By about 0900, the Creeks had been driven from the field, and at about the same time, both towns become infernos when about 400 houses are set afire. The Creeks sustain about 200 killed, including the king of Tallase and the king of Auttose. The Americans sustain 11 killed and 54 wounded. The Indians aligned with the Americans sustain only a few casualties.

During the engagement, the cavalry contingents (Irwin's cavalry and a detachment of Steel's cavalry) under Major Freeman play a prominent part in the victory. Quarter Master Terrill sustains a severe wound and his horse is shot from under him; however, he escapes death. Another officer, Lieutenant Strong, also has his horse shot from under him, but he too survives. Following the victory, General Floyd takes the time to bury his dead troops before departing for Fort Mitchell, where his exhausted men can replenish their supplies, which have become dangerously low. Fort Mitchell, along the Chattahoochee River, stands about 60 miles from Floyd's position. It is near an old Spanish fort (Fort Apalachicola) and present-day Fort Benning along a primary Indian trail leading to the Tombigbee River. During the early part of the march to Fort Mitchell, some of the Creeks that survived the battle mount an attack against Floyd's column just as it is climbing Heydon's Hill, about one mile east of where the Creeks were defeated. The attack against the rear guard is lightning quick and for a while fiercely fought; however, the Americans immediately return fire and the Creeks vanish as quickly as they appear. Chief William McIntosh (Lower Creeks) participates with the U.S. forces at this battle. When Floyd's army resumes its advance, the column moves toward Tuckabatchee, Alabama, arriving there in late January 1814.

November 29 (Monday) *In naval activity,* the American privateer *Sparrow* out of Baltimore is captured by the HMS *Plantagenet* at Long Branch, New Jersey, after the *Sparrow* is forced to run ashore. The point of capture is about six miles from the position of an American squadron. A contingent of about 100 men is drawn from the squadron and they attack the British-held vessel, despite receiving heavy fire from the 74-gun warship. Nevertheless, the boarders are driven from the *Sparrow* and it is returned to American control. A contingent of British troops close upon shore in barges, but they are repelled by the Americans before they can land on the beach, and they are compelled to return to their ship. During the operation to recapture the *Sparrow*, the Americans sustain one fatality. The entire cargo is saved and the *Sparrow* later arrives at its destination, New York.

On the 30th, Commodore Jacob Lewis at New York writes to the secretary of the Navy informing him of the recapture:

> Sir, I have to inform you, that on the 29th, the flotilla force recaptured from the *Plantagenet*, a schooner from New Orleans, loaded with cotton and lead. The enemy had chased the schooner on shore about 13 miles from where the flotilla lay at anchor; however, before the enemy had time to get the vessel off, or to unlade the cargo, they were attacked, beaten off and the vessel taken possession of. The enemy sent a flag to demand a ransom for the schooner and cargo, stating she was in their power, and unless we consented to ransom the vessel, he would destroy her, also all the houses on the shore. All his threats did not answer his purpose; the vessel and cargo are ours. I have the honour to assure you of my consideration and respect. J. Lewis.

In an earlier letter to the secretary, Commodore Lewis stated: "The saving of the cargo of the *Sparrow* was a very gallant affair. The 74 came near enough to fire grape shot at our people, having no sort of shelter, they laid down on the sand, and presented their heads to the enemy; and when his barges neared the shore, they rose and beat them off." Also, before its ordeal, the *Sparrow* under Captain Burch had captured a schooner, the *Meadow*, and after removing some items, the crew released it. They also captured another schooner, the *Farmer*, which was also released.

December **In Washington, D.C.,** President Madison, having been inundated by complaints from states regarding British vessels supplying blockading squadrons, urges Congress to take action. Congress passes legislation on the 17th that produces a new embargo prohibiting the exportation of many items, either by land or water. Earlier the House passed similar legislation; however, it failed to pass in the U.S. Senate.

In naval activity, by this time the United States Navy has captured the following British ships: the frigates *Java*, *Guerriere* and the *Macedonian*, along with the sloops *Alert*, *Duke of Gloucester* and the *Frolic*, and the brigantines *Boxer*, *Detroit*, *Dominica* and the *Peacock*. The schooner *Highflyer* is also captured. British vessels lost are the frigates *Barbados* and *Southampton*; the brigantines *Avenger*, *Emulous*, *Falcon*, *Magnet*, *Moselle*, *Persian* and *Plumper*; and the schooners *Chub* and *Subtle*. They have lost 489 guns carried by the 22 ships captured or lost.

The United States has lost the ships *Chesapeake* and *Wasp*, the brigantines *Nautilus*, *Viper* and *Vixen*, and the schooners *Growler* and *Julia* (both recaptured). The American losses have totaled seven vessels and 117 guns.

While engaged at the Battle of Lake Erie, the British lose two ships, the *Detroit* (separate from the brigantine *Detroit*) and the *Queen Charlotte*, the brigantine *Hunter* and the schooners *Chippeway* and *Lady Prevost*, along with the sloop *Little Belt*. The losses on the lake increase the number of vessels lost or captured from 22 to 28, with a new total at 549. In addition, the Americans lose the *Hamilton* and *Scourge* to storms and the *Lawrence* is lost on the lake.

December 1 (Wednesday) *In naval activity,* a British squadron, comprising the HMS *Endymion*, HMS *Loire* and the HMS *Ramillies*, takes possession of the schooner *General Marion*. The squadron also seizes the sloop *Rising Sun* (C.B. Hussey, master). The *Rising Sun* is separate from the schooner *Rising Sun* seized on 21 March 1813 and the schooner *Rising Sun* captured 31 March 1813.

December 2 (Thursday) *In naval activity,* two British warships, the HMS *Albion* and the HMS *Nimrod*, intercept and capture an American ship, the 260-ton *Chili* (R. Gardner, master), which is returning to Nantucket after completing a whaling voyage.

December 3 (Friday) *In naval activity,* the HMS *Nimrod* intercepts and seizes the sloop *Manhattan*. Also, the privateer *America* sails from Bath, Maine. It remains at sea until April 1814.

December 4 (Saturday) *In naval activity,* two British warships, the HMS *Loire* and the HMS *Ramilles*, while on patrol intercept and capture the ship *Gardiner*.

December 5 (Sunday) **In Alabama,** on or about this day, General Claiborne writes to General Jackson to extend his congratulations on his recent victories over the Creeks. He also brings Jackson up to date on the operation under Claiborne's command in the southern sector. General Jackson is also informed that large stores of corn and miscellaneous supplies are at Fort Claiborne. Another letter from Claiborne is dispatched to Governor Willie Blount of Tennessee. It details the situation in Pensacola where additional British warships have arrived.

General Claiborne remains concerned about the conditions at Mobile. Earlier he had dispatched a detachment under Major Kennedy to Mobile to meet with Colonel Bowyer regarding the British at Pensacola. Upon their return, not surprisingly, General Claiborne receives intelligence that the number of British troops had greatly increased and that the Indians continue to receive supplies to aid their terror raids which are now including Baldwin County, where the Creeks had destroyed the Kennedy mills and Byrns' mills. Lt. Colonel George Henry Nixon, successor of Colonel Russell at Mount Vernon, has also received command of Fort Pierce, which is close to where the Creeks are concentrating their raids.

In Rhode Island, Commodore Rodgers, aboard the USS *President,* sails for Barbados. The *President* seizes four British merchant ships before sailing for home. It defies the blockading squadron and successfully breaks through to arrive at Sandy Hook on 18 February.

In naval activity, the British warships HMS *Majestic* and *Junon* intercept and capture the schooner *Catherine* (J. Church, master). The *Catherine* is separate from the letter of marque *Catherine* captured July 1812 and the brigantine *Catherine* overtaken 2 May 1813.

December 6 (Monday) ***In naval activity,*** two British warships, the HMS *Junon* and the HMS *Majestic* while on patrol intercept and seize the 65-ton sloop *Jane,* which is going to Boston from Cape Cod Bay. The *Jane* is separate from the ship *Jane* seized on 27 August 1812, the schooner *Jane* seized 10 December 1813, the sloop *Jane* seized on 2 August 1814, the sloop *Jane* captured 10 September 1814, the brigantine *Jane* captured 9 November 1814, and the sloop *Jane* overtaken on 12 November 1814.

December 7 (Tuesday) **In Washington,** President James Madison, having anticipated announcing great gains in Canada during his annual address to Congress, is unable to do so because of the dismal failure of the campaign. The president addresses Congress with no mention of the campaign. Nonetheless, the press is not bashful. Newspapers across the country publish headlines that emphasize the failure, to the dismay of the president, Congress and the military commanders.

December 7 to February 12 **In Canada,** at the town of Malone, American General James Wilkinson is recuperating from his illness. He established headquarters there following the defeat at Chrysler's Farm in November. On December 7, Wilkinson dispatches a letter to Secretary of War John Armstrong in which he includes a proposal for seizing Isle aux Noix during the winter of 1813–1814 by launching an assault from Plattsburgh. The plan apparently finds no traction in Washington. During January 1814, Wilkinson proposes a new plan, but it too apparently is received in Washington as being implausible. And, he issues another plan by which Kingston could be taken followed by an attack in the spring to seize Montreal. He also informs Washington of the poor conditions of his force. By 20 January, the secretary of war directs Wilkinson to dispatch General Brown and 2,000 troops supported by artillery to Sackets Harbor.

He is also ordered to abandon his positions at Malone about 15 miles from French Creek and return to Plattsburgh.

December 8 (Wednesday) ***In naval activity,*** the USS *Little Belt* encounters a strong storm and is pushed into shore at Black Rock, New York. Efforts to refloat it fail. The sloop is discovered by the British, who destroy the ship by fire. Also, the HMS *Wolverine,* while operating off the East Coast, intercepts and seizes the schooner *Enterprise* (J. Plumpley, master), which is taking a cargo of salt from Boston to Philadelphia. The prize is taken into port at Liverpool.

In other naval activity, the HMS *Martin* seizes the schooner *Julian* (E. Foster, master). The *Julian* is separate from the *Julian* seized on 13 November 1812, the *Julian* seized on 6 August 1814 and the *Julian* captured on 17 November 1814. Also, the schooner *West Indian* is captured by two British warships, the HMS *Loire* and the HMS *Ramillies.*

December 9 (Thursday) ***In naval activity,*** Captain David Porter departs from Nuka Hiva (Nooaheevah) in the Marquesas Islands (Polynesia); however, Porter, who had erected a fort since his arrival there during the previous October, directs part of his squadron — the *Greenwich, Seringapatam* and the *Sir Andrew Hammond*—to position themselves beneath the guns of the fort. Porter appoints Lt. John M. Gamble as commander of the force and leaves instructions for him to depart in five and one-half months. Gamble is also the commander of the *Greenwich.* Once Porter sails, the friendly islanders begin to cause some problems, which compels Gamble to send a contingent ashore to restore order.

(The date for Porter's departure varies from source to source. The date used for this entry comes from the memoirs of Commodore Porter. However, in a letter from Porter to the secretary of the Navy, dated 3 July 1814, Captain Porter mentions his date of departure as 12 December. The latter appears to be in error. In Porter's book (published 1823), *A Voyage to the South Seas,* Captain Porter also states 9 December as his date of departure.)

A gregarious Otaheitan named Tamaba sails with Porter and the man is well liked by the men. However, for an unknown reason, he is punched by the boatswain's mate and he is not one accustomed to being hit. The man breaks down and cries, but the effects of the blow are more serious than thought. During the night, he jumps overboard at a point about 20 miles from land. Captain Porter is saddened deeply by the loss and he believes that the chances of Tamaba surviving are quite slim. Nonetheless, he does reach land safely "after swimming and floating two nights and a day."

December 10 (Friday) American Brigadier General George McClure, under threat from a British force under General Sir Gordon Drummond, issues the order to prepare to evacuate Fort George, New York. Drummond, due to the failure of Wilkinson's campaign to seize Montreal, is closing on the fort with a force of about 470 men, including more than fifty Indians. McClure's force stands at about 75 to 100 able-bodied men because of militia terms expiring this day. The Americans, prior to returning to New York, burn the town of Newark (Niagara) and a portion of Queenston. At Queenston, the civilians find themselves homeless during an unusually bitter and wet December. Of about 150 homes, only one remains standing.

While the Americans hold Newark, a group of Canadians under Major Mallory, formerly a member of the Assembly, and another, Joseph Wilcox, branded traitors by the late General Brock, operate out of the town. These mounted troops, including some from the U.S., act independently and perform duties such as guiding Americans through unfamiliar territory. The band, known as the "Canadian Volunteers," is under constant pursuit by a contingent under Captain William Merritt. Eventually, some are captured, tried, convicted and hanged. This group, considered renegades by the British, suffer heavily at the Battle of Lundy's Lane. On 4 October, Secretary of War John Armstrong issued instructions to General McClure: "Understanding that the post committed to your charge may render it proper to destroy the town of Newark, you are hereby directed to apprise its inhabitants of this circumstance and to invite them to remove their effects to some place of greater safety. I am, JOHN ARMSTRONG."

At the time, McClure realized that the changing weather in Newark would soon prevent any chance of crossing the river due to floating ice, and this would keep his small force trapped. Armstrong's orders to burn the town were aimed at preventing British troops from establishing winter quarters in the homes.

In naval activity, the *Betsy* (E. Tibberts, master), a 98-ton sloop en route from Waldeborough, Maine, to Boston, is intercepted and captured by the British privateer *Wolverine,* which takes it into port at Liverpool. The *Wolverine* also intercepts and seizes the 75-ton sloop *Charles* (J. Andrews, master), which is going from Kennebeck, Maine, to Boston. The *Charles* is separate from the *Charles Fawcett* captured on 6 September 1812, the 95-ton sloop *Charles* seized on 4 October 1813, the schooner *Charles* captured 26 June 1814, and the brigantine *Charles* overtaken 5 November 1814.

The British privateer *Wolverine* seizes the schooner *Jane* in the vicinity of Cape Ann. No crew members are aboard the *Jane* when it is captured; it is taken into port at Liverpool. The *Jane* is separate from the ship *Jane* seized 27 August 1812, the sloop *Jane* captured 6 December 1813, the sloop *Jane* seized 2 August 1814, the brigantine *Jane* captured 9 November 1814, and the sloop *Jane* seized 12 November 1814. Also, the British privateer *Wolverine* intercepts and seizes the 78-ton schooner *Laura Jane.* On this day, the *Wolverine* also captures the 69-ton schooner *Trent* and the 88-ton schooner *Polly,* which is transporting a cargo of fish and lumber. The prize and its cargo are taken into port at Liverpool.

Also, the HMS *Loire* intercepts the privateer schooner *Rolla* off Long Island. The British frigate is able to sever one of the *Rolla*'s masts, which ensures its capture. During its time at sea, the *Rolla* had become one of the most successful American privateers (*see also*, **December 12–15, 1812**).

December 11 (Saturday) *In naval activity,* the 76-ton schooner *Erie* (John Hearn, master), while en route from Havana, Cuba, to Baltimore with a cargo of coffee and sugar, is halted and seized by the HMS *Sophie*. The British confiscate the cargo and forward it to Bermuda. The *Erie* is taken into the service of the Royal Navy and utilized on the Chesapeake as a tender to the squadron operating there.

December 12 (Sunday) **In Alabama,** on or about this day, General John Cocke, who has joined General Jackson at Fort Strother with his force of about 1,400 Tennesseans, is ordered by Jackson to return to East Tennessee to raise an additional 1,500 troops. Many of the men who came down with Cocke are at the end of their enlistments. Cocke returns to Tennessee with a contingent of those who are completing their terms.

In Canada, the Americans abandon Fort George. The evacuation occurs quickly, and while the column returns toward Niagara, the supplies, stores and even the guns are abandoned. Afterward, British General Vincent's force at Chippewa occupies the fort. The British plan retaliation. By late December, they launch an attack across the river to assault Niagara.

In Connecticut, Captain Stephen Decatur, with his three-ship squadron having moved back down the river during the early part of the month, takes advantage of the cold weather to break out of New London Harbor. After sunset on a very dark night, the vessels opposite Market Wharf make last minute adjustments just before heading toward the open sea in hopes of slipping through the British blockading squadron. Despite the great secrecy of the plan, boats from the *Hornet* and *Macedonian*, which had been out front, return to notify Decatur that the British had been informed of the movement. The crew reports that the "blue lights" had been lit along both sides of the river to signal the British that the squadron was on the move. The operation is aborted. Those who betrayed the squadron are never caught or identified. The Federalists deny that they had been responsible; however, they do receive the blame for being traitors and become known as the "Blue-light Federalists." A letter from Decatur to the secretary of the Navy, dated 20 December, states: "Notwithstanding these signals have been repeated, and have been seen by twenty persons at least in this squadron, there are men in New London who have the hardihood to affect to disbelieve it, and the effrontery to avow their disbelief."

The *Macedonian* and the *United States* are dismantled in spring 1814. The crews depart New London by overland routes to join with other squadrons. The *Hornet* remains seaworthy; however, it does not embark from New London until 1815, when it evades the blockading squadron and makes it to New York.

December 13 (Monday) **In Alabama,** General Ferdinand Claiborne prepares to depart from Fort Claiborne en route to attack the Indian stronghold at Econochaca. His force is composed of about 1,000 men. The objective stands west of Montgomery along the Alabama River. The column arrives close to the village on the 23rd. General Claiborne this day advances toward Double Swamp about eighty miles distant.

In other activity, Colonel George Henry Nixon, who had succeeded Colonel Russell at Mount Vernon, is also given command of Fort Pierce, established this year in Clarke County along the Alabama River near another fort established this year, Fort Montgomery.

In naval activity, the HMS *Curlew* intercepts and seizes the sloop *Calmar* (D. Maloney, master). Also, a British squadron, comprising the HMS *Loup Cervier*, HMS *Rover*, HMS *Statira* and HMS *Valiant*, encounters a lone American sloop, the 44-ton *Emeline* going from New York to Rhode Island with a cargo of flour. The *Emeline* is seized.

December 16 (Thursday) *In naval activity,* the British privateer *Shannon* spots the American 119-ton schooner *Enterprise* (R. Stevens, master), which is transporting a cargo of ballast from Boston to Bath, Maine. The schooner is seized and taken into port at Liverpool.

December 17 (Friday) **In Washington, D.C.,** Congress, at the strong but secret urging of President Madison, passes the Embargo Act, which immediately becomes a matter of serious concern to the Federalists. It is essentially condemned in the New England states. The legislation is carved to halt the New Englanders from interacting in commerce with the British naval squadrons. It is believed in Washington that the New Englanders are providing the British with supplies as a trade-off to prevent their seacoast towns from being bombarded. The act forbids the exportation of goods, livestock and produce, along with specie, by either land or sea. The act immediately becomes over-burdensome, particularly because of its timing. The towns along the coast meet the New England winter without fuel and many other necessities. The New Englanders become irate, perplexed, and in a sense, revolutionaries, as Washington soon learns that New England dangles a possibility that a separate peace, outside of the Union, will be negotiated with Great Britain. New England states have already prohibited their respective state troops from being placed under federal control, and they forbid their militias from leaving their home states.

Even the clergy is affected by the legislation. The clamoring from some of the pulpits is thunderous. One clergyman proclaims: "If the rich men persist in furnishing money, war will continue till the mountains are melted with blood—till every field in America is white with the bones of the people." A pointed message from another minister states: "Let no man who wishes to continue the war by active means, by vote or lending money, dare to prostrate himself at the altar, for such are actually as much partakers in the war as the soldier who thrusts his bayonet, and the judgment of God will await them."

Resistance to the act builds continuously until the avalanche of protests coerces Congress to repeal it in February 1814.

In New York, the British capture Fort Niagara from the Americans. The British attack force led by Colonel Murray captures hundreds of American soldiers. Having evicted the Americans from the Niagara district in Canada, the British continue their retaliation in response to the Americans having destroyed Newark, Canada, and part of Queenston by fire earlier in the month. The British, after seizing Niagara, operate out of the fort to further penetrate American territory. British-Indian forces attack and burn other nearby places, including Black Rock, Buffalo; Fort Gray, Lewiston; and Manchester, New York. In addition, the British and their Indian allies attack and destroy Tonawanda Blockhouse outside of Buffalo and Tuscarora. The area encompassing Tonawanda is later divided as part of two counties, Tonawanda in Erie County and North Tonawanda in Niagara County. Also, at or about

Captain Stephen Decatur.

A view of Fort Niagara from Fort George, Canada.

this day, the British come upon the USS *Trippe*, which is grounded near Buffalo Creek. The British destroy it by fire.

In Vermont, a British contingent (Frontier Light Infantry) under Captain Barker attacks the American post at Derby and seizes it at dawn. Later, on 9 January 1814, the adjutant general's office in Quebec reports that the strike had culminated with the destruction of a recently built 1,200-man barracks. The troops also destroyed the "stables and storehouses, and a considerable quantity of valuable military stores has been brought away." Barker also reports that "Captain Curtis and Taplin, Lieuts. Messa and Bodwell and Ensign Boynton of the Township Battalions of Militia [had] been most active in the execution of this judicious and spirited enterprise."

In naval activity, the British privateer *Shannon* seizes the schooner *Rubicon* (J. Lassel, master), which is on its way to Belfast from Boston with a cargo of ballast. The prize is taken into port at Liverpool.

December 18 (Saturday) In Canada, Lt. General Gordon Drummond writes to Sir George Prevost that the "disasters which were reported to have befallen Commodore Chauncey's squadron has proved but too just, the Madison only having sustained some damage by being ashore for 48 hours. But she is now, as well as the other vessels of the enemy's fleet, in safety at Sackets Harbour." He also informs Prevost that Major-General Vincent had been on this day relieved of command and ordered to return to Kingston, and that he has been succeeded as commander of the Right Division by Major-General Riall. Drummond's letter also requests that General Stovin be permitted to depart from Montreal and that General Proctor remain in command at Kingston, which he describes as a post of "little importance." Also, Drummond, intending to attack Fort Niagara, informs Prevost that he has "placed a force under the command of Colonel Murray, Inspecting Field Officer, for that purpose."

In New York, a separate British force, bolstered by about 500 Indians, crosses the Niagara River to attack Lewiston. The post there is defended by a light complement of troops under Major Bennett. The British, commanded by General Riall, encounter heavy resistance; however, their superior numbers finally succeed in encircling Bennett's force. Nonetheless, Bennett refuses to capitulate. He leads his contingent out of the trap and the troops break through the British lines to reach safety. Nevertheless, eight men in the command are killed. After Bennett's troops break out, the British plunder the village and the Indians wreak havoc on the civilians. Following the destruction of Lewiston, General Riall advances to several other towns, including Manchester (Niagara Falls), Tuscarora and Youngstown, and each one is destroyed. During this period of mass destruction, the British also destroy homes and farms of the people living on the outskirts of the villages. Troops under Major General Hall arrive from Buffalo on 26 December; however, by that time, the path of destruction has been devastating and Hall's militia troops are neither seasoned nor well armed. Also, at Buffalo, Brigadier General George McClure delivers an address to the citizens of Chautauqua, Genesee and Niagara:

> The present crisis is alarming. The enemy are preparing to invade your frontier and let their savages loose upon your families and property. It is now in your power to avoid that evil by repairing to Lewiston, Schlosser and Buffalo. Every man who is able to bear arms is not only invited, but required to repair to the above rallying points for a few days or until a detachment of militia arrives. The enemy are now laying waste their own country. Every man who does not take up arms, or who are disposed to remain neutral, are inhumanly butchered, their property plundered and their buildings destroyed.... Think of the consequences; be not lulled into a belief that because you live a few miles from the river that you are secure; no, fellow-citizens, the place to meet them is on the beach; there you will have it in your power to chastise them; But should they be suffered to penetrate into the interior with their savages, the scene will be horrid. If, then, you love your country and are determined to defend its rights; if you love your families and are determined to protect them; if you value your property and are determined to preserve it, you will fly to arms and hasten to meet the enemy should they decide to set foot on our shores.

McClure's address also indicates that intelligence has placed the time of attack on the following night (19th).

In naval activity, the British privateer *Liverpool Packet* intercepts and seizes the sloop *Nancy Sanders*.

December 18–26 In Canada, a British force, composed of about 550 men under Colonel Murray (Lt. General Sir Gordon Drummond's command) crosses the Niagara River at Five Mile Meadows to attack Fort Niagara (18th). The troops land at Five Mile Meadows at about 0400. At the time of the landing, the commander of Niagara, General McClure, is away from the post. He had information that an attack was probable, prompting him to travel to Buffalo to acquire reinforcements. In McClure's absence, Captain Leonard is in temporary command; however, at this time, he is also away from the post and staying at a farm several miles distant.

The post is not on the alert and the gates of the fort are open. The troops at Niagara number about 450; however, most are on the sick list. The British approach the fort and to their surprise, they do not need their scaling ladders due to the unprotected gates. Sentries are quickly taken out before they can sound the alarm and the Redcoats walk into the fort and unleash their vengeance for the earlier burning of Newark (Canada). Some resistance is raised by guards in a blockhouse at the southeast sector of the fort and it inflicts casualties. Colonel Murray is among the wounded; however, the British swarm across the post with fixed bayonets. The Americans, most of whom are asleep, are attacked and slain. The bayonet spare neither sick nor able bodied. About 65 men die in their beds. About 15 others who are discovered in cellars meet the same fate. As the rampage ends, fourteen troops survive but with wounds and the remainder of the garrison, just under 350 troops, are captured. Only about 20 Americans escape. The British sustain six killed, including one officer. Another few, including a British surgeon, are wounded. Some contemporary accounts of the attack report that women in the fort receive cruel treatment by their captors.

General Drummond, having secured Fort Niagara, decides to build a new fort at Mississauga Point, opposite Fort Niagara. It becomes the only star point fort constructed in Canada. The post was to be named Fort Riall; however, it is later named Fort Mississauga. It is completed during spring 1814, and with two others posts, it is one of the points which forms a defensive triangle. The Canadians utilize much of the debris, including chimneys, hearths and stone, from Newark as material for the fort. The construction of the post is overseen by Colonel Le Vigoreux and some other engineers, and it is to be capable of quartering several hundred troops. The British guns at the new post will dominate the channel at the mouth of the river. The formidable threesome—Forts George and Fort Mississauga in Canada and Fort Niagara in New York—seemingly prepare the British for any offensive that might be mounted by the United States.

General Sir Gordon Drummond, having been appointed governor of Upper Canada earlier, devotes a lot of his time at Newark to reorganizing the militia, which by now has gained valuable experience in combating the American forces that have invaded. By spring, Drummond's efforts have paid off in a more confident militia. The Lincoln militia based at Newark is commanded by Colonel William Claus. The units include the 1st, 2nd, 3rd, 4th and 5th Regiments. His regulars are the 8th, 41st, 49th, 89th, 100th and the Royal Scots. Drummond is also bolstered by contingents of the Royal Artillery, several squadrons of the 19th Light Dragoons and other artillery

Interior of Fort Niagara.

detachments. His force also contains many Indians under various chiefs, including Blackbird, John Brant and Oneida Joseph. The Caughnawagas and the Seven Nations tribes also augment Drummond's army. They are led by French Canadian officers DeLorimier and Ducharme.

The Americans' situation on the Niagara frontier remains bleak. Confidence in the militia is greatly diminished, so much so that the U.S. is compelled to prepare to field only regulars, and they would be commanded by generals expected to turn the increasing setbacks into victories. All the while, some of the New England states continue to refuse to commit troops to the federal cause. The U.S. government's recent embargo on shipping has severely curtailed foreign trade, and the British naval blockade actually causes the U.S. Navy to increase its numbers. The government in Washington, in addition to trying to find the right leaders to bring about victory, remains concerned that New England's adamant opposition to the war could ignite open rebellion and push certain states into trying to secede.

By spring of 1814, British Forts George, Niagara and Mississauga stand nearly as one giant fortification, with the guns of each within range of one another and capable of laying down a crossfire to prevent the Americans from launching an attack against any one of them. They hold near-invincible positions in their iron triangle. The British also get support on the water by the appearance of the HMS *Royal George*, which arrives from Kingston. At the first sign of the disappearance of the ice on the waterways, more reinforcements arrive, including the British 103rd and 104th Regiments and the Canadian Glengarry Regiment and other units.

Jonas Harrison, collector of customs for the district of Niagara, mentions in one of his letters (held by the Buffalo Historical Society) that some thought Captain Leonard, who was visiting with his family when the fort was seized, had become a traitor and sold out to the British, but no evidence is ever produced.

December 19 (Sunday) **In New York,** Lt. General Drummond in writes to Sir George Prevost concerning the progress at Fort Niagara:

> DEAR SIR,—I have the satisfaction to inform you that the Fort of Niagara fell into our hands at 5 o'clock this morning. It was carried in a most gallant manner by assault at the point of the bayonet by the troops, as per margin ("Grenadier Co'y Royal Boots Regt. Flank companies 41st, 100th Regt. Royal Artillery") I had selected and placed under the command of Colonel Murray. The enemy have suffered some loss in killed; that on our part is comparatively small. There have been taken about 150 prisoners, amongst whom is Capt. Leonard, the commandant, and several officers. I neglect to say that Lt. Nowlan of the 100th Regt. has been killed and that Colonel Murray has been wounded severely in the wrist. There are several pieces of ordnance mounted in the fort and about 3,000 stand of arms, a large quantity of clothing, salt and other stores.

In related activity, several hundred Indians attack an American militia contingent deployed at Lewiston Heights during the morning. The Americans, commanded by Major Bennett, are easily surrounded; however, Bennett is unwilling to consider surrender. He orders a charge, which succeeds. The detachment breaks through; however six or eight men, including two sons of Captain Jones, an Indian interpreter, are killed.

While the British continue their raids on American soil, other towns, including Lewiston, Manchester and Youngstown, along with the Indian Tuscora village become targets that are destroyed. People who are unable or unwilling to abandon their homes are, according to a letter of 22 December from General McClure to the secretary of war, "inhumanly butchered by Indians, led by British officers." McClure tells the secretary that the Canadian volunteers under Major Mallory had engaged the British in a two-day skirmish in which the volunteers "contested every inch of ground to the Tonawanda Creek," and that Lt. Lowe, attached to the U.S. 23rd Regiment, and eight of the Canadian volunteers had been killed.

In naval activity, the British privateer *Liverpool Packet* intercepts and seizes the 49-ton sloop *Patriot*, which is transporting a cargo of flour and candles from New York to Rhode Island. The *Patriot* is separate from the schooner *Patriot* seized 7 September 1812.

December 20 (Monday) **In Washington,** a motion is submitted in the House of Representatives to set up a committee that will design an "adequate and permanent provision" in support of all officers and enlisted men in the armed forces who become disabled by wounds while in the military service of the United States. The motion also includes government support for widows of the servicemen, as well as the education of children of the disabled veterans. It is tabled and the House never revives it.

In Canada, British General Stovin reports that an American contingent of about 130 men is spotted as it passes Arnold's mill en route back to Detroit. The troops are carrying flour and grain that had been seized. The column also destroys Arnold's barn. Later, on the 22nd, a contingent of cavalry that is trailing the column also passes through Arnold's mill. A British force under Lt. Colonel James at Delaware town, according to a report from General Gordon Drummond, is not able to intercept the column due to impassable roads, which would "have precluded all hope of success."

In naval activity, the American privateer *Saucy Jack* arrives in Charleston after completing a cruise in which it captured the brigantine *Agnes* and the sloop *John*. Also, the American privateer *David Porter* sails from Charleston en route to Bordeaux, France, with a cargo of cotton. The departure had been delayed two days due to bad weather, and Captain Coggeshall had another concern. Word had been received in Charleston that the U.S. Congress was at any moment going to issue an embargo that would create financial ruin for the owners and officers of the privateer. Coggeshall, trying to avoid getting clamped down if the legislation passes before he gets out of port, had nudged his vessel to the very fringes of the harbor and prohibited the crew from going ashore. On this night Coggeshall sprints out of the harbor and heads for the open seas.

December 21 (Tuesday) **In New York,** General McClure writes to the chiefs of the Six Nations:

> BROTHERS,—I am about to take leave of you for a short time. I cannot depart without expressing my satisfaction for the faithful services rendered your Great Father the President, for your faithful observance of orders and willing obedience to my commands. BROTHERS,— Many of your white brothers deserted me in the hour of difficulty, which you know, and which is the cause of our disaster. You have been faithful in the hour of danger, when your white brothers were in a state of rebellion against me. You spurned indignantly at their mutinous conduct.... BROTHERS,— Your Red Brothers and the British, who live on the other side of the Niagara River, have invaded your country; they have massacred in cold blood unoffending women and children; they have murdered or taken prisoners the two sons of your friend and interpreter Capt. [Horatio] Jones; they have laid waste the village of your Red Brothers the Tuscaroras, and carried off all their property. I have restrained you from this kind of warfare; I will no longer restrain you. Avenge yourselves on the authors of such barbarities, and all whom you find in arms against you, but show mercy to unoffending women and children. The enemy pay no attention to private property. You are at liberty to follow their example. Invite your Red Brethren every where to join you and drive them from our soil. There is no safety in remaining at home.... BROTHERS,— When I join you again I will bring regulars and militia who will never desert you or myself. Meanwhile I send to join you all the regular troops I can collect at present under a brave Chief, Major Riddle.

December 22 (Wednesday) *In naval activity,* the British privateer *Liverpool Packet* intercepts and seizes the 50-ton sloop *Mary* (E. Lewis, master), which is transporting a cargo of flour from New York to Rhode Island.

December 23 (Thursday) **In Alabama,** a force commanded by General Ferdinand Claiborne attacks Econachaca ("Holy Ground") on the east bank of the Alabama River slightly below Powell's Ferry. The Indian stronghold built on a bluff and protected by swamps and ravines contains about 200 houses and has no paths leading to it. The Indians under Red Eagle (William Weatherford), having been told by their prophets that they hold holy ground that cannot be penetrated by white men, are unprepared for an attack. Nevertheless, the American force, along with the allied Indians, finds the obscure village without being detected. The Creeks have been storing much of their plunder and they hold Americans captive as well as Indians who are friendly to the United States. Unknown to either the Indians or some captives that are to be burned to death, Sophia Durant and other half-breeds have been taken to the square and surrounded by the fires. Meanwhile, Claiborne's force is closing in three columns.

General Claiborne rides in the center at the point with Colonel Russell's regulars; Colonel Carson's column advances on the right. Wells' dragoons and Lester's guards advance as Claiborne's reserve corps. By the time the right column under comes into sight, the Creeks strike first and fiercely; however, the Americans overcome the resistance and drive the Creeks into retreat. The attack suffers a setback due to the terrain, which prevents pursuit. A contingent of cavalry under Major Cassels had been ordered to deploy slightly west of the village on the bank of the river; however, he fails to complete the move and retires to join with Carson. Meanwhile the 3rd Regiment under Carson falls properly in place. Despite the failure of Cassels to follow his orders, the victory is still complete.

The prophets had proclaimed that any white man who entered the sacred ground would not live; however, Claiborne's troops converge on the village and rout the Creeks at their stronghold. The Indians manage to get the women and children to the opposite bank of the river. They abandon their village and scatter. Some bolt for the river and reach safety on the opposite bank, while the others vanish in the swamps.

The next day, the Americans torch another town that contains about 60 houses, including that of Weatherford. Weatherford, according to reports, after finding himself lacking his warriors, evades capture or death by jumping with his horse from a high cliff into the Alabama River. He crosses to the opposite bank and escapes.

General Clairborne permits the Choctaws under Pushmataha to keep all of the spoils, and he forbids his troops to engage in pillaging. According to reports, most of the blankets and clothing had been taken by the Creeks at Fort Mims. Also, more than 1,000 bushels of corn are confiscated. The army keeps what it requires and the remainder is destroyed. One other item is a letter from Spanish Governor Manrique to the Creek chiefs, in which he sends his congratulations for their victory at Fort Mims. The village is burned the next day.

Major Cassels later receives a court-martial and it is determined that a guide caused the error. It is discovered that the supplies provided to the force had been inadequate for the arduous mission. Also, a battalion of militia under Major Benjamin Smoot participates in the engagement. Other participants include Captain Samuel Dale, Captain Heard, and Lt. Gerard W. Creagh. The force is also bolstered by about 150 Choctaws led by Chief Pushmataha.

The Americans' one fatality is Ensign Luckett. Twenty others are wounded; casualties may have been few due to the Creeks being low on ammunition and forced to fight with bows and arrows. According to a report sent by Claiborne to Secretary of War John Armstrong, the enemy Indians and Negroes sustain 30 killed, and "many were wounded."

The Negroes had been slaves who were coerced to fight. The Choctaws scalp all of the dead Creeks; however, the scalps of the Negroes are not kept; rather they are thrown away. The battle at the Holy Ground is the only battle during the conflict in which the Creeks used Negroes to fight against the Americans. General Claiborne also details his losses, stating: "The loss on our part was 1 corporal killed; one ensign, two sergeants, one corporal and two privates, wounded. We destroyed their town, (Econocacha,) consisting of 200 houses, and one other town of 60 houses."

December 24 (Friday) **In Alabama,** General Claiborne completes the destruction of the "Holy Ground." His cavalry is ordered to move farther up the Alabama River to a point known as Ward's place. While en route, the column intercepts and kills three Shawnee who had fought alongside the Creeks on the previous day. The gunfire is heard back in camp, prompting Claiborne to order his force to prepare to move out and head toward the sound of the guns. By now the troops are exhausted and their meat supply had been depleted for about nine days. Claiborne establishes night camp at Weatherford's place and his army is greeted on Christmas Eve with rain and cold.

In 1814 General Ferdinand Claiborne settles in Mississippi. He becomes legislative councilor and afterward presides over the deliberations of the legislature. Claiborne initially entered the service as an ensign in 1793. He was promoted to lieutenant the next year and captain in 1799. He resigned from the U.S. Army during 1802 but was appointed brigadier general of the Mississippi militia on 5 February 1811. He is the brother of Governor William Claiborne of Louisiana.

In New York at Batavia, General Amos Hall, after being told that a force of about 1,000 British and several hundred Indians had been detected, orders Lt. Colonel Lawrence to "take the command of all the militia which have marched, or are to march to Lewiston from Batavia, and also of the troops now there under the command of Lieut. Col. Achinson [Atkinson], who will be second in command." The next day, Lawrence is directed to advance to Lewiston, and if possible, he is to jump from there to the town of Manchester (Niagara Falls) and Black Rock.

December 25 (Saturday) **In Alabama,** General Claiborne's force, including Carson's volunteers from Mississippi, spend part of Christmas at Weatherford's place, but the command lacks food except for some corn. Nevertheless, the troops continue to search for Weatherford's warriors until the following day before marching back to Fort Deposit en route to Fort Claiborne. By the time General Claiborne arrives at Fort Claiborne, his army drastically shrinks. The enlistments of the Mississippi volunteers under Colonel Carson and the cavalry expire. Both units are released from service. General Claiborne's force is reduced to about 60 men and their time in service expires within one month. Claiborne writes to the secretary of war to inform him of the condition of the force; he makes it known that some of the troops departed without shoes and naked. He also informs the secretary that he is leaving for home once he receives permission from General Flournoy.

Major Cassels receives a court-martial and is acquitted. It is determined that his guide (Sam McNac) was at fault for not deploying at his assigned position. Another court of inquiry convenes to discover why the command did not have sufficient food during the expedition and it finds blame with the army contractor. Also, Colonel Russell receives sole command of Fort Claiborne.

In New York at Batavia, General McClure writes to the secretary of war with some details regarding the loss of Fort Niagara:

> It is a notorious fact that on the night on which Fort Niagara was captured Captain Leonard was much intoxicated and left the fort about 11 p.m. I am assured that he has since given himself up; that he and his family are now on the Canadian side of the strait. It was not without some reluctance that I left him in immediate command of the fort, but there was no alternative as he outranked every other officer. His uniform attachment to British men and measures, added to the circumstances of his not effecting his escape when in his power, strengthened me in a suspicion there was a secret understanding with regard to this disgraceful transaction. Permit me to suggest to you, Sir, that unless regular troops are sent to this frontier immediately the enemy will penetrate into the interior of the country and lay waste all before them. The militia will do to act with regulars but not without them. In spite of all my exertions to ensure subordination my late detachment ultimately proved to be very little better than an infuriated mob. It was not, however, the fault of the privates but of such officers as were seeking popularity and who on that account were afraid of enforcing subordination and introducing strict discipline. I have collected from the different recruiting rendezvous about one hundred and twenty soldiers and put them under the command of Lieutenant Riddle of the 15th United States Infantry, an excellent and deserving officer. I cannot conclude this communication without reporting the conduct of Doctor Cyrenius Chapin, (late Lieutenant-Colonel of volunteers). To him in a great measure ought all our disasters to be imputed. His publications in the Buffalo Gazette that the enemy had abandoned Burlington I fear had the desired effect. I have found him an unprincipled disorganizer. Since dismissing him and his marauding corps he has been guilty of the most outrageous acts of mutiny if not of treason. When I came to Buffalo, accompanied only by my suite, he headed a mob for the purpose of doing violence to my feelings and person, and when marching to the Rock at the time of an alarm, five or six guns were discharged at me by his men.

Also, General Amos Hall at Batavia orders a 150-man contingent of infantry under Lt. Colonel Lawrence to move toward Lewiston to join with a militia force under Lt. Colonel Achinson, which is deployed along the Ridge Road at Forsyth's, about 15 miles east of Lewiston. Lawrence is directed to gather ammunition that had been taken from Lewiston's arsenal and move to Buffalo and beyond by water to Black Rock. Lawrence's infantry is escorted by cavalry under Captain Marvin. Colonel Achinson is directed to remain at Forsyth's as a reserve corps. General Hall also directs the remainder of the militia at Batavia to repair to Buffalo, leaving regulars at

Batavia. Also this day, General Hall departs from Batavia for Buffalo.

December 26 (Sunday) In New York, General Hall arrives at Buffalo from Batavia and assumes command of the 2,000 volunteers there. Hall is disappointed in the condition of the militia and describes the scene as being "disorganized and confused." In a later report to Governor Tompkins, said the entire department is destitute. He also informs the governor of the situation at Fort Niagara, seized by the British on 18 December: "Our loss in the capture of Fort Niagara has been immense. What number of brave men have been sacrificed, we have not yet been able to learn. It must have been great. Several inhabitants have been killed at Lewiston, among whom it is not ascertained there are any women or children."

In naval activity, the American privateer *Herald* arrives in New York from Charleston. While en route, it had engaged a British schooner, with neither vessel able to prevail by dusk. Afterward, the *Herald* lost the enemy vessel during the night. The following June (or possibly July), the *Herald* captures the ship *Friendship* while it is en route to Lisbon from London. The *Friendship* at the time of its capture is flying Swedish colors, and according to the *Friendship,* carrying a British cargo valued at thirty thousand pounds. Other prizes seized by the *Herald* during its time at sea include the *Ellen,* a schooner transporting a cargo from Belfast, Ireland, to Lisbon, which is diverted to Beaufort. It also captures one brigantine and one schooner, both of which are taken into port at Ocracoke Inlet, North Carolina. Another American privateer named *Herald,* operating out of New York and commanded by Captain J. Miller, is a 17-gun schooner. It is not known to have captured any prizes during the conflict. It is seized during the latter part of the war by two British warships.

Other privateers out of New York that score successes late in the war include the *Invincible,* the *Jonquille* and the *Marengo.* The *Invincible* during its time at sea seizes a merchant ship out of Liverpool that is en route for Antigua, and diverts it to Wilmington, North Carolina. Its other prizes include the brigantine *Nimble,* carrying a cargo of produce out of the West Indies, which is taken into port at Tenerife in the Canary Islands; the 10-gun schooner *Prince Regent,* which is stripped of its guns; and the cutter *Lyon,* carrying dry goods and hardware, which is halted and its cargo removed before being released. The *Invincible* also captures the brigantine *Margaretta* with a cargo of wine, along with another brigantine, the 10-gun *Conway,* carrying dry goods. It also seizes a schooner, the *Francis and Lucy,* which is transformed into a cartel after its cargo is transferred. The *Jonquille* scores some success during April 1814. Also, the *Marengo* during its time at sea captures eight prizes; seven are taken into friendly ports and one is destroyed at sea.

December 27 (Monday) In Canada, Lt. Colonel J. Harvey, at British Headquarters of Upper Canada, Niagara Frontier, under direction of Lt. General Drummond, writes to General Hall:

> SIR: I am directed Lieut. General Drummond to acknowledge the receipt of your letter addressed to Major General Vincent on the subject of the excesses said to have been committed by the Indians at Lewiston. That some excesses were committed the Lieut. General admits and sincerely laments, at the same time he has the satisfaction of knowing that every effort was made and every exertion used by Major General Riall, and the officers and soldiers of the British force under his command to restrain those excesses. You sir, cannot but be aware of the difficulty or rather the impossibility of effectually controlling an infuriated band of savages. Major General Riall and the officers under his orders did however afford effectual protection to all who remained in their houses. A British soldier, a sentinel, lost his life in defending a female, an inhabitant of Lewiston, and no less than nine women and eighteen children saved by the intrepidity of the Major General and the troops from the savage fury of the Indians, and now in safety on our frontier sufficiently attest the anxious [? anxiety] of the British troops and their commander to alleviate as much as possible to the peaceful inhabitants the dreadful evils of a mode of warfare, to which the example of the American government had compelled us to have recourse. I allude as well to the employment of Indians by the American Generals beyond their own frontier as to the burning in which a number of old and infirm persons and children were left to perish in the snow, an act which, the season of the year and all other circumstances considered, is unexampled in barbarity. I have the honor to be, Sir, with respect, Your Humble Servant, HARVEY.

The next day, General Hall writes to General McClure that he has "ascertained that no women or female children have been butchered in the late affair at N[iagara] and Lewiston." Also, at Buffalo, General Hall orders a review of all units under his command at Buffalo and at Black Rock. He names the units as:

> Buffalo-Lieut.-Colonel Boughton, of the cavalry and mounted volunteers, 129; Lieut.-Colonel Blakeley, of the Ontario exempts and volunteers, 433; Lieut.-Colonel Chapin, of the Buffalo militia, 136; Lieut.-Colonel Mallory, of the Canadian volunteers, 97; Major Adams, of the Genesee militia, 382 and at Blackrock: Brigadier General Hopkins, 382 effective men, composed of the corps commanded by Lieut.-Colonel Warden and Lieut.-Colonel Churchill, exclusive of a body of 37 mounted infantry, under command of Captain Ransom, 83 Indians, under command of Lieut.-Colonel Granger, and one piece of field artillery, a six pounder, and 25 men commanded by Lieut. Seeley, making my aggregate force on the 27th to be 1,711 men.

Two days later, a regiment of Chautauqua militia composed of about 300 troops, commanded by Lt. Colonel McMahon, arrives at Buffalo.

In naval activity, the American privateer *David Porter* (Captain Coggeshall) intercepts a British vessel during a period of especially nasty weather, which makes it to dangerous to board the prize. Orders are given to the British to follow the privateer and that failure to comply would cause severe harm by the stern guns. The British reluctantly comply. At about midnight (27th-28th), the weather begins change drastically when the winds pick up and the skies become pitch dark. The British prize manages to break away unnoticed and escape.

December 28 (Tuesday) In New York at Buffalo, Major General Amos Hall reviews the troops, and he assesses them as being "extremely well and all equipped."

December 29 (Wednesday) In Canada, Lt. Colonel John Harvey writes to Major General Riall:

> SIR,— Finding that the enemy is assembling a large force on the opposite frontier, the object of which can only be to attempt the recovery of the fort of Niagara, or the prosecution of his atrocious system (began at Fort George) of laying waste our peaceful frontier, Lieutenant General Drummond has considered it his duty to push over to the opposite shore the disposable troops for the purpose of dispersing this force, and destroying the villages of Buffalo and Black Rock in order to deprive the enemy of the cover which these places afford. The Lieutenant General desires that you will accordingly take under Your command the troops now assembled on this line, and in conjunction with the whole body of the Indians proceed to execute the service above mentioned by crossing the river in the course of this night, so as to be ready to commence the attack on Black Rock at daylight to-morrow morning.

General Riall is also ordered to destroy three American armed schooners, all of which are "on shore high and dry on the beach — two below the Buffalo Creek and one above it."

In New York at Headquarters (Buffalo), Major General Amos Hall issues General Orders in which he congratulates the militia under his command on the Niagara frontier and rings praise upon them for having left their homes and families during the nasty winter season to defend against an invading enemy: "Their alacrity in flying to arms at the first alarm of danger merits and will no doubt receive the thanks of their country. At least they will have the consolation of reflecting that they have done their duty, although others may have forgotten theirs."

General Hall writes to Brigadier General McClure that "no women or female children have been butchered in the affair at Niagara and Lewiston." His letter to McClure says "it will be absolutely necessary to keep at least 2,000 men on the frontier," however, he also states, "The detachment you will please to order on as expeditiously as possible. The enemy makes considerable movements on the opposite shore and [we] keep strict watch by night by sentinels and patrols. I, however, do not believe they will attempt to cross unless they find our force is wasting, which will of course be the case in a few days unless the detachment should supply their places."

December 29–30 In New York, General Amos Hall, who arrived in the vicinity of Lewiston from Buffalo on the 26th, now has about 2,000 troops since a reinforcing regiment of about 300 men has joined him. Nonetheless, the British, who have been ravaging the region since they seized Fort Niagara, are well armed and more seasoned. British General Drummond had reconnoitered the American positions on the 28th and concluded that he would launch an attack. During the evening of the 29th, a force of just under 1,500 troops, primarily regulars drawn from the British 8th, 41st, 89th, Royal Scots and grenadiers of the 100th Regiment, prepare to strike Black Rock. The regulars are bolstered by one company of the 1st Lincoln Militia, commanded by Captain John D. Servos, and about 400 Indians under Chief Blackbird and a few other chiefs.

At around midnight on the 29th-30th, no doubt remains about the suspected attack when General Hall is informed that a mounted patrol operating below Black Rock near Conjockatie's Creek is under fire and Lt. Boughton's horse has been shot from under him. Shortly afterward, the British advance and seize Sailors' Battery, which is also close to the creek. General Hall orders the forces at Black Rock under Colonels Churchill and Warren (due to the absence of General Hopkins) to advance and retake the battery; however, he remains concerned that the primary British objective is Buffalo and that Black Rock is merely a diversion designed to drain Buffalo of its troops.

Nonetheless, the militia falters at the first sounds of the British guns and scatters in all directions. Meanwhile, General Hall orders a second attack to regain the battery. Two corps, under Major Adams and Colonel Chapin, advance; however, the combined force merely duplicates the first assault and again the British fire demoralizes the militia within a short time, and these troops also flee. By dawn, Hall's 2,000-man force is reduced to about 1,200. Undaunted by the massive flight of the militia under him, General Hall remains confident. He directs yet another corps, commanded by Colonel Blakeslee, to storm the battery and simultaneously, he orders the remainder of his force to close upon Black Rock. Just as the column is advancing along the road to the town, Hall is greeted by the break of day. At the same time, he sees a wave of enemy boats closing on the shoreline near the home of General Porter. Hall's thoughts begin racing at the speed of light. He countermands his orders to Colonel Blakeslee and sends orders for him to abandon the attack on the battery on the British left and turn his attention to the shoreline. He is to strike the British center where they intend to land.

The force under General Riall lands within striking distance of the American camp and opens the attack at dawn on the 30th. One contingent debarks slightly below Black Rock, and it encounters heavy resistance before the boats reach shore. The other British contingent (Royal Scots and militia), led by General Gordon Drummond, lands between Black Rock and Buffalo under the protective fire of a battery on the Canadian side of the river. The British left wing is to be attacked by the Indians under Lt. Colonel Granger and by a contingent of Canadian volunteers under Colonel Mallory to protect the American right wing.

The British are stung by a 6-pounder commanded by Lt. Seely, which is deployed below General Peter B. Porter's residence, along with three guns (one 24-pounder and two 12-pounders) under Lt. Farnum of the U.S. 21st Infantry, who is a volunteer during this engagement. Simultaneously, Colonel Blakeslee's infantry continues to pour fire into the boats. The Royal Scots sustain about 50 killed before the boats reach shore. Nonetheless, the British defy the fire and continue to press forward. Meanwhile, Hall discovers that the friendly Indians have failed to attack the British left wing, which imperils the entire right flank of the Americans.

Attempts by Lt. Riddle to place his regulars at the front are ignored by General Hall, who by this time has lost the ability to command. Riddle then asks permission to move to the village with a force of about 200 troops, including his 80 regulars, to save the village and rescue the women and children before the Indians can arrive. Hall again denies the request. Despite Hall's refusals, Lt. Riddle moves into the village with his regulars and they empty the arsenal to keep the arms and ammunition from falling into the hands of the British.

Suddenly, the small band of Americans who have fought steadfastly become imperiled. Hall calls upon his reserve force under Colonel McMahon and orders an attack against the British flank, but McMahon finds that nearly his entire corps has become terrified and unwilling to fight. The ranks begin to thin as the demoralized troops take flight and the officers are unable to halt the stampede. Nonetheless, some of the troops rally; however, the situation by this time has moved beyond critical. General Hall's force has rapidly depleted. His cavalry and the mounted infantry are of no value and unable to participate, but not due to cowardice but because of the terrain, which is unsuitable for the horses.

Hall, having only a Spartan force left on the field and nearly encircled by well disciplined regulars, is compelled to order a retreat to prevent the annihilation of those who chose to do their duty rather than run. After pulling back to a more tenable position, he attempts to regroup and launch an attack against the long line of Redcoats which is en route to Buffalo, but all is in vain. By dusk, General Hall, unable to mount a cohesive force, orders his remnant army to retire to Eleven Mile Creek. The massive desertion by the militia leaves Black Rock and Buffalo undefended. After arriving at the creek, Hall is able to gather only 200 to 300 troops.

With no meaningful resistance, the British move into Black Rock and Buffalo. Both towns are plundered and reduced to ruins. Inhabitants who are unable to escape are tortured and killed, except for a few who remain unharmed. In Buffalo, one house and the jail survive. The town of Black Rock receives identical treatment. One house where some women and children had taken refuge is spared. No documentation explains why some of the houses are spared.

During the fierce skirmish, one man, Job Hoisington, takes it upon himself to singlehandedly hold his ground at the present-day intersection of Porter and Plymouth Avenues. His steadfastness provides time for the rest of his militia unit to retire to safety. His family and other villagers are able to escape before their homes are burned. Job, who dies defending his position, remains undiscovered until spring of 1814.

British retaliation for the destruction inflicted by General McClure at Newark and the surrounding area in Canada had been swift and destructive; however, most of the civilians had abandoned their homes at the first words of the British landing. The citizens from a large region stretching inland flee to positions farther inside the interior. All roads are suddenly crammed with wagons loaded with possessions, along with livestock and horses, but many others abandoned everything to avoid the onslaught. Nonetheless, for most their trepidation had been unnecessary. The British destroy only property close to the river.

The new year for the residents in the part of New York that had been plundered becomes a period of desperation. The American military successes along the northern frontier are wiped away, except for the recovery of the Michigan Territory. The American losses at Black Rock and Buffalo combined totals about 300 to 400 killed or wounded. In addition, the British capture about 130 prisoners. Militia casualties are light, three privates killed and five wounded, along with one officer, Captain Servos, who sustains a wound. General Amos Hall, in a letter to Governor Tompkins dated 13 January 1814, states that casualties were higher than expected and that when the Americans retook the ground, they discovered "fifty bodies and probably there are some yet undiscovered in the woods." In the same letter, Hall notes that the British had admitted to 300 casualties.

December 30 (Thursday) **In Maryland,** the British vessel *Bramble* sails into the harbor at Annapolis under a flag of truce. The vessel is transporting peace dispatches from England. As 1813 is ending, both sides are aware of the damage to commerce and the toll on the respective navies. The British, since the beginning of the conflict, have captured seven U.S. warships with a combined total of about 119 guns; however, to the utter dismay of the British, the young and less experienced U.S. Navy has during the same period seized 26 warships of the Royal Navy, with a combined total of more than 550 guns.

On the ground, the British continue to thwart the Americans. As the year closes, all the initial U.S. gains against Canada have been wiped out, with the lone exception of the campaigns to recapture Detroit and the Michigan Territory.

In addition to the warships of the U.S. Navy, which is small compared to the Royal Navy, the Americans had authorized privateers to help interfere with British commercial vessels and engage small British warships when the opportunity arises. Privateering is not well thought of by many due to earlier times when pirates and privateers were indistinguishable. Nevertheless, for the U.S. during this conflict, it is essential to make use of the skills of the innumerable seamen in the nation, though it is impossible to incorporate them into the navy.

One of the most prominent advocates for using the services of privateers is former President Thomas Jefferson. Just after war had been declared, Jefferson published his opinion on the matter:

> In the United States, every possible encouragement should be given to privateering in time of war with a commercial nation. We have tens of thousands of seamen that without it would be destitute of the means of support, and useless to their country. Our national ships are too few to give employment to a twentieth part of them, or retaliate the acts of the enemy. But by licensing private armed vessels, the whole naval force of the nation is truly brought to bear on the foe; and while the contest lasts, that it may have the speedier termination, let every individual contribute his mite, in the best way he can, to distress and harass the enemy and compel him to peace.

In New York, the British attack Black Rock and Buffalo. In a letter from Lt. General Drummond to Sir George Prevost, dated this day, Drummond reports on the invasion:

> DEAR SIR,— I have the satisfaction of acquainting Your Excellency that the attack which was made at daylight this morning on the enemy's troops at Black Rock has been completely successful, Major General Riall having in the most gallant style defeated, after a short but severe contest, a body of upwards of 2,000 men advantageously posted. The corps employed on this service were detachments of the Royals, King's and 41st Regiments with the flank companies of the 89th and 100th. After having driven the enemy from Black Rock Major General Riall immediately pursued them toward Buffalo, from whence after a few rounds from his field guns he again rapidly fled toward the Eleven Mile Creek. The number of the enemy killed and wounded was very great. Our loss has been severe. Not having as yet received any official report I can only say generally that the conduct of the troops, not only in the field but in their patient suffering of great privation, &c., was above all praise — that the circumstances of carrying on military operations in such a climate is sufficient proof of the zeal of the troops.... Very few prisoners were made except such as were wounded, a circumstance which marks very clearly the rapidity of the enemy's flight. About seventy prisoners are in our hands, amongst whom is the famous Dr. or Colonel Chapin, whom, in consequence of his former escape, I have sent off toward Quebec by an officer and two dragoons. We have taken seven pieces of ordnance of different calibres and destroyed four of the enemy's armed schooners and sloops. The town of Buffalo has been burnt, as well as that of Black Rock previous to its evacuation by the troops. Many valuable stores have been taken.

Also this day, General Hall writes Governor Tompkins:

> SIR,— December 30th, 1813, 7 o'clock p.m. I have only a moment to acknowledge the receipt of your letter of the 25th inst. and to add that this frontier is wholly desolate. The British crossed over, supported by a strong party of Indians, a little before day this morning near Black Rock. They were met by the militia under my command with spirit, but overpowered by the numbers and discipline of the enemy the militia gave way and fled on every side; every attempt to rally them was ineffectual. The enemy's purpose was obtained and the flourishing village of Buffalo is laid in ruins. The Niagara frontier now lies open and naked to our enemies. Your judgment will direct you what is most proper in this emergency. I am exhausted and must defer particulars till to-morrow. Many valuable lives are lost.

December 31 (Friday) **In New York,** Colonel Winfield Scott writes to Secretary of War John Armstrong that as ordered by General Wilkinson, he departed from Fort George in Canada on 13 October 1813, and that Fort George "as a field work, might be considered as complete at that period. It was garnished with ten pieces of artillery, (which might easily have been increased from the spare ordnance at the opposite fort,) with all ample supply of fixed ammunition." Scott also explains in the letter that on 14 October Fort Niagara "was under the immediate command of Captain Leonard, 1st Artillery, who, besides his own company, had Captain Read's of the same regiment; together with such of General McClure's brigade as had refused to cross the river. Lieutenant-Colonels Fleming, Bloom and Dobbins of the militia had successively been in command of this fort [Niagara] by order of the Brigadier General, but I think neither of them was present at the above period" (*see also*, **October 13**).

1814

In Alabama, Fort Bainbridge is established by General Floyd near Tuskegee.

In Georgia, a frontier post (Fort Gaines) is established along the Chattahoochee River to guard the zone separating the Indians and settlers according to the Treaty of Fort Jackson. The task of keeping the area free of encroaching Indians is delegated to an Indian agent, Colonel Benjamin Hawkins, and William McIntosh, a Coweta chief, born of a Creek mother named Senoya and Captain William McIntosh from Savannah. Fort Gaines is near a Seminole village at Fowltown. In addition, the Georgia militia and U.S. regulars will temporarily garrison Fort Early, which is constructed this year at Coney, Georgia. Fort Hawkins at Macon, built during 1805, does not come under attack during the war but is used as a supply depot.

In Maine, the British seize Fort Madison (later Fort Porter) at Castine. In addition, the British reoccupy nearby Fort George, which they had held during the American Revolution. The forts remain under British control until April 1815. Fort Allen is established by the militia at Portland in southern Maine. It remains active until several years after the war. Fort Lawrence is established at Munjoy Hill in present-day Portland. It remains active until about the end of the war.

Major General George Cobb had been in command of the 5th Division (Maine militia) for a few years; however, this year, he is succeeded by General John Blake. Later during the 1840s Henry Wadsworth visits the area and writes a poem about the hill and Fort Lawrence, "My Lost Youth."

In Massachusetts, Fort Sewall is established near Marblehead. A fort was initially built here at Gale's Head during 1742 and through the years it was expanded. At this time it is named in honor of Judge Samuel Sewall. The USS *Constitution* comes under the custody of the fort during 1814 when the British attempt, but fail, to destroy it. Also, Fort Strong is established on Long Island. It is designed by Loammi Baldwin, the man who designed the Bunker Hill Monument. It is fortified beginning in the late nineteenth century and continuing through the twentieth century, expanding with eight batteries (deployed 1874 and 1906). The final battery to remain operational is Long Island Head Battery, which ceases during 1947.

In Michigan, Fort Gratiot is established at Port Huron, where during the 1680s, the French had manned Fort Ste. Joseph.

In New York, Fort Clinton is established in New York City at a site known as McGown's Pass (present-day Central Park at about 5th Avenue and 107th Street). This Fort Clinton is separate from Fort Clinton in Saratoga County, Schuylerville, 1746; Castle Clinton in Manhattan, about 1811; Fort Clinton of Orange County, Fort Montgomery, 1777; and Fort Clinton in Orange County, West Point, 1778.

In Western New York, due to the threat of an invasion of Rochester by a British fleet that had arrived near the mouth of the Genesee River, the Americans establish Fort Bender at Rochester in Monroe County.

In Pennsylvania, Fort Gaines is established on Middle Bank a few miles from Fort Mifflin in the vicinity of Philadelphia. By the following

Fort Sewall, Massachusetts.

year, Fort Mifflin is abandoned. Its sister fort, Gaines, is only built for temporary use. Fort Gottenburg at Essington, also near Fort Mifflin, had been built there during the 1640s by the Swedes when the area was considered part of New Sweden.

In Tennessee, Fort Marr is established in the vicinity of Old Fort.

In Wisconsin, Fort Shelby (Fort Crawford) is established in the vicinity of Prairie du Chien. It is later captured by the British and renamed Fort McKay.

January–February   In Alabama, Colonel Russell, leading his regiment and two companies of volunteers, departs Fort Claiborne to intercept the Indians and push them from the area near the Cahaba River. Russell sends a barge carrying provisions up the Alabama River with orders to move into the Cahaba and proceed to Old Towns, where it is to join with the army. The barge, protected by an artillery piece and commanded by Captain Denkens, fails to make the rendezvous. A small party is dispatched in a canoe to find it; however, the canoe, carrying Lt. Wilcox and five men, overturns. Two of Wilcox's guns are lost and the ammunition is ruined. The canoe is uprighted but Wilcox's party is now defenseless. Later on the second night out, the party is intercepted, fired upon by Indians and seized. Only two men, both named Wilson, escape; however, they nearly starve to death in the woods. Matthew Wilson is found and rescued and the other eventually finds his way back to the fort. Lt. Wilcox and the other three men are taken down the Cahaba toward the Alabama River.

In the meantime, Denkens' barge, which had taken a wrong turn, arrives at the mouth of the Cahaba, but too late to make the rendezvous. Denkens reverses course to return to the fort, and the Indians who captured Wilcox's party spot the barge near the mouth of Pursley Creek. Rather than risk losing their captives, the Indians turn their tomahawks on Wilcox and the others. All four men are scalped and killed except Wilcox, thought dead but remaining alive. Shortly thereafter, Denkens' party nears the canoe, and as the barge comes alongside, they see that Wilcox is alive. He is too far gone to provide any details.

Colonel Russell remains at Old Towns for about two days but his force has no provisions. Russell orders his force to form for the return march to Fort Claiborne. In an effort to forestall starvation, the troops use some of their animals for food. Colonel Russell's horse is the first of 12 animals sacrificed to save the command. During the arduous march, the column is met by a supply train at Bradford's Pond. Afterward, the column arrives at the crossroads and the militia is disbanded. The regulars continue to march to Fort Claiborne. A funeral for the dead is held at Fort Claiborne on 7 January.

In other activity, General Floyd's Georgia militia establishes Fort Hull about 40 miles west of Fort Mitchell. The post is built to support Floyd's campaign against the Upper Creeks (Red Sticks).

Early January   In Washington, D.C., the president informs Congress of a British proposal for peace negotiations that reached Washington in November. England, which had rejected mediation by a third party, had agreed to direct talks with the United States. The British propose that the talks be held in London; however, they also include Gottenburg, Sweden, as an alternative place. The Americans, who unlike the British had previously accepted a third party in the talks, agree to the negotiations and select Gottenburg. John Quincy Adams, Albert Gallatin and James Bayard, previously chosen as negotiators, are retained. Henry Clay and Jonathan Russell are selected to join the negotiating team.

The American negotiators are directed to remain adamant in their demand that the British stop impressing Americans into the Royal Navy, and in return the U.S. will prohibit British sailors from serving on American ships. The negotiators are also authorized to inform the British that deserters will be returned them as part of the agreement.

In Alabama, the campaign initiated by General Jackson the previous fall has depleted his forces. Despite having only about 12 men who served during the campaign and about 900 new recruits at Fort Strother, Jackson plans to penetrate the Creek territory. The force will be supplemented with about 200 friendly Indians. The Creek Indians attack on 22 January.

In New York, the first war steamship, *Fulton the First*, is built at Noah Brown's shipyard. The vessel is designed for the defense of the harbor. Essentially a floating battery, it is capable of traveling six miles per hour. It is built under the supervision of Robert Fulton, inventor of the first commercially successful steamboat, and named in his honor.

In naval activity, the American privateer *Roger* (Captain R. Quarles), which recently sailed out of Norfolk, seizes the schooner *Henry* and its cargo of fish. The prize is taken into port at Charleston. At about the same time (January), the schooner *Maria* is also captured by the *Roger*, but finding the prize of no value, Captain Quarles orders it burned.

January 1 (Saturday)   In New York, the British, having completed their mission, which included the destruction of Black Rock and Buffalo, move back into Canada. An article in the *New York Evening Post* issue of January 19 notes:

> They left no buildings standing at Black Rock and Buffalo except they are blacksmith's shop, used as an armory, and a small house of a Mrs. St. John. They came out of Buffalo about two miles and burnt all as far as the brick house of Mr. W. Hodge inclusive, in which were 6 or 8,000 dollars worth of goods that were also lost. Of the Americans killed at Black Rock the bodies of 35 have been found. The enemy have also in their possession 69 prisoners.... The schooners Ariel, Little Belt, Chippawa and sloop Trippe, lying near Buffalo Creek, fell into the enemy's hands and are probably destroyed. The tavern house of Major Miller at Cold Springs and the house of Lieut.-Colonel

Fulton the First.

Granger at 4 Mile Creek are, not burnt as reported. The conduct of a portion of our militia during the awful scenes at Buffalo is reported as more rapacious than that of the enemy, (excepting perhaps the British Indians.) Many of them have been seen engaged in plundering our unfortunate sufferers of what the enemy did not take.

January 3 (Monday) **In Connecticut** at New London, Commodore Decatur and Captains James Biddle and J. Jones jointly sign a letter after inspecting a model of Robert Fulton's steamship:

> We, the undersigned, have this day examined the model and plans of a vessel of war, submitted to us by Robert Fulton, to carry 24 guns, 24 or 32 pounders, and use red hot shot, to be propelled by steam at the speed of from 4 to 5 miles an hour, without the aid of wind or tide. The properties of which vessel are: That without masts or sails, she can move with sufficient speed; that its machinery being guarded, she cannot be crippled; that its sides are so thick as to be impenetrable to every kind of shot and in a calm or light breeze, she can take choice of position or distance from an enemy. Considering the speed which the application of steam has already given to heavy floating bodies, we have full confidence, that should such a vessel move only four miles an hour, she could, under favourable circumstances, which may always be gained over enemies' vessels in our ports, harbours, bays and sounds, be rendered more formidable to an enemy than any kind of engine hitherto invented. And in such case she would be equal to the destruction of one or more 74's, or of compelling her or them to depart from our waters. We, therefore, give it as our decided opinion, that it is among the best interests of the United States, to carry this plan into immediate execution.

Robert Fulton.

In New York at Albany, Governor Daniel D. Tompkins, having been advised of the British progress on the Niagara frontier, writes to General Amos Hall with instructions: "I beg that you will endeavour to check that panic which I am informed exists amongst the Militia and Inhabitants, and endeavor to animate them with feelings and courage more worthy of their professions and of the character of the Militia of the State of New York."

In Ohio, a 40-man contingent, led by Lieutenants Davis, Fisk and Larwell, is attacked by a British force, while on a reconnaissance mission near the La Tranche River. Only two men escape. Three of the troops are killed and the rest are captured. The incident is reported by the *New York Evening Post*, in its issue of January 15, 1814.

In Pennsylvania, Major General David Mead dispatches a letter to Lieutenant Jesse D. Elliott: "Sir,—I have ordered out the whole of this brigade, and one thousand men from the lower brigade, for the defence of Erie and the fleet. A long and severe indisposition, which has confined me to my room and bed, renders me unable to go to Erie at present. I have no doubt you will give to General Kelso the benefit of your experience and skill, in erecting works for the defence of the town and place. I sent on your despatches to Pittsburgh."

January 3 to March 23 **In New York** at Albany, the court-martial of General William Hull for his surrender of Detroit without raising any resistance begins 3 January. He is charged with "treason, cowardice and neglect of duty and conduct unbecoming an officer." The members of the court are Major General Henry Dearborn, president, Brigadier General Bloomfield, Colonel Robert Bogardus, Lt. Colonel Samuel S. Conner, Lt. Colonel S.B. David, Lt. Colonel Richard Dennis, Colonel J.B. Fenwick, Lt. Colonel James House, Colonel William N. Irvine, Colonel Peter Little, Lt. Colonel John W. Livingstone, Lt. Colonel William Scott and Colonel William Stewart. Martin Van Buren is the special judge advocate (he is later vice president under President Andrew Jackson and the 8th president of the U.S.).

Colonel Lewis Cass is the first witness. His letter written 10 September 1812, while General Hull remained a prisoner of the British, describes the surrender of Detroit. Detractors charge that Colonel Cass was biased because he was in line to be Hull's successor. Nevertheless, there seems to be no testimony from any of the other officers to support Hull's action. At the time of the surrender, some called it treason. (*See also,* **August 16** [1812] **(Sunday)** THE SURRENDER OF DETROIT.)

With regard to the charge of cowardice, General Hull responds:

> But, gentlemen, upon the charge of cowardice, I am bold to say, I have no dread. I have fought more battles than many of the young men who have impeached me of this crime have numbered years. I appeal to the history that bears record of those who were engaged in the bloody contests for our liberty; there you shall find my name,—but not as a coward! I have brought before you the testimony of the few who remained of those, who were my companions in arms in times that tried men's souls. Do they say I am a coward? I invoke the spirits of the departed heroes who have died at my side by the sword of the enemy, to say if I am a coward. I would call the shades of Gates, Wayne, Schuyler and of Washington to tell you how often they have led me into battle and to say if they found me a coward. Will you believe that the spirit which has so often prompted me to risk my life for my country should now have so far forsaken me as that I have become a traitor and a coward? Will you believe that the years in which I have grown gray in my country's service should so far have changed my nature as that I could have been the base and abject thing my enemies have represented? No, gentlemen; that blood which animated my youth, age has not chilled. I at this moment feel its influence, and it makes me dare to say that no man ever did or can think me a coward.

General Hull insists that he surrendered to prevent his force from being massacred, as threatened by General Brock.

At the end of the trial, General Hull is found guilty of cowardice in the face of the enemy and sentenced to death. President Madison, although not in disagreement with the sentence, intervenes and spares General Hull's life through a pardon. General Hull's name is stripped from the rolls of the U.S. Army. Efforts continue to this day by some to exonerate the general's reputation.

January 4 (Tuesday) **In Georgia,** Governor Peter Early informs General David Blackshear that he is to assume command of the army. Blackshear succeeds General John Floyd. General Floyd resumes service after he recuperates and will be back in service late in the month.

January 5 (Wednesday) **In New York,** Major General Amos Hall begins reorganization. A contingent of 1,800 troops is activated. Several days later, it is split into two separate regiments. A contingent drawn from the 7th and 24th Brigades (militia) will form one of the new regiments, which will be commanded by Colonel John Harris. The other will be established from a contingent drawn from the 1st, 6th, 38th and 39th Brigades, to be commanded by Colonel Hugh W. Dobbin. The regiments will be combined into a new brigade commanded by Brigadier General William Burnett.

January 5–9 *In naval activity,* the USS *President*, sailing in the West Indies, captures three British vessels: *Wanderer, Edward* and *Jonathan*.

January 6 (Thursday) **In New York** at Genesee, General James Wadsworth, after being notified that General Hall had abandoned Eleven Mile Creek and that he had re-established his headquarters at Batavia, writes to Governor Tompkins to offer his appraisal of the situation on the frontier:

> SIR,—When I heard that General Hall had removed his headquarters to Batavia and that 11 Mile Creek was abandoned, I thought it high time to rally. I sent out circulars to put in motion a thousand men, started myself, met General Hall returning to Bloomfield. He thought

the frontiers were safe and disapproved of volunteers going on irregularly. The convictions of my mind were very different, but I instantly acquiesced and sent expresses to stop the volunteers. I continued on myself. The enemy re-crossed the Niagara River Saturday and Sunday except about sixty men, who were sent to burn all before them between Black Rock and Lewiston. Dr. Brown, who went with a flag to dress our wounded was informed that the force which crossed the river consisted of six hundred regulars and 50 Indians. There are about 200 men at 11 Mile Creek and about the same number at Batavia. Colonels Davis and Brooks are good citizens but feeble men. Major Mallory, (I think his name is,) of the Canada Volunteers, being more efficient, has in effect the command of our frontier. In fact the consternation of the militia is so great that they cannot be reduced to tolerable (order) for some time. A hundred regulars and fifty Indians would now march to Batavia without serious opposition. The frontier is now dependent for its safety on the clemency of the English, Butler's Rangers and the Indians. General Hall is detaching and organizing fifteen hundred militia. You will be deceived if you expect any effective service from them. General McClure (who is a mere coxcomb) by his bad management and the disaster at Buffalo has spread fright and consternation among all ranks, broken down the ardor and spirit of the militia, and it will require some time for it to recover. The frontier will remain defenceless until a regiment of regulars is sent on…. It is essential you should be apprized of the real situation of the frontier, this is my apology for addressing (you.) I beg you to consider this letter as confidential and not to be communicated to any person. Most of the inhabitants have left Batavia. The population west of Batavia are flying in all directions in great distress.

In naval activity, the British privateer *Wolverine* captures the *Aurora* (R. McKenzie, master) on its way from Boston to Mount Desert, Maine. The prize and its cargo of wood are taken into Liverpool. The British privateer *Wolverine* intercepts and captures the 91-ton sloop *Mary*, going with a cargo of wood from Penobscot, Maine, to Boston. The prize is taken into port at Liverpool.

In other naval activity, the British privateer *Wolverine* seizes the 114-ton schooner *Ten Brothers*, re-routing it and its cargo of wood into port at Liverpool. Also, the British privateer *Wolverine* intercepts and seizes the 52-ton schooner *Victory*, which is carrying a cargo of cord wood and timber. The *Victory* is separate from the brigantine *Victory* seized on 19 March 1813, the schooner *Victory* seized on 7 August 1814 and the ship *Victory* seized in September 1814.

January 7 (Friday) In Canada at Malone, Maj. Gen. Wilkinson writes to the secretary of war about the conditions of the troops at French Mills: "Sir, the mail route by Burlington has become dilatory and uncertain. I therefore send this to Utica by express to advise you that we are still safe from the enemy, and I understand snug from the weather but our troops die at the French Mills owing, as all ranks avow, to the bad quality of the flour, medicines and hospital stores." The troops' rations at French Mills are down to "about seven days and those at Chatcauguay to less than three."

He also presents his plans for an offensive:

I propose to march on the 3d or 4th of next month [February] a column of two thousand men from Chateauguay and the same from Plattsburgh, with the appropriate attirail and the necessary sleighs for transport; the first to move by the route of General Hampton to sweep the enemy to the St. Lawrence, then to turn to the right and march for St. Pierre, while the second will march by the route of Hemmingford and La Torlue to form a junction at St. Pierre, from which point the united corps will proceed against the posts of St. Philip, L'Acadie and St. John, and, having beaten, routed, or captured the detachments at these defenceless cantonments, shall be governed by circumstances whether to occupy their quarters and hold the country and reduce the Isle aux Noix or return to our cantonments. Simultaneous with these movements four thousand men from the French Mills will cross the St. Lawrence, attack Cornwall, capture or rout the corps of the enemy's regular troops in that vicinity, disperse the militia, fortify and hold possession of the village, and then effectually cut off the intercourse between the two provinces…. Should the double operations proposed be deemed too hazardous, then will you be pleased to point out that which may be preferred, either to take possession at Cornwall or to break up the posts or cantonments in our front; we are certainly competent to either, and I am desirous the troops under my command should not eat the bread of idleness.

January 8 (Saturday) In New York, about 70 troops, led by General John Swift and Lt. Colonel C. Hopkins, surprise a British contingent out on a detail collecting wood. The British sustain four killed and the Americans sustain one man killed. The British prisoners are taken to Canandaigua. Later, General Amos Hall, upon being informed of the skirmish, cautions Smith about being too overconfident in executing raids until reinforcements arrive at his station.

January 10 (Monday) In New York at Batavia, a contingent of cavalry departs from the camp to bolster the force under Lt. Colonels Swift and Hopkins on the frontier. General Hall had been informed that the British were closing against their command.

January 11 (Tuesday) In New York, Marines and sailors bolster their positions at Fort Tompkins at Sackets Harbor to prepare for an anticipated assault by the British. Shipbuilding has been continuing through the bitter winter that has taken a severe toll on equipment and men. Today, Henry Eckford, supervisor of the shipbuilding, and Naval Master Commandant William Crane check the planking of the nearly finished Brigantine *Jefferson*. Two other vessels, the *Jones* and *Superior*, are also under construction. The British plan to attack is aborted and the *Jefferson* and *Jones* are seaworthy by early April. The frigate *Superior* joins the other two on the Great Lakes during the summer, participating with the lake squadron against the British at Kingston and Niagara.

In other activity, General Hall writes to Lt. Colonels Swift and Hopkins at Batavia, regarding a British force that is approaching their position on the frontier: "I have only to direct that, should you not be able to meet the enemy in fair fight, that you give him every annoyance in your power, covering your retreat in the best manner your force will warrant." General Hall also informs the colonels that he will arrive at their camp in a few days.

January 12 (Wednesday) In Canada at Kingston, Lt. General Drummond, in a letter to Sir George Prevost dated this day, states: "It has also been reported to me from a person who crossed over at Fort Erie ferry on Saturday last, that the enemy have brought on to Buffalo 15 pieces of cannon and that they intend taking possession of Fort Erie again as soon as the weather permits; that they are raising two regiments of colour, and that Sergeant Powell of the 19th Light Dragoons is at Eleven Mile Creek in a most deplorable state, extremely anxious, either by exchange or parole, to be permitted to come to Canada."

In New York, General Lewis Cass writes to Secretary of War John Armstrong at Williamsville:

I passed this day the ruins of Buffalo. It exhibits a scene of distress and destruction such as I have never before witnessed. The events which have recently transpired in this quarter have been so astonishing and unexpected that I have been induced to make some inquiry into their causes and progress, and, doubting whether you have received any correct information upon the subject, I now trouble you with the detail. The fall of Niagara has been owing to the most *criminal negligence*. The *force* in it was fully competent to its defence. The commanding officer, Captain Leonard, it is said, was at his own house, three miles from the fort, and all the officers seem to have rested in as much security as though no enemy was near them. Captain Rodgers and Captain Hampton, both of the 24th, had companies in the fort. Both of them were absent from it. Their conduct ought to be strictly investigated. I am also told that Major Wallace of the 5th was in the fort. He escaped and is now at Erie. The circumstances attending the destruction of Buffalo you will have learned before this reaches you. But the force of the enemy has been greatly magnified. From the most careful examination I am satisfied that not more than *six hundred and fifty men* of regulars, militia, and Indians landed at Black Rock. To oppose these we had from *two thousand five hundred to three thousand* militia. All except very few of them behaved in the most cowardly manner. They fled without discharging a musket. The enemy continued on this side of the river until Saturday. All their movements betrayed symptoms of apprehension. A vast quantity of property was left in town uninjured, and the Ariel, which lies four miles above upon the beach, is safe. They continue in possession of Niagara and will probably retain it until a force competent to its reduction arrives in its vicinity.

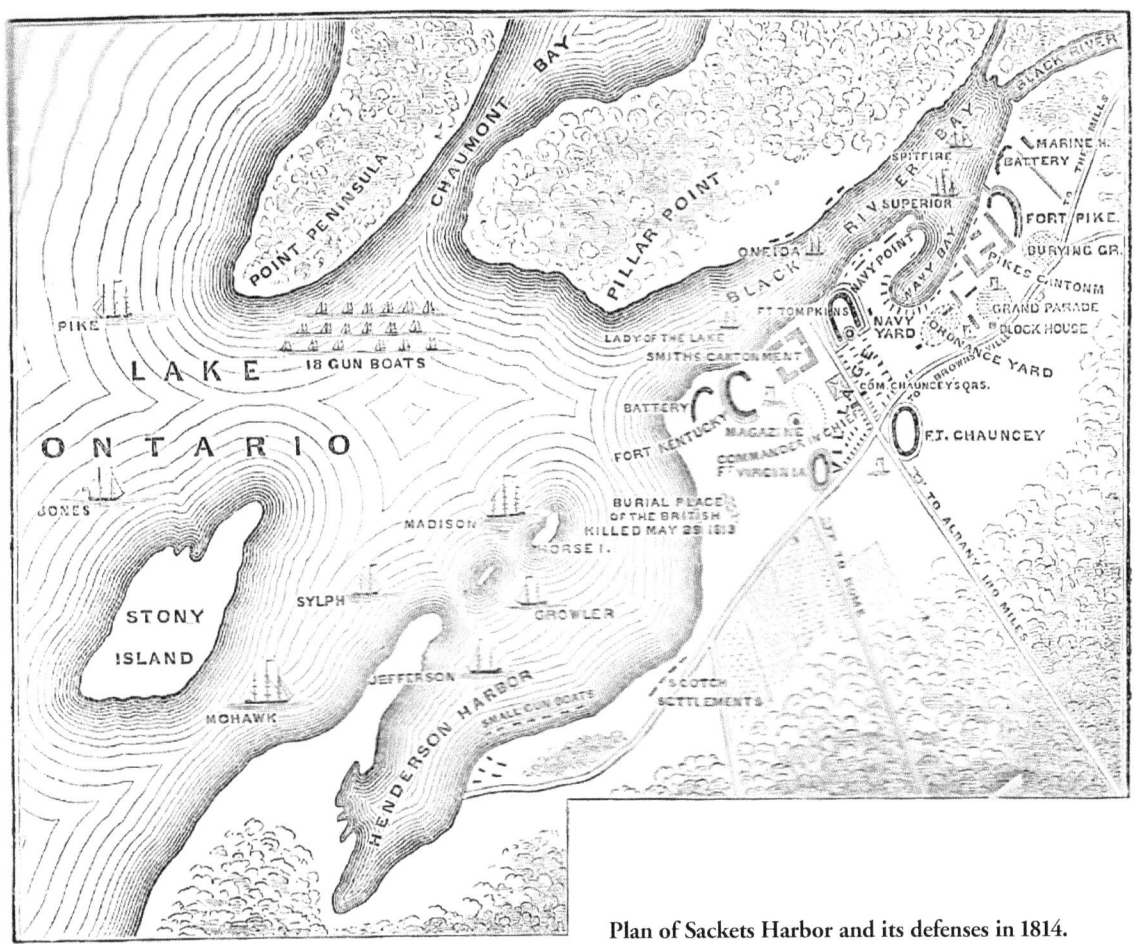

Plan of Sackets Harbor and its defenses in 1814.

January 13 (Thursday) **In Georgia,** General Blackshear at his camp slightly south of the Flint River writes a letter to Governor George Troup in response to a dispatch he received earlier this day. He informs Troup that when he initially arrived at Camp Hope, the Miccasukie Indians were identified as hostile, and he reports that the number of British at the Apalachicola River stands at only a small force. He also states that about 300 hostile Creeks (Red Sticks) in the area number about 300. However, he explains that while at Perryman's he was informed that the Miccasukies were identified as friendly and the Seminoles as hostile. Blackshear mentions: "I endeavored to find out who were the Seminoles; but all the information on that subject was so vague and evasive, and contained so many ambiguities, the same reports at different times explained differently, the same Indian towns represented at different times by different names, all calculated to mislead any officer who was credulous enough not to suspect some design." Blackshear also states that he received an order from Major General Thomas McIntosh based on another report that claimed 14,000 British troops were at the mouth of the river.

In naval activity, the British privateer *Hare* intercepts and seizes the sloop Hero (George Fishley, master) and takes it into port at St. John's, New Brunswick. The *Hero* is separate from the schooner *Hero* seized 12 June 1813, the schooner Hero overtaken 29 August 1813, the schooner *Hero* seized 14 November 1813, the schooner *Hero* captured on 3 July 1814 and the sloop *Hero* seized in early November 1814.

January 14 (Friday) **In Alabama,** two fresh regiments raised in Tennessee under Colonel Nicholas Perkins and Colonel William Higgins arrive at Fort Strother to provide General Jackson some relief. His force is dangerously reduced because of desertions and expiration of enlistments. However, the infusion of the new force of about 850 troops is not for the long term. The volunteers had enlisted only for sixty days. Nevertheless, Jackson is pleased to see the new regiments. At the time of their arrival, Jackson's army numbers only about 100 men. The situation had become so critical that General Jackson is forced to garrison Fort Armstrong with Cherokees to maintain that post on the Coosahatchie and to guard various places where stores are kept. Nonetheless, General Jackson remains positive and inexhaustible with regard to the new army being raised in Tennessee for service under him. Jackson continues to ensure that his army has the provisions to carry it to victory. He personally shuttles between Fort Strother and Ditto's Landing to shepherd the operation to speed the supplies to the fort. Meanwhile, Jackson immediately moves out with his fresh troops. Jackson's column crosses the Coosa River and marches to Talladega, where he arrives on the 16th.

In Michigan, Sailing Master Stephen Champlin writes to Lt. Jesse Elliott regarding conditions at Put-in-Bay and the protection of the ships: "I have every thing in complete order at this place. I have the guns mounted in the block house; I have mounted on board of the Detroit 21 guns, and on board of the Queen Charlotte 19. I have mounted those 32 pounders and 24 pounders that were left on board of the Detroit. I can bring 12 guns to bear in every direction. The ice is constantly kept open. I think if they attack us, they will meet with a pretty warm reception. The sailors are all well, the soldiers are very sick. We have provision enough to last till the first of April. The beef is very bad."

January 15 (Saturday) **In Ohio,** Lt. Champlain and surgeon of the Navy Eastman, after conferring with Major General John S. Gano at Lower Sandusky, depart from there for Put-in-Bay. Gano had been informed that about 40 cannon are deployed there "to give the enemy a warm reception should they visit them."

In naval activity, the British privateer *Hare* intercepts and seizes the 190-ton brigantine *Recovery*

Captain Stephen Champlin.

(D. Dunbar, master) which had been carrying a cargo of ballast and some specie from Bermuda to Castine, Maine; however, the specie had been taken ashore before it is captured.

January 16 (Sunday) **In Alabama,** General Andrew Jackson arrives at Talladega, where he is joined by Cherokees and friendly Lower Creeks. The Indians are startled when they notice that the American force is not very strong. Nonetheless, with the addition of the allies, Jackson moves out and advances toward the Tallapoosa River. Chief Wauhatchie of the Cherokee tribe participates in this campaign. He serves in a company composed of Cherokees commanded by Captain John Brown.

In Ohio, General John S. Gano (Ohio militia) at Lower Sandusky writes to Governor Return Meigs: "I have the pleasure to inform you that after repeated solicitations, and much delay, the paymaster has succeeded in obtaining two months' pay for the troops under my command. I have sent him on to Detroit as the men there are in great want of money to purchase necessaries, etc." General Gano also informs Meigs about Put-in-Bay and states that he will send them the regulars at Fort Seneca to reinforce the contingents there. The letter also informs the governor that the militia under him is exhausted and they have "begun to count the days" left in their enlistments.

General Gano's troops are moving logs because many of the animals have died due to the lack of forage. He had requested funds from Quartermaster Gardiner the previous November to buy forage from a place about 300 miles distant, but the money had not arrived. In the letter, he stated: "If three hundred dollars could have been sent on, I think it would have saved the United States three thousand; and I assure you I have used every exertion to preserve and protect the public property. As I before observed, nothing will induce the militia to remain after their term of service expires, which will be the last of next month." In closing, Gano mentions the scarcity of provisions: "Flour is very scarce at all the frontier posts. I have been between 'hawk and buzzard'—the commissary and contractor; and between the two, as is usual, must fail. What a wretched system of Warfare."

General Gano adds a P.S. regarding his force and thoughts on British actions: "My troops are so scattered, I have no disposable force without evacuating some of the posts that contain considerable military stores. I wrote some time since to General Harrison, recommending him to send on the recruits. They certainly will be wanted as soon as the British can move on the ice or by water to Detroit or the Islands. I fear we shall lose all that has been gained, unless great exertions are used to reinforce; and supply of provisions is much wanted."

January 17 (Monday) **In Ohio** at Lower Sandusky, General John Gano writes to General Harrison that he is concerned about the vessels in Put-in-Bay. Ten sailors and 40 troops are aboard the vessels and at a small blockhouse there. Gano intends to send about 30 reinforcements (regulars) once the ice becomes thick enough to hold their weight. Gano also mentions that if necessary, he can spare troops from the fort at Portage, where about 100 militia troops are deployed, if necessary; however, their enlistments terminate on 28 February 1814. Before his letter is sealed, a message arrives by dispatch from Put-in-Bay in which 200 reinforcements are requested.

January 18 (Tuesday) **In Canada** at Kingston, with the permission of Lt. General Drummond, Aeneas Shaw, adjutant general of militia, retires due to poor health. He is succeeded by Lt. Colonel Nathaniel Coffin.

In New York at Batavia, General Amos Hall writes to General David Mead at Fort Erie:

I am happy to learn that you are on your guard against supposed movements of the enemy threatening Erie and the fleet stationed in that harbor, and at the same time regret that it will not be in my power to lend you any material aid in the event of an attack. The forces under my command are small and barely sufficient for covering the frontier and quieting the apprehensions of the inhabitants. Large detachments and those frequent have been made from my division, and the militia in this quarter are now exceedingly harassed with duty. I shall take care to apprise you by express of any information that may be in my possession relative to the enemy's movements which may be material for you to know. As at present advised, I think there is some reason to apprehend an attack on your post should the ice become sufficiently strong and your post not be strongly guarded… . It would give me great pleasure to have such a force under my command as would enable me to co-operate with you in the meditated plan of defence and attack, without at the same time exposing the frontier to further devastation.

January 18–20 *In naval activity,* the USS *Enterprise,* supported by the brigantine *Rattlesnake,* seizes the Spanish brigantine *Isabella* from the British who had claimed the vessel as a prize. The two American vessels with their sailor and Marine contingents board and seize a Swedish vessel, the *Sincerity,* engaged in transporting British cargoes across the Atlantic.

January 19 (Wednesday) **In Washington, D.C.,** President Madison, compelled by overwhelming opposition to the Embargo Act passed in December, backtracks. He recommends that Congress repeal the law. Congress takes action in mid–April.

In Canada at Kingston, Lt. General Drummond writes to Sir George Prevost regarding an incident on 9 January:

A party that was sent out on the morning of the 9th to cut wood, under protection of a sergeant's covering party, was attacked by a body of the enemy, reported to consist of about 150 men, and driven in. The sergeant was severely wounded and nine men of the working party, it is supposed, taken prisoners, for no account was received of them so long after as the following night. It appears very extraordinary that any individuals of so small a fatigue party should not have been able to effect their escape, and particularly as it appears they were not furnished with arms to assist the covering party in repelling the attack or in effecting a slow and cautious retreat…. Major General Riall also states to me that the troop of Provincial Dragoons commanded by Captain Merritt have become extremely unserviceable from the wretched state of their horses, and that the most effective means of getting them in order for service in the coming spring would be by the appointment of an Inspecting Field Officer of Provincial Cavalry from the line and of known experience to visit their several posts frequently and issue such instructions as would ensure a certain if not speedy amendment in so useful a body.

Drummond's statement of the attack occurring on the 9th is in conflict with a statement by General Hall that it occurred on 8 January.

In another letter sent this day to Prevost, General Drummond, in an apparent answer regarding Buffalo and Sackets Harbor, states:

I found it totally impracticable to push the troops of the Right Division beyond Buffalo, and fortunately I did not even attempt it, for with every exertion I had only sufficient time to repass them across the river previous to it being blocked up with ice. With regard to Sackets Harbor any information I have received from thence has been so unsatisfactory that I cannot form any just opinion of the practicability of any attempt upon it at present, but Your Excellency may rest assured that I will not lose sight of any favorable opportunity that may offer of aiming a heavy stroke at so vital a spot of the enemy's resources in this neighborhood. Your Excellency is at the same time well aware of the inadequacy of the force I can command in this vicinity for an operation of any magnitude.

January 19–20 *In naval activity,* the American privateer *David Porter* (Captain Coggeshall) encounters a terrific storm which by about 0800 the winds rise to the strength of a hurricane. The ships battle the storm to forestall disaster, but at about 1200, a powerful wave plows into the ship and collapses "one of the stanchions, and splits open the plank-sheer." The vessel becomes imperiled, and for a while, it is uncertain whether the ship, which is close to going under, will be able to right herself. At about this time, the foresail splits and the water rips the lee bulwark from its base, which causes the enormous pressure to ease and permits the ship to right itself.

Nevertheless, the perilous moments had prompted other emergency actions to try to save the ship. One such action was to toss two guns overboard. Meanwhile, Captain Coggeshall struggles to find a way to ensure his vessel is able to outlive the storm. Using his ingenuity, he devises a contraption by modifying a boom. He "takes a square sail boom. Spanned at each end with a four-inch rope, and with the small bower cable made fast to the bight of the span, the other end being made fast to the foremast, the boom was thrown overboard and was run out some sixty fathoms." Coggeshall's device was described as having a "miraculous effect." His boom is credited with instantly breaking the "force of the waves and keeping the schooner's head to the sea." The crew and the ship survive the storm, which continues to bash the vessel into the following day. On the 18th, the *David Porter* resumes its voyage, which changes from its initial plans. The privateer makes into port at La Teste, France, on the 24th.

January 20 (Thursday) In Washington, D.C., John Armstrong, secretary of war, pursuant to order of President Madison, issues orders for General Wilkinson to abandon his camp on the Salmon River. Wilkinson's orders direct him to send General Jacob Brown with 2,000 troops and some cannon to Sackets Harbor, while he leads the remainder of his force to Plattsburgh. Armstrong's orders also direct Wilkinson to have the soldiers that are either sick or wounded transported to Burlington.

In Alabama, General Jackson's force arrives near a Hillibee village, Enitachopco. He establishes camp there for the night.

In New York, at General Hall's headquarters at Batavia, general orders are issued directing the contingent of militia from the 6th, 7th and 38th Brigades to be mustered into companies by Major Riddle and afterward, the troops are to march toward Lewiston to join with General John Smith's force, which is encamped close to the town along the Ridge Road.

General Hall writes Governor Tompkins about the situation at British-held Fort Niagara:

Sir,— Nothing important has occurred since I last wrote you. Our scouting parties from the camp near Lewiston occasionally approach within musket shot of Fort Niagara. It is ascertained the enemy keep no guards without the fort. The garrison from the best information that can be obtained, consists of 250 or three hundred men commanded by Colonel Young of the [British] 8th Regiment. There has been but little appearance of force seen of late opposite Black Rock and Buffalo. The whole force of the enemy, from information recently received, and their disposition were as follows;— Say, 200 at Burlington Heights — Major Glegg, 300 at Ft. Niagara — Colonel Young, 300 at Queenston Heights — Col. Hamilton, 1,200 from Chippawa to Erie, 300 or 400 Indians of the Six Nations, 800 or 1,000 Indians commanded by Colonels Elliott and Claus; the whole said to be under the command of Major General Riall.

There are no militia now in service on the British side of the Niagara River, according to late accounts from that side. It is reported that Lieut. General Sir Gordon Drummond has gone to Lower Canada, accompanied by Colonel Murray, who commanded at the capture of Fort Niagara and received a wound in the wrist. I have recently received letters from Major General Mead of Meadville and Captain Elliott commanding the navy at Erie stating the apprehension of an attack at the latter place as soon as the ice becomes sufficiently strong to pass over, which generally happens by 10 February. They have requested me to co-operate with them by stationing a force at Ohautauqua. In answer I was obliged to state that my force on this station will be small and barely sufficient to guard the frontier and quiet the fears of the inhabitants.

General Hall adds that his force actually stands at about 1,800 men, and that they will be deployed in equal numbers at Williamsville and near Lewiston. The regulars, about 150 strong, along with one officer, Lt. Riddle, on the frontier have received orders from General Wilkinson to repair to French Mills to join the regulars already there.

January 21 (Friday) In Alabama, General Jackson's scouts detect fresh tracks that point toward a heavy concentration of Indians. He establishes his camp before dusk. Patrols are sent out to reconnoiter and fires are lit just outside the perimeter of the camp, which has been formed into the shape of a square. During the night at about 2200, one of Jackson's pickets spots several of the enemy braves encroaching his position. He fires and one is killed. About one hour later, Jackson's scouts discover a strong Creek encampment several miles from Jackson's lines. The scouts report that the Indians are celebrating; however, they are also moving the women and children out of the camp.

In Canada at Kingston, General Drummond responds in a letter to an inquiry from Sir George Prevost regarding the destruction of the American vessels on Lake Erie:

The security of the right flank of the army and the preservation of the intercourse with and influence over the Western Indians being objects of the very first importance, it is proposed to undertake an expedition against Detroit and the enemy's vessels in that quarter as the only means by which these ends can be obtained. In making arrangements for the service due regard must be had to the immediate security of the Niagara frontier, the force which the enemy has at Detroit, and the means necessary to transport and provision the force which it may be thought necessary to employ. From the destruction of the enemy's boats and craft on the Niagara, no apprehension of an attack need be entertained on any part of that line below Fort Erie, and a very small force will suffice to prevent their crossing on the ice. By blocking up the roads leading from Sugar Loaf and from Haun's, all the routes except that immediately on the bank of the river, will be closed, and therefore our line of defence will be shortened and greatly strengthened. Under these circumstances, I should consider twelve hundred men as amply sufficient for the defence of this line, which will leave a sufficient number for performing the other service [destruction of ships at Put-in-Bay].

Drummond estimates that Detroit is defended by about 400 troops, with another 200 distributed between Amherstburg and Sandwich as well as some other outposts. He also concludes that the expedition will require 750 regulars, 100 Royal Marines if available, a detachment of Marine artillery (two 6-pounders and one 51-inch howitzer), 250 militia and 400 Western Indians. The force is also to include a Provincial troop under Captain Coleman, composed of 20 men and 200 seamen, with the latter being the primary component in the operation against the vessels in the bay. The report is meticulously done and includes the weight of the rations required for 21 days, as well as the amount of sleds (132) needed to carry provisions. Allowing for unforeseen circumstances, including carrying troops that falter on the arduous journey, Drummond calls for 500 sleighs. He believes that Detroit must be seized before attempting to destroy the vessels in the bay. His calculations place Put-in-Bay about 40 miles from Amherstburg; he believes the entire trek will be on ice. "The sooner it is undertaken the better, as the enemy will doubtless make great exertions to reinforce and provision Detroit, which delay on our part will perfectly enable them to effect," Drummond writes. "I am aware there are several minor arrangements to be made, but which easily can be, provided the general plan be approved of, I propose moving with this expedition myself, and Commodore Sir James Yeo has expressed his intention to accompany me. I shall be most happy to avail myself of his services if it meets Your Excellency's approbation." Prevost responds to Drummond's letter on 29 January.

In naval activity, two British privateers, the *Liverpool Packet* and the *Retaliation*, pounce upon and seize the schooner *Falun*, which is taken into Liverpool.

January 22 (Saturday) In Alabama, Indians halt the Tennessee militia at Emuckfaw along the Tallapoosa River. At about 0600, they attack General Jackson's force, initially by feigning a full-scale push against Jackson's right; however, Jackson, convinced that the actual attack would strike his left flank, had taken precautions to bolster his left. His instincts prove correct. The Creeks unfold their genuine intention and pound the left flank and a portion of Jackson's rear in a vicious attempt to collapse the lines. The intensity increases rapidly for about one-half hour, but the timely arrival of General Coffee, Adjutant General Sitler and Inspector General William Carroll quickly brings discipline and order back into the battle. The Indians fight tenaciously; however, Jackson's Tennesseans are not intimidated. They pour incessant fire into the enemy, and after about one-half hour of savage combat, the Creeks are driven back.

Meanwhile, infantry under Captain Terrill reinforces the left flank. While the Indians are in retreat, Jackson orders pursuit. It soon becomes necessary for Coffee to halt due to a lack of artillery. While waiting for more artillery to arrive, Jackson's right wing had come under attack. Coffee initiates a charge; however, inexplicably, only about 45 men join in the charge. The Creeks sense an opportunity to destroy Coffee's command. They charge Coffee's position, but allied Indians arrive to bolster his force, and at about the same time, more Tennesseans further reinforce the vanguard. The Creeks there choose to retire while Coffee's men dismount and pursue the enemy as they race toward a swamp by the creek.

In the meantime, the other Creeks remain indefatigable and persistent. They charge against Jackson's left flank, bellowing their war cries as they advance. Captain Terrill's infantry moves into position to galvanize the line. Furious firing commences and to add to the thunderclap, General Carroll leads a bayonet charge, which prompts the Creeks to escape the deadly blades. General Coffee remains steadfast at the swamp, keeping the Creeks there pinned down. Friendly Indians, led by Jim Fife, arrive to bolster Coffee, which gives him another opportunity to launch yet another bayonet charge. The Creeks are again compelled to flee from the bayonet. Coffee continues the chase for several miles before aborting the chase. The Creeks had been stymied at every point; however, they had raised ferocious resistance.

The stiff resistance combined with the mounting casualties and acute supply shortages cause Jackson to halt the operation. Before returning to Fort Strothers, a detail is assigned to recover the dead and bury them. Meanwhile, the camp is fortified in the event the Creeks launch a new attack, but the night passes peacefully.

In naval activity, two British privateers, the *Liverpool Packet* and the *Retaliation*, operating together, intercept and seize the 88-ton brigantine *Gustava* (Justin Nelson Berg, master), which is en route from St. Bartholomews to Boston with a cargo of coffee, molasses and sugar. The prize and its cargo are diverted to Liverpool. The *Gustava* is separate from the *Gustavia* seized 22 June 1813.

January 23 (Sunday)   In Alabama, General Andrew Jackson's force reaches Enotachopco late in the day, having had no encounters with the Creeks, sometimes referred to as Red Sticks. Nonetheless, Jackson remains cautious in anticipation of another assault. He is uncomfortable at the creek crossing due to the high probability that the opposite embankment holds a good ambush site. He dispatches scouts to select another place to ford the river, and they discover a safer spot about 600 yards from their camp.

In New York at Batavia, Lt. Colonel John Harris is ordered to repair to Hardscrabble, where Colonel Philetus Swift is encamped. Once there, he is to assume command of the contingent assigned to him by earlier division orders of 8 January. He is directed to take responsibility for the exterior post and maintain constant patrols between the camp and Lewiston to prevent the camp from coming under a surprise attack and to patrol as far as Manchester and Schossler. Also, headquarters orders Brigadier General William Burnett to repair to the encampment at Eleven Mile Creek (Williamsville) and assume command of the troops there.

January 24 (Monday)   In Alabama, at Enotachopco (Battle of Enotachopco), General Jackson resumes his march to Fort Strother at about 1000. The wounded, including General Coffee, who are unable to walk or ride are carried in litters made from the hides of dead horses. The troops move out in two columns with the right under Colonel Nicholas Perkins and the left under Colonel Stump. The rear guard is commanded by General Carroll and holds responsibility for reeling around and holding the ground if an attack occurs, while the two columns under Perkins and Stump swing out to strike the flanks of the attacking Creeks. The plan seems flawless; however, theory often differs with practical application. During the crossing, the Creeks attack the rear guard, but by then the wounded and the vanguard had completed the crossing. Colonel Russell's spies receive the brunt of the assault at nearly the same time an alarm shot is fired. General Carroll brings his force to a halt to form his defense, but to his surprise, the columns on the left and right fall into confusion and the panic causes both columns to flee even before firing a single shot.

The pandemonium spreads. The center of the lines begins to take flight, with Colonel Frederick Stump leading the parade. Troops haphazardly roll down the bank. Unfortunately for Stump, he gains the dubious honor of landing within the reach of General Jackson's sword and barely escapes the wrath of the general, who restrains his anger. Nevertheless, General Carroll, with only 25 men under Captain Quarles, holds the line and halts the charge of the Creeks. Meanwhile, the artillerymen under Lt. Armstrong, armed with muskets, ascend the hill, while the artillery commander, Captain David Deadrick, and a small detachment retrieve a six-pounder that is stranded in the middle of the creek. The gun is recovered just in time to defend against a large Creek force that outnumbers the artillerymen about ten to one.

Lt. Armstrong arrives with another gun to bolster Deadrick's besieged position. Complications develop when it is discovered that the rammer and pricker had been left behind; however, the gunners improvise without wasting a minute. Two of the gunners, Constantine Perkins and Craven Jackson, remain oblivious to the sheets of shells that continue to whiz by their heads and ready the gun. Perkins detaches the bayonet from his musket and uses the former as a rammer to load the cartridge. Simultaneously, Craven Jackson "uses his ramrod as a pricker, priming with a musket cartridge." The ingenuity of Perkins and Jackson provides the additional firepower just as the Creeks near point-blank range. A few of the artillerymen are slain; however, the pernicious shower of grape and shot takes the overconfidence out of the attackers. After the second blast, the artillerymen charge the attacking Creeks.

Meanwhile, Gordon's spies, who were at the front of the army at the initiation of the attack, had by now circled around to a point from which they strike the left flank of the enemy, while other contingents, including rear guard and the troops on the flanks, had regrouped after being rallied by General Jackson, and they too take the offensive. They cross back over to the other embankment and rush into the fight. The Creeks, sensing that Jackson's force had rebounded, lose their confidence. The Creeks disengage and depart without removing their dead. Twenty-six Indian bodies remain on the field.

Pursuit is initiated, but after advancing about two miles, the chase is terminated. This battle and the recent fight on the 22nd at Emuckfaw has cost Jackson twenty men killed and about seventy-five wounded. After the battle, General Jackson returns to Fort Strother. Once there, the sixty-day volunteers are directed to move to Huntsville, where the troops will receive their honorable discharges. General Jackson also authorizes General Coffee and his officers to return to their respective homes until they are needed again. The actions of Colonel Perkins and Colonel Stump cause both to receive court-martials. Colonel Stump is found guilty of cowardice and is cashiered from the army. Colonel Perkins also accused of cowardice is acquitted. Several chiefs, interviewed subsequent to the battles of Emuckfaw and Enotachopco, claimed that they "whipped Captain Jackson, and run him to the Coosa river."

Sergeant (later lieutenant) Robert Armstrong participates in this campaign and at the Battle of New Orleans. Later during the Creek War (1836), Armstrong is commissioned a brigadier general by President Jackson.

In New York, at General Amos Hall's headquarters in Batavia, a deserter from Fort Niagara, James Fox (8th King's Regiment), who abandoned the post on the 20th, is questioned about the circumstances at the fort. He informs the Americans that the post is well stocked with about a 3-month supply of wood and that the garrison is composed of about 700 men, bolstered by about 70–80 artillerists. The deserter also explains that Colonel Hamilton is expected to succeed the commander, Colonel Young.

In other activity, following this action, Brigadier General Jacob Brown and Brigadier General George Izard will be promoted to the rank of major general. Also, afterward, Colonels Macomb, Thomas Adams Smith, Daniel Bissell, Winfield Scott, Edmund Pendleton Gaines and Eleazar Wheelock Ripley will be appointed brigadier generals. The British continue to hold Generals John Chandler, James Winchester and William Henry Winder as prisoners. General Henry Dearborn left the service due to ill health.

Another general officer, Wade Hampton, departs from the army. Various sources list different dates for General Hampton's departure during spring. According to *Lamb's Biographical Dictionary*, Volume III, he left 6 April 1814. Afterward, General Hampton returns to South Carolina to his plantation, where he becomes an extremely affluent planter who is involved in land speculation. General Hampton's son, also named Wade, remains in the army. He participates with General Jackson at New Orleans. Confederate Lt. General Wade Hampton is the son of Colonel Wade Hampton and the grandson of Major General Wade Hampton. Major General Wade Hampton dies in South Carolina during 1835.

In Canada, General Drummond writes to Sir George Prevost:

Sir,—I have the honor to acquaint Your Excellency that I have received a report from Major General Riall dated the 14th inst., stating that two militia men, Isaac Ryan and Andrew Hearn, taken prisoners about 7 months since, had arrived at Niagara, having made their escape from Greenbush, where they had been confined with about 320 other regular and militia soldiers. They passed through Sackets Harbor last Thursday week. They confirm the account of the march of troops from that place to Salmon River and say that there are no troops at Sackets Harbor but the seamen and carpenters employed in building three brigs, as they were told, and they declare there is no other force than what they mention. About 50 or 60 other prisoners made their escape from Greenbush at the same time by undermining the prison.

Drummond on this day receives new intelligence which he includes in his letter:

> I received this day, viz:—That sleighs are collecting at Sackets Harbor to the number of 200 and to rendezvous there on Saturday at an early hour for the purpose of loading provisions for the army at Salmon River, at least such was the report. But better informed persons believe that they were collected for some military movement and think it more than probable that the evacuation of the position at French Mills is in contemplation, and that the troops and stores will be sent from thence to Sackets Harbor to secure the ships to be built there. The effective force at the former place is said to be about 2,000, at the latter it does not exceed 600 men.

In New York, General Hall writes from Batavia to Major General John Swift:

> SIR, I have this moment received your letter of 8 o'clock last evening. I regret very much that you have not a force equal not only to meet but to hunt the enemy back to the fort. There are four companies of 100 men each on their way to your relief, one of which must undoubtedly arrive this morning, another in the Course of this day, probably two. That will give you a handsome reinforcement. One other company will march today and Col. Harris will move this morning. They are all well equipped. I have no doubt that you will do everything to repel the enemy, should they attempt to attack you, that your force would justify. Your judgment will direct your immediate operations. I have to request that you would stay with Col. Harris for a few days after his arrival, if possible. You will be of great service to him.

In Ohio at Lower Sandusky, Brigadier General Gano tells General Harrison in a letter dated this day that a detachment sent earlier to Put-in-Bay had not been able to cross the ice; however, they are at the point of the peninsula and should be crossing soon. He also informs General Harrison that a contingent of militia under Major Crooks has also been ordered to cross, which will bolster the force. Gano remains concerned that the provisions will be running out before the ice breaks up to permit fresh provisions to be delivered. He is equally concerned about the supplies at Portage.

General Gano also informs Harrison that officers from Buffalo arrived with intelligence that the British are plotting a "secret expedition, their destination unknown." Nevertheless, Gano has some suspicions, and he tells Harrison that Detroit, Malden and Sandwich are prepared to "defend those places to the last extremity." Also, ammunition remains in short supply. General Gano has dispatched a contingent to Fort Meigs to acquire some from that garrison, which contains an abundance. However, the roads remain impassible, which prevents any transporting of the supplies until the ice melts. Gano is aware that the vessels in the bay contain 6,000 stand of arms, but the ice also prevents it from being moved.

In naval activity, the badly battered American privateer *David Porter* limps into port at La Teste on the west coast of France. The crew is less than jubilant. Despite being thankful that they had survived a terrible storm, the news that the village has no capability of repairing ships quells their optimism. The villagers, though, are ecstatic because they have learned that the Allies are closing on Paris and British forces under Wellington are inching toward Bordeaux. The news is not well received by Captain George Coggeshall, who realizes the British might soon occupy La Teste and Bordeaux, which would probably terminate the activity of the privateer. Nonetheless, the crew is told other ships and crews had perished in the recent storms, including five British vessels that were lost near La Teste.

Meanwhile, the British do seize Bordeaux. Coggeshall had traveled by horseback to Bordeaux and worked out an arrangement by which the consignees for his cargo agree to acquire for him a cargo of wine and brandy and have it taken to La Rochelle rather than Bordeaux. After a harrowing delay at La Teste due to the uncooperative weather, the *David Porter* barely sails before the British arrive, but on 13 March, just in time, the privateer departs from the harbor.

January 26 (Wednesday) **In Alabama,** General John Floyd's command, composed of more than 1,200 Georgian volunteers, bolstered by one company of cavalry and about 400 allied Indians, establishes camp on some high ground above the swamp at Calibee (Calebee) Creek in Macon County, about fifty miles from Fort Mitchell. Preparations are taken in case of attack by the Creeks, but the area remains tranquil until the following morning. However, the are Creeks nearby, preparing to launch their attack before dawn.

January 27 (Thursday) **In Alabama,** before dawn, the Creeks who had concealed themselves in the swamp near General John Floyd's positions (Camp Defiance) at Calibee (Calabee or Chalibbee) Creek spring from their positions and strike the flank and immediate front of the American lines at about 0520. The Americans are caught by complete surprise; however, they rebound quickly. The sentinels, unable to hold, retire to the main body. By then, the Creeks begin to pound against the front while striking both flanks. Nonetheless, the ferocity of the Creeks is matched by the persistence of the Yanks, who hold the line at every point despite sustaining heavy casualties. At the front, the Creeks penetrate to nearly 25 yards from the artillery, but to their dismay, Captain Thomas' guns pour effective fire upon them and the position is bolstered by Captain Adams' riflemen, who unleash effective streams of fire. The speed of the assault succeeds in isolating one of the picket posts, but the commander, Captain John Broadnax, receives some unexpected help when one of the friendly Indians, Timpoochy Barnard, a half-breed, and a few Uchees manage to guide them to safety.

The Creeks maintain the pressure, but the Americans remain adamantly opposed to surrendering ground. General Floyd prepares his cavalry for a charge, while he readjusts his positions. At about dawn, the battalions of Major Watson and Major Freeman on the left redeploy at right angles, while the battalions of Major Booth and Cleavland on the left wing receive identical orders. By the time the maneuver is completed, the cavalry has repositioned behind the right wing. Suddenly, the Creeks, who sensed victory, find themselves in an uncomfortable situation when the signal to charge is given. The infantry bolts forward with fixed bayonets, which deflates the Creeks' attack and forces them to retreat, with the infantry and the cavalry causing more chaos during the chase that continues after the Creeks reach the swamp. Captain Samuel Butts is killed during the charge.

After the battle, General Floyd ponders his options. His losses had been 17 killed and about 132 wounded, along with the Indians' losses of 5 killed and 155 wounded. However, he is also faced with having no defensive fortifications. Another concern is that the Creeks had been on the verge of victory, despite the tenacity of his troops until the bayonet turned the tide. He decides that his casualties had been too severe and that the Creeks might soon be reinforced. He directs his force to prepare to depart Camp Defiance. After remaining at the camp for about one week, the Georgians head back to Fort Hull. Once there, General Floyd leaves a small contingent to garrison the post before moving to Fort Mitchell, where his volunteers are discharged honorably at the end of their service. This expedition is the final one by Georgian troops against the Creeks. Meanwhile, the Creeks, who had gained refuge in the nearby swamps, return to the battlefield on the day following the battle.

In Ohio, General Gano at Lower Sandusky continues to be plagued with shortages of flour and other provisions. The other posts struggle with the same problems. Gano writes to General Harrison about the situation and mentions his sentiments regarding the contractors and quartermasters: "I think I would hang half of the quartermasters and all the contractors if I was to remain in service much longer; and I am astonished how you have managed with them to effect the objects you have, for there appears no system or regularity with any of them."

January 28 (Friday) **In New York** General Wilkinson writes from Plattsburgh to Sir George Prevost:

> SIR,—I am commanded by the Executive of the United States to disavow the conduct of Brigadier-General McClure of the militia of the State of New York in burning the town of Newark and in irrefragable testimony that this act was unlicensed to transmit to Your Excellency a copy of the order under color of which that officer perpetrated a deed abhorrent to every American feeling. From this testimonial Your Excellency will perceive that the authority to destroy the village was limited expressly to the defence of Fort George, a measure warranted by the laws of modern war and justified by precedents innumerable.

The outrages which have ensued the unwarrantable destruction of Newark have been carried too far and present the aspect rather of vindictive fury than just retaliation, yet they are imputed more to personal feeling than any settled plan of policy deliberately weighed and adopted, and I hope I shall receive from Your Excellency an assurance that this conclusion is not fallacious, for although the wanton conflagrations on the waters of the Chesapeake are fresh in the recollection of every citizen of the United States, no system of retaliation which has for its object the devastation of private property, will ever be resorted to by the American Government but in the last extremity, and this will depend on the conduct of your royal master's troops in this country.

General McClure lost any chance of further command.

January 29 (Saturday) **In Canada,** Governor Sir George Prevost, in a letter marked secret and dated this day to Lt. General Drummond, responds to a letter from Drummond:

SIR,— I waited the arrival of Sir James Yeo to reply to your letter of the 21st, containing your opinion upon the practicability of an attempt to destroy the enemy's vessels and craft on Lake Erie. The Commodore's sentiments respecting this highly important service appeared to me to fully accord with your own. The consequences which would result from the complete success of such an expedition are obvious, in fact, that feat only seems wanting to the brilliant issue of the campaign, as it would place us in the proud attitude of again reoccupying the widely extended frontier of the Canadas, an event exceedingly to be desired.

Unless a sudden change should occur in the enemy's disposition of his force, the troops you propose to remain would give sufficient security to the Niagara frontier, and the force intended for the proposed service seems adequate; still there are obstacles of magnitude to be encountered, but the principal arise from the very advanced state of the season, the little time left to mature preparations, and which, were they even now complete, the impossibility of advancing for the want of snow.

These considerations, with the uncertainty of the western shore of Lake Erie being sufficiently frozen to render their ships in Put-in-Bay assailable, and the thorough conviction on my mind that to give a chance of success the possession of Sandwich and Amherstburg should be obtained by the 24th Feby, and the destruction of the five vessels, reported by the Commodore, accomplished by the 25th.

I consider such serious embarrassment as rendering doubtful the attainment of what is proposed, and the more so if either Amherstburg or Detroit must previously be reduced. The delay which would be caused by this operation would, I apprehend, render the subsequent and all important attack upon the remote vessels impracticable, from the decay and insecurity of the ice at a later period.

It is allowed that in all great enterprises some risk must be run and something left to fortune. In this instance success depends on a sufficiency of snow and the expeditious assemblage of the force to be employed, and the possibility of obtaining the number of sleighs for conveying it rapidly to the point of attack accompanied by an ample supply of provisions. Should circumstances so far favor you as to permit the whole to move from Burlington or Ancaster by the 12th of Feby, and the snow on the ground at that time be sufficient, there appears a reasonable expectation of accomplishing a part of this important plan, but all depends on its being carried into execution with promptitude, celerity and secresy.... Whilst the enemy continues to concentrate a large disposable force near the frontier of Lower Canada situated between Lakes St. Francois and Champlain, thereby indicating his intention that the pressure of the approaching campaign should fall upon that Province, you must be sensible of my total inability of augmenting your present force. I give you this information that you may regulate your measures accordingly.

January 31 (Monday) **In Canada,** an American detachment operating near the Thames River springs a surprise raid and seizes a small guard detachment in the Delaware area. British Lt. Colonel Baby (assistant quartermaster general) and militia Captain Brigham are among those captured. One of the men, Westbrook, had gone over to the side of the Americans. During the raid, it is Westbrook who burns the buildings down.

In New York, General Amos Hall establishes his headquarters at Williamsville.

February *In naval activity,* the British vessels HMS *Phoebe* and HMS *Cherub* arrive at Valparaiso and blockade the port until they take vengeance on American Captain David Porter and his ship, the *Essex,* which has devastated British whaling ships in the Pacific for more than a year. The British ships close for the kill on March 28. Also, the *Roanoke,* a schooner attached to the Treasury Department, is transferred to the navy during this year, but the exact time is unknown. Details of its service have not survived; however, it is known that it was sold at Wilmington, Delaware, after the war.

In other naval activity, the American privateer *Governor Tompkins* intercepts a whaler on its way to Polynesia in the South Seas. The vessel is seized and transformed into a cartel. Also, the American privateer *Mars,* out of New York is intercepted by a 74-gun British warship and then runs ashore with the British in hot pursuit. Forty of the Americans escape with a large amount of cash but thirty others are seized. The British also rescue 43 English prisoners. Earlier in the war, the *Mars* had seized a brigantine, the *Superb,* and had it taken into port at Charleston. Nonetheless, during this last cruise, it had escaped capture by eluding pursuers eleven times.

In other naval activity, the American privateer *Morgiana* out of New York captures the schooner *Sultan* and a ship, the *City of Limerick.* The cargo considered valuable on the *City of Limerick* is transferred to the *Morgiana,* and afterward the prize is taken into an American port. The *Sultan* is taken to Wilmington, North Carolina. When the *Morgiana* completes its cruise and returns to its home port, the cargo is valued at $250,000.

February 1 (Tuesday) **In Alabama,** elements of the 3rd U.S. Regiment move out on a mission that takes them toward the Old Towns along the Cahaba. They are commanded by Colonel Russell bolstered by Captain Evan Austill and Lt. Creigh, along with a cavalry company under Captain Foster. Captain Samuel Dale also participates. A keel-boat transports the provisions while the column advances. However, the Indians detect the movement, and when the troops arrive at the objective, they discover that the towns are abandoned.

In the meantime, the troops desperately need the provisions, but the keel-boat fails to arrive. A small party of three men under Lt. Wilcox, a regular, volunteer to search for the boat. Misfortune strikes the party when their pirogue overturns and ruins their ammunition. The troops get separated but later they come together. Afterward, Indians spot the raft which the men had used to cross the river. They land and discover Wilcox and his two men. One Indian is quickly taken out by a paddle; however, one of the men, Simpson, is shot and Wilcox is seized. Armar, the other man, goes deeper into the cane, where he is able to observe. Wilcox and Simpson are scalped and left to die. Armar escapes after the Indians depart from the scene.

Meanwhile, the expedition had discovers no enemy, and Russell's command expends its provisions. Captain Dale later states that the force subsisted on "acorns and hickory nuts, rats and mice." Captain Dale and Colonel Russell each buy a horse, which are consumed by the troops to forestall starvation. The command finally makes it back to Fort Claiborne. Captain Dale's old wound sustained at Burnt Corn was also acting up, but a surgeon, Doctor Neal Smith, successfully removes the ball and finally ends his pain.

February 2 (Wednesday) **In New York** at Williamsville, General Amos Hall writes to Governor Tompkins that the militia contingent from his division that was formed into companies had reached the vicinity of Lewiston; however, rather than 1,900 troops, the force stands at only 1,100 men. General Hall's forces "have not been able to discover any late movements of the enemy, but believe a part of their force is gone on a secret expedition." He also speaks of the condition of his troops: "The troops under my command are healthy though badly furnished with camp equipage, there is not a camp kettle, not [a] tin pan to twenty men. I have been anxiously expecting the arrival of those necessary articles for the use of the troops, but have as yet been disappointed."

At British-held Fort Niagara, an American arrives at the post and informs the British that General Amos Hall's force is encamped about seven miles in the rear of Lewiston and the troops are constructing barracks. He also informs the British that American strength at Batavia stands at about 2,000 troops.

In naval activity, the USS *Ferret,* commanded by Lt. C.E. Crowley, encounters turbulence in Stono Inlet while it is en route from Port Royal to Charleston. It becomes grounded and afterward overwhelmed as the unruly surf literally breaks the ship apart. Despite the great peril, the entire crew makes it to shore.

February 3 (Thursday) **In Chile,** after arriving at Valparaiso, a neutral port, Captain David D. Porter directs the commander of the *Essex Jr.*, commanded by Lt. Downes, to lurk outside the port and maintain a vigil for British merchant ships that can be seized; however, Downes is also ordered to send immediate word if he detects any approaching British warships. While the *Essex Jr.* remains on patrol, Captain Porter attends to getting the *Essex* repaired so it can re-embark. Captain Porter goes ashore to pay his respects to the governor, and on the following day, the governor and his wife visit the ship.

February 5 (Saturday) **In Canada** at Kingston, Lt. General Drummond writes to Sir George Prevost that "there are about 1,000 fighting men, about 800 sailors and 300 ship carpenters, at Sackets Harbor at present; that no movement of troops has taken place; that all the sleighs lately collected have been dismissed; that Colonel Smith commands. Three vessels are positively to be built (their dimensions will be known by the next opportunity). It had been generally supposed that Major Forsyth was to have crossed over at or below Cornwall to intercept some of the convoys of stores and render the guns useless. But this place it would appear has been given up for the present." Drummond's P.S. notes that new intelligence has increased the number of troops at Sackets Harbor to 2,000.

In naval activity, the USS *President*, commanded by Commodore Rodgers, following a successful cruise in the West Indies, arrives back in the States. It crashes through the blockade and enters New York harbor.

February 6 (Sunday) **In Alabama,** the 39th U.S. Infantry under Colonel John Williams arrives at Fort Strother. Although the troops who had been with Jackson at the recent battles have been honorably discharged, thousands of other Tennesseans replace them by the end of the month. In East Tennessee, about two thousand troops move toward Jackson, while in West Tennessee at Huntsville, a comparable number of volunteers is also heading toward Alabama. In addition, Jackson is bolstered by Coffee's mounted troops as well as some dragoons from Eastern Tennessee. These troops plus the friendly Choctaw cause his force to swell to approximately 5,000 men with which to mount an offensive against the Creeks and their allies. Although the force is high in number, the supplies are insufficient. Jackson takes steps to gain food, and he directs the troops to construct flat-boats with which to transport the supplies down river. In the meantime, intelligence received from friendly Kialigee Indians stipulates that a large force of Indians is converging on the Tallapoosa River at a point known as Horseshoe Bend. The intelligence also names the tribes that are gathering, which include Creeks (Red Sticks), Fish Ponds, Hillibees, New Yaucas, Ocfuskes and Ufaulas. In the meantime, while Jackson's final plans are being formulated, the Creeks, having gained enormous confidence from the recent battles, continue to fortify their positions at Horseshoe Bend, thanks in great part to the aid of white men from Pensacola, Florida.

In Canada, a small British detachment departs from Cornwall and lands on shore in New York to regain some earlier lost property. It includes one subaltern officer, two sergeants, twenty Royal Marines and ten troops of the Royal Militia (under Captain Kerr), led by Captain Sherwood. The detachment lands during the evening. After midnight (6th-7th), the column moves through the village of Hamilton and advances from there nearly fifteen miles to a spot along the Grass River, where the items had been stored. While en route, Sherwood confiscates all available sleighs and horses with which to transport the goods back to the boats. By 0400, still without any opposition, the British complete the repossession operation and begin the return march to their boats. Once again, the troops pass through Hamilton. They meet no resistance and no property is disturbed. Nevertheless, about twenty of the sleighs are left behind due to the inability to bring them back.

At about 1400 on the 7th, the contingent reaches the boats, and after loading the items, the detachment recrosses the river. Before they embark, some American militia arrives; however, the Royal Marines deal with the militia and compel them to retire, leaving the detachment to complete the loading process and embark without further disruption.

February 7 (Monday) **In Pennsylvania,** at Harrisburg, Governor Simon Snyder orders: "In compliance with a requisition from the President of the United States, I do order into the service of the Union one thousand men, rank and file, of the Pennsylvania Militia, and a competent number of officers, to be composed of the First and Second Brigades of the Seventh Division and of the Second Brigade of the Fifth Division, designated for the service of the United States under General Orders of the 12th of May 1812, to rendezvous at Erie on the 5th day of March, then, or as soon thereafter, to be organized into one regiment and to be officered agreeable to law."

In naval activity, at Valparaiso, Chile, Captain David D. Porter entertains the governor and other prominent citizens on board the *Essex*. Porter, however, remains on the alert in the event a British warship appears. The *Essex Jr.* is anchored near the *Essex*, but positioned from where Lt. Downes' lookouts have a full view of the sea. At about midnight (7th-8th), Lt. Downes returns to his vessel and moves back out beyond the harbor to resume his patrol. Shortly thereafter, Porter gets an urgent message: "Two enemy's ships in sight."

The arrival of the British interrupts the ongoing celebration aboard the *Essex*. Porter focuses on preserving his ships. About one-half of the crew is still on shore and those men are recalled. Porter directs Downes to position his vessel near the *Essex* so they can support each other. Within about an hour and a half, the crews of both American ships are at their respective battle stations. On the morning of the 8th, at 0800, the British warships *Cherub* and *Phoebe*, both frigates, enter the harbor.

The HMS *Phoebe*, commanded by Captain Hillyar, slides in between the *Essex Jr.* and the *Essex* and pulls alongside of the *Essex*. Coincidentally, Porter and Hillyar had become acquaintances at Gibraltar way before the war erupted. Greetings are exchanged; however, the *Phoebe* begins to come even closer, prompting Porter to remind Hillyar that he was not in compliance with the laws of neutrality and underscores his complaint by informing Hillyar that the *Essex* is prepared to commence fire, but only if attacked. Hillyar's response reeks of condescension: "Oh sir, I have no intention of getting on board of you." Porter again cautions Hillyar, stating that if the *Phoebe* does "fall foul of the *Essex*, there would be much blood shed." By this point, Porter is becoming increasingly annoyed by both Hillyar's tone and his cavalier attitude.

At about the same time, the jib boom of the *Phoebe* swings across the forecastle of the *Essex*. Porter's annoyance increases to infuriation. He bellows an order to his boarding party, directing them to board the *Phoebe* at the instant its hull touches the hull of the *Essex*. Captain Porter is acutely aware that the *Phoebe* is poorly positioned and is unable to fire upon either the *Essex* or the

The USS *Essex* engages the HMS *Cherub* and the HMS *Phoebe*.

Essex Jr., while both American ships are poised to rivet the decks of the *Phoebe*. He also realizes that the HMS *Cherub* is too distant to provide any support.

Captain Hillyar is caught totally off guard. Before barging in on the *Essex*, he had been informed by a separate British ship in the port that Porter's crew was unprepared for a fight because Porter was throwing a large party aboard the ship and many of his crew members were celebrating onshore. Nevertheless, it is Hillyar that is unprepared as well as astonished — Americans are their battle stations and the boarding party is armed and anxious to move aboard his ship. Captain Hillyar's sly and cunning scheme, having been foiled, prompts him to vehemently protest, while he repeatedly states that he has no intentions of trying to seize the *Essex*, while exclaiming that the contact with the *Essex* had been accidental.

Porter, to the amazement of the government officials and other citizens of Valparaiso, spares the *Phoebe*. Afterward, the British frigate manages to slip free and move back beyond the range of the guns of the *Essex*. When questioned, Porter maintains that he was duty bound to "respect the neutrality of the port." The British, while maintaining their ruse of peaceful intent while at the neutral port, meet with Porter on the night of the 8th when they call on him at the home of Mr. Blanco, where he is staying while in Valparaiso. In turn, Captain Porter later visits Captain Hillyar.

While the days pass at Valparaiso, the two sides remain friendly but with some taunting. However, Hillyar is under orders to destroy the *Essex* wherever it is discovered, even if it is a neutral port.

Meanwhile, the British even use flags to taunt the Americans. Soon after its arrival, the *Phoebe* hoists a flag which displays the words "God and Country, British Sailors' Best Rights, Traitors Offend Both." That flag receives a response from the *Essex*, which hoists a flag at the masthead: "God, Our Country and Liberty, Tyrants Offend Them." Another nerve-rubbing incident occurs when Captain Hillyar inquires what Porter will do with his prizes and receives the response that at the first opportunity, the prizes would be burned. Hillyar in turn dares Porter to do it when the *Phoebe* is nearby, but Porter, not to be outdone, retorts: "We will see."

In other activity, the enterprising *Enterprise* and *Rattlesnake* continue their exploits and engage the HMS *Rambler*, a brigantine, defeating and capturing the British vessel after a sea battle in the Caribbean. Later in the month, these two daring vessels confront and capture two more British vessels, the letter of marque schooner *Mars* and the *Eliza*. On 25 February, an unidentified British warship is spotted. The *Rattlesnake* and the *Enterprise*, after determining the enemy ship is too strong, separate. The *Enterprise* tosses many of its guns overboard to gain speed and it succeeds in outrunning the British ship. It arrives at Wilmington, North Carolina, on 9 March. Afterward, the *Enterprise* serves off the coast of Charleston for the duration. It remains in service until July 1823, when it gets wrecked on Little Curaçao Island in the West Indies. The crew sustains no casualties. The *Enterprise* had been built during 1799 and served during the Quasi-war with France and the Barbary Coast War. The *Rattlesnake* also arrives back at Wilmington on 9 March. Shortly afterward, the *Rattlesnake* embarks on another cruise. Heading for La Rochell, it encounters a well-armed British transport, the *Mary*, and after an engagement of about 20 minutes, the British strike their colors. The *Mary*'s voyage to England is cut short in the Bay of Biscay, to the delight of about 60 Frenchmen held on board as prisoners. A prize crew sails it into a French port, where the French prisoners debark in their home country. The British sustain three killed, including the captain and three others wounded. The Americans sustain one man wounded, a Marine officer. The *Rattlesnake* also moves into La Rochelle, but its timing is less than impeccable. It evades the British blockade ships. The wounded Marine declines the medical advice to have his leg amputated, which becomes a fatal mistake. He dies within a few weeks. The prize *Mary* is later recaptured by the British.

February 8 (Tuesday) In Canada at Kingston, Lt. General Drummond writes to Sir George Prevost dated this day, informs the governor of the current situation: The letter in part:

> "SIR,— I have the honor to acquaint Your Excellency that I propose setting out to-morrow for the purpose of meeting the Provincial Legislature at York on the 15th instant. From the information I have received from Prescott, and which no doubt has been communicated to Your Excellency from thence, of the movement of the enemy's guns and stores from Salmon River, from the departure of the Newfoundland Regiment from hence, the deficiency of artillerymen and particularly of officers of that corps and the want of the 80th Regiment, which I had expected here, I consider the garrison to be so insufficient for the defence of this place that I have thought it necessary to order the effectives of the 41st Regiment from York without delay. The garrison will be left, as well as the Centre Division, under the command of Major General Stovin, who arrived here on the 6th inst. I regret to report to Your Excellency the great deficiency of forage in this neighborhood, particularly of oats. Although hay is abundant the Deputy Commissary General will not, I am apprehensive, without a recurrence to martial law, be able to procure a supply beyond the month of April. The farmers hold back their stock on hand so very rigidly that, although I am extremely averse to using such means, I believe I shall ultimately be under the necessity of issuing a proclamation to that effect.... I have ordered Major General Riall to organize a small force, consisting of the light companies of the Royals and the 89th Regiment with the Kent Volunteers and a strong body of Indians and push forward to Oxford, and "according to information advance thence to Delaware town or even towards the mouth of the Thames. I hope this force will be able to circumscribe the bounds of the enemy, to collect what supplies the country affords, (which I fear, however, has been well drained already,) and at all events provide for themselves and the Indians with them for a short time...."

In other activity, Sir James Yeo, also at Kingston, writes to Sir George Prevost:

> SIR,— I deferred writing to Your Excellency until I had communicated with General Drummond, who has no doubt made known his sentiments and decision respecting the expedition above. I am also of opinion, and fully aware that the season is not only too far advanced but the enemy's movements on that frontier will not allow the enterprise to be undertaken with reasonable hopes of success. From information obtained thro' two men sent from this yard, I am inclined to believe the enemy have already laid down a forty gun frigate, have the timber and keels cut for another frigate and a brig of 26 guns, the latter is named such on purpose to deceive. One of the men went on to Oswego and reports that they are building a great number of boats at that place, some for gunboats, that they have removed the sails, cables, guns, &c., of the Pike and Madison to Watertown. Under these circumstances I feel it my duty to recommend our building another frigate.... I believe that Your Excellency will agree with me that the more concentrated our force the better. She may be ready by July, when we shall most likely have sufficient seamen to man her; if not I can take the seamen out of the small vessels for so desirable a ship. The *Aeolus*'s guns will exactly answer.

February 12 (Saturday) In Canada, General James Wilkinson at the town of Malone issues the order to break down the camp. He orders General Brown to repair to Sackets Harbor, while he prepares to retire from Canada with the rest of his force and repair to Plattsburgh. Wilkinson also orders that his boats, bateaux and gunboats, all of which are frozen in the ice, to be set afire. All the camp buildings, including barracks and blockhouses, are demolished. During the retreat, Wilkinson, already demoralized by the failure of the campaign, gets no reprieve. A British force, minus the 49th Regiment, which had returned to Montreal in December, harasses Wilkinson's rear guard. The force, commanded by British Colonel Scott, is composed of about 1,100 troops, including a contingent of cavalry (*see also*, **December 7** [1813] **to February 12**).

February 14 (Monday) *In naval activity,* in Chile at Valparaiso, Captain Porter of the *Essex* honors Captain Hillyar's dare to burn one of his prizes in sight of the *Phoebe*. The *Hector*, one of the prizes, is towed out within the range of the guns of the *Phoebe* and the *Cherub* and set on fire. The British act quickly, but still they are unable to cut off the *Essex*, which returns to port unscathed.

February 14–19 The USS *Constitution*, operating in the waters off the West Indies and South America, has a successful voyage when it encounters and defeats the British vessels *Lovely Ann*, *Phoenix* and Brigantine *Catherine*. While off South America near *Surinam*, it captures the *Pictou*, a British sloop of war. The *Constitution* initiated the cruise, following repairs, during the latter part of 1813. The *Constitution* arrives back in New England at Marblehead after evading two British warships, but it does not sail again until December 1814.

February 15 (Tuesday) In Alabama, General Andrew Jackson at Fort Strother is informed by friendly Kialigee Indians that many warriors had formed together at the Tallapoosa near a bend in the river and on a nearby island in the vicinity of Emuckfaw. The friendly chiefs also inform Jackson that they intend to fight "to the last extremity." By this time, General Jackson's force has been rebuilt, and he has also received the 39th U.S. Regiment, providing him with regulars, one of whom is Sam Houston, who holds the rank of ensign. Jackson continues to be plagued with supply problems, due in great part to the atrocious roads in the region that stretch between Fort Strother and Fort Deposit, the latter standing only about 40 miles distant.

Meanwhile, on this day, soldier John Woods is shot by firing squad for insubordination and for attacking an officer. Jackson requires strict discipline to keep his army intact. This incident is used against him during his presidential campaign in 1828. Transporting supplies by wagon from Fort Deposit to Fort Strother takes about one week along the primitive route. Jackson's army at Fort Strother gets the required supplies by about mid–March and, once on the move, the columns arrive at the Creek encampment, about 55 miles distant, on 27 March.

February 16 (Wednesday) In Canada, a party of chiefs en route to Quebec to meet with Sir George Prevost arrive at York (Toronto). Tecumseh's sister and son, along with about twenty-six young warriors, are also with the party. The chiefs of the Western Nations who arrive include Kishkiwabik (Chippewa); Naiwash (Ottawa); Mitass (Saakies); Walisseka (Fox); Kenailounak (Fox); Waikitai (Kickapoo); Pamamai (Delaware); John Gray (Munsey); Wabachkweela or Whitehorse (Munsey); Ounagechtai (Six Nations); Twalwa or Isaac Peters (Six Nations) and Wassasskum (Winibiegoe). Captain Elliot is escorting the Indians; however, Lt. General Drummond provides assistance to support the Indians, and he sends word to General Stovin at Kingston and General De Rottenburg at Montreal to provide as much assistance as they can. Also this day, British Captain W.H. Merritt at Twelve Mile Creek writes to Major General Riall to inform him of the condition of his command, and he requests other duty:

> The state of my troop, and as the system is so very imperfect beg you will recommend it being put on another establishment. Our horses are furnished by the men @ 6d per diem, in consequence of which we have not more than twelve good horses in the troop. As our clothing and appointments have arrived, providing the Government will furnish twenty horses and deduct the sixpence, the troop will be effective in a very short time. I have thirty rank and file, which, if on the same establishment as Capt. Coleman's, (whose men are raised on the same terms and for the same period,) I trust will be of the most essential service the ensuing campaign, as they have a thorough knowledge of the country and their fidelity has been well tried since their first formation.

February 17 (Thursday) In Canada at Quebec, Governor Sir George Prevost writes to Lt. General Drummond regarding several matters, including the chiefs of the Western Nations: "Having no employment at this moment in the Lower Province for the Western Indians, it would be highly impolitic under existing circumstances to place them where you suggest, to the annoyance of the Canadians and to the irritation of the hitherto peaceful American borderers. Experience has taught me that Indians are not a disposable force and far from a manageable one when brought into action. Their cooperation is never to be relied on. From these considerations I am apprehensive they cannot be turned into an enemy's country as a free corps, there to feed themselves, while food is to be obtained. It is therefore proper you should ascertain the correctness of my objections before you adopt any plan for removing them from their present situation."

Prevost also informs Drummond that the force at Batavia and one other converging on Lewiston under General Hall does not seem to pose an immediate threat to the Niagara frontier, "provided our troops are vigilant and that a proper spirit of discipline is cherished among them."

February 18 (Friday) *In naval activity,* the sloop of war USS *Frolic,* launched 11 September 1813, sails from Boston en route to the West Indies.

February 21 (Monday) In Canada, Lt. General Drummond writes to Sir George Prevost to say he arrived at Burlington Heights this day. General Drummond also states: "I have received a report handed to me by Major General Riall of the arrival of the light company of the 89th Regiment with Lieutenant McGregor's Volunteers and some Indians at Tilbury, near the mouth of the River Thames, in consequence of a party of the enemy which had appeared near Chatham driving about 40 or 50 head of cattle, but which had abandoned the cattle and made a precipitate retreat, intelligence of the arrival of Captain Basden's detachment having been communicated to them by a family of the name of Hitchcock. A Captain Rowe of the militia has been taken prisoner, and a Mr. P. Blodget apprehended, on suspicion of acting for the enemy. Twenty-six stands of arms and a thousand rounds of ball-cartridge have fallen into the hands of the pursuers."

Also this day, in another letter to Prevost, General Drummond informs him that eight troops each a foreigner attached to the Royal Scots Regiment at Queenston had deserted and another four troops of the King's Regiment, based at Fort Niagara, had also gone over to the Americans.

February 23 (Wednesday) *In naval activity,* the HMS *Epervier,* a sloop, and the frigate HMS *Junon* capture the American privateer *Alfred,* which has been attacking British shipping since August 1812.

February 24 (Thursday) In New York at Sackets Harbor, Commodore Chauncey writes to the secretary of the Navy: "SIR,— I arrived here yesterday and found the station in excellent order, and everything in a fine state of preparation. Captain Crane is entitled to very great praise for his extraordinary exertions and indefatigable industry in preparing everything for service. The three ships first ordered are in a great state of forwardness; the largest has all her ribs up and the two smaller ones all planked and nearly half caulked, and will be ready to launch before the ice breaks up. My letter to Mr. Eckford did not reach him in time to make the alteration in the two small ships as proposed. They will be the same as the *Peacock,* as you first ordered. The larger one has been increased in the beam two feet. This vessel will be ready to launch about the first of May. The roads are dreadful, and if the present mild weather continues we shall experience difficulty in getting on our stores. I, however, hope for cold weather yet. I will in a day or two transmit to a view of the whole station."

February 25 (Friday) In Canada at Quebec, Sir George Prevost responds to a recent secret letter from Lt. General Drummond:

> The Military Secretary has laid before me your confidential letter of the 14th inst., containing information of the enemy's movements in the neighborhood of the River Thames, where it is reported that Lt. Colonel Baby, Captain Brigham and Springer, with a detachment of militia, have been made prisoners. I should wish that the Indians attached to the Right Division may be thrown forward, supported by militia and light troops, to check the excursions of the enemy in that direction and to re-occupy the ground recently lost. The report you have received of the disposition of the enemy's naval forces on Lake Erie has appeared to me important and satisfactory, proving, however, that the previous intelligence of the situation of those vessels was incorrect. I confidently trust that such precautionary measures may be adopted by our troops on the Niagara frontier as will prevent the advance of the enemy by that line of communication, and I recommend a peaceable disposition being promoted in the inhabitants of the neighborhood of Buffalo as best calculated to appease the wrath of the more violent characters amongst them, and to frustrate any attempt to carry into execution the threats to burn and destroy. I enclose for your information the copy of some secret and valuable intelligence which has just reached me, showing that if another campaign takes place the energies of the enemy will be displayed on Lakes Ontario and Champlain.

February 28 (Monday) In Washington, D.C., Secretary of War John Armstrong writes to Major General Jacob Brown:

> It is obviously Prevost's policy and probably his intent to reestablish himself on Lake Erie during the ensuing month. But to effect this, other points of his line must first be weakened, and these will be either Kingston or Montreal. If the detachment from the former be great, a moment may occur in which you may do, with the aid of Commodore Chauncey, what I last year intended Pike should have done without aid, and what we now all know was very practicable, viz.: to cross the river or head of the lake on the ice and carry Kingston by a *coup de*

main. This is not, however, to be attempted but under a combination of the following circumstances: practicable roads, good weather, large detachments (made westerly) on the part of the enemy, and a full and hearty co-operation on the part of our own naval commander. If the enterprise be agreed upon, use the enclosed letter (No. 2) to mask your object, and let no one into your secret but Chauncey.

The second letter states:

Sir,— Colonel Scott, who is in nomination as a brigadier, has orders to repair to the Niagara frontier, and to take with him a corps of artillerists and a battering and a field train, &c.; Major Wood of the engineers, and Dallaba of the ordnance will accompany or follow him. Four hundred Indians and about four thousand volunteer militia are under similar orders. The truth is that public opinion will no longer tolerate us in permitting the enemy to keep quiet possession of Fort Niagara. Another motive is the effect which may be expected from the appearance of a large corps on the Niagara in restraining the enemy's enterprises westward of that place. But will a corps so constituted be able to reduce Niagara or long impose on an enemy as well informed as itself? This is not to be expected — whence it follows that the President orders you to assemble means for conveying, with the least possible delay, the brigade you brought from French Mills to Batavia, where other and more detailed orders await you. Our advices from M[ontreal] state that large detachments are under orders for K[ingston] westwardly, and that no intention exists of attacking the harbor. Should, however, new movements from M[ontreal] indicate a different design, they will be promptly known to General [Wilkinson], and will produce a counter movement.

In Canada at Kingston, Commodore James Yeo writes to Sir George Prevost:

Dear Sir,— I had the honor of Your Excellency's note with the agreeable intelligence of 200 seamen being on their way. From the information obtained thro' the Qr. Master-General, I am decidedly of opinion that the enemy will use every exertion to establish a formidable force on Lakes Ontario and Champlain. It is the only measure at this moment likely to be popular in America. I pledge myself to Your Excellency that every exertion of my mind and body shall be devoted to defeat the enemy's views, and that the force entrusted to my command never shall surrender to the enemy while I have life. I feel persuaded at the same time that Your Excellency will agree with me, that to ensure such an important object as the naval superiority on the lakes, as little ought to be left to chance as possible. I therefore request Your Excellency will urge the Commander-in-Chief or Admiral at Halifax to forward the sails, rigging and cables with all possible despatch.

Also, Prevost writes to Lt. General Drummond: "As it is possible our naval ascendency on Lake Ontario may only have a short duration, the Federalists and Democrats agreeing cordially on the propriety of the exertions or the American government to preserve their superiority on the lakes, it becomes doubly necessary that you should resort to every practicable expedient for procuring provisions."

In naval activity, the HMS *Epervier* intercepts and seizes the privateer *Alfred* (P. Bessom, master), a brigantine carrying 94 men and 16 guns. The *Alfred* had been operating out of Salem.

Late February **In Canada,** an American contingent of 160 troops nder Captain Jeremiah Holmes, transporting two 6-pounders, advances to attack Fort Talbot about 100 miles from Detroit along the north shore of Lake Erie. Upon their arrival, they determine the British post is too fortified. The assault is aborted; however, later on 3 March, the Americans engage a superior force near the Thames River at the Longwoods. The skirmish erupts about dusk and continues for about one hour until both sides withdraw. The Americans sustain seven killed and wounded. British casualties are unknown.

March The Allied Armies capture Paris, France, signaling the end of Napoleon's reign. He abdicates the throne the next month. Also, the British squadron under Admiral George Cockburn reinitiates its raids along the lower part of the Chesapeake. At this time, Cockburn's squadron is composed of one 74-gun ship of the line, two frigates, one brigantine and one schooner. However, the squadron continues to receive additional vessels. The Marylanders pull together to meet the constant threats, but Admiral Cockburn is cunning, his strategy is solid and his movement with regard to selection of targets is difficult to predict. He is also quick to order a village or town burned if the citizenry fails to quickly submit; however, for those who acquiesce, the towns usually escape destruction.

As the number of farmers and merchants who lose their livelihoods increases dramatically, the people's cries for American naval support become incessant. All during this period, men are absent from their work due to their service in the militia, which leaves farms unattended. And with no naval force to neutralize the British, they continue to strike at will. Meanwhile, Commodore Joshua Barney, authorized during the previous year to raise a naval force, is nearly prepared. The next month, Barney is ready to sail, having acquired 26 barges and gunboats, along with about 900 men and a hearty band of shipmasters from Baltimore. In late May, Barney moves down the Chesapeake to regain Tangier Island, which the British have turned into a Negro encampment.

In naval activity, the American privateer *Governor Tompkins* seizes the *Henry*, a brigantine. The *Governor Tompkins* also ventures into the English Channel, where it captures ten vessels. During its career in the war, the privateer seizes a total of 20 vessels. Also, the 5-gun schooner *Hawk* (Captain W.H. Trippe) a privateer out of Wilmington, North Carolina, embarks on its first cruise, during which it seizes its only prize, the schooner *Phoebe*. The prize and its cargo of molasses and rum are sent into port at Wilmington.

March 1 (Tuesday) **In Canada** at Quebec, Military Secretary Noah Freer informs General Drummond by letter dated this day that Chief John Norton has been "commissioned as captain and leader of the Five Nations, Grand River Indians or Confederates." The letter also informs Drummond that Sir George Prevost has requested

> that no interference may be allowed from the officers of the Indian Department between these tribes and Captain Norton, and all communications to those tribes are to be made through the medium of Captain Norton. That Captain Norton may have it in his power to reward the faithful services of the warriors acting with him, and also to give countenance to the leading war chiefs who assist in preserving good order in the Five Nations[;] it is His Excellency's desire that an ample proportion of presents be put up separately for the Indians of the Five Nations, to be distributed under Captain Norton's directions.

March 3–4 **In Canada** near Longwood (Longwoods), a British ranger contingent, commanded by Captain Caldwell, encounters an American contingent on the night of the 3rd. British reinforcements (flank companies of the Royals and the British 89th Regiment) reach the scene at about 1700 on the 4th. The British discover that the Americans hold high ground, and their position is bolstered by breastworks of logs. Nevertheless, the British launch an assault which strikes at the left and right flanks in support of a direct assault against the front. Rangers and Kent Militia plow against the right. Indians assault the left, while the front is hammered by the Royals and the 89th Regiment. The Americans are pounded time and time again; however, the British on the flanks fail to gain the rear, and the front line staggers the attackers. The failure to penetrate compels the British to abort the attack and retire. During the heated engagement, every British officer, except Ensign Mills (89th Regiment) is either killed or wounded.

On 5 March, Lt. General Drummond informs Sir George Prevost of the skirmish: "I regret that our loss is very considerable." Drummond includes a detailed list of the casualties provided by Ensign Mills for each unit engaged:

> Royal Scots Light Company, one captain, nine rank and file killed; one lieutenant, 3 sergeants, 31 rank and file wounded; one bugler missing; 89th Light Company, one lieutenant, three rank and file killed; one captain, one sergeant and seven rank and file wounded and Volunteer Pigot wounded and taken prisoner; Loyal Kent Volunteers, one lieutenant, one sergeant and five rank and file wounded. Names of officers killed and wounded: Captain D. Johnston, Royal Scots, killed; Lieut. P. Oraeme, 89th Regt., killed; Captain Basden, 89th Regt., wounded and Lieut. A. Macdonald, Royal Scots, wounded.

March 4 (Friday) **In Canada,** at Kingston, an American sailor attached to the USS *Lady of the Lake*, having deserted, arrives at Kingston and delivers classified information regarding the plans for the upcoming naval offensive. Also, Colonel Matthew Elliott, at Delaware (Upper Canada) writes to Lt. Colonel Stewart regarding a conference he held with allied Indians: "Sir,— I have this day had a meeting with the Indians on the subject of carrying ammunition to their friends within the American territory. The result is that they refuse to proceed with the ammunition on the ground that our regular troops do not advance further than the settlements on the River Thames, and of course would be of no use in protecting their friends in the enemy's country. The Americans might hear of these supplies being sent to the Indians, and the consequence would be fatal, perhaps, to their whole tribes. They would, therefore, rather suffer for want of ammunition than endanger themselves or their families."

In other activity, an American contingent of about 160 rangers and mounted infantry under Captain Holmes (24th U.S. Infantry) skirmish with a British contingent of the Royal Scots and the British 89th Regiment at the De French River about 100 miles from Detroit. The British initiate the attack; however, Holmes' command holds extremely formidable positions that ensures the British will sustain heavy losses. The Americans prevail and inflict high casualties on the British, who end up with 84 either killed or wounded. The Americans sustain four killed and four wounded. According to intelligence gained from prisoners, the British contingent of about 256 troops was moving cattle toward either Burlington or Long Point.

In New York at Sackets Harbor, Commodore Chauncey, aboard the USS *General Pike*, writes to Secretary of the Navy William Jones regarding difficulties in receiving guns:

> I have the mortification to inform you that I have this moment received information that all our heavy guns are stopped at and below Poughkeepsie, in consequence of the badness of the roads, and that the teamsters have abandoned them there. I have wrote to the navy agent at New York upon the subject, and I have also directed Mr. Anderson to proceed immediately to the place where the guns are stopped, and send them to Albany, either by land or water. I presume that the latter will be the most preferable mode, as in all probability the North River will be completely open in ten days. If these guns should not arrive in Albany before the 20th of this month, I shall direct them to be sent up the Mohawk to Oswego, where I will have boats to receive them. By this route I can calculate on receiving all the guns by the first week in May. If they come by land, no calculation can be made when they can be delivered here.

In naval activity, the American privateer *Viper*, which left Charleston on 28 February, arrives at New Bedford, Massachusetts. During its short cruise, it seizes three prizes, the 10-gun British ship *Victory*, en route to Liverpool, England, from Jamaica with castor oil, coffee, cotton, indigo, white lead and logwood. The other prizes are the schooner *Nelson*, transporting a cargo of rum when it sailed from St. Thomas, and a Spanish schooner, the *Rosa*, carrying sugar and sailing under a British license when it left Bermuda. The *Viper* sends the trio into American ports, and upon its return, it is holding 14 prisoners.

March 4–5 The USS *Adams*, a sloop patrolling the waters in the vicinity of Africa and the West Indies, encounters the HMS *Nayntine Fairy*. The Marines and sailors on board the *Adams* seize the British vessel. The *Adams* consequently takes successful actions against the British vessels *Roebuck* and *Woodbridge*, capturing both.

March 5 (Saturday) **In Canada,** Commodore James Yeo writes to Admiral Sir John Boriase Warren, commander-in-chief of the North American Station, about an American deserter who arrived at Kingston the day before with intelligence about preparations at Sackets Harbor for an offensive:

> I have the honor to enclose for your information a copy of the deserter's deposition and a comparative statement of the two squadrons as they are likely to meet in battle. You will regret with me that the enemy's preparations are so great, and yet so short a time back as the 20th January not a keel was laid at Sackets Harbor. Now they have 400 shipwrights and two of their new ships nearly ready for launching, and a third will be ready by the 1st of May and a fourth by the end of that month. The roads from Albany, Boston and New York are covered with ordnance and stores for these vessels, and which when added to their old squadron will be far superior to anything I can bring against them. It therefore becomes my duty to acquaint you that unless I receive *immediate* reinforcements of guns, long 24 and 32 pounders, men and stores of every description, Upper Canada will, in my opinion, be lost to His Majesty. In the meantime I shall use every exertion to collect the shipwrights in this country and build (if possible) to be on something like equal terms with the enemy, altho' their resources are so much nearer to them than ours are to us that if they exert themselves it will be *impossible* for us to get an equal force. You, however, may rely that this squadron will do all in its power to uphold the honor of the British flag, nor shall it ever be surrendered to the enemy under any circumstances whatever.

In England, Earl (Henry) Bathurst writes from Downing Street to Sir George Prevost: "His Royal highness entirely approves of your having retaliated all the inhabitants of the United States the harsh measures which the American government had adopted with respect to that part of the Canadas which had been in their temporary occupation. You will not fail to inflict a similar retaliation whenever the conduct of the enemy will render it necessary. It is, however, the anxious wish of His Royal Highness that the example which has so properly been made of the destruction of Lewiston, Black Rock and Buffalo, may be sufficient to deter the enemy from the repetition of outrage so much at variance with the practice of war as carried on between civilized nations, for nothing can be more painful to His Royal Highness than to be under the necessity of extending inhabitants the aggravated miseries to which such a system, if persevered in on the part of the enemy, must infallibly give rise to."

Another letter from Bathurst to Prevost written this day mentions reinforcements requested by Prevost: "I am happy to have it in my power to acquaint you that the expectation which I held out to you in my dispatch of 10th August, of placing at your disposal four regiments by the spring of this year, is on the point of fulfillment."

In naval activity, the HMS *Prometheus* encounters an American privateer, the *Lizard* (B. Cook, master), operating out of Salem. The privateer is a 60-ton schooner carrying two guns and 32 men. It is captured.

March 7 (Monday) **In Michigan** at Detroit, Lt. Colonel H. Butler writes to General Harrison with details of a recent engagement against a British contingent:

> DEAR SIR,—By Lieut. Shannon of the U.S. Infantry I have the honor of informing you that a detachment of troops under my command, led by Captain Holmes of the 24th U.S. Infantry, has obtained a signal victory over the enemy. The affair took place on the 4th inst., about a hundred miles from here, on the River La Tranche. Our force consisted of not more than 160 rangers and mounted infantry. The enemy, from their own acknowledgment, had about 240. The fine light company of Scots Greys is totally destroyed; they led the attack most gallantly, and their commander fell within ten paces of our front line. The light company of the 89th has also suffered severely, one officer of the company fell, one is a prisoner, and another said to be badly wounded. In killed, wounded and prisoners the enemy lost about eighty whilst on our part there was but four killed and four wounded. The great disparity in the loss on each side is to be attributed to the very judicious position occupied by Captain Holmes, who compelled the enemy to attack him at a great disadvantage. This, even more than his gallantry, merits the laurel. Captain Holmes has just returned and will furnish a detailed account of the expedition, which shall be immediately transmitted to you. Enemy's forces as stated by prisoners: Royal Scots—101; 89th Regt—45; Militia—50 and Indians—40 to 60.

March 8 (Tuesday) **In Canada,** Lt. John Le Breton at Delaware (Upper Canada) writes to Captain C. Foster, military secretary to Lt. General Drummond:

> DEAR SIR,—As the report of our unfortunate and truly lamentable expedition has reached the general you are no doubt acquainted with the circumstances, I shall therefore forbear making any comments and only send you a sketch of the ground as nearly as I could take it on the spot. The American enclosure is only a brushwood fence with an abattis on the outside to prevent a charge, no defence in front but almost inaccessible except by the road. I regret very much not being authorized to raise a company. Since I am here I might have got several men. McGregor's company are dissatisfied with him and are about leaving him. Three of them have engaged in Coleman's dragoons and the remainder wish to join Caldwell's Rangers. I have seen several persons from the River Thames and Amherstburg, who all say that the inhabitants are anxiously expecting and a great many ready to join us. The Wyandots or Huron Indians are also at the back of the lake settlement anxiously expecting us. However, I fear our expedition to westward is now completely frustrated. In consequence of Colonel

Elliott being sick and the want of Indian chiefs the Indians who came up latterly are all returned back to the head of Lake Ontario. A man arrived from the River Thames today says that 500 Americans had crossed from Detroit to come to the assistance of those engaged on the 4th inst. I have learned that the first party came out with the intention of going to Port Talbot. They have brought with them 3 field pieces which they were obliged to leave at the Round O.

In Pennsylvania, Governor Simon Snyder, at Harrisburg, issues general orders which are sent to Colonel James Fenton:

> The detachment of one thousand men, Pennsylvania Militia of which you are constituted and appointed colonel commandant, having arrived, or the major part of it, at Erie, the place of general rendezvous, you will, as soon as practicable, organize (and any that may subsequently to a commencement of an organization arrive,) into one regiment, to consist of two battalions, and each battalion to consist of five companies. The officer in command is to be a lieutenant colonel. Each battalion is to be commanded by a major. Each company is to be officered as follows: One captain, one first lieutenant, one second lieutenant, one ensign, four sergeants and four corporals, and each company is to consist of one hundred men, rank and file. The officers to rank and be constituted and appointed according to law. As soon as you shall have organized the regiment as commanded you will report yourself and the number of men under your command to the nearest general officer commanding for the United States, and you are ordered and commanded to yield complete obedience to any orders issued by your superior officer in command at Erie or elsewhere for the United States.

March 9 (Wednesday) In U.S. Army activity, Colonel Daniel Bissell is promoted to brigadier general.

March 10 (Thursday) **In Canada,** General Riall details his situation on the Niagara frontier in a letter to General Drummond dated this day:

> SIR,—As the season for active operations is now advancing, and from the preparations and appearance of the enemy it is probable that an attempt may be made on this frontier, it is time that I should give confidential instructions to the officers in command of the different posts for their conduct in case of attack, but in order that my measures may be subordinate to your general intentions, I have thought it advisable previously to make a communication to you on this subject, and to request that you will be pleased to give me such information of your general plan of defence as may be necessary for my guidance in this respect. As my position is assailable in its front and on both flanks, I have to request that you will favor me with your directions for the line of conduct I should adopt in case of attack upon any of those points, referring more particularly to the right, where there is a possibility the enemy by effecting a landing at Long Point or its vicinity or by advancing along the western road may get into my rear and consequently cut off communication with you. I feel it my duty to represent to you that it is decidedly my opinion that the very small disposable force on this line is not by any means adequate to its defence in front, and to meet the probable movement of the enemy upon its flanks, and that unless I receive a good and sufficient reinforcement the situation of this division of the army may become extremely critical.

March 12 (Saturday) *In naval activity,* the USS *Peacock* leaves New York en route to deliver supplies to the naval station at St. Mary's, Georgia. Afterward, the *Peacock* goes on patrol off the Florida coast.

March 13 (Sunday) *In naval activity,* the American privateer *David Porter*, more or less stuck at La Teste, France, since late January, is anxious to get out of port. Nevertheless, the weather remains inclement and the Americans are quite concerned that a British squadron will arrive before they can sail. The minutes begin to pass as if they are hours, and although the time of departure is finally set for 1700, the pilot becomes nervous. He is fearful that once the ship leaves the harbor he will not be sent back to shore, and he does not want to be compelled to leave his family to go to the United States.

Captain George Coggeshall repeatedly tries to persuade the pilot to get the privateer out of the harbor. He even promises the pilot that he would remain in the area for an extra week to guarantee he would be landed and repatriated with his family. Still, the pilot is too fearful to agree. Coggeshall, aware that his pleas, including paying triple the pilot's fee, are in vain, tries another tactic to get his ship out of the harbor. In his next conversation Coggeshall states: "If you will not go to sea, just get the schooner underway and go down below the fort and anchor there within the bar." Surprisingly, the pilot agrees, and when the *David Porter* arrives at the designated spot, it is the pilot who receives a surprise.

Coggeshall, unwilling to risk getting nabbed by the British if the ship does not pass the bar, puts the barrel of a loaded pistol against the pilot's head. He tells the pilot that if he does not get the ship over the bar, he will be shot. The pilot is also warned that if he grounds the schooner, the results would be the same. The departure goes smoothly and the pilot is relieved that his life is spared. Captain Coggeshall had only intended to get his ship out of harm's way; the pilot was not in real danger of being shot.

During the morning of the 14th, according to Captain Coggeshall's account: "At eight o'clock in the morning, my second officer, with four men, took Mr. Pilot on shore. I gave the officer of the boat positive orders to back the boat stern oil to the shore, and let the pilot jump out whenever he could do so with safety. I took a spy-glass, and had the pleasure to see the man land, and scamper up the beach. The boat soon returned, and was hoisted on board, when we made sail and stood off in a N. W. direction." The *David Porter*, however, remains vulnerable to the British warships.

March 14 (Monday) **In New York** at British-held Fort Niagara, Colonel Robert Young writes to Major General Riall: "MY DEAR SIR,—Two steady well behaved grenadiers deserted last night. I am grieved and desponding at the circumstances and absolutely ashamed of the corps. I am, alas, too well persuaded that many more will go. The balances they are receiving will, I fear, have a great influence with them and yet the money has been so long due them that it was impossible, and at any rate highly impolitic to have withheld it upon any pretext whatever. There is yet a great deal of arrears due the men and when it shall be paid I am confident I shall have more desertions. I am puzzled how to act and what to think of the cursed scheming and general dissatisfaction which prevails in the regiment."

March 15 (Tuesday) **In Canada,** Lt. General Drummond writes from York to Sir George Prevost with details on a number of problems that are hindering progress:

> SIR,—I have the honor to transmit the copy of a letter from Captain Stewart of the Royal Scots light company to Major General Riall, whereby Your Excellency will perceive that much dependence cannot be placed on our Indian allies' co-operation. Major General Riall has reported to me that the enemy have lately shewn themselves in strong parties along the Niagara line and have been heard at work frequently at night at Lewiston Heights. The major general, under the supposition that he would have full employment for all the effectives of the Right Division the ensuing campaign and that his force will become more effective by the acquisition of the greater part of the garrison of Fort Niagara, has suggested the idea of destroying that fort with the exception of the north eastern square tower or stone building and the rampart on the land side, which should be continued to the river and well picketted as a cover to the communication to the tower. The weather has been so excessively severe on the Niagara frontier lately that it has been impossible to proceed with any of the works at Queenston and Mississauga Point. I am sorry to report to Your Excellency that sickness is prevalent in the King's Regiment, principally ague and dysentery, and the senior medical officer of the regiment recommends their immediate removal from Niagara.

General Drummond also informs Prevost that the supply of salt is dangerously low and the "fresh meat has nearly failed altogether."

March 15–16 *In naval activity,* the American privateer *David Porter*, having recently sailed from La Teste, France, to avoid being trapped by a British squadron, finds itself in a new precarious position when a British warship is spotted on the 15th. Captain Coggeshall becomes concerned; however, he expects to be able to outmaneuver and outsail the enemy pursuer. Unexpectedly, the British warship had apparently become familiar with the privateer's maneuvers, used often by other privateers, and remains on a course that permits it to gain steadily on the privateer. The Americans realize that in short order, the warship will be upon them. In a hastily called meeting, Captain Coggeshall proclaims to his officer that the only good option would be to run the gauntlet and receive the British fire as they speed past it in the attempt to catch the wind and escape or face capture.

The officers are also informed that British broadsides could disable the ship. In a flash, the crew runs up the square sail and catches the British off guard. They become stunned as the *David Porter* defies the odds and passes their frigate as if gliding with the wind. By the time the British rebound, the *David Porter* has gained about one mile. Meanwhile, Captain Coggeshall tries to gain an insurmountable lead. He directs the crew to use the water in most of the casks to wet down the sails to enable them to hold the wind. He also orders the sand ballast to be thrown overboard. The work succeeds and the *David Porter* bolts far ahead of the frigate.

By about 1600, the frigate is barely in view. Nevertheless, different danger jeopardizes the ship. In the confusing maneuvers to outrun the British, only two untouched casks of water remain instead of the four that Coggeshall had ordered to be held in full. And by throwing ballast overboard, too much had been tossed, which is further jeopardizing the vessel. The situation is becoming grave. The only food aboard for the crew of 35 men is a small amount of bread. The night passes slowly and the crew remains uncertain what the following day will bring.

On the morning of the 16th, only a few loaves of bread for breakfast is less than exciting. But the winds are favorable and before long the day grows more promising. At about dawn the lookouts spot several sail, presenting a full lunch for the crew. The ships are merchantmen, and to the beleaguered crew, it is as if the convoy had been sent to them in response to prayers devoutly said on the previous night. Suddenly, the crew disregards its lack of food and swings into action.

The *David Porter* moves alongside a brigantine and seizes it. The prisoners inform Captain Coggeshall that the several vessels had been with a convoy en route to St. Sebastian, Spain, with provisions and supplies for the British army fighting the French on the Spanish peninsula. Under the circumstances, the cargo of provisions are much more needed than the vessel. Captain Coggeshall convinces the captain of the vessel to use his crew to transfer the cargo to the *David Porter* in exchange for retaining his vessel.

With both crews handling the transfer, the cargo is aboard the privateer in about two hours. Meanwhile, the British captain, still preoccupied with watching his cargo vanish, finds some solace in maintaining his brigantine and avoiding becoming a prisoner. The Americans, having eliminated the possibility of famine, are again vibrant and in good humor. The British captain requests that Captain Coggeshall give him the brigantine and the cargo not seized that he could place it in his private account. Coggeshall agrees and presents the captain with a certificate stating that the ship had become an American prize and that it was voluntarily given to him as a present.

After a small break to dine on their recently acquired provisions, the crew of the *David Porter* begins to chase the other merchant ships of the convoy, which are breaking in every direction. Within a short time, due to the winds, the escapees are unable to outrun the privateer. The Americans quickly capture two brigantines and one ship. All three of the captured vessels receive an identical offer from the Americans and each of them agree, deciding that losing a cargo to save their ship and avoid becoming prisoners was worthwhile.

The British, after assisting in transferring the respective cargoes, are released, while the *David Porter* is beginning to bulge because of the amount of goods it has seized. Most of the items seized are related to the military, and they include uniforms, hats and small arms. During the operation to transfer the cargoes, the weather begins to deteriorate and suddenly the rain begins to pelt the men.

By about 1700, a British warship is spotted and Captain Coggeshall identifies it as the ship which had chased him earlier. The *David Porter* begins to maneuver between the merchant ships, and he instructs them to light their lanterns. They follow the instructions without realizing the warship is in view. In the meantime, all lights on the privateer are doused, while the Americans prepare to abscond. Using the darkness to his advantage, Captain Coggeshall slips away without incident and afterward the crew enjoys a feast. The merchant ships, however, soon become recipients of British fire from the frigate, which concentrates its guns on the burning lanterns.

March 16 (Wednesday) **In Alabama,** General Andrew Jackson prepares for his attack against the Creeks. A contingent of about 450 troops under Colonel Steele stays behind to garrison Fort Strother, while the army advances toward Horseshoe Bend on the Tallapoosa. In the meantime, Jackson had sent his supplies on flat boats, under the protection of the U.S. 39th Regiment, down the Coosa River. After five tedious days of marching through rough terrain, General Jackson reaches the mouth of Cedar Creek. While there, he orders the construction of Fort Williams, which is named in honor of the commander of the 39th U.S. Infantry.

March 17 (Thursday) **In New York** at British-held Fort Niagara, Colonel Robert Young again writes to Major General Riall to inform him of the dreadful situation at the post:

> My Dear Sir,—I am heartbroken at the general spirit of defection which has evinced itself in the regiment. I cannot divine the cause. I have indirectly employed agents to discover the source of grievance and complaint, and the full result of my inquiries are that they have incessant fatigues independent of their military duties and no comforts of any kind. In fact the men seem generally dissatisfied, and that spirit once disseminated amongst them not all the exertions and rhetoric of the officers can counterbalance. I feel my personal situation with respect to the regiment more humiliating than I have language to express. The regiment has lost its wonted character, and the more mortifying circumstance to me is that the very best men in the corps have evinced the greatest disposition to desert. I am not myself. I do not know what to say upon the occasion. I am chagrined and desponding and can only most conscientiously aver that I am ashamed and feel disgraced by associating my name with what I formerly and *proudly* designated the King's Regiment. In the name of God remove us as unworthy of retaining the Post of Honour. My confidence in the regiment is now gone, and its villainous conduct will bring my grey hairs with sorrow to the grave. It is hard, nay cruel, that after more than twenty-two years service in the regt. I should live to witness the disgrace which has been brought upon it. In despair I remain.

On this day, General Riall contacts General Drummond regarding Young's message:

> Sir,—I am extremely sorry to have to report to you again the very alarming height to which desertion from the King's Regiment in Fort Niagara has arrived, it having lost nine men in the last five days. From the report made to me by the officer commanding that regiment a spirit of discontent and inclination to desert so plainly appears to have engrafted itself in it that I have determined to withdraw it from that garrison and have accordingly ordered the 100th Regiment to be in readiness to relieve it. I am decidedly of opinion that it will be the most expedient measure to abandon the place altogether and destroy it.

In naval activity, there is a sea battle between the USS *Frolic,* a sloop, and the British brigantine *Little Fox.* At battle's end the *Little Fox* is vanquished by the Yankee vessel *Frolic* and seized.

March 18 (Friday) *In naval activity,* the American privateer *David Porter,* having during this cruise escaped capture several times, is again the target of the British. Two warships, a brigantine and a frigate, spot it and initiate pursuit. Once again, the privateer outsails his pursuers and Captain Coggeshall decides to pause at a small island off the west coast of France not too far from St. Gilles.

March 20 (Sunday) *In naval activity,* the USS *Erie,* initially launched at Baltimore in November, embarks his day on a cruise. A British blockading squadron off Hampton Roads prevents the *Erie* from reaching the open sea. Consequently, its commander sails the ship back to Baltimore on 7 April 1814 and remains in port until early January 1815. After the war, the *Erie* leaves Baltimore and sails to Boston to join Commodore Bainbridge's squadron heading for the Mediterranean to deal with the Barbary pirates. Nonetheless, by the time the squadron reaches Algiers, the problem had already been solved by Commodore Stephen Decatur. The USS *Erie* remains in service until 1850.

March 21 (Monday) **In Canada,** the Americans, having controlled Malden since British General Henry Proctor abandoned it in September, depart from there and return to the United States.

March 22 (Tuesday) **In Canada** at Kingston, Lt. General Drummond tells Sir George Prevost in a letter that Commodore Yeo "asserts he cannot possibly carry on the duty of the Naval Department on the opening of navigation with a less number of Royal Marines than 350; and to fill up vacancies arising from every description of casualty he conceives it absolutely necessary that the entire battalion should be upon the spot at Kingston for that purpose."

Also, a Canadian resident of York, Robert Christie, in the United States since spring April 1812, makes it back to Canada this day. He provides the government with information summarized as follows:

> He lives at York. Left it in April 1812, to see his father and mother, who reside near Philadelphia, where he has been not having it in his power to return till six weeks ago, when he came to Sackets Harbor as a ship carpenter. He left Sackets Harbor the night before last, not having it in his power to make his escape sooner. Says there are two brigs building at Sackets. He expects they are calculated to carry 24 guns each. They are planked up to the bends but not calked and no part of the deck laid. The large ship building on the point he calculates is to carry 48 guns; says it is planked up to the bends, but, same as the brigs, not calked and no part of the deck laid. He heard Commodore Chauncey say the other night, (last Saturday,) to Captain Crane that they must give the large ship up as they had not sufficient water to launch it. They had tried by making sufficient holes in the ice, and could only find about eleven feet water. They have only got thirteen guns. There are some about eight miles off, cannot say how many. The whole of the rigging has arrived at Sackets. Eleven hundred and sixty seamen at Sackets. He saw the troops march from Sackets on Monday week last, said to be 4,000, under the command of two generals, toward Niagara. Says there are about 1,600 men at Sackets.

March 23 (Wednesday) *In naval activity,* the 190-ton brigantine *San Joaquin* (Jose R. De Torres) encounters a strong British squadron composed of the HMS *Albion,* HMS *Armide,* HMS *Dragon,* HMS *Jaseur,* HMS *Lacedonian* and the HMS *St. Lawrence.* The *San Joaquin*'s voyage is terminated and it becomes a British prize.

March 24 (Thursday) **In Washington, D.C.,** Congress authorizes the president to increase the U.S. debt and directs the borrowing of $25,000,000 to continue the war against Great Britain. The costs are great across the ocean as well. The timely acts of the U.S. Navy and privateers have damaged the British merchants considerably, and their losses in captured vessels has them pressing for Britain to cease hostilities.

In Alabama, at Fort Williams, General Andrew Jackson, after leaving a contingent to garrison the post, departs from the fort with his army of about 2,000 troops. The column pushes across a rugged ridge lying between the Cossa and Tallapossa Rivers and arrives close to where the Creeks established their stronghold at the Horseshoe Bend (Cholocco Litabixee) within three days.

In naval activity, the American privateer *David Porter,* at the island of Ille d'Yeu off the coast of France for about one week, is directed by Captain Coggeshall to return to the United States; however, he is remains in France. The ship sails under the command of his first and second officers, Samuel Nichols and Charles Coggeshall (Captain George Coggeshall's brother), respectively. During the return cruise, the *David Porter* racks up several more prizes. It arrives safely back at Gloucester, Massachusetts, and soon moves to Boston, where it is sold for $10,000. The *David Porter,* afterward commanded by Captain J. Fish, embarks on a new cruise during the summer of 1814 and remains at sea until September 1814.

March 25 (Friday) **In Canada,** British Colonel Elliott writes to the deputy superintendent general of Indian affairs. The letter is dated "Beach 25 March," and states:

> Two young men of the Potawamy nation arrived here last night from Maipock. They state that the Indians in that quarter are sitting on their war club waiting to take it up when an opportunity may offer, also that we may as soon as the weather gets warm expect many of the young men to join us and get ammunition, also that the Americans tell them that they intend to attack us by the way of Long Point as soon as the navigation opens, and that the Hurons, Delawares and Shawanese are to accompany them. Should this prove true these nations can send five or six hundred men and leave sufficient with their women and children. I shall send to the other nations to avert if possible this evil. The Heights appear to be their object.

Another letter, from British Lt. Colonel R.H. Bruyeres to Sir George Prevost, gives Bruyeres' opinion, solicited by Prevost, regarding General Riall's proposal to destroy some of Fort Niagara:

> I very respectfully beg leave to submit to Your Excellency that I am of opinion that any partial destruction of this fort would render the position totally untenable and could not be maintained with so small a number of men as proposed, particularly when it is considered that the work alone required for the security of this blockhouse is far beyond the means you can have to execute it in the presence of the enemy. Should it therefore be judged expedient and indispensable to reduce the present strength of that garrison for the purpose of increasing the active force to be employed in the field, I recommend the total and entire demolition of the buildings and the fort and to evacuate that position. At the same time I should be very unwilling to resort to this measure if there is any probability that our naval ascendency on the lake can be so far established at an early season after the opening of navigation that we can by that means ensure the safe communication of troops and stores to that frontier. In this event the advantage to be derived from the acquisition of the river Niagara as a harbor is of such material importance that I would maintain the Niagara fort with a strong garrison as long as possible, without diminishing its present defences, but should the ascendency on the lake be doubtful, or even retarded to a late period in the campaign, I am well aware and fully convinced you have not the means to maintain that position if attacked with energy and great superiority of numbers. In this case I would immediately decide to demolish the American fort and concentrate all our force on the west shore.

March 27 (Sunday) BATTLE OF HORSESHOE BEND (BATTLE OF CHOLOCCO) **In Alabama,** General Jackson's army, following a march through the wilderness of about 11 days, arrives at the encampment of the Creeks at Emuckfaw

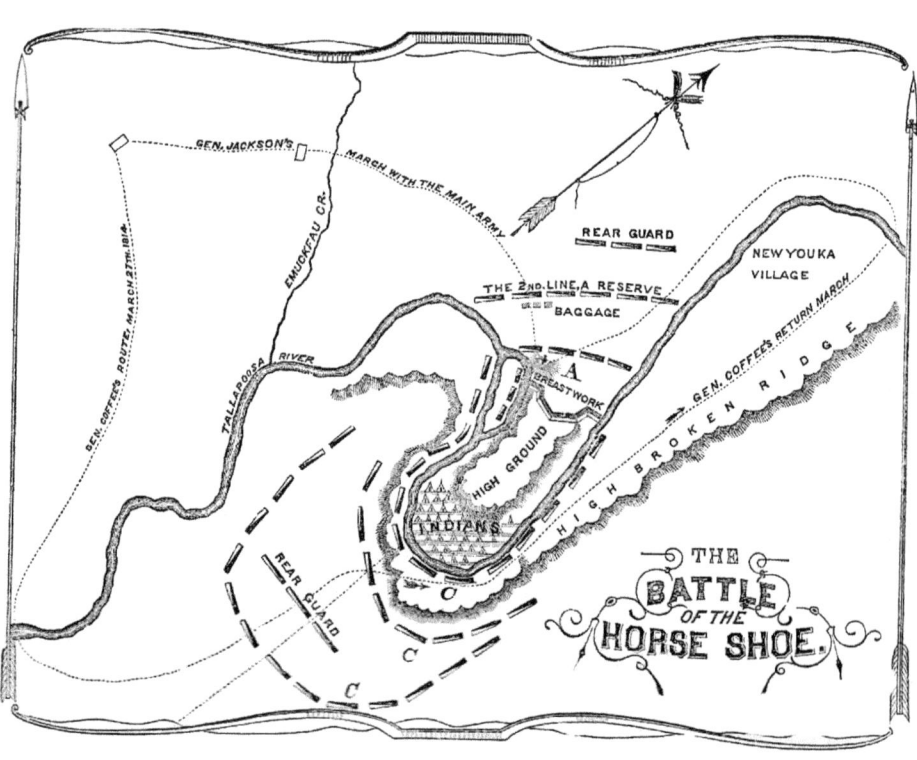

Battle of Horseshoe Bend.

(Horseshoe Bend), a peninsula at the Tallapoosa River at about 1000. The peninsula, composed of about 100 acres, has a slim neck that does not exceed 500 feet wide. Jackson scrutinizes the defenses of the Creeks and determines that the camp is well fortified and defended by about 1,000 warriors; however, he also believes that the Creeks' positions are untenable. His observations match his earlier perception when, in a letter regarding Horseshoe Bend, he states that "the Indians had penned themselves in for destruction." The leader, Chief Menawa, had deployed his force according to the advice of his medicine man, and the advice proves fatal.

Jackson discovers the poor positions and weakness of the perimeter, despite a formidable and near impenetrable breastwork extending about eight feet high. He discerns that his force can bypass the breastwork to avoid getting his troops snarled by a crossfire, thereby providing him with an advantage. He dispatches the mounted troops under General Coffee and the Indians with instructions to ford the stream about two miles below the main body. After crossing, Coffee is to swing back and deploy along the bank opposite the rear of the camp. Once Coffee's force deploys, a signal is sent to General Jackson, who orders the main body to advance. Jackson uses two artillery pieces to announce the presence of the army; however, the obstacles, including logs and earthworks that are stretched across the neck of the peninsula, absorb the bombardment without collapsing. After about two hours, it becomes evident that the artillery fire has been ineffective.

Initially, the Creeks shine with confidence. The fortifications seem as invincible as predicted by the medicine man. However, the forces under General Coffee and Chief William McIntosh ford the stream about two miles below the stronghold, and after reaching the east bank, Coffee initiates his assault against the enemy's rear. Soon after crossing, Coffee deploys two guns at a point less than 100 yards from the defenses. During this operation, some Cherokees with Coffee swim across the river, take control of the canoes and return to the west bank. Afterward, the canoes ferry the contingent under Colonel Morgan and allied Indians across to add to Coffee's strength. While the men crash through the village, they set the structures afire to totally confound the Creeks, who had no thoughts of being struck from the rear. The fires create rising plumes of smoke, and as the smoke rises, General Jackson becomes aware of Coffee's offensive.

At about the same time that Coffee's mounted infantry and the Indian allies spring their attack from the rear, General Jackson orders a bold bayonet attack. The combination is deadly, and as the horses plow into the Creek lines, the slashing bayonets of the Tennessee militia and the U.S. 39th Infantry converge upon the same points. Following about one-half hour of horrific close quartered fighting at the frontal defenses, regulars under Colonel Williams, including Major L.P. Montgomery and Ensign Houston, charge. Both Montgomery and Houston bolt to the top of the breastworks, followed by other troops, including militia attached to General George Doherty's brigade. No quarter is asked and none is given. The Tennesseans' bayonets bludgeon the Creeks without pause, forcing the Creeks to flee from their positions.

The Tennesseans relentlessly pursue the retreating Indians. Some are shot while hiding in the bushes and others are felled while they are running, and yet others who try to reach the river also find their escape route covered by marksmen. Some others find temporary safety by the bank amid some primitive breastworks and fallen trees.

General Jackson requests their surrender, but the Creeks remain defiant and kill the man sent to deliver Jackson's message. Jackson's artillery is put into action; however, once again, it fails to dislodge those at the bank. The Creeks also survive an attack launched to compel them to abandon their positions. Undaunted, Jackson turns to a more drastic tactic. He orders a detail to set the woods on fire.

The raging flames finally drive the Creeks from their positions and directly into the sights of waiting marksmen, who devastate those who flee from the flames. Chief Menawa, having sustained a serious wound during the melee, manages to evade being hit after abandoning the breastworks. He makes it to the river and submerges. Menawa clings to a root while under water and uses a reed that extends to the surface for breathing. Menawa remains undiscovered under water until dusk, then he escapes capture by swimming the river.

By dusk, the army prevails. More than 500 Creeks under Chief Menawa lay dead on the field. Monahee, a prophet, is among the killed, and two other prophets are killed. It is thought that many more had found their final resting place in the river. A report by General Jackson estimates that "only about ten had escaped." It is also reported that 250 prisoners are seized and that all but a few are women and children. A nearby island had been the positions of a contingent of Tennessee militia under Lt. Jesse Bean, and his marksmen had taken a high toll on any Creeks trying to escape by swimming the river to the island.

Jackson reports casualties at 26 killed and 106 to 146 wounded. Major Lemuel Montgomery of the 39th Infantry is among the killed. Montgomery, the first man to scale the breastwork, had been rallying his troops when he was shot in the head and killed instantly. Ensign Sam Houston is also among wounded, having sustained "two balls in his shoulder and fearful wounds in his thigh." Cherokee Indians aligned with Jackson sustain 18 killed and 56 wounded, and the Creeks aligned with Jackson sustain five killed and 11 wounded.

This decisive victory for the Tennessee militia and the army ends further Creek Indian resistance; in effect, ending the "Creek War." Jackson's troops are aided by several hundred Cherokee allies under Chief Whale and Lower Creeks under Chief McIntosh. Warriors of Chief Whale also take the Creek village of Tohopeka, where the families of the Creeks had stayed during the fighting. Another Cherokee chief, Wauhatchie, serving in an army company, sustains a severe wound. On 17 April, Chief Wauhatchie returns to Georgia. At Tohopeka, more than 300 women and children are taken captive.

Another nearby village, Newyaucau, is destroyed by Georgia troops under Major General David Adams prior to the assault against Horseshoe Bend. Chief William McIntosh (Coweta–Lower Creeks), for his service here as well as the Florida campaign, is later appointed brigadier general in the U.S. Army. William McIntosh (known also as Tustunnuggee Hutkee or White Warrior) was the son of a Scotsman, Captain William McIntosh of Savannah, and a Creek woman, Senoya.

The army departs for Fort Williams at Cedar Creek on the following day and arrives there on 2 April. Subsequently, the army moves deeper into the South to construct Fort Jackson, about 125 miles from Fort Mims, Alabama, near the ruins of an old French Fort (Toulouse). Forts Deposit, Williams and Strother have recently been established in Alabama. William Weatherford surrenders to General Jackson in April, but his life is spared. After being sent to Fort Claiborne, he is apparently permitted escape to avoid friends of those killed at Fort Mims from lynching him. Weatherford remains out of any future fighting and spends the rest of his life in Monroe County, Alabama, until his death in 1826.

Jackson's army had crushed the Creeks and simultaneously broken their spirit. Creeks who survive, about 200, begin to move north, and by summer, their circumstances become dire, so much so that they are fed by the U.S. government. The Creeks had been fighting not for themselves but as mercenaries for the British.

William Weatherford (right) surrenders to Jackson (*Battles of America by Sea and Land, Volume II*, Robert Tomes, 1878).

General Jackson notes in a letter: "While we fight the savage, who makes war only because he delights in blood, and who has gotten his booty when he has scalped his victim, we are, through him, contending against an enemy of more inveterate character and deeper design. So far as my exertions can contribute, the purposes, both of the savage and his instigator (English), shall be defeated." Also, the brigade of Brigadier General Thomas Johnson participates in this action.

Governor William Hawkins of North Carolina had ordered Brigadier General Joseph Graham to lead his brigade of troops from North Carolina and South Carolina to bolster General Andrew Jackson; however, the brigade does not arrive until after the victory. President James Madison had asked the governors of both states to commit a regiment to form Graham's brigade. The delay was blamed on the War Department, which did not expedite the arrival of supplies.

Graham's brigade participates in only a few skirmishes before returning home. The action terminates Graham's military service, which had included his service during the American Revolution.

Also, the North Carolina detached militia was composed of two brigades under the command of Major General Thomas Brown. Each of the brigades was composed of four regiments, five artillery companies and six rifleman companies. During this year in conjunction with a second levy, command is given to Major General Montford Stokes. Nevertheless, after the force is raised, they are not called to service. The troops return to their respective towns to await orders, which do not arrive. Consequently, General Stokes never takes active command in the field.

March 28 (Monday) In Chile at Valparaiso, the *Essex*, commanded by Captain David D. Porter, weighs anchor and attempts to break out into the open sea. He intends to pass the *Phoebe* and *Cherub* on the windward side; however, an unexpected squall pounds the *Essex* and severs the main top mast. As it tumbles, the some of the crew fall with it and they drown. Porter's chance of breaking out vanish when the mast falls. Aware of the peril, Porter attempts to get back into the neutral port, while the British close for the kill. Nonetheless, the severe damage makes it impossible for the *Essex* to re-enter the port. Porter heads for a small bay where he expects to be able to repair the damages. The *Essex* stands very close to the shore under a Chilean battery that is deployed less than one mile from Valparaiso and is considered to be within the boundary of the neutral port. The Chilean government, however, offers no assistance and more or less ignores its own position as neutral.

Captain Hillyar wastes no time in moving against Porter and his crippled ship. He ignores the port's neutrality, but the *Phoebe* and the *Cherub* advance slowly and with great caution. Just before 1600, the British commence fire. The *Phoebe*, which remains out of the range of the *Essex*'s guns, delivers a devastating barrage. The *Cherub* also commences fire with its guns, but it is closer to the *Essex*, and shortly afterward, it redeploys near the *Phoebe*. Despite the iron deluge, Porter's crewmen shift three long 12-pounders from the stern and redeploy them from where they can return effective fire.

Due to Porter's 12-pounders, the British are compelled to pull back to make repairs. Meanwhile, the Americans continue to struggle to get the springs on the cables to provide the Essex with the means to deliver a broadside. They succeed three times, but the British barrages sever the cables each time. After a short pause in the action, the British, having completed the repairs, return, and they renew the decimating bombardment. On the *Essex*, men are falling left and right in what is becoming a slaughter. The crew continue to return fire to the best of their abilities and display no inclination to surrender. Captain Porter, aware of his dire circumstances, realizes that he must attack or the ship and the crew will be destroyed.

The *Essex* by this time has been severely damaged and loss of life has been high. Porter is able to hoist only the flying jib as it begins its attack. The potent cripple moves into range of the *Cherub* and delivers effective fire which forces the heavily damaged *Cherub* to pull back out of the range of Porter's guns. From that point, it returns to the fight, but from a great distance. In the meantime, casualties aboard the *Essex* continue to worsen, with dead and wounded crew members lying everywhere. Despite the effective fire of the *Essex*, both British ships possess full sailing prowess as their masts remain intact. The *Phoebe* and the *Cherub* rely on their long guns to continue their battle with the crippled *Essex*. After about two hours of ferocious fighting, many of Porter's guns have been silenced, and he is unable to be favored by the wind, making it clear the escape path is closed. In addition, the British barrages had ignited several fires, one of which continues and threatens the magazine. Porter, having no options, decides to run the *Essex* ashore to permit the survivors to escape.

Porter's plan nearly succeeds; however, just before the *Essex* reaches shore, the winds change and the crew is unable to prevent the *Essex* from being carried toward the *Phoebe*, which again places it in line with more devastating fire. The Americans accept the misfortune and continue to refuse to think of defeat. The crew prepares to board the *Phoebe* once alongside it. At about this time, Lt. Downes moves from the *Essex Jr.* to confer with Captain Porter, but he is unable to get aboard. Nonetheless, Porter instructs him to return to the *Essex Jr.* and be prepared to destroy it if necessary to prevent capture by the British.

By this time the *Essex* resembles a death ship. It sustains hit after hit without being able to fire even a single gun. All the while, the Chilean government has refused to offer any assistance. And still Porter's boys refuse to quit. Porter directs the men to take some action, including cutting the anchor to cause the ship to swing around from where it is able to fire another broadside at its hunters; however, due to damages, the maneuver cannot be completed. Porter orders the *Essex* abandoned, but the only way to reach shore is to swim. The British fire had literally destroyed every boat on the ship. Astonishingly, of those who choose to swim to shore, some are seized in the water, while others succeed in making their escape; however, Porter is surrounded by the majority of the crew who refuse to abandon their ship or their commander. Nonetheless, by this time the crew is aboard a floating bomb that could blow at any moment. Those remaining aboard the *Essex*, oblivious the danger, fight the spreading fires succeed in extinguishing the flames before the magazine blows.

With one imminent threat rectified, the men move to the few operable guns and resume firing their long guns. The effort is gallant, noble, heroic and defiant, but their numbers have been shredded by the superior fire power of the *Phoebe* and *Cherub*. The troops, too few to turn the tide and with their vessel a sitting and crippled target, request that Porter surrender that the scores of wounded might be saved.

Captain Porter acknowledges that it is no longer possible to continue the fight. He calls for the officers to appear for a council. Only one, Lt. Stephen Decatur McKnight, remains able bodied. The others have been killed or wounded or are missing. First Lt. Wilmer had been struck by a piece of lumber and knocked overboard; Lt. Cowell had been knocked out of action after his leg was severed; Mr. Barnwell, the master, sustained a serious wound and was carried below deck; Lt. Odenheimer had also been tossed overboard; however, he survives and re-boards the vessel after it capitulates.

Porter realizes that his ship has sustained repeated hits that have penetrated the sides, but the ship's carpenters are either dead or among the wounded, making it highly probable that the *Essex* might soon sink. Consequently, at 1820, Porter reluctantly orders that the colors be struck.

Commodore David Porter.

At the time the Stars and Stripes is lowered, 75 officers and men remain standing, and of those, some soon die of their wounds. A few others die after the colors are struck when Captain Hillyar fails to call a cease fire. The appalling action by the British kills four men, each one standing near Captain Porter, who moves to re-hoist the colors and fight to the last man. Nonetheless after about 10 minutes of unconscionable fire, the British guns fall silent.

The American casualties for this battle vary from different sources. Commodore Porter's memoir enumerated 58 killed and 66 wounded. The British losses are light and reported as five killed. One American survivor, Davy Farragut, only 12 years of age, is saved, along with his pet pig "Murphy." Later, regarding the slaughter, Davy (Admiral David Farragut) stated: "I was standing near the captain when a shot came, killing four men and scattering the brains of one over both of us."

Afterward, the British repair the battered *Essex* and take it to England. In 1833, the *Essex* is utilized as a prison ship at Kingston. It is sold at auction in 1837. The *Essex Jr.*, after being captured, is transformed into a cartel to carry paroled American prisoners to New York. The ships departs on 27 April. While en route to the U.S., it is intercepted by the HMS *Saturn* (Captain Nash). The British commander examines the papers given to Captain Porter by British Captain Hillyar, and the ship is permitted to resume its voyage.

Soon after, the *Essex Jr.* is stopped again and by the *Saturn*. The encounter is not cordial, and this time Captain Porter and the others are held as prisoners. Porter makes it clear that he is now a prisoner and no longer bound to his parole. On the day following his recapture, while about forty miles off the eastern side of Long Island, while the *Essex Jr.* is right next to the HMS *Saturn*, Captain Porter decides he will make his escape. Using a boat, he takes off after leaving a message for British Captain Nash: "That Captain Porter was now satisfied that most British officers were not only destitute of honor, but regardless of the honour of each other; that he was armed, and prepared to defend himself against his boats, if sent in pursuit of him; and that he must be met, if met at all as an enemy." Porter's boat rows away with the *Essex Jr.* blocking the view from the Saturn. Soon the British do spot it and the *Saturn* gives chase, while at the same time, the breeze increases, slicing Porter's chances of escape. Good fortune also arrives in the form of a sudden dense fog. Porter uses the natural camouflage to modify his course and by so doing, his boat escapes capture. Meanwhile, during the ordeal, Captain Porter hears guns firing, and after the fog dissipates he observes the *Essex Jr.* being chased. It fares badly and is recaptured. Meanwhile, Porter's boat maintains its getaway. Later, after rowing for about 60 miles, Porter lands at Babylon, Long Island. His reception is less than enthusiastic. The Americans refuse to believe his tale and instead, perceive him to be a British officer. Captain Porter is able to end his interrogation and convince his American captors that he is a Yankee by presenting his commission.

After illegally recapturing the *Essex Jr.* on the day following Captain Porter's escape, the British ransack the ship and confiscate what money they find. The British also interrogate the crew and threaten repercussions, but following the outrageous actions, the British release the ship. After their ordeal ends, the *Essex Jr.* arrives in New York one day after Captain Porter does. The vessel is condemned and sold.

March 29 (Tuesday) *In naval activity,* the USS *Frolic*, commanded by J. Bainbridge, while cruising off the West Indies, encounters and destroys a British merchant ship. Late on this day, the *Frolic* intercepts and sinks an unidentified privateer.

March 30 (Wednesday) **In France,** word arrives at La Rochelle that the British and the Allies had captured Paris.

In New York, an American force of nearly 4,000 under General James Wilkinson departs Plattsburgh (Lake Champlain) and enters Canada. The Americans encounter resistance at Odelltown, but the advance continues. The British contest the advance and skirmishing ensues for about three miles. Nonetheless, the column reaches La Colle Mill at the Sorel River less than ten miles inside Canada at about 1500. The British and Canadians hold a blockhouse and are deployed in and about the mill on the opposite bank of La Colle Creek.

General Wilkinson, not overly concerned of the obstacles, moves up two guns to reduce the resistance. Wilkinson deploys his force at positions from where they can cut off the escape routes once the artillery reduces the walls of the mill. The guns begin to pound the target, and the bombardment continues for about two hours. Nonetheless, the mill withstands the attack and remains intact. Meanwhile, a force under General Macomb forms as Wilkinson's reserve.

The British display no signs of intimidation by the superior American force and the defensive positions remain steadfast. During the artillery attack, the defenders remain active and the British marksmen rip into the American positions, inflicting casualties and barring progress of Wilkinson's force. British fire wounds Captain McPherson, the commander of the battery; however, he remains in command. Soon afterward another shot strikes him in his thigh. McPherson is carried to safety and replaced by Lt. Larrabee. Shortly after Larrabee assumes command, a British marksman strikes him in the lung. Larrabee is replaced by Lt. Sheldon. Under the command of Sheldon, the artillery remains in action until the close of the lopsided action.

While Wilkinson's force is stalled at the mill, British major Hancock, the commander, is bolstered by a wave of fresh troops that increase his numbers from about 200 to about 1,000 men. Hancock, not satisfied with preventing Wilkinson from breaking through, decides to gamble on an attack to knock the American battery out of action. Hancock orders a charge, and the contingent drives toward the American guns; however, once the troops emerge from their fortified positions, they finally provide American riflemen with lucrative targets. The charge stalls due to the effective American fire, which forces the contingent to move back to the mill and blockhouse.

Hancock remains convinced that the battery must be captured. He orders a second attack. It too is met by a wave of fire, once again forcing the British to abort the assault and get back to their secure positions. Nonetheless, Hancock's force chooses not to retire. The British seal themselves in their formidable defensive positions and hold. Wilkinson is unable to dislodge them despite repeated attempts. The stalemate continues because Wilkinson is not able to bring up heavier guns due to the condition of the roads. Conse-

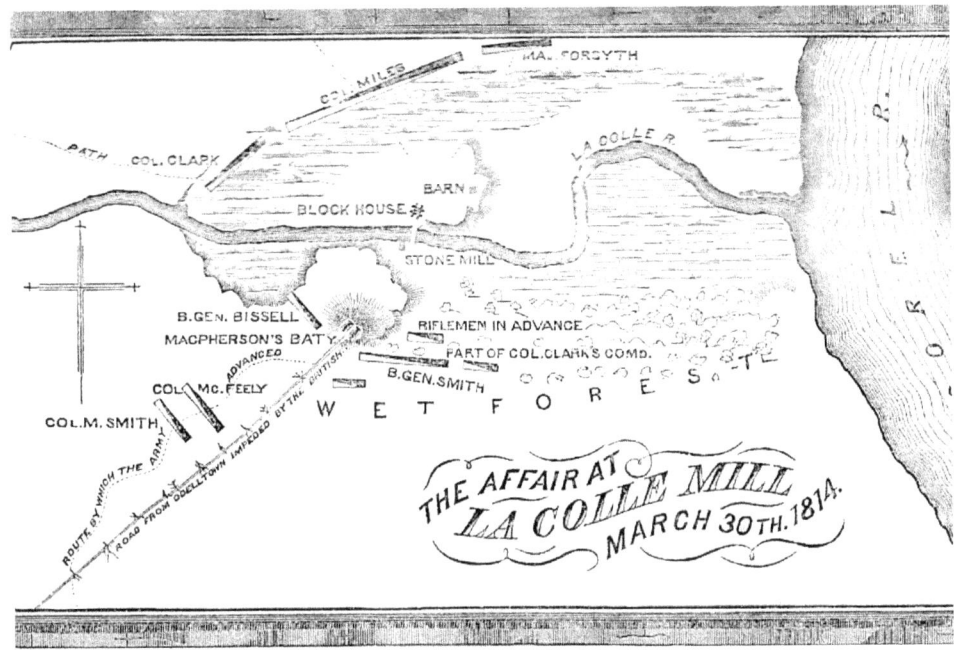

The affair at La Colle Mill.

quently, the British succeed in preventing passage. General Wilkinson cancels the operation. He orders Sheldon to retire.

The army returns to Plattsburgh. During the retreat, the troops face no further opposition; however, the elements remain an adversary. The trek is unpleasant, as the line of march is plagued by snow, rain and mud. Wilkinson's force sustains the loss of 154 men. The British lose 61.

Arriving at Plattsburgh, General Wilkinson requests a court-martial. He is acquitted but that does not salvage his career. The debacle at La Colle Mill ends General Wilkinson's military service. He is succeeded by General Jacob Brown, who is promoted to major general. Wilkinson is recalled to Washington but remains in the army until he is dismissed 15 June 1815. Afterward, he travels to Mexico to carry out a new scheme to acquire land and wealth. He dies in Mexico on 28 December 1825.

At about the same time as the change in command, Winfield Scott is promoted to brigadier general to command the Buffalo area. General Scott had been in Albany for the greater part of the winter following the dismal campaign of General Wilkinson. Also, Brigadier General George Izard is promoted to the rank of major general.

The humiliation that led to the replacement of Wilkinson is not the only embarrassment of the American army. Before summer's end, the British troops will stroll into Washington, D.C., without opposition. Fortunately, there are still enough good leaders to stem the British tide.

General Winfield Scott, in cooperation with Governor Tompkins, had been engaged in planning operations for the coming campaigns. Also, General Brown and General Scott had directed the army at Plattsburgh to advance to the frontier at Niagara; however, Brown traveled to Sackets Harbor rather than accompany Scott during the march. The route was through the wilderness and passed a solitary log cabin in one section that was inundated with rattlesnakes. Later, the area that contains the cabin becomes known as the city of Rochester.

The force that assembles in Buffalo includes the two brigades of regulars under General Winfield Scott and General Eleazar Wheelock Ripley, bolstered by General Peter B. Porter's militia brigade and an artillery battalion, commanded by Major Jacob Hindman.

At Buffalo, a rigid training period unfolds and the troops undergo incessant drilling, though progress on U.S. drilling has been slow since the close of the American Revolution when Baron Von Steuben introduced French tactics. Apparently, the command has only one book on the French tactics and it is written in French, complicating the task of teaching the instructors, most of whom speak no French. Nonetheless, the training continues.

During early July, the Americans cross the Niagara River and initiate a campaign in Canada. General Brown later receives intelligence that the British are preparing to launch an attack against Oswego. Brown dispatches Colonel Mitchell at Batavia to move his artillery battalion to Oswego to meet the probable threat. Mitchell, upon receiving the order, departs on the march, totaling about 150 miles. The column completes the movement in less than five days, only to find the post — which also acts as a supply depot for the army and for the fleet operating out of Sackets Harbor on Lake Ontario — unmanned and barely defensible. The barracks turn out to be habitable; however, the fort's guns are deemed inoperable. Nonetheless, Mitchell's battalion prepares for the attack. The British arrive off Oswego from Kingston, Canada, during early May.

March 31 (Thursday) **In Canada** General Drummond writes from Kingston to Sir George Prevost with a report from General Riall: "No progress had been made in any of the works on the Niagara Frontier in consequence of severity of the weather, there being more snow on the ground in that neighborhood now than there has been during the winter." Drummond also received a report that

> Major McKee of the Indian Department has been doing a great deal of mischief among the Indians upon the beach at the Head of the Lake, not only by getting shamefully drunk himself every day and speaking very improperly to them, but by permitting liquor to be sold to them in great quantities, which renders them outrageous and easy to be worked upon, and having understood that it might prove even dangerous to have him written to or spoken to with anger or displeasure on the subject as he has very considerable influence over them and might lead them astray, I thought it advisable to send for him to Kingston for the purpose of conversing with him on Indian affairs and propose soon after his arrival here to forward him to Montreal where Your Excellency will, I trust, find means to employ or detain him as long as we may find the service of the Indian tribes useful to the cause we are engaged.

He also informs Prevost that since the King's Regiment had been notified of their relief at Fort Niagara, desertions had totally stopped: "I have satisfaction in observing, a disinclination to the place only and not to His Majesty's service."

In France at La Rochelle, four American privateer captains — George Coggeshall (*David Porter*), Captain Brown (*Decatur*), David Maffitt (*Rattlesnake*) and Jeremiah Mantor (*Ida*) — meet at the Hotel des Ambassadeurs to discuss the present political situation in France. The British are inching toward Paris and some advance troops are probably within the city. While ground troops are close to seizing Paris, communications between it and La Rochelle have been cut off; however, the American captains have an equally pernicious situation off shore due to the formidable British squadron that has totally sealed the harbor at La Rochelle. The British essentially have paralyzed the American privateers and at least one other American vessel, which had been unable to run the blockade since the early days of the war. One of the privateers, the *David Porter* (Captain Coggeshall), had not entered La Rochelle. It remains on a small island off the coast. Coggeshall had arrived in La Rochelle on horseback. The meeting adjourns with the Americans deciding that an attempt to run the blockade is their only chance to avoid being captured.

Spring **In Canada**, General James Winchester, held by the British since his capture at the Battle of the Raisin River (*see also*, **January 21–23 Battle of Raisin River**), is among the officers exchanged. He returns to the United States and is ordered to repair to Mobile, Alabama, to assume command there. Apparently, his final official correspondence occurs on February 17, 1815, when he writes to Secretary of War James Monroe to inform the secretary that the British had seized Fort Bowyer in Mobile Bay. In March 1815, General Winchester resigns his commission and returns to Tennessee, where he remains until his death on 27 July 1826. Judge Laurent Durocher, a resident of Frenchtown who knew General Winchester, later told author Benson Lossing that Winchester was "a fussy man, quite heavy in person, and ill fit for the peculiar service in which he was engaged."

April **In Connecticut**, a British contingent of seamen and Royal Marines is carried up the Connecticut River. The troops debark just above Saybrook at Pettepaug Point. The British destroy some shipping there and afterward they destroy other vessels at Brockway's Ferry. The raiders then retire and pursuit is initiated by militia, bolstered by a detachment of U.S. Marines from the fleet, but no contact is made. The British damage caused during this raid is estimated at about $200,000.

In naval activity, a part of Captain David D. Porter's squadron prepares to embark. They have been at Nuka Hiva in the Marquesas Islands in Polynesia since the previous October. The commander of the force, Lt. Gamble, U.S. Marine Corps, is confronted by mutiny incited by his crew of mostly British seamen captured on whaling ships. Once Gamble detects the signs of the mutiny, he transfers all the arms onto his ship, the *Greenwich*. Nonetheless, the mutineers seize the *Seringapatam* on 7 May, and during the struggle, Lt. Gamble is wounded in his arm. After yet another attack by the mutineers, Gamble, his force reduced to 8 men, succeeds in getting to sea with the Sir Andrew Hammond. The ship sails toward Hawaii about 2,000 miles distant. The vessels arrive safely at the Sandwich Islands only to be captured by the HMS *Cherub* on 19 June 1814.

Also, Britain now blockades the New England ports, causing severe shortages in America. The United States reacts immediately and orders American ships to attack and seize British ships off England's coast. Their efforts are fruitful, capturing an enormous amount of British vessels by the summer. This type of concerted British pressure is straining the American cause. New Englanders, natural seafarers, are argumentative, and there has been talk of throwing in with the British, but it never materializes.

In other activity, the privateer *America* arrives back at Portsmouth to culminate a cruise that began during December 1813. During its time at sea, the *America* captured 12 prizes, including the 10-gun brigantine *Margaret*, which was cornered while sailing from Cadiz to Newfoundland with a cargo of salt. After its capture, the *Margaret* was taken into port at Salem. Other prizes include the *Sovereign*, a 300-ton brigantine that was taken into port at Portsmouth, New Hampshire; the brigantine *Brothers*, rerouted to a Spanish port; the 250-ton brigantine *Apollo*; the schooner *Hope*; and the schooner *Sylph*. A few of the prizes were destroyed at sea and several others became cartels to transport paroled prisoners. During the cruise, the *America* was commanded by Captain James Chever, who succeeded Captain Joseph Ropes.

Elsewhere, Captain George Coggeshall remains in France after ordering his privateer, the *David Porter*, to return to the United States. He had been there since the previous March to carry out some personal business for the owners of the privateer. At present, France is less than stabile due to the political circumstances and the advancing British Army, making it hard to find an American vessel, though a few are scattered around. The *Lion*, a schooner, is at L'Orient, along with the schooner *Spencer* and the *Leo*. The Americans in France are familiar with Captain Coggeshall, and they expeditiously work to find a swift vessel to get Coggeshall back to the States. All of the Americans still in France have concerns, including that France is expected to devise reasons to prevent American vessels from leaving. With that in mind, Captain Coggeshall works the crew around the clock to make it possible to get out of the country before the French interfere. On 6 November, the *Leo* prepares to sail.

In yet other naval activity, the American privateer *Midas*, an 8-gun schooner commanded by Captain Thompson, while cruising off the French coast, intercepts and captures the schooner *Francis*, which has a cargo of bullocks destined for the British Army. The prize is destroyed at sea. During this cruise, the *Perry* captures and destroys the schooner *Appallodore*, which is carrying fruit. During its time at sea, the *Perry* collects 14 prizes, including the British privateer *Dash*, defeated during December 1812. Also, the American privateer *Ultor*, an xebec (3-masted vessel) intercepts and seizes the 4-gun brigantine *Swift*. Earlier, the *Ultor* captured the brigantine *Robert*.

April 1 (Friday) **In naval activity,** off Cape Wrath, Scotland, the American privateer *Scourge* intercepts and seizes the British vessel *Symmetry*, which is transporting a cargo of salt and other items. During the same attack, the *Scourge* also seizes two other vessels, the ship *Winchester* and the brigantine *Union*. Captain J.R. Perry, commander of the *Scourge* transfers all of the British prisoners to a Swedish ship. After confiscating much of the cargoes, the three captured vessels are burned at sea. One other prize, the bark *Brothers*, carrying a cargo including salt, is sent into the United States.

In other naval activity, the American privateer *Galloway*, operating out of New York, at about this time intercepts and seizes the brigantine *Fanny*, out of London, which has a cargo of fish. It is taken as a prize and sent into port at Nantes.

April 2 (Saturday) **In Alabama,** General Andrew Jackson's force arrives at Fort Williams from Horseshoe Bend.

In Canada, General Drummond, at Kingston, sends a secret dispatch to Sir George Prevost:

> I have the honor to acknowledge the receipt of Your Excellency's letter of the 24th ultimo. marked private and confidential, enclosing the copy of a letter from Mr. Monroe to Brigadier General Winder of the United States Army on the subject of an armistice, on which Your Excellency desires my sentiments. I beg leave respectfully to submit as my opinion that the object of Mr. Monroe's letter is two-fold. First, to gain time for organizing their naval and military force. Second, to cause the proposal for the armistice, (the discussion of which is to afford that time,) to originate with Your Excellency. Unless Your Excellency is in possession of some other pledge than General Winder's assurances of the sincerity of his Government, I should place but little faith in them, as I have-ever understood that officer to be one of the most strenuous supporters of the war and withal the most plausible. therefore the more dangerous agent the American Government could employ in this country. It is impossible at present to ascertain to which side the naval superiority on the lake will preponderate on the opening of navigation unless full credit can be attached to the enclosed deposition, when, if so, the superiority will be decidedly on our side, and, at all events, we have, in my opinion, as much right to look for its possession as the enemy. The latest information I have received respecting the enemy's squadron has been from the accompanying document. Our two new ships, Sir James Yeo informs me, he is in hopes to launch on the 9th instant if the ice permits, and they will be in readiness with the other vessels immediately after the opening of navigation. It is highly satisfactory to know that the interests of the Indians will not be forgotten in any arrangement which may take place.

In naval activity, the American privateer *Scourge* intercepts and seizes an unidentified sloop which had sailed from Liverpool. The crew of the *Scourge* places some prisoners aboard it and permits the sloop to resume its voyage.

April 3 (Sunday) **In New York** at Albany, Governor Tompkins responds to a letter of 15 December 1813 from Jacob O'Dell that was filled with anger and complaints regarding O'Dell not being able to raise a battalion of cavalry. The governor informs O'Dell that the United States "had never called militia cavalry into service." He also eloquently rips O'Dell for the nastiness of the letter, then explains the trouble he had gone to in the process of raising O'Dell in rank. Tompkins also says that he continues to be his friend, includes his commission as brigadier general and encloses the original letter: "I am sure when you reflect on the propriety & perfect friendliness toward you of those arrangements, that you will feel mortified at having written the peevish letter above alluded to & would wish that you had it back to commit to the flames. I return you the original letter for that purpose."

In naval activity, the USS *Frolic* encounters two British warships, the HMS *Orpheus* and the HMS *Shelbourne* (formerly the American privateer *Racer*), in the Florida passage. Commander J. Bainbridge, aware that his ship is too weak to engage both vessels simultaneously, decides to run. Pursuit is initiated by the British, while the *Frolic* heads southward and sails toward Cuba. Though the *Frolic* tosses guns and other items overboard to increase speed, the chase ends off Matanzas in about six hours and the *Frolic* surrenders. The British rename it *Florida*. The *Florida* remains in British service until 1819, when it is dismantled.

In other activity, the USS *Constitution* encounters two British warships, the HMS *Tenedos* and the *Endymion*, which initiate pursuit. Captain Bainbridge of the *Constitution*, aware that he is outgunned, heads for the harbor at Marblehead, and with the help of a local pilot, the *Constitution* is safely guided into the harbor while the guns of the fort provide protection.

Also, the American privateers *Decatur*, *Ida* and the *Rattlesnake* begin to move down the harbor at La Rochelle to prepare to break through the blockade. On this day, official orders arrive declaring the government of King Louis XVIII. The fear of being detained by the French and the recent news that Paris had fallen makes it imperative that the Americans run the risk or face a future as guests of the British.

Later this day, the privateers encounter the British blocking passage. Two of the ships pull back, but the *Ida* creeps along the east end of the island where it lurks only for a short while before dashing out in full view of a disbelieving squadron at anchor off La Rochelle, which because of the tide is unable to reposition their guns. The *Ida* defies the odds and speeds past a waiting schooner that propels shots from every available gun. The *Ida* sustains some serious damage but shows no signs of capitulating. Other warships open fire, but the agile *Ida*, although taking more hits, breaks through the storm of fire and while moving as quickly as possible with about ten warships giving chase. Some of the crewmen throw unnecessary items overboard to lessen the weight, while others, most of whom emerge from the hold, make repairs. Upon fall of night, the *Ida* vanishes in the dark.

Although nearly all of its lights had been extinguished, some are necessary, and one of those is accidentally exposed, which marks its position. Three ships attempt to trap the *Ida*, but their plan fails. The darkness again preserves the privateer. Nonetheless, the huge hunting party maintains the search and at about dawn, two British frigates are spotted and they are also avoided. The *Ida* finally resumes its voyage and without further incident, it safely arrives at Boston in 26 days.

April 4–17 **In Alabama,** General Jackson departs from Fort Williams en route to the Hickory Ground. Jackson's force is inhibited by a shortage of supplies. The supplies are being carried by the troops because it was determined that the provisions could not be transported by water and the terrain is too harsh for the exhausted horses to transport them. Jackson is counting on the vanguard of the eastern army under Colonel Milton at Fort Decatur to provide supplies. The column moves slowly due to heavy rains. At Fooshatchie they seize a small number of Creeks. From there, Jackson resumes the march, while the Creeks abandon Hoithlewaule and other villages across the Tallapoosa River.

More problems emerge because Colonel Milton fails to support Jackson and the river floods, which prevents the army from continuing its pursuit. The column moves to the place where Governor Bienville had built the French post Fort Toulouse while the territory was still part of Louisiana, near the convergence of the Coosa and Tallapoosa Rivers. The American flag is planted and Fort Jackson is established. On 20 April, General Thomas Pinckney arrives at the post and assumes command.

April 4 to June 20 In France on April 4, Napoleon abdicates his throne. Two days later on the 6th, his unconditional abdication occurs. The following month, he sails to Elba. Although it appears that the war has ended by the abdication, freeing up British forces for the war with the United States, Napoleon later escapes from exile at Elba. He begins his return to France in February 1815 and arrives back at Paris on 20 March 1815. On 22 June, the Duke of Wellington defeats the French under Napoleon at Waterloo, finally ending Napoleon's reign. He is taken to St. Helena, where he arrives on 16 October, and where he remains until his death on 5 May 1821.

April 6 (Wednesday) In Washington, D.C., James Monroe writes to General Joseph Bloomfield at Philadelphia regarding a threat of attack by the British: "It is the decided opinion of the president, that preparation for the defense of the city of Philadelphia should be made without delay, and on all enlarged scale, looking, nevertheless to important and essential points, and carrying the measures adopted into effect with the utmost degree of economy. Gen. Swift, aided by Gen. Williams will be able to decide on the proper plans in each instance, and to execute what may be decided on."

In Canada, Sir George Prevost writes to General Drummond:

> SIR,— Earl Bathurst in a communication bearing date the 28th of January just received, having stated to me the desire of the Lords Commissioners of the Admiralty that the 2nd Battn. of Royal Marines, excepting the Artillery Company, should be placed immediately at the disposal of Commodore Sir James Yeo to enable him to fulfill their Lordship's orders for manning the squadron under his command, I propose to order on to Kingston the detachment of that corps now at Fort Wellington, which will be relieved by five companies of the 89th Regt. under Lieut. Colonel Morrison as soon as the navigation admits of their moving in that direction. The 89th will therefore be divided between Fort Wellington and Cornwall, and the post at Coteau du Lac will be occupied by a detachment of Embodied Militia.

In England, the British, having defeated Napoleon, have more troops available for service in the war against America. A 14,000-man army is available for duty in the United States.

April 7 (Thursday) In New York, the USS *Jefferson* (second) is launched at Sackets Harbor. Its crew is drawn from the USS *Erie*, a sloop of war, which is unable to sail from Baltimore due to the British blockading squadron that has the harbor sealed. Captain Charles G. Ridgely receives command.

In naval activity, the American privateer *Scourge* spots a Greenland whaler off the coast of England and initiates an attack by firing about ten broadsides. Nevertheless, the whaler is spared from capture when a British sloop of war that is near shore begins to pursue the *Scourge*. After a chase that lasts for about six hours, the *Scourge* finally outruns its pursuer. It later arrives at Chatham in Cape Cod, Massachusetts, to conclude a cruise that lasted for more than one year. During its time at sea, the *Scourge* seizes 27 British vessels and 420 prisoners.

April 8 (Friday) In Connecticut, some 240 British soldiers under the command of Lieutenant Coutts land at Essex at 0400. The raiders destroy the vessels in port. Over 20 U.S. ships are lost. Coutts, after the war, would describe his raid on *Essex* as "most unpleasant duty." This raid causes alarm along the entire New England coast, and as far away as Portsmouth, New Hampshire, there are increasing fears of British raids.

April 9 (Saturday) In Canada, Lt. Colonel John Harvey, at Kingston, writes a "secret and confidential letter" to Sir James Yeo:

> SIR,— The season for naval operations being at hand Lt. Genl. Drummond considers it advisable to communicate to you his ideas as to how the squadron under your command may be best employed on the opening of the navigation. Assuming that your superiority of force will be in the first instance decidedly secured by the accession to your former squadron of the two new vessels, the service that appears to Lt. General Drummond of the greatest importance to the defence of the Province is the reinforcement of the Right Division by the 103d Regiment and the conveyance at the same time of a supply of stores and provisions to Fort Niagara and Fort George. The Lieut. General would therefore wish that you would be pleased to make arrangements for executing this service at the earliest practicable period; the troops to be landed at the head of the lake, the stores and provisions at Fort Niagara and Fort George. After landing the stores, &c., at Fort Niagara and communicating with M. Genl. Riall it might be desirable if you find the M. General has no material assistance or co-operation to require from the squadron, that you should proceed down the American shore, looking into the different creeks and particularly reconnoitering Oswego, when, if you find it an object and consider the marines of the squadron sufficient for the service, you might land and bring off or destroy whatever stores, craft or public buildings the enemy might have there. It is also recommended that after the operation at Oswego, Commodore Yeo is directed to reconnoiter Sackets Harbor to determine whether or not an attack is practical.

In other activity, Lt. Colonel John B. Campbell (11th Regiment) is promoted to full colonel.

April 10 (Sunday) In New York at General Amos Hall's headquarters in Williamsville, following what turned out to be relatively quiet period, the recent arrival of United States regulars, general orders are issued: "The arrival of some battalions of United States troops enables the Major General to discharge the regiment of detached militia commanded by Lt. Col. Smith on Monday the 11th inst. Col. Smith will cause the several companies to be mustered preparatory to their discharge, as well as the field."

In other activity, General Edmund P. Gaines arrives at Sackets Harbor to assume command. Also on this day, Commodore Chauncey launches his new brigantine, which he christens the *Jones*. The HMS *Barbados* intercepts and seizes the American privateer *Polly*.

April 11 (Monday) In New Hampshire, Commodore Isaac Hull writes a second letter to Governor Gilman regarding his fears that Portsmouth is vulnerable to attack and the ships are in danger. At about the same time, Major General Storer also sends an urgent letter to the governor regarding the same subject. On the 15th, the governor directs General Storer to send a detachment "of not over 100 men" from the 1st and 35th regiments of his division, to be stationed at Fort Washington and Little Harbor. The order is executed immediately.

In New York, Commodore Isaac Chauncey writes from Sackets Harbor to Secretary of the Navy William Jones about British strength:

> Sir,— The agent that I sent a few days ago to the other side has this moment returned, with information that the enemy has all his fleet ready, (with the exception of the new vessels,) in the stream, he has 12 to 14 gunboats and a number of small craft, and 3,000 troops ready to embark for this place, and it is said they are only waiting for a favorable time to make the attack. My own impression is that they have understood that we are going to York and that they have prepared this force for the purpose of attacking the harbor the moment our fleet leaves it. The enemy, however, may be determined to make the attack at all hazards, as the object to them is of immense importance, and I am sorry to say that our force is but little adapted to the defence of this place. There are not a thousand effective men here besides the sailors and marines. General Gaines arrived here yesterday and assumed the command, and we shall endeavor to defend the place as long as we can with the means we possess.

Chauncey also mentions that 21 men have arrived at Sackets Harbor from Utica and that their journey of 80 or 90 miles took eight days.

In naval activity, the USS *Saratoga* (second) is launched. It carries eight long 24-pounders, six 42-pounder carronades and twelve 32-pounders. The arrival of the *Saratoga* on Lake Champlain makes the sea power of the U.S. on the North American lakes superior to that of the British.

The British are working tirelessly to outdistance the U.S. in naval power on the lakes, which they believe is essential for a successful invasion of the United States through New York. The planned invasion is in the works. Due to the appearance of the *Saratoga*, commanded by Master Commandant Thomas Macdonough, the British suspend the invasion until they can increase their sea power. In August, the British launch a large frigate that they expect to provide the firepower needed to gain superiority.

In other naval activity, the privateer *Grand Turk* seizes the vessel *Catherine*.

April 13 (Wednesday) **In Canada,** British Lt. Col. Glegg establishes headquarters at Fort George. A heavy snowstorm strikes on the 14th, and on the 15th, a schooner, the HMS *Netley*, transporting the 103rd Grenadier Company and some guns for the post, arrives from Kingston.

Also, Commodore James Yeo responds to a letter from Sir George Prevost:

SIR,—I have the honor to acknowledge the receipt of Your Excellency's letter of the 7th inst. requesting my opinion respecting an overture for an armistice offered by the American Government, together with the information recently obtained from a person from Sackets Harbor, which Your Excellency is disposed to consider as correct, which you wish me to compare with my former statement to you, (I perceive it corroborates the statement,) and which you wish should assist my judgment in the answer I am about to give. After the most deliberate consideration I am of opinion that as far as relates to naval operations it is by no means certain that the enemy will have the advantage at the commencement of the campaign, and the reinforcement of seamen and supply of stores which His Majesty's Government mean so frequently to assist us with, will, I have no doubt, enable us to acquire the ascendency on the lake. The third ship now building is, I believe, of far greater force than any the enemy can launch at Sackets Harbor and doubts have arisen as to the practicability of launching the large ship now ready, as will appear by the accompanying deposition of the carpenter of the *Madison*. But even admitting the enemy are able to launch their large ship and have received the whole of their guns and stores, (of which I entertain a doubt,) we never have been so competent to engage them with a reasonable prospect of success as at present. For although the enemy have a greater number of guns of heavy calibre, yet my having two ships of such effective strength as the Prince Regent and the Prince Charlotte closely to support each other, may give me an advantage in the early part of the action which I feel confident the talents of the officers an the spirits of the men under my command would immediately avail themselves of. I perceive two of the enemy's new vessels are brigs, and however formidable they may be as to *weight* of metal should any accident befall their gaff or main boom they become for the time unmanageable. Brigs have never been esteemed so effective as ships in battle. In short, Sir, I am fully persuaded that with the means I now possess with those the Government mean to place at my disposal, I shall be able either to bring Chauncey to a decisive action, or should I find him too superior, (for I cannot rely on his strength until I see his squadron,) manouvre with him until the third ship is ready, and which vessel I look upon to be of a description to look down all opposition. In the interim of this ship being ready, the reinforcements of seamen can be placed in heavy gunboats that may effectively assist me during the calms at the commencement of the season. These considerations induce me to be decidedly of opinion that were Your Excellency to accept of the proposed armistice it would neither conduce to the credit of His Majesty's Government or the honor of his arms, while it would enable the enemy to gain time for launching and equipping more ships, augmenting and concentrating his forces and bringing them to bear, (should a rupture of the armistice come, a measure I fear from the known enmity and insincerity of the American Government too likely too occur,) with redoubled force against us.

In other activity, in Canada, Lt. General Drummond writes to Sir George Prevost to inform him about Fort Niagara:

SIR,—I have the honor to acknowledge the receipt of Your Excellency's despatches by Captain Tasché of the militia. I avail myself of this opportunity to acquaint Your Excellency that Major General Riall has taken measures for levelling and destroying the batteries of the enemy which still existed in the neighborhood of Fort Niagara, one of them in particular being a very heavy work, immediately opposite to Fort George, required a considerable degree of labor and time. The quantities of ice which have come down the Niagara River have been so great as to cut off all communication with the opposite shore for some days. But the Major General hopes in the course of a week to have the Mississaga so far advanced as to mount four guns. He had directed Major Deane to fall back to Burford, having the Rangers in advance at Campfield's house, as the roads from Oxford are at present so excessively bad that should the enemy land at Long Point they could with ease arrive at the Grand River before Major Deane and cut off his passage of that river. I am concerned to report to Your Excellency the desertion of nine men of the 100th Regiment from the working party in destroying the batteries of the enemy before mentioned. One of them has since returned and declares that he had been taken prisoner and made his escape, but his story is not credited. The Shawanese Indians have elected the Prophet to be their war and Tecumseh's son their village chief. Thirty-five warriors with 90 women and children have arrived at Burlington from the River St. Clair. They report that vast numbers are awaiting our arrival at Detroit.

In naval activity, the privateer *Grand Turk*, a brigantine operating out of Salem, seizes a vessel, the *Indian Lass*. On this day, it also captures the vessel *Thomas and Sally*. The *Grand Turk* had seized another vessel on the 11th. At an undetermined time, it had captured an English cannon built in 1798. The cannon is acquired by a group of fisherman in Swampscott in 1835. It is initially used as a fog signal and is fired for the final time on 4 July 1857. It is then retired as a memorial to the fisherman in the town.

April 14 (Thursday) **In Washington, D.C.,** Congress, feeling the heat from constituents all across the country, had repealed the detested Embargo Act of the previous December. It becomes effective this day.

April 15 (Friday) Colonel Eleazar Wheelock Ripley is promoted to the rank of brigadier general. Ripley is breveted major general on 25 July 1814.

April 17 (Sunday) **In Canada,** Commodore James Yeo writes to Secretary of the Admiralty John Wilson Croker detailing the situation at Kingston regarding the fleet: "I have the heartfelt satisfaction to announce to you for the information of the Lords Commissioners of the Admiralty that His Majesty's frigates *Prince Regent* of fifty-eight and the *Princes Charlotte* of thirty-six guns were launched in safety at this yard yesterday evening. The *Royal George* has been hove down and repaired; the *Moira* and *Sir Sidney Smith* cut down to improve their sailing and the whole squadron put in an efficient state, and I hope to have all ready to take the lake by the 25th or 30th inst."

In naval activity, the American privateer *Scourge*, which had sustained some damage to its fore top mast during a recent running escape from a British warship off Scotland, sustains severe damage when both of its top masts are severed in a fair breeze. During the unexpected accident, one crewman is killed and three others are injured.

April 18 (Monday) **In Washington, D.C.,** Congress authorizes the purchase of vessels seized from the British on Lake Erie during the previous September. In addition, Congress appropriates $255,000 to be distributed as prize money among the officers and men (and their heirs) of the fleet under Captain Oliver H. Perry for their victory on Lake Erie. Captain Perry, in addition to his share of prize money, is awarded $5,000. Records of the U.S. Treasury account for a distribution of only $242,250.

In Alabama, General Andrew Jackson sends a letter to Governor Blount of Tennessee to inform him that the campaign against the Creeks "is drawing to a prosperous close." Jackson also explains that some of the Indians escaped over the Tallapoosa River and moved toward Pensacola. He says: "The Tallapoosa king is here confined. The Tostahatchie king of the Hickory ground, has delivered himself up. Weatherford has been with me, but I did not confine him. McQueen was taken but escaped. Hillinghagee, their great prophet, has absconded, but we will catch him."

Also, General Thomas Pinckney, the senior officer in the U.S. Southern Army, arrives at recently established Fort Jackson, Alabama. He assumes command as the senior officer in the Southern Army. Colonel Hawkins arrives with Pinckney. On the following day, the troops from West Tennessee under Andrew Jackson head home, while other troops, including those from the Carolinas and East Tennessee, remain. The hostilities with the Creeks have essentially ended, but still about 500 troops from East Tennessee will garrison Fort Williams, which was recently established while General Jackson was en route from Fort Strother to Horseshoe Bend. Other troops initiate operations around the Cahaba and Chattahoochee Rivers to seek out Creeks in an attempt to get them to surrender. General Jackson will return to his residence, the Hermitage in Tennessee, but in July he returns to the area. Fort Jackson was established where Fort Toulaise stood near the convergence of the Coosa and Tallapoosa Rivers when the area was still Louisiana.

In New York at Albany, Governor Daniel D. Tompkins, concerned that the British might strike, writes to Brigadier General Micahja Petit:

> Dear Sir: I am apprehensive from information received from the Westward, the British squadron on Lake Champlain may attempt some expedition up the Lake before ours will be ready; & that an attempt at the destruction of the establishment on the outlet of Lake George & of the village of Whitehall may be made. I will therefore thank you to be on the alert, & direct Col. Adams of your Brigade to be in readiness to repel any invasion of the District commanded by him. Should anything be wanting which I can supply, please to inform me of it without delay. I would advise you to go to Whitehall & take Col. Adams with you & there concert measures for obtaining & spreading the earliest information of the enemy's approach toward the head of the Lake & make arrangements to repel them in a manner which will do honor to the character of the Militia & of those who may command them.

In Canada, Lt. Colonel Robertson (King's Regiment) arrives at Halifax aboard the HMS *Manly*. One of the vessels in the convoy, the transport *Lord Somers*— carrying a contingent of the regiment along with the women, children and the baggage — had gotten separated from the convoy during a period of fog. While sailing alone, the *Lord Somers* came under attack by an American privateer at a point off the Halifax lighthouse. The privateer fails to capture it, but during the engagement one British sailor is killed and two others are wounded. In addition, 13 soldiers, including Captain James Agnew (British 8th Regiment), are wounded.

In naval activity, the HMS *La Hogue* seizes the 69-ton schooner *Sarah* going with a cargo of molasses and other items from St. Bartholomews to Boston. The *Sarah* is separate from the *Sarah* seized 19 February 1813 and the schooner *Sarah* captured on 28 September 1814. Also, the American privateer York, commanded Captain E. Staples, encounters a British transport, the *Lord Somers*, off Nova Scotia, and the transport proves to be capable of defending itself. The two antagonists pound each other incessantly, and after a while, the York has heavy casualties. The captain and six others are killed, while 12 others sustain wounds. The York, after assessing its losses breaks off and leaves the transport to continue its voyage.

Later, the York strikes again and intercepts the schooner *Diligence*, which is en route to St. John's from Halifax. The York absolves its recent failure to snatch the transport by capturing the *Diligence* and destroying it at sea. It then seizes a brigantine, the *Betsey*, during summer of 1814 while it is en route to Barbados with a cargo of fish. The York diverts it to Boston.

April 20 (Wednesday) *In naval activity,* the privateer *Grand Turk* seizes the *Thetis*.

April 21 (Thursday) *In naval activity,* the HMS *La Hogue* intercepts and seizes the 55-ton brigantine *Minerva* (A.C. White, master). The *Minerva* is separate from the brigantine *Minerva* seized 6 July 1812, the ship *Minerva* captured 8 September 1812, the brigantine *Minerva* captured on 30 June 1813, the sloop *Minerva* seized on 5 August 1813, the schooner *Minerva* seized 30 August 1813, the schooner *Minerva* captured on 11 August 1814, and the schooner *Minerva* captured on 26 September 1814.

April 22 (Friday) *In naval activity,* on or about this day, the American privateer *Scourge* intercepts and seizes the British ship *Caledonia*, which is en route to Nova Scotia. Twenty-six prisoners are transferred to the *Caledonia* and it is permitted to resume its voyage. Several days later, the *Scourge* seizes a brigantine that is en route from Dublin, Ireland, to Quebec. The brigantine, carrying a cargo of salt and other items, is destroyed at sea. Later the same day, the *Scourge* comes upon another British vessel carrying women and children, along with a cargo of lumber and other items. The Americans disable some of the sails and rigging, and they also place some prisoners aboard before permitting the vessel to resume its voyage.

April 23 (Saturday) In Canada at Montreal, Sir George Prevost writes Lt. General Drummond:

> It is difficult to foretell the next offensive measure of the enemy, as their policy has become notoriously miserably shallow since the intelligence of the great and glorious events which have occurred in Europe arrived at Washington, but if a flow of enterprise is rekindled and a descent on Long Point should be combined with an attack on Fort Niagara, it appears to me advisable that Major General Riall should concentrate his force between Chippewa and Fort George in order to crush the enemy marching upon Burlington. You will decide under what circumstances of danger Niagara [should] be blown to the moon.

April 25 (Monday) In Canada, troops attached to the Newfoundland Regiment, along with a party of sailors and naval artificers, depart from Kingston en route to York before moving beyond toward Michilimackinac. The contingent moves across Lake Huron in bateaux, and following an arduous journey finally reaches the post on 18 May to the jubilation of the garrison, which had been waiting for reinforcements. Upon their arrival the garrison also begins to further fortify the positions. On 18 June, Colonel McDougall reports that the post is prepared for an attack by any size force that the Americans might send against him.

In naval activity, the privateer *Lawrence*, a schooner, seizes the vessel *Cerez*. The vessel and prisoners are taken to Portland, Maine.

April 26 (Tuesday) *In naval activity,* the HMS *Pique*, a frigate, intercepts and seizes the privateer *Hawk*, which had only left port at Wilmington, North Carolina, the previous month.

April 28 (Thursday) *In naval activity,* the privateer *Grand Turk* seizes the *Catherine*, separate from the vessel *Catherine* captured by the *Grand Turk* on 11 April.

April 29 (Friday) In Washington, D.C., General William Henry Winder, after his release by the British, arrives in the capital.

In naval activity, the USS *Peacock*, while patrolling of the coast of Florida, spots a three-ship convoy being escorted by the HMS *Epervier* (Captain Wales) at about dawn. It initiates pursuit and after about four hours, it intercepts the *Epervier*. The British prepare to engage, and at about 1055, the *Peacock*, at nearly point-blank range, commences fire, which the *Epervier* returns. The two antagonists remain locked in a close-quartered battle; however, the British vessel sustains hits that sever its fore top mast and shreds the fore rigging. Meanwhile, it sustains about 20 devastating hits, some of which are below the water line. The *Epervier* has waist high water in the hull and every gun except three is out of action, forcing the crew to strike the colors. The British had also inflicted serious damage to the *Peacock*, but its guns remain operational and it is manageable, despite heavy damage to one of its masts. The British, according to the report of the U.S. commander, Captain Lewis Warrington, sustain eight killed and 13 wounded out of a crew of 123. The Americans sustain two wounded and no fatalities. The *Epervier* is taken as a prize. It also yields a bonanza, about $160,000 in gold bullion.

The Americans repair the ship the next day. That evening, both ships sail off moving northeasterly. They arrive near Amelia Island on 1 May.

April 30 (Saturday) In Canada at Montreal, Sir George Prevost sends another "secret and confidential" letter to Lt. General Drummond regarding Sackets Harbor:

> In your despatch of the 26th, which has this moment been brought to me, I perceive a more decided opinion on the contemplated movement against Sackets Harbor. You consider the land forces to be employed on this service should not be less than 4,000 effective rank and file to afford a reasonable hope of success. In order to render so many men disposable at Kingston, I ought to augment your present force there to at least 5,000 effectives, an increase little calculated to diminish the great difficulties which you are laboring under for provisions and forage to maintain a much smaller force. But the fact is that the force in this country is insufficient to enable me to concentrate at anyone point in Upper Canada the number of regulars you require for this important service without stripping Lower Canada of nearly the whole of them that are at present in it, and committing its defence to Provincials and militia.
>
> The views of His Majesty's government respecting the mode of conducting the war with America, do not justify my exposing too much at one stake. It is by wary measures and occasional daring enterprises, with apparently disproportionate means, that the character of the war has been sustained, and from that policy I am not disposed to depart.
>
> But a presumption that the government of the United States is animated by a sincere de-

sire of an armistice from a firm belief that the negotiation commenced at Gottenburg will terminate in peace has induced me to accede to the president's proposal to appoint an officer of rank to discuss and arrange to-morrow, on the part of H.M.'s government, with a similar person on the part of the American gov't the articles of a suspension of arms, at the village of Champlain.

This circumstance renders it inexpedient that an extensive offensive movement against any of the enemy's positions should be undertaken until you shall again hear from me on the subject. I do not feel disposed to give credit to the whole of Mr. Constant Bacon's deposition. The circumstances may be true but they are exaggerated, and in one instance I see much improbability in the statement. However, it is satisfactory to know that M. Genl. Riall is fully prepared against any enterprise. The Commiss'y Genl. has the most positive orders to forward provisions to Upper Canada as expeditiously as possible.

You will please to communicate to Commodore Sir James Yeo the subject of this letter, but I do not wish it to restrain him from any operation he may have in view until the armistice is officially announced.

In New York, Lt. Colonel James Mitchell arrives at Fort Ontario in Oswego. His artillery battalion, dispatched by General Jacob Brown, is armed as infantry rather than artillerymen, and they are tasked with meeting a British attack, which is expected shortly. The column arrives this day, having marched about 150 miles in less than five days. The fort is in terrible condition. The five guns are inoperable due to the absence of carriages, and three of the five pieces lack trunnions. Mitchell immediately orders his troops to construct modified carriages sufficient to get the guns working before the British arrive. Those not engaged with the project are involved in making repairs to the post.

In naval activity, the *Saucy Jack*, an American privateer operating out of Charleston, intercepts the vessel *Pelham* off Cape Nocola Mole in the Dominican Republic. A tenacious naval battle ignites. The British resist fiercely; however, they are finally compelled to surrender after fighting on the decks of the *Pelham* for at least fifteen minutes of the two-hour battle. The cargo includes dry goods, hardware, Irish linens, leather goods, wines, lead, gunpowder and many other items, making the *Pelham* the most lucrative prize of the *Saucy Jack*'s career on the seas. The British sustain four killed and 11 wounded. Captain Boyd of the Pelham sustains a grievous wound to the chest; however, he survives. The Americans sustain two killed and eight wounded.

May In New York, Major General George Izard is placed in command at Plattsburgh. In related activity, Brigadier General Scott receives command of the Niagara frontier.

In naval activity, Napoleon has abdicated the French throne and the British begin to focus on their remaining foe, the United States. Without the burden of fighting the French, the British Royal Navy has a huge force with which to finally terminate the war with America. At this time, the United Kingdom of Great Britain has 1,120 ships of the line, 130 frigates, no less than 120 brigantines and about 100 sloops.

In other naval activity, the American privateer *Yankee* sails at about this time (May–June) on another cruise, its fourth, again under Captain Elisha Snow. The *Yankee* remains at sea for only about four weeks, but it is a lucrative voyage. It intercepts and captures four vessels, the ship *Sir Hugh Jones*, en route to Guadalupe from Belfast, Northern Ireland, the brigantine *Maria Wirman* en route to Scotland from Havana, and the ship *Berry Castle*, carrying six guns. Captain Snow deems the *Berry Castle* of no value and orders it released, but the Americans relieve it of a cargo of barilla and wine before letting it proceed. The Yankee closes out its cruise with the seizure of the ship *San Jose Indiano*, and it becomes a bonanza for the crew after arriving at Portland when the value of the vessel and its cargo are valued at just under $600,000. The Yankee sets out on its fifth cruise on 1 October 1814.

In other naval activity, the American privateer *Roger* intercepts a vessel flying the Russian flag, and upon closer inspection, it is the ship *Fortuna*, carrying a cargo of British items. The *Fortuna* is seized and taken into port at Beaufort, South Carolina. During this same cruise, the *Roger* seizes another vessel laden with a cargo of rum, destined for England from Jamaica. It is diverted to an American port. The *Roger*, in August during same cruise, seizes the schooner *Contract*, which is carrying a cargo of salt, and diverts it to North Carolina. In December the *Roger* intercepts the *L'Aimable*, which is flying a Spanish flag and sailing from Havana, Cuba to England. After inspecting the cargo and discovering British property, the vessel is seized. One other vessel is snagged by the *Roger* before its cruise ends. It is packet *Windsor Castle*, en route to Halifax from Falmouth.

Also, the American privateer *Pike*, operating out of Baltimore, having gone to sea during the latter part of the conflict, makes up for lost time. While cruising this month, it seizes the brigantine *John* as it sails to Tenerife from London. Despite being within range of the long guns of a British warship, the *John* is destroyed at sea. The British attempt but fail to capture the *Pike*. Other seizures by the *Pike* include the schooner *Hope*; the schooner *Pickerel* (*Pickrel*), captured en route to Quebec from Dartmouth, England, with a cargo including dry goods and tea (the cargo is transferred and the vessel is destroyed); the schooner *Lord Nelson*, which is taken into port; the schooner *Venus*, taken into port; and the brigantine *Jane*, with a cargo of dry goods and provisions. Some of its cargo is seized, and afterward the *Jane* is made a cartel. The *Pike* also seizes the ships *Samuel Cummings*, carrying coffee and sugar, and the *Mermaid*, with coal and salt. The *Samuel Cummings* is sent into a southern port, but it gets wrecked on the coast. Nonetheless, some of its cargo is saved. The *Pike* seizes more than 20 prizes, including the British privateer *Pike* (burned at sea) and the *Industrious Bee* (burned at sea).

Following this cruise, at about September of this year, a flotilla of British boats chase it ashore. Some of the crew escapes; however the British do seize 43 members of the crew. During its time at sea, the *Pike* captures 250 prisoners; each one receives parole.

May 1 (Sunday) *In naval activity,* the recently commissioned USS *Wasp* (fifth), commanded by Master Commandant Johnston Blakeley, leaves Portsmouth, New Hampshire, en route to the waters at the western approaches to the English Channel. Also, the USS *Peacock*, commanded by Captain Warrington, and its recently captured prize, the HMS *Epervier*, arrive near Amelia Island, just below St. Mary's, where they encounter a British blockading squadron composed of two British frigates and one brigantine. The Americans immediately decide to separate. A frigate pursues the *Peacock*, but it evades the peril and arrives safely at Savannah on 4 May. The prize ship *Epervier*, having a crew of only 17 men, also escapes harm and arrives at Savannah. Congress later awards Captain Warrington a gold medal; his commissioned officers each receive a silver medal and a sword.

After arriving at Savannah the *Epervier* receives extensive repairs. It is then assigned to Commodore Stephen Decatur's Mediterranean Squadron. It participates in the action against the Barbary pirates at Algiers. Afterward, Commodore Decatur assigns the *Epervier*, commanded by Lt. John T. Shubrick, the honor of returning to the United States to deliver a copy of the treaty that Decatur consummated with Algiers, along with some captured flags.

The American privateer *Yankee Lass*, while on its first cruise, has an unfortunate encounter with the HMS *Severn*, a frigate. It is captured on its 20th day at sea. In other naval activity, the American privateer *Scourge* intercepts a brigantine that had sailed from Dublin, Ireland, with a cargo that includes cordage, fishing equipment and

Captain Johnston Blakeley, U.S. Navy.

other items, intended for consignees in Newfoundland. It is captured and sent into port in the United States.

May 1–2 **In New York** at Sackets Harbor, the *Superior*, a 66-gun frigate, having been constructed in 80 days, is launched on 1 May. Afterward, the sailors and the carpenters that completed the task begin a celebration that includes massive over-indulging that explodes into hostilities against soldiers the next day. Several of the carpenters beat a dragoon, who seeks help from a sentinel. One of the carpenters is shot by the sentinel, which causes more provocation. The carpenters and sailors form a mob and chase the sentinel. Other troops form a protective square to shield him from the mob. When the carpenters and sailors, carrying axes and cutlasses, are less than five yards from the troops, Commodore Chauncey and General Brown arrive to stop the fight. The sentinel is afterward sent to Watertown, and after an inquiry is held, the man is transferred to a point far from Sackets Harbor to prevent any further contact with those who came close to killing him.

May 2 (Monday) *In naval activity,* the HMS *Jaseur*, while operating in the Chesapeake, sends out one boat with a contingent of seven men under Lt. West of the Royal Navy. The party succeeds in capturing the privateer *Grecian* and getting it out and away from a battery. The prize is afterward placed in service in the Royal Navy. In other activity, the *Commerce* (James Ives, master), a 195-ton brigantine, is intercepted and seized by the HMS *Superb*. The *Commerce* is separate from the *Commerce* captured on 30 May 1813.

May 3 (Tuesday) **In Canada** at Kingston, Lt. General Drummond informs Sir George Prevost in a letter dated this day that the fleet is ready to sail:

> SIR, I have the honor to acquaint Your Excellency that I propose embarking on board the squadron as soon as the wind is fair, the following troops. viz: Royal Artillery, 24; Rocketteers, 6; Sappers, 20; Regiment De Watteville, 450; Glengarry Light Infantry, 50, which, with the Royal Marines (350) will make a disposable force of 900 men for the purpose of destroying, if possible, the enemy's magazines and stores at Oswego, and along the southern coast of Lake Ontario, bringing off, however, such quantities as it may be practicable for the relief of the Right Division.
>
> To satisfy myself that as much is done on this occasion as can be, I propose embarking myself with Commodore Sir James Yeo, but the immediate command of the troops I have entrusted to Lieutenant Colonel Fischer of De Watteville's Regiment.
>
> By the enclosed copy of information from Sackets Harbor, dated the 28th ultimo, Your Excellency will perceive that a new ship is to be laid down there and finished in six weeks. If such be the case it is impossible for us to keep pace with such exertions. I must again beg leave to repeat my opinion that the only way to completely secure the Upper Province is a vicious combined attack of army and navy against the enemy's chief means of annoyance, their fleet and stores at Sackets Harbor.
>
> But on this occasion the most ample measures must be taken to ensure success, and the small force which the Upper Province can afford must be assisted by a regular force from Your Excellency of certainly not less than 800 effective men from the Lower Province. In all these opinions I am joined by the naval commander, Sir James Yeo. Major General Riall has reported that the enemy are encamped at Buffalo with about 800 men, with three field pieces.

May 4 (Wednesday) *In naval activity,* the HMS *Curlew* captures the brigantine *Maria Francisca* (Nicholas Calveras, master) on its way from Havana to Boston. The *Maria* is separate from a ketch named *Maria* captured during 1812 and the ship *Maria* seized on 13 July 1812, the *Maria Windsor*, seized 29 March 1813, the brigantine *Maria* overtaken 24 June 1813, the brigantine *Maria Frederica* captured 14 July 1814 and the schooner *Maria* captured on 4 September 1814.

May 5 (Thursday) *In naval activity,* the British fleet under Commodore Yeo arrives in Lake Ontario several miles from Oswego. Commodore Sir James Yeo, having recently failed to destroy the new warship under construction at Sackets Harbor, moves to strike Fort Oswego, New York, where the rigging and other equipment, including the ship's guns, are presently stored. Commodore Yeo's force includes several thousand ground troops under the command of General Drummond. Yeo's massive fleet is observed by Mitchell as it approaches, and it becomes evident that his force is overmatched. With the post on one side of the river and the town of Oswego on the opposite bank, Mitchell realizes that to split his force would cause more problems. Consequently, he orders that tents be gathered and sent across the river to create an illusion that the American military presence is much greater. The ruse accomplishes what Mitchell had intended. The British are convinced that the village of Oswego is heavily protected. Consequently, they focus only on the fort rather than risk combat with a large force.

At about 1300, British boats begin to move toward shore. The Americans observe the landing force while it approaches, but the order to fire is withheld. Just as the fleet's gunboats move into close range, the American artillery under Captain James A. Boyle and Lieutenant Thomas C. LeGate, begins fire. Commodore Yeo and General Drummond initially send in a landing force transported by fifteen boats; however, Lt. Colonel Mitchell foils the landing by sending a small detachment and one piece of old artillery, a 12-pounder, to greet the invaders. The gunners wait until the boats move close to shore and at that point the British receive streams of fire that perplex the crews and cause some panic. The ancient artillery piece strikes one of the larger boats which is carrying three sails and 36 oars. The boat is splintered by the fire and the crew and troops are forced to abandon it. Other boats are also damaged.

Meanwhile, the remaining boats begin to return to the ships of the fleet. Mitchell's gun had repulsed the invasion force. Twice the gunboats are forced to turn back. The Americans lose one of their five cannon due to an explosion. The British launch a third attempt to land at about 2000, but again, the attempt fails. The winds turn unfavorable and the fleet is compelled to withdraw. General Drummond afterward contends that he did not intend to land; rather, his fifteen boats were only probing. The ships move back into position on the following morning.

May 6 (Friday) **In New York,** at Oswego, the Americans under Colonel Mitchell again prepare to defend the post at Fort Oswego. The British, thwarted on the previous day, begin to move in close to shore and enter the harbor.

At 0900, the operation unfolds. Seven British ships move closer to shore and into the harbor from where the guns pound Fort Oswego. While the more powerful vessels initiate the bombardment, the *Magnet* halts just to the front of the village. At the same time, the *Star* and the *Charinell* are towed to positions at the mouth of the Genesee River from where they can provide cover fire for the landing force (estimates vary from 900 to 1,200 troops), composed of contingents of De Watteville's regiment, commanded by Captain De Bersey, light infantry troops of the Glengarry Regiment, commanded by Captain M'Millan, one battalion of Royal Marines led by Lt. Colonel Malcolm, and a 200-man contingent of sailors, each armed with picks and cutlasses, led by Captain Mulcaster. Overall command is under Lt. Colonel Fischer. The British also maintain a reserve force aboard the fleet.

While the naval guns bombard the fort, the Americans raise tenacious resistance, despite having only four cannon. The shore guns ignite fires in the rigging on the HMS *Wolfe*, and these cause some of the ship's ropes to burn. By about noon, a contingent of Royal Marines under Lt. Colonel Fischer lands about 500 yards from the fort. Dur-

Attack on Oswego.

ing the landing, the British encounter some difficulty due to the unexpected depth of the water, which is well above waist high. The water destroys a large amount of the ammunition being carried by the troops. American militia troops are posted in the woods; however, the British Glengarry Light Infantry on the left flank is directed to sweep the militia from their positions. Meanwhile, the 2nd Battalion, Royal Marines, led by Colonel Malcolm, secures the right flank in conjunction with elements of the De Watteville regiment, commanded by Captain De Bersey, which advances in the center. Another contingent, composed of sailors, debarks near the mouth of the harbor.

The militia, recently arrived to bolster Mitchell's force, are unable to withstand the British thrust. Nonetheless, Mitchell is able to raise formidable resistance. He informs his officers that he intends "to fight as long as the honor of our arms and the interest of his country should require it." Mitchell commands two companies (commanded by Captain Melvin and Lt. Ansart, the latter in place of Captain Romayne, who is on a separate mission on the left bank of the river), which advance to engage. Captain McIntire and Captain Pierce hold the line against the light infantry.

When the British ascend the hill leading to the fort, the pressure forces Mitchell's defenders to withdraw to the ditch. The British succeed in overwhelming the artillery batteries and advancing to the bastions to the rear of Mitchell's left flank. Although the American line is driven back, it is a disciplined retreat with the defenders fighting while they withdraw. During the struggle, some Americans defiantly fight to prevent the British from seizing the fort's colors from a staff at the north end of the post. A few of the British troops are shot while trying to ascend the staff, and one defender is victimized by a British bayonet. Nonetheless, Lt. Hewitt of the Royal Marines captures the Stars and Stripes. When the peril mounts and Mitchell realizes the British have the fort, he orders his force to abandon the ditch and retire toward Oswego Falls. Mitchell had also taken the precaution of relocating the greater part of the fort's stores to prevent the British from confiscating them. In addition, Mitchell's troops destroy each of the bridges, once the retreating troops cross.

During the fighting, Mitchell, the only man mounted upon a horse, had been a conspicuous target, however, their sharpshooters had been unable to take him out. On the way to the falls, Mitchell dismounts to permit two men — one of whom is sick from exhaustion (Captain Pierce) and a sergeant who is wounded — to mount his horse and a spare horse to prevent them from becoming captives of the British or victims of the bayonet.

After driving Mitchell's force from the fort, the British take possession of it. They ransack the post and carry away whatever can be moved. They then burn the barracks down. The next morning, the fleet withdraws; however, before it sails, the British raise a vessel, the *Growler*, which contains some of the guns for the new vessel and had been intentionally sunk by the Americans at first sight of the fleet. The British raid spares the village due to Mitchell's phantom army tents, and their success had not been without cost.

The American force, composed of about 300 men, including about 30 sailors under Lt. Pearce, U.S. Navy, sustains five or six killed, including Lt. Blaney, U.S. Navy, of Delaware, 38 wounded and 25 missing. On the following day, seven of the wounded die. British casualty estimates are about 19 killed and 75 wounded. Captain Mulcaster (HMS *Princess Charlotte*) sustains a serious wound and Captain Popham (HMS *Montreal*) sustains a minor one.

Following the raid, Commodore Yeo again blockades Sackets Harbor in an effort to prevent the Americans from getting armaments to the new vessel. The Americans bypass the blockade by moving the supplies by an overland route.

May 7 (Saturday) In New York at Oswego, the British fleet under Commodore Yeo, having taken Fort Oswego on the previous day, weighs anchor at 0500 and sails toward Kingston. On the previous day, Commodore Yeo was on scene when the British were removing the stores, including salt and other confiscated items. He confronted Mr. Bronson and told him to supply pilots; however, Bronson replied that all pilots had departed the village. Yeo became irritated and bellowed: "Go yourself and if you get the boat aground, I'll shoot you." British Colonel Harvey, atop the bank, yells to Yeo informing him that Bronson is the village storekeeper and that he could be "useful to us." Yeo takes Bronson prisoner and Captain O'Connor is directed to take him aboard the *Prince Regent*. Bronson, who also refused to provide Yeo with intelligence regarding stores distributed to the Army and Navy, receives harsh treatment while he is held, but he does return to New York in a few months.

May 9 (Monday) In Canada, British Captain Daniel Pring sails from Isle aux Nois to attack the Americans and either seize or destroy the American warships that had recently been launched at Vergennes. Pring's mission is also tasked with intercepting provisions and supplies intended for the new vessels. On 14 May, the British squadron, which is carrying a contingent of Royal Marines, arrives off the mouth of Otter Creek. Pring's command is composed of eight galleys, several sloops, one new brigantine and one bomb ketch. The British announce their arrival with a bombardment; however, elements of the U.S. Navy under Lt. Cass and some potent artillery under Captain Thornton are thoroughly prepared to return the salutations. Those at the battery are augmented by a ground force under Colonel Aquila Davis and poised to intercept any landing force that might attempt to hit the beach.

The British shelling pounds the fortification, but without inflicting any severe damage or injury to the troops. Captain Pring continues to fire at the target for about one and one-half hours before he decides the attack is in vain. No landing is attempted and he retires. During his return to Isle aux Nois, American shore batteries at Burlington, Vermont, fire at the squadron while it is in a narrow part of Lake Champlain, and the British also come under fire by troops that are deployed along the shoreline. The squadron makes it through the gauntlet, but in the process, two of the rowboats, attached to the barges, are shot free and easily retrieved by the Americans. Pring also pauses at Gilleland's Creek to try to seize flour from some of the mills in the area. During the precarious mission to confiscate flour, the British take casualties. The militia kills or wounds a large number of British troops who are in two of the galleys. When Pring finally gets back to Canada, he is not well received. He is summoned to Montreal, where he receives a court-martial for misconduct. He loses his rank as commander of the naval forces on the North American lakes.

In naval activity, the brigantine *Dantzic* (J. Reid, master), en route from Bath, Maine, to Bermuda, is captured by the HMS *Fantome* and taken into port at St. John's, New Brunswick. Also, the American privateer *Scourge*, during its voyage home to the States from off the coast of Scotland, seizes the brigantine *Nancy* (sent into New York), carrying a cargo of oil, marble silks, sulphur and other items; the ship *Lord Hood*, en route from Quebec to London (burned at sea); and the brigantine *Trident*, also en route to London from Quebec, burned at sea. Two other vessels, the brigantine *Haddock* and the brigantine *Belfield*, also en route to London from Quebec, are captured and burned at sea. The *Scourge* arrives back at Chatham, Cape Cod, Massachusetts, during May to conclude a cruise that had lasted about one year. During the cruise, the *Scourge* captured 420 prisoners.

May 10 (Tuesday) In Michigan, a British relief force under Colonel McDougall arrives at Fort Michilimackinac, known as Fort George while held by the British, to bolster the garrison. The post, seized by the British during the early days of the war, stands as a guard to protect an attack against Canada from the rear.

May 11 (Wednesday) *In naval activity,* the American privateer *Holkar* is intercepted by the HMS *Orpheus*, and unlike some other vessels run ashore and captured by the *Orpheus*, the privateer's commander, Captain Rowland, manages to get his vessels to shore and his cargo and 25 prisoners safely on land. The British, however, continue their pursuit. Captain Rowland, unwilling to become a guest of the British, oversees a hurried defensive position once British boats are spotted heading for shore. Despite the odds, the Americans succeed in repulsing the attack and forcing the British to return to the ships. Afterward, about 15 corpses are carried to shore by the tide. After repelling the attack, Captain Rowland, realizing he cannot salvage his ship, orders his crew to escape The entire party evades capture. The British, however, move in closer and the *Holkar* is destroyed by the guns of the *Orpheus*.

Before the harrowing incident, while the *Holkar* was cruising in search of British shipping, it had captured a number of vessels, including the *Emu* in November 1812. Other prizes seized by the *Holkar* included a pair of trading ships and one 14 gun brigantine, which was taken into port at New York, along with a schooner, the *Richard*, that was sailed into Savannah.

May 12 (Thursday) **In New York,** the town of Charlotte at the mouth of the Genesee River becomes threatened when a British squadron arrives. The town's defenses number only 60 men, and they are bolstered by one piece of artillery. An urgent message is sent to General Peter B. Porter to inform him of the peril. General Porter arrives with reinforcements on the following morning in timely fashion. The British demand surrender; however, due to the arrival of the reinforcements, the demand is refused. Nonetheless, the British increase the pressure. Two gunboats proceed into the river and their guns commence a bombardment. In anticipation of the naval attack, all women and children have been escorted out of harm's way. Militia, about 300 strong, is gathered, and it is decided to seize the gunboats if they advance farther. Meanwhile, the British again demand that the town capitulate; however, despite a threat to land 1,200 troops, with orders to reduce the town, General Porter refuses to be intimidated. He declines the ultimatum. The British remain in place and on the 15th, they resume the bombardment that, identically to the initial attack, lasts for about one and one-half hours. During the evening, a landing force is debarked at Poultneyville. Here, too, the town is not heavily defended; however, word of the raid is delivered to General John Swift, who immediately responds. He arrives with a contingent of militia, and although the British had confiscated some stores, the militia forces the raiders to hurriedly head back to their boats.

In naval activity, the schooner *Mammoth,* a privateer, seizes the brigantine *Camelion.*

May 13 (Friday) *In naval activity,* the HMS *Superb* intercepts the 160-ton brigantine *Catalina* (J.F. Cerrero, master) on its way to New Bedford from St. Domingo with hides and molasses. Also, the sloop *Experiment* (Z. Lovell, master) is en route to New York from Barnstable, Massachusetts, with a cargo of fish and oil when it is intercepted and seized by the HMS *Bulwark* before it reaches its destination. The *Experiment* is separate from the schooner *Experiment* seized 11 April 1813 and the sloop *Experiment* captured 24 June 1813. In other naval activity, a British squadron, composed of the *La Hogue, Maidstone, Nimrod* and *Sylph,* encounters and seizes the brigantine *Victor,* which is transporting a cargo of sugar from Haiti to New London, Connecticut.

May 14 (Saturday) **In Canada,** on or about this day, an American contingent, having crossed Lake Ontario and landed at Longport, raids several villages including Dover and Port Ryerse along the lake shore. At the latter location, the widow of Captain Ryerse requests from the commanding officer, Colonel John B. Campbell, that her property be spared. The Americans do spare her home; however, all of the remaining structures, including the mills, are destroyed by fire. A militia force under Colonel Talbot, usually in the area, is at the time of the raids away at Brantford.

In naval activity, the sloop *Fame* (Aron Clarke, master) is seized by the British privateer *Liverpool Packet.* The *Fame* is separate from the sloop *Fame* seized on 1 April 1813, the 85-ton sloop *Fame* seized 31 May 1814, and the 48-ton sloop *Fame* captured 23 July 1814.

May 15 (Sunday) **In New York** at Poultneyville, the town, under threat since early May, had been reinforced on the 14th. On this day, the British fleet initiates a bombardment. The fleet is not immediately spotted due to a thick early morning fog; however, the fog also provides the militia some cover. Once it dissipates, the militia immediately detects the fleet and heads for the woods to avoid the naval gunfire. Afterward, some type of negotiations occur and the villagers agree to provide a specific amount of flour for the British. Apparently, the British go beyond the agreement by taking more flour, and the villagers take offense that the British also move into other sections of the village and inflict damage. The militia reacts by firing upon the British. The British return fire; however, it does not build into a major skirmish. The British, having gained the flour, move back to their boats and return to the ships. Two Americans snagged by the British are also taken back to the fleet. The two prisoners, Prescott Fairbanks and Richard White, are detained for a few months before they are returned to their homes.

In naval activity, the HMS *Bulwark* seizes the sloop *Amelia* (R.G. Cornwall, master) while it is sailing from New York to Providence, Rhode Island. The prize — with its cargo of bread, flour, ham, and pork — is taken into port at Liverpool. The *Amelia* is separate from the sloop *Amelia* that was captured on 5 August 1813. Also, the HMS *La Hogue* seizes the 160-ton ship *Tejo.* At the time of its capture, the *Tejo* has a cargo including flour, molasses and rum.

May 18 (Wednesday) *In naval activity,* the British privateer *Shannon* intercepts and seizes the sloop *John* (J.L. Stover, master). The *John* is separate from the brigantine *John* seized on 16 August 1812 and the brigantine *John* overtaken 5 April 1813.

May 19 (Thursday) **In Washington, D.C.,** Brigadier General William H. Winder, U.S. Army, is appointed as adjutant and inspector general, and as chief of staff of the Northern Army; however, by early July, he relinquishes the post to assume command of the 10th Military District.

In Canada at Kingston, Commodore James Yeo's, fleet having completed repairs following

The USS *Superior.*

British Commodore Sir James Lucas Yeo.

the attack against Oswego, departs. The USS *Lady of the Lake,* Commodore Isaac Chauncey's lookout vessel, is forced to run into Sackets Harbor. Afterward, the British resume the blockade. Meanwhile, Chauncey is attempting to get the USS *Superior* to sea. However, its guns have not yet arrived from Oswego Falls. Captain Woolsey volunteers to repair to the falls and get the guns to Chauncey by carrying them to Stoney Creek only a few miles from Sackets Harbor. Once at the creek, the guns are to be transported by an overland route to completely bypass the blockade and provide Chauncey the opportunity of getting the *Superior* on the lake to deprive Yeo of domination. To confuse the British, false intelligence is planted.

In naval activity, a sloop, the 67-ton *Ann* (Samuel Drinkwater, master), transporting a cargo of copper, hardware and tin from East Port to Boston, is intercepted and seized by the privateer

Shannon. The prize is taken into port at Liverpool. In other activity, the HMS *Superb* intercepts the sloop *Candaleria* (Eman Fernandez) while it is en route from Havana to Boston.

The British privateer *Shannon* intercepts and seizes the schooner *Defiance* (S. Marshal, master) and takes it into port at Liverpool. The *Defiance* is separate from the 118-ton sloop *Defiance* seized on 31 March 1813, the 104-ton sloop *Defiance* captured 4 April 1813, the 62-ton sloop *Defiance* taken on 3 June 1814, and the 46-ton sloop *Defiance* captured 3 August 1814. One other sloop named *Defiance* is seized by the HMS *Superb* and the HMS *Sylph* at an undetermined time during 1814. Also, the British privateer *Shannon* intercepts and seizes the sloop *Sally* (Moses Lowe, master). The prize is taken into port at Liverpool.

May 20 (Friday) **In New Hampshire,** Governor John Taylor Gilman orders more reinforcements sent to Portsmouth and Little Harbor due to the ongoing threat of a British attack. The governor calls for six companies from the 1st Division and two companies of the 2nd Division to move to Portsmouth within the next five days. The contingent, led by Major Edward J. Long, who assumes command on 27 May, deploys primarily at Fort Washington; however, it also spends time at Fort Sullivan and at Fort Constitution. The unit is dissolved on 26 July 1814.

Major Long, an aide to Governor Gilman since earlier in the year, is appointed major of the artillery detached for the defense of Piscataqua Harbor during September 1814. The next month, Long is appointed major of the 2nd Battalion, 1st Regiment, New Hampshire Militia. After the war, Major Long moves through the ranks and is named brigadier general of the New Hampshire Brigade during 1820. General Long succumbs on 27 February 1824 from falling on ice. Also, Colonel George Sullivan, the son of General John Sullivan, who served in the state legislature and the state senate, is appointed aide-de-camp to Governor Gilman. Sullivan remains in the post until June 1816.

May 22 (Sunday) Andrew Jackson is promoted to major general of the United States Army. His new command, the 7th Military District, includes the troops in Louisiana, Tennessee and Mississippi Valley. He succeeds Brigadier General Thomas Flournoy. On 31 May, the *National Intelligencer* in Washington, D.C., publishes the following announcement: "ANDREW JACKSON, of Tennessee is appointed Major General in the Army of the United States, vice WILLIAM HENRY HARRISON, resigned."

In naval activity, the schooner *Dominica* (F. Beaufew, master), carrying a cargo that includes wine, rice, muskets and other items, is intercepted and seized by a British squadron including the HMS *Dotterell,* HMS *Majestic* and the *Morgiana.*

May 23 (Monday) *In naval activity,* the HMS *Nieman* seizes the schooner *Clara* (J. Newman, master). The *Nieman* also seizes the 250-ton schooner *Model* (John Austin, master) while it is in port at Little Egg Harbor, New Jersey, and a third prize, the 214-ton schooner *Quiz,* which is en route from St. Iago to Philadelphia with coffee, molasses and sugar.

May 24 (Tuesday) **In New York,** the British increase their efforts to interrupt the American war operations at Sackets Harbor. Commodore Yeo initiates a naval blockade of the port to prevent supplies from reaching Captain Macdonough's squadron.

May 25 (Wednesday) *In naval activity,* the HMS *Saturn* intercepts and seizes a privateer, the schooner *Hussar* (F. Jenkins, master), along with the crew of 97 men. Also, the HMS *Curlew* seizes the ship *Ontario.* Also, the HMS *Curlew* and the HMS *Martin,* while operating together, encounter the vessel *Two Brothers,* a bark, and recapture it. The *Two Brothers* is separate from the schooner *Two Brothers* seized on 27 March 1813, the schooner *Two Brothers* seized 6 July 1813, the schooner *Two Brothers* captured 7 July 1813, and the schooner *Two Brothers* seized 4 September 1814.

May 28 (Saturday) **In New York,** the Americans have been struggling to discover a way to get guns to Sackets Harbor for the new vessel *Superior,* but Commodore Yeo has successfully blockaded the port. The Americans have abandoned any thoughts of transporting the guns and other equipment overland due to the difficulties involved, including an exorbitant cost. Success of a plan concocted by Captain Woolsey, U.S. Navy, depends in great part on story told to the British that the guns would be transported by way of Oneida Lake. Meanwhile, on this day, Captain Woolsey, with a flotilla of nineteen boats, passes through the rapids and arrives at Oswego at about dusk. The precious cargo includes twenty-two long 32-pounders, ten 24-pounders three 42-pound carronades along with twelve cables. During the mission, Woolsey determines that trying to reach Sandy Creek is too risky. He modifies his plan and instead will move down the lake and swing into Big Sandy Creek.

Captain Woolsey's force, escorted by about 125 riflemen, commanded by Major Daniel Appling, moves down the lake and reaches the mouth of the Big Salmon River, where about 125 Oneida Indians are waiting to join with the flotilla. During the night, one of the boats vanishes and heads for Sackets Harbor, where it is intercepted by Yeo's squadron. The captives tell Commodore Yeo the details of Woolsey's flotilla, which invigorates the commodore, who has been relentless with his quest to capture the guns. Meanwhile, on the morning of the 29th, while a British contingent is sailing to intercept Woolsey, it is discovered that one of the boats had departed. The flotilla advances and at about noon on the 29th, it reaches Sandy Creek.

On the following day (30th), six British vessels, including two gunboats, move up Sandy Creek, intent on surprising and capturing or destroying the American flotilla before it reaches its destination. However, as the British finally sight the flotilla, it is the Americans who hold the surprises. The British anxiously open fire as soon as the flotilla is within range of its guns, and at nearly the same time a British landing force debarks. Nonetheless, unknown to the overconfident Redcoats, they fail to spot Appling's sharpshooters, who are deployed in concealed positions awaiting their arrival.

The overconfident British advance in anticipation of a quick victory and an effortless maneuver to acquire the naval guns in the flotilla. The initial British fire scatters the Indians; however, Appling's sharpshooters stand firmly and quietly until the Redcoats move into close range. Appling's sharpshooters suddenly commence firing, striking the British flank and rear, then, to add to the fury of the blistering rifle fire, another surprise is lurking nearby. A squadron of light cavalry led by Captain Samuel D. Harris, and a company of light artillery, bolstered by infantry and two artillery pieces, commanded by Captain Melvin, had arrived from Sackets Harbor to meet Woolsey's flotilla; it is deployed close to Woolsey's boats. The reinforcements spring yet more firepower on the British ranks by pounding their front.

The leader of the advance, Ensign Hoare, is among the first to fall; he is struck by eleven balls. The American order to charge rings out and the riflemen bolt forward holding their weapons as if with fixed bayonets. In about ten minutes of incessant fire, the British are decimated and drained of any thoughts of continuing to fight. As soon as they surrender, the Indians allied with the Americans, who did not participate in the fight, begin to pounce upon the unarmed prisoners. The Americans stop them from murdering any of the captives. Nevertheless, it is thought that the Indians had been able to mortally wound at least one of the British officers.

The British force was commanded by Captains Popham and Spilsbury. The British sustain 17 to 19 men killed and another 50 wounded. Some of the British had landed on the south bank and had attempted to flee; however, they were captured, preventing anyone in the force from returning to report on the defeat.

During the ambush, the Oneidas that had joined the flotilla do not engage the British. After the surrender, the Americans under Woolsey find themselves with six additional vessels and a large number of British prisoners, including 27 Royal Marines, 106 sailors, two post captains, four naval lieutenants, one captain of Marines, two lieutenants, and two midshipmen. The captain of Marines and one of the midshipmen die of their wounds. Captain Popham moves forward to surrender his sword and is spotted by Woolsey, who bellows: "Popham, what are you doing in this creek?" He in turn spots his old acquaintance and remarks, "Well, Woolsey, this is the first time I ever heard of riflemen charging bayonets."

Captain Woolsey's plan and successful strategy also gains seven guns that were mounted on British vessels. The Americans sustain no fatalities; however, two men are wounded. Following the stunning victory, Captain Woolsey is unhindered in unloading the guns and cables; however, the task is nearly impossible. The guns are transported to Sackets Harbor; however, the cable for the *Superior* is enormous. It has a circumference of 22 inches and weighs 9,600 pounds, well over the capacity of any wagons. After about a week of trying to find a way to move the cable, a regiment under Colonel Allan Clark, having been informed of the British pursuit of Woolsey, arrives at the creek and comes up with a novel solution. The men will carry the cable.

Two hundred troops are selected for the task. The troops carry the massive cable on their shoulders and they pay a price. The giant rope cuts into their shoulders and they are battered with bruises; however, at Sackets Harbor, upon their arrival on the day after the march began, they are greeted with incessant cheers and a military band. They also receive a bonus that helps them forget the arduous march. A barrel of whiskey is also there to greet the troops as they gleefully drop the cable.

Meanwhile, Commodore Yeo is once again foiled. His embarrassing loss causes him additional problems. While the Americans are able to launch the *Superior* on 11 June, Yeo had been compelled to sail back to Kingston where he remains until he can acquire fresh troops and a new ship. With the *Superior* finally entering active service, Commodore Chauncey's fleet increases to nine ships that carry a total of 250 guns. Chauncey's fleet is prepared to sail on 1 August. Also, Major Appling, a Georgian who joined the army during 1808 as a lieutenant, is promoted to brevet lieutenant colonel in August for his heroic actions during this operation to get guns to Sackets Harbor.

In naval activity, the 150-ton *Diomede* (John Crowninshield, master), a privateer operating out of Salem, Massachusetts, is captured by the HMS *Rifleman.* The *Diomede* is separate from the brigantine *Diomede,* seized on 10 May 1813.

May 29 (Saturday) *In naval activity,* the HMS *Charybdis* intercepts and recaptures the 78-ton brigantine *Success.*

May 31 (Tuesday) *In naval activity,* the HMS *Endymion,* while operating off the North Carolina coast, intercepts and seizes the 85-ton sloop *Fame* on its way from Newport to Ocracoke, North Carolina, with a cargo of "spermaciti oil." The *Fame* is separate from the sloop *Fame* seized on 1 April 1813, the sloop *Fame* captured 14 May 1814, and the 48-ton sloop *Fame* seized on 23 July 1814.

June American naval vessels still scout the seas for British vessels that are fair game. The sloop *Wasp* engages and captures the British vessel *Neptune* in the North Atlantic on the 2nd. This is followed by the successful capture of the brigantine *William* in British waters on the 13th. The *Wasp,* confident after its two recent victories, continues its string by daringly engaging and capturing the HMS brigantine *Pallas,* at the entrance to the English Channel. The British have little success against the valiant *Wasp* during this venture into English waters. It finishes the month with the devastating capture of the *Henrietta* on the 23rd, the seizure of the vessel *Orange Boven* in French waters on the 26th, and then, the most devastating blow on the 28th, when the *Wasp* stings the HMS *Reindeer* in the North Atlantic.

In other activity, President James Madison deems it necessary to alter the instructions previously given to the peace commissioners by the secretary of state, making the cessation of impressment of American seamen a contingency of reaching a settlement with Great Britain. Because of changing circumstances, including the defeat of Napoleon, he instructs them to omit this item and one other, the issue of freedom on the seas. Madison's new orders arrive in Ghent during August on the first day the negotiators convene. His omissions give the British an early advantage, but the president is concerned that the United Kingdom of Great Britain, without France as a foe, might overwhelm the U.S. with its superior strength.

June 1 (Wednesday) BATTLE OF CEDAR POINT In Maryland, a squadron of eighteen light-draft gunboats commanded by Joshua Barney, which had earlier sailed from Baltimore, engages a British blockading force in the Chesapeake Bay. Barney's force moves out of the mouth of the Patuxent River and sails southward toward Tangier Sound, where it is believed the British are establishing a staging area. While en route Barney's squadron encounters a British contingent engaged in a reconnaissance mission. The Americans give chase; however, they become less anxious for a major confrontation when the HMS *Dragon,* carrying 74 guns, is spotted. After a short exchange of fire off Cedar Point, Barney expeditiously orders his force to retire to the Patuxent, with elements of the Royal Navy in pursuit. After reaching the river, the Americans move up about four miles to evade capture. On the 7th, Barney is informed that the British blockading force is at the mouth of the river. He changes his strategy by moving into St. Leonard's Creek instead of farther up the river.

In Washington, D.C., Brigadier General A.Y. Nicoll, inspector general, resigns. He is succeeded by Colonel John R. Bell on 20 October 1814.

In naval activity, the HMS *Martin* intercepts and recaptures the ship *Mary.*

June 2 (Thursday) *In naval activity,* the USS *Wasp* (fifth), commanded by Master Commandant Johnston Blakeley, encounters the vessel *Neptune,* a bark. The crew is taken prisoner; however, the *Neptune* is not seized as a prize. The Americans burn it.

June 3 (Wednesday) *In naval activity,* the 62-ton sloop *Defiance* (E. Sterling, master) is captured by a party from the British privateer *Liverpool Packet.* The *Defiance,* carrying a cargo of flour and other items, is in port at New Haven when seized. The *Defiance* is separate from the 118-ton sloop *Defiance* captured 31 March 1813, the 104-ton sloop *Defiance* seized 4 April 1813, the schooner *Defiance* taken on 19 May 1814, and the 46-ton sloop *Defiance* taken on 3 August 1814. One other sloop named *Defiance* is seized by the HMS *Superb* and the HMS *Sylph* at an undetermined time during 1814.

In other naval activity, the American privateer *Rattlesnake,* which had spent the winter 1813–1814 in Europe, is intercepted and seized by the HMS *Hyperion.* Captain Maffitt and his *Rattlesnake* had been blocked in port by a British squadron; however, following the escape of another American vessel, the *Ida,* Maffitt also made it to sea. The crew of the *Rattlesnake* and Captain Maffitt receive the dubious honor of being transferred to Dartmoor Prison near Plymouth, England, where they become subject to the incessant cruelty of the present commander, British Major Thomas George Shortland.

June 4 (Saturday) *In naval activity,* the USS *Peacock* sails from Savannah on its second cruise. It moves to the Bahamas and beyond, sailing eastwardly along the trade route toward Spain and Ireland. The cruise is lucrative. The *Peacock* seizes 14 prizes, two of which are transformed into cartels. The other twelve are destroyed at sea. The *Peacock* ends its cruise at New York on 29 October. In other activity, the HMS *Recruit* intercepts and seizes the schooner *Betsy,* which has a cargo of flour. The 90-ton brigantine *Francisca De Paula* (Frederica Arenos), en route from Havana, Cuba to Boston, encounters the HMS *Nimrod,* which seizes the brigantine and its cargo of molasses.

June 5 (Sunday) *In naval activity,* the HMS *Martin* intercepts and seizes the *Magdalena* (J. Nyman, master), a 62-ton schooner going from Boston to Halifax with a cargo of bread and flour. In other naval activity, the American privateer Decatur, after completing an uneventful 80-day cruise, is back out at sea. The HMS *Phin* intercepts the *Decatur* and initiates pursuit in a long-running chase that last about eleven hours. Nonetheless, the *Decatur's* career as a privateer ends when it is seized in Mona Passage between Puerto Rico and the Dominican Republic and links the Atlantic Ocean to the Caribbean Sea.

June 6 (Monday) *In naval activity,* the HMS *Nimrod* intercepts the 111-ton brigantine *Herculean,* which had left Haiti bound for either Boston, Massachusetts, or Madeira, Portugal. Nevertheless, the voyage is terminated before it reaches its destination with a cargo of molasses and sugar. The prize is seized by the *Nimrod.*

June 7 (Tuesday) *In naval activity,* the HMS *Jaseur*—operating on the Patuxent River with the HMS *Albion* and the HMS *Dragon*—again encounters the American naval force under Commodore Joshua Barney. British attempts to draw the Americans out fail. The sloop *Flash* (J. Barstow, master) is intercepted and seized by two British warships, the HMS *Nieman* and the HMS *Saturn.* The British privateer *Shannon* intercepts and seizes the 70-ton sloop *Lively,* which is en route from North Yarmouth to Boston with a cargo of wood. The prize is taken into Liverpool. The *Lively* is separate from the schooner *Lively* seized on 22 July 1812, the schooner *Lively* captured on 20 July 1813, the sloop *Lively* seized 24 July 1813, and the sloop *Lively* captured on 26 October 1814.

June 8–10 FIRST BATTLE OF ST. LEONARD'S CREEK In Maryland, the British, having recently failed to destroy Joshua Barney's squadron on the Chesapeake Bay, initiate a tumultuous bombardment of Barney's force at St. Leonard's Creek.

The British force, composed of about 20 barges and two schooners, use everything in their arsenal including rockets, but the Americans fail to yield despite the battering of the 8th and 9th. On the 10th, the British increase the intensity of their attacks. Moving under the sounds of British martial music, twenty-one barges, a schooner and a rocket boat move into the creek, and the craft are carrying about 800 troops intent on demolishing Barney's makeshift squadron, composed of two gunboats, 13 barges and his sloop, with a combined force of about 500 men. His two gunboats remain at anchor slightly above his squadron due to their inability to operate in the shoal water. The British schooners fire first, but the Americans immediately return fire. Barney's son, Major William B. Barney, defies the danger while he remains in a small boat and rows from vessel to vessel passing out his father's orders. Despite the British superiority, without explanation, after a prolonged duel, the British begin to disengage and sail back to the ships that are covering the attacking contingent. Enthusiasm builds within the American force as it gives pursuit trying to intercept the retiring force before it reaches the protection of the ships at the mouth of the creek. Nonetheless, the enthusiasm suddenly dissipates when an 18-gun schooner blocks further progress. Barney remains undaunted and orders his squadron to concentrate their fire upon the schooner. The powerful barrages force the schooner to withdraw under the guns of a frigate and a sloop of war. It makes it to its protectors; however, Barney's gunners had severely damaged it, which compels the British to run it ashore before it sinks.

By this time, the British aboard the frigate and sloop of war have become infuriated. Both ships open fire to destroy Barney's force and avenge the loss of their schooner. Barney's squadron is struck by a cyclone of fire in which the British propel at least 700 shots toward the squadron. Nonetheless, they fail to inflict any serious damage. During the furious bombardment, the rest of the British attack-craft arrive back under the protection of the ships' guns; however, Barney's guns are not silenced. They continue to return fire while the enemy returns to the ships. Afterward, Barney disengages and returns to his position in the creek.

On the following day, in his official report to Secretary of the Navy William Jones, Barney states:

> The large schooner was nearly destroyed, having several shot through it at the water's edge; its deck torn up, guns dismounted, and mainmast nearly cut off about half way up, and rendered unserviceable. It was otherwise much cut; they ran her ashore to prevent its sinking. The commodore's boat was cut in two; a shot went through the rocket boat; one of the small schooners carrying two thirty-two pounders had a shot which raked her from aft forward; the boats generally suffered, but I have not ascertained what loss they sustained in men.... On Saturday evening, they burnt the property of Mr. Patterson and Skinner.

Following the engagement, the British made no further attempts to dislodge Barney from the creek; however, they continue their terrifying mischief by striking plantations and burning property, along with constant plunder. The secretary of the Navy takes action. He dispatches 100 U.S. Marines and with three artillery pieces under Captain Samuel Miller to "relieve Commodore Barney from the blockade." Another contingent of artillery with two 18-pounders under Colonel Wadsworth and about 100 regulars are also sent to aid Barney. In the meantime, General Philip Stuart had called out militia, and they are en route to support Barney.

June 11 (Saturday) *In naval activity,* the 42-gun frigate *Mohawk* is launched at Sackets Harbor and taken into U.S. service. Also, the sloop *Morning Starr* is seized by a British squadron. The *Morning Starr* is separate from the sloop *Morning Star* seized on 13 June 1813 and the schooner *Morning Star* seized 18 August 1813. In other naval activity, a party drawn from the HMS *Bulwark* and the HMS *Nymphe*, using boats, enters a harbor close to Boston and captures the schooner *Orient*. The British privateer *Shannon* seizes the schooner *Two Friends*. The prize is taken into port at Liverpool. The *Two Friends* is separate from the schooner *Two Friends* seized 17 December 1812.

June 12 (Sunday) *In naval activity,* the British privateer *Retaliation* seizes the schooner *Armistice*, while it is en route from Boston to East Port and Machias, Maine. The prize and its cargo, which includes food, liquor, gunpowder, soap, leather and tobacco, are taken into port at Liverpool.

June 13 (Monday) **In Massachusetts,** Fort Phoenix at Fairview is attacked by a British warship, the HMS *Nimrod*, but the vessel is driven away and the landing is aborted.

June 14 (Tuesday) *In naval activity,* the USS *Wasp* (fifth), while cruising in the vicinity of the English Channel, encounters a British brigantine, the *William*. The vessel is seized but not taken as a prize. The Americans set the *William* afire. In other naval activity, the British privateer *Liverpool Packet* intercepts and seizes a 77-ton sloop, the *Janus* (P. Justin, master), which is en route from New York to Newport, Rhode Island, with a cargo of flour. The HMS *Nieman* seizes a sloop named *Janus* that is separate from the *Janus* seized this day. Also, the HMS *Saturn* intercepts and seizes the 65-ton sloop *Tickler* which is en route to Machias, Maine, from New York. The *Tickler* is separate from the *Tickler* seized on 4 October 1814.

June 15 (Wednesday) *In naval activity,* the British privateer *Liverpool Packet* captures the *Adventure*, commanded by master J. Martin, which is transporting a cargo of coffee, hides, molasses and sugar. The *Adventure* had been en route from Haiti to Bristol, Rhode Island, when it was intercepted. Elsewhere, the HMS *Narcissus* arrives on the Patuxtent River. Captain Barney advances up the river in a flotilla of 12 boats carrying Royal Marines and other troops. The force raids the town of Benedict and succeeds in confiscating one piece of artillery and a small number of muskets. Afterward, the British move to Marlborough, less than twenty miles from Washington, D.C., where they obtain supplies. In other naval activity, the British privateer *Shannon*, while on the prowl for easy targets, spots the schooner *Four Friends* (W. Shackleford, master) and seizes it. The *Shannon* also captures the schooner *Strong*, a privateer.

June 16 (Thursday) *In naval activity,* the HMS *La Hogue* intercepts and seizes the 156-ton brigantine *Voador*, which is en route to Boston from St. Salvador with a cargo of sugar and wood. The *Voador* is separate from the brigantine *Voador* seized on 28 June 1814.

June 18 (Saturday) *In naval activity,* the USS *Wasp* (fifth) intercepts and seizes the British armed brigantine *Pallas* as it cruises in the vicinity of the English Channel. Despite being armed, the *Pallas* capitulates without a fight. The *Pallas* is not seized as a prize; rather, the Americans destroy it at sea. In other activity, the 57-ton sloop *Eunice* (E. Hill, master) encounters the British privateer *Shannon* and the *Eunice* is seized before it can arrive at Boston with the cargo of wood it is transporting from North Yarmouth. The prize is taken into port at Liverpool. The *Eunice* is separate from the schooner *Eunice* captured 18 June 1813.

Also, the American privateer *Grampus* (Captain John Murphy), a schooner in company with two other privateers, the *Patapsco* out of Baltimore and the *Dash* out of Boston, are spotted by the HMS *La Hogue* while it is operating off Boston. The British initiate pursuit, but the warship is not up to the task of snatching any of the fast-sailing privateers. All three escape. It is later learned that Captain Capel of the *La Hogue* becomes infuriated after his failure to capture even one of the American vessels and experiences a minor temper tantrum on the deck of his ship. The privateer *Patapsco*, commanded by Captain Mortimer, is credited with three prizes during its time at sea. Meanwhile, the *Grampus* sets a course for the Canary Islands, and while cruising in that region, it seizes only an insignificant vessel, the brigantine *Speculator*, which is transporting a cargo from Lanzarote to London; the vessel is released. Afterward, the *Grampus* mistakes a sloop of war for a merchant ship, and when the British vessel is approached and ordered to surrender, it reveals its guns and begins to plaster the *Grampus*. The Americans sustain the barrage and Captain Murphy, aware of the danger, begins to break away. The *Grampus* does succeed in escaping from the British warship, Captain Murphy and one other man die from mortal wounds. During its time at sea, the *Grampus* is credited with the seizure of eight vessels.

June 19 (Sunday) **In Washington, D.C.,** a fresh alarm reaches the city when a British squadron again enters the Patuxent River in the vicinity of Benedict, Maryland. General Van Ness orders various units out to meet the threat, including the Georgetown Artillery and Riflemen, the Georgetown Dragoons, and a troop under Captain Thornton (Alexandria) and a contingent under Captain Caldwell (Washington, D.C.).

The command is given to Major George Peter. The units arrive at Nottingham on the following day and from there they are ordered to report to General Wadsworth at Benedict.

In naval activity, the *Sir Andrew Hammond,* attached to Captain David Porter's squadron, is seized by the HMS *Cherub* in the Sandwich Islands (Hawaii).

In other naval activity, a small American detachment encounters a gunboat that is suspicious in Alexandria Bay in the vicinity of Bald Island. The eighteen men and Lieutenant Gregory, and two sailing masters, Captains William Vaughan and Samuel Dixon, believe the Americans to be Canadians. The British send a skiff to inspect the strangers; however, the British party is captured. Meanwhile, the activity is observed back on board the gunboat. The British open fire. Gregory's detachment seizes the gunboat, the *Black Snake* (also gunboat No. 9), commanded by Captain Landon. All 18 men aboard, mostly Royal Marines, are captured. While returning to New York with their prize, another British gunboat

Captain William Vaughan.

intercepts the Americans just below French Creek. The British interception has the Americans trapped; however, Gregory's men take the prisoners ashore and scuttle the prize. Afterward, the British attempt to give chase, but to no avail. The detachment, along with the prisoners, makes it to Grenadier Island late in the night. On the following day, the detachment arrives at Sackets Harbor. On 4 May 1834, Congress awards Lt. Gregory and his men $3,000 for their actions.

Also, the schooner *William* is intercepted and recaptured by the HMS *Wasp.*

June 20 (Monday) *In naval activity,* the USS *Guerriere,* the first frigate to be built in the United States since 1801, is launched at the Philadelphia Navy Yard. It becomes the flagship of Stephen Decatur, and on 20 December 1815 it sails from New York en route to terminate the hostilities against the U.S. merchant ships by pirates operating out of Algeria and other Barbary states.

June 21 (Tuesday) *In Maryland,* a British force is reported to have landed at Benedict. A contingent of cavalry under Major John Peter departs from the capital en route to the town. The cavalry reaches the hills near the town at about 1700 and discovers that General Philip Stuart is already there with a militia infantry company and a small detachment of cavalry. Shortly afterward a British detachment is detected along the road in the distance, and at nearly the same time, the cavalry is ordered to charge. The chase nets several prisoners; however, the rest of the British bolt over a fence and make it into a field. The cavalry clears an opening and continues its pursuit. Afterward, a few more prisoners are seized during a skirmish and one other is killed. Meanwhile, the others make it back to the boats. American Francis Wise of the Alexandria militia is killed. After pushing the British detachment back to their boats, the Americans form to move into the town. The British naval force initiates its fire and the column comes under a heavy barrage. Nevertheless, the advance is not halted. Fire is returned by the two pieces of artillery, and the exchange continues for about one-half hour. The infantry does not participate. By this time, the Americans conclude that the British ground troops had made it aboard the waiting barges and a schooner. The attack is halted and General Stuart orders the force to withdraw. On the following day, the British vessels depart from Benedict.

June 22 (Wednesday) *In naval activity,* the 14-gun USS *Rattlesnake,* originally built as a privateer, acquired by the Navy during 1813, is captured by the 50-gun frigate HMS *Leander* after a long chase. The *Rattlesnake* is finally intercepted off Cape Sable, Nova Scotia. In other activity, the HMS *Tenedos* intercepts and captures the schooner *Deslesdernier* (J. Shackford, master) while it is en route from Boston to St. Andrews, West Indies.

June 23 (Thursday) *In naval activity,* the USS *Wasp* encounters a vessel, the *Henrietta,* a galiot (galley). The commander of the *Wasp,* Master Commandant Johnston Blakeley, permits the prisoners taken during the cruise to take possession of the *Henrietta.* In other activity, the sloop *Ex Bashaw* (M. Robinson, master) is seized by the HMS *Bulwark.*

June 24 (Friday) *In Europe,* the American peace negotiators arrive in Ghent, Belgium. They receive plenty of time to prepare to meet with the British, who seem intent to delay their arrival. Many people in the United Kingdom, particularly merchants, are anxious to see the war come to an end. But there is a boisterous faction known as the war party that begins to push for action to prove the superiority of the British over the Americans. The war party members, most of whom had never been to America, perceive the country as conquerable by encircling it with the Royal Navy. One of the cries of the faction is as follows: "Let us make Madison resign and follow Bonaparte to some transatlantic Elba." Their strategy: "Distress the coasts all the way from Maine to New Orleans, invade New York through Lake Champlain and Lake Ontario, and strike New York City by approaches from the sea." This strategy has the blessing of the *London Times,* which leads the charge.

Nevertheless, the British negotiators do not arrive until 6 August.

In naval activity, in the North Atlantic, the British brigantine *Hunter* becomes the hunted as it falls prey to the USS *Adams.* The *Adams,* still stalking the waters of the Atlantic, engages and seizes the brigantine HMS *Mary* on the 28th.

June 24–26 *In Maryland,* Colonel Decius Wadsworth arrives at St. Leonard's Creek on June 24. He confers with Commodore Barney and Captain Samuel Miller, U.S. Marine Corps, to decide on the strategy to deal with the British blockading squadron. They conclude that a battery must be constructed on a bluff lying between the creek and the Patuxent River, and that the position would also require a furnace to heat the shot. It is also decided that Wadsworth's two 18-pounders on traveling carriages will be deployed on the bluff. The guns are to support an attack by the flotilla, scheduled for the morning of the 26th. Commodore Barney assigns twenty of his men and Sailing Master Geoghan under Colonel Wadsworth to manage the battery. The project runs on schedule and the attack is launched at daybreak on the 26th.

Barney's barges and Wadsworth's battery simultaneously commence fire upon the British vessels anchored about 400 yards distant. The British react quickly, and return fire is catapulted toward Barney's squadron. The battle continues for about two hours, when unexpectedly, Wadsworth's battery falls silent. The crew spikes the two guns and abandons the position, leaving Barney's squadron in great peril, well within range of the British grape shot and without support fire while facing a far superior force with numerous barges and more importantly, two frigates, a brigantine and two schooners. Barney's options are stand and face annihilation or run. He chooses the latter, and the decision is made within several minutes.

The British, following Barney's hurried departure, also retire due to their apprehension that Barney's land battery might still harass or even devastate the squadron. The squadron redeploys near Point Patience. Following the absence of the blockaders, Barney moves out of the creek and up the Patuxent River. He repositions his squadron along the Western Branch close to Upper Marlborough. During the engagement, Barney's command, according to his report, sustains three killed, including Midshipman Asquith, and eight wounded.

In naval activity, the American privateer *Diomede,* commanded by Captain Crowninshield, is intercepted and captured by the British after it gets snagged during a heavy fog. It is diverted to Halifax, Nova Scotia. The *Diomede,* before its capture, had broken through the blockade at Salem and seized a large number of vessels. Its prizes included the ships *Cod Hook, Hope, Mary and Joseph, Traveller, Upton* and *William,* along with the brigantines, *Friends, Harmony, Providence* and the *Recovery.*

June 26 (Sunday) *In naval activity,* the USS *Wasp* (fifth) intercepts and captures the vessel *Orange Boven,* while operating in the vicinity of the English Channel. The Americans destroy the prize. Elsewhere, Commodore Joshua Barney's naval force, bolstered by a detachment of artillery and a contingent of Marines, engages a British blockading flotilla in St. Leonard's Creek. The Americans compel the British to end the blockade, permitting Barney to advance farther up the Patuxent River. In other activity, at Sackets Harbor, Commodore Chauncey, enthused about the recent success of capturing the *Black Snake* because of how it irritated the British, dispatches Lt. Gregory and sailing masters Dixon and Vaughn on another mission. The party embarks in two large gigs en route to Nicholas Island, which lies near Presque Isle. The detachment is tasked with lying in ambush for a group of British transports traveling from Fort George to York (Toronto).

The orders include instruction to modify the mission if no contact is made with the transports within three to four days by landing at Presque Isle and destroying a schooner that is under construction. The detachment executes the alternative plan after a British gunboat at Presque Isle appears just before an attack is to be sprung on a vessel. The Americans make contact with someone at Presque Isle who informs Gregory that the British have been made aware that his detachment is in the area. Gregory moves into action by acting before reinforcements might arrive from Kingston. The Americans debark and place some guards at selected houses to prevent any alarms from being sounded, while others in the party destroy the vessel, which carries 14 guns and appears to be nearly prepared for launching. After completing the destruction, the detachment rows to Oswego, and from there the troops return to Sackets Harbor on 6 July.

In naval activity, the British privateer *Rolla* intercepts and captures the schooner *Charles* (John Brown, master). The *Charles* is separate from the *Charles Fawcett* captured on 6 September 1812, the 95-ton sloop *Charles* seized on 4 October 1813, the sloop *Charles* seized on 10 December 1813, and the brigantine *Charles,* captured 5 November 1814. In other activity, the HMS *Fantome* spots a brigantine, the Cida De Leiria (J.J. Claudio, master) while it is en route from Lisbon, Portugal, to Boston. The brigantine is intercepted, captured and taken into port at St. John's, New Brunswick, along with its cargo that includes salt, wine and wool.

June 28 (Tuesday) *In naval activity,* the USS *Wasp* (fifth) commanded by Johnston Blakely, spots the HMS *Reindeer* around 0400 at a point about 225 miles west of Plymouth, England. The volatile encounter ignites a fury-filled duel from a distance of only about 60 yards when the *Wasp* initiates fire that rivets the British vessel. The British return heavy fire, and as the two vessels maneuver for advantage, the British twice are repelled from boarding the *Wasp.* The Marines aboard the *Wasp* add the pernicious sting of their fire to inflict heavy casualties upon the *Reindeer*'s crew. Nevertheless, for about 20 minutes the antagonists trade incessant fire until finally, the Yanks succeed in boarding the *Reindeer* and compelling the British to surrender. Although the *Wasp* prevails, it also sustains severe damage, including about six hits to its hull and heavy damage to its rigging and sails. Meanwhile, the *Reindeer*'s crew is transferred to the *Wasp.* Afterward, the Americans destroy the *Reindeer* by setting it on fire.

After seeing the *Reindeer* explode, the Americans, with their prisoners aboard the *Wasp,* set sail for L'Orient, France. En route the *Wasp* captures two more vessels. According to the commander's report, the Americans sustain five killed and 21 wounded. The British aboard the *Reindeer* sustain 25 killed and 42 wounded.

Also, the HMS *Nymphe* intercepts and captures the 180-ton brigantine *Voador,* which is carrying molasses and other cargo from Cuba to Boston. The *Voador* is separate from the brigantine *Voador* seized on 16 June 1814.

June 29 (Wednesday) *In naval activity,* the British privateer *Rolla* intercepts and recaptures the brigantine Hope (J. Strang, master). The *Hope* is separate from the ship *Hope* captured on 2 August 1813, the brigantine *Hope* seized 28 August 1813, the schooner *Hope* seized on 16 August 1814, the sloop *Hope* seized on 4 December 1814, and the shallop *Hope for Peace* seized on 18 July 1813.

June 30 (Thursday) *In naval activity,* the HMS *Martin* intercepts and seizes the schooner *Snap Dragon,* a privateer.

July As the war persists into its last months of confrontation, U.S. vessels maintain their standards as a new and fighting fleet and score further successes against the mighty Royal Navy. The Marines, who play a gallant part in support of the Navy in confiscating British vessels, participate in the capture of the British brigantine *Regulator,* which is defeated handily by the *Wasp* on the 4th. The USS *Peacock* takes the advantage the following day, seizing four British vessels in English waters.

While American diplomats wait in Ghent to begin peace talks with representatives from Great Britain, a huge force of British reinforcements, no longer needed by Wellington against Napoleon, who has been defeated and sent into exile, is en route to the United States. The coy British anticipate news of further progress which they can use to dictate terms rather than negotiate a settlement. Finally, on August 8, the British negotiators arrive and the talks begin.

In naval activity, the American privateer *Revenge,* a 14-gun schooner out of Baltimore (sometimes referred to as operating out of Norfolk) intercepts and captures the brigantine *Silena* and another vessel, the sloop *Friendship,* with the latter transporting a cargo of dry goods. The cargo and prisoners are removed and the *Friendship* is destroyed at sea. The *Revenge,* commanded by Captain R. Miller, had initially gone to sea early in the war. Other prizes credited to it include the ship *Betsy,* which was seized before it arrived at Glasgow and was diverted to Wilmington, North Carolina; the four-gun ship *Manly,* seized carrying wine and other cargo from the West Indies to Halifax and taken into port at Charleston; the schooner *Fanny,* captured after it departed Trinidad with a cargo of sugar and taken into port at Charleston, and another vessel, the schooner *Mary Ann,* which is spared. The prisoners of the *Revenge* are transferred to it and the crew is directed to sail to an English port.

Elsewhere, the American privateer *Ultor,* while in Long Island Sound, comes under attack. Two boats carrying British troops launch an assault to seize the *Ultor.* The American crew is prepared and the British are repulsed. One of the boats is captured and the other retires. The Americans capture eight men in the boat that could not retire. The captured boat, its commander having been killed during the attack, is taken into New London where the prisoners are transferred to the authorities. The deceased man is interred at New London. During its time at sea the *Ultor* seizes a total of 15 prizes.

Early July **In Missouri,** a relief force commanded by Captain John Campbell of the 1st U.S. Infantry and fitted out by General Benjamin Howard, governor of the Missouri Territory, departs for Prairie du Chien to bolster the garrison holding recently established Fort Shelby. Campbell's command is composed of 42 regulars and 66 rangers; however, 21 others accompany the contingent. They include women, the sutler's as-

The USS *Wasp* and the HMS *Reindeer* (*The History of the United States Navy [Biographical Sketches of American Naval Heroes],* Charles J. Peterson, 1860).

sociates, and the boatmen who manage three keel-boats, one carrying the regulars and the other two transporting the rangers, with those two boats commanded by Captain Stephen Rector and Lieutenant Riggs. When the flotilla reaches Rock Island, Illinois, an Indian ambush is waiting to be sprung.

The Sac and Fox Indians succeed in pulling off a ruse while they pretend to be friendly and cordial. Frenchmen with the flotilla inform Campbell that the Indians are being cunning and that they expect an attack, but Campbell disregards the warning. The French had actually been urged by the Indians to desert the Americans and return to St. Louis, because the Indians had a long-lasting affinity for the French and were reluctant to slay them. Nonetheless, the Frenchmen remain and the night passes peacefully. On the following morning, the flotilla embarks with the Americans believing the remainder of the journey would be uneventful. Shortly thereafter, the winds pick up and the lead boat with Campbell's regulars is pushed into shore at an island, which comes to be known as "Campbell's Island." It is out of sight of the other boats that had been in the lead; however, it does not take long for the others to know trouble had come upon them when they spot rising smoke. Meanwhile, the troops with Campbell debark and prepare to eat breakfast before trying to rejoin the flotilla. Guards are posted in case of an assault; however, the troops are not anticipating what unfolds. The small group is struck by a force of at least several hundred Indians under Black Hawk.

Smoke from the small arms fire spirals upward, and it is the signal to the other boats that Campbell is being attacked. The boats of Rector and Riggs change course and attempt to aid Campbell. The winds interfere and the intensity of the storm makes it impossible to reach the imperiled boat. Meanwhile the horde of Indians closes on the boat and encircles it. The Americans resist tenaciously, but the odds are too great and the contingent nears annihilation. Campbell is among the wounded. He is close to death while lying on his back on his boat, which is being consumed with fire. The troops from the other two boats, which had not been able to overcome the winds, finally arrive to join the survivors and rescue them from certain death. The rangers in Rector's command, mostly Frenchmen, had thrown many items overboard to lessen the weight to permit them to attempt to rescue Campbell.

Many of the rangers bolt from the boat into the water using the boat as a shield between them and the firing by Black Hawk's menacing band, while they shove their boat toward Campbell's burning craft, held by the enemy. To the dismay of the Indians, the boat reaches the imperiled craft and the rangers begin to extricate the survivors, including the wounded. The successful rescue of the survivors, including Campbell, while under attack by what some claim was close to 1,000 braves is literally a death-defying act. After being transferred to a boat manned by a skilled navigator named Hoadley, the wounded are safely taken out of harm's way. Rector's boat, carrying the wounded, heads back without stopping to St. Louis. For awhile, Riggs' boat seems to be trapped and captured, but the Americans remain in control of the vessel, which is so well fortified that the troops remain safe. Later, the ravaging winds that have impeded the boats subside and Riggs' crew is able to break free and head for St. Louis.

Upon his arrival, Riggs and the other troops are greeted with celebration despite their condition. The mission had been grueling and even those who did not sustain wounds are emaciated. The success in the rescue is hailed in St. Louis, but they failed to reach Prairie du Chien. The *National Intelligencer*, in its August 1814 issue, lists the casualties at 36 either killed or wounded. Doctor Abram Steward, a surgeon's mate, is among the wounded.

At this time there is no knowledge of the danger facing the small force at Fort Shelby. Meanwhile, the deadly ambush of Campbell's flotilla caused outrage in St. Louis, and plans are immediately underway to retaliate. Major Zachary Taylor of the 7th Infantry is designated commander of a large force that is to be sent to Rock Island to punish the Indians who launched the attack. His contingent is composed of about 334 officers and men, primarily militia and rangers; only forty regulars are assigned.

July 1 (Friday) *In naval activity,* two British warships, the HMS *Armide* and the HMS *Endymion*, while on patrol, intercept and seize the 100-ton schooner *Eliza*, which is en route from Wilmington to Halifax with a cargo of flour and tar. The *Eliza* is separate from the two *Eliza*s captured during 1812, a brigantine captured 31 March 1813 and a schooner seized on 3 July 1814, and a sloop, *Eliza Ann*, captured 31 October 1814.

July 2 (Saturday) **In Washington, D.C.,** Brigadier General William H. Winder, a native Marylander and nephew of Maryland's governor, Levin Winder, is appointed commander of the 10th Military District, a new command that encompasses Maryland and the District of Columbia. He is soon facing the British at Bladensburg, the entrance to Washington, where his leadership proves unsatisfactory. John Armstrong, the secretary of war, is disappointed by the choice of Winder rather than his preference, General Moses Porter. Armstrong from this point distances himself further from the president and the administration. Nevertheless, despite his obstinacy and lack of co-operation with the administration, he remains for a while as Secretary of War. General Winder will be scheduled to receive about 15,000 troops drawn from Maryland (6,000), Pennsylvania (5,000), Virginia (2,000) and the District of Columbia (2,000). This militia force is to be bolstered by about 1,000 regulars.

In naval activity, the sloop *Eclipse* is seized on the Chesapeake by the British.

July 3 (Sunday) **In Canada,** a 3,500 man American force under General Jacob Brown crosses the Niagara River to initiate a campaign. During the pre-dawn hours a brigade of regulars under General Winfield Scott, bolstered by Major Hindman's artillery battalion, crosses from Black Rock and lands at a point below British Fort Erie. Soon afterward, General Ripley's brigade of regulars crosses the river and lands at a point above the post. After final preparations, the attack is launched; however, it is of short duration. During the brief exchange of fire, four Americans and one of the defenders are killed, and at that point, the fort capitulates. The garrison, composed of 170 troops (8th Regiment) under Major Thomas Buck are seized and transported to New York.

The British main body under General Riall stands slightly more than fifteen miles below Fort Erie at Chippewa, above the Great Falls. General Riall had dispatched a contingent under Lt. Colonel Pearson which advances nearly to Fort Erie to maintain observation of the American force. Meanwhile, General Brown prepares to move against the British main body at Chippewa. Once Fort Erie falls, General Brown proclaims martial law. Brown's proclamation states that "men found in arms, or otherwise engaged in acts

General Winfield Scott.

General Eleazar Ripley (*The Illustrated American Biography, Volume III*, New York: J. Milton Emerson and Company, 1855).

of hostility, should be dealt with as enemies, while those demeaning themselves peaceably, and pursuing their private business, should be treated as friends." The proclamation also stipulates that "private property should be in all cases held sacred"; however, public property would be destroyed. Brown's proclamation forbids plundering.

In naval activity, the 41-ton schooner *Eliza* (A. Merrit, master), transporting a cargo of corn from New York to East Port, is intercepted and seized by the HMS *Rifleman*. The *Eliza* is taken into port at St. John's, New Brunswick. It is separate from the two *Elizas* captured during 1812, the brigantine *Eliza* seized on 31 March 1813, the schooner *Eliza* seized 1 July 1814, and the sloop *Eliza Ann* captured on 31 October 1814.

In other activity, the British privateer *Retaliation* encounters and captures the schooner *Hero* (Peter Lurvey, master). The prize is taken into port at Liverpool. The *Hero* is separate from the schooner *Hero* seized on 12 June 1813, the schooner *Hero* seized on 29 August 1813, the schooner *Hero* taken on 13 January 1814, and the sloop *Hero* seized during early November 1814.

July 4 (Monday) In Canada, General Jacob Brown accompanies General Winfield Scott's force when it departs Fort Erie en route to attack British General Phineas Riall at Chippewa. Not unexpectedly, the brigade encounters resistance from Lt. Colonel Thomas Pearson's contingent, which causes Scott's column to fight its way during the entire advance. In an effort to further hinder progress, Pearson destroys each of the bridges that span small streams as his force retires toward Chippewa, but the primary bridge that spans the Chippewa River remains standing. Nonetheless, General Brown believes it was destroyed, causing him to delay his attack. Despite the opposition, Scott's brigade advances to the Chippewa River by about dusk. The Americans pause about two miles below the river and establish night positions at the south bank of Street's Creek. Brown, unaware that the bridge was spared destruction, intends to repair it before the attack is launched; however, General Riall had already decided that a retreat would not be ordered. He intends to attack the Americans. Meanwhile, Lt. Colonel Pearson fords the river and rejoins Riall's main body at Chippewa.

In naval activity, the USS *Wasp* (fifth), having sustained severe damage during a battle with the HMS *Reindeer*, a 21-gun sloop of war, encounters the British brigantine *Regulator*. Despite its poor condition, the *Wasp* succeeds in capturing the *Regulator*, and another vessel, the schooner *Jenny*, on 6 July. Afterward, the *Wasp* reaches L'Orient in France, where the ship receives repairs and the crew acquires provisions and medical attention, those who need it. The *Wasp* sails again on 27 August.

July 5 (Tuesday) BATTLE OF CHIPPEWA In Canada, British General Phineas Riall, unwilling to retire in the face of the American force at Chippewa under General Jacob Brown, takes the offensive rather than wait for the Americans to attack. The American troops and their Indian allies under Chief Red Jacket (a long-term ally of the Americans stretching back to the American Revolution) come under harassing fire during the first part of the day. The British fire infuriates the pickets, and rather than remain the recipients of the Redcoats' musket fire, they move to action. Militia under General Peter Porter and the Indians redeploy deeper in the woods on the left from where they can flank the British that continue to fire upon the American lines.

The redeployment is observed and word is sent back to General Riall. He dispatches a seasoned force of regulars to strike the militia. Initially the militia holds its own during the skirmishing; however, the Redcoats charge and nearly effortlessly ignite a stampede. The militia falters, then completely collapses. The British accelerate their pace, and while the chase continues, General Riall orders his main body to advance. The intense activity on the British left causes huge clouds of dust to ascend; it attracts the attention of General Brown. He rides toward the dust clouds and sees the main body of the British as it drives forward. By this time, General Riall is becoming more confident, knowing that his regulars will maul the American militia.

General Brown, wasting no time, rides beyond General Scott's positions and reaches General Ripley's regulars who are lagging far behind Scott. General Brown directs Ripley to speed up his pace. All the while, General Scott remains unaware of the British attack. Scott is preparing for a dress parade on the plain between the Chippewa and the Niagara Rivers. General Brown intercepts Scott while he is marching toward the plain. Brown's message is direct and succinct: "The enemy is advancing. You will have a fight."

The British reach the plain before the Americans arrive. Riall deploys his force in concealed positions in the brush and patiently awaits the approach of the Americans, whom he intends to shred and force to run. Riall, as with most British

Chief Red Jacket.

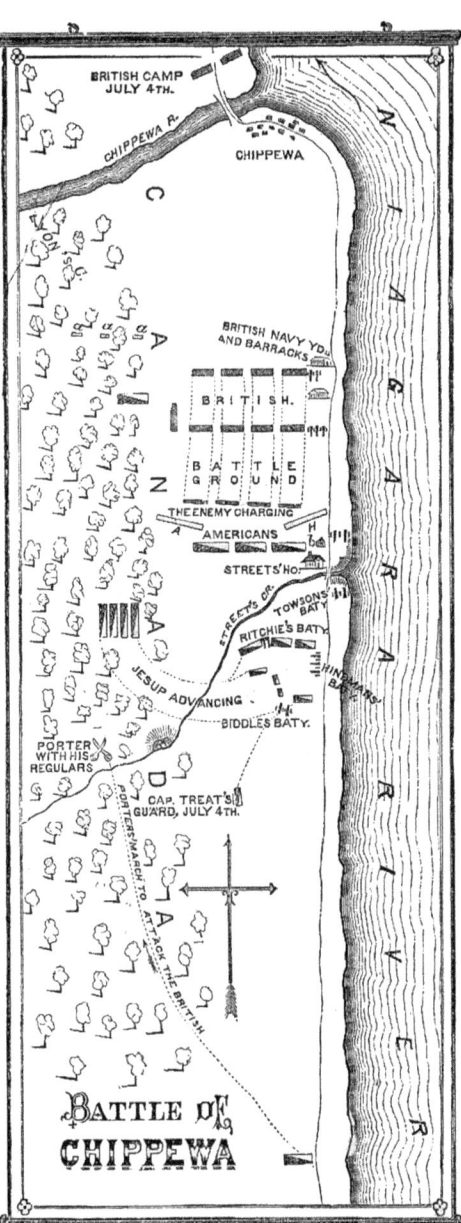

Battle of Chippewa.

officers, has no respect for the American militia, which has a reputation of charging to the rear when faced with regular British troops. Riall, once the American column is spotted, proclaims: "Nothing but Buffalo militia!"

Just as the Americans begin to cross the bridge, the British artillery, nine guns, begins to catapult shell after shell, but to Riall's immense surprise, there is no panic in the American ranks and the advance continues, despite the iron rainstorm. Suddenly, the troops described as "Buffalo militia" have seemingly been transformed into fearless warriors who disregard the heavy incoming fire. Riall suddenly discovers that the approaching enemy are not militia, as he excitedly remarks: "Why, these are regulars!"

The Americans deploy with great discipline. One of Scott's battalions, commanded by Major Thomas S. Jesup, holds the left, while Major

Leavenworth's battalion swings to the right and Major McNeil, with the third battalion, deploys in the center. The skirmishing intensifies immediately; however, General Scott is concerned that due to the retreat by the militia, his left flank might be endangered. Major Jesup is directed to shift his position to reinforce that side. Jesup is also ordered, once he realigns, to strike the British positions in the woods at the far right of their line.

Jesup's attack against the British right succeeds beyond expectations. Jesup's force, by defying the heavy fire, is able to isolate the British right wing, which simultaneously leaves the right of the main body defenseless. Riall's misfortune is compounded because General Scott immediately spots the vulnerable position and seizes the advantage before Riall can adapt and modify his lines. Scott orders Major John McNeil to lead his battalion through the hole. At the same time, Scott also orders Major Henry Leavenworth's battalion to crash into the British left. Both battalions charge and the momentum continues to build as they receive even more heavy fire. Undaunted, the battalions find themselves closing upon each other while battling the Redcoats from a distance of only about 80 paces.

All the while, Major (recently breveted) Nathaniel Towson's artillery, deployed in some high ground, supports the attacks, but one of Towson's guns had been knocked out of action, leaving only two artillery pieces against nine British guns. Nevertheless, Towson's duo rattles the British lines with a final devastating volley just before the Americans plunge into the British lines to ignite a gruesome bayonet attack. The effectiveness of the final volley begins to shatter the confidence of the British. The line begins to falter by 1800, just as the Americans unleash their bayonets. Pandemonium erupts as the British begin a haphazard retreat, while under heated pursuit by Scott's infantry. During the retreat, Major Jesup's battalion on the British right repulses a counterattack.

The British, having been solidly defeated, continue their retreat. The entire force flees across the bridge that spans the Chippewa River. Nevertheless, it is not an unchallenged retreat. The Americans initiate pursuit and succeed in capturing some of the British stragglers. The enemy begins to acknowledge that trained regulars in the American army are no longer inferior to the British regulars. In retrospect, the intense drilling and training that General Scott conducted for several months prior to the attack paid huge dividends. General Riall moves to Burlington Heights; however, he orders a contingent to move to the forts on the Lower Niagara. The Indians allied to the British failed to gain even one scalp and they took heavy casualties, about 87 killed. Indians who were allied with Riall are now disillusioned and begin to desert.

The number of troops engaged at Chippewa has never been accurately determined; however, it is known that both sides sustained heavy casualties, due primarily to the battleground, a plain that provided little cover for either side. General Ripley's force arrived too late to participate and the militia under General Porter absconded at about the first sounds of the guns. It is thought that fewer than 1,900 troops under General Scott were in the field and in turn, the British force had been composed of about 2,100 men. The Americans sustained 327 killed, wounded and missing. General Brown had two wounds but returns to work within a few weeks. Lt. Colonel John B. Campbell (11th Regiment) is among the wounded; however, he is unable to return to service. He dies of his wounds in late August. Colonel Campbell was the nephew of General William Campbell, who served in the Revolutionary War. The British sustain about 503 killed, wounded and missing. The figures are drawn from official after battle reports; however, they do not include Indian casualties. General Brown, in a letter to John Armstrong, secretary of war, dated 6 July, states that the British "left on the field, 400 killed and wounded."

Colonel Miller at Chippewa (*Battles of America by Sea and Land, Volume II*, Robert Tomes, 1878).

American General Winfield Scott's decisive victory over a superior British force—including the Royal Scots, and the King's, the 103rd and 104th Regiments—becomes a morale booster for the Americans. This tremendous victory of Scott over British General Phineas Riall is still remembered today at West Point. The gray uniforms of the cadets are in honor of the victory at the Battle of Chippewa. The U.S. 9th, 11th and 21st, 22nd Regiments are among the participants.

Following the battle, General Brown writes to the secretary of War regarding the actions of Winfield Scott: "I am indebted to Scott more than to any other man for this victory; he is entitled to the highest praise our country can bestow. His brigade has covered itself with glory." General Scott praises the actions of his troops, and in particular, several officers from New York, Gerard D. Smith, George Watts (first cousin of General Izard and Stephen Watts Kearny), and William Jenkins Worth. Worth gets special credit when Scott states in his correspondence: "He was bravery itself, and by remarkable coolness and courage saved my life at a moment in the beginning of the battle when the Indians were striving to obtain my scalp."

Also, the British contend that after the battle, the Americans bury their dead; however, they claim that the British dead are gathered in a pile and burned. This incident, similarly to the burning of Newark, enrages the British.

Colonel Thomas Jesup participates at this battle. He entered the army as 2nd lieutenant of the 17th Infantry and rose to the rank of colonel for his service at this action and the Battle of Niagara. He was also taken prisoner at Detroit during the early days of the war. After the war, he is named quartermaster general, and following ten years at the post, he is breveted major general. Col. James Miller participates at this battle.

July 6 (Wednesday) *In naval activity,* the schooner Bee is seized by the HMS *Nymphe*. The *Bee* is separate from two other schooners named *Bee*, captured on 8 July and 28 August 1814.

July 7–8 *In Canada,* the forces of General Brown initiate a move against Fort George. The column crosses the Chippewa River and advances toward the British post. During the march, a contingent under Lt. Colonel Isaac W. Stone of the New York militia enters the town of St. David and torches it. Stone's actions are condemned by the American government. He receives a court-martial and the board dismisses him from the army. Nonetheless, the operation continues. The Americans reach the post and initiate a siege; however, General Brown discerns that heavy artillery will be required to reduce the fort. He dispatches a party to Sackets Harbor to acquire guns. At Sackets Harbor, Commodore Chauncey is ill when the party arrives to request the artillery. Inexplicably, Chauncey does not delegate another naval officer to transport the guns.

In the meantime, General Brown discovers the wisdom of General Gordon Drummond's order to build Fort Mississauga as part of the triangle. The guns of that post bolster those of Fort George, which also is protected by the artillery of British-held Fort Niagara. Lacking artillery, Brown halts his force at Oak Bush. He refuses to enter the plain and expose his troops to what would be a pernicious cross-fire. The Americans are unable to discover an opening through which Fort George can be struck. The farms and houses are undefended and some of the American troops are reported to have taken great advantage by plundering the farms, which for the most part are inhabited only by women and children.

Lacking the arms that he believes necessary to guarantee the reduction of Fort George, General Brown terminates the siege. The Americans retire to Queenston and Brown arranges to transport his wounded to New York. Having abandoned the operation to seize Fort George, General Brown focuses on seizing Burlington Heights, followed by the capture of York and then Kingston. Success, however, depends upon the fleet under Commodore Isaac Chauncey. Nevertheless, to the great disappointment of Brown, Chauncey's fleet does not become available, which derails his master plan.

July 8 (Friday) *In naval activity,* the British privateer *Rolla* intercepts and captures the schooner *Bee* (J.L. Coleby, master). The *Rolla* takes its prize into port at Liverpool. The *Bee* is separate from two other schooners named *Bee,* captured 6 July and 28 August. Elsewhere, the *Rolla* captures the schooner *Boxer* (G.N. Davis) on this day. And, the British privateer *Retaliation* captures the American schooner *Constellation* and takes it into port at Liverpool.

July 10 (Sunday) *In Alabama,* Major General Andrew Jackson arrives back in Alabama at Fort Jackson from his home in Tennessee. He assumes command of the Southern Army. Jackson is also directed to consummate a treaty with the Creeks.

In Illinois, Indians launch a raid near Fort Butler and massacre one woman and six children. They strike during the afternoon and catch the victims while they are moving from one house to another. Rachael Reagan and her two young children are killed and two children of Captain Abel Moore, along with two children of his brother, William Moore. Mrs. Reagan's children are both killed by the tomahawk and then scalped. The Indians also strip the clothes from each of the victims. William Moore arrives back at his house following militia duty at the fort, and not seeing his children, he begins to search for them. Others join in the search and they discover one of the children, a three-year-old that had survived; however, her wounds prove fatal. The saddening news is sent to Fort Russell and from there to Fort Butler. At Fort Russell, the commander, Captain Able Moore, and the commander at Fort Russell, Captain Whiteside, take action.

A contingent of about 70 rangers on this day speed to Moore's Blockhouse (Wood River Township) where the massacre occurred, and by dawn on the 11th, the rangers are in full pursuit. The perpetrators are intercepted in Morgan County near Springfield. Ten Indians are spotted and shortly thereafter, their numbers are trimmed to one, the only Indian who escapes. The Indians are slain at a stream known as La Belleause (later Indian Creek). The place where the surviving Indian escaped becomes known as Cracker Bend. The victims of the incident remembered as the Wood River Massacre are interred in Vaughn Cemetery; however, because no men are available, each of them is interred without a coffin. Later, a monument is placed along the Fosterburg Road across from the Alton State Hospital in memory of the victims.

In naval activity, the HMS *Bulwark* intercepts and recaptures the schooner *Nelly.* Also, the HMS *Acasta* intercepts the 18½ ton schooner *Prudence* (L.G. Crocker, master) while it is en route to Washington, North Carolina, from Barnstable, Massachusetts, with a cargo of turpentine, varnish and other items. The *Prudence* is separate from the schooner *Prudence* seized 11 August 1812.

July 11 (Monday) *In Massachusetts-Maine,* a British squadron commanded by Sir Thomas Hardy, which had been standing off New London, Connecticut, arrives at Moose Island in Passamaquoddy Bay. Hardy's force is composed of five warships, including the HMS *Ramillies,* and some transports with the latter carrying about 1,500 troops under the command of Deputy Adjutant General Pilkington. The American garrison at Fort Sullivan has only about 50 men (40th U.S. Regiment) under Major Putnam, and they possess six pieces of artillery. Another force of about 250 militia on Moose Island is not capable of resisting a large force of British regulars. Nevertheless, one of the civilians, Benjamin Crown (later secretary of the Navy) informs Major Putnam that he will participate in defending the post. Putnam, realizing resistance would be fruitless, surrenders the fort. The British afterward rename it Fort Sherbrooke. While under British occupation, the post's guns are increased to sixty. Subsequent to seizing Eastport, the British seize the entire island along with Allen's Island and Frederick's Island, all located within the bay.

By 14 July, Commodore Hardy issues a proclamation that the citizens can either take an oath of allegiance to the king or leave the region. About 75 percent of the residents agree to take the oath; however, their impression that they would be treated as if they were British citizens is incorrect. Meanwhile, Britain gains possession of a hefty chunk of Massachusetts effortlessly, and they retain it for the duration. About one month after capturing the islands, the Provincial Council of New Brunswick, Canada, declares that the captured territory is to be considered as a conquered province, and the directive places the territory under martial law. While at Easton and the surrounding area, the British who gained the territory without resistance continue to have severe problems with deserters. The problem becomes a crisis and it is not uncommon to observe officers spending time as guards.

In naval activity, the HMS *Leander* seizes the brigantine (about 280–300 tons) *Rattlesnake.* In other naval activity, the HMS *Bulwark* intercepts and seizes the schooner *Thorn* (A. Hathaway, master). The *Thorn* is separate from the brigantine *Thorn* seized on 31 October 1812 and the schooner *Thorn* captured 8 November 1813.

July 12 (Tuesday) *In Washington, D.C.,* John Armstrong, the secretary of war, sends a letter to some governors advising them that they are to raise militia troops, who are to be equipped and on call for duty.

In Canada, a contingent of about 130 Americans under General John Swift (New York militia) skirmishes with a British detachment near Fort George while on a reconnaissance mission. General Swift had resigned his militia commission in February 1812, but now he is serving as brigadier under General Peter B. Porter's volunteers. The Americans under Swift seize an outpost and its picket, composed of one corporal and five troops. The prisoners had asked for and receive quarter; however, after being spared, one of the captives shoots General Swift in the chest and inflicts a mortal wound. He is taken to the home of James Thompson, where he dies. It is reported by a British source (*Annals of Niagara*) that General Swift, the brother of General Joseph Gardiner Swift, had earlier plundered the house in which he died.

In New York, an operation to regain Michilimackinac, seized by the British during July 1812, is initiated. Five naval vessels under Captain Arthur St. Clair (Sinclair) are transporting about 550 regulars and 250 militia, commanded by Lt. Colonel George Croghan, the hero of Fort Stephenson, Ohio. The flotilla is composed of the *Niagara, Caledonia, Scorpion, St. Lawrence* and *Tigress.* The vessels pause at Fort Gratiot, Michigan, recently built at Port Huron along the St. Clair River at the place where the French had manned Fort Ste. Joseph. The post was built by Captain Charles Gratiot, a West Point graduate (Class of 1808), the 16th man to graduate there. While at the fort, Croghan's force is bolstered by a regiment of Ohio volunteers under Colonel William Colgreave.

After leaving Fort Gratiot, Captain St. Clair moves to attack a recently established British post on Matchadach Bay; however, the vessels are unable to maneuver through the slim channels due to fog and a lack of pilots familiar with the channels. The mission is aborted. The flotilla then moves toward British-held Fort Ste. Joseph (Canada), where they discover it abandoned. Some troops remain to destroy the fort's structures, while the rest of the expeditionary force moves to the Sault Ste. Marie. The flotilla arrives there on 21 July, too late to intercept John Johnson, a "renegade magistrate from Michigan, and agent of the British Northwest Company." Johnson had absconded along with his assistants, and they had emptied the stores, taking everything available with them. Nonetheless, the Americans pause long enough to extinguish a burning sloop left behind that belonged to the British Northwest Company. After examining the vessel, to the men decide to destroy it by restarting the fires. The Americans also demolish the building there before returning to Fort Ste. Joseph. From there St. Clair's flotilla finally arrives off the objective on 26 July.

July 12 to November 16 *In naval activity,* the brigantine USS *Siren* (earlier *Syren*) (Captain J.D. Daniels), which had sailed out of Baltimore in spring, spots the British cutter HMS *Landrail* on the 12th. British Lt. Lancaster, commander of the *Landrail,* moves to evade the privateer to ensure that the dispatches aboard arrive at their destination. Nonetheless, the 7-gun *Siren* catches up with it to ignite a running battle that lasts for more than an hour. The vessels then exchange tenacious blows at close range for almost another hour, then the British surrender. The *Landrail* is sent back to the United States, but before it arrives, the British recapture it and sail it into Halifax. The *Siren* returns to the States.

Later, on 16 November 1814, the *Siren* encounters the HMS *Medway,* a 74-gun ship of the line. The *Siren* attempts to flee and the *Medway* initiates pursuit. The crew tries to gain speed by tossing its guns into the sea. It also cuts its anchor and disposes of its extra spars. In desperation, its boats are also thrown overboard. After a chase that lasts about eleven hours, the *Siren* runs ashore. The crew destroys the *Siren* and escapes.

The *Syren* was built for the U.S. Navy during 1803 and launched on 6 August of that year, then commissioned the *Syren* during September of 1803. It is a veteran of the Barbary Coast Wars; however, during the War of 1812, the Navy has very little detail of its service other than the day of its capture.

July 13 (Wednesday) *In naval activity,* two British warships, the HMS *Narcissus* and the HMS *Saturn*, intercept the 185-ton schooner *Governor Shelby*, which is en route from New York to Amsterdam with a cargo of tobacco. Also, the HMS *Superb* seizes the 33-ton schooner *Ranger*, which is transporting a cargo of flour from New York to Providence, Rhode Island. The *Ranger* is separate from the schooner *Ranger* seized 5 November 1814.

July 14 (Thursday) *In naval activity,* the brigantine *Maria Frederica*, moving from Amsterdam to Boston with a cargo of gin and other items, is intercepted and seized by two British warships, the HMS *Peruvian* and the HMS *Sea Horse*.

July 15 (Friday) In Washington, D.C., the House of Representatives (according to the *Annals of Congress*, 1813–1814), while in secret session, receives a resolution and a preamble by General Philip Stuart, the representative of the First Maryland District. Stuart underscores the danger in his district and calls for the government to issue arms to all able-bodied men. The resolution is sent to the military affairs committee, which completes its secret discussion on the matter by the following day. The committee states it had "examined into the state of preparation, naval and military, made to receive the enemy, and are satisfied that the preparation is, in every respect, adequate to the emergency, and that no measures are necessary on the part of the House, to make it more complete."

At the time of the committee's report there are no organized militia units close to Washington, nor are there any seasoned regular units. The only regulars in the area are several hundred green recruits of the U.S. 36th and 38th Regiments. The president, his cabinet and Congress are thoroughly convinced that the British will not attempt to attack the capital, even though the British fleet continues to conduct frequent raids and at times, they are so close that the sounds of the guns nearly reach the capitol.

In naval activity, the HMS *Nieman* intercepts and recaptures the 399-ton ship *Sir Alexander Ball* while it is en route to Malta.

July 16 (Saturday) *In naval activity,* the HMS *Acasta* intercepts and seizes the 71-ton schooner *Stephanie*, which is en route to Havana, Cuba, from Philadelphia with a cargo of flour, lard and onions.

July 17 (Sunday) **In Wisconsin,** a British force more the 400 regulars and about 400 Indians launches an attack at Fort Shelby. Troops under General William Clark (of the Lewis and Clark Expedition to the West Coast) had established Fort Shelby in the vicinity of Prairie Du Chien on St. Feriole Island earlier this year to entrench American presence and prevent the British from capturing the fur trade in the upper Mississippi region. The post, defended by about 150 troops, holds out for several days while both sides apparently remain far apart; however, the British eliminate the Americans' only available gunboat, which gives them the advantage. The siege continues until 9 August, when the garrison is compelled to capitulate. The British take possession of the post on the 20th and rename it Fort McKay.

After hostilities end, the post is relinquished to the Americans. Before the British evacuate the island in 1815, they destroy the fort. The British seizure of Fort Shelby is the only action that occurs in Wisconsin during the conflict. A relief force under Captain John Campbell (1st Infantry) had left St. Louis during early July; however, Indians under Black Hawk attacked the flotilla near Rock Island and prevented the contingent from reaching the post.

July 18 (Monday) *In naval activity,* the HMS *Tenedos* intercepts the schooner *Antelope* while it is taking flour and tar from Elizabeth City, North Carolina, to Portland, Maine.

July 19 (Tuesday) **In Canada,** a skirmish erupts at St. David's. The defenders are unable to prevent the American contingent from setting fire to the town.

In naval activity, the sloop *Diana* (William Paynter, master), en route to Havana, Cuba, from Philadelphia with a cargo of flour, is intercepted and captured by the HMS *Acasta*. The *Diana* is separate from the ship *Diana* seized on 20 September 1812.

July 20 (Wednesday) **In Canada,** an American contingent raids Sault Ste. Marie. Some pillaging occurs.

July 21 (Thursday) *In naval activity,* the HMS *Bulwark* intercepts and recaptures the 173-ton brigantine *Tyger*, which is en route from Malaga, Spain to Stattin, Prussia.

July 22 (Friday) U.S. officials sign the Treaty of Greensville with the Delaware, Miami, Seneca, Shawnee and Wyandotte Indian tribes. A stipulation of the treaty is that the natives declare war on the British.

July 23 (Saturday) **In New York,** General Jacob Brown awaits the arrival of a battering ram and fresh riflemen on the Niagara frontier; however, he receives word this day from General Gaines at Sackets Harbor that there will be a delay because Commodore Chauncey is ill. The fleet does not sail until the end of the month.

In naval activity, a British squadron composed of the HMS *Leander*, HMS *Nymphe* and the HMS *Spencer* converge on the 48-ton sloop *Fame* and seize it, while it is en route from Boston to Nantucket with a cargo of beef and pork. The *Fame* is separate from the sloop *Fame* seized on 1 April 1813, the sloop *Fame* overtaken 14 May 1814 and the sloop *Fame* seized 31 May 1814.

In other naval activity, the American privateer *Surprise*, out of Baltimore and commanded by Captain Barnes, arrives back at Newport, Rhode Island. It had just completed an adventurous and profitable yet harrowing cruise primarily in enemy waters off England, Ireland and Scotland, during which time it seized about 13 enemy vessels, while simultaneously escaping from pursuing British warships on sixteen separate occasions. After completing repairs at Newport, it embarks on a new cruise that keeps it out at sea until it arrives at Brest on Christmas Eve of this year. Upon its arrival in France, the French greet it with an eleven-gun salute. After spending the Christmas holidays in Brest, the *Surprise* re-embarks on 9 January 1815. The following are the known prizes of the *Surprise*: the brig *Queen Charlotte*; the ship *Milnes*, the brigantine *Lively*; the schooner *Prince Regent*, the brigantine *Willing Maid*, the brigantine *Polly* and the schooner *Sally*, all of which were burned at sea. Others that were transformed into cartels included the one-gun English privateer *Lively* (taken into Salem, Massachusetts); the ship *Caledonia* en route to Quebec from Cork, Ireland; the brigantine *Eagle*, the brigantine *Traveller*; the four-gun brigantine *Wellington*, and the *Eliza*. The *Surprise* is also known to have seized the brigantine *Albion* and the schooner *Charlotte Ann*; it is also credited with the recapture of the boat *Ann*.

Elsewhere around this time, the zebec *Ultor* out of Baltimore encounters two British boats in Long Island Sound. One of the boats, carrying eight men, is captured, but the other gets away. The British prisoners are taken to New London, Connecticut. The commanding officer of the boat is killed; however, his body is also taken ashore. He is interred at New London.

July 24 (Sunday) **In Canada,** General Brown, having been unable to launch an attack against British positions at Burlington Heights and other points due to the unavailability of Commodore Chauncey's fleet, retires toward Chippewa. Brown's strategy includes baiting General Riall to move against his army. However, the British are simultaneously moving against American positions in New York. General Brown receives intelligence on the following day that a British contingent of about 1,000 men had crossed the Niagara River at Queenston and landed near Lewiston.

In New York, British General Sir Gordon Drummond arrives at Niagara.

In naval activity, the HMS *Acasta* seizes the 30-ton schooner *Hazard* (D. Gorham, master) while it is en route from Matomken, Maryland, to Boston with a cargo of corn and flour.

July 25 (Monday) BATTLE OF LUNDY'S LANE (BATTLE OF NIAGARA, BATTLE OF BRIDGEWATER) **In Canada** during the afternoon, General Brown's ongoing advance against Chippewa is interrupted when Brown is informed that the British had landed troops near Lewiston, New York. General Brown absorbs the intelligence and discerns that the objective is Fort Schlosser and the supply depot. Brown decides to divert the British from their intent to seize the magazine there. He chooses to again move against the British forts at the mouth of the Niagara River in hopes of forcing the British to withdraw from New York.

General Winfield Scott advances with four battalions — Brady's, Jesup's, Leavenworth's and McNeil's. The column is bolstered by Major Nathan Towson's artillery and a cavalry contingent led by Captain Samuel D. Harris. The total number of men stands at about 1,300. The column initiates its advance at about 1700. While en route to the falls, the column reaches the home of a widow, Mrs. Wilson, in the vicinity of Table Rock, where British officers had been observing the column's movement. The Americans spot the British mounting their horses during the approach.

Mrs. Wilson freely informs General Scott that the officers were Riall and his staff; however, she purposely misleads Scott by telling him the British force under Riall amounts to about 1,100 troops, including about 300 militia, and that the force is supplemented by only two pieces of artillery. Her figures undercut Riall's strength by nearly 50 percent. After gaining the erroneous information, Scott sends word back to General Brown of the strength of the British and that they are located to Scott's front. General Scott advances with his main body; however, he directs a contingent to swing out to the left.

Scott's column reaches a clearance at Lundy's Lane and it becomes evident that Mrs. Wilson had provided false information regarding Riall's strength. Just as the troops enter the field, they discover a formidable British line of about 1,800 troops. Suddenly, the Americans discover also that widow Wilson's account of only two guns has since grown to nine guns, deployed on a slope right in the center of the Redcoats' positions. The guns dominate the entire field.

Scott quickly decides it is too risky to retreat and concludes that the only option is to take the offensive. Scott's decision to attack is solidly based on his trust in General Brown, whom he believes will expeditiously send up reinforcements to neutralize the British advantage. By this time, the forces are separated by about 150 paces. While the Americans are forming for the fight, the firing begins and neither side is considering defeat.

Scott's artillery, Major Towson's three guns, return fire; however, the diminutive battery is overmatched by Riall's nine guns, all of which deliver effective fire. The left wing of the British line is deployed west of the road that was near the river, and its positioning leaves the entire wing unattached to the remainder of the line, which stands about 200 yards distant. The ground separating the left wing contains brush, which the Americans use to help conceal the brigades of Jesup and Brady. The combination of the brush and the dwindling sunlight prohibits the British from properly assessing the strength of the two brigades.

Using the twilight to their advantage, Majors Jesup and Hugh Brady bolt from their positions and charge the left wing, igniting a ferocious exchange. Following some exhausting close-quartered fighting, the British are driven from their positions and pushed back to the center of the British line. During the donnybrook, the British are stunned when General Riall and some of his staff officers are captured. After seizing Riall, Majors Jesup and Brady halt their offensive movement and move back to their positions on the line.

In the meantime, the more powerful right wing on the British line swings into action to destroy Scott's left wing. Nevertheless, the British attack is foiled by Scott, who reacts to the British charge by ordering Major John McNeil to intercept the advancing force. The two sides collide and begin to bludgeon each other. Heavy losses occur to both sides; however, the British attempt to outflank Scott's left wing is crushed. All the while, activity to the rear of both sides is intense. Scott's runner reaches General Brown; however, Brown already knows of the battle through the ringing sounds of the artillery.

General Brown orders Ripley's brigade and Porter's militia to speed to the field of battle. Brown is at the point when the reinforcements advance to support Scott. Ripley and Porter reach the scene of the fighting, but not until the sun is setting. While Brown is reinforcing Scott, the British also receive fresh troops. Despite darkness, the combatants continue to pound each other.

Colonel James Miller at Lundy's Lane (*A Gallop Among American Scenery*, Augustus E. Silliman, 1881).

Ripley's brigade jumps into the fray and almost immediately determines that the British guns on the slope are the key to victory.

The 21st Regiment is selected for the extremely dangerous task of destroying or capturing the slope, to ensure defeat for the Redcoats. Colonel James Miller of New Hampshire (later governor of Arkansas), commanding the 21st, receives the order from Ripley to take the slope and responds: "I'll try, Sir." Miller's simple response becomes famous. Miller immediately moves out, using the cover of darkness to conceal his movement. The troops silently advance and reach a fence at the foot of the slope without being discovered by the British at the battery. Amazingly, they are able to slide the barrels of their muskets through the fence without causing an alarm to be sounded. While the Americans prepare to fire, they receive some unexpected support when the stark darkness on the slope is illuminated just as British troops light matches, giving the Americans perfect visibility.

The signal to fire is quietly given and the marksmen fire simultaneously. Each one of the British gunners is taken out. In an instant, Colonel Miller's troops topple the fence and charge up the slope, drive the remaining British troops from the hill to take control of the slope and the British artillery. General Scott's command continues to be embattled; however it maintains its original position. Casualties rise alarmingly on both sides as the incoming and outgoing fire remains incessant.

The savage combat that refuses to subside causes some units to expend all of their ammunition. Major McNeil is killed during the bloodbath and every captain in his command is also killed. After running out of ammunition, McNeil's battalion is compelled to fall back from the field. Despite the ominous darkness, the flying bullets continue to increase the number of casualties. Colonel Brady sustains a severe wound. Brady's battalion, after expending all of its ammunition, also is forced to retire. Nevertheless, the remaining regiments steadfastly hold their

General Edmund P. Gaines (*The Illustrated American Biography, Volume III*, 1855).

ground. Some troops from McNeil's command and from Brady's command, after acquiring ammunition, head back and join the line. Meanwhile, adjustments are made in the line to ensure that the recently captured British artillery remains in the hands of the Americans. The lines are redrawn to form at nearly right angles to the original position. The lines face westwardly and the troops are deployed from where they can firmly retain the slope.

Meanwhile, the British remain persistent in their quest to regain the lost ground and the guns. Brutal combat ensues for about two hours in the contest to determine the fate of the hill. The opposing forces fire at gun-flashes rather than visible targets. The blazing guns and the small arms fire at times transforms the stark darkness into artificial daylight. The combat is not confined to the guns and muskets. Often the two sides are engaged in close-quartered fighting in which the sounds of the clashing bayonets in the darkness add an even more ominous aura to the battlefield.

Rather than phasing out the fighting, both sides continue to add reinforcements. General Eleazar Ripley's force refuses to surrender any ground. Finally, after being repeatedly repulsed at the slope, the British relent. The attacks are aborted and the British retire. Prior to the cessation of hostilities, General Brown and General Scott both sustain wounds, and in the case of Scott, he had two horses shot from under him. His shoulder wound is debilitating, which ends his service in the field for the duration of the conflict. General Ripley assumes command after Scott and Brown are wounded. Brown actually has two wounds, but he refuses to dismount. He remains in command until the battle ends. His aide, Colonel Ambrose Spencer of New York, is killed.

As the British retire and the Americans remain on the field, it becomes apparent that the high cost of gaining and holding the slope brought with it some unintended consequences. All of the horses attached to the artillery had been killed. General Ripley, aware of the absence of fresh water and without interference from the British, begins to gather the wounded about one hour after their departure. Nonetheless, while he is able to move to Chippewa and have his camp completed before dawn on the 26th, he is unable to transport the captured guns. They are left in place and operable on the slope. Both sides claim victory.

On the following day, with Ripley in command, he does not take the offensive. The Americans retire to Fort Erie. Up to that point, General Brown had not enjoined a cordial relationship with General Ripley. Afterward, the pair become more estranged and relations between the two never improve. During 1895, the Canadian Parliament erects a monument on what became known as Drummond Hill. The inscription reads: "Erected by the Canadian Parliament in honour of the victory gained by the British and Canadian forces on this field on the 25th July 1814, and in grateful remembrance of the brave men who died on that day fighting for the unity of the [British] Empire."

During the morning of the 26th, the British return to the scarred battlefield. They recover their guns and they establish camp on the ground for which they fought on the previous day. The British fielded about 4,500 troops, well above the number earlier fed to General Scott by the widow, Mrs. Wilson. In turn, the American force under General Brown totaled about 2,600. Both sides had heavy casualties. The Americans sustain about 174 killed, 470 to 565 wounded and about 115 to 120 missing. Those killed or were wounded include Colonel Hugh Brady, Lt. Colonel Henry Leavenworth (breveted lieutenant colonel at the Battle of Chippewa), Major John McNeil and Major McFarland. Also, Lt. Colonel Leavenworth is breveted colonel for his actions at Lundy's Lane. British casualties stand at about 84 killed, 557 wounded and 235 missing or captured. British General Riall is among the captured. He is succeeded by General Sir Gordon Drummond.

The Canadian independent unit under Major Mallory and another officer, Wilcox, fighting alongside the Americans, is devastated at this battle. The band of mounted troops known as the Canadian Volunteers had been a primary target of the British since they began to operate in Canada as guerrillas. Wilcox had been shot by the British near Fort Erie on 20 July. Major Mallory makes it to the United States, his native country. The British bury their dead in the field, but in retaliation for the treatment of the British dead at Chippewa (5 July), the British pile the American dead in layers and burn most of them. Nonetheless, the body of Captain Abraham F. Hull, the son of General William Hull, is spared the cremation. The British bury him with full honors.

Also, General Peter Porter receives a gold medal from Congress in appreciation of his service during the war and a sword from New York. In 1815, President James Madison appoints General Porter as commander-in-chief of the U.S. Army; however, Porter declines. Also, General Porter, in Congress until the start of the war, when he chose to resign his seat, initially declined accepting a general commission, but afterward, he accepted command of a division of New York and Pennsylvania volunteers. He also participates at the siege of Fort Erie in August and September 1814.

Congress gives Colonel Miller a gold medal and a sword for his bravery on the slope. General Brown later makes this statement about Miller's action: "You have immortalized yourself! My dear fellow, my heart ached for you when I gave you the order, but I knew that it was the only thing that would save us." The British captives also refer to the attack launched by Miller: "It was the most desperate thing we ever saw or heard of."

Lieutenant John A. Dix, later U.S. Senator, major general in the Civil War and governor of New York, participates at this battle. Also, Colonel (later general) Thomas Jesup participates at this battle. He became quartermaster general, a post he held for more than 40 years until his death in 1860.

July 26 (Tuesday) **In Canada,** General Ripley, pursuant to his orders from General Brown, initiates action which places his command of about 1,800 men on the Queenston Road, however, he is informed that a large British force stands in his front. Consequently, in disobedience to his orders, he breaks camp at Chippewa and retreats. General Ripley orders the span over the Chippewa River destroyed, and once the task is accomplished, the force retires; however, General Brown directs Ripley to divert and move to Fort Erie in Canada. The British, about 5,000 strong, shadow the column. At a point several miles from Fort Erie, the British make camp and they initiate a siege of the fort. Meanwhile, during the march, an American detachment destroys Burch's Mills (built during 1786), a grist and saw mill on the west bank of the Niagara River slightly above Niagara Falls.

In Michigan, the flotilla under Captain Arthur St. Clair, U.S. Navy, arrives off Michilimackinac, which has been held by the British since July 1812. The ground troops under Lt. Col. Croghan remain aboard the vessels while an attack strategy is determined to seize the post, which is commanded by Lt. Colonel McDonall. Captain St. Clair is reluctant to move in close to bombard the post because it stands on high ground, and he fears that the fort's guns could easily devastate his vessels. Finally, on 4 August, Croghan's force lands at a spot on the northern sector of the island, from where it will strike the rear of the post. The lapse permits the British to prepare for the assault. Lt. Colonel McDonall empties the garrison force and deploys his troops to the rear of a small ridge that dominates the rear path to the fort. He also deploys two artillery pieces to bolster his fire power, while at the same time, his allied Indians are directed to take positions in the woods.

Meanwhile, Croghan's force lands unopposed and advances toward the fort, initially oblivious to the trap. Nevertheless, the Americans detect the British presence. Croghan moves to collapse the left side of the British line; however, the Indians, who remain undiscovered, unleash a devastating volley that takes out two officers, Major Holmes (killed) and Captain Desha, which creates instant indecision. However, Croghan orders an attack against the center of the British line. The solid thrust buys time, and the persistence during the plunge evicts the British from their positions and compels them to bolt from their breastworks to new positions in the woods to their rear.

The British regroup and prohibit further progress. After concluding that the line is impenetrable, Croghan orders a retreat. His column returns to the boats and the flotilla withdraws, leaving the coveted post under British control. The Americans lose 13 killed. The 52 wounded include Captains Van Horn and Desha and Lt. Jackson. Two others are reported missing. British casualties remain unknown. St. Clair then sails to the Nautawassaga River. About three miles from the mouth of the river, the Americans seize a blockhouse, but too late to claim the furs of the British Northwest Company. The furs had been transferred to a safer location.

Afterward, the *Tigress* (Captain Stephen Champlin) and the *Scorpion* (Captain Daniel Turner) are directed to remain to blockade any ships trying to deliver supplies of provisions to the garrison at Mackinaw, while the remainder of the force returns to Detroit. The two vessels assigned to blockade duty encounter difficulty on 3 September.

July 28 (Thursday) *In naval activity,* the British privateer *Lively* intercepts and seizes the 64-ton sloop *Nancy,* which is en route from New York to Providence, Rhode Island, with a cargo of corn and flour. The *Nancy* is separate from the ship *Nancy* seized on 17 August 1812, the schooner *Nancy* captured 28 May 1813, the schooner *Nancy* seized on 28 June 1813, the brigantine *Nancy* seized about 1–18 September 1814, and the brigantine *Nancy* captured on 13 September 1814. In other naval activity, the HMS *Asia* intercepts and seizes the 36-ton sloop *Unity* (J.C. Swain, master), which is transporting a cargo including turpentine and tar from Washington, North Carolina, to Philadelphia.

July 29 (Friday) *In naval activity,* the British privateer *Liverpool Packet* intercepts the 31-ton sloop *Logan* (Charles Willoughby, master) while it is en route to New London, Connecticut, from New Haven with flour. The *Logan* and its cargo are diverted to Liverpool. In other naval activity, the British privateer *Lively* intercepts and seizes the 44-ton schooner *Sukey,* which is carrying a cargo that includes beer and cider.

July 30 (Saturday) *In naval activity* in Connecticut, the British naval forces in Long Island Sound spot a privateer out of Stonington that is disguised as a merchant ship. The British send a barge under the command of Lt. Thomas Barret Powers to investigate. The privateer has only a few men on deck to maintain the ruse. Powers' barge closes, but unexpectedly, he is faced with a superior force. Powers removes his hat to inform the Americans that he is surrendering. Nevertheless, one of the men on the deck of the privateer, without orders or provocation, shoots Lt. Powers in the head and kills him. Once the captured barge is taken into port at Stonington Borough, the Americans make arrangements to give Lt. Powers a Christian burial with military honors. During the ceremony, Reverend Ira Hart, chaplain of the 30th Connecticut Regiment, gives a eulogy to honor the English officer who was only 18 years old at the time he was killed. Before the British fleet leaves American waters, British Captain Piget and the other officers attached to the HMS *Superb* erect a monument to Lt. Powers at his grave. In 1815, the lieutenant's father arrives from England, and after speaking with Captain Thomas Swan, a witness to the slaying, visits the gravesite of his only son. Mr. Powers makes it known that he is grateful that the people of Stonington gave his son a Christian burial.

In other naval activity, the schooner *Three Friends* (known also as the sloop *Pictou*) is captured by the British. The *Three Friends* is separate from the schooner *Three Friends* seized on 18 December 1812 and the *Three Friends* seized on 12 November 1814. Also, the HMS *Rifleman* intercepts the 22-ton schooner *Union* (W. Bradford, master), which is transporting a cargo of beef, butter and other items from Camden to Moose Island. The *Union* is separate from the brigantine *Union* seized on 14 August 1812, the ship *Union* seized on 16 August 1812, the schooner *Union* seized 14 October 1812, the schooner *Union* captured on 19 October 1812, the schooner *Union* seized 3 April 1813 and the ship *Union* overtaken 26 June 1813.

July 31 (Sunday) *In naval activity,* Commodore Isaac Chauncey, having recuperated from his illness, departs Sackets Harbor. The fleet is composed of the 62-gun *Superior* (Commodore Chauncey and Lt. Elton); 42-gun *Mohawk* (Captain Jacob Jones); 28-gun *General Pike* (Captain Crane); 24-gun *Madison* (Captain Edward Trenchard); 22-gun *Jefferson* (Captain Ridgely); 22-gun *Jones* (Lieutenant Woolsey); 14-gun *Sylph* (Captain Elliot); 16-gun *Oneida* (Lieutenant Brown) and *Lady of the Lake*. The *Jefferson* is making its initial cruise. The squadron moves up Lake Ontario in search of the British squadron under the Sir James Yeo and arrives off Niagara on 5 August. In company with the USS *Oneida* and the *Sylph*, it seals the river, preventing British vessels there from breaking through. Meanwhile, Chauncey moves with the main body to entice the British to engage his squadron. Meanwhile, the *Jefferson* remains on station for slightly more than one month before rejoining the main body. While en route from Niagara to Kingston, the *Jefferson* encounters a nasty storm on 12 September that nearly overwhelms it. To try to save the vessel, the crew tosses ten of its guns overboard. They fight the tempest for three days, but survive and rejoin the squadron on 17 September. In late November, the *Jefferson* goes out of service until spring; however, peace arrives in the meantime. Consequently, the *Jefferson* remains in ordinary until it is sold in April 1825.

Also, the 42-gun frigate *Mohawk* initiates its first mission. Another vessel, the USS *Ranger* (third), a 14-gun brigantine, joins Chauncey's fleet at an undetermined time during this year; however, the vessel, to be utilized only as a supply ship and transport, is later rendered unfit for service. The *Ranger* is sold in May 1832.

August *In naval activity,* the USS *Peacock*, during a mission in the waters off the coasts of England and Ireland, scores success with the capture of several British vessels, including the sloops HMS *William and Ann,* HMS *Leith Passket,* and the HMS *Peggy and Jane*. The *Peacock*, assisted by its Marine contingent, also seizes the *Sir Edward Pellen* off the Irish coast, as well as the vessel *William*. The USS *Adams* and the USS *Wasp*, both operating in waters in the vicinity of England and Europe, achieve success with victories over the British vessels *Paris* and the *Maria* by the *Adams*, a sloop. The *Wasp* continues its victory streak by catching and capturing the British brigantine *Lettice* on the 30th, followed by success and victory over the brigantine *Bon Accord* the following day. Two additional brigantines, including the HMS *Triton*, fall to the Yankee crew of the *Peacock* on the 21st and 23rd. Also, the American privateer *Harrison* out of Baltimore arrives at Savannah. Under its commander, H. Perry, the *Harrison* embarks on a second cruise during 1815. It seizes a total of six prizes.

August 1–31 *In naval activity,* the British, including naval forces and ground forces, capture several American vessels, the schooners *Elipse,* the schooner *Madison* and the schooner *Peacock,* each carrying cargoes of tobacco, during operations on the Patuxent and Potomac Rivers.

August 2 (Tuesday) **In New York City,** Mayor DeWitt Clinton calls for the citizens to volunteer to help finish the city's fortifications in response to a threat of a British invasion.

In naval activity, the 79-ton schooner *Delaware* (Joseph Merrihew, master), carrying a cargo of flour, soap and other items, is intercepted and seized by two British warships, the HMS *Acasta* and the HMS *Menelaus*, while it is en route from Wilmington to Cuba. In other activity, the HMS *Acasta* (George Gramsby, master) intercepts the 70-ton sloop *Jane,* which is transporting a cargo of hides and sugar.

August 2 to September 21 SIEGE OF FORT ERIE The British under General Drummond initiate an assault against Fort Erie, hitting Black Rock, New York, and then turning their attention toward the soldiers and the artillery at the post. The attack falters and the defenders under General Gaines hold out. General Brown, having no confidence in General Ripley, had appointed General Gaines as commander at Fort Erie. Dur-

Night attack against Fort Erie (*A Gallop Among American Scenery,* Augustus E. Silliman, 1881).

ing mid–August, British troops succeed in their assault to capture the Fort Erie blockhouse, only to be driven out with catastrophic losses when the ammunition magazine explodes. The Americans boldly attack British positions, delivering many more casualties. Both armies suffer severely but the Stars and Stripes continues to fly over the fort on 21 September, when the British abort the siege and retire toward Chippewa. General Gaines will be breveted major general for his actions.

In naval activity, the USS *Wasp* intercepts a British vessel and seizes it. Afterward, the Americans, to their jubilation, discover that their prize is actually the American privateer *Silo* that was captured by the British during January 1813.

August 3 (Wednesday) The British cross the Niagara River in force in what becomes an unsuccessful attempt to seize Buffalo, New York, from the Americans. Two hundred and fifty American sharpshooters commanded by Morgan drive the British back to Canada.

In naval activity, A British contingent attached to Admiral George Cockburn's squadron lands at Munday's Point and skirmishes with a contingent of General John P. Hungerford's command. The Americans are compelled to retreat and there is some pursuit. While on shore the British destroy some property. In other activity, the 46-ton sloop *Defiance* (Mulford Howes, master), carrying a cargo of salt and other items, is intercepted and seized by the British privateer *Lively*. The prize is taken into port at Liverpool. The *Defiance* is separate from the 118-ton sloop *Defiance* seized on 31 March 1813, the 104-ton sloop *Defiance* seized on 4 April 1813, the schooner *Defiance* captured 19 May 1814, and the 62-ton sloop *Defiance* taken on 3 June 1814. One other sloop named *Defiance* is seized by the HMS *Superb* and the HMS *Sylph* at an undetermined time during 1814.

August 4 (Thursday) **In Michigan,** Colonel George Croghan leads a force of soldiers and Marines in an attack against Fort George (Fort Michilimackinac). During the assault, Major Andrew Holmes is killed. Initially, the attack progresses as the landing succeeds; however, as the column advances toward the fort, a force of British and Indians, holding concealed positions, unleashes an ambush. Croghan is compelled to retire. The Americans regain the post the next year and rename it Fort Holmes.

In other activity, another contingent of Americans debarks at the mouth of the Nautauwasaga River at Lake Huron and will successfully attack and capture an enemy blockhouse.

August 5 (Friday) *In naval activity,* Commodore Chauncey's squadron arrives off Niagara. Upon reaching the mouth of the Niagara River, Chauncey orders Lt. Elliott, aboard the USS *Sylph,* to intercept the 14-gun *Beresford,* a schooner that had been transformed into a brigantine. Elliott's vessel runs the British ship ashore at a point slightly west of Fort George. It had been transporting troops from York to Niagara. The *Sylph* moves in closer and prepares to destroy the beached ship; however, before it can open fire, the crew self-destructs it. Lt. Elliott remains in service following the close of hostilities; however, on more than one occasion he leaves active service. During 1840, Commodore Elliott receives a court-martial and is removed from the Navy for four years; however, during October 1843, he is restored to rank and given command of the Philadelphia Navy Yard. Commodore Elliott dies during 1845.

In other activity, the HMS *Leander* intercepts and captures the 224-ton *Dalkablen* (Johan Magnus Berg, master), which is en route from Amsterdam to Boston with a cargo of iron and steel.

August 6 (Saturday) *In naval activity,* the HMS *Boxer* intercepts the 38-ton schooner *Julian,* which is transporting a cargo of beef, candles, flour, gin, soap, tobacco and other items from Boston to Machias, Maine. The *Julian* is captured and taken into port at St. John's, New Brunswick. The *Julian* is separate from the *Julian* seized on 13 November 1812, the *Julian* seized 8 December 1813, and the *Julian* captured 17 November 1814.

August 7 (Sunday) *In naval activity,* a Swedish brigantine, the 180-ton *Enigheton* (J.A. Doltz, master), having departed from St. Andrew's, is intercepted and seized by the HMS *Nieman* before it reaches its destination at Philadelphia. Elsewhere, the HMS *Spencer* intercepts and seizes the 22-ton schooner *Old Carpenter,* which is en route to Boston from Halifax with a cargo of dry goods. The 45-ton schooner *Victory,* carrying a cargo of green fish, is seized by the HMS *Leander.* The *Victory* is separate from the brigantine *Victory* captured 19 March 1813, the schooner *Victory* seized on 6 January 1814, and the ship *Victory* taken as a prize in September 1814.

August 8 (Monday) In Washington, D.C., President James Madison, concerned by the massive collection of British warships in Long Island Sound and the immediate threat of invasion, issues a proclamation that calls for an extra session of Congress: "Whereas great and weighty matters claiming the consideration of the Congress of the United States form an extraordinary occasion for convening them...." The British by this time have the ports in Connecticut sealed and only very infrequently does a privateer manage to squeeze through the blockade. Long Island Sound is not the only location receiving additional British warships. The British are preparing to launch a massive attack on the heart of the U.S. government, the capital at Washington, D.C. British General Robert Ross, a veteran of the war against France, has been selected to lead the campaign.

During mid–August, his force, composed of three 3,500 elite troops of Wellington's command, arrive in the Chesapeake Bay from Bordeaux, France. Once he arrives, his force will be increased with 1,000 Royal Marines from Admiral Cockburn's blockading squadron. The British also impress about 100 Negroes from plantations in the area. The Negroes receive a brief period of military training.

The District of Columbia, having been designated part of the newly created 10th Military District, comes under the command of General William H. Winder; however, his force is composed of only about 500 regulars, bolstered by about 2,000 militia troops. Nonetheless, once British General Ross arrives in Maryland, more militia are called upon. Winder will receive several thousand men from Maryland. Virginia, however, encounters a snafu with its contributing troops. The Virginians fail to receive flints for their weapons on a timely basis. Consequently, the delay causes them to arrive after the fighting had ended.

In Belgium at Ghent, the peace commissioners are Lord Gambier, William Adams and Henry Goulbourn representing England and John Quincy Adams, James A. Bayard, Henry Clay, Jonathan Russel and Albert Gallatin representing the United States. The Americans had expected to face high caliber negotiators on the British side of the table, but instead, London has dispatched commissioners who conspicuously lack experience. The Americans now believe the British are not taking the talks seriously.

While these talks get underway, London is also very involved in negotiations scheduled for Vienna, where the Allies will redraw the map of Europe subsequent to the recent defeat of Napoleon Bonaparte. Lord Castlereagh and the Duke of Wellington will handle the British end of the negotiations, not lower level diplomats, which reinforces the American opinion that the talks at Ghent are not a priority.

The American commissioners, once presented with British proposals that infer demands rather than compromise, immediately turn them down. The British propose that the United States must relinquish for all time constructing or maintaining any forts on the Great Lakes and that no American warships be permitted to sail the Great Lakes. Additionally, the British insist upon receiving huge amounts of land from several different sections of the country, including a parcel lying west of Lake Superior stretching to the Mississippi River, a portion of northeastern Maine and yet another in New York State, each designed to shrink the power of the U.S. and construct a protective zone in front of Canada. Then to further press the patience of the Americans, the British mandate that as a condition to a settlement, the U.S. must forfeit segment of land to be carved from the area which would be the states of Illinois, Indiana, Ohio, Michigan and Wisconsin. At this time, the demands would be the equivalent of the U.S. demanding that the United Kingdom cede Scotland to the United States. The British negotiators state that the area is necessary to provide the Indians with a separate state, which of course would also provide the Canadians dominance of the fur trade in the area, as well as an enormous buffer area.

One U.S. negotiator, Henry Clay, senses a ruse by the British rather than a firm commitment to war, but the majority of U.S. representatives prepare to terminate the negotiations rather than engage in frivolous talks. Clay's assessment proves true. London is experiencing tremendous pres-

Henry Clay.

sure from its citizens to end the hostilities and can ill afford to break off the talks. The British representatives receive a harsh message from the Foreign Office in reaction to the jack-hammer fashion in which they presented the British proposals to the Americans in Ghent, and it instructs them to maintain the negotiations.

The British representatives have inadvertently bolstered the American cause. Their stance as victors dictating to the vanquished accomplishes what the U.S. government has been unable to do, unite the republic. President Madison, once informed of the British demands, has them published and distributed to the American people, much to the dismay of the British, who are then placed between angry Americans and infuriated British citizens, who have tired of keeping a stiff upper lip. The talks continue and by October, the British again believe they hold the upper hand.

August 9 (Tuesday) **In Washington, D.C.,** the British fleet closing against the capital stands at the mouth of the St. Mary's River. It is composed of the 74-gun HMS *Albion*, two ships, two brigantines, three frigates, several sloops of war, thirteen schooners and one razee. Also present are the HMS *Severn*, the HMS *Prince William* and one brigantine. By 19 August, additional vessels arrive to bolster the British fleet, bringing it to 46 sail in the vicinity of Point Lookout and five frigates off St. George's Island.

In Alabama, Americans and one portion of the Creek Indian tribe subscribe to the Treaty of Fort Jackson (sometimes referred to as the Treaty of Conquest). This treaty cedes approximately twenty million acres of land in the area of Georgia and Mississippi Territory to the United States. Another part of the treaty has the Creeks agreeing to abandon sections of Alabama. The treaty creates a line separating the Mississippi Territory from the Creek lands. This boundary line begins at a point ten miles from the mouth of the Ofucshee Creek and runs directly to the mouth of the Summochio Creek, which lies at the mouth of the Chattahouchee River. In Alabama, the Poarch (Creeks) are protected by the treaty and the Creeks are directed to cede land to tribes that had been friendly to the U.S. Thirty-six humbled Creek chiefs sign the pact, imposed upon them by General Jackson. Others who attend include Adjutant General Robert Butler, Benjamin Hawkins, U.S. agent for Indian affairs, and the agent for the Creek Nation, Return J. Meigs.

In New York City, a huge crowd gathers in City Hall Park in response to a call from Henry Rutgers and Oliver Wolcott. The group decides to select a committee of defense drawn from the Common Council, which will be authorized to oversee the project to bolster the defenses of the city. The committee comprises George Buckmaster, Colonel Nicholas Fish, Peter Mesier, John Nitchie and Gideon Tucker. On this day, the work begins at Brooklyn Heights under the supervision of General Joseph Gardiner Swift. Within several days, it is reported that about 3,000 volunteers are participating.

In other activity, three New Yorkers, Abram Shoemaker, his brother, and Mr. Sergeant, while traveling by boat from Oswego to Sackets Harbor, are intercepted and captured by a British barge. The British commander, a Royal Marine lieutenant, snags the boat off Stony Point. Once the boat is secured, following resistance, the British troops, except four men, and the lieutenant, transfer to another boat. Meanwhile, when the lieutenant is off-guard, Abram Shoemaker shoves him out of the boat and regains control of it after knocking down a sailor. The British in the other craft spot the action, which prompts the Americans to abandon their prize. The trio jumps aboard a small boat and safely reaches Sackets Harbor.

In naval activity, the Spanish brigantine *Anita* (Frans Ornes, master) is intercepted by the HMS *Leander* while it is en route from Boston to Havana, Cuba. Also, the *Ida*, a 180-ton brigantine, carrying a crew of 64 men and transporting ten carriage guns and eighteen 16-pounders, is seized by the HMS *Newcastle* while en route from Boston to France.

August 9–11 **In Connecticut,** to the surprise and dismay of the citizens of Stonington, a British squadron — including the 74-gun HMS *Ramillies*, 44-gun *Pactolus*, the brigantine *Dispatch*, and the bomb-ship *Terror*, along with a number of barges and launches — is spotted moving into Fisher's Island Sound, despite the danger to the large ships on account of its water depth and reefs. It is an ominous sign that signals imminent danger. Commodore Sir Thomas Hardy, pursuant to orders to destroy the town, arrives off the target, Stonington. Hardy's command had recently captured Moose Island and other territory in Maine without resistance. He expects that this mission will be short. The harbor suddenly fills with townspeople who are learning of the threat. A boat, attached to the HMS *Pactolus*, approaches shore to deliver a message. It is met by a party of Americans who move out from the harbor to receive the message:

> HIS Majesty's Ship "Pactolus," 9th of August 1814, half-past 6 o'clock p.m.
> Not willing to destroy the unoffending Inhabitants residing in the town of Stonington, one hour is given them from the receipt of this to move out of town. T.M. HARDY, Captain H.B.M. Ship Ramllies To the Inhabitants of the Town of Stonington.

Hardy's succinct message informs the townspeople that his naval guns intend to reduce the town beginning in one hour. From the shoreline, the citizens easily see the warships, two frigates, one brigantine and a bomb vessel. The British threat does not intimidate the people. Using the available time, the women and children are escorted to safety at a place outside of Stonington, while the men race to raise a force and defend their town. Riders gallop to nearby villages to sound the alarm and acquire militia. Other men inform General Cushing, who is at New London, while another rider informs Colonel William Randall, who is the closest and arrives quickly. Colonel Randall, Captain William Potter, Lt. Hough and Lt. Lathrop intend to resist rather than capitulate. In the meantime, tar barrels are lit and their flames also telegraph the emergency, spreading the word to militia who live as far as 15 miles away.

The British spot the sudden appearance of breastworks, a conspicuous show of defiance, and

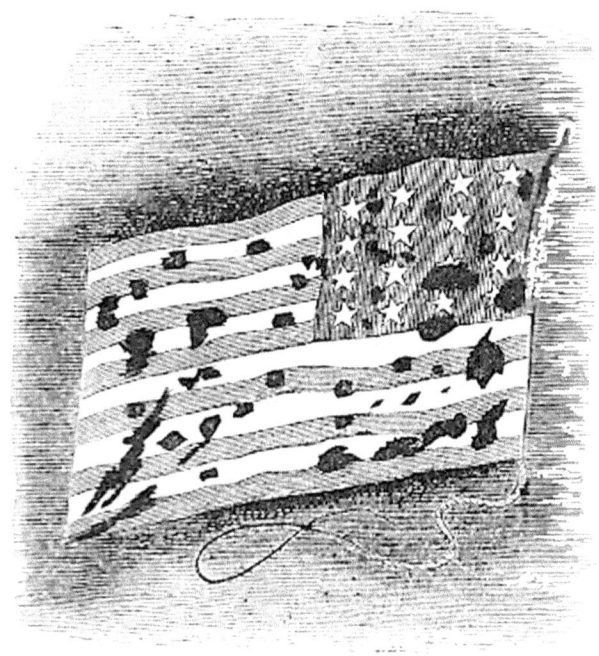

The Stonington flag.

shortly thereafter the British see a primitive flagstaff upon which the Americans nail the Stars and Stripes, which signals a fight to the last man. Other reinforcements under Captain Jeremiah Holmes arrive from Mystic. Holmes, a skilled gunner, handles an 18-pounder. During the attack, his accuracy is effective, so much so, that the HMS *Dispatch* escapes sinking only by cutting its cables. At one point, the situation becomes desperate when the ammunition becomes depleted and some in the town consider surrender. Holmes, upon hearing the word surrender, emphatically gives his response. His voice bellows as he points to the flag nailed to the mast and yells "No! That flag shall never come down while I am alive." The citizens determine for themselves that they preferred "being buried in the rubble" to capitulation.

Commodore Hardy seems unconcerned about the temporary obstacle, and he expects to eliminate it while reducing the town. In the meantime, before the British commence the attack, the defenders install some artillery, two 18-pounders and one six (or four) pounder. The men trained to handle artillery, including two strangers from Massachusetts, deploy at the guns, while the others prepare to meet the British with their muskets. Nevertheless, the Americans have additional handicaps against such a British force, and at the top of the list, there is a shortage of ammunition.

Colonel Randall arrives in Stonington before the sun sets and the activity to prepare for the invasion gets underway. Randall, anticipating a British landing during the predawn hours of the 10th, issues his orders: "To the 30th Regiment Connecticut Militia: In consequence of an attack on Stonington Borough, and in pursuance of orders received from the Brigadier, this Regiment is called into active service and will assemble at the Public House of Oliver York forthwith, and officers and soldiers will attend to this order and warn others and assemble accordingly." Troops continue flooding into the village and flaming tar barrels spread the word in lightning-fast fashion. General Isham arrives with his command. Afterward, the men form in companies out of the range of the British guns, then move into their respective positions.

As threatened by Hardy, at 2000, the bombardment commences and the British catapult many types of projectiles, including "round-shot, grape-shot, canister, bomb-shells, carcasses (iron cylinders covered with canvas that contain combustibles), rockets, and stink-pots. The British expect the town to be transformed into burning debris. In an attempt to quicken the destruction, a British landing party, carried in five boats, lands at about 1900. The landing is unopposed, creating an illusion that the militia had fled, leaving the town to the Redcoats. The British also land several guns without interference, which increases their confidence. Once ashore, the British move inland to complete the destruction. Except for the crackle of the fires, and the noise made by the British themselves, an eerie silence greets the British as they begin to advance.

The silence is abruptly broken when the British reach close range and the artillery begins to rivet the column. The Americans, commanded by Colonel Randall, rise from behind the breastwork and the riflemen increase the punishment. The bombardment had inflicted much damage to the buildings; however, rather than frighten the men, the British action had galvanized them. Within a short while, the British are driven back to their boats.

Commodore Hardy, having failed to subjugate the Americans, remains determined to take his objective. Continuing in his belief that the militia could not resist for too long without collapsing, withdraws, but only so he can swing his force around to the opposite (eastern) side of the peninsula, where his landing force can debark at an undefended location. The scheme seems foolproof; however, the Americans stay a step ahead of the commodore. The 6-pounder is taken over a difficult route to the other (eastern) side of the peninsula and deployed at a spot where another ambush could be sprung. The gun commanded by Ensign Frink (Captain Potter's company) and the muskets hold the ground until the men can lug one of the 18-pounders to the same location. The barges carrying the landing force arrive only to again be struck with unexpected fire. The British again are repelled. Expeditiously the raiders are forced to return to their ships.

Despite two unexpected setbacks, Commodore Hardy refuses to abort the mission. His retaliation remains incessant. The bombardment of Stonington continues until 2300. The following day, when Hardy resumes the bombardment at 0700, he receives some additional firepower when another frigate, the 21-gun *Nimrod*, arrives. His five ships advance closer to shore to inflict more devastation. The daring *Dispatch* moves extremely close to shore to cover the landing force that is advancing in five boats and two large launches; however, the *Nimrod* comes too close to the battery, placing the crew within range of a pistol shot. Unconcerned, the British intend to reduce the battery and then pull back out of harm's way. As the gunners on the *Nimrod* prepare to fire, they receive a volley from the 18-pounders that rips through the vessel and inflicts severe damage, forcing the brig to hurriedly pull back.

The British have yet to find a way to subdue the militia. Hardy dispatches yet another landing party to eliminate the pesky but deadly battery. The barges encroach the shoreline; however, the landing fails, and once again, the seasoned regulars hit a wall of fire that prohibits further progress. For the third time, the British are repulsed at the shoreline, and in the process of attempting the assault, the American 6-pounder scores a devastating hit on one of the barges and blows it to pieces. By this time, Commodore Hardy is becoming more infuriated at his inability to prevail. Nonetheless, he does not consider aborting the mission.

Once the troops get back to the ships, the squadron withdraws to get beyond the range of the artillery. Afterward, the bombardment is reinitiated and the battered town receives no reprieve. Hardy's guns pummel the place throughout the entire day and still, Hardy remains unsatisfied with his destruction. The British guns, after resting during the night begin to bellow once again in his attempt to turn Stonington into rubble.

Finally, on the 12th, while the American flag remains nailed to the primitive staff, the British guns cease firing. They had pounded the town, but not the spirit of its indefatigable defenders. The British squadron retires without having reduced the town or capturing a single defender. The British sustain 21 killed and at least 50 wounded. The Americans sustain one man lost to a mortal wound. Six others sustain minor wounds. Of the hundred or so houses in the town, the British incessant shelling totally destroys a few homes, while ten others are heavily damaged and about 25 others have only minor damage.

During the horrendous bombardment, one of the homes toward the rear of the town sustains heavy damage from shells passing through the structure. An elderly woman there, Huldah Hall, who was in poor health and not taken to a safe location, dies. Her daughter ignores the hurricane of incoming shells and walks to where the defenders are fighting to get help. The troops are stunned once they spot her. She informs the troops of her mother's death and requests help. A detachment accompanies the daughter back to the house and the woman is carried to the "old Robinson burial place." The land had been so battle scarred that the troops actually inter Mrs. Hall in a deep hole that was caused by artillery. The burial is quickly handled as the bombs continue to fly while the men and her daughter are at the cemetery.

August 10 In Canada, American General Izard receives orders from Secretary of War Armstrong to march toward Fort Erie with his force of 4,000 men to assist the besieged defenders. Izard's troops arrive on October 5.

In naval activity, the British privateer *Liverpool Packet* intercepts and seizes the 45-ton schooner

General George Izard.

Polly, which is en route from New Haven, Connecticut, to New York. Also this day, the *Liverpool Packet* in conjunction with another British privateer, the *Shannon*, also seizes the 65-ton sloop *Victress* (S. Pennoyer, master) which is en route from Bridgeport to New York with a varied cargo including butter, cheese, oats and liquor.

August 11 (Thursday) **In Alabama,** General Jackson, after consummating a treaty with the Creeks, departs from Fort Jackson en route to Mobile. Colonel Arthur P. Hayne accompanies the party. Jackson and some troops embark in boats. Jackson is aware that the probability of a British attack against Mobile is high. Upon his arrival, Jackson reverses a decision of General Flournoy, who had ordered Fort Bowyer at Mobile Point dismantled. Jackson inspects the post and directs that it be garrisoned. Jackson also sends out messages that are taken to Tennessee. On 9 September, Colonel Butler receives one of his letters in Nashville. Butler is directed to speed to Fort Bowyer, and he is also to have part of his volunteers move to New Orleans. Shortly thereafter, Butler sends militia under Colonel Lowery to join with Jackson's army. At about the same time, Jackson's close friend, General Coffee, departs to join with Jackson. Other forces that depart from Tennessee for Alabama include regulars under Captain Baker and Captain Butler.

Meanwhile, British forces are arriving at Pensacola, Florida. The British colors will be hoisted at Fort Barrancas and at Fort St. Michael. Colonel Nichols will establish his headquarters at the governor's house (Governor Manrique). After his arrival in Pensacola, Nichols offers the Indians $10 for each American scalp, including those of women and children, that they deliver to him.

In naval activity, two British privateers, the *Shannon* and the *Liverpool Packet*, intercept and capture the 48-ton schooner *Minerva*, which is carrying a cargo of fish, flour and other items. The prize and its cargo are taken into port at Liverpool. This *Minerva* is separate from like named vessels also captured: a brigantine, 6 July 1812; a ship, 8 September 1812; a brigantine, 30 June 1813; a sloop, 5 August 1813; a schooner, 30 August 1813; a brigantine, 21 April 1814; and a schooner, 26 September 1814.

August 12 (Friday) *In naval activity,* the USS *Ohio* and the USS *Somers*, while on patrol on Lake Erie, are seized by a British force under Captain Dobbs. At the time of their capture, both vessels are just off Fort Erie.

August 13 (Saturday) **In Maryland,** General Levin Winder, the governor of Maryland, writes to Secretary of War John Armstrong concerning General Smith's 2nd Division. Rather than place the Eastern shore in jeopardy by drawing militia from that region, it would be safer to leave the militia there in place, and accepting about 1,000 of the state troops in federal service. Winder also proposes that one regiment be requested from Pennsylvania, which would place his militia at about 3,000 troops. Armstrong responds and authorizes Winder to place the troops into U.S. service.

August 14 (Sunday) **In New York** at Albany, Governor Daniel D. Tompkins has been working to get reinforcements to New York due to a threat against the city. On this day, the governor issues his instructions in a letter to Lt. Colonel John Townsend: "Dr. Sir: Troops will assemble at Coxackie, Catskill, Hudson, Kingston, Rhinebeck, Poughkeepsie, New Burgh & New Windsor on Thursday next at 10 O' Clock in the forenoon from whence they will proceed to New York."

August 14 to September 21 SIEGE OF FORT ERIE In Canada, the British, having spent about two weeks establishing batteries while sporadically bombarding American-held Fort Erie, launches a full scale assault to regain the post. It begins under stark darkness and a nasty storm at the stroke of midnight (August 14th-15th). Lt. General Gordon Drummond signals the attack, and his orders mandate that the assault troops remove the flints from their muskets to help maintain silence. His orders also emphasize that no quarter be given. He has also pushed heavily for the troops to carry the fort by using their bayonets. Prior to springing what they expect to be a surprise attack, British troops advance in the darkness to deposit scaling ladders near the walls of the post. The British have included great details in their plans, which incorporate a three-pronged assault. Despite their careful planning and their secretive movement, the defenders in the fort are fully prepared and the guns are manned in preparation for the attack that has kept the garrison on full alert. The troops each have their musket nearby and ready for action.

Towson's battery, reduced to only 40 men, but well seasoned following the major contests at Chippewa and Lundy's Lane, holds the left side of the fort, along with about 250 troops of the 21st Regiment under Major Wood. One of the three attacking columns, Colonel Fischer (right column) strikes there; however, sentinels pick up the sounds of the moving column, composed of about 1,500 men, and in time for a reception committee to prepare a surprise for the British, who find that they are moving through a storm of fire from Towson's guns and the infantry posted there.

General Gaines speeds to the front, and while with major Wood, he was able to observe the British column. The British line was checked, but not until it reached a point about ten feet from the U.S. Infantry.

The British attempt to maneuver around the abattis by wading through chest-high water, prompting Gaines to order reinforcements of infantry and riflemen to support Wood's command; however, Wood assures General Gaines that his troops would hold without the reinforce-

The Siege of Fort Erie (*A History of the War of 1812 Between the United States and Great Britain*, Rossiter Johnson, 1882).

ments. Nonetheless, the British persist. They mount additional assaults, only to be repulsed each time. Nevertheless, the British are not persuaded to abort the attack; rather, they push harder and some scale the ladders and encounter defenders who have their bayonets fixed. The charges on the left are repelled, but the British persist in mounting another attempt to clear the walls. Again Yankee fire molests the attackers. Towson's guns are firing so rapidly that the nonstop flashes illuminate the area, providing the Americans with more visible targets. The artillerymen under Towson perform extraordinarily and the battery afterward receives the nickname "Towson's Lighthouse."

Meanwhile, General Gaines moves quickly to the American right, where a second British column (left) under British Colonel Scott storms the right side of the fort, defended by the 9th Regiment, under Captain Foster and Captain Broughton, two companies of volunteers (New York and Pennsylvania) and Lieutenant Douglass' artillery. The British encounter a defense that is impenetrable. The defenders under Lieutenant Douglass had scrutinized the ground to their front so intensely, that despite the darkness that conceals the exact location of the approaching enemy, Douglass' gunners are able to cover the approaches with deadly accuracy. To add to the dismay of the British column, Douglass' guns are loaded with bags of musket balls, and the sweeping fire rivets the ground, turning it into a killing field. Unknown to the column that is striking Douglass' position, the first column against Towson's side is repelled five separate times.

Meanwhile, the British column (center) under General Drummond that strikes the center reaches the parapet without discovery. Scaling ladders are swung onto the wall of the main fort, but here, too, the American defenders remain steadfast. A bayonet battle unfolds and brutal hand-to-hand combat also ensues, and it unfolds under clouds of smoke created by the cannon fire that hovers overhead. Both sides defiantly attempt to crush the other; however, the Americans manage to drive the column back. Undaunted, the British mount another attack and it too is repulsed, but still, the center column remains intent to break through. It mounts yet another assault only to be thrown back yet again. By this point, the defenders have repelled every assault, but still the British refuse to abort the attack.

The center column disregards its three failed attacks, diverts and strikes at a new point along the walls. They move swiftly and gain success initially when the scaling ladders are attached to the wall. In a flash, the troops fly up the ladders and gain entrance to the bastion before defenders can intercept them. Drummond is with the troops that enter the bastion. He urges his troops to act boldly and underscores his orders by continually bellowing: "Give the Yankees no quarter."

The British are soon met by more defenders and the fighting remains bloody and at close quarters, transforming the bastion into a ghastly cauldron. Drummond adheres to his order rigidly. Lieutenant Patrick McDonough, an artillery officer wounded during the struggle in the bastion, is approached by Drummond. McDonough asks for quarter and Drummond ignores the request by reiterating his command to give no quarter. McDonough defiantly clutches a spike and uses it to ward off the British; however, Drummond terminates the stand-off. Using his pistol, he shoots Lieutenant McDonough. Another American soldier, Jacob Plank (19th Regiment), who witnesses the shooting instantly fires at Drummond and strikes him in the chest, then uses his bayonet to stab Drummond. The blade of the bayonet pierces a copy of General Drummond's order and it rips precisely through the sentence that contains the words that urged a "free use of the bayonet." (The document carried by Drummond is later given to the New York Historical Society.) Two other officers, Captain Williams and Lt. Watmaugh, receive fatal wounds during the assault.

As dawn emerges on the 15th, the British still control the bastion. Major Hindman, bolstered by troops under Major Trimble, rush the British, but the attempt fails to evict them. Reinforcements under Captain Birdsall (4th Regiment) and a detachment of riflemen and infantry, ordered by General Gaines and sent by Generals Ripley and Porter, lunge forward through the gateway to support Hindman and Trimbleo, but the British hold the position. Captain Birdsall sustains a severe wound during the attack. Nonetheless, maintaining control is draining the holding force and fresh troops that arrive to bolster the force are of some help, but the American fire continually inflicts more casualties, forcing the British to send in their reserves. Major Douglass, deployed on the right, redirects his guns to plaster the route that the reserves must travel to reach the bastion. At the same time, the British that are still attempting to reach the fort are being targeted and hit with extremely effective fire by Captain Fanning's battery. Meanwhile, American troops under Captain Foster (11th Regiment) launch another attack, led by Major Hall, assistant inspector general, but the passageway is too slim, which prevents the contingent from spreading more than a few men abreast. This attack also fails.

The American fire continues to pummel the British, but it fails to force the reserves to pull back. The reserves are poised to advance, until without warning, the fate of the bastion is settled by a thunderous explosion that occurs in the magazine. The sight is horrifying. When the detonation occurs it is so powerful that the platform, which contains many men, is catapulted like an uncontrolled rocket to a height of about 200 feet. The sky is momentarily consumed with debris, including stones and lumber along with troops. The descent is equally gruesome, as the dead and wounded plummet to the earth over a large distance.

The British and the Americans are flabbergasted after observing the ghastly tragedy. The reserves make no move toward the devastated bastion. They retire. In turn, the British forego control of the ruins of the bastion and the surviving men of the three attacking columns retire to the British camp. Meanwhile, Captain Biddle is ordered to deploy an artillery piece from where it can place enfiade fire on the plain and the salient Glacis. At the same time, Fanning's battery fires in conjunction with Biddle's piece. No precise cause of the explosion has ever been determined. Some of the American officers say it was an accidental explosion; however, others contend that Lieutenant Patrick McDonough, who was wounded when shot by General Drummond after asking for quarter, lit the ammunition with a match in revenge for his treatment by Drummond.

Casualty reports are also cloudy. General Drummond lists 905 killed, wounded or missing, including his count of only 58 killed. Later, the Americans physically count 221 or 222 deceased British troops on the field. The Americans also seize 174 wounded who remain on the field, along with another 186 prisoners. The Americans lose 45 men during the bombardments that preceded the attack, and they sustain another 84 killed during the attack. The British losses prevent any immediate action to attempt to reduce the fort.

General Gaines, the commander at Fort Erie, uses the lull to undertake a major construction operation to restore the devastated bastion. Gaines also orders that his complete line of defenses be bolstered. General Gaines afterward gives special credit to Generals Eleazar Ripley and Peter B. Porter in a general order of 23 August: "To Brigadier General Ripley much credit is due for the judicious disposition of the left wing previous to this action and for the steady disciplined courage manifested by him and his immediate Command. Brig. General Porter commanding the New York and Penna. Volunteers manifested a degree of vigilance and judgement in his preparatory arrangements, as well as the military skills and courage in action which proves him to be worthy [of] the confidence of his country and the brave Volunteers who fought under him." In a letter to the secretary of war, Gaines states: "Major Hindman and the whole of the artillery under the command of that excellent officer [Captain Towson] displayed a degree of gallantry and good conduct, not to be surpassed."

Meanwhile, the British await reinforcement before launching yet another assault to recapture the fort. After the fresh troops arrive, General Drummond initiates a siege, and he eventually advances his parallels to positions close to the fort, providing the British positions from which to bombard Fort Erie on a daily basis. During one of the bombardments, a shell drops right through the roof of General Gaines' headquarters while he is there. The shell detonates close to the general and inflicts serious injuries which prevent him from remaining in command. General Brown, unwilling to give the command to General Ripley, assumes personal command of the fort. Afterward, General Gaines returns to Buffalo.

While the British continue to build their forces, fresh American troops arrive to bolster General Brown. The reinforcements reassure Brown that he can hold the post; however, the British bombardments continue to cause him concern. General Brown makes a decision to forestall the imminent attack by moving out to destroy the British works that contain the batteries. Brown concocts a plan to carve an obscure path through the woods to give the Yanks a route to deliver the columns to the right side of the British works. The construction continues without being discovered by the British, who maintain their strategy of committing only one third of the force to work on the parallels, with the main body remaining in camp about two miles to the rear.

General Drummond continues to prepare for the assault, but there is no apparent threat of an attack by the Americans, who appear to be confined to the fort.

During the night of 17 September, Brown unfolds his plan. About 2,000 troops divided into two columns creep out of the fort and silently trek toward the point from which the attack will begin. One column, led by General Peter B. Porter, travels along the hidden road, while the other column, led by General Miller, advances in a ravine. Shortly thereafter, the Yankees strike with swiftness to deliver a thunderous blow. The column, using the woods as cover, suddenly bolts from the brush and slams into the right, while those in the ravine drive straight into the center, causing pandemonium. The lightning strike leaves the British no time to prepare, and the reinforcements are too far in the rear to assist.

The Americans who appear seemingly from thin air plow into the siege works and inflict irreparable damage. All of the British guns are dismounted and rendered useless. At the same time, ferocious fighting occurs and each side inflicts high casualties; however, the Americans also succeed in detonating the ammunition magazines, causing a massive explosion. The operation terminates and the Americans vanish in the darkness and make it back to the fort, bringing about 380 British prisoners with them. The bold attack proves successful, but at a high cost. The Americans sustain about 527 casualties—79 killed, including General Daniel Davis; 232 wounded and 216 missing.

The British sustain about 673 casualties—115 killed, 178 wounded and 380 missing. Besides high casualties, Drummonds' plans are foiled with the destruction of the siege works and the loss of the British artillery and ammunition. Within a few days, General Drummond, unable to reduce the fort, aborts the operation on 21 September. He lifts the siege and withdraws heading toward the Chippewa River. After the departure of the British, General Brown makes plans to abandon the fort on his own terms.

The next month, the Americans knock down the British post and afterward, they depart from the debris of Fort Erie and return unmolested to New York. General Ripley had sustained a severe wound in the neck by a ball that passed through it, "while making a charge upon the enforcement of the enemy; and thus terminating a siege of 53 days of constant cannonading, when every day was a battle."

August 15 (Monday) In New York City, newspapers contribute manpower to the ongoing work to bolster the city's defenses. About 200 men, including journeymen and printers, exchange their printing skills for picks and axes. Others include a group of about 200 weavers and even a large number of butchers as well as men from various manufacturing firms.

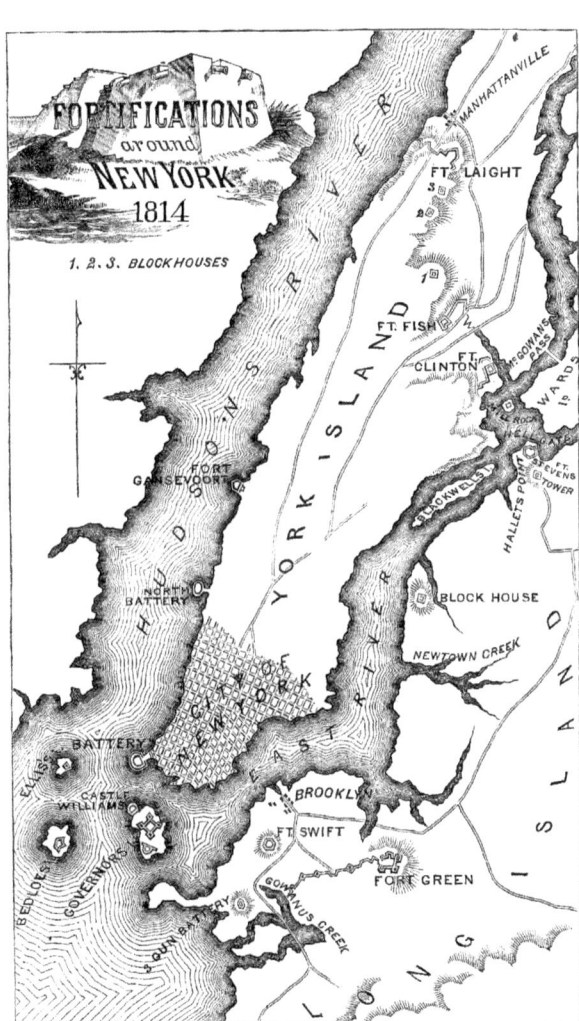

Fortifications around New York.

In naval activity, on or about this day, the USS *Mohawk,* commanded by Captain Jacob Jones, along with the *Madison, Pike* and *Superior,* establishes a blockade off Kingston, Canada. The flotilla also provides support to the force under General Jacob Brown during his Niagara campaign. The blockade continues until the latter part of September. In other activity, the 231-ton schooner *Herald* (John Miller, master), a privateer carrying 60 men and eight guns, is intercepted and captured by two British warships, the HMS *Armide* and the HMS *Endymion.*

August 16 (Tuesday) In Canada, a contingent of troops under Colonel John B. Campbell, having departed Detroit, launches an attack against a settlement at Port Talbot. The violence and monstrous activity devastates the townspeople and causes outrage in the British ranks. According to reports of the time, the attack left "upwards of 234 men women and children in a state of nakedness and want." Campbell, who takes full blame and states that he acted on his own, receives a reprimand.

In New York at Albany, Governor Daniel D. Tompkins becomes concerned about the defenses of Sackets Harbor. In a letter to Major General Widrig, he writes: "Dr. Sir: If the Commanding officer of Sacketts Harbour should make a requisition for Militia to defend that place, I beg you to order out the number required from Oneida, Herkimer, Madison or Montgomery Counties without waiting to consult me upon the subject; & you will please to instruct the Brigades of your Divisions to the same effect with respect to detachments from their respective Brigades." Also on this day, the governor writes to his brigadier generals (Dodge, Haile and Hurd): "Dr. Sir: You will please to comply immediately with any requisition upon the Militia of your Brigade, which may be made by the Commanding Officer at Sacketts' Harbour, & will report to me thro' the Major General of your Division the manner & extent of your compliance therewith."

In naval activity, the HMS *Wasp* intercepts and recaptures the 237-ton ship *Helen* (Thomas Holmes, master) while it is en route from Havana, Cuba, to Greenock, Scotland, with a cargo of sugar and wood. Elsewhere, the British privateer *Liverpool Packet* intercepts and seizes the 33-ton schooner *Hope,* which has a cargo of flour, pork, tobacco and some other items.

The *Invincible Napoleon,* originally a French privateer that has been bouncing back and forth between the British and the Americans, is on a cruise when encountered by the HMS *Armide.* The privateer breaks for safety, and during the pursuit, the Americans toss ten of its guns into the sea to gain speed, but to no avail. After about ten hours, the British again recapture it.

August 17 (Wednesday) In Alabama, a contingent of 53 Choctaw Indians — led by Pushmataha with Moshulatubbee named as second in command — is mustered into the U.S. service as a company. This company is afterward attached to the command of Major Uriah Blue. The Choctaw company participates in the final phase of bringing the Creek War to an end. Subsequently, on 27 January 1815, the company is mustered out of the service at Fort Stoddert.

August 18 (Thursday) In Maryland, General William Winder is informed that the British fleet had received reinforcements on the previous day. Action is immediately taken to counter the enemy force that is on the advance. Requisitions are sped to the governors of Maryland and Pennsylvania, and the general call goes out to militia at all points. Also, General John Peter Van Ness orders General Robert Young to "call out, en masse," his brigade, including the militia at Alexandria, Virginia. As part of this call-up, two troops of cavalry receive orders to repair to Bladensburg and join together after they arrive. On the 20th, General William H. Winder orders the cavalry to ford the Potomac opposite Alexandria, and once across, the command is to establish their camp while awaiting new orders. Young's brigade is composed of about 450 men, and it is bolstered by two brass 6-pounders and one brass 4-pounder.

August 19 (Friday) In Maryland, 4,000 British troops commanded by Major General Ross arrive at the Patuxent River to initiate raids on Alexandria, Virginia, and Washington, D.C. Ross' force debarks at Benedict, Maryland, against no resistance. The landing place stands about 40 miles southeast of the capital. Ross's naval force has 27 vessels.

General William H. Winder is working feverishly to gather the necessary troops to intercept the advancing British army, which is en route to the capital. He sends plans regarding the defense of the city to the secretary of war. The secretary, John Armstrong, sends back word that the plans had been forwarded to President James Madison. Secretary Armstrong also instructs Winder to contact the Navy Department to inquire about what type of support the Navy can provide.

Meanwhile, Commodore Joshua Barney, soon after receiving intelligence about the British strength at the Patuxent River, rushes a letter to William Jones, secretary of the Navy: "Dear SIR: One of my officers has this moment arrived from the mouth of the Patuxent, and brings the enclosed account. I haste to forward it to you; the Admiral [Cochrane] said he would dine in Washington on Sunday, after having destroyed the flotilla, etc." The list of British strength: "One eighty or ninety gun ship, flag at the main. Four seventy-four gun ships, one flag at mizzen. Six frigates. Ten ships about thirty-two guns. Five small ships. Two brigs. One large schooner, sixteen guns. Two smaller schooners about ten guns. Thirteen large bay craft." The secretary sends a quick response and orders Barney to "retire with his flotilla as high up the river as he could get, and if the enemy landed, to set fire to the boats, and join General Winder with his men."

In naval activity, the HMS *Tenedos* intercepts and recaptures the 168-ton vessel the *Snow Wanderer.*

August 19–24   In Maryland, American units begin to converge upon Bladensburg. The American forces at or near there on the 23rd include a brigade from D.C. of about 1,070 men, composed of two regiments (militia and volunteer companies of Washington and Georgetown) commanded by Colonel Magruder and Colonel William Brent. The D.C. regiments are supported by two light artillery companies, commanded by Major George Peter and Captain Benjamin Burch, supported by two rifle companies commanded by Captains Doughty and Stull, and General Walter Smith, of Georgetown. Also in the area are a brigade of about 500 men under General Robert Young, also from D.C., composed of companies drawn from Alexandria and the surrounding area, a cavalry company under Captain Thornton, and one company of light artillery commanded by Captain Marsteller; however, Young's brigade does not participate because it was deployed to defend Fort Washington; a brigade out of Baltimore under General Tobias Stansbury, composed of a 550-man regiment under Lt. Colonel Ragan (formerly captain in U.S. Rifles) and a regiment of about 850 men under Lt. Colonel Schutz; a contingent under Lt. Colonel Joseph Sterrett, composed of the 5th Baltimore Regiment (volunteers), a rifle battalion under Major William Pinckney and two volunteer artillery companies from Baltimore under Captain Meyers and Captain Magruder; two regiments composed of about 750 men under Colonel William D. Beall, a veteran of the American Revolution, and Colonel Hall; a 240-man contingent under Colonel Kramer; two battalions totaling about 150 men, commanded by Majors Maynard and Waring; Virginia militia under Colonel George Minor, composed of a regiment of about 600 men and a 100-man contingent of cavalry; several hundred infantrymen (regulars) and one company of about 80 men of the U.S. 12th Regiment, under Lt. Colonel William Scott; and Commodore Barney's force composed of about 400 seamen and 150 Marines, the latter accompanied by two 18-pounders.

Other units include about 300 Maryland cavalrymen under Lt. Colonel Tilghman, Major Otho H. Williams and Major Charles Sterett; the Bladensburg Troop of Horse, commanded by Captain J.C. Herbert; and a 125-man contingent of U.S. Cavalry, commanded by Lt. Colonel Lavel. Also, pursuant to orders from President Madison, General Samuel Smith at Baltimore has a third brigade at the ready, prepared to march at a moment's notice. The total American force, including some who arrive on the 24th and 25th, stands at about 7,000 troops.

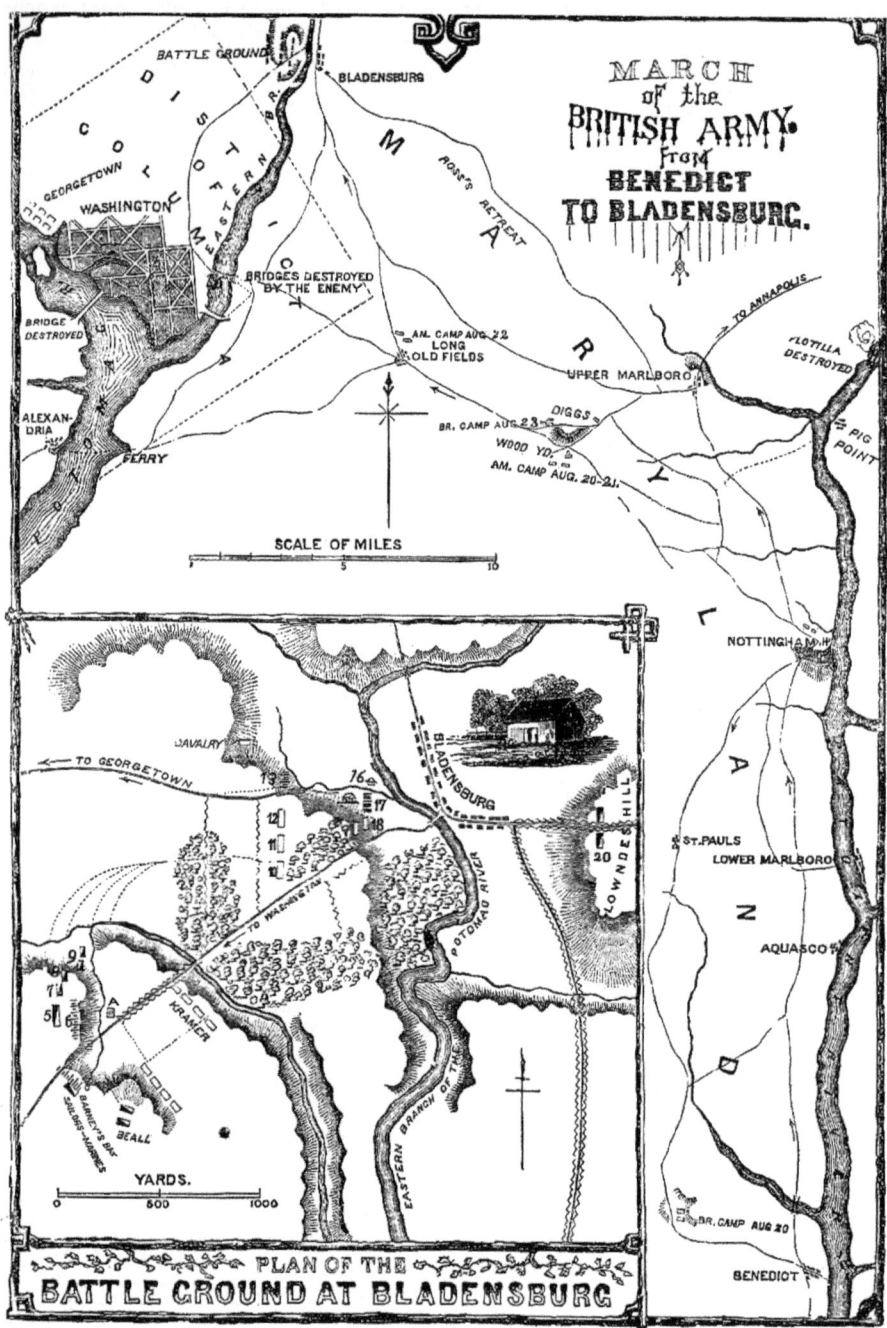

Bladensburg.

General Samuel Smith.

August 19–25 THE BATTLE OF BLADENSBURG
The British are coming, but not to Concord. This time, after landing on the 19th, they intend to march right into the White House and their intent is not to take tea with the Madisons. The trepidation is great for the citizenry as the Redcoats in fine attire accompanied by regimental music move swiftly through Maryland, the band filling the air with melodious tunes as they march in cadence against the anticipated defenders. In Washington, preliminary action is taken; however, not defensive. Pursuant to orders from the Secretary of War John Armstrong, the magazines and the vessels are destroyed to prevent capture.

General William H. Winder establishes his headquarters at the Eastern Branch bridge. He dispatches a succinct note to John Armstrong suggesting that the situation upriver is "threatening." He proposes that Commodore Barney's contingent should move to Greenleaf's Point to command the batteries there and also occupy the Washington Navy Yard. If that is not possible, another contingent should be ordered there. Armstrong said he "saw no necessity for ordering Barney to Greenleaf's Point or Navy Yard—advised the Commodore to join the army at Bladensburg, and ordered Minor's regiment to that place." Cavalry patrols move out in all directions to shadow the British and to gather intelligence as the Redcoats continue their advance to the capital. In addition, plans are made to destroy the bridge if necessary.

British General Ross, in an attempt to prevent the anticipated heat of the day from interfering with his advance, sets out from his camp at Melwood during the early predawn hours. By 0400, the columns are passing near the American camp at Old Fields. Duplicating his ruse used at Nottingham, the army reaches the fork in the road about two miles past the American camp. Ross orders the column to take the fork running westward directly to Washington, which lies about seven miles distant; however, after advancing only a short distance, leaving time for any American patrols to observe the rear echelon to turn at the fork, General Ross cunningly reverses directions and advances northward heading directly toward Bladensburg, about ten miles distant.

On the 22nd, Commodore Barney had been ordered to destroy his fleet and afterward move to Nottingham. Upon his arrival there on the morning of the 24th, General William H. Winder directed Barney to lead his force of about 500 sailors and Marines, with the latter under the command of Captain Samuel Miller, to positions along the main road where Barney's two 18-pounders are deployed, between the forces of Colonel Beall and Colonel Hood. Beall had just arrived following a grueling 16-mile march. General Winder places Barney's battalion in command of the guns, which are manned by his seamen, while the Marines and Barney's remaining seamen, under Captain Samuel Miller, acting as infantry, form a protective ring around the artillery. A militia battalion under Colonel Kramer deploys off in the woods to the front of Barney's position and those of Beall and Hood. Another regiment, under Colonel Brent, along with Major Waring's battalion and a few other units deploy as the left flank of the second line at a point in the rear of Major George Peter's artillery.

Meanwhile, the regulars under Lt. Colonel Scott form their line in front of Magruder's artillery, which leans from the left toward Peter's artillery. The artillery (six 6-pounders) under Magruder and Meyers hold ground at a makeshift breastworks that dominates the road and the bridge. Near the artillery, a battalion of riflemen deploy on the right and hold positions close to the river near the intersection of the two roads. On the left of the artillery, Major Pinckney deploys the remainder of his riflemen behind a barn near the Georgetown Road, and they are bolstered by two militia companies under Captain Gorsuch and Captain Ducker (Colonel Schutz's regiment). To the rear of Pinckney's positions, Colonel Ragan posts his command, with his right leaning against the Georgetown Road. The line continues with the remainder of Schutz's regiment; however, a small gap exists between Ragan's position and that of Schutz. The far left flank of the infantry is held by Colonel Sterrett's regiment.

On the morning of the 24th, General Stansbury's command deploys in some heights close to the old bridge between the old post road and the Washington Road. All of the positions are complete by about noon on the 24th. Meanwhile, militia troops out of Baltimore under General Tobias arrive, and they are directed to deploy near present-day Cottage City, along the Bladensburg-Washington Road. Initially, General Winder had deployed his forces at Wood Yard, anticipating the British columns would march straight into his positions; however, General Ross advanced to Nottingham, then swerved to the right, taking his force toward Marlborough to link with Admiral Cockburn, who is accompanied by seamen and Royal Marines. At about 1100, General Winder, receives word at his headquarters that the British are closing on Bladensburg.

After leaving a small artillery to demolish the bridge at the Eastern Branch, Winder orders his entire force to advance to the town. As soon as he arrives, Winder confers with General Stansbury and Colonel Monroe, and he informs them that he "approved the dispositions which had been made." The British can be seen on a hill opposite their positions, and the general also sees President Madison, who arrives with a party that includes Secretary of War Armstrong, and a lawyer, Francis Scott Key, a volunteer in Major Petr's artillery. Key had received permission from President Madison to go out to the fleet to try to secure the release of a prominent physician from Marlborough, Doctor Beanes. Congressman Alexander McKim arrives on his horse and proclaims that he had voted for the war and "he could not find it in his conscience, if not to fight for it, at least to stand by those who did." General Winder, who is staring at the enemy as the column is moving into Bladensburg, begins to receive strong suggestions on where to redeploy his troops from the visitors. The arm-chair suggestions work on Winder's demeanor; however, he remains calm and realizes there is no time to realign his positions even if the secretary of war was among those making the suggestions.

In line with the British route change, General Winder had initially retired to the Battalion Old Fields before sprinting to Bladensburg. The trek for the British, despite having no opposition, is dreadful due to the blistering heat, which punishes the troops and causes a large number to falter from exhaustion. Nevertheless, the column arrives at Bladensburg at about 1200 on the 24th. Meanwhile, the British, while approaching, spot a huge cloud of dust, and shortly thereafter, they spot the American army just as the column passes a plantation. The Americans are formed in three lines along a hill, with their flanks protected by the Anacostia River and a steep ravine. The site of the defenses is solid, advantageous high ground, with an array of artillery that dominates the approaches and the bridge. In addition to the three lines, the cavalry is posted nearby in a field. However, the British remain unsure whether the town itself also contains troops. The column is halted to permit a reconnaissance patrol to determine the American strength within the town. Upon its return, the patrol reports that Bladensburg is free of troops, and those who were there had also been redeployed on the opposite bank of the river.

The advance is resumed, and within a short while, the British enter into the range of the American artillery, then suddenly, the Americans observe a sea of red descending Downes' Hill. It is an overwhelming sight to the militia posted west of the Anacostia River. The British press forward with the usual rigidity of British regulars, and they come under heavy fire. Initially, the British spread out and take positions in and around some houses, but they only pause there while General Ross assesses the situation. It is determined that a delay in finding a ford would be more costly, and that the only practical route is to cross the bridge. By about 1300, the British move at double-quick toward the bridge that spans the Anacostia River.

The attackers hit a hurricane of fire from artillery on their left and afterward from a two gun battery which holds its fire until the British are on the bridge. The British take severe casualties

Francis Scott Key (*History of Maryland [1812–1880], Volume III*, Thomas J. Scharf, 1879).

and their attack stalls. By this time American riflemen deployed in the woods open fire to inflict more casualties; however, the artillery fire becomes less effective. At this time the light brigade advances toward the bridge and pushes across, passing over and around dead and wounded comrades who fell during the charge. They succeed in gaining a foothold on the opposite bank. Once across, the brigade strikes the first line of defense and compels the defenders to retreat without firing a shot. The hasty retreat leaves two guns in the field for the British.

Despite having no backup troops, the vanguard disposes of their "knapsacks and haversacks" and lunges forward to collapse the second line, but as the impetuous advance begins, General Winder observes that the remainder of the enemy force is still on the opposite bank. He orders the 5th Baltimore regiment to counterattack, and the regiment is joined by regiments of Ragan and Schutz, who align on the right and center of the line. With the support of artillery, the British are pushed back, and at the same time, the Americans advance with fixed bayonets. Meanwhile, the British line had been too widely extended, which prevents them from being able to hold their positions. They are pushed to the river bank, but the attack fails to drive them back across the river. Shortly thereafter, General Ross succeeds in pushing a brigade across the bridge to reinforce the vanguard and take the point. With a more solid force on the opposite bank, Ross sends the 44th Regiment to strike Winder's left. The attack is synchronized with a rocket attack which inflicts terror into the militia, which is receiving its baptism under fire. The militia troops, not realizing the rockets are pyrotechnics, panic and take flight. Major Pinckney is wounded during the fighting at the bridge, but he is able to rally his men, who reform and fight alongside the 5th Baltimore Regiment. All the while, the British fire upon the retreating Americans.

The militia on the left flank vanish in quick retreat; however, for a while, Winder is able to hold his ground on the right until the British 4th Regiment arrives to bolster the attack. Shortly thereafter the American line there falters when more British troops join the attack. To their left, the Americans observe the entire line had collapsed, and then they see the attacking British 44th Regiment closing upon their rear, causing the right to follow suit. The militia retreats haphazardly, permitting the British regulars to turn the other flank to place Winder in an untenable position while he orders a retreat. Sterrett's riflemen hold their ground to provide cover fire for the troops under Ragan and Schutz. The regiment, bolstered by Burch's artillery, succeeds in pushing back the British light brigade. At about the same time, reinforcements from Annapolis arrive from the east. Nonetheless, they become fearful of not getting any support from Winder's force. Consequently they end up in the rear. By this time, the British are close to surrounding Sterrett's 5th Regiment and Burch's artillery. Winder orders both units to retreat in order to reform. Nonetheless, the epidemic of panic overcomes the regiment when they sense they will be surrounded. Discipline vanishes and a stampede begins. Colonel Sterrett's efforts to halt the flight and restore order are in vain. The British, after forcing Winder to relinquish more ground, turn their attention on the remainder of the American force, the second line.

Colonel Kramer's militia takes the brunt of the attack and they resist tenaciously, but only for a short time. Outnumbered by about two to one and with no signs of any reinforcements on the move, they are shoved back. Meanwhile, General Walter Smith's force — composed of the Georgetown militia, the Washington militia and the regulars commanded by Lt. General Scott — up to this point has remained in place to the rear of the second line. The British on the opposite side (left) of the road advance to turn Scott's flank, protected by Colonel Brent. They are met by Magruder's artillery; however, the barrage is ineffective and the British maintain the pace.

The British prepare to advance to seize the capital, expecting no more opposition, except for one stubborn group that remains in place at the guns. While the British pause on the right side of the road in a field, the artillery under Major Peter begins to bombard the field; however, it does not deter the British. The British left wing, commanded by Colonel Thornton, pushes down the road directly toward Barney's position, which contains two 18-pounders. Commodore Barney, along with his seamen and contingent of Marines, had not been frightened of the Redcoats or their rockets. The guns had been stinging the British throughout the battle and now as the final strong point, the British receive unexpected effective fire that stuns the British who had so easily overrun the army and now find themselves under fire by troops that refuse to surrender an inch. Nevertheless, when the militia absconded, the teamsters joined in the race to the rear still hitched to the ammunition wagons, leaving Barney's sailors and Marines with only a small amount of ammunition. Commodore Barney's command, however, soon convinces the British that they are not moving against militia. Commodore Barney and Captain Samuel Miller, U.S. Marine Corps, lead the troops during a spectacular example of engaging a superior force. The British are pounded by the guns of the defiant band. Repeatedly, the British lunge forward and each time they are handily repulsed.

The sailors and Marines boldly engage the attackers and hold their ground, and then mount a counterattack that drives the British back. Nevertheless, after the militia under Beall had fled, Barney's force loses its flank protection, giving the British the opening to eventually encircle the Spartan force. Up until just before the dubious retreat of the army, President Madison, John Armstrong and James Monroe had been at the scene of the battle until President Madison directed the party to leave and let the army handle the British. General Armstrong and James Monroe, himself an officer during the Revolution, had actually interfered by having Winder rearrange some of his forces.

As the capital is being abandoned, First Lady Dolley Madison refuses to leave the White House until the president returns. It is Mrs. Madison who shows strength in this time of desperation. With the Army gone, it is Mrs. Madison who saves George Washington's portrait. At about 1500, two messages arrive at the White House. Both warn of the pending disaster, and Mrs. Madison is urged to depart immediately, but she ignores the danger. Earlier, George Washington Parke Custis arrived at the White House. He was extremely concerned about the portrait of George Washington, which would certainly become a prize of the British. Just before she departs to escape, with no time to spare, she directs a servant to pull the frame from the wall. The canvas is removed from the frame and Washington's portrait, painted by Stuart, is taken to safety at Georgetown. She carries it herself as she departs the deserted capital. Mrs. Madison also saves an original copy of the Declaration of Independence.

Back at Bladensburg, by the time encirclement becomes imminent, Commodore Barney had received a debilitating wound, but still, he has not lost his fighting spirit. Barney orders his men to disable the guns and break away. He also refuses to allow his troops to carry him off. Before retiring under orders of Barney, his battalion had felled about 225 British troops. Commodore Barney is no stranger to the British. During the Revolution, the indomitable commodore had literally been captured four times, including once when he escaped from the infamous Mill Prison at Plymouth and outwitted the British to escape from England and make it back to the United States. Having an apparent propensity to be a guest of the British, Barney was again seized by them during 1793, and as improbable as it seems, Commodore Barney, who retired after the Revolution, was reactivated during 1812 and captured again at that time.

The British, after to seizing Commodore Barney for the seventh time, hold him only for a short while. Although he has a wound to his thigh and continues to carry the ball, he resumes command of his squadron during October 1814 and remains in command until his squadron is deactivated during October 1815. In 1818, Commodore Barney is preparing to move to Kentucky, but dies in Pittsburgh on 1 December.

General Robert Ross wins a decisive victory over the Americans under General Winder at Bladensburg, but not without cost. British Colonel William Thornton's brigade, which pursues the Americans, has high casualties. The British seize at least half of the American guns and many muskets. They also capture 120 prisoners. The Americans sustain about 150 casualties. According to a British officer's report, the British lose about 500 killed or wounded. Colonel Thornton, commanding officer of the light brigade, is seriously wounded; Lt. Colonel Wood of the 85th Regiment is also gravely wounded along with another officer, Major Brown, who commanded the advance guard. General Ross escapes injury; however, his horse was shot from under him. The United States Army and American governmental officers evacuate Washington, taking with them important documents, including secret journals of Congress. President Madison and his cabinet had been emphasizing the Canadian campaign, yet unwittingly they did not properly prepare a defense of the capital.

During the American retreat, after pulling back about 500 or 600 yards, the column halts and reforms; however, they are ordered to resume the retreat. Winder then orders for his entire force to converge on the high ground west of the turnpike gate less than two miles from the capital. While General Smith and other officers begin to gather the scattered troops, the Virginia regiment, commanded by Colonel George Minor, delayed due to a snafu in acquiring weapons, arrives to join Smith. Colonel Minor's fresh regiment is delegated to provide cover fire for the army as it retreats. Nevertheless, although it is Winder's intent to march to Washington to defend the city, the militia had scattered with most fleeing toward Montgomery Court House, Maryland. He confers with Secretary Armstrong and it becomes obvious that Washington cannot be defended. A decision is made to assemble the troops in the heights of Georgetown. However, it is soon determined that that militia is too widely scattered. By the following day (25th), the orders are changed and the army is instead to be assembled at Montgomery Courthouse.

British troops led by Admiral Sir George Cockburn and General Ross occupy Washington, D.C., against no opposition on the 24th. They move to the White House and set it afire. They also burn the Capitol building and many other structures. Only bad weather prompts the British to call off the attack and return to their ships on the Patuxent River. A sudden storm as frightening to the British as the British fireworks were to the defenders of Bladensburg saves Washington and the cause. In addition, the British occupy Fort Washington at Greenleaf's Point, which had been self-destructed by the Americans. An accidental explosion occurs while demolition crews are destroying the powder, killing quite a few British troops and wounding many more.

The British spare very few buildings in the capital. Doctor Thornton persuades the British to spare the patent office, which also contains the post office, on the grounds that the building contains items and documents that have "value for the whole scientific world." Other buildings that escape harm include the jail, one hotel and several private homes.

The British also capture the Marine Corps barracks; however, the British also spare it and the commandant's house. It is uncertain why, but the two reasons most talked about were the British respect for the Marines' actions at Bladensburg and because the British had initially intended to permanently occupy the city and use the barracks. The British, pushed out of Washington by the storm, leave their fires burning on the night of the 25th to divert the Americans' attention and march back to the ships at Benedict along the Patuxent River. The British had set the USS *Boston* afire, while in D.C., but it had been moored at the navy yard since 1802, and due to being in poor condition, it was not scheduled to participate in the conflict.

The Americans have little to celebrate following the rout at Bladensburg, but in retrospect, the federal government had done little to prepare for the invasion and the government's expectations of having untrained militia hold off a seasoned British army was folly. One of the British officers who chronicled the battle stated: The fact is, that, with the exception of a party of sailors from the gunboats, under the command of Commodore Barney, no troops could behave worse then they did. The skirmishers were driven in as soon as attack[ed], the first line gave way without offering the slightest resistance, and the left of the main body was broken in within half an hour after it was seriously engaged. Of the sailors, however, it would be injustice not to speak in the terms which their conduct merits. They were employed as gunners, and not only did they serve their guns with a quickness and precision which astonish their assailants, but they stood till some of them were actually bayoneted, with fuses in their hands: nor was it till their leader was wounded and taken and they saw themselves deserted on all sides by the soldiers, that they quitted the field.

The British savor the victory, while plans are being readied for the capture of Washington, Baltimore and Fort McHenry, which they believe is probably defended only by militia. With this multiple thrust, which includes the capture of Lake Champlain by Commodore Downie and domination of New York by General Prevost, who is coordinating with Downie, the British expect the Americans to fold. The full fury of the Crown must crumble Fort McHenry and humble Baltimore, while the Royal Navy drains Lake Champlain of the Yankee impersonation of a genuine fleet. Once Baltimore is taken, they expect Philadelphia to fall along with New York, and the war shall quickly cease, and all this by September if the British have their way.

This exciting news of the victory and the burning of the capital is dispatched to London, which prompts new messages to be delivered to the British negotiators in Ghent. They are instructed to prepare to demand that Britain shall retain all territory that it presently occupies as a condition of a settlement. The representatives are informed that much more good news is about to unfold, as other British victories are close at hand. The news is disheartening to the Americans, who anxiously await some positive word from the battlefields of the United States.

August 20 (Saturday)   In Maryland, General William H. Winder is informed that a British force has arrived at Benedict. Winder dispatches troops under Colonel Tilghman and Captain Caldwell to harass the line of march to slow the progress. The troops are also ordered to destroy provisions when possible.

In New York, the massive work project to bolster the defenses of New York City continues while the threat of a British invasion haunts the region. A group of about 500 men arrive at Harlem Heights to begin their participation and another group of about 1,500 Irishmen move into Brooklyn to participate there. Seemingly, everyone is helping in one way or another. Young boys, too small to participate in the strenuous work, volunteer to use shingles to carry dirt. Others come from nearby towns to help. One group arrives from Bushwick, Long Island, and they are accompanied by their pastor, who begins their participation with a prayer. Afterward, the Long Islanders spend their time distributing food and refreshments to the workers. All the while, the aura of pending disaster hovers. Startling alarms continue to arrive, regarding British actions against various New England coastal towns.

Circumstances change on the 27th, when word arrives that the British had seized and burned the capital. Tension mounts; however, the British later are stymied at Fort McHenry when those defenders forestall any invasion of New York. Nonetheless, the projects on the fortifications surrounding New York continue. The works include Fort Fish; Fort Laight; Fort Swift, constructed near the site of the Revolutionary post, Fort Stirling at Brooklyn Heights, and another, Fort Lawrence in the same vicinity, which overlooks Gowan's Bay and Governors Island; Fort Stevens on Hallet's Point, Long Island, named in honor of Major General Ebenezer Stevens; fortifications at Mill Rock; and Fort Clinton at McGowan's Creek, near Harlem Creek. To the rear of Brooklyn the works include Fort Greene, Cummings Redoubt, Masonic Redoubt, Washington Battery and Fort Firemen.

In naval activity, a British squadron under Sir Peter Parker, aboard the 34-gun HMS *Menelaus*, sails up the Chesapeake and arrives off Rock Hall, Maryland, where he drops anchor and plans to launch several destructive raids. In other activity, a British squadron — the HMS *Forth*, HMS *Loire* and the *Saturn* — intercepts the *Condedos Arcos*, a 210-ton ship carrying mixed items including iron, sugar and tea. Elsewhere, the HMS *Espoir* on or about this day seizes the vessel *Judith*, which is transporting a cargo of brandy, coffee, cotton and other goods.

August 21 (Sunday)   In Maryland, during the morning, General William H. Winder's militia force assembles. Later this day, U.S. Marines under Captain Miller arrive to join with the army. Winder is also reinforced by the U.S. 86th and 88th Regiments, which arrive at the Wood Yard between Upper Marlborough and Washington, about five miles in front of the main body and about ten or twelve miles from Upper Marlborough. Meanwhile, Commodore Joshua Barney is informed that the British had landed a force at Benedict and that they are advancing toward Washington, D.C. Barney, accompanied by most of his officers and about 400 men, speeds to join with the other American defenders. Lt. Frazier is left in charge of the flotilla and a small contingent with orders to destroy the vessels if the British approach in force. He arrives at Upper Marlborough during the evening, and on the following day, he is instructed by General Levin Winder to join him at the Wood Yard. Barney's force arrives there at about noon.

Winder receives intelligence in a letter from Colonel Monroe that he had reconnoitered the British near Benedict and that he "enumerated 27 square rigged vessels, some bay craft and barges." A second letter from Monroe urges Winder to dispatch 500 or 600 troops to launch an attack. During the night, Monroe and another officer, Colonel Beall, arrive at Winder's camp and provide him with more details. Colonel Beall reports that he had observed about 4,000 troops; however, he emphasizes that he had not seen the entire force. Winder's report from Colonel Monroe is not reassuring. Monroe estimates the British force at 6,000; however, that is high. The Americans in or around Bladensburg total about 7,000 and the British force totals about 4,500 (see also, **August 19–25 THE BATTLE OF BLADENSBURG**).

In naval activity, the HMS *Nieman*, while on patrol, intercepts and captures the 69-ton schooner *Hibernia* which is transporting a cargo of various items from Philadelphia to Boston.

August 22 (Monday) **In Washington, D.C.,** Secretary of War John Armstrong issues the following order: "WAR DEPARTMENT, 22d August 1814.–12 o'clock. General Order. General Douglass will assemble his brigade at Alexandria, and hold it there subject to orders." On the 23rd, Armstrong issues new general orders: "Lieutenant Colonel Minor will repair to Washington with the regiment under his command, with the utmost despatch; he will report on his arrival to Colonel Carberry of the 36th regiment, and make a requisition for arms and ammunition." His second general order: "All the militia now in and marching to Alexandria, besides Colonel Minor, will march immediately to Washington; these orders will be communicated by Colonel Taylor."

Armstrong also sends a message to General William H. Winder to inform him that General Douglass had been directed to advance directly to the capital and disregard his orders to rendezvous with General John Hungerford.

In Maryland, an American contingent advances toward the British positions at Nottingham. It is composed of the 36th and 88th Regiments under Lt. Colonel William Scott, bolstered by three companies drawn from General Walter Smith's brigade under Major Peter, who also commands his artillery company and Captain Davison's light infantry and Captain Stull's corps. While the column advances, General William H. Winder and Colonel Monroe are far in front on a reconnaissance mission, which takes them close to the British camp to enable them to observe the enemy advance. Meanwhile, the main body advances slightly and deploys in some high ground. An American contingent of cavalry encounters the British and is compelled to retire. In turn, the advanced corps deploys to meet the spear of the British advance; however, it is ordered to retire to join the main body, which is deployed to meet the advance. Nevertheless, the British fail to take the suspected route to reach the capital and instead advance along the road that leads to Nottingham. The unexpected maneuver leaves the Americans about three miles from where the British modified their march and swerved away from the American defensive line.

General Winder quickly adjusts his strategy and withdraws his entire line to the old field, about eight miles from the capital and an equal distance from Marlborough. During this maneuver, an explosion coming from the direction of Pig's Point captures the attention of everyone in the area, and it becomes evident that Commodore Barney's little squadron has been destroyed. The 16 gunboats and 13 schooners, including Barney's sloop *Scorpion*, are self-destroyed by order of the secretary of war to prevent capture by the British. At the time, Barney is en route to join General Winder, while a detachment of five men on each of Barney's vessels remain aboard until the order is given to destroy the craft.

Meanwhile, the British arrive at Nottingham, where they establish a camp. In the evening, General Winder receives some prominent visitors. President James Madison, Secretary of War John Armstrong, Secretary of the Navy William Jones, and Attorney General Richard Rush arrive at the battalion Old Fields and remain with the commander until the night of the 23rd.

General Stansbury arrives at Bladensburg on this day. By this time General Winder has ordered the army to withdraw to the capital. At about midnight (23rd–24th), Colonel Monroe arrives at Bladensburg, while he is en route to Washington. He directs Stansbury to launch a strike against the rear of the British; however, Stansbury is reluctant to depart from Bladensburg because he is under orders to hold there. However, he had another problem; the troops under Colonel Sterrett had been overcome by exhaustion, which compels him to remain at Bladensburg.

In Virginia, General Young, pursuant to orders from General Winder, breaks camp at Alexandria and advances toward Piscataway Creek. There the brigade deploys in the heights a few miles to the rear of Fort Warburton (later Fort Washington).

August 23 (Tuesday) **In Washington,** Colonel George Minor's Virginia militia regiment arrives in the evening. Minor reports directly to the president and requests his orders. President Madison, however, directs him to John Armstrong. While meeting with Armstrong, Colonel Minor is informed that his regiment, composed of about 600 infantry troops and 100 cavalry, cannot be provided with arms until the following morning. Minor is to receive the arms from Colonel Carberry; however, on the following day, despite hours of searching, Colonel Minor cannot find him. Finally, late in the day, Colonel Minor rides out to General William H. Winder's headquarters at the Eastern Branch bridge outside of the capital to inform him of the problem. After receiving orders from Winder for the arsenal to provide the arms, he returns to his regiment and moves to the arsenal, only to be held up by the person responsible for handing out the weapons, who continued to waste time. Once the officers of the regiment counts the cartridges, the man insists upon recounting them. The elusive Colonel Carberry (88th Regiment and a veteran of the American Revolution) arrives in time to untangle the mess. He offers his apologies for his absence and explains that he had returned to the county seat on the previous night.

The regiment, once armed, moves to Capitol Hill; however, for Minor, the nightmare does not immediately end. He has to remain behind to sign receipts for the arms he acquired. If the delay had lasted a little longer, the British could have signed for the arms.

In Maryland, outside of Washington at the battalion Old Fields, General Winder's army assembles during the morning and the president reviews the troops. Meanwhile, the recent appearance of the British has caused rumors to fly and much conversation about their objective, whether it is Washington, or possibly Annapolis or Fort Washington. The rumors about the size of the British force also circulate rapidly with the estimates ranging from below 5,000 up to about 12,000. Although the estimates of British manpower vary, it is known that the force lacks cavalry and its complement of artillery stands only at about two field pieces and one howitzer.

Also this day, an American contingent seizes a small amount of prisoners. Using intelligence gained from the captives, combined with intelligence gained by observing the British advance, General Winder concludes that the British are not yet ready to resume their advance. He decides to unify his forces with those at Bladensburg.

General Winder sends a messenger to General Stansbury with instructions for his force and others there to repair to Upper Marlborough. Meanwhile, after leaving command of his force with General Smith, Winder departs from his camp, and with a cavalry escort, he rides toward Bladensburg to intercept Stansbury. Back with the main body, General Smith is under orders, which include moving to cover Winder's flank if he moves against Bladensburg. Smith is also to direct his advance corps to strike the British along their line of march; however, if they remain in place, the lines should be attacked. In the afternoon, Captain Stull's contingent skirmishes with the British; however, it is short lasting and the Americans retire, while the British, whom Winder believes will remain in place for the day, are vigorously on the advance.

Meanwhile, the British continue to unfold their master plan to seize the capital. During the afternoon, pursuant to orders from General Ross, Admiral Cockburn dispatches orders to his naval and Royal Marine forces at Pig's Point, which direct them to move to Mount Calvert, where the Marines are to debark along with their artillery. One contingent is to join Ross at Upper Marlborough. When Ross departs from Upper Marlborough, he leaves Captain Robyns with his Marines to hold the position, while he advances to Melwood, several miles from the American encampment at Old Fields.

August 24 (Wednesday) **In Washington, D.C.,** following the victory over the American army under General William H. Winder, the British take possession of the capital against no opposition. However, a hurricane strikes and compels the British to withdraw. In addition to the damage the British inflicted to the city, the hurricane destroys buildings they overlooked. By the following day, the hurricane has evicted the British (see also, **August 19–25 BATTLE OF BLADENSBURG**).

In naval activity, the British launch the HMS *Confiance*, a powerful 36 gun frigate. They immediately begin to fit it out as quickly as possible. The British, having defeated the French under Napoleon, are able to spare elite troops for service against the United States and large numbers are sped from Spain to the St. Lawrence to permit them to bolster the pending invasion of New York through Lake Champlain. Also, the cutter *Landrail* (Lt. John Hill, master) is recaptured by the HMS *Wasp*.

August 25 (Thursday) **In Maryland,** General William H. Winder continues to gather stray troops. The decision to defend the capital had been canceled on the previous day and the attempt to regroup at the heights of Georgetown had also been aborted. Instead, the American forces decide to assemble and regroup at Montgomery Courthouse in Maryland to prepare to defend Baltimore, expected to be the next objective of the British. Baltimore must be held or Philadelphia will follow.

August 25–29 **In Washington, D.C.,** a report by a British chronicler includes the following:

> Our troops were this day kept as much together as possible upon the Capitol Hill. But it was not alone on account of the completion of their destructive labors, that this was done. A powerful army of Americans already began to show themselves upon some heights, at the distance of two or three miles from the city; and as they sent out detachments of horse, even to the very suburbs, for the purpose of watching our motions, it would have been unsafe to permit more straggling than was absolutely necessary. The army which we had overthrown the day before, though defeated, was far from annihilated; and having by this time recovered [from] its panic, began to concentrate itself on our front, and presented quite as formidable an appearance as ever. We learnt, also that it was joined by a considerable force from the back settlements, which had arrived too late to take part in the action, and the report was, that both combined, amounted to nearly twelve thousand men.

The British first observe the American presence at about noon. Nevertheless, shortly thereafter, as if out of nowhere, the skies begin to darken and in a flash, a hurricane whips through the city; however, not at a quickened pace. The storm punishes buildings and people alike for about two hours in which the terror is a described by an English officer who was there:

> Of the prodigious force of the wind, it is impossible for you to form any conception. Roofs of houses were torn off by it, and whisked into the air like sheets of paper; while the rain which accompanied it, resembled the rushing of a mighty cataract, rather than the dropping of a shower. The darkness was as great as if the sun had long set, and the last remains of twilight had come on, occasionally relieved by flashes of vivid lightning streaming through it, which, together with the noise of the wind and the thunder, the crash of failing buildings, and the tearing of roofs as they were stript from the walls, produced the most appalling effect I ever have, and probably ever shall witness. This lasted for nearly two hours without intermission; during which time, many of the houses spared by us, were blown down, and thirty of our men, besides several of the inhabitants, buried beneath their ruins. Our column was as completely dispersed, as if it had received a total defeat; some of the men flying for shelter behind walls and buildings, and others falling flat upon the ground to prevent themselves from being carried away by the tempest; nay, such was the violence of the wind, that two pieces of cannon which stood upon the eminence, were fairly lifted from the ground and borne several yards to the rear.

Once the storm abates, General Ross makes the decision to abandon the city. He issues orders that all inhabitants must be off the streets by 2000. He concludes that he cannot accomplish more in the city, and of the rejuvenated Americans attack, he could face defeat. In the darkness of night, camp fires remain lit while the British, under orders to remain absolutely silent, begin to depart from the city. The Third Brigade is the first to depart, followed by the artillery and the Second Brigade. The rear, assigned to cover the retreat, is the Light Brigade, which had been the vanguard during the attack at Bladensburg. At 2130, the column silently moves out. Even the officers had relinquished their horses to help ensure the silence. The withdrawal is flawless. The city is evacuated undiscovered, and while the campfires burn, it seems only that the British had settled in for the night.

After departing from the city and passing other campfires, including what appeared to be those of a string of pickets, the column treks toward the scene of the battle; however, for anyone glancing to the rear, the fires had been so well established that the troops are unable to discern whether all the troops had departed. Upon reaching the scarred battlefield, the column is greeted by the unexpected sight of a glistening moon which spotlights the grotesque consequences of the horrendous clash of the previous day. Bodies, battered by the violent rains of the horrific storm had added grotesque elements to the battlefield, transformed into a graveyard that also contained some who had not yet succumbed. One of the British officers described the scene: "The dead were still unburied and lay about in every direction, completely naked. They had been stripped even of their shirts; and, having been exposed in this state to the violent rain till the morning, they appeared to be bleached to a most unnatural degree of whiteness. The heat and rain together had likewise affected them in a different manner, and the smell which arose upon the night air was horrible."

After the column moves into the town of Bladensburg, it is halted to permit the men of the Light Brigade to head out to search for the knapsacks and haversacks left during the fight at the bridge. Some of the officers seek out the wounded that had been in a makeshift hospital in one of the houses. Realizing the main body would be departing without them, they expressed great anxiety about their fate being up to their American captors. Nonetheless, their tremendous fears are baseless. Later, when the Americans arrive back in Bladensburg, the British wounded receive excellent treatment and even a generous dose of kindness.

Following the pause of about one hour or so, the march is resumed; however, in addition to leaving their wounded behind, only some of their dead are buried. At least 200 British soldiers are buried by Americans. The troops, already overexhausted from lack of rest, march throughout the night, but they are so sleep deprived that troops begin to fall out of rank, unable to maintain the pace. By 0730, their endurance had totally collapsed and a halt is ordered. The weary troops hardly reach the ground before the entire brigade, except for a few who are assigned as sentinels, fall into a deep sleep. The officer chronicling the campaign describes the scene: "The entire army resembled a heap of dead bodies on a field of battle, rather than living men."

General Ross continues to be concerned about the return of the Americans. At noon, the troops are awakened, and shortly thereafter, the march to the ships at Benedict resumes and continues until about dusk, when they reach their former camp at Marlborough. Ross establishes night quarters there. During the day's march, no American forces intercept the column; however, the British encounter a large number of slaves that propose joining with the British in exchange for their freedom. However, General Ross, known for his propensity to protect private property, considers the slaves as property and declines all except a few of the offers. Although no American forces strike the column, American cavalry shadows the army as it makes it way back to the ships and along the way, the Americans are able to pick up stragglers. General Ross finally arrives at Benedict on the 29th.

August 26 (Friday) **In Washington, D.C.,** while the British remain in the capital, prior to the arrival of a hurricane, a 200-man detachment is dispatched to the Washington Navy Yard to destroy whatever had not been disposed of by the Americans before they abandoned it. While there, unknown to the British, the Americans had dumped a huge supply of ammunition into a well. One of the men in the contingent, intending to douse a match, drops it into the well atop the hidden ammunition dump. The match ignites the powder, which intern causes an explosion that catapults flames into a nearby magazine, which is loaded with powder and causes yet another explosion. The results are devastating. Bricks, mortar, shot and shells, along with ammunition and numerous other items shoot toward the sky and descend rapidly. Twelve British soldiers are killed and more than 30 others are wounded.

In Canada, a British fleet departs Halifax en route to land a force in Maine. The fleet arrives at its destination on 1 September.

In Maryland, General William H. Winder at Montgomery Courthouse orders the army to advance to Baltimore.

August 27 (Saturday) **In Washington, D.C.,** General Walter Smith leads his brigade into the city.

In Alabama, General Jackson's Army arrives at Mobile and immediately prepares for an antici-

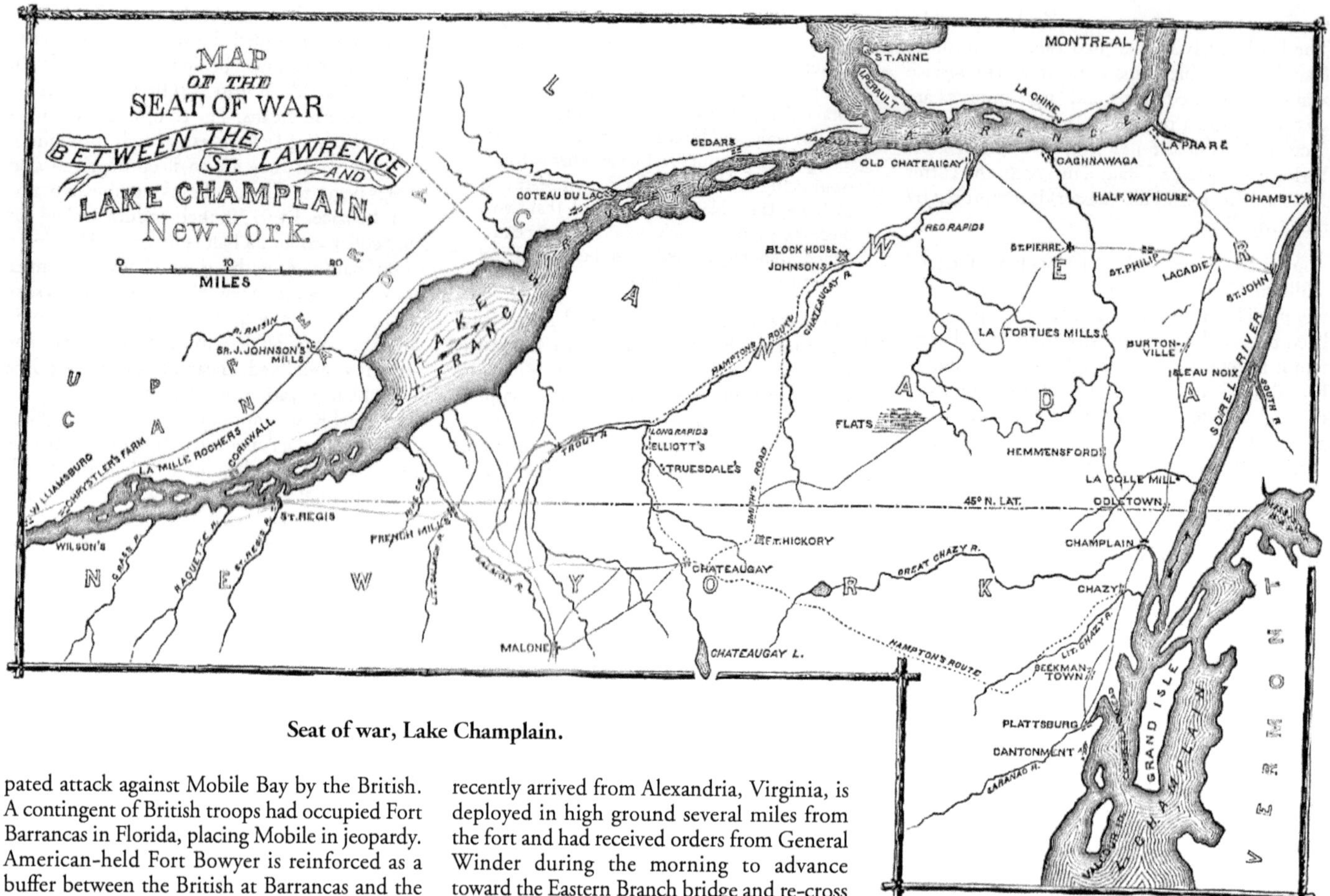

Seat of war, Lake Champlain.

pated attack against Mobile Bay by the British. A contingent of British troops had occupied Fort Barrancas in Florida, placing Mobile in jeopardy. American-held Fort Bowyer is reinforced as a buffer between the British at Barrancas and the Americans in Mobile.

In Maryland, a British squadron commanded by Captain James Gordon advances up the Potomac moving toward the capital. The men seize Fort Warburton (Fort Washington), which contains 49 troops under Captain Dyson and 26 guns. Nine of the guns are positioned to dominate the river; however, Dyson, under orders to destroy the fort if a British ground force approaches, chooses to abandon the post upon the approach of the naval squadron. The garrison, overwhelmed by fear, takes flight without firing even one gun. The British take possession of the fort, which remains intact. They destroy it the next day. However, while in the process of destroying the ammunition left behind by the defenders, an accidental explosion occurs and the British sustain some casualties.

In related activity, General Young's brigade, recently arrived from Alexandria, Virginia, is deployed in high ground several miles from the fort and had received orders from General Winder during the morning to advance toward the Eastern Branch bridge and re-cross the river to the Virginia bank. General Winder had established his headquarters at the bridge on the 24th.

In naval activity, the USS *Wasp*, having completed repairs, sails from L'Orient, France. On the 30th, it intercepts and seizes the brigantine *Lettice*, then on the following day, the *Wasp* intercepts and seizes a second brigantine, the *Bon Accord*.

In Pennsylvania, the Philadelphia Light Troop (Philadelphia city cavalry), commanded by Captain Charles Ross, enters into federal service for the period up to 20 December of this year. The unit is attached to the Light Brigade (Pennsylvania volunteers) commanded by Brigadier General Thomas Cadwalader.

August 28 (Sunday) *In naval activity,* Sir Peter Parker's squadron operating in the Chesapeake opens a bombardment on Worten. In conjunction with the naval attack, a raiding party debarks and destroys the property of Henry Waller. The squadron plans another raid for the 30th to continue the terrorization of the Eastern shore.

Fort Washington.

In other activity, the 20-ton schooner *Bee* (Elisha Burnham, master), while en route from Halifax to Cape Ann, is intercepted by two British vessels, the *Rifleman* and the *Peruvian*. The prize, along with its dry goods cargo, is taken into St. John's, New Brunswick. Elsewhere, the 31-ton schooner *Dove* (D. Gorham, master), while transporting a cargo of corn and flour from New York to Rhode Island, is intercepted and seized by the British privateer *Lively*. The *Dove* is diverted into port at Liverpool. The *Dove* is separate from the *Dove* seized 17 December 1812, another captured on 27 November 1813, and yet another captured on 21 September 1814.

August 29 (Monday) **In New York,** pursuant to recent orders, General Izard departs Plattsburgh to succeed General Brown as commander of the Niagara frontier. General Izard leads about 4,000 troops to Buffalo; however, about 1,200 troops remain at Plattsburgh under the command of General Alexander Macomb. Later, he receives reinforcements. Subsequent to his arrival at Buffalo, General Izard moves out for Fort Erie with reinforcements during early October.

In other activity, the British, having been greatly bolstered with troops and additional ships made available since the defeat of Napoleon, are preparing to launch their second invasion into the United States in an attempt to conquer new territory before peace negotiations might be consummated at Ghent. A massive force under Gen-

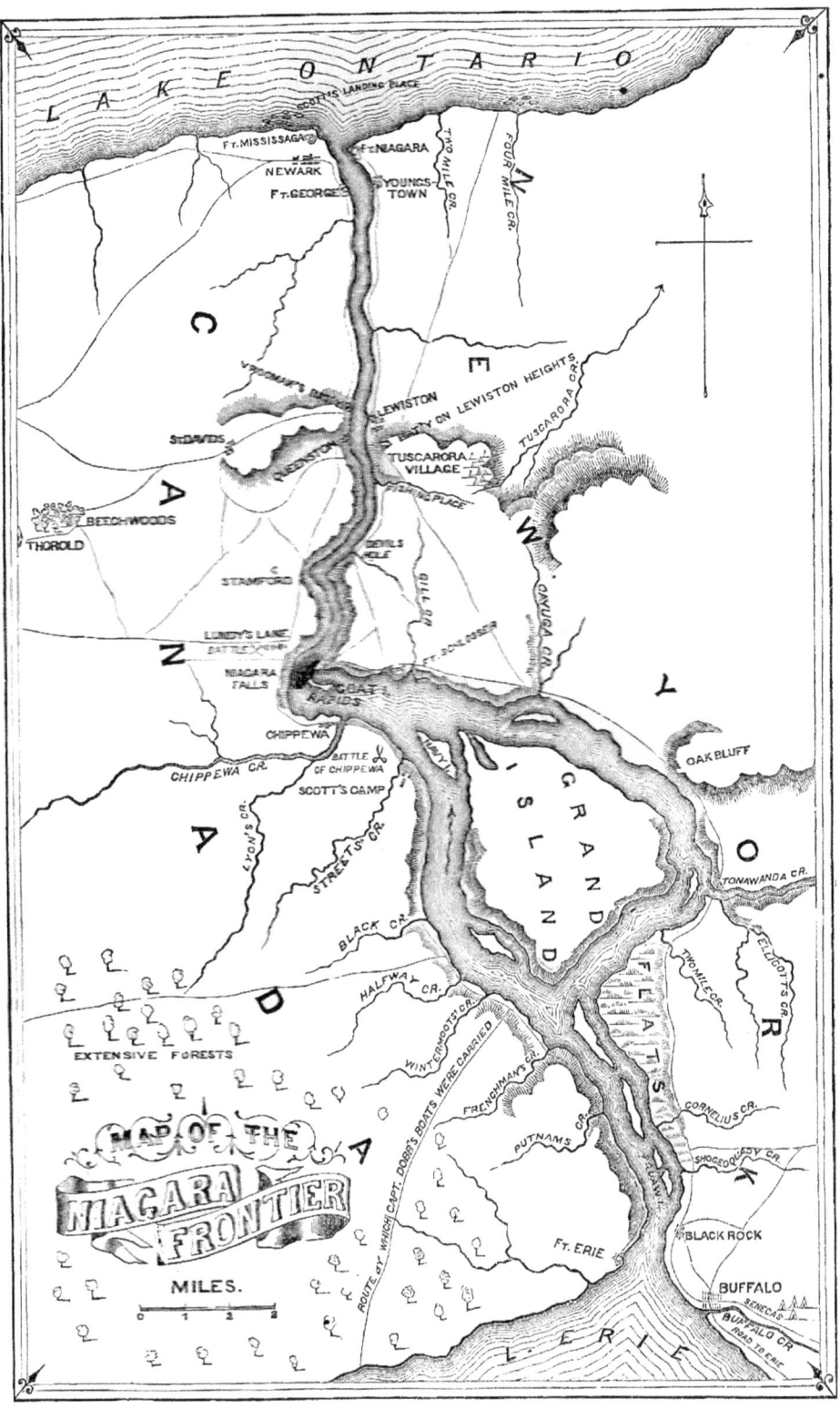

Map of the Niagara Frontier.

eral Prevost stands at the foot of Lake Champlain. Prevost has been ordered to trace the path General Burgoyne used during 1777. The main objective is Plattsburgh, thought to lack a large force due to General Izard's departure for Buffalo and afterward Fort Erie.

Before moving against Plattsburgh, General Prevost informs the citizens in the lake region that they must toss aside their allegiance to the United States and that they will have to pledge their allegiance to King George and the United Kingdom. The proclamation is not well received. Prevost also mandates that the residents must provide the British army with provisions, which also infuriates the people. Nevertheless, the region is not heavily populated, leaving Prevost for the time being unmolested, and for the same time, New York's geography remains unchanged. Prevost's quest of striking hard and seizing domination of the St. Lawrence and hopefully Lakes Champlain and Ontario depend on the Royal Navy, which Prevost believes will carry the victory in what becomes known as the Second Invasion of the United States.

General Prevost initiates his march on this day and reaches the border with the United States on 1 September. Meanwhile, General Alexander Macomb places no weight on the words of General Izard, who informed him prior to departing Plattsburgh that the British would most probably evict him from Plattsburgh, or he would become a prisoner of the British. Macomb apparently believed more in his own abilities and the skills of his force than of the dreadful prophesy of General Izard. By the time the British are poised to strike, Macomb's force increases to about 3,500, including 2,000 militia prepared to hold the town against Prevost's 14,000 men.

General Macomb also augments his defenses by directing his troops to construct several blockhouses as well as three redoubts on the peninsula where the Sarnac River converges with the Cumberland Bay (Plattsburgh Bay). The town's protections against a British attack include Fort Brown, positioned on the north bank (thirty feet high) of the river to thwart an assault from the Saranac River; Fort Moreau, positioned between the other two to protect from an attack from Plattsburgh; and Fort Scott, atop a high cliff that dominates Lake Champlain and the American right flank. The guns of Fort Scott are turned from the bay toward the approach of the British ground forces.

In naval activity, the British privateer *Lively*, while prowling off the Atlantic coast, intercepts and seizes the 18-ton sloop *Highland Hill* and its cargo of Indian corn while it is en route from New York to Newport, Rhode Island. The prize is taken into port at Liverpool.

August 29–30 *In Maryland,* a British squadron arrives at Annapolis on a journey to Washington. The inhabitants offer no resistance, and on the following day, the town surrenders. The British demand supplies, provisions and even vessels, and the citizens acquiesce. Afterward, in Washington, the U.S. forces take action to halt the squadron from acting at will without challenge. Sailors are assembled and placed under the command of Commodores John Rodgers, Oliver H. Perry and David D. Porter and Captain Creighton. Three fire boats and four barges are also committed to ensure the British do not continue to have free passage in the region. According to design of the recently established force, the rear of the British squadron comes under continual harassment. Meanwhile, Commodore Porter, supported by Captain Creighton and other naval officers oversee the construction of a battery along the Potomac (west bank) at the White House (separate from the president's residence in the capital). The battery is built by sailors and U.S. Marines. The position is also bolstered by Virginia militia (General John P. Hungerford's brigade) and other units. Meanwhile, on the east bank of the river, Commodore Perry and Captain Reed, U.S. Navy, oversee the construction of a battery at Indian Head.

August 30 (Tuesday) BATTLE OF CAULK'S FIELD (BATTLE OF MOORESFIELD) **In Maryland,** the British frigate *Menelaus* and the other vessels in Sir Peter Parker's squadron launch another raid on the Eastern Shore against the town of Fairlee and destroy the farm of Richard Frisby. Before leaving the property, they take four of his "colored men." However, after they return to the ship, a celebration begins, and from too many spirits, they decide to land again and attack a militia camp, commanded by Captain Reed. About 260 troops, split into two divisions under Captain Henry Crease and Lt. Pearce, under the overall command of Sir Peter Parker move against the camp near Moorefields, less than ten miles from Chesterton (Kent County) at a spot only about one-half mile from the beach. The men taken at Frisby's farm act as pilots and take the raiding party toward the camp by a circuitous route in hopes of gaining surprise. The American camp is held by about 170 troops of the 21st Maryland Regiment under the command of Lt. Colonel Philip Reed, a Revolutionary War veteran (captain) and a U.S. Senator representing Maryland (1806–1813). Word of Parker's impulsive plan leaks and the intelligence reaches Reed before the British arrive, giving him time to prepare. Without delay, all of the baggage is carried to the rear, while his troops redeploy in some high ground near Captain Caulk's residence, with their left on the road, next to the center where three artillery pieces are planted and prepared to fire.

Meanwhile, the British boats arrive. Just after landing, they seize two sentinels, which increases their enthusiasm and builds their confidence in the belief that they have not been detected. Upon their arrival at the camp, which had been vacated, the British are told that the troops relocated to the rear. Sir Peter orders the advance and the march resumes. Following a trek of about four or five miles, the American positions are spotted on a plain, which is encircled by woods. The troops, however, are out in front of the camp, and although the British see Reed's command, they do not see a contingent of riflemen under Captain Wickes and a lieutenant that are posted at the road where the Americans expected the attack to originate.

The British see Reed's line form, and at about the same time, the British initiate the assault. Reed counters by drawing in his riflemen, who stiffen the line when the British are only about "70 paces" out, but still the Americans are greatly outnumbered. According to Reed's report, fire erupts "along the whole line, and was sustained by our troops with the most determined valor. The enemy pressed our front; but foiled in this, he threw himself on our left flank, which was occupied by Captain Chambers' company. Here too, his efforts were equally unavailing. His fire had nearly ceased, when I was informed that in some parts of our line the cartridges were entirely expended, nor did any of the boxes contain more than a very few rounds." Nonetheless, Reed remains calm. Once the artillery cartridges are gone, he orders his force to fall back to regroup and redistribute the remaining ammunition, which is done. However, as the ammunition becomes fully depleted, the British, aware that the Americans had pulled back, make no further advance. The British, rather than pushing forward, halt the assault and return to their boats.

The fighting had lasted for about one hour; however, the results were much more costly than anticipated. None of the Marylanders, except the two lookouts, are seized. The British leave behind 10 killed and five wounded, and about 17 other wounded troops are taken back to the boats. Sir Peter Parker is among the casualties; his wound is fatal. Some reports say Parker died after being taken back to his flagship; however, the British officer who chronicled the campaign stated:

> He received a ball in the thigh. Not suspecting that the wound was dangerous, he continued to push forward, till he fell, exhausted from loss of blood; when, on examining the hurt, it was found that the femoral artery was cut, and before any proper assistance could be afforded, he literally bled to death. Seeing their leader killed, and the enemy retiring, apparently with the design of drawing them away from the coast, the sailors now halted, and, taking up their dead commander, returned to the river, without having been able to effect anything which might, in any degree, console them for their loss.

Sir Peter Parker was the son of Admiral Christopher Parker and the grandson of Admiral Sir Peter Parker. His remains are later transported to Halifax, along with those of Major General Ross, who is killed during the campaign to seize Baltimore. Also, Lt. Colonel Reed reports that based on intelligence he received from the British, their force sustained 40 to 43 casualties during the raid.

Sir Peter Parker.

In Virginia, a squadron of eight vessels attached to British Admiral Cockburn's fleet moves up the Potomac River to strike Alexandria. After arriving and receiving no resistance, the British move ashore. The garrison at a minor post, Fort Warburton, self-destructs the post at first sight of the British. A landing party goes ashore and threatens the citizens. The town is given an opportunity to save Alexandria from destruction at high cost. The British demand the "immediate delivery of all public and private naval and ordnance stores; of all shipping, and the furniture necessary to their equipment then in port; of all the merchandise of every description, whether in the town or removed from it since the 19th of the month; that such merchandise should be put on board the shipping at the expense of the owners; and that all vessels which might have been sunk upon the approach of the fleet should be raised by the merchants and delivered up with all their apparatus." Despite the outrageous demands, the citizens choose to comply rather than resist. The British remain at the town until 6 September undisturbed by the army or militia. Upon its departure, the squadron does come under fire from two separate batteries, at Indian Head and at White House, commanded by Captain Perry and Captain Porter respectively; however, the British sustain little damage as they depart with an enormous amount of American property and supplies.

In less than two weeks, General Ross and Admiral Cockburn have destroyed the capital, scattered the government and terrorized the surrounding region with a force of fewer than 3,000 troops. Word of the exploits of Ross and Cockburn is sent back to England, but by the time the story reaches London, the significance of the campaign is enormously exaggerated. The printed word in the *London Times* gives the impression that a major city had been wiped out, but at the time Washington is little more than a small village. Nonetheless, the headline reads: "The ill-organized association is on the eve of dissolution, and the world is speedily to be delivered of the mischievous example of the existence of a government founded on democratic rebellion." In the 9 October issue, the *Times* states: "The American Government must be displaced, or it will sooner or later plant its poisoned dagger in the heart of the parent state."

In naval activity, the 26-ton schooner *Enterprise*, en route from Barnstable, Massachusetts, to Washington, D.C., is intercepted and captured by the HMS *Nieman*.

August 31 (Wednesday) *In naval activity,* the HMS *Wasp* intercepts an American brigantine, the *Charlotte*, which is transporting a cargo that includes coffee, molasses, rum and sugar. The *Charlotte* (Ezekiel Allen, master) is caught and captured while moving from Antigua to Port Glasgow, Scotland.

September **In Pennsylvania,** while the British are beginning to focus on seizing the capital and Baltimore, Lt. Colonel Thomas Cadwalader is encamped just outside of Philadelphia. However, the forces there have no commander. Cadwalader is appointed commander. The brigade, composed of artillery, cavalry, infantry and some militia, is later reinforced with riflemen from several sections of Pennsylvania, bringing the total number of men to about 3,500. By year's end, the brigade is dismissed from federal service.

In New York, the hospital at Crab Island receives a huge amount of troops suffering from a variety of illnesses, including victims of an acute outbreak of dysentery and typhus. Although the facility is already overwhelmed, more arrive on September 10, some ill and others wounded from fighting at Culver Hill and Halsey's Corners. And on the 11th, the little island north of Valcour Island receives even more victims as the fighting becomes heavy at the nearby Battle of Plattsburgh. About 400 of the sick and injured are removed and taken to Burlington, Vermont.

The vessels that participate include the USS *Saratoga*, the USS *Eagle*, a brigantine, the USS *Ticonderoga*, a schooner, the sloop USS *Preble*, and the gunboats *Allen*, *Aylwyn*, *Ballard*, *Borer*, *Burrows*, *Centipede*, *Ludlow*, *Viper* and *Wilmer*. Also, the ship *Victory* is seized by a combine British naval-land force while it is at anchor at Penobscot, Maine.

In naval activity, the American privateer *David Porter* returns toward its home port after a cruise that began earlier in the summer under the command of Captain J. Fish. During its time at sea, the privateer captures a number of vessels carrying valuable cargoes. They include the brigantine *Cornwallis*, the brigantine *Horatio*, the brigantine *Mars* and the ship *Vester*. During its return to the States, three British warships encounter it and they initiate pursuit. The chase continues for nearly 1,000 miles, but in vain. The swift privateer outmaneuvers the royal trio and finally leaves them in its wake. It safely arrives back in port at New York. In other naval activity, the American privateer *York* arrives at Boston following a 13-week cruise in which the crew sustained no loss of men. Nonetheless, while cruising primarily off Brazil, the *York* captures a number of vessels, and the combined value of the cargoes amounts to one and one-half million dollars. Subsequently, on its final cruise during the war, the *York*, which remains at sea until April 1815, seizes only one vessel and only temporarily. The prize is soon after recaptured by the British. Also, the American privateer *Argo* intercepts and seizes a brigantine, the *Mary and Eliza*, after it embarks from Halifax with a cargo of lumber. A prize crew is assigned to take it into an American port, but while en route, a British warship drives it ashore at Barnegat, New Jersey, and destroys it.

September 1814 to June 1815 CONGRESS OF VIENNA The various European powers gather in Vienna subsequent to the defeat of Napoleon, who is in exile. The conference is to redraw the map of Europe and to reinstate the monarchies that had been ended by Bonaparte's conquests. Although war with France had come to an end, the United Kingdom remains at war with the United States and without Napoleon as a nemesis, the British are now able to send more force to the United States. But in the meantime, the British participate with the other three primary European powers on this diplomatic operation. Austria, Prussia, Russia and the U.K. expect to jointly make the primary decisions, but the French, through the skill of Talleyrand, succeed in getting a major voice during the deliberations. Spain and other smaller nations, however, do have representation at the conference. The key negotiators are Prince Klemens von Metternich, Austrian minister of state, who acts as president of the assembly; Arthur Wellesley, Duke of Wellington, on behalf of Britain; Robert Stewart, Viscount Castlereagh, of England; Prince Karl August von Hardenberg, Prussia; and Charles Maurice de Talleyrand-Perigord, France.

During the conference, the French Empire is neatly re-carved to the satisfaction of the attending parties. Just before it ends, explosive news will arrive at the conference and laughter at first, followed by somber moods and raised anxiety. Word of Napoleon's escape from Elba during February of 1815 fails to cause any immediate concern, but soon after, when it is further learned that Napoleon has arrived back in France and is marching on Paris, it becomes apparent that once again Napoleon must be stopped or there will be no peace in Europe, nor will the results of the conference have any validity. The Allies react quickly and the stage is set for a major confrontation.

Ferdinand VII of Spain regains his throne and he is less than tactful with Spain's possessions in South America. The colonies objecting to his policies defy his rigid rule and then they ignite rebellion; however, unlike the revolution of their neighbors to the north in the United States, there will be no permanent union of states. Nevertheless, there is a yearning for independence that cannot be easily quelled. Also, Mainz in the western part of Germany, which was earlier ceded to France, is given to the Grand Duchy of Hesse-Darmstadt.

September 1 (Thursday) In New York, General Prevost's 14,000-man army arrives at the border with Canada. He continues the advance toward Plattsburgh; however, unlike the march through Canada, the columns encounter obstacles that hinder progress. The British encounter destroyed bridges and frequently come upon fallen trees that block the roads. The delays do not annoy Prevost because he is out in front of fleet under Commodore George Downie, which is to support the attacks. The British arrive outside Plattsburgh on 6 September.

In Tennessee, General James Robertson, Indian agent, becomes ill and dies. His remains are later taken to Nashville to be interred.

In naval activity, the USS *Wasp*, which has been thrashing British shipping in the vicinity of the English Channel, spots a British merchant ship convoy, composed of 10 vessels, during the pre-dawn hours. The merchantmen are under the protection of a powerful ship of the line, the 74-gun *Armada*. The *Wasp* disregards the superior strength of the HMS *Armada* and moves directly toward one of the merchant ships, the brigantine *Mary*. In short order, the prize is gained without interference from the British warship. The British crew is rapidly transferred to the *Wasp*, and once the prisoners are safely aboard, the Americans set the *Mary* on fire. Once the *Mary* is taken, the *Wasp* continues to defy the *Armada*. It moves to seize another on the convoy ships; however, the HMS *Armada* begins to close on the *Wasp*, prompting the Americans to make a speedy departure. Nevertheless, having lost its second target and having avoided a battle against the *Armada*, the *Wasp* remains on the prowl. Later this day, lookouts spot a sail on the horizon and the *Wasp* initiates pursuit. At about 2130, the *Wasp* has closed the distance and suddenly the British vessel comes under fire.

Unknown to the Americans, the British vessel is not a merchant ship; rather, it is the HMS *Avon*, one of the British warships that has been on the hunt for the Yankee intruder. The British return fire and a duel ensues for about 30 minutes. At about 2200, the British guns cease fire. The Americans incorrectly suspect that the cessation points to capitulation. The guns on the *Wasp* are silenced and a call is made demanding that the unknown vessel strike its colors. The response is forthcoming, but there is no surrender. The targeted vessel, the 18-gun *Avon*, reinitiates its fire, prompting the guns of the *Wasp* to resume firing. The guns of the *Wasp* rake the *Avon*, and shortly thereafter, the British guns again become silent. American fire had pummeled the *Avon*, leaving it unable to continue the fight.

More surprises occur just as the prize crew is preparing to board the *Avon*. The lookouts aboard the *Wasp* spot another British warship that is closing, prompting the prize crew to abort the boarding of the prize. In the meantime, the crewmen of the *Wasp* remain at their battle stations, prepared to battle the approaching warship; however, suddenly the *Wasp* finds itself facing a British trio as two other warships are spotted on the horizon. The plan to destroy the *Avon* is aborted. The *Wasp* prepares to depart the

General James Robertson.

area rather than fight three enemy ships. Meanwhile, the British vessel on site chooses not to engage the *Wasp*; however, it does open fire with a broadside that inflicts some damage to the rigging and sails.

The *Wasp* sails off without completing the destruction of the *Avon*; however, the earlier inflicted damage had been quite severe and the *Avon* sinks soon after the *Wasp* departs. The British warships fail to intercept the *Wasp*, permitting it to continue to pounce upon British shipping. It encounters another British vessel on 12 September.

In other naval activity, the brigantine *Nancy*, at about this time (1 September to 18 September), transporting a cargo of lumber and timber, is captured by a joint British naval-ground force. Elsewhere, the 14-gun American privateer *Harpy*, commanded by Captain William Nichols and operating out of Baltimore, intercepts and captures the 10-gun *Princess Elizabeth*, a British packet. During the brief engagement, the British sustain three killed and a few others wounded. One American is killed. The *Harpy* carried a crew of 100 men and the crew of the *Princess Elizabeth* numbered 38 men. After the prize is seized, the Americans discover that the passengers include the Turkish ambassador to England and several English army officers. The Americans also relieve the vessel of about $10,000 in specie and four of its guns, while tossing the remainder of its guns overboard. After paying a ransom of $2,000, Captain Moon releases the vessel and lets it continue its voyage.

September 1, 1814, to April 15, 1815 **In Maine,** a British fleet arrives in the Back Cove and seizes Fort Madison (Fort Porter) at Castine

British General John Cope Sherbrooke.

and Fort St. George (Thomaston). The fleet comprises three 74-gun warships, the HMS *Dragon, Spellcer* and *the Bulwark*, accompanied by two frigates, the HMS *Burhame* and *Tenedos*, two sloops, the *Sylph* and *Peruvian*, and the schooner HMS *Pictu*, along with a tender and ten transports, the latter carrying 3,500 men. The troops are attached to the British 29th, 62nd, 98th Regiments and two companies of the 60th Regiment. The ground troops are bolstered by a contingent of the Royal Artillery. The naval squadron is commanded by Rear Admiral Richard Griffith (of the White).

The American shipping in the harbor (Eaton's Thomaston, South Thomaston and Rockland) including a revenue cutter also falls victim to the Royal Navy. The ominous presence of the fleet had apparently inflicted fear in the garrison at Fort Madison. The troops fire their artillery, then they blow up the fort's magazine before absconding to Portland. Fort Madison is renamed Fort Castine by the British.

The British also seize Fort St. George, established during 1719. The guns are destroyed, but the British afterward rebuild the post and mount about 60 guns. Other seizures include the courthouse and the customs house. After the British seize the main objectives, they inform the civilians by proclamation that "if the people would remain quietly at their homes and continue to pursue their usual avocations, would surrender all their arms, and would refrain from communicating intelligence to the Americans, they should have protection and safety ensured to them." Meanwhile, the British utilize the courthouse as a barracks. The British also construct defenses, including batteries and a blockhouse. Nevertheless, they also commandeer some of the prized private residences for officers. A barn owned by Mr. Hooke is utilized as a military hospital, while a contingent is deployed at the old church in North Castine.

The home of Otis Little becomes the quarters of a group of officers — Captain Coker, Captain Gell, along with Lieutenants Evans and Sands, and their servants. Unknown to the British, the Americans had concealed a large amount of ammunition and 100 muskets in the barn. Although the British hold the town for the duration, the arms, hidden by town officials, are never discovered. The British secure their positions and initiate patrols. The activity increases as British troops expand their patrols by advancing upriver. The towns of Hampden, Bangor, Frankfort and Bucksport are seized. During the missions, the British confiscate some horses, oxen and sheep, and six American vessels are seized. They include the *Hancock*, which is regained, and the *Lucy*, which is lost. The *Bangor Packet* and *Oliver Spear* are taken; the *Polly* is ransomed; and one known as "the beautiful boat," the *Cato*, could not be recovered. Some other vessels are destroyed, including the *Liverpool Trader*.

The British continue to bolster their defenses, and they initiate a project to increase the size of the fort's trench, transforming it into a canal that serves a dual purpose, as an obstacle for the Americans, but also to prevent desertions, a new problem that continues to get worse. After completing the work on the canal, the British discover that it does not deter the disgruntled troops from deserting. In a more drastic action, the British who capture two deserters, use them as an example. The men are tried and after being convicted, both are executed by firing squad. One other soldier is shot before he reaches the opposite side of the canal.

The Americans make no attempts to regain the forts, leaving the British to control the area for the duration of the conflict. Meanwhile, on 12 September, about one-half of the force, under General Sherbrooke and Admiral Griffith, depart to capture Mathias. Admiral Milne and General Gerard Gosselin remain in command of the forces that stay to control the forts.

In naval activity, the *Cod Hook* is captured at an unknown time during September by a combined force of the enemy, including ground troops and naval forces. The British take the prize into port at British-held Castine, Maine.

September 2 (Friday) **In Illinois,** a force under Major Zachary Taylor, which had departed from St. Louis to avenge the recent attack against Captain Campbell's flotilla, arrives at Fort Independence near Troy, a post used to monitor the Indians in that region of the Mississippi Valley. From there, Taylor reaches his objective on the 4th.

In naval activity, a British fleet under the command of Captain Gordon, consisting of 21 vessels, departs Alexandria, anticipating an American attack in retaliation for the devastation inflicted by the British upon Washington.

In other activity, the *Lively*, a British privateer, encounters the *Betsy* (B. Parker, master), an 88-ton sloop that had sailed from Nantucket. The *Betsy* and its cargo of fish, oil, salt and other goods are taken into port at Liverpool. The 89-ton sloop *Drake* (R. Middlebrook, master), carrying a cargo of liquor, turpentine and other items, is confiscated by the HMS *Belvedira*. The British burn the *Drake*. Also, the British privateer *Lively* captures the 27-ton schooner *Dromo* (J. Parker, master) and takes it into port at Liverpool. At the time of its capture, the *Dromo* is carrying a cargo that includes fish and salt.

Elsewhere, the 158-ton brigantine *Favourite* (W. Ayton, master) is intercepted and seized by the HMS *Alban* while it is en route from Calcutta to Port Jackson (New South Wales, Australia). At the time of its capture, the *Favourite* has a cargo that includes rice, sugar and tea. The *Favourite* is separate from the schooner *Favourite* seized on 5 April 1813. Also, the 48-ton schooner *Planter* is intercepted and seized by the British privateer *Lively*. At the time of capture, the *Planter* is carrying a cargo of fish, oil, salt and other items. The *Planter*, separate from the ship *Planter* seized on 2 September 1812, is taken into port at Liverpool.

September 2–5 Commodore Rodgers' fleet catches and engages the British along the Potomac; but the British guns are too much for the tenacious Rodgers. The American fleet breaks the engagement and withdraws.

September 3 (Saturday) **In Louisiana,** on or about this day, a British squadron, including the sloop HMS *Sophia*, arrives off the island of Grand Terre near the headquarters of Jean Lafitte at Barataria. Lafitte, previously an owner, with his brother, of a blacksmith shop in New Orleans, had sold the business to become involved in smuggling. He has a large force and a fleet of ships. The British had sent Captain Nicholas Lockyer of the *Sophia* to persuade Lafitte to side with the British in a massive attack against New Orleans. Lockyer is accompanied by a naval lieutenant and an army officer, Captain McWilliams.

Lafitte rows out toward the ship and is met by Lockyer's boat. The British inquire about Lafitte, but he fails to identify himself, although he does escort the officers to his headquarters. Before reaching shore tells the party that he is Lafitte. The British are not well received when they reach shore; however, Lafitte is able to control his men. Lafitte listens attentively as the British try to lure him into their plans after they give him a proclamation issued by Lt. Colonel Edward Nicholls, the commander of the British ground troops operating along the coast of Florida.

Lafitte is offered a captain's commission in the Royal Navy and they offer him $30,000 in gold. In addition, he is promised a large grant of land, including tracts for each of his men once the Americans are evicted and the territory comes under the British flag. Captain Lockyer then delivers his close, which avoids any congeniality. Lockyer informs Lafitte that if the British offer is declined, the squadron will return with sufficient strength to demolish the fort, and he states that Lafitte's buccaneers would be annihilated. Lafitte absorbs everything said by the British but, rather than signal his intentions, he informs the British that he will require some time to make his decision.

Despite being considered a pirate by the government in Louisiana, Lafitte is not in favor of New Orleans being attacked by the British. He takes the documents, including notes which he had taken, and delivers them to Governor William C.C. Claiborne, while informing him of the British plan. At the time, Lafitte is also aware that the Americans are in the process of striking his headquarters. Nonetheless, Claiborne and other officials who distrust Lafitte erroneously conclude that the documents are not genuine. Lafitte is rebuffed. To make matters worse, Claiborne authorizes a naval attack against Barataria.

Lt. Colonel Nicholls' proclamation reads:

> Native of Louisiana! on you the first call is made to assist in liberating from a faithless imbicile government, your paternal soil: Spaniards, Frenchmen, Italians and British whether settled or residing for a time in Louisiana, on you also I call to aid me in this just cause: the American usurpation in this country must be abolished and the lawful owners of the soil put in possession. I am at the head of a large body of Indians, well armed disciplined and commanded by British officers — a good train of artillery with every requisite, seconded by the powerful aid of a numerous British and Spanish squadron of ships and vessels of war. Be not alarmed, inhabitants of the country at our approach; the same good faith and disinterestedness which has distinguished the conduct of Britons in Europe, accompanies them here; you will have no fear of litigious taxes imposed on you for the purpose of carrying on an unnatural and unjust war; your property, your laws, the peace and tranquility of your country, will be guaranteed to you by men who will suffer no infringement of theirs; rest assured that these brave red men only burn with an ardent desire of satisfaction for their wrongs they have suffered from the Americans, to join you in liberating these southern provinces from their yoke and drive them into those limits formerly prescribed by my sovereign.
>
> The Indians have pledged themselves in the most solemn manner not to injure in the slightest degree the persons or properties of any but enemies to their Spanish or English fathers; a flag over any door whether Spanish, French or British will be a certain protection, nor dare any Indian put his foot on the threshold thereof, under the penalty of death from his own countrymen; not even an enemy will an Indian put to death, except resisting in arms, and as for injuring helpless women and children, the red men by their good conduct and treatment to them (if it be possible) make the Americans blush for their more inhuman conduct lately on the Eseambia, and within a neutral territory.
>
> Inhabitants of Kentucky, you have too long borne with grievous impositions — the whole brunt of the war has fallen on your brave sons; be imposed on no longer, but either range yourselves under the standard of your forefathers, or observe a strict neutrality; if you comply with either of these offers, whatever provisions you send down will be paid for in dollars and the safety of the persons bringing it as well as the free navigation of the Mississippi guaranteed to you.
>
> Men of Kentucky, let me call to your view (and I trust to your abhorrence) the conduct of those factions which hurried you into this civil, unjust and unnatural war at the time when Great Britain was straining every nerve in defence of her own and the liberties of the world when the bravest of her sons were fighting and bleeding in so sacred a cause — when she was spending millions of her treasure in endeavoring to pull down one of the most formidable and dangerous tyrants that ever disgraced the form of man — when groaning Europe was almost in her last gasp — when Britons alone showed an undaunted front — basely did those assassins endeavor to stab her from the rear; she was turned on them renovated from the bloody but successful struggle — Europe is happy and free, and she now hastens justly to avenge the unprovoked insult. Show them that you are not collectively unjust; leave that contemptible few to shift for themselves, let those slaves of the tyrant send an embassy to Elba, and implore his aid, but let every honest, upright American spurn them with united contempt. After the experience of twenty-one years, can you any longer support those brawlers for liberty who call it freedom when themselves are free; be no longer their dupes — accept of my offers — everything I have promised in this paper I guarantee to you on the sacred honour of a British officer.
>
> Given under my hand at my *head-quarters,* Pensacola, this 29th day of August 1814. EDWARD NICHOLLS.

In naval activity, the American Commodore Rodgers, in pursuit of a British fleet, pauses while passing Alexandria, Virginia. He is incensed that the townspeople have not yet re-hoisted the Stars and Stripes.

In other naval activity, a British expeditionary force composed of about 1,000 men, dispatched from Castine, Maine, arrives at Hampden, which is about 35 miles from the British base. Their objective is the USS *Adams*, which had recently completed a cruise in European waters. The British intend to capture the *Adams* while it is receiving repairs. The ship's commander, Captain Morris, in anticipation of a British attack, had ordered the construction of batteries. He gathers militia, but the troops lack weapons. Morris uses the ship's supply to provide the militia with muskets. Nonetheless, as soon as the British regulars come into view, the militia abandons its positions and scatters. The flight of the militia makes it impossible for Captain Morris' seamen and Marines to repulse the Redcoats who have arrived in great numbers; however, Morris does not consider surrender. He orders the crew and his Marines, except for a small detachment, to escape. After the men depart, Morris and the others who remain behind set up the *Adams* for destruction by lighting a slow-match. The British by this time have posted men at the bridge to cut off escape. Undaunted, Morris and the others jump in the water and swim to safety to deny the British their prisoners. The British at about the same time have also failed to capture the frigate, which suddenly explodes, leaving them no options except to return to Castine.

On 8 January, a court of inquiry is held regarding the action of the militia commander General John Blake (1st Brigade and 10th Division), a veteran of the Revolutionary War, and Lt. Colonel Andrew Grant. Major General Henry Sewall acts as president of the inquiry. It ends with a decision that the charges do not appear to warrant a court-martial.

Also, in Michigan, near Fort Michilimackinac, where the USS *Tigress* and *Scorpion* have been assigned blockade duty since the previous August to prevent supplies and provisions from reaching the garrison at Mackinaw, a British force awaits darkness, then creeps up and by total surprise, captures the *Tigress*. Keeping the American flag flying, the British now on the *Tigress* come alongside the *Scorpion* and board it.

Elsewhere, the privateer *Decatur* out of Maine under Captain E. Brown is seized by a British squadron, however, the prize is later lost at sea. The *Decatur* is separate from the privateer *Decatur* out of Charleston commanded by Captain Dominique and the privateer *Decatur* under Captain Nichols of Newburyport.

September 4 (Sunday) **In Washington, D.C.,** James Monroe, in a letter dated this day to Pennsylvania Governor Simon Butler, discusses probable objectives of the British force on the Patuxent River in Maryland: "The city of Philadelphia, I am aware, offers by its wealth a strong induce-

Captain Charles Morris.

General John B. Blake (*The Maine Historical and Genealogical Recorder, Volume III*, 1886).

ment to the enemy to make an attempt on it. Its population, however, being great, its organized and well trained force considerable, much confidence is entertained that it will make a defence worthy the high character which it sustains with the nation. To repel such danger, it will be necessary for you to have your force in the best possible preparation for action; to watch the enemy's movements in every direction, and to communicate to me without delay every circumstance deserving of attention."

Also this day, Monroe writes to N.B. Boileau, the secretary of the Commonwealth of Pennsylvania: "Your letters of August 27th and 28th, have been received. Orders have been given for depositing at Carlisle, ten thousand stand of arms and equipments, to meet the exigencies of the times in supplying such militia as may be called into the actual service for the defence of the sea board. These will be made subject to the requisition of the Governor of Pennsylvania, with the provision that such as may be received must be receipted for conformably to the provisions of the act for arming the whole body of militia."

In Louisiana at Grand Terre Island, Jean Lafitte pens a letter to Representative John Blanque in the Louisiana House of Representatives to advise him of the British intent to attack New Orleans and their proposal to have Lafitte receive a captain's commission in the Royal Navy if he and his band join the British campaign. Lafitte, who speaks English, French and Spanish fluently, also delivers a separate letter for Governor Claiborne to Blanque. Blanque, Claiborne, Major General Villere, Colonel Ross and Commodore Patterson meet and decide to dismiss the documents as fraudulent and to decline the support of Lafitte. Nonetheless, the word of an imminent attack spreads quickly and the citizens' anxiety increases. The attendees except General Villere vote in the negative; however, the governor is unable to vote because he presides at the conference. Lafitte, whose brother Pierre is in jail at this time, is not only rebuffed; he is also going to be attacked at his stronghold.

In Maryland, men are rushing from all directions to form for a defiant stand at Baltimore. If the British are to gain access, they must crush the fired up resistance, including the 56th Virginia, 38th U.S. Infantry and five companies from Pennsylvania. Baltimore must hold if the British are to be stopped. Total manpower mounts to over 15,000 but they are not all regular army and they must face British regulars.

In New York, the main body of General Prevost's army arrives at a point about eight miles from Plattsburgh. Several gunboats move closer to the objective and establish a battery on the east side of Isle la Motte, from where the British guns can provide cover fire for the invasion force when the attack against Plattsburgh is launched.

In Pennsylvania, Governor Simon Butler writes to Major General Bloomfield:

> SIR: It is of importance at this eventful crisis to know how much of the ordnance, small arms, ammunition, military stores, and camp equipage now deposited in the United States arsenal near this city, can, in case of emergency, be furnished on your order for the Pennsylvania militia, in conformity to any order you may have received from the Secretary at War. If, as is represented, there are in the arsenal a quantity of rifles, the best weapon in the hands of undisciplined men, it is desired to know whether any of them and how many can be had on loan, or on any other terms, for the use of such of our militia who are now or that may eventually be ordered into service.

In naval activity, the HMS *Nimrod* intercepts and seizes the schooner *Maria*, which is moving from Newport, Rhode Island, to New York with a cargo of fish, oil and salt. In other naval activity, the HMS *Nieman* intercepts the schooner *Two Brothers*, which is en route to Havana, Cuba, from Philadelphia with a cargo including corn, flour, onions and other items.

September 4 to October 16   In Illinois, Major Zachary Taylor's force arrives at the Rock River on September 4th from Fort Independence (Cap au Gris Fort) on the Illinois side of the Mississippi River near Troy. No interference from Indians had been encountered during the journey, and according to a report from Major Taylor, the contingent did not spot even one Indian. Nonetheless, the invisible Indians suddenly make their appearance known as the flotilla passes the Rock River and proceeds up the Mississippi. Taylor concludes that his large boats cannot enter the extremely narrow mouth with his large boats. At about the same time, a large number of horses stand conspicuously on an island that begins just opposite of the mouth, and more horses are detected along the western bank of the Mississippi. Taylor immediately discerns that the horses were intentionally placed as another cunning trick by the Indians to fool the Americans into dispatching small contingents ashore.

Taylor, rather than being snagged by an ambush, merely modifies his strategy, originally suggested by General Benjamin Howard to pass by the Indian villages to leave the impression that the flotilla is moving directly to Prairie du Chein. Taylor's intent is to draw the Indians from their villages down toward the rapids, which would give him the opportunity to destroy them before they had time to return. Unexpectedly, nature alters his plans. The winds begin to become unfavorable, and by the time the flotilla reaches the head of the island upon which the horses had been spotted, Taylor's entire force becomes imperiled, not by Indians but by the elements. His force is struck by a powerful hurricane. After a prolonged struggle, the flotilla finally manages to reach a tiny island in the middle of the river. Unable to safely proceed, Taylor's force debarks at about 1600 to wait out the storm. The view is less than pleasant as on both sides of the river; the number of Indians continues to increase. All the while, even more Indians are spotted as they ignore the stiff winds and currents to cross the river at various places in their canoes. Nonetheless, the only terrifying noise originates from the howling winds. No gunfire is exchanged and the night passes without a fight.

At about daybreak, the Indians fire at Captain Whiteside's boat from close range and a corporal who is outside of the boat suffers a mortal wound. Taylor, having been prepared to fight, but on his terms, had issued orders stating that "if a boat was fired on to return it, but not a man to leave the boat without positive orders from myself." Taylor waits for the sunlight to totally emerge before taking action. Before moving against his foe, a guard is assigned to protect each of the vessels. Immediately thereafter, the Americans take the offensive, ignoring the possibility that they might be greatly outnumbered. The troops swarm across the diminutive island and reach the opposite shore; however, the Indians who fired upon the boat had evaded a fight; rather they were able to wade from the island to another island just below Taylor's encampment. Troops under Captain Whiteside spot the Indians as they reach the other island and a brief but heated exchange of fire erupts. Two Americans sustain wounds. Captain Rector, who had survived the attack against Captain Campbell's flotilla at Prairie du Chien, is ordered by Taylor to "drop down with his boat to ground and to rake the island below with artillery." Rector is also directed to open fire on every canoe he sees trying to cross the river. The firing continues for about one hour without any visible results. During that time, no Indians ventured out in the river on a canoe.

After Whiteside ceases fire, he moves downstream about 60 yards to destroy a group of canoes that are visible stationary targets. During this operation, a British contingent, holding concealed positions, commences firing with artillery. Taylor's boats, the recipient of the artillery, remain completely vulnerable. Taylor reacts immediately by deciding to return fire at the position that stands, according to Taylor, about 350 paces from the boats. However, he quickly countermands his order after concluding that the British fire would destroy the boat before his 6-pounder would correctly strike the concealed positions of the British. Meanwhile, British fire strikes Lt. Hempstead's boat, causing major damage. Instead, Taylor orders his boats to move down, and despite coming under direct fire, while traveling only one-quarter mile, the boats pass. Meanwhile, the Indians on both banks of the river fire haphazardly.

Rector's boat, having been under heavy fire since the first British round was catapulted, comes under direct attack by the Indians while it is close to shore. Nonetheless, through the skill of the troops on board, after about fifteen minutes of heavy pressure, the Indians are driven back, helped in great part by Rector's effective delivery of grape shot. In the meantime, Whiteside brings his boat close to Rector's craft to deliver additional punishment from his swivel gun. At about the same time, the Americans begin to move downstream, and for the next two miles, Indians along the banks fire incessantly at the boats. Nonetheless, return fire from the boats keeps the Indians from any attempt to board. Finally, after moving about three miles, Taylor finds a suitable place to land where the boats, most of which have anchors too weak to hold in the river, can remain anchored.

British boats initiate pursuit and shadow Taylor's flotilla to its landing place, where the wounded can be treated and the boats can receive repairs. Once Taylor's troops deploy on a prairie and prepare to engage, the British observe the actions of the Americans and immediately reverse course and retire. After the British retire, Taylor convenes a meeting with his officers to determine if they possess enough strength to move against the villages to destroy them and their crops. It is determined that they are outnumbered by at least three to one, and that it would not be practical to make the attempt, particularly because provisions are becoming dangerously low. The boats retire to Warsaw, Illinois, to carry out another priority of the mission, to construct a fort (Fort Edwards) that could dominate the river in that region of the Mississippi.

While constructing Fort Edwards, named in honor of Ninian Edwards, the first governor of Illinois, the troops destroy Fort Johnson, a few miles above the new post. After the war, the fort becomes also a trading post. The troops remain in the area for nearly one month; however, many descend the river to return to St. Louis, where they receive their discharges on 16 October 1814.

Major Taylor, in his report to General Howard, states that three of his men received mortal wounds during the mission and that eight others sustained serious wounds. In praise of his command, Taylor also states:

> I am much indebted to the officers for their prompt obedience to orders, nor do I believe a braver set of men could have been collected than those who compose this detachment. But, sir, I conceive it would have been madness in me, as well as a direct violation of my orders, to have risked the detachment without a prospect of success. I believe I should have been fully able to have accomplished your views if the enemy had not been supplied with artillery, and so advantageously posted as to render it impossible for us to have dislodged him without imminent danger of the loss of the whole detachment.

During 1815, treaties of peace are signed with the Sacs and Fox Indians at Portage des Sioux on the 13th and 14th of September. During the signing of the pacts, it become clear that some of the Sacs had never strayed from a previous treaty made during 1804, and that they never engaged in hostilities against the Americans. They chose to remove themselves from Black Hawk and relocate along the Missouri River.

In 1816, the Americans establish Fort Armstrong at Prairie du Chien, constructed with logs and stones. The post also contains block houses. Fort Armstrong remains active during the Black Hawk War and beyond until 1836. During 1832, the Treaty of Fort Armstrong is signed there by General Winfield Scott and Governor John Reynolds on behalf of the United States. The Sac and Fox Indians, by terms of the treaty, agree to peace with the United States, and they agree to move to a reservation. During the Civil War, the Rock Island Arsenal is established there in 1862, and from 1863 through 1865, the post is also used to hold Confederate prisoners. At present, the U.S. Army operates the Rock Island Arsenal Museum, which covers the history of the fort from the Black Hawk War. Other points of interest at the former fort include a Confederate cemetery and the Rock Island National Cemetery.

September 5 (Monday)   In New York, at Albany, Governor Tompkins writes to General Lewis seeking assistance for a recently organized unit: "Sir: The Corps of Sea Fencibles destined for the Block Houses in Gravesend bay is organized and ready to take possession of their quarters. Will you have the goodness to give the necessary orders for them to take possession, to be finished with ammunition & rations, & to give them directions with respect to their reporting to Colo. Bogardus or at Headquarters."

In naval activity, the schooner *James* (Eli Crawford, master) is intercepted and seized by the HMS *Niemen*. At the time of its capture, the *James* is transporting a cargo of flour.

September 5–11   In New York, General Sir George Prevost and his force of about 14,000 men (most had served with Wellington) reach the vicinity of Plattsburgh. Prevost pauses to await the British fleet to attack the American force of approximately 4,000 to 4,500, under General Alexander Macomb. Prevost has proclaimed his intent to conquer the area of New York stretching southward to Ticonderoga. He also demands that the inhabitants discard their allegiance to the United States, and the edict demands that the people give his force supplies. Meanwhile, Commodore Downie's squadron, constructed on the Sorel, is moving onto Lake Champlain.

Prevost's force, advancing in two columns, led by Major General Manley Powers and Major General Thomas Brisbane, encroaches the town. A contingent of regulars and militia led by Major (later major general) John E. Wool, deployed the previous night, meet the attack as it advances along Beekmantown Road. Wool's riflemen commence fire and Prevost's vanguard (right wing) is driven back to the main body. Shortly thereafter, a British surge forces Wool's contingent to pull back to the opposite (south) side of the Saranac River. The Americans demolish the bridges after crossing. Wool redeploys at a stone mill near Culver's Hill, and when the British move to bolt across the river, riflemen forbid passing. A contingent of young men and boys,

John E. Wool.

General Alexander Macomb.

known as Aiken's volunteers, had been offering resistance by firing from the woods and behind fences. They deployed at the mill after the Americans were driven back across the river. During the skirmish, British Lt. Colonel James Wellington and Ensign P. Chapman are killed. Wool's force also sustains some casualties. He decides his positions might become untenable if the British move to strike his flank. The contingent withdraws to Halsey's Corner. Once there, Wool is reinforced by Captain James Leonard's command, which is accompanied by two pieces of artillery. The British resume their advance, and once again, the column comes under heavy fire from the cannon, which catapults three shots that strike effectively. However, despite sustaining more casualties, the British have not yet resigned themselves to halt.

The bugles blare and they initiate a charge that compels Leonard to retreat hurriedly. One British officer, Lieutenant Kingsbury, sustains a severe wound. He is carried to a farmhouse belonging to Isaac C. Platt; dies on the following day. Lt. Kingsbury is interred on the farm, but later during 1844, his remains are re-interred in the village cemetery. Meanwhile, during the fighting, militia under General Mooers arrives. On the following morning, Colonel David B. McNeil arrives to bolster Wool with his contingent of militia. Prevost blinks. He halts his advance, orders supplies to be brought up and initiates work on establishing batteries that can eliminate the obstacle on the south bank. In the meantime, while Wool halts the progress of Prevost's right wing, his left wing encounters a contingent of riflemen and cavalry under Lt. Colonel Daniel Appling. The 13th Regiment under Captain John Sproul, deployed at Dead Man's Creek, intercepts Prevost's left wing. Lt. Colonel Appling, supported by a contingent of New York cavalry and a detachment of riflemen, take the point to observe the British advance. The contingent under Appling is supported by gunboats, and the British column moving on the left along a road close to the lake comes under heavy effective fire. Nevertheless, the British react by deploying riflemen in some houses along the north bank of the river; however, the Americans terminate their fire by destroying the houses by hot shot. The resistance succeeds in derailing Prevost's progress, and he remains unwilling to launch his full-scale attack until the squadron arrives.

During the waiting period, Prevost, while at his headquarters at Allen's farmhouse, begins to construct batteries, and he finalizes his plans for the seizure of Plattsburgh. Prevost's headquarters stand on the opposite bank of the Saranac River about a mile from Fort Brown; however, he refuses to cross the river for the main attack without the presence of the British squadron. Nonetheless, there is some contact with the Americans on the 7th and the 9th. Later, on the 11th, Commodore Downie's fleet arrives and Prevost becomes jubilant.

The young troops in Aiken's volunteers continue to participate until the battle for Plattsburgh terminates. Afterward, General Alexander Macomb promises each of the boys a rifle. The promise is kept; however, Congress does not get around to fulfilling it until May 1826.

Major Wool is promoted to brigadier general in 1847 and major general in 1862. He serves in the Mexican War and the Civil War, retiring during the latter on 1 August 1863. He dies on 10 November 1869 at age 85.

September 6 (Tuesday) In Maryland, American guns are entrenched at Indian Head as the British fleet passes en route to Baltimore, but they escape unharmed. Gordon's British fleet is still around to aid the assault against Fort McHenry and Baltimore. Meanwhile, at Baltimore, work on fortifying the city continues for the attack that is expected. Even British newspapers and politicians have been boasting about the doom intended for the city. One statesman proclaimed that Baltimore is "the great depository of the hostile spirit of the United States against England." One of the newspapers in London printed: "The American navy must be annihilated; their arsenals and dock yards must be consumed; and the truculent inhabitants of Baltimore must be tamed with the weapons which shook the wooden turrets of Copenhagen." And another newspaper in London had declared its opinion by printing: "If any towns are to suffer, they should be the objects, in order to crush a large body of privateer shipping in Baltimore, and in Washington to destroy a pretty well supplied arsenal, and thus prevent Congress meeting there again, an event much and generally wished for by the people of New York, Philadelphia and the Eastern States."

Nonetheless, in Baltimore, the inhabitants had galvanized. The military and civilian volunteers have been working non-stop to guarantee that the British do not establish winter quarters in Baltimore as General Ross had proclaimed; rather that they do not even spend a night in the city. The fortifications include two lines of breastworks that stretch northward from Harris Creek to a point beyond Loudenslager's Hill (known also as Hamstead's Hill). The length of the line is about one mile, and at close intervals, half-moon batteries are erected in which artillery pieces on field carriages are deployed. Slightly behind the two lines on higher ground, the Americans construct several other batteries, one of which becomes known as Rodger's Bastion, which stands above Fort McHenry on the harbor side of Paterson Park. On the north side of the city, the border line is dotted with rifle pits. Nearby other bastions and batteries are built to provide protection for the riflemen. The defensive measures also include the water approaches. Batteries are located at Lazaretto Point and Canton, as well as another between Canton and the fort.

Other precautions include having vessels intentionally sunk at the mouth of the harbor off what later becomes Winan's Point. The approach to the rear of the fort is guarded by two redoubts, Fort Covington (named in honor of Brigadier General Leonard Covington, killed on 13 November 1813) and the City Battery. The defenses there are further bolstered by another battery (Circular Battery) of seven guns, deployed in the rear of the two redoubts on high ground near the foot of Light Street (later Battery Square). And yet other precautions are taken, including Water Battery directly in front of Fort McHenry. The 42-pounder guns at the Water Battery had been acquired on loan from the French consul.

Nonetheless, the fate of Baltimore still rests upon the ability of the Americans to hold the above mentioned defenses. Commodore Rodgers, commander of the batteries and entrenchments, states in his official reports:

> In the general distribution of the forces employed in the defence of Baltimore, with the concurrence of the commanding general, I stationed Lieutenant Gamble, first of the *Guerriere*, with about one hundred seamen, in command of a seven-gun battery, on the line between the roads leading from Philadelphia and Sparrow's Point.
> Sailing-Master De La Zouch of the *Erie* and Midshipman Field of the *Guerriere*, with twenty seaman, command a two-gun battery fronting the road leading from Sparrow's Point. Sailing Master Ramage of the *Guerriere*, with twenty seamen, in command of a five-gun battery, to the right of the Sparrow's Point Road. And Midshipman Salter, with twelve seamen, in command of a one-gun battery, a little to the right of Mr. Ramage. Lieutenant Kuhn, with the detachment of marines belonging to the *Guerriere*, was posted in the entrenchment between the batteries occupied by Lieutenant Gamble and Sailing-Master Ramage. Lieutenant Newcomb, third of the *Guerriere*, with eighty seamen, occupied Fort Covington, on the Ferry Branch, a little below Spring Gardens. Sailing-Master Webster, of the flotilla, with fifty seamen of that corps, occupied a six-gun battery on the Ferry Branch known by the name of Babcock. Lieutenant Frazier, of the flotilla, with forty-five seamen of the same corps, occupied a three-gun battery near the Lazaretto.

In naval activity, the USS *Scorpion*, commanded by Midshipman Henry E. Turner, which has been operating on Lake Erie and Lake Huron since May, is caught off guard. The British, having seized the USS *Tigress* several days ago, approach the *Scorpion* on Lake Huron and seize it. Afterward, the *Tigress* and the *Scorpion* are taken to Mackinac. The *Scorpion* is taken into the Royal Navy as the 4-gun schooner *Confiance*.

There is no supporting evidence to the legend reported by the U.S. Navy that the *Scorpion* and *Tigress* are later sunk in Georgian Bay in Lake Huron, off Penetanguishene, Ontario. In other activity, the brigantine USS *Surprise*, built during the summer of 1814 for service with Commodore Thomas Macdonough's squadron, is renamed the USS *Eagle*. Also, the HMS *Wasp* recaptures the 207-ton vessel *Snow Alexander*.

September 6–9 *In naval activity,* the British squadron transporting General Ross' army departs Benedict, Maryland, at dawn, but Baltimore is not the destination. The fleet attempts to disguise its target by sailing toward the Chesapeake from the Patuxent and entering the Potomac on the 7th. They move upriver for two days to confuse the Americans, and on the 9th of September, they change course and sail back to the Chesapeake, from where the ships move toward the mouth of the Patapsco. It is a cunning scheme; however, at Baltimore, there is no doubt that the British are coming.

September 7 (Wednesday) **In New York** at Plattsburgh, General Prevost dispatches a column to probe the American positions on the opposite side of the Saranac River. The column, under Captain Noadie, selects a crossing about five miles west of Plattsburgh. A contingent of Colonel Miller's regiment under Captain Vaughn intercepts the column and forces it to abort the mission.

In naval activity, the 333-ton ship *Betsy* (W.H. Bennett, master), carrying a cargo of pepper and betel nuts, is intercepted and recaptured by the HMS *Pylades*.

September 8 (Thursday) *In naval activity,* a British squadron — including the HMS *Bacchante,* HMS *Pictou,* HMS *Rifleman* and the HMS *Tenedos* — captures the schooner *Fox* at Machias, Maine. During the raid, the British confiscate a variety of meat, including beef and pork, which is loaded onto the *Fox* before they sail the prize to St. John's, New Brunswick. The *Fox* is separate from the sloop *Fox* seized 5 December 1814.

September 9 (Friday) **In Massachusetts,** the defenders at Old Stone Fort in Rockfort are caught by surprise when the HMS *Nymph,* standing near the edge of Cape Ann at dawn, sends a contingent ashore to seize the post. Two barges carry the raiding party ashore at Bearskin Neck. Once the Redcoats are spotted, the bell in the church rings incessantly to sound the alarm. The British on one of the barges react by firing at the belfry. One of the shells strikes a post of the steeple, where it remains as a permanent visible sight. The British seize the fort.

In Pennsylvania, Thomas Cadwalader is commissioned as brigadier general of the Pennsylvania 1st Brigade, 1st Division. He succeeds General George Bartram, who resigned.

In New York at Plattsburgh, during the ongoing siege, a contingent of the 15th Regiment under Captain George McGlassin departs Fort Brown opposite General Prevost's positions. The Americans ford the Saranac River and launch a surprise raid that catches a British work party off guard. The British sustain one officer and six troops killed. Several others are wounded. The British abandon their project, leaving the Americans the opportunity of destroying the works and spiking the guns of the battery without any heavy skirmishing. Once the area is destroyed, the Americans return to the fort with no casualties.

In naval activity, the privateer *General Armstrong* sails from Sandy Hook, New York, at about midnight (9th–10th). It is commanded by Captain Samuel Reid, U.S. Navy, and his officers include 1st Lt. Frederick Worth (brother of William Jenkins Worth); 2nd Lt. Alexander O. Williams, and 3rd Lt. Robert Johnson. The vessel moves out to sea at Sandy Hook and succeeds in penetrating the British blockade. For about two weeks the cruise is uneventful; however, it encounters a British squadron in the Azores on the 25th.

September 10 (Saturday) **In Maryland,** the Americans gain intelligence that a British fleet of about 50 sail had been spotted in Chesapeake Bay moving toward Baltimore. General Winder dispatches a force to the city and militia begin to arrive from neighboring areas. Command of the forces is given to General Samuel Smith, a Revolutionary War veteran, who was made a brigadier general of Maryland militia at the close of the war. Fort McHenry becomes crowded. Over 1,000 men are crammed inside the walls awaiting the imminent British assault, and thousands more are deployed at Baltimore to meet the threat.

In Pennsylvania at Philadelphia, Governor Simon Butler writes to Acting Secretary of War James Monroe regarding the defenses of the city to inform him that about 600 volunteers had arrived and others are en route, and that General Bloomfield is organizing a camp at Marcus Hook slightly outside the city.

In naval activity, the schooner *Betsy* (H. Geyar, master) en route from Boston to Machias, Maine, with flour and provisions, is halted and captured by the HMS *Alban*. In other naval activity, the British privateer *Lively* seizes the schooner *Industry* (Moses Brown, master), while it is en route from Halifax to New England. The prize and its cargo of dry goods are taken into port at Liverpool. The *Industry* is separate from the schooner *Industry* captured 20 August 1813, the schooner *Industry* seized 3 November 1813, and the sloop *Industry* captured on 16 January 1815.

Also, the British privateer *Lunenburg* seizes the *Sandbird* (Nathaniel Pearley, master). Also, the American privateer *General Armstrong,* one day out of Sandy Hook, spots an unidentified vessel and chases it for about nine hours. Once the vessel is intercepted, it is found to be the unarmed American privateer *Perry* (Captain John Coleman) out of Baltimore. Captain Coleman explains that his guns were thrown overboard while outrunning a British blockading vessel after it departed from Philadelphia six days before. The *General Armstrong* resumes its cruise, while the *Perry* returns to port to acquire new arms. Departing again under the command of Captain R. McDonald, the *Perry* succeeds in 22 prizes, primarily in the West Indies, including two brigantines, four schooners and 16 sloops. Of the prizes, one is transferred to the prisoners and 18 are destroyed at sea. The others are taken into port with prize crews.

September 11 (Sunday) THE BATTLE OF LAKE CHAMPLAIN (BATTLE OF PLATTSBURGH) **In New York** at Plattsburgh, the American defenders brace for a full scale attack by General Prevost's

Forts and batteries at Plattsburgh.

General Thomas Macdonough.

General Benjamin Mooers.

army; however, the dire circumstances become more grave when a British fleet under Commodore Downie arrives off Cumberland Head near the entrance to Plattsburgh Bay. General Alexander Macomb remains cautious but optimistic that the British can be repulsed. Up to this day, Macomb's forces have held Prevost's army from crossing the Saranac River, but General Prevost breathes a little easier as the British ensign comes into view as it approaches Cumberland Head and Prevost spots the formidable British fleet. Prevost immediately orders his force to prepare to launch the assault. He orders two brigades to cross the Saranac.

The American defenders include about 3,400 men; however, about 1,400 of the troops are either invalids or considered non-combatants. Some of Macomb's infantry are deployed aboard Macdonough's ships and are being used as Marines. The units involved include contingents of the 6th, 29th, 30th, 31st, 33rd and 34th Regiment, along with one company of the 15th Regiment. Other units include a company of light artillery under Captain Leonard and a small contingent of the 13th Regiment. Macomb is also bolstered by a series of forts, including Fort Moreau, Fort Brown, a redoubt known as Fort Scott, a battery and a pair of blockhouses. Fort Moreau is commanded by Colonel Melancton Smith, the son of Judge Smith. Fort Brown is commanded by Lieutenant Colonel Storrs and Fort Brown is commanded by Major Vinson. General Macomb has also taken other precautions by dispatching a messenger to Vermont to request that Governor Martin Chittenden speed reinforcements, and he had ordered Captain John Sproul with a contingent of the 13th Regiment, bolstered by two artillery pieces, to deploy at Dead Man's Creek. Lt. Colonel Appling, supported by a contingent of New York cavalry and a detachment of riflemen, is ordered to the front to observe the British advance. In addition, General Macomb requests that General Mooers call out the New York militia. (*See also*, **September 5–11**.)

The British armada under Commodore George Downie, equipped with massive firepower, closes. The British remain aware of an American naval force to the front; however, they consider the squadron to be only a puny ensemble of floating driftwood, manned by inferior seamen incapable of standing up to the Royal Navy.

Lieutenant Thomas Macdonough, the commander of the American squadron, composed of fourteen vessels, holds his force in place at the southern portion of the lake. MacDonough, seasoned by the Tripolitan pirates and taught by the likes of Stephen Decatur and Edward Preble, possesses no fear of the superior force. He also has no qualms about seeking divine assistance.

Plan of action, Lake Champlain.

Macdonough gathers on deck with his officers, and just before his guns begin to roar, the group prays for help from God.

The American squadron is spread out, making it impossible for the British fleet to move into the bay without victimizing Macdonough's naval force. The entire enemy fleet is susceptible to being broadsided during the advance to break through. Every U.S. ship has its bow pointing to the north, with the 20-gun USS *Eagle* holding the point, accompanied by the 26-gun *Saratoga*, 17-gun *Ticonderoga*, followed by the 9-gun (seven 12-pounders and two 18-pounders) USS *Preble*. The *Preble* is deployed extremely close to a shoal, blocking any opportunity for a British vessel to sail around it. Macdonough has also deployed his ten gunboats within his line near the intervals that separate the larger warships. Macdonough's fourteen vessels carry a total of 86 guns and about 850 men. In contrast, the British fleet is composed of four large warships carrying 75 guns, and it is bolstered by 12 gunships with 20 more guns. The crews of Commodore Downie's fleet number about 1,050 men.

Battle of Plattsburgh.

Lt. Macdonough at the Battle of Lake Champlain (*Battles of America by Sea and Land, Volume II*, Robert Tomes, 1878).

Meanwhile, in the bay, Macdonough has his ship, the *Saratoga*, positioned somewhat peculiarly by "laying a kedge anchor broad off each of her bows and carrying the hawsers to the quarters." By manipulating its hawsers, the ship's stern is effortlessly and quickly turned in any direction, while the cable controlling the main anchor holds the ship bow in a stationary position. Consequently, the *Saratoga* is poised to deliver a broadside at any point in an instant.

As the conflict reaches the point of ignition, two of the British warships are firing as they close; however, the 36-gun HMS *Confiance* holds until it is less than one-half mile away, then it drops anchor commences fire. Meanwhile, the gunners aboard the USS *Eagle* have become over anxious. They fire without having been given the signal. The shots fall short of the targets. Anxiousness spreads to a caged rooster aboard the *Saratoga*. The bird manages to get out of his cage and shortly thereafter, as a cannon fires, the rooster lands on a gun slide, and as if trying to rally the crew, he begins to crow while rapidly flapping his wings. The bird turned entertainer brings a flash of levity into the desperate encounter. The crew reacts to the bird's antics by raising three cheers while they erupt in laughter.

While the diversion gives the crew a good laugh, Macdonough has retained his focus on the enemy. A long gun sighted by Macdonough bellows and the shell is propelled directly toward the *Confiance*. It strikes with deadly accuracy as it plows into the deck, severs its anchor cable and demolishes its helm. Once the *Saratoga* fires, the remainder of his squadron follows suit. Meanwhile, the *Confiance* fires a broadside at the *Saratoga* from point-blank range. The *Saratoga* sustains damage and fatalities; however, the some of the crew brave the danger to get the wounded below deck before returning to their stations. The British gunners are not yet seasoned and after discharging the first broadside, they neglect to reset the elevation of the gun barrels. Consequently, the shots that follow reach higher elevation. The *Saratoga*'s rigging takes a beating, but not the ship's structure. Nonetheless, the British return fire remains heavy and the engagement is elevated from the preliminaries to a full-scale conflagration. The broadside from the *Confiance* inflicts about 40 casualties upon the *Saratoga*. The sea becomes obscured by smoke and fire. The thunderous roar of the opposing guns adds more fury to the battle; however, within about 15 minutes, it becomes clear that Macdonough's line had held.

The lead British vessel, HMS *Finch*, having incurred severe damage, strikes its colors and drifts onto a shoal close to Crabland. The Americans also gain the *Chub*. Macdonough's force also suffers. British weapons on the 16-gun HMS *Linnet* sever the *Eagle*'s springs and are set to inflict more damage until the *Saratoga* intervenes and plasters the *Linnet*'s deck, forcing its commander, Captain D. Pring, to strike its colors. The commanding officer of the *Eagle*, Lt. Henley, makes some adjustments, then positions the *Eagle* to the rear of the *Saratoga*, between it and the Ticonderoga. During the blistering combat, the *Preble* does not escape harm. British gunboats focus on it and they knock the *Preble* from its position, placing some additional temporary pressure on the remainder of the line. However, the gap is immediately blocked when the other ships make adjustments.

In the meantime, the British guns continue to pummel the *Saratoga*, and every gun on the starboard side is knocked out of action. Nonetheless, because of the way Macdonough has rigged the *Saratoga*, he is able to maneuver the cables to swing the vessel around to commit his operational guns. The maneuver is completed in a short span of time, permitting Macdonough to race back into action. The British see the *Saratoga* swing like a merry-go-round and within minutes the *Confiance* is shellacked with fresh broadsides that inflict more heavy damage.

The *Confiance* attempts to duplicate Macdonough's actions; however, the attempt is unsuccessful. After about two hours, the crew of the HMS *Confiance* strikes the colors. With the capitulation of the *Confiance*, the remaining British ships also capitulate; however, the British galleys are able to move away and escape down the lake before the Americans can board them to take possession. The Americans' inferior squadron suddenly dominates the sea, to the dismay of British General Prevost, who sees his grand vision of victory dissipate at the instant the colors are lowered on the *Confiance*, the same instant that boisterous resounding cheers of the Americans ring in Prevost's ears. Throngs of people watch from the Vermont shoreline.

Back on the ground, General Prevost orders about 8,000 men to advance toward the fort on the north bank. The British are delayed at three separate points where two bridges had been destroyed. They attempt a crossing at a fourth point, known as Pike's Cantonment. British artillery is activated to provide cover fire. Nonetheless, the troops find it extremely difficult to advance toward the bank. Americans on the opposite bank unleash a steady stream of fire to confound the Redcoats. The British encounter a wall of fire originating from the forts and blockhouses near the lower bridge, and at the upper bridge, American riflemen also prevent a crossing.

At Pike's Cantonment, the thrust by regulars against the militia finally grants some success on the fourth attempt to ford the river. The Redcoats gain the other bank and presume that the militia as usual had fled toward the Salmon River, giving Prevost a path to the objective. However, the British receive an unpleasant surprise. The militia, after being driven back, reorganizes and is reinforced by volunteers under General Samuel Strong from Vermont that had been sent by the governor. By then the militia is also augmented by two artillery pieces under Lieutenant Sumpter. After regrouping, the Americans prepare to launch their counterattack. At the same time, they receive good news. Chancellor Walworth, adjutant general of General Benjamin Mooers' division, arrives with word that the U.S. fleet had defeated the British and had capitulated. The militia, rejuvenated after learning of the tremendous victory in the bay, bolts forward and begins to thump the British.

Nearly all of the British who fail to surrender lose their lives. Those who survive the iron wave of driving militia flee back across the river. Meanwhile, British artillery maintains its steady fire, but General Prevost fails to make another attempt to cross the river. This assures total victory for General Macomb. An artillery exchange continues between the British and the guns at Fort Brown until about dusk.

The British scheme to conquer territory in New York and Vermont is foiled, and the American militia plays a key part in defeating the enemy. The British gunboats head back to Canada and General Prevost immediately terminates the campaign and initiates the long march back to Canada. McDonough's victorious seamen pay a price to preserve the state. The navy sustains 52 killed and 58 wounded. The British report losing 57 killed, including Commodore Downie, and they also have 72 wounded. However, Lieutenant McDonough's report lists British casualties at 84 killed and 110 wounded.

According to a report of General Alexander Macomb: "The loss of the enemy in killed, wounded, prisoners and deserters, since his first appearance [at Plattsburgh on 6 September] cannot fall short of 2,500, including many officers, among whom is Colonel Wellington of the Buffs." General Benjamin Mooers, later this year, is awarded a sword for his actions at Plattsburgh (*see also*, **December 24 In New York**).

Also, news of McDonough's stunning victory is sped to the U.S. negotiators in Ghent, Belgium, to provide them with the political ammunition they need to equalize the British arrogance. The British had raised the stakes, but their gamble failed. Consequently, the American victory on Lake Champlain increases the negotiators' bargaining power.

At Ghent, the British reluctantly listen to the Americans dispel any thoughts of relinquishing territory to Britain. The U.S. negotiators also insist upon a settlement that retains the territory as it stood prior to the outbreak of war. Also, the captured *Linnet*, built earlier this year, was initially named the *Niagara*. It is taken into service by the U.S. Navy; however, by the time its repairs are completed, the war is over. It remains in ordinary at Whitehall, New York, until it is sold in 1825. The *Preble*, which had sustained major damage, remains out of service following the battle. It is sold at Whitehall, New York, during July 1815. The USS *Saratoga*, laid up until after the war, is sold during 1825. Also, Joseph Smith, promoted to lieutenant (later rear admiral), participates aboard the *Eagle*.

September In New York, Following the battle at Plattsburgh, the Americans will establish Fort Tompkins and Fort Gaines, named for Governor Daniel D. Tompkins and General Edmond Gaines. They join three other forts built prior to the siege. Fort Tompkins is built southwest of Fort Brown and Fort Gaines is positioned south of Fort Scott between Lake Champlain and Tompkins. The British headquarters during this period are near the mouth of the Saranac River on the property of the Kent-de Lord House.

September 11–14 SIEGE OF FORT MCHENRY In Maryland at Baltimore, a British fleet of about 50 vessels arrives off North Point, placing General Ross' army about 14 miles by land from Baltimore and the fleet about 12 miles from the harbor. At 0300 on the 12th, the ships lower the boats and the ground troops are carried to shore under the protection of several brigantines, which are at anchor close to the beach. The entire landing force is ashore by 0700. The morale of the troops remains high due to their anxiousness to be rewarded with plunder. The officers, too, are eager to fly the British colors over Fort McHenry, once they dislodge the militia as they did at Bladensburg. Each man in the columns is provided with cooked provisions intended to last three days. They also carry 80 rounds of ammunition, a spare shirt and one blanket. Meanwhile, riders are en route to the city. Upon their arrival, the alarm is spread. At the courthouse green, three cannon shots signal the danger. Simultaneously, church bells begin to ring. The Reverend John Gruber of the Light Street Methodist Church, upon hearing that the British are close, states: "May the Lord bless King George, convert him, and take him to heaven, as we want no more of him."

In and around the city, the defenders have been working feverishly to bolster the defenses. By the time British arrive later this day, about 5,000 troops are deployed in the defenses. About 1,000 troops are packed into Fort McHenry.

Major General Samuel Smith, commander of the Baltimore defenses, orders General John

General George Armistead.

General John Stricker.

Stricker to move out on a reconnaissance mission. Stricker's brigade, composed primarily of Baltimore militia, includes the 5th Regiment (550 troops under Lt. Colonel Joseph Sterrett); 6th Regiment (620 troops under Lt. Colonel William McDonald); 27th Regiment (500 troops under Lt. Colonel Kennedy Long); 39th Regiment (450 men under Lt. Colonel Benjamin Fowler); and the 51st Regiment (700 men under Lt. Colonel Henry Amey). Stricker's brigade also includes 150 riflemen led by Captain William B. Dyer, along with a 140-man cavalry contingent led by Lt. Colonel James Biays and the Union artillery commanded by Captain John Montgomery. Montgomery's artillery men add 75 troops to the brigade, and they possess six 4-pounders.

General Stricker's mission is to reconnoiter the route leading to North Point and to assign the cavalry the responsibility of moving in close to observe the British positions. The brigade departs Baltimore at 1500 and treks along the old Philadelphia Road to the intersection with Long Log Lane (later North Point Road). Once there, Stricker leads the brigade to the vicinity of Bear Creek, where night quarters are established at the Methodist meeting house. However, Stricker pushes his cavalry ahead to spy on the British camp. He also directs Dyer's riflemen to deploy near some pine woods about two miles beyond the meeting house. The militia is poised to intercept General Ross, but Baltimore also faces a severe threat from the sea. Admiral Alexander Cochrane's naval force is preparing to attack Fort McHenry from the sea.

The night is consumed with uncertainty for the Americans and the British alike. Baltimore must be held, for if it falls, the British scheme to link the forces of Ross and Cochrane with those in New York under Commodore Downie and General Prevost in a massive pincer movement to strangle the American resistance and regain their lost colonies. The temporary tranquility combined with the darkness seemingly increases the anxiety of the defenders.

Meanwhile, the British at North Point experience similar tension as the invasion force awaits dawn to debark and roll into Baltimore. Admiral Cochrane encounters problems because of the low depth of the water approach to Fort McHenry, which will hinder the operation. The frigates and bomb-ships will have to force their way through any obstacles to gain domination on the river and commence the attack. Cochrane directs the larger vessels to anchor off North Point. Nevertheless, among the British command, enthusiasm is high, and as a follow up to Bladensburg and the invasion of the capital, the troops, who sleep with their clothes on, enthusiastically await dawn to deliver the final blow.

General Ross remains extremely optimistic and even has time to enjoy his breakfast.

In the meantime, a small party of Captain Biay's cavalry inadvertently strays into British lines. The British order them to surrender, but the Americans refuse, and suddenly their horses bolt over a fence, permitting the detachment to escape. Nonetheless, the ground is unfamiliar to them. The troops (William B. Buchanan, James Gittings, and Richard Dorsey) encounter a Negro man near a church. They offer him money if he will direct them to the Baltimore Road. He accepts the offer and tells the men he will return shortly. Unfortunately, he keeps only half of his promise. The man does quickly return; however, he is accompanied by British regulars who trap the American cavalrymen, and at the point of muskets and bayonets, they are compelled to surrender.

By this time, about 0800, the Redcoats, each carrying 80 rounds of ammunition, begin to roll forward. The splendid uniforms and near-perfect formation at times is sufficient to cause militia to scatter, but in his instance, General Stricker's men stand ready to test their mettle against Britain's elite troops.

Ross directs a light brigade, commanded by Major Jones (4th Regiment), to take the point as vanguard. An artillery unit transporting six horse-drawn guns trails, with the 2nd brigade just behind the artillery, and it is followed by the sailors, with the third brigade holding the rear. It is an amazing sight to behold as the seemingly unending red wave flows uninterrupted toward Baltimore.

The vanguard spots what is obviously breastworks at a slim part of the peninsula. The obstacle causes the British to use caution. From the front, facing the works, the British ascertain that it extends across for a distance of about one mile between the river and a creek and that the flanks are naturally protected by water and dense woods. The column halts to ensure the rear is not lagging too far behind. Nonetheless, while the British prepare for action, it becomes unnecessary. The works are incomplete and the Americans had abandoned the position.

At about the same time, the squad that earlier captured the three American cavalry troops arrives with their prisoners, and they are immediately taken to General Ross, who interrogates them. The prisoners seem unintimidated by the general and retain the presence of mind to falsify their responses. In regard to Ross' inquiry about troop strength, they inflate the number to 20,000 defenders. Ross is unimpressed, and with a sniff of condescension responds: "But they are mainly militia I presume." Ross's expectations rise when the troops inform him that his assessment is correct. Triumphantly, Ross declares that he will "take Baltimore if it rains militia." To underscore his intent, Ross also proclaims that he would "eat dinner tonight at Baltimore, or in hell."

British morale begins to soar when they realize the obstacle is abandoned. They anticipate a rerun of Bladensburg; however, unknown to the British, the ground had been abandoned due to being untenable if utilized only as a defensive position, and the American strategy is defense with no intent to take the offense. Nonetheless, for the time, the illusion that fear caused the abandonment inflates the British, who expect a quick victory and a double celebration when the British ensign is nearly simultaneously hoisted in Baltimore and over Fort McHenry.

The column resumes the march, but after advancing only about one mile, the British quite unexpectedly discover that the Americans surely had not fled. The vanguard comes under heavy fire. In a flash, a rider races to the rear with orders to have the trailing brigades accelerate their advance. Meanwhile, as the British are forced to adjust their plans to meet the threat, their nemesis, General Stricker, is unfolding his battle plan. The British, who still cling to their rigid European formations, are under fire from troops in the woods. The terrain is flat, which prohibits the officers farther back from determining the strength of the American force, leaving for the moment suspense as to whether this is a minor skirmish or a full-scale attack.

The British speed toward the front; however, the merriment has dissipated. During this period, while the forward rush is underway, yet another rider arrives from the front to deliver solemn news. General Ross, who only recently proclaimed that he would either have dinner in Baltimore or in hell, would not be dining in the city. An American sharpshooter had struck him with a mortal wound. The word of Ross' demise reverberates through the column as if lightning had struck.

The shock is powerful and suddenly the sea of Redcoats, rocked by the death of their general, realizes that the quest for Baltimore will not be a rerun of Bladensburg. For some, the news of Ross' death does not immediately sink in; however, it becomes an indelible memory when Ross' riderless horse passes by and the troops see his blood-covered saddle. The sniper took aim just as Ross responded to the sounds of the fire and rushed to the point. Soon after, the troops that reach the point are also able to see the general along the side of the road during his final moments. Colonel Arthur Brooke immediately assumes command. He is an outstanding soldier; however, he is also much more cautious than Ross, and his new responsibility is accepted reluctantly.

Desperate efforts are undertaken to get General Ross back to the fleet. Nonetheless, the wound to his thigh takes his life before those transporting him can reach the boats. For the British, it was as if a cloud of gloom descended upon the entire army; however, there is no time to mourn. Colonel Brooke of the 44th Regiment resumes operations to evict the blocking force and proceed to Baltimore.

The British army remains under observation by the Americans. Their commander, General Stricker, remains composed and disciplined, and he seems to possess an uncanny ability to know Brooke's next move before it is executed. There is a short lull in the battle as the American riflemen on the line are pushed back; however, the primary line stands resolute and stretches across the terrain on ground that is similar to the abandoned works, giving the Americans natural protection on both flanks, each of which is leaning upon small lakes. Their positions are also near woods for additional protection.

Colonel Brooke signals the advance and the Redcoats begin to close on Stricker's line. British artillery delivers its volleys during the advance and the American guns return fire. All the while, the American riflemen hold their fire. A nearby farmhouse is left unoccupied by Stricker, as are some other buildings, and during the deployment of the troops, he neglected to plant any troops to hold the barn. Stricker's left becomes his weakest link. Meanwhile, the British guns ignite fires in some of the buildings, including the barn. During this ongoing exchange of fire, the ground troops have yet to use their guns. The thunderclap created by the cannon and the flames from the fires create a colossal panorama of the horrors of war.

Stricker's artillery targets the British 21st Regiment with two of his guns, while others plaster the British guns and yet others pour into the 85th Regiment, along with British light companies. The path to Baltimore, thought to have been an easy trek, becomes a flaming smoke-choked highway, inundated with Americans that so far exhibit courage. The British ground troops await the order to plunge forward to collapse the line. Colonel Brooke, once aware that a contingent had reached the woods as ordered, signals the advance, which unleashes the Redcoats. British buglers from one end of the column to the other begin to blare, and suddenly the attack commences. During this crucial period, the British artillery and rockets finally affect the militia.

The British become recipients of a whirlwind of fire from Stricker's guns. Some fall, but the troops ignore the firestorm and push forward. The dogged advance brings the British to within 100 yards of the Americans; however, the militia holds in place. The exchange between the ground troops has yet to begin, leaving the British to continue to expect the militia to run. Finally, the Americans deliver a volley and continue firing incessantly. The British return fire; however, they are unable to bait Stricker into mounting a charge to provide the British with the opportunity to bludgeon the militia with fixed bayonets on the open field. All the while, General Stricker continues to scrutinize the battlefield to discern Brooke's strategy. After failing to pull Stricker into an open battle, the British continue the advance until only about twenty yards separates the two sides.

Despite the mounting British pressure from close range, the militia, to the surprise of the British, is still formed in a solid line. The British also observe that the line resembles regulars due to the precision of the movements. In a flash, the vision of the opposing troops becomes blurred. The area instantly becomes a huge cloud of smoke, reducing visibility to zero. The muskets roar and the skirmishers are compelled to fire blindly through the dense smoke. At irregular intervals during the deadly exchange, the breeze clears the smoke, but only briefly do the opponents catch a glimpse of their enemy.

By this time, General Stricker can see that his left is in jeopardy. There is some confusion there and the British succeed in making progress; however, Stricker orders a retreat. To the British, it appears as if victory is at hand. There is no disorder nor lack of discipline as the Americans withdraw. Stricker's force makes and orderly retreat to the next line of defense, the fringes of Baltimore. Stricker is able to carry out his artillery, except two pieces which are captured when the British kill the two commanding officers. Had the officers not been killed, those guns would also have been taken to Baltimore. Meanwhile, the British conclude that immediate pursuit would be in vain. While the Americans head for their fortified lines at the city, the British claim the day and establish camp, postponing their advance until the following day.

In the meantime, the other prong in the attack, Admiral Cochrane's fleet, is still a pernicious threat to Fort McHenry. Nonetheless, Major George Armistead, the commander of the fort, remains confident. He has been monitoring the British ships and discerns that the British will launch an attack this day (12th). Armistead's calculations are slightly off. Cochrane's guns remain silent throughout the night (12th-13th); however, at 0700 on the 13th, the British guns unleash a thunderous man-made storm that propels exploding projectiles that each weigh about 190 pounds.

Meanwhile, back at Baltimore, General Stricker's force regroups and prepares to again engage Colonel Brooke's army on the following day. The night passes quietly, but on the morning of the 13th, the bombardment of Fort McHenry is so powerful that it is felt at Stricker's positions. Some reports actually state that the sounds of the exploding shells of the British could be heard more than 100 miles away at Philadelphia. Back at the British camp, the troops, who had slept on the ground, were peppered throughout the night by a pesky rainstorm that began at about midnight and intensified as the night passed, causing alarm. The violent storm threatened to soak the troops' fire-locks. The troops get little rest. Reveille sounds during the predawn hours. By dawn, Brooke's column resumes the march anticipating fresh American resistance, prompting the British to proceed with caution. They encounter obstacles such as fallen trees, but the route remains free of American riflemen.

The lack of resistance increases the confidence of the advancing troops. Despite the absence of the enemy, the march of less than ten miles is tedious due to the difficulty in removing the fallen trees that block the road. By the time the column arrives within sight of General Stricker's positions, evening has arrived.

Colonel Brooke now has a good view of American positions. He does not require a second glance. The full force of General Samuel Smith is deployed and Brooke realizes that the army he faced on the previous day was only a corps. He also discerns that the figure of 20,000 defenders given to him from the captured cavalrymen appears to have been accurate. From his position to the front of the Americans' line, Baltimore is not visible due to a series of hills that form a prolonged ridge. That ridge now contains Smith's army, along with a conspicuous line of formidable breastworks that stretch along the entire ridge to its terminus at a fort with guns that dominate the river.

General Smith had bolstered these positions by constructing a series of redoubts that protect the right flank, while simultaneously giving the Americans dominating positions that control the entire path of ascent. Smith's defenders have about 100 pieces of glistening cannon poised to shred an attack force, besides having the ability to trap assault troops in a crossfire.

The ground standing between Brooke's positions is barren due to an operation that cleared the lumber to provide the Americans with what could be described as a killing field, waiting to claim its victims. Brooke realizes that a frontal attack in broad daylight would be suicidal. Brooke, with Admiral Cochrane, devises a scheme by which the fleet, after dark, would create a diversionary action to permit Brooke to launch his attack.

The modified British strategy is pragmatic compared to the consequences of a daylight assault without any naval support. The British still consider the Americans inferior fighters and they believe that if the Navy can silence the guns of the fort at the river, they can gain the position. The presence of the Redcoats, they contend, will be sufficient for them to roll over the defending column. Once accomplished, they expect the militia to abscond rather than face the British in close-quartered fighting on the ridge. They envision a flawless operation by the Royal Navy to ensure success and finally give them passage into Baltimore.

Nevertheless, communications with Admiral Cochrane make it unpleasantly clear to Colonel Brooke that the water is too shallow for the vessels to encroach the American positions, and the lighter ones would be prone to damage by vessels that had been sunk in the channel to block the fleet. Nonetheless, Cochrane sends a flotilla of barges and some other vessels to strike the western portion of the American lines. They create a half moon formation and begin a bombardment. Meanwhile, another contingent of craft, carrying about 1,200 troops, moves up the cove to a position past Fort McHenry to land the force and strike the rear of the fort; however, the diversionary action fails. The guns at Fort McHenry and those of City Battery and Fort Covington concentrate their combined power on bludgeoning the flotilla. The scheme fails and it also fails to provide Brooke with any support.

During this same period, Fort McHenry, Fort Covington, City Battery and other defensive positions continue to come under constant bombardment. Streams of powerful shells, rockets and mortars have been smashing into the fort for the entire day, and on one occasion, a solitary shell nearly brought victory to the British. Just after 1400, a British shell crashes into the magazine at the fort, which is holding one quarter of a million pounds of ammunition. Except for the fact that the shell failed to detonate, Fort McHenry would have been blown into oblivion.

By this time, the night sky is solid black; however, the ongoing storm continues to illuminate the darkness with irregular and frightful streaks of lightning, while the blazing naval guns create incessant flashes of light, and the soaring rockets add additional color to the grim darkness. The defenders at Fort McHenry are unable to see the ships; however, the Royal Navy remains outside of the range of the fort's guns, making it impossible for the Americans to return fire against the fleet.

The British gunners focus upon gun flashes to seek out their targets. The burnt orange streaks of fire that soar through the air, combined with the earth shattering noise of the guns, increases the terror even for the inhabitants who are able to watch the monstrous bombardment. The British guns pound the fort, but the bombardment is so powerful and violent that many homes in Baltimore are literally shaken. The British, however, are stymied. They have been halted on the ground and Fort McHenry continues to resist the monstrous bombardment. So far, the flag is still flying and at times can be spotted in the stark darkness nearly as a silhouette when the bombs and mortars explode.

To some, it would appear that the fort will resemble debris when dawn arrives and to others, including a lawyer, Francis Scott Key, the unharnessed fury of the guns is an optimistic sign. Key is aboard an American peace ship. He had been taken out to the British fleet to attempt the release of one of his friends, Dr. William Beanes and the British bombardment had commenced before he could get back to shore. Key remains anxious about whether the flag will be flying at dawn.

Meanwhile, back on shore at the British lines outside Baltimore, Colonel Brooke is compelled to call a war council. At about 0300 on the morning of the 14th, he issues the order to retreat, following the council's conclusion that an attack against the ridge, without the aid of the fleet, would by folly. The British and force retires but the campfires are left burning to create the illusion that their camp is active. The march back to the ships is not accompanied by any jubilance; however, en route, the storm that has pounded the troops since the night of the 12th finally relents. The skies clear and the moon reappears. During the somber retreat, the troops recross the battlefield. The scene is gruesome. Those who fell during the tenacious contest remain in place exactly where they were slain.

The British pause on the silent battlefield for about one hour before resuming the march. The pause is not without incident. The British spot a few Americans that appear motionless as they hang from the branches of trees. The men had climbed the trees and tied themselves to the tree to avoid falling. The British refuse quarter and the riflemen are shot and killed. Just after the march resumes, at about noon on the 14th, the column arrives at the spot where General Ross had been slain. At about the same time, a bugler sounds the alarm to signal an approaching enemy force. The troops prepare to engage and simultaneously, gunfire is heard. An American cavalry detachment had been dispatched to search for the retreating column. The cavalry strikes the rear-guard and captures two British troops; however, British artillery prompts the cavalry to retire with the prisoners. After the incident the retreat resumes and the column arrives at the boats on the morning of the 15th.

Back at Fort McHenry, the British bombardment continues until 0300 on the 14th. The British had propel about 1,500 to 1,800 of the gargantuan shells upon the fort. In addition, mortar boats constantly pound the fort. Generals Smith and Stricker hold on the outskirts of town, but throughout the remaining darkness, the fate of Fort McHenry remains in doubt. Outside the fort, the anxiety is rampant and the suspense agonizing. Nonetheless, when the sun begins to spring up from beyond the horizon, there is a huge sigh of relief. The Stars and Stripes is still flying.

Off in the distance, Francis Scott Key spots the flag when the morning mist evaporates. By that time, Major Armistead had replaced the fort's storm flag with the enormous flag that had been made for the post. It inspires Key to write a poem, initially untitled and first printed under the title "Defense of Fort McHenry;" however, it later is titled "The Star Spangled Banner." The poem is transformed into a song that afterward inspires millions of Americans. In 1931, it becomes by act of Congress the national anthem.

The Battle of Fort McHenry is sometimes referred to as the Battle of North Point or as the Battle of Long Log Lane. The successful repulse of the British fleet takes a toll on Major Armistead. He becomes ill and unable to even submit his after-action report. He recuperates and is able to return to duty in about two weeks.

The British report losses on land as 46 killed and 300 wounded. The Americans report 20 killed, 90 wounded and 47 missing; however the British also claim that when the fleet departed, it carried with it 200 Americans. Other sources give 290 British casualties and the Americans 213, with 50 captured.

September 12 (Monday) **In Maryland** at Baltimore, once it is ascertained that the British have retreated, orders are issued, most probably by General Smith, to dispatch the baggage wagons to the battlefield to gather the dead and the wounded. Word of the mission spreads, and by the time the wagons return, people are consumed with anxiety and their faces reflect extreme anguish as they search for their loved ones. The scene is indescribably agonizing as the bodies are placed on the ground alongside one another inside the entrenchments.

While the people scan the rows of the deceased troops, some women faint, while others are openly shedding tears and expressing their grief with cries, screams and sighs, blending in with the sounds of pained grief that can be heard all across the field. In one instance, an elderly man, described as being in his 70s or 80s, who arrives in search of his sons, discovers both among the dead. He does not faint, nor is he screaming; however, he is trembling as he bends over their bodies. A bystander inquires of the man if he had lost someone. The man replies while tears are flowing profusely down his face: "Yes sir, in the Revolution, I lost my father and two brothers, and here lie my two sons, but they have died in a good cause." (*See also,* **September 11–14** SIEGE OF FORT MCHENRY.)

In naval activity, the crew of the American privateer *Midas,* commanded by Captain Alexander Thompson, raids Royal Island in the Bahamas. A contingent transported to the beach in two boats attacks four separate settlements. The motive for the attack is thought to have been revenge for the British rampage in Washington, D.C., when much of the capital was burned by the British under General Ross. The raiders literally destroy everything in sight, leaving only one building standing. In addition, the Americans confiscate personal items and valuables from the citizens who had not been able to escape to safer positions further inland. The people that do make it into the woods include about 20 children.

The raiders even display arrogant disrespect for the dead by disturbing the tomb of the wife of the most well known planter on the island, Benjamin Barnett, for the sole purpose of obtaining booty. Even the terrorized civilians' fear gains no sympathy. While on the rampage, the Americans also make it known that had they been able to seize Benjamin Barnett, he would have been decapitated and that they would have incinerated his body. After the unconscionable raid, colonial British authorities dispatch official complaints to the American authorities.

Secretary of War James Monroe sends an official apology for the actions of Captain Thompson and his crew. The license (letter of marque) of Captain Thompson and of the privateer *Midas* is cancelled by President Madison. Until the time of the raid, Captain Thompson had been regarded as a reputable officer and his crew had not previously engaged in any uncivilized activity. Thompson had earlier seized enemy vessels off the Bahamas and all prisoners captured received good treatment.

September 12–15 SIEGE OF FORT BOWYER **In Alabama** at Mobile Point, a large British-Indian force composed of more than 500 Indians and other troops, including about 125 Royal Marines, is spotted near the fort on 12 September. The post is garrisoned by 160 troops under Major William Lawrence. After dark on the 12th, four British warships, carrying 92 guns, arrive in the area. On the 13th at about noon, the British and the Americans exchange fire, but no major ground assault is launched. During the afternoon of the 15th, the British again move against the fort, supported by the warships, with the *Hermes* commanded by Captain William Henry Percy (senior naval officer in the Gulf of Mexico) at the point. The other ships that participate are the 20-gun HMS *Carron* (Captain Robert Churchill Spencer), 18-gun *Sophie* (**Captain** Nicholas Lockyer), and the HMS *Childers* (Captain John Brand Umfreville).

While the American guns concentrate on the vessels, a contingent of ground troops and Indians advances, but the artillery halts its progress after only firing a few volleys. Meanwhile, the Americans also take a heavy pounding, and at one point, the flag is apparently hit and downed from its staff. While the Americans are replacing it, the British mistake the absence of the Stars and Stripes as the opportunity for victory. The charge is renewed, but to the dismay of the British, a new flag emerges and fresh fire derails the advance.

The HMS *Hermes* sustains damage during the contest and becomes a captive of the channel's current, which begins to carry it away from the fort. All the while the guns concentrate on the involuntary retirement of the vessel. The attack is aborted and the British warships retire, preserving Mobile Point. Late in the night, the British set the *Hermes* on fire and its magazine explodes. Another of the British ships sustains damage; the fort's guns compel it to withdraw. Shortly thereafter, the remaining two ships also retire.

After aborting the attack, the British also discontinue the plan to seize Mobile and instead move against New Orleans. The British, who are

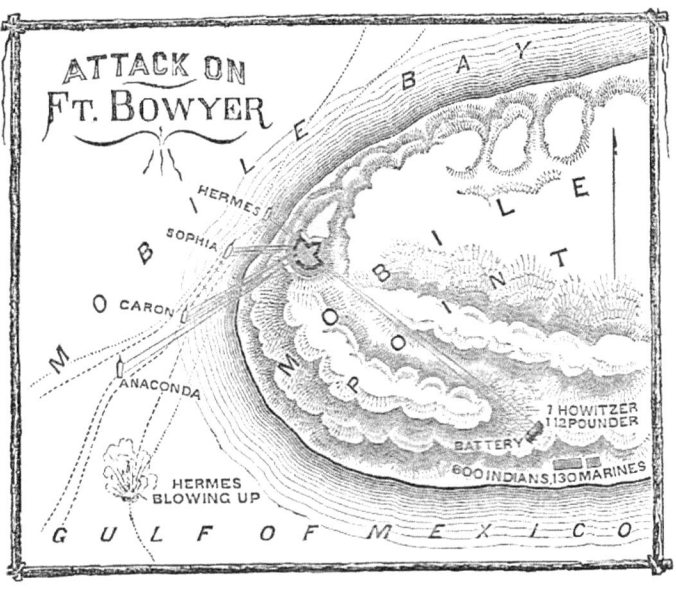

Attack on Fort Bowyer.

using Pensacola, Florida (Spanish territory), as a jump off point to strike U.S. positions at Mobile, Alabama, and New Orleans, Louisiana, return to Mobile early the next year. The Americans sustain four killed and four wounded. The British casualties total about 32 killed and 40 wounded.

September 12–26 The Yankee captains are still delivering decisive blows against the Royal Navy. The USS *Wasp,* elusive as ever, stings the British brigantine *Three Brothers* in the North Atlantic, taking it captive, then speeds against the HMS *Bacchus,* another Royal brigantine, seizing it as well. The British, well aware of this sloop, are unable to destroy it. Later, on the 21st, the *Wasp* engages and captures yet another British vessel, the brigantine *Atlanta.* Not to be undone, the privateer *General Armstrong* gives the British a special day when they believe it trapped at the Azores on the 26th. The British, hoping to make it to New Orleans to handle Andrew Jackson, are unexpectedly detained.

September 13 (Tuesday) *In naval activity,* the privateer *Dash,* a brigantine, is commissioned this day in Maine. Also, the HMS *Pylades* recaptures the brigantine *Nancy.* This *Nancy* is separate from like named vessels also captured: a ship, 17 August 1812; a schooner, 28 May 1813; a schooner, 28 June 1813; a sloop, 28 July 1814; and a brigantine, seized about 1–18 September 1814.

September 14 (Wednesday) **In Georgia,** General Blackshear, confident that for now the frontier in Georgia is safe, writes to Colonel Wimberly with orders: "SIR:— The danger of an immediate invasion on the frontier appears to have subsided for the present. A detachment of troops having marched out to Flint River will, in my opinion, give security to the frontier. You will therefore discharge the men ordered out on the frontier of your county."

In Washington, D.C., Secretary of War Armstrong turns in his resignation to President Madison. James Monroe, who earlier took the position on a temporary basis, once again becomes the secretary of war.

In naval activity, the USS *Wasp* (fifth) encounters and destroys a British merchant ship, *Baccus.*

September 15 (Thursday) The last few weeks have been frustrating for the British during this crusade against the United States. The elite Royal Navy is humbled on Lake Champlain, costing them the revered Captain George Downie in addition to the mighty fleet. The unexpected defeat on the lake also costs them the Hudson Valley and New York as Sir George Prevost, who diligently sought to reclaim British honor in the wake of the defeat of General Burgoyne during the American Revolution, is foiled by American ingenuity. His procrastination allows the Americans to prepare and build their confidence. Prevost, without naval support, must return to Canada. The British also had their hopes tied to the imaginary thought that Washington, Baltimore and the entire area must collapse at the mere sight of the Redcoats and their reputation.

The Yankees take their lumps at the capital but pay retribution at Baltimore and Fort McHenry, where the British lose General Ross, yet another general to be shipped to England in a barrel of rum. After the British pour every possible amount of firepower at their disposal on Fort McHenry without conquest, coupled with the disaster on Lake Champlain, it is clear that the Americans can hold for the duration. Britain is compelled to negotiate in earnest with the Americans, as the disillusioned fleet under Admiral Cockburn departs and subsequently sails for Jamaica.

The British merchants at home are also feeling pressure, as American privateers have jostled the merchant convoys at will on the high seas, costing the British a royal fortune. The U.S. fleet may have been quarantined at port by the massive British blockade, but while the king's sails hold the U.S. Navy in check at home, the sea roving knights are clearing the king's bishops and pawns.

James Monroe, secretary of state, secretary of war and later president of the United States.

General John Armstrong (*The American Generals*, John Frost, 1850).

These ocean-going cavaliers, or privateers known to the English as "bloody Yanks," raid relentlessly and their seamanship is tremendous.

These vessels are agile and aggressive, unafraid to tackle the giant British warships. It is their contribution that maintains pressure on the Crown by keeping the king's treasury from overflowing. By the latter part of the war, these rambling, lightning-fast, full-fisted privateers with swivel guns number in the hundreds. That's a lot of Yanks and a lot of Stars and Stripes to tangle with, even if you are king. The British had attempted to persuade the Duke of Wellington to assume command of the troops in Canada, but he declines, informing the Ministry that lacking control of the Great Lakes, success would be extremely difficult. The candid assessment by Wellington and his additional statement that he believed Britain, having failed to make the necessary territorial gains in the United States, would have no valid claim to unconquered ground, puts the situation in the proper perspective. The decision to invade the U.S. from Canada is aborted.

In naval activity, the ship *Vestal* is intercepted and recaptured by the HMS *Dragon.*

September 15 (Thursday) *In naval activity,* the British fleet under Admiral Cockburn is anchored at North Point, Maryland. The troops who served under the late General Ross begin departure from the area and join the main body of the British fleet. The body of General Ross is on board the HMS *Royal Oak,* preserved in a barrel of Jamaican rum. This is the customary way of returning the remains of fallen leaders.

September 16 (Friday) **In Louisiana,** a naval squadron under Commodore Patterson attacks Grand Terre Island, Louisiana, the headquarters of Jean Lafitte and his buccaneers. Lafitte had recently informed Governor Claiborne of the British plan to attack and seize New Orleans; however, his story was not believed. The Americans have orders to destroy the pirates' cove at Barataria. A contingent of Americans including Marines land at the objective, but few of Lafitte's men are there. Lafitte is also away at the time of the attack. Commodore Patterson reports the capture of 8 schooners, six of which had no flag and two sailing under flags of the Cartagenian Republic. The force also seizes one brigantine and one felucca. Before departing with their several prisoners, the Americans set the stronghold on fire. Afterward, Lafitte and his men remain in hiding until General Jackson arrives in New Orleans during early December.

In New York, General George Izard arrives at Sackets Harbor from Lake Champlain with his force of about 4,000 troops. The force had traveled by the Mohawk and Black River valleys.

In Pennsylvania, militia under Major General Nathaniel Watson is ordered to assemble at York, prior to departing for Baltimore. The force is composed of four regiments and one battalion, divided into two brigades. The 1st Brigade is commanded by Brigadier General John Forster and the 2nd Brigade is commanded by Brigadier General John Addams.

September 17 (Saturday) **In Canada,** American troops initiate an attack on the batteries of the British, who are holding Fort Erie under siege. The spearhead penetrates the British lines between Battery No. 2 and Battery No. 3 under a hurricane of fire. General Ripley, sensing the peril, sends up a contingent of the U.S. 21st Regiment (Lt. Colonel Timothy Upham's regiment) to bolster the attack, and within about one-half hour from jump off, both batteries are seized, along with two blockhouses and the adjoining entrenchments. The British, under immense pressure, abandon battery No. 1. The Americans disable each of the guns, and they detonate a magazine in Battery No. 3. The Americans also seize about 24 prisoners. The British withdraw on the 21st.

After the victory, which forces the British to lift the siege within a few days, General Brown states: "Thus, one thousand regulars, and an equal number of militia, in one hour of close action, blasted the hopes of the enemy, destroyed the fruits of fifty days' labor, and diminished his effective force 1,000 men at least." Colonel Eleazar D. Wood, a graduate of West Point (1806, Cadet #17) is killed. Wood had been adjutant general with Harrison during fall of 1813, and he was a participant in the Battle of Lundy's Lane and the Battle of the Thames.

Lt. Colonel Bedel's 11th U.S. Regiment acts as vanguard of General James Miller's column. Subsequent to this action, Lt. Colonel Moody Bedel is promoted to colonel of the regiment. The date of his commission is 4 September 1814. After the war, Colonel Bedel returns to New Hampshire; however, his fortunes begin to change. He becomes a brigadier general of Vermont militia; however, by the time he dies on 13 January 1841, at Bath, all the land and wealth accumulated by his family, including his father, Colonel Timothy Bedel, is gone and he dies in poverty. At one time, Bedel had owned more than half of Bath township and a large part of Haverhill.

Also, at the conclusion of this campaign, Lt. Colonel Upham, due to ill health, is transferred to recruiting service. At the close of hostilities, Upham resigns from the service; however, on 15 May 1819, he is appointed brigadier general of the 1st Brigade, 1st Division (New Hampshire militia). The next year he is named major general of the 1st Division as successor to Major General Clement Storer. Following his resignation in May 1823, Upham becomes navy agent at Portsmouth for a short time, appointed by President William Henry Harrison. Afterward, he relocates in Boston and then to Charlestown, Massachusetts, where he dies 2 November 1855 at age 72. Also, Brigadier General Daniel Davis of the New York militia is killed during this day's action.

In naval activity, the ship *Galloway* is captured by a British naval force bolstered by ground troops at Penobscot, Maine. The British also confiscate wine and liquor from other American vessels, including the *Decatur*. They destroy these vessels at Penobscot, then load the booty on the *Galloway* before departing.

September 18 (Sunday) In Canada, a survey team working along Talbot Road West near Port Talbot discovers two field pieces and ammunition wagons that had been left behind by an American force under Major Holmes during an expedition against Port Talbot that was aborted. The Loyal Essex Rangers retrieve the guns and ammunition and burn the wagons. The guns and ammunition are taken to a swamp and hidden.

In Maryland, the guns of Fort McHenry fire a tumultuous salute in honor of the American victory on Lake Champlain. The triumphant flag that flew over this legendary fortress has been preserved and is on display at the Smithsonian Institution in Washington, D.C.

In England and in Canada, various newspapers proclaim that a fleet will sail from England to reinforce the British troops already in America. The reinforcements are drawn from the army under the Duke of Wellington that engaged the French on the Peninsula. Nonetheless, the Duke (Arthur Wellesley) declines command of the force. The boastful press actually pinpoints New Orleans as a target. General Sir Edward Michel Pakenham, the brother-in-law of Lord Wellington, receives command of the force. On 24 October, Pakenham receives his commission from Lord Bathurst with orders to move to Plymouth and sail from there for Louisiana.

In naval activity, the HMS *Niemen* spots a schooner, the *Daedalus*. The *Niemen* seizes it while it is en route from Port au Prince to New York with a cargo of coffee. Also, the HMS *Bacchante* intercepts and seizes the 188-ton *Perseverance* (Robert James, master), which is en route to Castine from Moose Island, Maine, with a cargo of dry goods, molasses, rum and other items.

September 19 (Monday) In Washington, D.C., James Monroe writes from the War Department to Pennsylvania Governor Simon Snyder: "SIR: The enemy, having left Baltimore and passed down the bay, I have deemed it advisable to alter the destination of the Pennsylvania militia assembled at York. General Watson has been ordered to march those troops to the neighborhood of Philadelphia and dispose of them, agreeably to such arrangements as may have been made for the defence of that city, should it be attacked by the enemy. It is hoped, however, that our late brilliant success on Lake Champlain and pressure on the enemy, on that frontier generally may contribute to relieve our eastern frontier."

September 20 (Tuesday) In Canada, an American contingent operating out of Detroit again raids settlements in upper Canada. About 27 families are subjected to great suffering due to the cruel action that includes the burning of private residences.

September 21 (Wednesday) British General Drummond's forces lift the siege at Fort Erie after suffering massive losses.

In naval activity, the USS *Wasp* encounters and captures a British brigantine, the 8-gun *Atlanta*. They decide to keep the *Atlanta* as a prize. A prize crew, under Midshipman Geisinger, sails it to Savannah, Georgia. The *Wasp* continues its cruise, which had begun in May; however, no further word is heard from it. The *Atlanta* arrives back in the United States at Savannah on 4 November. The *Wasp*, last spotted by a Swedish merchant ship during early October, is thought to have been lost during a storm on its way to the Caribbean.

In other activity, the USS *Mohawk*, while on blockade duty off Kingston, is diverted for another mission. It participates with other vessels from Commodore Chauncey's fleet to move General Izard's force of about 3,000 troops from Sackets Harbor to the Genesee River. After completing the mission, it returns to the flotilla off Kingston and remains there until the latter part of the month. By spring of 1815, the war ends and the *Mohawk* remains in ordinary at Sackets Harbor until 1821. At that time it is rendered unfit for service and sold. Elsewhere, the 24-ton schooner *Dove* (John Procter, master), carrying a cargo of oil and fish, is captured off Salem by the British privateer *Lunenbury*.

September 22 (Thursday) In New York, General Izard's force arrives at the Genesee River. He lands and from there the column advances to Batavia, which it reaches on the 26th.

In naval activity, the HMS *Statira* captures a sloop, the *Ambition* (C. Vandine, master). The *Caledonia* (W. Macfarlane, master), on its way from Greenock to Montreal, is recaptured by the HMS *Nymphe*. The *Caledonia*'s cargo includes bread, coal and flour.

September 26 (Monday) *In naval activity,* the privateer *General Armstrong*, manned by about 90 men including officers, while in the neutral port of Fayal in the Azores to acquire supplies, is confronted by a nasty and well armed British armada commanded by British Commodore Lloyd. At about noon, the *General Armstrong* anchors. Captain Samuel Reid meets with the American consul, John B. Dabney. The consul takes care of getting fresh water delivered to the *General Armstrong*. He also assures Reid that the British squadron that arrived will inflict no harm while his ship is moored in neutral waters under the jurisdiction of Portugal. Captain Reid anticipates weighing anchor on the following morning; however, the British under Commodore Lloyd have their eyes on the privateer with intent to seize it and use it in the campaign to seize New Orleans.

Before dusk, Reid, Dabney and a few other men leave shore and move out to the *General Armstrong*. After a while, the British squadron appears in the distance and Reid observes six warships. The British ships anchor in the roads and their positioning totally cuts off any escape route of the *General Armstrong*, with its seven guns. It faces a total force of about 2,000 men who are en route to join Admiral Cochrane at Jamaica. Three of the British vessels, the flagship *Plantagenet* (Captain Robert Lloyd), the brigantine *Carnation*, and the frigate *Rota* (Captain Philip Somerville), combined carry 136 guns. Commodore Lloyd's eagerness to seize the *General Armstrong* overrides the international law that requires the neutrality of a nation to be respected. Three of his warships close upon the American vessel and the British demand surrender. The British expect the Americans to immediately comply due to the overwhelming firepower lurking close enough to decimate their vessel; however, the British receive a totally unexpected response: "Surrender Hell!"

Reid's response seems to reverberate throughout the British squadron. The British, flabbergasted by the audaciousness of the Yanks, prepare to board and seize the obstinate crew and the ship by sheer force; however, with some respect for the neutrality of the Azores, Lloyd's guns remain silent. He remains confident that with a lightning-quick strike, the boarders will take the ship and raise the British colors aboard it.

After darkness blankets the harbor, the British move in to surprise the Americans, but Reid's

Captain Samuel Reid, U.S. Navy.

crew is prepared and lying in wait for the four British boats under Lt. Robert Faussett to creep up on them. With the assistance of the moonlight, Lloyd's actions are observed by Reid. Calmly and quietly, the Americans prepare their guns and the rest of the crew are all at their battle stations waiting to greet the boarders. Essentially, Reid's crew has established an ambush.

At about 2000, four British boats carrying about 160 men approach the *General Armstrong*. Once they are spotted, the *General Armstrong*, which had been moving, drops anchor. The boats are hailed several times; however, the British ignore the calls. The boats approach the *General Armstrong*, which by this time had maneuvered closer to the castle. Captain Reid, in a low voice, instructs his crew: "Hold your fire until I give the word, boys. Wait till they get within range, and then teach 'em better manners."

Just as the British begin to board, Reid bellows: "Now, boys! Let 'em have it for the honor of the flag!" At that instant, the Marine detachment opens fire and instantly, rather than gaining the deck, the British receive withering effective fire, turning their visions of an easy kill into a tragic nightmare. Even the ship's cook, a Negro and his assistant, join in the fighting. The two men team up and dump boiling water upon the boarding party. The British attempt to overcome the resistance, and for a while, the fighting becomes vicious, but the British thrust is soon quashed. The British are thrown back and the survivors call for quarter. The boats pull away to return to the ships, but they too get pummeled. During the attack, one American is killed and Reid's 1st officer is wounded.

The *Armstrong*'s guns commence firing just as the boats pull away, and in a flash of thunderous fire, the harbor is filled with debris from the shattered vessels.

The British commander becomes more determined to take the prize. Simultaneously, Captain Lloyd's impatience to get his flotilla to New Orleans increases along with his anger. He decides to assault in force. During the lull, the governor of Fayal dispatches a strong message to Commodore Lloyd to inform him that the American vessel is under the protection of Portugal. Lloyd's frustration by this point is overwhelming. He answers the governor by stating that if the guns of the castle intervene, the British warships would bombard the town. Meanwhile, the illumination from a full moon has permitted the townspeople to watch. The shoreline is jammed with apprehensive but curious spectators.

Back on the *General Armstrong*, neither the spectators nor the British are able to determine the situation. It remains seemingly dead in the water. No crewmen are visible and no sounds are detected. Meanwhile, the British remain aware of their casualties from the first attack, but do not know how badly the Americans had suffered. The *General Armstrong* could easily be identified as a death-ship. By about 2100, once again, British boats are seen approaching the *General Armstrong*. The force totaling about 400 troops carried by 12 or 14 boats closes as one tightly linked line, and as the distance is rapidly decreasing, British confidence rebuilds after receiving no fire. Just as the attacking boats move into point-blank range, they are bombarded by the *General Armstrong*'s long tom and the fire of Marine sharpshooters. The deluge descends upon the boats continuously. The British remain oblivious to the cascading shells, while they return fire and converge to mount their next attack. At about midnight (26th–27th), Lloyd launches his second attack with a huge boarding party. Initially, the flotilla heads for a tiny reef of rocks, and once there the boats form in single file as if forming a spear. From the decks of the *General Armstrong*, there is only absolute silence until the boats are hailed.

Captain Reid's calls, having been ignored, brings his crew to life. The silence is broken as the men bolt from their concealed positions and commence firing. The British are jolted by the thunderclap that batters the advancing column. Nonetheless, the British recover from the shock and fire is returned. The boats come alongside the *General Armstrong* and with their craft having encircled the privateer, the distinct sound of "no quarter" rings out as Redcoats begin to climb aboard from all points. They are greeted as before. The American fire riddles the boarders, and Captain Reid, left-handed, is not a spectator. He fires pistols (handed to him by a group of powder boys) with his right hand, while he skillfully uses a cutlass with his left hand to fend off the enemy. The close quartered bloody combat ensues for about forty minutes. Lt. Williams is killed and Lieutenants Worth and Johnson sustain wounds; however Reid is in the thick of the donnybrook from start to finish. Despite the determination of the British and their undaunted persistence, they are repulsed at every point, unable to sustain a foothold on the decks. At one point, the British make it onto the deck, but Reid leads an attack to bolster the faltering line and the British are pushed back over the sides.

The price paid for the failed attack is exorbitant and the ramifications for the British are far reaching. During the hard-fought second attempt to board the *General Armstrong*, British casualties skyrocket. Three of their boats are sunk, and in one of the boats, which carried fifty men, only one officer evades death. Some of the remaining boats are left with only a few rowers and some others have lost all of their rowers. The area in the vicinity of the battle is ghastly. Four of the British boats are washed ashore by the surf and each of them contains only dead troops. Even the *General Armstrong* had become consumed with British dead and wounded.

In what becomes known as an astonishing feat, the crew of the *General Armstrong* had repulsed two attacks and inflicted more than 300 casualties upon the British. The American casualties figures are initially hard to believe: two killed, including Lieutenant Williams, and seven wounded. One Englishman, an eyewitness to the battle, later wrote: "God deliver us from our enemies, if this is the way they fight."

On the morning of the 27th, Captain Lloyd, still unable gain his prize, orders the brigantine *Carnation* to pulverize the *General Armstrong*. The guns are unleashed; however, the *General Armstrong*, which is beginning to look invincible, returns fire, and when the guns cease, Lloyd suffers yet another failure. The privateer remains afloat, while the battered and riddled *Carnation* is compelled to withdraw for repairs. By this time, Captain Reid concludes that the *General Armstrong* cannot be saved. Nevertheless, he remains unwilling to let the British take it. The crew scuttles the ship and heads for shore. Afterward, the British set it afire.

Commodore Lloyd, still stinging from his failure to gain his prize, threatens the governor. He delivers an ultimatum to turn over the Americans or face an invasion. Lloyd informs the governor that he will land 500 troops to take them. His demand is declined. Meanwhile, Captain Reid and the crew had moved to an ancient convent and demolished its drawbridge to bolster their defensive position if attacked. Lloyd, however, had issued a hollow threat. His casualties had been too severe and include many of his officers. The threat is not carried out. Meanwhile, back at Fayal, the bodies of British troops continue to be washed ashore by the surf. The squadron is delayed for ten days.

Later, two British sloops of war, the HMS *Thais* and the HMS *Calypso*, arrive. They pick up fifty wounded and take them back to England; however, the captains are ordered not to mention the engagement with the *General Armstrong*. Reid's crew had held up the squadron, which is anxiously awaited by Admiral Cochrane. When Lloyd finally arrives in Jamaica and Cochrane is informed that one privateer had delayed the voyage and caused horrific casualties, Commodore Lloyd is censured by Cochrane. In contrast, the extraordinary heroism of Reid's crew receives praise throughout the States, and the *General Armstrong* receives credit for aiding the defenders in New Orleans by their courageous feat in the Azores. Captain Reid later learns from the British consul that the second assault to seize the *General Armstrong* cost the English 120 killed and about 130 wounded. Captain Lloyd was among the wounded. He sustained a severe leg wound that required amputation. The English killed include 1st Lt. William Matterface (*Rota*) and 3rd Lt. Charles R. Norman (*Rota*); the wounded include 2nd Lt. Richard Rawle (*Rota*); 1st Lt. Thomas Park (*Rota*); and Purser William Benge Basden (*Rota*).

In other naval activity, the HMS *Loire* intercepts and seizes the schooner *Good Hope*, which is transporting a cargo of shingles and turpentine. The prize and its cargo are taken into port at Liverpool. Also, the privateer *Lunenburg* seizes the 136-ton schooner *Minerva*, which is en route to Boston from Wiscasset, Maine.

September 28 (Wednesday) *In naval activity,* the HMS *Maidstone* seizes the schooner *Sarah*, which is carrying fish and lumber from St. John's to Barbados.

September 30 (Friday) *In naval activity,* a boat containing five men, attached to the USS *Superior*, while operating near the head of the St. Lawrence River, intercepts a small flotilla of a few boats that are en route to Kingston. All of the craft are seized and taken to Sackets Harbor.

October 1814 **In Maryland,** some Maryland militia officers have by this time accumulated personal grievances that prompt them to retire. Major General Samuel Smith, a Revolutionary War veteran, resigns. He is succeeded by General Robert Goodloe Harper. The appointment of Harper causes Brigadier General Stricker, who is the senior brigadier in the division, to feel slighted, and he too resigns. The commander of the militia announces the resignation of Stricker on 11 November. The letter also states that Lt. Colonel James Sterett (5th Regiment) is appointed to brigadier general of the Third or City Brigade to replace Stricker. Sterett is jumped over Colonel William Donald, at present, the senior officer of the brigade. After resigning, General Stricker becomes the manager of the Bank of Baltimore. He dies on 23 June 1825 in Baltimore.

In Belgium, news of the British occupation of Washington and of their destruction of the city reaches the negotiators, inflating the desires of the British and prompting apprehension among the Americans. The British anticipate more startling news concerning what they consider to be imminent victories in New York State and in Louisiana at New Orleans; however, news of the premature evacuation of Washington and the steadfast defense at Fort McHenry has not yet crossed the Atlantic. Details of the spectacular American naval victory on the Great Lakes, guaranteed to deflate the egos of the British representatives, are still en route. When the news arrives, the British dreams of acquiring about one-half of Maine, Fort Niagara and much of the immediate territory and the coveted Fort Michilimackinac are suddenly transformed into a nightmare. The Americans, having pondered the extraordinary demands, now abruptly state that the demands are unacceptable. The British had envisioned a bonanza by gaining the territory in Maine, which would have provided them with a land route from Quebec, which becomes isolated during the winter months when the St. Lawrence River freezes, to their naval facility at Halifax, Nova Scotia. Nevertheless, with the unexpected setbacks, the British are compelled to negotiate to terminate the war.

In naval activity, the American privateer *Shark* out of New York captures the schooner *Mary*, which is transporting a cargo of dry goods intended for San Domingo in the Dominican Republic. The *Mary* is diverted to New Orleans. The *Shark* also seizes five other prizes while at sea, two of which are taken into American ports and the remainder destroyed at sea. In other naval activity, the 8-gun American privateer *Whig*, a schooner, arrives at New York at about this time (September–October). Twenty-three prisoners are aboard when it enters the harbor. Some other prisoners seized during the cruise had returned to England on one of the *Whig*'s prizes, a sloop the *Enterprise*, which was captured while en route to Madeira from Guernsey. The vessels *Brunswick* and the *Race Horse*, both brigantines, and the schooner *Britannia*, although captured by the *Whig*, do not reach port. They are burned at sea.

October 1 (Saturday) *In naval activity,* the British privateer *Liverpool Packet* intercepts and seizes the 40-ton sloop *Fylinda* (Peter Burr, master), which is moving to deliver a cargo of Indian corn and rye to Rhode Island. The prize and its cargo are diverted to Liverpool. In other naval activity, the American privateer *Yankee* out of Rhode Island, commanded by Captain William C. Jenkes, who succeeds Captain Elisha Snow, embarks on its sixth cruise, this one lasting until late January 1815. The *Yankee* seizes the brigantine *Courtney*, the brigantine *Lady Prevost* and the brigantine *Speculator*, along with the ships *General Wellesley* and the *St. Andrews*. It also seizes one schooner, which is transporting a cargo of flour from Bermuda. During the cruise, Captain Jenkes loses one of his legs. He is succeeded in command by Captain B. K. Churchill. The Americans release the *Speculator* to the prisoners. The *Courtney* is taken into port at New Bedford and the *General Wellesley* is ordered into Charleston, South Carolina. The *General Wellesley*, with its cargo is valued at $250,000, wrecks on a bar as it tries to move into the harbor. The losses are great. The entire British crew of 36 men and 50 Lascars are killed, along with two Americans assigned to the prize crew.

The *Yankee*, during its six cruises, had captured 40 British vessels (25 brigantines, five schooners, nine ships and one sloop). It had either captured or destroyed an estimated $5,000,000 in British property.

October 4 (Tuesday) *In naval activity,* the HMS *Loire* and the HMS *Niemen*, cruising together, intercept and capture the 41-ton schooner *Tickler*, which is has a cargo of bread, flour and other items. This *Tickler* is separate from the schooner *Tickler* seized on 14 June 1814.

October 5 (Wednesday) **In Canada,** General George Izard arrives at Fort Erie with reinforcements. These troops remain until the fort is destroyed by the American defenders on November 5. Izard then removes all American soldiers from Canadian soil.

In New York, at Sackets Harbor, Colonel Washington Irving, aide-de-camp to Governor Tompkins, arrives with a response from the governor regarding a request to strengthen the town due to a threat that the British might launch a new offensive to gain it. The governor authorizes the commanding officer to call out the militia in any number that he believes necessary. After a meeting with Colonel Mitchell, General Oliver Collins calls upon militia from all points within Herkimer, Oneida, Lewis, and Jefferson Counties. Militia has often been called upon when Sackets Harbor is threatened; however, this time the militia overruns the town. About 2,500 troops respond. The infusion of the militia pushes the number of defenders to more than 5,000 men. Other militia generals in the area include General Walter Martin of Martinsburg (Lewis County). Martin's brigade participates in this call-up. Nevertheless, the threat dissipates and no attack occurs. During this period of uncertainty, two frigates are under construction, the *New Orleans* at Navy Point (Sackets Harbor) and the *Chippewa* at Storr's Harbor, but neither vessel is completed before the end of the conflict.

October 6 (Thursday) *In naval activity,* the HMS *Wasp* intercepts the 92-ton schooner *Mary* and recaptures it.

October 9 (Sunday) **In Michigan,** a force of about 700 mounted troops under General Duncan McArthur arrives at Detroit in response to hostile Indians that have been creating problems around Lake Michigan. McArthur's troops have been drawn from Kentucky and Ohio. His intent is to penetrate Canada on a bold raid that is intended to relieve some of the pressure on General Jacob Brown's forces that are heavily pressured on the Niagara frontier by drawing some of his British opponents toward his force. Later in the month, he departs from the city and rides northward with his column, which has grown to about 750 troops and includes five artillery pieces. The column sweeps through various towns and villages after moving around Lake St. Clair and fording the St. Clair River on 26 October. It arrives on 4 November at Oxford, where a force of militia is quickly captured, disarmed and paroled; however, those who attempt to raise opposition find that their houses are burned down. Afterward, the column advances through several other villages and reaches the Grand River, where the area is defended by British, militia and Iroquois Indians. After some skirmishing there, General McArthur moves southward toward Malcolm Hill, also along the Grand River, and engages the militia based there. McArthur sustains one man killed and six wounded. His troops inflict seven casualties, including killed and wounded, and capture of 131 militia troops. Before departing, the Americans demolish a flour mill. On the way to Dover, located on Lake Erie, the column passes a few other mills and they too are destroyed. The destroyed mills create problems for the British, because they were primary sources for troops operating against the central army of the Americans.

During the last phase of the mission, the Americans roll through Simcoe and St. Thomas as they head for Sandwich, pursued by Redcoats. Nonetheless, the British force of more than 1,000

General Duncan McArthur.

Thomas Worthington, governor of Ohio, 1814–1818.

troops fails to intercept General McArthur. He arrives at Sandwich on 17 November. At Sandwich, some of his force is dismissed and afterward, General McArthur returns to Ohio.

On 13 December 1814, in a private letter to Governor Thomas Worthington (successor to Governor Meigs), General McArthur states his thoughts on the situation at Detroit:

> The contractor failed in November to supply the troops at Detroit with the flour part of the ration, and they are now subsisting upon the immediate resources of the adjacent country. The advanced state of the season precludes the hope that any flour can be forwarded by lake transportation, should it have been collected at Erie, of which there is no authentic account. A considerable supply is reported by the contractor to be in readiness to be taken down the St. Mary and Miami of the Lake [Maumee] as soon as practicable, of which there can be no certainty until April. Three or four thousand hogs are reported by the contractor to be in readiness to proceed to Detroit by the route of the Auglaise or Hull's Road. Subsequent information as to the number collected, and the price allowed to sub-contractors, induces a belief that not more than one thousand will reach that place. These facts have been communicated to the government with a request that funds might be transmitted to this place to enable a special commissary to endeavor to supply the troops of the frontier. There is reason to presume that a delay for an arrangement of this kind would be fatal; more especially as it is the intention of the government to increase the military force of the Northwestern frontier.

McArthur urges the governor to request that the legislature become involved: "The loan of thirty thousand dollars would probably enable a person duly authorized to forward to Detroit by way of Sandusky five hundred barrels of flour, and fifteen hundred hogs."

October 11 (Tuesday) *In naval activity,* the HMS *Armide* intercepts and recaptures the brigantine *William.*

October 11–15 *In naval activity,* on the 11th, the American privateer *Prince de Neuchatel* (Captain Ordronaux), having sailed from Boston several days ago, arrives at a point close to Nantucket Shoals. Its captain senses imminent danger when he spots a ship in the distance near Gay Head that is unquestionably beginning to close upon his privateer. He is confident that the vessel is a British warship because of his knowledge that few American ships are in the vicinity. The *Prince de Neuchatel* immediately begins to run, but progress is impeded due to the absence of fair winds. Captain Ordronaux is equally concerned about being captured because he is towing a British merchant vessel, the ship *Douglas,* which had not yet reached an American port. Tensions aboard ship begin to rise, but the crew remains committed to saving themselves and their prize.

By about 1500 some stiff winds arrive to finally intervene. The two vessels under the Stars and Stripes work to lose their pursuer. By about 1900, a new calmness descends on the area and the Americans observe the British warship, which earlier had been about twelve miles in the rear. Meanwhile, the current is forcing both vessels toward shore. Captain Ordronaux's ship and his prize drop their anchors at a distance of about one quarter mile from each other.

With darkness having arrived, the crew of the privateer prepares for the worst, a night attack. Shortly thereafter, the prize crew spots the inevitable, British barges moving toward the privateer. A signal is sent and the crew scrambles in the darkness to prepare to meet the attack. Once the British are spotted coming toward them, the ship's guns roar bolstered by small arms fire. Nonetheless, the British remain oblivious to the barrages and the musket fire as they inch closer to their target. Lt. Abel Hawkins, of the HMS *Endymion,* while ignoring the fire, directs his contingent to maintain the advance and encircle the privateer to permit boarding from all points to overwhelm the insolent Americans. Once in place, the British attempt to board, but they have not anticipated the reception awaiting them.

There are no signs of chivalry. The contest from the beginning is barbaric as the British begin their ascent at every possible point. The Americans spare no method of defending their ship. Bare knuckles pound the intruders, who also face pistols and swords. Anything capable of bashing the British is committed. Chains, spikes and even vicious bites are used. The British manage to grasp a short-lived stay on the decks, and bringing them to believe they will gain the ship from its rear, only to become disillusioned when they are repelled and violently driven off the ship. In the meantime, the British receive incessant small arms fire. Captain Ordronaux remains in the center of the brawl. He personally fires about 80 shots at the boarding party.

At one point, the British, who continue to give as much as they receive, begin to gain the decks as the Americans show some signs of faltering under the relentless pressure. At the same time, Captain Ordronaux gives his crewmen a vivid reason to get their adrenalin flowing. Before the attack, he had made it clear that the ship would not be taken. and if he was unable to prevent boarding, the ship would be blown up with the colors flying and all hands aboard. Suddenly, while the crew is trying to regain the momentum to expel the boarding party, they watch their captain hustle over to the magazine while holding a lighted match. Faced with certain death if they fold, while listening to the captain yelling that he "would blow up the ship if they retreat further," the men instantly become rejuvenated, as if the lit match had injected them with additional strength.

While their aggression reaches a pinnacle and they discover additional animal instincts, the Americans refocus and an extraordinary burst of fury explodes. The Americans drive the British back and the survivors bolt for the barges, ending the wildly fought contest after twenty minutes of exhausting, close-quartered fighting. Nonetheless, at battle's end, the Americans, ecstatic that they had preserved their ship and permitted their captain to extinguish the lighted match, find additional pride when voices in the darkness from British troops yell out for quarter. These gallant privateers, looked upon by the Royal Navy as inferior seamen, had inflicted an embarrassing defeat upon the king's finest. The British, numbering 120, including Royal Marines and a few boys, had been repelled by 37 crewmen who left the impression to the British survivors that they had entered a cauldron of death rather than a puny privateer.

Of the five barges that approached the privateer, three had been driven off by the current with no one onboard and alive. One other was sunk and of 43 men aboard, only two are rescued. It is thought that those carried away by the current had drowned in the darkness too far away to be saved by either the Americans or the British. The remaining barge was captured by the Americans. At the beginning of the assault, it was carrying 36 men and of those, eight were killed and 20 sustained wounds, leaving fewer than ten unscathed. Despite the horrific fight, the Americans sustain seven killed and 20 wounded, leaving only ten crewmen standing without injury at the culmination of the battle. Lieutenant Hawkins, who commanded the boarding party, was killed during the struggle.

Although the Americans prevailed, great danger continues to lurk. Captain Ordronaux needs no reminder that he is holding too many prisoners and even a minor mistake could wipe out the victory. The 30 British prisoners are stripped of their arms, and he refuses to bring them aboard the privateer to eliminate any chance of them overwhelming his able bodied men. However, a few men, thought incapable of causing harm, are transferred. Three of those brought aboard are midshipmen and two are seriously wounded. A master's mate, also wounded, is brought aboard, along with the second lieutenant of the *Endymion*. The others are detained in a launch that contains no oars. On the following day, the British taken on board, representing all the prisoners, agree to terms that prohibit them from participating in any action against the United States until officially exchanged.

After concluding the agreement, the prisoners are taken ashore at Nantucket and transferred to a U.S. marshal. Afterward, the *Prince de Neuchatel* sails to Boston without interference from the HMS *Endymion*, which had effortlessly been evaded during the voyage. The privateer and its prize arrive at Boston on 15 October.

Following the heart-thumping mission, Captain Ordronaux relinquishes command of the privateer but buys a part-ownership in it. Captain Ordronaux himself is not easily identified as a ship's captain. He was described by one of his crew: "A Jew by persuasion, a Frenchman by birth, an American for convenience, and so diminutive in stature as to make it appear ridiculous, in the eyes of others, even for him to enforce authority among a hardy, weather-beaten crew should they aught against his will."

October 17 (Monday) **In Pennsylvania,** Brigadier General Samuel Smith, at Camp Marcus Hook, certifies that the Delaware County Fencibles has been mustered into federal service. Also, Andrew Mitchell is commissioned major general of the 11th Division of militia (Cumberland and Franklin Counties). General Smith had not accepted any pay for his service during the entire war, nor did any member of his staff.

In naval activity, two British warships, the HMS *Narcissus* and the HMS *Dispatch,* operating in Long Island Sound, intercept and seize the 70-ton schooner *Eagle,* which is transporting a cargo of eight mounted guns and some pistol stocks.

October 19 (Wednesday) **In Canada,** a brigade composed of about 1,000 men under General Daniel Bissell, attached to General Izard's command, engages a British force at Lyon's Creek (also known as Cook's Mills). The British under Colonel Christopher Myers had been deployed by General Drummond to protect the mills. Initially, the American vanguard is driven back across the creek, preventing them from advancing to the objective, the mill; however, the British who initiate pursuit encounter stiff resistance once they ford the creek. Bissell's troops hold steadfastly and the British are compelled to recross the creek with the Yankees in pursuit. The main body's counterattack becomes too strong for the British to drive back. They are forced to retire, but the British retain their discipline. After the British disengage, the Americans destroy the mill and confiscate the stockpile of wheat. This skirmish terminates the fighting on the Niagara frontier.

General Bissell, born in Connecticut during 1768, entered the militia during the American Revolution as a fifer before he was ten years old. He joined the U.S. Army during 1788 and afterward held command at Fort Massac, where French troops had earlier established Fort Massiac (and previously Fort de L'Ascension), near Cairo, Illinois, along the Ohio River. In 1809, Bissell, with the rank of lieutenant colonel, held command of Cantonment Belle Fontaine (later Fort Belle Fontaine) in Upper Louisiana along the Missouri River at Waterloo, Illinois. When the War of 1812 erupted, Bissell attained the rank of full colonel. After the war, he returned to St. Louis where he built his estate known as Franklinville. Bissell retired from the army during 1821. In early 1826, President John Quincy Adams re-nominated Bissell as colonel of the 2nd Artillery, following the senate's failure to confirm; however, the Senate also rejects it for a second time.

The Bissell home remained in the family for more than 150 years. At present, the home is owned by the County of St. Louis (donated to the county during the 1960s). General Bissell died during 1833 and was survived by his wife, Deborah, and their four children.

October 20 (Thursday) *In naval activity,* the HMS *Saracen* on or about this day spots the vessel *Saucy Jack* while it is grounded in the Potomac River. The British seize the vessel and its cargo of corn and sweet potatoes.

October 21 (Friday) **In Georgia,** the governor (commander in chief of the militia), pursuant to a letter from Secretary of War James Monroe, requesting 2,500 militia troops (in accordance with orders from the War Department on the previous 4th of July), directs the troops be raised. A regiment under Colonel Davis S. Booth is detached from General Allen Daniel's division, along with a regiment under Colonel Ezekiel Wimberly (General Blackshear's brigade). The other units are two companies detached from Brigadier General Lee's brigade (Jones County) and one volunteer artillery company commanded by Captain James Saffold. The force, to be commanded by Major General McIntosh and Brigadier General Blackshear, is to proceed to Mobile to bolster General Andrew Jackson.

In the meantime, the British sustain a defeat in New Orleans and the column is recalled due to a British force that lands in Georgia in January 1815. On 4 February 1815, General Blackshear, after learning of Jackson's victory at New Orleans, sends a message to Captain Mathias:

> CAMP, 182 MILES BELOW HARTFORD, Gen. Blackshear has the honor to inform Capt. Massias that the detachment under his command will arrive this evening at Barrington, and also that a gentleman of high respectability arrived in camp last evening with the pleasing intelligence that on Monday last a *feu-de-joie* of nineteen guns was fired at Fort Hawkins in celebration of the signal victory gained over the British, by General Jackson, at New Orleans. The report is that Gen. Jackson killed one thousand dead, and took five hundred prisoners, with only the loss of twenty men. Too good to be entirely true, I fear. Gloria Dei I Gloria Jacksoni [signed by Thomas Hamilton, aide to Blackshear].

October 22 (Saturday) *In naval activity,* the vessel *Amazon* (John Raines, master), carrying a cargo of bread and flour, is intercepted and recaptured by the British ship HMS *Bulwark*. In other activity, the 28-ton schooner *Dolphin,* carrying a cargo from Boston to Bath, Maine, is intercepted and captured by the privateer *Lunenburg*.

October 23 (Sunday) *In naval activity,* the HMS *Bulwark* encounters and seizes the privateer *Harlequin,* a 232-ton schooner operating out of Portsmouth, Maine, with a crew of about 115 men and 10 guns.

October 24 (Monday) *In naval activity,* the HMS *Maidstone* encounters and captures the 125-ton brigantine *Black Swan* (Jacob McDaniel, master) while it is carrying dry goods and lumber from Boston to Havana.

October 25 (Tuesday) **In Alabama,** General John Coffee arrives in the vicinity of Mobile, on the western bank of the Tombigbee River with a force of just under 3,000 men. General Andrew Jackson arrives the next day.

October 26 (Wednesday) **In Alabama,** General Coffee's mounted dragoons arrive to bolster General Andrew Jackson's forces. Jackson is preparing to attack British-held Pensacola, Florida, which is Spanish territory. Jackson's army includes the U.S. 3rd, 39th and 44th Infantry Regiments, bolstered by one battalion of volunteer dragoons, Tennessee militia and allied Indians. The army fords the Tombigbee River, crosses Nannahubba Island and reaches Mim's Ferry. From the ferry, the entire contingent moves overland and reaches Montgomery, Alabama, on 4 November. By 6 November, Jackson is on the fringes of Pensacola.

In naval activity, the privateer *Dash* seizes a vessel, the *Thinks to Myself.* In other naval activity, the HMS *St. Lawrence* intercepts and seizes the 88-ton sloop *Lively,* which is en route to Georgetown from New Bedford with a cargo of potatoes and salt.

October 27 (Thursday) *In naval activity,* the HMS *Maidstone* intercepts the 227-ton ship *Mentor* and recaptures it. The *Mentor* is separate from the sloop *Mentor* seized on 11 July 1813.

October 28 (Friday) **In New York,** at Albany, Governor Tompkins writes to James Monroe, Secretary of War: "Sir: I have the honor to report to you that in pursuant to the direction of the president, I have this day assumed the command of the Third Military District. Not having received the books, papers or other Articles belong-

General John Coffee.

ing to the command, nor taken possession of Head Quarters which are still occupied by Major General Lewis, I am under the necessity of postponing answers in detail to your several communications of the 19th and 22nd instant until to morrow evening, but in the mean time shall exert myself to meet your views as well with respect to Sacketts Harbour as to the affairs of this district."

October 30 (Sunday) *In naval activity,* the HMS *Bulwark,* while on patrol, intercepts and recaptures the ship *Halifax* and its cargo of various items including dry goods and flour.

October 31 (Monday) *In naval activity,* the sloop *Eliza Ann,* carrying a cargo of Indian corn, is halted and seized while it is en route from New Bedford to New York. The prize is taken into port at Liverpool.

In other naval activity, the American privateer *Saucy Jack,* while operating off the western tip of the Dominican Republic, encounters the HMS *Volcano,* a bomb-ship, and two transports. Captain Chazel of the privateer, believing he has intercepted three merchant ships, advances to seize them. At about 0100 on the following morning (1 November), as he reaches range, the *Saucy Jack* commences fire with its long tom and shortly thereafter the British warship returns fire. At about 0600, Captain Chazel is able to get a better look at the foe, and he observes that one of the ships has 18 guns mounted and another has 16 guns mounted. However, Chazel has no knowledge of the British troops on board the *Volcano.* By 0700, the *Saucy Jack* maneuvers into position from where a boarding party is poised to seize the *Volcano,* which is the ship nearest the privateer. Captain Chazel discovers the soldiers in the vessel and quickly aborts the order to board. The *Saucy Jack* pulls away and tries to outrun the British. Two ships are in pursuit, the *Golden Fleece* and the *Volcano.* The British succeed in inflicting damage to the *Saucy Jack,* which sustains eight killed and 15 wounded, but the British fail to catch it.

The British report on the same engagement:

Kingston, Jamaica, Nov. 2d.— Yesterday morning, the Volcano, bomb-ship, Captain Price, and transport ship Golden Fleece, from the Chesapeake, having on board 250 troops, appeared in the offing, but from the baffling winds were not enabled to reach Port Royal, at the time this paper was put to press. On Sunday night, about 12 o'clock, off Navassa Island, the Volcano perceived a schooner standing toward it, which fired several shot, which were returned. The Volcano shortened sail, in order that the schooner might approach it. At about eight o'clock the following morning, it was ascertained to be a large black vessel, with white streaks; it ran alongside, and attempted to board, but finding the Volcano was not a merchantman, it endeavored to sheer off, at which time several volleys of musketry and great guns were discharged at it, that swept its deck, and killed most of those who endeavored to board, when the remainder were seen to run below. The Volcano then chased it for three miles, but perceiving no probability of coming up with it, relinquished the pursuit. During the contest a very enterprising officer of the marine-artillery, lieutenant W.P. Futzen, and two seamen were killed, and two men wounded. The privateer had in company a Balahoo schooner, which did not attempt to afford her any assistance; she mounted six carriage guns, and one on a pivot, and was full of men.

Early November **In Canada,** a strong force of mounted Kentuckians and a contingent of Indians led by General Duncan McArthur initiates a mission that takes the column through part of the western district and the London district. The troops destroy mills and provisions, while they subsist by acquiring food from the people. The troops engage in only slight pillage due to the inability to carry items back to Detroit. In Nova Scotia, at about this time, a contingent of militia at Yarmouth seizes the privateer *Fame.*

In naval activity, the sloop *Hero* is unexpectedly encountered and captured by the HMS *Tenedos.* The *Hero* is separate from the schooner *Hero* seized on 12 June 1813, the schooner *Hero* seized 29 August 1813, the schooner *Hero* taken on 13 January 1814, the schooner *Hero* captured on 3 July 1814 and the sloop *Hero* seized on 13 January 1814. In other naval activity, the privateer *America* embarks on its fourth cruise and sails directly for Europe.

November 1 (Tuesday) *In naval activity,* the privateer *Thinks to Myself,* a schooner, is commissioned this day in Maine. The vessel had been captured by the privateer *Dash* on 26 October. In other naval activity, the privateer *Macdonough,* a 180-ton brigantine operating out of Portsmouth, is intercepted and seized by the HMS *Bacchante.* At the time of its capture, the *Macdonough* is carrying a crew of 60 men and armed with five mounted guns.

In Virginia, Brigadier General Thomas Parker resigns from the service. At this time, he is stationed at Norfolk. General Parker, a veteran also of the American Revolution, dies at his estate, "Soldier's Retreat," in Frederick on 24 January 1820.

November 2 (Wednesday) **In New York,** Governor Daniel D. Tompkins, in his capacity of general and commanding officer of the Third Military District, has an accident. He falls from his horse while at Fort Greene.

November 3 (Thursday) **In Washington, D.C.,** Congress passes a resolution requesting that President Madison "cause a gold medal to be struck, with suitable emblems and devices and presented to Major General Scott, in testimony of the high sense entertained by Congress of his distinguished services in the successive conflicts of Chippewa and Niagara [Lundy's Lane], and of his uniform gallantry and good conduct in sustaining the reputation of the arms of the United States." The medal is issued; however, there is a prolonged delay. General Scott does not receive it until the end of his successor's term, on 26 February 1825.

In Maine, a flotilla of merchant ships, under escort by the HMS *Fantine,* arrives at Castine from Eastport. One of the vessels, an unarmed schooner (previously the privateer *Snap Dragon*), which is transporting a contingent of Royal Marines, is hailed by a boat operating out of Waldoboro. The Americans come under small arms fire and sustain four casualties, including two killed. Afterward, the boat returns to its port. In other naval activity, the British privateer *Rover* intercepts and seizes the 120-ton brigantine *Rachel* (John Patterson, master), which is en route to Wilmington, North Carolina, from Portland, Maine, with potatoes and salt.

November 4 (Friday) **In Alabama,** General Andrew Jackson arrives with his army at Montgomery en route to Pensacola, Florida, the port which the Royal Navy is using to strike American positions in Alabama and Louisiana.

November 5 (Saturday) The Americans, holding out since the siege of September 17, begin their evacuation from Fort Erie, destroying the fort themselves to prevent British occupation. General Izard now removes all American troops from Canada.

In naval activity, the brigantine *Charles* (J. Everett, master) is intercepted and recaptured by the HMS *Saturn* while it is en route from St. John's, New Brunswick, to Barbados with a cargo of fish and lumber. The *Charles* is separate from the *Charles Fawcett* seized 6 September 1812, 95-ton sloop *Charles* seized 4 October 1813, the 75-ton sloop *Charles* captured 10 December 1813, and the schooner *Charles* seized on 26 June 1814. Also, the British privateer *Lunenburg* intercepts and seizes the 85-ton schooner *Ranger* (John Burton, master). The *Ranger* is separate from the schooner *Ranger* seized 13 July 1814.

November 6 (Sunday) **In Florida,** General Jackson, standing at the entrance to Pensacola, issues an ultimatum to the Spanish Governor of Florida for the surrender of Forts Barrancas and St. Michael. The Spanish do not comply. Jackson will commence his attack to eradicate the British threat to Mobile the next day. (Spain although neutral, permits the British to hold the fort.)

In related activity, Lieutenant Alexander Murray of the Mississippi Dragoons is killed by an Indian while leading a mounted reconnaissance patrol during a time he was isolated from the contingent. Also, Jackson dispatches a messenger, Major Pierre, under a flag of truce to Fort St. Michael, a Spanish fort held by the British. The fort disregards the white flag and fires upon Major Pierre. Jackson, upon receiving word of the incident, dispatches a heated note to the governor demanding an explanation for the insult to his messenger and the flag. The governor denounces the action and at about midnight, Major Pierre returns to the fort, but the governor rejects turning over Forts St. Michael and Barrancas to the Americans. The governor is informed by Pierre that the alternative is that the Americans will take them by force.

Meanwhile, Jackson is informed by a man who had returned from a mission that took him into Pensacola that the town is occupied by about 5,000, including the Spanish, British and allied Indians, and that a battery had been erected to intercept any American advance that attempts to bypass Fort St. Michael.

November 6, 1814, to May 9, 1815 *In naval activity,* the American privateer *Leo* has been completely repaired and is ready to sail from France to the United States. On November 2, the 320-ton vessel was purchased by a group of Americans in France at this time from another American, Thomas Lewis, presently residing in Bordeaux. Captain George Coggeshall receives command of the vessel, which is rated as a superior sailing ship. Coggeshall, on the 2nd, received its commission as a letter of marque authorized by William H. Crawford, U.S. minister at Paris. Nonetheless, Captain Coggeshall is not enthralled by its armament. He later remarks: "We were miserably armed; we had, when I first took command of the schooner, one long brass 12-pounder, and four small 4-pounders, with some fifty or sixty poor muskets. Those concerned in the vessel seemed to think we ought, with so many men, to capture prizes enough."

Coggeshall also remains concerned that the French might begin to detain American vessels before it sails. As a precaution, the *Leo* is moved down in the harbor. Meanwhile the French action that was dreaded unfolds. Captain Coggeshall receives instructions demanding that all vessels return to the dock and that once there the privateer is to be stripped of all of its small arms and its guns except one, which is permitted to remain on board. The Americans comply sheepishly, but later after dark, between 20 to 30 muskets are smuggled onto the ship to bolster its one gun, a 12-pounder.

On the 8th, the *Leo* finally gets underway. A British brigantine is spotted off the Isles of Scilly on the 13th, and after firing only one shot, it surrenders to the Americans. Captain Coggeshall assigns a prize crew to take the vessel into an American port. The weather, having been nasty since the *Leo* departed from France, continues without change. The *Leo*'s course is modified to attempt to get out of the inclement weather. It sails southward, and although the weather improves, the crew has little time to rejoice. On the 18th, it is chased by a British brigantine off the coast of Spain. Later on this day, the crew sees a merchant ship, but due to the menacing brigantine, which has continued the pursuit, the vessel gets a pass and the *Leo* maintains its race to outrun the British warship. The *Leo* continues its run throughout the night and by dawn on the 19th, there is no longer any sight of the brigantine.

The *Leo* spots a vessel at about 0700 and without the pressure of the brigantine trying to close for the kill, Captain Coggeshall orders the crew to chase and seize the prize. By about 1000, the vessel, a British cutter, the *Tenerife*, carrying a cargo of wine and en route to London, is overtaken and captured. The Americans remove 20 casks of wine and they transfer the crew to the *Leo*. The vessel is destroyed.

Afterward, the *Leo* experiences more harrowing incidents when discovered by British warships, but on each occasion it evades capture. On 24 November two British frigates spot it and initiate a chase, yet again, the *Leo* remains out of reach. Also on the 24th, two merchant ships come into view, but the *Leo*, focused on self-preservation, lets them pass without incident. It maintains course, and during the afternoon of the 25th, it spots a vessel and moves to seize it. Within about one-half hour, it is revealed that the ship is a frigate. At about the same time, the *Leo* comes under fire and the American flag is hoisted. The *Leo* responds by hoisting its colors, and once the frigate's crew sees the Stars and Stripes, they haul the American flag down and they catapult the English colors to the top of the mast. Nonetheless, the British fire fails to halt the *Leo* and after dark it outdistances its pursuer.

On the following day (26th), unimpeded by any British warships, the *Leo* intercepts and seizes a merchant ship. Captain Coggeshall assigns a prize crew and the vessel, along with its cargo, including brimstone and rags, is taken into port in the United States. The prisoners are transferred to the *Leo*. By December 1, circumstances begin to brighten when the *Leo* arrives off the Rock of Lisbon; however, at about 1300 the lookouts spot a formidable frigate that is closing fast. Captain Coggeshall takes steps to evade the warship until the *Leo* sustains an accident. At about 1400, part of the foremast breaks off and a short time later another section gets severed. At the time, there remains a large distance between the *Leo* and the British warship, leaving the Americans the confidence that they can make port at Lisbon before it can be intercepted. During the night and into the 2nd, the crew struggles to reach port. Success seems to be at hand. By 1300 on the 2nd, a pilot from Lisbon is brought aboard after the *Leo* reaches (by towing) the mouth of the Tagus River. At nearly the same time, a British frigate, the HMS *Granicus*, emerges from the river and the *Leo* is trapped. Captain Coggeshall is compelled to capitulate.

British captain W.F. Wise and his crew afford their prisoners extraordinary kindness and essentially treat them as passengers while the sail toward Gibraltar. Once at Gibraltar, Captain Coggeshall prepares to escape. While sitting in the courtroom of the Admiralty office awaiting the start of proceedings, Coggeshall notices a man (Mr. Allen) motioning for him to come over to where he is standing. Coggeshall responds and once there, he sees that the British lieutenant had left his post. Coggeshall after diverting the attention of a sergeant, hurriedly exits the building and shoots across a park and safely passes through the Land Port Gate standing at the northwest tip of the town.

From there, once outside the walls, he makes it to a Norwegian vessel and receives the cooperation of its captain, who provides Coggeshall with a Norwegian uniform. From there Coggeshall moves to the house of a smuggler (Antonio) in Algeciras, where he remains for several days. Afterward, he hires a mule and using provisions for about two days, which were given to him by his new friends, heads for Cadiz with the help of a guide. He finally arrives there on 28 December. Captain Coggeshall remains there until 15 February 1815, when he boards a Portuguese vessel with a captain who mandates that his crewmen gather on the quarterdeck three times a day; they all kneel down and he leads them in prayer. On 20 February the ship reaches Cape St. Vincent at about 1600. The captain, according to Captain Coggeshall, unabashedly calls for all hands and addresses them stating: "Officers and men, it has pleased God to bring us in safety thus far on our voyage; now let us all kneel down and thank him for his goodness and mercy to us poor sinners, and beseech him to conduct us in safety to our destined port."

The ship enters the harbor at Lisbon, Portugal, on 23 February. While in Lisbon, Captain Coggeshall encounters a friend from New York, James L. Kennedy, who is also anxious to get back to the States. Although pleased to have a friend with him, more importantly, Captain Coggeshall builds a relationship with some Portuguese who operate a wine-trading company, and they own a brigantine, the *Tres Hermanos*. Coggeshall, after discussing passage aboard the brigantine, strikes a deal, but passage includes Coggeshall's consent to offer his experience and advice to the ship's captain, apparently a very young and quite inexperienced man. Captain Coggeshall agrees, but he has reservations, including the caliber of Portuguese seamen and their conspicuous trait of avoiding soap. Another item that annoys Coggeshall is that he is reluctant to sail under the Portuguese flag. Nonetheless, after realizing no American vessels would be sailing for at least several weeks, Coggeshall and Kennedy depart on the Portuguese vessel on 13 March.

Soon after departing from the harbor, the captain essentially ignores Coggeshall, despite his promises to the owners. Captain Coggeshall later notes: "The little, narrow-minded captain did not consult me at all on the course of the vessel, and absolutely appeared so jealous of me, that my position was almost insupportable; and had not my friend Kennedy been on board, and the brig bound to New York, I should probably have been worse treated by these wretches. Although I scarcely exchanged a word with one of his men during the passage, I once overheard them say they should like to knock me in the head and throw me overboard." He also later relates: "The brig was in such a filthy condition, that Mr. Kennedy and myself suffered out of measure with one of the plagues of Egypt. The probability is, that before leaving Lisbon the sailors were allowed to sleep in the berths in the cabin, and thus every part of the vessel was overrun with vermin."

Finally, after an infamous voyage of 58 days, the ship arrives off Sandy Hook and soon enters New York Harbor to deliver Captain Coggeshall back to the States following his absence of sixteen months and twenty-one days. Describing his experience and offering some advice, the captain states. "I cannot leave this brig without warning my friends and countrymen never to take passage across the Atlantic in a Portuguese vessel of any description."

November 7 (Monday) **In Florida,** a contingent of troops under Captain Laval attacks and seizes a battery that stands in the path of General Jackson's route into Pensacola. During the assault, some accompanying artillery is unable to keep up due to the sandy beach. Nevertheless, while the Spaniards commence firing, Laval, at the head of the troops, bolts upon the battery and receives a devastating wound to one of his legs. The defenders of the battery abandon the position under the heavy pressure, but the officer in command decides to hold singlehandedly; he is captured. The Americans lose seven killed and eleven wounded. The Spanish defenders lose four killed, six wounded and some captured.

After eliminating the obstacle, Jackson moves against Pensacola. Three columns close quickly, and suddenly the approach of several thousand Americans prods Spanish Governor Manrique to have a change of heart. A white flag is offered by Manrique, who is suddenly anxious to agree to Jackson's terms and surrender Forts St. Michael and Barrancas. The offer turns sour when the commander at Fort St. Michael refuses to capitulate. Jackson, in the meantime, instructs Major Pierre to use 800 troops to ensure American occupation by the end of the day. Meanwhile a battery (St. Rose) outside Fort Barrancas is destroyed by the Spanish.

The British, so far unfazed by Jackson's presence, initiates a naval bombardment of Jackson's main body as it withdraws to the camp at the fringe of Pensacola. To deter the British from landing troops from the ships offshore, Jackson deploys about 500 troops along the beach, and in another tactical maneuver, he deploys some artillery on a dominant point, Mount St. Bernard, from where three pieces of artillery focus on the stubborn garrison under Colonel Sotto in Fort St. Michael. And to underscore the intent of Jackson, two companies deploy alongside the artillery. Apparently, Captain Denkins' artillery projects the proper incentive to bring about surrender.

At about 1800 hours, the Spaniards offer to capitulate, with the stipulation that they will be unable to depart until the morning of 8 November. This falls short of Jackson's intent, which is to control the fort prior to dawn to prevent the British warships from enjoying freedom of the sea. The delayed surrender proves unacceptable to the Americans and modifications occur. Denkins prepares to descend from the heights of Mt. St. Bernard to storm Fort St. Michael. Denkins' moves bring about a sudden change to Colonel Sotto, who decides that relinquishing the fort immediately is in his best interest. The Americans without incident take possession at about 2300.

Although Jackson has secured Pensacola, Fort Barrancas remains in the hands of the enemy. On the following morning, the Spanish governor still refuses to order the garrison to capitulate. Brigadier General William Colbert, a Chickasaw chief, who had fought alongside the Americans during the Revolution and afterward during the frontier wars in the northwest, has served for about nine months in the infantry during this conflict before joining in the fight against the Red Sticks. He is known to have pursued hostile Creeks from Pensacola nearly to Apalachicola.

November 8 (Tuesday) **In Florida,** at Pensacola, the Spanish governor, Manrique, still refuses to relinquish Fort Barrancas. This causes General Jackson to launch an assault, but before it commences, the Spanish self-destruct the fort. The British troops under Colonel Nicholls return to the ships, which sail for safer waters outside of the range of the fort's guns. Once the British re-embark the Creeks also hurriedly abandon the area. They move into the woods to evade capture by Jackson's troops. Subsequently, pursuit of the Red Sticks Creeks commences. Mounted forces under Major Blue, supported by friendly Indians, including Creeks, Chickasaws and Choctaws, criss-cross the swamps between Escambia and the bays in West Florida. The contingent essentially carries out the mop-up operations of the Creek War. All prisoners seized are taken to Fort Montgomery.

In naval activity, the HMS *Leander* captures the privateer *General Putnam* (J. Evans, master), a schooner operating out of Salem and carrying a crew of 41 and four guns.

November 9 (Wednesday) **In Florida,** General Andrew Jackson returns from Pensacola to Montgomery, Alabama. From there, Jackson departs for Mobile after placing much of the army under the command of Major Uriah Blue (39th U.S. Infantry). In Mobile he is briefed, and after a short stay, he heads for New Orleans, Louisiana. While in command, Major Blue constantly sends out mounted patrols that search the swamps along the Escambia and the bays in western Florida. Blue's troops are accompanied by friendly Creeks, along with Chickasaws and Choctaws. The patrols engage renegade Creeks and many, including women and children, are captured and taken under heavy guard to Fort Montgomery.

In naval activity, the HMS *Maidstone* intercepts and seizes the 224-ton brigantine *Jane,* which is en route from Liverpool, England, to New Brunswick, Canada, with a cargo of salt. In other naval activity, the British privateer *Rover* intercepts and seizes the 21-ton schooner *Ruth* (Ambrose Jones, master), which is transporting a cargo of dry fish.

November 11, 1814, to January 27, 1815 *In naval activity,* the American privateer *Lawrence,* commanded by Captain E. Veasey, intercepts and captures the brigantine *Eagle* on 11 November. While the prize crew is sailing it into an American port, several prisoners attempt to regain the ship. Two Frenchmen and one Negro, after collaborating with the former commander, strike on 7 December. The prize master, John Snow, is killed, along with the man at the helm and one other. The prisoners close the hatch to confine the other Americans. During their captivity, the Americans plan to take their prize back. Three days later, they spring their attack. They pry the hatch open and quickly overwhelm and disarm both of the Frenchmen; however, the Negro, named Manuel, while being confronted, decides to jump overboard with his cutlass in hand. Once the ship is regained, it resumes its voyage, which is again interrupted on 27 January 1815. The HMS *Saturn* intercepts the *Eagle* just as it approaches New York and recaptures it for the second time. Nonetheless, the British are unable to maintain possession for long. Shortly after being recaptured, the *Eagle* is lost at sea by shipwreck. The *Lawrence* arrives in New York on 25 January 1815.

November 12 (Saturday) *In naval activity,* the privateer *Fly* is commissioned in Maine this day. Also, the British privateer *Rover* intercepts and seizes the 65-ton schooner *Jane,* which is transporting a cargo of ballast from Boston to Harpswell, Maine. The prize is taken into port at Liverpool. In other naval activity, the British privateer *Lunenburg* intercepts and seizes the 25-ton schooner *Three Friends* (John Philips, master), which has a cargo of ballast going from Kittery, Maine to Boston. The *Three Friends* is separate from the schooner *Three Friends* seized 18 December 1812 and the schooner *Three Friends* captured 30 July 1814.

November 14 (Monday) **In New York City,** Governor Tompkins writes to Commodore Macdonough:

> Sir: I have reflected for a few hours upon the subject of the confidential Letter of the Secretary of the Navy which you communicated to me this afternoon. The steam frigate building in this harbour is, I presume, intended to act as a moveable Battery for harbour defence; & is expected to operate most advantageously in a calm, when ships of the ordinary construction would be unmanageable; & she of consequence enabled to choose her position. The experiment of her utility is still to be tried though I think it probable she will answer the end proposed. I do not believe however that Vessels of this description would be formidable on the ocean, or on broad waters; or that they would be the most advisable armament for lake Ontario. Ships of the line & frigates form the naval force, upon which alone I should place reliance; either for blockading the enemy fleet on that lake or for conquering it in open fight.

November 15 (Tuesday) **In New York,** Governor Tompkins issues orders to Captain Tyler regarding Sandy Hook: "Sir: Brigadier Genl. [Joseph] Swift is preparing the light House at Sandy Hook for defence. Four nines or twelves, one 51-inch Howitzer &. ten small pieces are required to equip it. You will please to call on General Swift the Chief Engineer, for information as to the places in which they are to be mounted & prepared the Cannon, Howitzer & small pieces for the purpose as soon as possible."

In naval activity, the HMS *Saturn* intercepts and recaptures the 237-ton brigantine *Theodore;* the prize is taken into port at Liverpool.

November 16 (Wednesday) *In naval activity,* the pilot of the American privateer *Syren* runs the vessel ashore along the New Jersey coast while sailing toward the Delaware after culminating a cruise. Afterward, the vessel comes under attack by a British force carried by three barges. The Americans repel the attackers during a contest that lasts about two hours before they conclude their position is untenable. Nevertheless, the crew disregards the option of surrender. They get to shore with their six prisoners and leave the burning *Syren* to the British. The *Syren* had captured a British privateer, the *Sir John Sherbroke*, which is en route to an American port; however, the prize crew is intercepted and chased off of New Jersey during December. Also, the *Syren* had seized two vessels off the coast of England, and both were destroyed at sea. Another prize, the *Emulation*, is abandoned by the crew in the Western Isles.

November 17 (Thursday) *In naval activity,* the American-held 70-ton schooner *Julian* (John Darah, master), carrying a cargo of rum, is recaptured by its own crew while the vessel is moving from St. Vincent's to Liverpool. The *Julian* is separate from the *Julian* seized on 13 November 1812, the *Julian* seized 8 December 1813, and the *Julian* captured 6 August 1814. In other naval activity, the American privateer *Leo* intercepts and seizes a Spanish brigantine, the *Alonzo*. The Americans board it at about 1500 to abruptly terminate its voyage to London. A prize crew is assigned to the *Alonzo* and it is taken into port in the United States.

November 19 (Saturday) **In Tennessee,** General William Carroll departs Nashville en route to New Orleans with a division of Tennessee militia volunteers to join with General Jackson, who is threatened by a British army. The troops travel by barges, flat-boats and even rafts, each of which is crammed with men. Nevertheless, Jackson's call for reinforcements causes difficulties. Gathering the craft had been complicated, and due to the time of year, the Cumberland River usually is not navigable. The distance to New Orleans is about 1,500 miles, a most difficult march. Carroll receives some unexpected assistance when the region is struck by successive storms that raise the water level, allowing them to use the river. But Carroll's force has another major problem. Most of his volunteers lack weapons.

Fortuitously, after the flotilla enters the Mississippi River, Carroll encounters some U.S. government vessels that had departed Pittsburgh, Pennsylvania and were transporting weapons and ammunition. Suddenly, the Tennesseans find themselves fully armed with a substantial amount of ammunition. The flotilla arrives near New Orleans on 22 December, coincidentally on the eve of a British attack against Jackson's positions. General Carroll, like General Coffee, is a long-time friend of General Jackson.

In Georgia, Major General David Adams, who earlier was directed to raise a division (5th), informs General David Blackshear that he will require 75 of the troops to be drawn from Blackshear's brigade. Blackshear is also directed to erect blockhouses on his frontier line at a space of between ten to twenty miles. General Blackshear retains his commission until 1826. On 21 February 1826, Governor G.M. Troup states in a letter to General Blackshear: "It would be ungenerous, after you had filled so many offices of trust and honor, civil and military, and all to the satisfaction and advantage of your country, to deny to you, in the decline of life, the privilege to retire from your military command. I regret, notwithstanding, that the infirmities of age, or any other cause, should deprive the public of your usefulness in any sphere of action. It is known to me that, if your strength has departed, your patriotism remains unquenched, and that in any peril or danger threatened to the country we can still confidently appeal to that first of virtues which has never failed you in the worst of times, and which you will carry with you to the grave. Your resignation is accepted, with a sincere hope that many days of happiness remain for you."

General Blackshear had married Fanny Hamilton during 1802. Together they had eleven children: Mary Hamilton (December 1, 1803, died in infancy); James Hamilton (November 1805, married Caroline, daughter of General John Floyd); William Thweatt (November 14, 1807), Edward Jefferson (June 1810, married Mary Jane, daughter of Col. James J. Pittman); Ann Eliza (April 1812, died in infancy); Eliza Ann (December 1813, died in infancy); David, Jr. (February 1816); Everard Hamilton (June 1818, married Isabella Maria C., daughter of Colonel Everard Hamilton); Joseph John Floyd (October 1821); Elijah Francks (September 1822, married Mary Ann L., daughter of Colonel Everard Hamilton) and John Duke (January 1824, died within one year of birth). General Blackshear dies on 4 July 1837. His wife died at age 43 on 28 February 1824.

November 18–19 *In naval activity,* the American privateer *Leo* (Captain Coggeshall) is chased by a British warship. At about 2000 on the 18th, the lookouts on the *Leo* spot a sail that when identified is a brigantine; however, with the warship close behind, the *Leo* bypasses it. At about midnight (18th-19th) nasty weather arrives, prompting Captain Coggeshall to order the sails adjusted to cope with the elements. By about 0700 on the 19th, the lookouts spot another vessel and the pursuing warship is nowhere in sight. By 1000, the vessel, a cutter out of Tenerife en route to London with a cargo of wine, becomes a prize of the *Leo*. The crew removes twenty casks of wine, with the prize's sails and rigging, and takes prisoners aboard the *Leo*. The prize is destroyed.

After a while, the *Leo* is greeted by another sail; however, the incoming salutations are shells being catapulted by a 16-gun warship. Captain Coggeshall orders return fire by his 12-pounders. Nevertheless, the *Leo* is not anxious to engage in a standing battle. After receiving more than thirty shots in its general direction, with one them striking the *Leo*, Coggeshall focuses on losing the British and quickly sails off to escape any further damage.

November 21 (Monday) *In naval activity,* the American privateer *Leo* spots an unidentified vessel and initiates pursuit. After closing to within about three miles, Captain Coggeshall orders the crew to hoist the British colors. The vessel, a frigate, hoists a Portuguese flag. The vessel while continuing to evade the *Leo* apparently is trying to trick the *Leo* into moving within range of its guns. The British colors are replaced by the Stars and Stripes and Captain Coggeshall, confident he can effortlessly outrun the frigate if it is a British warship, adjusts the sails and the *Leo* soon loses sight of it.

November 22 (Tuesday) **In Alabama,** General Jackson on or about this day departs Mobile, heading toward New Orleans. He leaves a detachment that can be rushed in several different directions, depending upon where the British assault will occur. Reinforcements also depart Nashville on the 20th to meet Jackson at New Orleans. Coffee's force heads toward Baton Rouge, where he is stationed, and from where he can move back to Mobile or on to New Orleans, wherever his men are needed most.

In naval activity, the American privateer *Leo*, en route from France to the United States, encounters a British schooner taking a cargo of fruit from Malaga to Dublin, Ireland. The Americans remove some of the fruit and transfer the prisoners to the *Leo*. A crew is assigned to the prize with orders to take it into an American port. Also, at about midnight (21st-22nd), the *Leo* encounters a Danish vessel, and during the brief pause, Captain Coggeshall transfers 10 prisoners to the Danes.

November 23 (Wednesday) *In naval activity,* the *Firmina* (Antonio Jose Feleira, master), a 260-ton ship going from Boston to Amelia Island, is cut off by a British squadron comprising the HMS *Arab*, the HMS *Curlew*, the HMS *Junon* and the HMS *Maidstone*. The British seize the ship and its cargo of ballast.

The American privateer *Leo* encounters a brigantine; however, it is a Prussian vessel. Soon after at about 1200, the *Leo* spots two other vessels, and it becomes obvious that they are British warships, once the chase begins. The *Leo* is too fast for the British to have any chance of catching it.

November 24 (Thursday) *In naval activity,* the British assemble a large fleet at Jamaica. The force includes seamen and reinforcements (Wellington's army). Other British troops that had participated in the Baltimore campaign join the force later. The force is commanded by British General Keane. Meanwhile, General Pakenham is still at sea en route from England. Optimism permeates the entire operation and the British are so confident of seizing Louisiana that the fleet is also transporting a staff that will "rule over the Crown Colony of Louisiana." In other naval activity, the HMS *Spencer* seizes the 120-ton *Superb*, a brigantine en route to Philadelphia from Charlestown with a cargo of rice.

November 25 (Friday) *In naval activity,* the privateer *Cumberland*, a schooner, is commissioned in Maine this day. In other naval activity, the American privateer *Leo* spots an unidentified sail at about 1500 and initiates a chase. The ship fires at the *Leo*, and at about the same time, the Stars and Stripes are hoisted, but only momentarily before the colors are lowered and replaced by British colors. Once the British colors are flying, the vessels fires another four or five shots, none of which reach the *Leo*. By about dusk, contact is lost.

November 26 (Saturday) *In naval activity,* the American privateer *Leo* (Captain Coggeshall) encounters an unidentified sail at about 1300. It initiates pursuit and at 2130 comes up alongside and seizes its prey, without incident. The prize is a 6-gun 200-ton British ship, carrying a mixed cargo including brimstone, mats and rags. On the following day, the crew is transferred to the *Leo* and a prize crew is assigned. The ship out of Palermo, Italy, en route to London, is diverted to a U.S. port. In other naval activity, it is reported in London that the British ship *Adele* (East India vessel) had been seized by an American privateer off Pontana (Indonesia).

November 26–27 A British fleet leaves Jamaica with four regiments from the Chesapeake Campaign and additional fresh troops from England. They are joined at sea by additional vessels and men.

November 27 (Sunday) *In naval activity,* the American privateer *Leo* encounters an unidentified sail, but the encounter turns friendly when it is discovered to be a Portuguese schooner. Later in the day, at about noon, the Rock of Lisbon comes into sight.

November 28 (Monday) *In naval activity,* the privateer *Armistice* is commissioned in Maine.

November 29 to December 2 (Tuesday) *In naval activity,* the 12-gun American privateer *Kemp*, commanded by Captain Jacobs, departs from Wilmington, North Carolina, en route to the West Indies. On 1 December, the privateer's lookouts spot a convoy that appears to include at least one British warship. The *Kemp*, carrying a crew of 130 men, shadows the convoy from a distance and maintains contact throughout the night (1st-2nd). On the morning of the 2nd, the Americans are able to see that eight merchant ships are sailing under the protection of a frigate. Captain Jacobs senses an opportunity to be able to pick off the merchant ships by lurking to the rear. At about 1200 on the 2nd, the frigate, which has been maintaining surveillance on the *Kemp*, tires of the annoyance and swings away from the convoy to dispose of the privateer.

The British frigate confidently pursues the *Kemp*, to the glee of Captain Jacobs, who intentionally sweeps it away from the convoy for a prolonged chase. After nightfall, while the British frigate struggles to keep up with the superior sailing vessel, the *Kemp*'s crew extinguishes its lights and without discovery changes course and sails back toward the convoy while the frigate searches blindly for the privateer. By the following morning at about 1100, sails are spotted, and after closer examination, Captain Jacobs realizes that the frigate had not yet returned. The privateer, expecting to strike before the frigate can return, moves directly toward the convoy.

Meanwhile, the British, who immediately realize they are coming under attack by a privateer, rally to combine the 46 guns of their eight merchant ships, which also have a total of 134 men. Anticipating the attack, the merchant ships form in a line with their guns facing the path of attack, and before the closing *Kemp* can strike, the British take the offensive and move to converge on the privateer, each delivering a broadside as they pass the *Kemp*.

Captain Jacobs, while absorbing the initial enemy fire, orders return fire withheld. And then as he passes through the line, while at extremely close quarters, the *Kemp* fires two deadly broadsides that drains the British from maintaining effective action and causes them interfere with one another. Captain Jacobs, taking advantage of the undisciplined British merchantmen, keeps one enemy vessel between the *Kemp* and the other enemy ships as a shield, while the Americans begin to pick off the vessels one at a time. By his cunning strategy and the sailing skills of his crew, one of the vessels, the brigantine *Portsea*, manned by 26 men and mounting 8 guns, is taken, along with its cargo, which includes coffee and sugar. One American is wounded during the capture of the first ship in the convoy.

Less than one hour later, a boarding party of eight men springs from the *Kemp*, takes the British crew by surprise and adds the 16-gun ship *Rosabella*, manned by 35 five, men as a prize, following a brief fight on its decks. At nearly the same time, a boarding party led by Captain Jacobs bolts upon one of the schooners and seizes it without encountering any resistance, giving the *Kemp* three prizes and still, there is no sight of the frigate. The next target becomes the biggest brigantine in the convoy. Captain Jacobs, undaunted by its size, springs the attack. The boarding party does meet some fierce resistance, but it is overcome after about 15 to 20 minutes of combat. After seizing the fourth prize, Captain Jacobs realizes that he must spare the remaining four, but not because the British warship is within sight; rather because his crew has been severely diminished by the assignment of prize crews and no additional men can be spared without great risk to the *Kemp*.

Captain Jacobs and his crew have stripped the convoy of one-half of its vessels and had sustained one man, John Irwin, killed and four others wounded. The prizes carry some valuable cargoes, primarily coffee and sugar. The *Rosabella*, with a cargo valued at $300,000, arrives safely at Charleston, then accidentally gets caught on the bar and is totally lost. About one week after its arrival, a British brigantine assigned to the blockading squadron arrives and destroys the *Rosabella*. During its entire service at sea, the *Kemp* seizes a total of fifteen vessels. The *Kemp* sets sail for home, unaware of the location of the frigate it lost in the darkness. No further contact is established, permitting the *Kemp* an uneventful voyage. The prizes are sent into various southern ports.

December *In naval activity,* the American privateer *Syren* out of Baltimore, commanded by Captain J.D. Daniels, captures the 12-gun British privateer *Sir John Broke* (*Sir John Brook*). The prize is driven ashore in New Jersey at Rockaway to escape recapture by British blockading ships. The American prize crew removes its armaments and other items before they burn it.

December 1 (Thursday) **In Louisiana,** Jackson arrives in Baton Rouge. This is where he will stage his defense and hopefully prevent a British victory, if the assault comes by way of the Mississippi River.

In naval activity, the American privateer *David Porter* embarks on another cruise. During its short fifteen days at sea, the privateer captures the brigantine *Hiram*, with a cargo valued at $100,000, and another vessel, the *Ann Dorothy*, which had been an American vessel earlier captured by the British. After a short stay in port, the privateer embarks on another cruise during January 1815, unaware that the war had ended. During this final cruise, the *David Porter* searches far and wide for British shipping off such places as Brazil, the Canary Islands, Madeiras, Portugal and the Western Isles. During the cruise, which lasts 80 days, it is able to seize only three ships, the *Flying Fish* with a rich cargo valued at $200,000, the 3-masted schooner *George*, which is deemed of no value and released, and the brigantine *Legal Tender*, bringing its total prizes during the conflict to fifteen. The brigantine *Legal Tender* does not make it to an American port. The 74-gun ship HMS *Spencer* intercepts it and it is recaptured on 7 March.

In other naval activity, the American privateer *Leo*, commanded by Captain Coggeshall, encounters an unidentified sail rapidly approaching. Just after 1400, while preparing to take action if necessary, the *Leo* unexpectedly sustains a crippling accident. The wind snaps its foremast at a point about one third from the top and at nearly at the same time, it is again severed down near the deck. During the confusion of the moment, to the dismay of Captain Googeshall and the crew, the British vessel passes nearly close enough to touch. Captain Coggeshall notes:

> While in this situation, I had the mortification to see the ship pass us, within pistol-shot, without being able to pursue it. I believe she was an English packet, just out of Lisbon, and bound for England; and, I doubt not, if this unfortunate accident had not occurred, we should have captured her in less than one hour from the time she was first seen. At this time the packets transported large quantities of specie to England, and this ship would, in all probability, have proved a rich prize to us. I have no doubt the mast was defective, and that it should have been renewed before leaving port. From this untoward circumstance resulted all the misfortunes attending the cruise.

Captain Coggeshall becomes concerned because of the condition of his ship and focuses on getting into Lisbon or into St. Ubea before dawn of the following day or risk capture by the British. By 1600, after rushing temporary repairs, the *Leo* heads for Lisbon.

December 2 (Friday) General Jackson, accompanied by only his staff, arrives at New Orleans, following a ride of eleven days. The general and his party pause at the J. Kilty Smith estate in a village near where the Canal Carondelet meets the Bayou St. John. Smith had been expecting General Jackson, and for the occasion he had engaged the services of his neighbor, a Creole woman, to prepare for the visit. Jackson and the others with him are treated royally; however, his

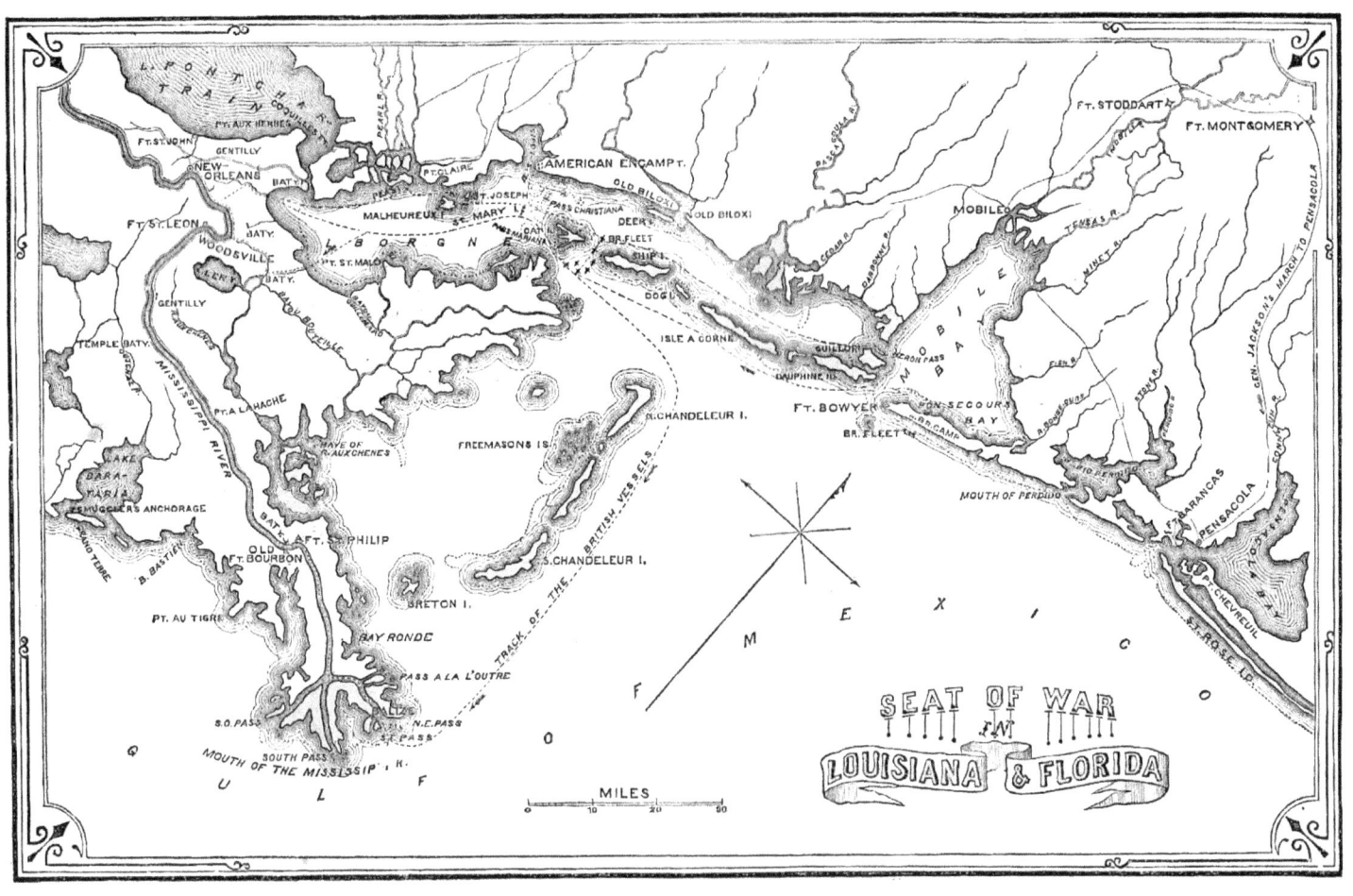

Seat of war, Louisiana and Florida.

uniform is ragged and he looks exhausted. Later, the woman gets Smith aside and privately burns his ears, stating: "Ah, Mr. Smith! How could you play such a trick upon me? You asked me to get your house in order to receive a great General. I did so. I worked myself almost to death to make your house *comme il faut* and prepared a splendid *dejeuner*, and now I find that all my labor is thrown upon an ugly old Kaintuck-flatboatman instead of your grand General, with plumes, epaulettes, long sword and mustache." Smith's repeated attempts to convince his neighbor that it was Jackson were in vain.

Following breakfast, the party departs in carriages and proceeds into the city. Their horses, too exhausted to continue, are left at the Smith estate. A welcoming committee, including Governor Claiborne and the mayor of New Orleans, Nicholas Girod, are there to greet him. Jackson gives a brief speech about preserving the city. Most people there speak little or no English; however, Edward Livingston, a prominent attorney who speaks both English and French, translates. Jackson's words, despite the translation, mesmerize and electrify those present, and General Jackson begins to be referred to as the "Savior of New Orleans."

Following his introduction to the citizens of New Orleans, General Jackson is taken to his headquarters in a brick building, one of the few such buildings in the city, at 106 Royal Street. Shortly thereafter, the Stars and Stripes is unfurled from the third floor of his headquarters. His presence, speech, demeanor and strength of character became instantly effective and the dreadful fear that had permeated the city soon vanishes. Jackson immediately prepares to fortify the city's defenses against a British assault. He also appoints Edward Livingston as his aide-de-camp.

Jackson also learns of the plight of Lafitte by intermediaries. Interestingly, Lafitte is usually remembered as a pirate, yet he only went to sea twice in his life, once when he sailed from France to America and his second time at sea, which turned fatal, when he sailed back to France. General Jackson accepts the services of Lafitte and his entire band of buccaneers. Jackson assigns them to the artillery. General Jackson takes some other unusual steps. He releases some prisoners from jail, those who have two months or less to finish their sentences.

The Louisiana militia is called up for service at the city, and he requests the services of free Negroes. Jackson also sends word to Baton Rouge to direct General Coffee to lead his 2,000 troops to New Orleans to further bolster his forces. Nonetheless, as the defending force increases, General Jackson is also awaiting another force, volunteers from Kentucky and from Tennessee, all of whom are being transported by vessels. In an effort to maintain absolute control of the city during this period of uncertainty, General Jackson declares martial law.

During his initial days in New Orleans, General Jackson attends a dinner at the residence of the Livingstons. Unlike his earlier pause at J. Kilty Smith's home, as described by Mr. Livingston, "The General was in the full-dress uniform of his rank — that of major general in the regular army. This was a blue frock-coat with buff facings and gold lace, white waistcoat and close fitting breeches, also of white cloth, with morocco boots reaching above the knees. To my astonishment this uniform was new, spotlessly clean and fitted his tall, slender form perfectly. I had seen him before only in the somewhat worn and careless fatigue uniform he were on duty at headquarters. I had to confess to myself that the new and perfectly fitting full-dress uniform made almost another man of him."

General Jackson is reluctant to speak about the imminent invasion, a subject which was of great interest to all of the ladies present; however in that regard, Jackson does say to Mrs. Livingston and the others, "while possibly the British soldiers might get near enough to see the church-spires that pointed to heaven from the sanctuaries of your religion, none should ever get even a glimpse of the inner sanctuaries of your homes."

Following the departure of General Jackson from the dinner, it becomes evident that he had won a major battle with eloquence and charm rather than bullets and steel. Livingston is immediately encircled by the women in attendance, who exclaim nearly in unison, "Is this your savage Indian fighter? Is this your rough frontier general? Shame on you for deceiving us so. He is a veritable *preux chevalier!*"

In naval activity, the schooner *Cynthia*, transporting a cargo that includes cotton, flour, grain and lumber from New York to New Providence in the Bahamas, is seized by the British privateer *Rolla*. In other naval activity, the American privateer *Leo*, damaged by an accident on the previous day, is trying to limp into port at Lisbon before getting caught by a British warship, but the winds become unfavorable during the early morning hours, impeding progress. At about 0500, the *Leo* arrives near Cape Esparttel and the Rock of Lisbon, and the winds totally subside. The men man two boats and begin to tow the *Leo* toward port. The men struggle with the task, but by about 1400, the *Leo* stands only four miles from shore, and so far, no enemy warships are in sight. At that same time, a pilot from Lisbon reaches the ship. The crew also detects a British warship moving out of the Tagus River. Suddenly the crippled *Leo* is threatened by a 38-gun frigate, the HMS *Granicus*, commanded by Captain W.F. Wise. The Herculean effort to get the Leo into port falls short. The British capture it and the crew is taken aboard the frigate. The British take the *Leo* into Gibraltar.

December 3 (Saturday) *In naval activity,* the navy acquires a vessel, the *Leader*. It is afterward commissioned the USS *Flambeau*. It sees no action during the conflict, which is coming to a close; however, it departs New York on 20 May 1815 as part of Commodore Stephen Decatur's squadron, which sails to participate against the Barbary pirates at Algiers. The *Flambeau* sails back to the United States from Gibraltar with the squadron on 6 October, but en route it gets separated during a storm. Nonetheless, the *Flambeau* safely arrives at Newport, Rhode Island, on 9 November. Within a few weeks it is placed in ordinary at New York. It remains there until it is sold in April 1816.

In other activity, the *Gleaner* (Timothy Chapman, master), a 70-ton sloop which started out from New York, is intercepted and seized before it reaches its destination at East Haddam, Connecticut, with a cargo of flour, rye and other items. The British privateer *Rolla* takes its prize into port at Liverpool. The *Gleaner* is separate from the privateer *Gleaner* seized on 23 July 1812.

In naval activity, the *Lucia*, a sloop en route from New York to Bedford, Massachusetts, is intercepted and seized by two British privateers, the *Liverpool Packet* and the *Rolla*.

December 5 (Monday) *In naval activity,* the British privateer *Rover* intercepts the schooner *Fox* (Samuel Swasy, master) while it is en route to Elizabeth, North Carolina, with a cargo including salt and potatoes. The prize is taken into Liverpool. The *Fox* is separate from the schooner *Fox* seized on 8 September 1814. In other naval activity, the HMS *Granicus,* carrying the crew of the American privateer *Leo*, arrives at Gibraltar. Captain Coggeshall and two of his officers are held aboard the *Granicus* until they can be taken to the Admiralty Board. Meanwhile, the British split up the crew to have them sent back in smaller groups to England in separate ships. Within a day, the *Granicus* sails from Gibraltar and makes a stop at Morocco opposite Gibraltar to acquire fresh water. While in port at Morocco, the *Granicus* also undergoes a fresh paint job. During this pause, American Captain Coggeshall is treated more like a passenger than a prisoner and the two officers with him are also treated extremely well. Captain Coggeshall later remarks: "We messed in the ward-room. I had a stateroom to myself, and was as comfortable and happy as I could be under the circumstances. I used to dine with Capt. Wise almost daily; he frequently said to me, 'Don't feel depressed by captivity, but strive to forget that you are a prisoner, and imagine that you are only a passenger.'" Coggeshall later writes in his book (1856) *The History of the Privateers* that Captain Wise had told him while aboard the *Granicus*:

> You Americans are a singular people as it respects seamanship and enterprise. In England, we cannot build such vessels as your Baltimore clippers; we have no such models, and even if we had them, they would be of no service to us, for we never could sail them as you do. We have now and then taken some of your schooners with our fast sailing frigates. They have sometimes caught one of them under their lee, in a heavy gale of wind, by out-carrying them. Then, again, we have taken a few with our boats in calm weather. We are afraid of their long masts and heavy spars, and soon cut down and reduce them to our standard. We strengthen them, put up bulkheads, etc., after which they lose their sailing qualities, and are of no further service as cruising vessels.

Captains Wise and Coggeshall have frequent conversations while aboard the *Granicus*. Captain Wise, while discussing the duel between the USS *Constitution* and the HMS *Guerriere,* mentions that Captain Dacres of the *Guerriere* is his cousin and Captain Coggeshall informs Wise that Captain Isaac Hull of the *Constitution* is his relative (first cousin to his father).

Another interesting conversation centered around a British captain's wife who was aboard ship while an American schooner, thought trapped, managed to escape. As Captain Wise related the incident, he pointed out how the encounter would be written by a "nautical man," who would probably say: "The ship got into the wind and made a stern board, and before we could get sufficient steerage way upon her to tack after the schooner, the little craft had already made three or four tacks right in the wind's eye, and was soon out of reach of our shot, and thus made her escape, to our great surprise and mortification." Captain Wise continued his story, which turned upon the captain's wife after the ship returned to England. She, having watched the entire operation from the quarter deck, began to relate the encounter to her friends and explained that her husband's ship could not catch the American schooner. When someone inquired why it was not caught, she succinctly responded: "Because we could not turn around soon enough."

During the voyage, one of the confident and enthusiastic midshipmen, anxious to defend the honor of England by engaging an American frigate, mentioned his sentiments at dinner in company with Captain Wise and Captain Coggeshall. Captain Coggeshall, while listening, hears Captain Wise respond with what might be called an eloquent reprimand: "Don't boast, youngster, perhaps if you should, you might get handsomely whipped."

December 6 (Tuesday) *In naval activity,* two British privateers, the *Liverpool Packet* and the *Rolla*, cruising together, close on a schooner, the 29-ton *Fairtrader*, which is en route from New Bedford to New York with a cargo of candles, fish, salt, rice and wine. The privateers overpower the *Fairtrader* and take it into port at Liverpool. The *Fairtrader* is separate from the privateer *Fairtrader* seized on 16 July 1812.

December 7 (Wednesday) *In naval activity,* after being at sea for 15 days, the British arrive at Stip Island, less than 50 miles from General Jackson's forces at New Orleans. The British intend to get the ground troops across Lake Borne and Lake Pontchartrain, neither of which are thought to be defended.

December 8 (Thursday) *In naval activity,* the HMS *Nimrod* intercepts and recaptures the 146-ton brigantine *Lady Prevost* (Alexander Strang, master), which is en route from Lisbon, Portugal, to St. John's, Newfoundland.

December 9 (Friday) *In naval activity,* a British fleet that includes some small vessels arrives off the Gulf of Mexico from the West Indies. The weather is poor but it eventually clears, which provides an opportunity for the troops to get a glimpse of land. The fleet, including the HMS *Tonnant*, formerly a French warship before its capture at Abouquir, leads the way, trailed by the *Sea Horse* and the remainder of the force. The land which is spotted is Dauphine Island, Alabama. The British skirt past the island and sail westwardly toward Lake Borgne, which is north of New Orleans. While passing Dauphine Island, the British notice two U.S. gunboats along the shoreline that seem to be positioned to shadow the massive fleet. Nevertheless, the British ignore the American vessels and continue their voyage. The weather again changes and the British decide it would be too dangerous to risk entering Lake Borgne until the following morning.

Meanwhile, the two U.S. vessels, Gunboats No. 23 and No. 163, commanded by Lt. Isaac McKeever (later commodore) and Lt. Ulrick, return to Biloxi Bay after they determine the British had halted for the night. There they join their squadron, commanded by Lt. Catesby Jones (later commodore). Jones' orders from Commodore Patterson had been to post his force, composed of his six gunboats and two other vessels, and to deploy to block the fleet's barges from reaching shore.

December 10 (Saturday) **In Louisiana,** the British fleet, which had arrived from the West Indies with reinforcements, waits for the morning fog to dissipate before entering Lake Borgne. The fleet is under observation by Lt. Catesby Jones' squadron. Jones redeploys his force at Pass Christian to block passage. Meanwhile, the British hit an obstacle, but not the U.S. gunboats; rather, after entering the lake, the ships encounter shallow water, which prevents the larger ships from any further advance. The British make adjustments to their plan. Troops are transferred to the smaller vessels. Nevertheless, the gunboats must still be eliminated before the vulnerable transports and other vessels can attempt to make a landing. While the troops are held back, Captain Lockyer is assigned the task of ridding the lake of the gunboats. Lockyer is familiar with the coastline due to his earlier visits to Grand Terre Island when the British attempted to persuade Jean Lafitte to side with them. The boats, about 45 of them, are gathered, and on the night of the 12th, Lockyer advances. The boats carry a total of 42 guns, and his ground troops, including sailors and Royal Marines, number about 1,000.

December 12 (Monday) **In Louisiana,** British Captain Lockyer leads his flotilla away from the fleet and toward the small U.S. naval detachment that is holding positions at Christian Pass on Lake Borgne. The pass is the British gateway to New Orleans. While Lockyer moves to engage the Americans, Admiral Cochrane's fleet remains at anchor off Ship Island, Mississippi. A two-day chase ensues and the two forces finally clash on the 14th.

December 13 (Tuesday) **In Louisiana,** the Americans at Baton Rouge are ordered to New Orleans by Andrew Jackson to defend the city against the invasion. The British have landed about 40 miles outside of New Orleans.

In naval activity, a flotilla of about 45 boats attached to the British fleet under Admiral Cochrane closes on Lt. Catesby Jones' diminutive force of gunboats. Several of the barges are sent to seize one of Jones' vessels, the schooner *Sea Horse,* commanded by Sailing Master William Johnson, which is on a mission to acquire supplies. The British move close to the *Sea Horse* to board it; however, it makes no attempt to escape. The crew appears to be making no effort to resist. Nonetheless, just as the three barges move into range, the guns of the *Sea Horse* roar into action. The British who come under fire unexpectedly are further dismayed when a shore battery of two 6-pounders also erupts. The barges are deluged with flying steel. The boats retire. Meanwhile, the *Sea Horse,* more difficult to corral than thought, remains operable.

As the British retire, the Americans, still confronted with facing the entire force, refuse to consider capture. The ship's commanding officer orders the crew to destroy all supplies on shore and orders the ship to be set afire.

In the meantime, Catesby Jones and his Spartan force continue to disregard the immense odds they face. Jones' naval detachment sails toward Petit Coquilles, a predetermined point where the Americans have minor fortifications. Nonetheless, reaching the destination becomes a futile maneuver. His detachment is unable to overcome the strength of the currents, which pull his vessels away from the Rigolets, a diminutive strait in Orleans Parish, and pushes them toward a slim channel that lies between the mainland at Point Clear and Malheureux Island. The shallow water snags several of Jones' vessels, which bog down in the sand. Jones, however, shows no inclination to destroy his vessels and escape capture. At dawn the next day, the entire British flotilla comes into view. Nonetheless, Jones continues to disregard the insurmountable odds; he intends to engage the enemy.

December 14 (Wednesday) **In Louisiana,** Catesby Jones' naval detachment remains stranded in a channel separating the mainland from Malheureux. At dawn, spotters observe the British flotilla at anchor less than ten miles from Jones' gunboats. The British troops are leisurely relaxing following their long journey and enjoying their morning meal before the rowers once again set out to capture or destroy the American gunboats. The view from the channel is overpowering, and it would neither be ungallant nor cowardly for Jones to avoid calamity by scuttling his vessels and escaping to shore. Jones, however, possesses no thoughts of avoiding a fight. He summons his officers and once they are together on his ship, the officers are given the battle plan. Without dissent, the officers return to their respective vessels and prepare for the floating army under Captain Lockyer, whose flotilla is composed of about 45 boats carrying no fewer than 1,000 seamen and Royal Marines. The British force is bolstered by more than 40 guns.

In the meantime, the British, having finished their breakfasts, prepare to dispose of Jones' pesky blockade. While the Americans can see the movement of the flotilla, Lockyer is able to observe the activity in the channel. Lockyer, commanding an overwhelmingly superior force, is disappointed when he does not spot the Americans attempting to escape the inevitable. Instead, he sees bristling activity as they are forming for battle rather than taking flight. For the British the astonishing sight looks more suicidal than courageous. Nonetheless, Jones' commanders are anchoring their respective sterns with springs on the cables. Five gunboats, No. 156, Jones' flagship, No. 5, No. 169 and No. 163, alone stand against the advancing flotilla, which is aligned in near perfect formation stretching from bank to bank.

The British wave moves forward, but still, the Americans show no signs of flinching; however, the British Commander Lockyer undergoes a period of deciding the risk of attacking such an audacious band that displays an obvious willingness to fight to the last man. Meanwhile, Jones' gunners are poised to fire as the barges are just coming into range. Nonetheless, they observe something unexpected. A detachment of the boats begins to break away and row westwardly, arousing the curiosity of Jones' men. Soon it becomes obvious. A sail is spotted and it becomes the target of the British. Another U.S. vessel, the *Alligator,* is desperately attempting to evade the British and join Jones in the channel. Lockyer, on the other hand sees an easy kill. The *Alligator,* not quite a ship of the line, is a small tender. Nonetheless, its commander, sailing master Richard S. Sheppard, and his crew expect to help hold the line in the channel.

Four of the barges, transporting about 400 troops, move against the *Alligator.* At about the same time, the British get some outside assistance when the winds vanish and the *Alligator* gets stalled, leaving it stranded. The British move in quickly and seize it, along with its solitary gun and 8-man crew. The prize brings jubilation to Lockyer, who, having earlier been repelled at Fort Bowyer, shares his jubilation with the men in the entire flotilla. While totally ignoring Jones' floating barricade, he halts his advance. He orders his force to take a meal, permitting each of them to receive an extra portion of rum to relax them before returning to the task of bulldozing through the obstacles in the channel. In his after action report, Captain Lockyer lists the *Alligator* as an armed sloop. The vessel *Alligator* had been acquired and commissioned by the navy at New Orleans during 1813. There is no record of the *Alligator* after being seized by the British.

By about 1030, the flotilla resumes its advance and the deep red uniforms become more brilliantly colored by the descending rays of the sun. The absence of overcast skies also causes the Marines' bayonets to sparkle, and in totality the British force creates a picture of a colossal killing machine. Nonetheless, as the flotilla advances, the Americans seemingly are oblivious to the might of the force that is about to pounce on them.

The British are poised for a most devastating thrust and the vagabonds in the gunboats remain unnerved. To the British, they appear docile and lifeless, as if the decks are manned by scarecrows. The crews of the gunboats display no signs of igniting a battle, nor any visible signals that the gunboats are being self-destroyed. Lockyer begins to believe that the Americans had realized the futility of raising opposition and would capitulate without raising resistance; however, Lockyer's thought process is suddenly jolted and everyone aboard each of the barges becomes wide-eyed as the motionless gunboats spring to life and propel a devastating series of shots that soar on a trajectory that batters the perfectly formed line of barges, causing the British line to expeditiously become rather irregular and infuriated after being greeted initially by the 32-pounder on Gunboat No. 23.

Following Lt. Isaac McKeever's opening barrage from that gunboat, the other vessels commence fire. The raking fire causes damage to the barges; however, the shelling also inflicts casualties and interferes with Lockyer's quick kill. He faces only five gunboats; however, it is evident that the commanders (Lt. Catesby Jones, No. 156; Sailing-master John D. Ferris, No. 5; Lt. Isaac McKeever, No. 23; Sailing Master Ulrick, No. 163, and Lt. Robert Spedden, No. 169) have galvanized their entire force to create formidable resistance. The British quickly realize that despite their slim numbers, the Americans hold dominating positions from which the American guns can pulverize the barges.

Captain Lockyer observes that two of the gunboats are out farther than the other three. He devises a plan to crack the line. He forms his flotilla into three separate divisions and afterward begins his advance. The gunboat at the point is approached by four barges and two gigs; however, its commander, Catesby Jones, remains prepared. His gunners find the range and propel successive rounds that rivet the barges in concert with streams of musket fire that rake the troops. Suddenly the four attack-barges shrink to two. The two barges that sustain fatal damage capsize, and it takes a Herculean effort by other barges to save the survivors. The British aboard the barges sustain horrific casualties; however, Lockyer intends to prevail. Nevertheless, Jones' remains afloat and he continues to dole out punishing fire.

Lockyer resumes the attack to clear the channel and Jones' gunboat comes under yet another attack. Undaunted, Catesby Jones is in the forefront standing brashly on the deck as a conspicuous target and unwilling to give the British victory. Shells and bullets soar back and forth from close range. Jones spots a British officer who appears to be the one directing the fire of both the seaman and the Marines. The barge is extremely close to Jones' gunboat. While Jones himself is dodging bullets, he takes aim with his pistol and strikes the officer, inflicting a mortal wound. The death of the officer, Lt. Pratt, injects more intensity into the firestorm. At about the same time Pratt is killed, Captain Lockyer, who is standing nearby, receives one of his three wounds.

The British seek instant retaliation. Jones becomes the recipient of a savage burst of fire from a large number of troops aboard Lockyer's barge who fire in unison. Most of the shots miss the mark; however, one of the troops scores and wounds Jones in his shoulder. The wound is serious but not fatal. Jones is unable to continue the fight due to the excessive pain. Crewmen manage to get him below deck. Later, it is determined that the British officer shot by Jones had been with the force under General Ross that moved into the capital. By the time Jones is taken below deck, the heroic fight in the channel is almost over. Lt. Parker assumes command and he hears Jones yell, "Keep up the fight" and responds affirmatively. Nevertheless, a British bullet takes him out before he actually takes command.

The British ramp up the effort to seize Gunboat No. 56, and despite the valiant defense, unbreakable nerves and absolute defiance, the British troops pour upon the deck from various points to overwhelm the crew. Nonetheless, the capture of Jones' flagship had been at high cost. The British sustain heavy casualties and even their commander, Captain Lockyer, had sustained three separate wounds which cause him to bleed profusely. Shortly after taking possession of the U.S. gunboat, Lockyer collapses from loss of blood. Troops rush to his side and he too is carried below deck and placed right next to Lt. Jones. Meanwhile, the other divisions concentrate on the remaining for gunboats.

British Lt. James Barnwell Tatnall assumes command of the battered division. In the meantime, Jones' other gunships become heavily embattled. The second division under Captain Henry Montresor closes against Lt. Ulrick's gunboat (No. 163) and here, too, the British encounter murderous fire which prevents the British from closing and boarding. Ulrick's crew remains calm under fire and relentless in their quest to forestall the British advance. After being stymied, Tatnall is reinforced by the remaining division under Captain Samuel Roberts. The combined pressure succeeds in gaining Ulrick's gunboat, but yet again at high cost, as the resistance is stubborn and the defenders remain cantankerous. Relentlessly, the Americans catapult incessant effective fire, despite the British having increased their firepower.

Suddenly, British gunners aboard the two captured gunboats direct their fire toward the three holdouts that continue to bar passage.

The British focus on Gunboat 169, commanded by Lt. Spedden. Two British barges launch their attack, but yet again, despite the exhaustion of his crew, the Yanks become rejuvenated rather than submissive at the sight of the closing craft. Whatever fears might be lurking among the crew on Lt. Spedden's ship are well concealed. Spedden's men, while under heavy attack, remain oblivious to the streaming shells and continue returning fire. The hurricane of flying steel forces the British to move their barges to the rear of the captured vessels to prevent disaster. Nonetheless, the mounting carnage does not cancel out the British insistence that they will crush the remaining force regardless of cost.

The two British divisions coordinate a combined attack. During the tenacious attack, Lt. Spedden sustains a wound as he and his crew attempt to exchange blows; however, his craft is besieged by more than ten barges. Spedden, similarly to Catesby Jones, leads from the point of the battle. He boldly bellows orders from his position on the deck, to the dismay of the British. Royal Marines target him. Having already lost the use of his left arm after being hit by grapeshot, he is struck by musket fire in his right shoulder. Suddenly, Spedden is standing in a pool of his own blood and he no longer has use of either of his arms. Still he refuses to strike the colors. Nonetheless, the British swarm onto the gunboat and overpower the crew. Spedden, however, despite his inability to defend himself with his sword or pistol, refuses to cooperate with his captors, who forcibly get him below deck.

The British use their captured guns to finish off the remaining gunboats, No. 5, commanded by Sailing-master John D. Ferris, and No. 23, commanded by Lt. Isaac McKeever, the latter having been the first to fire upon the flotilla. McKeever, the last to remain in the fight, is finally compelled to surrender at about 1230 to terminate the fiercely contested battle on Lake Borgne. About one-third of Catesby Jones' force is either killed or wounded and four of the five commanders are among the wounded. Only Lt. Ulrick evades injury. The British sustain 17 killed and 77 wounded.

Following the victory, the flotilla returns to Ship Island to prepare for the next phase of the campaign, the seizure of New Orleans. The flotilla is met on its return with resounding cheers and tremendous jubilation; however, the men aboard the barges are subdued because of the cries of anguish and pain coming from the wounded. Captain Lockyer, however, had cleared the waterway into New Orleans and his victory assures Admiral Alexander Cochrane that no U.S. naval vessels stand between him and his objective. Once back at Ship Island later this day, all wounded, including the American prisoners, are transferred to the HMS *Gorgon*.

While Lt. Catesby Jones and his fellow captives burden themselves with the thought of the loss of New Orleans, which appears imminent, the British ready the final steps in the campaign. The ground troops afterward begin to land on Pea Island; however, the island is ill suited for a landing. The British immediately encounter difficulties due to the shallow waterways. The landing operation takes an inordinately long time. Most troops are finally landed by December 22. From the landing place, the troops proceed to the Villere Plantation, where the British establish quarters for the strike against Jackson at New Orleans.

Once word of the demise of the squadron reaches New Orleans, Commodore Patterson sends two men—Mr. Shields, a purser in the U.S. Navy, and Doctor Murrell—under a white flag to reach the British fleet to request permission to treat the U.S. wounded. Admiral Cochrane is less than overjoyed when introduced to them off Cat Island. The Americans' request is declined, but worse, Cochrane informs them that they will be detained. The action by Cochrane is appalling; however, the men have no options. Cochrane detains them on his flagship where he places a guard at their cabin. Subsequently, the reluctant guests of the admiral use every opportunity to feed the British inflated information regarding the defenses at New Orleans, with the intent of placing doubts in the mind of the admiral and other high ranking officers. Both American captives remain in British custody on 12 January 1815.

In Connecticut, Federalists gather under a cloak of secrecy at the Hartford Convention to draft a string of proposals intended to collate their grievances against their opposition in Congress, the War Hawks of the Southern and Western States. Several of their suggested initiatives involve amendments to the Constitution. The twenty-six representatives, all holding anti-war positions, originate from the New England States of Connecticut, Massachusetts, New Hampshire, Rhode Island and Vermont, with the latter not participating until late December.

The convention concludes on January 5, 1815, but the resolutions become unnecessary due to the end of the war. The representatives assemble at the alderman's chamber of City Hall; however, the public is not permitted to be present. During the ongoing sessions, rumors begin to spread and the U.S. government dispatches a regiment under Major Thomas S. Jesup to Hartford supposedly for recruiting purposes; however, Jesup is under orders to maintain a watch on the convention, based on reports that the convention is an "unpatriotic conclave."

Each day, the session begins with a prayer; however, one Episcopalian priest declines taking part, saying that he "knew of no form of prayer for rebellion." The resolutions include amendments to the Constitution that stipulate "representation and taxation should be based on free persons"; a requirement that "the power of Congress was to be limited; and a vote of two-thirds of its members being required to admit a new state, to declare war, or to interdict commerce, "except in case of an actual invasion." Other resolutions include "the disbarring any but already naturalized citizens from eligibility to Congress, or from holding any civil office under the authority of the United States"; and a recommendation that "the presidential office should be restricted to one term, and that no State should furnish two Presidents in succession." Some other minor resolutions are also adopted before the convention ends on 5 January.

December 15 (Thursday) *In naval activity,* construction of the 58-gun USS *Plattsburgh* gets underway, pursuant to a contract signed this day; however, once word of the conclusion of the war arrives back in the United States, the construction project ends and the incomplete *Plattsburgh* remains on the stocks until it is sold at an undetermined time prior to 1824. In other naval activity, the 21-gun American privateer *Warrior,* commanded by Captain Guy R. Champlin (formerly of the *General Armstrong*), while cruising off Fayal, encounters a British frigate at anchor in the harbor. Captain Champlin, after noticing the frigate, changes course. Instead of entering the harbor he sails off to escape the warship. However, at about the same time, the Americans are spotted by the British and a chase begins. After about eight hours of trying to outrun the British, the *Warrior* realizes that capture is becoming more imminent, prompting Captain Champlin to decide to take a dangerous risk. With several hours of daylight remaining, the *Warrior* maneuvers to position itself as if a battle is at hand, and once the British see its starboard guns, they take the bait. While the British adjust their sails to engage, Captain Champlain's crew tosses a large number of its guns overboard on the port side, out of the view of the British. As part of the ruse, the Americans also dispose of some other items to lessen their weight. Suddenly, while the British guns are preparing to destroy the *Warrior,* it takes off at full sail, and by dark, it loses the frigate.

The *Warrior* seizes some prizes before it returns to port. They include the brigantine *Hope* en route to Buenos Aires from Glasgow (sent into port in the United States); the 10-gun ship *Francis and Eliza,* en route to New South Wales from London with more than 100 convicts (male and female); the 8-gun ship *Neptune,* en route to Bahia from Liverpool, and a brigantine, the *Dundee,* with a cargo and $15,000 in specie.

December 16 (Friday) **In Louisiana,** the British invasion force under General Keane debarks at Des des Poix Island (Pine Island) near the mouth of the Pearl River. The landing operation continues until 20 December. The elements remain nasty and the troops suffer, having no tents for shelter. A cold wave moves in just after a nasty rainstorm and the uniforms become soaked, then to make the situation more grave, the rain is trailed by a deep frost that brings deadly results. The troops' wet uniforms freeze and literally cause a large number of troops to succumb. The hardest hit units are those of the colored troops that have arrived from the West Indies.

In New Orleans, General Andrew Jackson proclaims martial law. Also, some men described as renegades arrive at the British camp and British expectations increase after being informed by the men that New Orleans is poorly defended. They also tell the British that there is great wealth in the city, and that the populace is anxious for the British to arrive and would join with them. On the 22nd, the British head for the Bayou de Catiline (later Bayou Bienvenue).

December 17 (Saturday) *In naval activity,* the USS *Constitution,* commanded by Captain Charles Stewart, sails from Boston, evades a blockade and gets out to sea en route to cruise off the coasts of Portugal and Spain. Meanwhile, the British, focused on keeping it penned at Boston, learn that Old Ironsides has again eluded capture. A massive search begins with all available ships committed to terminating its days at sea.

Captain Charles Stewart, U.S. Navy.

December 18–22 **In Louisiana** at New Orleans, General Jackson is still anxiously awaiting reinforcements to provide him with enough troops to withstand an invasion and prevent the British from getting domination of the Mississippi River. At this time, his force includes only Louisiana militia troops and some regular units, the U.S. 44th Regiment, commanded by Colonel George Ross, and the U.S. 7th Regiment, commanded by Major Henry Peire, along with an artillery contingent under Lt. Colonel William MacRea. Jackson appears confident that the desperately needed reinforcements will arrive in time. Spirits begin to improve this day (18th). Mississippians under Major Hinds arrive, and soon afterward, Jackson enjoys another sigh of relief when General Coffee's brigade arrives. When Coffee arrived at Baton Rouge, a message from Jackson was handed to him. The urgency was clear. Coffee's column, composed of about 800 of his most fit troops, races from Baton Rouge without bringing any baggage. The column had just completed an 800-mile march to reach Baton Rouge, but rest would have to wait. Coffee's column travels about 150 miles to reach the fringes of New Orleans in two days.

Finally the men get an opportunity to rest when the column halts at the Avart Plantation. Coffee rides into the city to inform Jackson of the arrival of the column, which adds another 800 men to the defending force. More troops begin to flood the area when General Carroll arrives with division of Tennessee volunteers during the night of the 22nd. The Tennesseans under Carroll bolt from their barges and flatboats following a journey that began on 19 November. Their arrival is timely. On the following day, Jackson receives intelligence that the British are at the doorstep of New Orleans. Carroll's troops are not seasoned regulars, but they are skilled with their rifles and tales are told that they could shoot squirrels from trees before they could walk.

December 20 (Tuesday) **In Louisiana,** General Keane is finalizing his plan to strike New Orleans. Since his arrival, parties had moved out to reconnoiter and the men decide which bayou to use. Keane has dissolved the Light Brigade, which had participated in the Maryland campaign, by splitting it into three battalions (4th, 85th, and 95th) and the force commanded by Colonel Thornton (85th Battalion). The vanguard is bolstered by a contingent of rocket men and two light 3-pounders. The remaining units are formed into two brigades. Colonel Brooke receives command of the first brigade, which is composed of the 21st Fusiliers and one colored regiment. The second brigade, commanded by British Colonel Hamilton (7th West India Regiment), is composed of the 93rd Highlanders and the remaining colored units. One other unit, the 14th Dragoons, remains unattached. It is assigned to General Keane. The British arrive at the Villere Plantation outside of New Orleans on the 23rd.

December 21 (Wednesday) *In naval activity,* the American privateer *Prince de Neuchatel,* fresh off its momentous victory over a superior boarding party, sails from Boston on a new cruise, and it evades the blockading squadron to make it to the open seas. No enemy contact is made with either merchant ships or warships. It does, however, get caught in a terrific storm after being out for about five days, and the weather remains nasty for several days. When the weather finally becomes favorable, the privateer looks like it been badgered by the enemy.

Due to the inaction of the third officer with a reputation of being negligent, the night-watch had not been handled properly. The incident proves costly. A man is ordered to climb to the masthead to put a lookout in place. Nonetheless, it is too little, too late. The view is unwelcome.

As soon as the lookout reaches his position, he reports a warship that is closing fast. He increases the number to three when two additional ships are seen closing upon the privateer.

The squadron, part of Admiral Sir George Collier's command, had departed from the Massachusetts coast to join in the search for the USS *Constitution*. The privateer, having beaten the storm, is not in excellent condition, and there has been no time to make repairs. Making matters worse, the lack of a lookout for much on the night prevented the squadron from being discovered earlier, which would have given the ship more time to escape.

The privateer runs, but not far. It is intercepted by the HMS *Acasta*, HMS *Leander* and the HMS *Newcastle*, all of which are more able to confront the rough seas. The *Prince de Neuchatel*, after being cut off, is seized as a prize; however, gaining possession is difficult due to the rough seas. One party gets aboard, but no others can. The Americans conspire to re-seize the ship. Just before midnight (28th–29th) the captives get to the deck, but once there they realize the spars and sails are in too poor a condition to permit them to escape. They abort the attempt.

On the following morning they are transferred to the *Leander*. After boarding the *Leander* they discover that the USS *Constitution* has gained a reputation with the British when they read a sign that is posted: "Reward of £100 to the man who shall first descry the American frigate Constitution provided she can be brought to, and a smaller reward should they not be enabled to come up with her." The HMS *Leander* had been specifically selected to search for and capture the elusive *Constitution*, known also as Old Ironsides, the nemesis of the Royal Navy. The crew of 500 men had each been selected for service aboard the *Leander* during its quest to terminate the career of the primary target of the Royal Navy. Some of the crew members delight in boasting of the upcoming demise of the *Constitution*, but some of the veterans are not so confident and they inject some realism: "If you had seen as much of the *Constitution* as we have, you would give her a wide berth, for she throws her shot almighty careless, fires quick aims low and is altogether an ugly customer."

The prisoners are for the most part held in the very bottom of the ship where they share space with the anchor cables. After a horrid voyage, the *Leander* arrives at Fayal in the Azores, where the prisoners are transferred to the sloop HMS *Pheasant*, which transports them to England, leaving the *Leander* to resume its search for Old Ironsides.

December 22 (Thursday) *In naval activity,* the privateer *Lucy*, an armed schooner commanded by Perez Drinkwater, is commissioned this day. However, the document is unsigned. It lacks the signatures of President Madison. Nevertheless, the war comes to a close in two days on Christmas Day.

December 22–23 *In Mississippi,* the vanguard of British General Keane's army, commanded by Colonel Thornton, sails for New Orleans. The boats depart at about 0900 on a less than enjoyable voyage. Two Choctaw chiefs are aboard the flotilla, along with General Keane and his staff officers. Keane has also brought two of the men from Fisherman's Village in Louisiana who chose to betray the Americans. No enemy forces are encountered; however, a natural enemy of all armies hovers overhead. The skies look ominous as heavy blackened clouds signal an imminent cloudburst. Nevertheless, the crews and the 1,800 troops ignore the signs and focus on the prize at the end of the journey: New Orleans. The thoughts of dominating the city ease the stress of exhaustion and even the pains of the body. However, despite the perfection of the rowers, who maintain successive rigid lines of ten boats across, there is an uncanny aura that permeates the entire force. The drums are silent, and although there is no indication of any enemy presence, the entire complement of troops is as quiet as the drums. As the advance continues, two cutters hold the point, while the flanks are similarly protected and three other cutters guard the rear to prevent any surprises.

After a while, the silence is shattered as the clouds burst and a pounding rain descends upon the flotilla. The crews continue to row in perfect order and their oars remain synchronized to create an illusion that the British are waterproof. Nevertheless, the crewmen and the troops find their clothes soaked from the deluge. The Redcoats ignore the pelting rain as the boats continue toward New Orleans. Finally, about the latter part of the morning, the drenched troops get a glimpse of the sun as it emerges and the clouds begin to dissipate. Suddenly, the sky becomes cloudless and the troops are then greeted with gushing cool winds that sweep into the area to compound the misery of the men. They also have an unpleasant reminder of the passing storm, because it had dumped water into the boats, leaving the men's legs at least ankle-high in water.

The conditions in the boats compel the flotilla to pause to give the men a rest and permit them to try to get their clothes dry and to warm themselves. Afterward, the flotilla resumes the journey and the seamen row non-stop throughout the night. At about sunrise on the following day, the advance forces are able to see the Louisiana coastline, which does not offer optimism or enthusiasm. The view is that of swampland. Nonetheless, the flotilla arrives without incident and the Americans in New Orleans have not yet been informed that a British force is forming for attack ten miles from the city.

December 23 (Friday) THE NIGHT BATTLE *In Louisiana,* after arriving outside New Orleans, the British debark and advance toward the Villere Plantation. The route is unprotected, permitting the British to effortlessly approach and surround the main house. Major Gabriel Villere, the son of General Villere, while resting on his porch, spots the British in motion down by the river. Stunned by the unexpected visitors and lacking troops, Villere darts to the rear of his house in an attempt to escape capture and rush into the city to sound the alarm. Nonetheless, the British by that time have the property encircled. Villere,

Colonel Dennis de la Ronde.

after reaching his back door, discovers a line of Redcoats awaiting his exit. Colonel Thornton, himself, with his sword drawn, calls for the major to surrender. After he is seized, Gabriel Villere also discovers that his brother Celestin had been seized. Both men are confined to the house under heavy guard. General Keane arrives at the plantation at about 1030; however, Major Villere, despite his desperate situation, remains determined to break out. Villere, in addition to being concerned about New Orleans, is also overly concerned that if he remains a captive, some will perceive that the Creoles lack faith in the cause.

While the British relax their concentration momentarily, Villere impetuously dashes to a window by barreling over a few of the unsuspecting guards, flies through the opening and races toward a tall picket fence, while bullets are whistling by his ears. He bolts over the fence, to the astonishment of a large number of Redcoats who could not have duplicated his feat. The British immediately chase Villere; however, Villere's familiarity with the terrain works to his advantage. He darts into the cypress forest that adjoins a swamp and for a while, he stays out in

Major Francis Plauche.

front. The British continue the hunt and nearly stumble upon him. Villere's dog had spotted him when he bolted through the window and over the fence, but Villere was unaware of the dog's chase until he discovers the dog as it comes beside him. The arrival of his dog brings about an extremely difficult moment. Realizing that the dog would innocently reveal his location if he hides in a tree, he realizes that the dog must be slain. Afterward, he descends the cypress tree and the British abort the chase. Villere reaches a nearby plantation, where he encounters an officer, Colonel de la Ronde.

Major Villere and the colonel acquire a boat, which they row to the opposite bank of the Mississippi. There they encounter P.S. Dussau de la Croix, an official of New Orleans. In a flash, the three men mount horses and gallop in the direction of the city to inform General Jackson that the British had landed. The riders are spotted by General Keane, and from the rising dust, Keane has no doubt of their destination. Nonetheless, Villere's escape compels General Keane to accelerate his plan.

General Keane deploys his vanguard in a field to the front of the plantation house. Those three regiments spread out and hold positions between the road and the river. Other troops are pushed farther along the road that leads into the city. The troops deploy along a fence and a protective ditch. Keane utilizes his rocket contingent to protect his rear by positioning it along the bank of the river. The Villere Plantation house is selected by Colonel Thornton as headquarters, and to fortify it, the British post three light artillery pieces outside. All the while, scouts are dispatched in search of any advancing American troops. All returning patrols report no U.S. activity; however, General Keane, having been fed intelligence from some Americans that had been earlier detained, continues to fret about the size of Jackson's force. Nevertheless, the British are prepared to meet an attack, yet Keane is unwilling to launch an assault against the city. At this time, the main body of the British force had not yet arrived.

Back at New Orleans, General Andrew Jackson, after being informed that the British had landed at Villere Plantation, states: "By the eternal, they shall not sleep on our soil." Immediately thereafter, Jackson assembles his force to launch an attack. The decision to attack the British to some seems imprudent, but Jackson is convinced that an attack is imperative and must be carried out before the British can overrun the defenses. Jackson's forces are scattered about the area. The battalion under Major Francis Plauche stands about two miles from Jackson's headquarters at Bayou St. John, and Jackson's regulars are two places, the barracks within the city and at Fort St. Charles (San Carlos) in present-day French Quarter, where a U.S. Mint is later built (400 block of Esplanade). The remaining troops include those under Generals Coffee and William Carroll.

Coffee's force, which had arrived the night before, is dispatched to Bienvue Bayou to block passage there. Meanwhile, Coffee's command is camped at the Avart Plantation. The Louisiana militia and about one-half of the free colored battalion are posted along the Gentilly Road. General Coffee's command, the dragoons under Major Hinds, the Orleans Rifles and the battalions under Plauche and Daquin receive orders to break their encampments and converge upon Montreuil's plantation just below the city. Once there, the combined commands are to link with Jackson's regulars. The scenes all along the lines display non-stop motion; however, there are no signs of desperation despite the graveness of the threat.

The uniforms of the militia and volunteers are neither inspiring nor do they in any way instill even the slightest fear into the hearts of the British, who continue to maintain a condescending attitude; however, the American militia and volunteers who don peculiar looking clothes have not been awestruck by the presence of the British with their impeccable, resplendent crimson uniforms, glistening bayonets and their awesome reputation of being skilled warriors who humbled Napoleon. The attire of the Kentuckians and Tennesseans is perhaps best described by Alexander Walker, author of *Jackson and New Orleans*: "Their appearance, however, was not very military. In their woollen hunting-shirts, of dark or dingy color, and copperas-dyed pantaloons, made, both cloth and garments, at home, by their wives, mothers and sisters, with slouching wool hats, some composed of the skins of raccoons and foxes, the spoils of the chase, to which they were addicted almost from infancy — with belts of untanned deer-skin, in which were stuck hunting-knives and tomahawks — with their long unkempt hair and unshorn faces." Nonetheless, the troops realize they arrived not to attend a British ball; rather to assure victory for Jackson and the citizens of New Orleans. Their quest is to best those who had vanquished Napoleon and terminate once and for all King George's obsession with regaining his lost colonies.

The clanging bells of St. Louis Cathedral signal the 3 P.M. hour as the various units, including a contingent of Choctaw Indians led by Captain Jugeat, converge upon Fort St. Charles, from where they will move as one force toward the plantation. The volunteers join with the regulars and there is great contrast in their dress as well as their military behavior; however, the finely dressed regulars enthusiastically welcome the volunteers and militia. There is an overwhelming aura of confidence as they eagerly advance to meet the foe.

The vanguard, which had advanced earlier, includes Peire's 7th Infantry composed of more than 325 men, a 60-man contingent of U.S. Marines and an artillery detachment. They hold the road slightly below the city. Jackson had also dispatched a New Orleans volunteer company (Beale's Rifles) of skilled marksmen, who went out in front of the vanguard. During the initial part of the advance, clouds of rising dust could be seen in the distance. Shortly thereafter, as the dust encroaches Jackson's force, the cause becomes visible. The long column of dragoons which had sped from the opposite part of the city arrives to add more strength to the force, Major Hinds' Mississippians and their proud steeds and another column of horsemen are close behind, those of General Coffee's mounted Tennessans. In a flash, Coffee's column comes to a halt, and after he and Jackson exchange a few words, the general is off again. The Tennesseans move out at a full gallop, creating yet another cloud of dust. By this time, Jackson's chest is about to burst from the pride he possesses regarding these men who selflessly and knowingly are riding and marching into a cauldron to intercept what at the time is considered the world's finest army. Nonetheless, while Jackson is momentarily touched by the magnificent sight, yet again his emotions rise even higher when he spots the Creole battalion racing at full speed to join the column. At about the same time, the column bulges even more as the battalion of freemen arrives.

The troops depart with an added incentive to transform the British invasion into a brief and deadly sojourn. In a city about to be attacked or be placed under siege, the women and children are usually evacuated to a place of safety; however, the women in New Orleans adamantly oppose any such action. They line the streets and peer through windows with tear-filled eyes while the men march out to engage the British; however, they intend to be there to greet them upon their return. The courage and determination of the stout-hearted women silently transmits a canopy of resoluteness that hovers over the column. The Creoles under Plauche and the freemen of color under Dacquin, holding the rear, march out of the city. Soon after, the final element of Jackson's strategy appears when the USS *Carolina* is spotted as it maneuvers into position. At about the same time, General Jackson mounts his horse and jumps off in a gallop to reach the head of his column. He is accompanied by his staff.

Back in the city, there is some apprehension due to the insufficient defenses that have been hurriedly erected; however, the spectacle of the moving column and in particular, the presence of Jackson overrides the fears of the citizens who believe that with Jackson in command, they will prevail. One of the women had a question and it was delivered to Jackson: "What were [we] were to do, in case the city was attacked?" The general immediately responded: "No British soldier shall enter the city as an enemy, unless over my dead body."

The British at the Villere Plantation remain on high alert; however, up to this point none of the numerous patrols sent out to reconnoiter had reported even a detachment. The various approaches to the camp are guarded by pickets, and they report no enemy activity. Meanwhile, a strong contingent of the British 95th Rifles are way out in front, but they too detect no signs of an imminent attack. The tranquility is eerie. Nevertheless, British General Keane remains short two brigades that have not yet arrived due to difficulties with the boats in the canal. Nonetheless, Colonel Thornton, still irritated because the commander had halted rather than driven directly into New Orleans, is convinced that by halting, their camp had become vulnerable. Thornton is also convinced that despite the fact that no Americans had been spotted, that the encampment would be struck before dawn.

While the British troops continue to establish their camp, parties are authorized to ride throughout the area in search of private homes where they can confiscate food and spirits. The troops return with food for a feast after pillaging, and the items from plantations ensure a fine meal, particularly for the officers, who choose for themselves before the food is distributed to the rank and file. After the meals are finished, the troops are prepared to finally get some rest. Nonetheless, off in the distance, a sentry at one of the outposts spots some dust from a small detachment of horsemen. The guards conceal themselves, and as the riders approach close range, they are fired upon. It is reported that one man is killed and two others wounded; however, none are captured. The detachment hurriedly retires. The riders involved are attached to the Feliciana Dragoons, an elite Louisiana unit. Nonetheless, the incident makes it clear that another restless night is at hand. For a while there are no further interruptions. But after about an hour passes, the British discover more of the elusive Americans when a sizable column is spotted as it advances smartly and in conspicuous view.

The British temporarily are unsure of the purpose of exposing themselves, when suddenly, Major Hinds gives his order and the column spreads out like a fan and the British become startled to see the dragoons charging their outpost positions. The defenders are easily driven from their positions as the cavalry maintains its charge and closes on the main British line, where the 95th Rifles are waiting for the horses to come into range. Unexpectedly, Hinds calls a halt to the charge at a distance of about 100 yards from the rifles, to the disappointment of the British marksmen. After a brief pause, the dragoons raise the dust as the troops gallop back toward General Jackson. The British are amused at the apparent cowardice of the American cavalrymen who retreat rather than engage. However, unknown to the British, the daring mission succeeds.

One of the riders with Hinds had been Colonel Arthur P. Hayne, Jackson's inspector general. His task is to scan the British positions and determine the size of their force and to absorb as much information on their defenses as possible. After the dragoons retire, the British begin to relax and enjoy their evening meal. Nevertheless, for many, exhaustion has taken a toll and those troops skip the meal to get some sleep.

British thoughts of a perfectly quiet night get interrupted at about 1900, when several officers notice a vessel cruising down the river. The sense of danger begins to lessen when the British mistake the USS *Carolina* for a British warship and their confidence rises sharply thinking that naval support had arrived and was placidly nudging close to camp. Some suspense builds when repeated requests to respond are ignored by the crew. The crew also ignores a burst of rifle fire. The darkness only deepens the mystery, yet no alarms are set off. After swinging into position close to shore, the British finally get a response. Lighted matches on deck sparkle and the flashes are followed by an officer bellowing: "Give this for the honor of America!"

Simultaneously, the *Carolina* delivers a broadside and the riflemen aboard the vessel shower the camp with shot after shot. The storm of fire strikes blindly in the darkness; however, the air is so thick with flying shot and shell that casualties, including many who are sleeping, mount quickly. The killing fire of unknown origin creates pandemonium and the circumstances prevent any quick restoration to order; however, Colonel Thornton orders the troops to evacuate the camp to seek safety under the levy. While they suffer from the hurricane of fire, the British remain unaware that the guns of the *Carolina* had ignited Jackson's land attack.

After restoring calm and discipline to his force, Colonel Thornton begins to react to the attack. Reinforcements (85th and 95th Regiments) speed to bolster the pickets, while Thornton orders the 4th Regiment to establish a line to the front of headquarters (Villere house) to maintain communications between the plantation and the lake, while remaining in reserve until needed at any point. Nevertheless, while the British are rebounding from the initial shock of the attack, they are still greatly hindered by the darkness and the inability to assess the size of the attack or from where the next barrage will originate. Major Gubbins of the 85th maintains order on the right, while Major Samuel Mitchell holds command on the left without either of them knowing what might be next to descend upon them.

While the British brace for the unknown, Jackson's force had already arrived at the Rodriguez Canal no more than two miles from the British lines, and his forces had dug out a ditch running at an angle of about ninety degrees that extends from the river to the swamp. Simultaneously, the wing under General Coffee had swung into motion, and it is advancing on the left directly toward the swamp to a point between the Lacoste Plantation and the La Ronde Plantation, the pre-appointed place to leave their horses. Although the Americans are also impeded by darkness, the enthusiasm continues to build, while the anxiety increases along the British lines. The suspense on the part of the British is due in great part to the fact that General Keane has not been able to determine Jackson's strength, which he believes could be as many as 20,000, according to unverifiable information.

The wing under General Coffee is poised to maneuver his Tennesseans toward the British right flank, from where they can plunge into the rear. While Coffee moves into position, Jackson advances to launch a direct frontal assault. The moves are coordinated and the two forces are set to attack on the signal, which is to be fired by the USS *Carolina*. At 0700, with Commodore Patterson aboard, the *Carolina*, commanded by Captain Henley, initiates its fire to set the attacks in motion. While the naval barrage interrupts the activity in the British camp, General Coffee's brigade, deployed near the swamp, springs into action. The Tennesseans, augmented by Beall's Rifles, plunge forward to batter the rear while simultaneously working to sever communications between the camp and the lake. However, the dragoons are held back on the La Ronde Plantation after it is decided the terrain contains too many obstacles such as fences and ditches, making it impossible for the horses to operate freely.

Meanwhile, the forces under Jackson — composed of his regulars, the battalions of Plauche and Daquin, MacRea's artillery and the Marine contingent — drill straight ahead from their positions on a narrow strip between the Mississippi and the morass to pound General Keane's frontal defenses. Both forces had the added element of being guided by men familiar with the terrain. Major Villere accompanies Jackson, and Coffee is guided by Colonel De La Ronde.

Shells pound the camp in a bitter contest which is fought nearly blindly due to the conditions. The sky is starless and the heavy overcast of thick, ominous clouds conceals the moonlight. The two sides are confined to bludgeoning each other in stark darkness. Often it is impossible to tell friend from foe, and at times, as one party encounters another, friends mistake each other as the enemy. The fighting becomes close-quartered and vicious. The British regulars, well seasoned from the Napoleonic Wars, are skilled with their bayonets; however, the Americans are armed with only a few bayonets. Nonetheless, many of the Kentuckians and the Tennesseans are armed with long-knives, which inflict equally gruesome wounds. Conditions are so poor that if either side ventures forth in search of the opposing side and if the encounters ignite a contest, other units are restricted from rushing to provide support. Nevertheless, neither side relents, and the bloody confrontation continues for about three hours under illumination provided solely from the flashes of the guns. Even the artificial light is obscured by suffocating smoke.

On the British right, the suspense terminates rather quickly when about 800 men (dismounted) under Coffee arrive near the British line. After leaving about 100 men with the horses, the remaining 700 smash into the flank. Reaction is immediate as the British deploy to repulse the nearly invisible foe. While the right line tightens and the crackle of small arms intensifies, the night air carries and amplifies the sounds to also inform Jackson that Coffee's part of the operation is underway.

Coffee's contingent is able to successfully maneuver themselves into positions from which they can drive straight ahead to strike at the heart of the British positions. Swiftly and silently, during the initial moments, the Tennesseans, under orders to withhold their fire until at nearly point-blank range, encounter and eliminate a few guards at the outposts before the British realize they are under attack in the rear. The Americans, by the time they are discovered, are in the process of slicing through the camp itself. Meanwhile, elements of the elite 85th Regiment arrive to block any further passage. The Tennesseans, however, refuse to be humbled by the Redcoats, and the British intend to eliminate the pesky backwoodsmen. Nevertheless, the British soon possess a new and reluctant opinion of the Tennesseans when the donnybrook ignites. Coffee's long guns equal and overmatch the British sharpshooters, while at close-quarters, the British are introduced to the Tennesseans' tomahawks and long-knives.

The British are unable to maintain a rigid formation in the darkness, giving the less disciplined Tennesseans extra leverage, and they are also able to instill respect for their long guns. The British can attest to the effectiveness of the fire. Several of the British officers are victimized, including Brigade Major Harris. The contest more resembles a series of street brawls than a usual skirmish, and the savageness is escalated due to the grim blackness of the sky. Both sides are compelled to use trickery to attempt to discern friend from foe, but the method is less than foolproof, making it impossible to know how many casualties come from friendly fire.

While Coffee's Tennesseans continue to pressure the rear, they pick up familiar sounds that command their attention. One segment of Coffee's force is snarled by a steady line of fire originating from the area containing the quarters of the Negroes. The distinctive sound is the unique crack of the British Rifles. Once the exact origin of the fire is determined, the Tennesseans in a snap converge on the objective. Lieutenant Colonel Lauderdale is killed during the attack. The British bolt from their concealed positions and a tenacious struggle ensues when the antagonists become so closely intertwined that hand-to-hand combat determines the victor.

The British find their rifles to be perfect clubs; however, the Tennesseans' savage weapons of choice during this gruesome encounter are their tomahawks and long-knives, both of which inflict horrific wounds. After sustaining a severe battering, the British Rifles are compelled to withdraw from the grove in the Lacoste Plantation to regroup, while the Tennesseans maintain their romp through the British encampment. Coffee's progress has carried his force well into the range of the guns of the USS *Carolina* and at the newly formed British line, but not without cost.

During the final thrust, a large contingent of his force, Beall's Rifles and about 200 of his Tennesseans commanded by Colonel Gibson and Colonel Robert Dyer, respectively, lose contact with Coffee. Despite the darkness, the British detect the gap created when the separation occurs. They grasp the opportunity and funnel troops into the hole. Shortly thereafter, Dyer moves to reinitiate contact; however, when he is asked the identity of his unit, he responds, "The Second Division of Tennesseans." At about the same time, it becomes obvious that the inquiry had come from the British. Dyer and Gibson immediately reverse course and break for the river while under a storm of fire.

During the rush to the river, Colonel Gibson trips and is immediately pounced upon by a British soldier who jabs him with a bayonet. Gibson, suffering only a superficial wound, relieves the soldier of his rifle and delivers a powerful blow that leaves the trooper in Gibson's recent prone position and hurries off to rejoin the retreat. For Dyer, the retreat is also harrowing. British fire had wounded him and his horse. As the horse tumbles, Dyer is unable to free himself. Other Tennesseans directed by Dyer halt their retreat and deliver a volley toward the pursuing British.

The Tennesseans effectively compel the British to suspend the chase, and in those few desperate moments, the men extricate Dyer and the retreat resumes. Soon they are reunited with General Coffee. The other isolated unit, a large part of Beale's Rifles, became separated during the intense struggle in the heart of the British camp, when General Coffee had swung his force toward the right. The Rifles on the far left fail to notice the shift and get themselves stranded in the middle of the camp. The troops scatter in small detachments and attempt to use the darkness to help them reach their lines, but the British are able to capture many by deception.

By this time, General Coffee has reached a point by which any further penetration will endanger his command. He faces vicious British fire, however further progress will carry his troops straight into the range of the guns of the *Carolina*, which continue to bombard the British positions. Rather than risk calamity, Coffee sends word to Jackson regarding the situation, and he receives a quick response in which Jackson orders him to cancel his attack and rejoin Jackson's division.

In Jackson's sector, his force (right division or wing) had advanced briskly and confidently. The lead company of the 7th Regiment under Lt. McClelland becomes the first unit to plow into the British lines. From its position on Jackson's far right, McClelland's command reaches the point dividing the Lacoste and La Ronde Plantations and the troops cross into the latter, where they encounter severe fire from elements (about 80 troops) of the British 95th Regiment. The British, commanded by Captain Hallem, hold solid positions at the outpost, and they fire from within a ditch that is behind a fence. Nevertheless, the Americans become irritated, not because of coming under fire; rather because Colonel Piatt with the company is unable to prod the defenders to extricate themselves from the ditch to meet his force in close-quartered fighting. Undaunted, the company (7th Regiment) drills ahead, evicts the defenders after some ferocious fighting and then they occupy the outpost. During the fierce exchange, Lt. McClellan and a sergeant are killed and Colonel Piatt, while at the head of the command, sustains a wound in his leg.

In the meantime, the situation at the captured outpost remains fluid. The British, their pride bent after being shoved out of the outpost, have regrouped to mount a counterattack to reclaim the coveted position. At the same time, Lt. Bellevue's Marine contingent is escorting the artillery as it nears the outpost. While the guns begin to pound other British outposts, the counterattack gets underway and once again, the near-zero visibility adds confusion to the confrontation. The British focus on capturing the guns at all hazards, while the artillerymen and the Marines are attempting to recover from the intense fire that has wounded some of the artillery horses.

Nearby, General Jackson, unable to see the combatants, rushes to the sounds of the guns to discover the British had effectively broken the cohesion of the artillerymen and the Marines. Having already crashed through a raging fight without being harmed by the streams of shells, Jackson remains oblivious to the danger while he rallies the men. Jackson bellows: "Save the guns, my boys at every sacrifice." He and his aides suddenly find that the unit recovers from the temporary shock and the Marines and one company of the 7th Regiment reform as a galvanized unit. The British fail to seize the guns.

All the while, the British, while defending the points under assault, continue to try to out-think Jackson by fortifying their lines thought to be the next target. Jackson's other forces, including the remaining troops of the 7th Regiment and the 44th Regiment deployed to the left of the 7th, relentlessly shove their way through the darkness and arrive at the river to transform the sporadic fire fights into a huge conflagration. Both sides exchange steady and heavy fire from their opposing positions, each formed in a perpendicular line. The flanks of both sides have only one protective element, darkness, leaving either side the opportunity to turn their opponent's flank. The Americans' left flank becomes vulnerable when the British extend their line to provide maneuverability for them to strike the rear of the 44th Regiment. Pressure forces the 44th Regiment to swing its line to the left at about the same time as the Creole and Freemen battalions are arriving on scene. Both advancing battalions encounter extremely heavy fire, but the advance continues. As the Creoles begin to deploy to the left of the 44th, a part of the battalion detects the positions of the 44th and mistakenly believes them to be British. The Creoles inadvertently fire upon the 44th and inflict casualties. A catastrophe is averted by Major Francis Plauche's quick action. He untangles the confusion before the 44th and the Creoles annihilate each other.

Plauche then leads his battalion straight through heavy fire and into the British line. The thrust begins to gain momentum and the freemen under Colonel D'Aquin who are trailing closely maintain the pace. The advance is also reinforced by the 44th, which has recovered from the friendly fire incident. As the British line begins to falter, the Americans' confidence soars and they are eager to mount a full scale charge to dismantle the continuity of the British defenses and permit the Americans to isolate a segment of the British army. Nevertheless, Colonel George Ross, commander of the volunteers, inexplicably directs Plauche to cancel the charge and hold his position. The order, considered imprudent, eliminates any possibility of the two divisions linking up to cut off the entire left side of the British force.

During the fast-moving action as the battle winds down, the British themselves, not immune to misidentification, have some difficulty recognizing an approaching unit. Major Samuel Mitchell of the 95th Regiment moves to ensure that the troops are part of the 93rd, which he is awaiting. After nearing the advancing column, he asks whether the troops are part of the 93rd, and he is greeted with a response, "Of course." Nonetheless, he fails to detect a Southern accent, and shortly afterward he is encircled by Americans who take him as a prisoner.

Although the ongoing fighting seems to have

lasted for days, it is only about 2000, when the British (on the right) on their own volition decide to withdraw to their initial positions at the plantation. At about the same time a dense fog rolls into the region. The battle essentially terminates as General Jackson orders a retreat. The Americans withdraw to a point about four miles from the city. The British positions remain fixed on the plantation; however, headquarters is abandoned and the Villere house becomes a hospital. Casualties for the Americans are reported as 24 killed, 115 wounded and 74 missing.

The British under General Keane, according to his official report, sustain 46 killed, 167 wounded and 64 missing. However, an account of the battle written by British lieutenant Glieg states: "Not less than five hundred men had fallen, many of whom were our finest soldiers and best officers; and yet we could not but consider ourselves fortunate in escaping from the toils, even at the expense of so great a sacrifice." The Americans later recover a journal, retrieved from a dead British officer who participated at the battle. The journal lists the number of British casualties as "two hundred and twenty-four killed, and an immense number wounded."

After the battle, the British troops get little rest. The weather is nasty and the area comes under a dense fog, leaving the troops who have no shelter to sleep under intolerable circumstances. In addition, the sounds coming from the pain-stricken wounded adds to already trying conditions.

For the next several days, Jackson continues to bolster his defenses. Fresh British reinforcements arrive, commanded by General Gibbs and General Edward Pakenham. After debarking, General Pakenham examines the terrain of the British positions, and he becomes highly concerned after discerning that the troops have settled upon a dreaded morass. He is equally dismayed at the sight of the American fortifications to their front which appear to him to become stronger as the hours pass, but his displeasure does not stop with the soggy ground and poor defenses. Pakenham takes note that there are no British warships on the river to support the army. The flat ground upon which the British must advance appears to Pakenham as a quagmire waiting to snare his force. The terrain upon which the encampment had been made, however, has protection, swampland on the right and the river on the left. Nonetheless, his positions remain vulnerable to attack from naval vessels and also by artillery posted on the opposite bank of the river.

While the British lack naval support, two American vessels, the USS *Louisiana* and the USS *Carolina*, maintain a steady bombardment of the British lines. The British positions are also harassed by the elements. While the naval barrages continue unabated, the troops are pelted by pesky rain and penetrating frost. Nonetheless, Pakenham unfolds his strategy by ordering a contingent to bring up heavy artillery and a furnace. The items are transported during darkness, deployed on a levee and prepared for action.

December 24 TREATY OF GHENT ENDS THE WAR The Treaty of Ghent is signed by American and British officials, ending the War of 1812. This news does not reach America in time to prevent the siege of New Orleans. The agreement is received in the United States with celebration, but in England, the British press smacks the English commissioners with a bloody cat-o-nine tails, lashing out at the results and branding it as a sell-out. However, at the time of the scathing press articles, the British are still unaware of Jackson's spectacular victory at New Orleans. For the Americans, the British have agreed to put off the talks about fishing rights and British navigational rights on the Mississippi. The treaty does not cover nor even mention the rights of neutral shipping, nor the impressment of American seamen, the principle cause of the American declaration of war. However, the latter point has become moot since the elimination of Napoleon. Essentially, both sides have fought to a point of over-exhaustion, permitting the treaty to proclaim a truce beneficial to both antagonists. The Americans, subsequent to their upcoming triumph at New Orleans, proclaim victory and the administration does not attempt to change the people's opinion. The British had held the upper hand, but were unable, despite superior numbers in ships and men, to subdue the Americans, due in great part to the astonishing achievements of privateers.

In Louisiana at New Orleans, the British are directed to redeploy at more tenable positions. During the night of Christmas Eve, the levee is abandoned except for a detachment of pickets that remain posted there and along the riverbank. The remainder of the force establishes a new camp at the Lacoste plantation in a field on the land lying to the rear of a sugar house and other structures. The weather remains disagreeable and continues to cause problems for the troops, who have no shelter and are forced to remain extremely uncomfortable. In the aftermath of the previous day's fighting, there is still disbelief in the boldness of the American attack and concern about how the British regulars had not swept the rabble from the field. Nonetheless, the new encampment provides additional protection if another assault is launched.

General Jackson is of the belief that his raw troops, having had their baptism under fire, are better prepared for the next violent encounter. He also remains adamantly opposed to extending even the slightest advantage to the enemy. Jackson's next line of defense remains directly in front of the British, and it involves the La Ronde Plantation. His primary line is drawn at the Rodriguez Canal. The 7th Regiment, bolstered by one company of dragoons, remains out front on the plantation, while the others deploy at the main line. Work parties construct dirt mounds, while others zealously increase the depth and width of ditches. The work progresses nonstop. All the while parties are moving back and forth among the fortifications and the city as tools and equipment are brought out to increase productivity. By day's end, the Americans complete a prolonged line of mounds, averaging from three to four feet high, described as their "castles" by those who construct them. At the far right, Jackson deploys two 6-pounders with which to dominate the road. Jackson's troops forego any holiday festivities and focus on preventing the British from spending Christmas in New Orleans. Nonetheless, General Pakenham is not yet prepared to launch his offensive.

In New York, Governor Daniel D. Tompkins writes to General Samuel Strong of Vermont:

> Sir: The Legislature of the State of New York in contemplating the zeal & alacrity manifested by the citizens of Vermont when this State was menaced by a powerful army; & the eminent services rendered by them, have unanimously resolved that you their leader are entitled to the gratitude of your country, & that the Volunteers who shared with you in the glory of the battle of Plattsburgh have justly merited the thanks of this State. In obedience to the joint resolution of our Legislature (a copy of which is enclosed.) I shall hereafter have the honor of present you a sword, as a memorial of the proud victory in which you took so distinguished a share. It is with the liveliest feelings that I convey to you the high sense entertained by this State of your patriotism, talents & conduct. And I must pray you to communicate to the gallant Volunteers of Vermont, both officers & men, who, under you, stepped forth in a moment of peril, in defence of this State, the thanks of a grateful people.

Tompkins also writes to Major General Benjamin Mooers to inform him of action by the legislature regarding his deeds at Plattsburgh:

> Sir: I have the honor to transmit to you an unanimous resolution of the Senate and Assembly of this State expressive of their high sense of your conduct at the battle of Plattsburgh on the 11th of September last. In addition to this expression of their sentiments, I am charged to present to you a sword as a trophy of that memorable day. It is with pride & satisfaction that I have become the organ of public sentiment on this occasion & while I unite my individual feelings, I pray you to receive for yourself & to communicate to the officers & soldiers of the Militia who fought under you, the thanks of the legislature & the high sense entertained by that body of the patriotism, talents & conduct.

Tompkins writes similar congratulatory letters to Generals Jacob Brown, Edmund Gaines, James Miller, Eleazer Wheelock Ripley and Winfield Scott, informing each of them that they have been awarded swords. General Miller subsequently becomes governor of Arkansas (1819–1826) and afterward, collector of the port of Salem, Massachusetts. He was born at Peterborough, New Hampshire during April 1778.

Colonel James Miller (21st Infantry), who was commissioned major of the U.S. 4th Infantry during 1808, was breveted brigadier general for his "distinguished service" at Niagara, according to the state historian on 25 July 1814. He became known as the hero of Lundy's Lane. During the war, he served as colonel of the U.S. 6th Infantry until transferring to the 21st Infantry during March 1814. Also, by resolution of Congress on 3 November 1814, he was awarded a gold medal for his "gallantry and good conduct at Chippewa,

Niagara and Fort Erie, Canada." General Miller died at Temple, New Hampshire, on 7 July 1851.

Governor Tompkins writes to Alfred Davis, a son of General Daniel Davis, who was killed at Fort Erie:

> Sir: You will perceive by the enclosed document that the Senate & Assembly of the State of New York are sensible of the distinguished merit & conduct of your lamented Father, Brigadier General Davis, in the sortie from Fort Erie, & sincerely deplore his death. They have charged me to present to you a sword as a mark of public gratitude for his generous & gallant services. I shall hasten to convey to you the memorial which a grateful people consecrate to the memory of one of their most illustrious defenders. I beseech you to bear in mind that it is the need of patriotism & of virtuous self devotion & should ever a crisis arise, which shall require you to unsheath it, emulate the deeds of your heroic sire, & think no sacrifice too great in the cause of a beloved country. May you follow his footsteps in the path of virtue & of glory, & be prosperous & happy.

Governor Tompkins writes a similar letter to Asa R. Swift, the son of Brigadier General John Swift, killed near Fort George on 12 July 1814.

In naval activity, the HMS *Junon* intercepts and seizes the 104-ton schooner *Armistice* (John Williams, master), after it sails from Charleston en route to New York with a cargo of copper, cotton and rice. The *Armistice* is separate from the schooner *Armistice* seized on 12 June 1814.

December 25 **In Louisiana** at New Orleans, the British continue to ponder why they have been stymied by the Americans. The second guessing among the troops includes questioning the strategy and ability of their commander, General Keane. Nevertheless, Keane also has supporters; however, rather than accept the fact that Jackson's troops have neutralized their superior experience and numbers, the blame is easier placed on the commander. The camp has been subdued since the fighting on the 23rd, but Christmas brings a surprise that raises the spirits of the entire camp when General Pakenham arrives to assume command. He is accompanied by General Samuel Gibbs, another seasoned officer who participated in the Napoleonic Wars. The arrival seemingly erases the gloom and doom hovering over the camp and the troops for the moment forget the misery of the dismal conditions as well as the annoying frost and fog. It becomes a scene of mass euphoria when the troops conclude that with Pakenham, the brother-in-law of the Duke of Wellington, victory is at hand. Pakenham, himself, is consumed with confidence and eager to perform flawlessly, since this becomes his initial operation as overall commander. With the arrival of the additional seasoned troops, Pakenham now commands an army that ranks among the finest to be fielded by Great Britain. The entire complement of troops except the 93rd Highlanders and the Black regiments had served on the Peninsula and while Wellington marched into France. The British force at the plantation includes the Rifles, 21st, 44th, 85th and the 14th Dragoons, none of which have sustained a defeat on the field, and other units are still en route, including the 7th Fusiliers (Pakenham's own), the 40th and the 43rd Regiments. The camp is overcome with good cheer. The artillery is fired in tribute to the general and the boisterous noise is heard at the American outposts, which immediately causes curiosity. Scouts are able to determine the reasons for the celebration and post-haste, word is rushed to General Jackson.

Meanwhile, General Pakenham, after assuming command from a relieved General Keane, re-establishes headquarters at the Villere Plantation house and holds a conference with the officers. The reports are less than encouraging and Pakenham is not impressed. He had already discerned that the positions are poor, and during the conference he is disappointed that the vanguard did not drive straight into New Orleans. For a while, Pakenham is prepared to re-embark and choose a separate landing place until he is persuaded by Admiral Cochrane that victory could still be achieved. Cochrane is so consumed with the inferiority of Jackson and his troops, he boasts that if the British regulars were incapable of destroying the defenders, he would "bring up the sailors and marines from the fleet, and storm the American lines, and march into the city." He adds: "The soldiers could then bring up the baggage."

Similarly to British General Ross at the gateway to Baltimore when he declared that he would eat dinner in Baltimore, shortly before he was killed, a prisoner of the Americans (captured on the 23rd) had informed General Jackson that Admiral Cochrane had proclaimed that he would eat dinner in New Orleans on Christmas Day. General Jackson quickly retorted: "Perhaps so, but I shall have the honor of presiding at that dinner." Before the conference ends late in the night, Pakenham splits his army into two brigades to be commanded by Generals Gibbs and Keane.

In naval activity, the crew aboard The USS *Constitution,* "Old Ironsides," finally ends its year or so of internment by crashing through the British blockade. Under the command of Captain Charles Stewart, the *Constitution,* after entering the Atlantic Ocean, follows a course that takes it to the Portuguese Islands to search for the British. In February 1815, it encounters a British squadron and ignites the final sea duel of the War of 1812.

December 26 (Monday) **In Louisiana** at New Orleans, rumors about a British general's arrival on Christmas Day abound and spread rapidly throughout the American lines. In the usual fashion of rumors, as they pass from man to man, the exaggerations grow steadily. Some of the tales have placed the Duke of Wellington as the new commander. Meanwhile, General Jackson would not be diverted from the task at hand even if King George had landed. He maintains his normal exhausting schedule, encouraging the men at the canal to continue strengthening the defenses, not by issuing directions; rather by riding from one end of the line to the other to personally rally the troops. If some of his defenders had begun to over worry, he makes it clear that he has no fear of them faltering in the face of the enemy. He informs the troops of his confidence: "Here we shall plant our stakes, and not abandon them until we drive these red-coat rascals into the river, or the swamp."

British General Pakenham, along with his staff and some other officers, ride out of camp on a reconnaissance mission to assess the strength of the enemy. No regular forces are detected and Pakenham is amused by the activity of some undisciplined detachments of cavalry that are observing the British encampment and at times firing at the outposts. Pakenham remains unimpressed with their appearance and pays little mind, due to the tremendous contrast with his previous enemies who, like the British, fought in the rigid European style. The absence of a strong opposing army, represented only by the woodsmen on horses operating in defiance of the British lines, give Pakenham no instant thoughts on strategy; however, the audacious woodsmen strongly suggest they are supported by more than a phantom army. Pakenham concludes that the path to victory can be gained only by a full-scale attack to whack and collapse the entire defending line.

Meanwhile, the other visible signs of Jackson's force have continued to bombard the encampment. Pakenham realizes that both American vessels must be destroyed before he launches the assault. To bring about the desired results, heavy guns are requested from the fleet. By the night of the 26th, the British receive some 12-pounders and 18-pounders with which to destroy the vessels.

December 27 (Tuesday) **In Louisiana** at New Orleans, the USS *Carolina* and the USS *Louisiana,* both of which have been plastering the British positions, become targets of the recently arrived heavy artillery at dawn. The U.S. vessels return fire, and for about one-half hour, the morning sky seems inundated with opposing streaming projectiles that create a massive show of destructive firepower that can be easily heard back at the American lines. The duel of the guns draws throngs of people to the river banks to witness the astonishing spectacle. The British gunners are seasoned, and they catapult shell after shell that delivers thunderclaps of effective fire. Meanwhile, the British positions, under attack since the day the camp was established, receive identical deadly fire. The British are compelled to judge their outgoing fire by the incoming firestorm, and based on the gun flashes of the ships, the British race for cover to evade death or injury and afterward bounce back into position to resume their fire.

During the ferocious exchange, emotions of both antagonists slip onto a roller-coaster of ups and downs. Back in the city, General Jackson observes the contest from a window at the Macarte House by peering through a telescope he had acquired on loan from a local Frenchman. On the British lines, General Pakenham has a front row seat at the battery, from where he inspires and encourages the gunners. Despite the ground shaking barrages and deafening sounds of exploding shells, the shouting and cheering can also be heard from the British and from the American crewmen. The British envision the demise of the two ships as their guarantee of success; however, on both vessels, the crews, seemingly encircled by rings of fire and immediately under the innumerable burst of shells, do not have the luxury or burden of shifting emotions. To a man, they are focused only on silencing the menacing artillery to ensure British failure. Nonetheless, during the tumultuous exchange, it becomes evident that the artillery has inflicted damage to the *Carolina*.

British hearts pound with excitement when the guns aboard the *Carolina* fall silent. Enthusiasm builds when it appears that pandemonium has erupted aboard the vessel; however, there is no confusion nor indecisiveness. The crew maintains its discipline when the order to abandon ship is given. Nonetheless, excitement increases in the British camp when the troops observe the Americans descending onto their boats.

While the crewmen remain aware that their abandonment of the *Carolina* is delivering thrill to the Redcoats, they begin to shout their good-byes to the British. All hands are safely in the boats before the fires spread and consume the entire ship. The cheers from shore rise to a crescendo as the vessel is transformed into a colossal fireball just before the magazine explodes. In an instant, the ship is blown into pieces and the horrific sounds reverberate as they are carried up and down the river. For those back behind the American lines who fail to hear the explosion, they become aware of it when the ground begins to shake. In the meantime, the ship's commander, Captain Robert Henley, succeeds in reaching shore safely, and despite the avalanche of fire, his casualties amount to one man killed and six others wounded.

The loss of the ship causes some trepidation within the city; however, Jackson's earlier prophesy that the British would not enter the city continues to keep the spirits high, not so much because of the promise but because of the general who made the promise. The British become overwhelmed by their success. General Pakenham, having eliminated a major nemesis, sets his sights on the city itself; however, the concentration on the *Carolina* provided the *Louisiana* the opportunity to evade destruction by pulling back beyond the range of the guns. With the loss of the gunboats on Lake Borgne followed by the loss of the *Carolina*, Jackson is left with one vessel. Its commander, Lt. Thompson, hastily raised a crew and had the *Louisiana* equipped for battle in just a few days. Finally the British guns turn on it; however, the *Louisiana*, precariously positioned, absorbs the storm of fire with only some minor damage inflicted when one of the shells explodes on the deck. A few men are wounded, but no fatalities occur. The ship is also fighting an unruly current and poor winds; however, despite the inexperience of the crew, Thompson manages to pull off a harrowing escape. Shortly thereafter, the *Louisiana* reaches the American lines about four miles outside of the city and it is met with resounding cheers.

The British hear the cheers of the Americans, but they remain optimistic after having secured their flanks. The success of the British guns boosts morale, while Generals Gibbs and Keane are forming their respective brigades in preparation for driving over the defenders and moving into the city. Admiral Cochrane's plans for eating Christmas dinner in New Orleans had been delayed, but with the liquidation of the *Carolina*, he intends to enjoy a victory dinner in the city.

Later this day, the British take advantage of the absence of the naval barrages and begin to assemble on open ground. The two brigades await the signal to advance from their dreadful camp. During the early part of the evening General Pakenham gives the word to advance and a rocket soars upward. The two brigades under Keane and Gibbs, on the left and right respectively, move out heading toward the American fortifications. Keane's column moves along the road which runs along the river, while the other brigade treks through the woods which provide cover for the advance. American patrols shadow the advance. Both brigades reach a point about six hundred yards or less from the stiffened American lines; however, no immediate attack is planned, particularly because of the lessons learned on the 23rd.

The troops are directed to break formation and get rest in preparation for the following day, which is expected to be an exhausting but exhilarating experience. Morale is high as the troops prepare for a night's sleep without the worry of a continual naval barrage, but to their great surprise, Major Hinds' dragoons, earlier thought to be cowardly due to their retreat without a fight, reappear as if sleepless phantoms who emerge out of thin air. The British pickets get no reprieve, nor do the outposts, both of which come under rifle fire. Then to add to the night-terror, Hinds' dragoons operate as shuttles. Detachment after detachment gallops directly toward the outpost, pausing only long enough to propel a volley before dashing away. The thunderous sounds of the galloping, the crack of the guns and devilish yells and screams of the dragoons in absolute darkness inject some additional trepidation for the British during the uncertainty of the harrowing night. The Redcoats, unable to discern whether the Americans are simply unfolding harassment raids or unleashing the preliminaries prior to a full-scale attack, find it nearly impossible to get to sleep from which they might not arise. Meanwhile, the Americans involved with the operation enjoy their lack of sleep. For the British, it is becoming obvious that their European style of warfare is of no value against the Americans, whom they consider uncouth and even barbaric.

The British are appalled by the raids against their outposts, something they had not encountered during the Napoleonic Wars due to a mutual unwritten agreement that outposts were safe from attack unless a post was positioned as an obstacle during a full-scale attack against a main body. This rule is irrelevant to the Americans; the British have arrived to conquer their territory, and a Redcoat is a designated target. The Yanks' strategy, gained after successive generations of fighting Indians as well as the British during the American Revolution, proves to be an excellent neutralizer when facing superior numbers of seasoned troops. Although the Americans while attached to military units are capable of fighting in formation, they are equally if not more dangerous while acting as guerrillas. With regard to the chivalry that the British had expected, it is held in reserve for General Jackson to use after he repulses the invasion. For the time being, the matter at hand is to kill the invaders rather than display sophisticated manners and becoming once again a British colony.

While the British anxiously await dawn to unleash their bayonets against the Americans, General Jackson continues to oversee the operations. His military instincts continue to be nearly flawless in determining the next move of the British and deciding upon countermeasures to ensure failure by the invaders. With his borrowed telescope, he succeeds in scrutinizing the British deployments. With the intelligence, he adjusts his defenses and strengthens the section he suspects the British will plow against at first light on the following day. The Americans also become sleep-deprived, but while the work continues, the troops are not harassed by the Redcoats. Jackson redeploys additional artillery at the expected point of contact. The welcoming committee on the road, originally two 6-pounders, later includes a 12-pounder and 24-pounder, and by dawn on the 28th, yet another 24-pounder lurks by the roadway to greet the advance. Jackson also ensures that the dormant naval guns of the USS *Louisiana* are prepared to bolster his ground troops. Meanwhile, as the lull in the battle on the ground continues, the British remain concerned that Jackson will launch a second attack before they are fully prepared to advance to take the city. British Admiral Malcom sends a message to Admiral Cochrane: "The general [Pakenham] proposes to move tomorrow at daybreak."

December 28 (Wednesday) **In Louisiana** at New Orleans, the British, completely irritated by the actions of the Americans who harassed the outposts and pickets the night before, are awaiting the order to advance to retaliate. The offensive is designed to test the strength of the American lines and is designated a reconnaissance in force. In the meantime, the Americans, by modifying their lines as ordered by General Jackson, are prepared for the onslaught, particularly at the points where Jackson expects the strongest thrust. The regulars under General Coffee remain on the project. Jackson has also directed the Louisiana 1st Regiment to deploy on the right, and he orders the 2nd Louisiana Regiment sent to the left to augment the farthest point along that line (Coffee's sector), considered less strong than the right.

General Jackson had also worked on the levee by cutting it below the line to have a plan whereby the road would flood, if necessary, drowning the British during their advance. The troops under General William "Willie" Carroll, poorly equipped, move to the Rodriguez Canal. Lacking proper weapons, the troops strengthen the entrenchments that stretch along the far left of the American defenses. Jackson's force has nearly doubled, as reinforcements have continued to arrive, giving him more than 4,000 troops, including Lafitte's band.

Before dawn a large contingent is spotted as the men are racing from the city toward Jackson's line. The disheveled lot are the men under Lafitte, and they have run from Fort St. John to join in the fight. The Baritarians, known also as pirates or buccaneers, enthusiastically take command of one of the 24-pounders. Meanwhile, crew members of the ill-fated USS *Carolina* arrive, and those troops take control of a howitzer and another 24-pounder. The British, however, are unaware of the increased strength along the American line. Nonetheless, troops under General Pakenham are seasoned, and they number about 8,000.

Keeping with his usual strategy, Jackson continues to monitor the British positions from his headquarters, and similarly to a professional gambler, his facial expressions remain unchanged, displaying a serious demeanor. Meanwhile, the British get a pleasant surprise which seems to be a good omen. As the morning mist dissipates, the skies are especially clear and the weather is extremely favorable under the bright sunlight beaming down on their scarlet uniforms and bouncing off their bayonets in absolute contrast to the miserable weather they have lived with since they landed. The birds and the animals find themselves being serenaded by the drummers and the boisterous blare of the bugles as the brigades form for the attack under the perceptive eyes of Jackson, who scans the entire British line to counter whatever action is initiated by Pakenham.

General Pakenham signals the advance, and both brigades move out in two separate columns. General Gibbs' brigade, composed of the 4th, 21st, and 44th Regiments along with a black corps, advances with immense precision, keeping close to the swampland on their right, while the 95th Rifles stretch out across the plain until they nudge up against the right of General Keane's column, composed of the 85th, 95th and one black corps, which is marching along the main road and keeping close to the levee. Keane's column is trailing the artillery, which is moving straight down the road. A contingent of the 14th Dragoons escorts General Pakenham and his staff. Pakenham maintains a watch over both columns. The British remain convinced that their opponents are unprepared to match the awesome power that is approaching their positions. While the main body is closing on the American defenses, a separate unit, commanded by Colonel Robert Rennie and composed of some light infantry and skirmishers, maneuvers to reach positions to the rear of the American camp. Meanwhile, morale soars as the British see the American scouts hurriedly ring off a few rounds, then retire after shouting disparaging remarks to further provoke the British rank and file.

Rennie's contingent, while Gibbs' column is at a halt, reaches positions about 100 yards from General Carroll's Tennesseans after driving back the outposts. Carroll dispatches Colonel James Henderson with a 200-man contingent with orders to get to the rear of Rennie to isolate his command from the main body of the column.

Nevertheless, Rennie had posted a detachment in concealed positions, and while the Tennesseans are in the process of reaching their objective, a wave of fire cuts into the column with nasty results. Colonel Henderson is among the five troops who are killed; however the British fire also wounds several other troops. The unexpected volley causes the column to lose its discipline. The troops abort the advance and haphazardly rush back toward their lines. Rennie, aware of the panic and knowing that Carroll possesses no artillery, seizes the advantage and orders his column to drive straight into Carroll's positions. Nevertheless, at about the same time, a messenger from General Gibbs delivers orders which direct Rennie to immediately halt his advance and return to the main body. Although Rennie had been poised to collapse Carroll's line, he is unaware of the peril of Keane's column; however, after the column returns to join with Gibbs, the troops are positioned from where they observe Keane's column being mauled.

The British operating on the left are able to determine some weakness; however, on the right, General Keane's column encounters invulnerable defenses. The column begins to close on the defensive line, and soon after passing Bienvu's house, American artillery intentionally reduces the Chalmette house, which is loaded with combustibles. After the explosion, burning timbers fly in all directions. Immediately afterward, Keane pauses to examine the enemy line, and the view through his glass is not what he was anticipating. New and heavy artillery had been deployed off Jackson's weak link, the left side of his line, and the guns dominate the approach to the extent that the front of Keane's column is subject to being shredded by an avalanche of fire from the guns manned by Lafitte's buccaneers under the leadership of Dominique You and another Baritarian known as Bluche. The Baritarians' skill with artillery has been gained at the expense of vulnerable ships at sea. During the approach, British artillery had been active; however, it did not achieve the objective of collapsing the line to force the militia to flee. In fact, other American artillery had been exchanging blows with the attackers. At about the same time, the battery manned by the seamen of the *Carolina* begins to roar; then to increase the pressure, the USS *Louisiana* reappears and it also opens fire.

The British get caught between a hurricane of artillery and naval fire as well as fires from the burning structures. Keane's column attempts to break through, but the effort is in vain. All the while, the casualties continue to soar dangerously due to the effectiveness of the artillery. While the guns pour volley after volley, the *Louisiana* catapults about 800 shells into their ranks. To their front, the British are blocked by an impassible ditch in which the troops get snagged by waist-high mud. The expanding fires from the structures with the combustibles that are exploding create intolerable heat and flames that also threaten the column. The smoke becomes so dense that visibility is reduced to zero. The unexpected disaster brings the mission to a succinct halt. The entire force is recalled and the two artillery pieces brought forward to blow a hole in the line cannot be withdrawn due to the American fire. After the British are compelled to retreat, a courageous detachment of seamen under Sir Thomas Troubridge of the Royal Navy brave the fire and creep up to the stranded artillery. Ropes are attached to the guns and the men pull them to safety.

Once again, Jackson has foiled the British scheme, and without requiring his infantry, except for Colonel Henderson's failed attempt to trap Colonel Rennie. The British, however, do conclude that Jackson's left is the vulnerable point. After the British return to their line, more artillery is requested from the fleet to ensure that the main attack will finally succeed. Meanwhile, the Yanks continue to build upon their defenses, while the British, having discovered the weak link in the line, prepare to establish a siege before they launch their major attack. Pakenham, however, is shocked by the results of the mission and thrashing Keane's brigade received and frustrated that for the first time, troops under his command had been compelled to evade enemy fire by seeking cover.

The Americans lose nine killed, including Captain Carrick, a U.S. Marine who is hit by a rocket and sustains wounds to his arm and head that prove fatal. His horse is shattered into pieces. The number of British casualties has never been authenticated. Estimates place the casualties at about 200 killed or wounded, including a large number of men killed during the general retreat. An official report, excluding the casualties during the retreat, are listed as 16 killed and 43 either wounded or missing. Among the British officer losses, Captain Collings (British West India Regiment) attached to the 93rd Regiment, failed to seek shelter at the ditch, despite being ordered to lie down. He is struck with a cannon ball that decapitates him. The Americans had used only their artillery, and the injuries inflicted were ghastly, unlike a clean shot from a rifle. The number of men who survive their injuries are extremely low. The USS *Louisiana*, which focused its guns primarily on the British batteries while it remained under incessant fire itself, sustains one man killed.

The humiliating defeat for the British has an instant demoralizing effect on the commanders as well as the men. The recent visions of a grand rout of the ragtag Americans sinks into oblivion. General Pakenham anxiously awaits the brigade under General Lambert, who has not yet arrived from England, despite having sailed from Plymouth simultaneously with Pakenham. By this time, Pakenham is desperate to welcome Lambert to replenish his beleaguered force.

The British myth of invincibility is crushed and the Americans had accomplished what Napoleon had failed to do. Jackson's gunners had humbled the British regulars and provoked the commander to order them to retreat. The guns had splintered the advancing battalions, forcing the harrowing retreat to be uncharacteristic by British standards. The retreat could not unfold by companies with rear guard cover; rather, orders are issued to hurriedly retire in small parties to avoid even more devastation by Jackson's guns. All throughout the day, an elevated

British head was subject to being blown off by grape and shot, and during the haphazard retreat it is estimated that about 60 troops are killed or wounded. It would be rare to find a comparable dishonorable retreat in the annals of British history.

General Pakenham's losses create major complications; however, other difficulties arise due to the planning of the invasion. There were no thoughts of any major opposition to the invasion, and Jackson, derogatorily described as the "ignorant Indian fighter," was presumed to be a pushover. Consequently, the food supplies have been dangerously depleted. Coupled with the failure to take New Orleans on a timely basis, the British are compelled to remain in their camp on open ground, which makes them captives of the elements. Disease, particularly dysentery, strikes the army, taking a high toll on men who are already beyond exhaustion. They are able to confiscate some livestock from the surrounding plantations, but animals in the region are scarce. The horrors of their circumstances are magnified because of their location, which has them only a few miles from their prize, and yet because of the obstinate and defiant Americans, the city might as well be a mirage to the struggling British army.

December 29 (Thursday) In New Orleans, the Americans continue to maintain their defenses while the British, having again been repulsed on the previous day, remain exasperated. During the night (29th-30th), snipers continued to harass the British outposts. The British have convinced themselves that the city can still be taken, once they deploy additional firepower acquired from the fleet that is capable of knocking out Jackson's artillery. The British are confident that Jackson's left is the most vulnerable spot along the line. However, Jackson, once again instinctively convinced that the British will strike his left, modifies his line and redeploys some artillery to dominate the suspected route of advance.

Two 12-pounders under Lt. Spotts are placed near the woods, and another piece, also a 12-pounder, is deployed between the previously mentioned guns and the center of the line. Jackson directs a volunteer, French general Garrique, to command the latter piece, and he also brings in two additional guns (6-pounder and 18-pounder) under Colonel Perry, who places his guns in the same general area. More strength is put in place when Commodore Patterson unloads a 24-pounder and two 12-pounders from the USS *Louisiana* and establishes his Marine battery on the west bank of the Mississippi River at Jourdan's Plantation at a spot to the rear of the levee, providing Jackson with artillery placed to dominate the frontal approaches to the line. Patterson designates some of his crew to handle the battery. To further bolster his force, Patterson dispatches Lt. Thompson into the city to round up anyone who even looks like a seamen. Thompson expeditiously sweeps into the city and jumps from one boarding house to another until he finds sufficient manpower. Not one man speaks English. Despite the language barrier, the battery is tested on the following day.

December 30 (Friday) In Louisiana, the British, having received some additional guns from the fleet, activate their batteries to attempt to eliminate Jackson's batteries. They initially intend to destroy the USS *Louisiana*. Nonetheless, Commodore Patterson's land battery on the opposite bank proves too powerful. The gunners at the British batteries, after sustaining a bombardment for several hours, are forced to evacuate their positions. The incessant fire also drives other British troops from their houses at Chalmette's and Bienvu's. Patterson's battery rivets the area with cascading shells that clear the threat on Jackson's right. The British sustain such heavy fire that it becomes too dangerous to venture near the river to conduct reconnaissance patrols. Meanwhile, with the added security of Patterson's battery, the right appears to be secure, leaving General Jackson to ensure his left sector, where General Carroll and General Coffee continue to increase the depth of the ditches, a nasty but necessary project. Back in the British camp, plans are being finalized to launch what is expected to be the final assault that carries the British ensign straight into New Orleans.

After dusk, the Americans resume their usual harassment raids to keep the British outposts unnerved. The Tennesseans seemingly enjoy interrupting the British, and in turn the British are forced to remain alert. The intruders are often heard as horses gallop toward the outposts, but individuals maneuver within rifle shot to pick off any unsuspecting guards. The regulars under Major Hinds also remain active, particularly on special missions for Jackson. Once Jackson is informed of a new British position, he dispatches Hinds to close upon the battery or redoubt to gather intelligence. For the British, the appearance and disappearance of Hinds' dragoons is becoming constant. The column suddenly appears in the distance and the British are familiar with the routine. After Hinds reaches a point several hundred yards from the position, the horses swing into a full gallop and they maintain their stride, despite British fire. Hinds' troops, on the fly, are able to assess the strength and position of the artillery before galloping off to deliver the intelligence to Jackson. Other units also participate in these nightly raids that never fail to disrupt the British camp, because it is always unclear whether the raid is part of a major night assault. At about midnight, the raiders return to camp; however, the British spend the rest of the night wondering when the next alarm will be sounded.

December 31 (Saturday) In New Orleans, within the city itself and at the defenses just outside the city, the fear and anxiety caused by the arrival of the British has been eradicated. Jackson's troops, many of whom had been young and untrained militia when the Redcoats landed on 23 December, have been able to halt the British convincingly. In less than one month, the Americans have stripped the British of their swagger, outfought their finest, overmatched their artillery, exasperated their commanders, and prevented them from acquiring sufficient food supplies. Jackson's guns had compelled the British to cower under fire and become frozen in place during an attack in which they had to retreat in small parties to avoid being annihilated. Every tactic tried by the British up to this point has been foiled by Jackson's flawless strategy and his uncanny ability to foretell what the enemy's next move would be.

In the city, the daily routines continue without interruption by British artillery, which has been unable to get within range. As 1814 is fading into the new year, there is a stark difference in the two camps. Although some historians have penned sanitized descriptions of the opposing camps to create what would usually be the conditions in a British encampment that is poised to destroy its foe, there are no signs of jubilation under the British ensign. The conditions continue to be dreadful and the troops still lack tents. The British, standing only several hundred yards from the American defenses, can observe the Americans, who exhibit no timidity, and in fact the British threat, although severe, does not prevent the Americans from enjoying some relaxation. Several bands, particularly that of the Orleans Battalion, provide music which along with a near steady beating of the drums is easily heard within the British lines, where the mood is somber and the British musicians uncharacteristically silent. Even bugle calls are rare in the camp, and when a bugle does blare it is most likely a signal that Americans are again threatening the outposts. The British camp appears to be under a canopy of gloom and desperation, as if the usual British confidence had been mysteriously transferred to the American lines, where there are endless rows of tents and an abundance of food. While the British maintain their theory that the next attack will succeed, they are constantly reminded of their failures by the sight of the American flag fluttering in the breeze above the American lines, which further infuriates the rank and file. The flag that prevailed at Fort McHenry now holds resolutely at the Mississippi River.

Admiral Cochrane and General Pakenham, seemingly oblivious to the grave conditions in the camp and still unimpressed with the superlative actions of the Americans, once again beam with illusions of grandeur as the guns from the fleet are in the process of being deployed for the purpose of finally overrunning Jackson's defenses after their guns reduce the fragile parapets. The commanders, however, aware of the accuracy of Jackson's guns, remain cautious and prudent in an attempt to outfox Jackson before launching the attack. No activity to place the guns begins until after dark. Although the British are planning to startle Jackson with the powerful display of artillery at dawn on the 8th, the day is not tranquil. Artillery from both sides exchange fire and the Americans continue to harass the British. Jackson, who has maintained near constant vigil, once again picks up a signal that the British are preparing yet another attack. He observes the increase in activity and their initiation of patrols as well as a massive redeployment of troops.

During the night of the 31st into the predawn hours of New Year's Day, the British engage in planting the guns which have been brought up from the fleet. The noise created by hammers, shovels and other tools is carried by the night air and heard by guards along the American lines. The camp of the British suddenly coming back to life causes curiosity at the American defenses. All signs point to a new attack, and Jackson has discerned that Pakenham is ready to try again to take his prize. The British complete the project and get the big guns in place before dawn.

Late December   In Georgia, Captain Samuel Dale, while at the Indian agency, is entrusted with documents from the secretary of war at Washington that need to get to General Jackson at New Orleans. Dale is persuaded by Colonel Hawkins and General McIntosh to make the dangerous journey through hostile territory. He completes the trek in eight days and arrives just as General Jackson's army is in the process of defeating the British. Dale, inquiring of the whereabouts of the general, is told that he is with his troops at Chalmette. Dale observes the battle; however, he does not get to hand the papers to General Jackson until after midnight. Jackson opens the packet without speaking, then responds: "Too late; too late; they are always too late at Washington." Jackson is amazed that Dale had completed the arduous journey in only eight days.

1815

In Alabama, Fort Jonesboro is established in the north central sector of Alabama slightly west of Birmingham. The post is required to defend the region against hostile Upper Creek Indians, known also as "Red Sticks."

In Florida, the British abandon Fort Blount, which had been constructed during the ongoing war. They leave the fort and its supplies and ammunition for their allies in the area, Negroes and Indians, including Seminole and Choctaws. The remaining weapons include artillery pieces. The fort becomes known as "Negro Fort." From here, the leaders initiate raids into Florida and Georgia.

In Georgia, the British attack and destroy the American position at St. Mary's (Battery at Point Peter), about sixty miles above Savannah.

In Louisiana, Fort Petites Coquilles in New Orleans is reconstructed by the Americans and renamed Fort at the Rigolets. During 1827, the fort is again reconstructed, but the site is moved to a better location and within one mile of the original fort built during 1793. The fort at that time will be renamed Fort Pike. The British under Pakenham attack the fortifications defending New Orleans; however, over-powering American artillery drives the British back and Jackson still holds the city. The British cannons miss their mark, but return fire by American batteries commanded by Enoch Humphrey, Patterson and the pirate Dominique level the British batteries.

In naval activity, the American privateer *Diamond,* commanded by Captain W. Davidson, intercepts and seizes a brigantine, the *Lord Wellington,* which is en route from Halifax to Havana. The vessel is carrying passengers including some who are Spanish. At the request from the Spanish, the *Lord Wellington* is released and permitted to resume its voyage.

January   In Georgia, the British attempt to launch their first actual invasion when a force of about 1,500 troops prepare to land at Point Peter. Major General Thomas Pinckney had placed Major Massias' unit at the point to defend it. Nonetheless, the British conclude that Point Peter is more formidable than they had thought and the decision to attack is aborted. The troops return to the fleet. Earlier the British had conducted small-scale raids against Beaufort, South Carolina, but nothing of consequence. Also, General Pinckney retires from the service during the following June and retires at his residence (Eldorado) in Charleston, where he died on 2 November 1828 at the age of 79. During his funeral, his body was escorted by companies of the 16th and 17th regiments, as well as a squadron of cavalry and a contingent of federal troops based at Fort Moultrie. General Pinckney's saddled horse also participates in the procession, which moves from his residence on Legare Street to St. Philip's Church (Episcopal).

General Pinckney had married Elizabeth, a daughter of Jacob and Rebecca Motte. His wife died while he was in England as the American minister. They had two sons and two daughters. Later he married a second time, taking Mrs. Frances Motte Middleton, the widow of an Englishman who emigrated to join the American cause during the Revolutionary War. His second wife was the sister of his first wife. General Pinckney was the brother of another Revolutionary War veteran, General Charles Coatesworth Pinckney, a signer of the U.S. Constitution. General Pinckney's three swords, which he used during the Revolution and the War of 1812, were inherited by his sons with a caveat that "they never be drawn in any private quarrel, and never remain in their scabbards, when their Country demanded their service." According to one historian, "fourteen of his descendants served in the Confederate army; one was a major-general, one was killed in battle at Chancellorsville, one at [Fort] Sumter, and others shared the fate of captives."

In North Carolina, Colonel William S. Hamilton, U.S. Army, on recruiting duty in North Carolina since April 1813, receives new orders. He is relieved of recruiting and directed to repair to his new duty station at Fredericksburg, Virginia. He is scheduled to move to the New York frontier at the arrival of spring; however, by then word that the war was over had arrived and the move becomes unnecessary.

January 1 (Sunday)   In Washington, D.C., James Monroe writes to Governor Simon Butler of Pennsylvania:

> SIR: I have just had an interview with Mr. Roberts and Gen. Lacocke, and find, with great regret, that an order issued by Gen. Scott has been understood to have a bearing on Gen. Worrel, which has wounded his feelings. They seem to apprehend that this order may have interfered with your own views relative to the command of the militia of Pennsylvania, in the service of the United States, in that district. With the information which I possess, not having as yet heard from Gen. Scott, it is not in my power to give any explanation of the means alluded to. I can only remark that, when Gen. Bloomfield withdrew from the command of the district, it was committed to Gen. Gaines, as well to prevent local collision, as to secure to the city of Philadelphia and the district the aid of his acknowledged talents; that the same motives had influence in transferring the command to Gen. Scott, after the departure of Gen. Gaines for New Orleans; and that Gen. Scott, on going to Philadelphia, was instructed to take measures for palliating and removing any unpleasant sensations, in any of the officers, which might have been excited, and particularly in Gen. Worrel. In pursuing which, he was to communicate and harmonize with you. Your absence from the city, and the necessity of his early return to Baltimore, have, I find, rendered this impossible. In the talents of Gen. Scott, and in full disposition to obtain a strict impartiality in the discharge of his public duties, I have the greatest confidence. Should be, by any orders, have given just cause for such excitement, I am satisfied that it had been unintentional.

General Abner Lacocke had been a brigadier general of the Pennsylvania militia prior to the war (1807). He had been elected to the U.S. Senate in 1812, following his service in the State Senate from 1808 to 1810. He also served as Congressman during the Twelfth Congress.

In Louisiana, the British, despite an all-night work party that included about one half of the troops, have suddenly recovered a bounce in their step and their missing swagger has returned. As dawn breaks, the Americans still can't pinpoint the source of all the noise during the night due to a dense fog; however, directly in front of their defenses about 400 yards distant, the British have erected works and deployed thirty pieces of artillery, twenty long 18-pounders and ten 18-pounders. The project had been under the supervision of Colonel (later general) John Burgoyne, whose father had fought the Americans during the American Revolution until his capture at Saratoga during 1777.

The work is completed at dawn and the ground troops pull back to await the order to charge after the big guns silence Jackson's artillery and demolish the redoubts. General Pakenham is beginning to believe his imminent victory will elevate him to an earldom, and Admiral Cochrane senses he is closer to his well publicized remarks about dinner in New Orleans. The day in the British camp unfolds with a tinge of brilliance even though the sun is thoroughly blocked by a dense fog that shows no signs of dissipating. Back at the American lines, the joviality of New Year's Eve continues and the troops are more prepared for a parade to celebrate the new year than to receive an attack. The peril remains invisible due to fog that conceals the British camp and the recently erected redoubts. Actually both sides are essentially blind beyond a distance of about 20 or 25 yards. The premonitions of the veterans that the British would attack at dawn had caused concern, but with no British guns roaring, the troops fall into a holiday mood.

Jackson had authorized the friends and family members from the city to enter the camp to celebrate with the troops, who with their chests bulging with pride are even preparing for a parade, all the while having no knowledge that matches are being lit and the British gunners can hardly wait to avenge their humbling defeat of the 28th. The engineers under Colonel Burgoyne have supposedly constructed the batteries to ensure that their guns will be invulnerable from Jackson's artillery and from the Marine battery that has been pummeling their ranks. Nonetheless, the British bands remain silent, creating the impression that they have not yet recovered from their recent drubbing. Finally, the fog lifts and the sun dominates. The clear, unobstructed view provides the Americans with a sobering and deadly sight — thirty heavy artillery pieces elevated and prepared to pulverize their camp.

The celebration in the American camp comes to a succinct close as the shells are propelled rapidly by some of the army's finest gunners. Civilians begin to rush from the camp, while the troops, stunned by the bombardment and still in their freshly cleaned clothes, head post-haste to their battle stations. The parade field is suddenly inundated with descending artillery shells and exploding Congreve rockets. Nonetheless, thanks to the British, who forced the raw militia to become savvy troops over the past month, the militia does not become rattled. Similarly to the seasoned regulars, they rebound from the shock of the surprise bombardment and with good discipline prepare to meet the attack.

While the British troops to the rear of the batteries peer at the hurricane of fire, they expect to jump off in a triumphant charge toward the inoperable guns of the Americans, surely destroyed by the firestorm. Meanwhile, the gunners perk up when they observe General Jackson's headquarters become the recipient of their marksmanship. From the distance, it appears as if the building had been hit by a demolition team. Inside the building, the destruction is overwhelming and furious. Walls and furniture are hit, split and shattered with dust and debris flying everywhere. Clouds of plaster dust permeate the rooms and even bricks are dislodged and transformed into flying weapons. To anyone outside, it appears as though no one inside could have survived. Although many of Jackson's staff resemble ghosts or zombies due to their layers of dust, none sustain injuries, and the most severe casualty of the British bombardment had been Jackson's half-finished breakfast. Later estimates put the number of balls and shells that disrupted the general's breakfast at 100. Nonetheless, General Jackson, although fearless in the face of his enemies, wisely concludes that his headquarters should be relocated. Shortly thereafter, Jackson moves to the front lines.

The British positions are again obscured, not by a returning fog, but from the thunderclap of the 30 monstrous guns. The British are waiting for the smoke to dissipate so they can evaluate the devastation they inflicted. Nevertheless, Jackson's guns had remained unscathed, and his redoubts, described as "feeble" by the British, had absorbed the pounding, thanks in great part to the soft Louisiana dirt. Jackson, with his usual calm demeanor and stern expression, arrives near the battery commanded by Humphrey, easily noticeable because of the cigar which appears to be sewn to his lips. His men, similarly to the British, are waiting for the intense smoke to vanish; however, the British are not expecting any severe retaliation.

Meanwhile, Jackson puts the situation in perspective: "Ah, all is right. Humphrey is at his post and will return their compliments presently." Afterward, Jackson moves to a nearby battery to encourage his troops there, and in response to their vociferous cheers as he jumps from battery to battery, he perceives some apprehension due to the whizzing rockets. Jackson tells his troops not to be concerned: "Don't mind these rockets, they are mere toys to amuse children." The British used the same type rockets (pyrotechnics) at Bladensburg, and they instilled fear into the militia, but here, the militia has no intentions of running.

At the instant the smoke clears, Humphrey's 12-pounders initiate the return fire and the British, familiar with the types of cannon, discern that the fire is originating from light artillery, which to them verifies that the massive bombardment did its destruction as predicted. The infantry is relieved that their advance will not be struck by another wall of fire. Nevertheless, the comfort zone is of short duration. While the British came under fire by Humphrey's battery on the right, the remainder of the guns on the line had not yet opened fire. Within a short while, a ghastly series of violent blasts occurs when the other batteries join with Humphrey's. Suddenly, the guns thought to have been decimated catapult volley after volley into the British positions. The guns under Dominique, Norris and Spotts stream heavier shells upon the British, then at nearly the same time, more firepower is committed when the 12-pounder under the French General Garrique begins to pound the enemy position to his immediate front and the colossal gun under Crawley propels its devastating fire toward the redoubts considered to be invincible.

The waves of fire arcing toward the British ensures a delay in the ground attack, as the infantry once again is reluctantly confined to their positions behind the batteries. Any attempt to advance during the ongoing artillery battle would be absolute folly. Back at the American lines, confidence remains steadfast along the line and the incessant fire fails to deflate the morale. For any of the troops along the line inquiring where their commander was holding his headquarters, they needed to only glance to the left or right and they might find his arm on their shoulder. Jackson remains in the thick of the battle, encouraging the troops as he floats all along the line. Dominique, the Baritarian, defies the British fire and the odds by impetuously standing in full view of the British, while directing the fire and screaming his salutations in French to the British.

The earth shattering bombardments continue unabated, and despite the violence and deadly fire, civilians are attracted to the riverbanks to observe the raging battle. Burgoyne's engineers had built up the works sufficiently to provide the British gunners an advantage, and their fire remains effective; however, the damage inflicted to Jackson's batteries does not silence his guns. Nevertheless, one of Dominique's sustains damage when a shell strikes its carriage and the 32-pounder commanded by Crowley is hit and damaged, along with one of Garrique's guns. In another effective strike, a British shell hits two caissons, which causes a huge explosion when 100 pounds of gunpowder detonates. The Americans' remaining guns continue to blast the British positions despite the incessant fire they are facing. After more than an hour of non-stop explosions, the British fire begins to fall off. From the American lines, it is impossible to detect the precise reason until the smoke clears, but the assumption is that the British have also sustained damage.

All along the American line, which stretches for about 1,000 yards, eyes are straining in vain to get a look at the British redoubts, but the smoke is formed like a stone, leaving the Americans to wonder. After a while, the smoke clears and the Americans clearly see the results of their gunners. The redoubts become visible and the view, depending on the vantage point, is either invigorating or total frustration. The redoubts erected by the army engineers had totally collapsed, leaving the guns exposed.

The British commanders, concerned that the troops are exposed and vulnerable to the American guns, order them to take cover in the ditches. The promise that the fleet's guns would decimate Jackson's ramparts to open the way to New Orleans fails. All the while, there is no remorse along the American lines. They escalate the fire patterns to deliver even more flying destruction. The British sustain what seems to be an ordinary hit; however, it tears through the wall of the redoubt and shatters, with pieces shooting directly into the hogsheads filled with sugar. The hogsheads, after being irrigated, cause the guns to collapse from their carriages. The collapsed guns kill some crew members. It becomes a hard lesson for the British, who discover that having sugar, rather than sand or dirt, in the hogsheads caused the tragedy. British shells continued to plaster Jackson's redoubt throughout the engagement, but the American redoubts had been constructed only of Louisiana dirt (despite some erroneous reports that Jackson's lines were bolstered by bales of cotton). The British shells cause no damage to the embankment; the dirt wall absorbs them like a sponge.

The American guns continue to plaster the damaged works and the British there are compelled to abandon the positions. The boldness of the Americans increases as the remaining operable guns are knocked out of action. While the British are scampering from the redoubt, the Americans begin to yell insults. The British focus on reaching a ditch rather than returning the insults. The remaining British redoubts come under the thunderclap, and the iron storm also cripples those. The British are pinned by the incessant fire until about 1200, when the American fire is suspended. The British receive a temporary reprieve because the guns require a pause to permit the overheated weapons to cool down.

The British guns are beyond repair, but the results of the American barrages remain concealed by the dense clouds of smoke. As the smoke begins to vanish, the British redoubts come into view, but they are nearly unrecognizable. The redoubts more resemble the aftermath of a violent storm that had cast a fleet upon the rocks. Destroyed, damaged, disfigured remnants of the artillery that had gained countless laurels for the British during the struggle to defeat Napoleon are scattered about in what has become a royal scrap yard. Cochrane's fleet guns, despite their might, had failed to gain him access to New Orleans. From the American lines, the British are observed while they move to extricate the guns that survived decimation in conjunction with what appears to be the beginning of another general retreat. Nonetheless, the Yankee gunners exhibit no compassion for the faltering enemy. The guns continue to blast the British positions and the effectiveness is equal to that of 28 December. British troops who pop up from a ditch become subject to decapitation. The British had thrown wave after wave of fire into the Americans; however, the number of casualties reported is 34, including killed and wounded. The fatalities were primarily civilians who had been toward the rear of the camp and near the riverbank to observe the battle.

The British, repulsed yet again, are compelled to revisit the plantations they thought had been vacated for the last time. General Pakenham, after arriving back at the Villere Plantation, re-establishes his headquarters in the house he departed earlier in the day. Meanwhile, the brigades of Generals Gibbs and Keane re-establish their respective camps at Bienvu and Lacoste. The British are forced to again come up with a new plan to seize their prize; however, the troops, having become disgruntled come to consider the talk of victory to be pure cackle. Conditions within the British lines continue to deteriorate as dysentery plagues the troops and they continue to lack proper food. Subsequent to a council, the officers conclude that the new plan concocted by Pakenham is foolproof. The British plan calls for a twin attack which will pound the American lines on both banks of the river, with the first objective being the guns on the right bank, which once secured can be used against Jackson's main line. They have convinced themselves that by dividing their army, the thrust will sever communication between Jackson and the city and the American redoubts will crumble. Nevertheless, the efforts to get the troops and equipment in position is tedious, as is bringing up barges for the crossing. The task is not completed until 7 January.

In naval activity, the American privateer *Grand Turk*, commanded by Captain Nathan Green, departs Salem, Massachusetts. After departing from the harbor at about 1230, the ship reaches Baker's Island by 1400. Except for some sporadic long-range contact with a British flag, the cruise remains uneventful until the afternoon of 17 February 1815, when the Americans are able to acquire information regarding the location of British merchant ships.

January 2 (Monday) In Louisiana at New Orleans, the Americans, having forestalled a full-scale attack by repelling the British on the previous day, resume their work projects to further bolster the fortifications outside the city. Subsequent to the close of action on New Year's Day, Jackson resumes the details to strengthen his lines. He also draws a second line about one and one-half miles behind the first, which nudges his force closer to the city. Meanwhile, the British begin to get a flotilla of barges moved up to their positions. Some officers and troops suggest that the barges could be moved more quickly dragged on rollers, but the idea, despite having been successful in bringing up the guns, is rejected. Consequently a major project to modify the canal is undertaken. In the meantime, Jackson continues to anxiously await the arrival of more reinforcements. His concerns fade on the 3rd, when cheers are heard upon the arrival of Kentuckians, Tennesseans and Louisiana militia.

Two additional seasoned British regiments under General John Lambert finally arrive on the 6th. The new regiments boost the number of Redcoats and lift the spirits of the troops who so far have not been able to crush the resistance. The British, unlike the Americans, are not pondering the results of the ultimate battle; rather, they are wondering only how long it will take to capture the city and gain control of the Mississippi River, which will provide them with the ability to link directly with the troops in Canada. General Pakenham prepares to launch an attack to overrun the battery of Commodore Patterson without destroying the guns, which he believes can be redeployed to fire upon Jackson's line.

In naval activity, the American privateer *Harpy* intercepts and captures the British ship *William and Alfred*, commanded by Captain William Drysdale. Later, Captain Drysdale writes about his captivity and states his thanks to Captain Nichols, the commander of the *Globe*: "To the commander of the said brig, and all his officers for their great civility, indulgent lenity and humane usage while on board, and generously delivering up all his private property. And should at any future time, Captain Nichols or any of his officers come to London, Captain Drysdale will be happy to see them at his house, Stepney Green, near London. Given under my hand, on board the *Harpy* at sea, this day, January 6, 1815." The British officers add a similar testimony as a supplement to Drysdale's testimonial. The *William and Alfred* is taken into port in the United States. Also, the *Harpy* captures the ship *Jane*, which is en route to Antigua from London. Captain Nichols transfers the cargo and afterward releases the vessel as a cartel. Another prize of the *Harpy* is the ship *Garland*. It along with its cargo of rum, is taken into port at Salem. The *Harpy* arrives back at Salem during April 1815.

January 3 (Tuesday) Silence is still in effect in the vicinity of New Orleans, as no actions develop between the British under Pakenham and Jackson. Kentucky reinforcements under General Thomas arrive, causing excitement in Jackson's camp. The Kentuckians arrive with no guns at their sides, causing Jackson to exclaim: "I have never seen a Kentuckian without a gun and pack of cards and a bottle of whiskey in my life!"

In naval activity, the *Guerriere*, a 169-ton brigantine (Francis A. Burnham, master), carrying a crew of 60 men and four guns and operating out of Portsmouth, Maine, is intercepted and seized by the HMS *Junon*.

January 6 (Friday) In Louisiana at New Orleans, the British continue to bring up the barges with which the two-pronged attack will be launched to eradicate Jackson's defenses and give the British their prize, New Orleans, which for more than one month has been successfully defended by General Jackson. Meanwhile, the British continue to struggle with the acute food shortages. That which is available is extremely poor. Nonetheless, the troops, seasoned veterans, prove their mettle by enduring the miserable conditions with only the usual complaints. Meanwhile, General Pakenham becomes animated when his desperately needed reinforcements arrive this day. The 7th Regiment (Fusiliers) and the 43rd Light Infantry, commanded by Lt. Colonel Blakeney and Lt. Colonel Patrickson, respectively, build up the camp. The contingent is under the overall command of General Lambert. Both of the newly arrived regiments have been severely battle tested and proven to be among the finest in the British army; however, their first glance at Pakenham's exhausted force does not inspire optimism. Nonetheless, the appearance of his old regiment, the Fusiliers, momentarily causes Pakenham to slip into a sentimental mood as he greets many of his friends and recollects their victorious days on the old battlefields. However, the time for reminiscing is premature. Pakenham begins to tie up the loose ends and form his army, which now totals about 10,000 seasoned veterans, for the task ahead. He also utilizes the seamen and Royal Marines that have arrived with the fleet.

Pakenham delegates Colonel Thornton's 85th Regiment, bolstered by sailors, Royal Marines, a detachment of rocketeers, along with several carronades as the unit to protect his flank. Thornton is to cross the river on barges on the following night (7th), launch a surprise attack and seize the guns of Patterson's Marine battery before dawn. General Gibbs' brigade, composed of the 4th, 21st and 44th Regiments, is to strike what Pakenham has determined Jackson's weakest link, his left, while General Keane is to ignite a diversionary move by shifting toward the right side of Jackson's line to convince Jackson that his right is the main objective. Once Jackson takes the bait, Keane's force (93rd and 95th Regiments, light companies 7th and 43rd Regiments, and a contingent of West Indian troops) is to be prepared to pounce upon the line at the first opening. The main attack is to commence during the predawn hours of 7 January.

The resiliency of Jackson's forces is displayed by some of the crewmen of the squadron earlier destroyed on Lake Borgne by the British. Lt. Johnson, commanding three boats, creeps out of Chef-Menteur, evades contact with the British squadron and intercepts a British brigantine that is en route to deliver a supply of rum and biscuits to Pakenham's forces at Bayou Bienvu. The Americans seize ten crew members and safely return them to Jackson's headquarters. Through interrogation, the Americans learn that the British attack is imminent, and as Jackson had surmised, the prisoners inform Jackson that the British have been digging a canal to permit them to conduct a landing on the opposite bank of the Mississippi.

January 7 (Saturday) **In Louisiana,** the British are completing the final steps before launching their major full-scale attack to reduce the American redoubts which continue to bar passage into New Orleans. There are no thoughts of failure, only of adding to the laurels of the regiments, but still, there remains one seemingly perpetual stumbling block, the indefatigable General Andrew Jackson, who has molded a hardened army out of raw militia and volunteers in little more than one month. Jackson has repeatedly repulsed some of the finest troops in the British army. Although the greater part of the people in New Orleans continue to have absolute confidence in the general, a small minority, including some crony politicians, are beginning to worry more about themselves than of the fate of the city; however, it is only a minority, and reports to the contrary are due more to the imagination of the authors who perceived genuine opposition against Jackson. The general is still constantly observing the British movements from his battered headquarters.

By this day, Jackson has received more reinforcements, including about 500 men (militia) under General Philemon Thomas, who arrived on 1 January. Since the arrival on 3 January of about 1,500 Kentuckians under General John Thomas who mostly lack weapons and proper clothing, the women of New Orleans have worked tirelessly to sew the clothing for the men. The legislature authorizes $16,000 for them and people in the region raise $100,000. One source that does not contribute is the U.S. Congress. The Kentuckians had traveled on their own for the sole purpose of doing their part to save New Orleans. They get their opportunity on the following morning, but for the present, there is still an enormous amount of preparation for the upcoming attack. Jackson, having learned the British plan from prisoners on the previous day, spends his entire day ensuring that troops are prepared and that his defenses can continue to withstand the British attacks.

The American line is not uniform from one end to the other. The height and thickness of the walls varies, leaving some weak spots; however, the walls for the entire length have been built solely with Louisiana soil. There are no cotton bales at any point. The lines extend from the river to the woods and from the latter, the line is pushed into the swamp. Captain Humphrey's artillery is placed on the road less than 75 yards from the river near the levee. His regulars dominate the road and provide protection for the flank of the redoubt with their pair of brass 12-pounders, manned a U.S. artillery contingent, and one 6-pounder, manned by dragoons attached to Major St. Geme. The other batteries are spaced out along the line as follows: Battery No. 2, manned by crew men of the USS *Carolina* under Lt. Norris, contains one 24-pounder, which is deployed less than 100 yards from Humphrey's battery; Battery No. 3, manned by Dominique You and the Frenchman Bluche, along with a detachment of Baritarians and a contingent of French privateers, contains two 24-pounders; Cominique's battery stands only about 50 yards from the guns of Battery No. 2; and Battery No. 4, manned by crew members of the USS *Carolina* under Lt. Crawley, contains one 32-pounder and is nearly within touching distance of Battery No. 3.

The remaining batteries along the line—No. 5, No. 6, No. 7 and No. 8—are separated by just under 200 yards. Battery No. 5, commanded by Colonel Perry and Lt. Kerr, contains one 18-pounder and two 6-pounders. Next along the line, Battery No. 6, which contains one brass 12-pounder, is manned by a contingent of the D'Orleans Battalion, led by Lt. Berbel and under the overall command of General Garrique. The French general had fought against the English during the Napoleonic Wars. Garrique's battery stands only about 35 yards from Battery No. 5; however, a large gap exists between it and Battery No. 7, which is deployed just under 200 yards distant. Battery No. 7, commanded by Lt. Spotts and Chameau, contains one long brass 18-pounder and one 6-pounder, whose commands are attached to the U.S. Artillery. About sixty yards beyond Battery No. 7, a small carronade is posted; however, it had been poorly mounted and little is expected of it. The battery is commanded by an artillery corporal and manned by a contingent of General William Carroll's force.

General Jackson's remaining artillery is under Commodore Patterson and deployed on the opposite (right) bank. Patterson's Marine Battery contains nine artillery pieces. Combined, Jackson has 25 artillery pieces, and he is depending on the continuing effectiveness of the Marine battery, which is charged with flanking the British on the left bank. Jackson, thinking ahead, has also chosen to establish a safety net in the event the British might penetrate his redoubts. A new line is established less than two miles from the primary defenses to provide a back-up defensive position in front of the city. Jackson utilizes those in his force who remain either poorly armed or those who have no weapons to hold that position. They will defend their position with axes, shovels, and their personal knives. The shovel brigade is reinforced by the cavalry under Major Hinds, which continues to be confined to reconnaissance raids due to the lay of the land, which is not suited for usual cavalry operations. Nevertheless, Hinds' command is prepared to race forward at the instant the British penetrate. Jackson has Hinds in reserve to beat back the British and cover the withdrawal, if necessary, as the defenders pull back to the second line of defense. And still, Jackson had ordered yet a third line established on the outskirts for added insurance against any of the British being able to plow their way into the city.

Jackson's ground troops are deployed all along the redoubt and beyond. To the extreme right, a 30-man contingent of Beale's Rifles is posted between Captain Humphrey's battery and the river bank. Back at the far right of the redoubt, Lt. Ross is deployed with one company of the 7th Regiment, and there is also a detachment of the 44th Regiment led by Lt. Marant in the redoubt. The main body of the 7th under Major Peire is posted to the left of Beale's Rifles and covers the ground from there to Battery No. 3, to provide protection for the guns of Captain Humphrey and those of Lt. Norris, but also to guard the magazine in that sector. The line stretching between the two guns of Battery No. 3 is protected by a company of the carboneers and a contingent of Plauche's Orleans Battalion. Next in line, the battalion of free men of color are posted between Batteries No. 3 and 4. Battery No. 5 is under the protection of the 44th Regiment under Captain Baker.

Nearly all of the remaining line is under the protection of General Carroll's command; however, this day, General John Thomas Adair arrives with a command of 1,000 more Kentuckians to complete General Thomas's division. Adair, a native South Carolinian, had relocated to Kentucky. Of the new arrivals, 600 of the troops are commanded by Colonel Gabriel Slaughter (later, during 1816, governor of Kentucky) and the remaining 400 are under Major Reuben Harrison. Adair's command eases the strain of Carroll's responsibility on the line. One other unit, a 50 man Marine contingent led by Lt. Bellvue, is posted to the right of Battery No. 7. Finally, beyond the Marines, General Coffee's command holds responsibility for Jackson's extreme left and the conditions there are deplorable. Coffee's troops are surely going to be cantankerous. Their positions force them to remain standing in the water, and for sleep, the only available beds are floating logs that are trapped and tied to trees.

The remaining American troops are scattered about. Major Hind's squadron is posted at Delery's Plantation and another cavalry unit of 50 men under Ogden is deployed close to Jackson's headquarters. To the rear of the American lines, the Louisiana militia battalion under Colonel Young is deployed close to Pierna's canal to intercept any British unit that might attempt to attack by that route, while other detachments are holding outposts about 500 yards to the front. Jackson's force, which holds the line in front of New Orleans on the east bank of the river, includes only about 800 regulars; however, his militia forces and volunteers have been performing as well as regulars. About 3,200 of his 4,000 troops are actually deployed along the line. The consolidated report in the adjutant general's office gives Jackson, on 8 January, a force of 5,045 on the left bank of the river, not including Major Reuben Harrison's Kentucky battalion of about 400 troops.

Throughout the day on the 7th General Jackson appears to be indefatigable; however, the responsibility of preserving the city as well as the weight of preserving his army is taking a toll on his health. As he dashes from unit to unit to prepare his forces for the attack, he does not have intelligence on the number of British troops preparing to demolish his line. However, he is aware that General Pakenham has recently received more reinforcements. Jackson is relying heavily on his commanders, Acting Brigadier General Ross, who controls the line from right to left of the 44th, and Major General Carroll and Brigadier General Coffee, on his left. The Americans continue to work on their defenses; however, the next phase, the ignition of the battle, depends upon Pakenham's readiness to launch his assault. Jackson expects the offensive will begin at dawn on the 8th.

Back in the British camp, the assault force continues to become more restless as they anxiously await the order to attack. Except for the recently arrived reinforcements, the British are still determined to avenge their successive failures and prove their superiority in the field. The British plan is not completely on schedule because of the tedious task of bringing up the boats, which will play a primary role in the operation. Nonetheless, as the day passes, the suspense and anxiety increases for both antagonists. The British ponder their calculations regarding the weak points in Jackson's lines, and they remain deeply concerned about having all of the boats in place in time to strike Commodore Patterson's battery. Meanwhile, Jackson, aware of the non-stop activity within the British lines, is not yet sure where the main attack will strike. He deliberates whether his weak right side is the target or if the British have been emboldened sufficiently to strike his positions on both banks simultaneously with their full strength. Reconnaissance patrols are dispatched to discover the plan. Colonel John R. Grimes, while scouting British lines at the Villere Plantation, easily spots activity which indicates the British intent to cross the river, but he simultaneously concludes that General David Morgan must redeploy his force at the levee across from the Villere Plantation, which will have his troops in place to intercept the boats before the troops can land. Morgan, however, essentially ignores the advice of Grimes. He retains his main body in place and pushes his vanguard, composed of about 120 militia troops, ahead but not to a strategic point; rather at a point at least three hundred yards from when the boats will touch shore, but still directly to the front of Morgan's positions.

After dusk, Commodore Patterson, accompanied by R.D. Shepherd, a volunteer serving as an aide, creep down the right bank of the river and from their positions directly opposite from where the British intend to cross the river, they are able to observe the activity. Patterson can hear the noise of boats being dropped into the water and even some of the orders being given by officers. While returning to his battery, Patterson confers with General Morgan and informs the general that his positions are vulnerable. Patterson and Morgan have concluded the main attack would be against the right bank. Patterson sends his aide to Jackson's headquarters with the intelligence and an urgent request for reinforcements for Morgan. Shepherd makes it to Jackson's headquarters and delivers the message.

Jackson had been resting, but not sleeping like his staff. After listening to Richardson, General Jackson instructs him to head back to General Morgan's positions and tell him that he is mistaken. "The main attack will be on this side, and I have no men to spare." Shepherd is also directed to inform Morgan that he "must maintain his position at all hazards." Before Shepherd departs, General Jackson glances at his watch, sees that it is past 0100 and in a flash, his staff, spread out on the floor, gets the word: "Gentlemen, we have slept enough. Arise. The enemy will be upon us in a few minutes; I must go and see Coffee."

January 7-8 BATTLE OF NEW ORLEANS **In Louisiana,** the Americans holding the line outside the city are bracing for what is expected to be the most powerful assault by the British since their arrival in Louisiana in early December. Technically, the city is under siege, but General Jackson and his commanders and troops have repeatedly and handily stopped the British from gaining entry to the city. Consequently, the British invaders have depleted most of their supplies, and they still lack even tents. Many of the troops are also suffering from dysentery. Nonetheless, throughout this day (7th), General Pakenham is finalizing details before ordering the attack. The ground troops have discarded their somberness. The gloom which has hovered over the camp dissipated with the arrival of two additional seasoned regiments that had participated in the Napoleonic Wars. Thanks to the arrival of fresh food supplies, the troops even celebrate with a grand feast to lift their spirits. Strangely, however, the British band continues to remain uncharacteristically silent.

General Andrew Jackson.

Music has been absent in the British camp since Pakenham's forces arrived in the United States.

Back at the American lines, the troops await the assault. Based on acquired intelligence, Jackson is aware that the British will launch a two-pronged assault, and there is some question as to where the primary attack will strike. The general, who has so far outfought and outthought the

General Edward Pakenham is mortally wounded at the Battle of New Orleans (*Battles of America by Sea and Land, Volume II*, Robert Tomes, 1878).

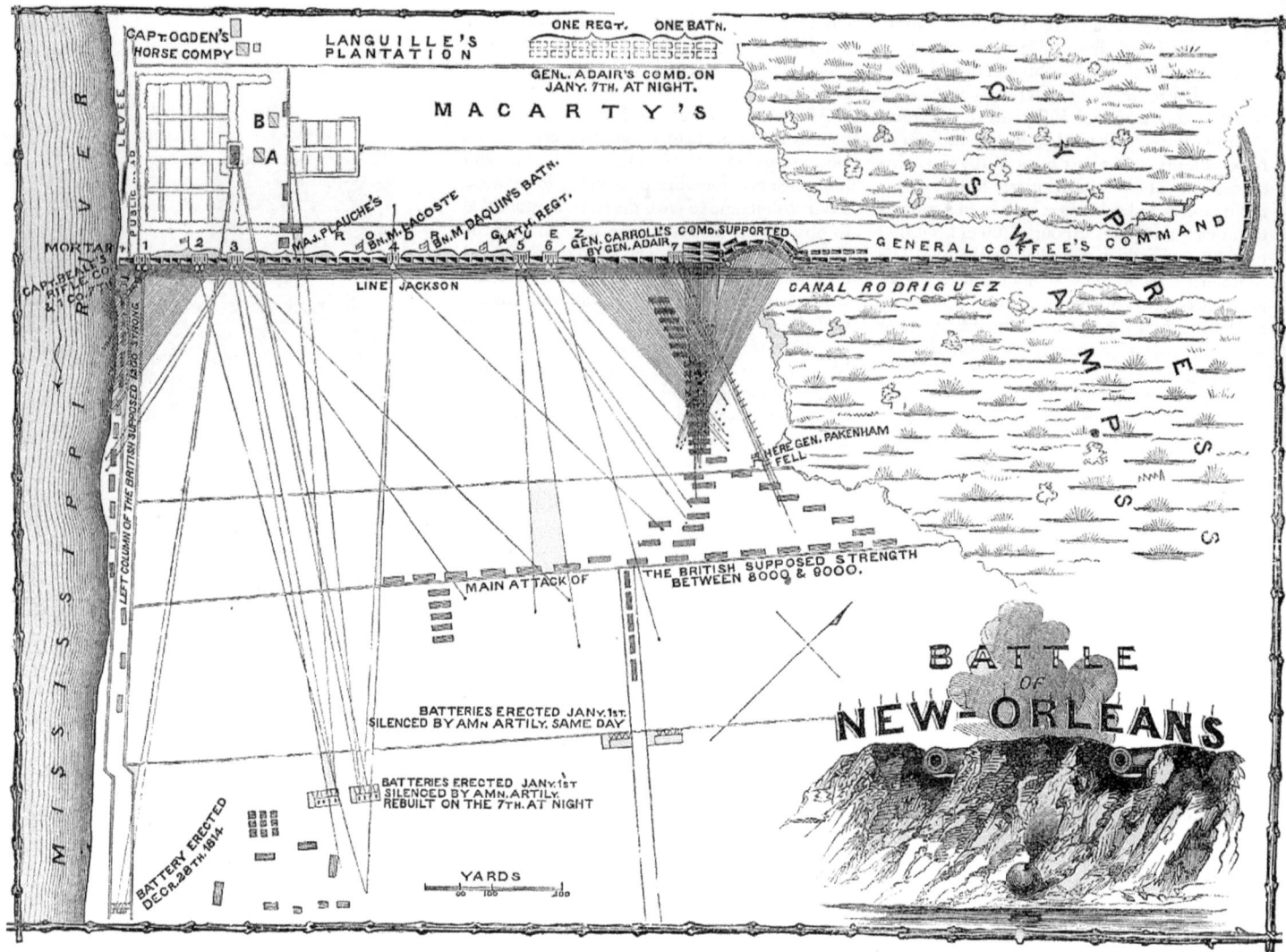

Battle of New Orleans.

British at every turn, is convinced the positions on the opposite bank of the Mississippi will be struck by a diversionary attack to draw attention away from his main positions. Nonetheless, requests from Commodore Patterson and General David Bannister Morgan for reinforcements had been rejected by Jackson, who assured both officers that their positions were not the main objective. Jackson does order about 500 troops to bolster the opposite bank.

As midnight (7th–8th) approaches, the British plan to have boats available is behind schedule. Water levels in the canal had dropped and the walls at certain points collapse, which makes it necessary for the seamen to drag and pull the boats. Colonel Thornton, charged with crossing the river and capturing the Marine battery under Commodore Patterson and turning the guns on Jackson's positions, is paramount to the success of the operation. By about 0300 on the 8th, Thornton realizes that he is short about 75 percent of his boats.

The lack of the proper number of boats compels Thornton to prepare to embark with only about one-half of the troops assigned to the mission. With about 700 men, including a contingent of seamen and one company of Royal Marines, Thornton gives the signal for Captain Roberts to shove off. From shore the river appears extremely calm, and as the crews begin rowing, the flotilla encounters an unexpected surprise. The current, although appearing tranquil, is too strong for the rowers to maintain control. Rather than the short jump to the right bank, the ole Mississippi sweeps the entire flotilla downstream until finally the crews are able to get the boats to shore. However, they are more than one mile from where they expected to debark. The setback is costly, because the force loses the darkness of the night. As the troops bolt from the boats, the first signs of dawn have already arrived.

At about 0400, Thornton's boats finally reach shore. The troops move ashore without encountering any resistance. Under the protection of a flotilla of gunboats commanded by Captain Roberts, the column moves toward General Morgan's positions. Once the column approaches the advanced line, a contingent of the 85th is separated from the main body and directed to strike the positions of Tessier, while the remainder of the column drills directly toward Davis, coming under fire by carronades aboard Captain Roberts' gunboats. The unseasoned Kentuckians under Tessier abscond almost as quickly as the British begin to fire. Shortly thereafter, Thornton's column (sailors, Royal Marines and the 85th Regiment) initiate a charge. The small detachment hurriedly abandons the line and races back toward Morgan's main body. The retreat is haphazard, and Morgan hears the commotion. He advances on horseback and intercepts Colonel Davis, then instructs him to post his troops to the right of the Louisiana militia. Morgan prepares his line for the imminent attack with his force of only about 600 troops. The advancing force under Thornton comes into full view in a line of the 85th stretched across the plain, along with the contingent of sailors on the road and the Royal Marines under Major Adair being held in reserve.

The 85th under Colonel Gubbins and the sailors led by Captain Money initiate the charge at the sound of the bugle, while the waiting Americans meet the sailors with their guns, a 12-pounder under Philibert along with two 6-pounders under the adjutant-general, John

Nixon. The fire is effective and the sailors sustain casualties, including Captain Money, who is hit while leading the assault. Captain Money's command is slowed by the heavy fire; however, Colonel Thornton observes the faltering sailors and pushes the 85th forward. It too comes under fire from Morgan's ground troops. Thornton, who sustains a wound, disregards it and plunges ahead. He sends a contingent under Captain Shaw with instructions to plow into the center. Simultaneously, two other contingents of the 85th strike the far right and the center of Davis' positions. The maneuver receives more support when the carronades on the gunboats propel shells onto Morgan's batteries at the far left of his line. Thornton's presence of mind turns his strategy into a master stroke. The lightning-fast attacks include other contingents of the 85th that slam against Davis' positions.

The Kentuckians along Davis' positions observe the wave of troops approaching, and they panic. These raw troops fear being trapped between two forces. Rather than stand and fight, they race to the rear. General Morgan instructs Colonel Davis to halt the stampede, but the effort is futile. Morgan persists and manages to persuade a small group to return to face the enemy; however, before they arrive back in position, a series of British rockets descend upon them and they again panic and race like jack rabbits in the direction of Morgan's left. All the while, the Louisiana militia holds steadfastly and delivers streams of effective fire into the advancing ranks. Nevertheless after hasty departure of the frightened Kentuckians, the militia has no protection on its right. Immediately, the British take the advantage. They bolt over the ditch, ascend the parapet and gain positions within the lines of Morgan.

The militia, now holding untenable positions, is compelled to abandon their ground or face capture. By the time they become imperiled, they had already fired their final cartridge. Steps are taken to disable the guns before they pull back. There is neither disorder nor lack of discipline. They retire as a unit, while under fire from the British. During this desperate period, Commodore Patterson observes Morgan's predicament and orders his guns, which have been supporting General Jackson's line on the opposite bank all through the morning, turned to bolster Morgan. The race to the rear is also observed by Patterson, and as the horde is running full speed toward his positions several hundred yards to the rear of Morgan, he becomes enraged. Patterson orders a midshipman, the commander of a 12-pounder, to fire upon the "damned cowards." The midshipman, unwilling to question the commodore, complies. He raises the lit match and prepares to fire, but the commodore has a change of heart and the order is cancelled, preserving the Kentuckians. By this time, Thornton is threatening Patterson's battery. He orders the guns spiked. Afterward, the troops toss the ammunition into the Mississippi, withdraw in orderly fashion and head toward the USS *Louisiana* several hundred yards to the rear.

Colonel Thornton's command continues its advance; however, he has no knowledge of the progress or lack thereof on the opposite bank. Nonetheless, his late arrival on the opposite shore made it obvious that his target, Patterson's battery, had not been supporting the advance of the brigades of Gibbs and Keane. While Patterson is moving toward the *Louisiana*, the militia is trailing close behind. Once Patterson's party arrives at the ship, they are unable to get it underway. The militia, although executing a retreat, remains cohesive and prepared for a fight if Thornton catches up to them. The militia, after noticing Patterson's dilemma, suspend their pullback to free the vessel. They succeed and Patterson moves out beyond the reach of the British guns. Meanwhile, the militia resumes marching until they reach the Boisegeveau canal, where they regroup. By the time the militia prepares to receive Thornton's command; however, momentous events beyond the control of Morgan, Patterson and even Thornton have occurred on the opposite bank.

Thornton's force arrives at Patterson's battery. At nearly the same time, an artillery officer, Colonel Dickson, sent to intercept Colonel Thornton, arrives at the battery and informs Thornton of the disaster on the left bank. Thornton tells Dickson that with his reinforcements (contingents of sailors and Royal Marines), he can hold the battery. Dickson, however, insists the positions are untenable. Thornton holds, but Dickson hurries back to report to General Lambert, and without a moment's thought, Lambert orders him to abandon the battery and report to him.

While Thornton is preparing to re-cross the river, General Jackson is sending reinforcements to bolster Morgan; however, Jackson's choice as commander of the relief force, a Frenchman, General Humbert, is offensive to the militia officers. They procrastinate due to not wanting to serve under Humbert, which causes a prolonged delay in getting reinforcements to Morgan. In the meantime, Thornton's efforts to re-cross the river take a large part of the day. Due to his recall, which occurs in conjunction with an agreement between Jackson and Lambert, the progress of the British on the right bank is halted. Consequently, the Redcoats never advance to the militia's positions at the canal.

On the left bank, the main body of the attack force has not yet heard reveille, but word of the misfortune regarding Colonel Thornton's crossing of the river had gotten back to the officers, most of whom have not slept. The jovial conversations surrounding their soon to be victory suddenly turns somber. The officers who take the news as a bad omen show no signs of cowering. A question is tossed at Colonel Dale, a stouteous officer and the commander of the 93rd Highlanders. He is asked about his opinion with regard to the boats being delayed. Rather than directly respond, Colonel Dale looks to his regimental physician, Doctor Dempster, then

A scene from the Battle of New Orleans (*Valor and Victory [The Age of Vindication], Volume X*, Edwin Markham, 1912).

The Battle of New Orleans (*Valor and Victory [The Age of Vindication], Volume X*, Edwin Markham, 1912).

hands him a letter and his watch: "Deliver these to my wife. I shall die at the head of my regiment," essentially a declaration that despite his thoughts that the battle is lost, his duty to British shall not be derailed even at the cost of his life. The profound effect that his words have on the younger officers can only be guessed, but surely chills must have run down their spines.

Another officer, Colonel Thomas Mullens of the 44th Regiment, the unit delegated to lead the charge against Jackson's redoubts, is equally fatalistic; however, his words speak of no heroic allegiance to Britain. To the contrary, he comes rather close to expressing contempt when he states that his regiment would essentially be executed and their corpses would become a bridge for the trailing troops to pass over as they advance to a similar fate. Meanwhile, for the officers involved in the dreadful conversation, there would be no sleep whatsoever. The grim news had also been delivered to General Pakenham as soon as he arrived at the canal. Nonetheless, the general makes no move to alter his strategy. The operation continues and Pakenham remains absolutely sure that his heroic and courageous troops will surmount the unexpected setback and carry the day against all odds. At a distance of about 500 yards from the American redoubts, Generals Gibbs and Keane (neither aware of the delay of Thornton) form their columns and the troops are raring to jump off; however, the brigades remain motionless because the signal from Colonel Thornton is late. The troops become edgy, but there is still no fire by Thornton on the opposite bank. Actually, Thornton and his boats are still fighting the current on the Mississippi.

Back at the positions where the main attack force is formed, there is apprehension due to the absence of Thornton's fire; however, the column under Gibbs begins its advance under cover of yet another fog. The brilliant colors of the British uniforms are obscured by the mist; however, the Americans are waiting and prepared for the assault. All across the line, men are peering into the dense canopy of fog in search of even the slightest presence of the British to seize the honor of firing the first shot. The gunners at Battery 7, under Lt. Spotts, are convinced that they detect a slim red line that becomes visible at a point directly to their front at a distance of about 300 yards. Shortly thereafter, the fog begins to lift and the British column is totally exposed. Suddenly, the American gunners are staring at a sea of scarlet that is stretched nearly from one side of the plain to the other.

The British fire a rocket from a position close to the river, just before another rocket is fired from a position near the swamp. The rockets temporarily divert the gunners, and by the time they are about to fire, the British column momentarily vanishes, causing confusion at the American lines. Nevertheless, the activity had only been a maneuver by which the column had reformed into a column of companies. The British ground troops are not accompanied by their musicians or even their drummers. The companies, however, are greeted by the music of an American band which begins to play at first sight of the Redcoats. Their choice of music specifically selected to taunt the British is "Yankee Doodle," a name the British gave to those ragtag troops of George Washington during the American Revolution. The British as they advance have a clear view of the Stars and Stripes, which is on a high staff at about the mid-point of Jackson's line. The British have already been angered by their earlier defeats and are more determined to demolish the redoubts. They continue their advance with precision.

Meanwhile, as Gibbs' brigade is advancing toward the right, General Keane's brigade pushes against the left with about 1,000 men, including companies of the West Indian brigade under Colonel Rennie. The British encroach the American outpost without being detected, and they catch the guard completely unaware. Effortlessly, the British drive them back toward the redoubt. During the hurried retreat, Captain Humphrey observes the British in pursuit; however, he holds his fire out of fear of striking the Americans as well as the British. The Americans make it back to the main defenses, but the vanguard of Rennie's force is on their heels. The British burst through and ignite close-quartered combat with elements of the defending 7th Infantry. The vicious hand-fire, and those British holding the redoubt suddenly become anxious to relinquish the redoubt. At the same time, a 56-man Marine contingent under commanded by Lieutenants de Bellevue and de Grandpre withstand an attack by the 93rd Highlanders. The Scottish regiment is totally unsuccessful and forced to retreat after sustaining high casualties. The Marines hold the redoubt without the loss of a man. Nevertheless, the threat rather than being terminated becomes more grave, as the main body is closing in a formation of two solid columns, moving separately, with one moving along the river and the other marching directly down the road.

During their approach, Captain Humphrey has no concern about hitting friendly troops. The British suddenly come under fire from the men of the 7th Regiment and the guns of Captain Humphrey's battery (No. 1) less than 75 yards from the river. The British along the road are overcome by the devastating fire but the troops by the levee remain unscathed. Commodore Patterson's Marine Battery detects the contingent that appears safe and he rectifies the situation by getting the range, and then his battery plasters the levee with grape. The commander, Colonel Rennie, has sustained a severe wound when he is struck in the thigh by grape; however, the pain does not deter him. He continues to press forward. With a small detachment, he arrives at the ditch on the far right and then reaches the crest of the redoubt. The conquest is glorious for the British, who have been jinxed at nearly every move. Rennie and two others, Captain Henry and Major King, take sole possession of the redoubt from the contingent of the Orleans Rifles, which falls back. Rennie's jubilance is premature. He raises his sword and swings it back and forth while proclaiming: "Hurrah boys, the day is ours." Nonetheless, the detachment of the Orleans Rifles had not retired; rather, they pulled back to give themselves better targets. The three British officers soon after claiming victory are killed by the Orleans sharpshooters. Consequently, the remainder of the force retreats, heading toward the safety of the levee. During the retreat, a young bugler who observed the entire advance by positioning himself in a tree and blowing his bugle, which was heard despite the constant burst of shells, is left behind. Apparently, his position had been spotted, but the boy remained unscathed. After the British are gone, a soldier captures the boy and takes him into the American lines, where they treat him royally and shower praise upon him for his courage.

The bodies of Colonel Rennie and the other two officers are carried into the American lines. A discussion develops about who struck down the colonel. A man named Withers states: "If he isn't hit above the eyebrows, it wasn't my shot." Shortly thereafter it is determined that Colonel Rennie had been hit slightly above the eyebrow and Withers receives recognition as the marksman who killed Rennie. In the meantime, as the threat to the left is finally terminated, the column on the right under Gibbs is encountering severe difficulty.

General Gibbs maneuvers his column toward the woods to gain some protective cover with the 44th under Colonel Mullens at the point, trailed by the 21st and 4th Regiments respectively. It is an awesome sight as the Redcoats quicken their pace and zoom past the redoubt on the far right of the British positions. As they reach the swamp, the 44th Regiment, composed primarily of Irish troops, is under orders to stack their arms and carry the facines and the ladders.

By this time, several of the American batteries have the column in their sights. Batteries 6 and 7 and the howitzer at No. 8 open fire. Grape and shot arc toward the advancing line as the rattle of thunder signals the avalanche of fire, which causes a disruption of the cohesion of the force. Suddenly, yet another snafu interferes with the advance. While on the run from death, men of the 44th along with other troops manage to pick up some of the ladders and facines as the advance resumes, however, the guns of Spotts and Garrique, along with the howitzer prevent success in bringing up the necessary equipment. Word that the ladders and facines had not arrived spreads through the column, while the troops advance with their weapons on their shoulders under a fire storm of grape and shot.

Once Pakenham learns of Mullen's failure to carry out his order, he becomes incensed and races to the point to verify the rumors, which prove to be true. Mullens is castigated by Pakenham, who by this point is infuriated. He orders Mullens to expeditiously return to the rear, gather the ladders and facines, then hurry back with his regiment. The remainder of the column is affected by the confusion and the advance temporarily stalls. Nonetheless, the American batteries remain unaffected. They catapult round after round into the ranks to wreak havoc. General Gibbs is faced with watching his troops begin to fall from the iron storm. He reacts angrily and yells at the top of his voice: "Let me live till to-morrow and I'll hang him [Mullens] to the highest tree in that swamp."

If Gibbs remains where he stands, his chances

of being alive at dawn on the following day are slim. Rather than have his forces slaughtered in place, while waiting for the ladders, he issues his order: "Advance!" Once again, the American gunners observe a perfectly spaced column of Redcoats moving straight toward the redoubt. British rockets carrying combustibles zoom overhead; however, the distraction does not impede either the rapidity or the effectiveness of the American guns, which deliver incessant volleys of death and destruction.

The path of advance is turning scarlet from the layers of dead and wounded, while the advance continues. As the British soldiers are blown out of the formation huge gaps are created in the column, but others quickly fill in the spaces. As if on parade rather than under the enfilade, the British remain oblivious to the fire and move directly toward the line where Spotts' pernicious 18-pounder at Battery No. 7 is still pounding the brigade.

The situation for the British, already grave, suddenly deteriorates when they find themselves in a deadly quagmire. Choices seem few. Stand and die, advance and die, or retreat and risk death. Gibbs' brigade bravely attempts to forge ahead only to enter a cauldron in which the heat is provided by the incessant waves of artillery fire. Still the British refuse to quit. Onward they trek, unaware that the battery commanded by Spotts is protected by the Tennesseans under General Carroll and a large contingent of Kentuckians.

Up to this point the British have faced wave after wave of withering fire primarily from Battery No. 7; however, as they inch closer to the redoubt, the ground they stand upon is instantly transformed into a blazing inferno. The other batteries, nearly in unison, unleash their terrifying fire upon the beleaguered brigade at just about the time they come into the range of the Tennessean sharpshooters. In rapid succession, the Tennesseans deliver a devastating volley, and almost as soon as the muskets are discharged, a second line opens fire. After their volley, a line of Kentuckians replaces them to deliver more punishing blows. Once the first wave of Kentuckians fires, they step back only to be replaced by a second line of Kentuckian marksmen. The blinding smoke conceals the carnage, and as Patterson's Marine Battery joins the fight, the entire front of the redoubt is swept by a flash flood of iron that causes the ground to quiver.

The Americans maintain their fire and receive non-stop encouragement from General Jackson, who bellows: "Stand your guns. Don't waste your ammunition. See that every shot tells."

And then the general adds: "Give it to them, boys; let us finish the business to-day." Despite the agonizing thrashing, the British reach a point about 200 yards from the ditch in front of the redoubt, but there is neither safety nor concealment here, nor a pause in the punishment being heaped upon them. The British are greeted with the order "Fire! Fire!" being bellowed by General Carroll. In an instant, as if the sky had opened with a gargantuan cloudburst, the entire line delivers riveting fire, and in rapid succession another volley follows without pause as four separate lines, two of the Tennesseans and two of Kentuckians, rotate seamlessly as if on a revolving wheel. The British are absolutely astonished to watch their ranks become shredded. The combined noise created by the muskets and the cannon reverberate, and as if bouncing off the clouds, the sounds become amplified as the whirling thunderclaps inflict indelible marks into the memories of the survivors.

The fire is so thick that it could be said that a Louisiana mosquito could not survive. Nonetheless, those under Gibbs who are able-bodied remain determined to gain the ditch, but still they lack the ladders and facines. British officers still standing ignore the sheets of fire to lend encouragement by gaining the front of the stymied column. However, it is common knowledge that the 44th had not yet come up with the necessary equipment, prompting the troops to ask, "Where is the 44th?"

Gaining ground to reach the ditch without the equipment is sure folly, but a calming voice, that of General Gibbs, begins to yell: "Here come the 44th," soothing words to the desperate but persistent brigade. As calmness regains its position over the disorder, the troops spot the 44th, but it is only a contingent and to their great surprise, Colonel Mullens is not leading it; rather the commander, General Pakenham, arrives with the troops. Pakenham had run the gauntlet with his Irish troops carrying the equipment. Just before he reaches the column, his bridle arm is struck by American fire and at the same time, a ball strikes and kills his horse. Pakenham pays little attention to the incoming fire. He quickly mounts the pony of his aide, Captain McDougall, and reaches the front; however, by the time he arrives the column has hit an impenetrable wall of fire that checks the advance.

The British officer corps by this time has been decimated. Nearly all the regimental officers have been eliminated or wounded, leaving the troops with mass confusion and unable to penetrate the walls of fire. Cohesion breaks down due to the insufficient number of officers to maintain discipline. Some of the troops valiantly but in vain struggle to reach the ditch, while others, essentially the greater part of the brigade, attempt to make their way to the swamp. Momentarily, the field directly in front of the American positions is free of advancing British troops until they regroup at the ditch where they discard their knapsacks and reinitiate their advance. General Keane, expected to remain in reserve, decides to ignore his instructions to threaten but not attack the redoubt. He orders his brigade to join in the attack. Suddenly, a fresh wave of crimson pours onto the field with the 93rd Regiment in front of the column. The troops advance in good order with the rays of the sun beginning to penetrate the hovering smoke to bounce off their uniforms and seemingly increase the brilliance of their bayonets. The front line, composed of about 100 troops abreast, moves forward with added boldness, as if they believe themselves to be immune from the unfolding living nightmare. Nonetheless, neither the splendor of their impeccable uniforms, nor the swagger in their step or their menacing bayonets impress the Tennesseans and Kentuckians, who remain perfectly still while the artillery pours fire upon the approaching line.

The 93rd Regiment plows forward at an accelerated pace determined to gain the ditch. The effort is both gallant and noble; however, they are driving straight toward General Carroll's command. Suddenly, the order is given and the British line is shredded by an inescapable avalanche of fire. Colonel Dale, who earlier mentioned his premonition of death, is killed by grapeshot while at the front of his 93rd Regiment. The spectacular display of unharnessed violence does not prompt the British to retire; rather, the remnants of Gibbs' brigade become inspired by the daring of the 93rd. They rush to their aid to snatch victory from defeat by a powerful thrust directly into the American lines that up to now have been invincible. Major Andrew Creagh, having assumed command of the 93rd, glances to the left and spots Pakenham. To his right, General Gibbs is back in the thick of the fight. The British are still vulnerable to the incessant fire, but the column reaches a point about 100 yards from the coveted ditch. All the while the grape and shot descends upon them to inflict more deadly punishment, while the thickening smoke obscures vision all the more.

General Pakenham is still on his aide's pony but his right arm has been rendered useless. Nevertheless, while his aide leads the pony, the general continues to brave the fire. He conceals his injury by removing his hat with his left hand, then he waves it back and forth to rally his troops, yelling: "Hurrah brave Highlanders!" But his cheers are short lasting. At about the time he completes his words of praise, a flying shell from an American gun scores a direct hit that kills or mangles nearly all who are close to the impact. Pakenham survives the massive explosion with a severe wound to his thigh; however, he is tossed from the horse which had died instantly. While being assisted by other officers and men, yet another American shell crashes. Pakenham, while being lifted from the ground, sustains another wound, this one in his groin. The latest hit is debilitating and fatal. General Pakenham, paralyzed, is somehow safely carried back through the whirling shells to the rear and laid by an oak tree. His condition is beyond medical aid. A surgeon is rushed to his side, but to no avail. Almost at the same time the doctor makes it known that his wound is mortal, General Pakenham dies.

Just before General Pakenham had died, he had the strength to direct Sir John Tyndell, a staff officer, to call for the reserves under General Lambert. A bugler is summoned, and as he begins to signal for Lambert to advance, the invisible cloud of doom that has been plaguing the British since they landed strikes again. The bugler is struck in his arm by an American ball. This causes him to drop his bugle, and the unintended consequence is that the reserves remain in place until it is too late to be of any value.

The British, despite their indomitable spirit and their brash courage under fire, are unable to discover a weak link in the American defenses, while the indefatigable Americans continue to riddle the British ranks with menacing fire. Officers continue to fall along with the rank and file and the generals are not immune to the fury. General Gibbs and General Keane remain active on the field after Pakenham falls, but American fire soon inflicts a mortal wound upon General Gibbs. He suffers with agonizing pain into the following day before he dies. Meanwhile, the remaining general officer in the field, General Keane, sustains a dangerous wound to the neck, and he is carried to the rear.

The Americans have cleared the table, eliminating all the British field officers, which causes additional insurmountable problems. Still, the Redcoats refuse to accept defeat. Major Wilkinson, the brigade major, assumes command of the fragmented brigades and calls for the troops to follow him as he bolts forward leading a near-suicidal charge into the mouths of the American artillery and the lines of sharpshooters. About 20 of the troops and Lt. Lavac accompany Wilkinson. The little band makes it to the ditch and beyond to the redoubt. Wilkinson actually begins to climb the wall of the redoubt, then, just as his head and shoulders become visible, he instantly becomes the point-blank target. The major is blasted by the fire of no less than ten muskets, and the results are gruesome. He is riddled with bullets and yet he survives for the moment with agonizing pain.

The scene is heartbreaking even for the hardened Kentuckians and Tennesseans. Major Wilkinson to the very end is concerned only about his duty. An American officer and Kentuckian attempts to befriend Wilkinson during his final time on earth and tries to cheer his spirits: "Bear up, my dear fellow, you are too brave a man to die." Wilkinson, well aware that he is fading fast, responds with little more than a whisper: "I thank you from my heart. It is all over with me. You can render me a favor; it is to communicate to my commander that I fell on your parapet, and died like a soldier and a true Englishman." Meanwhile, the British just behind Wilkinson see him being sliced up with American bullets, but a few troops attempt to reach the top of the redoubt in vain. They are spared being cut down by the muskets because they fail to reach the top. Most of the detachment had already sought safety in the ditch.

By the time Major Wilkinson initiates his charge, most of the surviving men of the decimated brigades are hurriedly falling back. Usually it is the British watching their foe fleeing from British muskets and bayonets. This time, the American militia and volunteers in support of the regulars have reversed the roles. The field is still permeated with smoke as the retreat unfolds, leaving the Americans in suspense with regard to the depth of their success and no knowledge that they have destroyed about two-thirds of two British brigades by either death or wounds. During the retreat, General Lambert, still holding the reserves in place, finally hears of the death of Pakenham and the wounds of Gibbs and Keane. He proceeds with extra caution to provide some protection for the retreating remnants of the brigades. In retrospect, the failure of the bugler to signal General Lambert to reinforce the besieged brigades most probably preserved his command.

During the tumultuous contest, the troops holding the opposing ends of the American redoubt have tirelessly met and repelled each advance by the British, and their successes have inadvertently caused the troops holding the center to become frustrated. The center of the line is not challenged and the guns posted there remain dormant. The ground troops—including the 44th Regiment, Daquin's battalion, Major Lacoste's battalion and Plauche's battalion, numbering about 800 men—get no opportunity to directly engage the attacking force. The units specified are under orders to refrain from firing for two specific reasons, the advancing British are out of the range of their muskets and secondly, Jackson forbids wasting ammunition. Nevertheless, while the troops are shut out of the action, the officers remain on the alert due to the overwhelming temptation to slip away momentarily either to the left or right to get into the fight. Meanwhile, in the middle of the line, the band that began to play "Yankee Doodle" at first sight of the Redcoats has been as active as the guns. The music continues during the entire engagement to provide patriotic songs as an added inspiration to the men on the line.

On the far right of the redoubt at the swamp, the British had sent a contingent led by Lt. Colonel Jones (4th Regiment) against the positions of Major General Coffee. Coffee's Tennesseans had been posted in the water, and the appearance of the British provides them with some exercise in addition to intercepting the intruders. The British are totally outclassed in the mud and water. The Tennesseans bounce from log to log, and they easily adapt to skirmishing in the mud. The incursion fails miserably and the attacking troops are either killed or captured. The troops of the West Indian Regiment begin to feel comfortable after becoming prisoners, because in their minds, they had surrendered to troops "of their own color and blood." The captors are Caucasians, but their prolonged time in the swamp and their lack of razors and soap had fooled the captives.

At 0800, the Americans and British had been in constant combat for two hours when the fighting begins to subside because the ground troops have difficulty spotting targets. Shortly thereafter, orders to cease fire get passed down the entire line. General Jackson is moving along the line to personally congratulate his troops for their outstanding feat in the defense of the city and the Stars and Stripes. The troops realize they have been victorious; however, due to the hovering smoke from the guns, which have not yet been silenced, they remain unaware of the depth of the victory. There is concern that the British might be regrouping to mount another attack. While passing the band, which continues to play, Jackson is greeted with "Hail Columbia." At the same time, the troops instantaneously break out with their congratulatory chants and hurrahs to the general in recognition of his leadership.

When the smoke clouds begin to vanish and the celebrating troops look out upon the field, the joy of the victory is suppressed by the horrific scene from one end to another. The Americans clearly see Redcoats at every point, but not one is standing and those who are alive are stretched out in agonizing pain among the layers of dead troops. The plan destined to capture New Orleans had become a calamitous event, the worst defeat for the British army in the annals of the United Kingdom. The scene is beyond grotesque. Irregular red lines of deceased troops are lying everywhere. At some spots entire platoons are massed together and to the front of General Carroll's positions, the rows of the lifeless troops extend out at least 200 yards. Locating a standing live British soldier becomes extremely difficult; however, after a while, through the use of telescopes, General Lambert's reserves are located when a thin red line is observed far in the rear at a ditch.

The horrendous scenes on the battlefield are so breathtaking that the joy of victory is subdued and replaced by sympathy and outreach as the horrors of war are absorbed by the victors. The voices of the wounded, easily heard in the redoubt, cause some troops to ignore orders. They carry canteens and slip down the parapet to give the wounded some comfort. Nevertheless, some of them are wounded or killed by wounded British troops who do not realize the men are only trying to give aid. The powerful British army that defeated Napoleon lies shattered at the gateway to New Orleans, humbled by General Andrew Jackson.

The general, however, remains ever on the alert, and although he is more relaxed, he ensures that the line remains prepared for a new assault. By about noon, it becomes evident that no attack is being prepared. During the operation to capture the wounded, one British officer resents being captured by a Tennessean. The officer ignores the order to surrender and tries to walk away until the Tennessean informs the officer that if he takes another step, he will be dead. As he surrenders, he remarks: "What a disgrace for a British officer to have to surrender to a chimney-sweep."

Word of the spectacular victory arrives back at the city and celebrations break out throughout. Even the youngsters are anxious to participate. A group of boys gather and with a drum and fife they begin to march through the streets. Before the day is out, the British do enter the city; however, most are being transported to the hospitals for medical aid. The hospitals, however, are overcrowded from Americans either sick or wounded. Nevertheless, the British are not abandoned. They are taken into private homes, and they receive the help of the families in addition to the services of physicians. The British able-bodied prisoners also enter the city, but not as conquerors. They arrive under the guard of a contingent of General Carroll's command.

In the meantime, a small detachment of Americans had moved out beyond the front lines. They report to General Jackson at about noon that a party of British troops are arriving at the lines under a white flag. Three riders approach and one is an officer. The party halts about 300 yards from Jackson's lines. Colonel William O. Butler and two other officers ride out to meet with the British. The officers accept the communication and take it back to Macarte's, where Jackson had established headquarters. The British message requests an armistice to permit time to bury the dead. The Americans take the message to Jackson's headquarters. Jackson immediately notices the absence of General Pakenham's signature. The signature on the message designates no rank and states only "Lambert." The message is taken back to the British party and the Americans inform them that no armistice can be concluded until the authority of the commander in chief is affixed to the document. Jackson, again one step ahead of the British by his reply, forces General Lambert to re-sign with his rank as commander-in-chief. This informs Jackson that Pakenham is deceased. The modified document is returned within about one-half hour.

General Jackson proposes that hostilities cease on the left bank only to permit the burials; however, he allows no cessation on the right bank, with a restriction that neither side is permitted to send reinforcements to the right bank on the 9th during the armistice. Jackson is aware that the British have made inroads on that bank. Lambert requests time and agrees to respond by 1000 on the 9th. Meanwhile, he sends word to Colonel Thornton and orders him to abandon his positions at Patterson's Marine battery and report back to the main body. During the night of the 8th, after destroying some sawmills and other equipment and supplies, he arrives back on the left bank. Although Thornton had inflicted a defeat upon Morgan's force, the British sustain higher casualties. The 85th Regiment sustains two killed and 39 wounded, and the contingent of sailors and Royal Marines sustain four killed and 49 wounded. Morgan's command sustains one killed and five wounded. The missing Kentuckians are later discovered in the rear.

That same night, Commodore Patterson moves to regain his battery and completes the task during the early morning hours of the 9th. At dawn on the 9th, Jackson receives a round-about message from Patterson that the position is back under American control. The British are also informed that the battery is back in action when Patterson's guns deliver a series of shots into their outpost positions.

Casualty figures for the British vary. American reports place the casualties at 700 killed, 1,400 wounded and 500 captured. British reports indicate 291 killed, 1,951 wounded and 488 captured. The British figures regarding killed are confined to those killed in the field, but they do not include those who died from their wounds. The most tragic part of battle has not yet been learned. Later the participants will discover that every death, disfigurement and injury during the struggle for New Orleans on 8 January had occurred after the war ended, but before the word arrived in the United States.

Also, during the British campaign, the *Tchifonta*, a corvette, remained incomplete in New Orleans. Construction was started during either late 1813 early 1814, and it was to play a part in the defense of the city, but the project was halted by Secretary of the Navy William Jones. The ship remains incomplete after the war. It is sold about 1820.

Also, Colonel William O. Butler of Kentucky had joined the army as a private and participated at the Battle of the Raisin River, where he survived capture and later fought at the Battle of the Thames. During the Mexican War, he is appointed major general, where he serves under General Zachary Taylor. During 1848, he is the Democratic nominee for vice president on the ticket with General Lewis Cass; however, Zachary Taylor, a Whig, wins the presidency along with his vice presidential candidate, Millard Fillmore. Also, Robert Armstrong, a captain of Tennessee artillery under General Jackson during the Creek War, in which he sustained a serious wound at the Battle of Talladega, participates in this battle. In 1829, he is appointed postmaster at Nashville; however, during the Second Seminole War (1836), he commands cavalry with the rank of brigadier general. He held the position of postmaster until 1845, when he was appointed as consul to Liverpool, England, by President Polk. After his diplomatic service, General Armstrong established a newspaper, the Washington *Union*. He died in Washington, D.C., on 23 February 1854.

January 9 (Monday) In Louisiana, during the early part of the morning, General Lambert agrees with the terms of Jackson that were proposed on the previous day regarding an armistice to permit the burial of the dead. A line is drawn several hundred yards to the front of the American redoubt. The American troops delegated to the somber task of delivering the deceased British troops to the British sector begin to retrieve the bodies, which are at nearly every step. The Americans use the improvised ladders that the British had brought to scale the walls. Once the remains are transferred, they are interred at a designated place on the Bienvenu property that is marked off as "the cemetery of the Army of Louisiana." The British become agitated by an American officer who is counting the number of dead while smoking a cigar. The British perceive that they are being humiliated when the officer repeatedly emphasizes that American losses had totaled eight killed and 13 wounded on the left bank.

One British officer, Major H.O. White, while speaking with Captain Maunsel White, states: "It is a mere skirmish — mere skirmish!" Captain White, noticing the unending rows of deceased British troops, retorts: "One more such skirmish and devilish few of you will ever get back home to tell the story." On the same field where exploding shells not long before caused deafening sounds, there is stone silence as the officers, the first of the troops to be transferred to the British, are delivered. No words are spoken; however none are needed as the Americans observe their brave foe accepting their dead, while their eyes become tear-filled. Separately from the others, the remains of the officers are carried back to the Villere Plantation where, subsequent to dusk, they (except a few) receive a Christian burial in the garden of the Villere house. Some others, thought to be British colonels Rennie and Dale, similarly to Generals Pakenham and Gibbs, are prepared for transportation back to England in the customary barrels of rum.

January 9–18 In New Orleans, the distant sounds of artillery are heard in the city. The consensus is that the British are attacking Fort St. Philip on the left bank of the Mississippi River about 80 miles below New Orleans. The post has been reinforced since the arrival of General Jackson, who anticipated a British attempt to reduce it. Nevertheless, the British instead moved against New Orleans without gaining domination of the river. In the meantime, Jackson's foresight is instrumental in preparing for an assault. The fort's magazine is camouflaged and two smaller magazines had been erected. A detachment had also been posted down river to signal the fort once a British squadron is detected. The post is bolstered by 29 guns, including two 32-pounders. The garrison, commanded by Major Overton, stands at 366 troops, composed of two companies (163 men, led by Captain Brontin and Captain Waide) of the U.S. 7th Regiment along with two U.S. artillery companies (117 men, commanded by Captain Wolstonecraft, Captain Murray and Captain Walsh), along with a 54-man contingent of Lagan's Louisiana Volunteers and a 30-man contingent of the free men of color under Listeau. Also, Gunboat No. 8 is moved into the bayou and its crew joins with the garrison.

The boat posted to await the arrival of the Royal Navy spots the approaching sail at about noon. Immediately thereafter, the detachment heads back to the fort to inform Major Overton that five vessels — the sloop-of-war HMS *Herald*, the brigantine HMS *Sophia* and a tender, along with two bomb-ships — are encroaching the fort. The garrison, shut out of the major battle of the previous day, remains eager to contribute its services to the preservation of the city. Activity within the walls of the post accelerates at a rapid pace when the troops race to their battle stations. The two 32-pounders are quickly surrounded by Cunningham and his crew from Gunboat No. 8. Captain Wolstonecraft assumes command of the center, while Captain Murray's contingent assumes responsibility for the left bastion and Captain Walsh's force takes the right bastion. Other troops under Captain Brontin deploy to the rear, from where they can spring to whichever point requires their assistance. At about 1500, the vanguard of the British squadron reaches a point about one and one-half miles from the fort. The two vessels in the lead, both bomb ships, are greeted by an artillery barrage, which prompts both vessels to reverse course.

The vessels find concealment at a point slightly less than 3,800 yards from the fort. The anchors are dropped and the flags are hoisted at nearly the same time the bombardment is initiated. The shells are catapulted toward the fort but without accuracy. A shell flies over the fort, followed by one that detonates over the fort, but the remaining volleys fail to reach the post. Shells continue to be propelled toward the fort with impeccable timing. One shell is fired every two minutes straight through the night; however, except for the incessant noise, the fort is undisturbed. During the night, small parties are sent in boats from the vessels to reconnoiter, and they approach so close to the fort that the night air carries their conversation within earshot of the sentinels.

The British make no attempt to storm the fort; however, the bombardment continues on the 10th and into the 11th. Finally, on the 11th, one of the British shells inflicts some damage when fragments strike the flag mast. In reaction, the flag is nailed to a halyard, only to be downed again when another hit severs the halyards. A sailor on the crosstree re-affixes the Stars and Stripes to ensure that the British realize it still waves.

Meanwhile, the British remain equally persistent. They continue their relentless bombardment for the next three days, the shell bursts accompanied by torrential rains. On the 11th, one man is killed and one other wounded when a British shell hits the contractor's house, erroneously thought to be the fort's magazine. The garrison remains engaged with the British while other troops continue to make repairs.

Ammunition and supplies arrive at the fort from New Orleans on the 13th. By now the post is inundated with water from the constant rain, making it more difficult to operate effectively. Nonetheless, the troops seemingly ignore their soaked clothes to remain focused on the squadron that is intent on taking the fort. Casualties remain low despite the nonstop shelling. The British do succeed in damaging one of the 32-pounders; however the fort's guns are not silenced. The guns score some success after receiving the ammunition. Shells explode over one of the bomb ships and the crew gets rattled. Nevertheless, the squadron maintains its bombardment, which becomes more accurate on the 17th when some of the shells strike the parapet. At dawn on the 18th, the Americans prepare for yet another storm of fire, but to their surprise the guns of the British are silent. From the walls of the fort, the squadron becomes fully visible, and the troops observe the squadron as it retires after failing to accomplish its mission.

While the British begin their departure, there is a huge outburst along the walls of Fort St. Phillip when the garrison sends the squadron a ring of three cheers along with a goodbye volley. The fort had survived the naval attack which had begun on the 9th and delivered about 1,000 shells upon it. Total American casualties amount to two men killed and three others wounded. Also, Fort St. Philip is also known as Fort San Felipe, Fort Plaquemine and Fort Ste. Philippe.

January 9 to February 26 *In naval activity,* the American privateer *Surprise* departs from Brest, France, where it had been in port since 24 December. After being at sea for about five days, a British warship spots the surprise and initiates pursuit. The *Surprise*, which had been so frequently chased during the previous year, takes the threat in stride as it maneuvers its sails to outsmart its latest nemesis. While on the run, the British warship fires about fifty shots at the *Surprise*, but to the crew's dismay none inflict any harm. By dark, the *Surprise* loses its pursuer.

On the 28th, the lookouts on the *Surprise* detect what seems to be a British warship on its leeward side. The privateer begins to initiate yet another escape from harm. The warship continues to close, and by about 1230 the British colors are hoisted in conjunction with a broadside. Unimpressed and unintimidated, Captain Barnes responds by hoisting the Stars and Stripes in concert with a broadside fired by the privateer. Meanwhile, the British accept the broadside as American insolence, prompting them to increase their fire, while the *Surprise* remains focused on maneuvering into an advantageous position from which it can prevail. Captain Barnes's crew, using the sweeps, skillfully gains a position from which its guns propel a devastating broadside that succinctly terminates the battle. Suddenly, the British ship *Star* strikes its colors. The British privateer's cargo is partially transferred to the *Surprise*. A prize crew is assigned and it is taken into port at New York. The two ships encounter a severe blizzard on 26 February, when the vessels are close to the United States. The *Surprise* loses sight of the prize, but both vessels reach port safely.

During its service at sea, the *Surprise* captures a total of 34 British prizes, including its last cruise, during which it seizes 20 British merchant ships, one of which is a privateer. The crew seizes a total of 197 prisoners; however, only 37 are taken into the United States. The others are released. During one encounter, the *Caledonia* is seized and afterward recaptured by the prisoners, only to again get intercepted and captured by the *Surprise*. The British crew is taken aboard the *Surprise* and the prize is taken into port at Salem, Massachusetts.

January 11 (Wednesday) *In naval activity,* the privateer *Union,* a schooner, is commissioned in Maine this day.

January 12 (Thursday) *In Louisiana,* a navy purser named Shields and Doctor Morrel, sent under a white flag to attempt to give aid to the Americans captured on Lake Borgne the previous December, are finally released this day. Admiral Cochrane had refused to permit them to meet with the prisoners, and he actually held them as prisoners on his flagship. Both men arrive back at Jackson's lines this day. Within about a week, Shields and Morrel initiate a mission to attempt to capture stray British boats on Lake Borgne.

January 13 (Friday) *In naval activity,* the schooner *Comet,* en route to Elizabeth City from New Bedford, encounters the British privateer *Liverpool Packet,* and it is unable to escape capture. The prize, carrying a cargo of salt and other items, is taken into port at Liverpool.

January 14 (Saturday) *In naval activity,* the American privateer *Arrow,* a 14-gun brigantine, sails from New York on a cruise to the West Indies. The privateer carries a crew of 150 men. Once it departs from the harbor it is never heard from again.

January 14–15 The USS *President* under Captain Stephen Decatur attempts to run the British blockade off Long Island during inclement weather on the night of the 14th, but as the vessel is breaking for open seas after weighing anchor off Staten Island, it gets hooked on a sandbar. The crew, by about 2200, gets the vessel over the bar, but due to damage to the rudder and the winds, the *President* cannot return to port. It glides along the Long Island shore for about fifty miles before heading southeast by east. During the early morning hours at about 0500, lookouts spot three sail. Decatur evades them in the darkness, but at dawn, the danger intensifies when four British warships are spotted. Two of them are to the rear with the other two divided, one on each quarter. The lead vessel, a 74-gun razee, commences fire, but causes no damage. Nonetheless, the chase continues. By noon, another ship closes from the rear and the crew of the *President* takes steps to lighten the load by tossing items, including anchors and provisions, overboard to gain more speed.

By 1500, a brigantine is flying toward the *President,* while the 50-gun *Endymion* arrives at close range and it commences fire, which is immediately returned by the *President.* At about 1700, the *Endymion* is at about half-point range, prompting the *President* to maneuver into a position from which it could deliver a broadside; however, the *Endymion* fails to take the bait. By this time, the *President* is sustaining more damage, including the rigging and the sails. Nevertheless, the *President* continues to forestall disaster. At the arrival of dusk, Decatur changes course in an attempt to draw off one of the pursuers. The battle ensues and after trading broadsides, the British guns of the *Endymion* are silenced; however, the remainder of the squadron is closing fast, prompting Decatur at about 2000 to forego his prize and break away.

At about 2300, two more ships, the *Pomone* and the *Teneuos,* arrive. The *President* receives even heavier fire. By this time, about 20 percent of the *President*'s crew had become casualties, and it was cut off from escape. Decatur, aware that his ship is too badly damaged to escape or even match the fire power of the British, decides that he must surrender. Lieutenants Babbit, A. Hamilton and Howell are killed.

Lieutenants Shubrick and Gallagher receive praise from Decatur (in a report written while aboard the HMS *Endymion* on the 18th) for their actions during the battle. Decatur also praises Lieutenant Twiggs and his entire complement of U.S. Marines, which fired about 5,000 rounds. Others among the crew that receive praise are Midshipman Randolph and a volunteer, Mr. Robinson.

The Americans sustain 26 killed and 60 wounded. The British ships that capture the *President* are the 74-gun *Majesty,* 60-gun *Endymion,* 60-gun *Pomome,* 38-gun *Teneuos* and the 18-gun *Despatch.* Total British casualties are 11 killed and 14 wounded according to their report; however, Commodore Decatur later states that he was taken aboard the *Endymion* 36 hours after the battle, and at that time, he witnessed the burial of ten British crewmen. Decatur surrenders his sword, but only to the entire squadron and to the British commander-in-chief. It was forwarded to Captain Hayes of the *Majestic;* however, Hayes who had arrived after the battle, chooses to have it returned.

Decatur is among the wounded, but in his official report he does not mention this. During the fighting, while in a conspicuous position, he had been hit in the chest by a splinter that knocks him down. Crew members rushed to his aid, but after a short while he snapped back into action. Later a second splinter struck his forehead. Decatur had been given command of the *President* during the summer of 1814, along with the *Peacock* (Captain Warrington), *Hornet* (Captain James Biddle) and the store-ship *Tom Bowline*. Crews of the other ships in Decatur's squadron remain unaware of the capture of the *President*.

Commodore Decatur arrives at Bermuda on 26 January. The weather had been extremely nasty and he thinks that the captured *President* had been lost, but it arrives on the 30th. Although the *President* had engaged multiple warships, the British embellish the reports and conceal many of the facts. In England, the praise for the victory goes to the *Endymion*, one of the four warships that participated; however, during the fighting between the *President* and the *Endymion*, the latter had been totally vanquished and was compelled to drop back to await the remainder of the squadron. To the illusion, illustrations (engravings) that follow portray only the *Endymion* as the victor and the *President* as the vanquished, while the other ships are completely eliminated from the scene. These illustrations that are spread rapidly throughout Great Britain and its colonies do not even mention the remainder of the squadron in the accompanying captions or articles.

Decatur is paroled shortly after his capture. He arrives at New London on 22 February and by the following May, he returns to the sea. Captain Decatur earlier served aboard the USS *United States* under Commodore John Barry as a midshipman, when he was promoted to the rank of lieutenant aboard the USS *Essex* during 1801. It was Decatur who entered Tripoli harbor during 1804 and destroyed the USS *Philadelphia*, which was being held hostage by the Barbary pirates. He received a gold medal from Congress for his actions at Tripoli. During this conflict (which had actually ended before this action), he was commanding Commodore Barry's *United States*. During May of this year, Decatur returns to the Barbary Coast to deal with the pirates and during the summer, he and his naval squadron persuade the pirates at Algiers, Tripoli and Tunis to sign treaties. During April 1816, Decatur becomes a member of the Board of Navy Commissioners, which operates out of Washington, D.C. Stephen Decatur is also known for the legendary quote: "Our Country! In her intercourse with foreign nations may it always be in the right; but our country, right or wrong." In 1820, Commodore James Barron challenges Decatur to a duel. On 22 March at Bladensburg, Maryland, the two men face off. Both Decatur and Barron sustain wounds; however, Decatur's wound is mortal and he dies. Barron survives. Commodore Barron resumes his naval career. His commands include the Philadelphia Navy Yard. He dies while on active duty as the senior officer in the U.S. Navy on 21 April 1851 at Norfolk, Virginia.

January 16 (Monday) *In naval activity,* the 41-ton schooner *Gift*, having departed from Boston with a cargo including beef, pork, salt and other items, is intercepted and seized by the British privateer *Rover* before it reaches its destination at Charlestown. In other naval activity, the British privateer *Rover* intercepts and seizes the sloop *Industry* (Oliver Slate, master) while it is transporting a cargo including cider, flour and gin from New York to Sag Harbor. The prize is taken into port at Liverpool. The *Industry* is separate from the schooner *Industry* seized on 20 August 1813, the schooner *Industry* seized 3 November 1813 and the schooner *Industry* captured on 10 September 1814.

January 17 (Tuesday) **In Louisiana**, an agreement between the Americans and the British is reached regarding a prisoner exchange. The time is set for the following day. On the 18th, the 95th Rifles escort the Americans to their receiving units, and once exchanged, they are escorted into the American lines, accompanied by military units and a military band. They are received with tumultuous cheers.

January 18 (Wednesday) **In Louisiana**, the British await darkness to abandon their encampment outside New Orleans. The British troops, already dejected due to their unexpected and unprecedented defeats by General Jackson, initiate their march toward Lake Borgne. The trek in the darkness through the swampland does little to raise their spirits. Nonetheless, the column arrives at Lake Borgne at about dawn. By then, the men had also suffered from the chill of the night, and upon their arrival at the lake, they are greeted with an unkind westerly wind. General Lambert, who succeeded General Pakenham as commander-in-chief upon the death of the latter, remains in some jeopardy. The entire command is poorly positioned, being 60 miles from the British fleet, and the safety of his command depends upon the timely arrival of the boats from the fleet. The troops have not had tents since their arrival in December. They lack the fuel to provide heat for the troops and have an acute shortage of provisions. The army is compelled to undergo these conditions until 27 January, when they are evacuated.

January 19 (Thursday) **In Louisiana**, the British retreat that began the previous night has not been detected by the Americans; however, rumors begin to fly through the lines hat the British had retired. Jackson is skeptical. He and other officers see flags still conspicuously flying and some guards visible in the encampment. General Jackson calls upon General Humbert, the Frenchman, to give his opinion. After viewing the camp through the telescope, he informs Jackson that the camp is deserted. When asked why he is certain, Humbert tells Jackson that once he takes another look, he will see a crow hovering near one of the guards, which is actually a stuffed uniform, not a soldier. The fake soldier is so poorly done that even the crow is not fooled. As Jackson is preparing to send out patrols, a British physician approaches under a white flag. The message he is carrying confirms General Humbert's statement. The message informs General Jackson that the British army had departed, and it includes a request that the sick and wounded left behind receive care and medical treatment. Eighty British troops unable to travel are still in the British encampment.

The American lines burst with jubilance when the rumors prove true; however, General Jackson, aware of British tactics, refuses to relax his caution. A patrol led by Colonel La Ronde and accompanied by Colonel Reuben Kemper and a contingent of Major Hinds' dragoons is sent to reconnoiter the Villere Plantation with instructions to remain alert in the event rear-guard troops are manning obstacles. Jackson also dispatches a separate detachment under Major Villere to search the woods that surround his family's house. Meanwhile, some of the officers try to convince General Jackson to initiate a full-scale pursuit. Jackson, however, is cognizant of the fact that his militia could be overwhelmed by Lambert's regulars in an open battle. He rejects the suggestions.

Later, Doctor Kerr, surgeon general of Jackson's force, accompanies the British surgeon on a ride to the British hospital at Jumonville's plantation to check on the invalids there. In the meantime, General Jackson moves out to the abandoned British camp. He discovers that in addition to leaving his wounded behind, General Lambert had been unable to transport all of his supplies and artillery. Jackson discovers 14 pieces of heavy artillery still in the camp. Although aware of the British retirement, Jackson remains concerned that Lambert might still make another attempt to return. He ensures that his troops are in place to meet the threat if it occurs before he returns to New Orleans on the following day.

Timothy Pickering, formerly a U.S. senator representing Massachusetts and a leader of the disunion party, is known to have penned a letter on 23 January which read: "If the British succeed in their expedition against New Orleans — and if they have tolerable leaders I see no reason to

Commodore James Barron.

doubt of their success — I shall consider the Union as severed. This consequence I deem inevitable. I do not expect to see a single Representative in the next Congress from the Western States." Also, Lord Castlereagh, while speaking with the king of France just before the date of Pickering's letter, was also resolved to the demise of Jackson and the citizens of the entire nation when he said: "Sire, I expect that at this time most of the large seaport towns in America are laid in ashes — that we are in possession of New Orleans and have command of all the waters of the Mississippi and the lakes; so that the Americans are now little better than prisoners at large in their own country."

January 20 (Friday) In Louisiana, General Jackson departs his headquarters and returns to New Orleans for the first time since he left the city on 28 December to meet the threat of the British invasion. Upon his arrival, the residents break out in tumultuous celebration. Jackson remains concerned that the British can still reappear. He asks that Abbe Dubourg, the apostolic prefect of the state of Louisiana, proclaim 23 January as a day of public prayer and thanks to God for preserving the city.

In other activity, Mr. Shields and Doctor Morrel, recently released from captivity by British Admiral Cochrane, on this day, while on the hunt for stray British boats on Lake Borgne, succeed in seizing a barge transporting a contingent of 37 troops of the 14th Dragoons under Lieutenant Brydges. The American flotilla, composed of four boats when it moved from Bayou St. John onto the lake, had been joined by two additional boats at Petites Coquilles. The British troops, en route from Bienvenu's Plantation, are intercepted before they can reach the fleet. The prisoners are taken to Chef Menteur while Morrel and Shields continue their mission in search of other boats. The flotilla encounters several additional boats and one schooner. All are seized and the Americans find themselves with 63 additional prisoners. Not long after gaining the new prisoners, the winds become unfavorable and the boats become separated. The captured schooner becomes too difficult to control when the captives become obstinate. The men decide to set it afire. However, problems develop when British boats spot the flames and close against Morrel and Shields. The Americans make it to land near the mouth of the Rigolets.

Meanwhile, the British debark a landing party above the point where the Americans debarked, and the party sets out to cut off the Americans. The scheme is foiled when about 20 of the volunteers under Morrel open fire and prompt the British to retire. Nonetheless, the small American contingent remains in danger of being caught by the British. Morrel heads for Petites Coquilles to get reinforcements while the prisoners remain with Shields. Shortly after Morrel departs, a British gunboat appears. Shields reacts quickly by paroling his prisoners. He and his party make it back to Petites Coquilles, along with 23 prisoners.

January 21 (Saturday) *In U.S. Army activity,* a court inquiry convenes regarding General William H. Winder's actions during the Battle of Bladensburg and the British capture of Washington. General Winfield Scott presides. On 25 February, the court rules unanimously:

> The Court, with great attention and much labor, have perused the numerous papers and documents referred to them, from whence they collect — that Brigadier General Winder was appointed to the command of the 10th Military District, of which Washington was a part, on the 2d of July 1814; that immediately thereafter he took every means in his power to put that District into a proper state of defence; that from the period when well-grounded apprehensions were entertained that the enemy meditated an attack upon the Capital, his exertions were great and unremitted; that through these exertions he was enabled to bring into the field, on the 24th of August 1814, the day on which the battle of Bladensburg was fought, about five or six thousand men, all of whom, excepting four hundred, were militia; that he could not collect much more than one-half of this force until a day or two previously to the engagement, and six or seven hundred of them did not arrive until fifteen minutes before its commencement; that from the uncertainty whether Baltimore, the City of Washington, or Fort Washington would be selected as the point of attack, it was necessary that Brigadier General Winder's troops should frequently change their positions, owing to which, and alarms causelessly excited on the night of the 23d of August, they were all much fatigued, and many of them nearly exhausted at the time when the hostile army was crossing the bridge at Bladensburg; that the officers commanding the troops were generally unknown to General Winder, and but a small number of them had enjoyed the benefit of military instruction or experience.
>
> The members of this Court, In common with their fellow-citizens, lament deeply the capture of the Capital; and they regard with no ordinary indignation the spoliation of its edifices, those public monuments of art and science, always deemed sacred by a brave and generous foe; but amidst these mingled and conflicting sensations, they nevertheless feel it to be their duty to separate the individual from the calamities surrounding him, and to declare that to the officer upon whose conduct they are to determine, no censure is attributable. On the contrary, when they take into consideration the complicated difficulties and embarrassments under which he labored, they are of opinion, notwithstanding the result, that he is entitled to no little commendation; before the action he exhibited industry, zeal and talent, and during its continuance a coolness, a promptitude, and a personal valour highly honorable to himself, and worthy of a better fate.

In naval activity, the British privateer *Lunenburg* intercepts and seizes the 91-ton sloop *Experiment*, which is en route to Nantucket from New York with a cargo of candles, corn, flour, oats and other items. The prize is taken into port at Lunenburg. The *Experiment* is separate from the sloop *Experiment* seized 24 June 1813 and the schooner *Experiment* seized on 13 May 1814. Also, the HMS *Bulwark* intercepts and seizes the 202-ton schooner *Tomahawk*.

January 22 (Sunday) *In naval activity,* the American privateer *America*, while operating in European waters, intercepts the schooner *Arrow*, which is transporting various types of nuts from Catalonia to London. A prize crew sails it into port at Salem, Massachusetts. At about the same time, the *America* also captures the schooner *Adeona*, which is carrying a cargo of broadcloth, and it, too, is taken to Salem.

January 23 (Monday) In Louisiana at New Orleans, the day of prayer and thanksgiving to God for the preservation of New Orleans (as requested by General Jackson on the 20th) is celebrated. The St. Louis Cathedral is prepared for the day of thanks and the arrival of the throngs expected to participate. The artillery fires a salute when General Jackson arrives at the gate of the plaza. From the plaza to the cathedral, the prettiest young girls of the city form in two rows representing the various states and territories, and as Jackson passes them he is greeted by two young children, each standing on a pedestal, anxiously waiting to place a laurel wreath upon him. After ascending the arch Jackson is greeted by the girl representing Louisiana. Afterward, General Jackson is escorted into the cathedral, where he is met by Abbe Dubourg and a large number of Catho-

Andrew Jackson statue, New Orleans.

lic priests. Following the conclusion, General Jackson heads back to his headquarters.

In naval activity, the USS *Peacock*, accompanied by the USS *Hornet* and the *Tom Bowline*, the latter a storeship, leave New York. Later off South America, they encounter a British frigate. The American vessels separate to avoid an engagement. The *Peacock* rounds the Cape of Good Hope and searches in the Indian Ocean for British merchant ships. During its time in the Indian Ocean, the *Peacock* captures and destroys three vessels. On 4 June, well after the close of hostilities, it encounters a 14-gun vessel, the *Nautilus*, attached to the East India Company in the Straits of Sundra.

January 24 (Tuesday) **In Louisiana,** by this date, the defenders at New Orleans finally receive arms and ammunition from the federal government. Despite the late arrival, they are heartily received because the British are still in Louisiana and they have also been reinforced, making the perceived threat of renewed hostilities possible. Another problem that has emerged since the defeat of the British is that the militia is beginning to falter and desertions have begun. Frenchmen, not yet naturalized, are disinterested in fulfilling camp duties. They attempt to get support from the French consul. Jackson in turn directs that all Frenchmen who try to use the consul as an excuse not to do their duty are to be escorted out of the city. Consequently, the legislature, already displeased with the popularity of Jackson, attempts to tear down his reputation, not an unusual tactic for politicians.

In naval activity, the HMS *Bulwark* intercepts and seizes the 267-ton brigantine *Joseph and Mary* (Stephen Stanton, master), while it is en route from Prince Edward Island, Canada, to Falmouth with a cargo of lumber.

January 25 (Wednesday) *In naval activity,* the American privateer *Lawrence*, operating out of Baltimore, after arriving in New York on this day, reports that during its cruise, thirteen prizes, including eight large ships, had been seized, and of those eight received prize crews with orders to bring the respective vessels into American ports. Captain Veasey also reports that 106 prisoners had been captured, and of those 15 were ordered back to the United States.

January 31 (Tuesday) *In naval activity,* the American privateer *Macdonough*, a brigantine out of Rhode Island carrying six guns, encounters an unidentified sail, which gives the appearance of having a double row of port guns. Later the Americans discover the additional row on the bottom is not real. The *Macdonough* takes the offensive, and at just about 1400 while arriving within close range, hoists the Stars and Stripes. The British vessel seemingly enthusiastically awaits returning fire. By 1430 both vessels are intensely engaged within pistol shot range. Although the British are using fewer than ten guns for their broadsides, the Americans simultaneously come under enormous pressure from a huge number of muskets from British troops, whom the Americans had not realized were on board until the incessant fire begins to heavily strike the decks of the *Macdonough* about 1530. The British small arms fire is extremely effective, causing damage and inflicting casualties. By this time, the Americans become imperiled, as the ship had absorbed damage at the water line, which threatens to cause the vessel to sink.

The crew works feverishly to control the leaks; however, the chances of seizing the British vessel have passed, particularly because of the great number of Redcoats aboard. Captain Wilson, having observed his casualty list increasing by the minute, concludes that the time has come to disengage and save his ship. Although Wilson's decision is pragmatic, he is unaware of the extent of damage inflicted upon the British by his crew. As the *Macdonough* pulls away, his crew sees the British are extremely busy trying to repair American-inflicted holes along their water line, indicating that they had sustained too much damage to consider pursuit. The Americans sail off en route to Savannah, Georgia, while the British ship is also under sail on a course that the Americans believe is the Canary Islands.

February 1 (Wednesday) *In naval activity,* the 6-gun American privateer *Perry* out of Baltimore returns on or about this day to the Delaware River after displaying to the British that it apparently had more lives than a proverbial cat. It had escaped pursuing British warships about ten times, including one encounter that nearly destroyed it at sea due to fire from a razee that devastated its rigging and sails.

During the cruise, which lasted ninety days, the *Perry* had destroyed 18 vessels at sea and four others had been taken into American ports. In addition to the captured merchant ships, the *Perry* had also engaged and captured a 4-gun British gunboat, the HMS *Ballahou*, commanded by Lt. Norfolk King and carrying a crew of 30 men. Nonetheless, while the *Ballahou* is close to entering the port at Wilmington, a British warship intercepts it, drives it into shore and destroys it.

February 4–13 **In Louisiana** at New Orleans, General Jackson dispatches to the British fleet three representatives to propose talks on a new prisoner exchange and to attempt to get the British to return to their owners the slaves they had taken. Edward Livingston, aide to Jackson, Captain Maunsel White of the Louisiana Blues, and R.D. Shepherd, aide to commodore Patterson, arrive off the fleet on 7 February. Their presence is not welcomed because the British have just decided to try again to take Fort Bowyer, where they were repulsed during September 1814.

During their time aboard Cochrane's flagship, the HMS *Tonnant*, a cordial relationship develops, and one incident includes the return of a sword that had been claimed by General Keane, although it is generally believed by many of the British that the sword belonged to General Pakenham, who was wounded in his sword arm just before being killed on 8 January. After accepting the sword, Keane speaks about the importance of a man's sword on the battlefield. Some of the younger officers, none of whom had been at the battle, begin to tease the general for losing his sword in the field, but Keane immediately retorts: "My young friends, if you had been where I was on the 8th of January last, you would have lost your heads as well as your swords."

While the American negotiators are holding talks with the British commanders, a British squadron is on the attack against Fort Bowyer in Alabama. The post, ill-prepared for a powerful land attack, is compelled to surrender on 11 February. At Fort Bowyer, Colonel Lawrence, the commander, held a garrison of less than 400 troops and was besieged by an entire British brigade, including the 4th, 24th, and 44th Regiment, along with the 95th Rifles. All land routes had been severed, preventing any reinforcements from arriving to lift the siege. After surrendering, the Americans are afforded the honors of war. The British, however, do not initiate an attack to seize Mobile. In recognition of the seizure and the British intent to overvalue their prize, they hold a grand dinner aboard the *Tonnant* and the American negotiators are in attendance. Following the dinner, while the guests are receiving their wine and some dessert, some curtains are pulled back, giving those at the table a view of Fort Bowyer at the instant the Stars and Stripes is being replaced by the British ensign. As the American flag descends from the top of the staff an artillery barrage can be heard. Admiral Edward Codington, resting in the seat at the head of the table, speaks to Colonel Livingston while he points to the British flag being hoisted: "Well, Colonel Livingston, you perceive that our day has commenced." Livingston, while raising his glass and touching it to the admiral's glass, responds: "We do not begrudge you that small consolation."

The British, their chests expanding with pride after seizing the post, hardly have time to savor the victory, the sole victory of the dreadful campaign, when a boat arrives alongside the *Tonnant* on the 13th. A naval officer moves aboard the *Tonnant* and hands a packet to Admiral Malcolm, who at the time is on deck speaking with R.D. Shepherd. Admiral Malcolm opens the packet and begins to read the message, then suddenly, his voice becomes especially jovial as he grasps Shepherd's hand while he exclaims, "Good news! Good news! We are friends. The *Brazen* [HMS] has just arrived outside, with the news of peace. I am delighted!" Armed with the news of the end of the war, the three Americans return to New Orleans to inform General Jackson. The news is well received, but Jackson cautions that the Americans must remain vigilant because until the U.S. ratifies the treaty, there remains a chance of renewed hostilities.

February 9 (Thursday) *In naval activity,* the *Atlas*, a 40-ton schooner (Alexander Livingston, master), while en route from Elizabeth City, North Carolina, to Newberry (Newbury Port, (Massachusetts, New Hampshire or Rhode Island) is intercepted and captured by the British privateer *Dove*. The *Atlas* and its cargo of flour and rice are taken into port at Liverpool.

February 11 (Saturday) **In Alabama,** Fort Bowyer, located in the vicinity of Mobile and garrisoned by fewer than 400 men commanded by Colonel Lawrence, is stunned when a fleet of 13 British vessels transporting 5,000 troops arrives following the abandonment of New Orleans. The garrison troops, like the British, are unaware that the war is over. The Americans conclude they are unable to withstand such a combined force intent on attacking by both land and sea. The garrison, which numbers 360 troops, marches out in cadence to the beat of drums and with the colors in full display. The Americans are placed about several British ships as prisoners; however within several weeks, due to the end of hostilities, Fort Bowyer is re-occupied by the United States. Later, during 1818, Fort Bowyer is replaced by Fort Morgan. (*See also,* **February 4–13.**)

February 12 (Sunday) **In Georgia,** General Blackshear receives orders from General Floyd to dispatch a company to Sapelo Island, where it is to bolster militia under Major Hopkins. It is thought that the British might launch an attack against the island.

February 13 (Monday) News of the Treaty of Ghent reaches Washington this day. Celebrations break out around the country, even in New England, which had staunchly disapproved of the war. Only a short while ago, New England was still discussing secession, and many Americans seemed overburdened with melancholy, thinking that the peace conference had ended in failure and that the war would continue to rage. But, the news during the beginning of February regarding Jackson's tumultuous victory over the British in New Orleans began the process of optimism and the news of the consummated treaty incites spontaneous joy.

Nonetheless, the time of danger is not completely gone. The Canadians feel as if they have been hung out to dry, despite their enormous contribution to the war effort. The most serious problem is that they believe Canada should have the authority to control its fisheries, and this is followed by Canadian concerns that no land had been preserved as a protection area to forestall American encroachment. At this time, the Canadians have at their disposal a large number of warships scattered about the Great Lakes; however, the U.S. has also deployed sizable numbers of vessels. The distant standoff creates a possible clash. The British, accepting an American proposal, will begin negotiations with the U.S. in hopes of both countries agreeing to make the lakes neutral by disarming all ships. An agreement will be reached during April 1817.

February 14 (Tuesday) **In Washington, D.C.,** Secretary of War James Monroe writes to Major General Pinckney at Savannah: "SIR:— It is with great satisfaction that I have to inform you that a treaty of peace was concluded between the United States and Great Britain, at Ghent, on the 24th December last. A copy of this treaty was received to-day, by Mr. Carroll, has been examined by the President, and will, I have no doubt, be ratified. I give you this information that hostilities may immediately cease between our troops and those of Great Britain. It will be proper for you to notify this to the British commander in your vicinity."

In Georgia, General Pinckney at Savannah issues General Orders for General Blackshear: "The militia troops of Cuthbert's brigade, called into the service of the United States, and assembled at Sisters' Ferry, including the two companies of riflemen under marching-orders, will be discharged as soon as mustered. Any part of these troops not joined are hereby countermanded. The senior officer at Sisters' Ferry will take the most prompt and effectual means to publish this order." Also, the orders stipulate: "Lieutenant-Colonel Austin, an officer commanding a regiment of South Carolina infantry called into United States service and ordered to rendezvous at Two Sisters' Ferry, will obey the requisition of Brigadier General Floyd, commanding troops in the United States service in Georgia to move into Georgia, and, on his arrival there, will report to Gen. Floyd and obey his orders."

Following the close of his service, Floyd retires to his plantation, known as the Fairfield on the Satilla River. Upon the death of General Floyd on 24 June 1824, per his request, his body is wrapped "in the folds of the beloved flag for which he fought." Later, his son, General Charles L. Floyd, is interred at Fairfield next to his father. Another son, Richard, serves with the Confederacy as a lieutenant on the CSS *Florida*. Also, General John Floyd's father, Charles, a veteran of the American Revolution, was captured by the British and spent a prolonged time as a prisoner. Reports of his service state that he had the following words written on a "silver crescent on his hat … the motto 'liberty or death.'"

February 16 (Thursday) *In naval activity,* the *Dove,* a British privateer, intercepts the 172-ton brigantine *George,* which had sailed from George Town for New Bedford. The *George* and its cargo, including rice and molasses, are taken to Liverpool. The *George* is separate from brigantine *George* seized 8 July 1812, the brigantine *George* seized on 17 July 1812, and the brigantine *George* captured 22 July 1812. In other naval activity, the American privateer *Macdonough,* which arrived at Morlaix, France, on 7 February, gets an unexpected visitor, a British warship that enters the harbor and drops anchor close to the *Macdonough.* The British attempt to intimidate the Americans by ordering them to surrender their prizes. The Americans respond quickly, but in the negative. All hands prepare to defend their ship and their prizes. Nevertheless, the British decline pressing the issue. After the threat diminishes, the *Macdonough* prepares to return to the United States.

February 17–18 President Madison officially declares an end to the War of 1812. The next day the U.S. Senate ratifies Treaty of Ghent (December 24) with a unanimous vote, ending the war with the United Kingdom. After the war, an exhausted Europe settles down and the Americans glide into a period known as "The Era of Good Feelings" (1815–1823), as the United States transforms itself into a more flexible nation and natural changes take place. Regionalism remains a mainstay of the Union as one sector maneuvers for positioning atop the other, but it is a family affair; the nation as a whole receives a free flowing spirit of nationalism. However, by about 1830, the internal tranquility sustains a few cracks as differences between various sections of the country take issue with legislation, depending upon how it would affect their area. The bickering becomes nasty and the gloves come off as the ever-burning issue of "states' rights" jumps to the front of the stage and begins to control the spotlight.

In naval activity, the American privateer *Grand Turk,* commanded by Captain Nathan Green, while off Pernambuco, Brazil, spots a catamaran. The vessel is halted and the officers are questioned about British merchant ships. The Americans are informed that eight British ships are in port and some are prepared to sail. Captain Green enthusiastically receives the fresh intelligence from a vessel that had just left the port. The *Grand Turk* lingers in the area in expectation of pouncing upon targets as they depart from the harbor. Later in the day, the privateer nudges closer to the harbor to ascertain the types of shipping there. The first potential victim comes into sight on the 19th.

February 19 to March 10 *In naval activity,* at about 1730, a British vessel sails out of the harbor at Pernambuco, Brazil, to the delight of the American privateer *Grand Turk,* which has lurking in the region anxiously anticipating a target. A slow-paced chase is initiated, and by the following morning the ship is intercepted and boarded. The vessel, the *Joren Francisco,* is sailing under a Spanish flag, but to its misfortune, it is carrying a cargo of cinnamon, coffee, sugar and tea. Captain Nathan Green is convinced that the cargo is heading to British consignees and the colors had been flying fraudulently. The prize and its cargo are taken into an American port. After sailing northward to seize its prize, and shortly after successfully capturing it, the *Grand Turk*'s lookouts spot a new sail to the south, and to their jubilation the vessel appears to be sailing directly toward the *Grand Turk,* which essentially holds in place until it arrives. On the 21st, the Americans halt the vessel, the ship *Active Jane* out of Liverpool, at about 1830. The prize is carrying specie worth about $17,500 from Rio de Janeiro to Maranham, Brazil. Captain Green holds the prize close until the morning of the 22nd to give it a more thorough search, but nothing more of value is discovered. The crew and the specie are transferred to the privateer, and then the vessel is destroyed. Following its seizure of the two prizes, the *Grand Turk* continues its cruise inflicting damage to British shipping as it moves. Meanwhile, British warships begin to converge on the area in an attempt to short circuit the cruise. The British make contact on 10 March.

February 20 (Monday) U.S. Captain Charles Stewart, unaware that peace is made with the British, engages the 32-gun HMS *Cyane* and the 21-gun HMS *Levant* in the Atlantic under a darkened sky. The British warships carry a combined 53 guns versus 45 on the *Constitution,* "Old Ironsides." Captain Stewart trades round for round and with some expert withering fire. The *Cyane* (Captain George Falcon) strikes its colors while it still has a mast. There is an attempt by the *Levant* (Captain George Douglas) to rescue the crew of the disabled ship and continue the fight, but its guns are not even close to equaling the firepower of "Old Ironsides." The Americans lose four killed and ten wounded. By about 2200, the *Constitution* is preparing to sail to Port Praya with its two prizes. Neither side is aware that a peace treaty has been signed.

Captain Stewart had served as lieutenant under Captain (later Commodore) John Barry aboard the USS *United States* before he was promoted to captain during July 1800 and given command of the USS *Experiment*. In 1812, he received command of the *Constellation*, and during 1813, Stewart became commander of the USS *Constitution*.

February 26 (Sunday) **In New York City,** Commodore Stephen Decatur arrives in the city from New London, Connecticut, following his return from Bermuda after being released by the British. A court of inquiry is convened regarding the loss of the USS *President* the previous month. Commodore Murray presides. Commodore Decatur and all of his officers are cleared of all blame (*see also*, **January 14–15**).

In naval activity, the HMS *Bulwark* intercepts and recaptures the 129-ton schooner *Rhoda* on its way to England from Bermuda. Elsewhere, the American privateer *Chasseur*, while cruising about 35 miles from Cuba, spots a schooner. Captain Boyle immediately initiates pursuit. Upon closer inspection, it is determined to be a warship in company of a convoy. By about 1230, the *Chasseur* fires one shot and the Stars and Stripes is hoisted. The schooner ignores the warning shot and attempts to avoid an engagement. Nonetheless, the *Chasseur* continues pursuit, and in the meantime, the schooner suffers an accident that causes the fore top mast to be severed, giving the Americans time to gain on it. By 1300, the schooner, which is the HMS *St. Lawrence* (formerly American privateer *Atlas*) hoists the British ensign; however, Captain Boyle believes the schooner is not well armed and he thinks the crew is small in number because very few men are spotted on the decks. Rather than prepare for a full-scale battle, the crew of the *Chassseur* prepares only for a quick seizure before the ship can make it to port in Havana. About one-half hour later, the *Chasseur* moves alongside the schooner, and to their surprise, the British ring out three cheers and display their concealed weapons. Simultaneously, the Americans discover the crew members are regular navy. The British had been able to fool Boyle, but his demeanor remains cool as the *Chasseur* is raked with fire.

Boyle once again is faced with a choice of whether to fight. Characteristically, within seconds, the decision is made. The Americans return fire, confident that they can rebound and prevail. Boyle moves in close for an opportunity to prevent disaster. Both vessels maneuver to gain the advantage while exchanging heavy close-range fire. At about 1340, Captain Boyle leads a boarding party. The first Americans succeed in boarding; however, surprisingly, there is no struggle. The British surrender to the boarding party. The fire from the *Chassseur* had devastated the *St. Lawrence*.

Numbers vary regarding casualties. The Americans list British casualties at 15 killed and 25 wounded. The British commander lists six killed and 17 wounded. American casualties amount to five killed and eight wounded, including Captain Thomas Boyle. Captain Boyle releases the *St. Lawrence* as a cartel to ease his problem of having too many prisoners. The British are permitted to sail into Havana.

Neither the Americans nor the British realize their engagement occurred after the war had ended. The British officers, however, are overwhelmed by Boyle's kindness and consideration. British Lt. Gordon issues the following:

> At Sea, February 27, 1815, on board the United States Privateer *Chasseur*: In the event of Captain Boyle's becoming a prisoner of war to any British cruiser I consider it a tribute justly due to his humane and generous treatment of myself, the surviving officers and crew of His Majesty's late schooner *St. Laurence* to state that his obliging attention and watchful solicitude to preserve our effects and render us comfortable during the short time we were in his possession were such as justly entitle him to the indulgence and respect of every British subject. I also certify that his endeavors to render us comfortable and to secure our property were carefully seconded by all his officers, who did their utmost to that effect.

The *Chasseur* arrives in port on 15 April.

February 28 (Tuesday) *In naval activity,* the HMS *Bulwark* intercepts and recaptures the 119-ton brigantine *Margaret*, which has a cargo of fish, lumber and staves. The *Margaret* is separate from the schooner *Margaret* seized on 16 March 1813 and the sloop *Margaret* captured on 10 October 1813.

March 2–3 **In Washington,** in conjunction with declaring war with Algiers, Congress authorizes President Madison to equip warships for the cause. The United States declares war against Algiers in response to their demands for money in exchange for the USS *Edwin* and crew, the *Edwin* having been captured during the war with Great Britain. The American fleet departs the United States during May to visit the dey (Omar, Son of Mohammed) of Algiers. Immediately thereafter, two squadrons are fitted out for sea. Commodore William Bainbridge receives command of one squadron and the other squadron is to be commanded by Commodore Decatur.

March 5 (Sunday) **In Louisiana** at New Orleans, General Jackson, infuriated at a local judge for assisting Frenchmen who were unwilling to support the defense of New Orleans, issues the following order at 1900: "To COLONEL ARBUCKLE, Headquarters Seventh Military District: Having received proof that [Judge] Dominick A. Hall has been aiding and abetting and exciting mutiny within my camp, you will forthwith order a detachment to arrest and confine him, and report to me as soon as arrested. You will be vigilant; the agents of our enemy are more numerous than was expected. You will be guarded against escapes."

March 6–7 *In naval activity,* the American privateer *Ino*, attempting to get to the wharf at Charleston, gets snagged by a reef. The British send a party in boats to seize it, but the effort fails. Later during the night the *Ino* becomes further imperiled and seems to be close to breaking up. The British make another attempt to seize it, but it also fails. Afterward, the crew descends into rafts at about the same time they set it afire. At 1400, the *Ino* explodes. Nonetheless, the men are far from safety. Their rafts are battered by the surf and shredded. While men are trying to swim to shore, British boats again arrive. Two men are captured. A small schooner arrives and gets the men to shore. It is later learned that the crew of the British warship HMS *Severn* had been aware that the war had ended when the attacks were made on the *Ino*.

March 7 (Tuesday) *In naval activity,* the HMS *Spencer* intercepts and recaptures the 116-ton brigantine *Legal Tender* while it is en route from Newfoundland to Lisbon, Portugal.

March 10 (Friday) *In naval activity,* the USS *Constitution*, commanded by Captain Charles Stewart—along with two prizes, the 32-gun

The privateer *Chasseur* (*History of American Privateers [and letters of marque]*, George Coggeshall, 1856).

HMS *Cyane* and the 21-gun HMS *Levant*—arrives at the Cape Verde Islands. Stewart spots a vessel, the *Swan*, which is at Porto Praya on San Jago, the largest island in the Cape de Verde archipelago. At about 1200, British warships are spotted near the mouth of the harbor. Initially, despite a fog, one sail is detected, but shortly thereafter it becomes clear that there are three warships—50-gun *Leander*, 50-gun *Newcastle* and the 40-gun *Acasta*. The Americans are in a neutral harbor; however, Captain Stewart has serious doubts about the British respecting the neutrality of the port. Rather than risk a fight with the squadron, commanded by Captain Sir George Collier, Captain Stewart decides to weigh anchor. In less than ten minutes, the *Constitution* and its prizes are sailing out of the harbor. Just as the Americans pass through the mouth of the harbor, the British squadron spots them and initiates pursuit.

The British begin to close on the two prizes; however, the *Constitution* remains at a safe distance. Stewart signals the *Cyane* and orders the prize crew to sail northwest to complicate the British operation by forcing it to split up or at least to permit the *Cyane* to escape. Nevertheless, the British remain in formation and continue to focus on the *Constitution*. Stewart orders the remaining prize, the *Levant*, to also break off and follow the *Cyane*. Once the *Levant* changes course, the British squadron remains in formation; however, it too changes course and follows the *Levant*, leaving the *Constitution* on its own. The British capture the *Levant* while still in the neutral harbor, but the *Cyane* escapes. The British inexplicably lose the opportunity to gain the *Constitution*, a prize that the British had at the top of their list. The *Constitution* arrives back at New York on 15 May 1815, where the crew learns that the war with Britain had ended. However, they also are informed that a new conflict had begun with the Barbary pirates.

March 10–18 *In naval activity,* the American privateer *Grand Turk*, having inflicted punishment upon British shipping during this cruise, is aware that the Royal Navy is searching for it. Nevertheless, the *Grand Turk*, while cautiously maintaining a vigil for enemy warships remains on the hunt. At about dawn, the lookouts spot a sail in the distance; the order for all hands to stations is issued. The privateer moves slowly toward the vessel expecting it to be a merchant ship, but prepared if it is a warship. Meanwhile, at about 0630, another strange sail is spotted, but it is left unscathed after being identified as a Portuguese ship. Nevertheless, within less than one hour, a third vessel is spotted. The latter appears more likely to be a British warship; however, Captain Nathan Green is not discouraged. The privateer proceeds with caution and resumes its chase of the vessel first spotted.

By about 1000, Captain Green is able to discern that his prey is a warship that is attempting to be cunning; it is merely trying to draw the *Grand Turk* into the range of its guns. The British, anxious to deliver a fatal blow to the *Grand Turk*, discover that there scheme has been foiled when the *Grand Turk* suddenly tacks and absconds. The British, however, intend not to be denied the opportunity to capture or destroy the insolent privateer. They initiate pursuit at full sail, only to observe their prey, with superior speed, leaving the British frigate far behind after about one-half hour. As an unofficial farewell to the frigate, Captain Green orders the Stars and Stripes hoisted, while the privateer fires a lone shot to celebrate the separation. However, the British on the frigate do not relent. They maintain the chase despite the great distance between them and their prey.

The winds change to favor the frigate, which is pushed ahead, while the privateer becomes snarled by the calmness of its winds, leaving the frigate to come up close by about 1130. Captain Green, remaining confident, directs the crew to get all of the sweeps out, and after completing the operation, it again begins to pull away to the dismay of the British. Meanwhile, the British are slowed by the winds, and they are compelled to get all of the boats out front to begin towing it. During this operation, British gunners fire without inflicting any harm. While the privateer is getting away, the British repeatedly attempt to tack without success. Captain Green again orders the colors hoisted, while at the same time, his long tom commences fire in an attempt to damage the frigate's rigging and sails.

Just as the *Grand Turk* has escaped yet again, the lookouts spot new danger. Another British ship arrives to join the chase. Captain Green reacts immediately by swinging his ship around, permitting it to sail northwardly with both British ships giving chase. The *Grand Turk* remains on the run into the following day (11th), but the British refuse to abort the chase, which continues into the 12th. At dawn it appears as if the privateer has finally outsailed its pursuers. Nonetheless, the reprieve lasts only a while. At about 1330, the two British brigs that had vanished from sight reappear, and they are receiving some stiff winds, while the *Grand Turk* out front is unable to catch any strong breezes. At about 1700, the British progress is checked when the winds subside, once again permitting the *Grand Turk* to lose its pursuers.

The *Grand Turk* sails without interruption until about 1400 on Monday, the 13th, when the lookouts spot a sail to the northwest. A while later, at 1600, another vessel is detected. The *Grand Turk* in the meantime had been making repairs, including the replacement of the fore top mast, which had taken a beating from the elements during its attempts to evade the British frigates; however, by 1700 all the work is completed and the *Grand Turk* sets its sights on the latter vessel detected. The Americans halt it and board it at about 1900 to discover the ship is Portuguese and transporting a cargo of salt. Relieved that there is still no sign of his pursuers, Captain Green resumes his cruise, which remains uneventful until 18 March.

March 11 (Saturday) **In Connecticut,** it is a momentous day. The British fleet, which has maintained an effective blockade for more than two years, salutes the colors at Fort Trumbull and departs Long Island Sound.

March 13 (Monday) **In Louisiana** at New Orleans, General Jackson receives official word that the treaty with Britain had been ratified by the U.S. Congress. Jackson forwards the news to British General Lambert. In addition, Jackson informs the army through a general order that martial law in New Orleans is terminated. Jackson also grants pardons to all those having committed military offenses. On the following day, General Jackson pays tribute to his militia and afterward, they are released from duty. Although the hostilities have concluded, both sides are faced with another enemy, an epidemic of dysentery. The Americans in New Orleans are affected similarly to the British camp on Dauphin Island.

March 16 (Thursday) **In Louisiana** at New Orleans, the American troops, including all those volunteers still in the city, assemble at the plains of Chalmette, where General Jackson reviews the troops. The 3rd, 7th and 44th U.S. Regiments, led by General Edmund Pendleton Gaines and trailed by the uniformed troops of New Orleans, pass in review. Afterward, General Jackson again pays tribute to their bravery and courage during the defense of the city. It is Jackson's final official duty. He transfers command to General Gaines and prepares to return to his home in Nashville, Tennessee.

Ironically, Jackson, the man responsible for saving the city of New Orleans and preventing the British from gaining a hold on the mighty Mississippi River, is later thanked by the entire nation except for the legislature in Louisiana, which thanks all except Jackson. During the days that martial law had been in effect, the governor, at the urging of Jackson, had actually deployed troops to observe the action of the legislature due to suspicions that plans were in the works to surrender the city. Although the legislature despises Jackson, the rumors of treason had been later proven unfounded. A judge, Dominick Hall, had clashed with Jackson's declaration and in turn, Jackson had Hall jailed (*see also,* **March 5**).

Just prior to Jackson's departure, the judge retaliated and fined Jackson $1,000 for contempt of court. Jackson, rather than cause a commotion, wrote a check for the fine. The judge's action does not sit well with the people who raise the sum to cover the check in mere minutes; however, Jackson declines the money. He instructs those behind the gesture to use the money for the orphaned children of the men who gave the ultimate sacrifice to save the city.

After returning to Tennessee, General Jackson continues to recuperate by getting some genuine rest at his residence, the Hermitage. After remaining there for about four months, he travels to the capital. By that time, the U.S. Army had been reduced to about 10,000 men. General Jackson commands the southern division, and the northern division is commanded by General Jacob Jennings Brown. While en route to Washington, General Jackson attends a dinner in his honor at Lynchburg, Virginia, and former President Thomas Jefferson attends. General Jackson remains in Washington until early 1816. During his return trip to Tennessee, he pauses at various tribes, including the Cherokee, Chickasaw, Creek and Choctaw, accomplishing some success by consummating treaties. Upon his return to the Hermitage, he is able, thanks to his salary as a major general, to free himself of his remaining debt, and he is also able to prepare a new gift for his wife, Rachael. Construction of a brick house is begun to replace his double-log cabin. In addition to the new home, he also orders the construction of a very small church on the property.

Jackson, although not a practicing Christian for much of his life, retained always a great respect for the clergy. On one occasion at Nashville, a Reverend Cartwright was about to give his sermon when Jackson entered the church. The minister, known for his unique style of preaching, was urged "to be on his best behavior," which did not get received with exuberance. Glancing at the people in the pews and at the general, who was leaning against pillar, Reverend Cartwright bellowed: "Who is General Jackson? If he don't get his soul converted, God will damn him as quick as he would a Guinea Negro." The consensus was that the minister would son receive Jackson's wrath; however, on the following day, when Jackson and the minister spoke, it was actually the beginning of a lifelong friendship. Jackson said Reverend Cartwright "was a man after his own heart, that he highly approved his independence, and that a minister of Jesus Christ ought to love everybody and fear no mortal man."

March 17 (Friday) **In Alabama,** the British army under General Lambert abandons Dauphin Island and joins the fleet, which sets sail for Europe. About mid–May, the British fleet arrives off the coast of France, and they are stunned to see the French flag flying over the castle at Brest, which had been flying the British ensign when the army sailed to seize Louisiana. Shortly afterward when they arrive home in England they are informed that Napoleon, whom they defeated before sailing to the United States, had escaped captivity at Elba, returned to France and had reassumed his power. The exhausted troops, expecting to gain some rest and relaxation, barely enter English waters when they are informed that their services are required immediately and that they will be moving to Belgium to bolster Wellington's army. General Lambert is also notified that he is to be knighted for his gallant leadership at New Orleans. He too joins Wellington as commander of the 10th Brigade, composed of the British 4th, 27th, 40th and 81st Regiments. Subsequently, at the decisive Battle of Waterloo, Lambert's brigade sustains the highest number of casualties in the army. After this service, Lambert is governor of Jamaica in place of General Keane. Lambert (Sir John) dies while in Jamaica during 1848.

One particular British officer, Colonel Mullens, receives no laurels at Waterloo. He instead receives a court-martial for his actions at New Orleans on 8 January, and he receives the bulk of the blame for the defeat. His court-martial is held in Dublin, Ireland, during the summer of 1815. After being convicted he is dismissed from the service. His problems originated with his failure to get the ladders and facines in place to permit the British to scale Jackson's parapet. The British never reached the parapet, so the absence of the ladders actually had no bearing on the results of the battle. Had the ladders been brought to the front, there were no troops to use them.

Also, the other regiments that participated at New Orleans are assigned recruiting service. The ranks of the 93rd had been badly battered and resembled only a shell of its former strength. Nevertheless, it does eventually come back to full strength and will participate in the Crimea. General Keane becomes governor of Jamaica and later serves in India, and for his service at the latter, he achieves knighthood and later he becomes Lord Keane. General Keane dies in Ireland about 1845.

March 18 (Saturday) **In naval activity,** the American privateer *Grand Turk* remains concerned that the British frigates giving pursuit have not been spotted for some time and might yet reappear. The lookouts spot a sail, and at about 1400, it is halted and discovered to be a Portuguese vessel, carrying slaves from Africa to Rio de Janeiro. While alongside the ship, another sail is spotted northwest of the *Grand Turk*'s position. It darts away from the slave runner and pursues the second vessel. At 1630, the vessels hoists the British colors while its stern guns fire upon the *Grand Turk*. The privateer ignores the fire and holds its own fire, but maintains its pursuit. Less than one hour later, the unidentified British vessel fires at the privateer which had come into range, only to receive devastating return fire from the gunners on the *Grand Turk*. The British, overwhelmed by the effective barrage catapulted by the port guns, is unable to match the firepower.

Within ten minutes after firing its ineffective broadside, the British strike their colors. The *Grand Turk* takes possession of the brigantine *Acorn*, which had left Liverpool with a cargo of dry goods destined for Rio de Janeiro. The vessel is also mounting 14 guns. The Americans, aware that the area is an operating region for British warships, immediately begin to transfer the cargo, but it becomes tedious and the operation continues into the following day. On Sunday morning before the operation is completed, the same pesky but deadly frigates arrive at about dawn to disrupt the operation. Captain Green halts the transfer of goods, rushes a 12-man prize crew under Joseph Phippen onto the *Acorn* and directs the crew to get off straightaway for the United States.

In the meantime, the *Grand Turk* prepares for yet another marathon race to escape. Once again the British fail to seize their prey and the *Grand Turk*, after losing sight of the cruisers, vanishes in the darkness, never to encounter them again. Captain Green has new concerns, the condition of his ship and his conviction that the treaty signed at Ghent will be ratified. Closing out the cruise on a successful note, the privateer sails for home. During the voyage, it encounters another Portuguese slave-runner. Captain Green transfers his eleven British to the vessel after releasing them on parole. Later, on 16 April, the *Grand Turk* encounters an American schooner, the *Comet*, which is sailing to Barbados and at that time, the crew learns that the war had ended. It sails into Salem, Massachusetts, on 29 April to culminate a 118-day cruise, during which the privateer captured 30 vessels; the prizes were 12 brigantines, seven schooners, three ships and eight sloops. On 30 May, the *Grand Turk* is sold and transformed into a merchant ship.

March 19 (Sunday) **In naval activity,** the HMS *Cossack*, a sloop, intercepts and recaptures the 100-ton schooner *Thistle* from an American prize crew while it is off Cape Sable in Nova Scotia. The *Thistle*, carrying a cargo of fruit and wine, had recently been seized by the American privateer *America*. The *Thistle* is taken into Halifax and then returned to the United States because the war had ended. Also this month, the privateer *America* encounters a British privateer, the 8-gun *Elizabeth*, carrying a crew of 31 men. Despite being greatly overmatched, the British privateer engages and raises ferocious resistance. Nonetheless, the superior firepower of the *America* terminates the battle within about 20 minutes. The *Elizabeth* sustains "700 shot holes." After taking possession of the prize, the Americans disarm it, and because it is not carrying a valuable cargo, the vessel is returned to the survivors. American fire had killed two men and wounded thirteen, increasing the casualties to about one-half of the crew.

March 23 (Thursday) **In naval activity,** the sloop of war USS *Hornet*, commanded by Master Commandant James Biddle, encounters the 16-gun HMS *Penguin* near Tristan d'Acunha in the South Pacific just before noon. However, neither the Americans nor the British had received word that the hostilities had ended. Both vessels close upon each other and the battle ignites at 1340,

Privateer *America* (*A History of American Privateers*, Edgar Stanton Maclay, 1900).

Captain James Biddle.

when opposing broadsides are launched. The battle rages for only about fifteen minutes before the commanding officer of the *Penguin* receives a mortal wound. The *Penguin* gets snarled by the rigging of the *Hornet* and while in the process of extricating itself, its foremast is severed, leaving the *Penguin* crippled. Meanwhile, the guns of the *Hornet* have maintained their fire. The *Penguin* is compelled to strike its colors at just after 1400. The crew is transferred to the *Hornet*. Meanwhile, the battered *Penguin* has sustained too much damage to be saved. The American crew suffers one dead and 10 or 11 wounded. The British have 14 dead and 28 wounded. The war has been over for three months.

Shortly after the defeat of the *Penguin*, the sloop of war USS *Peacock* and the schooner USS *Tom Bowline* arrive on scene. The British prisoners are transferred to the *Tom Bowline*, which transports the prisoners to Rio de Janeiro accompanied by the *Peacock*. For about three weeks, the *Peacock* and the *Hornet* continue to operate without the knowledge that the war had ended. Afterward, they sail to the East Indies.

March 26 (Sunday) *In naval activity,* the HMS *Maidstone* intercepts and captures a 65-ton brigantine the *Louisa* (William Newel, master) which is en route to Greenock, Scotland, from Gibraltar with a cargo that includes wine, raisins and other items. The *Louisa* is separate from the sloop *Louisa* seized 3 August 1813.

April In Florida, Captain George Woodbine, an Englishman, moves down the Apalachicola River and establishes a fort from which he instigates the Indians and informs the U.S. that he represents the forces of the king of England in Florida. In addition, Woodbine transports Negro slaves earlier seized from planters by English forces during the recently ended war. Woodbine and others work to convince the Creeks that their lands should be restored according to their interpretation of the Treaty of Ghent.

In naval activity, the American privateer *Amelia,* a 6-gun schooner out of Baltimore, arrives at Philadelphia following its third cruise. On its initial cruise it had captured 80 prisoners along with shipping valued at one million dollars. On its second cruise, the Amelia captured 112 prisoners and about 2,200 tons of enemy shipping. During this its final cruise, it captured ten prizes, one of which was transformed into a cartel, and its prisoners were transferred to it. Some of the others were destroyed at sea. While en route back to the States, it was well received at L'Orient by the authorities and the population; however, during a later pause at St. Bartholomews where it entered port to acquire fresh water, the governor is belligerent. He refuses the Americans their request for supplies and arrogantly demands that its captain leave the port post-haste.

April *In naval activity,* the American privateer *York* arrives at Boston to culminate a frustrating and unsuccessful cruise in which it captured only one prize and lost it soon afterward when it was recaptured. During the cruise its enemy turned out to be the elements rather than the British. During one particular squall, four men were washed overboard. It had been bashed by several separate squalls that inflicted damage and cost it some of its guns and anchors.

April 6 (Thursday) In England at Dartmoor Prison, the commandant, Major Thomas George Shortland, after arriving back at the prison after a day in Plymouth where he consumed a large quantity of spirits, discovers that one of the inner walls of the prison has a hole in it. Shortland overreacts due to the belief that a major prison break was imminent and that the masses might move through the minute opening. He calls out the guard, about 1,000 men, who receive orders to fire upon the masses who are more or less trapped in the yards without cover. At this time, the British are aware that the war had ended. The British officers refuse to order the troops to fire; however, Shortland gives the order and the slaughter begins. Meanwhile, some British troops warn the Americans of the imminent order to fire and most to try to get back to their cells. The firing commences but most of it hits high on the walls, it is assumed that the troops reluctantly obeyed the order to fire and simultaneously followed their consciences and did not fire for effect. Shortland, conspicuously inebriated, draws his sword and leads an inglorious charge against the prisoners still in the yards. Neither man nor boy are spared the bayonet and many of the captives are stabbed in the back. Even stragglers who try to hide in the yards are searched out. Their pleas for mercy go unheeded. As a testament to the regular British soldier involved in the barbaric actions of Shortland, and proof that they intentionally fired to miss, only seven men are killed and 60 wounded. If the British had completely followed the dishonorable order, thousands might have been killed. One isolated British guard had been caught in between the prisoners. He had awaited massive retaliation and surely death at the hands of his captors as the only Redcoat held by the Americans. The Americans inform the terrified soldier that he would not be harmed. They keep their word and to the astonishment of the British, when they reopen the gates, he walks back to his regiment unscathed.

April 10 (Monday) *In naval activity,* the privateer *America* arrives back at Salem, Massachusetts, to culminate its final cruise of 134 days. The privateer, during the course of the war, provided its owners a net of about $600,000.

April 15 (Saturday) In Maine, the British evacuate Fort George after having controlled it since the previous September.

In naval activity, the privateer *Casseur* under Captain Thomas Boyle arrives at Baltimore. While passing Fort McHenry, the men salute the post. The crew is informed that the war had ended. The following is a partial list of prizes it seized during three months at sea: the sloop *Christiana* out of Kilkadee, Scotland, turned into a cartel; the brigantine *Reindeer* out of the island of Lanzarote en route to London; brigantine *Marquis of Cornwallis,* also out of Lanzarote en route to London, turned into cartel; brigantine *Alert,* out of Poole, en route to Newfoundland, destroyed at sea; brigantine *Harmony,* turned into cartel; the ship *Carlbury,* out of London; 14-gun brigantine *Eclipse;* brigantine *Commerce;* brigantine *Antelope;* schooner *Fox;* 12-gun ship *James,* out of London; 8-gun brigantine *Atlantic,* out of London (the *James* and the *Atlanta* were seized at the same time); 8-gun ship *Theodore* out of Liverpool; and the brigantine *Amicus* out of Liverpool.

Captain Boyle during the cruise had captured a total of 18 vessels; however, some were recaptured. During the cruise, Boyle paroled 150 prisoners and an additional 143 were brought back to the United States.

April 17 (Monday) In New York at Albany, Governor Daniel D. Tompkins relinquishes command of the Third Military District, a post he assumed temporarily on 2 November 1814. He writes to General John P. Boyd: "Sir: I transmit, enclosed, the copy of a communication from the acting Secretary of the War department, Alexander Dallas, relieving me from the command of the Third Military District. If orders to the contrary should not have been given, you will on the receipt of this letter assume the absolute command of the district & will announce the same in orders." Alexander Dallas, secretary of the treasury, at the request of the president, succeeded James Monroe to permit the latter to return to his primary responsibilities as secretary of state. Dallas remains at the post from 2 March until 15 August.

Tompkins, on 24 February 1817, resigns as governor: "Gentlemen of the Senate and of the Assembly of the State of New York. Having received official information of my election to the office of Vice President of the United States, I surrender, through their representatives, to the People of this State, the office of their Chief Magistrate." Governor Tompkins serves in President Monroe's administration from 4 March 1817 through 4 March 1825.

April 27 (Thursday) *In naval activity,* the USS *Hornet* and the USS *Peacock* encounter the

HMS *Cornwallis* while they are en route to the East Indies, still unaware that the war is over. The Americans mistakenly identify the vessel as a merchant ship rather than a 74-gun warship. Both American vessels initiate pursuit, and when they begin to close and recognize their prey, positions reverse and the *Hornet* and *Peacock* resort to trying to outrun the superior vessel. The British gunners are inaccurate during the chase. Both vessels outrun the *Cornwallis*, but in the process of making their escape, the *Hornet* had donated nearly all of its guns to the sea, followed by tossing the ammunition supply overboard, its spare bars and other equipment to allow it to gain more speed. It made its escape without harm due to the fact that nearly all of its boats were also thrown overboard. The *Hornet* arrives in New York on 9 June.

May 2 (Tuesday) *In naval activity,* the American privateer *Macedonian* enters port at Portsmouth, culminating a cruise during which it captured several vessels, the brigantine *Margaret and Trevis*, the 260-ton ship *Somerset*, carrying four guns and a cargo of brandy and wine, and the brigantine *Mercury*, with a cargo of wine and other items.

May 17 (Wednesday) Colonel Hugh Brady receives command of the U.S. 2nd Infantry Regiment. Brady, seriously wounded at Lundy's Lane in July 1814, had returned to duty in September and was given command of the 22nd Infantry. Later he receives command of Fort Pike in Sackets Harbor, New York, where he remains until 1826. Meanwhile, on 6 July 1822, he is promoted to the rank of brigadier general. Subsequently, he participated in the Black Hawk War. During 1847, he assumes command of the 7th Military District with his headquarters at Detroit. During the following year, he is promoted to the rank of brevet major general. During April 1851, on the 15th, at the age of 83 and still on active duty, in command along the Canadian border, General Brady is thrown from his carriage and injured fatally. He is interred at Elmwood Cemetery in Detroit.

May 20 to June 30 The United States, which had declared war on Algiers on 3 March, sends a naval fleet commanded by Commodore Stephen Decatur to deal with the Algerians. The squadron sets sail on May 20 with the *Guerriere* as flagship, followed by the USS *Constellation*, *Epervier*, *Macedonian*, *Ontario*, *Saranac*, *Spark* and *Torch*. The squadron moves swiftly to reach the Mediterranean to deal with the pirates. Decatur arrives at Gibraltar on 15 June. Shortly after arriving off Cape Gata, Spain, the Algerian vessel *Mashuda* is spotted during the early morning on 17 June. Decatur orders his men to their battle stations. As the squadron attempts to close, the Algerian vessel makes no attempt to run. Commander Lewis requests authorization from Decatur to "make sail." Commodore Decatur, however, has noted that the Algerian ship by not trying to flee has probably identified the squadron as British because Algeria is not anticipating the arrival of the United States Navy. Decatur's instincts prove true. He instructs Lewis: "Do nothing to excite suspicion; she lies well as she is now." Nevertheless, Decatur's attempt to totally surprise the enemy ship gets foiled when the USS *Constellation* prematurely hoists the Stars and Stripes. An attempt to fix the mistake is quickly unfolded. Decatur raises the British ensign on the *Guerriere* and the other ships also hoist the British flag. The Algerians on the warship, however, realize the Americans are at their doorstep.

The frigate *Mashuda*, commanded by Admiral Rais Hammida, tries to evade the squadron by running toward safety at Algiers. The *Mashuda* seemingly begins to fly; however, the USS *Constellation*, only about one mile away and the closest to the pirates, gives chase. Other vessels trailing closely join in the hunt to intercept the *Mashuda* before it reaches port. The *Epervier*, *Guerriere*, and the *Ontario*, the only ships close enough to support the *Constellation*, race toward the enemy ship. The *Constellation* closes the gap and begins to fire. The *Mashuda* returns fire as it runs. Nonetheless, the barrage from the *Constellation* proves sufficiently effective to prompt the Algerians to modify their escape course. Admiral Hammida, convinced that his fate is sealed if he tries to make it to Algiers, instead moves toward the Spanish coast.

During the maneuver to change course, the *Mashuda* sails directly toward the *Ontario*. In response, the *Ontario* passes within about one-quarter mile of the *Mashuda*'s bow, while the other American ships had altered their courses and arrive on scene. The *Guerriere* moves into position between the *Constellation* on the starboard and the *Epervier* on its larboard. The *Guerriere* defiantly moves into close range and sustains musket fire that inflicts several casualties. Decatur remains aware of the wounded; however, he defies the fire and moves in closer, then unleashes a deadly broadside that inflicts horrific devastation.

The effective fire is immediately followed by another powerful broadside. Admiral Hammida had already been killed. He had suffered a wound from a shot fired by the *Constellation*, but at the time of the first broadside, Admiral Hammida was sitting in a chair on the quarter-deck, which had him elevated so he could observe from above the rail. He was split in half by a 42-pound shell. Other officers had also been killed, but the second broadside terminates the contest. The crew, having lost its commanders, also lose heart and the will to continue. They abandon their battle stations and try to escape by hiding in the hull. Some of the crew continue to resist, but in vain, despite their loyalty. Marines and sailors aboard the *Guerriere* liquidate them quickly. Nonetheless, the Algerians fail to signal the surrender of the ship.

Although the Algerians fail to strike the colors, Commodore Decatur senses the immense devastation and he orders the *Guerriere* to cease fire. He maneuvers the *Guerriere* into position from which a boarding party can take possession of the prize. During the maneuver, a gun on the main deck of the *Guerriere* explodes, causing some confusion. At the same time, the *Epervier* arrives on the starboard quarter of the *Mashuda* and the *Guerriere* is no longer between it and the *Mashuda*. The *Epervier* observes suspicious activity on the *Mashuda*, when its helm is raised as if making another attempt to escape. The commander of the *Epervier* and his crew rush into action to take on the 46-gun *Mashuda*. Downes' 16-gun brigantine opens fire and immediately receives fire from the *Mashuda*; however, Downes' skills overcome the deficiency in fire power and his crew delivers nine consecutive broadsides that pulverize the *Mashuda*.

Finally, the Americans spot the signal that it had surrendered. Decatur delegates Captain Lewis to lead the boarding party to gain possession of the *Mashuda*. Two other officers, Midshipmen Hoffman (Decatur's aide) and Howell, accompany the party. The scene aboard the prize gruesome. Admiral Hammida's body is splattered about along with thirty other crewmen. Four hundred and six others remain alive and are taken prisoner. In contrast, the *Guerriere* sustains four wounded from the initial musket fire and of those, one died of his wounds. In addition, three others are killed and seven wounded when the gun of the *Guerriere* exploded. The *Mashuda*, under guard by the USS *Macedonian*, is taken to Cartagena.

On the following day, Commodore Decatur summons the captains of the squadron to his flagship. Upon their arrival, the officers move to Decatur's quarters, where he had arranged souvenirs of war on a table. They included "cimeters, attaghans, and Turkish daggers and pistols." He invites the officers to choose for themselves; however, he suggests that Captain Downes should get first choice due to his spectacular leadership on the *Epervier*. Subsequently, Commodore Decatur sails eastward to cruise along the coast of Spain to search for and destroy or capture the remainder of the Algerian squadron. Decatur believes that two frigates and a few smaller ships are still operating in that area.

Two days later (19 June), Decatur encounters another pirate ship off the coast. He strikes quickly and effortlessly destroys the vessel *Estedio*. Once the *Estedio* is eliminated, Decatur sets his sights on Algiers, and his intent is to reach the troublesome city before the remnant Algerian fleet can arrive there to ensure that his squadron can intercept it and either capture or destroy them before they can enter the port. While en route, Decatur holds a council with his officers to detail his master plan which calls for a full scale attack designed to destroy the shipping and the city's batteries if the dey fails to accept his terms. The squadron arrives at Algiers in late June.

June 20 (Tuesday) *In naval activity,* Commodore Decatur's squadron, having eliminated two Algerian warships, arrives at Algiers to demand the dey sign a treaty that will be upheld. The last time Decatur was in the harbor of Tripoli to do battle was when he ventured in and fired the captured USS *Philadelphia*. This time the Yankee warships glide in unhurriedly and announce their arrival, stating they bring guns instead of money, and it will be absolute pleasure for the Navy to level the city of Omar, Son of Mohammed the Conqueror and Great, unless the Americans being held captive are released immediately.

The *Guerriere* holds the point when the squadron comes into view. The warship is flying a white flag, and it also has the Swedish colors flying as a sign that the Americans seek to communicate with the Swedish consul, Mr. Norderling. An American diplomat, Mr. Shaler, is aboard the USS *Guerriere*. At about noon on the 29th, a party from Algiers arrives alongside the *Guerriere* and the men, including Norderling and the Algerian captain of the port, are invited to board. During the meeting, Commodore Decatur asks the port captain about the location of their fleet and receives the response, "By this time it is safe in some neutral port." Decatur retorts: "Not the whole of it," to the surprised captain, who is then informed of the fate of the *Mashuda* and the *Estedio*, along with the demise of Admiral Hammida. The captain is in disbelief until a captive lieutenant still aboard the *Guerriere* is brought forward to confirm what Decatur had stated.

The port captain immediately loses his confidence and concentrates on the fate of Algiers. He inquires what is necessary to consummate a treaty with the United States. The response further deflates the captain's confidence, as he is informed that Algiers must cease any thoughts of tribute and all American prisoners must be released to the squadron. The American representatives also hand the port captain a letter from President Madison that explains the choices for Algiers, either war or peace, and the president's statement makes it clear that the squadron had arrived to enforce the war option if that is what Algiers chooses. Another element of the letter makes it emphatically clear that the representatives, William Shaler and Commodores William Bainbridge and Stephen Decatur, had been authorized to conclude the treaty. The captain also receives a similar letter signed by the American representatives.

After accepting the letters, the captain of the port attempts to stall negotiations to permit time for the Algerian fleet to return, but the tactic is immediately detected and rebuffed. He also tries to convince the representatives to debark and under a pledge of security to conduct the talks in Algiers and that proposal is also declined. Afterward, the Swedish consul and the captain of the port return to the city. On the following day (30 June), both men return to the *Guerriere*, and they are euphoric as they explain that they are authorized to consummate a treaty. Nonetheless, the terms, particularly that Algiers must return all American property they had plundered, are found objectionable. Other terms insist upon the release of all Christians being held by the Muslim pirates and yet another term demands that "in case of war, citizens and subjects should mutually be allowed to embark with their effects; and should any prisoners of either country be captured by the cruisers of the other, they should not be made slaves, nor forced to hard labor, or confined beyond what might be necessary to secure their safe keeping, until exchanged; that if any of the Barbary States, or other powers at war with the United States, should send any American vessel as a prize into an Algerine port, such prize should not be allowed to be sold there, but compelled to depart after receiving necessary refreshments; but vessels of war of the United States should be allowed to resort to the Algerine ports with their prizes, and to sell them there."

The Algerians seek other stall tactics and claim that the dey who declared war against the United States was Hadji Ali (The Tiger); rather than the present dey, and the Algerians proclaim that The Tiger had been assassinated on 23 March. Furthermore, the Algerians proclaim that his successor, the prime minister, was executed on 8 April. They essentially plead the case for the present dey, Omar Pacha, but to no avail. The Americans refuse to consider any modifications to the treaty. Still, the Algerians try to stall by suggesting a truce until the treaty is finalized, only to again be find their proposal rejected.

A proposal to hold off for three hours is also rejected with the following response: "Not a minute; if your squadron appears in sight before the treaty is actually signed by the dey, and sent off with the American prisoners, ours [squadron] will capture it." However, the Americans agree that if the treaty is signed and all American prisoners are aboard boats that are returning to the *Guerriere*, they would not fire. In the meantime, an Algerian warship is spotted as it nears the harbor. Decatur prepares to capture the ship, but he also spots a boat moving toward his flagship and it is flying a white flag, which causes him to suspend action against the approaching pirate vessel. The captain of the port arrives with the signed treaty within the specified three hours. Decatur verifies that the treaty is signed. He also inquires: "Are the prisoners in the boat?" He receives the response, "They are." Nonetheless, Decatur again inquires, "Every one of them?" and he receives an affirmative answer. Decatur ends the war, and to the jubilation of more than 500 American captives, they are freed by the commodore and reunited with their American flag.

The American consul arrives in Algiers on the 30th and the treaty is finalized. The dey makes available $10,000 in payment for the brigantine *Edwin* and its cargo earlier seized by the pirates. Some remarks are delivered the English consul just after the treaty is consummated, regarding Britain's involvement with the Algerians' declaration of war against the Americans. The dey's prime minister, speaking to the British consul, states: "You told us that the Americans would be swept from the seas in six months by your navy, and now they make war upon us with some of your own vessels, which they have taken." Commodore Stephen Decatur and his squadron had successfully completed the mission within forty-one days after leaving America's waters.

The dey, Omar, had difficulty believing that no money would be forthcoming; however, after some verification, he realized his navy had been obliterated and that his palace was the next target. The brigantine USS *Edwin* and its crew members, captured during the war with Britain, were instantly released. The pirates were so relieved that they could give back their American captives that the generous dey gave the Americans pouches full of gold and the treaty to boot, ending tribute payments to Algiers on 30 June 1815. The Stars and Stripes sails unhampered in the Mediterranean, thanks to Decatur and the navy.

The brigantine USS *Saranac*, originally laid down during the previous year but not completed before the close of hostilities, sailed from New York as part of Commodore Stephen Decatur's squadron, one of two squadrons being dispatched to the Mediterranean to deal with the Barbary pirates at Algiers. The privateer *Spark*, a brigantine, built at Sackets Harbor during 1813 and acquired by the U.S. Navy during 1814 at Baltimore, also sailed with Decatur's squadron. Lt. Thomas Gamble received command of the *Spark*. Initially it was scheduled for service on the Lakes; however, hostilities ceased before the *Spark* was sent to sea. The *Spark* returns to the States on 6 October with Commodore William Bainbridge's squadron. The *Spark* remains in active service until 1825. The schooner *Torch*, previously a privateer, had been acquired by the navy during 1814 at Baltimore, but hostilities had ceased before it got to sea. Subsequent to this campaign, the *Torch* returns to the United States, where it remains until sold during April 1816.

June 24 (Saturday) **In Pennsylvania**, the resignation of Major General John Phillips, commander of the 16th Division (militia), is accepted by the governor. He is succeeded by Charles Martin.

June 30 (Friday) *In naval activity,* the USS *Peacock*, operating in the Straits of Sundra between Java and Sumatra, encounters the 14-gun *Nautilus*, a ship attached to the East India Company. Once contact is made, the British inform Captain Warrington of the *Peacock* that the war is over and a treaty had been signed in Ghent, Belgium. Nonetheless, Warrington is skeptical and believes it British mischief. He demands that the *Nautilus* lower its colors. The British reject the ultimatum and the *Peacock* delivers a broadside that kills or wounds 15. The Americans board the *Nautilus* and to his embarrassment, he discovers that the British had not tried to fool him and that the war really is over. The *Peacock*,

Captain Lewis Warrington.

however, sailing alone, had never received word of the termination of the hostilities. Captain Warrington immediately releases the *Nautilus*, then sets his course for the United States. The *Peacock* arrives in New York on 30 October 1815.

During the following year, an official court of inquiry convenes and at its conclusion, it is determined that Captain Warrington had been totally blameless. The *Peacock* continues in service until July 1841, when it is wrecked in the Pacific Northwest. The *Peacock* gets tossed upon a reef by the surf while trying to cross the bar at the mouth of the Columbia River on the 17th. All attempts to save it fail. The crew escapes harm and important documents are also saved; however, by the morning of the 20th, the *Peacock* sinks.

July 3 (Monday) *In naval activity,* the USS *Independence*, at the head of the first contingent of Commodore Bainbridge's squadron, sails from Boston en route to the Mediterranean. Decatur's squadron joins Bainbridge at Gibraltar on 13 September. Commodore Bainbridge, during his time as commander at the Boston Navy Yard, could not get the *Independence* to sea before the war ended.

The USS *Lynx*, built the previous year but not completed until after the war had ended, heads for the sea this day. The *Lynx* sails out of Boston as part of the nine-ship squadron under Commodore William Bainbridge. The squadron is en route to the Mediterranean to terminate the ongoing interference with U.S. shipping by the Barbary Coast pirates. The *Lynx* remains in active service until January 1820, when it comes to a mysterious and tragic end. The *Lynx* departs St. Mary's, Georgia, on 11 January 1820, en route to Kingston, Jamaica. The *Lynx* and its crew of 50 men vanishes and is never heard from again.

July 14 (Friday) *In naval activity,* the USS *Epervier* is en route from the Mediterranean to the United States on a mission to deliver a copy of the treaty gained by Commodore Stephen Decatur with Algiers. The *Epervier* is also carrying flags captured from the now non-existent navy of the dey of Algiers. Once the *Epervier* moves through the Straits of Gibraltar, it vanishes without a trace. The entire crew, 132 sailors and two Marines, is never heard from again.

Lt. Thomas T. Shubrick, the commander, initially entered the navy during 1806. He was aboard the USS *Chesapeake* when it was compelled to strike its colors by the HMS *Leopard* in June 1807. Afterward, he served aboard the *Argus* and the *United States*, the latter during 1810. However, shortly after transferring to the *United States*, Shubrick refused to acquiesce to Captain Decatur to agree not to fight a duel with another officer. Decatur had intervened to halt the first duel. Shubrick is transferred to the *Viper*, which permitted Decatur to keep him with the squadron. During early 1812, Shubrick was commissioned a lieutenant and assigned to the *Constitution*. During the contest against the *Guerriere*, 80 men were wounded, but Shubrick, who commanded the guns on the quarterdeck, was unscathed. Later during the fight with the *Java*, again Shubrick escaped injury. On the *Hornet*, Shubrick evaded injury. He inadvertently built a reputation for bringing luck to any ship on which he served. His luck continued while on board the *United States* and again on the USS *President*, again under Decatur. On 15 January 1815, the *United States* was captured by the British, and during the fight, three other lieutenants were killed and Decatur was wounded, yet Shubrick was unhurt. After being held a short time, Shubrick and the others were released.

He received command of the USS *Guerriere* and sailed with Decatur to Algiers. During a contest with an Algerian warship, a gun aboard the *Guerriere* exploded and still Shubrick's extraordinary luck continued. He was unhurt; however, a gun fragment shot through his hat. Although the British were unable to wound the lieutenant, he could not evade the tragedy of a hurricane. He was en route to deliver the copy of the treaty; however, he was also anxious to rejoin his wife, whom he had married just before his squadron sailed. Two other officers, both married at about the same time as Shubrick, Captain Lewis (of the *Guerriere*) and Lieutenant Benedict J. Neale, also lost their lives on that fatal voyage.

July 15 (Saturday) *In naval activity,* Commodore Decatur, still operating in the Mediterranean, arrives at Cagliari on the southern tip of Sardinia after sailing from Algiers. Decatur had decided his crew required some rest. Decatur's orders to subdue Algiers had been completed in record time. Despite no direct orders regarding Tunis and Tripoli, he had learned that both countries had been in violation of treaties with the United States, and he intends to use his squadron to terminate their hostile actions. The squadron remains in port until 25 June, when it heads for Tunis. The squadron arrives in the Bay of Tunis on the 26th.

July 26 (Wednesday) *In naval activity,* Commodore Decatur's squadron arrives off Tunis. It anchors in a conspicuous spot to underscore the American intent to compel Tunis to adhere to the treaty it had earlier signed with the United States. Tunis, a neutral port during the late war between the U.S. and Great Britain, had permitted the British to enter the port and capture two prizes that had been taken into that port by the American privateer *Abellino*. The value placed on the two vessels was $46,000. Decatur dispatches a party with instructions to seek out the American consul (M.M. Noah) to enlist his assistance in convincing the bey to pay that amount. The party is also carrying an ultimatum stating that if the amount is not paid within twelve hours, the naval squadron will bombard the city. During the meeting with the bey, he instructs the consul to tell Decatur to land and come to his palace. The consul then informs the bey that Decatur will not come until the debt is settled, and the matter is to be settled aboard ship. The bey responds: "I know that admiral; he is the same one who, in the war with Sidi Yusef of Trablis burnt the frigate [*Philadelphia*]." As the conversation continues, the bey implies that Americans lie: "You went to war with England, a nation with a great fleet, and said you took their frigates in equal fight. Honest people always speak truth."

Nevertheless, the consul immediately responds by telling the bey that it was a truthful statement, just as he directs the bey's eyes offshore toward the *Guerriere*, the *Macedonian* and the *Peacock*, while informing him that they had been in the Royal Navy until captured by the United States. After peering through an eyeglass and scanning the bay, the bey discovers British warships flying the Stars and Stripes. He slips back to some cushions where he sits down and begins to comb his beard. After some pondering, the bey concludes that he will pay the debt, but not until the end of the year. In the meantime, Decatur, dressed in sailor's garb, had approached shore in a boat. He determined that the place was difficult to approach and that it was heavily defended, by vessels in the harbor and batteries. Nonetheless, Decatur begins to prepare his attack. The delayed payment is declined and the bey decides to pay immediately. Commodore Decatur lands, and while he is in conversation with the British consul, the money is delivered to satisfy the debt for the two prizes of the privateer *Abellino*.

Decatur's visit, similarly to his visit to Algiers, brings an end to Tunis' hostile actions against the U.S. Stephen Decatur's American armada convinces Tunis to sign an agreement similar to that signed by the dey of Algiers, ending tribute to that country also. Decatur's squadron departs from Tunis for Tripoli on 2 August.

August 2 (Wednesday) *In naval activity,* Commodore Decatur's squadron sails from Tunis en route to Tripoli to compel that nation to adhere to their treaty with the United States and to terminate their piracy against U.S. shipping. The squadron arrives on 5 August. In what had become a pattern, Tripoli, similarly to Algiers and Tunis, had permitted Britain to disregard the neutrality of its port to seize two vessels that had been taken there by the American privateer *Albellino*. The British had informed the bashaw that the Royal Navy would quickly eliminate the United States as a naval power. Nevertheless, the British consul in Tripoli has no explanation for the arrival of Decatur's squadron, which includes several former British naval vessels.

After arriving in the harbor, Decatur issues an ultimatum that demands payment of $30,000 in payment for the loss of the two vessels. He also demands that the American flag be re-hoisted at the American consul in conjunction with a 31-gun salute fired from the castle of the bashaw. The bashaw is unimpressed by the threat. Rather than acquiesce, he assembles a huge force, including about 20,000 Arabs. He also returns the threat by claiming he is prepared to declare war against the United States. Nevertheless, before he proclaims his declaration, the bashaw is informed of Decatur's recent visits to Algiers and Tunis, which causes an instantaneous change of heart. The bashaw dispatches the governor of Tripoli to meet with Commodore Decatur aboard the *Guerriere*. The American consul informs Decatur that the bashaw has agreed to pay $25,000. Decatur responds by instructing the consul to inform the bashaw that he would accept $25,000 on the condition that he include the release of ten Christian slaves.

Decatur's demand is met. Two Danish youths

and eight Sicilians (one family, husband, wife and children) are released. The Muslim pirates have been capturing Christians to be used as slaves for centuries. It is a moment of great jubilation for those Christians who expected to be captives for the remainder of their lives. They are expeditiously taken aboard the *Guerriere*. Commodore Decatur, however, had not forgotten the remainder of his demands. The American flag is rehoisted at the American consul and it is not done without fanfare. The *Guerriere*'s band debarks and marches to the consul and enthusiastically breaks out with the tune "Hail Columbia," while the guns of the palace serenade the flag-raising with a 31-gun salute. Commodore Decatur and his entire squadron are responsible for regaining the honor of the Stars and Stripes on 7 August, while simultaneously persuading Tripoli to honor their treaty and restoring peace between Tripoli and the United States.

It had been 71 days since the squadron sailed from New York. In that time, the United States Navy had subdued Algiers, Tunis and Tripoli and compelled each of them to sue for peace, while forcing them to terminate their piracy against U.S. shipping. Commodore Stephen Decatur later states: "I trust that the successful result of our small expedition, so honorable to our country, will induce other nations to follow the example, in which case the Barbary States will be compelled to abandon their piratical system." Subsequent to his triumph, Decatur departs from Tripoli on 9 August. The squadron sails toward a friendly port and arrives at Syracuse on 12 August; however, due to a quarantine, the crew is unable to go ashore. On 15 August, after receiving fresh water and supplies, the squadron heads for Sicily and arrives off Messina on the 20th. Upon his arrival, a pilot comes aboard the *Guerriere*; however, due to the unruly winds, he refuses to guide the ship into the harbor. Decatur, however, is determined to enter the port. He excuses Captain Downes from the responsibility and takes over, first by verifying the accuracy of the chart. Once the fearful pilot concurs with its accuracy, Decatur personally moves the vessel into port, where the crew is well received. The return of the family that had been seized as slaves startles the townspeople, who greet them as if they had returned from the dead. The Sicilians, who have been perpetually victimized by the pirates, are elated. They praise Decatur and call him the "Champion of Christendom."

August 5 (Saturday) *In naval activity,* the USS *Java*, under command of Commodore Oliver Hazard Perry, leaves Baltimore. It pauses at Hampton Roads and New York to acquire additional rigging before moving to Newport, Rhode Island, where it acquires the remainder of its view. Construction had been initiated during the previous year, but not completed until after the close of hostilities. The USS *Java* is separate from the HMS *Java* captured and later destroyed by the USS *Constitution* off Brazil during 29 December 1812; however, it is named in honor of that victory by Commodore Bainbridge.

August 7 (Monday) The naval squadron under Stephen Decatur secures a treaty with Tripoli, ending their piracy of American vessels. At about the same time, Commodore Bainbridge arrives in the Mediterranean. Finding that hostilities had ended, he pens a letter to the secretary of the Navy: "Peace having taken place with the regency of Algiers, it only now remains for me to obey your instructions, by exhibiting the squadron off Tunis and Tripoli, and by leaving one frigate and two smaller vessels near the Gulf of Gibraltar, and then return to Newport, with the remainder of the squadron, where I shall expect to arrive some time in November next." During 1816, the dey sends an eloquent blackmail letter to the president of the United States, James Madison, insisting on reinstating the old terms of paying tribute. The letter, dated 24 April 1816, reaches the White House, infuriating and amusing the president. The request states that the Algerians did not actually see Stephen Decatur in their country so it could be said that President Madison did cooperate with a portion of the demand by not sending him. In his stead, Commodore Chauncey, the 74-gun ship-of-the-line USS *Washington* and an escort are sent to insure the treaty of 1815 is kept by the Algerians. The American warships arrive off Algiers and need fire not one shot. Warships from Britain and Holland have virtually destroyed the city. The gregarious dey ends his piracy, promises no more of it and assures Commodore Chauncey that the treaty is in effect.

September *In naval activity,* Commodore John Shaw, prevented from getting to sea from the Thames River in Connecticut, since spring 1814, finally departs. He is aboard the USS *United States* bound for the Mediterranean. Later, when Commodore Bainbridge returns to the U.S., Shaw receives command of the squadron. Subsequently, he is relieved by Commodore Chauncey. Shaw returns to the United States aboard the USS *Constellation* during November 1817. Upon his return home, Shaw receives command of the Boston Navy Yard followed by command of the Charleston Navy Yard. He dies during September 1823 during a visit to Philadelphia.

October In Florida and Alabama, although the war with the Creeks had terminated the previous year and the War of 1812 had also ceased, some British still in the vicinity of Pensacola continue to work against the Americans by provoking Indians. Again the frontier between Fort Mitchell and Fort Jackson comes under harassment by Creeks still in the area.

October 6 (Friday) *In naval activity,* following a successful coordinated effort with commodore Stephen Decatur to establish the Mediterranean Squadron, Commodore Bainbridge returns to the United States. Captain Shaw receives command of the Mediterranean Squadron. While en route, the *Independence* pauses at Malaga and a seamen deserts. He is captured but claims to be a Spanish citizen. He is taken to the headquarters of the general of Marine. Once informed, Bainbridge moves to see the governor, who sends him to the general of marine. Both men decline Bainbridge's demand that the seaman be returned. Commodore Bainbridge becomes irritated. After returning to see the governor, Bainbridge makes it clear that because the Spanish government is protecting a seaman and not a private citizen, it is an insult to the American flag. Bainbridge gives the governor one-half hour to return the deserter to the *Independence*, and if he is not returned, Bainbridge informs the governor that 500 men will debark and seize the deserter. He also cautions the governor that if his contingent encounters resistance, the naval guns will commence firing upon the town. Shortly thereafter, a detachment of Spanish troops arrive to transfer the deserter. Captain Bainbridge departs for Gibraltar. Bainbridge's command arrives at Newport, Rhode Island, on 15 November 1815.

One of the warships that returns to the States, the *Saranac*, is decommissioned on 12 December 1818 and afterward condemned. It is later sold at New York City. Commodore Bainbridge continues in the service at various posts, including the president of the board of navy commissions, a position he received from the president upon the resignation of Commodore Rodgers. In 1831, Commodore Bainbridge is superceded by another officer by Mr. Branch, secretary of the Navy, an unexpected and unjustified action. By that time, Bainbridge, having moved his family 26 times and had decided that there would be no more moves. Nevertheless, during autumn 1832, Bainbridge is restored to command by President Andrew Jackson through the new secretary of the Navy, Mr. Woodbury. While his family remains in Philadelphia, Bainbridge repairs to his new command, the Boston Navy Yard. Nonetheless, his health deteriorates. During January 1833, he becomes ill from pneumonia and in March he is compelled to return to Philadelphia. He dies July 28.

He is survived by his wife and four daughters (his only son predeceased him). He is interred on 31 July at Christ Church in Philadelphia. His remains are escorted by a contingent of United States Marines and a brigade of U.S. infantry commanded by Colonel Watmough.

1816

In Alabama, Fort Crawford is established in Escambia County upon orders by General Andrew Jackson. The fort, manned by Alabama militia and units of the U.S. 7th Infantry Regiment, is used to observe Spanish operations in West Florida. It is deactivated the next year.

In Georgia, a contingent of the 4th U.S. Infantry led by Lt. Colonel (later brigadier general) Duncan L. Clinch establishes positions southwest of Lake Seminole in Decatur County. The encampment, named Camp Crawford, is fortified during September and renamed Fort Scott. Troops from Fort Scott are dispatched during July to destroy a fort in Florida, known as "Negro Fort," due to frequent raids upon settlers from the Negroes and Indians there.

In Illinois, Fort Armstrong is established at Rock Island. The fort is manned by the army until 1836. After that, the Illinois militia maintains a presence there until 1845. Also, Fort Handy is built in the vicinity of West Union in Clark County near the French Fort Creve Coeur, the first French fort in Illinois, built during 1680.

In Louisiana, Fort Selden is established in Natchitoches Parish. Troops occupy it from 1816 to 1817, and later it is again occupied from 1819 through 1822. The troops receive responsibility for protecting the area near Bayou Pierre and the Red River as well as the southwestern frontier.

In Virginia, the Bellona Arsenal is established in central Virginia near Richmond along the James River on Old Gun Road near the Huguenot bridge. It remains in operation until about 1837, but later during the Civil War, the Confederate States acquire it.

In Wisconsin, Fort Howard is established near the mouth of the Fox River at Green Bay.

Spring In Kansas, a large force of Pawnee Indians attacks a party of hunters along the Arkansas River on an island later known as Chouteau's Island. Despite the odds, the hunters repel the assault. One is killed during the attack.

April The USS *Boxer*, a brigantine, intercepts a pirate ship, the *Comet*. Marines and sailors capture the vessel.

April 24 (Wednesday) Thomas Jefferson writes to DuPont de Nemours: "Enlighten the people generally and tyranny and oppression of body and mind will vanish like evil spirits at the dawn of day."

June 30 (Sunday) At this time the active duty strength of the U.S. Marine Corps stands at 472 men, including twenty-one officers and 451 enlisted men.

July 27 to August 26 In Florida, the U.S. sends troops from Fort Scott at Chattahoochee under Colonel (later general) George Lamont Clinch of Georgia to destroy Fort Apalachiola (known as Negro Fort). It was established the previous year by British Captain Woodbine, who claimed to represent the forces in Florida of the king of England. Woodbine is harboring slaves and hostile Indians. Marines, serving aboard the gunboats No. 149 and 154, participate in the capture and destruction of the fort on 26 August. Captain Zachary Taylor (later general and president) participates in this expedition. During the assault, a shell strikes a magazine within the fort. It causes a huge explosion that kills many, including women and children. During 1818, the army constructs Fort Gadsden at this site.

August 27 (Tuesday) There are no hostilities between the United States and Spain, but Spanish guns from an armada off the coast of Vera Cruz commence firing on the American vessel *Firebrand* as it sails past the Spanish fleet.

September The cadets at West Point receive gray uniforms to honor the regulars who had worn gray at the battles of Chippewa and Lundy's Lane. West Point still wears these colored uniforms and its cadets are referred to as "The Long Gray Line."

September 14 (Saturday) In Georgia, a treaty is agreed upon between the United States and the Cherokee at the Chickasaw Council House. Sequoyah and fourteen others represent the Cherokee. U.S. representatives include General Andrew Jackson, General David Meriwether (Georgia militia), General David Adams (Georgia militia) and Jesse Franklin. The treaty is ratified by the entire Cherokee nation on 4 October at Turkey Town. Cherokee chiefs and warriors who sign are Richard Brown, Chickasawlua, Chulioa, Dick Justice, Path Killer, The Boot and The Glass.

Autumn In Oregon, some hostilities break out between the Indians and a group of trappers when the Indians demand that the fur trappers abandon what they considered their lands; however, the ultimatum is disregarded and a fight ensues. After the skirmish the trappers move to Fort George (Astoria Post).

December In Georgia, Fort Scott in the southwestern part of Decatur County is evacuated. Consequently, hostile Seminoles and Red Sticks (Creeks) plunder the fort.

December 11 (Wednesday) Indiana is admitted to the Union as the 19th state.

BIOGRAPHIES OF GENERAL OFFICERS

Adair, Major General John John, the son of Baron William and Mary Moore Adair, was born in Chester County, South Carolina, on 9 January 1757. John's parents were Scottish immigrants. He attended school in Charlotte, North Carolina, then entered the state militia during the American Revolution. He was captured by the British and subjected to some harsh treatment while incarcerated. After the revolution, John married Katherine Palmer during 1784. They had twelve children, and of those, ten were daughters.

During 1786 or 1787, John settled in Mercer County, Kentucky. He served in the Kentucky military, initially as a captain under St. Clair, and later he received the rank of lieutenant colonel while serving under General Charles Scott. He also entered politics. He was elected as a state representative and served for a period of eight years between 1793 and 1803 (1793–1795, 1798, and 1800–1803). He also served as a delegate to the Kentucky state constitutional conventions (1792 and 1799), along with being the speaker of the House in 1802 and 1803. Kentucky entered the Union on 1 June 1792.

During the hostilities that ensued along the Northwestern Frontier (Northwest Territory), Adair participated as an officer in the mounted infantry under General Arthur St. Clair. On 6 November 1792, a band of Indians led by Chief Little Turtle attacked the encampment near recently established Fort St. Clair (twenty miles south of Greenville, Ohio). Major Adair's command participated in the battle and the attackers were met with great tenacity. Adair moved to turn the Indians' flanks. He ordered Lt. George Madison to strike the right flank, but Lt. Hall, directed by Adair to strike the left flank, had been killed. Adair led the attack himself. The effective pressure drove the Indians out of the camp; however, at a point about 600 yards distant, the Indians regrouped to ignite another furious battle. The Indians pressed Adair's right flank. About 60 warriors drove forward, but Adair, sensing the precariousness of his positions, ordered a disciplined retreat. The Americans regrouped and formed a solid line at the camp. Nonetheless, the Indians crashed into the defensive line to cause yet another violent contest. After a period of tenacious fighting, the Indians, having sustained severe casualties, were compelled to retire. Adair's contingent sustained six killed, five wounded and four missing. Lt. Madison and Colonel Richard Taylor were among the wounded.

Adair was raised to brevet brigadier general during 1797 and to major general during 1799. Later, Major Adair was appointed register of the U.S. land office in Frankfort, Kentucky, and served in that capacity in 1805–1806. During his term as register, Adair met with Little Turtle, who was passing through Frankfort with a large party of Indians, accompanied by Captain William Welle, Indian agent. During their meeting, General Adair mentioned that he had been defeated by Little Turtle because he had been surprised. Little Turtle retorted, saying: "A good general is never taken by surprise." General Adair was also caught up in the Aaron Burr conspiracy, due to accusations made by General James Wilkinson, himself considered a co-conspirator. The allegations caused great harm to Adair's reputation. Consequently, he was viewed by some with high suspicion; however, as time passed, it became more clear that Adair's actions as well as his opinions were founded on the belief that plans of Burr had been condoned by the government, which was at the time was preparing for war with Spain. Adair, who was ordered arrested by Wilkinson when he arrived in New Orleans, was later cleared of having done anything wrong or illegal. General Wilkinson was directed to issue an apology to Adair and pay him damages. Nonetheless, due to the incident, Adair remained out of public life for about ten years.

Adair was elected to the U.S. Senate to complete the term of John Breckinridge, who resigned his seat to become the U.S. attorney general. Adair, elected as a Democratic-Republican, served in the Senate from 8 November 1805 to 18 November 1806. He failed to win a full term. During the War of 1812, General Adair participated in the campaign in which General Isaac Shelby moved into Ohio to join with General William Henry Harrison's Canadian campaign, which culminated with the victory at the Battle of the Thames in 1813. Adair's actions during the campaign were admirable, and he was afterward breveted brigadier general by Shelby, who also appointed Adair as adjutant general of the Kentucky troops. General Adair participated as commander of Kentucky troops at the Battle of New Orleans. One unintended consequence from that seminal victory was a running debate between Jackson, who accused the Kentuckians of cowardice during the fight, and Adair, who defended the actions of the Kentuckians.

Following the fighting at New Orleans, Adair's reputation was resurrected and he regained popularity. He again served in the Kentucky legislature during 1817. In 1820, Adair was elected eighth governor of Kentucky for a term of one year. He successfully achieved victory by running on a platform that promised relief to the Kentuckians, who suffered heavily during the Panic of 1819. Adair held the governor's post until 1824. Subsequently, during 1831, Adair, running as a Jacksonian, was elected to the U.S. House of Representatives, where he served from 4 March 1831 until 3 March 1833. He did not run for re-election.

General Adair retired and lived out his life on his estate in Harrodsburg, until his death at age 83 on 19 May 1840. He was interred on his estate, Whitehall. In 1872, he was re-interred in the state cemetery (Frankfort Cemetery) in Frankfort. The state of Kentucky later dedicated a monument in his honor within the grounds of the cemetery.

Adams, Brigadier General David David was born on 28 January 1766. He may have served in the military in a unit that was attached to General Henderson's command in South Carolina during the latter part of the American Revolution. However, based on his date of birth, it is more probable that the person who participated was a relative rather than David, who would have only been about fifteen years old. After the war, David's family relocated to Shoulder Bone Creek, Georgia. At the time, there was great turmoil in the region between the settlers on the frontier and the Creek Indians, the latter having been determined to rid the whites from their lands.

The settlers along the frontier joined together to construct blockhouses and forts to enable them to withstand what became incessant attacks. Still, the powerful Creeks were able to launch frequent attacks and establish innumerable ambushes that inflicted high casualties and often annihilated entire families. David Adams became a major in the Georgia militia. He was initially elected as major; however, his leadership ability became apparent while he acted as a scout for about ten years. The Georgia legislature elevated him to the rank of brigadier general, and afterward, he was appointed as a major general.

On 13 November 1813, General Adams ordered Brigadier General Blackshear to initiate a drive to enlist recruits to construct a series of blockhouses along the frontier. During 1814, Adams prepared to join with General Andrew Jackson's army in the campaign to terminate the Creek hostilities. The Americans pushed into Creek territory along the Tallapoosa River and began a dedicated effort to destroy the strongholds. The campaign culminated in victory at the Battle of Horseshoe Bend on 27 March 1814, when Jackson's force mauled the Indian force of about 1,000 warriors under Chief Menawa during a tenacious battle.

General Coffee, Chief William McIntosh (later brigadier general) and Sam Houston participated. In his after battle report, General Jackson estimated that "only about ten [warriors] had escaped." At Tohopeka, where the families of the warriors had remained during the battle, more than 300 women and children were seized. Before the fighting at Horseshoe Bend, General Adams' Georgian troops devastated the village of Newyaucau; however, Adams' force encountered difficulty at the river, which had flooded, preventing Adams from crossing to join in the primary battle. His force retired and encamped. Adams had ordered that no fires were to be started to ensure that the Creeks would not be able to estimate the size of his isolated command.

After the War of 1812, General Adams acted as a commissioner, along with General Jackson, General David Meriwether and Jesse Franklin, who successfully consummated a treaty with the Cherokee on 14 September 1816 at the Chickasaw Council House in Georgia. In 1820, he participated in concluding a treaty with the Creeks. In addition to his military service, General Adams had served in various civilian positions in the Georgia government, including more than 25 years in the state legislature. Details of his death are unknown. It is thought that General Adams died between 1830 and 1840.

Appleton, Brigadier General James James, the son of Samuel and Mary White Appleton, was born on 14 February 1785 at Ipswich, Massachusetts. He served in the Massachusetts legislature while still a young man. He served in the militia during the War of 1812 with the rank of colonel. At the conclusion of the war, he was appointed brigadier general. Later, Appleton relocated in Portland, Maine. He was elected in 1836 to the state legislature of Maine, where he served for one term. Appleton, a dedicated temperance reformer and an advocate for the end of slavery, ran unsuccessfully for governor. Afterward, he returned to Ipswich, where he died on 25 August 1862.

Armistead, Colonel George George, the son of John and Lucinda (Lucy) Baylor Armistead, was born in Virginia at New Market on 10 April 1780. John and Lucinda had eight other children, five boys and three girls. George joined the army as a 2nd lieutenant on 8 January 1799. On 1 November 1806, he was promoted to captain, followed by another promotion on 3 March 1813, when he became a major in the 3rd U.S. Artillery.

He participated in the campaign to capture Fort George in Canada during May 1813. In the meantime, he married Louisa Hughes of Baltimore on 26 October 1810. They had the following children: Mary (born December 1812, married John Bradford, died in 1885); Margaret Hughes Armistead (born September 1814 in Gettysburg, while her father was defending Fort McHenry, married Lewis Howell of New Jersey); Christopher Hughes Armistead (born April 1816); Georgiana Louisa Frances Gillis Armistead (born November 1817, married William Stuart Appleton, died July 1878).

During the summer of 1814, after the British captured and sacked the capital, they moved against Baltimore to launch a two-pronged assault. Major Armistead received the brevet of lieutenant colonel from President Madison after the decisive American victory for his extraordinary leadership. It was effective 12 September 1814. He remained tireless during the siege, and to taunt the British fleet, he ordered a huge flag to fly over the fort. In a letter to General Samuel Smith, commander at Baltimore, during the summer, Major Armistead stated: "We sir, are ready at Fort McHenry to defend Baltimore against invading by the enemy, and it is my desire to have a flag so large, that the British will have no difficulty seeing it from a distance." That flag was made famous by a lawyer, Francis Scott Key, who was aboard a British warship attempting to win the release of Doctor Beanes during the bombardment. He penned an untitled poem that later became known as "The Star Spangled Banner."

Despite the incessant bombardment, the naval attack also failed. The attack, which began on 11 September when the British fleet arrived off North Point, ended in failure on the 14th. Baltimore had been saved and in all probability Philadelphia and New York were also preserved because of the victory gained by the overall commander, General Samuel Smith, and Major Armistead. The British found that the militia at Baltimore were not going to provide the British army with a rerun of Bladensburg. The gallant victory took a high toll on Colonel Armistead. He developed a heart problem which took his life on 25 April 1818.

The citizens of Baltimore showered praise on Colonel Armistead after the victory, and citizens all along the Atlantic coast were relieved thanks to his heroic leadership, which they believed saved the East Coast from invasion. He was given a silver bowl, formed to resemble a British bombshell, along with goblets. Later, during 1882, a monument to honor Colonel Armistead was constructed on Federal Hill overlooking downtown Baltimore. Afterward, another monument in honor of the hero of Fort McHenry was built on the grounds in September 1914 when the city celebrated the Centennial of the Battle of Baltimore.

Confederate General Lewis Addison Armistead, born in North Carolina, was the son of brevet brigadier General Walker Keith Armistead and his wife, Elizabeth Stanley Armistead. He was also the nephew of Colonel George Armistead.

Barney, Commodore Joshua Joshua Barney was born in Baltimore, Maryland, on 6 July 1759. He received experience on the sea while still a teenager, and by the time hostilities broke out with Britain as the American Revolution was getting underway, Joshua sided with the Patriots. He became a crew member of the *Hornet* and participated in the mission of invading New Providence during February–March 1776, when Marines landed and confiscated military stores. Later, on his birthday, 6 July, he was appointed a lieutenant in the Continental Navy, following his actions while engaged against the British in Delaware Bay. He became executive officer on the captured vessel *Sachem* (formerly HMS *Edward*).

In spring 1777 he was stationed on the *Andrew Doria*, one of the vessels assigned to defend Philadelphia. He sailed on 23 October en route to St. Eustatius to pick up military supplies, and on the return trip, the *Andrew Doria* seized the 12-gun HMS *Racehorse* and a British snow, the *Thomas*. Barney was placed aboard the *Thomas* as prize master, but it never reached port. The British recaptured it on 4 January 1777. After being exchanged on 20 October 1777, Barney transferred to the *Virginia*, but almost immediately he was captured for the second time when the vessel ran aground in the Chesapeake Bay near Annapolis on 30–31 March 1778.

The captain of the *Virginia*, James Nicholson, abandoned the ship so fast that he left his trousers behind. Joshua Barney attempted to control the ship and maintain order among the crew, but many of them had become inebriated and Barney was overpowered by them before the ship was seized. Nicholson actually returned to the captured vessel under a white flag to request that his trousers be returned.

During August, Barney was again exchanged. Undaunted, he again went to sea, but yet again, while serving on a privateer in 1779, he became a temporary guest of the British. After being exchanged that year, he resumed his naval career. He served aboard the *Saratoga*, which was launched in 1780. During that tour of duty, while in charge of a prize, Barney was captured yet a fourth time; however, in retrospect, serving in a British prison saved his life. The *Saratoga* disappeared without a trace at some point beyond 18 March 1781.

The British, after seizing Barney, chose no exchange. He was transported to New York and for a while received good treatment, including being permitted to venture ashore with the stipulation that he had to return to the *Ardent* at night. But the British officer responsible for his fair treatment was transferred, leaving Barney to a different fate. He, seventy other officers and some enlisted men were squeezed aboard the *Yarmouth* in December 1780 and taken to England. During the voyage the officers were held in dungeon-like conditions, cramped in a space with a height of only three feet, and given putrid water and terrible food. No doctors were permitted to check on them, and before the ship reached England, following 53 days at sea, eleven officers had perished after losing their senses.

One of the officers who survived along with Barney was Silas Talbot. And for the others, the conditions were equally deplorable. The British informed them that they were to be hanged. About eleven men died en route to Mill prison in Plymouth. Nonetheless, the young and agile naval officer began to plan a daring escape. The British suspected Barney was a high risk, and for some time he was placed in solitary confinement, but rather than break his spirit, this made him more determined to break out, despite a double wall and high security.

Barney faked an injury and began to use crutches to lessen the scrutiny placed upon him. His ruse worked to perfection. While he hobbled about, he detailed in his mind how the security worked and in the process, by some luck, he encountered a British guard who had earlier been a captive of the Americans and, having been treated well, he naturally reciprocated, giving Barney the opportunity to befriend him. The guard condoned the escape. With the help of a few other Americans, the escape plan unfolded on 18 March 1781, while the guard had duty at the spot between the double wall.

The guard signaled "Dinner," meaning the jailers would be at dinner at 1300, leaving only sentinels on guard. While a few prisoners distracted the other guards in the yard, Barney passed by the friendly guard, then bolted upon a very tall American at the wall and catapulted to the top and from there landed to begin the great escape in the clothes of a British officer.

An Englishman, known to be an American sympathizer, was stunned to answer a knock at his door and discover a British officer, and he was more startled when he found out the Barney was an American escapee, knowing that harboring a prisoner could have gotten him hanged. Nevertheless, arrangements were made to conceal him temporarily, and then Barney was hurried to the man's father, a minister and friend of the Americans. All the while, the British had not yet discovered that Barney had been gone for a second day.

Under the pretense of being a fisherman, Barney was put aboard a vessel and still no alarm had been sounded as the craft moved past the British fleet. However, after the vessel reached the open sea, a privateer pulled alongside to question the men on the fishing boat. Barney discarded his fishing attire, donned his British uniform and met the officer from the privateer with great authority, demanding that the privateer let him pass due to a secret mission that could not be interrupted without great peril. The astute officer required proof and Barney continued his rant, exclaiming that he could not expose the mission, but he would be glad to head back to Admiral Digby for him to explain.

The officer was not too keen about that idea for fear the British Navy would press some of his crew in to service. Nonetheless, the officer insisted that they return to Plymouth. Still showing no signs of stress and continuing his impersonation of a British officer, Barney agreed, and both vessels moved toward port, reaching shore on the following morning. With Barney remaining aboard, still thought to be a British officer on a secret mission, the officer headed for Admiral Digby's fleet. In the meantime, Barney was able to grab a rope and slide down the vessel and into a boat, injuring himself in the process, but he made it to shore, and after a precarious encounter with a British customs officer, made it safely back to the house of the minister, where he met two other former prisoners (Colonel Richardson and Doctor Hindman). At about that time, Barney's ruse was discovered and the alarm was sounded. Barney remained at the minister's home without being discovered for several days, and from there he was again given assistance. Having changed his appearance and dress, his coach was permitted to pass through the gate of the town and proceed to Exeter.

From there, Barney continued his escape by riding a public stagecoach to Bristol and, still without being discovered, he was able to travel to London, bid it a fond farewell and sail to France. From there he went to Holland and boarded the privateer *South Carolina*. After a turbulent voyage, Barney and some others boarded the privateer *Cicero*, out of Beverly, Massachusetts. Finally, Barney completed his bold escape and reached America. At Boston, he met other Americans who had also escaped from Mill prison.

After his return to the U.S., Barney married Ann Bedford in 1781. He declined offers to command a privateer and traveled to Philadelphia, where he took command of the 16-gun *Hydor Alley* (armed by Pennsylvania) during March 1782. Although Lord Cornwallis had surrendered at Yorktown, Virginia, in October and the major fighting in the North had ended, Pennsylvania was concentrating on terminating the British privateers that had been operating on the Delaware River. On 8 April, Barney vanquished the HMS *General Monk* (formerly the *George Washington*) in Delaware Bay after a brief but tenacious battle that compelled the British to strike their colors. An accompanying privateer, the *Fair American*, offered no assistance to the *General Monk*. Congress promoted Lieutenant Barney to captain following the victory.

The *General Monk*, operating in the vicinity of the Delaware Capes since 1780, had devastated or captured about 60 vessels while under command of Captain Josiah Rodgers, until Barney knocked it from the British service. Barney became the commander of the prize, renamed the *General Washington*, and sailed for France during November 1782. Upon his return, he carried dispatches from Benjamin Franklin indicating the imminent termination of hostilities, following the recent signing of preliminary peace terms. Nonetheless, Barney seemed unable to lose his propensity for capture. During 1793, he again spent some time in captivity after being seized by the British on charges of piracy. Subsequently, Barney served as a captain in the service of France, coincidentally during the Quasi War with France, but he returned to the United States in 1800.

When war again erupted with Britain in 1812, Joshua Barney spent time as a privateer. His exploits in the *Rossie*, beginning on 15 July 1812 when he sailed from Chesapeake Bay, resulted in the seizure of 18 vessels; one was the HMS *Princess Amelia*. The successful cruise ended on the 21 November 1812.

After becoming aware of the British warships in the Chesapeake, Barney proposed on 4 July 1813 constructing a small fleet of gunboats that could be flexible enough to take on the Royal Navy's blockade of the Chesapeake Bay. His blueprint included gunboats that could also be rowed, to permit his men to navigate the rivers and outmaneuver the large warships. His blueprint was approved by William Jones, the secretary of the navy, making Barney's fleet a temporary part of the U.S. Navy. Consequently, Barney, who had retired after the American Revolution, was reactivated. He received the rank of commodore.

A naval battery at St. Leonard's Creek, Maryland, was established to protect the gunboats on the Patuxent River. The fleet was constructed and was activated at Baltimore during May 1814. The following month, Barney's squadron of 18 light-draft gunboats engaged the British, but soon after, the outmatched Americans disengaged and broke for the Patuxent River. On 8–10 June, the British, having failed to destroy Barney's squadron on the Chesapeake Bay, moved to destroy it at Leonard's Creek. Despite the unyielding pounding, Barney's squadron refused to capitulate and the British once again failed to eliminate the threat. Barney broke through the blockade and headed farther up the Patuxent River.

At Pig's Point on 22 August, Barney ordered the squadron—16 gunboats and 13 schooners, including Barney's sloop *Scorpion*—destroyed to prevent capture by the British. Barney afterward moved with his force to the defense of Bladensburg, where the British were pressing toward Washington.

At Bladensburg, the British introduced a new and mysterious weapon — rockets — that caused panic among the American defenders, most of whom were fresh troops with no experience. The Americans, numbering about 6,000 men against 2,600 of the enemy, deserted their positions and headed back to Washington, but without pause they kept moving into Virginia, leaving the capital without defense except for one battalion of U.S. Marines, who held their ground at Bladensburg, and the contingent of sailors under Captain Joshua Barney, which also was prepared to fight.

As it turned out, the British had not introduced a pernicious weapon; rather, they had catapulted pyrotechnics (fireworks) that exploded in midair but caused no harm. The ruse had not fooled either the Marines or Barney's men. The British attempted to overrun the thin line of Americans, but Captain Samuel Miller, U.S. Marine Corps, and his force held the line and inflicted more than 225 casualties upon the British. Finally, after two hours of preventing passage, the Marines and Barney's force withdrew. However, the time bought allowed President James Madison to get back to the White House and get his wife to safety. British General Robert Ross was able to move into Washington, but he failed to nab the president.

During the attack at Bladensburg, Captain Barney was wounded in the thigh, making it difficult to escape. He once again became a reluctant guest of the British, but he was soon released. The fighting at Bladensburg ended Captain Barney's service in the field; however, following his recuperation, Barney again took command of his squadron during October of 1814 and retained it until October of 1815, when it was deactivated. Although the British took Washington in the War of 1812 and burned parts of it, they were driven from the town, not by the American army; rather by a tremendous storm that terrified the British as much as their rockets had scared the Americans.

Captain Barney carried the ball that struck him in the thigh until his death. During 1815, he traveled to Europe, but he was compelled to cut his mission short due to his health. During 1818, Captain Barney had been in the process of relocating from Elkridge, Maryland, to Kentucky, but while traveling, he became seriously ill at Pittsburgh, Pennsylvania. He succumbed there on 1 December 1818.

Beall, Brigadier General Reasin Reasin was born in Maryland on 3 December 1769. While he was young, his family relocated to Washington County, Pennsylvania. In 1790, Reasin, having joined the army, served under General Harmar against the Indians on the frontier. After the ill-fated campaign, Reasin returned to Pennsylvania. He did not participate in General St. Clair's campaign; however, he did later serve with General Anthony Wayne. He resigned from the army while holding the rank of ensign in 1793, and after returning to Pennsylvania he married Rebecca Johnson.

During 1801, Beall relocated his family to Ohio, initially at Steubenville, and around 1803 he moved to New Lisbon (Columbiana County). By the time war with Britain erupted in June 1812, Beall had risen to the rank of brigadier general in the Ohio militia. Once General Beall was informed of the surrender of Detroit by General William Hull, he gathered his forces to advance and provide protection for settlements in Richland and Wayne Counties. The troops were attached to several regiments from Harrison and Jefferson Counties, along with another regiment from Columbiana and a contingent from Stark County.

The combined force made their rendezvous in Canton, then departed and advanced westwardly. During August, General Beall established a blockhouse at Wooster, and his camp there was known as Camp Christmas. While there, reinforcements, about three companies, joined Beall's force. Meanwhile, on 10 September, a band of Indians allied with the British attacked two families in Mifflin (Ashland County). Frederick Zimmer and his family along with a neighbor, Martin Ruffner, were killed. Nevertheless, troops attached to Beall's command were unable to locate the Indians, who vanished after the massacre.

A new camp, Camp Musser, was established in the northern sector of Vermillion Township. While the troops were there, an alarm was sounded and the men prepared to defend against an assault. As the attackers closed, the defenders discovered that the approaching enemy was not Indians but cattle which had broken out of a corral and stampeded. The incident is remembered as the Second Battle of Cowpens, with the first one being genuine and having been fought at Cowpens in South Carolina during the American Revolution.

The force later advanced and established Camp Whetstone. The army again moved and established yet another camp, called Camp Council. By then the troops were subsisting on half-rations. Morale was deteriorating and some were preparing mutiny. During that period, while at Camp Council, a sentry halted an unknown rider, accompanied by a small group of Indians. They were approaching the camp by way of the Huron Road coming from the south.

Initially, the sentinel refused to permit the rider to pass, and he demanded the countersign; however, the stranger could only respond that he did not know the password. Despite being told he could not pass, the rider began to advance until the sentry cocked his weapon and advised him that "if he moved another step he was "a dead man." Shortly thereafter another sentry was called and he informed the officer of the guard. As soon as the officer arrived, there was some embarrassment noticeable on the sentry's face when the officer addressed the stranger as General William Henry Harrison. The general was actually well pleased with the sentry (Hackethorn). General Harrison spoke to the sentry: "That's right, young man. Let no one pass without the countersign; it is the only way to keep 'em at gun's length."

On the morning after General Harrison arrived in the camp, the troops who were planning mutiny were preparing to march out of camp; however, to their surprise, they were suddenly introduced to the stranger that arrived on the previous night. General Harrison stepped up on a tree stump and addressed the troops. Harrisons rallying speech concluded, "Fellow-soldiers, cultivate a spirit of subordination, patriotism and courage, and ere long the recent victory gained at Detroit by the enemy shall be refunded with double interest, and ultimately the haughty British Lion shall be subdued by the talons of the American Eagle." The speech was effective. Troops who were ready to leave camp began to drop their knapsacks and blankets. From that day forward, the threat of mutiny vanished.

At the time, the troops were state troops, not in federal service. The commander of the division was Major General Wadsworth. Using state law, he proclaimed that movement of Beall's brigade was controlled solely by himself. Nonetheless, Wadsworth directed Beall to march his brigade to Cleveland, where he had his headquarters. Beall refused the order by discerning that his paramount responsibility was to protect the settlers on the frontier against Indian raids. Afterward, General Wadsworth, a veteran of the American Revolution and by now elderly, dispatched General Perkins to Beall's camp to arrest him and bring the brigade to Cleveland.

Upon the arrival of General Perkins, as requested, General Beall surrendered his sword. The brigade arrived in Cleveland at Camp Avery two days later and a trial was set for General Beall. After hearing the evidence, the court acquitted him. He was ordered to take his brigade to reinforce General Winchester. En route to the Raisin River, orders arrived directing General Beall to return because the enlistments of his force had expired. During the operation, Beall's troops cut a road through the wilderness that became known as Beall's Trail. It ran from Wooster to the state road at Planktown.

General Beall was elected to Congress as a representative from Ohio. He served 1813 to 1814. He resigned his congressional seat in 1814 to accept the position of register at the land office in Wooster. He retained the post until 1824, when he retired to private life. He died in Wooster at his residence on 20 February 1843.

Benson, Major General Perry Perry, the son of James and Hannah Benson, was born in Talbot County, Maryland, on 6 August 1757. He was a descendant of Doctor James Benson, one of the early settlers who established his residence along the St. Michaels River between Royal Oak and the town of St. Michaels. He received only a fundamental education and there are no records of his early youth. Benson served during the American Revolution as a captain. During July 1775, while the Annapolis Convention was in session, it was decided that forty companies of Minutemen would be established to secure the safety of Maryland.

Perry's name was not among the officers of the 1st Talbot Company, which was commanded by Captain James Hindman. On 25 June 1776, in response to a request from the Continental Congress, the Convention of Maryland acted to raise a Flying Camp to be composed of 3,405 troops. Talbot County was called upon to supply one company. Within four days, the company officers were appointed, with Greenbury Goldsborough named captain. Perry Benson was appointed ensign. No documentation verifies that the unit was ever established; however, it is known that Captain Goldsborough was not in active service as part of the Flying Camp under General Washington and that he did not serve actively in the militia of his home county. Although it remains unknown who Benson's captain was, it is certain he did serve during 1776 in the Flying Camp under General Washington. Benson probably joined the army either as a private or as a non-commissioned officer in a unit that became part of the Maryland 4th Battalion, drawn from Caroline, Cecil, Dorchester, Kent, Queen Anne's and Talbot Counties, commanded by Colonel William Richardson of Caroline County.

Reports by a contemporary historian stated that the 4th Battalion arrived in New York on 8 September, after the fighting on Long Island. The Eastern Shore Company under Captain Veasey and other Maryland units did participate in the fighting on Long Island. The 4th Battalion under Colonel Richardson arrived in time to participate at the Battle of Harlem Heights and at the Battle of White Plains, but again, there is no documentation that Benson participated in the two engagements. Actually, it is only known that Perry Benson served with that "Old Virginia Line" that had gained a reputation for its "courage in battle." By the close of 1776, the Line had constantly been in action and the battalion had nearly been annihilated. By early the following year, the enlistments of the men of the Flying Camp were about to expire.

During March 1777, the Maryland forces underwent reorganization when the legislature acted to form a unit of regulars, which when divided amounted to seven battalions, commanded by Brigadier General William Smallwood. The fifth of these battalions was organized with men residing on the Eastern Shore. The 5th Battalion was commanded by Colonel William Richardson. Perry Benson was appointed first lieutenant of the 5th Company, 5th Battalion. About January 1777, the Maryland 5th Battalion, deployed as part of the main army at Staten Island, was ordered to repair to Delaware to eliminate the problems being caused by Loyalists in Sussex County. After a short time in Delaware, the battalion was sent into Philadelphia, which was threatened by the British. Lieutenant Benson participated at the Battle of Brandywine, where he sustained a minor wound, and he fought at the Battle of Germantown. In June 1778 or 1779, he was promoted to the rank of captain in the Continental Army. In 1780, Benson served in the Southern theater under General DeKalb and later under General Lincoln and General Gates. Benson participated in the debacle known as the Battle of Camden in August 1780, and his company was among those Maryland and Delaware units that remained on the field while Gates was in flight. Benson also participated in the Battle of Cowpens under General Daniel Morgan.

After General Gates was succeeded by General Nathanael Greene, Benson remained in the South, and by the beginning of 1781, the Virginia Line was reorganized and drastically reduced because of the large number of casualties sustained. The seven regiments were reduced to only one, under the command of General Otho H. Williams. However, back in Maryland, the crisis was handled and enough men were recruited to rebuild the number of regiments to five, with Captain Benson being attached to the 5th Regiment, commanded by Colonel Benjamin Ford. Captain Benson also participated at the Battles of Guilford Court House and Hobkirk's Hill. At the Battle of Fort Ninety-Six in 1781, while leading the 1st Virginia Regiment, Captain Benson sustained a severe wound. A musket ball that hit him "entered his left arm, passed through his shoulder and neck, and lodged in his face. A fellow soldier, Thomas Carney, a colored man, who fought by his side, took him upon his shoulders, carried him out of the ditch into the American lines, and laid him before the surgeon."

Benson's wound was thought to be mortal, but he survived. His service essentially ended due to the wound. He was honorably discharged in 1783. He retired and resided on the family estate in Talbot, where he focused on farming. He also got married. During the Whiskey Rebellion in Pennsylvania (1794), Benson re-entered the service with the rank of lieutenant colonel to participate in squashing the short-lived rebellion ignited by Pennsylvanians incensed by the tax on liquor. The Maryland brigade was commanded by John Eccleston of Dorchester (general of brigade); however, the Maryland troops never advanced beyond Frederick. Before 1800, Colonel Benson was appointed brigadier general of Maryland militia.

During 1812, General Benson, a Federalist who never lost his propensity to despise the British, unlike many Federalists, began to organize the Talbot County militia shortly after war was declared to ensure Maryland would be prepared if a British force arrived at its shores. Maryland did receive a temporary reprieve during the first part of the war. Nevertheless, during March of 1813, a British fleet arrived in the Chesapeake Bay.

General Benson worked to keep the militia prepared for an attack, which he believed would be against St. Michaels. Additional troops were deployed there. On 10 August, as he believed, the British sent a contingent aboard eleven boats that moved toward shore at Parrott Point, defended by Dodson's 4-gun battery. The British were greeted also by a flag the women of St. Michaels had presented earlier to the company. While the boats were landing troops, two guns were fired, but the defenders at the fort retired, leaving their muskets behind. The British paused, then changed their plan and moved to positions from which they could fire at the town from the river. The effective fire from artillery compelled them to abort the attack before they could take the town. The boats returned to their ships, which were anchored off Kent Point. Late on 26 August, a second attempt to seize the town was launched, but was also repelled. By the 30th, the threat ended when the British squadron retired.

After the war, General Benson's military career also came to a close. Governor Charles Goldsborough appointed Benson a major general, effective 1 November 1819. Benson had been raised a Methodist, but later in life, he claimed to be an Episcopalian.

He was a member of the Masonic fraternity, a member of the Board of Trustees of the Maryland Agricultural Society for the Eastern Shore, and a member of the Society of the Cincinnati (his certificate, signed by General Washington regarding the diploma of the society, showed a date of 27 July 1793). He was married two times. His wives were sisters, Elizabeth and Mary Johnson, the daughters of Henry Johnson. No children were born during his first marriage; however, General Benson and his second wife, Mary, had children, three of whom survived him: Elizabeth Johnson (married Thomas Bond, and secondly Louis Pascault), George Robert Benson, and James Henry Benson.

General Benson died on 2 October 1827 and was buried at Wheatland. The Daughters of the American Revolution chapter notes in its records that General Benson's remains were in 1901 re-interred at another "Benson graveyard at Newcomb [Maryland], just off the St. Michael's Road where it is marked by a large flat stone in an unmarked grave." The DAR also notes that "his tombstone is incorrectly marked October 21st."

Bissell, Brigadier General Daniel The son of Ozias and Mabel Roberts Bissell, Daniel was born in Connecticut in 1768. His parents had eight other children, four sons and four daughters: Elijah, Leverett, Ozias II, Russell, Belle, Freedom, Hannah and Mabel. During the American Revolution, he served as a drummer boy. He joined the army during 1788. In September 1791, he was appointed as a cadet, and he was advanced to the rank of ensign on 11 April 1792. By January 1794 he held the rank of lieutenant, followed by his promotion to captain during January 1799. Meanwhile, Daniel married Deborah, the daughter of Jacob Seba, a resident of Middlebrook, Connecticut, originally from Holland, about 1793. Daniel and Deborah's children were Eliza (married William Morroson of Kaskaskia); Mary (married Risdon H. Price of St. Louis); Cornelia (married Major Douglass, U.S. Army); James (died in infancy), and James Russell Bissell (born in 1808, while General Bissell and his wife were in Connecticut).

During 1804, while attached to the U.S. 1st Infantry, he held command at Fort Massac along the Ohio River near Cairo, Illinois. During his tour at the post, Bissell became acquainted with Daniel Boone, who had relocated to Missouri, and the two men became good friends. While he was in command at Fort Massac, the Lewis and Clark Expedition was underway. Captains Meriwether Lewis and William Clark paused there during November 1803. Captain Bissell was unable to raise a large number of volunteers as requested by the government, which was disappointing to Lewis and Clark; however, George Drouillard, the son of Pierre Drouillard, a French-Canadian and his wife, a Shawnee, joined the expedition, primarily as an interpreter. Due to his skills as a "frontiersman, hunter-trapper, scout, master of sign language, interpreter, and expert in Indian ways," George was considered "indispensable by Lewis and Clark."

In 1807, in reaction to the death of Major Russell Bissell, the commander of Fort Belle Fontaine (St. Louis), Daniel Bissell was ordered to the post to succeed his brother as commander. In 1808, he was promoted to the rank of lieutenant colonel, the rank he held until the outbreak of the War of 1812. After acquiring Missouri as part of the Louisiana Purchase, General James Wilkinson had sought a post which would provide the opportunity to deploy U.S. troops in St. Louis and establish a post where trade with the Indians could begin. Fort Belle Fontaine was the first post established by the United States in the territory purchased from France (Louisiana Purchase). It was constructed by the 1st U.S. Regiment under Lt. Colonel Jacob Kingsbury. During 1809, when it was determined that the post could become vulnerable due to its location on low ground, its recently arrived commander, Lt. Colonel Daniel Bissell, within about one year was authorized to relocate it. After the project was concluded, during 1811, the fort stood high atop a cliff and contained 30 log buildings, each having a stone foundation. Under Bissell's direction, the post also was more heavily fortified with blockhouses and palisades. One other major change, the trading post, established when the fort was first built, was eliminated, confining it to military affairs. Fort Belle Fontaine remained an active post until 1826, when Jefferson Barracks Post was established in the southern sector of St. Louis County.

Bissell was promoted to full colonel on 15 August 1812, a rank he held until named brigadier general in March 1814. On 19 September 1812, Colonel Bissell observed that the "Yankees" in the Northeast displayed "a spirit amongst them, so unlike Americans, Yes, a sprit almost of Rebellion that will not do, in times like these, the Citizens to a man, after the Declaration of War ought to subscribe the Soldiers Creed, viz. not to ask why or wherefore they are to fight; it is the will of the Government, and I think absolutely necessary, it is true I would have liked to have had the Declaration been against the French also, but whatever is, is right with our Government."

During the war, Bissell served in various parts of the country and in Canada, including Mobile, Alabama, and in Louisiana at Baton Rouge and New Orleans. On 19 October 1814, a force under General Bissell, composed of about 1,000 men, attacked an enemy force under Colonel Christopher Myers at Lyon's Creek (Cook's Mills). Myers had been ordered there to protect the mills. Initially the British held firmly against the vanguard and succeeded in driving it back to the opposite bank of the creek; however, Bissell's main body compelled the British to retire soon after they crossed the creek. The Americans destroyed the mills. Bissell's victory became the final engagement on the Niagara frontier.

After the War of 1812, General Bissell returned to St. Louis. He reverted to his full rank of colonel. He also began to construct his estate, which became known as Franklinville. In May 1815, General Bissell became colonel of the U.S. 1st infantry with the brevet of brigadier general. On 10 September 1824, pursuant to a meeting held in St. Louis, Bissell, the chairman of the committee that planned to welcome Lafayette to St. Louis, sent the invitation, which Lafayette accepted. While Lafayette was in Philadelphia accompanied by his son, George Washington arrived in St. Louis aboard the vessel *Natchez* on 29 April 1825. A grand reception was held at the mansion of Major Pierre Chouteau. On 16 January 1826, Bissell was transferred to the U.S. 2nd Artillery. The U.S. Senate twice declined to confirm President John Quincy Adams' appointments of Bissell as colonel of the U.S. 2nd Artillery.

General Bissell died of pneumonia on 14 December 1833. He was survived by his wife, Deborah, and their four children. Mrs. Bissell died on 15 November 1843. The Bissell home remained in the family for more than 150 years, before it was donated to the County of St. Louis in the 1960s. At one time, the Bissell property amounted to about 2,300 acres. Daniel's son, James R., donated the land where the original Methodist church was built in the town about 1854. The Daniel Bissell House is open to the public.

Bloomfield, Brigadier General (Governor) Joseph The son of Doctor Moses and Sarah Ogden Bloomfield was born on 18 October 1753 at Woodbridge, New Jersey. His mother was the daughter of Robert and Phebe Baldwin Ogden. Joseph's father was a surgeon and hospital physician for the Continental Army in the American Revolution who was captured and exchanged. Doctor Bloomfield had also been a member of the legislature and the Provincial Congress during the American Revolution, and served in the New Jersey Assembly representing Middlesex County during 1784.

Joseph did not follow his father into the medical field. He received his basic education at a classical school in Deerfield Township, run by the Rev. Enoch Green, who was also pastor of the Presbyterian church there. He studied law at Perth Amboy under Cortlandt Skinner, attorney general of New Jersey and a Loyalist, while maintaining an interest in politics. He received his license to practice on 12 November 1774. He began his practice in Bridgeton. Joseph, like his father, was a veteran of the Revolution. He received a commission as a captain of the 3rd New Jersey Regiment, commanded by Colonel Elias Dayton, during February 1776. He participated in the ill-fated invasion of Canada; however, after the regiment received orders to repair to Canada, the army was retreating. The regiment spent some time at Fort Stanwix and afterward at Ticonderoga. While at Ticonderoga, Joseph Bloomfield was appointed judge advocate of the Northern Army. In 1777, he was promoted to the rank of major. Bloomfield participated in various actions, including defense of Philadelphia at the Battle of Brandywine during September 1777 and the Battle of Monmouth in June 1778. He was wounded at either Brandywine or Monmouth.

He resigned from the service on 29 October 1778, and soon afterward married Mary McIlvane, the daughter of Doctor William McIlvane of Philadelphia, on 1 December 1778. It is thought that they had a child who died within two weeks. After the death of his wife, Bloomfield remarried, taking Isabella Ramsey as his second wife. After the war, he was appointed to the Board of Admiralty in 1783, and the same year, subsequent to the resignation of William Patterson, was elected attorney general of New Jersey, a post he retained until 1792. During the Whiskey Rebellion (1794) in Pennsylvania, Bloomfield participated as a brigade commander with the rank of brigadier general. General Bloomfield had also served as a member and for a time, president, of the New Jersey Society for the Abolition of Slavery. During 1795 he was elected mayor of Burlington, New Jersey, the town to which he relocated after the close of the war. He retained the post until 1800. During the period he held the office of mayor, he was also a member of the Board of Chosen Freeholders of Burlington County. In 1801 he was elected governor; however, the following year (1802) there was a tie vote and the state existed without a governor for the entire year. Duties of the executive office were carried out by John Lambert, the vice-president of the council. During 1803, Bloomfield was again elected by the legislature, then he served (being elected annually) as governor until 1812.

He was appointed brigadier general in the U.S. Amy on 13 March 1812, just a few months before war was declared against Britain. He served for a while in New York State along the border with Canada, and he participated in the attack against Fort George in Canada at the mouth of the Niagara River. Afterward, he was transferred to Philadelphia, where he remained until his active service ended on 15 June 1815. After the war, he was elected to Congress during 1817 and re-elected in 1819.

General Bloomfield died on 3 October 1823, and two days later, he was interred in the cemetery of St. Mary's Episcopal Church in Burlington. Bloomfield's political affiliation was Democratic-Republican (modern-day Democrat). He became a close friend of Thomas Jefferson, and like Jefferson he had a large collection of books in his library. General Bloomfield was described as a brave officer who was respected greatly by his friends, and he was known to possess some tendencies of eccentricity. General Bloomfield also served as a trustee of Princeton College (later university).

Boyd, Brigadier General John Parker John, the son of James and Susanna Coffin Boyd, was born at Newburyport, Massachusetts, on 21 December 1764. In addition to John, his parents had the following children: Robert (born 13 November 1758); Joseph (born 23 July 1760);

Margaret (born 25 January 1762); Frances (born 14 August 1766); Ebenezer Little (born 6 July 1768); Charles Coffin (3 February 1770, died 19 August 1770); William (born 20 March 1776); and Mary Lee (born 22 January 1778). Boyd joined the army in 1786 at a time which he believed was not a suitable to be a soldier. He resigned from the army and later sailed for India, where he arrived in Madras during July 1789. While in India, Boyd was in the service of the Mahratta, and he organized a force of mercenaries that he hired out to various princes. At one time, he commanded about 10,000 troops. Later, after completing his service in the East Indies, Boyd departed from India and sailed for Paris, and from there he returned to the States during 1808. That year, Boyd returned to service in the U.S. military. He received his commission as colonel of the U.S. 4th Infantry regiment on 7 October 1808.

During 1811, the U.S. 4th Regiment under Colonel Parker was at Pittsburgh, Pennsylvania, when orders arrived from Washington for the regiment to repair to Vincennes, Indiana, to join General William Henry Harrison. Colonel Boyd and his regiment departed on flatboats on which they traveled to the Falls of the Ohio, Kentucky, where they debarked and marched overland to reach their destination. The distance they traveled was about 400 miles. Reportedly, the regiment completed the journey in such a short time that it was considered an amazing achievement. Boyd's regiment arrived in time to participate in the Battle of Tippecanoe in November 1811, the triumph that terminated Indian hostilities in the region.

Later, on 1 June 1812, General William Hull, governor of Michigan, departed from Dayton, Ohio, en route for Urbana. He was joined at the latter by the 4th Regiment under Colonel Boyd, which arrived there from Vincennes. On 26 August, Colonel Boyd was appointed brigadier general. On 13 April 1812, the country was divided into nine militarty districts, with a tenth district established in June. General Boyd was assigned to the 8th District, which encompassed New York from the Highlands and Vermont. The commander was General Henry Dearborn. In addition to General Boyd, General Dearborn was assisted by Major Generals James Wilkinson and Morgan Lewis, along with Brigadier Generals John Chandler, Zebulon M. Pike and William H. Winder. Lt. Colonel Winfield Scott served as adjutant general.

General Boyd participated in various engagements, including the attack that seized Fort George, Canada, on 26–27 May 1813 and the Battle of Chrysler's Field in November 1813, where General Wilkinson's campaign to seize Montreal was derailed. In the meantime, on 23 June, General Boyd, in command at Fort George in the absence of General Morgan Lewis (temporary successor to General Henry Dearborn), dispatched a contingent under Lt. Colonel Charles G. Boerstler, 14th U.S. Infantry, to capture a British supply depot at Beaver Dam, which stood about 15 miles outside the fort. The British, with an inferior-sized fort, pull off a ruse and capture the contingent after establishing an ambush at the town of Thorold. Initially, the column absorbed the shock caused by about 400 Indians, but when the Americans charged into the woods, the Indians in their usual manner vanished; however, they changed tactics and only withdrew to establish yet another ambush. The Americans also held their own and afterward tried to repair to an open field.

Meanwhile, a small 47-man contingent of Canadian militia arrived and demanded surrender after splitting up to give the illusion that their force was larger than it was. Boerstler, informed that 1,500 troops of the main body were close behind and that 700 Indians were nearby, surrendered. The British commander, Lt. Fitzgibbon, had informed Boerstler that his statement was true and based on "the honor of a British soldier."

After Boerstler's force surrendered on the guarantee that they would receive parole, the agreement was broken and the Indians began their plunder. This was more or less the final incident leading to the dismissal of General Dearborn as commander of the district. He was succeeded by Major General James Wilkinson on 6 July 1813. At the time, Dearborn was at Fort George. After his departure, General Boyd assumed command there, which caused additional problems. Secretary of War John Armstrong's faith in Boyd had limitations. Armstrong believed that Boyd should not command higher than a brigade. Despite commanding about 4,000 men, Armstrong's orders prohibited Boyd from acting, ending further land action except for some minor skirmishes for the remainder of the year. On 20 September 1813, General Wilkinson met with General Boyd and other officers at Fort George. They decided to abandon the post and return to New York.

At Sackets Harbor on 17 October 1813, General Wilkinson initiated the campaign to seize Montreal. General Boyd was one of his brigade commanders. The operation included another force under Major General Wade Hampton joining with Wilkinson's command; however Hampton and Wilkinson despised each other. On 11 November, the American advance hit opposition at Chrysler's Farm. On the day of the engagement, Generals Wilkinson and General Morgan Lewis were both ill, which placed General Boyd in command. When the fighting was over, both sides claimed victory. Although it was a stalemate, General Boyd was criticized for the way he commanded at the battle and his reputation was never fully recovered.

On 17 April 1815, Governor Daniel D. Tompkins, at Albany, relinquished command of the Third Military District. He wrote on that day to General Boyd: "Sir: I transmit, enclosed, the copy of a communication from the acting Secretary of the War department, Alexander Dallas, relieving me from the command of the Third Military District. If orders to the contrary should not have been given, you will on the receipt of this letter assume the absolute command of the district & will announce the same in orders." After the war, General Boyd returned to Boston and became involved in private enterprise endeavors. He was one of the founders on the towns of Orneville and Medford, Maine. He did not seek any public office. In 1816, he authored *Documents and Facts Relative to Military Events During the Late War.*

He was appointed as naval officer of the port of Boston during March 1830, a post he held until his death a few months later. General Boyd, who never married, died on 4 October 1830. He was interred at Copps Hill Burying Ground in Boston.

Brown, Major General Jacob Jennings
Jacob, the son of Samuel and Abi White Brown, was born at Penn's Manor in Bucks County, Pennsylvania, on 9 May 1775. His mother was the daughter of a Quaker preacher, Joseph White, and her brother, Benjamin White, was also a Quaker preacher. Jacob's parents had eight children. Jacob was a descendant of Quakers who arrived in Pennsylvania with William Penn. The first of the Browns to arrive in America were George and Mercy Brown. They were married during 1679 and had fourteen children, ten boys and four girls. Of the boys, three were named Samuel, and it is thought that two of them died in childhood. John, one of the sons of Samuel and Ann, married Ann, the daughter of Benjamin Field, during 1750, and they had eight children (possibly nine). They were Samuel (father of General Brown); Sarah (married Samuel Allen); John (married Martha Harvey); Benjamin (married Jane Wright); Charles (married Charlotte Palmer); Joseph (married Marry Butcher); Elizabeth (married Mailon Yardley); and David (died young and unmarried).

As a young man, Brown made his living as a teacher. In 1796 he was employed in Ohio as a surveyor, a position he retained for about two years. Upon returning to New York, he went back to teaching after being placed in charge of a "Friends school." He began to meet various influential Americans, including Gouverneur Morris, the man responsible for persuading Brown to relocate to New York. Brown acquired a vast tract of land in the St. Lawrence frontier close to Sackets Harbor, and from it, the town of Brownsville emerged about 1799. Brown is thought to have received his initial military experience while serving as secretary to General Alexander Hamilton. Some others doubt the story, because Hamilton claimed he never had a secretary. Also, in some early biographies of General Brown, written shortly after the War of 1812 ended, no association between Alexander Hamilton and Jacob Brown were included.

During December 1802, Brown married Pamela Williams, a sister of one of his friends. At the time of their marriage, she was only about 17 years old. They had nine children: Gouverneur; Jacob (married Frances Austin); Nathan (married Virginia Duval); William (married Elizabeth Barnes); Eliza (married Edmund Kirby); Katherine (married Larkin Smith); Margaret (married John Brown); Mary (no information available); and Pamela (married David Vinton).

Brown was appointed colonel of his local

militia in 1809. He also served in a judicial capacity after being elected a county judge. In 1808 he dabbled in smuggling potash into Canada in violation of the Embargo Act of 1808, one of a series of acts initiated by President Jefferson during his second term. Brown accumulated wealth while engaged in his enterprise, but by the following year, he terminated the activity when he entered the military. In 1810 Brown was promoted to the rank of brigadier general of militia. During 1812, General Brown raised a brigade that served under him in the region of the frontier which became his responsibility. His sector stretched for about 200 miles from Oswego to Lake St. Francis, and some sources set the sector at about 300 miles, between Oswego and St. Regis. In early October 1812, the British launched an attack on Ogdensburg; however, General Brown's forces repelled the assault. Afterward, General Brown's service terminated. He returned to Brownsville to be with his family, but the next spring he was back in the field. On 28–29 May 1813, with Brown in command at Sackets Harbor, again the British launched an assault to seize it with a force estimated at about 1,300 men. The Americans prevailed and the British sustained about 300 killed and wounded. General Brown was commissioned brigadier general in the U.S. Army on July 19. In October he participated in General Wilkinson's failed campaign to seize Montreal.

In early November 1813, General Brown deployed artillery at French Creek in New York while his force acted as vanguard for General Wilkinson's army. The American artillerymen compelled British gunboats to withdraw. On 10 November, Brown's command was stalled at Hoople's Creek, but the militia was eventually driven back. On the following day, Brown's force was away from Chrysler's Farm, which prevented Brown from being with his superior officers at the devastating defeat that sealed the fate of Wilkinson's campaign to seize Montreal.

Brown's force remained deployed at French Mills, New York, during the bitter winter; however, his record in the field had not been overlooked in Washington by Secretary of War John Armstrong. On 24 January 1814, General Brown received another promotion. He was raised to major general in the U.S. Army and given command of the Niagara frontier, Left Division, 9th District. His force was composed of two regular brigades, commanded by Generals Eleazar Ripley and Winfield Scott, along with a volunteer brigade under General Peter B. Porter.

Later General Brown received new orders to advance his army across the Niagara River and seize the terrain in the Niagara peninsula up to York. By summer 1814, he was racking up a string of victories over the British, including the Battle of Chippewa, where he was wounded twice, but retained command until the battle ended. After recuperating General Brown was back in command of the army at Fort Erie, which had been seized by the Americans. Brown also participated at the Battle of Lundy's Lane, also claimed as a victory by the British. During September 1814, his force repelled a British assault against Fort Erie. The British then retired from the vicinity of Fort Erie and returned to Fort George.

General Brown was acknowledged in November 1814 officially by Congress, which gave him a gold medal in recognition of his outstanding service. After the war, General Brown remained in the army in command of the Northern Military District. In 1821 he was named commanding general of the United States Army. Brown became the senior officer in the army following the resignation of General Andrew Jackson. During his term, Brown worked with Secretary of War John C. Calhoun to reform and modernize the army, and he was known to be an advisor to President James Monroe and President John Quincy Adams.

He continued to suffer from a disease that struck him while he was at Fort Erie during the late war. It was given as the cause of his death on 24 February 1828, which occurred while General Brown was still in office. He was interred at the Congressional Cemetery in Washington, D.C. A monument was later built there in his honor. General Brown's sudden death at his residence in Washington, following a brief illness of only several days, caused deep sadness in the capital. On 25 February 1828, funeral honors are prepared and published by the Adjutant's Office:

> The senior officers of the General Staff of the Army and the Commanding General of the Militia of the District of Columbia, will convene at the Adjutant General's Office this morning, at nine o'clock, to make suitable arrangements for the funeral honors of the distinguished and lamented Major General Brown. "By order of the Secretary of War, R. Jones, Adj. Ben. Pursuant to the foregoing instructions, the officers charged with the arrangement, direct the following order of procession, as the last and mournful duty to be paid the mortal remains of the late General-in-Chief of the United States Army. The funeral escort will be composed as follows: A Battalion of Infantry; A Division of Artillery; A Squadron of Horse; General Staff of the District Militia; Officers of the Militia; Officers of the Navy and Marine Corps; Officers of the Army; Marine Music [Marine Band]; Major General Macomb. Order of Procession: The Clergy of the District and Surgeon General of the Army; General's Horse; Pall Bearers (Brig. Gen. Thompson; Col. Towson; Brig. Gen. [John] Wool; Brig. Gen. Gibson; Brig. Gen. Jesup; Comm. Warrington; Major Gen. Smith; Brig. Gen. Bernrad; Comm. Rodgers; Major Gen. Gaines; Gen. Harrison; Major Hamilton); The relatives of the deceased; His Aids and General Staff of the Army; The Marshal of the District; The President of the United States (John Quincy Adams); Committee of Arrangements of the Senate and House of Representatives; Sergeant-at Arms of the Senate; Vice President and Secretary of the Senate; The Senate of the United States; The Sergeant-at-Arms of the House of Representatives; Speaker and Clerk of the House of Representatives; The House of Representatives; The Heads of Departments; Chief Justice, and Associate Justices of the Supreme Court; Foreign Ministers, their suites, and Consuls of Foreign Powers; The Postmaster General, and Comptrollers of the Treasury; Auditors and Treasurer; The Register of the Treasury, Commissioner of the General Land Office and other Civil Officers of the Government; Judges and Attorney of the District of Columbia; Members of the Bar; Mayors and other civil officers of Washington (Gales), Georgetown and Alexandria. Masonic Societies and such other Societies as may join in the procession Citizens and Strangers. Major General Macomb will command the military escort and Colonel Jones will officiate as officer of the day. Major Cross and Major Hook, Colonel Andrews and Major Randolph, are appointed the marshals of the day."

On the day of General Brown's interment, Wednesday, 27 February, guns were fired every half-hour from dawn to dusk.

Jacob's wife, Pamela Williams Brown, born in 1775, survived her husband.

Burbeck, Brigadier General Henry, the son of Colonel William and Jerusha Glover Burbeck, was born in Boston on 8 June 1754. Henry's father was an English officer, born in Boston and stationed on Castle Island, Massachusetts, at Castle William (later Fort Independence), the fifth of eight forts built there. In late 1775, he succeeded Colonel Richard Greely as commander of the Massachusetts Artillery. Initially, William married Abigail Tuttle and they had two children, Abigail and Edward. After Abigail died, William married Jerusha, the daughter of John and Susannah Ellison Glover. William and Jerusha had nine children, including Henry. The other eight were William (baptized March 1749, died young); Jerusha (baptized June 1751, married Captain John Cathcart); Mary (baptized April 1752, died in infancy); John (baptized August 1755); Joseph (baptized November 1756); Thomas (baptized August 1758); Mary (2nd, baptized July 1762) and Susannah (baptized April 1765). Henry's mother died in Boston during July 1777 and his father died in the same city in July 1785. Apparently, William Burbeck was also a skilled wood carver, and some of his work can still be found in Boston.

Henry's early years were spent at the castle. His schooling was handled by his father. Shortly after the Battles of Lexington and Concord, Henry received his commission on 19 May 1775 as a lieutenant of artillery. It was signed by the president of the Massachusetts Provincial Congress, Doctor Joseph Warren. Burbeck served actively during the siege of Boston, and on 1 January 1776, he was promoted to first lieutenant of artillery. He served under Colonel Richard Gridley (first chief engineer and artillery commander of the army). On 12 September 1777, Burbeck was promoted to the rank of lieutenant captain of artillery. He continued to serve under General Henry Knox. He participated at various actions during the war, including the defense of Philadelphia at the Battle of Brandywine in September 1777 and the Battle of Germantown fought after the British occupied Philadelphia during October 1777. Burbeck went into winter quarters at Valley Forge with General Washington. In the spring, he participated in the pursuit of the British after they abandoned Philadelphia and at the major clash at the Battle of Monmouth in June 1778. Meanwhile, Burbeck was promoted to the rank of captain lieutenant on 1 January 1777 and given command of the 3rd Artillery Regiment. He remained in the north when General Washington headed south. Burbeck's command was part of the defensive force that defended the Highlands. After the British abandoned New York (final elements departed during November 1783), Burbeck's regiment was among the units that advanced into New York City. Captain Burbeck was promoted to the brevet rank of major on 30 September 1783. Following the evacuation of New York, Major Burbeck repaired to West Point, where he remained until he was honorably discharged on 1 January 1784.

In 1786, Burbeck was re-commissioned captain of artillery. The next year he received command of West Point, a post he retained until 1789. During 1790, Henry married Abigail Webb of Bath, Maine; she died on 9 July 1790. Afterward he married Lucy E. Rudd of New London, the widow of Captain Henry Caldwell. They had the following children: Susan Henrietta (born September 1815, married Lt. Epaphras Kibby); Charlotte Augusta (born March 1818); Henry William (born May 1819, died February 19, 1840); Mary Elizabeth (born March 1821); William Henry (born October 1823); and John Cathcart (born February 1826).

Burbeck was General Anthony Wayne's chief of artillery from 1792 to 1794, while Wayne was quelling the Indian hostilities in the Northwest Territory. Next he commanded Fort Mackinac on Mackinac Island in Michigan from 1796 until 1799. From 1798 to 1802, Burbeck was the senior regimental commander of artillerists and engineers in the army. He was promoted to lieutenant colonel on 7 May 1798 and to full colonel on 1 April 1802. Meanwhile, during 1800, he assumed command of the Department of the East. On 10 July, according to the Daughters of the American Revolution, Burbeck was promoted to the rank of brevet brigadier general. He received command of the 2nd military district (Rhode Island and Connecticut). Burbeck arrived at New London in July 1813 to assume command in the name of the U.S. government. Burbeck discovered that about 800 men of the militia were on active duty; however, Connecticut militia was under the orders of Governor John Cotton Smith, a Federalist, who assumed the office in October upon the death of Governor Roger Griswold. The state government had prevented its militia from being controlled by the federal government to guarantee that the men would not be used outside of the state. Burbeck, pursuant to instructions from Secretary of State James Monroe, dismissed the militia on 12 July 1814. However, he retained the guard under Lt. Horatio G. Lewis at Stonington. The dismissal of the militia left Fort Griswold and Fort Trumbull defenseless. The British learned of the release of the militia, and by the following day, a naval squadron arrived in the harbor and bombarded Stonington.

Burbeck was breveted brigadier general on 10 September 1813. He retired from the army during 1815 and took up residence at New London. He died on 2 October 1848 at age 94. At the time of his death, he was president of the Massachusetts Society of the Cincinnati. He was interred at Cedar Grove Cemetery.

Cadwalader, Brigadier General John The son of General John and Williamina Bond Cadwalader was born on 28 October 1779 in Maryland. His father died on 10 February 1786. Afterward, John's mother moved the family back to Philadelphia. John was admitted to the bar there in 1801. He applied for an officer's commission during 1799 when it was thought that war with France was becoming imminent; however, the conflict known as the Quasi War with France was fought only on the high seas. Nevertheless, John served as a private in a cavalry troop. During 1801, Thomas married Mary Biddle on 25 June. They had the following children: John (later judge); George (later major general, U.S. Army); Thomas (born August 1808–, died unmarried January 1844); Henry (born January 1817, died unmarried June 1844); and William (born October 1820, died unmarried October 1875).

When the War of 1812 commenced, John Cadwalader served as a captain and then lieutenant colonel of a volunteer cavalry regiment. During September 1814, while the British were intent on capturing Baltimore, Lt. Colonel Cadwalader was encamped just outside of Philadelphia, and the cavalry volunteers had no commander. Cadwalader, the highest ranking officer in the camp, was appointed commander of what was a light brigade, composed of artillery, cavalry, infantry and some militia (without uniforms), about one battalion. The brigade was reinforced with riflemen from several sections of Pennsylvania, bringing the total number of men to about 3,500. General Cadwalader focused on training and tactics. Nevertheless, before the end of 1814, the brigade was dismissed from federal service. During 1815, General Cadwalader was given command of the division encompassing Eastern Pennsylvania, Delaware and sections of Maryland and New Jersey. His command was given on a temporary basis, which lasted about two months. During January 1815, Congress decided to add two divisions to the U.S. Army. General Cadwalader was thought to be the choice for commander of the Pennsylvania division and that the governor, Simon Snyder, would appoint him major general; however, it was also thought that he would be offered appointment as brigadier general in the federal service and commander of one of the two new divisions. Nevertheless, peace had arrived, which made the two new divisions unnecessary. General Cadwalader subsequently became major general of the Pennsylvania 1st Division (militia). During 1826, he was a member of the board, along with others including Lt. Colonel (later general and president) Zachary Taylor and General Winfield Scott, charged with reviewing and modifying tactics. The section of the report pertaining to cavalry tactics is thought to have been authored solely by Cadwalader.

General Cadwalader died on 26 October 1841.

Calmes, Brigadier General Marquis Marquis, the son of William Calmes, who married Lucy Neville, the daughter of Captain George Neville, was born in 1755. His grandfather, also named Marquis (Marquis De La Calmez, anglicized into Calmes), a Huguenot, emigrated from France to England during 1724. In 1726, he traveled to America and settled in the vicinity of Greenway Court, south of Richmond in Virginia. The young Marquis served as an officer with the rank of captain in the American Revolution. At the outbreak of the war, Marquis had been attending school in Europe; however, he returned home to join the service and began his military life with the rank of captain. He raised a regiment at his own expense; it was attached to the 3rd Virginia Regiment commanded by Colonel Thomas Marshall, also a Virginian. Marshall's son John (future chief justice) also served as an officer in the regiment. At the Battle of Brandywine, Colonel Marshall was wounded, and Calmes, by then a lieutenant colonel, assumed command.

Calmes participated at the Battle of Monmouth and various other actions, including the Yorktown campaign when Washington, with the support of the French fleet under Comte De Grasse and the French ground troops under Rochambeau, forced the surrender of General Charles Cornwallis. On 4 February 1777, Calmes had been promoted to the rank of lieutenant colonel. Later, on 4 August 1779, Colonel Calmes resigned from the service. While serving during the Revolution, Calmes became friends with Lafayette and their friendship continued well after the war. After the war ended, Calmes moved to Kentucky. He led a company of men to Kentucky, which at the time was still a frontier of Virginia. The party traveled by keel boats that carried them down the Ohio River to the region at the mouth of Cabin Creek. Calmes afterward moved across the creek to Indian Fields (later Clark County). He remained there and established a farm; however, later he relocated in Fayette County (later Woodford County, named in honor of Brigadier General William Woodford). Calmes established his residence at "Caneland," close to "Buck Pond," the residence of Colonel Thomas Marshall. Both Marshall and Calmes constructed brick homes. During the War of 1812, he was named brigadier general on 31 August 1813.

He received command of the 1st Brigade of Kentucky riflemen. The brigade was composed of the regiments of Colonel Trotter and Colonel John Donaldson. Calmes' brigade served in the northwest under General William Henry Harrison, and the brigade participated in the invasion of Canada. During the Battle of the Thames, General Calmes became ill and unable to command. Nonetheless, he did get carried and was present during the Battle of the Thames.

Colonel George Trotter commanded the brigade during the battle. After the war, he returned to his estate in Kentucky.

In 1825, Lafayette, while touring the country, visited Versailles and was greeted by General Calmes and many others at the Watkins Tavern, where a grand party was held in Lafayette's honor. General Calmes continued to dress in the colonial style throughout his life. He "wore his hair in a queue and neatly tied with a black ribbon, a broad cocked hat, sweeping blue cloth coat with metal buttons, velvet knee pants, and stockings, and shoes with large silver buckles." He was not interested in politics; however, during 1795, General Calmes did serve in the legislature. He is known to have owned slaves, and he saw to it that they learned various trades. He also made his own brandy and whiskey.

General Calmes, who founded the town of Versailles, had a stone mausoleum constructed on the family plantation. Upon his death during 1834, he was interred there. His wife, Priscilla Heale Calmes, was also interred there. As the years passed, the condition of the tomb deteriorated; however, during 1990, it was restored. The tomb is still on the property in the middle of a paddock. General Calmes and his wife had nine children, five sons and four daughters.

Carroll, Brigadier General William "Willie" William, the son of Thomas and Mary Montgomery Carroll, was born in Pennsylvania near Pittsburgh on 3 March 1788. Little information exists about his parents. However, it is known that his family was related to Charles Carroll of Carrollton, a signer of the Declaration of Independence. William's grandfather, Daniel Carroll, was also the grandfather of Charles Carroll of Carrollton. William and his son, Charles, at the invitation of their cousin Charles Carroll, journeyed to the Carroll residence in Maryland and arrived there during November 1832. Upon their arrival they were informed that Charles had died shortly before their arrival.

During 1810, William Carroll traveled to Nashville, Tennessee, to establish a new branch of the business in Pittsburgh in which he was a partner. Subsequently, he became friends with General Jackson; however, William, known more as Willie, was not a native of Tennessee and was also unfamiliar with the ways of the natives, particularly dueling. He was reluctant to resort to such a method of settling an argument, although not in any way fearful of such activity. He was challenged by Jesse Benton and the challenge was accepted. General Jackson acted as second for Carroll, who prevailed. Benton was wounded, but he survived. Carroll was also wounded but only superficially in his thumb.

Carroll first entered the military as a brigade inspector; however, General Jackson, having great expectations, had him quickly moved through the ranks. William married Cecilia Bradford during September 1813. They had four children, one of whom was William Henry Carroll, who joined the Confederate service.

When General Jackson was ordered to move into the Indian country, Willie Carroll was away in Pittsburgh, but once informed he sped back to Tennessee and arrived in time to join the column just before it entered the Indian Territory. On 9 November 1813, at the Battle of Talladega, Carroll, with the rank of colonel, led the vanguard and deployed from where the Indians could be cut down when they attempted escape.

On 22 January 1814, at Emuckfaw, Indians struck Jackson's force twice. During the fighting, General Carroll led a daring bayonet charge that drove the Indians from the field, and on the 24th, at the Battle of Enitachopco, while Jackson was en route back to Fort Strother, the Indians launched another attack. Some panic overcame parts of Jackson's force. Carroll attempted to form a defensive line only to discover the columns on his left and his right fled in panic, leaving Carroll and 25 men under Captain Quarles to halt the attacking Creeks, who were forced to retire.

Pursuit was initiated, but after moving about two miles, the chase was aborted.

During October 1814, Jackson was commissioned as a major general in the regulars. Afterward, General Carroll was promoted to major general of Jackson's Tennessee division. On 14 November, Carroll's force at Nashville prepared to depart for New Orleans to join Jackson. The troops departed on 19 November and met up with government boats carrying arms and ammunition along the way in Mississippi. The flotilla resumed the journey and arrived in the vicinity of New Orleans on 22 December just before the British launched an assault against Jackson's positions. During the last part of the journey, General Carroll used the time to train his men on the use of their weapons.

In New Orleans, the primary battle was fought on 7 January 1815 and the Americans won a decisive and spectacular victory in which the British sustained a horrific defeat. General Jackson received a gold medal.

Generals Carroll and John Coffee were each given swords. One side of the blade of General Carroll's sword was inscribed: "New Orleans, Jany. 8, 1815, Talladega, Emuckfaw, Enotachopco and Tohopeka." The other side read: "Presented by the State of Tennessee to Maj. Gen. Wm. Carroll, as a testimony of high respect for his public services."

After the war, General Carroll returned to Nashville and resumed his life as a businessman. He owned the steamboat the *General Jackson*, which passed down the river under the bluffs at Nashville.

During the depression of 1818–1819, he suffered a devastating financial setback that essentially ended his business enterprises; however, his name by that time had become widely known in Tennessee due to his military record during the war. He was elected governor of the state in 1821, beating out his opponent, Edward Ward, by about a 3-to-1 vote. He served three consecutive terms, which made him ineligible for re-election in 1827. Nonetheless, he ran again in 1829, won the post and afterward he was twice re-elected and served a total of six terms.

Despite limits of three consecutive terms, General Carroll disregarded the law and ran for a fourth term; however, the people of Tennessee, using the three-term limit, rejected his bid for the governorship in 1835.

General Carroll pressed forward with his goals, including amending the state constitution to bring about a fairer system of taxation and placing the election of officials into the hands of the people. Those goals were achieved, but another, building a state capital, ran behind. It was achieved but construction did not commence until the year after he died. Other achievements included the construction of a hospital for the insane and the building of a state penitentiary.

General Carroll died on 22 March 1844. The state of Tennessee erected a monument in his honor. The inscription read: "As a gentleman he was modest, intelligent and courteous; as an officer, brave and daring; as a statesman, firm, wise and just."

Cass, Brigadier General Lewis Lewis, the son of Jonathan and Mary (Molly) Gilman Cass, was born on 9 October 1782 in Exeter, New Hampshire. His ancestors immigrated to America with the first settlers to arrive in that part of the country. Lewis was the oldest of six children born to Mary and Jonathan. Lewis' father was a veteran officer of the American Revolution who joined with the Americans in April 1775, on the day following the battles at Lexington and Concord. He participated at various actions including Bunker Hill, Trenton, Princeton, Saratoga, Germantown and Monmouth. After the Revolution, he served as a major under General Anthony Wayne against the Indians in the Northwest.

Lewis' father, Jonathan, noticed Lewis' abilities that included a capacity to learn that seemed to be beyond his age. Lewis was placed in the Phillips Exeter Academy during 1792 when he was only ten years old. Despite his age, Lewis was able to keep up with the older students. He remained at the academy for seven years studying the classics and mathematics. In 1799, Lewis taught school in Wilmington, Delaware, where his father was stationed. During 1800, the Cass family relocated to Ohio, where Jonathan had earlier served on the frontier. Jonathan, as a brevet major, commanded Fort Hamilton until the Treaty of Greenville was consummated. The family established residence at Marietta in southern Ohio, which was founded by the Ohio Company. General Rufus Putnam, brother of General Israel Putnam, was involved as a representative of the Ohio Company as the overseer of the project to establish the settlement. Lewis had arrived in Ohio about one year before the family relocated. It was there that he began to study law. About one year after the family moved to Ohio, they re-established themselves at Zanesville. Lewis remained in Marietta to continue his studies under Return Jonathan Meigs (governor of Ohio, December 1810 to March 1814).

On 1 March 1803, Ohio officially entered the Union as the 17th state. Lewis Cass became the first man admitted to the bar under the new Constitution during autumn 1802. Afterward, he began to practice law in Zanesville. Cass, with the aid of his political and influential friends at Marietta, was able to build his reputation rapidly as a fine attorney. In 1806, Lewis married Elizabeth, the daughter of Major General Joseph Spencer (Revolutionary War era). They had the following children: Lewis Jr. (born 1814); Isabella (known also as Belle —, married Baron Theodore Marinus Roest Von Linburg); Elizabeth (Eliza); Mary Sophia; Matilda Frances; Ellen (born 1821 and died 1824); and Spencer (born June 1828, died October 1828).

Cass was elected to the Ohio state legislature in 1806. During his term of office, he served on the committee that was investigating Aaron Burr. Cass drafted the law which authorized the Ohio authorities to seize and arrest the men involved with Burr's scheme which was intended to divide the Western states from the Eastern states. The law made it possible to nab the boats involved when they passed down the Ohio River. Cass' involvement in derailing Burr's scheme did not go unnoticed in Washington. The following year, President Jefferson appointed Cass as U.S. marshal for the state of Ohio, a position he retained until 1813.

During 1812, just before war against Great Britain was declared, Ohio was asked to provide its quota of men. Soon 1,200 volunteers converged on Dayton. The Third Regiment was commanded by Colonel Lewis Cass. The Ohio regiments came under the command of General William Hull, the governor of the Michigan Territory. Colonel Cass served with Hull during the invasion of Canada. When General Hull surrendered Detroit and all of the Michigan Territory without a fight, Colonel Cass was outside of the city on special duty, trying to assist a train bringing supplies to Detroit; however, Cass' command was included in the surrender. Earlier, Cass was credited for the first victory in Canada during late July when the Americans skirmished with Indians at a bridge at the Riviere ux Canards, which was called the Tar-ontee (Tarontee) by the Indians. He was called by some "the hero of Tarontee." On the 28th, the Americans failed to seize the bridge, but on the following day, bolstered by Colonel Duncan, the men took the objective. Nevertheless, Duncan and Cass were ordered by General Hull to retire to Detroit, despite their contention that they could hold until reinforcements arrived.

After being paroled, Colonel Cass repaired to Washington, D.C., to give his report on the surrender. Afterward, Colonel Cass was appointed major general of the Ohio militia. He was still on parole at the time, which prevented him from participating in the war until he was exchanged. By early 1813, President Madison directed Colonel Cass to raise two regiments. Soon after, during February 1813, he was appointed colonel in the U.S. Army at about the same time he was exchanged. On 13 March 1813, he was breveted brigadier general. General Cass was ordered to the West, where he was attached to General William Henry Harrison and received command of the U.S. 27th Regiment. General Cass participated with General Harrison at the victorious Battle of the Thames on 5 October 1813. Harrison placed Cass in command of the Michigan Territory and afterward, on 29 October, President Madison named him governor of Michigan, which at the time was primarily inhabited by French settlers. The next year, General Cass purchased a tract of 500 acres for the sum of $12,000. He maintained his headquarters at Detroit. He held the post for eighteen years under Presidents James Monroe, John Quincy Adams and Andrew Jackson. During 1815, General Cass brought his family to Detroit.

On 22 July 1814, the governor and General Harrison met with a group of hostile Indians at Greenville, Ohio. The group agreed the army would protect the Indians and in turn, the Indians would provide their assistance to General Cass. One band of the Indians had apparently been impressed with the governor. When he returned to Detroit, they accompanied him. General Cass cooperated with General Duncan McArthur during 1815 to work out arrangements with the Indians at Fort Meigs at the time the northwestern part of Ohio was acquired by the United States. The next year, General Cass negotiated with the Indians at St. Mary's to follow up on the Treaty of Fort Meigs and add some modifications. At the same time, the government was engaged in acquiring Indian lands in Indiana. Later, during 1819, General Cass participated in the treaty that was consummated at Sagano, by which the United States acquired large tracts of land in Indiana and Michigan.

Although the war had ended, the British continued meddling in the Northwest. The Webster-Ashburton Treaty, consummated during 1842, ended some of the difficulties that had existed between the two countries. In the meantime, as governor, General Cass, who also acted as superintendent of Indian affairs, focused on improving the territory by having roads constructed and by erecting forts. He was also known for his fairness when dealing with the Indians. One of his strategies aimed to eventually open up the wilderness for white settlements. General Cass was also responsible for the erection of lighthouses on the Michigan shore. Another of his civic contributions was his involvement in the establishment of laws which became known as the "Cass code."

General Cass did not confine himself as governor by remaining in the capital.

In 1820, Cass and his party, including Henry R. Schoolcraft and Captain David B. Douglass of the Army Corps of Engineers, traveled by canoes and traversed about 5,000 miles to explore the region that comprised the upper lakes and to discover the source of the Mississippi River. Another primary purpose of the expedition was to create a map for the region; however, there was also a military purpose. General Cass was tasked with informing the Indians at Sault Ste. Marie that the United States was going to construct a fort in the area. Captain Douglass, a topographer and a teacher of mathematics at West Point, was charged with drawing the map and surveying the plant life and animals encountered during the expedition.

On 6 June, the expedition arrived at Michilimackinac. After receiving supplies, it departed on the 13th on a barge for Sault Ste. Marie. The Ojibway tribe there was not receptive, as their loyalties remained with the British. One of the chiefs, known as "The Count" and dressed in a British uniform, displayed his disapproval of the Americans by hoisting a British flag near the Americans' camp. In a flash, the British flag was ripped from its staff by Cass, who trampled it under his boots. Cass informed the Indians, through his interpreter, that they were within the United States and only one flag would be flown, the U.S. flag. Shortly thereafter, the Ojibway ceded a tract of 16 square miles along the St. Mary's River.

General Cass' bold action of hauling down the British colors paid a huge dividend. Fort Bradley followed when it was constructed by an American contingent under Colonel Hugh Brady in 1822. The post replaced the old French post, Fort de Repentigny, which had been seized by the British. Afterward the Stars and Stripes flew on the Upper Peninsula. The Americans, in addition to meeting with the Ojibway tribe, had also secured a treaty in 1820 with the Chippewa (Treaty of the Sault). The establishment of Fort Brady cemented American domination of the region around Lake Superior.

Cass's expedition did not terminate after the meetings with the Ojibway and Chippewa. He and two others traveled up the Ontonagon River, where they observed the massive amount of copper known as the Copper Rock. Afterward, the expedition advanced to the western tip of Lake Superior and from there it proceeded to the post of the American Fur Company at Fond du Lac. Afterward the party split into two groups that took separate routes to another American Fur Company post at Sandy Lake. Afterward, on the way back to Detroit, the expedition paused at the Falls of St. Anthony in Minnesota, where they encountered the 5th U.S. Infantry Regiment under Lt. Colonel Henry Leavenworth. Later, the expedition arrived at Fort Crawford at Prairie du Chien, at the western tip of the Michigan Territory.

After the expedition departed from Fort Crawford it proceeded to Fort Howard at Green Bay, where the fort welcomed the expedition with a hearty salute from its guns. While at Fort Howard, the soldiers that had accompanied the expedition were dismissed. Cass also arranged to have all of the specimens gathered by the scientists taken back to Detroit. Afterward, General Cass and those remaining with the expedition traveled down the western shore of Lake Michigan to Chicago. From there, he mounted a horse and returned to Detroit. Later, during 1828, he published an article in the *"North American Review"* that detailed the expedition.

During 1823, General Cass consummated a treaty with the Delawares which resulted in the Indians ceding tracts of land along the Muskingum River in Ohio. In 1825, he teamed with Governor (General) William Clark of St. Louis to consummate a treaty at Prairie du Chien with the northwestern tribes. During 1827, he participated in getting new treaties at Green Bay and at St. Joseph's; however, at the former, he was surprised to discover that the Winnebagoes did not attend. They were mounting forces to raise the hatchet against the white people. Cass took a canoe and sought the camp of the Winnebagoes. He discovered their village along the banks of the Wisconsin River. Acting alone, he walked into their village and attempted to persuade them, but to no avail. Upon his departure, one of the Indians fired his rifle at the general. It was never determined if the rifle misfired or whether the weapon was empty. On his return trip, he learned of one family massacred and a river boat that was attacked. The crew of the river boat repulsed the assault. Cass made it to St. Louis and from there U.S. troops repaired to the area and terminated the problem and most probably eliminated all out warfare before it began.

Yet again in 1828, General Cass participated in consummating new treaties at Green Bay and at St. Joseph's. General Cass, who could have been dubbed the "canoe governor," remained active for his entire eight years in the office and was responsible for adding millions of acres to the United States. Also in 1828, he was elected president of the Historical Society of Michigan.

During 1831, after President Jackson had eliminated his cabinet to rid himself of members he considered disloyal, he selected General Cass to be in his new cabinet as secretary of war; Cass accepted the post. He succeeded Senator (Major) Eaton. During 1832, while Cass was secretary of war, the Black Hawk War erupted when Chief Black Hawk attempted to regain lands. The conflict was short-lived and futile for Black Hawk and his followers. The hostilities erupted in Illinois in March and ended in August.

General Cass was a proponent of a strong U.S. Navy, but he was equally in favor of a strong army. He pushed for a series of formidable coastal fortifications to protect the country from a naval assault. In late 1836, Cass was appointed envoy extraordinary and minister plenipotentiary to France by President Jackson, and he retained that diplomatic post until 1842. His health forced him to relinquish his post at the War Department, though he remained well liked and appreciated by President Jackson. In 1837, General Cass, using a war ship provided by the government, took time to tour the East. He visited Sicily, Italy, Malta, Greece, Egypt, Bethlehem Jerusalem and Nazareth.

While serving as minister to France, General Cass, during 1842, adamantly opposed the "Quintuple Treaty" that Britain purported to be the means to dissolve the slave trade; however, the treaty had a clandestine purpose. It allowed the British to search without reason any ships on the high seas. The French signed the document, but General Cass' tireless efforts halted the treaty from being ratified by the French government. His opposition riled the British to a boiling point. He was told it would be extremely dangerous for him to pause in England on his return trip to the States. The threat had no effect. He did stop in England before sailing for the States, where he arrived in December 1842. President Jackson said in a letter General Cass dated 8 July 1843:

I have the pleasure to acknowledge your very friendly letter of the 26th May last. It reached me in due course of mail, and such has been my debility and afflictions, that prevented me from the power of acknowledging it until now, and even now it is with great difficulty I write.

In return for those kind expressions with regard to myself, I have to remark that I shall ever recollect my dear General, with great satisfaction, the relations, both private and official which subsisted between us during the greater part of my administration. Having full confidence in your abilities and republican principles I invited you to my Cabinet, and I never can forget with what discretion and talents you met those great and delicate questions which were brought before you whilst you Presided over the Department of War which entitled you to my thanks and will be ever recollected with the most lively feelings of friendship by me. But what has endeared you to every true American was the noble stand you took as our Minister at Paris against the Quintuple Treaty, and by your talents, energy and fearless responsibility defeated its ratification by France a treaty intended by Great Britain, to change our international laws and make her mistress of the seas, and destroy the national independence, not only of our nation but all Europe, and become the tyrant on every ocean. Had Great Britain obtained the sanction of France to this treaty, with the late disgraceful treaty of Washington so disgraceful to our national character, and injurious to our national safety in war &c &c then, indeed we might have hung our harps upon the willows and resigned our national independence to Great Britain. But to your talents, energy, and fearless responsibility we are indebted for the shield you threw over us from the impending danger [which] the ratification by France would have brought upon us. For this act of yours the thanks of every true American is yours, and the applause of every true republican; and for this noble act I tender you my thanks.

After Cass returned to the U.S., he was to have a reception at Faneuil Hall in Boston, but he was unable to attend. When he arrived in New York City, he was given a large, friendly welcome there, and shortly thereafter a large reception awaited him in Philadelphia. For a while there were thoughts that General Cass would be nominated as the Democratic candidate for the presidency. He was opposed to the annexation of Texas; however, as his chances of candidacy increased, he realized that he would have to favor annexation. Consequently, he changed his position and proclaimed that he favored annexation. Nonetheless, Cass lost to James K. Polk' and gave Polk his support. Polk, a Tennessean, was elected in 1844 to become the 11th president of the United States.

General Cass was elected to the U.S. Senate, where he served from 4 March 1845 until 29 May 1848. He resigned to run for the presidency as the Democratic party candidate, with General William O. Butler, a Kentuckian, running as his vice president. He was defeated by General Zachary Taylor, a veteran of the War of 1812 and the hero of the Mexican war. Afterward, General Cass was again elected to the Senate to fill the vacancy he created when he resigned to seek the presidency. General Cass remained in the Senate until 3 March 1857. He was president pro tempore of the Senate during the Thirty-third Congress.

In 1857, President James Buchanan named Cass secretary of state. He resigned from this position in 1860 due to government's failure to reinforce Fort Sumter and other fortifications in Charleston, South Carolina, that were under threat by the Confederates who were preparing to secede and take the posts. General Cass had been allied with Henry Clay and in support of his bid to seek compromises. General Cass departed from the capital and returned to Detroit. His sympathies during the Civil War were with the Union. On 24 April 1861, less than two weeks after the surrender of Fort Sumter, General Cass, while back in Detroit, was requested to address the people. It was just after the Board of Trade of Detroit unfurled the Stars and Stripes over their rooms. He proclaimed the Constitution, the Union and the flag should be defended: "In the midst of this prosperity, without a single foe to assail us, without a single injury at home caused by the operations of the government to affect us, this glorious Union, acquired by the blood and sacrifice of our fathers, has been disowned and rejected by a portion of the States composing it — a Union which has given us more blessings than any previous government ever conferred upon man."

He also served as the first president of the American Historical Society. While he was minister to France, he penned the work "*France, its King, Court and Government.*" General Cass received an honorary law degree from Hamilton College in New York. He was also admitted as an honorary member of the American Philosophical Society in Philadelphia, New Hampshire and Rhode Island. He was an honorary member of the Indiana Historical Society, the American Antiquarian Society and the Columbian Institute.

General Cass died in Detroit on 17 June 1866 at age 83. He was interred in Elmwood Cemetery.

Chandler, Brigadier General John John, the son of Joseph and Lydia Eastman Chandler, was born on 1 February 1762 at Epping, New Hampshire. In addition to John, the Chandlers had the following children: Nathaniel (born 22 September 1748, married Anna Prescott); Molly (born 20 April 1751, married Major James Norris); Lydia (born 15 May 1753, married Joseph Whittier); Joseph (born 29 July 1755, married Sarah Haynes); Sarah (born 5 August 1757, died 4 November 1774); Hannah (born 22 September 1759 —, married David Maloon); Olla (born 16 March 1704, died 10 July 1783); Jemima (born 7 December 1766 —, died 1 November

1785); and Jeremiah (born 26 March 1769, married Dolly Runlett, died on 10 September 1806).

John's father served as captain in the French and Indian War and in the American Revolution. On 2 January 1775, Captain Chandler was chosen as one of the members of the Committee of Inspection and Correspondence at Epping. On 22 July 1776, he became a member of the New Hampshire Committee of Safety. Nevertheless, John's father's service was terminated on 17 September 1776 when died from disease, not combat, at Mount (Fort) Independence. On 25 February 1778, Captain Chandler's youngest children, Olla, Jeremiah and Jemima, were placed under the guardianship of Jeremiah Eastman. John's mother married John Bartlett on 19 November. Upon the death of her second husband, she moved into the home of her son Jon and his wife at Monmouth, Maine, where she lived until her death on 9 March 1820 at age 84.

In the meantime, John Chandler followed in his father's footsteps and joined the military when he was only about 15 years old, just after his father was killed. Chandler had little if any formal education. His enlistment was for three months and at its end, his mother refused to let him re-enlist. While he was on active duty he was at Saratoga when British General Burgoyne surrendered his army. Chandler acquiesced to his mother's fears of him going back into the army; however, without seeking her permission, he went to sea on a privateer, the *Arnold*, and afterward, he found himself a prisoner of the British on a prison ship at British-held Savannah. Chandler and other prisoners managed to escape by boat and split into small parties. Chandler and two others attempted to walk back home. One of them died in North Carolina and another died when they reached New Jersey; however, Chandler succeeded in walking all the way back to New Hampshire. His time on a privateer had ended, but after arriving home, John did again join the army, and he remained in the service for the duration of the war.

After the war, in 1783, Chandler married Marry Whittier of South Hampton. Their children were Caroline Elizabeth (born 20 August 1784, married Doctor Benjamin Prescott of Bath, Maine); Clarissa (twin of Caroline Elizabeth, born 20 August 1784, died several days later); Clarissa II (born 7 June 1786, died 13 October 1792); John Alonzo (born 19 May 1791, married Delia E. West and later Eunice P. Robinson); Anson Gonzalo (born 14 October 1793, married Elizabeth Ann Pike in 1825 and Annie Eliza Bradbury in 1852); Clarissa Augusta (born 12 July 1797, married Doctor Amos Nourse); and William Henry Augustus (born 24 April 1803, died 7 January 1805).

Chandler had few resources; however, an opportunity emerged when he came under the guidance of General Henry Dearborn, who later became secretary of war. Chandler, after borrowing $400, through his friendship with the Dearborns, acquired 200 acres and through those same connections, he began to prosper. He was one of the initial settlers in Monmouth, Maine. He was a member of the Maine Senate from 1803 until 1805, when he was elected to the U.S. Congress, where he served from March 1805 until March 1809. He resigned from the Senate to become the high sheriff of Kennebec County. He served in the War of 1812 with the Maine militia, and he also became a brigadier general in the U.S. Army.

Chandler was appointed a brigadier general in late January 1812, along with Joseph Bloomfield (New Jersey), John Armstrong (Pennsylvania), James Winchester (Tennessee), William Hull (governor of Michigan Territory), Thomas Flournoy (Georgia), Morgan Lewis (New York), and Alexander Smyth (Virginia). On 10 March 1813, General Dearborn, concerned about his ability to defend Sackets Harbor, directed General Chandler to repair to Sackets Harbor with the 9th, 21st and 25th Regiments.

In April 1813, General Chandler was assigned to the 9th military district, which encompassed New York extending north from the Highlands and Vermont, and was under the command of Major General Henry Dearborn. By June 1813, American forces were pursuing British troops after they abandoned Fort George in Canada. On 5 June, the American vanguard (two brigades and cavalry) arrived at Stoney Creek. General William Henry Winder requested reinforcements, and General Chandler's command arrived. Although the British were outnumbered and on the run, British General Vincent halted at Burlington Heights to prepare a defense. The Americans at the time dominated the entire area extending from Fort George to Stony Creek.

On 6 June, a British force of only about 700 men, which had departed from Burlington heights at midnight (5th–6th), moved quietly through the woods. Officers had ordered the troops to remove the flints from their weapons to eliminate the chance of an accidental firing. The British anticipated some stiff opposition. Generals Chandler and Winder had taken no precautions because they believed the British would not launch an attack. The British struck while the troops slept. One of the pickets was able to fire a warning shot, but still, the British captured some artillery, but with no artillerymen in their contingent, the guns were not turned on the Americans. They also captured Generals Chandler and Winder. The attack also brought General Dearborn's advance to a halt. The Americans retired to Fort George. The British attack achieved no decisive victory, but it did convince the Americans that the British forces were far stronger than thought; however, despite the element of surprise, they sustained about 150 casualties.

A report by General Dearborn, who was not present, said Generals Chandler and Winder were seized after attacking an artillery position, the British were driven from the field and General Vincent had been killed. The generals did not charge any artillery, but on the following day, Chandler and Winder had dinner with General Vincent at the British camp. General Chandler's career in the field on the frontier essentially ended following his capture. After his exchange he finished out the war in Portland, Maine, which at the time was part of Massachusetts.

After the war, he became a member of the Massachusetts General Court in 1819 and served as the first president of the Maine Senate.

General Chandler also served as a member of the Maine constitutional convention (1819–1820). After Maine entered the Union as the 23rd state on 15 March 1820, General Chandler was elected to the U.S. Senate as a Democratic-Republican. Later, he became a Crawford Republican and afterward a Jacksonian. He served in the U.S. Senate (1820–1829). While in the Senate, Chandler was instrumental in the establishment of the federal arsenal at Augusta, Maine, and was a proponent of the construction of the military road that stretched from Bangor to Houlton. He resigned from the Senate in 1829 to accept the appointment as collector of customs at the port of Portland. He held the post for about eight years before retiring.

General Chandler spent the rest of his life in Augusta, Maine, where he died at age 79 on 25 September 1841. He was interred at Mount Pleasant Cemetery. He was survived by his wife, Mary, and one of their children, Anson Gonzalo.

Clark (Clarke), Major General John The son of General Elijah and Hannah Harrington (Arrington) Clark, John was born in North Carolina during 1766. Elijah and Hannah had several young children when the family relocated in Georgia; the names and number remain uncertain. It is known that in addition to John, they included Elijah Jr.; Gibson; and three daughters, who became Mrs. Thompson, Mrs. Benajah Smith, and Mrs. Walton. Although John had been unable to receive his formal education due to the American Revolution, the other siblings each attended school. When John's father relocated about 1774, he had not been committed to the Patriots' cause, but at some point, he became deeply committed. His son John, with the rank of major, is thought to have participated in the war (his father's command) with Britain during the siege of Augusta in 1781. John is also mentioned as participating with his father at the Battle of Jack's Creek during 1787. However, there is some controversy because of John's young age (16) during 1781. The participant may have been a relative rather than John.

Nonetheless, John Clark did become a dedicated military man who rapidly rose in rank to become a major general in the Georgia militia. He received command of the state forces designated to guard the seacoast of Georgia during the War of 1812. In 1819, General Clark was elected governor of Georgia, then won re-election. During 1827, General Clark relocated in West Florida, where he died on 15 October 1832.

Clay, Major General Green Green, the son of the Rev. Charles and Martha Green Clay, was born on 14 August 1757 in Powhatan County, Virginia. Green traveled to Kentucky while he was young. He became a surveyor, although his education was only basic. Initially he spent a few years in the militia during a time when there was turbulence with the Indians. During that time he also began to acquire large tracts of land. He also served as a delegate to the General Assembly of Virginia before Kentucky was admitted to the Union as the 15th state on 1 June 1792. On 14 March 1795, Green Clay married Sally Lewis. They had seven children: Elizabeth (born March 1798); Sidney Payne (born July 1800); Paulina Green (born September 1802); Sally Ann (born September 1804); Brutus Junius (born July 1808); Cassius Marcellus (born October 1810); and Sophia (born March 1813).

During the War of 1812, Green Clay was a major general in the Kentucky militia. On 26 April 1813, General Clay's force was en route to relieve Fort Meigs, which was under siege by Colonel Proctor. A messenger on that day was dispatched from General William Henry Harrison to inform Clay to speed up his advance. During the early part of May, Clay's columns arrived, and during the operation to lift the siege, Colonel Dudley's contingent was nearly annihilated due to Dudley's impetuous actions. However, Proctor's attack failed and the siege was lifted. Afterward, General Harrison departed from Fort Meigs en route to Lower Sandusky, leaving the fort under the command of General Clay. In June a man who had escaped from Canada arrived at the post to forewarn General Clay that a large British force was en route to capture Fort Meigs. On 8 July, some enlistments had expired at Fort Meigs. General Clay decided to lighten the mood. He gave the following order: "The commanding General directs that the Old Guard, on being released, will march out of camp and discharge their guns at a target placed in some secure position; and as a reward for those who may excel in shooting, eight gills of whiskey will be given to the nearest shot, and four gills to the second. The officer of the guard will cause a return, signed for that purpose, signifying the names of the men entitled to the reward." Afterward, those troops whose enlistments terminated departed for their homes. One group of fourteen men was ambushed at a spot between Fort Meigs and Fort Winchester. Only two survived.

That month, the British again launched an assault to seize Fort Meigs. They tried to fool the Americans by destroying a relief column that did not exist; however, General Clay did not take the bait and rush reinforcements from the fort. The gates remained closed and secure, and the enemy poised outside the gates waiting to pounce on the column once the gates were opened were disappointed. The attack, which began on the 26th, ceased on the 27th and Colonel Proctor retired without gaining his prize. The troops at Fort Meigs were dismissed at the end of their enlistments. General Clay moved with the regulars as far as Detroit. The troops were preparing to participate in the invasion of Canada; however, General Clay returned to his residence in Madison County.

He retired and spent the remaining years of his life in private, working his farm and his estate. He died on 31 October 1826 at age 72. General Clay's son, Cassius served in the Mexican War as an officer. During the Civil War, he attained the rank of major general of volunteers. He resigned from the service on 11 March 1863 and afterward he served as minister to Russia.

Coffee, Brigadier General John John, the son of Joshua Coffee, who emigrated from Ireland, was born in Prince Edward County, Virginia, on 9 June 1772. Sometimes he is confused with his cousin John Coffee, the son of Peter Coffee (brother of Joshua, born in Virginia 1784 and later removed to Georgia, where he became a brigadier general in the Georgia militia. In 1798, John (subject of this sketch) moved to Davidson County, Tennessee. Initially, Coffee set out to be a merchant, but in 1807 his interests changed dramatically when he became a surveyor. In 1809 he married Mary Donelson, a relative of Rachel Donelson, the wife of General Andrew Jackson. They had the following children: John (born 1815); Elizabeth Graves (born 1817); Alexander Donelson (born 1821); Catherine Harriett (born 1826); Emily (born 1828, died the next year); and William Donelson (born 1830).

Coffee served with General Jackson in 1813, and during that year, on 24 September, Coffee was promoted to brigadier general of Tennessee militia. General Coffee had raised a cavalry regiment during the early days of the War of 1812, and after the massacre at Fort Mims on 30 August 1813, he raised two additional regiments. While serving with Jackson during the Creek War (1813–1814), General Coffee participated at the Battles of Tallushatchie, Emuckfaw, Enitachopco and Horseshoe Bend. He was seriously wounded at Emuckfaw, but he recovered and participated in the campaign to seize Pensacola. In December 1814, Coffee arrived in time to reinforce General Jackson. He participated during the siege and the spectacular victory over the British at the Battle of New Orleans on 8 January 1815. After the war, General Coffee resided in Alabama, where he became a planter. He died on 7 July 1833.

Covington, Brigadier General Leonard Leonard, the son of Levin and Susanna Magruder Covington, was born on 30 October 1768 in Aquasco, Maryland. Leonard's parents had one other child, Alexander, born on 25 October 1771. Leonard received an excellent education, including the study of English, mathematics and some Latin. Upon the death of his father, he was nudged toward a life of husbandry by his mother. Following the defeat of General Arthur St. Clair by the Indians in 1791, Covington joined the army on 14 March 1792 and became a cornet of cavalry. The next year, he was appointed as a lieutenant of dragoons. He served under General Anthony Wayne in the Northwest Territory during the campaign which avenged St. Clair's loss by the decisive victory over the Indians. During June 1794, on the 30th, a severe clash occurred near Fort Recovery, Ohio, after a contingent of troops had departed the fort with a significant number of packhorses. The column was struck by about 1,000 braves. It sustained a casualty rate of about 50 percent, and the Indians were able to seize all of the horses. The Indians, including Chippewa, Ottowa and Potawatomi, became over confident after the successful raid and decided to reduce the fort. Nonetheless, the garrison, composed of skilled riflemen and artillerymen, decidedly repelled the attack and essentially caused a rupture of the cohesion of the various tribes, injecting friction between the northern tribes and the Delaware, Shawnee and Wyandot. Chief Blue Jacket, a Shawnee, after being accused of cowardice, led his tribe back to their territory.

Captain Covington displayed great valor. He sustained no wounds, but his horse was shot from under him. After the campaign, Covington resigned from the service on 12 September 1795. He returned to his farm in Maryland. During the following year, he married Rebecca Mackall, his cousin. They had six children, including Rebecca and Levin. As his reputation grew, he was elected to the Senate of Maryland (1802); however, he declined taking his seat. In 1805, he was elected to the 9th U.S. Congress, where he served until 1807. That year, he relinquished his seat after being elected unanimously to the Maryland Senate.

Covington also served as a presidential elector who supported Thomas Jefferson. While relations with Britain were quickly deteriorating, he accepted an appointment on 9 January 1809 as lieutenant colonel of the Light Dragoons, the sole regiment of dragoons in the army at that time. Shortly thereafter, he was promoted to full colonel. In 1810, he received command of Fort Adams at Loftus Heights, Mississippi, less than 40 miles south of Natchez. After traveling down the Ohio and Mississippi Rivers, Colonel Covington and his family arrived in Mississippi during January 1810. He purchased a property known as "Propinquity." While in Louisiana and the Mississippi Territory, he participated in taking possession of Baton Rouge (December 1810) without incident. During March 1811, Covington was directed to repair to Fort Stoddard along the Alabama River. Nevertheless, the Spanish continued to hold Mobile. General Wilkinson arrived in New Orleans on 9 July 1812. He assumed command in New Orleans and the Mississippi Territory. On 4 August that year, Wilkinson placed Colonel Covington in command at Pass Christian, Mississippi, where his force was ordered to be prepared to move at a moment's notice if needed.

Colonel Covington was appointed brigadier general on 1 August 1813. After arriving in Louisiana he was pleased with the region, so much so that he purchased a plantation near Natchez, Mississippi, and along the banks of the Mississippi River. He was on active duty in the South when war with Great Britain erupted, and at the time, he held the rank of colonel. There was a great deal of time spent preparing for an attack by the British; however, it did not materialize. Once the threat against Mobile or New Orleans passed, Colonel Covington was transferred to the northern frontier at the same time General Wilkinson was ordered to repair to western New York.

On 13 May 1813, Colonel Covington, in conjunction with General Wilkinson's orders to move to western New York, after saying his goodbyes to his family, departed from New Orleans by horseback and rode to Washington, D.C. After spending a while in the capital, Covington also repaired to New York. By autumn 1813, Colonel Covington, by then a brigadier general, commanded one of General Wilkinson's brigades during the ill-fated campaign to seize Montreal. By 17 October, General Wilkinson sailed from Sackets Harbor. His brigade commanders were General Covington and Generals John Parker Boyd, Robert Swartwout and Jacob J. Brown, bolstered by a reserve brigade under General Alexander Macomb.

On 11 November 1813, at the Battle of Chrysler's Field (Battle of Williamsburg), while on a flanking maneuver intended to seize the British artillery, General Covington received a fatal wound while riding his white horse and waving his saber during a charge against the British right. A British soldier posted at Chrysler's barn shot him and the wound was mortal. He died two days later at French Mills, where he was interred. He was survived by his wife and six children.

A report by the commander-in-chief said this about General Covington: "It would be presumptuous in me to attempt to give a detailed account of this affair, which certainly reflects high honor on the valor of the American soldiers, as no example can be produced of undisciplined men with inexperienced officers, braving a fire of two hours and a half without quitting the field or yielding to the antagonist. It is due to his rank, his worth and his services that I should make particular mention of Brigadier General Covington, who received a mortal wound through his body while animating his men and leading them to the charge. He fell where he fought, at the head of his men, and survived but two days. He died lamented by the whole army from the commanding General to the private soldier, as well for his private virtues as for his valor as an officer."

General Covington's remains were taken to Sackets Harbor, New York, on 14 August 1820 and re-interred at what was later known as Mount Covington. Of General Covington's six children, three were boys; however, none left a son, which caused his name to become extinct during 1915 when the final Covington died. General Covington's widow and the children, following the death of General Covington, lived with his brother, Alexander.

Croghan, Lt. Colonel George The son of Major William and Lucy Clark Croghan, George was born in Kentucky near the Falls of the Ohio (Louisville) in November 1791. His father was from Ireland and served in the American Revolution. George's mother was the sister of George Rodgers Clark and General William Clark. George received an excellent education in Kentucky, and at age seventeen, he entered William and Mary College in Virginia, from where he graduated in July 1810. After graduation, George entered the law school of William and Mary. The next year he entered the service as a private. Afterward, he was selected as aide-de-camp to General Boyd. He participated in the Battle of Tippecanoe. Following the expedition on the Wabash River, Croghan was appointed captain in the provisional army to be established in spring of 1812.

Shortly after war with Great Britain erupted during June 1812, Captain Croghan departed from Kentucky with a contingent under General James Winchester en route to Detroit, where General William Hull was threatened by a British army under General Isaac Brock; however, Detroit was surrendered without a fight before Croghan's unit arrived. Later, during a march toward the Rapids he received command of Fort Winchester. Following the defeat at the Raisin River, Captain Croghan joined with General Harrison at the Rapids. He was at Fort Meigs when it was attacked during May 1813, and his actions aided in the repulse of the British under Colonel Henry Proctor. Later that year, Captain Croghan was promoted to major and then to lieutenant colonel. He also received command of Fort Stephenson in Ohio.

In the meantime, the garrison at Fort Meigs had again repelled a British assault. Having failed to reduce Fort Meigs, the British set their sights on a fort that seemed less formidable, Fort Stephenson. General Harrison, aware of the British intent, sent a messenger to the fort to order Major Croghan to abandon it, but by the time the messenger arrived, Croghan believed it to be too late to evacuate. The British, about 5,000 strong, including Tecumseh's Indians, bolstered by four gunboats, attacked. Croghan, with only one artillery piece and 160 men, repelled the assault. Croghan's riflemen and their one gun, which is shortly after the victory nicknamed "Ole Betsy," had added one more defeat to Proctor's record. He retreated on 4 August. Croghan's losses during their defense of the post amounted to one man killed and seven others with minor wounds. Major Croghan (17th U.S. Infantry) was awarded a gold medal by the U.S. Congress, which also gave a sword to each of the officers who participated in the defense of the post.

On 12 July 1814, Lt. Colonel Croghan led a contingent to recapture Fort Michilimackinac. The naval squadron carrying Croghan's contingent first arrived at Fort St. Joseph and found it abandoned. The flotilla arrived at its objective on 26 July. Nevertheless, the British repelled the assault. After the mission, Croghan returned to Detroit. He remained on active duty until the end of the war, and afterward when the army was being downsized, he resigned from the service. During 1817, he married Serina, a daughter of John Livingston of New York. Subsequently, he served again during the Mexican War. He died on 8 January 1849 from cholera, while in New Orleans with the army.

Cushing, Brigadier General Thomas Humphrey Thomas, the son of Nehmiah and Sarah Humphrey Cushing, was born in 1755 in Pembroke, Massachusetts. Thomas' father died while serving as a captain at Crown Point on 12 January 1762. Thomas joined the army during the American Revolution, initially as a sergeant. From January until December 1776, he was attached to the 6th Continental Infantry Regiment. On 1 January 1777, he was appointed as a 2nd lieutenant and served with the 1st Massachusetts Regiment. He was later promoted to the rank of first lieutenant. Sergeant Cushing was captured on 14 May 1781. On 30 September 1783, he was promoted to the rank of brevet captain. He served in a Continental regiment from November 1783 until 20 June 1784. Captain Cushing became attached to the 2nd U.S. Infantry on 4 March 1791 and afterward, on 4 September 1792, he was assigned to the 2nd Sub-legion. He was transferred to the 1st Sub-legion in conjunction with his promotion to the rank of major in March 1793. On 27 February 1797, Captain Cushing was named inspector of the army, a post he held until 22 May 1793. Later, on 1 April 1802, he was promoted to the rank of lieutenant colonel and assigned to the 2nd U.S. Infantry Regiment. While serving in the Mississippi Territory, he commanded the American troops along the Mississippi and Tombigbee Rivers. He supervised the construction of a series of forts, particularly Fort Stoddart.

On 26 March 1802, Cushing was appointed inspector general on 26 March 1802. He retained the post until 9 May 1807, and was promoted to the rank of full colonel on 7 September 1805. Colonel Cushing was responsible during the Neutral Ground Dispute in 1806 to protect the American territory east of the Sabine River to ensure that the Spanish did not enter U.S. territory. Hostilities did not erupt. Later, on 2 November 1806, General Wilkinson signed the Neutral Ground Treaty to end the dispute. During early 1812, William North, former adjutant general of the Army, was again placed in nomination and afterward confirmed as adjutant general; however, he did not accept. On 6 July, Colonel Cushing was installed in place of North. He was promoted to the rank of brigadier general effective 2 July.

During April 1813, the country was divided into nine military districts with a 10th district established in July. General Cushing received command of the 1st District, which encompassed Massachusetts and New Hampshire. The next year he was transferred to the 2nd Military District, where he made his headquarters in New London, Connecticut. Connecticut was one of the New England states that was uncooperative with the federal government with regard to the state militia. The situation remained tense; however, General Augustine Taylor, commander of the militia, had many more troops than Cushing's regulars, which essentially prohibited Cushing from ever gaining complete control. On 2 September 1814, General Cushing wrote to Governor John Cotton Smith:

> Whether I have understood the views of the government [Connecticut] respecting the

detachment lately organized or not, is in my estimation, a question of no importance at the time, since by referring to my letter of the 10th of August, your excellency will there find the conditions on which the draughted militia, now in service were asked for, and have been received into the service of the United States. If these conditions did not accord with the "views of this Government"; it is not for me to assign the motive which induced your Excellency to make the detachment; but while I regret that any misunderstanding should exist on this subject, I feel confident that my communications have been too explicit to leave a doubt as to the course authorized and enjoined by the Government of the United States.

On the following day, a letter from Governor Smith to the secretary of war provides another example of the tension between the state and the federal government:

> In consequence of the exposed and defenseless situation of the town of New Haven and borough of Bridgeport, I have thought proper, by the advice of the Council, to order into service six hundred men, for the protection of these places. The general officer [General Cushing] of the United States, located at New London, has been advised of this procedure, and has also been requested to cause the troops to be duly mustered and supplied. He admits the propriety of the measure, but as I understood, refuses to comply with the request, and on grounds, which, in my view, are wholly inadmissible. It is my duty, sir, to inform you of these circumstances, and to express the assurance I feel that you will order the requisite supplies to be immediately furnished.

The feud between General Taylor and General Cushing continued for the duration. General Cushing left the service in June 1815. Subsequently, in January 1816, he was appointed collector of customs at the port of New London. He also engaged in a duel with a Virginia congressman, William J. Lewis. The congressman hit Cushing, but Cushing's watch sustained the hit and he was spared. Afterward, the two men settled their differences. Congressman Lewis said to General Cushing: "I congratulate you, General, on having a watch that will keep time from eternity."

General Cushing received a court-martial based on charges placed by General Wade Hampton during 1811. He was acquitted. General Cushing never married. He died at New London on 19 October 1822.

Dearborn, Major General Henry Henry, the son of Simon and Sarah Marston Dearborn, was born in Hampton, New Hampshire, on 28 February 1751. Initially, his ancestor, Godfrey Dearborn, and his son Henry emigrated from Exeter, England, and arrived in Exeter, New Hampshire, during 1639. They subsequently relocated in Hampton after staying only about ten years at Exeter. As a young boy Henry attended school in Epping, then later he began to study medicine under Doctor Hall Jackson at Portsmouth, New Hampshire. Henry was one of twelve children. His siblings were Simon, Levi, Deborah, Sarah, Benjamin, Hannah, Abigail, John (born 1732), John (born 1736), Eliphalet, and Ruth.

In 1771, Dearborn began his medical practice at Nottingham Square, and at about the same time, he married Mary Bartlett. They had two children, Sophia (born 1773, married Dudley B. Hobart), and Pamela Augustus (married Judge Allen Gillman). Pamela, who married in 1799, died that same year. Henry took Dorcas Osgood Marble (widow of Colonel Isaac Marble) as his second wife during 1780. They had three children, Julia Cascaline (born 1781, married Joshua Wingate, Jr.), Henry Alexander Scammel (born 1783, married Hannah Swett) and George Raleigh (born 22 October 1784, died unmarried, 3 December 1806). After marrying Dorcas, General Dearborn became stepfather to her two daughters, Dorcas and Mary (married Doctor James Parker). During 1813, he married yet again, taking Sarah Bowdoin (widow of her cousin and husband, James Bowdoin, the son of Governor James Bowdoin of Massachusetts) as his third wife. No children were born of Henry's third marriage.

During 1775, Dearborn shelved his medical practice as the American Revolution was getting underway. After raising a force of about 60 volunteers, he led them into Massachusetts to bolster the other American volunteers at Cambridge. The column was part of Colonel John Stark's New Hampshire regiment. The arrival of Dearborn's unit coincided with the British attempt to vanquish the rebels at Bunker Hill (Breed's Hill). Before reaching Stark's positions, Dearborn's volunteers came under heavy fire as they advanced across Charlestown Neck.

In September, Dearborn participated in the campaign to seize Quebec. The march into Canada was exhausting and many failed to complete it. The elements were harsh and provisions were often unavailable. A dog belonging to Dearborn had to be killed due to desperation caused by the shortage of food. Dearborn stated in his journal: "My dog was very large and a great favorite, I gave him up to several men of Capt. Goodrich's company on their earnest solicitation; they carried him to their company, killed and divided him among those who were suffering most with hunger; they ate all but the bones and these they broke to make a broth for another meal; but one other dog was with the detachment, this was small and had been privately killed and eaten. Old moose-first settlement in Canada, many men died with exposure, hunger and fatigue."

Dearborn, himself, became too ill from fever

Major General Henry Dearborn's house.

to maintain the pace. He remained behind at a shack near the Chaudire River and there was neither medicine nor medical help. Essentially, he was left there to die. Nonetheless, after about ten days of touch-and-go regarding his chances of surviving, his fever broke and he lived. After regaining his strength, Dearborn set out by sleigh to join his company, which he did just before the attack on Quebec. However, the Americans were repulsed and during the assault, Dearborn, holding the rank of captain, was captured and transferred to Halifax, Nova Scotia. During May of the following spring, he was paroled; however, his official exchange did not occur until March 1777.

Meanwhile, on 19 March 1777, Dearborn was promoted to major and attached to the 3rd New Hampshire Regiment, commanded by Colonel Alexander Scammel. In September he was transferred to the 1st New Hampshire Regiment, commanded by Colonel Joseph Cilley (successor to John Stark). Major Dearborn participated in various actions, including Ticonderoga against British General Burgoyne. He also struggled with the army at Valley Forge (winter 1777–1778) and served under General Washington at the Battle of Monmouth (June 1778). As a lieutenant colonel, he led a successful charge against the British right wing and succeeded by a bayonet charge in collapsing the line. At the time, General Washington, having observed the attack, inquired of Dearborn: "What troops are those?" Dearborn responded excitedly, "Full-blooded Yankees from New Hampshire."

Colonel Dearborn also participated in General Sullivan's Indian campaigns (Six Nations, in central New York), including the Battle of Newtown, in which Sullivan's forces inflicted a severe defeat upon the Indians under Brant and the Loyalists under Sir John Johnson. He also went south with General Washington when the army slipped away unnoticed by the British and moved to Philadelphia, from where Washington repaired to Virginia and finally gained that momentous victory at Yorktown when General Cornwallis was trapped by a French fleet offshore and the American and French land forces which had drawn a net around the town. British reinforcements either by land or sea could not arrive and the French fleet prohibited any chance of evacuation. During the Virginia campaign, Dearborn was on General Washington's staff and served as deputy quartermaster.

Following the victory at Yorktown, Colonel Dearborn served at Saratoga in 1782 on garrison duty until the close of the war.

Afterward, he returned to New Hampshire, but he did not permanently return to medicine. He engaged in farming on his land, which was along the Kennebec River in Maine. He did receive an appointment during 1784 (or possibly 1787) as brigadier general of militia and afterward he was promoted to the rank of major general in the Maine militia. About 1787, Dearborn was appointed by President George Washington as U.S. marshal for Maine. From March 1793 to March 1797, he served in Congress as a representative from Maine. During his terms, he was anti-administration or anti–Federalist (Democratic-Republican, present-day Democrat).

In March 1801, Colonel Dearborn received a huge promotion when President Thomas Jefferson named him secretary of war. After a term of eight years, Colonel Dearborn was named collector of the port of Boston, Massachusetts. Nonetheless, his connection with the military was not finished. With the imminent approach of the War of 1812, Colonel Dearborn was back in uniform, although it was a different one. During February 1812, he was named first major general in the U.S. Army. He received command of the Northern Department, from the Niagara River east to the New England coast. Soon after, Thomas Pinckney, a South Carolina Federalist, was appointed second major general. He received command of the Southern Department and Brigadier General James Wilkinson was dispatched to New Orleans to replace General Wade Hampton (grandfather of Confederate General Wade Hampton). During May 1812, Dearborn established headquarters for the Northern Department at present-day Greenbush opposite Albany. The next month, he encountered resistance after requesting troops from Governor Strong of Massachusetts. The governor, similarly to other New England governors, would not permit their militia to serve outside their respective states. Dearborn, in Boston when war was declared, remained there for a while trying to acquire coastal defenses, and he spent time on recruiting. While he was in Massachusetts, the British captured Detroit, and they defeated an American force at Queenston, Canada, on the Niagara River. Afterward, General Dearborn led a force out of Plattsburgh, New York, but no contact was made with any British forces. The column returned to Plattsburgh.

During August 1812, General Dearborn consummated an armistice with British General Sir George Prevost, governor of Upper Canada. During the temporary truce, American troops continued to funnel into the region, and by September General Van Rensselaer's force amounted to about 8,000 troops (regulars and militia) stretched from Fort Niagara and Buffalo. On 19 November, General Dearborn aborted his intended attack against Montreal, specifically because the militia refused to cross into Canada. By the 23rd, the units already in Canada withdrew. Dearborn at no time personally led any of his troops into Canada. General Wilkinson, promoted to major general during February 1813, later succeeded General Dearborn as commander of the Northern Department (9th Military District).

Meanwhile, York (in Toronto), held only by Canadian militia under Colonel Chewitt, was seized by the Americans during late April. In late May, Fort George was seized by the Americans; however, again, General Dearborn was not at the front of his troops. He remained aboard ship until the post, commanded by British General Vincent, was captured. General Morgan Lewis on 27 May wrote to General Dearborn:

> Fort George and its dependencies are ours; the enemy, beaten at all points, has blown up his magazines, and retired. It is impossible, at this time, to say any thing of individual gallantry; there was no man who did not perform his duty in a manner, which did honor to himself and country. Scott's and Forsyth's commands, supported by Boyd's and Winder's brigades, sustained the brunt of the action. Our loss is trifling; not more than 20 killed, and twice that number wounded. The enemy has left in the hospital 124, and I sent several on board of the fleet. We have also made about 100 prisoners of the regular forces.

General Dearborn, in an official letter, lent no factual substance to the circumstances of the assault. He claimed Indians had participated and none were there. He also reported General Vincent as being killed, along with Dearborn's statement that the British requested time to bury their dead; however, it was the British who buried the American dead. General Vincent was not present at the beginning of the attack.

By early June 1813, General Dearborn, already over-stressed, was rattled when the British squadron under Commodore Yeo appeared, and shortly thereafter, General Morgan Lewis was installed as temporary commander of General Dearborn's command.

Before the end of June, General John Boyd replaced General Lewis, the latter having departed Fort George in Canada for Sackets Harbor, New York. Meanwhile, President Madison, bordering on replacing General Dearborn, reacted quickly following an incident in Canada which involved the capture of a contingent under Lt. Colonel Charles G. Boerstler, 14th U.S. Infantry, on 22–23 June, which followed the debacle at Stoney Creek on 6 June, which included the capture of Generals John Chandler and William H. Winder. General Dearborn was replaced by General James Wilkinson on 6 July, and according to orders, the command change was to be temporary until General Dearborn regained his health. Nonetheless, he did not regain the command, and despite requesting an inquiry, none was ever convened, leaving the actual reasons for his being relieved of command without an answer.

Dearborn wrote one letter to the president, which was answered on 8 August 1813 without the president saying anything substantive. Dearborn wrote again on 17 August: "To suspend an officer of my grade and situation in command, except by the sentence of a court-martial, or the opinion of a court of inquiry, is such a strong measure, as on general received principles, could only be justified by the most unequivocal and outrageous misconduct of the officer; and I cannot permit myself to doubt but that on reflection, it will be considered proper to afford me a hearing before a suitable military tribunal, previous to my being again ordered on duty." General Dearborn received a letter, dated 24 December 1813, from the War Department ordering him to repair to New York City to assume command there.

He reported to New York as ordered, but the inquiry never convened. In June 1814, a letter from Secretary of State James Monroe informed Dearborn: "My own idea is that you require no vindication in the case alluded to; that public opinion has already done you justice." General Dearborn was honorably discharged from the Army on 15 June 1815.

At one point, President Madison attempted to re-appoint General Dearborn to the position of secretary of war; however, opposition was so aggressive that Dearborn's nomination was withdrawn by the president. During July 1822, having been appointed minister plenipotentiary to Portugal, Dearborn sailed for Portugal. He apparently was dissatisfied with his mission as a diplomat and resigned after serving about two years. He returned to the United States and resided in Roxbury, Massachusetts. He died there on 6 June 1829 and was interred at Forrest Hills Cemetery outside of Boston.

Desha, Brigadier General Joseph Joseph, the son of Robert and Eleanor Wheeler Desha, was born in Monroe County, Tennessee, on 9 December 1768. During 1781, he moved to Kentucky with his father, then the next year moved to Tennessee. In 1789, he married Peggy Bledsoe. In 1792, Desha returned to Kentucky and settled in Mason County. He served in the military in 1794 and participated in the campaigns of General Anthony Wayne and General William Henry Harrison. He served in the Kentucky legislature from 1797 to 1806. During 1813, Desha was appointed a major general of volunteers. He participated in the Battle of the Thames in which General William Henry Harrison delivered a decisive defeat upon the British. After the war, General Desha was elected to Congress. He served from 1816 until 1819, then was elected governor of Kentucky in 1824.

After completing his term, General Desha retired to private life. He remained on his farm in Harrison County until his death on 11 October 1842, which occurred at Georgetown. He was the brother of Brigadier General Robert Desha, who married Nellie Shelby, the daughter of David and Sarah Bledsoe Shelby.

Flournoy, Brigadier General Thomas Thomas, the son of Matthew Flournoy, a veteran of the American Revolution, was born in North Carolina during 1775. Thomas' father was born in Prince Edward County, Virginia, and served there as sheriff during 1756. Matthew moved to Kentucky in 1785 and was killed in an engagement with hostile Indians at Orchard Springs. There is very little information relating to Thomas' early years; however, it is known that he arrived in 1795 in Georgia, where he practiced law. It is thought that Thomas had experience with the military because he was appointed as a brigadier general in Georgia during January 1812, before war was declared against Great Britain in June.

During April 1813, General Flournoy was appointed commander of Military District No. 7, which encompassed Louisiana, Mississippi and Tennessee. Later, about the end of July, General Flournoy refused to authorize General Claiborne's request to strike "for the heart of the Creek nation." At the time, Flournoy believed that the Creeks would make war against only themselves. His response to Claiborne: "Your wish to penetrate into the Indian country, with a view of commencing the war, does not meet my approbation; and I again repeat, our operations must be confined to defensive operations." Claiborne also requested that General Flournoy protect the settlements in Alabama by activating the militia, and he received the following response: "I am not authorized to make the call." General Claiborne, although turned down by Flournoy, took it upon himself to provide protection by dispatching troops to Fort Mims, Fort Madison and other places believed to be threatened by the Creeks. On August 2, Claiborne requested reinforcements (7th U.S. Infantry) to stabilize his force which had been greatly reduced by sending the contingents to protect the settlements; however, General Flournoy again declined the request. He was reluctant to cut his force due to his fears that the Spanish might launch an attack.

During October 1813, a party—including a prominent Choctaw chief, Pushmataha, and George S. Gaines—traveled to Mobile to speak with General Flournoy and offer their services to join in the fight against the Creeks; however, General Flournoy declined their offer due to his reluctance to accept Choctaw Indians as soldiers in the U.S. Army. Nevertheless, to the great relief of the settlers, Flournoy changed his mind and agreed to accept them. The Chickasaws were also persuaded to become allies of the Americans.

On October 12, General Flournoy made a complete turnaround. He ordered General Ferdinand Claiborne to initiate offensive action against the Indians that had joined with the British. Flournoy's order, as described by himself, were "contrary to that of civilized nations, but the conduct of Great Britain and the acts of her Indian allies fully justify it." The order, intended to protect the settlers by running the hostile Indians out of the region, included the following: "Follow them up to their contiguous towns, and to kill, burn and destroy all their Negroes, horses, cattle, and other property, that cannot conveniently be brought to the depots." During the operation, the Indians, thought to have gathered in large numbers, remained elusive except for some small clashes. Meanwhile, General Flournoy continued to have less than congenial relations with Claiborne and other American officers. His steadfast positions alienated many and not only those in the military. He was known to dislike the Louisianians in general.

By 1814, General Flournoy's command style had ruffled too many feathers. General Andrew Jackson was selected to succeed him in May 1814, and the decision was not well received. General Flournoy resigned from the service in September. The change of command had a profound effect on the operation in the South. Jackson countermanded an order from General Flournoy to dismantle Fort Bowyer at Mobile and directed that it be fortified. And there appears to be complete agreement that the destiny of New Orleans might well have ended differently if General Flournoy had been in command.

During 1820, General Flournoy was appointed as U.S. commissioner to the Creek Indians. He remained in the post until 1836, during that period when the Creeks were removed from the territory. General Flournoy died in North Carolina on 24 July 1857. He was survived by his wife, Catherine A. Howell Flournoy, the daughter of Major Reading Howell, a veteran of the American Revolution. Mrs. Flournoy returned to Philadelphia after the Civil War. The family estate in Augusta, Georgia, had been destroyed during the war. At some point after arriving back in Philadelphia, she donated her father's sword to the Philadelphia Chapter of the Daughters of the American Revolution. Mrs. Flournoy, who was born on 21 August 1800, died in Philadelphia on 21 November 1900.

General Flournoy's first wife, Sophia Davies Flournoy, who married him during 1801, died on 29 January 1829. They had the following children: Robert Flournoy (born May 1802, died August 1816); Sarah Ann Flournoy (born March 1804, married Charles Dixon Williams, died at unspecified time prior to 1830); Julia Charlotte Flournoy (born 1807, married Thomas Moore Berrien, died November 1836); Martha Milledge Flournoy (born March 1806, married John Carter, died April 1872); Elizabeth (born January 1809, died at an unknown time); Mary M. (born January 1810, married David Fairchild Halsey, died February 1837); Emily Agnes (born June 1813, married Joseph A. Camfield, died September 1844); John James (born June 1815, died April 1886); Maria Frances (born October 1818, married John Howard Snider, died at an unknown time); Sophia T. (born May 1821, married Henry Hora, died at an unknown time); and Thomas (born August 1824, died 1866).

Floyd, Brigadier General John of Georgia John, the son of Charles Floyd, a native of Virginia who resettled in Beaufort, South Carolina, was born in Beaufort on 3 October 1769. John's father, a veteran of the American Revolution, is known to have worn silver crescent with the words "Liberty or death" inscribed on it. He was captured during the war and imprisoned for a long period of time, which in turn broke him financially. John, while a young man, worked as an apprentice for a carpenter. About 1791, John accompanied his father to Georgia and settled in Camden County. He established himself as a boatwright, which quickly extricated him from poverty and placed him in a position of affluence. From that, he branched out and began to build houses. John Floyd built a plantation, the Bellevue Plantation House for his parents. For his family, he built the Fairfield Plantation House. In addition, Floyd was elected to the Georgia Assembly. In 1793, John married Isabella Maria Hazzard on 12 December. They had 12 children. Also, he was appointed as captain of militia about 1804, followed by his appointment as brigadier general about 1806, with command of the 1st Brigade. He was later promoted to major general of the Georgia 1st Division. When the United States declared war against Great Britain, General Floyd was prepared for action; however, the British made no immediate offensive moves against Georgia. Nevertheless, during September 1813, the federal government requested more than 3,000 troops. General Daniel Stewart, holding seniority, was given command; however, he declined due to his age and the condition of his health, which made the command go to General Floyd.

On 29 November 1813, General Floyd led a force of Georgians, a contingent of the U.S. 39th Infantry, and several hundred friendly Indians toward a Creek stronghold at Auttose along the east bank of the Tallapoosa, at the mouth of Calebee (Chalibbee) Creek. Following a march of about 120 miles, the column arrived within 20 miles of the objective. The Creeks were handily defeated and Floyd's force killed about 200 Indians and burned about 400 houses. His force sustained 11 killed and 54 wounded. General Floyd was among the wounded. After the victory, Floyd led his command to Fort Mitchell (near present-day Fort Benning, Georgia). While the column proceeded to Fort Mitchell, the Indians attacked about one mile from where they were defeated. Again they were defeated. Chief William McIntosh (Lower Creeks) participated with the U.S. forces at this battle.

Soon after the battle the terms of enlistments ended. Another army was raised to protect Savannah from a British invasion; however, it did not occur. When Floyd's army resumed its advance, the column moved toward Tuckabatchee, Alabama, reaching the vicinity in late January 1814. General Floyd's Georgia militia established Fort Hull at a point about 40 miles west of Fort Mitchell. The post was built to support Floyd's campaign against the Upper Creeks (Red Sticks).

Subsequent to his service, General Floyd retired to his plantation, The Fairfield on the Saltilla River. He served in the U.S. Congress 1827–1829. He died on 24 June 1839. His body, per his request, was wrapped "in the folds of the beloved flag for which he fought." His son, General Charles L. Floyd, is interred at Fairfield next to his father. Another son, Richard, served with the Confederacy as a lieutenant on the CSS *Florida*.

Floyd, Brigadier General John of Virginia
John, the son of Colonel John and Jane Buchanan Floyd, was born on 24 April 1783 near Louisville, Kentucky, at Floyd's Station, which at the time was part of Virginia. On 12 April 1783, Colonel John Sr., and his brother Charles, were ambushed by Indians while returning to their homes from the Salt River. John was wearing a bright scarlet coat, which made him a conspicuous target. He was fatally wounded and died on the following day, leaving two small children, William and George Rodgers Clark, and a wife who was expecting her third child. William died young; however, George Rodgers Clark grew to maturity and followed in his father's footsteps, becoming an Indian fighter who served in the Indian Wars including the Battle of Tippecanoe. There are few records on his later life until his death in June 1823.

John's birth came twelve days after his father was killed by Indians. John's mother later married Captain Alexander Breckenridge, but he died during 1801. John received an excellent education, beginning on his mother's knee, where he learned how to read and write. At age thirteen, through the efforts of Senator John Brown of Kentucky, he entered Dickinson College in Carlisle, Pennsylvania, and he graduated from the medical department of the University of Pennsylvania in 1806. Afterward, he became a member of the Philadelphia Medical Society and the Philadelphia Medical Lyceum. During 1804, John married Letitin Preston, the daughter of Colonel William Preston, who had been a close friend of his father. John and Letitin had the following children: George (died in infancy); Susan (died in infancy); Thomas (died in infancy); Mary (died at age 6); Coralie (died at age 11); John Buchanan (governor from 1848 to 1862, secretary of war in President Buchanan's cabinet, and Confederate brigadier general and major general of Virginia state troops); William Preston (later a surgeon); George Rodgers Clark (secretary of the Wisconsin Territory, member of the West Virginia legislature); Benjamin Rush (lawyer); T. Jetty Preston (married William S. Lewis); Elizabeth Lavelette (married George Frederick Holmes); and Nicketti Buchanan (married Senator John Warfield Johnston).

John Floyd practiced medicine for a while in Christiansburg, Montgomery County. During 1807, he became a justice of the peace, and in 1807, he was appointed a major in the militia. Floyd acted as surgeon with the rank of major during the War of 1812, until he was promoted to the rank of brigadier general. During 1814, General John Floyd was elected to the state House of Delegates; the next year, he was elected to Congress serving from 4 March 1817 to 3 March 1829. However, in 1828, he did not run for re-election. He was governor of Virginia from 1830 to 1834.

General Floyd died on 17 August 1837 at Sweet Springs, Monroe County, Virginia (later West Virginia). He was interred in an unmarked grave in the Sweet Springs Cemetery.

Gaines, Brigadier General Edmund Pendleton Edmund, the son of James and Elizabeth Strother Gaines, was born on 20 March 1777 in Culpeper County, Virginia. Edmund's father was a veteran of the American Revolution. During the conflict, James Gaines resided temporarily in North Carolina; however, after the war, he returned to Virginia. James' financial circumstances deteriorated due to the issuance of valueless Continental paper money. The family moved to Sullivan County (later eastern Tennessee), at the time a region in which the Cherokee were constantly raising the hatchet against white settlers.

Edmund had reached age 13–15 when the family relocated, and it was natural for boys his age to become skilled with weapons with which to help defend the settlements. Although Edmund worked on the family farm, he found time to become an expert rifleman, and he also studied military tactics. When he reached age 18, Edmund was elected captain of a local militia company. In 1799, he was appointed as an ensign in the U.S. 6th Infantry Regiment. The next year, when the regiment was dissolved, Edmund was transferred to the U.S. 4th Regiment.

Subsequently, during 1801, he was involved with surveying a road from Nashville, Tennessee, to Natchez, Mississippi. Colonel Thomas Butler, commander of the 4th Regiment assigned Gaines to initiate the topographical survey for the purpose of constructing a military road. The project continued into 1804. At the time, relations with Spain were again deteriorating. Spain declined abandoning their military posts at Mobile and Baton Rouge. The Spanish also failed to relinquish the territory stretching from the isle of Orleans to the Iberville River in Mississippi and the Perdido River, included in the Louisiana Purchase. President John Adams appointed Lieutenant Gaines as the military customs collector at Mobile.

At the time, Lt. Gaines was posted at Fort Stoddart, about 35 miles from Mobile; however, the president remained confident that Gaines would be taking possession of Mobile. Having achieved the rank of captain, he was appointed postmaster in 1806, giving him additional responsibilities as commander of Fort Stoddart, namely to protect the mail. This included using as many troops as he believed necessary, and he was also tasked with providing protection for the various revenue inspectors within his jurisdiction, a stretch of 600 miles, nearly all of which was wilderness, between New Orleans, Louisiana, and Athens, Georgia.

On 17 January 1807, Captain Gaines, commander of Fort Stoddart, appointed also as U.S. marshal by President Adams, intercepted and captured Aaron Burr, former vice president of the U.S., who had become a fugitive. Burr was seized at McIntosh Bluff in Alabama. Burr, ordered captured by President Jefferson for engaging in activities that threatened the security of the U.S.,

was tried and acquitted. Nonetheless, he fled from the country before he could be tried on charges that he murdered Alexander Hamilton.

Captain Gaines, about 1811, considered resigning from the army, but with the clouds of war gathering, Gaines decided instead to take a leave of absence from the army to practice law. Gaines started his law practice in the territory and practiced in the counties of Baldwin and Washington. However, after toiling in the legal profession for just barely more than one year, war was declared and Gaines wasted no time in returning to his army uniform.

During early 1812, Captain Gaines was promoted to the rank of major, and in July he was promoted to lieutenant colonel. In January 1813, he was promoted to full colonel. He was for a while stationed at Fort Meigs while it was threatened by the British (July 1813). Colonel Gaines became ill prior to General Harrison's victory at the Battle of the Thames in October 1813, but shortly thereafter, during the following November, Colonel Gaines participated in the Battle of Chrysler's Farm as commander of the 25th U.S. Infantry. His regiment covered the retreat. In early 1814 Colonel Gaines was among several who were promoted to the rank of brigadier general.

During April 1814, General Gaines arrived at Sackets Harbor to assume command. Major General Brown, having no confidence in General Eleazar Ripley, placed General Gaines in command of Fort Erie in Canada. A superior British force initiated a siege there August 2 to September 21. During mid–August, the British assaulted the Fort Erie blockhouse and penetrated it; however, they sustained catastrophic losses when an ammunition magazine exploded. The Americans increased their losses by driving them out of the post. Nonetheless, the siege failed. The British retired on 21 September, leaving the Stars and Stripes to wave over the post. On 15 August, General Gaines was breveted major general and received a gold medal from Congress.

During one of the bombardments, a shell dropped right through the roof of General Gaines' headquarters, and when it exploded, Gaines was severely wounded. He was compelled to relinquish command; however, General Brown continued to retain his lack of confidence in General Ripley. Rather than pass command to Ripley, General Brown assumed personal command of the post.

General Gaines returned to Buffalo. He saw no further active service during the war. He was ordered to New Orleans; however, he arrived too late to participate in the defense of the city. On 16 March, the American troops assembled on the plains of Chalmette, the scene of their victory over the British that preserved New Orleans. The 3rd, 7th and 44th U.S. Regiments, led by General Edmund Pendleton Gaines and trailed by the uniformed troops of New Orleans, passed in review. General Jackson, after paying tribute to the troops, transferred command to General Gaines and began to prepare to depart from New Orleans and return to Nashville.

General Gaines remained in the service beyond the close of hostilities. He acted as a commissioner to the Creek Indians in the South during 1817, and he participated in the conflicts with the Creeks and the Seminole Indians. Afterward, he was named commander of the Eastern Department. Later, during 1832, he led a campaign in which he defeated Black Hawk. In 1836, he commanded at Camp Sabine and Fort Jesup in Louisiana.

General Gaines was appointed commander of the Department of the West during 1839. Difficulties emerged in 1846 when he was stripped of command for dispatching American troops into Texas during the Mexican War when he became aware that General Zachary Taylor was at Fort Brown, Texas, and surrounded by a Mexican army. Gaines dispatched a large force of volunteers to relieve Taylor. His actions were seen in Washington as "exceeding his authority."

General Gaines received a court-martial, which was held in Virginia at Fortress Monroe on 20 July 1846. General Gaines acted as his own defense attorney. The court found that "there was no direct authority for the course pursued by the general, except an honest conviction that he was acting in accordance with the dictates of duty." An appendix (recommendation) was added to the verdict: "Having now reported their finding and opinion, the court recommend to the favourable consideration of the president, the good and patriotic motives, and the public zeal by which, as the court believe. General Gaines was actuated in all these transactions, and therefore they recommend that no further proceedings be had in this case."

General Gaines married three times, but no children were borne by any of his wives. They were Frances Toulmin, Barbara Blount (daughter of Tennessee's Governor William Blount) and Myra Clark Whitney. Gaines married his third wife, Myra, when he was about 62 years old. General Gaines devoted his latter years (about ten) as a litigant in his wife's suit against the city of New Orleans. He died in New Orleans on 6 June 1849. He was interred at Mobile, Alabama, in the "Church Street Graveyard."

General Gaines' service and memory were honored by various places being named after him. These included Gainesville, Florida, Gainesville, Georgia, and Gainesville, Texas. Others included Gainesville Township in Michigan, Fort Gaines on Dauphin Island in Alabama, and another Fort Gaines established in New York during September 1814.

Graham, Brigadier General Joseph Joseph, the son of James Graham, was born on 13 October 1759 in Berks County, Pennsylvania. Joseph's father emigrated from Ireland. James' first wife died, leaving six children; however, he remarried, taking a widow, Mary McConnell Barber, as his second wife. She was the mother of Joseph and four other children, with Joseph being the youngest. Joseph's father died during 1763. Afterward, Mrs. Graham and her children accompanied a party of people who traveled to the Carolinas, where she resettled in Mecklenburg County, North Carolina, in a home just outside of Charlotte. Mary was able to send her children to excellent schools, including Queen's College (later Liberty Hall) in Charlotte. Joseph, who became a skilled swordsman, also excelled in engineering and surveying. He was also an avid reader who enjoyed history and geography.

Joseph Graham served time in the militia during the American Revolution, and he sustained a wound that nearly took his life while leading a company of cavalry. He participated at the Battle of Stono on 29 June 1779. During July 1779, while serving as quartermaster, he became ill from fever, which disabled him for about two months. He was forced to take a temporary discharge. He participated against Lord Rawdon in command at Charleston. Graham again sustained severe wounds, six from saber swords and three from lead bullets. He was left in the field and thought to be dead when the Americans retreated; however, he regained consciousness during the night and crawled to the home of Susannah Alexander, who gave him aid and later got him to a hospital, which saved his life. Once he recuperated, Graham raised a company of 55 men. General Davidson placed him in command. His company engaged the British at Cowan's Ford and at other places until the British abandoned North Carolina when Lord Cornwallis moved to Virginia. Graham was ordered to raise a troop of cavalry from the men of Mecklenburg and he succeeded. Robert Smith was appointed colonel and Graham was named major. They defeated a contingent of Tories near Wilmington, and his contingent defeated a British force at Waccamaw to close out his active service during the Revolution.

He returned to his farm, where his mother lived. In 1787, Graham married Isabella Davidson, the daughter of John Davidson, a signer of the Mecklenburg Declaration of Independence. After his marriage, he moved to what was called the Red House, near the Catawba River. They remained there for about four years. He and his brother began to manufacture iron with his father-in-law. They erected furnaces in Lincoln County. Mrs. Graham took in the orphaned son of her brother-in-law, General William Lee Davidson (her sister's husband), who was killed at the Battle of Cowan's Ford. Major Graham, the fearless soldier, had a soft spot in his heart for his wife, Isabella, and when she became too ill to walk, he would carry her to her favorite spot in the garden where she could enjoy the summer sun. Isabella died in 1807. They had three children: Violet Wilson, John Davidson and Mary.

During the War of 1812, the Creek war also erupted. President Madison requested troops from North Carolina and South Carolina, each of which provided a regiment. The combined regiments amounted to a brigade, and Governor Hawkins appointed Joseph Graham to the rank of brigadier general as commander of the brigade. However, not unusually, the War Department failed to furnish supplies for the brigade. Consequently, the troops arrived in Alabama after Jackson had defeated the Creeks at the Battle of Horseshoe Bend to end the war. The brigade engaged only in a few minor skirmishes. General Graham's active service ended; however, he served several terms as major general of the North Carolina militia. After the war, General Graham also served as the sheriff of Mecklenburg County, and he was a member of the Court of Common Pleas and Quarter Sessions.

By 1834, General Graham's health had deteriorated, forcing him to relinquish the business to his sons. On 13 October 1836, General Graham, a Presbyterian, entered the following into his day-book: "This day I am seventy-seven years of age and in good health, *Dei Gratia*." On 12 November, he died from apoplexy. He was interred in the cemetery of Machpelah Church.

Hampton, Major General Wade Wade, the grandfather of Confederate General Wade Hampton (1818–1902), was born in Virginia during 1752. Wade's parents, Anthony and Elizabeth Preston Hampton, relocated in South Carolina from Virginia during the mid-1750s, where they began to build a home and a family on the frontier. The settlers in South Carolina all were aware of the great dangers facing them; however, their desire to conquer the wilderness outweighed the fear of Indian attacks. Nevertheless, the differences between the settlers and the Cherokee continued to deteriorate as the settlers began to expand their holdings, while the Indians took offense at what they considered treaty violations. After the American Revolutionary War erupted, the dreams of the Hamptons were upset tragically during 1776 when Cherokee raids were causing pandemonium in the back country. A Cherokee band struck the Hamptons' property at a time when five of Anthony's sons were not at the residence. Prior to these Indian attacks, many South Carolinians supported the Crown rather than the Patriots' cause, until the British began to incite the Cherokee in coordination with the British naval attack against Charleston. The Indians killed Anthony, his wife Elizabeth, their son Preston and a grandson, child of their daughter Elizabeth and her husband James Harrison. There were at least seven. The five sons absent from the massacre required no further incentive to join with the American rebels in their fight for independence.

Wade (I) served with the rank of lieutenant colonel in a regiment of light dragoons, which was attached to General Sumter's brigade (state troops). He participated in various actions during the war, including a successful engagement against a British cavalry contingent on 1 December 1781 at Dorchester, South Carolina. At the time, the British under Cornwallis had already surrendered (September 1781) at Yorktown, Virginia. Following the action, General Greene continued to push the British back toward Charleston. After the war, Colonel Hampton was elected to the South Carolina Assembly, where he served from 1799 to 1786 and again in 1791. In 1795, he was elected to Congress and served from March 1795 to March 1797. He was not re-elected, but in 1802 he again was elected to Congress and served from March 1803 until March 1805. He entered the U.S. Army in 1808 with the rank of colonel. Colonel Hampton was appointed brigadier general the next February.

In January 1812, while in command at New Orleans, he was replaced by General James Wilkinson. During September 1812, subsequent to General Joseph Bloomfield departing for New York, General Wade Hampton assumed command at Lake Champlain. He established headquarters at Burlington, Vermont, and by summer, his command amounted to about 4,000 troops. On 31 December 1812, Congress authorized six new major generals in conjunction with twenty new regiments. The officers promoted in addition to Wade Hampton were William Henry Harrison, James Wilkinson, Morgan Lewis, William R. Davie and Aaron Ogden, who never served. Major Hampton received command of the Fifth U.S. Military District. It comprised Virginia beginning at the Rappahannock River and extending south. He was assisted by Brigadier General Thomas Parker.

On 16 August 1813, General Wilkinson sent orders to General Hampton regarding Wilkinson's campaign to seize Montreal and General Hampton exploded with anger. Hampton wasted no time in contacting Secretary of War Armstrong and making it clear that would not be subordinate to Wilkinson. Hampton also submitted his resignation. Secretary Armstrong became personally involved in the dispute as an arbitrator, but without much success. General Hampton eventually agreed to participate in the campaign before resigning. The tension among the commanders seeped down into the ranks, making a bad situation worse. Nevertheless, Armstrong seemingly maintained working relationships with Wilkinson and Hampton. General Armstrong oversaw the campaign from Buffalo, but too many problems were connected.

During early October, General Hampton advanced from Chateauguay; however, his destination remained a secret, known only to him. Meanwhile, Wilkinson arrived near Kingston with about 10,000 men, still anticipating that Hampton's 10,000 men would link with him before the combined forces struck Montreal. While en route, Hampton's army was intercepted at the Chateauguay River in late October by about 500 men, including Indians. Hampton's army was stalled and he returned to New York, leaving Wilkinson's force on its own; however, General Wilkinson remained unaware of Hampton's failure at the river until 12 November. Once informed, Wilkinson conferred with his officers and it was decided to abort the attack and return to New York. Afterward, Wilkinson retired, leaving Montreal unscathed and Secretary of War Armstrong's plan to conquer Montreal a total failure.

General Hampton resigned his commission on 6 April 1814 and returned to South Carolina, where he continued to accumulate land and wealth, along with ownership of about 3,000 slaves. He became one of the most affluent planters in the nation. General Hampton (I) died on 4 February 1835. General Hampton's son, also named Wade, born in 1791, served during the war as a lieutenant in the light dragoons. Later he became aide-de-camp to General Andrew Jackson at New Orleans, and he was Jackson's deputy inspector general. Wade Hampton (II) was the father of Wade Hampton (III), born on 18 March 1818. Wade (III) joined the Confederate Army as a private. He rapidly rose in the ranks and commanded General Robert E. Lee's cavalry and then Confederate General Johnston's cavalry. After the Civil War, General Wade Hampton (III) became governor of South Carolina in 1878 and spent time in other public service positions.

Harrison, General (later president) William Henry, the son of Benjamin (signer of the Declaration of Independence) and Elizabeth Bassett Harrison, was born in Charles City County, Virginia, on 9 February 1773 on the Berkeley Plantation. His parents had three sons and four daughters who lived past infancy. In addition to William Henry, they were Benjamin III (married Anne Mercer and later Susannah Randolph); Carter Bassett (married Mary Howell Allen and later Jane Byrd); Lucy (married her cousin Peyton Randolph, a nephew of Peyton Randolph, the first president of Continental Congress, and then Anthony Singleton); Elizabeth (1752, married Doctor William Rickman and later John Edmondson); Anne (1758, married David O. Copeland); and Sarah (married John Minge). William Henry was a voracious reader as a youngster, and the family library was of great use for him. Later, he entered Hampden-Sydney College in southern Virginia. There is no record of when he entered or graduated, although he did study medicine. His father, Benjamin — who served in Congress, was a signer of the Declaration of Independence, and had served as a three-term governor of Virginia — was a man of affluence when he entered politics; however, at the time of his death on 4 April 1791, he was close to poverty. "William Henry had not been of age at the time of his father's death, but he was under the guardianship of Robert Morris. William Henry, against the wishes of Morris, decided to leave college to enter the army and participate under Governor St. Clair during his campaign in the northwest. Morris discussed the personal dilemma with President Washington; however, Washington failed to agree with Morris, and in fact Washington commissioned William Henry as an ensign in the 1st Artillery Regiment, at the time based near Cincinnati at Fort Washington. Although only nineteen years old, William Henry Harrison seemed to have found a perfect fit for his abilities.

Harrison arrived at the post soon after the defeat of St. Clair by Chief Little Turtle (Miamis) and the Delaware chief, Buckongahelas. Harrison's perilous duties during the winter had been so well handled that St. Clair had him promoted to lieutenant. He became an aide-de-camp to General Anthony Wayne and participated with Wayne's Legion in his victorious campaign of 1794, in which he avenged the defeats of Harmar and St. Clair to bring peace to the frontier. "Within a short while Harrison was promoted to the rank of captain. He received command of Fort Washington, Ohio.

During 1795, on 29 November, William Henry married Anna Symmes, the daughter of Supreme Court Justice John C. and Anna Tuttle Symmes. William Henry had met Anna while at Fort Washington. Anna's father did not attend the marriage and later, upon meeting Harrison, the judge with a heavy tone of sarcasm, said: "I understand you have married Anna." Harrison responded: "Yes Sir." The judge then prodded: "How do you expect to support her?" Harrison snapped back saying: "By my sword and my own right arm." The reply was apparently more than satisfying because afterward, the relationship between Harrison and his father-in-law began to warm. William Henry and Anna's children were William Symes; Benjamin; John Scott (father of General Benjamin Harrison, who became the 23rd president of the United States); Anna (married Colonel Taylor); Carter; Betsey (married Mr. Short); Maria (married Mr. Thornton); Lucy (married Mr. Estey) and Mary.

General Wayne died during 1797 and Captain Harrison resigned his commission during 1798. However, he was appointed secretary of the vast Northwest Territory that year. Later, the Northwest Territory was split with one part becoming the Ohio Territory (later a state) and the remainder the Indiana Territory. From 4 March 1799 to 14 May 1800, William Henry served as a representative to the 6th Congress from the Northwest Territory. During 1801, Harrison was named governor of the Indiana Territory, which initially included Michigan, Illinois, Indiana, Iowa, and recently acquired Louisiana. At the time Harrison was only 25 years old, yet he had been handed great powers of authority which in some cases was "absolute."

Harrison had the authority to draw maps by creating townships and counties, and he possessed the authority to create and enact laws of the territory regarding civil matters as well as criminal, along with the power to adapt them to the circumstances of the territory. His powers also extended into the military. He had the authority to appoint officers, except for general officers. Harrison had also been given the power to distribute land grants and who would receive the grants rested entirely on him. No one superseded his authority and his signature on the title was not subject to challenge. It is a testament to his integrity and character that such a young man was able to withstand the temptation to use the power for his own gain. No charges of unfairness or favoritism were lodged against him.

Harrison was also superintendent of Indian affairs. During 1809, Governor Harrison concluded the Treaty of Fort Wayne, by which the Indians who inhabited southern Indiana ceded additional territory. Nonetheless, relations with the Indians began to deteriorate due in great part to the prodding of the British in Canada, who continued to resent Americans after the

American Revolution. The British took advantage of two equally ambitious Indian brothers, Tecumseh, known also as the "Crouching Panther," and Elkswatawa, known also as the "Loud Voice or Prophet." Tecumseh and the Prophet had plotted to unite all of the tribes in an effort to drive the whites from their lands, and they had been told by the British that the "Father [King George III] from beyond the Great Lake [Atlantic Ocean]" would support the effort. The Indians, assured of an alliance with the British, initiate their plans; however, Harrison did not stand idle. Hostilities ignited by Tecumseh took a toll in the region and the Indians began to terrorize the Americans. The scalps of women and children were hanging from a string outside of Tecumseh's wigwam.

Harrison assembled his forces and personally led them into battle. The Indians, under the Prophet, struck on 7 November 1811 to ignite the Battle of Tippecanoe. Harrison's troops rallied and inflicted a devastating defeat upon them, elevating Harrison in the eyes of all the Americans in the territory. Private Adam Walker, who maintained a journal, noted that "General Harrison received a shot through the rim of his hat. In the heat of the action, his voice was frequently heard, and easily distinguished, giving his orders in the same calm, cool, and collected manner, with which we had been used to receive them on drill or parade. The confidence of the troops in the General was unlimited."

The next day, Harrison topped off his victory by destroying Prophets Town. The triumphant victory, however, had its detractors, particularly William Eustis, secretary of war, who displayed conspicuous animosity toward Harrison from what seemed to have originated from envy. Nonetheless, to bypass the jealousy of the secretary, Harrison was appointed as brigadier general and commander of the Kentucky militia. Later, on 1 September, Harrison was officially commissioned brigadier general, U.S. Army, by the president, and he received command of all U.S. forces in the Territory of Indiana and in the Illinois Territory. Governor Scott of Kentucky, unaware of the president's intentions, had appointed Harrison as major general of the Kentucky militia on 25 August. Subsequent to his appointment by President Madison, General Harrison remained undefeated in the field. He defeated the British at the Battle of the Thames (5 October 1813) and with the seminal victory, Tecumseh was killed, which effectively terminated his confederacy.

Harrison's victory forced the British to abandon Detroit, which in turn gave Harrison the honor of avenging General Hull's humiliating defeat there, along with regaining Michigan for the United States. John Armstrong resented the laurels received by General Harrison. On 23 October 1813, Harrison was informed by the War Department that "he had "permission to return to his family." General Harrison's admirable service record, combined with regaining Michigan for the United States, exposed the underhanded decision by the War Department; nevertheless Harrison complied. He returned to Cincinnati to rejoin his family and established headquarters there. On 11 May 1814, General Harrison, who had become known as the "Father of the Northwest," resigned his commission effective on 31 May.

Despite the severe blow inflicted upon Harrison by the War Department, his deeds had not been forgotten by the people of Ohio, who elected him to the Fourteenth U.S. Congress to complete the term of John McClean. He was re-elected and served in the Fifteenth Congress from 8 October 1816 to 3 March 1819, when he entered the state Senate and served until 1821. During his term in the Senate he ran an unsuccessful campaign for governor in 1820. In 1822 he became a presidential elector in the state of Ohio and unsuccessfully ran for Congress. Following that setback, he ran for the U.S. Senate during 1824 and won. He served in that office from 4 March 1825 until 20 May 1828, when he resigned to become the U.S. minister to Colombia, a post in which he served 1818–1829. In addition, during his service in the Nineteenth Congress (4 March 1825 to 3 March 1827), and Twentieth (4 March 1827 to 3 March 1829), Harrison was chair of the Committee on Military Affairs.

During 1836, Harrison, the Whig candidate for president, was defeated for the presidency by Martin Van Buren. Undaunted, he ran again during 1840 and won the election to become the 9th president of the United States. He was inaugurated but contracted pneumonia and died shortly after on 4 April 1841. His vice president, John Tyler, succeeded him. President Harrison was interred in William Henry Harrison Memorial State Park in North Bend, Ohio. He was interred in William Henry Harrison Memorial State Park in North Bend, Ohio.

During his lifetime when not in the military or in public service, President Harrison worked his farm. His wife, Anna, survived him; however, she was ill at the time of his inauguration and remained in Ohio. After his death, she moved in with her only surviving son, John Scott, during 1855, where she remained until her death on 24 February 1864.

Henry, Major General William William, the son of the Rev. Robert Henry, was born on 12 April 1761 in Charlotte County, Virginia. At age 17, he entered the army during the American Revolution as a private. He served under Colonel Henry "Lighthorse Harry" Lee and participated at various engagements, including Guilford Courthouse and at Yorktown. During 1781, William relocated in Kentucky in Lincoln County; however, after a while, he moved to Flournoy Station in Scott County. After the war, William served under General James Wilkinson in his campaign on the northern frontier in 1791. William married Elizabeth Julia Flournoy on 12 October 1786. They resided initially at Henry's Mills, which William built on North Elkhorn River between Georgetown and Lexington, Kentucky. About 1800, the family moved to Cherry Spring. Their children were Elizabeth Julia (born October 1787, died January 1788); Robert Pryor (born November 1788, member U.S. Congress, married Gabriella Frances Pitts); Matthews Winston (born January 1790, married Juliette Frances Pitts); William II (born July 1791, married Cornelia V. Gano of Georgetown, Kentucky, died February 1847); John Flournoy (born January 1783, married Mary Wilson Duke, died November 1873); Thomas (born June 1796, married Susan Dudley, later married Mary Ford, died October 1841); Daniel (born June 1796, married Eliza Viriles Gano, later married Lucy W. Green, died July 1837); Benjamin Franklin (born December 1797, died January 1798); Patsy Caroline (born June 1799, died October 1814); Patrick (born July 1801, married Elizabeth Julia Flournoy, died March 1864 at Brandon, Mississippi); Gustavus Adolphus (October 1804, married Marion [Marian] McClure, died September 1880); Eliza (born July 1805, died November 1805) and Lucretia (born October 1808, died October 1811).

In 1803, William Henry became a member of the first synod of the Presbyterian Church in the state of Kentucky. He also served in the Kentucky legislature in 1793–1794, 1801 and 1809. He was a state senator from 1796 to 1800. During 1813, he was defeated by Colonel Robert Johnson, Sr., in a race for the state legislature and afterward, he declined ever running again for political office.

While the Kentuckians were in Ohio during the War of 1812, the commander, General Isaac Shelby appointed Henry a major general and second in command. General William Henry participated at the Battle of the Thames on 5 October 1813. He was also frequently engaged against hostile Indians who ventured into Kentucky. Afterward, President Madison appointed Henry as assessor in the Third Kentucky District. In 1816, General Henry moved to Hopkinsville, Clark County, where he lived privately in retirement until his death on 23 November 1824. He was interred in a private family cemetery on his brother's farm about ten miles outside of Hopkinsville. Of his thirteen children, five sons participated in the War of 1812. Two of General Henry's children served in the U.S. Congress as representatives of Kentucky, and a third son, Gustavus A. Henry, served in the Kentucky legislature (1831–1832).

Howard, Brigadier General Benjamin Chew Benjamin, the son of John Howard, a veteran of the American Revolution, was born in 1760 in the part of Virginia that later became Lexington, Kentucky. After receiving his regular education, Benjamin began to study law. After passing the bar, he initiated his law practice in Lexington, Kentucky. In 1800, he became a member of the House of Representatives in Kentucky. Afterward, he was elected to Congress, where he served in the Tenth and Eleventh Congresses (4 March 1807 to 10 April 1810) until he resigned to accept the post of governor of the Upper Louisiana Territory, a position he held from 1810 until 1812. Benjamin Howard succeeded Governor Meriwether Lewis, who died under mysterious circumstances on 9 October 1809. Officially, Governor Lewis' death was ruled suicide; however, he sustained a shot to the head and a shot to the chest. At the time of his death, pistols were single-shot weapons.

Governor Howard married Mary Mason on 14 February 1811. Mary died prematurely on 21 March 1813, leaving no children. Meanwhile, Governor Howard became the first governor of the Missouri Territory (1812–1813). On 12 March 1813, Howard was named brigadier general in the regular army, when he received command of the Eighth Military District, which encompassed the territory west of the Mississippi River. He did not participate in any major actions during his time in service; however, he was involved in dealing with Indians in his region. General Howard's life was cut short when he died unexpectedly in St. Louis on 18 September 1814. He was initially interred in the Old Grace Church Graveyard; however, he was later re-interred in Bellefontaine Cemetery.

Hull, Brigadier General William William, the son of Joseph and Eliza Hull, was born in Derby, Connecticut, on 24 June 1753. William received a fine education and graduated from Yale during 1772. He became a close friend of Captain Nathan Hale, also a Yale graduate, who was captured by the British and hanged as a spy. While growing up, William also worked on the family farm. He attended law school in Litchfield, Connecticut, and after passing the bar in 1775, there was little time to practice law. William's parents had been leading him toward a life in the ministry; however, his decisions were beginning to move him further away from entering the ministry.

Before William Hull became a lawyer, for a while he was a tutor at a school, and for a while he did begin to study for the ministry. Nevertheless, by the time he became a lawyer, the war clouds were already gathering. War with Britain was imminent. Hull was captain of a Connecticut militia company and shortly thereafter joined with other volunteers from Connecticut who joined General George Washington at Cambridge, Massachusetts.

In the American Revolution, Captain Hull participated in the Battle of Trenton on 26 December 1776 and in the Battle of Princeton during early January 1777. He remained in New York, attached to a Massachusetts' regiment, until the surrender of British General John Burgoyne at the Battle of Saratoga (2nd) during early October 1777.

Major Hull joined with General George Washington in time to spend the dreadful winter at Valley Forge, while the British controlled Philadelphia. In June 1778 he participated in the Battle of Monmouth, New Jersey. He also participated with General Anthony Wayne in the successful capture of Stony Point (15 July 1779).

Subsequently, on 21 January 1781, Lt. Colonel Hull participated with General Parsons in a successful assault against Loyalists' positions (Delancey's Refugee Corps) at Morrisania and at Throg's Neck, New York. During the operation, about 50 prisoners were taken, and at a point near Delancey's Bridge, Hull ignored the danger and led an attack that rescued 32 Americans. Afterward, Hull was compelled to retire under heavy fire with the British in pursuit for about two miles before his contingent rejoined the main body, which retired toward the Highlands and arrived back at camp about midnight (22nd–23rd).

That year, 1781, Hull married Sarah Fuller, the daughter of Judge Abraham Fuller. Their children were Abraham, Anne, Anne Hickman, Caroline, Cornelia Page, Eliza, Julia Wheeler, Maria, and Rebecca. Also, General William Hull's nephew, Isaac (later captain, U.S. Navy) the son of Joseph (William's brother) and Sarah Bennett Hull, lived with General Hull as a young boy, and he was later adopted by William. Isaac became the first captain of the USS *Constitution*, which engaged and defeated the HMS *Guerriere* just before his uncle surrendered Detroit.

Following General Cornwallis' surrender at Yorktown, Virginia, the war began to wind down. After the close of hostilities, the British refused to relinquish a series of forts on the frontier. Colonel Hull was dispatched to Quebec as a U.S. government representative to insist that the forts be turned over to American forces; however, despite the conditions stipulated in the peace treaty of 1783, the British continued to stall. Colonel Hull also participated with General Washington in New York when the British had abandoned their posts.

In 1786, Colonel Hull participated in the short-lived (Daniel) Shay's Rebellion that erupted in western Massachusetts (1786–1787). Afterward, he was engaged in some diplomatic activity that involved working with Britain to bring about a treaty with the Western Indian tribes. In 1798, he went to France and England. Upon his return, Colonel Hull was appointed a judge of the Court of Common Pleas in Massachusetts, and at about the same time, he was commissioned a major general of Massachusetts militia. General Hull remained in public service, and it included being elected to the Senate of Massachusetts.

In 1805, during the administration of President John Adams, General Hull was appointed governor of the Michigan Territory. It was here that he committed the act he is most remembered for, surrendering a large section of the United States to the British without a fight.

At the outbreak of war with Great Britain, Major General Hull (Massachusetts militia) was commissioned as a brigadier general in the regular army.

On 12 May 1812, General Hull, at Dayton, Ohio, assumed command of the Ohio troops (three regiments) that were provided by Governor (Colonel) Return Meigs. The columns departed from Dayton and advanced to Detroit. During the journey, General Hull directed that a series of blockhouses be constructed to provide security for invalids and for protecting convoy trains. The next month, war was declared against Britain; however, letters from the War Department failed to inform Hull. Nonetheless, he did receive word from unofficial sources.

General Hull arrived at Detroit on 5 July 1812. His intent was to invade Canada; however, his plans were aboard a vessel that was captured by the British, giving General Isaac Brock a complete blueprint of Hull's campaign. The army advanced on 12 July, but the campaign was short-lived.

At Detroit, General Hull remained unaware that the British had captured Fort Michilimackinac. General Hull also refrained from attacking his main objective, Malden, except for a reconnaissance force that approached it on the 19th.

Hull was compelled to retreat and return to Detroit. During early August, Hull wrote to William Eustis, secretary of war, that he had to abandon Canada because of "the defection of the Wyandotte Indians, the fall of Mackinac, the advance of British reinforcements from Niagara and the resultant interruption of communication with Ohio." Circumstances deteriorated following the failed campaign and General Hull, looked upon as a renowned officer during the American Revolution, found his reputation on a rapid downward slide. He attempted repeatedly to locate a supply train at the Raisin River and escort it into Detroit without success.

Meanwhile, General Brock was moving quickly to attack Detroit, which General Dearborn had sworn to defend. By 13 August, the British began to construct batteries. Nonetheless, while the British were poised to strike, General Hull, against the sentiments of his officers, surrendered the city without a fight. General Hull gave up the entire Michigan Territory.

With the capture of General Hull, Brigadier General Simon Perkins of the Ohio militia received command of the entire northwestern frontier.

Once the British took possession of Detroit, the American militia troops received parole; however, the regulars, including General Hull, were taken to Montreal and from there to Quebec. General Hull was later exchanged for thirty British troops, but he received no accolades. A court-martial convened on 3 January 1814 and ended on 23 March. He was charged with "treason, cowardice and neglect of duty and conduct unbecoming an officer." The members of the court included the president, Major General Henry Dearborn, and Brigadier General Bloomfield, Colonel Robert Bogardus, Lieutenant Colonel Samuel S. Conner, Lt. Colonel S.B. David, Lt. Colonel Richard Dennis, Colonel J.B. Fenwick, Lt. Colonel James House, Colonel William N. Irvine, Colonel Peter Little, Lt. Colonel John W. Livingstone, Lt. Colonel William Scott and Colonel William Stewart. Martin Van Buren (later vice president under President Andrew Jackson and the 8th president of the U.S.) was the special judge advocate.

The first witness was Colonel Lewis Cass, who wrote a letter on 10 September 1812, while General Hull remained a prisoner of the British. The charges against Hull noted in his original letter are reiterated by Cass in his testimony, but were challenged because Cass was considered a candidate to become Hull's successor.

Nevertheless, there seemed to be no testimony from any of the other officers in the command supporting Hull's action, and by some at the time of the surrender, it was called "treason."

In his defense, General Hull called upon his previous service in the American Revolution and his bravery in previous battles. He insisted that he surrendered to prevent his force from being massacred, as threatened by General Brock. He maintained that had he defended the fort, his supplies would not have lasted and that the entire territory would have been ravaged by Indians once the fort fell. He also placed the blame on the Madison administration, which was the cause of his inferior numbered force. General Hull was found guilty of cowardice in the face of the enemy and sentenced to death. President Madison, although not in disagreement with the sentence, intervened and spared General Hull's life through a pardon. Nevertheless, General Hull's name was stripped from the rolls of the U.S. Army.

General William Hull died on 29 November 1825.

Izard, Major General George George, the son of Ralph and Alice Delancey Izard, was born near London at Richmond on 21 October 1776, where his parents were temporarily living. In addition, Ralph and Alice had the following children: Henry (the oldest); Margaret (born in Charleston 12 February 1768); Elizabeth (born 22 February 1769, died 13 August 1769); Charlotte (born 16 February 1770); Ralph (born in London, 5 August 1772, died 13 October 1772); Charles (born 15 September 1773, died 19 July 1784); Elizabeth (born at Paris, 11 October 1777, died 1 November 1784 at Charleston); Anne (born in Paris 1 February 1779); Ralph II (born 26 February 1785); Caroline (born in Charleston, 24 September 1786; died 22 June 1788); Henrietta (born 15 May 1788, died 24 May 1788); William (born New York, 1 June 1789, died November 1789) and Charlotte Georgina (born 16 September 1792).

George's family was affluent, powerful and influential in South Carolina. General Izard's father, Ralph, was appointed as commissioner to Tuscany on 7 May 1777, while he was in France. He succeeded Benjamin Franklin. During his stay in Paris, Ralph Izard experienced some difficulty with Benjamin Franklin and Silas Deane because he agreed with Arthur Lee, the other commissioner. Ralph Izard was recalled, but his letters of explanation after reaching Congress were met with approval. He arrived back in America in August 1780, and shortly thereafter, he arrived at General Washington's headquarters, where he worked to get General Nathanael Greene as the successor to General Horatio Gates as commander of the Southern Army.

Meanwhile, his wife and their younger children remained in France. George attended school there until 1783, when he returned to Charleston, South Carolina. Ralph Izard, like some other Patriots, had put up his estate in South Carolina as payment for warships during the war, and later he would be compelled to return to South Carolina to try to salvage the estate. In 1789, while New York was the capital of the nation, Ralph, having been appointed to the U.S. Senate representing South Carolina, moved his family there. George was sent to a preparatory school prior to attending Columbia. The next year, Congress began to meet in Philadelphia and another location change for the Izards occurred. George entered the University of Pennsylvania as a junior during the winter of 1790–1791 and graduated in 1792.

After college, he traveled to England, where he came under the care of a family friend, Thomas Pinckney, the American minister to England. "The only school then immediately available was the Prince of Wales' Royal Military Academy of Kensington Gravel Pits." The school, illustrious by appearance, according to George Izard, was poorly run. Without consulting with Pinckney, George withdrew. In 1792, at Minister Pinckney's suggestion, George traveled to Germany to attend a private military school in Hesse Cassel. George remained there for two years and after believing he had as much as he could, he departed. There was friction between him and the principal, Beauclair, the latter responsible for sending a vindictive and calumnious report regarding George's conduct. From Marburg, George traveled with a group by wagon to northern Germany. While he was in northern Germany, his father remained concerned about his further education and contacted James Monroe, the American minister to France. Afterward, George received a letter from his father and shortly thereafter repaired to Paris and met Monroe, who intervened and arranged for George to enter a military school for engineers at Metz.

During 1795, George, at age 19, received a commission as lieutenant in the U.S. Corps of Artillerists and Engineers, which was dated 4 June 1794. Nonetheless, George remained in France until 1797. He arrived in Baltimore during November 1797.

As ordered, he repaired to Charleston to assume command of the defenses at Castle Pinckney. To deal with the crisis emerging with France, the U.S. Army was rebuilt with George Washington named commanding general. Nevertheless, Washington was not called upon to lead the army in combat. The conflict, known as the Quasi War with France, was contained to sea action. No land forces were engaged and the war was settled by the Treaty of Morfontaine in September 1800.

Washington's three major generals were Alexander Hamilton, Charles C. Pinckney, and Henry Knox; however, Knox declined, leaving a vacancy. A second regiment of artillery and engineers was also established. Captain Izard received command of one company, and it was assigned garrison duty at Fort Pinckney. Izard remained there until January 1800, when he transferred to New York to become an aide to General Hamilton. Later, Hamilton repaired to Albany to handle a lawsuit with which he had been involved prior to the rebuilding of the army. Meanwhile, Captain Izard went to Philadelphia to join a board of artillery convening there.

In January 1801, Izard received a leave of absence from the service and returned to England, where he stayed for a short while before moving to Paris where he remained until July, then returned Baltimore. Upon his return to the States, Captain Izard received orders to report to Fort Mifflin in Philadelphia to assume command of a company. Afterward, he was stationed at West Point until he resigned from the army in April 1803.

Also in 1803, Captain Izard married a widow, Elizabeth Carter Shippen of Bucks County, Pennsylvania. George and Elizabeth had three children, Ralph Farley and George, both of whom were born during early 1803 and who died unmarried. Their third child, James Farley, was born in Pennsylvania during 1811. James graduated from West Point, Class of 1828, Cadet #524. He was mortally wounded during the Seminole War at Fort Izard, Florida, on 5 May 1836. He was buried on the battlefield.

After the death of George Washington on 14 December 1799, General Alexander Hamilton was appointed commander-in-chief of the army. Captain George Izard was assigned to his staff.

On 12 March 1812, Captain Izard was named colonel of artillery. By the following year, he was promoted to the rank of brigadier general. During April 1813, Congress divided the country into nine military districts and later added one more. General Izard received command of the Third District (New York–New Jersey), which extended from the sea to the Highlands and a sector of New Jersey. During September of 1813, sickness of epidemic proportions struck Sackets Harbor; the 700 men on the sick list included General Izard and other officers.

During March 1814, General Izard was promoted to the rank of major general and two months later he received command of Plattsburgh at the same time General Winfield Scott received command of the Niagara frontier.

On 10 August 1814, General Izard received orders to advance to Fort Erie in Canada to lift the siege there. His force arrived in early October. Meanwhile, General Brown assumed command of the Niagara frontier after General Scott received a debilitating wound at the Battle of Lundy's Lane (25 July 1814). After General Izard arrived at Fort Erie, he succeeded General Jacob J. Brown as commander of the Niagara campaign. His army remained at the post until it was totally destroyed. On 5 November 1814, with the siege that began on 17 September over and Fort Erie demolished, General Izard began to withdraw his entire force from Canada. General Izard, the senior major general on the Canadian frontier during late 1814 and January 1815, is blamed by some historians for underperforming, and yet others support him for having accomplished what he could with the means at his disposal provided by the government. Nonetheless, his record withstood the scrutiny.

After the war, General Izard resigned from the service. In 1816, he published his official correspondence with the War Department, and it underscored his actions while vindicating his conduct during the war. This was followed by other works, including his account written while governor of Arkansas of his years in Europe while getting educated on battle tactics. Equally important, General Izard kept a private journal that documented the period during which he commanded a brigade under General Hampton, the Canadian campaign of 1813. The results of his work clearly explained his actions, detailed his movements and verified that he was a competent and admirable commander, not the person depicted by his detractors "a slave to routine and not able to make use of the material at hand when nothing better could be furnished by the government."

After he left the army, General Izard settled in Philadelphia on Spruce Street between 9th and 10th Streets. He also had a summer home in nearby Bristol in Bucks County, just outside of Philadelphia.

On 4 March 1825, General Izard was named military governor of Arkansas and superintendent of Indian Affairs. He succeeded General James Miller, the first governor of Arkansas. The year before Izard was appointed governor, Major Edward W. Duval was named Indian agent. He essentially ignored Governor Izard, reporting instead directly to Washington. Nevertheless, within one year, the practice ended and Izard prevailed. From that point, Duval kept Izard informed.

General Izard was well thought of by most, including Heckaton, the chief of the Quapaws, who described him as "a white man of the right kind and worthy of everybody's confidence." Later, the Choctaws were removed westward "without a particle of friction, and south Arkansas was entirely clear of Indians." Governor Izard was also instrumental in the subsequent removal of the Cherokee. Governor Izard was not a pretentious individual and was comfortable with himself. He is known to have been an impeccable dresser, with a vast knowledge of the ways of the world, due to his early years when he received his education.

During his lifetime, with one exception, he refused to accept gifts. Being a man who chose to always be clean-shaven, he did accept razors. One of his practices might be considered eccentric by some. Governor Izard brought seven razors with him when he repaired to Arkansas. Each one had his name on it and a particular day of the week. Unlike many men of the period, he would never enter his office in the morning without having shaved. However, he was known to be quite comfortable under any circumstances, whether he was in attendance at a royal palace in Europe or the humble tent of an Indian.

While serving as governor, General Izard initiated the organization of the state's militia, and he urged that an arsenal be constructed in Little Rock due to his concern that hostilities with the Indians were imminent. It was during his administration that the Indians, including the Choctaws, Quapaws and other tribes, were relocated on reservations. Similar to his military career, as governor Izard had detractors. Some described him as "an aristocrat and a martinet." Nonetheless, close scrutiny of his record as governor points to a pragmatic man. While he was in Arkansas, his family remained in Philadelphia. Tragedy struck during 1827 when his wife died. He traveled to Philadelphia, and when he returned to Arkansas, his health continued to deteriorate because of a previous disease from which he never fully recovered.

General Izard died while in office on 22 November 1828. He was interred in Little Rock at Mount Holly Cemetery and a monument was built in his memory by Senator Chester Ashley.

Jackson, Major General Andrew Andrew, the son of Andrew and Elizabeth Hutchinson Jackson, was born in Waxhaws in a disputed sector of the Carolinas on 15 March 1767. His parents and his two older brothers, Hugh and Robert, emigrated to America during 1765. In 1767, Andrew's father died, just before Andrew was born, leaving his wife to raise the children on her own. As a youngster, Andrew lived on his uncle's farm in a sector claimed by North and South Carolina, with Andrew believing he was in North Carolina and in those times, the boys from North Carolina were often at odds with the boys from South Carolina. Nevertheless, when the boundary dispute was settled, Andrew found that without moving, his uncle's property was in South Carolina. In 1780, when Andrew was 13, he and his brother Robert joined the militia. Hugh was killed while fighting as a Patriot at Stono River. However, because of his age, Andrew was employed only as a messenger and after quite a conversation, he was able to persuade Major Davie to appoint him as an aide. During that time, Andrew and Robert were both captured by the British and afterward exchanged.

The brothers received only fundamental educations; however, Andrew's mother had high expectations that he would enter the ministry. He attended an academy in the Waxhaws settlement overseen by Mr. Humphries. Nevertheless, the British under Lord Rawdon, Duke of Camden, had been intent on stripping the Waxhaws of all its inhabitants. The British raid scored some success, but many, including Andrew and his brother, were among those who escaped. Later both were captured. One of the British officers demanded that Andrew clean his boots, but Andrew absolutely refused, which caused the officer to draw his sword. Andrew, young and unarmed, was able to use his hand to divert the blade from striking his head; however, he did sustain a wound, one that would leave an indelible mark on his memory and cement his dislike of the British. Robert was wounded much more severely. Because of the mistreatment by the British and the lack of medical aid, Robert Jackson died of his wound due to an inflammation of the brain after he was exchanged on 27 April 1781. Andrew's mother died during November 1781. She was interred in Charleston.

Andrew, having lost his entire family, was able to cope. He resumed his education, but his mother's aspirations of Andrew becoming a man of the cloth were not to be realized. For a while, he was employed in a saddler's store and taught school; however, he also renewed his studies under the tutelage of Mr. McCulloch and refocused on languages, literature, mathematics and other subjects which would gain him entrance into a university. In 1784, Andrew began to study law under Spruce McCay at Salisbury, North Carolina, and completed his studies under John Stokes. He began to practice law during 1786 and the year was appointed as solicitor for western North Carolina (later Tennessee). Two years later, Jackson accompanied Judge McNairy to what later became Tennessee. The two men arrived in Nashville during October 1788. Later, Jackson was named attorney general of the territory, which he used to deepen his reputation. On 17 January 1794, Andrew married Rachael Donelson, the daughter of John and Rachael Stockley Donelson. She was the tenth of eleven children.

Rachael had previously been married to Lewis Robards. There were complications regarding whether Jackson and Rachael had married without a divorce being in effect. To further complicate the issue, Andrew and Rachael married in Spanish held Mississippi where only Catholic marriages were legal, and neither was Catholic; both were Protestant. Afterward, Robards was granted the divorce and Rachael was found guilty of adultery and abandonment. The Jacksons remarried in Tennessee.

After Tennessee entered the union on 1 June 1796 as the 16th state, Jackson served on the Constitutional Convention. His participation was active and probing, which highlighted his talents and skills, both of which made it clear that he had received an excellent education. Jackson's reputation became more widespread and the people of Tennessee were apparently impressed with his attributes. They elected him to be the first representative from Tennessee to enter the U.S. Congress. He served in the Fourth and Fifth Congresses, 5 December 1796 until September 1797. During 1797, Jackson was elected to the U.S. Senate, where he served until April 1798.

Jackson's demeanor and character kept him from becoming involved with the mischievousness that had become common in the halls of Congress. During 1798, after resigning from the Senate, he returned to Tennessee and was appointed as a judge to the Tennessee Supreme Court. Although he had not sought the position, he did accept it; however, his time on the bench was short. He resigned during 1804 and afterward retired to his residence along the Cumberland River, where he had long before resided with his family.

Back in Tennessee, Jackson became engaged in some mercantile endeavors and became a planter. He encountered some personal difficulty during 1806, when another lawyer, Charles Dickinson, a formidable marksman, boasted that he would kill Jackson. Jackson, not prone to hiding from danger, engaged in a duel with Dickinson on 30 May 1806 and prevailed. Dickinson was killed and Jackson initially believed that he himself had been mortally wounded. Jackson sustained some broken ribs, but the shot did not penetrate. He survived and resumed his private life until 1813, when hostilities with the Creeks erupted into open war.

While the conflict with the Creek Indians was running concurrently with the War of 1812, Andrew Jackson was appointed commander of all Tennessee forces. In June 1812, General Jackson committed his entire force of Tennessee volunteers for service with U.S. forces in the war against Great Britain. General Jackson, during 1813, had also gotten involved in an altercation in Nashville with two brothers, Thomas and Jesse Benton. At that time, Jackson was seriously wounded and he nearly died, but he did survive.

After a Creek attack on Fort Mims, Alabama, that killed 500 people, Jackson led a campaign by volunteers from Georgia, Mississippi and Tennessee. The experienced Indian fighters arrived at Huntsville, Alabama, on 11 October. Two of the volunteers were Davy Crockett and Sam Houston. The Americans initiated action to retaliate for the massacre of Fort Mims by destroying their strongholds. The village of Littefutchee along Canoe Creek was reduced early on the 29th by cavalry. Other Creek villages destroyed included Tallasehatche (later Jacksonville).

On 8 November, General Jackson's force defeated 1,000 enemy Creeks who surrounded a fortified house containing friendly Creeks.

Jackson's engagements with the Creeks continued at Fort Strother, and when his force increased to about 5,000 with the arrival of reinforcements, he was ready to launch his major offensive at Horseshoe Bend. It was struck on 27 March 1814 and Jackson's troops devastated the Creeks. The victory catapulted Jackson to even more prominence when word spread that he ended the Creek war.

General Jackson's actions at Horseshoe Bend were duly noted by Congress, which commissioned him a major general in the U.S. Army in May 1814. In July he assumed command of the U.S. Southern army.

From there Jackson planned to drive the Spanish from Pensacola, Florida. On 6 November, General Jackson sent an ultimatum to the Spanish governor demanding the surrender of Forts Barrancas and St. Michael. In the Battle of Pensacola, the forts surrounding Pensacola were surrendered except for St. Michael, which was self-destructed by the Spanish.

By 9 November, with Pensacola secure, General Jackson departed for Mobile, Alabama, where he remained only for a short while.

General Jackson arrived at Baton Rouge on 1 December and immediately began to bolster the defenses to prepare for a British attack by way of the Mississippi River. On the following day, he arrived at New Orleans. There, in the Battle of New Orleans about a month later, his 5,000 soldiers defeated 7,500 British and sealed Jackson's status as a national hero.

During 1817, General Jackson returned to the military during the First Seminole War in a campaign against Seminole and Creek Indians. He seized Florida, which belonged to Spain but was subsequently ceded to the U.S. in a treaty. He was appointed as governor of the new territory during 1821.

Nonetheless, General Jackson quickly became "disgusted" while holding the post as governor. He resigned within four months after his appointment and returned to Nashville to continue his life outside of politics. Nonetheless, circumstances in the country and his continued popularity more or less compelled him to return to public life in answer to those who maintained that the country needed him. He finally consented to run for president. Nevertheless, the presidency would for a while elude him.

Jackson was re-elected to the U.S. Senate and served from 4 March 1823 until 14 October 1825, the day he resigned. Afterward, he ran unsuccessfully for president during 1824, losing to John Quincy Adams; however, four years later (1828) he was elected as the 7th president of the United States, and his term in office became known as the "Jacksonian Era." Jackson received 178 of the 261 electoral votes and John Quincy Adams received 83.

With Jackson having become president-elect, Nashville was planning a huge celebration and dinner to honor the Jacksons and the date was set for 23 December. Nevertheless, the campaign was grueling and those opposing Jackson drew his wife's character into the campaign and they pounded upon her marriage to Robards and the circumstances revolving around her marriage to Jackson. The anti–Jackson press "sensationalized" her marital history and caused her enormous shame. During that tumultuous campaign, their son Lyncoya died suddenly. Rachael suffered a severe heart attack during that autumn. For a while, it appeared likely that she would gain full recovery, so much so that she purchased "a gown and white slippers" which she intended to wear to Andrew's inaugural ball. However, she did not live long enough to attend. Rachael died just before Christmas on 22 December 1828 at age 61. Not too long after dawn on the 23rd, the jubilant aura in the city was crushed by an avalanche of deep sadness when it was announced that Mrs. Jackson had died on the previous night.

Andrew Jackson, known also as "Old Hickory," never really recovered from the loss of his wife. He placed a miniature portrait of her in a locket that he wore and placed every night on his bedside table. Jackson also visited her grave site every night while at the Hermitage. During 1834, on 3 July, a figurehead of President Jackson was placed aboard the USS *Constitution*, but later that night an unknown party boarded Old Ironsides and decapitated the figurehead. At the time, the anti–Democrats were incensed and demanded the figurehead be replaced.

On 30 June 1835, President Jackson eluded death by assassination when the assassin, Richard Lawrence, fired two pistols, both of which misfired, at the president. Lawrence was captured and placed in a mental asylum. Also that year, President Jackson, a traditionalist, ordered that the U.S. Army and the U.S. Marine Corps change their uniforms by reverting back to the style worn during the Revolutionary War.

Jackson's second term had not been uneventful. The Seminoles continued to cause problems, and in the Southwest, relations with Mexico were deteriorating as Texas was moving toward independence. On 21 January 1836, President Jackson dispatched General Winfield Scott to take command of all U.S. troops near Texas, and a few weeks later the Mexicans slaughtered the garrison at the Alamo. In April, Sam Houston defeated the Mexicans at the Battle of San Jacinto. War between Mexico and the United States was forestalled for about ten years.

President Jackson's second term ended on 3 March 1837. Afterward, he retired to his estate, the Hermitage, located outside of Nashville. Andrew Jackson died on 8 June 1845. He was interred on his estate along with his wife.

The Jacksons had two adopted sons, Andrew Jackson, Jr., a twin born to Rachael's brother Severn Donelson, and Lyncoya Jackson, an Indian child found by General Jackson while on the battlefield next to his dead mother. The Jacksons were also legal guardians for six boys and two girls. They included John Samuel Donelson, Daniel Donelson, and Andrew Jackson Donelson, sons of Rachael's brother Samuel (died 1804). Andrew Jackson Donelson worked in the White House when Jackson was president. The others were John Donelson, Andrew Jackson Hutchings, Caroline Butler, Eliza Butler, Edward Butler and Anthony Butler (the Butler children had belonged to Colonel Edward Butler, Revolutionary War era).

Johnson, Brigadier General Richard Mentor Richard, the son of Colonel Robert and Jemimi Suggett Johnson, was born in Jefferson County, Kentucky, at "Beargrass" just outside of Louisville, on 17 October 1780. Richard's parents had ten other children: Elizabeth (Betsy), James (later senator), William, Sarah (Sally), Benjamin, Robert, John Telemachus, Joel, George W., and Henry. Richard received his education in the common schools; however, he also attended Transylvania University in Lexington, where he studied law and gained admittance to the bar in 1802. Afterward, Johnson practiced in Great Crossings, Kentucky. He served in the Kentucky House of Representatives (1804–1806) and served in Congress from 4 March 1807 until 3 March 1819. In 1813, Johnson was appointed as a colonel of Kentucky volunteers. On 26 June 1813, Colonel Johnson led a contingent from Fort Winchester to Fort Meigs. Simultaneously, forces under Colonel William P. Anderson and a contingent of cavalry under Major George Croghan were also en route. On the 28th, General Harrison arrived at Fort Meigs and found that Colonel Johnson had already arrived with about 150 cavalrymen. On 4 July, Johnson arrived at Fort Stephenson and gave a riveting speech that uplifted the entire garrison.

On 25 September, Harrison ordered Johnson, at Fort Meigs, to repair to the Raisin River. On the following day, Johnson's regiment was shocked when they came upon the remains of Kentuckian troops that had been massacred the previous January at the river. On 4 October, Harrison's army reached the forks of the Thames River, and the next day, the Americans thrashed the British under General Proctor. During the raging battle, Colonel Johnson was wounded while leading a charge against Tecumseh's Indians at the marsh. Colonel Johnson received personal credit for killing Tecumseh; however, there is no evidence to verify it.

General Johnson served in the U.S. Senate from 10 December 1819 to 3 March 1829. He served as vice president (chosen by the Senate) of the United States from 8 February 1837 to 3 March 1841, under President Martin Van Buren. He served in the Kentucky state House in 1850.

General Johnson died in Frankfort, Kentucky, on 19 November 1850. He was interred in the Frankfort Cemetery. General Johnson had a common law wife, Julia Chinn, a mulatto slave. Julia had two children that Richard claimed as his own. Johnson's relationship with Julia hurt him politically. In 1840 the Democrats declined re-nominating him as vice president. President Van Buren ran for re-election with no vice president on the ticket. He lost the election to William Henry Harrison.

Kenton, Brigadier General Simon Simon, the son of Mark and Mary Miller Kenton, was born in 1755 (contemporary sources differ on the month, including March and May). Little is known about his parents other than his father was from Ireland and his mother was of Scottish descent. As a young man Simon worked in farming and did not attend any type of formal schooling. He reached maturity without being able to read or write.

While still a young man, Simon lost the girl he loved to a neighbor's son. It led to a confrontation and Simon was beaten. He retaliated and beat one of his attackers, named William Veach. This occurred during 1771. Simon erroneously believed that he killed him. He ran away and after reaching Ise's Ford, on the Cheat River, he changed his name to Simon Butler, but it did not change his circumstances. By that time, he was fearful of getting caught and hanged for the murder of his former friend. Simon became paranoid, thinking that even strangers were pursuing him.

Simon traveled to Fort Pitt, where he met the infamous Simon Girty, who at one time saved Simon's life. He also came into contact with John Strader and George Yeager, two men who were well acquainted with the wilderness and the Indians. Simon Kenton accompanied them down the Ohio River, where few whites ventured. They spent the winter 1771–1772 together on a hunting expedition. During spring of 1772, they sold their pelts to a French trader and afterward resumed their hunting. In 1773, they were attacked by Indians and Yeager was killed. Strader and Kenton escaped, but barely, and they were subjected to great deprivations.

During 1774, Kenton returned to Fort Pitt and joined the army. He participated in Dunmore's War as a spy. After being fired upon by Indians, Kenton got separated from his party and did not get back to Fort Pitt. He arrived at another post on the Monongahela River, and the commanding officer did not believe his story. Kenton was arrested as a spy for the Indians. A messenger was sent to Fort Pitt, and upon his return, Kenton was released and allowed to return to Fort Pitt. During 1775 and 1776, Kenton was in Kentucky fighting off Indian attacks against various stations, including two sieges against Boonesborough. Kenton also remained employed as a spy until 1778. That June, he joined with George Rodgers Clark on the campaign against Kaskaskia. Following the campaign, he returned to Harrodsburg.

Later that year, Kenton accompanied Clark on an expedition to Chillicothe. He was captured by Indians, and just before he was to die at the stake, Simon Girty intervened and his life was spared. He was taken to the British at Detroit, where he remained until summer of 1779, when he escaped with the aid of Mrs. Harvey, the wife of a trader, who inconspicuously purchased items, including powder and dried beef, that would be required to effect their escape. On the night of their escape, Mrs. Harvey took three rifles from a stack while the Indians were engaged in a drinking spree. The items were hidden in a tree. Simon and two others, Nathan Bullitt and Jesse Coffer, after traveling about 400 miles, arrived at Louisville during the summer of 1779.

During spring of 1780, Indians again began to ravage Kentucky settlements, including Ruddell's and Martin's. Kenton commanded a company of volunteers under General George Rodgers Clark, who undertook a campaign to avenge the raids that succeeded in destroying a large number of Indian villages. During autumn of 1782, General Clark initiated another campaign against the Indians and again, Kenton participated. From 1788 until 1793, Kenton continued to participate in engaging the Indians, who continued to attack Kentucky settlements. In 1793, he led a contingent of Kentuckians against a band of marauding Indians as they crossed the Ohio River. The Indians were soundly defeated and the victory terminated further Indian attacks in the region.

That same year, holding the rank of major, Kenton accompanied General Anthony Wayne, who had arrived near Cincinnati with his army. However, winter arrived to stall the campaign. During that period, Fort Greenville and Fort Recovery were built, the latter on the site where General St. Clair was defeated. Meanwhile, at the onset of winter, Major Kenton was discharged, ending his military career until the War of 1812. During the early 1800s, about 1802, Kenton arrived in Urbana, Ohio, where he remained for several years after a rough time in Kentucky, where his lack of knowledge on the law cost him heavily. He departed from his home penniless and without his property.

While in Ohio, Kenton was elected a brigadier general of militia. About 1810, he was received into the Methodist Church. During 1813, when General Isaac Shelby of Kentucky arrived in Ohio at Urbana, Kenton joined his fellow Kentuckians, not as a general but as a private, although closely associated with the commanding general. Kenton participated in the victory at the Battle of the Thames. In 1820, he relocated near the head of the Mad River in Logan County. At the time, Kenton, who never accumulated any riches, was again in poverty. Through the efforts of Senator Bumet and General Vance (later governor of Ohio), a pension of twenty dollars a month was gained for General Kenton to aid him during his final years.

During his final months, too weak to walk, he would have a friend take him to attend church services. General Kenton died in April 1836. General Kenton married Elizabeth Jarboe, who survived him until her death in 1842. They had the following children: Simon (born 1793, died 1844); Sarah (born 1795 died 1862); Mary (born 1803, died 1864); and Clara (born 1829, died 1889).

Lee, Colonel Henry Henry Lee, known as "Light Horse Harry," the son of Henry and Lucy Grimes Lee, was born on 29 January 1756 on the family estate in Westmoreland County, Virginia. In addition to Henry, their oldest child, his parents had the following children: Charles, Richard Bland, Theodorick, Edmund Jennings, Lucy (b. 1774, died unmarried), Mary (birth date unknown, second wife of Philip Richard Fendall about 1792), and Anne (b. 1776, married William Byrd Page).

Henry, having been born in an influential family, received an excellent education. At about age 13, he entered the College of New Jersey (later Princeton) and graduated during 1773. Following graduation, he returned to the family estate and began to manage the plantation in the absence of his father, who was engaged in negotiating treaties with various Indian tribes. At age 19 Henry entered the service. He was commissioned as a captain of a company of dragoons on 18 June 1776.

Captain Henry Lee participated in the New York campaigns of 1776. On 31 March 1777, Lee's company was attached to the 1st Continental Dragoons. He participated in the defense of Philadelphia, including the Battle of Brandywine on September 9–11, 1777, and the Battle of Germantown in October 1777. During the contest at Germantown, General George Washington designated Lee's cavalry as his bodyguard. After the fighting at Germantown, the British retired to Philadelphia, while General Washington established winter headquarters at Valley Forge.

On 20 January 1778, a contingent of British troops, having received intelligence of the whereabouts of Captain Lee, launched a raid and converged on Eagle Tavern near Valley Forge. Nevertheless, the Americans in the tavern, including Lee, did not surrender. The doors were bolted and the British force, which included Banastre Tarleton, were repelled. Several British troops were killed during the exchange. Lee was later promoted to the rank of major commandant. Congress also resolved "that he be empowered to augment his present corps by enlistment of two troops of horse to act as a separate corps." This was later increased to three and then four.

On 18 August, Captain Lee led his corps to the final British stronghold in New Jersey: Paulus Hook (Jersey City). The British were surprised and overwhelmed. The attack succeeded in capturing 159 British troops. The British also sustained 50 killed. After the lightninged immediately and took no time to disable the guns. Some officers, apparently jealous of Lee's success, lodged charges against him. Lee received a court-martial, but the scheme failed. He was exonerated and his actions received accolades.

On 21 October 1779, his battalion was named "Lee's Partisan Corps." Major Lee's corps deployed at Burlington, New Jersey, during the winter of 1779–1780. Later Washington directed Lee to move south to join with and bolster General Nathanael Greene, the latter having been ordered south to replace General Horatio Gates. Lee was promoted to the rank of colonel on 6 November 1780 and remained in the field for the duration. On 24 January 1781, a contingent of Patriots led by Colonels Francis Marion and Henry Lee attacked a British stronghold at Georgetown, South Carolina. No fighting occurred. The Americans in retreat, following their victory at Cowpens on 17 January 1781, chose not to take casualties and the British offered no resistance. The British, led by Lt. Colonel George Campbell, were given parole. Afterward, the Americans headed for the Catawba River.

On 7 February Colonel Henry "Lighthorse Harry" Lee's cavalry, which had been operating in South Carolina with Francis Marion, the Swamp Fox, arrived at Guilford Court House with General Isaac Huger's force and joined with General Greene. At the time, British General Lord Charles Cornwallis was in pursuit of Greene, attempting to intercept the Americans before they reached the Dan River and Virginia. Part of Colonel Lee's corps covered the rear of the column. The British vanguard under General Charles O'Hara felt the sting of Lee's cavalry.

Meanwhile, the Americans reached Virginia safely. On the 19th, Colonel Lee was dispatched by General Greene to gather intelligence on the British and to join other forces. On 25 February 1781, a column of Loyalists under Colonel John Pyle, was advancing to join with Cornwallis, but it encountered Colonel Lee's command. The Loyalists were jubilant, believing they had met militia troops under Cornwallis, and upon sight of the Patriot cavalry, they shouted, "Long live the king." Lee temporarily continued the ruse, but as the Loyalists moved closer and began to pass by the supposedly friendly militia, the true colors become known as the Americans initiated a furious attack, leaving the relaxed Loyalists no time to react. About 200 to 300 Loyalists were killed by the sword, while large numbers were wounded and the remainder captured. The incident is remembered as "Pyle's Massacre."

On 15 April, Colonel Lee joined with Marion in South Carolina, where they captured British Fort Watson, Fort Motte, Fort Galpin, and Fort Cornwallis at Augusta, Georgia. On 17 July, Lee's force, combined with those of Marion and Sumter, clashed at Quimby Bridge (Berkeley County, South Carolina). The British raised heavy resistance and repulsed the attack, but they were compelled to retire after sustaining heavy casualties. On 8 September, Colonel Lee's corps participated at the Battle of Eutaw Springs, the final major battle in South Carolina. Later, on 13 December 1782, Colonel Lee was with the force of General Anthony Wayne outside Charleston when word arrived that the British would be abandoning Charleston on the following day.

In spring of 1782, Henry married Matilda Ludwell, his cousin and the daughter of Philip and Elizabeth Steptoe Ludwell. Matilda's sister, Flora, married another cousin, Philip Ludwell Lee, the son of Richard Henry Lee. Henry and Matilda had four children: Nathanael Greene (b. about 1784, died in infancy); Philip Ludwell (b. about 1785, died during 1795); Lucy Grymes (b. during 1786, married Bernard Moore Carter); Henry (b. 1787). After the war, Colonel Lee was elected to the Virginia legislature, and then in 1786 to Congress. Although he was not a delegate to the Constitutional Convention in Philadelphia during 1787, when the United States Constitution was adopted on 17 September, Lee did serve as a delegate to the state ratification convention of 1788. Virginia ratified the Constitution on 25 June 1788 to become the tenth state.

During 1790, Henry's wife, Matilda, died (about May). Henry Lee was elected governor of Virginia the following year. He succeeded Beverly Randolph and served from 1791 through 1794. In the meantime, Lee had been pondering whether to travel to France to serve in the French Army with a commission as a major general. He sought advice from General Washington, who advised against the trip based on conditions in France, and he also remarked: "Because it would appear a boundless ocean I was about to embark on, from whence no land is seen. Those in whose hands of the government [of France] is intrusted are ready to tear each other to pieces, and will more than probably prove the worst foes the country has."

Lee also received an opinion from Charles Carter of Shirley. Besides going to France, Lee was also working toward marriage to Anne Hill Carter, the daughter of Charles and his second wife, Ann Butler Moore Carter. Carter's earlier opinion is thought to have bolstered Washington's advice, because if Henry went to France, Anne Hill's parents would not consent to the marriage. Carter said in a letter to Henry Lee, dated 20 May 1793: "The only objection we ever had to your connection with our beloved daughter is now done away. You have declared upon your honor that you have relinquished all thoughts of going to France, and we rest satisfied with that assurance. As we certainly know that you have obtained her consent, you shall have that of her parents most cordially, to be joined together in the holy bonds of matrimony, whenever she pleases; and as it is determined on, by the approbation and sincere affection of all friends, as well as of all the parties immediately concerned, we think the sooner it takes place the better."

Henry Lee got married and avoided getting entangled in the French Revolution. He married Anne Hill Carter on 18 June 1793. They had six children, one of whom was Robert E. Lee, an officer (West Point graduate 1829) in the United States Army until the outbreak of the Civil War, when he refused to take up arms against Virginia. Robert E. Lee was appointed commanderd, Henry and Anne had the following children: Algernon Sidney (born at Stratford, April 1795); Charles Carter (born at Stratford, November 1798); Anne Kinloch (born at Stratford, June 1800, married Judge William Louis Marshall); Sydney Smith (born September 1802 at Camden, New Jersey, while Mrs. Lee was on a visit there; married Anna Maria Mason); and Catherine Mildred (born at Alexandria, Virginia, in February 27, 1811, married Edward Vernon Childe).

On 19 July 1798, Colonel Lee was commissioned as a major general of the United States Army. The next year he was elected to the U.S. Congress. During his service there, George Washington died (14 December 1799) at this home in Mount Vernon. Henry Lee was delegated by Congress to deliver the eulogy in honor of President Washington to the House of Representatives. Lee's eulogy on 26 December 1799 was spellbinding and has continued to be considered a classic of American oratory. The most remembered part is that Washington was "first in war, first in peace and first in the hearts of his countrymen; he was second to none in the humble and endearing scenes of private life."

Henry Lee retired from public life during 1801 and afterward suffered some severe financial setbacks by involving himself in bad choices in land speculation. He was compelled to move from the estate (Stratford) to Alexandria and relied on a trust of his wife to maintain the family. During his retirement, he authored *The Memoirs of the War of '76 in the Southern Department* in 1809. In 1814, he was badly wounded while confronting a political mob in Baltimore, Maryland, and he was never able to completely recuperate.

Lee's health by 1817 deteriorated further, prompting him to take a voyage to the West Indies in an attempt to regain his health; however, he found no success. While he was en route back to his home in Virginia during spring of 1818, he paused in Georgia to visit one of General Nathanael Greene's daughters, Louisa Shaw, who resided on Cumberland Island, but he never completed the trip to his home. General Henry "Light Horse Harry" Lee died while at Mrs. Shaw's residence on 25 March 1818. At the time of Henry Lee's death, Robert E. Lee was about eleven years old.

Lewis, Major General Morgan Morgan, the son of Francis Lewis (signer of the Declaration of Independence) and his wife, Elizabeth Annesley, was born 16 October 1754 in New York City. Morgan's parents had two other children, Francis and Ann. Morgan received his education at the Elizabeth Academy and College of New Jersey (Princeton College), class of 1773. After receiving his degree, he began studying law in the office of John Jay. In 1774, he joined a company of volunteers. Subsequent to the Battle of Bunker Hill (Breed's Hill), Lewis traveled to

Boston to join the army as a volunteer. He served in a rifle company commanded by Captain Ross of Lancaster, Pennsylvania. Meanwhile, Lewis was elected captain of the New York City Volunteers. He remained with the siege of Boston until he returned to New York in late August. On the 25th, after dusk, Lewis was ordered to provide protection for those who were removing the arms and ammunition from the arsenal on the battery due to the appearance of the HMS *Asia.*

Captain Lewis' contingent spotted a boat with muffled oars approaching, and calls for the craft to respond were ignored. Meanwhile, the British crew had a small blue light "under the bow of the boat, near the surface, unaware that it was a reconnaissance boat acting as a guide for the warship, which began to bombard the arsenal. American riflemen, after hearing no response, fired at the boat, inflicting some casualties. Nevertheless, the arms and ammunition were saved.

The New York militia was established in November 1775. John Jay was initially appointed colonel of the 2nd Regiment of Foot; however, the organization and the discipline of the regiment was actually handled by Major Lewis because Colonel Jay never joined.

During June of 1775, Major Lewis accompanied General Horatio Gates to the northern frontier in Canada as his chief of staff. After the American army abandoned Canada and returned the States during 1776, he was elevated to the rank of colonel and appointed quartermaster general of the Northern Department, a post he retained for the duration of the war. While on the frontier, he participated in the expedition against Ticonderoga, and he served with General Schuyler during the two Battles of Saratoga (Stillwater, 19 September, and Saratoga, 7 October 1777), which culminated in the surrender of British General Burgoyne.

In 1779, he married Gertrude, the daughter of Robert R. and Margaret Beekman Livingston, making him part of the influential Livingston family. He participated with General Van Rensselaer during autumn 1780 in the Mohawk valley against General Sir William Johnson and Chief Joseph Brant when the British attacked Fort Keyser at Palantine (Stone Arabia) and afterward ignited the Battle of Klock's Field, near Utica. The Americans sustained large losses due in part to decisions made by Rensselaer. Colonel Lewis afterward participated with General (governor) George Clinton on the expedition to Crown Point during 1780.

After the war, Colonel Lewis returned to studying law. He and his wife initially resided at Rhinebeck and afterward at Hyde Park. Back in New York, Colonel Lewis was appointed as colonel commandant of a renowned corps of volunteer militia in New York City. After George Washington was elected as the first president of the United States, Colonel Lewis' corps escorted Washington at his inauguration in April 1789.

Colonel Morgan Lewis was a member of the New York Assembly 1789–1792, initially from New York City and in 1790 from Duchess County, where he had moved. He was also appointed as a common pleas judge and then attorney general of the state of New York during 1791, where he served into 1792, the year that he was named to the state Supreme Court. He became chief justice during 1801. He remained on the bench until 1804, when he was elected governor of the state, defeating Aaron Burr. That same year, General Lewis appointed Maturin Livingston, his son-in-law, as recorder of New York, which ignited charges of nepotism. During 1806, DeWitt Clinton, the mayor of New York, terminated Maturin as recorder, only to receive political payback in 1807 when he was removed as mayor by the governor. Nonetheless, the same year, Governor Lewis lost his bid for re-election after being defeated by Daniel D. Tompkins.

Although the country was at peace during his term as governor, he was still guided by his military experience, and he maintained close scrutiny of the militia. He pressed for the implementation of horse-drawn artillery and was responsible for introducing it to the militia, which he believed was of paramount importance to ensure the defense of the state. Earlier, horse-drawn artilley had been considered by some as folly; however, during the Revolution, artillery outlasted its detractors and proved its importance. Governor Lewis also ordered that every county in the state contain a magazine, a move that proved invaluable after the outbreak of war with Britain.

He was elected to the state Senate in 1810 by a wide margin described as "a larger majority than had ever before been given."

When war with Britain was considered imminent, Lewis reverted back to his military service when he was appointed quartermaster general of the army and given the rank of brigadier general in May 1812. Soon after assuming his new duties, General Lewis became involved in arranging prisoner exchanges. Some difficulties emerged, but just after the Battle at Queenston (October 1812), General Lewis forwarded letters of credit to a personal friend in Montreal and each of the drafts were honored. He was able afterward to dispatch an officer, and using the same system, succeeded in gaining the release of some prisoners. They arrived in Boston during December 1812. The government in Canada declined accepting bills drawn from the U.S. government; however, the house of McGilvany agreed unequivocally to accept and cash any bills drawn on Morgan Lewis as an individual.

During March 1813, General Lewis was raised to the rank of major general. At that time, he was separated from his previous post as quartermaster general and ordered to repair to the northern frontier. He took command of his division on 17 April. Most of his force was deployed in the vicinity of Fort Niagara. Lewis' command was under General Henry Dearborn.

On 27 May, during the pre-dawn hours, the American force led by General Lewis landed on the Canadian bank of the Niagara River and seized Fort George. On the following day, the American pursuit was halted, leaving the British retreat to continue without interference. Although the order to halt is usually attributed to General Lewis, there is some indication that General Dearborn had initiated the order and directed Lewis to carry it out. Nevertheless, the abandonment of the chase was considered to be a bad decision that caused problems for the American campaign.

Following the seizure of Fort George, Generals John Chandler and William H. Winder set out to attack the British at Burlington Heights and the operation was turned into a debacle. Both generals were captured by the British; however, the British attack was eventually repulsed. After the engagement, General Lewis was ordered to assume command. By September 1813, General Lewis was directed to take command of the forces at Sackets Harbor and prepare to accompany the new commander of the frontier, General James Wilkinson, on a campaign to seize Montreal. Nevertheless, the campaign was aborted after the defeat at Chrysler's farm on 11 November. Both the British and the Americans declared victory; however, Wilkinson's failure to break though the British defenses compelled him to abandon his quest to seize Montreal. Wilkinson and Lewis were ill and command fell to General John Parker Boyd. General Lewis related his thoughts later in a letter his wife:

> The impetuosity of Boyd, it is said (but you must not say it), threw our lines into disorder, broke their ranks, and the enemy drove us in turn. Covington's ammunition was exhausted, and our artillery just arrived in the field as our troops gave way. The enemy did not choose to try us again, though his force was at least equal, if not superior, to ours, as we had just sent away many detachments. Our loss is heavy. We have not as yet the whole of the returns. General Covington and several other officers fell gloriously. He was a very gallant soldier. I have never in my life suffered as much as I have done in this expedition. When on shore, lying under canvas in cold and boisterous weather equal to January on the Hudson; when on board, confined to a hole three feet high, with a constant dysentery, which sets blackberry jelly and every other remedy at defiance, I several times thought I should bid adieu to you all without the aid of the enemy. I am now, thank God, on shore in a house, though not a comfortable one. I am far from well, but in hopes of being re-established shortly by the aid of a milk and vegetable diet. I hope that Armstrong will order me to Washington to settle my accounts, that I may have once more an opportunity of embracing you all. Till then and forever, God preserve you all.

By the 13th, Wilkinson's forces crossed the St. Lawrence River and returned to New York, where they established winter quarters. In 1814, General Lewis assumed command of the defenses of New York City. Nonetheless, New York was spared because the British chose New Orleans, Louisiana, as their primary objective. He separated from the army with an honorable discharge on 15 June 1815.

When General Lewis returned from Canada,

he had brought an unusual guest, the dog that had belonged to British General Isaac Brock, who requested before he died that his servant take the dog back to the Brock family in England. Nevertheless, inexplicably, the servant embarked without General Brock's dog. The dog, which was called Brock, after his master, remained with the Lewis family for a while before General Lewis arranged to have the animal transported to England so it would, as General Brock requested, be returned to his family.

During his years of retirement, General Lewis often had visitors, and one of those was Louis Napoleon Bonaparte, who initially visited the general during 1835. By that time, General Lewis had become deaf. His wife, Gertrude, died the previous year at age 76. The general and Gertrude had been married for 55 years. General Lewis's health began to fail but he never lost his faith. Frequently he prayed. At age ninety, he is known to have said, "I know that He who has taken care of me for ninety years will not desert me now."

General Lewis died at age 90 on 7 April 1844. His funeral was held at St. Paul's Chapel (Episcopal). Officers of the Army and Navy attended, along with New York military units, the Society of the Cincinnati, officials of New York City and members of the Masonic Lodge. On the following day, the general's remains were taken from New York to Hyde Park, where he was interred, according to his request, next to his wife. He was survived by his daughter Margaret, the only child of General and Mrs. Lewis.

Macomb, Major General Alexander Alexander, the son of Alexander and Catherine Navarre Macomb, was born on 3 April 1782 in Detroit, Michigan. Alexander's grandfather John Macomb emigrated from Ireland and his mother's family was of French descent. Alexander's father, a fur trader, returned to New York while Alexander was still a baby. In the meantime, after the close of the American Revolution, Alexander's father acquired a large tract of land known later as "Macomb's Purchase." When Alexander was eight years old, his father placed him in a school under the Rev. Doctor Uzual Ogden in Newark, New Jersey. The Reverend Ogden was the pastor of the Episcopal church in Newark and at the time, he was also the bishop-elect for the Episcopal Diocese of New Jersey. Alexander received a fine education that included the classics, mathematics and French.

On 28 May 1798, when Macomb was 18 years old, he was elected into a unique company, the New York Rangers, commanded by Lieutenant Commandant Edward Laight, which had its roots back in the French and Indian War (1755–1763) and was known to be composed of the elite troops of every British commander along the border with Canada and the Lake George region. The rangers were attached to the 3rd New York Regiment (militia), commanded by Colonel (later major general) Jacob Morton, a veteran of the American Revolution. However, Macomb remained with the rangers only a short while. During January 1799, he was appointed as cornet of light infantry, effective on 10 January. Later that year, General North, adjutant general of the Northern Army, assigned Colonel Macomb to his staff as assistant adjutant general. Also about that time, Macomb visited Montreal to examine British discipline in the army. He met with British General Napier Christie Burton, along with other officers.

Upon his return, although there had been cutbacks in the military, Macomb, with the rank of second lieutenant, was attached to an old troop of dragoons, which by that time contained part of his old regiment. Macomb received his commission on 10 February 1801. It was delivered to him by President Jefferson. He was dispatched to Philadelphia on duty with recruiting. On 12 October, he was promoted to 1st lieutenant and assigned to the Corps of Engineers. Shortly afterward, pursuant to orders, he repaired to West Point, which at the time was in its infancy and commanded by Superintendent Lt. Colonel Williams.

The following year, on 23 July, he married Catharine Macomb, his 16-year-old cousin. Catherine was the daughter of William and Sarah Jane Dring Macomb. Later that year, he traveled to Fredericktown, Maryland, to attend the court-martial of Colonel Thomas Butler, a Revolutionary War veteran who was accused by General Wilkinson of disobeying orders regarding the length of his hair when he refused to cut it. He had been wearing the style used by most men still in service who served during the Revolution. The court sustained the regulation. Macomb served as judge advocate during the trial and for a few others held at that same time. Afterward, he returned to West Point. It was suggested that he "write a treatise as a general guide for courts-martial," something he later accomplished.

During 1805, Lt. Macomb was promoted to the rank of captain (Corps of Engineers), effective 11 June 1805, by General Dearborn, who was secretary of war at the time. He was assigned to the eastern seaboard to inspect the fortifications along the coast. After his promotion, he repaired first to Portsmouth, New Hampshire. During 1806, Macomb was appointed as superintendent of the project underway on the Catawba River at Mount Dearborn in South Carolina about 35 miles above Camden. The project was to establish a federal armory and a depot for use by the southern states. During that time, he wrote his treatise on courts-martial. Two Revolutionary general officers, William R. Davies and Charles Cotesworth Pinckney, were both shown the treatise, and they contributed to fine tuning the piece. It was afterward presented to the government authorities. The secretary of war and the president both approved of Alexander's piece, and it was adopted and became the "standard for the guidance of courts-martial."

Macomb remained at Mount Dearborn until 1807, when he was directed to take the position of chief engineer of the fortifications and other military projects in the works for the defense of the harbors and seacoast of North Carolina, South Carolina and Georgia. The seacoast fortifications in the south had deteriorated greatly since the close of the Revolutionary War. Meanwhile, tensions with the United Kingdom were accelerating, and some fear was building as to the ability of the U.S. to defend itself if the British ignited any adversarial action. Macomb repaired to Charleston to construct some temporary batteries at Fort Johnson. He also modified other harbors and erected some temporary works between Ocracoke Inlet and the St. Mary's River.

In 1808, Captain Macomb was elevated to the rank of major, effective 3 February 1808, and he was given responsibility as superintendent of the seacoast fortifications. On 25 February 1811, he was promoted to the rank of full colonel. Later that year, despite his friendship with General James Wilkinson, Macomb acted as judge advocate at the court-martial of Wilkinson at Fredericktown, Maryland. Wilkinson was acquitted. Just before war was declared against Britain in 1812, Major Macomb was appointed as adjutant general on 28 April.

On 6 July 1812, Colonel Macomb received command of the U.S. 3rd Regiment of Artillery, composed of "twenty companies of one hundred and eighteen each." Essentially, he had received command of a division, but without the rank of a division commander. In November, Macomb led his force to the New York frontier, where it spent the winter of 1812–1813 at Sackets Harbor. His command missed the attack on Kingston; however, it did participate at Niagara and at Fort George. He also participated in the ill-fated campaign of General James Wilkinson to seize Montreal.

On 24 January 1814, Colonel Macomb was promoted to the rank of brigadier general and appointed to command on the east side of Lake Champlain. Initially, he was based at Burlington, Vermont, but after a period of relative quiet, General Macomb was back in the midst of combat when the British under Sir George Prevost launched an attack against Plattsburgh during September 1814. At that time, Macomb had been left in command at Plattsburgh by General Izard, who had marched to Fort Erie in Canada.

On 1 September, the British army under Prevost arrived at the Canadian border with New York. By the 6th, the 14,000-man army was on the outskirts of the objective. General Macomb's defending force stood only slightly above 4,000 men; however, the troops were prepared.

Major (later major general) John Wool had arrived on the previous night with regulars and militia to intercept the British. After an extended battle, General Macomb's defenders saved Plattsburgh, while the U.S. Navy prevailed offshore.

The British plan to seize territory in New York and Vermont was foiled. General Prevost was compelled to march back to Canada. The victory greatly aided the American negotiators at Ghent.

Following the victory, the Americans built additional forts; however, the war was nearly at an end after the battle for Plattsburgh. General Macomb promised each of the young men and boys (Aiken's volunteers) a rifle for their service.

The U.S. Congress acted on General Macomb's promise, and eight years later, in May 1826, Congress fulfilled it.

General Macomb was promoted to major general, effective 11 September 1814, the day of the victory. General Macomb dismissed the militia but remained in command at Plattsburgh. He did receive leave to visit his family at Belleville, New Jersey. After peace was restored, the army retained two major generals and four brigadier generals. Macomb was selected as one of the four brigadiers. President Madison directed Macomb to repair to the capital to become a member of the board tasked with organizing the Peace Establishment. The difficult assignment was completed on 17 May 1815. Afterward, General Macomb was assigned to 3rd Military Department. He established his headquarters in New York City.

After a while, General Macomb was transferred to Michigan to assume command of the 5th Military Department. He established his headquarters at Detroit, the city in which he was born; however, at the time of his birth, Detroit was only a frontier town. He remained at the post until 1821, when he was ordered to Washington, D.C., to become the chief of the Engineer Department. On 8 June, General Macomb, his wife, his nine young children and his mother-in-law departed from Detroit. Their departure was a combination of sadness and joy. The throngs of people, including Catholic and Protestant clergy, were happy for him but sad to watch him leave. His party arrived in Washington on the 20th of the same month.

Alexander and Catherine had twelve children. Catherine died in childbirth on 19 September 1822. General Macomb called upon his elderly parents who were residing in New York to come and live with him. His parents, who had been affluent in their early lives, had been reduced to poverty. In May 1826, General Macomb remarried, taking Harriet Balch Wilson as his second wife. She was the daughter of the Reverend Balch of Georgetown. Upon the death of Major Jacob Jennings Brown in 1828, General Macomb was appointed as commander-in-chief of the army. He retained the post until his death on 25 June 1841.

Madison, James James Madison, the son of Colonel James and Nelly Conway Madison, was born on 16 March 1751 in Port Conway (King George County), Virginia. At the time of his birth, James' mother was visiting her parents. After the birth of James, his mother returned to the family plantation, Montpelier. James' father was the son of Ambrose and Frances Taylor Madison. James' mother was the daughter of Francis and Rebecca Catlett Conway Moore. In addition to James, his parents had the following children: Francis (born June 1753); Ambrose (born January 1755, later major); Catlett (born February 1758, died March 1758); Nelly (born February 1760); William (born May 1762); Sarah Catlett (born August 1764); a son (born 1766, died in infancy); Elizabeth (born February 1768, died May 1775); infant son (born July 1770, died at birth); Reuben (born September 1771, died June 1775); and Frances Taylor (born October 1774).

James received his early education from his mother as well as private tutors and attendance at a private school. He attended the College of New Jersey (later Princeton), from where he graduated in 1771 at age seventeen. After graduation, James remained an extra year to study for the ministry. Afterward, he returned home, but still, James was uncertain of which career he would pursue. But in the meantime, conditions in the colony had shifted and the colonists were beginning to seriously question the policies of the Crown and Parliament. The strained relations began at about the same time Parliament passed the Stamp Act during 1765. By the early 1770s, James had aligned himself with the Patriots' cause.

By 1775, his course was certain. James Madison became involved with local politics when he was appointed to the Orange County Committee of Safety. The following year, he was a member of the Virginia Convention. During the convention, Madison was instrumental in helping to frame the Virginia constitution. Also in 1776, Madison was elected to the House of Delegates, a position he held through 1777. In 1778, he became a member of the Council of State, where he served into 1780, when he was elected to Congress. Madison remained in Congress until 1783, and during the following year, he was returned to the Virginia House of Delegates, serving there until 1786, when he was returned to Congress until 1788.

The struggle for independence culminated in victory while Madison was serving in Congress. The bulk of the fighting terminated with the surrender of General Lord Charles Cornwallis at Yorktown during October 1781, but the preliminary peace treaty wasn't signed until 1782, with the official end to the war occurring during 1783 with the Treaty of Paris. Afterward, during 1785, while the nation was involved with various postwar problems, Madison attended the Mount Vernon Conference, which was called to find a way to increase navigation on the Potomac. It had been determined earlier that the boundary between Maryland and Virginia was the Virginia shoreline, not the middle of the Potomac. Maryland and Virginia concluded an agreement; however, according to the Articles of Confederation, the agreement was deemed invalid because the articles forbid a treaty of any kind between separate states without authorization by Congress. Consequently, a new convention (Annapolis Convention) was called to find solutions to increase interstate navigation, including linking the interior with the sea. It was expected that delegates from every state would attend, but only a few states sent delegates, which caused the convention to conclude without success; however, it did determine that a Constitutional Convention was required to either modify the Articles of Confederation or to design a new government.

The Constitutional Convention was called and scheduled to convene in Philadelphia during May 1787. James Madison was a delegate and aligned with Alexander Hamilton and John Jay in creating a series of 85 essays, *The Federalist Papers*, that were published in various newspapers in New York prior to the convention. They spelled out the dangers faced by the new nation because of foreign influence, and they validated the necessity of a new constitution. The essays were published under the name "Publius" and continue to be a primary reference source to better understand the Constitution.

While a delegate at the Constitutional Convention, Madison's knowledge of the weaknesses of the Articles of Confederation bolstered his position in support of adoption of the Constitution and made up for his inability to master the art of rhetoric. Madison was a primary force during the discussions and debates, in which he spoke about 150 times. Only Gouverneur Morris and James Wilson spoke more often. On 17 September 1787, the Constitution was adopted, effective upon ratification by nine states.

During his state's ratification convention, Madison again was pressed to the forefront of the defenders to ensure ratification over the objections of some other very prominent and powerful Virginians, including Patrick Henry, Richard Henry Lee and George Mason. Nonetheless, those aligned with Madison prevailed. Virginia ratified the Constitution on 25 June 1788 to become the tenth state to join the union. The new Congress convened during early March 1789, and on 30 April, General George Washington was inaugurated as the first president of the United States.

Madison was a member of Congress in the House of Representatives from 1789 until 1797. During that period, he was instrumental in the adoption of the Bill of Rights (first ten amendments to the Constitution), and he participated as one of the congressmen who formulated the federal system of taxation; however, he had great differences with the administration, particularly the policies of the Treasury Secretary Alexander Hamilton. Others who shared Madison's ideology included Thomas Jefferson. Madison and Jefferson were responsible for founding the Democratic-Republican Party (present-day Democrats) as the opposition party to the Federalists.

During 1794, Madison abandoned his life as a bachelor when he married Dolley Payne Todd, the daughter of John and Mary Coles Payne. Dolley was about sixteen years younger than James. She had been married to John Todd, a Quaker, but he died within two years, leaving Dolley with a son. Her marriage to James was childless. By about 1797, James Madison's public activity began to wind down as he slipped into a period where his private life dominated his day, but later, during 1798, he became rejuvenated and authored the "Virginia Resolution" in opposition to the Alien and Sedition Acts, which were heavily favored by the Federalists and opposed by the Democratic-Republicans. At the time, the nation was imperiled by spies and others intent on harming the security of the United States. After the election of Thomas Jefferson, he bolted back into public life when he received a presidential appointment as secretary of state and served in that post from 1801 until 1809. Then he succeeded Jefferson to become the fourth president of the United States.

As the newest leader of the United States, President Madison inherited much of the foreign intrigues that plagued the previous administration. Britain and France continued to create problems and similarly, on the domestic front, the nation was locked in a financial crisis. American vessels on the high seas were still being intercepted. Diplomacy failed to resolve most of the problems. After a concentrated effort, the situation with France leveled off, but with the former nemesis of the United States, relations continued to become more strained and then, finally, but not unexpectedly, the War of 1812 commenced with Britain. Simultaneously, American forces were involved in a conflict (Patriots' War) in Florida, where the Indians were incited by the Spanish, and the British continued to impress American sailors into the Royal Navy.

Once again, America was compelled to fight, but during the War of 1812, it was to keep its sovereignty, not to gain it. President Madison, on 1 June 1812, urged Congress to declare war against Britain and soon after, on the 18th, war was declared. A vote that month to also declare war against France failed in the Senate by only two votes. Initially, the United States sustained some setbacks, including the loss of Fort Michilimackinac and Detroit during August 1812. During October 1812, President Madison, who had called up 100,000 militia troops in April, called up an additional 1,500 troops from Tennessee to launch an offensive against the Creek Indians in Florida. That December, Major General Andrew Jackson led the expeditionary force, composed of about 2,000 troops, into Florida and the campaign continued until 6 May 1813. While the American land forces were struggling during the first year of the war, the United States Navy experienced great success, despite the more powerful Royal Navy.

In 1814, the British moved against the capital. As they advanced, the opposition, mostly militia, fled, leaving only a contingent of Marines and sailors under Commodore Joshua Barney at their front. Barney's Marines and sailors held the line at Bladensburg during August, and while they stood steadfastly, Congress joined the militia and fled into Virginia. Although Washington had become a ghost town, Dolley Madison refused to evacuate until the president returned to the White House. At the time, he was at Bladensburg observing the battle. Dolley, while waiting for her husband, rescued vital records and a portrait of George Washington, according to popular legend. After the president returned, the Madisons calmly departed the capital. The British soon after occupied Washington and before leaving burned the White house. They were forced to abandon the capital, but not by U.S. troops; rather, a terrible storm arrived and that caused them to depart.

The war was brought to an end with the signing of the Treaty of Ghent on 24 December 1814, but back in the United States, no one yet knew that the war had ended. The British were preparing to take New Orleans, while the Americans were preparing to defend. Shortly after the start of the New Year, on 8 January, the British attacked under cover of a fog and their ranks were decimated. Both sides claimed victory, but the Americans, despite their unpreparedness, were able to prevent the British from prevailing.

After the war, President Madison completed his term with less stress until he retired during 1817, when he was succeeded by one of his trusted allies, James Monroe. James and Dolley Madison returned to Montpelier, but he did continue to be active in politics, and he toiled with his journal from the Constitutional Convention, a valuable work that was published by the government after his death. In addition to his political activity, President Madison also served as rector of the University of Virginia from 1826 until 1836, the year of his death. He was co-chairman of the Virginia constitutional convention between 1829 and 1836.

President James Madison succumbed on 28 June 1836. He was survived by his wife and stepson. Later, during 1844, Mrs. Madison sold the family plantation, Montpelier. In 1984, the property was given to the National Trust for Historic Preservation and it is open to the public as a museum, operated by the Montpelier Foundation.

Massie, Major General Nathaniel Nathaniel, the son of Major Nathaniel and Elizabeth Watkins Massie, was born in Goochland County, Virginia, on 28 December 1763. Nathaniel's grandfather Charles emigrated from England. His parents had three other children, two boys and a girl. He was their eldest child. Nathaniel's brother Henry founded the city of Portsmouth in Scioto County, Ohio. Nathaniel's mother died when he was eleven years old. As a youngster, Nathaniel had a fine education and was taught surveying. He also joined the military, serving in the Virginia militia during the American Revolution in 1780–1781. After the war, Nathaniel Massie moved to Kentucky in 1783. Like many other Kentuckians, he became skilled in fighting Indians; however, he also became interested in becoming a merchant. Consequently, he began to make a fine living by becoming a salt trader.

While he engaged in business, Massie also initiated expeditions into Ohio, and during 1790, he decided to found a settlement there. Accompanied by nearly twenty families, he departed from Kentucky to establish Manchester, Ohio. Families who accompanied Massie received 100 acres. Massie selected 1,000 acres for himself and established Buckeye Station; it was purchased by his brother-in-law Judge Charles Willing Byrd in 1807. Meanwhile, Massie had explored Paint Valley, and during spring of 1795, his party engaged a band of Shawnee at Reeve's Crossing at Paint Creek, the final exchange prior to General Wayne consummating the Treaty of Greenville, which brought peace to the region. During 1796, he moved to Chillicothe and the party began to build their cabins at a place called Station Prairie. The next year, although he had no training in law, Massie was appointed judge of Common Pleas Court in Adams County, and he was made a colonel in the Adams County militia.

During 1799, Massie served as a representative of Adams County in the initial Territorial Legislature. He also was a member of the second Territorial Legislature representing Ross County. He served in the state Senate as a representative of Ross County through its first and second sessions. During 1800, he married Susan Everard Meade, the daughter of Colonel David Meade of Chaumiere, Kentucky. Their children were Nathaniel, Elizabeth, Richard, Anne, and Henry. Subsequently, on 11 January 1804, the state legislature elected Massie as major general of the Ohio militia with command of the 2nd Ohio Division. During 1806, he served in the state House of Representatives and in 1807 ran for the governor's seat, only to be defeated by Return J. Meigs. However, Meigs was declared ineligible and the post was offered to Massie, but he declined. Thomas Kirker, the speaker of the Senate, assumed the office of governor.

General Massie reverted to his private business ventures and accepted other employment. In addition to selling parcels of his land, he invested in the construction of sawmills and grist mills. General Massie during 1813 raised a contingent of 500 men who were rushed to bolster General William Henry Harrison at Fort Meigs; however, it was his final public duty. His successful life and career came to a close after he came down with pneumonia in autumn of 1813. He died on 3 November 1813 and was interred in front of his home. General Massie's wife, Susan, survived him and lived until 1837. She was buried alongside of her husband. During June 1870, the citizens of Chillicothe arranged for both of them to be reinterred at the cemetery in Chillicothe.

Mathews, Brigadier General George George, the son of John and Betsy Ann Archer Mathews, was born on 30 August 1739. He was cocky as a young man when he was engaged in fighting Indians and afterward during the American Revolution against the British. George was close to being illiterate; however, he did read aloud when at home," and he had a photographic memory. He also had a propensity to discount authority and is known to have acknowledged only two whom he felt were his superiors, General George Washington and the Lord. George dressed in period style, including "knee breeches, fair topped boots, a shirt ruffled at bosom and wrists and his sword dangling at his side." George Mathews for awhile was employed as sheriff of Augusta County, Virginia. He participated as a volunteer in the French and Indian War and fought at the Battle of Point Pleasant during Dunmore's War in 1774. During the American Revolution, he was a colonel of the 9th Virginia Regiment. He participated in the Battle of Brandywine and the Battle of Germantown, both fought in 1777 in the defense of Philadelphia. He was wounded and captured at the latter and held aboard a British prison ship in New York harbor. Thomas Jefferson, at the time the governor Virginia, wrote to Colonel Mathews: "We know that the ardent spirit and hatred of tyranny which brought you into your present situation, will enable you to bear up against it, with the firmness which has distinguished you as a soldier, and look forward with pleasure to the day when events shall take place against which the wounded spirit of your enemies will find no comfort, even from reflections on the most refined of the cruelties with which they have glutted themselves." Colonel Mathews was not exchanged until 1781.

After his exchange that December, Colonel Mathews became attached to General Nathanael Greene's army as colonel of the 3rd Virginia Regiment. During that time he acquired a tract of land in Georgia. After the war, Colonel Mathews invested in farming. He moved his family to his farm in 1785 in Oglethorpe County. In 1786, he was elected governor of Georgia, then served in the U.S. Congress from 4 March 1789 to 3 March 1791. He was again governor of Georgia, 1794 to 1795. Acutely aware of his inability to read and write properly, while he was governor Mathews employed a schoolmaster to ensure that his communications were properly written and spelled correctly. However, his name was associated with the Yazoo Land Fraud, in which Georgia land was sold to speculators at low prices. Although he was not accused of the fraud, because he signed the legislation as governor, his reputation suffered severely.

In 1797, he left Georgia and settled in the Mississippi Territory. During 1798, President Adams nominated Mathews for the post of governor of the Mississippi Territory, but withdrew his name from consideration because of the Yazoo Fraud incident. Mathews traveled to the capital to personally confront the president; however, following some harsh words, the president soothed Mathews' ego by informing him that his son, John, would be appointed supervisor of public revenue in the state of Georgia. In 1811, with the rank of brigadier general, he participated in the expedition into West Florida, but was recalled before an attack was launched against St. Augustine. General Mathews took his recall personally and decided to confront President Madison, but during the journey to the capital, he became ill and died at Augusta, Georgia, on 30 August 1812. He was interred at the cemetery of St. Paul's Churchyard.

Mathews was married three times. He married Anne "Polly" Paul in 1762 and they had eight children: John, William, George, Charles Lewis, Anne, Jane, Margaret and Rebecca. After Polly's death, he married Margaret Cunningham Reed, a widow, in 1793. About 1796, Margaret traveled alone to Virginia and afterward, she contacted the governor and requested that he come to Virginia to get her so she would not have to again travel alone. Governor Mathews was quick to respond. He informed his wife that he did not take her to Virginia, "nor was he going to trouble himself to go there and bring her back." They remained separated for more than two years and the legislature settled the differences by granting each of them a final divorce. He married Mary Flowers Carpenter as his third wife in 1804; they only lived together sparingly.

McArthur, Major General Duncan Duncan, the son of John and Margaret Campbell MacArthur, was born in Duchess County, New York, on 14 January 1772. Duncan's parents had emigrated from Scotland to America in the late 1740s. Young Duncan later dropped the first "a" from his name and spelled it McArthur. Duncan's mother died when he was only about three years old. Subsequently, Duncan's father remarried, and during 1780, the family relocated in western Pennsylvania. As a youth, Duncan worked on various farms in the area. His family was rather poor. Duncan never received a formal education due to the absence of schools in the Pennsylvania frontier. Nonetheless, he taught himself how to spell and read by the time he was a teenager.

As a young man he worked with pack trains that traveled the primitive trails of the Allegheny Mountains to deliver supplies and provisions to various settlements. He also joined the military and participated in various campaigns, including General Josiah Harmar's ill-fated operation against the Indians in 1790. That year, Duncan McArthur moved to Kentucky, where he worked for a while at a sawmill. He also found employment with Nathaniel Massie, who was at the time surveying the Scioto valley. He found the area near Chillicothe, Ohio, favorable and later settled in Ohio. In the meantime, he was employed by the state of Kentucky as an Indian ranger. He was assigned to patrol the Ohio River. In 1795, McArthur was back with Nathaniel Massie, but not in his former menial position. He was hired as an assistant surveyor. By the following year, McArthur was involved with surveying the town of Chillicothe.

During 1797, following his marriage to Nancy McDonald, he moved into his cabin near Chillicothe. Later, McArthur, who was raised in a poor family, began to accumulate wealth until he became one of the most affluent men in Ohio. In time, his cabin was replaced by a mansion which became known as "Fruit Hill." He and his wife had the following children: Nathaniel (born October 1798, died July 1799); Margaret (born may 1800, died February 1823); Thomas Jefferson (born April 1802, died February 1832); Effie (born October 1804, died March 1807); Allen Campbell (born December 1805, died April 1858); James McDonald (born July 1808, died August 1840); Henrietta (born in 1810, died in 1813); Nancy (born in 1813, died in 1829); Eliza Ann (born November 1813, died September 1856) and Mary (born February 1818, died December 1842).

In 1804, McArthur was elected to the state legislature of Ohio. The next year, he served in the state Senate until 1814, part of the time running concurrent with his service in the military during the war. McArthur acted as speaker of the House in 1809–1810. Meanwhile, in 1805, he was engaged in the effort to organize the Ohio militia and was commissioned as a colonel. Later, during 1808, General McArthur was elevated to the rank of major general of militia.

During 1812, General McArthur raised a regiment of volunteers and was commissioned a colonel in the regular army. On 25 May 1812, General Hull assumed command of the Ohio troops. McArthur commanded one of the three Ohio regiments (1st Ohio). While the 1st Regiment was advancing from Urbana, Ohio, to Detroit, it was cutting a road through the wilderness. At a point along the Scioto River, near Kenton, Ohio, the regiment paused to erect a post, composed of two blockhouses linked together by palisades. The post was later named Fort McArthur.

At Detroit, General William Hull surrendered the city to the British without the support of his officers and without raising any resistance. A movement had been underway to replace General Hull with McArthur, but he was not in the compound when the capitulation was taking place. McArthur was also elected to the Thirteenth Congress; however, according to the Congressional Records, he never qualified and resigned on 5 April 1813. Shortly before his resignation, McArthur was commissioned as brigadier general of volunteers in the U.S. Army during March 1813. Also that year, General McArthur succeeded General Green Clay as commander at Fort Meigs. On or about 13 September 1813, General McArthur crossed over the Detroit River at Detroit and moved into Sandwich to assume responsibility for it. On the day before his arrival, forces under General Harrison had occupied it.

General McArthur's brigade participated with General Harrison at the Battle of the Thames on 5 October 1813. On 6 October, General McArthur, at Sandwich, Canada, dispatched a detachment to rid the region of a band of Indians that had been plundering the town. On that same day, he wrote to the secretary of war to inform him that some Indians were seeking peace: "Since General Harrison's departure, five nations, of Indians, viz.— Ottowas, Chippewas, Pottewatamies, Miamies, and Kickapoos, who were but a few miles back have come in for peace; and I have agreed that hostilities should cease, for the present, on the following conditions: they have agreed to take hold of the same tomahawk with us, and to strike any who are, or may be enemies to the U. States, whether British or Indians; they are to bring in a number of their women and children and leave them as hostages, whilst they accompany us to war. Some of them have already brought in their women; and are drawing rations."

During spring of 1814, when General Harrison left the service, he was succeeded by General McArthur, commander of the Northwestern Army. During October 1814, General McArthur led a force of about 700 Kentuckians and Ohioans out of Detroit and into Canada to conduct a series of raids as a diversion to draw the attention of the British away from General Jacob Brown from a major operation on the Niagara frontier. The operation lasted about one month and succeeded in destroying a large amount of public property. McArthur's column swept through a series of towns and villages after rounding Lake St. Clair. On 4 November, the column encountered opposition at Oxford, which was quickly overcome. Afterward, heavier resistance, including regulars, militia and Indians, was encountered at the Grand River. The British raised a force of about 1,000 men, but the force failed to intercept McArthur's column. It arrived at Sandwich on 17 November. Some of the force was dismissed there. General McArthur returned to Ohio.

After the war, General McArthur again served in the Ohio House of Representatives (1817–1818) before returning to the state Senate from 1821 until 1823. Afterward, he was elected to the Eighteenth Congress (4 March 1823 to 3 March 1825). He chose not to run for re-election in 1824; however, he did yet again return to the Ohio state House of Representatives in 1826, then served again in the Senate from 1829 until 1830. He was governor from 1830 until 1832. During 1834, he ran unsuccessfully for a seat in the Twenty-third Congress.

General McArthur's wife, Nancy, died on 23 October 1836. General McArthur died at Chillicothe on 29 April 1839.

Meriwether, Brigadier General David The son of Colonel James (son of David) and Judith Burnley Meriwether, David was born in Virginia (Albemarle County) at Cloverfield, which is close to Charlottesville, on 10 April 1755. Some sources list David's place of birth as Louisiana County during 1754. David had two younger siblings, James and William. David was the grandson of Nicholas Meriwether, who arrived in Virginia from Wales and became an affluent planter who acquired large tracts of land, including one grant from King George II that gave him just under 18,000 acres near Charlottesville.

During the American Revolution, David Meriwether joined the military as a lieutenant. Subsequent to his death, a commission as lieutenant in the Continental Army was discovered in his papers. The commission, under General Washington, was dated 15 May 1779. Meriwether participated in various actions during the war, which included New Jersey while Washington's army was driven into Pennsylvania. He was in the Battles of Brandywine, Trenton and Monmouth, along with the siege of Charleston. Lt. Meriwether also participated in the siege of Georgia toward the latter part of the war when a contingent of Virginians under Colonel Posey was sent there. Lieutenant Meriwether was captured at Savannah and paroled.

He used his time on parole to return to Wilkes County, Georgia, and while there he married Frances Wingfield in 1782. David and Frances had eight children: John, James (later major), William (later doctor), Fannie, George, David, Thomas and Judith. After the war, David relocated in Wilkes County, Georgia (1785). On 21 September 1797, Meriwether was appointed brigadier general of militia by Governor Jared Irvin and given command of the 3rd Division. He also served in the state House of Representatives and was speaker (1797–1800). Later, he was elected to the U.S. Congress to complete the term of Benjamin Taliaferro, who resigned. Meriwether served in Congress from 6 December 1802 until 3 March 1807. During that time, he aligned himself with his friend President Jefferson during the controversy with Aaron Burr.

General Meriwether chose to retire at the end of his term. He returned to his plantation in Athens. In the meantime, he was appointed as a commissioner to the Creek Indians during 1804. Afterward he was continually reappointed and tasked to deal with other tribes. General Meriwether did not participate in combat during the War of 1812, but he did conduct his business as an Indian agent. After the war, General Meriwether was one of the commissioners, along with Jesse Franklin and General Andrew Jackson, who concluded a treaty with the Cherokee during September 1816 at the Chickasaw Council House.

General Meriwether concluded a treaty with the Creeks during 1807, through which he succeeded in opening a route (post road) from Washington, D.C., that ran directly through Creek Territory to New Orleans. The route was used by Sam Dale, who rode along it from the Creek Agency to deliver government dispatches to General Andrew Jackson during the British campaign to seize the city. General Meriwether, along with General David Adams and John McIntosh, concluded a treaty with the Creeks during 1820.

General Meriwether died on 16 November 1822. He was interred on his plantation; however, the exact location of his unmarked grave remains unknown.

Miller, Brigadier General James James, the son of James and Catherine Gregg Miller, was born on 25 April 1776 in Peterborough, New Hampshire. It is thought that James' father was a farmer. James received an excellent education. He attended an academy in Amherst, Massachusetts, and afterward entered Williams College. After passing the bar, he began to practice law in Greenfield during 1803. James married Martha Ferguson and they had one son, James Ferguson Miller, who later became a U.S. naval officer. Subsequent to his wife's death, James married Ruth Flint.

At about the same time he started his law practice, Miller joined the militia and received command of an artillery company. His conduct became conspicuous and brought him to the notice of General Benjamin Pierce, a veteran of the American Revolution. General Pierce recommended that Miller be promoted to the rank of major and assigned to the U.S. 4th Regiment at Fort Independence (Boston Harbor). Pierce's recommendation was accepted and Miller was commissioned a major, with his commission bearing the date 3 March 1809. He participated in the advance of his regiment from Newport, Rhode Island, to Vincennes, Indiana, during August 1811, during that time of turbulence with the Indians. While en route to Indiana, Major Miller was promoted to the rank of colonel.

In May 1812, Colonel Miller received orders to advance his regiment to Detroit to bolster the American forces already there.

Miller's force encountered the British, and for a while, the situation began to deteriorate. Nonetheless, Miller's command rebounded with some artillery fire and a bayonet attack, forcing the British-Canadian-Indian force of more than 1,000 to retire. The engagement, known as the Battle of Monguagon, was the only victory of the Americans over the British in Michigan. Miller's water-logged column arrived back at Detroit on 12 August. At Detroit, the troops were preparing to meet a British attack, expected at any time. To their disappointment and dismay, after first being told that Hull informed Brock "the town and fort would be defended to the last extremity," they saw Hull surrender his entire army without a fight when the British closed and were met by only a white flag. Colonel James Miller, one of about 2,000 men who were taken prisoner, had been urged by other officers to take command, but he declined, saying "matters had gone too far, but had Hull signified to me his intention of surrendering, I would have assumed command and defended the fort to the last."

Colonel Miller was exchanged during 1813. His first full-scale action after exchange was the Battle of Chippewa, while he commanded the U.S. 21st Infantry. That was followed by the Battle of Lundy's Lane at Fort Erie. At Lundy's Lane on 25 July 1814, Colonel Miller was catapulted into prominence when General Ripley asked: "Can you take that hill?" Miller replied, regarding a formidable battery: "I'll try sir!" He led two attacks that failed. Nonetheless, Colonel Miller launched a third attack, thought insurmountable by some, that has probably been best described by George Barstow's *History of New Hampshire* (1842):

> The British artillery, posted on a commanding height, had annoyed our troops during the earlier part of battle. "Can you storm that battery?" said General Ripley to Miller. "I'll try, sir," replied the warrior; then turned to his men, and, in a deep tone, issued a few brief words of command: "*Twenty-first,* attention. Form into column. You will advance up the hill to the storm of the battery. At the word, *Halt*," you will deliver your fire at the portlight of the artillerymen, and immediately carry their guns at the point of the bayonet. Support arms-forward-march." Machinery could not have moved with more compactness than that gallant regiment. Followed by the *twenty-third,* the dark mass moved up the hill like one body, the lurid light flickering on their bayonets as the combined fire of the enemy's artillery and infantry opened murderously upon them. They flinched not, faltered not. The stern, deep voice of the officers, as the deadly cannon-shot cut yawning chasms through them, alone was heard—"Close up-steady, men-steady." Within a hundred yards of the summit, the loud' *Halt"* was followed by a volley, sharp and instantaneous as a clap of thunder. Another moment, rushing under the white smoke, a short, furious struggle with the bayonet, and the battle was won. The

enemy's line was driven down the hill, and their own cannon mowed them down by platoons. This brilliant success decided the fate of the conflict, and the American flag waved in triumph on that hill, scorched and blackened as it was by the flame of artillery, purpled with human gore and encumbered by the bodies of the slain.

Congress awarded Colonel Miller for his leadership and gallantry under fire by promoting him to the rank of brigadier general. Miller became known as the "Hero of Lundy's Lane".

General Miller was appointed the first governor of the Arkansas Territory on 3 March 1819. He resigned from the army but postponed leaving New England until the summer had passed. He departed during September, but his family remained in New Hampshire. Nevertheless, his route was circuitous. From New England, General Miller traveled to Washington, D.C., where he learned that in addition to being appointed governor, he was also made superintendent of Indian affairs for the Arkansas Territory. After completing his business in the capital he repaired to Pittsburgh, Pennsylvania. By that point, after having acquired arms and other supplies, General Miller went down the Ohio and Mississippi Rivers and arrived at Arkansas Post, Arkansas, on 19 December 1819.

Prior to his arrival, the secretary of the Territory, Robert Crittenden, had been running the Territory. In Miller's absence, Crittenden had used his authority to appoint allies to various positions. Subsequent to his arrival, General Miller assumed his duties as governor. He encountered difficulties regarding land claims of the Cherokee, Choctaw and Quapaw Indians and the intent of white settlers to gain the land claimed by the tribes. In 1821, he encountered problems when hostilities between the Cherokee and the Osage Indians erupted. General Miller did not accomplish any great successes during his term of office. In April 1821, he left Arkansas for New Hampshire to visit with his family and avoid the torrid heat in Arkansas. He returned to Little Rock during November. Later, during June 1823, Miller again returned to New Hampshire, and he stayed there for the remainder of the year. He resigned as governor during December 1824. That autumn, he was elected to the U.S. House of Representatives in New Hampshire, but he declined taking the seat.

Upon his return to New Hampshire, he was appointed as customs collector at Salem and Beverly, Massachusetts. He suffered a stroke during 1849, which compelled him to relinquish his post. He suffered another stroke and died on 7 July 1851. General Miller worked with Nathaniel Hawthorne at the port of Salem and Hawthorne dedicated part of one chapter ("The Custom House") of his classic work "*The Scarlet Letter*" to General Miller. Miller County in Arkansas and Miller State Park in Peterborough, New Hampshire, were named in his honor.

Monroe, President James James Monroe, the son of Spence and Eliza Jones Monroe, was born in Westmoreland County, Virginia, on 28 April 1758 on the family estate located where Monroe Creek flows into the Potomac River. James entered William and Mary College during 1774, but the following year, he joined the military after the clashes at Lexington and Concord on 19 April 1775. James was commissioned as a 2nd lieutenant in the 3rd Virginia Regiment. The next year he participated in the New York campaigns and was with General George Washington during the retreat through New Jersey when British General William Howe was attempting to vanquish the Continental Army.

That same year, James Monroe was promoted to the rank of first lieutenant. He was wounded during the Battle of Trenton on 26 December. He also participated in the defense of Philadelphia, including the Battle of Brandywine in September and the Battle of Germantown in October. On 20 November 1777, Monroe was promoted to the rank of major and assigned to the staff of General William Alexander (Lord Stirling). He remained in the Continental Army until December 1778 and participated in the Battle of Monmouth in June 1778. After he resigned, he returned to Virginia where in 1780 he studied law under Thomas Jefferson.

During 1782, Monroe was elected to the assembly and was appointed to the executive council. The following year, he entered national politics when he was elected to Congress, where he remained until 1786. That year, he married Eliza Kortwright, the daughter of Lawrence Kortwright. He met her while attending sessions of Congress in New York. James and Eliza had two children, Eliza (married Judge George Hay), and Maria (married Samuel L. Gouverneur). James and Eliza settled in Fredericksburg, where James established his law practice.

James Monroe was again elected to the Virginia Assembly during 1787; however, he was not a delegate to the Constitutional Convention that year in Philadelphia. The following year, he was a delegate to the Virginia ratification convention. Monroe sided with those who raised opposition to ratification, but his allies did not prevail. Virginia ratified the U.S. Constitution on 25 June to become the tenth state. Monroe was elected as one of the first senators from Virginia. He was in office when President George Washington was inaugurated. Monroe remained in the Senate until he was appointed minister to France during 1794 as successor to Gouverneur Morris. In 1796, Monroe was recalled by President Washington.

After returning to America, Monroe resumed his law practice, but two yeas later he returned to public life when he was elected governor of Virginia; he retained that post for three years. After his term ended, his friend and ally, President Thomas Jefferson, appointed Monroe and Gouverneur Morris as special envoys to the French Court, which at the time was under the domination of Napoleon. While working with Gouverneur Morris, the pair negotiated with Napoleon for the acquisition of Louisiana, which Napoleon was prepared to sell to the United States to ensure that it would not be gained by Britain. Following the conclusion of his diplomatic mission in France, Monroe moved to Spain and worked with Charles Pinckney in negotiations with Spain regarding boundary conflicts. Prior to returning to the United States, Monroe was in England again working with Pinckney to consummate a treaty. The pair succeeded, but the treaty was declined by Congress.

After his return, Monroe was elected governor of Virginia during 1811, at a time when the United States and Britain were on a collision course. By that time, President James Madison had been in office for about two years, and like his predecessor, Thomas Jefferson, Madison was a Democratic-Republican and an ally and friend of James Monroe. President Madison named Monroe secretary of state, and concurrently for a period of time (27 September 1814 to 2 March 1815), he was also secretary of war. In 1815, Monroe was again named secretary of state, and he retained the post until 1817, when he became president of the United States (4 March 1817 to 4 March 1825).

During Monroe's two terms as president, the United States still faced problems with hostile Seminole Indians in Florida who were incited by the British and the Spanish. During his first year, he also had to deal with pirates operating in Florida, but by May of 1818, General Andrew Jackson seized the Spanish garrison at Pensacola to terminate that Indian War. Afterward General Jackson deported the Spanish to Havana, Cuba. Other expeditions against the Seminoles would be launched, but the Seminoles never signed a peace treaty with the United States. Although progress was made against the pirates, the U.S. Navy did not totally terminate the problem until about the time the Civil War erupted.

President Monroe was succeeded by President John Quincy Adams, the son of John Adams, during 1825. After completing his term as president, James Monroe again returned to his home. He is remembered mostly for the Monroe Doctrine, which he issued on 2 December 1823. It said, in part: "The American Continents by the free and independent condition which they have assumed, are henceforth not to be considered as subject for future colonization by any foreign Power."

After the death of his wife, Eliza, President Monroe departed Virginia and relocated in New York, where he lived with his daughter, Maria, who had married Samuel L. Gouverneur. President James Monroe died there on the Fourth of July 1831.

Parker, Major General Alexander Alexander, the son of Judge Richard and Elizabeth Beale Parker and the brother of Brigadier General Thomas Parker, was born in Virginia about the late 1740s. Alexander was appointed as ensign in the 2nd Virginia Regiment (Continental Line) on 28 September 1775. On 24 January 1776, he was promoted to the rank of 2nd lieutenant, and later promoted to the rank of captain. He continued service in the South, and while defending against the British at Charleston, he was captured on 12 May 1780. Subsequent to his exchange, he resumed serving until the end of the war.

During 1808, Alexander Parker returned to the service and received his commission as colonel of the U.S. 5th Infantry on 3 May 1808; however, he again resigned on 31 December 1809. Three years later, when war was declared against Britain, Colonel Parker re-entered the military, but not with the regular army. He was commissioned as major general of Virginia militia. General Parker married Elizabeth Redman, a widow, on 18 March 1790. He died about 1820.

Parker, Brigadier General Thomas Thomas, the son of Judge Richard and Elizabeth Beale Parker, was born in Virginia about 1750. In addition to Thomas, Richard and Elizabeth had the following children: Richard (later colonel, died at Charleston in 1780); Alexander (later major general of militia); John; William Harwar (later captain in the Virginia state navy); Foxhall A. Parker (later captain, U.S. Navy) and Richard Elliott. He served in the Revolutionary War as 1st lieutenant (4 July 1776), captain (April 1778) of the 3rd Virginia Regiment, and with the 5th Virginia. On 8 January 1799 he was promoted to the rank of lieutenant colonel with the 8th U.S. Infantry. On 15 June 1800, Colonel Parker was honorably discharged.

On 12 March 1812, a few months before war was declared against the British, Colonel Parker was appointed as colonel in the 12th U.S. Infantry. Parker served under General Wade Hampton and participated in the actions on the northern frontier. On 12 March 1813, he was promoted to the rank of brigadier general. During April 1813, General Parker was assigned to Norfolk, where he served under General Wade Hampton, commander of the 5th Military District, which extended south from the Rappahannock River in Virginia. While at Norfolk, he resigned from the service on 1 November 1814.

General Parker married Sallie Opie. They settled on an estate known as Soldier's Retreat which he had constructed along the right bank of the Shenandoah River about 20 miles outside of Winchester, Virginia. General Parker died at the "Retreat" on 24 January 1820. The couple had one child, Eliza, who later married Colonel (later general) Armistead Mason, the son of Colonel (senator) Stevens Thomson and Mary Elizabeth Armistead Mason. General Parker died on 20 May 1820.

Pike, Brigadier General Zebulon Montgomery Zebulon, the son of Captain Zebulon Pike, Sr., a veteran of the American Revolution, was born in New Jersey on 5 January 1779. He was actually born in Lamberton (later Lamington) in Somerset County, though some historians claim he was born in Lamberton in Mercer County, New Jersey, or Solebury, Pennsylvania. The Pike family ancestors were among the first settlers to arrive in New Jersey. Captain John Pike was among them. Zebulon's siblings included George W., who was appointed to the Naval Academy during 1808 and died during the war in 1812, James B., and Maria H.

Zebulon did not receive an accelerated education; however, by his own merits, he studied French, Latin and Spanish, becoming fluent in each. He also became skilled in the sciences as well as mathematics. He entered the military when he was only about 15 years old. He served under his father as a cadet. Afterward, he served on the western frontiers. In 1801, against the wishes of his family and the family of his bride-to-be, Clarissa Harlow Brown of Cincinnati, Kentucky, the pair eloped. Zebulon and Clarissa had five children; however, only daughter Clarissa reached adulthood.

On 9 August 1805, while Lewis and Clark were en route to the Pacific Ocean, Zebulon Pike led a party of 20 men, with sufficient provisions for four months, from St. Louis on an operation to explore the Mississippi River to its source. The mission was initiated by President Jefferson. The expedition departed in a large boat but had to abandon their craft and resort to using canoes which they built and by marching overland. The expedition continued for eight months and 20 days. On 2 January 1806, the party came upon a British trading post (North West Company) at Lower Red Cedar Lake near present day Aitkin, Minnesota. The British had been operating on U.S. Territory and without paying "duty or license," and their activity had also essentially eliminated the competition of Americans in the region. Pike's primary mission was to discover the source of the Mississippi and to acquire treaties with the Indians in the region; however, his orders had also directed him to gather intelligence on British operations. The encounter was friendly and the expeditionary force remained at the post for a while.

On 8 January a detachment of Pike's contingent arrived at Sandy Lake. By 1 February 1806, Pike arrived at Leech Lake, where he again encountered the British Northwest Company. Pike immediately reminded the British that they were in U.S. territory and under the U.S. flag. He directed them to immediately stop inciting the Indians; however, Pike was aware that the U.S. was not yet prepared to literally control the region. The British cooperated, but only while the Americans remained at the lake. Once Pike departed from there, the British resumed their usual activity and re-hoisted the British flag.

Pike's contingent headed back for the St. Anthony Falls near Minneapolis where Fort St. Anthony (later Fort Snelling) was established on 11 April. Pike's command afterwards returned to St. Louis and arrived there on 30 April 1806, completing a journey which had begun the previous year. On 15 July, Lt. Zebulon Pike departed from Bellefontaine, Ohio, to explore the Southwest on a mission initiated by General James Wilkinson. Pike led another expedition to explore the interior of Louisiana and advance toward northern Mexico. His detachment departed from St. Louis, and they had with them about 40 Osage Indians who had been captives until rescued by the Americans. Pike was to escort them back to their territory. While en route, Zebulon passed through Kansas, and while there, on 29 September, his contingent compelled the Spanish flag at Pawnee to be lowered and replaced by the Stars and Stripes. In 1901 the state of Kansas erected a monument to recognize Pike's action at Pawnee. The expedition encountered extreme hardships once winter weather arrived. The men did not have proper clothing and their horses died, forcing the men to carry their supplies and provisions through the wilderness, often without sufficient food. The expedition reached what later became Pike's Peak in Colorado during November 1806. Pike initially named it "Grand Peak." The team's effort to climb the mountain was halted by a storm.

On 17 January 1807, only Pike and the doctor who accompanied the expedition were able to move out of the desperate camp to seek food. The others had been suffering from the frost. Pike and the doctor managed to strike a buffalo three times and still the animal refused to fall. He escaped, leaving the hunters without their prize. Two days later, on the 19th, while back on the hunt, three buffaloes were hit, but yet again none were brought down. On or about 24 January, when mutiny was beginning to creep into the party, finally a buffalo was shot and seized. Back at camp, the men enjoyed their feast.

On 7 February 1807, a Spanish force halted Lt. Pike's contingent while it was in the territory along the Arkansas and Red Rivers. Pike related in his journal that the Spanish informed him that he was at the River Del Norte, rather than the Red River and in Mexican territory. The Spanish caused the Americans no harm; however, they did escort them to Santa Fe, New Mexico, and from there to Durango, Mexico, before taking them through Spanish Texas to Louisiana. Pike's expedition arrived back at Natchitoches on 1 July 1807.

Shortly after he returned, he received the thanks of Congress and was promoted to captain, followed by promotion to major and afterward to lieutenant colonel. In 1810, Lt. Colonel Pike was promoted to the rank of full colonel in the U.S. Infantry. He was stationed on the northern frontier when war erupted with Great Britain during June 1812. In November, Colonel Pike, attached to General Dearborn's army, moved into Canada on the advance to York, where a short firefight erupted. The Americans returned to their camp and established winter quarters.

During April 1813, Colonel Pike was promoted to brigadier general. He was assigned to Military District No. 9, which included New York, extending north from the Highlands and Vermont. The district was commanded by Major General Henry Dearborn. On 25 April 1813, General Pike sailed with Commodore Chauncey's squadron from Sackets Harbor as part of the force charged with seizing York. Pike's force landed on 27 April against tenacious resistance from the British and their Indian allies. During the operation, an explosion occurred which caused a wall near a British battery to collapse. General Pike was mortally injured while he was attending a British soldier. He was taken aboard Commodore Chauncey's flagship and while en route, he remained coherent. He was told that the British colors were struck and the Stars and Stripes had been hoisted. Pike's condition made it difficult for him to speak, but he was able to request that the captured British colors "be placed under his head." General Pike died while the British flag was being made into his pillow. He was not yet 35 years old.

General Pike was embalmed at York. His remains were taken to Sackets Harbor and he was interred at Fort Tompkins. Pike's aide, Captain Nicholson, who was alongside of Pike when the explosion occurred and also killed, was interred beside General Pike. In 1818, General Pike's remains were re-interred nearby at Madison Barracks.

Pinckney, Major General Thomas Thomas, the son of Charles and Eliza Lucas Pinckney, was born in Charleston on 23 October 1850. Thomas was also the brother of Charles Coatesworth and Harriott (Harriet) Pinckney. Thomas' father was appointed chief justice of South Carolina to succeed Chief Justice Graeme; however, he only served one year due to political considerations in England which caused him to be replaced by Peter Leigh. Eliza, having earlier imported some eggs of silkworms, took her prize silk when the family traveled to England during 1753 and it was spun into several dresses. Eliza kept one of the dresses, but the other two were given away, one to the Princess of Wales and the other to Lord Chesterfield. When the family returned to South Carolina, Thomas and his brother Charles C., remained in England to complete their education. Thomas attended Westminster School and Oxford. While at Westminster, Thomas was known as the "best Greek scholar of his class."

Thomas, however, was focused on much more than the classics, Greek, Latin and the law. While in Europe, Thomas received instructions on horseback riding, and he was taught how to fence, but even that was insufficient to quell his thirst for knowledge. He traveled to Normandy before returning home, and while there for about one year, he studied military science at Caen. During the Creek War (1813–1814), it was discovered by an officer on his staff that the only book carried in General Pinckney's saddle bags "was a "pocket edition of the Greek poets." Throughout his life, General Pinckney was a voracious reader.

After studying at the Temple, he was admitted to the bar in 1774, and afterward he practiced law in Charleston. During 1775, Thomas was commissioned a lieutenant in the Continental Army. He served under General Benjamin Lincoln, General Horatio Gates and Count D'Estaing as an aide-de-camp. Pinckney participated in various actions including the Battle of Stono in June 1779, where he was second in command of Colonel Henderson's light infantry. Major Pinckney also participated at the siege of Savannah in September 1779 and at the Battle of Camden in August 1780. At Camden, Pinckney was wounded and captured.

Pinckney, who attained the rank of major by war's end, married Elizabeth Hotte, the daughter of Jacob and Rebecca Brewton Hotte, on 22 July 1779. Elizabeth, the daughter of Rebecca (heroine of the American Revolution), had been trained as a nurse. Her skills greatly aided Pinckney after he was wounded at Camden.

After the war, Pinckney returned to practicing law. In 1787, he was elected governor of South Carolina and served for two years. During 1789, he declined accepting a position as a U.S. District judge. In 1791, Pinckney was elected to the state legislature. During this time he drafted the act which established the South Carolina court of equity. Subsequent to an appointment by President George Washington, Pinckney served as minister to Great Britain from 1792 to 1796. He traveled to Spain in 1794 to set up the treaty of Ildefonso, which when secured free navigation of the Mississippi River for American vessels and gave the U.S. access to the Gulf of Mexico. After arriving back in the States, Pinckney ran unsuccessfully as a Federalist for the presidency in 1796.

He was elected in 1799 to the Sixth Congress and served from 1799 until 1801.

Subsequently, with war with the United Kingdom at hand, Thomas Pinckney exchanged hats and switched back to the military. He was appointed commander of the Southern Department (designated District No. 6 during April 1813) on 27 March 1812, with the rank of major general, the second major general appointed following General Henry Dearborn. The department included North Carolina, South Carolina and Georgia. General Pinckney participated with General Andrew Jackson during the hostilities with the Creeks. In February 1813, Congress authorized the occupation of Florida, west of the Perdido River, but the invasion was halted and Pinckney and Jackson received orders to dismiss their command and return.

On 16 April 1813, General Pinckney, in Georgia, in conjunction with President Madison's decision to evacuate East Florida, ordered the U.S. forces to withdraw from Camp New Hope and repair to Point Peter on the St. Mary's River. On or about 13 May, the final elements of the Americans at Fernandina abandoned the post. A 49-man Marine contingent under Lt. Sevier accompanied the army on the trek to Point Peter. General Pinckney had become so impressed with Lt. Sevier and his artillery that he ordered the Marines to remain with the southern army. Nonetheless, to the great disappointment of General Pinckney, orders that originated with the commandant of the Marine Corps directed Sevier and his contingent to return to Beaufort, South Carolina.

General Pinckney retired from the service in June 1815 and returned to his private life. He resumed his law practice in Charleston. He also succeeded his brother Charles Coatesworth Pinckney (signer of the U.S. Constitution), who died while serving as president-general of the Society of the Cincinnati. Thomas Pinckney, who was president of the Charleston chapter since 1806, when he succeeded General William Moultrie, assumed the post and retained it from 1825 to 1828. General Pinckney died at his residence (Eldorado) in Charleston on 2 November 1828 at age 79. During his funeral, his body was escorted by companies of the 16th and 17th Regiments, as well as a squadron of cavalry and a contingent of federal troops based at Fort Moultrie. General Pinckney's saddled horse also participated in the procession, which traveled from his residence on Legare Street to St. Philip's Episcopal Church.

General Pinckney's wife, Elizabeth, had died while he was in England as the American minister. They had two sons and two daughters: Thomas Jr. (later colonel, married Elizabeth Izard); Mary (unmarried); Charles Coatesworth (married Phoebe Wright Elliott); and Rebecca Motte (died young).

In 1797 he married a widow, Frances Motte Middleton. Their children were Harriett Lucas (married Francis Kinloch Huger); Edward Rutledge (1806–1832); and Mary (1804–1822).

General Pinckney's three swords, which he used during the American Revolution and the War of 1812, were inherited by his three sons with a caveat that "they never be drawn in any private quarrel, and never remain in their scabbards, when their Country demanded their service." "Fourteen of Thomas Pinckney's' descendants served in the Confederate army."

Pinckney's plantation, Eldorado, was located along the Santee River. Initially, Jackson resided at what was known as the Fairfield, but he signed that residence over to his oldest son when he acquired Eldorado, which he named after his Spanish mission and constructed with his own carpenters. Rebecca Motte, Pinckney' mother-in-law, had participated in the purchase of Eldorado. As a widow, she desired to be near her daughters, one of whom, Frances, was Pinckney's wife. Mrs. Motte sold her plantation on the Santee and contributed some of the money from the sale toward the purchase of the land and house. General Pinckney also owned other property in Charleston and on Sullivan's Island.

Eldorado resembled a French chateau due to "its wide corridors, its lofty ceilings, and its peaked roof of glazed tiles." Although General Pinckney had been a military man as well as a diplomat and a planter, he also had a natural mechanical ability and a curiosity for experimenting, much like his mother, who introduced indigo into South Carolina. General Pinckney continued working on improving the machinery used in the rice fields. He also possessed knowledge of hydraulics, and his knowledge of engineering which he used while engaged in fortifying the harbor at Charleston enabled him to implement experiment after experiment to improve the system that eventually led to making the rice fields in South Carolina the finest in the South and the world.

General Pinckney, subsequent to marrying Frances, his second wife, acquired a large tract of marshlands at the mouth of the Santee River, and the land was essentially considered valueless because it was alternately covered with fresh water and sea water. Nonetheless, General Pinckney immediately compared the ground to similar land in Holland and began to realize that he could transform it into workable land by using the "Van Hassel system of embankment. Pinckney contracted an engineer from Holland to undertake the challenge. After successive experiments, they conceived a plan that succeeded in eliminating the salt from the soil and began a prosperous venture that allowed Pinckney to market about 20,000 barrels of rice per year.

Pinckney had other talents as well as a quick-thinking mind. During the days of experimentation, the general was contacted by a local sheriff who informed him that part of his property was in the sheriff's jurisdiction and that taxes had to be paid or the sheriff would be compelled to sell that parcel off at a public auction. The sheriff received an unexpected response. Pinckney told the sheriff that if the sheriff could make the sale, he would pay him a commission for accomplishing what the general was unable to do, sell the land.

General Pinckney's constant quest for improvement did not confine itself to planting. Having spent many years in England, he was not content with the quality of the cattle in the region, which prompted him to begin importing cattle, some from England, but also from other European countries including Italy. After experimenting with the different breeds, he decided that those imported from England were the best for dairy products and meat; however, he also realized the English cattle desperately struggled with the torrid heat of the summer. The cattle imported from Italy (Tuscans), however, were better suited for the rice fields and they easily adapted to the plow and the wagon.

Pinckney's endeavors seemingly were tireless. He looked into the various types of farming used in different parts of the globe. His correspondence covers the various soils of different countries, modes of cultivation, rotation of crops, the different implements used in husbandry and even the collection of samples of dirt from different parts of the country and the world, in his efforts to improve agriculture in South Carolina.

Pinckney also enjoyed hosting guests and his plantation was known only infrequently not to have visitors. One of his guests was an affluent Englishman, Adam Hodgson, who remained in the United States for several years exploring the country. Upon his arrival at Eldorado, he was taken aback by the size of the windows in the house and the great number of them, which he wrote about in a volume of his work, "*Travels*," published in 1824. Hodgson noted that the windows were "enough to make an Englishman shudder when he recalled the tax upon each pane of glass to which he was accustomed at home."

Hodgson was also impressed by General Pinckney's extensive library, which included many works published in England. He noted that the library also contained a more "extensive collection of agricultural works than I had ever seen before in a private library. In works on botany and American ornithology (a part of zoology dealing with birds) the supply was large. The latter especially interested me, not having seen them before." Hodgson, although uncomfortable seeing the slaves, examined their houses as well as their food and acknowledged that Pinckney "would be regarded as second to few in Europe as a statesman, a scholar, and a gentleman."

General Pinckney did not keep his accomplishments to himself. The results of his experiments were generously shared for the good of every planter in the state and often he published articles in *The Southern Agriculturist*.

Pinckney and his more famous brother had a close relationship. The last time they appeared together in public was during April 1825, when the people of Charleston gave a grand welcome to Lafayette when he visited there with his son. Lafayette was jubilant upon seeing his old friends from the war and many people in the crowd, which was estimated at about 10,000, witnessed Lafayette embracing both brothers at the intersection of George and Meeting Streets.

General Pinckney attended the annual meeting of the South Carolina Agricultural Society in February 1828, and he reported on crops other than rice that had been cultivated on 20 acres, which he donated to the society. The experimental crops were "wheat, flax, garden peas, barley, oats, cow peas, French beans, slip potatoes." It was General Pinckney's last meeting. He died during the following year. Someone who signed his name as "A rice planter" wrote following:

> I was one of those who heard the lucid observations of General Pinckney, that lamented friend of his country, at the discussions of the agricultural society on rice and other crops. I fear we shall not look upon his like again. Where shall we find another with a mind so refined as his, with manners so polished, with a conception of his country's interests so perfect, with an intellect so capable of subjects of embracing the most comprehensive importance as well as selecting those of minor importance as they floated by and converting them all to the public good? Where shall we find a man of motives so pure, so deserving of the full confidence of his fellow-man, and so perfectly possessing it? Wise without conceit, and without the blemish of egotism. This is a character seldom met with in any country.

Porter, Brigadier General Moses Moses, the son of Benjamin and Rea Porter, was born in Danvers, Massachusetts, in March 1756. Porter joined the military as a lieutenant and served under Captain Samuel R. Trevett's artillery company at Bunker Hill (Breed's Hill) in June 1775. He served for the duration and remained in the army after the war. On 29 September 1789, Porter was appointed lieutenant of artillery. In November 1791, he was promoted to the rank of captain. Captain Porter participated with General Anthony Wayne during his victorious campaign over the Indians on the northwestern frontier in 1794. He also held command at Fort Harmar. On 2 June 1796, the British at Quebec ordered the evacuation of Detroit more than ten years after the end of the Revolutionary War. On 7 July 1796, Colonel John F. Hamtramck, commander at Fort Miami, dispatched a 65-man contingent of artillerymen and infantry, led by Captain Moses Porter, to take possession of Detroit. The British abandoned the fort on the 11th; however, before the evacuation, "the retiring garrison of English troops, to show their spite against the Americans, locked the gates of the fort, broke the windows in the barracks, and filled the wells with stones." Nonetheless, on the 11th at precisely 1200, the Stars and Stripes was raised over the garrison.

On 26 May 1800, Porter was appointed major of the U.S. 1st Artillery. He was promoted to colonel of light artillery on 12 March 1812. He participated in the campaign to seize Fort George in Canada in May 1813. Colonel Porter was breveted brigadier general on 10 September 1813. After participating in the seizure of Fort George, he also accompanied General Wilkinson on the ill-fated campaign to take Montreal. Porter's artillery was attached to General John Parker Boyd's brigade.

In 1814, he commanded at Norfolk, Virginia, until the close of hostilities. Porter remained in the army after the war. In March 1821, he was named colonel of the 1st Artillery.

General Porter died unmarried on 14 April 1822 in Cambridge, Massachusetts. General Porter, having been known for his "colorful language," became known as "Old Blowhard." Also, General Porter is separate from another Moses Porter, son of Moses Sr., and Sarah Kilham Porter, born in Danvers and later relocated in Vermont, who also was a veteran of the American Revolution and who died in 1803.

Ripley, Brigadier General Eleazar Wheelock Eleazar, the son of Sylvanus Ripley, was born on 15 April 1782 in Hanover, New Hampshire. Eleazar was one of six children in the family. He attended Dartmouth College, which was founded by his grandfather, also named Eleazar (Eleazer), and graduated in the class of 1800. He studied law and subsequent to passing the bar began to practice in Waterville, Maine, which at the time was still part of Massachusetts. During 1807, he was elected to the Massachusetts House of Representatives, where he served in 1807 and in 1811.

During 1812, Ripley moved to Portland, Maine, where he was chosen as a state senator. On 12 March he was commissioned as lieutenant colonel of the U.S. 21st Infantry. Shortly thereafter, General Dearborn directed Ripley to assume command of the fortifications and harbors along the eastern seaboard. During September 1812, he departed from Portland and afterward arrived at Plattsburgh during October. Upon his arrival, he joined the Northern Army under General Bloomfield. Following the conclusion of the campaign, Ripley led his regiment to Burlington, Vermont, to establish winter quarters. On 12 March 1813, Lt. Colonel Ripley was promoted to full colonel. He participated in the attack on York, where General Zebulon Pike was killed (April 1813), but he sustained only a minor wound.

Colonel Ripley was present at the capture of Fort George in Canada, but he was not at the Battle of Stoney Creek when Generals Chandler and Winder were captured by the British. Meanwhile, General Dearborn directed Ripley to escort the prisoners from Fort George to Oswego and from there he repaired to Sackets Harbor. During November 1813, Colonel Ripley participated at the Battle of Chrysler's Farm (General Wilkinson's campaign to seize Montreal), where General Leonard Covington was killed. After the engagement, General Wilkinson aborted the campaign, due in part because General Wade Hampton did not link his army with Wilkinson's force. On or about 15 April 1814, he was elevated to brigadier general, and he was breveted major general on 25 July 1814.

On 3 July 1814, General Ripley participated with General Jacob Brown's campaign, including the Battle of Lundy's Lane and the Battle of Chippewa. At Lundy's Lane, it was General Ripley who ordered Colonel James Miller to take a slope and it was Miller who replied with his famous response: "I'll try, sir." Miller's 21st Infantry took the hill and he was later promoted to brigadier general. During the battle, Generals Brown and Winfield Scott had sustained wounds, leaving General Ripley to assume temporary command; however, on the following day, Ripley did not take the offensive. General Brown's confidence in General Ripley dropped precipitously. He placed General Edmund Pendleton Gaines in command at Fort Erie rather than General Ripley. A British attack against the fort was repelled and General Gaines commended Ripley's actions during the siege. Nevertheless, General Gaines became disabled when a British shell came into his quarters through the roof, and General Brown, rather that turning command over to Ripley, assumed personal command of the fort. During the siege, General Ripley received a serious neck wound. On 3 November 1814, Congress awarded General Ripley a gold medal.

After the Americans abandoned Fort Erie, General Ripley, still recuperating, returned Albany in February 1815. He remained in the service until 1820, when he resigned on 1 February. After his retirement from the army, he settled in Jackson, Louisiana, and resumed practicing law. He also served in the Louisiana Senate. Afterward, he was elected to the U.S. Congress (24th) as a Jacksonian. He was then elected to the 25th Congress as a Democrat and re-elected yet again to the 26th Congress (serving in total from 4 March 1835 until 2 March 1839).

General Ripley died while in office on 2 March 1839 at West Feliciana Parish. He was interred in a private cemetery at St. Francisville, Louisiana.

General Ripley married his first wife, Love Allen, the daughter of the Rev. Thomas Allen, on 30 July 1811. They had two children, Henry (died while serving in the army of Texas during the struggle for its independence from Mexico), and a daughter, Elizabeth (born at an unknown time), who married Thornton Lawson. General Ripley's wife, Love, died during 1828 from yellow fever while she was at Bay St. Louis, Mississippi. He remarried in 1830, taking Aurelia C. Smith Davis, daughter of Courtland and Catherine Cooper Smith, as his second wife.

Scott, Major General Winfield Winfield, the son of William and Ann Mason Scott, was born on 18 June 1786 near Petersburg, Virginia. In addition to Winfield, his parents had one other son, James, and several daughters. Winfield's father died in 1791 when Winfield was only about 5 years old. His mother carried on the task of raising her children alone, but she also died before Winfield came of age, during 1803. Winfield was able to remain focused despite losing both parents. He attended William and Mary College after spending about one year in Richmond studying under Doctor Ogilvie. While at William and Mary, he studied law. Afterward, he entered the law firm of David Robertson in Richmond. In 1806, he began to practice law in Petersburg, where he "rode the circuit" and when possible, worked in the law office of Benjamin W. Leigh. During 1807, Winfield Scott moved to South Carolina to open a practice; however, state law mandated that a person live in the state for one year before being allowed to practice law. Unable to receive a waiver, he returned to Virginia. However, his career in law was beginning to fade away due to the circumstances "that were moving the nation close to war with France or England or both."

During 1807, Scott served as a volunteer in a cavalry troop, called out by the president to close the harbors to British warships; however, he did not enter the service until the following year, when he was commissioned as captain of artillery. Outright war was several years away, but the path seemed clear and hostilities at some point appeared inevitable. Scott was pro–Jefferson and pro-war. His various writings and speeches left no doubt as to where he stood. In the meantime, Captain Scott was dispatched to Louisiana where he was to join his Virginia company with General James Wilkinson's army. Captain Scott had been familiar with Wilkinson and his association with Aaron Burr, which did little to bring about a cordial relationship between the general and the captain. Scott's disdain for Wilkinson only intensified after he arrived in New Orleans. In turn, Wilkinson's sentiments regarding Scott were hostile from the beginning.

On 10 January 1810, Captain Scott received a court-martial on charges by Wilkinson that he withheld money from his command and that he used disrespectful language regarding his superior (Wilkinson). Captain Scott vehemently denied the first charge, but he admitted the second charge, stipulating that his accusations were justified. The court ruled the first charge to be dismissed. Nevertheless, on the second charge, the only option was to convict. Scott was sentenced, according to the Sixth Article of War, "to suspension from rank, pay and emoluments for one year." For Wilkinson it was what might be called a pyrrhic victory. The court had no options on the charge; however, Captain Scott suffered no harm from his peers. Before departing for home, Scott was given a dinner in his honor by other soldiers and even civilians as if to congratulate him for his actions. Although Scott would be absent form the service, he did not waste the time. After returning to Virginia, he spent enormous time at the home of Benjamin Leigh, where he studied various methods of warfare in all branches of the services.

Scott became lieutenant colonel of the 2nd Artillery around July 1812. Also, while Lt. Colonel Scott was in New Orleans he married Lucy Baker; however, she died early during 1816. Later, Lt. Colonel Scott assumed command of the regiment. He repaired to the New York frontier.

On 12 October, Colonel Scott arrived at Lewiston from Buffalo and requested permission to join the attack against Queenston scheduled for the following day. His request was denied. Nevertheless, Scott established a battery near the Lewiston Ferry from where his artillery could support the attack. The attack was postponed until the 13th and Scott did participate. General Wadsworth relinquished command to Colonel Scott. Meanwhile, militia back across the river refused to cross into Canada, while other reinforcements requested from General Smyth did not arrive.

All the while British reinforcements were arriving from Fort George. The Americans, essentially trapped, were compelled to surrender. The British had transformed defeat into victory.

In late May 1813, Colonel Scott participated in the attack against Fort George in Canada. During the assault, Scott barely escaped serious injury or death when a British magazine exploded and the debris rained down upon him on the 27th. Except for being knocked off his horse, Scott was unscathed. He retained command and was the first to enter Fort George. Rather than selecting one of his men, Scott, standing at about 6 5 , hoisted the Stars and Stripes himself. Colonel Moses Porter, who arrived just after Scott, bellowed: "Confound your long legs, Scott, you have got in before me!" Once the post was secured, Scott remounted and initiated pursuit of the retreating British; however, he departed without any cavalry. Twice he was ordered to halt the chase by General Boyd, but he continued. He told one of the messengers: "Your General does not know that I have the enemy within my power; in seventy minutes I shall capture his whole force." Nonetheless, the third messenger was Boyd himself, who caught up with Scott and ordered him to return to the captured fort. Colonel Scott remained at Fort George until he received orders from General Wilkinson. He departed from the post with his command and the invalids en route to Fort Niagara.

During spring of 1814, General Jacob Brown succeeded General Wilkinson as commander of the Northwestern Army. About the same time, General George Izard received command at Plattsburgh, and General Winfield Scott assumed command of Niagara Frontier. In July 1814, General Scott participated in General Jacob Brown's operation that pitted his force against the British at Chippewa and Lundy's Lane. The Americans departed from Fort Erie in Canada on 4 July. On the 5th, Scott scored a huge victory over the British under British General Riall at Chippewa.

On 25 July 1814, another major clash occurred at Lundy's Lane. The British retired, but both sides claimed victory. General Brown and General Scott both sustained wounds, and Scott had two horses shot from under him. His shoulder wound was debilitating and ended his service in the field for the duration of the conflict. The Battle of Lundy's Lane is also known as either the Battle of Niagara or the Battle of Bridgewater. General Scott was hit twice by balls; the latter one shattered the joint in his left shoulder. For a while, the surgeons believed he might not survive. General Scott was first taken to the American camp at Chippewa and then to Williamsville, a present-day suburb of Buffalo, where he recuperated at the house of a friend. General Scott had the company of British General Riall and his aide, Major Wilson, both of whom were wounded and prisoners. During that time, the men who had been enemies on the field became friends.

Once General Scott was able to travel he set out for Philadelphia to receive medical help from a surgeon, but the trip was slow going. While en route, President Madison promoted him to the rank of major general, stating at the time: "Put him down major general. I have now done with objection to his youth." Scott stayed in Batavia for a few weeks. From there he was carried on a litter to Geneva. Afterward, General Scott's journey continued with no end to volunteers attempting to participate in their hero's journey. When his carriage arrived at Princeton, New Jersey, the commencement exercises of New Jersey College (Princeton) were being held. He received royal treatment by the faculty, and the valedictorian paid tribute to the wounded patriot who managed to make it to the stage. Apparently, General Scott, essentially fearless while under enemy fire, was taken aback by the attention. He was given an honorary master of arts degree by the faculty.

After departing from Princeton, General Scott resumed his journey, and as he approached Philadelphia in September 1814, he was met by a division of militia and by Governor Simon Snyder. General Scott was over-exhausted and far from recovery; however, despite his contention that he was not well, he was named the "nominal head of the Pennsylvania and Maryland forces at a time when both cities were still under a severe British threat. The department leaders believed that General Scott would instill the confidence in the troops that would provide them with the inspiration needed to succeed against the enemy. He left Philadelphia and for Baltimore, where he was treated by Doctor Gibson. The surgery was successful, but not right away. He remained disabled for some time. Nonetheless, he repaired to Washington and assumed command in October 1814 of the 10th Military District.

General Scott remained there throughout the winter of 1814–1815. In February 1815, the Treaty of Peace arrived at the capital. Soon after, President James Monroe, who succeeded President James Madison, offered the position of secretary of war to General Scott, but he declined on the grounds that other officers with more seniority would be much more entitled. President Monroe countered by requesting that Scott become acting secretary until William H.C. Crawford made his return from Paris; however, Scott refused again on the grounds that he would not jump over other officers with more seniority.

President Monroe dispatched General Scott on a diplomatic mission to visit the governments of Europe, including France, England and Russia, to seek out their views on American policies. His mission was to also discern the European sentiments regarding the various ongoing revolutions in South America and Mexico. President Monroe remained concerned about possible intervention by a European government. He issued the Monroe Doctrine, which forbid all European nations from interfering in the hemisphere. The doctrine succeeded; however, at the time it was issued, the United States was actually unable militarily to back it up. Scott first arrived in Europe shortly after Napoleon failed in his bid to return to power.

General Scott received help from Tadeusz Kosciusko, an American general in the American Revolution, who had received introductory letters in advance of Scott's arrival. At the time Kosciusko was recuperating from illness in Switzerland. Through his efforts, Scott was able to meet with Napoleon's marshals. He also visited all military fortifications, including naval installations in Belgium, France and England. General Scott completed his mission and returned to the United States during the summer of 1816. Upon his return, General Scott received command of the Department of the Atlantic Seaboard with headquarters in New York City. He retained the post until 1831.

One child, John Baker Scott, was born to Winfield and his first wife, Lucy, in February 1816. During March 1817, General Scott married Maria Mayo, about 22 years old, from Virginia. They had the following children: Maria Mayo (born October 1818, died in 1833); John Mayo Scott (born in April 1819, died in September 1820); Virginia (born 1821, died in August 1845); Edward Winfield (born March 1823, died in May 1827); Cornelia (born in 1825, died in 1886); and Adeline Camilla (born January 1834, died in February 1882).

In November 1814, Congress passed a resolution requesting President Madison have a gold medal struck and presented to General Scott "in testimony of the high sense entertained by Congress of his distinguished services in the successive conflicts of Chippewa and Niagara [Lundy's Lane], and of his uniform gallantry and good conduct in sustaining the reputation of the arms of the United States." The medal was finally presented to General Scott on 26 February 1825 by President James Monroe during the final days of his second term as president." General Scott, upon receiving the medal, is known to have responded to the president:

> If, in the resolve of Congress, or in your address, sir, my individual services have been overestimated, not so the achievements of that gallant body of officers and men, whom in battle it was my good fortune to command, and of whom I am, on this interesting occasion, the honored representative. Very many of those generous spirits breathed their last on the fields which their valor assisted to win; and, of the number that happily survive, there is not one, I dare affirm, who will not be ready, in peace as in war, to devote himself to the liberties and the glories of the country.

General Scott had also received awards from Virginia and New York. During February 1816, the Virginia legislature, by unanimous vote, resolved that Governor William Cary Nicholas present General Scott with a sword in recognition of his service during the war, particularly at Chippewa and Lundy's Lane. He received it in 1825. New York gave him a sword on 25 February, the day the British finally evacuated New York City. Governor Daniel D. Tompkins made the presentation.

For a while, a rift occurred between General Scott and General Andrew Jackson which began over some correspondence that was passing between them (1819–1823). The ill feelings moved to the brink of violence, but the two settled their differences before it came to a duel. The two men then remained good friends. In the late 1820s, General Scott turned in his resignation after General Edmund Pendleton Gaines and General Alexander Macomb were promoted to major general over him. Scott claimed that his brevet major general had made him eligible. His resignation was never officially accepted.

On 10 November 1829, General Scott, in a letter dated at New York to Secretary of War Eaton, withdrew his resignation ". Several days later, on the 13th, General Scott received his response. He was ordered to report to the commanding general, General Macomb. He was assigned to the Eastern Department, where he remained until ordered to the West to deal with the hostile Indians in Illinois and Iowa that were led by Black Hawk.

During 1832, General Scott, leading a force of about 1,000 men, departed from the East Coast en route to Buffalo, New York, from where the contingent would head west to join with General Atkinson. Cholera broke out aboard the ships. Scott finally arrived at Prairie Du Chien, but his force was trailing and the war had just ended. Black Hawk's attempt to win territory east of the Mississippi River failed.

General Scott arrived back at New York in October 1832 and was soon called to Washington. Trouble had erupted in South Carolina when the state nullified the federal revenue laws. President Jackson was prepared to send an expeditionary force, but he first wanted to try to settle the dispute. Secretary of War General Lewis Cass dispatched General Smith to Charleston by order of 18 November 1832 to inspect the fortifications and to determine if reinforcements would be required. Scott was to coordinate his efforts with the port collector and the U.S. district attorney. Meanwhile the state was prepared to break away from the Union to form a new government. Scott's mission, however, was clandestine. His presence was not perceived for what it was because Scott had been visiting the seacoast fortifications on an annual basis. Once Scott had made all the preparations in the event of hostilities, he returned to New York, where he made preparations to send reinforcements if necessary.

Also in 1832, the Treaty of Fort Armstrong was signed in Illinois by General Winfield Scott and Governor John Reynolds on behalf of the United States. The Sauk and Fox Indians, by terms of the treaty, agreed to peace with the United States, and they agreed to move to a reservation. During January 1833, General Scott returned to South Carolina. He was at Fort Moultrie for a few days before the people in Charleston realized he had returned. Scott was there to take command and enforce the laws if it became necessary. Nevertheless, the problem was settled peacefully and the legislature rescinded the ordinance. General Scott received the credit for the peaceful resolution. Nevertheless, he was not destined for too long a period of tranquility.

During 1835, hostilities erupted with the Seminoles in Florida under Osceola, a half-breed Creek. On 28 December, the Indians ambushed and nearly annihilated an American contingent of 110 men in what came to be known as the Dade Massacre. Only two troops survived. Scott was sent to Florida and arrived on 22 February. Nonetheless, the Seminoles and the Negroes that were allies remained elusive. The campaign was aborted until the army could devise a plan that would include posts being built in the Everglades. In a report to the War Department, dated 30 April 1836, Scott noted: "To end this war I am now persuaded that not less than 3,000 troops are indispensable; 2,400 infantry and 600 horse; the country to be scoured and occupied requiring that number." He also recommended "two or three steamers, with a light draught of water, and fifty or sixty barges capable of carrying from ten to fifteen men each."

In July 1836, General Scott was recalled to Washington to respond to charges against him placed by General Thomas Jesup. An inquiry was held, but not until 3 October 1836. The court was composed of Major General Macomb and Brigadier Generals Hugh Brady and Henry Atkinson. Jesup charged that "Scott's "course [in Florida] had been destructive to the best interests of the country." General Scott was acquitted of any wrongdoing; however, he lost the command, despite the court's findings that he had processed the war properly. Nonetheless, without Scott's leadership, the president, Andrew Jackson, who refused to restore Scott to command, discovered that six years would pass before the Seminoles were suppressed.

General Scott became involved in what was known as the Patriots War (1838–1839) when Americans attempted to join with rebels in Canada. Scott's leadership essentially squashed the Americans' participation. Afterward, General Scott was involved with the Cherokee Relocation; however, during 1846, he was back in the field as a combat commander when war erupted with Mexico.

The Whig Party placed Scott's name in the hat for the presidential nomination during 1839 when the convention met at Harrisburg, Pennsylvania, on 4 December; however, the nomination went to General William Henry Harrison. Scott then supported Harrison. Harrison died on 4 April 1841, one month after ascending to the presidency. General Alexander Macomb died on 25 June 1841. Macomb's death left General Scott as the senior major general in the U.S. Army and its commander-in-chief.

During 1846, politics entered the scene when General Scott was reluctant to assume command of the army because he believed General Zachary Taylor had been doing a splendid job in the Mexican War. President James K. Polk tried to place a lieutenant general over Scott, but Congress refused to go along with his scheme. General Scott departed for the Rio Grande on 28 November 1846. In the meantime, the Mexican Army had crossed the Rio Grande into Texas during the previous May and afterward, Taylor and his officers learned of the plight of Scott. Taylor made it clear that Scott was welcome to assume overall command. After arriving in Texas, General Scott learned of President Polk's attempt to discredit him. Nonetheless, he continued with his responsibilities to bring the war to a conclusion.

Scott planned the United States' first major amphibious invasion, the invasion of Vera Cruz. Meanwhile, Santa Anna, during February 1847, demanded that General Taylor's force of fewer than 5,000 men surrender at the Battle of Buena Vista.

Shortly thereafter, Scott launched his invasion on 24 March. Commodore Matthew Perry commanded the naval forces. The city surrendered on the 29th. The Americans then raised the Stars and Stripes over the city of the True Cross. The Americans continued toward the Mexican capital. On 13 September, soldiers and Marines captured the castle of Chapultepec. On the 13th and 14th, General Scott's troops marched into Mexico City. U.S. Grant and Robert E. Lee, along with Jefferson Davis and other future general officers (Confederate and Union) participated in the campaign.

On 24 September 1847, General Scott, empathetic to the people in Mexico, a Catholic country, issued the following edict: "Here, as in all Roman Catholic countries, there are frequent religious processions in the streets, as well as in churches, such as the elevation of the Host, the viaticum, funerals, etc. The interruption of such processions has already been prohibited in orders; and, as no civilized person will ever wantonly do any act to hurt the religious feelings of others, it is earnestly requested of all Protestant Americans either to keep out of the way or to pay to the Catholic religion and its ceremonies every decent mark of respect and deference."

At the time of the outbreak of the Civil War, General Scott held the rank of brevet lieutenant general. In April 1861, he initiated a plan to fortify Washington, D.C. General Scott, a Virginian, had been approached about joining the Confederacy. His response: "I have served my country, under the flag of the Union for more than fifty years and so long as God permits me to live, I will defend that flag with my sword, even if my native state assails it."

On 1 November 1861, Major General George B. McClellan was appointed general-in-chief. He succeeded General Winfield Scott, who requested permission to retire. He took a short voyage to Europe. He lived to see the Union preserved. General Scott died at West Point on 29 May 1866. He was interred in the cemetery at the Military Academy.

Shelby, General Isaac Isaac Shelby, the son of General Evan and Letitia Coxe (spelling variations include Laeticia Cox) Shelby, was born on 11 December 1750 in the vicinity of Hagerstown, Maryland. Isaac's parents also had the following children: Susanna, John, Evan Jr., Moses, James, Catherine, Sarah, and Rachel. Isaac's father had immigrated to America about 1735, settled in Maryland and later relocated in the vicinity of present-day Bristol, Tennessee. In 1774, Isaac Shelby received a commission as lieutenant (Fincastle militia) from Colonel William Preston. Shelby served in his father's company. During October at the Battle of Point Pleasant (Dunmore's War), Shelby's father assumed command of a regiment after Colonel Andrew Lewis, the son of General Andrew Lewis, was fatally wounded. At that point, Shelby assumed command of his father's company. The Indians sustained a severe defeat, despite the fact that Governor Dunmore's force was not at the battle. Dunmore was away trying to broker peace. The situation created a conflict between General Lewis and the governor.

After the victory, Lieutenant Isaac Shelby remained deployed at Point Pleasant as commander until July of 1775. At that time, Lord Dunmore, concerned about the emergence of American resistance to the Crown, disbanded the force at Point Pleasant to prevent its joining the Patriot forces that were building. After his deployment ended, he traveled to Kentucky, and while in the employ of Henderson and Company, Shelby was engaged in surveying land there. During 1776, he was commissioned a captain of militia by the Virginia Committee of Safety. He participated in the Battle of Long Island Flats during the summer of 1776.

Governor Patrick Henry appointed Shelby in 1777 as commissary of the garrisons scattered across the frontier, including those of the Continental Army. In 1778, Shelby was elected to the Virginia legislature as a representative of Washington County and was appointed as a major by Governor Thomas Jefferson (successor to Patrick Henry) and attached to the guards assigned to protect the commissioners delegated to draw the border between North Carolina and Virginia. When the border was settled, Shelby, like his father and others, suddenly found himself no longer a Virginian. Shelby's property was within North Carolina.

Meanwhile, Governor Richard Caswell of North Carolina took advantage of Shelby's residency and appointed him colonel of militia for Sullivan County. During 1779, Shelby procured supplies using his personal credit for an expeditionary force commanded by his father,

Colonel Evan Shelby, at a time when government funds were not available. Colonel Evan Shelby concluded the campaign with great success against hostile Chickamauga Indians. In February 1780, the British moved against Charleston. Despite a large army with naval support under General Benjamin Lincoln, the city fell on 12 May 1780. Shortly thereafter, word of the surrender reached Colonel Shelby while he was in Kentucky on yet another surveying mission. Shelby cut short his surveying and returned to his home in North Carolina, and once there became aware of a call from Colonel Charles McDowell to assemble as many troops as possible due to the threat of a British invasion of North Carolina.

Shelby enthusiastically jumped back in the saddle. He raised a contingent of just under 250 troops, each a skilled rifleman, and the force set out to cross the mountains to bolster McDowell in South Carolina. Colonel Shelby's mounted riflemen participated in the victories over the British at Cedar Springs, Thickety Fort and Musgrove's Mill, the latter having erupted on 17 August 1780. He and his "Overmountain Men" played a key role in evicting the British from North Carolina during the American Revolution.

Colonel Shelby was elected to the North Carolina legislature after he returned home, and he was re-elected during 1782. Consequently, he departed from the army; however, prior to his departure, Colonel Shelby had proposed plans to attack Cowpens, another British stronghold.

At Cowpens on 17 January 1781, the forces of General Daniel Morgan (who had command of part of Greene's army) scored yet another decisive victory against the British, bringing the American army closer to total victory. Other battles followed, but British General Cornwallis departed the Carolinas for Virginia, where he failed to gain his objectives and was unable to get reinforcements due to a French naval blockade at Yorktown, forcing his surrender during October 1781.

During 1783, Colonel Shelby was appointed as a commissioner to survey land along the Cumberland River that had been set aside for soldiers who had fought during the American Revolution. When the responsibility was completed, Colonel Shelby settled and married in Boonesborough, Kentucky. He married Susanna Hart, the daughter of Captain Nathaniel Hart, during 1783 and settled near Stanford, Kentucky. They had the following children: James (married Mary Pindell); Sarah (married Ephraim McDowell); Evan (married Nancy Warren); Thomas Hart (married Mary McDowell and then Mary Bullock); Nancy (married S.K. Nelson); Isaac (married Maria Warren); John (died unmarried); Letitia (married Colonel Charles Stewart Todd); Catherine (died young); and Alfred (married Virginia Hart).

Once he became a Kentuckian, Colonel Shelby became a solid proponent of Kentucky entering the union. Some, including General James Wilkinson, favored breaking away and consummating an alliance with the Spanish. Kentucky entered the union on 1 June 1792 to become the fifteenth state. Colonel Isaac Shelby, having been a loyal Virginian and North Carolinian during the war, remained equally loyal to Kentucky and became its first governor. He was governor for four years, and although war with Spain did not erupt, the period at times was tumultuous with Spanish domination of the Mississippi River, the route to the Gulf of Mexico through New Orleans.

By 1795, the Spanish acquiesced and a treaty was consummated that opened up the river to the shipping of the United States. Colonel Shelby retired from office during 1795, refusing to run for another term. He returned to his estate to farm. He turned down various opportunities to resume in public offices, but he did accept an appointment as a presidential elector, and he participated six separate times under three presidents: Thomas Jefferson (1801–1909), James Madison (1809–1817), and James Monroe (1817–1825).

Colonel Shelby continued to enjoy his retirement, but when another war with Britain was imminent, he agreed to again become the governor of Kentucky. However, he offered more than his statesmanship. Colonel Shelby, several years beyond sixty, bounced back into the saddle when the frontier became endangered following the surrender of the army at Detroit on 16 August 1812 and the massacre at Raisin River on 21 January 1813, in which the British and their Indian allies killed about 100 and captured about 500 Kentuckians.

Colonel Shelby, although never having been commissioned as a brigadier general, as commander-in-chief of the armed forces of Kentucky raised a force of about 4,000 troops and rode to join with General William Henry Harrison at the Battle of the Thames on 5 October 1813. The Americans were victorious and a British ally, Tecumseh, was killed. Congress during 1818 awarded gold medals in honor of their leadership in the face of the enemy to General Harrison and Governor Shelby. Colonel Shelby later, during 1819, turned down an appointment from President Monroe, which would have made him the secretary of war. However, he did accept an appointment as a commissioner to deal with the Chickasaw Indians regarding the cession of territory in West Tennessee. He served with General Andrew Jackson. The mission was successful.

Colonel Isaac Shelby returned to his farm, where he died on 18 July 1826. Colonel Shelby's brother, General Evan Shelby, Jr. (North Carolina militia), resided in the vicinity of the Red River at Clarkesville. He was killed by Indians on 18 January 1793, when he was ambushed while in a boat on the river.

Smith, Brigadier General Thomas Adams Thomas, the son of Francis and Lucy Wilkinson Smith of Wilkes County, was born on 12 August 1781 at Piscataway in Essex County, Virginia. Georgia. Thomas' father was a member of the Virginia House of Burgesses. After receiving a fundamental education, Thomas attended William and Mary College. He entered the military in 1800 and received the rank of ensign. On 15 December 1803, he was commissioned as a 2nd lieutenant of artillery. He was promoted to 1st lieutenant on 31 December 1805. Later, on 17 September 1807, Thomas married Cynthia Berry White, the daughter of General James White of Knoxville, Tennessee. Their children were Lucy Anne, James White, Mary Lawson, Hugh Lawson, Reuben, Crawford Early, Troup, and Cynthia White.

Following his promotion to captain, Thomas Smith continued climbing up through the ranks. He made captain of the 1st Rifles on 3 May 1808, and on 31 July 1810, he was raised to lieutenant colonel. Just after war was declared on Great Britain, Smith was promoted to full colonel on 6 July 1812. Prior to the outbreak of war, Smith was based on the Florida frontier from 1808, when he commanded at St. Mary's until he was ordered to the Canadian theater during 1812. While he was on the Florida frontier, Smith's' force had frequent skirmishes with hostile Indians; however, there were no major engagements. During that time, his command also engaged Spanish forces. While on the frontier, Smith was at various places for the duration, including French Mills, Plattsburgh and Sackets Harbor.

On 24 January 1814, Smith was raised to brevet brigadier general, followed by his promotion to brigadier general on 25 January 1815. After the war, General Smith was appointed commander of the 9th Military District. He established his headquarters at Bellefontaine, Missouri. During 1817, Major S.H. Long of the topographical engineers was sent to Bellefontaine to join Smith's command. He led an expedition into the Arkansas valley. While there, Long established a post which was named Fort Smith in honor of General Thomas Adams Smith. General Smith remained in the service until he resigned in the autumn of 1816. Afterward, he became the "receiver of public moneys" at Old Franklin, Missouri. He also established a farm known as "Experiment" on Salt Fork in Saline County about 1824–1825, which was expanded after he and his wife inherited many slaves. General Smith died at his residence on 25 June 1844.

Smyth, Brigadier General Alexander Alexander, the son of Reverend James and Frances Stuart Smyth, was born in Ireland about 1765 on the island of Rathlin. During 1775, he arrived in America with his family and settled in Botetourt County, Virginia. After studying law and passing the bar, Alexander began to practice law in Abingdon. He moved to Wythe County and became a member of the state House of Delegates, where he served in 1792, 1796, 1801, and 1802, followed by continued service from 1804 until 1808. In 1791, Alexander married Nancy Brinkley. During 1808, Alexander Smyth was elected to the state Senate, where he served in 1808 and 1809. He joined the U.S. Army in 1808 and served until 1813.

During spring of 1812, Smyth was promoted to the rank of brigadier general. On 2 July, he was appointed inspector general. During autumn, while in western New York, General

Smyth, along with Lt. Colonel Winfield Scott, provided assistance to Lieutenant Jesse D. Elliott, U.S. Navy, and Captain Nathan Towson, U.S. Army, who departed 8–9 October from Black Rock Navy Yard to seize two British warships, the HMS *Detroit* and the brigantine HMS *Hunter*. On 13 October 1812, at the Battle of Queenston, General Van Rensselaer requested reinforcements from General Smyth, but none arrived. By 23 October, General Smyth succeeded General Van Rensselaer.

By 18 November, Smyth's command at Buffalo numbered about 4,000 troops, counting the recent arrival of 2,000 men from Pennsylvania. Smyth had boasted by proclamation on the 10th, "In a few days, the troops under my command will plant the American standard in Canada to conquer or to die. Men of New York, you deserve your share of fame. Then seize the present moment. If you do not, you will regret it; say the valiant bled in vain, the friends of my country fell and I was not there."

On the 19th, General Smyth informed the British at Fort Erie in Canada that the armistice agreed up earlier by General Stephen Van Rensselaer and British General Roger Sheaffe would terminate in 36 hours. The notice was in accordance with the pact that either side would give 36 hours notice before reopening hostilities. Smyth was inflated with confidence when he informed his troops on the 25th to be ready to march "on a moment's notice."

On 28 November, an American contingent attached to General Smyth's command crossed into Canada and demanded that Fort Erie be surrendered. His demand was declined. On the 19th, General Smyth ordered his total force to advance into Canada; however, he apparently suddenly became indecisive. While one contingent was in the river, Smyth countermanded his own order. He postponed the attack until 1 December. The decision halted the arrival of reinforcements that were en route to relieve the vanguard that invaded on the previous day.

The force that was in the river was commanded by General Porter was forced to return to base. Later, Porter accused Smyth of "cowardice and Smyth responded by accusing Porter of being a fraud. The disagreement led to a duel, but neither man was harmed. Afterward, the two antagonists reconciled their differences.

General Smyth's decision to abort the attack had immediate ramifications. Smyth's military career was terminated. The officers under his command became infuriated. They prepared to tar and feather him, but he departed from the post before the officers could carry out their intent. Subsequently, General Smyth's name was stripped from the rolls of the U.S. Army without a trial. He appealed to the U.S. Congress, which in turn handed his complaint to the secretary of war, but he was not reinstated.

In 1816, Smyth returned to the Virginia House of Delegates. He served there in 1816, 1817, 1826 and 1827. He also served in the Fifteenth U.S. Congress (March 1817 to March 1819) and was re-elected to the Sixteenth, Seventeenth, Eighteenth, Twentieth and Twenty-first Congresses. General Smyth died in Washington, D.C., on 17 April 1830. He was interred in the Congressional Cemetery.

Swartwout, Brigadier General Robert Robert, the son of Abraham and Mary North Swartwout, was born at Poughkeepsie, New York, in 1778. Robert was a descendant of Roeloff Swartwout, who emigrated from Holland in the mid-1600s. Robert's father, Abraham, was a veteran of the American Revolution. During 1793, Robert married Margaret Dunscomb. They had seven children: Catherine Hone (born January 1809); Henry (born January 1811, died in Florida while serving in the U.S. Army); Mary (born February 1813); Robert II (born April 1815); Margaret (born August 1817); Edward Dunscomb (born September 1818, served in the Union Army during the Civil War); and John (born February 1821, served in the Union Army during the Civil War). Meanwhile, Robert Swartwout became an ally of Aaron Burr, who attempted to establish a political party in opposition to DeWitt Clinton. During 1803, Swartwout engaged in a political quarrel with a lawyer, Richard Riker. The dispute accelerated into a duel, which was fought on 14 November. Both men survived, but Riker sustained a serious wound.

Swartwout followed in his father's footsteps by joining the military. He served initially in the War of 1812 as a militia colonel and then as a brigade commander of the U.S. 4th Brigade. He was appointed quartermaster general on 21 March 1813. After the death of General Leonard Covington at the Battle of Chrysler's Field in Canada on 11 November 1813, Swartwout was named as Covington's successor.

After the war, General Swartwout moved to New York City. He resumed his career as a merchant. His two brothers, John and Samuel, also served during the War of 1812. General John Swartwout served with the New York militia and Samuel was adjutant of the Irish Greens. After the war, General Robert Swartwout was navy agent (1818) in New York City and held the position for a few years. He also served in local politics as an elderman in Ward Five. He died in New York City on 19 July 1848.

Swift, Brigadier General Joseph Gardner Joseph, the son of Doctor Foster and Deborah Delano Swift, was born in Nantucket on 31 December 1783. Joseph's father was the son of Samuel Swift and his mother was the daughter of Captain Thomas Delano. At the time of Joseph's birth, his father was in Virginia, where he had gone to see General Washington with a letter of introduction from General Benjamin Lincoln. Foster took the trip to attempt to re-establish himself in Alexandria close to where his only brother, Jonathan, resided and resume his medical practice there. While in Virginia, Joseph's father's health took a downturn. Upon his return to Massachusetts, he cancelled his plans to relocate in Virginia and instead moved his practice to the town of Apponagansett, which was close to New Bedford. In 1792, the family moved to Taunton, which stands about mid-way between Boston and Providence, Rhode Island. Meanwhile, Joseph attended a school operated by Abner Alden and then a school on Taunton Green that was operated by Sally Cady. Afterward, Joseph attended an academy in Taunton where he studied Greek, Latin and geometry, the subjects which would prepare him for entry at Harvard.

During 1798, Joseph had a narrow escape with death when he fell through the ice on the Taunton River while ice skating and vanished. He was able to resurface through the hole in which he fell. Some Quakers who were nearby rescued him by extending a pole.

Later, many of the youth of Massachusetts were looking forward to becoming midshipmen, and General David Cobb, a veteran of the American Revolution, was involved with handing out applications. Nonetheless, Joseph's mother's family members were Quakers, which precluded Joseph from getting his mother's blessing regarding his entry into the military. She was set on Joseph becoming a doctor. During summer of 1799, Joseph was preparing to enter Cambridge College. At that time, the U.S. 14th Infantry, commanded by Colonel Nathan Rice, arrived at the Taunton River.

Joseph's father became the temporary regimental surgeon. During that time, an artillery contingent and a detachment of engineers under Captain Amos Stoddart arrived at the camp while en route to Rhode Island. The scene impressed Joseph, and when some of the troops, friends of Joseph's father, inquired whether he might want to become an ensign, Joseph became enthused and requested that his parents seek the help of General Cobb to secure a "cadet's warrant." Another family friend, John Gardner, intervened and through his connection with President John Adams, the warrant was forthcoming in spring of 1800. Joseph was ordered to report to Colonel Lewis Tousard, commandant of engineers at Providence, Rhode Island.

During 1798, Joseph Swift was getting more experience. He was appointed as superintendent for the construction of the "South Wing Battery" at Fort Wolcott in Newport, Rhode Island, on Goat Island. Later in the year, Swift returned home to Taunton to visit his mother, while his father was out of town at Nantucket. After his arrival, the family home was destroyed by fire on 16 September.

On 1 October 1801, Swift received orders from Secretary of War General Dearborn to report to West Point Military Academy. He arrived in October and reported to Lieutenant Osborn, commandant, and to Professor George Baron. Professor Baron sent a servant to direct Swift to carry out an order, which Swift refused to accept. Baron appeared, stating: "Do you refuse to obey my orders?" Swift responded: "No, sir, but I refuse to receive a verbal order by any servant," which infuriated Baron, who bellowed: "You are a mutinous young rascal." Swift in turn bolted over a fence to get at the professor, who hurriedly returned to his quarters with Swift on his heels. Baron bolted his door.

Swift came close to being expelled; however, after an examination of the facts, it was Professor Baron who was arrested. He was dismissed from the service. Swift was found "guilty of using disrespectful words" to his superior officer. Nonetheless, he was released and directed to report for duty. The next year, 1802, Congress passed legislation on 16 March to decrease the size of the U.S. Army. One of the officers affected by the cut was Swift's instructor, Tousard.

Swift became a cadet of engineers in July 1802, one of twelve at West Point. At the time, Colonel Williams was the commander of the corps of engineers. One of Swift's fellow cadets was Hannibal Montresor Allen, a son of Ethan Allen of Revolutionary War fame. During September 1802, the first public examination was given to the cadets and its first two graduates were Joseph Gardner Swift and S.M. Levy, Cadet No. 1 and Cadet No. 2.

In 1804, Swift spent some time with his uncle Jonathan, brother of his father. While in the capital, he also became acquainted with Luther Martin (framer of the U.S. Constitution) and General William Eaton. He also had the pleasure of dining with President Jefferson. Afterward, he returned to West Point.

In late April, he received orders to repair to North Carolina to inspect the harbor at Cape Fear and to "direct the execution of a contract with General Benjamin Smith of Belvidere, to construct a battery at the site of old Fort Johnson, in Smithville, of a material called tapia." He reported to General Dearborn at the War Department on 31 May, and while there he again met with the president and the secretary of state, James Madison.

By January 1805, Swift received command of Fort Johnston at the mouth of the Cape Fear River. He succeeded Lt. Fergus and remained in command there into the following year.

On 6 June 1805, Swift married Louisa Margaret Walker at her father's (James) residence, known as "The Barn." On June 22, while attending a party in honor of the marriage, Lt. Swift was informed by letter that he had been promoted to the rank of 1st lieutenant of engineers.

On 14 July 1806, Swift was succeeded at Fort Johnston by Lieutenant William Cox, also of the engineers. However, Lt. Swift was too ill from fever to travel. By 8 September, he was able to travel to Wilmington, North Carolina. During October, Lt. Swift was promoted to captain.

During February 1807, Lt. Swift received orders to repair to West Point. At that time, he had served in North Carolina just under three years. He departed from his post in North Carolina on 20 March, aboard the packet *Venus*. His wife and their child, James, along with his mother-in-law and a servant, Nancy, accompanied him. They arrived in New York City on the 28th. Afterward, he arrived at West Point on 6 April and assumed command.

On 16 March 1808, Major Swift (promoted to major during February 1808) repaired to Boston to examine Boston Harbor and to determine new locations for defensive fortifications along the Massachusetts' coast. At about the same time, Colonel Moses Porter was executing identical duties in Maine. During this time, Joseph's wife Louisa had a second child, Jonathan Williams Swift, who was born on 30 March. The child was named in honor of Colonel Williams, the chief of the Corps of Engineers. In May, Swift moved his family from Taunton to Fort Independence (Castle Williams).

During March 1809, the administration of President Jefferson began to break up with the resignation of General Dearborn, who relinquished his post as secretary of war to accept the post of collector at the port of Boston; however, at the outbreak of war with Britain in 1812, General Dearborn was named senior major general. In October 1809, Major Swift departed from Boston and returned to North Carolina aboard the brigantine *Short Staple*. He arrived at Federal Point near Cape Fear on 6 November. He joined his family at Wilmington, where he remained at "The Sound" until 10 November.

On 4 March 1810, another son, Alexander Joseph, was born while Louisa was at the home of her mother. In late 1809, the North Carolina legislature donated Fort Johnston to the federal government. During May of 1810, Major Swift returned there to assume command. On 20 July, Major Swift was ordered to repair to Fredericktown, Maryland, to join as a member of the board at the court-martial of General James Wilkinson.

On 1 August, command of Fort Johnston was turned over to Lieutenant Roberts, and Swift departed from the fort and headed to Maryland. The court-martial convened on 1 September 1810, regarding charges that extended over the years 1789 through 1810 and included "treason, conspiracy with Colonel Burr, corruption with the Spanish governor of Louisiana, Manuel Gayozo de Lemos and Baron Carondelet, disobedience of orders and neglect of duty." The trial continued for about four months and ended on Christmas Eve 1810. Wilkinson was acquitted.

Afterward, Major Swift stopped in Washington, D.C.; however, due to the acquittal of General Wilkinson, his reception was quite different from earlier visits. The verdict of acquittal was not received well in the capital by the secretary of war, the president and many others. Afterward, Major Swift returned to North Carolina and discovered that Lt. Roberts, who had been in command, had died during November of 1810, leaving his family in dire circumstances. Later, on 30 June 1812, Major Swift arrived in Charleston and reported to General Thomas Pinckney to introduce himself as the chief army engineer of the his department (Southern) of the Army. Major Swift also served as aide-de-camp to General Pinckney. At about the same time, July 6, Swift was promoted to lieutenant colonel of engineers, then full colonel on 31 July.

On 10 November 1812, Colonel Swift was informed by General Samuel Smith and Governor Gilman of the Senate a plan was underway by Secretary of War Eustis to make Robert Fulton, a civilian engineer, the chief engineer over the candidacy of Colonel Swift; however, President Madison did not support the scheme and it failed. Swift was appointed chief engineer by a unanimous vote of the U.S. Senate on 4 December 1812. A few days later, on the 8th, Colonel Swift attended a festive celebration in Washington in honor of the victory of the USS *Constitution*, commanded by Captain Isaac Hull, over the British warship HMS *Guerriere* on 19 August.

On 31 December 1812, Colonel Swift received news that his wife, Louisa, had delivered another boy, Thomas Delano, on 23 November 1812.

During 1813, Colonel Swift continued in his duties and among those was inspecting the fortifications in the East, including Fort McHenry and other posts in Pennsylvania and in New York. On 6 April, Colonel Swift reported to General George Izard before assuming command at Staten Island. Swift had a brigade, composed of the 32nd Infantry (Colonel Hawkins) and the 41st Regiment (Colonel Alexander Deniston). As chief engineer, he was also responsible for the region's harbor forts and the series of blockhouses at Utrecht Bay at the western tip of Long Island, Princess Bay at Staten Island and Sandy Hook at Jamaica Bay to ensure the area was prepared to defend against a British squadron which was just off Sandy Hook. Militia troops attached to General John Swartwout's command at Perth Amboy, New Jersey, manned the blockhouses.

On 17 July, Colonel Swift's wife and family joined him in New York.

On 31 August, Colonel Swift, General Leonard Covington and other officers in the party arrived in Albany and repaired to Sackets Harbor for the campaign to seize Montreal. Many in the army had become ill due to spoiled bread.

On 6 September, Lieutenant James Gadsden and Lieutenant R. E. De Russy arrived at Sackets Harbor to join with Colonel Swift. Both officers set out to reconnoiter the waterways leading to the St. Lawrence River. Another engineer, Brevet-Major Totten, Swift's first assistant, also arrived to serve with Swift.

On 19 October, General Wilkinson ordered Colonel Swift and Major Totten to execute a reconnaissance mission on the St. Lawrence up to Prescott to gather intelligence and plan an attack to seize the post there. By 31 October, Colonel Swift forwarded his plan to General Wilkinson. Swift received a response from General Wilkinson stating that his army "should enter the river by 3d November."

By the first spark of dawn on the 7th, Wilkinson's force was on the American bank of the river, opposite Prescott. At the time, Wilkinson's force numbered about 7,000 men; however, he still expected the army under General Wade Hampton to arrive and bolster his force. On 11 November, Wilkinson's army was stalled at Chrysler's Farm. To make the situation worse, by the following day (12th), Wilkinson learned that General Hampton would not be joining him at St. Regis. The message was delivered to Wilkinson, who was at Barnhard's Bay by Colonel Henry Atkinson, Hampton's inspector general. The arrival of the message sealed the fate of the campaign. It was terminated and Wilkinson returned to New York.

Colonel Swift noted in his memoir that General Covington, mortally wounded at Chrysler's Farm, died on the 12th and was interred on the 14th. Before he died, General Covington requested that Colonel Swift give his (Covington) sword to his son and he also asked Swift to give his horses to his servant. Colonel Swift carried out the requests. Shortly thereafter, on the 17th, Colonel Swift was ordered by Wilkinson, at French Mills, to deliver a sealed letter to General Hampton. Swift was also ordered to send back a report of what he observed while delivering the message.

Afterward, still according to orders, Swift was directed to repair to Washington, D.C., to deliver the letter he had in his possession for the secretary of war. Wilkinson had also stated to Swift: "While you are in Washington, you will be able to learn what may be my destiny. Any communication you may make to me on this subject will be gratefully received. I shall also be glad to hear from you on your route through the great towns. "With unfeigned friendship, Your obliged and faithful James Wilkinson." Colonel Swift did meet with General Hampton and the latter informed Swift that he did not disobey Wilkinson's order. He said he had intended to join him, but his force was too depleted.

On 25 February 1814, Colonel Swift received his commission as brevet brigadier general from adjutant John B. Walbach. General Swift noted in his memoir that the date of the commission should have been November 1813. He stated that "this omission I have attributed to General Armstrong's dislike of my friendly regard for General Wilkinson."

On 3 April 1814, General Swift and his wife, Louisa, were confirmed at St. Ann's Episcopal Church in Brooklyn. Afterward, General Swift initiated a tour of all military installations east of New York to Maine. He used the tour to squeeze in some time with his parents. He arrived in Boston and visited with his father at his post as surgeon, and he visited his mother at the family residence in Boston. At the time, Joseph had not seen his parents in more than four years. From Boston, General Swift sailed with Commodore Isaac Hull aboard the USS *Constitution* on a short voyage to Portsmouth. He returned to Boston on 21 April. Afterward, General Swift stopped in Rhode Island and in Connecticut to inspect other posts before returning to Brooklyn on 7 May, when he departed from New Haven (Fort Hale).

Upon his return to his headquarters, General Swift received correspondence from the War Department regarding his request to be transferred to the frontier on the Lakes. His request for transfer was declined. General Jacob Jennings Brown had even requested that General Swift be transferred to Niagara. General Swift remained in New York, and he accompanied General Henry Dearborn on an inspection tour of all the defenses of the New York Harbor.

General Swift focused on fortifying the defenses due to a perceived threat of a British invasion; however, he also used other measures. He dispatched spies who were able to visit the squadron off Sandy Hook and acquire intelligence, including returning with sketches from the cabins of Sir John B. Warren and Sir Thomas Hardy that indicated an attack at some point between Rhode Island and Chesapeake Bay. Nevertheless, it was never determined if the sketches presented theoretical plans or precise plans.

Throughout July, work continued on the harbor defenses and countless civilians volunteered to help with the projects. Meanwhile, on 1 July 1814, General Swift and his family returned to West Point.

Additional work continued in August and throngs of citizens arrived in Brooklyn Heights where work began to construct Fort Green. The defending force of citizen soldiers built up to about 20,000 men, including about 1,000 militia under General Jeremiah Johnston from Long Island. General Swift cautioned the New Yorkers that unless absolutely necessary, no citizen should leave New York. Other precautions included establishing temporary hospitals and accumulating large numbers of doctors and nurses to handle casualties outside the city if the British launched their invasion.

General Swift, not known to boast, did brag about one thing, his horse, "Flim Nap." General Swift said that Flim Nap "carried me at half speed from and to Harlem and Brooklyn with ease, twice, and sometimes three and four times in a day, thus enabling me to forward the working parties of citizens." The general also frequently praised the officers and men who served under him. Nonetheless, the attack never came.

On 27 December 1814, General Swift was ordered to repair to Baltimore to become a member of a board delegated "to revise the present, and form a new system of infantry tactics for the United States Army." On 13 February 1815, word arrived that a peace treaty had been signed at Ghent, and that General Jackson scored a devastating defeat on the British at the Battle of New Orleans on January 8. Celebration began to break out, despite the fact that snow storms were blanketing parts of the East Coast.

General Swift returned to Brooklyn on 3 March. Throughout the summer, he maneuvered to keep West Point operating. Supplies were short and the banks were reluctant to loan money, based on their belief the government was not going to repay. He borrowed from a Mr. Barker the sum of about $65,000, which enabled him to prevent the academy from being dissolved.

On 30 March, the Swift family was increased with the birth of their first daughter, Sarah Delano, born while General Swift was away at West Point. The following month, the general received less welcome news. In Washington, Secretary of War Crawford decided that a French engineer should be brought into the Corps of Engineers as the commander. Communications erroneously indicated that General Swift concurred; however, he was adamantly opposed to the idea that a foreigner should lead the corps.

Behind the scenes, Lafayette and Mr. Gallatin had selected French General Bernard, who served with Napoleon, as their choice for chief engineer. He arrived in the summer of 1816 and met with President Madison and the secretary of war in the capital, without any notice being given to General Swift, who was instructed to confine himself to the duties at West Point. On 16 November, General Swift repaired to West Point where he relieved Captain Partridge on 25 November.

In another letter from the secretary, dated 19 November, Swift was informed that Bernard had been appointed brevet brigadier general and was to be second in command under Swift. Nonetheless, the scheme was leading to Bernard, to the dismay of the corps, becoming chief engineer. Bernard arrived at West Point on 2 December. Swift made it clear to Bernard that he was skeptical of informing any foreign officer, "however high and honorable might be the character of the individuals of any foreign nation so employed."

General Swift noted in his memoir:

> The government in this matter are that my talents as chief engineer are assumed to be inferior to those of General Bernard, which may be a correct opinion, for I have not had the experience of that distinguished man; in reference to which I had stated to the government that the benefit of that experience could, with some deference to the pride of a corps that had been created at the Military Academy, be secured to the country by placing General Bernard at the head of an engineer professorship at West Point. To be sure the corps of engineers is composed of young men, nevertheless, during the late war they had been found respectable in their vocation, and all of the corps who had been in the field had been honored by brevets. Whether the forts on the Atlantic coast had been judiciously located and constructed, it was a fact that all the principal forts had kept the enemy at bay during the late war. On the whole I come to the conclusion that it is due to my country, and to the corps, that I command, so to cooperate with General Bernard, under the law of 16th February last, as to prove to the country that I am influenced by a sense of duty and not by mere selfishness.

General Swift resigned from the service on 12 November 1818.

He next pursued a career as a civil engineer. On the day following his resignation General Swift informed the secretary of the treasury that he accepted the position as surveyor. One day later, on 14 November 1818, General Swift repaired to New York City to begin his duties on a project that was to be completed by the end of the coming winter. It was completed on 24 February 1819, and the plans were delivered to the secretary of war. General Bernard examined the plans and said they were good, but he "preferred his own." General Swift and Colonel McRee concluded that "Bernard was not the genius he had been reputed.

On 15 April 1819, yet another addition was born to the Swift family — McRee, a son named after Colonel McRee. In September 1819, General Swift relocated his family in Brooklyn Heights.

He spent this rest of his life as a civil engineer; however, he also remained closely associated with West Point. He worked on projects in New York and the Great Lakes. He was also involved with New Jersey legislature, which appointed him and Nathaniel Prime to "superintend the plan to open the Morris Canal improvement."

He was involved with projects on the Great Lakes, including surveying Oak Orchard Creek for constructing a harbor at its convergence with Lake Ontario. Another major project was building the Pontchartrain Railroad in Louisiana, which was to run from New Orleans to Lake Pontchartrain. For the latter project, he hired George Barclay and William Sentell, along with carpenters and other workers. At the time, he also came down with fever and nearly died.

General Swift lived to see the end of the Civil War. He died at his residence in Geneva, New York, on 23 July 1865. He was interred there in a family plot. General Swift was the brother of Brigadier General Jonathan Swift of the New York militia.

General Joseph Gardner and Louisa Swift had the following children: James Foster (born 15 May 1806, married Mary F. Jephson, died 18 March 1830); Jonathan Williams (born 30 March 1808); Alexander Joseph (born 4 March 1810, West Point 1830, killed during the Mexican War, 4 April 1847); Thomas Delano (born 23 March 1812, died 2 September 1829); Julius Henry (born 1 September 1814, died 6 February 1850); Sara Delano (born 30 March 1816, married Peter Richards in 1861, died 22 March 1876); McRee (born 15 April 1819); Louisa Josephine (born 30 April 1821, married Peter Richards in June 1843, died 16 January 1859); Harriet Walker (born 3 February 1824, died 7 December 1826); Charlotte Farquhar (born 5 April 1826, died 31 December 1840); and James Thomas (born 30 August 1829, married Margaret Weston).

Wilkinson, Major Brigadier General James
James Wilkinson, the son of Joseph and Betty Heije Wilkinson, was born in Benedict, Maryland, during 1757. James' father was a prosperous merchant, which enabled James to receive an excellent education. He studied medicine at the University of Pennsylvania and established a medical practice in Maryland; however, his career was interrupted by the outbreak of hostilities. He repaired to Massachusetts and joined the army at Cambridge. Wilkinson was attached in September 1775 to the expeditionary force of Colonel Benedict Arnold, which was preparing for the Canadian expedition, led by General Richard Montgomery. Wilkinson was a volunteer in the Pennsylvania Rifle Battalion (part of 1st Continental Regiment) commanded by Colonel (later general) William Thompson. While Wilkinson was initiating a friendship with Arnold, he also was befriended by another officer in the force, Captain Aaron Burr.

During the ill-fated expedition, Wilkinson was promoted to the rank of captain. At that time he was attached to the 2nd Continental Regiment. Wilkinson had served on the staff of General Nathanael Greene from November 1775 until April 1776. Afterward, on 2 June he was appointed to General Arnold's staff as aide-de-camp, a position he held until 17 July. Three days later, on 20 July, Wilkinson became a brigade major, and in that capacity he became a member of General Horatio Gates' staff on 13 December 1776. Wilkinson was present at the Battle of Princeton and was with General Hugh Mercer when he succumbed on 12 January 1777 at the Clark house. Wilkinson noted later: "Excited to brutality by the gallantry of his resistance, they stabbed him with their bayonets in seven different parts of his body and inflicted many blows on his head with the butt-ends of their muskets; nor did they cease their butchery until they believed him to be a crushed and mangled corpse."

Wilkinson was promoted to the rank of lieutenant colonel of Thomas Hartley's Continental regiment on 12 January 1777. He was appointed as deputy adjutant-general of the Northern Department on 24 May. In the meantime, British General John Burgoyne was completing preparations for an invasion of New York. During June 1777, the British began their campaign which was intended to plow through Ticonderoga and steam roll through the opposition to reach Albany to link up with General Henry Clinton, who was simultaneously going to advance from New York. Colonel Wilkinson was a participant at the crucial First Battle of Saratoga on 19 September 1777. During the ferocious contest, General Horatio Gates remained in his headquarters, never entering the field of battle. However, he dispatched Wilkinson to order Benedict Arnold to retreat. Arnold ignored the order to retreat and instead ordered General Learned to launch an attack. Arnold's strategy prevailed and Burgoyne sustained a defeat, but Gates retaliated. He omitted Arnold's name from the battle report and Arnold was stripped of command.

Later, while the two sides were about to ignite a second major battle, the Patriots came upon some luck. Colonel John Hardin, on a personal reconnaissance mission, crept into the British lines undiscovered and gathered intelligence regarding their defenses and the strength of the force. Hardin encountered Colonel Wilkinson and transferred the intelligence with a request that Wilkinson rush the information to General Gates. Wilkinson complied, but he neglected to tell Gates anything about Hardin having been the source of the intelligence, leaving the impression that it was himself who ventured on the midnight excursion. Afterward, at the Second Battle of Saratoga, again Gates remained in his headquarters. Arnold, forbidden to take the field again, ignored Gates. The British were thrashed and Burgoyne was later forced to surrender his entire army.

In September, a dispute between Gates and Wilkinson erupted. Wilkinson challenged Gates to a duel. However, it never occurred. Gates is known to have said that firing at Wilkinson would have been "like firing at his own son."

General Gates dispatched Colonel Wilkinson to Philadelphia to inform Congress of the victory, but he intentionally failed to send a dispatch to inform General Washington. Wilkinson delivered the letter (dated 18 October) from Gates to Congress on 31 October, and he also gave his version of event to Congress. Consequently, Congress, impressed by Wilkinson, promoted him to the rank of brigadier general on 6 November 1777. Arnold and Colonel Daniel Morgan won the day, but Gates received a gold medal. Wilkinson arrived in Philadelphia eighteen days after he left Saratoga and the news of the victory was late. A motion was made to have Congress award a sword to Wilkinson, prompting John Witherspoon to propose something else: "I think ye'd better gie the lad a pair of spurs." Witherspoon's straight-faced sardonic humor caused the motion to vanish.

Wilkinson did receive another reward. He was appointed secretary to the Board of War on 5 January 1778, which placed him in the company of another member, General Gates. During that time, the Conway Cabal was underway and Wilkinson was aligned with those who plotted to relieve General George Washington as commander-in-chief and replace him with Gates. General Wilkinson confided in Lord Stirling (General William Alexander), and by revealing the secret movement, the plot was soon foiled. Lord Stirling, a loyal friend of Washington, relayed the information to his commander-in-chief. General Thomas Conway, the chief instigator, later believing he was on his death bed, apologized to Washington, but he lived.

General Wilkinson immediately lost favor among his fellow officers. Nearly 50 officers demanded that Wilkinson be stripped of his commission. On 6 March 1778, Congress received a letter of resignation from Brigadier General James Wilkinson, which stated in part: "To obviate any embarrassment which may result from this disposition, by the consequent resignation of officers of merit, I beg leave to relinquish my brevet (of brigadier), as I wish to hold no commission unless I can wear it to the honour and advantage of my country. This conduct, however repugnant to fashionable ambition, I find consistent with those principles on which I early drew my sword in the present contest." Congress accepted his resignation. On 31 March 1778, Wilkinson resigned his position as secretary to the Board of War. The resolution accepting his resignation also stated "that his letter be returned as improper to remain on the files of Congress."

Also that year, James married Anne Biddle, the daughter of John and Sarah Owen Biddle of Philadelphia. The Biddle family was among the most prominent in the city. James and Anne had four children, but apparently, their first child died in infancy. The other three were John (died at about fourteen years old), James, and Joseph. On 24 July 1779, James Wilkinson was appointed as clothier general, a position he held until 27 March 1781, when he resigned.

In 1782, General Wilkinson was made a brigadier general in the Pennsylvania militia. He moved to Lexington, Kentucky, and at the time, the Spanish controlled navigation on that part of the Mississippi River leading to New Orleans and the Gulf of Mexico, and the Spanish prohibited U.S. shipping. Wilkinson concluded that if he could arrange an agreement with the Spanish to grant him shipping rights, he would strike it rich. During 1787, his scheme was been successful in part by bribing the Spanish commandant at Natchez with two thoroughbreds, and the produce grown in Kentucky was about to head down the river. Meanwhile, Wilkinson traveled by land, heading to New Orleans to meet the flatboat there. Prior to Wilkinson's arrival, the flatboat arrived in New Orleans and as usual, it was confiscated by the Spaniards. Once Wilkinson arrived, he and the governor worked out yet another deal that cost Wilkinson about $2,000 per year as a pension to the governor to gain exclusive shipping rights. The flatboat was instantly released.

Wilkinson's actions were against American policy, and in fact, created more problems. The blockage of the Mississippi River prompted some Americans to consider separating from the United States government to form a separate republic aligned with the Spanish. The settlers combined their complaints of the river blockage and the inability of the government to protect the settlements from Indian attacks as the primary reasons for trying to separate western Kentucky from eastern Kentucky. With immense funding of Spanish gold, Wilkinson, by June of 1788, had garnered the support of a majority in the region for the proposed separation. The stage was set and a convention was scheduled for 28 July 1788, at which time a new constitution would be established for the new state of Kentucky; however, complications developed when the Spanish representative, Diego Gardoqui, inserted a new condition. He demanded that east and west Kentucky be included in the secession movement. The Spanish sent dispatches to John Sevier, but Sevier in turn contacted Isaac Shelby and others, including Thomas Marshall and George Muter. Afterward, Wilkinson's scheme was foiled and the secession never occurred. Wilkinson afterward lost his golden touch and his business ventures were badly stalled.

During 1791, Wilkinson requested that Congress reinstate him to active service in the army. He was reinstated with the rank of lieutenant colonel commandant during December 1791. Colonel Wilkinson was ordered to join General Anthony Wayne in the Western Department. During 1790, the Virginia legislature appointed General Charles Scott as commander of the Kentucky militia. The next year, Scott led an expedition to the Wabash River to attack the Indians who were responsible for raiding the settlements and villages. General Wilkinson led an expeditionary force into the region, but neither Scott nor Wilkinson was able to vanquish the foe. Neither was General Arthur St. Clair in 1791. Finally, General Anthony Wayne terminated the Indian hostilities at the Battle of Fallen Timbers on 20 October 1794.

Despite his brush with treason, Wilkinson, while in the army, continued clandestine contact with the Spanish officials. It was subsequently discovered that Wilkinson received a pension from the Spanish at least during 1800. The Spanish continued to cause problems for about ten years, but ultimately, the United States prevailed. Wilkinson's military service in the West was considered favorable. Consequently, on 5 March 1792, he was promoted to the rank of brigadier general. Upon the death of General Wayne on 15 December 1796, General Wilkinson became Wayne's successor as the military governor of the Southwest Territory and supreme commander of the United States Army.

On 20 December 1803, the United States assumed control of the Louisiana Territory. At the time, Napoleon controlled Louisiana, and he was at war with Britain. Napoleon, fearful of the land falling into the hands of the British, sold Louisiana to the United States. During 1805, Wilkinson was appointed governor of the Louisiana Territory in conjunction with the establishment of the Louisiana-Missouri Territory on 3 March 1805. That autumn, Wilkinson informed the government of a new scheme, by Aaron Burr, who intended to build yet another empire in the Southwest. At the time of the disclosure, Wilkinson was well aware that the government was holding knowledge of the intrigue and later Burr implicated Wilkinson in the plot. Doubts remain as to whether Wilkinson was the chief instigator.

Wilkinson did receive a court-martial, on allegations of receiving money from the Spanish government and his relationship with the Aaron Burr conspiracy, but General Wilkinson was acquitted due to insufficient evidence against him. General Peter Gansevoort presided as chair at Wilkinson's court-martial which ended on Christmas Day, 1811, with a not guilty verdict.

General Wilkinson's wife, Betty, succumbed in 1807. Afterward, James married Celeste Laveau Trudeau and they had several children, including twins. General Wilkinson was appointed as a major general on 2 March 1813 and ordered to the Northern Department. Wilkinson fared poorly during an incursion into Canada against Montreal, and friction arose between him and General Wade Hampton. The difficulties led to a court of inquiry in 1815, and again, Wilkinson was exonerated.

General Wilkinson remained in the service, but he reverted to tactics he had used during the Revolutionary War, complaining about the commander-in-chief, the difference being, his present commander was the president, James Madison, and the conflict, although still against the British, was the War of 1812. Wilkinson's actions caused him to be recalled to the capital. General Wilkinson was dismissed from the army on 15 June 1815. General Wilkinson, influenced by new visions of adventure and wealth, traveled to Mexico in an effort to acquire land. He died while in Mexico on 28 December 1825.

Williams, Brigadier General David Rogerson
The son of David and Anne Rogerson Williams and the grandson of Reverend Robert Williams, David was born in Robbins Neck, South Carolina, on 8 March 1776. David's father died prematurely on 1 January 1776, a few months before he was born. David's mother married Captain Jeremiah Brown during 1782. David received his education initially in Wrentham, Massachusetts, and afterward, he entered Rhode Island College (later Brown University) in Providence, Rhode Island. It was the first Baptist college in America. During January 1795, David was informed that "the remittances from his plantation in South Carolina failed him and he went south to investigate the cause." He began his southward journey on 11 January, and upon his arrival in South Carolina he was told that his plantation was so far in debt that it held no value. He was urged to sell it. Nonetheless, David refused: "I will not buy another hat until my inheritance is redeemed." The financial crisis prevented him from returning to college; however, his circumstances were taken under consideration, along with his excellent scholastic record while in school. The college did award him his degree in 1801. Meanwhile, he was admitted to the bar during 1797.

Williams began to practice law in Providence and remained there for several years. In 1796, he returned to New England and married Sarah Power, the daughter of Captain Nicholas and Rebecca Corey Power of Providence. Their first child, John Nicholas Williams, was born on 2 July 1797. In December 1799, a second child, George Frederick, was born in Providence, but he died as a young boy in 1810. Sarah died in February 1803. During 1801, David became the owner of the *City Gazette* and the *Weekly Carolina Gazette* in Charleston, South Carolina, from 1801 to 1803. During 1803, the *Weekly Carolina Gazette* initiated a venture of raising cotton and manufacturing in Darlington County. Williams continued to be involved with the planting and manufacturing until he died. He also built the first cotton seed mill in the state of South Carolina about 1812; it was a five-story structure that extended about 200 feet in length. He was also thought to be the first planter in South Carolina to protect his fields from the river by "banking the river." His manufactured items included hats, hemp cordage and shoes. General Williams also constructed a machine "for the manufacturing of cotton seed oil."

In 1805, Williams was elected as a Republican to the Ninth and Tenth Congresses (4 March 1805 through 3 March 1809). In November 1809, he remarried, taking Elizabeth Witherspoon, the daughter of John and Mary Conn Witherspoon of Pee Dee, as his second wife. Later, he was elected to the Twelfth Congress (4 March 1811 to 3 March 1813). He entered the military and was appointed brigadier general on 9 July 1813. Nevertheless, his military career was short-lived. Initially he served in the South (Seventh District), but he was ordered to the North, where he became ill before the Battle of Lundy's Lane. General Williams resigned from the service on 6 April 1814. That year, General Williams was elected governor of South Carolina, a post he held until 1816. He then served in the state Senate from 1824 until 17 November 1830.

Elizabeth Williams owned a ferry that operated on Lynch's Creek. She received it from her Uncle Robert Witherspoon. In an effort to build a bridge at the crossing, General Williams personally supervised the project. However, on the opposite bank, while the trestles were being placed, the beams fell and Williams became trapped along with some of the Negro workers. General Williams insisted that his workers were to be rescued before him and they were. General Williams died from his injuries on the following day, 11 November 1830. General Williams was interred at the family cemetery.

While on the Niagara frontier, General Williams served under General Boyd. He had not participated in any major engagements and was anxious to command on the field of battle. He requested to be transferred to the Southern Theater to participate against the Creeks. Afterward, many of the details are unclear. He arrived in Washington on 29 September 1813. In November, the *Carolina Gazette* published an article stating that General Williams had departed from Charleston en route to join the Southern Army. At the time, it was thought that he would assume command of General Floyd's army; however, there were no troops for him to command. General Williams had actually tendered his resignation to Secretary of War John Armstrong on 8 December 1813, but it was not accepted until the 6 April 1814. There is no documentation that General Williams ever commanded any forces after he arrived in the South.

Winchester, Brigadier General James James, the son of William and Lydia Richards Winchester, was born on 6 February 1752. David's father arrived in America at Annapolis, Maryland, in March 1729. In addition to James, his parents had the following children: Katherine (born November 1748, married Edward Hotchkiss, died October 1815); William (born December 1750, married Mary Parks, died April 1812); Mary (born October 1755, married a Mr. Roberts, first name unknown —, died October 1799); George (born March 1757 —, died July 1794, unmarried); Richard (born April 1759, married Rebecca Lawrence); Stephen (born May 1761, married Sally Howard, died April 1815); Elizabeth (born August 1763, died unmarried during June 1847); Lydia (born December 1766, died unmarried in April 1849); David (born December 1766, died unmarried April 1849); and David (born April 1769, died unmarried in January 1835). James entered the service at the time the hostilities erupted.

During May 1778, James was appointed a lieutenant in the Maryland 3rd Regiment. He was captured by the British and exchanged on 22 December 1780. He participated in the Yorktown campaign and was present when Sir Charles Cornwallis surrendered his army to George Washington in October 1781. During 1782, he was promoted to the rank of captain. He resigned from the service in August 1783. After the American Revolution, James, along with his brother George, relocated in Tennessee in 1784. The two brothers built a mill and acquired a large tract in present-day Memphis. On 9 July 1794, George was killed by Indians when he was ambushed near present-day Gallatin.

James Winchester was commissioned as a brigadier general during March 1812. The following September, General Winchester arrived at Fort Wayne (Indiana) to succeed General William Henry Harrison as commander of the Northwestern Army. The change in command was not well received by the troops. Meanwhile, Governor Isaac Shelby of Kentucky had written to William Eustis on 5 September urging that General Winchester be replaced by General Harrison. On 24 September Harrison received a dispatch: "The President [Madison] is pleased to assign to you the command of the Northwestern Army which in addition to the regular troops and rangers in that quarter, will consist of the volunteers and militia of Kentucky, Ohio, and three thousand from Virginia and Pennsylvania, making your whole force ten thousand men."

Meanwhile, on 22 September, General Winchester, at Fort Wayne, wrote to Governor Meigs of Ohio to request reinforcements to bolster his force for an attack against British-held Detroit: "I rejoice at the prospect of regaining lost territory and with hope to winter in Detroit or its vicinity. You will please furnish two regiments of soldiers to join me at the foot of the lowest Maumee Rapids about the 10th or 15th of October, well clothed for a fall campaign. It is extremely desirous to me that no time be lost in supplying this requisition. The cold season is fast approaching, and the stain on the American character by the surrender of Detroit not yet wiped away."

On the night of 21 January 1813, the British moved to attack General Winchester's camp near the Raisin River. General Winchester, however, had been overconfident and despite warnings, he took no precautions and failed to post a sufficient guard. The British struck during the early morning hours of the 22nd and General Winchester was captured. Winchester was not even in camp. He was at his headquarters about one mile outside of the camp. Despite the debacle that had unfolded, some troops refused to capitulate. Colonel Proctor, the British commander, coerced Winchester to persuade those troops (Kentuckians, under Lt. George Madison) to surrender, but the reply was that with Winchester as a prisoner, his order was invalid. Eventually they surrendered on terms proposed by Madison; however, the Indians began to massacre many of the troops. The attack, remembered as the Raisin River Massacre, cost the Americans about 900 casualties, including about 400 killed or missing, with the remainder being captured. Fewer 35 troops escaped. The devastating loss compelled General Harrison to suspend his attack against Detroit. On the 23rd, General Winchester, while a prisoner, wrote a letter to John Armstrong: "However unfortunate may seem the affair of yesterday, I am flattered by a belief, that no material error is chargeable upon myself, and that still less censure is deserved by the troops I had the honor of commanding. With the exception of that portion of our force which was thrown into disorder, no troops have ever behaved with a more determined intrepidity."

General Winchester was exchanged during spring 1814. Upon his return to the United States he was ordered to assume command at Mobile, Alabama. His final communication from Mobile occurred on 17 February 1815 when he wrote to Secretary of War James Monroe that Fort Bowyer had fallen to the British. One month later, March 1815, General Winchester resigned from the army. He returned to Tennessee, where he remained until his death on 27 July 1826.

General Winchester and his wife, Susan Black Winchester, had the following children: Mabcus, Napoleon, Valebus, Caroline, Laura, and Maria. Susan died on 19 February 1809. She was interred at Westminster, Maryland. General Winchester, upon his death, was interred in the same churchyard.

Winder, Brigadier General William Henry William, the son of William and Charlotte Henry Winder, was born 18 February 1775 in Somerset County, Maryland. His mother was the sister of Governor John Henry (1797–1798). After receiving his elementary education, William Henry entered the University of Pennsylvania, where he studied law. Subsequent to his graduation and passing the bar, William began his law practice in the city of Baltimore in 1798. Just before war was declared against the British in 1812, William was appointed lieutenant colonel of the U.S. 14th Infantry; however, he had no military experience. In July 1812, he was raised to full colonel.

Colonel Winder participated in the actions on the Niagara frontier, and in March 1813, he was promoted to brigadier general. Meanwhile, on 28 November 1812, Colonel Winder, leading elements of the 12th, 13th, 14th and 15th U.S. Regiments and bolstered by a small naval contingent, sailed from New York at Black Rock as part of the attack to seize Fort Erie, defended by only about 80 British regulars (49th British Regiment) and about 50 troops of the Newfoundland Regiment and some militia. Nevertheless, the Americans were repelled. Later in the day, General Alexander Smyth demanded the surrender of Fort Erie, and prepared to launch his main attack; however, he changed his mind while troops were in the river and postponed the assault until 1 December. Nevertheless, elements of the American vanguard were left stranded. By aborting the attack, no reinforcements could reach the remainder of the vanguard. General Peter B. Porter accused General Smyth of cowardice and the accusation led to a duel. Colonel Winder and Lt. Samuel H. Angus acted as seconds. Neither antagonist was injured; Smyth and Porter reconciled their differences.

During April 1813, the country was divided

into nine military districts with a tenth district being established later. General Winder was assigned to the Ninth District — New York extending north from the Highlands and Vermont. The district was commanded by General Dearborn. In May 1813, General Winder participated in the attack to seize Fort George in Canada. He and General John Chandler were captured on 6 June at Stoney Creek when the British launched a surprise attack against the American camp. An after battle report by General Dearborn, who was not present, erroneously stated that Chandler and Winder were captured while attacking an artillery position. The report also stated that British General Vincent was killed; however, he was not present.

After his release, General Winder arrived in the capital on 29 April 1814. On 19 May, he was named adjutant and inspector general, and as chief of staff of the Northern Army. On 2 July, he relinquished the post to assume command of the 10th Military District, which gave him responsibility for defending the capital. The selection of Winder as commander caused a rift in the cabinet. Secretary of War John Armstrong became livid after his choice for commander, General Moses Porter, had been discarded in favor of Winder, the nephew of Governor Levin Winder of Maryland. During August, Winder's forces took a beating at Bladensburg, and on the 18th, the British occupied Washington without incident. Afterward, a hurricane forced the British to evacuate the capital; however, British General Ross was intent on taking Baltimore. Fort McHenry withstood the assaults, naval and land. It was during that struggle that Francis Scott Key penned his famous poem that later became the national anthem, "The Star Spangled Banner."

On 21 January 1815, a court inquiry was convened to deal with General Winder's actions at Bladensburg. On 25 February, the court ruled unanimously he was not guilty of any wrongdoing. After the war, General Winder resigned from the service on 24 May 1815, then served two terms in the Maryland Senate. He died on 24 May 1824 and was interred at Green Mount Cemetery in Baltimore. General Winder's son, John Henry, graduated West Point and served in the artillery during the Mexican War, then resigned from the U.S. Army to join the Confederacy.

Appendix A.
Generals, U.S. Army and Militia, War of 1812 Era

This list includes commodores, an honorary rank given to captains prior to the initiation of the rank of admiral during 1862 (BG: brigadier general; MG: major general).

Adair, General John
Adams, BG David, GA
Addams (Adams), BG John, PA
Allen, BG James, KY
Appleton, BG James
Armstrong, BG General John, U.S. Army
Ashley, BG William H., MO
Atcheson, MG Thomas, PA
Bainbridge, Commodore William
Banks, MG James, PA
Barnes, MG Hezekia, VT
Barringer, BG Daniel, NC
Barringer, BG John Paul, NC
Bartram, BG George, PA
Beall, BG Edward, GA
Beall, BG Frederick, GA
Beall, MG Joseph, OH
Beall, BG Reasin, OH militia
Bedel, BG Moody, NH
Benson, BG Perry, MD
Biddle, Commodore James
Bissell, BG Daniel, U.S. Army
Blackshear, General John
Blake, MG John Brewer, ME
Bliss, BG Jacob, MA
Bloomfield, BG (later MG) Joseph, PA
Boden, BG John, PA
Borrows, MG John, PA
Bower, BG Jacob, PA
Bowie, MG Robert
Boyd, BG John Parker, U.S. Army
Breckinridge, BG James, VA
Bright, BG Michael, PA
Brooke (Brooks), BG William, PA
Brown, MG Jacob Jennings, U.S. Army
Brown, BG John, MD
Brown, BG John, PA
Brown, MG Thomas, NC
Burbeck, BG Henry, U.S. Army
Butler, MG Henry, NH
Butler, MG William Orlando, KY
Byrd, BG William, GA
Cadwalader, BG John

Cadwalader, General Thomas, PA militia
Caldwell, BG Samuel, KY
Calmes, BG Marquis, KY
Carroll, General William
Cass, BG Lewis, U.S. Army
Chandler, BG John, ME
Chauncey, Commodore Isaac
Chiles, BG David, KY
Claiborne, General Ferdinand L.
Clark, MG John, GA
Clark, General William
Clarkson, General Matthew, NY militia
Clay, General Green
Cobb, General David Goldsborough, ME
Coburn, BG Simon, MA
Cocke, BG John H., VA militia
Cocke, BG William, TN
Coffee, BG John, GA
Coffee, BG John TN
Colfax, MG William, NJ militia
Collins, BG Oliver, NY militia
Courtlandt, BG Pierre William, Jr., NY militia
Covington, BG Leonard, U.S. Army
Cowles, MG Solomon, CT
Craig, BG Alexander, PA
Craig, MG Thomas, PA
Crane, MG Elijah, MA
Crooks, BG Richard, PA
Crosby, General John, ME militia
Cunningham, BG John W., PA
Curtenius, BG Peter, NY militia
Cushing, BG Thomas Humphrey, U.S. Army
Davis, BG Amasa, MA state troops
Davis, BG Aquila, NH
Davis, BG Daniel, NY militia
Davis, MG David, GA
Davis, BG Thomas, NC
Dearborn, MG Henry, U.S. Army
Decatur, Commodore Stephen
Derby, BG Samuel, MA militia
Desha, MG Joseph, KY
Desha, BG Robert, KY
Dickinson, BG Joseph, NC

Dicks, BG John, PA
Dinsmore, BG Samuel, NH
Dodge, BG Richard, NY
Doty, BG Ezra, PA
Dougherty, BG George, TN
Douglass, BG Hugh
Dudley, BG Peter, VT militia
Duncan, BG William, PA
Eaton, BG William, U.S. Army
Eddy, BG Gilbert, NY
Elliott, Commodore Jessie
Ellis, General John, NY
Elmer, BG Ebenezer, NJ militia
Evans, BG Lewis, PA
Eyster, General Jacob, PA
Farrington, BG Putnam
Felton, BG Boone, NC
Fish, BG Nicholas, NY militia
Flournoy, BG Thomas, GA, U.S. Army
Floyd, MG John, GA
Floyd, BG John, VA
Foote, BG Enoch, CT
Forman, General Thomas, MD
Forster, BG John, PA
Furber, BG Richard, NH
Gaines, BG Edmund Pendleton, U.S. Army
Gano, MG John S., OH militia
Gano, General Richard, OH
Gansevoort, BG Peter
Gettys, BG James, PA
Giles, MG Aquilla, NY cavalry
Gilliland, MG William, PA
Glascock, BG Thomas, GA
Godwin, BG Abraham, NJ
Goodwin, MG Nathaniel, MA
Graham, BG Joseph, NC
Graham, BG Thomas, PA
Gratiot, BG Charles
Haight, BG Samuel S., NY militia
Haile, BG James, NY militia
Hale, MG Samuel, NH
Hall, MG Amos, Niagara frontier
Hamilton, BG Thomas J., GA

354

Generals, U.S. Army and Militia, War of 1812 Era

Hampton, MG Wade, U.S. Army
Harper, BG Robert Goodloe, MD
Harris, BG Jeptha, GA
Harris, BG William, PA
Harrison, BG John, PA
Harrison, MG William Henry, U.S. Army
Hathorn, MG John, NY
Henry, MG William, KY
Hermance (Heermance), BG Martin, NY
Hetrick (Hetrich), BG Christian, PA
Hibshman, BG Jacob, PA
Hilghman, BG Jacob, PA militia
Hinman, BG Ephraim, CT
Holmes, BG David, CT
Hopkins, BG Francis, GA
Hopkins, BG Reuben, NY
Hopkins, MG Samuel, KY
Hopkins, BG Timothy S., NY militia
Hottenstine, BG David, PA
Hovey, MG Amos, MA
Howard, BG Benjamin Chew, MO
Howe, General Hezekia, CT
Hubbard, MG John, CT
Hull, Commodore Isaac
Hull, MG William, U.S. Army
Humphreys, BG David, CT
Hungerford, General John P., VA
Huntley, BG Elisha, NH
Hurd, BG Jabez N.M., NY
Hurst, BG Henry, PA
Irwin, BG John, GA
Isham, General Jirah, CT
Izard, MG George, U.S. Army
Jackson, MG Andrew
Jett, BG Thomas, GA
Johnson, BG Jeremiah, NY militia
Johnson, BG Richard Mentor, TN
Johnson, BG Thomas, TN militia
Johnston, BG Jeremiah, NY
Jones, Commodore Jacob
Kelso, BG John, PA
Kenton, General Simon
King, George Edward, KY
King, General John, KY
King, MG Nathaniel, NY
King, MG William, ME militia
Kreider, BG Conrad, PA
Lazell, BG Sylvanus, MA
Lee, General Henry" "Lighthorse Harry"
Leftwich, BG Jabez, VA
Leftwich, BG Joel, VA
Lewis, MG Morgan, U.S. Army
Light, BG Adam, PA
Lingan, General James Maccubin, MD
Lucas, BG Robert, OH
Lusk, BG Levi, CT
Macdonough, Commodore Thomas
Macomb, BG Alexander, U.S. Army
Marks, BG William, Jr., PA
Martin, MG Charles, PA
Martin, BG Walter, NY militia
Mason, General John, Georgetown
Mason, BG Thomas, PA
Massie, General Nathaniel
Matthews, BG George, GA
Matoon, BG Ebenezer, MA
McAfee, General Robert, KY
McArthur, General Duncan, BG
McClary, BG Michael, NH
McClelland, BG Alexander, PA
McClure, General George, BG
McComb, BG James, PA
McDonald, General Duncan

McDonald, BG John, ME militia
McIntosh, MG Thomas, GA
Mead, MG David, PA
Menary, BG James, OH
Merchant, BG David, PA
Meriwether, BG David
Merriman, BG James, CT
Mertz, BG Henry, PA
Metcalfe, General Thomas P., KY
Miller, BG Daniel, NY
Miller, BG Henry, MD
Miller, BG James, NH
Miller, BG Robert, PA
Millikin, BG Daniel, OH
Mills, BG James, OH
Montgomery, BG John, NH
Mooers, MG Benjamin, NY militia
Moore, BG Arthur, PA
Morgan, BG David Bannister, LA
Morris, Commodore Charles
Munger, BG Edmund, OH
Murray, Commodore Alexander
Murray, BG James, PA
Mynderse, BG Wilhelmus, NY
Newnan, MG, GA
Nicholl, BG A.Y., U.S. Army
Noble, BG John, PA
Odell, BG Jacob, NY militia
Ogden, MG Aaron, NJ, U.S. Army
Ogle, MG Alexander, PA
Paine, BG Edmund, OH
Paine, BG Eleazer
Paine, BG Joel, OH
Paine, BG John, KY
Parker, MG Alexander
Parker, General Daniel
Parker, BG Thomas, U.S. Army
Patterson, Commodore Daniel Todd
Patterson, BG Thomas, PA
Paulding, General William, Jr., NY
Pearce, MG Cromwell, PA
Pearson, BG Jesse A., NC
Pegram, General John, MG
Perkins, BG Simon, OH militia
Perlee, MG Edmund, NY militia
Perry, Commodore Oliver Hazard
Pettit, BG Micajah, NY
Phillips, MG John, PA
Philson, BG Robert, PA
Pike, BG Zebulon Montgomery, U.S. Army
Pinckney, MG Thomas, U.S. Army
Porter, Commodore David
Porter, BG Moses, U.S. Army
Porter, General Peter B.
Porterfield, BG Charles, VA
Porterfield, BG Robert, VA
Posey, BG Thomas
Preston, BG Francis, MD
Putnam, General David, MA
Ramsey, BG Jonathan, KY
Ray, BG James, KY
Rea, MG John, PA
Reid, Captain Chester, U.S. Navy
Richardson, MG Alfred, MA militia
Riddick, BG Joseph, NC
Ringgold, BG Samuel, MD
Ripley, BG Eleazar Wheelock, U.S. Army
Robertson, General James, Indian agent
Robinson, BG Asa, NH
Rodgers, Commodore John
Rose, General Abraham, NY militia
Ross, BG William, PA
Rush, BG Richard

Saylor, BG Jacob, PA
Scheetz, MG Henry, PA
Scott, BG Winfield, U.S. Army
Sewall, MG Henry, ME
Shackleford, BG Edward, GA
Shaw, MG Aeneas
Sheetz (Shietz), MG Henry, PA
Shelby, General Isaac
Shinn, MG William N., NJ militia
Slade, BG Jeremiah, NC
Smith, BG Gerrit (Gerritt), CT
Smith, BG John, NY militia
Smith, Leonard, NY militia
Smith, General Samuel, MD
Smith, BG Samuel, PA
Smith, BG Thomas Adams, U.S. Army
Smith, BG Walter, District of Columbia
Smyth (Smith), BG Alexander, U.S. Army
Snyder, BG Thomas, PA
Spering (Spiring), BG Henry, PA
Stansbury, General Tobias, MD
Steddiford, BG Gerard, NY militia
Steel, MG James, PA
Steel, BG John, NH
Steel, MG William, PA
Steele, BG John, PA
Stevens, MG Ebenezer, NY
Stevens, BG Ebenezer, PA militia
Stevenson, MG James, PA
Stewart, Commodore Charles
Stewart, BG Daniel, GA militia
Stokes, MG Montford, NC
Storer, BG Clement, NH
Stricker, General John, MD
Strong, MG Samuel, VT militia
Stuart, General Philip, MD
Sunbury, BG Suinbury
Swartwout, MG John, NY
Swartwout, BG Robert
Swift, BG John, NY militia
Swift, BG Joseph Gardner, U.S. Army
Tannehill, MG Adamson
Taul, General Micah
Taylor, MG Augustine, CT
Taylor, BG James, KY
Taylor, General Robert R.
Taylor, BG Robert V., VA
Terry, BG Nathaniel, CT
Terry, BG Nathaniel, KY
Thomas, MG Jett, GA
Thomas, General John, KY
Thomas, BG Philemon, LA
Thompson, BG David, CT
Thompson, BG David, KY
Thompson, MG Wiley, GA
Tingey, Commodore Thomas
Towson, BG General Nathan, MD
Trotter, BG George, KY
Tryon, BG Moses, Jr., CT
Tupper, General Edward W., OH militia
Turner, BG John, MA
Udree, MG Daniel, PA
Van Courtland, BG Pierre, NY
Van Orden, BG Peter S., NY
Van Ness, General John Peter, VA militia
Van Rensselaer, General Stephen
Varnum, MG Joseph B., MA militia
Villere, MG Jacques Philippe
Waddell, BG Thomas, PA
Wadsworth, MG Elijah, OH militia
Wadsworth, General William, NY militia
Walker, MG Valentine, GA
Warrington, Commodore Lewis

Watson, MG Nathaniel, PA
Welborn (Wellborn), BG James, NC
Welborn (Wellborn), MG William, NC
Wells (Welles), BG Arnold, MA
Wells, BG Henry, PA
Wells, BG Isaiah, PA
Westbrook, BG Frederick, NY
Wharton, BG Robert, PA
Whitcomb, MG Philemon, NH
White, General James
White, General William
Whitehill, MG James, PA
Wickham, BG George D., NY
Widrig, MG George, NY
Wilkinson, MG James, U.S. Army
Williams, BG David Rogerson, U.S. Army
Williams, BG Jonathan, CT
Williams, BG Robert, VA
Williams, MG William, CT
Williamson, BG John, OH
Wilson, MG John, PA
Winchester, BG James, TN, U.S. Army
Winder, BG Levin, MD
Winder, BG William Henry, U.S. Army
Wingate, BG John, OH
Winlock, BG Joseph
Woodward, General Thomas S.
Wool, General John E.
Worrall (Worrel), MG Isaac, PA militia
Worth, General William Jenkins
Wright, BG Daniel, NY
Wynn, BG Thomas
Wynns, BG Thomas

Young, General Robert, District of Columbia militia
Young, BG William, PA

Appendix B.
James Madison's War Message to Congress, June 1, 1812

To the Senate and House of Representatives of the United States:

I communicate to Congress certain documents, being a continuation of those heretofore laid before them on the subject of our affairs with Great Britain.

Without going back beyond the renewal in 1803 of the war in which Great Britain is engaged, and omitting unrepaired wrongs of inferior magnitude, the conduct of her Government presents a series of acts hostile to the United States as an independent and neutral nation.

British cruisers have been in the continued practice of violating the American flag on the great highway of nations, and of seizing and carrying off persons sailing under it, not in the exercise of a belligerent right founded on the law of nations against an enemy, but of a municipal prerogative over British subjects. British jurisdiction is thus extended to neutral vessels in a situation where no laws can operate but the law of nations and the laws of the country to which the vessels belong, and a self-redress is assumed which, if British subjects were wrongfully detained and alone concerned, is that substitution of force for a resort to the responsible sovereign which falls within the definition of war. Could the seizure of British subjects in such cases be regarded as within the exercise of a belligerent right, the acknowledged laws of war, which forbid an article of captured property to be adjudged without a regular investigation before a competent tribunal, would imperiously demand the fairest trial where the sacred rights of persons were at issue. In place of such a trial these rights are subjected to the will of every petty commander.

The practice, hence, is so far from affecting British subjects alone that, under the pretext of searching for these, thousands of American citizens, under the safeguard of public law and of their national flag, have been torn from their country and from everything dear to them; have been dragged on board ships of war of a foreign nation and exposed, under the severities of their discipline, to be exiled to the most distant and deadly climes, to risk their lives in the battles of their oppressors, and to be the melancholy instruments of taking away those of their own brethren.

Against this crying enormity, which Great Britain would be so prompt to avenge if committed against herself, the United States have in vain exhausted remonstrances and expostulations, and that no proof might be wanting of their conciliatory dispositions, and no pretext left for a continuance of the practice, the British Government was formally assured of the readiness of the United States to enter into arrangements such as could not be rejected if the recovery of British subjects were the real and the sole object. The communication passed without effect.

British cruisers have been in the practice also of violating the rights and the peace of our coasts. They hover over and harass our entering and departing commerce. To the most insulting pretensions they have added the most lawless proceedings in our very harbors, and have wantonly spilt American blood within the sanctuary of our territorial jurisdiction. The principles and rules enforced by that nation, when a neutral nation, against armed vessels of belligerents hovering near her coasts and disturbing her commerce are well known. When called on, nevertheless, by the United States to punish the greater offenses committed by her own vessels, her Government has bestowed on their commanders additional marks of honor and confidence.

Under pretended blockades, without the presence of an adequate force and sometimes without the practicability of applying one, our commerce has been plundered in every sea, the great staples of our country have been cut off from their legitimate markets, and a destructive blow aimed at our agricultural and maritime interests. In aggravation of these predatory measures they have been considered as in force from the dates of their notification, a retrospective effect being thus added, as has been done in other important cases, to the unlawfulness of the course pursued. And to render the outrage the more signal these mock blockades have been reiterated and enforced in the face of official communications from the British Government declaring as the true definition of a legal blockade "that particular ports must be actually invested and previous warning given to vessels bound to them not to enter."

Not content with these occasional expedients for laying waste our neutral trade, the cabinet of Britain resorted at length to the sweeping system of blockades, under the name of orders in council, which has been molded and managed as might best suit its political views, its commercial jealousies, or the avidity of British cruisers.

To our remonstrances against the complicated and transcendent injustice of this innovation the first reply was that the orders were reluctantly adopted by Great Britain as a necessary retaliation on decrees of her enemy proclaiming a general blockade of the British Isles at a time when the naval force of that enemy dared not issue from his own ports. She was reminded without effect that her own prior blockades, unsupported by an adequate naval force actually applied and continued, were a bar to this plea; that executed edicts against millions of our property could not be retaliation on edicts confessedly impossible to be executed; that retaliation, to be just, should fall on the party setting the guilty example, not on an innocent party which was not even chargeable with an acquiescence in it.

When deprived of this flimsy veil for a prohibition of our trade with her enemy by the repeal of his prohibition of our trade with Great Britain, her cabinet, instead of a corresponding repeal or a practical discontinuance of its orders, formally avowed a determination to persist in them against the United States until the markets of her enemy should be laid open to British products, thus asserting an obligation on a neutral power to require one belligerent to encourage by its internal regulations the trade of another belligerent, contradicting her own practice toward all nations, in peace as well as in war, and betraying the insincerity of those professions which inculcated a belief that, having resorted to her orders with regret, she was anxious to find an occasion for putting an end to them.

Abandoning still more all respect for the neutral rights of the United States and for its own consistency, the British Government now demands as prerequisites to a repeal of its orders as they relate to the United States that a formality should be observed in the repeal of the French decrees nowise necessary to their termination nor exemplified by British usage, and that the French repeal, besides including that portion of the decrees which operates within a territorial jurisdiction, as well as that which operates on the high seas, against the commerce of the United States should not be a single and special repeal in relation to the United States, but should be extended to whatever other neutral nations unconnected with them may be affected by those decrees. And as an additional insult, they are called on for a formal disavowal of conditions and pretensions advanced by the French Government for which the United States are so far from having made themselves responsible that, in official explanations which have been published to the world, and in a correspondence of the American minister at London with the British minister for foreign affairs such a responsibility was explicitly and emphatically disclaimed.

It has become, indeed, sufficiently certain that the commerce of the United States is to be sacrificed, not as interfering with the belligerent rights of Great Britain; not as supplying the wants of her enemies, which she herself supplies; but as interfering with the monopoly which she covets for her own commerce and navigation. She carries on a war against the lawful commerce of a friend that she may the better carry on a commerce with an enemy — a commerce polluted by the forgeries and perjuries which are for the most part the only passports by which it can succeed.

Anxious to make every experiment short of the last resort of injured nations, the United States have withheld from Great Britain, under successive modifications, the benefits of a free intercourse with their market, the loss of which could not but outweigh the profits accruing from her restrictions of our commerce with other nations. And to entitle these experiments to the more favorable consideration they were so framed as to enable her to place her adversary under the exclusive operation of them. To these appeals her Government has been equally inflexible, as if willing to make sacrifices of every sort rather than yield to the claims of justice or renounce the errors of a false pride. Nay, so far were the attempts carried to overcome the attachment of the British cabinet to its unjust edicts that it received every encouragement within the competency of the executive branch of our Government to expect that a repeal of them would be followed by a war between the United States and France, unless the French edicts should also be repealed. Even this communication, although silencing forever the plea of a disposition in the United States to acquiesce in those edicts originally the sole plea for them, received no attention.

If no other proof existed of a predetermination of the British Government against a repeal of its orders, it might be found in the correspondence of the minister plenipotentiary of the United States at London and the British secretary for foreign affairs in 1810, on the question whether the blockade of May, 1806, was considered as in force or as not in force. It had been ascertained that the French Government, which urged this blockade as the ground of its Berlin decree, was willing in the event of its removal, to repeal that decree, which, being followed by alternate repeals of the other offensive edicts, might abolish the whole system on both sides. This inviting opportunity for accomplishing an object so important to the United States, and professed so often to be the desire of both the belligerents, was made known to the British Government. As that Government admits that an actual application of an adequate force is necessary to the existence of a legal blockade, and it was notorious that if such a force had ever been applied its long discontinuance had annulled the blockade in question, there could be no sufficient objection on the part of Great Britain to a formal revocation of it, and no imaginable objection to a declaration of the fact that the blockade did not exist. The declaration would have been consistent with her avowed principles of blockade, and would have enabled the United States to demand from France the pledged repeal of her decrees, either with success, in which case the way would have been opened for a general repeal of the belligerent edicts, or without success, in which case the United States would have been justified in turning their measures exclusively against France. The British Government would, however, neither rescind the blockade nor declare its nonexistence, nor permit its non-existence to be inferred and affirmed by the American plenipotentiary. On the contrary, by representing the blockade to be comprehended in the orders in council, the United States were compelled so to regard it in their subsequent proceedings.

There was a period when a favorable change in the policy of the British cabinet was justly considered as established. The minister plenipotentiary of His Britannic Majesty here proposed an adjustment of the differences more immediately endangering the harmony of the two countries. The proposition was accepted with the promptitude and cordiality corresponding with the invariable professions of this Government. A foundation appeared to be laid for a sincere and lasting reconciliation. The prospect, however, quickly vanished. The whole proceeding was disavowed by the British Government without any explanations which could at that time repress the belief that the disavowal proceeded from a spirit of hostility to the commercial rights and prosperity of the United States; and it has since come into proof that at the very moment when the public minister was holding the language of friendship and inspiring confidence in the sincerity of the negotiation with which he was charged a secret agent of his Government was employed in intrigues having for their object a subversion of our Government and a dismemberment of our happy union.

In reviewing the conduct of Great Britain toward the United States our attention is necessarily drawn to the warfare just renewed by the savages on one of our extensive frontiers — a warfare which is known to spare neither age nor sex and to be distinguished by features peculiarly shocking to humanity. It is difficult to account for the activity and combinations which have for some time been developing themselves among tribes in constant intercourse with British traders and garrisons without connecting their hostility with that influence and without recollecting the authenticated examples of such interpositions heretofore furnished by the officers and agents of that Government.

Such is the spectacle of injuries and indignities which have been heaped on our country, and such the crisis which its unexampled forbearance and conciliatory efforts have not been able to avert. It might at least have been expected that an enlightened nation, if less urged by moral obligations or invited by friendly dispositions on the part of the United States, would have found its true interest alone a sufficient motive to respect their rights and their tranquillity on the high seas; that an enlarged policy would have favored that free and general circulation of commerce in which the British nation is at all times interested, and which in times of war is the best alleviation of its calamities to herself as well as to other belligerents; and more especially that the British cabinet would not, for the sake of a precarious and surreptitious intercourse with hostile markets, have persevered in a course of measures which necessarily put at hazard the invaluable market of a great and growing country, disposed to cultivate the mutual advantages of an active commerce.

Other counsels have prevailed. Our moderation and conciliation have had no other effect than to encourage perseverance and to enlarge pretensions. We behold our seafaring citizens still the daily victims of lawless violence, committed on the great common and highway of nations, even within sight of the country which owes them protection. We behold our vessels, freighted with the products of our soil and industry, or returning with the honest proceeds of them, wrested from their lawful destinations, confiscated by prize courts no longer the organs of public law but the instruments of arbitrary edicts, and their unfortunate crews dispersed and lost, or forced or inveigled in British ports into British fleets, whilst arguments are employed in support of these aggressions which have no foundation but in a principle equally supporting a claim to regulate our external commerce in all cases whatsoever.

We behold, in fine, on the side of Great Britain, a state of war against the United States, and on the side of the United States a state of peace toward Great Britain.

James Madison's War Message to Congress, June 1, 1812

Whether the United States shall continue passive under these progressive usurpations and these accumulating wrongs, or, opposing force to force in defense of their national rights, shall commit a just cause into the hands of the Almighty Disposer of Events, avoiding all connections which might entangle it in the contest or views of other powers, and preserving a constant readiness to concur in an honorable re-establishment of peace and friendship, is a solemn question which the Constitution wisely confides to the legislative department of the Government. In recommending it to their early deliberations I am happy in the assurance that the decision will be worthy the enlightened and patriotic councils of a virtuous, a free, and a powerful nation.

Having presented this view of the relations of the United States with Great Britain and of the solemn alternative growing out of them, I proceed to remark that the communications last made to Congress on the subject of our relations with France will have shewn that since the revocation of her decrees, as they violated the neutral rights of the United States, her Government has authorized illegal captures by its privateers and public ships, and that other outrages have been practised on our vessels and our citizens. It will have been seen also that no indemnity had been provided or satisfactorily pledged for the extensive spoliations committed under the violent and retrospective orders of the French Government against the property of our citizens seized within the jurisdiction of France. I abstain at this time from recommending to the consideration of Congress definitive measures with respect to that nation, in the expectation that the result of unclosed discussions between our minister plenipotentiary at Paris and the French Government will speedily enable Congress to decide with greater advantage on the course due to the rights, the interests, and the honor of our country.

Appendix C.
Prizes of American Privateers and Vessels Under Letters of Marque, Captured on Unspecified Days, 1812–1815

This list is not all-inclusive. Many other unnamed vessels were also taken by American privateers.

1812

The brigantine *Pursuit* seized by the *Rapid*; the brigantine *Tay* seized by the *Rapid*; the 6-gun ship *Britannia*, captured by the *Thrasher*; the 6-gun brigantine *Howe*, seized by the *Dart*; the brigantine *Elizabeth* (out of Liverpool), captured by the *Decatur*; the 7-gun brigantine *Ocean*, seized by the *Saratoga*; the 12-gun ship *Esther* captured by the *Montgomery* out of Salem; the 16-gun ship *Quebec* seized by the *Saratoga*; the ship *Richmond* captured by the *Thomas*; the 12-gun ship *Adonis*, of Greenock, seized by the *Montgomery*;

The 14-gun ship *Falmouth*, seized by the *Thomas*; the brigantine *Two Friends*, captured by the *Benjamin Franklin*; the 6-gun privateer *Snow Friends*, seized by the *Dart*; the schooner *Trial*, seized by the *Leader*, out of Providence; the schooner *John and George*, captured by the *Regulator*; the schooner *Mary Ann*, seized by the *Mack Joke* out of New York; the brigantine *Hannah*, captured by the *Montgomery*; the schooner *Mary*, seized by the *Mack Joke*; the 2-gun brigantine *Pomona*, seized by the *Decatur*;

The brigantine *Devonshire*, captured by the *Decatur*; the brigantine *Concord*, seized by the *Dart* and destroyed at sea; the brigantine *Hope*, seized by the *Dart*; the schooner *Minorca*, captured by the *Wasp* of Baltimore; the barque *William and Charlotte* seized by the *Decatur*; the 11-gun ship *Grenada* and the armed schooner *Shadock*, captured by the 1-gun privateer *Young Eagle* out of New York; the brigantine *Roebuck* seized by the *Rosamond* of New York; brigantine *Henry* seized by the *Yankee* operating out of Bristol; the 14-gun ship *Hopewell* captured by the *Comet*; 6-gun brigantine *Hazard*, captured by the *Dolphin* out of Salem and recaptured by the frigate *Eolus*, then taken into Boston by the USS *Wasp*;

The schooner *Forebe and Phoebe*, seized by the *Squando*; the brigantine *Thetir*, by the *Yankee* of Bristol; brigantine *Alfred*, taken by the *Yankee*; brigantine *Antelope*, seized by the *Dolphin* of Salem; the ship *Kitty*, captured by the *Rossie*; the schooner *Spunk*, captured by the *Fair Trade* out of Salem; the schooner *Providence*, seized by the *Wiley Reynard*, operating out of Boston;

The 8-gun ship *Guayana*, taken by the *Dromo* out of Boston; the 8-gun barque *Duke of Savoy*, captured by the *Decatur* operating out of Newburyport; the ship *Evergreen*, seized by the *Dolphin*; the 4-gun brigantine *New Liverpool*, seized by the *Yankee*; the 12-gun ship *Mary Ann*, seized by the *Highflyer* of Baltimore; the 10-gun ship *Henry*, seized by the *Comet*; the schooner *Alfred*, captured by the privateer *Spencer*, operating out of Philadelphia;

The brigantine *Resolution*, seized by the *Nancy*, operating out of Portsmouth, N.H.; the transport ship *Lord*, seized by the *Mars*; the transport ship *Canada*, captured by the *Paul Jones*; the brigantine *John and Isabella*, captured by the *Paul Jones*; the ship *Neptune*, seized by the *Saratoga*; the ship *Mentor*, seized by the *Saucy Jack*, operating out of Charleston;

The schooner *Huzzar*, captured by the *Liberty*, operating out of Baltimore; the brigantine *Antrim*, seized by the *Saucy Jack*; the ship *Marianna*, taken by the *Governor McKean* of Philadelphia; the brigantine *Isabella*, seized by the *Teazer*; the brigantine *Diana*, seized by the *Dart*; the 14-gun ship *John*, captured by the *Comet* out of Baltimore; the 14-gun ship *Commerce*, taken by the *Decatur* out of Newburyport;

The privateer-schooner *Frances*, seized by *Dolphin*; the brigantine *Tor Abbey*, captured by the *Thrasher*; the schooner *Jenny*, seized by the *Teazer*; the schooner *Adela* sailing under Spanish colors, taken by the *Rosamond*, out of New York; the brigantine *Brig Point Shares*, seized by the letter of marque schooner *Baltimore*;

The brigantine *San Antonio*, sailing under Spanish colors, captured by the *Marengo*, out of New York; the schooner *Single Cap*, seized by the *Matilda* of Philadelphia; the schooner *Fame*, taken by the *Nonsuch*, operating out of Baltimore; the 12-gun ship *Phoenix*, captured by the *Mary Ann*; the brigantine *Favorite*, seized by the *Industry*; the brigantine *Sir John Moore*, seized by the *Industry*;

The brigantine *Lord Sheffield*, taken by the *Marengo*; the schooner *Betsey Ann*, seized by the privateer *Fame*; the brigantine *Henry*, captured by the *John* out of Salem; the schooner *Four Brothers*, seized by the *Fame*; the schooner *Four Sons*, captured by the *Fame*; the schooner *Antelope*, seized by the *Rosamond*; the schooner *Dawson*, seized by the *Wasp*, operating out of Baltimore;

The sloop *Venus*, captured by the *Two Brothers*, out of New Orleans; the brigantine *Jane and Charlotte*, seized by the *Nonsuch*; the brigantine *Porgie*, seized by the *Highflyer*; the 10-gun ship *Ned*, seized by the *John and George*; the schooner *Robin*, taken by the *Revenge*, operating out of Salem;

The 10-gun brigantine *John*, seized by the *Benjamin Franklin* out of New York; the schooner *Three Sisters*, taken by the *Fame*; the schooner *Comet*, captured by the *Rapid* of Charleston; the schooners *Searcher* and *Mary*, seized by the *Rapid*; the 6-gun brigantine *Union*, captured by the *General Armstrong*, operating out of New York; the schooner *Neptune*, seized by the *Revenge* out of Salem; the barque *Fisher*, taken by the *Fox* of Portsmouth;

The brigantine *James Bray*, seized by the *Bunker Hill*; the brigantine *Lady Harriot*, seized by the privateer *Orders in Council*; the brigantine *Freedom*, seized by the *Thorn*; the schooner *America*, of Newburyport, captured by the privateers *Fame*, *Industry*, and *Dromo*; the brigantine *Fancy*, captured by the *Joel Barlow*; the schooner *John Bull*, forced to ground at Crooked Island by the *Rover* of New York; the 10-gun ship *John Hamilton*, seized by the *Dolphin*;

The schooner *Loreen*, captured by the *Revenge* of Philadelphia; the brigantine *Bacchus*, seized by the *Revenge*; the brigantine *Venus*, seized by the *Polly*, out of Salem; the packet *Townsend*, seized by the *Tom*, operating out of Baltimore; the brigantine *Burchall*, seized by the *High Flyer* of Baltimore; the sloop *Parmelia*, captured by the *Revenge*; the brigantine *Two Brothers*, captured by the *Benjamin Franklin*;

The brigantine *Active*, seized by the *High Flyer*, operating out of Baltimore; the vessel *Oria*, seized by the letter of marque *Leo*; the ship *Betsey*, captured by the *Revenge* of Baltimore; the 8-gun brigantine *Dart*, seized by the *America* out of Salem; the 16-gun ship *Queen*, seized by the *General Armstrong*, operating out of New York; the brigantine *Lucy and Alida*, captured by the *General Armstrong*, retaken by the British only to be recaptured by the *Revenge*;

The schooner *Swift*, seized by the *Rolla*, out of Baltimore; the *Rolla* also took the 14-gun ship *Mary*, the 10-gun ship *Eliza*, the 18-gun ship *Rio Nouva*, the 10-gun ship *Apollo* and the 6-gun brigantine *Boroso*; the sloop *Reasonable* chased ashore by the *Liberty*; the schooner *Maria*, taken by the *Liberty*; the 3-gun schooner *Catharine*, captured by the *Eagle* and the *Lady Madison*;

The schooner *Rebecca*, seized by *Jack's Favorite*; the 12-gun ship *Hope*, the ship *Ralph* and the 10-gun *Euphemia*, seized by the *America* operating out of Salem; the schooner *Meadow*, seized and released by the *Sparrow*; the schooner *Erin*, captured by the *Eagle*; the schooner *Mary*, seized by the *Eagle*; the brigantine *Peggy*, out of Barbados, captured by the *Hunter*; the 8-gun ship *Arabella*, seized by the *Growler*;

The 10-gun ship *Neptune*, seized by the *Decatur*; the schooner *Prince of Wales*, seized and released by the *Growler*; the 12-gun ship *Aurora* and the 10-gun brigantine *Emu*, captured by the *Holkar* of New York; the brigantine *Pelican*, seized by the *Mars*, operating out of New London; and the 10-gun brigantine *Ann*, taken by the *Growler*.

1813

The 4-gun sloop *Mary Ann*, 6-gun schooner *Alder*, the brigantine *Fly*, the 8-gun brigantine *Thames*, brigantine *Harriet*, the brigantine *Matilda*, the 10-gun brigantine *Shannon*, the 10-gun *Andalusia* and the schooner *George*, taken by the privateer *Yankee*; three unnamed vessels seized and destroyed on the Spanish Main and an unnamed sloop, seized and retained by the *Snap Dragon* out of New Bern, N.C.; six unnamed vessels seized by the privateer *Divided We Fall*;

The 10-gun letter of marque brig *Malvina*, seized by the letter of marque schooner *Ned*, operating out of Baltimore; the brigantine *Tartar* seized by the *General Armstrong*; the 3-gun schooner *Fox*, seized by the *Hero*, operating out of Stonington, Connecticut; the brigantine *London Packet* and the brigantine *Return*, captured by the *Paul Jones*; the schooner *Farmer*, seized by the *Sparrow*, operating out of Baltimore; an unnamed ship, valued at between $400,000 and $500,000, seized by the *True Blooded Yankee*, which seized five other unnamed prizes;

The brigantine *Charlotte*, captured by the *Montgomery*, operating out of Salem; the privateer schooner *Richard* and the privateer sloop *Dorcas*, seized by the *Holkar*, operating out of New York; the 8-gun brigantine *Edward*, an unnamed sloop and a 16-gun brigantine, taken by the *Alexander*, out of Salem;

The brigantine *Mars*, captured by the *Fox*; the ship *Nancy*, seized by the *Yorktown*; the schooner *Delight*, seized by the privateer *Fame* out of Salem;

The 12-gun king's packet *Mary Ann*, seized by the *Governor Tompkins*, operating out of New York; the 12-gun ship *Dromo* and an unnamed brigantine captured by the *Thomas*, operating out of Portsmouth; the 16-gun corvette *Invincible Napoleon*, the 10-gun packet *Ann* and the schooner *Greyhound*, seized by the *Young Teazer* out of New York;

The British packet *Express* and the 8-gun brigantine *Mary*, seized by the *Anaconda*, operating out of New York; the 10-gun ship *William*, seized by the *Grand Turk*, operating out of Salem; the brigantine *Harriet*, captured by the *Anaconda*; the schooner *Pearl*, captured by the *Liberty*, out of Baltimore; the schooner *Britannia*, captured by the *Grand Turk*; the 10-gun ship *Loyal Sam*, seized by the letter of marque schooner *Siro*, operating out of Baltimore;

The 14-gun ship *Venus*, taken by the *Globe*; the brigantine *David*, seized by the *Governor Plumer*; the 2-gun brigantine *Ajax* and the 2-gun brigantine *Hartley*, seized by the *Governor Tompkins*; the brigantine *General Prevost*, seized by the *Rolla* out of Baltimore; the schooner *Brown*, seized by the letter of marque *Bellona*, operating out of Philadelphia; the schooner *Liverpool Packet*, taken by the *Thomas* of Portsmouth;

The ship *Susan*, captured by an unnamed American privateer; the ship *Seaton*, seized by the *Paul Jones* and later destroyed at sea by the *Globe* due to being unseaworthy; the schooner *Elizabeth* and the ship *Pelham*, seized and destroyed by the *Globe*; the brigantine *Margaret*, seized by the *America* of Salem and sent into that port; the 12-gun brigantine *Morton*, taken by the *Yorktown*;

The 4-gun brigantine *Sally*, captured by the *Benjamin Franklin*; the brigantine *Hero*, captured by the *Teazer*; the brigantine *Resolution*, seized by the *Nancy*; the brigantine *Ann*, seized by the *Teazer*; the 2-gun brigantine *Thomas*, seized by the *Decatur*; the brigantine *Tulip*, flying American colors and transporting English goods, captured by the *Atlas*; the ship *Eliza Ann*, captured by the *Yankee*; the schooner *Success*, seized by the *Benjamin Franklin*; the schooner *Lady Clark*, captured by the *Bunker Hill*; the schooner *Sally*, from Sidney, Nova Scotia, seized by the *Wiley Reynard*;

The schooner *Blonde*, captured by the privateer *John*; the armed schooner *Dorcas*, seized by the *Liberty*, operating out of Baltimore; the brigantine *Union* and the ship *Aurora*, both from Ireland, seized by the *True Blooded Yankee*; the ship *Integrity*, seized by the *True Blooded Yankee*, which also seized and destroyed the schooner *Leonard* in Dublin Bay; the 12-gun brigantine *Avery*, seized by the *Yorktown*; the brigantine *Betsey*, captured by *Jack's Favorite*;

The schooner *Three Sisters*, captured by the *Saucy Jack*; the schooner *General Horseford*, captured by the *Decatur*; the brigantine *Nelly*, out of Cork, seized and burned by the *Fox*, operating out of Portsmouth; the sloop *Peggy*, the brigantine *Louisa*, the schooner *Brother and Sister* and the *Westport* are also captured by the *Fox*; the sloop *Fox* out of Liverpool taken by the American privateer *Fox*, along with the sloop *William and Ann*, the sloop *James and Elizabeth*, the brigantine *Chance* and the brigantine *Mary*;

The American ship *Venus*, transporting British goods, seized by the *Dolphin*; the 2-gun ship *London Trader*, seized by the *Decatur*; the brigantine *Good Intent*, brigantine *Venus*, the brigantine *Happy*, the bark *Reprisal*, and the schooner *Elizabeth*, seized by the *Snap Dragon*; the schooner *Flying Fish*, the sloop *Kate*, the 10-gun ship *Louisa*, the 10-gun brigantine *Three Brothers*, and the sloop *Catherine*, seized by the *Saucy Jack*;

The ship *Grotius*, the schooner *Susan* and the schooner *Vigilant*, seized by the *Frolic*; the ship *Reprisal*, out of Scotland, the brigantine *Friends* and the brigantine *Betsey*, captured by the *Frolic*; the *Galliot Guttle Hoffnung*, the 8-gun brigantine *Jane Gordon* and the schooner *Hunter*, seized and destroyed by the *Frolic*; the brigantine *Earl of Moira*, seized by the *Industry*; the 1-gun schooner *Louisa*, captured by the schooner *Expedition*, operating out of Baltimore;

Four unnamed vessels, seized and burned by the *Lovely Cordelia* of Charleston; the schooner *Lilly* and the brigantine *Mary Ann*, seized by the letter of marque schooner *Pilot*, operating out of Baltimore;

The British packet *Lapwing*, captured by the *Rattlesnake*; two unnamed English ships and the ship *Industry*, captured by the *True Blooded Yankee*; the sloop *Traveller*, captured by the privateer-boat *Lark*; the 14-gun ship *London Packet*, the brigantine *Jane* and the brigantine *Atlantic*, seized by the *Argus*, operating out of Boston; a separate brigantine *Jane*, seized by the *Snap Dragon*; the 18-gun packet *Morgiana*, captured by the *Saratoga*; fifteen unnamed vessels, seized and burned off Jamaica by the *Lovely Cordelia*, operating out of Charleston;

The schooner *Fame*, seized by the *Saratoga* and wrecked on Long Island; the ship *St. Lawrence*, captured by an Eastern privateer; nine unnamed vessels seized by the *Yankee*; three merchant ships, part of a convoy, seized by the letter of marque *Water Witch*; the brigantine *President*, seized by the *Polly*, operating out of

Salem; the brigantines *Ann, Mary, Despatch, Telemaebus, Favourite, Howe* and the 10-gun schooner *Katy*, seized by the *Yankee*;

Thirteen unnamed merchant ships, seized and burned by the privateer *Leo* of Baltimore; sloop *General Hodgkinson*, seized by the *Saratoga*; the brigadier *Edward*, seized by the *Fox*, operating out of *Baltimore*; the brigadier *Lloyd*, taken by the *Saratoga*; the 10-gun ship *Venus* and the schooner *Surinam*, captured by the *Saratoga*; the 10-gun brigantine *Sir John Sherbroke*, seized by the *Saucy Jack*; the 4-gun ship *Manly*, taken by the *Revenge*, operating out of Baltimore;

Fifteen to twenty vessels seized off the coasts of Portugal and Spain and destroyed by the privateer *Lion*, operating out of Baltimore; the schooner *Messenger*, captured by the *Comet*, out of Baltimore; the brigantine *Agnes*, seized and destroyed at sea by the *Saucy Jack*; the sloop *John* and a few small British vessels captured by the *Saucy Jack*; the brigantine *Abel* and an unnamed schooner out of *Martinique*, captured by the *Caroline* of Baltimore; the sloop *Resolution*, taken by the *General Armstrong*;

The brigantine *Phoebe*, seized and destroyed at sea by the *General Armstrong*; the brigantine *Commerce*, seized by the brigantine *Flirt*, operating out of *New York*; the schooner *Fanny* and the brigantine *Silena*, seized by the *Revenge*, operating out of Baltimore; the brigantine *Victoria*, captured by the privateer *Rapid* of Charleston; the British ship *Tryal* and an unnamed brigantine out of Lisbon, captured and burned at sea by the *Grand Turk*;

The brigantine *Cossack*, seized by the 2-gun *General Stark*, operating out of *Salem*; the schooner *Jasper* and the brigantine *Criterion*, taken by the *Caroline*; the schooner *Rebecca* and the schooner *Agnes*, captured by the *Grand Turk*; the schooner *Henry* and the schooner *Maria*, captured by the privateer *Roger*, out of Norfolk; the ship *Nereid* and two unnamed vessels, taken by the *Governor Tompkins*, operating out of New York;

Eight unnamed vessels that were burned, and the *Castor*, turned into a cartel, seized by the *True Blooded Yankee*; the *True Blooded Yankee* also captured the *Active, Watson, Cora,* and *Eliza*; the schooner *Traveller*, captured by the *Frolic* of Salem; the schooner *George* and the sloop *Experiment*, captured by the *Fly*;

The tender *Vigilant* and nine unnamed vessels, destroyed at sea when seized by the *Comet*, operating out of Baltimore; the brigantine *Young Husband*, captured by the *Governor Tompkins*;

The brigantine *Tullock*, the ship *Minerva* and an unnamed brigantine, seized by the *Fox*; an unnamed sloop, seized by the *General Stark*; the schooner *Harmony*, taken by the privateer boat *Terrible*, operating out of Salem;

six unnamed vessels seized by the privateer *Diomede*, the schooner *Mary*, seized by the *Macedonian*, operating out of Baltimore; an unnamed sloop out of Jamaica, seized by the *Hope*; the schooner *Curfew*, captured by the *Alfred* out of Salem; the brigantine *Tercilla*, seized and burned by the *Alfred*;

An unnamed 500-ton ship carrying British goods but flying Swedish colors, taken by the *Chasseur*, operating out of Baltimore;

An unnamed 400-ton 12-gun ship and an armed schooner (formerly the American privateer *Eldridge Gerry*), seized by the *True Blooded Yankee*; the schooner *Mary and Joseph* and the schooner *Hope*, captured by the *Diomede*; the brigantine *Bykar*, seized by the *Fox*; the schooner *Susan and Eliza*, taken by the *Mars*, out of New York; an unnamed schooner under the pretense of being Spanish but carrying British goods, and another unnamed schooner, captured by the *Viper*;

An unnamed schooner, seized by the privateer *Fairy*, operating out of Baltimore; an unnamed ship sailing under Russian colors, captured by the *Saucy Jack*; the brigantine *Superb*, seized by the *Mars*, operating out of New York; the brigantine *Friends*, captured by the *Diomede*, operating out of Salem; the schooner *Sea Flower*, seized and burned by the letter of marque schooner *Tuckahoe* out of Baltimore; the schooner *Hazard*, seized by the *Tuckahoe*; the brigantine *Sovereign*, captured by the *America*, operating out of Salem; and the schooner *William*, seized by the *Diomede*.

1814

British bark *Concord*, ship *Liberty*, brigantine *Jolly Bachelor*, 4-gun brigantine *Ruby*, the *Hartford* and the brigantine *Brunswick*, seized by the *Rattlesnake*; the 186-ton brigantine 4-gun *Betsey*, the brigantine *Thetis*, the 4-gun vessel *Diligent*, the sloop *Fame*, the vessel *Galliot Perseverance*, the *Friends' Adventure* and the brigantine *Pax*, seized by the *Rattlesnake*;

The vessels *Latona* and *Experiment* and the brigantine *Burton*, taken by the *Scourge*; the brigantine *Nottingham*, the brigantine *Britannia, The Brothers*, the *Westmoreland*, and *Prosperous*, captured by the *Scourge*; the ship *Brutus*, seized by the *Rattlesnake* and the *Scourge*; the 4-gun brigantine *Hope* and the 2-gun *Economy*, of 181 tons, taken by the Scourge;

The British brigantine *Brothers*, seized by the *America*, operating out of Salem, the brigantine *Elizabeth*, taken by the privateer *Caroline* out of Baltimore; the Swedish ship *Annette Catharine*, carrying British goods, seized by the *Saucy Jack*; the schooner *Nimble* and the schooner *Trinitaria*, seized by the *Saucy Jack*; the schooner *Jason*, seized by the *Caroline*; an unnamed schooner seized by the *Kemp*;

Fifteen unnamed British vessels, seized by the privateer *Prince of Neufchatel*, operating out of New York; the brigantine *Apollo*, the cutter *Patty*, and the brigantine *Ann*, seized by the *America*; an unnamed ship out of Liverpool, taken by the *Invincible* of Salem; the schooner *Encouragement*, seized and destroyed by the *Frolic*, operating out of *Salem*; the brigantine *Two Sisters*, taken by the *Wasp*; operating out of Philadelphia;

The schooner *Hope* and the schooner *Sylph*, seized by the *America*; the schooner *Eclipse*, seized by the *Wasp*, operating out of Philadelphia; the schooner *Cobham*, seized by the privateer *Jonquilla*, operating out of New York; the brigantine *Louisa*, seized by the *Kemp*, operating out of Baltimore; the ship *Hebe*, taken by the *Surprise* of Baltimore;

The brigantine *Nimble*, seized by the *Invincible*; the brigantine *Ceres*, captured by the *Grampus*, operating out of Baltimore; an unnamed schooner, seized by the *Saratoga*, out of New York; the schooner *Friends' Adventure*, seized by the *Fox*; the brigantine *Fanny*, seized by the *Galloway*, operating out of *New York*; an unnamed brigantine, seized by the *Fox*;

The schooner *Kentish*, seized by the *Saratoga*; the 10-gun schooner *Prince Regent*, seized by the *Invincible*; the cutter *Lyon*, captured by the *Saratoga*, the 8-gun brigantine *Portsea*, seized by the *Saratoga*; the 10-gun brigantine *Conway*, seized by the *Saratoga*; the schooner *Francis and Lucy*, seized by the *Saratoga*; the brigantine *Margaretta*, seized by the *Invincible*;

The 6-gun brigantine *Henry*, captured by the *Governor Tompkins*; an unnamed schooner taken by the *Snap Dragon*; the brigantine *James*, seized by the *Young Wasp*, operating out of Philadelphia;

The ship *Union*, seized by the *Rambler*, which was recaptured by the *Curlew* before being lost at sea; the brigantine *Fair Stranger*, seized by the *Fox*; an unnamed brigantine, seized by the *Expedition*, operating out of Baltimore;

The schooner *Miranda*, seized by the *Chasseur*, operating out of Baltimore; the sloop *Martha*, captured and turned into a cartel by the *Chasseur*, which seized and destroyed two other vessels; the American schooner *Adeline*, captured by a British frigate, then recaptured six days later by the privateer *Expedition*; the brigantine *Experience*, seized by the *Caroline* out of Baltimore; the ship *Experience*, seized by the *Rapid*; an unnamed schooner, taken by the *Perry* of Baltimore;

The schooner *Francis*, the schooner *William* and the sloop *Irwin*, seized by the letter of marque schooner *Midas*, operating out of Baltimore; the schooner *Appallodore*, seized and destroyed by the *Midas*; the brigantine *Bellona*, seized and destroyed by the *Globe*, operating out of Baltimore;

The sloop *Cygnet*, captured by the *Saratoga*; the schooner *Diligence*, seized and destroyed by the *York*; the sloop *Bonita*, seized by the *Delisle*, operating out of Baltimore; the brigantine *Robert*, seized by the zebec *Ultor* of *Baltimore*; the ship *Equity*, seized and destroyed by the *Rattlesnake*; the ship *Adston*, seized by the *Rattlesnake*; an unnamed brigantine, captured by the *Rattlesnake*; the ship *James*, seized by the *Young Wasp*;

The brigantine *Swift*, captured by the zebec *Ultor*; the brigantine *Camelion*, seized by the *Mammoth*, operating out of Baltimore; two unnamed vessels seized by the *Caroline*; the ship *Fortuna*, flying Russian colors but carrying British goods, seized by the privateer *Roger*, operating out of Norfolk; the schooner *Phoebe*, captured by the *Hawk* out of Washington;

The 6-gun brigantine *Kutozoff*, seized by the *Surprise*; the schooner *Young Farmer*, seized by the letter of marque *Henry Guilder*, operating

Prizes of American Privateers and Vessels Under Letters of Marque

out of New York; two unnamed vessels seized by the letter of marque *James Monroe*; the ship *Joanna*, seized by the *Chasseur*; the 540-ton ship *Pelham*, seized by the *Saucy Jack*; the schooner *Hope*, seized by the privateer *Pike* of Baltimore; the schooner *Pickrel*, seized and destroyed by the *Pike*;

The ship Askew, seized by the *True Blooded Yankee*; the 6-gun schooner *Brilliant*, captured by the *Scourge*; the brigantine *Dove* and the ship *Jane*, seized by the *Fox*, operating out of Portsmouth; the ship *Mermaid*, seized by the *General Pike*, operating out of Baltimore; the ship *Commerce*, taken by the privateer *Lawrence* of Baltimore; the ship *Upton* and the brigantines *Providence* and *Britannia*, seized by the privateer *Diomede*, operating out of Salem; the brigantine *Harmony* and *Recovery* seized and destroyed by the *Diomede*;

The 6-gun brigantine *Melpomene* and the brigantine *Britannia*, captured by the *Chasseur*, operating out of Baltimore; the ship *Henry Dundas*, taken and released by the *Rattlesnake*; the brigantine *Indian Lass*, seized by the *Grand Turk*; the brigantine *Catharine*, seized by the *Grand Turk*, retaken by the British brigantine *Bacchus*, only to be lost again to the *Grand Turk*, which destroys it; the sloop *Caroline*, taken by the *Grand Turk*;

The schooner *Traveller* and the ship *Cod Hook*, seized by the *Diomede*; the schooner *Victoria*, seized by the cutter sloop *Hero*, recaptured by the British until the crew sided with the Americans and took the vessel into an American port; the 6-gun brigantine *Jessie*, seized and burned by the *Hero*; the schooner *Ann*, seized by the *Hero* and turned into a cartel; the schooner *Robert Hartwell*, seized by the *Hero*; the schooner *Funchall*, captured by the *Hero*, of New York;

The brigantine *Liddelle*, seized and turned into a cartel by the *Amelia*, operating out of Baltimore; the schooner *Octavia*, captured by the *Harrison*, out of Baltimore; 22 British vessels seized and 18 of those destroyed by the privateer *Perry* of Baltimore; the 12-gun ship *London Packet*, seized by the *Chasseur*, out of Baltimore; the 10-gun brigantine *Astrea* and a privateer, the *Dash*, seized by the *Midas*; the schooner *Union*, captured by the *Amelia*, operating out of Baltimore;

The sloop *Friendship*, the schooner *Mary Ann* and the schooner *Alert*, seized by the *Revenge*; the sloop *Active*, seized and destroyed by the *Fairy* of Baltimore; the brigantine *Lord Nelson*, out of Belfast, seized and destroyed by the zebec *Ultor*; the schooner *Nancy* and two unnamed vessels, seized by the zebec *Ultor*; a Portuguese ship, the *St. Jose*, taken by the *Yankee*, out of Bristol; the 1-gun privateer schooner *Amnesty*, seized and destroyed by the zebec *Ultor*, of Baltimore; the sloop *Tickler*, also seized by the *Ultor*;

The schooner *Rambler*, captured by the *Perry*, operating out of Baltimore; the 2-gun schooner *Fairy*, out of Ireland, seized by the *Perry*; the 6-gun Britannic Majesty's schooner *Bulaboo*, seized by the *Perry*; the ship *Friendship*, flying Swedish colors, seized by the *Herald*, operating out of New York; the ship *Hugh Jones*, out of Belfast, seized by the *Yankee*; the schooner *Fox*, seized off the coast of Ireland and turned into a cartel by the *Surprise*;

The brig *James and David*, seized and released by the *Surprise*; the brigantine *Fidelity*, captured and destroyed by the *Surprise*; the schooner *Ellen*, out of Belfast, taken by the *Herald*, operating out of New York; the brigantine *Duke of York*, out of Greenock, seized by the *General Armstrong*; the sloop *George*, seized off the coast of Ireland and destroyed by the *General Armstrong*; the brigantine *Swift*, seized by the *General Armstrong*; the brigantine *Defiance*, taken and destroyed by the *General Armstrong*;

The brigantine *Friendship*, seized and destroyed by the *General Armstrong*; the brigantine *Stag*, seized and destroyed by the *General Armstrong*; the ship *Dorcas*, seized and destroyed by the boats of the *General Armstrong*; the 6-gun ship *Berry Castle*, seized and released by the *Yankee*; the schooner *Linnet*, seized by the *Snap Dragon* operating out of New Bern; an unnamed schooner seized and destroyed by the *Snap Dragon*;

Six vessels seized by the *Prince of Neufchatel*; an unnamed brigantine seized by the *Rambler* out of Boston; the frigate *Fortitude*, captured by the *Surprise*, out of Baltimore; the schooner *George Canning*, taken by the *General Armstrong*; the ship *Pizarro*, captured by the *Midas*, of Baltimore; the brigantine *Espiranza*, seized by the *Midas*, of Baltimore; the brigantine *Elsinore*, seized by the *Midas*;

The ship *Julia*, the brigantine *Mary Ann*, the schooner *John Duncan* and the vessel *Louisa*, seized by the privateer *Harrison*, operating out of Baltimore; the brigantine *Betsy*, seized by the *York*; the ship *Alfred*, taken by the *Harpy*, out of Baltimore; the ship *Antonia*, flying Russian colors, seized by the *York*; two unnamed brigantines captured and destroyed by the *York*; the ship *Hero*, out of Newfoundland, seized by the *Ida*, operating out of Boston;

The *Countess of Harcourt*, seized in the English Channel by the privateer *Sabine* of Baltimore; the cutter *Landraile*, seized in the English Channel by the *Syren*, out of Baltimore; two unnamed brigantines seized and destroyed by the *Syren*;

Fourteen unnamed vessels captured and destroyed in the English Channel and six other vessels captured by the *Governor Tompkins*, operating out of New York; the brigantine *Betsey and Mary*, out of Spain, seized and destroyed by the *Kemp* of Baltimore; the ship *Calypso*, flying Swedish colors, seized by the *Kemp*; the brigantine *New Frederick*, taken by the *Kemp* and released; the schooner *Contract*, taken by the *Roger*, out of Norfolk;

The brigantine (transport) *Doris*, seized by the *Grampus*, operating out of Baltimore; the ship *Hoppet* and the brigantine *Eliza*, taken by the *Saucy Jack*, operating out of Charleston; the schooner *Mary*, captured by the privateer *Shark*, operating out of New York; the brigantine *Maria Wirman*, seized by the *Yankee*;

The British brigantine *Pike*, seized and destroyed by the American privateer *Pike*, out of Baltimore; an unnamed schooner, seized and turned into a cartel by the privateer *Pike*; the British schooner *Industrious Bee*, seized and destroyed by the *Pike*;

The schooner *Venus*, the schooner *Lord Nelson*, and the brigantine *Jane* (destroyed), also seized by the *Pike*; the brigantine *Orient*, out of Portsmouth, England, seized and destroyed by the *Pike*; the brigantine *John* taken by the *Pike*; the ship *Samuel Cummings*, seized by the *Pike*;

The cutter *Wasp* and the brigantine *Dover*, seized and destroyed by the *Rattlesnake*; an unnamed British brigantine and an unnamed schooner, seized by the privateer *Herald*, operating out of New York;

The ship *Five Sisters*, seized and released by the letter of marque schooner *Dash*; the 6-gun ship *Vestern*, the brigantine *Horatio*, the brigantine *Mars* and the brigantine *Cornwallis*, seized by the privateer *David Porter*, operating out of Boston; brigantine *Endeavour* (transport), seized and destroyed by the *Surprise*;

The cutter *Jubilee*, seized by the privateer *Whig* and turned into a cartel; the schooner *Alexandria*, the brigantine *Irish Minor*, the brigantine *Eliza* and the brigantine *Princess Mary*, seized by the *Whig*; the British schooner *Esperance*, seized and destroyed by the *Whig*; the ship *Postethwell*, out of Cork, captured by the *Whig*; the brigantine *Nancy*, and the schooner *Columbia*, seized by the privateer *Portsmouth* operating out of Portsmouth; an unnamed sloop, seized by the *Portsmouth*;

The brigantine *Fire Fly*, seized by the privateer *Sabine*, operating out of Baltimore; the brigantine *Mary and Eliza*, out of Halifax, seized and burned by the privateer *Argo*, operating out of Baltimore; the brigantine *Argo*, out of Dublin, seized by the *Surprise*; the sloop *Farmer* and the brigantine *Britannia*, seized by the *Mammoth*, of Baltimore; the brigantine *Ceres*, out of Glasgow, taken by the *Mammoth*; and the brigantine *Harvest*, the 10-gun brigantine *William* and the brigantine *Rover*, seized by the privateer *York*, which also recaptures the American sloop *Regulator*.

Appendix D.
Proclamation Issued by General William Hull to the People of Canada on 12 July 1812

To inhabitants of Canada: After thirty years of peace and prosperity, the United States has been driven to arms. The injuries and aggressions, the insults and indignities of Great Britain have once more left them no alternative but manly resistance or unconditional submission. The army under my command has invaded your country, and the standard of union now waves over Canada. To the peaceful, unoffending inhabitant it brings neither danger nor difficulty. I come to find enemies, not to make them. I come to protect, not to injure you.

Separated by an immense ocean and an extensive wilderness from Great Britain, you have no participation in her councils, no interest in her conduct. You have felt her tyranny, you have seen her injustice — but I do not ask you to avenge the one or redress the other. The United States are sufficiently powerful to afford you every security, consistent with their rights and your expectations. I tender you the invaluable blessings of civil, political, and religious liberty, and their necessary result, individual and general prosperity — that liberty which gave decision to our councils and energy to our conduct in our struggle for independence, and which conducted us safely and triumphantly through the stormy past of the Revolution — that liberty that has raised us to an elevated rank among the nations of the world, and which has afforded us a greater measure of peace and security of wealth and improvement, than ever yet fell to the lot of any people.

In the name of my country, and by the authority of my government, I promise protection to your persons, property, and rights. Remain at your homes; pursue your peaceful and customary avocations; raise not your hands against your brethren. Many of your fathers fought for the freedom and independence we now enjoy. Being children, therefore, of the same family with us, and heirs to the same heritage, the arrival of an army of friends must be hailed by you with a cordial welcome. You will be emancipated from tyranny and oppression, and restored to the dignified station of freemen.

Had I any doubt of eventual success, I might ask your assistance; but I do not. I come prepared for every contingency. I have a force which will look down on all opposition, and that force is but the vanguard of a much greater. If contrary to your own interests and the just expectation of my country, you should take part in the approaching contest, you will be considered and treated as enemies, and the horrors and calamities of war will stalk before you. If the barbarous and savage policy of Great Britain be pursued, and the savages be let loose to murder our citizens, and butcher our women and children, this war will be a war of extermination. The first stroke with the tomahawk, the first attempt with the scalping knife, will be the signal of one indiscriminate scene of desolation. No white man, found fighting by the side of an Indian, will be taken prisoner — instant destruction will be his lot. If the dictates of reason, duty, justice, and humanity cannot prevent the employment of a force which respects no rights and knows no wrong, it will be prevented by a severe and relentless system of retaliation.

I doubt not your courage and firmness — I will not doubt your attachment to liberty. If you tender your services voluntarily, they will be accepted readily. The United States offer you peace, liberty, and security. Your choice lies between these and war, slavery, and destruction. Choose, then, but choose wisely; and may He who knows the justice of our cause, and Who holds in His hand the fate of nations, guide you to a result the most compatible with your rights and interests, your peace and happiness.

Appendix E.
General Isaac Brock's Response to General Hull's Proclamation on 22 July 1812

The unprovoked declaration of war by the United States of America against the United Kingdom of Great Britain and Ireland, and its dependencies, has been followed by the actual invasion of this Province, in a remote frontier of the western district, by a detachment of the armed force of the United States. The officer commanding that detachment has thought proper to invite His Majesty's subjects not merely to a quiet and unresisting submission, but insults them with a call to seek voluntarily the protection of his government.

Without condescending to notice the epithets bestowed in this appeal of the American commander to the people of Upper Canada on the administration of His Majesty, every inhabitant of the Province is desired to seek the confutation of such indecent slander in the review of his own particular circumstances. Where is the Canadian subject who can truly affirm to himself that he has been injured by the government in his person, his property, or his liberty? Where is to be found, in any part of the world, a growth so rapid in prosperity and wealth as this colony exhibits? Settled, not thirty' years, by a band of veterans exiled from their former possessions on account of their loyalty, not a descendant of these brave people is to be found who, under the fostering liberality of their Sovereign, has not acquired a property and means of enjoyment superior to what were possessed by their ancestors. This unequalled prosperity would not have been attained by the utmost liberality of the government or the persevering industry of the people had not the maritime power of the Mother Country secured to its colonists a safe access to every market where the produce of their labour was in request.

The unavoidable and immediate consequences of a separation from Great Britain must be the loss of this inestimable advantage; and what is offered you in exchange? To become a territory of the United States, and share with them that exclusion from the ocean which the policy of their government enforces; you are not even flattered with a participation of their boasted independence, and it is but too obvious that once estranged from the powerful protection of the United Kingdom you must be re-annexed to the dominion of France, from which the provinces of Canada were wrested by the arms of Great Britain, at a vast expense of blood and treasure, from no other motive than to relieve her ungrateful children from the oppression of a cruel neighbour. This restitution of Canada to the Empire of France was the stipulated reward for the aid afforded to the revolted colonies (now the United States). The debt is still due, and there can be no doubt but the pledge has been renewed as a consideration for commercial advantages, or rather for an expected relaxation in the tyranny of France over the commercial world. Are you prepared, inhabitants of Canada, to become willing subjects, or rather slaves, to the despot who rules the nations of continental Europe with a rod of iron? If not, arise in a body, exert your energies, co-operate cordially with the King's regular forces to repel the invader, and do not give cause to your children, when groaning under the oppression of a foreign master, to reproach you with having so easily parted with the richest inheritance of this earth — a participation in the name, character, and freedom of Britons!

The same spirit of justice which will make every reasonable allowance for the unsuccessful efforts of zeal and loyalty will not fail to punish the defalcation of principle. Every Canadian freeholder is, by deliberate choice, bound by the most solemn oaths to defend the monarchy, as well as his own property; to shrink from that engagement is treason not to be forgiven. Let no man suppose that if in this unexpected struggle, His Majesty's arms should be compelled to yield to an overwhelming force, the Province will be eventually abandoned; the endeared relations of the first settlers, the intrinsic value of its commerce, and the pretensions of its powerful rival to re-possess the Canadas, are pledges that no peace will be established between the United States and Great Britain and Ireland of which the restoration of these provinces does not make the most prominent condition.

Be not dismayed at the unjustifiable threat of the commander of the enemy's forces to refuse quarter should an Indian appear in the ranks. The brave bands of aborigines which inhabit this colony were, like His Majesty's other subjects, punished for their zeal and fidelity by the loss of their possessions in the late colonies, and rewarded by His Majesty with lands of superior value in this province. The faith of the British government has never yet been violated — the Indians feel that the soil they inherit is to them and their posterity protected from the base arts so frequently devised to over-reach their simplicity. By what new principle are they to be prohibited from defending their property? If their warfare; from being different to that of the white people, be more terrific to the enemy let him retrace his steps — they seek him not — and cannot expect to find women and children in an invading army. But they are men, and have equal rights with all other men to defend themselves and their property when invaded, more especially when they find in the enemy's camp a ferocious and mortal foe, using the same warfare which the American commander affects to reprobate.

This inconsistent and unjustifiable threat of refusing quarter, for such a cause as being found in arms with a brother sufferer in defence of invaded rights, must be exercised with the certain assurance of retaliation, not only in the limited operations of war in this part of the King's dominions, but in every quarter of the globe, for the national character of Britain is not less distinguished for humanity than strict retributive justice, which will consider the execution of this inhuman threat as deliberate murder, for which every subject of the offending power must make expiation.

Appendix F.
Thomas Boyle's Proclamation
By Thomas Boyle, Esquire,
Commander of the Private Armed Brig Chasseur, etc.

PROCLAMATION:

Whereas, It has become customary with the admirals of Great Britain, commanding small forces on the coast of the United States, particularly with Sir John Borlaise Warren and Sir Alexander Cochrane, to declare all the coast of the said United States in a state of strict and rigorous blockade without possessing the power to justify such a declaration or stationing an adequate force to maintain said blockade;

"I do therefore, by virtue of the power and authority in me vested (possessing sufficient force), declare all the ports, harbors, bays, creeks, rivers, inlets, outlets, islands, and seacoast of the United Kingdom of Great Britain and Ireland in a state of strict and rigorous blockade.

And I do further declare that I consider the force under my command adequate to maintain strictly, rigorously, and effectually the said blockade.

And I do hereby require the respective officers, whether captains, commanders, or commanding officers, under my command, employed or to be employed, on the coasts of England, Ireland, and Scotland, to pay strict attention to the execution of this my proclamation.

And I do hereby caution and forbid the ships and vessels of all and every nation in amity and peace with the United States from entering or attempting to enter, or from coming or attempting to come out of, any of the said ports, harbors, bays, creeks, rivers, inlets, outlets, islands, or seacoast under any pretense whatsoever. And that no person may plead ignorance of this, my proclamation, I have ordered the same to be made public in England. Given under my hand on board the Chasseur.

THOMAS BOYLE.

Bibliography

Abbot, Willis J. *Blue Jackets of 1812*. New York: Dodd, Mead, 1882.

Allen, Joseph. *Battles of the British Navy*, Vol. 2. London: Henry G. Bohn, 1852.

Allen, William B. *A History of Kentucky*. Louisville: Bradley and Gilbert, 1872.

Ambler, Charles H. *The Life and Times of John Floyd*. Richmond: Richmond Press, 1918.

American Historical Magazine, Vol. 2. New York: Americana Society, 1907.

American Historical Magazine, Vol. 7. Nashville, TN, 1902.

American Historical Magazine, Vol. 22. Nashville, TN, 1917.

American Historical Review, Vol. 20. London: Macmillan, 1915.

American Monthly Magazine (Daughters of the American Revolution), Vol. 18. Washington, D.C. Printed by the Society, 1901.

American Monthly Magazine (Daughters of the American Revolution), Vol. XLI. Washington, D.C. Printed by the Society, 1912.

American Vessels Captured by the British During the American Revolution and the War of 1812. Salem, MA: Essex Institute, 1911.

Ancestral Records and Portraits, Vol. 1. New York: Grafton Press, 1910.

Annual Report of the American Historical Society, 1906, Vol. 1. Washington, D.C.: Government Printing Office, 1906.

Appleton's Cyclopaedia, Vol. 1. New York: D. Appleton, 1888.

Army of the United States. New York: Maynard, Merrill, 1896.

Auchinleck, G. *A History of the War Between Great Britain and the U.S. of America (1812, 1813 and 1814)*. Toronto: Maclesar, 1855.

Bailey, Isaac. *American Naval Biography*. Providence: Isaac Bailey, 1815.

Baltimore: Its History and Its People, Vol. 3. New York and Chicago: Lewis Historical, 1912.

Bangor Historical Magazine, Vol. 2. July 1886–June 1887, 1887.

Barnes, James. *Naval Actions of the War of 1812*. New York: Harper, 1896.

Barney, Mary. *Biographical Memoir of Commodore Joshua Barney*. Boston.

Barstow, George. *The History of New Hampshire*. Concord: I.S. Boyd, 1842.

Barton, Wilfred M. *The Road to Washington*. Boston: Richard G. Badger, 1919.

Baughman, A.J. *History of Ashland County, Ohio*. Chicago: S.J. Clarke, 1909.

Bausman, Joseph H. *History of Beaver County, Pennsylvania*, Vol. 1. New York: Knickerbocher, 1904.

Bell, Andrew. *History of Canada*, Vol. 3. Montreal: John Lovell, 1860.

A Biographical Notice of Com. Jesse D. Elliott. Philadelphia: Printed for the author, described as "A Citizen," 1835.

Biography of General Lewis Cass. New York: J. Winchester, New World Press, 1843.

Blake, Jonathan. *History of the Town of Warwick, Massachusetts*. Boston: Noyes, Holmes, 1873.

Bonney, Catharina. *Legacy or Historical Gleamings*, Vol. 1. Albany: J. Munsell, 1873.

Boyd, William P. *History of the Boyd Family*. Rochester: John F. Smith, 1912.

Brackenridge, H.M. *History of the Late War*. Philadelphia: James Kay, Jun., 1845.

Brackett, Albert G. *History of the United States Cavalry*. New York: Harper, 1865.

Brannan, John. *Official Letters of the Military and Naval Officers of the United States (1812, 13, 14 and 15)*. Washington City: Way and Gideon, 1823.

Brice, Wallace A. *History of Fort Wayne*. Fort Wayne: D.W. Jones, 1868.

Brock, R.A. *Virginia and Virginians: Eminent Virginians*, Vol. 1. Richmond and Toledo: H.H. Hardesty, 1888.

Brown, G.W. *Historical Genealogy of a Branch of the Brown Family*. Philadelphia: John P. Murphy, 1885.

Browne, James Alex. *England's Artillerymen*. London: Hall, Smart, and Allen, 1865.

Browning, Charles H. *Americans of Royal Descent*. Philadelphia: Porter and Coates, 1891.

The Builders of a Nation: A History of the United States. New York: Stanley-Bradley, 1892.

Canada: An Encyclopedia of the Country, Vol. 1. Toronto: Linscott, 1898.

Cartmell, T.K. *Shenandoah Valley, Pioneers and Their Descendants*. Fredericksburg: By author, 1909.

Centennial History of Washington, D.C. Dayton, OH: W.J. Shuey, 1892.

Chandler, George. *Descendants of William and Annis Chandler*. Gloucester: Charles Hamilton, 1883.

Chapter Sketches, Connecticut Daughters of the American Revolution. New Haven: Connecticut Chapters of the Daughters of the American Revolution, 1904.

Christie, Robert. *The Military and Naval Operations in the Canadas*. Quebec: 1818.

Claiborne, J.F.H. *Life and Times of Gen. Sam Dale, the Mississippi Partisan*. New York: Harper, 1860.

____. *Mississippi as a Province, Territory and State*, Vol. 1. Jackson: Power and Barksdale, 1880.

Clark, Lewis H. *Military History of Wayne County, New York*. Sodus, NY: Lewis H. Clark, Hulett and Gaylord, 1883.

Cleaveland, Nehemiah. *History of Bowdoin College*. Boston: James Ripley Osgood, 1882.

Cobbett's Political Register, Vol. 22 (July to December 1812). London: Published by the author, 1881.

Coffin, William F. *1812: The War and Its Moral; A Canadian Chronicle*. Montreal: Printed by Job Lovill, 1864.

Coggeshall, George. *History of American Privateers and Letters of Marque*. New York: By the author, 1856.

Collins, Lewis. *Historical Sketches of Kentucky*. Maysville, KY: Lewis Collins; and Cincinnati: J.A. and U.P. James, 1850.

Compendium of History and Biography of Detroit and Wayne County, Michigan. Chicago: Henry Taylor, 1909.

Connard, Howard L. *Encyclopedia of the History of Missouri*, Vol. 6. New York, Louisville, and St. Louis: Southern History, 1901.

Connecticut as a Colony and as a State, Vol. 3. Hartford: Publishing Society of the State, 1904.

Connelly, William Elsey. *History of Kentucky*, Vol. 5. Chicago and New York: American Historical Society, 1922.

The Constitution and Register of Membership of the General Society of the War of 1812. Philadelphia: By the Society, 1899.

Cruikshank, Ernest Alexander. *The Documentary History of the Campaign Upon the Niagara Frontier*. Lundy's Lane Historical Society, 1908.

Cullum, George W. *Campaigns of the War of 1812–1815*. New York: James Miller, 1879.

Cushing, Thomas H. *The Trial of General Thomas H. Cushing Before a General Court Martial*. Philadelphia: Moses Thomas, 1812.

Dawson, Henry B. *Battles of the United States by Sea and Land*, Vols. 1 and 2. New York: Johnson, Fry, 1858.

Delafield, Julia. *Biographies of Francis and Morgan Lewis*, Vol. 2. New York: Anson D.F. and Randolph, 1877.

Dictionary of American Biography. Boston: James R. Osgood, 1872.

Dillon, John B. *A History of Indiana*. Indianapolis: Bingham and Doughty, 1859.

Dimitri, John. *Lessons in the History of Louisiana.* New York, Chicago and New Orleans: A.S. Barnes, 1877.

Documents Relating to the Revolutionary History of the State of New Jersey. Trenton: John L. Murphy, 1901.

Drake, Francis S. *Memorials of the Society of the Cincinnati of Massachusetts.* Boston: By the Society, 1873.

Dyer, Oliver. *General Andrew Jackson, Hero of New Orleans.* New York: Robert Bonner's, 1891.

Edgar, Matilda. *Ten Years of Upper Canada in Peace and War (1805–1815).* Toronto: William Briggs, 1890.

Eggleston, Edward, and Lillie Eggleston Seelve. *Brant and Red Jacket.* New York: Dodd, Mead, 1879.

Encyclopedia History of Missouri. New York, Louisville and St. Louis: Southern History, 1901.

Encyclopedia of Mississippi History, Vol. 2. Madison, WI: Selwyn A. Brant, 1907.

Evans, W. Nelson, and Emmon B. Stivers. *The History of Adams County, Ohio.* West Union: R.B. Stivers, 1900.

The Family Magazine. Boston: Otis; New York: Redfield and Lindsay, 1837.

Farmer, Silas. *The History of Detroit and Michigan.* Detroit: Silas Farmer, 1884.

Fay, H.A. *Collection of the Official Accounts (in detail of all the battles fought by sea and land).* New York: E. Conrad, 1817.

The Fire Lands Pioneer, June issue. Norwalk, OH: Fire Lands Historical Society, 1882.

Fortier, Alcee. *The History of Louisiana,* Vol. 3. New York: Manzi Joyant, 1904.

Foster, George E. *Sequoyah, the American Cadmus and Modern Moses.* Philadelphia: Office of the Indian Rights Association, 1885.

Fraser, John. *Canadian Pen and Ink.* Montreal: Gazette, 1890.

Frost, John. *The American Generals.* Hartford: Case Tiffany, 1850.

Garber, Virginia. *The Armistead Family 1635–1910.* Richmond: Wittet and Shepperson, 1910.

A General Register of the Navy and Marine Corps of the United States. Washington: C. Alexander, 1848.

Giddings, Joshua R. *The Exiles of Florida.* Columbus, OH: Follett, Foster, 1858.

Glover, Anna. *An Account of John Glover of Dorchester and His Dependents.* Boston: David Clapp, 1867.

Goodrich, S.G. *A Pictorial History of the United States.* Philadelphia: J.H. Butler, 1874.

Gould, J.C. *Old Times in Tennessee.* Nashville: Tavell, Eastman and Howell, 1878.

The Granite Monthly, Vol. 7. Concord, N.H.: John Norris McClintock, 1884.

The Granite Monthly, Vol. 47. Concord, N.H.: Granite Monthly, 1915.

Grant, James. *British Battles on Land and Sea,* Vol. 2. London, Paris and New York: Cassell, Petter and Galpin, n.d.

Greswell, William Parr. *History of the Dominion of Canada.* Oxford: Royal Colonial Institute, 1890.

Griffin, Martin I.J. *Commodore John Barry.* Philadelphia: Published by the author, 1903.

Griffith, Thomas W. *Sketches of the Early History of Maryland.* Baltimore: Frederick G. Schaeffer, 1821.

Guernsey, R.S. *New York City and the Vicinity During the War of 1812,* Vol. 2. New York: Charles R. Woodward, 1895.

Halbert, J.S., and T.H. Ball. *The Creek War of 1813–1814.* Chicago, IL: Donohue and Henneberry and Montgomery, AL: White, Woodruff and Fowler, 1895.

Hampton, William Judson. *Our Presidents and Their Mothers.* Boston and New York: Cornhill, 1922.

Hannay, James. *History of the War of 1812.* Toronto: Morang, 1905.

Hannings, Bud. *American Revolutionary War Leaders.* Jefferson, NC: McFarland, 2009.

_____. *Chronology of the American Revolution.* Jefferson, NC: McFarland, 2008.

_____. *Forts of the United States.* Jefferson, NC: McFarland, 2006.

_____. *Portrait of the Stars and Stripes,* Vol. 1. Glenside, PA: Seniram.

Hanson, J.W. *History of Gardiner, Pittston and West Gardiner.* Gardiner: William Palmer, 1852.

Hardy, Stella Pickett. *Colonial Families of the Southern States of America.* New York: Tobias and Wright, 1911.

Harper's Monthly Magazine, Vol. 28. New York: Harper, 1864.

Harris, Thomas. *The Life and Services of Commodore William Bainbridge, USN.* Philadelphia: Carey, Lea and Blanchard, 1833.

Hatch, William Stanley. *A Chapter of the War of 1812 in the Northwest.* Cincinnati: Miami Printing, 1872.

Hayden, Reverend Horace Edwin. *Virginia Genealogies.* Wilkes Barre, PA, 1891.

Headley, J.T. *The Lives of Winfield Scott and Andrew Jackson.* New York: Charles Scribner, 1852.

Herringshaws National Library of American Biography, Vol. 1. Chicago: American Publishers' Association, 1909.

Historical Collections, Vol. 35. Lansing: Michigan Pioneer and Historical Society, 1907.

Historical Encyclopedia of Illinois and History of St. Clair County, Vol. 2. Chicago: Munsell, 1907.

The Historical Magazine, Vol. 3. New York: Charles B. Richardson, 1859.

The Historical Register of the United States, Part 2, Vol. 4. Philadelphia: G. Palmer, 1816.

History of Fayette County, Indiana. Chicago: Warner, Beers, 1885.

History of Middlesex County, New Jersey. John P. Wall and Harold E. Pickersgill, eds. New York and Chicago: Lewis Historical, 1921.

History of Morrow County and Ohio. Chicago: O.L. Baskin, 1880.

History of New England, Vol. 2. Boston: Crocker, 1881.

History of the German Society of Maryland. Published by the Society, 1909.

History of the Great Lakes, Vol. 1. Chicago: J.H. Beers, 1899.

The History of Will County, Illinois. Chicago: William Le Baron, Jr., 1878.

Hord, Rev. Arnold Harris. *Genealogy of the Hord Family.* Philadelphia: J.B. Lippincott, 1898.

Hotchkiss, Fanny Winchester. *Winchester Notes.* New Haven: Tuttle, Morehouse and Taylor, 1912.

Hough, Frank B. *A History of Jefferson County, New York.* Albany: Joel Munsell; and Watertown: Sterling and Riddel, 1854.

Hull, General William. *Memoirs of the Campaign of the Northwestern Army, 1812.* Boston: True and Greene, 1894.

The Illustrated American Biography, Vol. 3. New York: J. Milton Emerson, 1855.

"In Memoriam: General Lewis Cass." *The Free Press,* Detroit, 1866.

Ingersoll, Charles. *Historical Sketch of the Second War Between the United States and Great Britain,* Vols. 1 and 2. Philadelphia: Lee and Blanchard, 1845.

Ingersoll, L.D. *A History of the War Department.* Washington, D.C.: Francis B. Mohun, 1880.

Irelan, John Robert. *History of the Life, Administration and Times of William Henry Harrison.* Chicago: Fairbanks and Palmer, 1888.

Irving, L. Homfray. *Canadian Military Institute Officers of the British Forces in Canada, 1812–1815.* Canada: Welland Tribune, 1908.

Jackson, Isaac Rand. *The Life of William Henry Harrison.* Philadelphia: W. Marshall, 1840.

James, William. *Military Occurrences of the Late War Between Great Britain and the U.S.,* Vol. 1. London: Black, Kingsbury, Parbury and Allen, 1816.

Jenkins, John S. *Jackson and the Generals of the War of 1812.* Philadelphia: J.L. Gihon, 1854.

Johnson, Rossiter. *A History of the War of 1812 Between the United States and Great Britain.* New York: Dodd, Mead, 1882.

Johnston, Henry P. *Yale and Her Honor Roll in the American Revolution.* New York: Privately printed, 1888.

Jones, A.D. *The Illustrated American Biography,* Vol. 3. New York: J. Milton Emerson, 1855.

Judson, Harry Pratt. *The Growth of the American Nation.* Meade, PA, and New York: Flood and Vincent, 1895.

Kelly, Howard A., and Walter L. Burrage. *American Medical Biographies.* Baltimore: Norman Remington, 1920.

King, Edward. *The Great South.* Hartford: American Publishing, 1875.

Kirby, William. *Annals of Niagara.* Lundy's Lane Historical Society, 1896.

Knight, Lucian Lamar. *Georgia's Landmarks, Memorials and Legends,* Vol. 1. Atlanta: Byrd, 1913.

Lamb, Martha J., and Mrs. Burton Harrison. *The History of New York City,* Vol. 3. New York: A.S. Barnes, 1896.

Latour, A. Lacarriere. *Historical Memoir of the War in West Florida and Louisiana.* Philadelphia: John Conrad, 1816.

Lewis, Virgil A. *History of Virginia from Settlement of Jamestown to the Close of the Civil War.* Richmond and Toledo: H.H. Hardesty, 1888.

Life of General Jacob Brown. New York: Nafish and Cornish, 1847.

Life of General Lewis Cass. Philadelphia: G.B. Zieber, 1848.

Lossing, Benson. *The American Historical Record (and Repertory of Notes and Queries),* Vol. 1. Philadelphia: Chase and Town, 1872.

_____. *Eminent Americans,* Vols. 1 and 2. New York: International Book, 1869.

_____. *The Empire State: A Compendious History of Commonwealth of New York.* Hartford: American, 1888.

_____. *Harper's Cyclopaedia of United States History,* Vol. 1. New York and London: Harper's, 1905.

_____. *Lives of Celebrated Americans.* Hartford: Thomas Belknap, 1869.

_____. *The Pictorial Field Book of the War of 1812.* New York: Harper, 1869.

Lovell's History of the Dominion of Canada. Montreal: Lovell, 1876.

MacDonough, Rodney. *Life of Commodore Thomas MacDonough.* Boston: Fort Hill Press, 1909.

Bibliography

Mackenzie, Alexander Slidell. *The Life of Stephen Decatur*. Boston: Charles C. Little and James Brown, 1846.

Maclay, Edgar Stanton. *A History of the American Privateers*. London: Sampson Low, Marston, 1900.

Magazine of American History, Vol. 15. New York: 1886.

Magazine of American History, Vol. 19. New York 1888.

The Magazine of History, Vol. 7. New York: William Abbott, 1881.

The Magazine of History, Vol. 8. New York: William Abbott, 1908.

Magazine of Western History, Vol. 12. New York: Magazine of Western History, 1890.

The Maine Historical and Genealogical Recorder, Vol. 3. Portland, ME: S.M. Watson, 1886.

Mansfield, Edward Deering. *The Life of General Winfield Scott*. New York: A.S. Barnes, 1852.

_____. *The Military Services of Lt. General Winfield Scott*. New York: N.C. Miller, 1862.

Marine, William M. *The British Invasion of Maryland*. Baltimore: The Society of the War of 1812. 1913.

Markham, Edwin. *Valor and Victory: The Age of Vindication*, Vol. 10. New York and Chicago: William H. Wise, 1912.

McAfee, John J. *Kentucky Politicians: Sketches of Representative Corn Crackers*. Louisville: Courier Journal, 1886.

McClay, Edgar Stanton. *A History of American Privateers*. London: Sampson Low, Marston, 1900.

McDonald, John. *Biographical Sketches of General Nathaniel Massie, General Duncan McArthur, Captain William Wells and General Simon Kenton*. Cincinnati: E. Morgan, 1838.

McGregor, John. *British America*, Vol. 2. London: T. Cadell, Strand; and Edinburgh: William Blackwood, 1833.

McMaster, John Bach. *A History of the People of the United States: From the Revolution to the Civil War*, Vol. 4. New York: D. Appleton, 1895.

McQueen, James. *A Narrative of the Principal Military Events During the Memorable Campaigns of 1812, 1813, and 1814*. Glasgow: Edward Khull, 1814.

Men of Mark in Georgia, Vols. 1 and 2. Atlanta: A.B. Caldwell, 1910.

The Mexican War and Its Heroes. Philadelphia: Grigg, Elliot, 1849.

The Military and Naval Magazine of the United States, Vol. 1. Washington: Thompson and Homas, 1833.

Miller, Stephen F. *The Bench and Bar of Georgia*, Vol. 1. Philadelphia: J.B. Lippincott, 1858.

_____. *Memoir of General David Blackshear*. Philadelphia: J.B. Lippincott, 1858.

Moore, Edward E. *A Century of Indiana*. New York, Cincinnati and Chicago: American Book, 1910.

Moore, John W. *History of North Carolina*. Raleigh: Alfred Williams, 1880.

Morgan, Forrest. *Connecticut as a Colony and as a State*, Vol. 3. Hartford: Publishing Society of Connecticut, 1904.

Morgan, Henry J. *Sketches of Celebrated Canadians*. Montreal: R. Worthington, 1865.

Morton, J. Sterling. *Illustrated History of Nebraska*. Lincoln: Western Publishing and Engraving, 1905.

Murdoch, Beamish. *A History of Nova Scotia or Acadie*, Vol. 3. Halifax: James Barnes, 1867.

A Narrative of the Campaigns of the British Army: Washington and New Orleans. London: John Murray, 1821.

The National Cyclopaedia of American Biography, Vol. 5. New York: James T. White, 1894.

The National Cyclopaedia of American Biography, Vol. 15. New York: James T. White, 1909.

The National Cyclopaedia of American Biography, Vol. 13. New York: James T. White, 1906.

The National Magazine, Vol. 1 (November 1884–April 1885). Cleveland, OH, 1885.

National Magazine, Vol. 27. Boston: America: 1903.

The National Portrait Gallery of Distinguished Americans, Vol. 1. New York: Monson Bancroft; Philadelphia: Henry Perkins; and London: O. Rich, 1834.

The National Portrait Gallery of Distinguished Americans, Vol. 2. New York: Monson Bancroft; Philadelphia: Henry Perkins; and London: O. Rich, 1835.

The National Portrait Gallery of Distinguished Americans, Vol. 3. Philadelphia: D. Rice and A.A. Hart, 1854.

The National Portrait Gallery of Distinguished Americans, Vol. 4. Philadelphia: Robert E. Peterson, 1853.

Neff, Jacob K. *The Army and Navy of America*. Lancaster, PA: John Pearsol, 1868.

The New American Encyclopedia, Vol. 15. New York and London: D. Appleton, 1862.

The New England Historical and Genealogy Register, Vol. 28. Boston: By the Society, 1874.

The New International Encyclopedia, Vol. 7. New York: Dodd, Mead, 1909.

Niles Weekly Register, Vol. 30. Baltimore: Franklin Press, 1826.

The North Carolina Booklet, Vol. 9. North Carolina Society, Daughters of the Revolution, 1909.

Notes and Queries: Historical, Biographical and Genealogical, Relating Chiefly to Interior Pennsylvania, Volume 1897. Harrisburg, PA: Harrisburg Publishing, 1898.

Nuckolls, B.F. *Pioneer Settlers of Grayson County Virginia*. Bristol, TN: King Printing, 1914.

O'Byrne, William R. *A Naval Biographical Dictionary*. London: John Murray, 1849.

_____. *The Biographical Dictionary of the Officers of the Royal Navy*. London: William Clowes.

The Old Northwest Genealogical Quarterly, Vol. 3. Columbus: Old Northwest Genealogical Society, 1900.

Owen, Thomas McAdory. *History of Alabama and Dictionary of Alabama Biography*, Vol. 3. Chicago: S.J. Clarke, 1921.

Paine, Ralph D. *The Fight for a Free Sea*. New Haven: Yale University Press, 1921.

Parton, James. *The Life of Andrew Jackson*, Vol. 1 and Vol. 3. New York: Mason Brothers, 1860.

The Past and Present of Plattsburgh. Troy, NY: Troy Printing House, 1891.

Paullin, Charles Oscar. *Commodore John Rodgers*. Cleveland: Arthur H. Clark, 1910.

Pennsylvania Archives, Vol. 4. Harrisburg, PA: Harrisburg Publishing, 1907.

Pennsylvania Archives, Second Series, Vol. 12. Harrisburg, PA: Lane S. Hart, 1880.

Pennsylvania Magazine of History, Vol. 21. Philadelphia: Historical Society of Pennsylvania, 1897.

Pennsylvania Magazine of History, Vol. 35. Philadelphia: Historical Society of Pennsylvania, 1911.

Peterson, Charles J. *History of the United States Navy: Biographical Sketches of American Naval Heroes*. Philadelphia: James B. Smith, 1860.

Peyton, J. Lewis. *History of Augusta County, Virginia*. Staunton: Samuel M. Yost, 1882.

Pickett, Albert James. *History of Alabama*, Vol. 2. Charleston: Walker and James, 1851.

Pictorial Life of Andrew Jackson. Philadelphia: Lindsay and Blakiston, 1845.

Pinckney, Reverend Charles Coatesworth. *The Life of General Thomas Pinckney*. Boston and New York: Houghton Mifflin, 1895.

The Pioneer and General History of Geauga County, New York. Published by the Historical Society of Geauga County, 1880.

Poore, Ben Perley. *The Political and Congressional Directory, 1776–1878*. Boston: Houghton, Osgood, 1878.

Porter, Admiral David. *Memoir of Commodore David Porter*. Albany: J. Munsell, 1875.

Porter, Captain David. *A Voyage in the South Seas: 1812, 1813 and 1814*. London: Sir Richard Phillips, 1823.

Porter, Joseph W. *Genealogy of Descendants of Richard Porter*. Bangor, ME: Burr and Robinson, 1878.

Powell, E. Alexander. *Some Forgotten Heroes and Their Place in American History*. New York, Chicago and Boston: Charles Scribner's, 1922.

Proceedings of the Biennial Meeting, Society of the War of 1812. Lancaster, PA: Published by the Society, 1911.

Proceedings of the Virginia Historical Society, December 1891. Richmond: Published by the Society, 1892.

Public Papers of Daniel B. Tompkins, Governor of New York, Military, Vol. 3. Albany: Published by the State of New York, J.B. Lyon, 1902.

Public Papers of Governor George Clinton, Vol. 2. Albany: Published by the State of New York, 1900.

Publication of the Buffalo Historical Society, Vol. 5. Buffalo: By the Society, 1902.

Publication of the Buffalo Historical Society, Vol. 7. Buffalo: By the Society, 1904.

Publications of the Mississippi Historical Society, Vol. 4. Jackson, MS: Printed for the Society, 1921.

Publications of the Nebraska State Historical Society, Vol. 20. Lincoln: Published by the Society, 1922.

Read, D.B. *Life and Times of Major General Sir Isaac Brock*. Toronto: William Briggs; Montreal: C.W. Coates; Halifax: B.F. Huestis, 1894.

Register of Debates in Congress, Vol. 12. Washington: Gales and Eaton, 1836.

Register of Kentucky State Historical Society, Frankfort, KY. Louisville, 1904.

The Register of the Kentucky State Historical Society, Vol. 18, No 53. Date of publication unknown.

Report of the Adjutant General, State of New Hampshire, The Year Ending June 1, 1868. Manchester: John B. Clarke, 1868.

Revolutionary Characters of New Haven. New Haven: General Humphrey's Branch of the Connecticut Society of the Sons of the American Revolution, 1911.

Reynolds, Cuyler. *Genealogical and Family History of Southern New York and the Hudson River Valley*, Vol. 3. New York: Lewis Historical, 1914.

Richards, George H. *Memoirs of Major General Alexander Macomb*. New York: M'Elrath, Bangs, 1833.

Richardson, Hester Dorsey. *The Patriotic Marylander*, Vol. 1, No. 1. Baltimore: The Maryland Daughters of the American Revolution, 1914.

Roosevelt, Theodore. *The Naval War of 1812*. New York and London: G.P. Putnam's, 1902.

Scharf, J. Thomas. *History of Baltimore City and County*. Philadelphia: Louis H. Everts, 1881.

———. *History of Maryland: 1812–1880*, Vol. 3. Baltimore: John B. Piet, 1879.

———. *History of St. Louis and County*, Vol. 2. Philadelphia: Louis Everts, 1883, 1812.

Scott, Winfield. *Memoirs of Lt. General Winfield Scott*, Vol. 1. New York: Sheldon, 1864.

Seaver, Frederick J. *Historical Sketches of Franklin and Its Several Towns*. Albany: J.B. Lyon, 1918.

The Sewanee Review, Vol. 4. Sewanee, TN: University Press, 1895.

Shaw, William F. *History of Essex and Hudson Counties, New Jersey*, Vol. 1. Philadelphia: Ecerts and Peck, 1874.

Sheads, Scott S. *Guardian of The Star-Spangled Banner: Lt. Colonel George Armistead and the Fort McHenry Flag*. Baltimore: Toomey Press, 1999.

Shinn, Josiah Hazen. *Pioneers and Makers of Arkansas*. Baltimore: Genealogical and Historical, 1908.

Schribner's Monthly. New York, 1872.

Silliman, Augustus E. *A Gallop Among American Scenery*. New York: A.S. Barnes, 1881.

Simpson, Henry. *The Lives of Eminent Americans*. Philadelphia: William Brotherhead, 1859.

A Sketch of the Adjutant General's Department, 1775 to 1875. New York City: Printed for private distribution by Colonel James B. Fry, 1875.

Sketches of the War Between the United States and the British Isles, Vols. 1 and 2. Rutland, VT: Fay and Davison, 1815.

Slocum, Charles Elihu. *The History of the Maumee River*. Defiance, OH: Published by the author, 1914.

Small, H. Beaufort. *Chronicles of Canada*. Ottawa: G.E. Desbarats, 1868.

The South Carolina Historical Magazine and Genealogy, Vol. 1. Charleston: The S.C. Historical Society, 1900.

Spears, John R. *The History of Our Navy, 1775–1897*, Vol. 1. New York: Charles Scribner's, 1897.

Spillane, Edward P. *Life and Letters of Henry Van Rensselaer*. New York: Fordham University Press, 1908.

Stearns, Ezra S. *History of Plymouth, New Hampshire*, Vol. 2. Cambridge: Cambridge University Press, 1906.

Stevens, Walter B. *St. Louis: The Fourth City, 1794–1911*, Vol. 2: St. Louis and Chicago: S. J. Clarke, 1911.

The Story of the Battle of New Orleans. New Orleans: Louisiana Historical Society, 1915.

Strait, Newton A. *Alphabetical List of Battles, 1754–1900, Compiled from Official Sources*. Washington D.C., 1905.

Strother, D.H. *Illustrated Life of General Winfield Scott*. New York: A.S. Barnes, 1847.

Thomas, R. *The Glory of America*. New York: Ezra Strong, 1834.

———. *A Pictorial History of the United States of America*. Hartford: E. Strong, 1847.

Thwaites, Reuben Gold. *Early Travels*, Vol. 4. Cleveland: Arthur H. Clark, 1904.

Tomes, Robert. *Battles of America by Sea and Land*, Vol. 2. New York: James S. Virtue, 1878.

Tomlinson, Everett T. *The War of 1812*. New York, Chicago and Boston: Silver, Burdett, 1906.

Treman, Ebenezer Mack, and Murray E. Poole. *The History of the Treman, Tremaine and Truman Families in America*. Press of the Ithaca Democrat 1901.

The Twentieth Century Biographical Dictionary, Vol. 8. Rossiter Johnson, ed. Boston: Biographical Society, 1904.

The Twentieth Century Biographical Dictionary, Vol. 10. Rossiter Johnson, ed. Boston: The Biographical Society, 1904.

Tyler, Lyon G. *Men of Mark in Virginia*. Washington, D.C.: Men of Mark, 1906.

United States Naval Institute Proceedings, Vol. 34, Part 2. Annapolis: Naval Institute, 1908.

The Universal Encyclopaedia, Vol. 2. New York: D. Appleton, 1890.

Van Rensselaer, Maunsell. *Annals of the Van Rensselaers of the United States*. Albany: Charles Van Benthuysen, 1888.

Van Rensselaer, Solomon. *A Narrative of the Affair of Queenston: War of 1812*. New York: Leavitt, Lord. Boston: Crocker and Brewster, 1836.

Victor, O.J. *Winfield Scott, Commander-in-Chief: Life and Military Civic Services*. New York and London: Eadle, 1861.

Virginia Magazine of History and Biography, Vol. 2. Richmond: House of the Society, 1895.

Virginia Magazine of History and Biography, Vol. 4. Richmond: House of the Society, 1897.

Waldo, S. Putnam. *Life and Character of Stephen Decatur*. Middleton, CT: Oliver D. Cooke, 1822.

Walker, Alexander. *Jackson and New Orleans*. New York: J.C. Derby, 1856.

Walker, Francis A. *The Making of the Nation*. New York: Charles Scribner's, 1905.

Wallace, Lew. *The Life of Benjamin Harrison*. Philadelphia, Chicago, Kansas: Hubbard, 1888.

Warfield, J.D. *The Founders of Anne Arundel and Howard Counties, Maryland*. Baltimore: Kohn and Pollock, 1905.

Watson, John F. *Annals of Philadelphia and Pennsylvania in the Olden Times*, Vol. 3. Philadelphia: Edwin S. Stuart, 1899.

Western Reserve and Northern Ohio Historical Society. Cleveland: Fairbanks, 1877.

Wheeler, George Augustus. *History of Castine, Penobscot and Brooksville, Maine*. Bangor: Burr and Robinson, 1875.

Wheeler, John H. *Historical Sketches of North Carolina, 1584 to 1851*. Philadelphia: Lippincott, Grambo, 1851.

Wheeler, Richard Anson. *History of the Town of Stonington*. New London: Press of the Day, 1900.

White, Truman C. *Our Country and Its People: Erie County, New York*, Vol. 1. Boston: Boston History, 1898.

Williams, John Lee. *The Territory of Florida*. New York: A.T. Goodrich, 1837.

Williams, John S. *History of the Invasion and Capture of Washington*. New York: Harper, 1857.

Wilson, Leonard. *Makers of America*, Vol. 2. City of Washington: B.F. Johnson, 1916.

Wilson, Thomas. *The Biography of the Principal American Military and Naval Heroes*, Vol. 2. New York: John Low, 1820.

Winborne, Benjamin B. *The Colonial and State History of Hertford County, North Carolina*. Published by the author, 1906.

Wiseman, C.M.L. *Centennial History of Lancaster, Ohio*. Lancaster, OH: C.M.L. Wiseman, 1898.

Wyatt, Thomas. *Memoirs of the Generals, Commodores and Other Commanders: American Revolution and War of 1812*. Philadelphia: Carey and Hart, 1848.

Yearbook of American Clan Gregor Society. Richmond: Appeals Press, 1916.

Young, Colonel Bennett H. *The Battle of the Thames*. Louisville: John P. Morton, 1903.

Young, John Russell. *Memorial History of the City of Philadelphia*, Vol. 2. New York: New York History, 1898.

Young, William T. *Sketch of the Life and Public Service of General Lewis Cass*. Detroit: Markham and Eldon, 1852.

Index

Abellino (privateer) 301
Abigail (vessel) 63
Able (brigantine) 174
HMS *Acasta* 40, 42, 48, 60, 73, 87, 123, 127, 128, 221, 222, 225, 270, 296
Achinson, Lt. Colonel 180
Acorn (brigantine) 297
Active (brigantine) 123
Active (privateer) 111
Active (ship) 63
Active (vessel) 31
Active Jane 294
Actress (privateer) 38, 39
Aculco 17
Adair, British major (Royal Marines) 284
Adair, General John 156, 282
USS *Adams* (sloop) 197, 216, 225, 243
Adams (US Army vessel) 27, 52
Adams, A. (master) 44
Adams, Captain (Genesee militia) 175
Adams, Captain (infantry officer *Alabama*) 191
Adams, Captain (USS *Georgiana*) 129
Adams, Colonel (General Petit's brigade) 208
Adams, Major General David 174, 201, 263, 303
Adams, Colonel George 60
Adams, John Quincy 20, 259, 37, 100, 168, 184, 226
Adams, Major 135, 181
Adams, Peter USN 123
Adams, William 226
Addams, Brigadier General John 254
Adel (British ship) 264
Adeline (American schooner) 86
Adeline (brigantine; seized 15 August 1812) 50
Adeline (brigantine; seized 21 August 1812) 56
Adeline (later USS *Asp*) 96
Adeline (privateer) 174
Adelphi (ship) 89
HMS *Adeona* 43
Aderton, British Captain Thomas 158
Adiona (British brigantine) 48
Adiona (schooner) 292

Adler's Post 86
Adventure (vessel) 215
Advocate (privateer) 31
HMS *Aeolus* 29, 35, 36, 38, 40, 63, 87
Aeolus (vessel) 110
Affleck, British captain 44
HMS *Africa* 29, 35, 36, 38, 53, 55
Agnes (brigantine) 179
Agnes (schooner) 112
Agnew, British Captain James 208
Agnew, Captain Samuel 25
Aiken's volunteers 246
Alabama Indians 135
HMS *Alban* 242, 247
Albany, New York 185
HMS *Albion* 165, 175, 200, 214, 227
Albion (brigantine) 222
Albion (British merchant ship) 94, 96, 97, 98
Albion (ship) 94
Alden, John (master) 50
Alder (vessel) 72
HMS *Alert* 36, 48, 49, 53, 87, 138, 175
Alert (brigantine) 102, 298
Alert (later *Decatur*) 89
Alert (sloop) 165
Alexander (privateer) 105, 115
Alexander, Joseph 38
Alexander, Major 113
Alexander I, Czar 13, 14, 33, 58, 100, 168
Alexis (brigantine) 95
Alfred (British brigantine) 35
Alfred (privateer) 50, 53, 195
Algeria 216
HMS *Algerine* 87
Algiers 291, 295, 299, 300, 301, 302
Alianza (ship) 157
Alicia (vessel) 159
Allcorn, Colonel John 168
USS *Allegany* (*Alleghany*) 39
USS *Allen* (gunboat) 241
Allen, Ezekiel (master) 240
Allen, General James 161
Allen, Lt. Colonel John 50, 58, 59, 60, 67, 87, 89, 90, 91, 92
Allen, Captain William Henry 147
Allen's farmhouse 246

Allen's Island 221
USS *Alligator* (armed schooner) 103, 131
USS *Alligator* (2) 131
Alligator (Gunboat No. 166) 131, 267
Alligator (vessel) 146
Alligator Indians 64
Allison, J. B. (master) 113
Almeda, Captain 174
Alonzo (Spanish brigantine) 263
HMS *Alpha* 57
Alson, J. 134
Altberg, E. (master) 63
Altham, T. (master) 103
Amazon (vessel) 259
Ambition (brigantine) 61
Ambition (sloop) 255
Amelia (privateer) 298
USS *Amelia* (schooner) 84
Amelia (sloop) 145, 212
Amelia Island 23, 24, 209
America (privateer) 60, 61, 64, 67, 77, 79, 80, 82, 88, 132, 175, 204, 205, 260, 292, 297, 298
America (vessel) 29
American Pacific Fur Company 18
Amey, Lt. Colonel Henry 250
Amherstburg (formerly Malden) 52, 157
Amicus (brigantine) 102
Anaconda (American privateer) 84, 89, 115, 121, 133, 136
Anderson, British Lt. 119
Anderson, Colonel John 92
Anderson, John (master) 48
Anderson, Mrs. 93
Anderson, Colonel William P. 131
Anderson's trading post 92
Andrews, J. (master) 176
Angus, Captain 140
Angus, Lieutenant Samuel H. 80
Anita (Spanish brigantine) 227
Ann (67-ton sloop) 212
Ann (120-ton brigantine) 165
Ann (142-ton schooner) 113
Ann (boat) 222
Ann (brigantine) 151, 156

Ann (brigantine; seized in 1812) 165
Ann (brigantine; seized 4 November 1813) 165
Ann (packet) 31
Ann (schooner; seized by the *Nonpareil*) 43
Ann (schooner; seized by the privateer *Globe*) 49
Ann Dorothy (vessel) 264
Ann Green (vessel) 42
Ann Kelly (schooner) 40, 43
Anna (125-ton brigantine) 126
Annapolis, Maryland 147, 182
Ansart, British lieutenant 211
Anson (schooner) 74
HMS *Antelope* 87
Antelope (brigantine; seized by the *Chasseur*) 102, 298
Antelope (brigantine; seized by the *Dolphin*) 40
Antelope (schooner) 222
Apollo (250-ton brigantine) 205
Apollo (ship) 34, 49
Apollo (sloop) 102
Appallodore (schooner) 205
Applegarth, British Captain 71
Appleseed, Johnny 62
Appling, Major (later Lt. Col.) Daniel 213, 214, 246
HMS *Arab* (18-gun) 87, 169, 263
Arab (schooner) 104
HMS *Arachine* 87
Arbuckle, Colonel Matthew 295
Archangel, Russia 138
Archibald Gracie and Sons 29
Arenos, Frederica 214
HMS *Arethusa* 87
Argo (brigantine) 60
Argo (privateer) 241
Argus (American privateer) 39, 43
USS *Argus* (formerly *Merrimac*) 27, 31, 68, 127, 133, 147
USS *Argus II* 147
USS *Ariel* 157, 158, 159, 184
HMS *Armada* 241
Armar (soldier) 192
HMS *Armide* 200, 218, 231, 258

Armistead, Major 125, 252
Armistice (104-ton schooner) 275
Armistice (privateer) 264
Armistice (schooner) 215
Armstrong, Henry B. (Army officer) 72
Armstrong, Brigadier General John 34
Armstrong, General John (Secretary of War) 22, 34, 45, 82, 87, 93, 95, 98, 99, 101, 102, 116, 134, 139, 146, 148, 159, 151, 152, 157, 158, 165, 176, 180, 183, 186, 189, 195, 218, 220, 221, 228, 229, 231, 234, 235, 236, 253; named secretary of war 81
Armstrong, Sergeant (later brigadier general) Robert 190, 289
Army Bill Act (Canadian) 84
Arnold's Mills 160, 179
Arrow (privateer) 290
Arrow (schooner) 292
Arundel, Robert (master) 68, 77
Ashford, James USN 55
Ashley, Lt. Colonel William H. 27
HMS *Asia* 225
Asken, J. (master) 134
Askew, J. (master) 59
USS *Asp* (formerly *Adeline*) 96, 136, 137, 146, 151
Aspinwall, Colonel 119
Astor, John J. 19, 57
Astoria, Oregon 86
Astoria Post *see* Fort Astor
HMS *Atalanta* 36, 82
HMS *Atalante* 104, 129
Atalante (British privateer) 106
Atchenson (Atkinson), Lt. Colonel 180
Atkins, J. (master) 169
Atkinson, Captain 105
Atkinson, Captain Thomas W. 153
Atkinson, Lt. 127
Atlanta (brigantine) 164, 253, 255
Atlanta (formerly *Siro*) 88
Atlantic (*Atlanta*) (brigantine) 102, 298

371

USS *Atlantic* (later *Essex Jr.*) 101, 129
Atlantic (letter of marque) 118
Atlas (3-gun schooner) 31
Atlas (privateer; later HMS *St. Lawrence*) 31, 33, 121, 133, 136, 138, 295
Atlas (schooner) 293
Atwater, Acting Governor Reuben 32
Auld, Colonel 148
Aurora (vessel) 186
Austill, Captain Evan 153, 173, 192
Austill, Jeremiah 173, 174
Austin, C. J. 87
Austin, John (master) 213
Austin, Major 60
Austin, Lieutenant Colonel William 294
Austria 241
Autauga Indians 135
Auttose, Alabama 174
Avart Plantation 269, 271
HMS *Avenger* 175
HMS *Avon* 241, 242
USS *Aylwyn* (gunboat) 241
Aylwin, Lieutenant 85
Ayton, W. (master) 242
Azores Archipelago 255

Babbit, Lieutenant 290
Baby, British Lt. Col. 192, 195
HMS *Bacchante* 247, 255, 260
HMS *Bacchus* 112, 253
Bacchus (brigantine) 153
Baccus (British merchant ship) 254
Backus, Lt. Colonel Electus 116, 118, 119, 120
Bacon, Captain (cavalry) 64
Bacon, Mr. Constant 209
Bailey, Captain Dixon 139, 141, 145, 147, 149, 150
Bailey, James 150
Bailey, Mrs. 150
Bailey, Peggy 150
Bainbridge (ship) 55
Bainbridge, Joseph 203, 205
Bainbridge, Captain William (commodore) USN 18, 20, 26, 27, 30, 42, 68, 76, 80, 84, 85, 87, 88, 93, 98, 122, 199, 295, 300, 301, 302
Baker, A. (master) 106
Baker, Captain 229, 282
Baker, Captain Daniel 47
Baker, G. B. (master) 126
Baker, Thomas 87
Bald Island 216
Baldwin, Loammi 183
Ball, John 134
Ball, Major (later colonel) James V. 67, 132, 134, 138, 156, 158
Ball, Peter 134
HMS *Ballahon* 87
HMS *Ballahou* 293
USS *Ballard* (gunboat) 241
Ballard, Captain Bland W. 64, 65, 90
Ballard, Edward J. USN 122
Ballard, Mr. 122
Ballenger, Major 147
Ball's farm 134

Baltic (262-ton ship) 164
Baltimore (American privateer) 86
Baltimore (American schooner) 68
Baltimore, Maryland 41, 105, 246
Bancroft, H. (master) 106
Bangor Packet 242
Banhouse, H. F. 87
Banks of Newfoundland 32
Barbados 175
HMS *Barbados* 206
Barbee, Colonel Joshua 64
Barber, D. 87
Barbour, Governor James 21
Barbour, Colonel Philip 154
Barclay (vessel) 118, 133
Barclay, British Captain Robert Heriot 117, 142, 144, 154, 155, 158
Barker, Benjamin (master) 174
Barker, Captain 178
Barlow, Joel 20
Barlow, Joseph (minister to France) 18, 20
Barnard, Timpoochy 191
Barnes, A. (master) 142
Barnes, Captain (privateer *Surprise*) 222
Barnes, Captain J. 86, 290
Barnett, Benjamin 252
Barney, J. T. (master) 103
Barney, Commodore Joshua 37, 39, 40, 42, 44, 48, 49, 57, 60, 62, 69, 75, 77, 133, 196, 214, 215, 216, 217, 231, 232, 234, 235, 236
Barney, Major William 215
Barnstable, Massachusetts 221
HMS *Barossa* 126
Barr, Major Thomas 157
Barret, Lt. Thomas 225
Barrette, British Lieutenant G. W. 144, 145
Barrie, Robert 87
Barron, Captain (Commodore) James 12, 13
Barron, James, Sr. (Commodore of Virginia Navy) 12, 291
HMS *Barrossa* 115, 127
Barry, Commodore John 11, 291, 295
Barry, Major William T. 157
Bartholomew, Colonel Joseph 83
Bartholomew, Lt. 65
Bartlett, W. (master) 165
Bartley, British Lt. 80
Barton, Lieutenant 170
Bartram, Brigadier General George (Pennsylvania) 247
Basden, British Captain 195, 196
Basden, William Benge (purser) 256
Bass Island 157
Bassano, Duc de (French foreign minister) 20
Bassett, Major 80
Bassett's Creek Valley 151
Basswood Cantonment 120
Bastard, Captain RN 29
Batavia, New York 180, 181, 186, 190, 195

Bates, Captain 174
Bathburst, Earl Henry 197, 206
Baton Rouge 100, 131, 264, 267
Battery at Point Peter 23, 279
Battle of Bridgewater *see* Battle of Lundy's Lane
Battle of Burnt Corn 140
Battle of Caulk's Field 241
Battle of Cedar Point 214
Battle of Chippewa 218
Battle of Cholocco *see* Battle of Horseshoe Bend
Battle of Chrysler's Farm (Battle of Williamsburg) 171
Battle of Fallen Timbers 33
Battle of Frenchtown 89
Battle of Horseshoe Bend (Battle of Cholocco) 200
Battle of Lake Champlain 247
Battle of Lake Erie 154
Battle of Lundy's Lane 222
Battle of Mississinewa 83
Battle of Mooresfield *see* Battle of Caulk's Field
Battle of New Orleans 283
Battle of Niagara *see* Battle of Lundy's Lane
Battle of Plattsburgh *see* Battle of Lake Champlain
Battle of Queenston 70
Battle of Raisin River (Raisin River Massacre) 90, 91
Battle of Sacket's Harbor 118, 119, 120
Battle of St. Leonard's Creek (first) 214
Battle of Slippery Hill 147
Battle of Sodus Point 126
Battle of Stoney Creek 124
Battle of Talladega 170
Battle of Tallusehatche (Tallasehatche) 168
Battle of the Canoes 173
Battle of the Thames 160
Battle of Tippecanoe 20
Battle of Williamsburg *see* Battle of Chrysler's Farm
Battle of York (Toronto) 106
Battle (Siege) of Fort Bowyer 252
Battle (Siege) of Fort Erie 225, 229
Battle (Siege) of Fort McHenry 250
Baupen, A. (master) 136
Bayard, James A. 100, 168, 184, 226
Bayonne Decree 15
Beale's Rifles 273, 282
Beall, General Reazin 56, 75
Beall, Colonel William 232, 235, 236
Beall's Camp at Canton 22
Beam's Blockhouse 22
Bean, R. O. (master) 141
Beanes, Doctor William 252
Bear Creek 250
Beasley, Major Daniel 141, 148, 149
Beatty, Lt. Colonel H. 127
Beaufew, F. (master) 213
Beauharnois, Quebec 165
Beaver Dam 117, 128, 134
Beckwith, General Sir Sidney

Royal Marines 94, 123, 130, 147, 148
Bedel, Brigadier General Moody (New Hampshire militia; also Lt. Col 11th Regiment, USA) 33, 254, 255
Bedel, General Timothy 33, 254
Bee (schooner) 220, 238
Beekmantown Road 245
Belfast (vessel) 105
Belfield (brigantine) 211
Belgrade (brigantine) 112
Bell, Colonel John R. 214
Belle (107-ton schooner) 125
Bellefontaine, Ohio 12, 17, 340
Belleisle (brigantine) 35
Bellevue, Lieutenant USMC 273
Bellinger, Colonel Christopher P. 22, 32, 40
Bellona Arsenal 303
Bellville Post at Bellville 22
HMS *Belvidera* 29, 32, 33, 35, 36, 38, 43, 45, 55, 56, 61, 87, 95, 101, 103, 104, 106, 157, 174, 242
Benedict, Maryland 216, 231, 247
Benedict, Colonel Thomas B. 32, 94, 97
Benevolent Blues 23
Benjamin (brigantine) 77
Benjamin Franklin (privateer) 41, 43, 75
Benjamin Franklin (vessel) 36
Bennet, Major 178, 179
Bennett, Captain Richard 154
Bennett, W. H. (master) 247
Benson, General Perry 21, 113, 148, 165
Bentley's battalion 78
Benton, Jesse 116, 151
Benton, Colonel (later U.S. senator) Thomas H. 116, 151
Berbel, Lieutenant 282
HMS *Beresford* 169, 226
Beresford, British Admiral Sir J. P. 87, 98, 123, 134
Berg, C. C. (master) 157
Berg, Johan Magnus 226
Berg, Justin Nelson 190
Berlin Blockhouse at Cheshire 22
Berlin Decree 13, 16
Bernadotte, Marshall Jean Baptiste Jules (changes name to Charles John) 16
Berry, Captain 160
Berry Castle (ship) 209
Berryman, Captain William 154
Bersford, British Captain John 103
Bertoddy, Charles (master) 43
Betsey (brigantine) 208
Betsey (brigantine out of Malaga) 34
Betsey (British brigantine) 147
Betsey (sloop) 44
Betsey Ann 70
Betsy (88-ton sloop) 242
Betsy (98-ton sloop) 176
Betsy (117-ton schooner) 137
Betsy (333-ton schooner) 247

Betsy (lookout boat) 116
Betsy (schooner) 214, 247
Betsy (ship) 217
Betsy (sloop; seized 26 March 1813) 103
Betsy (sloop; seized 31 March 1813) 103
Betsy and Jane (schooner) 165, 47
Biays, Lt. Colonel James 250
Biddle, Captain James 123, 185, 290, 297
Biddle, Captain John 230
Biddle, Lt. 73
Bienville, Governor 206
Bienvu Plantation 292
Big Salmon River 213
Big Sandy Creek 213
Bilbo, 1st Lieutenant Archibald 153
Binns, John 26
Bird (80-ton schooner) 106
Birdsall, Captain Benjamin 230
Bissell, Colonel (later brigadier general) Daniel 190, 198, 259
Bissell, Deborah 259
Bissett, Lieutenant Alexander 81
Bisshopp, Lt. Colonel (later colonel) Cecil 80, 117, 135
Black Fish Jr. (Shawnee) 108
Black Joke (privateer) 34
Black Rock Navy Yard (Buffalo) 68, 69, 135, 177, 182, 183, 225
Black Snake (gunboat No. 9) 216, 217
Black Swamp 78
Black Swan (brigantine) 259
Blackfeet Indians 13, 16
Blackshear, Ann Eliza 263
Blackshear, Caroline Floyd 263
Blackshear, Major (later brigadier general) David 81, 144, 174, 185, 187, 253, 259, 263, 294
Blackshear, David Jr. 263
Blackshear, Edward Jefferson 263
Blackshear, Elijah Francs 263
Blackshear, Eliza Ann 263
Blackshear, Everard Hamilton 263
Blackshear, Fanny Hamilton 263
Blackshear, Isabella Maria C. Everard 263
Blackshear, James Hamilton 263
Blackshear, John Duke 263
Blackshear, Joseph John Floyd 263
Blackshear, Mary Ann L. Hamilton 263
Blackshear, Mary Hamilton 263
Blackshear, Mary Jane Pittman 263
Blackshear, William Thweatt 263
Blackstone, Maryland 113
Bladensburg, Maryland 231, 232
Blair, Richard 169
Blake, General John 183, 243

Index

Blakeley, Master Commandant Johnston 209, 214, 216
Blakeley, Lt. Colonel 181
Blakeney, Lt. Colonel Sir Edward 281
Blakeslee, Colonel 182
Blanchard, C. (master) 104
Blanco, Mr. 194
Blaney, Lieutenant USN 211
Blanque, John 243
Blennerhassett, Harman 12
Blessed Mother 17
Bligh, British Lt. 87
Blockade (privateer) 123
Blockade (privateer 2-gun sloop) 31
Blodget, Mr. 195
Blonde (schooner) 34, 73
Bloodhound (dispatch boat) 36
Bloom, Colonel Henry 62, 183
Bloomfield, Governor (brigadier general; later major general of militia) Joseph (New Jersey) 22, 23, 61, 79, 103, 185, 206, 244, 247, 279
Blount, Governor (Tennessee) William "Willie" 169, 175, 207
Bluche (Baritarian) 277, 282
Blue, Major Uriah 231, 262
Blue Light Federalists 177
Blyden, N. D. 174
Blythe, British Captain Samuel 152
Boardman, J. (master) 129
Boddely, B. (master) 100
Bodley, Major 81
Boerstler, Lt. Colonel Charles G. 80, 128, 129
Bogardus, Colonel Robert 185
Bogman, B. (master) 158
Boileau, Lt. Colonel Nathan Brittan 53, 244
Boisegeveau canal 285
HMS *Bold* 87, 115, 129
Bolina (vessel) 48
Bon Accord (brigantine) 225, 238
Bona (American privateer) 44
Bonaparte, Joseph 105
Bonaparte, Napoleon *see* Napoleon
HMS *Bonne Citoyenne* 82, 85, 88, 93
Booth, Colonel Davis S. 259
Booth, Major 174, 191
Bordeau, Joseph 90
Bordeaux, France 191
HMS *Borer* 126, 147, 173
USS *Borer* (gunboat) 241
Borodino, Russia 58
USS *Boston* 142, 235
Bostwick, British Captain (later colonel) 80, 163
Boswell, Colonel William E. 109, 110, 113, 155
Botts, Captain George W. 153
Boughton, Lt. 181, 182
Bourne, F. (master) 36
Bowe, Erastus 132
Bowers, Doctor 92
Bowers, Captain Gustavus W. 153
Bowie, General Robert (governor of Maryland) 121

Bowlegs (Indian town) 95, 96
Bowyer, Colonel John 105, 175
HMS *Boxer* 131, 134, 139, 144, 151, 152, 169, 175, 226
USS *Boxer* 303
Boxer (schooner) 221
Boyd (British vessel) 42
Boyd, British captain 209
Boyd, Hannibal (seaman) 97
Boyd, Colonel (later brigadier general) John Parker 15, 20, 27, 56, 103, 117, 118, 125, 128, 134, 157, 165, 171, 298
Boyd, Major 170
Boyer, Colonel Samuel 104
Boyle, B. C. 87
Boyle, Captain James A. 210
Boyle, Captain Thomas 42, 83, 88, 89, 94, 102, 295
Boynton, Ensign 178, 298
Boys, William 31
Bradberry, Captain William 140, 164
Bradford's Pond 184
Bradley, Colonel Edward 170
Brady, Colonel (later brigadier general) Hugh 35, 223, 224, 299
Braganza (vessel) 41, 43
Bramble (British vessel) 182
Branch (78-ton schooner) 109
Branch, John (Secretary of the Navy) 302
Brandt House 124
Brandy Jack (Indian) 91
Brant, Chief Joseph *see* Chief Joseph Brant
Brant, John (the younger) 71, 72, 128, 179
Bray, British captain 126
Bray, Isaac (master) 47
Bray, British Lt. J. 87
HMS *Brazen* 87, 293
Brazier's Landing (later French's Landing) 173
HMS *Bream* 48, 87, 103, 104, 105, 106, 109, 115, 136, 137
Breckenridge, Lt. USMC 127
Breckinridge, General James 17
Brenow, Captain B. 34
Brent, Colonel William 232
Brenton (letter of marque) 153
Brenton, British Captain J. A. 38, 87
Brice, Robert 55
Brigham, Captain 192, 195
Brisbane, British Major General Thomas 245
Britannia (brigantine) 36
Britannia (schooner) 257
Britannia (ship) 59, 89
Britannia (vessel) 112
British Northwest Company 12, 221

British units—
1st British Lincoln Regiment (militia) 71, 178, 182
2nd British Lincoln Regiment (militia) 178
3rd British Lincoln Regiment (militia) 178
4th British Lincoln Regiment (militia) 71, 178, 282
4th British Regiment 138, 234, 272, 277, 282, 286, 293, 297
5th British Lincoln Regiment (militia) 178
7th British Regiment (Fusiliers) 275, 281, 282
8th (King's) British Regiment 31, 70, 107, 116, 119, 178, 182, 183, 190, 195, 199, 204, 220
10th British Royal Veterans Regiment 31
10th Veteran Battalion 91
13th British Regiment 141
14th British Dragoons 275, 292
19th British Regiment 22
21st British Regiment 242, 251, 275, 282, 286
24th British Regiment 293
27th British Regiment 297
39th British Regiment 171
40th British Regiment 275, 297
41st British Regiment 31, 37, 38, 42, 45, 51, 52, 71, 91, 113, 126, 137, 143, 161, 178, 182, 183, 194
43rd British Regiment 275, 281, 282
44th British Regiment 234, 251, 275, 277, 282, 286, 287, 293
49th British Regiment (grenadiers) 31, 71, 79, 80, 116, 124, 133, 169, 171, 178
62nd Regiment 242
64th British Regiment 125
69th British Regiment 242
81st British Regiment 297
85th British Regiment 234, 251, 272, 275, 277, 281, 284, 285, 289
89th British Regiment 169, 178, 183, 194, 196, 206
93rd British Regiment (Highlanders) 273, 275, 277, 282, 285, 286, 287, 297
95th British (Rifles) Regiment 271, 273, 275, 277, 282, 291, 293
98th British Regiment 242
100th British Regiment 31, 119, 137, 138, 141, 178, 179, 182, 183
103rd British Regiment 136, 141, 179, 206, 207, 220
104th British Regiment 38, 119, 126, 178, 220

Light Brigade 237, 269
Light Brigade (Pennsylvania volunteers) 238
Royal Artillery 178, 179
Royal Scots 178, 182, 194, 195, 220

HMS *Briton* 68
Broadnax, Captain John 191
Broadnax, Lt. 64
HMS *Brock* 107
Brock, British captain 77
Brock, Colonel (later major general) Isaac (president of Upper Canada) 19, 22, 35, 36, 37, 38, 45, 46, 48, 49, 50, 51, 52, 53, 56, 62, 69, 70, 71, 72, 73, 77, 176, 185
Brockway's Ferry 204
Broke (British privateer) 144, 146, 148
HMS *Broke* (formerly USS *Growler*) 141
Broke, British Captain Philip Bowes Vere 29, 37, 39, 67, 121, 122
Bronson, Mr. 211
Brontin (Broutin), Captain 289
Brooke, British Colonel Arthur 251, 252, 269
Brooke, George Mercer (later major general) 80
Brooklyn Height 227
Brooks, Colonel 186
Brooks, General John 31, 156
Brooks, Lt. John USMC 103, 156
Brooman's Point 70
Broome, Edward James USN 123
Brothers (bark) 205
Brothers (brigantine) 112, 205
Brothers (British vessel) 43, 44
Broughton, Captain G. 229
Brown, British major 234
Brown, Captain E. 243
Brown, Captain 69, 70
Brown, Captain (privateer *Decatur*) 204
Brown, Lt. Charles 87
Brown, Doctor 186
Brown, Brigadier General (later, general-in-chief USA) Jacob Jennings 25, 32, 42, 44, 62, 63, 66, 67, 69, 70, 118, 119, 120, 138, 148, 165, 168, 171, 173, 176, 189, 190, 194, 195, 204, 209, 210, 218, 219, 220, 221, 222, 223, 224, 225, 230, 231, 254, 257, 274, 296
Brown, Lt. (USS *Oneida*) 151, 225
Brown, Captain James 29, 39
Brown, Captain John 188
Brown, John (master) 217
Brown, John USN 55
Brown, Joshua 169
Brown, Lieutenant 120
Brown, Lt. (commander privateer *Governor Tompkins*) 77
Brown, Lt. (militia) 63
Brown, Moses (master) 247
Brown, British Captain Philip 87

Brown, Captain Return B. 46
Brown, Richard (Cherokee) 168, 303
Brown, S. (master) 165
Brown, Major General Thomas 202
Brown, William (master) 35
Browne, British Lt. C. D. 87
Bruce, J. (master) 114
Brunswick (vessel) 257
Brush, Colonel E. 51, 52
Brush, Captain Henry 45, 46, 52
Bruyeres, British Lt. Col. R. H. 200
Brydges, Lieutenant 292
Buchanan, William B. 250
Buck, Major Thomas 218
Buckmaster, George 227
Buckskin (privateer) 43, 47
Budd, Lt. Charles 122, 123, 145
Budwell, Lieutenant 178
Buffalo, New York 165, 177, 180, 181, 182, 183, 204, 226
Buffalo Creek 177, 181
Buffalo *Gazette* 80, 180
Bullock, Major James S. 81
HMS *Bulwark* 112, 212, 215, 216, 221, 222, 242, 259, 260, 292, 293, 295
Bunker Hill (29-ton schooner) 100
Bunker Hill (privateer) 43, 56
Bunker Hill Monument 183
Burbank, Lt. George W. 89
Burbank, Lieutenant 137
Burbeck, Brigadier General Henry 103, 131, 142
Burch, Captain Benjamin 232, 234
Burch, Captain (privateer *Sparrow*) 175
Burch, Colonel 172, 173
Burchall (British packet) 76
Burch's Mills 224
Burdett, British Captain George 87, 95, 144
Burgess, A. (master) 106, 156
Burgoyne, British General John 138, 162, 239, 254, 279
Burgoyne, Lt. Colonel John Fox 280
HMS *Burlame* 242
Burlington, Vermont 61, 126, 141, 151, 211, 241
Burlington Battery 126
Burlington Heights, Canada 118, 142, 163, 189, 220
Burn, Colonel James (cavalry) 117, 124
Burnett, Mr. 50
Burnett, Brigadier General William 185, 190
Burnham, F. A. (master) 41
Burns, Colonel 124
Burnt Corn 169
Burr, Aaron 12, 13, 14, 21
Burr, Peter (master) 257
USS *Burrows* (gunboat) 241
Burrows, Commander William 86
Burrows, Lt. William 152
Burton, John (master) 260
Bush, Lt. William S. USMC 54, 55
Butler, Colonel (later

brigadier general) Benjamin 115
Butler, Captain 229
Butler, Lt. Colonel H. 197
Butler, Percival 53
Butler, Adjutant General Robert 227, 229
Butler, Governor Simon 243, 244, 247, 279
Butler, Corporal (later major general) William O. 53, 78, 288, 289
Butler, Major General Henry (New Hampshire militia) 33, 138
Butler's Rangers 186
Butts, Captain Samuel 191
Byng, H. D. 87
Byrns' mills 176
Byron, Captain Richard RN 29, 87, 95

Cabell, Governor William H. 17
Cadet (privateer) 47
Cadwalader, Brigadier General Thomas 238, 240, 247
Caesar 173, 174
Cahaba River 184
Cahoone, Captain 147
Cairns, J. (master) 102
Caldwell, British captain 196
Caldwell, Captain Elias B. 65, 215
Caldwell, Captain 215, 235
Caldwell, General Samuel 153, 161
HMS *Caledonia* 68, 69
USS *Caledonia* 126, 154, 155, 221
Caledonia (British privateer) 93, 96, 97
Caledonia (British vessel) 208
Caledonia (ship) 222
Caledonia (vessel) 255, 290
Calhoun, John C. 27
Calibee (Calebee) Creek 191
Caller, Colonel James 139, 140
Caller, Robert (American officer) 140
Calloway, Colonel John 154, 161
Calmar (sloop) 177
Calmes, Brigadier General Marquis 151, 153
Calson (schooner) 134
HMS *Calypso* 256
Camden (105-ton schooner) 151
Camelion (brigantine) 36
Camp Avery 65
Camp Bull 156
Camp Council 22
Camp Crawford (later Fort Scott), Georgia 303
Camp Defiance, Alabama 191
Camp H (Ohio) 72
Camp J (Ohio) 72
Camp New Hope 29
Camp Number Three (Ohio) 72
Camp Russell *see* Fort Russell
Camp Whetstone 22
Campbell. Elizabeth Henry 31
Campbell, Captain John (1st Infantry Regiment) 222, 242, 245
Campbell, Colonel John B. 80, 83, 206, 212, 217, 218, 220, 231
Campbell, Colonel (later brigadier general) William 31, 220
Campbell's Island 218
Canada (transport) 93
Canadian Volunteers 176
Canary Islands 169
Candaleria (sloop) 213
Cannon, Colonel Newton 168
HMS *Canso* (previously privateer *Lottery*) 95, 156
Cantonment Belle Fontaine (later Fort Belle) 259
Cap au Gris Fort *see* Fort Independence, Illinois
Cape Henry 139
Cape Sable (Nova Scotia) 216
Capel, British Captain Thomas Blanden 116, 121, 215
Captain Bulkely (privateer) 58
Captain Isaacs 106
Captain Logan (Shawnee) 60
Caravan (brigantine) 146
Carberry, Colonel Henry 236
Card, John 75
Carden, British Captain John Surman 75, 76
Carey's Blockhouse 17
Carl Gustaff (874-ton ship) 126
Carlbury (ship) 102, 298
Carleton, General Guy 32
Carlotta (brigantine) 128
Carmick, Major Daniel USMC 19, 47
HMS *Carnation* 255, 256
USS *Carolina* 126, 148, 271, 273, 274, 275, 276, 277
Caroline (18-ton schooner) 106
Caroline (195-ton brigantine) 105
Caroline (American privateer) 174
Caroline (sloop) 112
Caroline (vessel) 36
Carpenter, D. 87
Carrick, Captain USMC 277
Carroll, Mr. 294
Carroll, Colonel (later brigadier general) William 170, 189, 190, 263, 269, 271, 276, 277, 278, 282, 283, 287, 288
HMS *Carron* 252
Carroway, Captain 36
Carson, Colonel Joseph 134, 141, 148, 152, 153, 173, 180
Cartagenian Republic 254
Cartwright, Captain David 140
Cartwright, Reverend 297
Cass, Colonel (later brigadier general) Lewis (Secretary of State under President Buchanan) 26, 32, 35, 36, 38, 39, 42, 46, 50, 51, 52, 85, 101, 103, 138, 159, 163, 164, 165, 185, 186, 289
Cass, Lieutenant USN 211
Cassels, Major 180
Casseur (privateer) 298

Cassin, Commodore John USN 94, 138
Cassin, Lt. USN 86
Castle of Ano 42
Castlereagh, British prime minister *see* Stewart, Robert
Cat Island 268
Catalina (160-ton brigantine) 212
Catalina Patriota (ship) 157
Catharine (brigantine) 194
Catherine (8-gun vessel) 129, 133
Catherine (brigantine; seized 1 May 1813) 112
Catherine (letter of marque) 41
Catherine (privateer) 43
Catherine (schooner) 176
Catherine (schooner; seized 4 December 1813) 41
Catherine (vessel) 101, 207
Cato (boat) 242
Cato's Fort 131
Caughnawaga (Indians) 128, 179
Caulk, Captain Isaac 240
Cedar Creek (Alabama) 199
Centipede (barge) 127
USS *Centipede* (gunboat) 241
Centurion (schooner) 104
Ceres (brigantine) 34, 43
Ceres (schooner) 133
Ceres (vessel) 57
Cerez (vessel) 208
Chadds, British Lt. 84, 88
Chalmette house 277
Chamberlain, Captain 105
Chamberlain, S. (master) 57
Chambers, British major 109, 143
Chambers, Captain Ezekiel 240
Chambliss, Lt. W. R.(Mississippi volunteers) 150
Chameau, Lieutenant 282
Champlain Town 141
Champlin, Captain Guy R. 100, 101, 104, 269
Champlin, Captain Stephen 154, 187, 225
Chance (brigantine) 147
Chance (privateer) 30
Chandler, Brigadier General John 22, 79, 100, 103, 124, 125, 190
Channing, Mr. 121
Chantier, Captain Le 94
Chapin, British Colonel (doctor) Cyrenius 136, 180, 183
Chapin, Lt. Col. (Buffalo militia) 181, 182
Chapin, Major 129
Chaplin, L. (master) 58
Chapman, British Ensign P. 246
Chapman, Timothy (master) 266
Chapman, William (master) 40
Charbonneau, Jean Baptiste 13
Charbonneau, Touissant 13, 35
USS *Charinell* 210
Charles IV of Spain, King 14, 105

Charles XIII of Sweden, King 16
Charles (brigantine) 116
Charles (brigantine; captured 5 November 1814) 260
Charles (schooner; captured 26 June 1814) 217
Charles (sloop; captured 3 October 1813) 160
Charles (sloop; seized 10 December 1813) 176
Charles Fawcett (ship) 60
Charles Stewart (privateer) 47
Charlotta (208-ton ship) 164
Charlotte (brigantine) 240
Charlotte, New York 212
Charlotte Ann (schooner) 222
Charlton (10-gun British ship) 101, 137
HMS *Charybdis* 214
Chase (schooner) 81
Chasseur (privateer) 102, 295
Chateauguay, Canada 165, 186
Chauncey, Captain (Commodore) Isaac 44, 57, 60, 62, 68, 74, 77, 84, 96, 99, 104, 106, 107, 108, 109, 111, 114, 115, 116, 118, 119, 139, 141, 142, 144, 146, 147, 148, 149, 151, 153, 156, 157, 158, 159, 163, 166, 169, 178, 195, 197, 206, 207, 210, 212, 214, 217, 220, 221, 222, 225, 226, 255, 302
Chauncey, Lt. Wolcott 68, 109, 119, 120, 126
Chautauqua militia 181
Chazel, Captain J. P. 31, 43, 260
Chazy Landing 141
Cheever, John (seaman) 85, 303
Chef Menteur (Louisiana) 292
Cherokee Indians 169, 188, 201, 296
HMS *Cherub* 134, 192, 193, 194, 202, 204, 216
USS *Chesapeake* 12, 13, 14, 27, 29, 98, 105, 121, 122, 146, 175, 301
Chever, Captain James 205
Chewitt, British Colonel 108
Chickasaw Council House 303
Chickasaw Indians 164, 262, 296
Chief Big Warrior 66, 111, 121
Chief Black Hawk 218, 222, 245
Chief Black Warrior 164
Chief Blackbird (Black-bird) 50, 134, 179, 182
Chief Blue Jacket 47
Chief Bowlegs 29, 64
Chief Chickasawlua 303
Chief Chuliaa 303
Chief Colbert 147
Chief Delgadito 16
Chief High Head Jim 135
Chief Isaac (or Isaac Peters) 195
Chief Isaacs 66
Chief John Gray 195
Chief John Norton 196
Chief Joseph Brant 128
Chief Josiah Francis 129, 135

Chief Kenailoounak 195
Chief Killer 303
Chief Kishkiwabik (Chippewa) 195
Chief Mad Dragon 175
Chief Major Riddle 179, 182, 189
Chief Marpot 56
Chief Menawa 201
Chief Mitass 195
Chief Mushelatubba (Moshulatubbee) 164, 231
Chief Naiwash 195
Chief Negro-legs 59
Chief Oneida Joseph 179
Chief Onoxse 61
Chief Oshawahnail 162
Chief Ounagecechtai 195
Chief Pamamai 195
Chief Payne 64
Chief Peter McQueen 135, 140
Chief Puckshenubbe 164
Chief Pushmataha 147, 164, 180, 231
Chief Red Eagle (William Weatherford) 149, 150, 158, 174, 179, 180; surrenders 201
Chief Roundhead (Round Head) 90, 91
Chief Shahaka 16
Chief Split-Log 78
Chief Stone-eater 59
Chief The Boot 303
Chief The Glass 303
Chief Wabachkweela 195
Chief Waikitai 195
Chief Walisseka 195
Chief Walk-in-the-water 46, 90, 161
Chief Wassasskum 195
Chief Wauhatchie 188, 201
Chief Whale 201
Chief White Horse 195
Chief White Pigeon 68
Chief William McIntosh (also known as Tustunnuggee, Hutkee or White Warrior — later brigadier general USA) 106, 175, 183, 187, 201, 279
Chief Win-e-mac 79
Child, A. (master) 165
Childers, British Captain John 252
Childers, British Captain Nicholas 253
Childers, Captain Thomas 153
Chile 148; refuses to help USS *Essex* 202
Chiles, General David 153, 161
Chili (260-ton vessel) 175
Chinese (privateer) 58
Chippewa (frigate) 257
Chippewa, Canada 208, 218, 220, 222, 224
Chippewa Indians 38, 163
Chippewa River 218
HMS *Chippeway* (*Chippewa*) 53, 154, 155, 156, 166, 175
USS *Chippeway* (*Chippewa*) 184
Chittenden, Governor Martin (Vermont) 248
Chivers, British captain 45

Index

Choctaw company 231
Choctaw Indians 19, 141, 164, 174, 180, 193, 231, 262, 271, 297
Chouteau, Pierre 147
Chouteau, Pierre, Sr. 15, 16
Christ Church (Philadelphia) 302
Christian, Samuel 65
Christian Pass 267
Christiana (brigantine) 126
Christiana (sloop) 102, 298
Christians (captives) 300
Christie, Robert 200
Christopher, Captain John 153
Chrysler, Captain John 171
Chrysler's Farm 171
Chrystie, Lt. Colonel John 70, 71
HMS *Chub* (*Chubb*) 45, 175, 249
Church, J. (master) 176
Churchill, Captain B. K. 257
Churchill, Lieut.-Colonel 181, 182
Cida De Leiria (brigantine) 217
HMS *Circee* 113
Circular Battery (Baltimore) 246
City Battery (Baltimore) 246, 252
City of Limerick 192
Claiborne, Brigadier General Ferdinand L. 100, 131, 132, 134, 136, 141, 143, 145, 147, 148, 149, 151, 153, 164, 168, 174, 175, 176, 177, 179, 180
Claiborne, Governor William C. C. (Louisiana) 25, 30, 180, 243, 244, 254, 265
Clara (schooner) 213
Clark, Colonel Allan 214
Clark, Captain (cavalry) 64
Clark, Doctor 59
Clark, Colonel Isaac 33, 164
Clark, British Lt. Col. Thomas (2nd Regiment, Lincoln Militia) 133
Clark, Captain (later general and governor) William (Lewis and Clark Expedition) 13, 15, 27, 222
Clarke, Aaron (master) 212
Clarke, Colonel Elijah 23
Clarke, Major General John 23
Clarke, S. (master) 83
Claudio, J. J. (master) 217
Claus, British Colonel William 178, 189
Clay, General Green 108, 109, 110, 111, 113, 114, 127, 128, 131, 134, 138, 139, 158
Clay, Henry 20, 56, 121, 168, 184, 226
Cleary, Captain R. 31
Cleavland, Major 191
Clerk, Major 124
Clewley, Captain W. 31
Clinch, Lt. Colonel (later brigadier general) George Lamont 303
Clinton, Cornelia 24
Clinton, Mayor De Witt 21, 45, 72, 225
Clinton, Governor (vice president) George 11, 15, 19, 24, 121
Clinton's Blockhouse at Clinton 22
Coates, Captain J. 31
Cobb, Major General George 183
Cochrane, British Vice Admiral Sir Alexander 250, 251, 252, 255, 256, 267, 268, 275, 276, 278, 280, 281, 290, 292, 293
Cockburn, British Rear Admiral George 87, 94, 104, 110, 113, 114, 123, 127, 129, 131, 135, 136, 196, 226, 235, 236, 240, 254
HMS *Cockchafer* 136
Cocke, Major General John 169, 171, 172, 173, 177
Cod Hook (vessel) 216, 242
Coddington, British Admiral Sir Edward 293
Coffee, Captain Jesse 153
Coffee, Colonel (later brigadier general) John 96, 150, 151, 157, 163, 164, 168, 169, 189, 190, 193, 201, 229, 259, 263, 265, 269, 271, 272, 273, 276, 278, 283, 288
Coffee, Lt. John 160
Coffin, British Lt. Col. Nathaniel 72, 188
Coggeshall, Charles 200
Coggeshall, Captain George 29, 39, 57, 165, 174, 179, 188, 191, 198, 199, 204, 205, 261, 263, 266
Coker, Captain 242
Colado, J. G. (master) 151
Colbert, Brigadier General William (Chickasaw chief) 262; *see also* Chief Colbert
Colbroth, J. (master) 134
Colby, J. L. (master) 221
Colcord, J. (master) 136
Cole, Stephen 14
Cole, William T. 14
Coleman, British captain 189, 195
Coleman, Captain (Florida) 64
Coleman, Captain John 247
Coles, Colonel Isaac 172
Colgreave, Colonel William 221
HMS *Colibri* (*Colibre* and *Collibrie*) 40, 41, 47, 48, 56, 57, 87
Collector (later *Pert*) 68
HMS *Collector* 36
Collier, British Captain F. A. 87
Collier, Captain (later admiral) Sir George 42, 270, 296
Collings, British captain 277
Collings, William 58
Collins, Captain James 77
Collins, J. (master) 136
Collins, Brigadier General Oliver (New York) 257
Collins, T. (master) 167
Colter, John 13
Columbia (39-ton schooner) 114
Columbia (39-ton brigantine; captured 10 May 1813) 114
Columbia (87-ton schooner; captured 18 December 1812) 83
Columbia (98-ton brigantine) 115
Columbia (brigantine) 115
Comanche Indians 16
Combs, Captain Leslie 87, 110, 111, 112
HMS *Comet* 164
Comet (American privateer; *Pride of Baltimore*) 42, 83, 88, 89, 94, 95, 102
Comet (pirate ship) 303
Comet (schooner) 290, 297
Commerce (185-ton brigantine) 120
Commerce (195-ton brigantine) 210
Commerce (brigantine) 41
Commerce (British brigantine) 102, 298
Commerce (schooner) 112
USS *Commodore Barry* 40
USS *Commodore Hull* 89
USS *Commodore Preble* 145; *see also* USS *Preble*
Concord (brigantine) 112
Concord Point 112
Concordia (vessel) 44
Condedos Arcos (ship) 235
Cone, Captain Peter 56, 57
HMS *Confiance* (36-gun frigate) 247, 248, 249
HMS *Confiance* (formerly USS *Julia*) 151
HMS *Conflict* 136, 163
USS *Congress* 27, 31, 68, 111, 142
Congress, U.S. 23, 24, 33, 35; authorizes raising ten regiments and officers 22; places embargo on all vessels in U.S. ports 24; vote to declare war against England 27
Congress of Vienna 241
Conner, Lt. Colonel Samuel S. 185
USS *Conquest* 68, 77, 146, 151
Consolation (sloop) 105
HMS *Constant* 68
USS *Constellation* 27, 42, 95, 127, 295, 299, 302
Constellation (schooner) 221
USS *Constitution* ("Old Ironsides") 27, 29, 30, 36, 37, 39, 43, 48, 50, 53, 54, 76, 77, 82, 83, 84, 85, 88, 97, 98, 142, 183, 194, 205, 266, 269, 270, 275, 295, 296, 301, 302; earns nickname 55
HMS *Contest* 136

Continental units —
1st U.S. Infantry Regiment 15, 46, 59, 111, 217
1st U.S. Light Dragoons 120
2nd U.S. Infantry Regiment 31, 299
2nd U.S. Light Dragoons 67, 124, 141, 156
3rd U.S. Artillery Regiment 24
3rd U.S. Infantry Regiment 28, 32, 174, 192, 259, 296
4th U.S. Infantry Regiment 15, 26, 27, 134, 148, 230, 303
5th U.S. Infantry Regiment 124, 186
6th U.S. Infantry Regiment 27, 111, 125, 248, 274
7th U.S. Infantry Regiment 143, 218, 269, 273, 274, 282, 296, 303
8th U.S. Infantry Regiment 22
9th U.S. Cavalry 148
9th U.S. Infantry Regiment 220, 229
10th U.S. Infantry Regiment 103
11th U.S. Infantry Regiment 33, 172, 220
12th U.S. Infantry Regiment 80, 232
13th U.S. Infantry Regiment 23, 80, 89, 111, 124
14th U.S. Infantry Regiment 80, 108, 124, 128
15th U.S. Infantry Regiment 80, 125, 180, 247, 248
16th U.S. Infantry Regiment 124, 172, 279
17th U.S. Infantry Regiment 53, 83, 101, 141, 142, 279
19th Light Dragoons 186
19th U.S. Infantry Regiment 83, 101
20th U.S. Infantry Regiment 102
21st U.S. Infantry Regiment 33, 137, 172, 182, 220, 223, 254, 274
22nd U.S. Infantry Regiment 35, 124, 220
23rd U.S. Infantry Regiment 124, 172, 299
24th U.S. Infantry Regiment 101, 147, 186
26th U.S. Infantry Regiment 148
29th U.S. Infantry Regiment 248
30th U.S. Infantry Regiment 248
31st U.S. Infantry Regiment 248
33rd U.S. Infantry Regiment 248
34th U.S. Infantry Regiment 248
35th U.S. Infantry Regiment 106
36th U.S. Infantry Regiments 222
38th U.S. Infantry Regiment 222, 244
39th U.S. Infantry Regiment 141, 164, 174, 193, 195, 199, 201, 259, 262
44th U.S. Infantry Regiment 259, 269, 273, 282, 288, 296
45th U.S. Infantry Regiment 94
86th U.S. Infantry Regiment 235
88th U.S. Infantry Regiment 235

Continental units by state —
Connecticut
1st Connecticut Artillery Battalion 87
1st Connecticut Cavalry Regiment 28, 87
1st Connecticut Division (1st and 7th Brigades) 28, 87; 1st Brigade (1st, 18th, 19th, 22nd Regiments and 1st Cavalry Regiment) 28, 87; 7th Brigade (6th, 15th, 23rd and 24th Regiments and 7th Cavalry Regiment) 28
1st Connecticut Infantry Regiment 28, 87
2nd Connecticut Cavalry Regiment 28, 87
2nd Connecticut Division (2nd and 4th Brigades) 28, 87; 2nd Brigade (2nd, 7th, 10th, 27th and 32nd Regiments and 2nd Cavalry Regiment and 1st Artillery Battalion) 28; 4th Brigade (4th, 8th, and 28th Connecticut Regiments and 4th Cavalry Regiment) 28, 87
2nd Connecticut Infantry Regiment 87
3rd Connecticut Cavalry Regiment 28, 87
3rd Connecticut Division (3rd and 5th Brigades) 28, 87; 3rd Brigade (3rd, 8th, 20th, 30th and 33rd Regiments and 3rd Cavalry Regiment) 28, 87; 5th Brigade (5th, 11th, 12th, and 21st Regiments and a Cavalry Regiment) 28
3rd Connecticut Infantry Regiment 87
4th Connecticut Cavalry Regiment 28, 87
4th Connecticut Division (6th and 8th Brigades) 29; 6th Brigade (14th, 17th, 25th, and 35th Regiments and 6th Cavalry Regiment) 29; 8th Brigade (8th, 13th, 16th, 26th and 29th Regiments and 8th Cavalry Regiment) 28, 87
4th Connecticut Infantry Regiment 87
5th Connecticut Cavalry Regiment 28, 87

5th Connecticut Infantry Regiment 87
6th Connecticut Cavalry Regiment 28, 87
6th Connecticut Infantry Regiment 87
7th Connecticut Cavalry Regiment 28, 87
7th Connecticut Infantry Regiment 87
8th Connecticut Cavalry Regiment 28, 87
8th Connecticut Infantry Regiment 87
9th Connecticut Infantry Regiment 87
10th Connecticut Infantry Regiment 87
11th Connecticut Infantry Regiment 87
12th Connecticut Infantry Regiment 87
13th Connecticut Infantry Regiment 87
14th Connecticut Infantry Regiment 87
16th Connecticut Infantry Regiment 87
17th Connecticut Infantry Regiment 87
18th Connecticut Infantry Regiment 28, 87
19th Connecticut Infantry Regiment 28, 87
20th Connecticut Infantry Regiment 87
21st Connecticut Infantry Regiment 87
22nd Connecticut Infantry Regiment 28
23rd Connecticut Infantry Regiment 87
24th Connecticut Infantry Regiment 87
25th Connecticut Infantry Regiment 87
26th Connecticut Infantry Regiment 87
27th Connecticut Infantry Regiment 87
28th Connecticut Infantry Regiment 87
29th Connecticut Infantry Regiment 87
30th Connecticut Infantry Regiment 142, 225, 227
32nd Connecticut Infantry Regiment 87
33rd Connecticut Infantry Regiment 87
35th Connecticut Infantry Regiment 87
Kentucky
1st Kentucky Division (1st, 3rd and 4th Brigades) 153
1st Kentucky Regiment 91, 153
2nd Kentucky Division (2nd and 5th Brigades and 11th Regiment) 153
2nd Kentucky Regiment 153
1st Kentucky Brigade (1st and 2nd Kentucky Regiments) 153
2nd Kentucky Brigade (3rd and 4th Kentucky Regiments) 153
3rd Kentucky Brigade (5th and 7th Kentucky Regiments) 153
3rd Kentucky Regiment 153
4th Kentucky Brigade (6th and 8th Kentucky Regiments) 153
4th Kentucky Regiment 153
5th Kentucky Brigade (9th and 10th Kentucky Regiments) 153
5th Kentucky Regiment 91
8th Kentucky Regiment 161
9th Kentucky Regiment 161
17th Kentucky Regiment 83
Louisiana
1st Louisiana Regiment 276
2nd Louisiana Regiment 276
Maine
1st Division Maine militia 183
Maryland
1st Maryland Division 229
4th Baltimore Regiment 234
5th Baltimore Regiment 234
21st Maryland Regiment 240
Michigan
1st Michigan Regiment (militia) 52
New Hampshire
1st New Hampshire Division 213
1st New Hampshire Regiment 94, 213
2nd New Hampshire Division 213
15th New Hampshire Infantry Regiment 115
31st New Hampshire Infantry Regiment 115
34th New Hampshire Infantry Regiment 115
35th New Hampshire Infantry Regiment 115, 206
New York
1st New York Division 24, 69
2nd New York Division 24
4th New York Brigade 69
6th New York Brigade 189
7th New York Brigade 189
38th New York Brigade 189
Ohio
1st Ohio Regiment 26
2nd Ohio Regiment 26
3rd Ohio Regiment 26
Pennsylvania
1st British Lincoln (militia) 71
1st Pennsylvania Division 33, 247
1st Pennsylvania Regiment 25
2nd British Lincoln (militia) 71
2nd Pennsylvania Regiment 25
3rd Pennsylvania Regiment 25
4th British Lincoln (militia) 71
5th British Lincoln (militia) 71
5th Pennsylvania Division 193; 2nd Brigade 193
7th Pennsylvania Division 193; 1st Brigade 193; 2nd Brigade 193
8th Pennsylvania Regiment 25
9th Pennsylvania Regiment 25
10th Pennsylvania Regiment 25
11th Pennsylvania Regiment 25
12th Pennsylvania Regiment 25
13th Pennsylvania Regiment 25
14th Pennsylvania Regiment 25
15th Pennsylvania Regiment 25
16th Pennsylvania Regiment 25
71st Pennsylvania Regiment 27
94th Pennsylvania Regiment 28
Virginia
56th Virginia Regiment 244

Contract (schooner) 209
Contractor (vessel; later USS *Trippe*) 115
Conway (brigantine) 181
Conway Cabal 22
Cook, B. (master) 101, 197
Cook, J. (master) 160
Cook's Mills 259
Cooksley, John 87
Coombs, J. (master) 73
Cooper, Captain cavalry 130
Cooper, H. (master) 114
Coosa Mountain 169
Coosa River 199
Coosa Town 121
Coosahatchie River 187
Copus, Reverend 62
Copus family 62
HMS *Coquette* 87
Cora (privateer) 31, 36, 40
Cordelia (brigantine) 38
Cornells, Mr. 26
Cornwall, Canada 171, 186, 193
Cornwall, R. G. (master) 212
HMS *Cornwallis* 299
Cornwallis (brigantine) 241
Cossac (schooner) 24
Cossack (brigantine) 34
Cossack (British vessel; later American privateer) 111
HMS *Cossack* (sloop) 297
Cossack (vessel) 112
Costilla, Father Miguel Hidalgo y 16
Cotgrove, Major 89
Cotton, Captain Joshua A. 65
Coulson, Samuel 97
Coulter, John 16
Coulter's Blockhouse 22
Courtlandt, Brigadier General Pierre W. Jr. 157
Courtney (brigantine) 257
Cousins, J (master) 115
Coutts, British lieutenant 206
Covington, Colonel (later brigadier general) Leonard 44, 115, 165, 171, 172, 246
Cowell, Lt. 202
Coweta Indians 175, 183
Cowles, Major General Solomon 87
Cox, Lt. W. S. 122
Crab Island hospital 241
Cracker Bend 221
Craig, Captain Elijah 160
Cranberry (schooner) 105
Cranberry Creek 137
Crandall, C. (master) 36
HMS *Crane* 87
Crane, Lt. (later captain) William 31, 38, 151, 186, 200, 225
Craney Island 127
Crawford, Eli (master) 245
Crawford, Ensign 141, 147
Crawford, William H. (minister to France) 127, 261
Crawley, Lieutenant John 280, 282
Crawley, Mrs. 93
Craycroft, Captain R. 174
Creagh, British Major Andrew 287
Creagh, Lieutenant Girard W. 140, 180
Crease, British Captain Henry 240
Cree Indians 38
Creek (Lower Creeks) 188, 201, 262
Creek Agency, Georgia 24, 26
Creek Indians (Red Sticks) 19, 149, 150, 151, 160, 168, 170, 175, 180, 187, 189, 190, 191, 193, 195, 201, 207, 221, 227, 262, 296, 298, 302, 303
Creigh, Lt. 173, 192
Creighton, Captain John O. 239
Creoles 271, 273
Crevie, John (British officer) 125
Criterion (vessel) 174
Crittenden, Major John J. 157
Crocker, J. (master) 57
Crocker, L. G. 221
Crockett, Colonel Anthony 135
Crockett, Davy 160, 164, 169
Croghan, Major (later Lt. Col.) George 140, 141, 142, 143, 221, 224, 226
Croker, John Wilson (Secretary of the Admiralty) 207
Cromwell, General Charles (Pennsylvania) 33
Crooke, British Captain James 71
Crooke, British Captain William 71
Crooks, Major 191
Crosby, Ebenezer 99
Crowel, E.W. (master) 138
Crowel, S. 100
Crowel, Zadoc 96
Crowley, British captain 72
Crowley, Lt. C. E. 192
Crown, Benjamin 221
Crown Solomon (British privateer) 106
Crowninshield, Captain Benjamin 105, 115
Crowninshield, Captain George 146
Crowninshield, Captain John 34, 111, 214, 216
Crutchfield, Major 129, 130
Cuampe Indians 16
Cuba (vessel) 125
HMS *Culloden* 88
Culver Hill 241, 245
HMS *Cumberland* (74-gun) 87
Cumberland (privateer) 263
Cumberland Head 141, 248
Cumberland Island 25
Cumby, W. P. 87
Cummings, E. (master) 134
Cummings, Acting Midshipman John C. 69
Cummings Redoubt 235
Cunningham, Captain Isaac 153
Cunningham, Captain James 153, 158
Cunningham, Lieutenant 289
Curaçao Island (West Indies) 194
Curfew 53
HMS *Curlew* 76, 87, 103, 105, 106, 116, 134, 135, 147, 148, 213, 263
Curlew (privateer) 40, 42, 210
Currie, J. (master) 173
Curtis, Captain 178
Cushing, Captain Daniel 133
Cushing, Brigadier General Thomas Humphrey (Adjutant General) 22, 25, 34, 42, 99, 103, 227
Custis, George Washington Parke 234
Cuthbert, Colonel Alfred 294
HMS *Cuttle* 87
Cuyahoga (vessel) 33, 34
HMS *Cyane* 87, 294, 296
Cynthia (schooner) 266
Czar Alexander I 13, 14, 33, 58, 100, 168

Dabney, John B. (American consul) 255
Dacres, Captain RN 29
Dacres, British Captain James Richard 55, 266
Dacres, British Vice Admiral James Richard 54, 55
Dale, Captain Richard 85
Dale, British Colonel Robert 285, 287, 289
Dale, Captain Samuel 140, 153, 173, 180, 192, 279

Index

Dalkablen (vessel) 226
Dallas, Alexander 298
Dalliba, Lt. James 46
Dalrymple, Joseph (seaman) 97
Dameron, Captain J. 44
Daniels, Major General Allen (Georgia) 259
Daniels, Captain J. D. 221, 264
Dantzic (brigantine) 211
HMS *Daphne* 138
D'Aquin, Colonel 273
Daquin, Major 271, 272, 288
Darah, John (master) 263
Dart (brigantine) 22
Dart (British brigantine) 80, 123, 124, 125, 129, 131, 141, 146, 147, 149, 151
Dart (privateer) 112
Dart (schooner) 146
Dartmoor prison (Dartmoor Depot) 125, 214, 298
Daschkoff, Mr. 100
Dash (British privateer) 82, 205
Dash (privateer out of Boston) 215
Dash (privateer out of Maine) 253, 259, 260
Dash (privateer out of Norfolk) 31, 36
Dashiel, Midshipman 129
HMS *Dauntless* 87
Dauphin Island 266, 296, 297
Davenport, Colonel Richard 153
David, Lt. Colonel S. B. 185
David Porter (privateer) 165, 174, 179, 188, 189, 191, 198, 199, 200, 204, 205, 241, 264
David's Creek 56
Davidson, Captain John 65
Davidson, Lt. 185
Davidson, Captain Michael 153
Davidson, Captain W. 279
Davidson, William (master) 40
Davie, Major General William R. 85
Davies, British captain 87
Davis, Alfred 275
Davis, Colonel (later brigadier general) Aquila 94, 211
Davis, Captain 132
Davis, Brigadier General Daniel 230, 255
Davis, G. N. (master) 221
Davis, John 83
Davis, Lt. Col. John 284, 285
Davis, Major 21
Davis Creek (Florida) 48, 61
Davison, Captain George 236
Dawson (vessel) 33
Dawson, Captain J. 106, 153
Day, J. (master) 221
Dead Man's Creek 246
Deadman's Island 127
Deadrick, Captain David 190
Dean, British private 42, 52
Deane, British major 307
Dearborn, Major General Henry 22, 28, 35, 53, 56, 62, 65, 72, 75, 78, 79, 86,
95, 98, 100, 103, 106, 109, 111, 114, 116, 118, 124, 125, 128, 129, 133, 134, 136, 157, 185, 190
De Azedido, Don Alexandre Jose 90
de Bellevue, Lieutenant USMC 286
De Bersey, British captain 210
Deborah (schooner) 151
De Cant, Captain 46
Decatur (privateer out of Charleston) 53, 89, 144, 145, 148, 174, 205
Decatur (privateer out of Maine) 53
Decatur (privateer out of Maine; under Captains S. N. Lane and Diron) 53, 89, 214, 243
Decatur (privateer out of Newburyport; under Captain Nichols; formerly the *Alert*) 89
Decatur (vessel) 255
Decatur, Captain (Commodore) Stephen 13, 26, 68, 74, 75, 85, 122, 123, 131, 177, 185, 199, 209, 216, 248, 266, 290, 291, 295, 299, 300, 301, 302
Decharme (Indian) 128
De Chaumont, Le Ray 21
HMS *Decouverte* 37
Decree of St. Cloud 20
Deesha, Major General Joseph 153
Defiance (62-ton sloop taken on 3 June 1814) 214
Defiance (104-ton sloop; seized 4 April 1813) 104
Defiance (118-ton schooner) 103
Defiance (schooner; seized 21 May 1814) 213
Defiance (sloop) 214, 226
Defiance (sloop; seized 1814 by HMS *Superb* and HMS *Sylph*) 104
Defiance (sloop; seized by the HMS *Bream*) 103
Defiance, Ohio 68
De Godoy, Manuel 14
De Grandpre, Lieutenant USMC 286
Degres, Captain J. 31
DeHaven, British Major P. W. 129
De Koven, Captain H. 47
Del Carmen (schooner) 126
De la Croix, Dussau 271
De la Ronde, Colonel 271, 272
Delaware (schooner) 225
Delaware County Fencibles 259
Delaware Indians 83, 134, 200, 222
De La Zouch 246
Delery's Plantation 282
Delight (schooner) 70
Delila (letter of marque) 31
DeLorimer (French Canadian officer) 179
Delphin (brigantine) 115
HMS *Demerara* 87
Deming, Major David 28, 87
Demmitt, Captain Moses 153
Democratic Press 26
Dempster, Doctor 285
De Nemours, Dupont 303
Denkens, Captain 184
Denkins, Captain James 262
Dennis, British captain 70, 171
Dennis, Lt. Col. Richard 185
Denny, Major James 26
Dent, Captain Benjamin 141, 148
Deqolodre, Captain Antoine 22
Derby, Vermont 178
Dering, Mr. 37
De Rottenburg, British major general 133, 169, 195
de Salaberry, British Lt. Colonel Charles 165, 166
De Selvia, A. C. (master) 115
Desha, Captain Benjamin 224
Desha, General (governor) Joseph 50
Deslesdernier (schooner) 216
HMS *Despatch* 290
De Torres, Jose R. 200
Detroit 50, 158, 162, 189
HMS *Detroit* 154, 155, 175
HMS *Detroit* (frigate; formerly USS *Adams* or *John Adams*) 52, 68, 69
USS *Detroit* 187
DeVall, Major 161
Devonshire (brigantine) 44
De Watteville, Major General Louis (German officer) 163, 210, 211
Dewley, Captain E. W. Or J. Dooley 82
HMS *Diadem* 127, 129
Diamond (12-gun brigantine) 53
Diamond (229-ton brigantine) 148
Diamond (privateer) 279
Diana (brigantine) 112
Diana (ship) 55, 63
Diana (sloop; seized 19 July 1814) 222
Diana (vessel) 55
Dickenson, Charles 12, 151
Dickinson, Brigadier General Joseph F. 128
Dickson, British Colonel Alexander 285
Diego, Juan 17
Diligence (schooner) 208
Diligent (American privateer) 60
Diligent (British brigantine) 43
Diligent (brigantine; seized August 1813) 147
Dill, Captain 31
Dimock, Captain 137
Dinsmore, Brigadier General Samuel (New Hampshire militia) 33
Diomede (238-ton brigantine) 114
Diomede (privateer) 111
HMS *Diomede* 129
Diomede (150-ton privateer; captured 28 May 1814) 214, 216
Diron, Captain Dominique 53, 144, 145
Democratic Press 26
HMS *Dispatch* 227, 228, 259
Dispatch (168-ton brigantine) 106
Dispatch (brigantine) 156
Dispatch (seized 25 October 1813) 165
Dithurbide, Captain D. 98
Ditto's Landing 187
Divided We Fall (privateer) 41
Divina Pastora (885-ton ship) 151
Dixon (British officer) 143
Dixon, Lt. (later U. S. Senator and major general) 224
Dixon, Captain Samuel 42, 137, 216, 217
Dobbin, Colonel Hugh W. 185
Dobbins, Captain Daniel (master) 61, 99, 135
Dobbins, Lieutenant-Colonel 183
Dobbs, British Captain Alexander 229
Dobson, Captain W. B. 121, 136
Dodge, J. (master) 106
Dodge, Brigadier General Richard 25, 60, 63, 69, 70, 231
Dodson, Captain Will 113
Doherty, General George 201
HMS *Dolphin* 35
Dolphin (28-ton schooner; seized October 1814) 259
Dolphin (American privateer) 34, 40, 43, 50, 56, 93, 98, 104, 174
Dolphin (schooner; seized 12 August 1812) 48
Dolphin (schooner; seized 28 July 1813) 141
Dolphin (seized 16 August 1813) 148
Doltz, J. A. (master) 226
HMS *Dominica* 59, 144, 145, 148, 175
Dominica (brigantine packet) 95
Dominica (schooner) 213
HMS *Dominico* 87
Don Carlos (schooner) 147
Donald, Colonel William 257
Donaldson, Colonel John 153
Doolan, James 139
Dorcas (2-gun schooner) 86
Dorcey, Richard 250
Doris (ship) 57
HMS *Dotterell* 213
Double Swamp 177
Doughty, Captain 232
Douglas (merchant ship) 258
Douglas, Captain George 294
Douglass, Lieutenant David 229
Douglass, Brigadier General Hugh 236
Dougle, Captain A. 31
Dove (24-ton schooner) 255
Dove (31-ton schooner) 238
Dove (77-ton schooner) 82
Dove (British privateer) 293, 294
Dove (seized 27 November 1813) 174
HMS *Dover* 131
Dover, Canada 212
Dowers, B. (master) 151
Downes, Lieutenant (later captain) John 110, 129, 133, 163, 167, 193, 202, 299
Downie, British Commodore George 235, 241, 245, 246, 248, 250, 254
HMS *Dragon* 87, 200, 214, 242, 254
Drake (89-ton sloop) 242
Drake's farm 160
Drew, T. (master) 39
Drinkwater, Captain Perez 270
Drinkwater, Samuel (master) 212
Dromo (27-ton schooner) 242
Drouillard, George 17
Droyer, Lt. Edward F. 87
Drummond (vessel) 163
Drummond, A. (master) 115
Drummond, British Lt. General Sir Gordon 176, 178, 179, 181, 182, 183, 186, 188, 189, 190, 192, 194, 195, 197, 198, 199, 204, 205, 206, 207, 208, 210, 220, 222, 224, 225, 229, 230, 231, 255, 259
Drummond Hill 224
Drysdale, British Captain William 281
Duane, Colonel 79
Dubois, Captain 20
Dubourg, Abbe (Bishop) 292
Ducharme (French Canadian officer) 179
HMS *Duchess of Portland* 35
Duck (ship) 115
Duck River Massacre 93
Duckworth, Admiral Sir John T. 49
Dudley, Lt. Colonel William 109, 110, 111, 114
Dudley's Massacre (Dudley's Massacre) 110
Duke (vessel) 44
HMS *Duke of Gloucester* 40, 77, 108, 120, 175
USS *Duke of Gloucester* 151
Duke of Wellington *see* Wellesley, Arthur
Dunbar, D. (master) 188
Duncan, Captain David 28
Duncan, Miss 17
Duncan, Brigadier General William 54
Dundee (brigantine) 269
Dundern Castle 117
Dunlap, Colonel 32
Dunn (American officer) 141
Durand, British Captain 71
Durant, Sophia 179
Durocher, Judge Laurent 204
Dwyer, Colonel 166, 170
Dyer, A. (master) 144
Dyer, Colonel Robert Henry 273
Dyer, Captain William B. 250
Dysart, Captain Johnston 154
Dyson, Captain Samuel T. 46, 52, 238

Eagle (70-ton schooner) 259
Eagle (brigantine) 222, 262
USS *Eagle* (brigantine) 241, 247, 248, 249
USS *Eagle* (gunboat; later HMS *Finch*) 123

Index

Eagle (privateer schooner) 31
Eagle (privateer sloop) 31
HMS *Eagle* (separate from the *Finch*) 134
Earl (vessel) 44
Earl Camden (British sloop) 127
HMS *Earl of Moira* 40, 48, 77, 118, 137, 151
Earle, British Commodore Hugh 77
Early, Governor Peter (Georgia) 185
Easely's Station 150
East Florida 23, 40
Eastern Star (vessel) 53
Eastman (surgeon of the navy) 187
Eastman, Lt. Jonathan 46, 47, 52
Easton, Maryland 102, 165
Eastport (Moose Island) 148
Eckford, Henry 57, 186, 195
Eclipse (brigantine) 102, 298
Eclipse (sloop) 218
Econochaca (Holy Ground) 177, 179, 180
Economy (80-ton brigantine) 79
Edward (brigantine) 115
Edward (vessel) 185
Edward (whaling ship) 137
Edward and Hiram (schooner) 78
Edwards, British major 120
Edwards, Territorial Governor Ninian 50, 76, 245
USS *Edwin* 295, 300
Elba 241, 297
Eldridge, Lt. 134
HMS *Electra* 87, 134
Electra (ship) 39
HMS *Elephant* 82, 87
Eleven Mile Creek (Williamsville, New York) 182, 183, 186, 190
Elipse (schooner) 225
Eliza (10-gun sloop) 58
Eliza (41-ton schooner) 118
Eliza (90-ton schooner) 85
Eliza (100-ton schooner; seized 1 July 1814) 218
Eliza (105-ton brigantine) 103
Eliza (British vessel) 194
Eliza (schooner) 37, 43, 174
Eliza (schooner; seized 23 July 1814) 222
Eliza Ann (vessel) 21
Eliza Ann (seized in August 1812 by *Yankee*) 43
Eliza Ann (sloop; captured 31 October 1814) 260
Eliza Gracie (vessel) 29
HMS *Eliza Swan* 138
HMS *Elizabeth* 87
Elizabeth (2-gun brigantine) 131
Elizabeth (brigantine) 34
Elizabeth (brigantine; seized 22 June 1813) 127
Elizabeth (brigantine; seized 20 November 1813) 174
Elizabeth (British brigantine) 148
Elizabeth (British privateer) 297
Elizabeth (merchant ship) 66

Elizabeth (privateer 3-gun schooner) 31
Elizabeth (schooner) 43, 151
Elizabeth (sloop) 77
Elizabeth (sloop; seized 25 August 1813) 148
Elizabeth and Esther (brigantine) 43
Elk Landing, Maryland 110
Elkton, Maryland 110
Ellen (brigantine) 134
Ellen (schooner) 181
Elliott, British captain 79
Elliott, Captain (son of Mathew Elliott) 52
Elliott, Lieutenant (Commandant) Jesse D. USN 60, 68, 69, 77, 144, 155, 157, 158, 159, 165, 166, 185, 187, 189, 195, 225, 226
Elliott, Senator John 81
Elliott, Martha Stewart 81
Elliott, British Col. Matthew 65, 196
Elliott, British Colonel William 143, 189, 200
Elliott, William 92
Ellstrom, B. (master) 164
Elmore, Captain Warner 154
Elton, Lieutenant 225
Elvira (sloop) 157
Elwell, Captain 44
Embargo Act (22 December 1807) 14, 15, 16
Embargo Act of 17 December 1813 177, 207
Embargo Act second 14, 15
Embargo Act third 14, 15
Emeline (sloop) 177
Emerson, Captain Arthur 127
Emery, J. (master) 149
Emperor (American schooner) 114
Emperor Alexander 20
Emperor Napoleon *see* Bonaparte, Napoleon
Empress (ship) 40
Empress Marie Louise 19
Emu (transport) 81, 211
Emuckfaw 189, 194
HMS *Emulous* 24, 35, 36, 37, 38, 39, 40, 42, 48, 53, 55, 56, 60, 105, 106, 113, 144, 175
Encampment Number 1 (Ohio) 66
Encampment Number 3 78, 79
Encouragement (vessel) 34
Endeavor (104-ton sloop) 148
Endeavor (sloop) 37
Endicott, Captain 40
HMS *Endymion* 103, 175, 205, 214, 218, 231, 258, 259, 290, 291
Enforcement Act 16
England (UK) 241
Enigheton (180-ton brigantine) 226
Enotachopco 189, 190
USS *Enterprise* 27, 47, 142, 152, 188, 194
Enterprise (26-ton schooner) 240
Enterprise (brigantine) 36
Enterprise (British schooner) 163
Enterprise (privateer) 111

Enterprise (schooner; seized 21 May 1813) 116
Enterprise (schooner; seized 8 December 1813) 176
Enterprise (schooner; seized 16 December 1813) 177
Enterprise (schooner; seized 30 August 1814) 36
Enterprise (ship) 34
Enterprise (sloop) 257
HMS *Epervier* 63, 138, 169, 195, 208, 209
USS *Epervier* 299, 301
Eposy Mina (schooner) 148
Epworth, E. P. 87
USS *Erie* 135, 148, 199, 206
Erie (76-ton schooner) 177
Erskine, David M. (British foreign minister) 16
Erskine, George 16
Esperanzo (70-ton schooner) 103
HMS *Espiegle* 97
HMS *Espoir* 235
Essex, Connecticut 206
USS *Essex* (frigate) 25, 27, 32, 35, 36, 45, 48, 49, 68, 76, 80, 82, 85, 87, 90, 93, 96, 101, 110, 114, 118, 125, 126, 127, 128, 129, 133, 136, 137, 139, 142, 148, 156, 163, 165, 192, 193, 202, 203, 291
Essex Jr. (formerly the whaler *Atlantic*) 101, 110, 129, 133, 193, 194, 202, 203
Essex militia 90
Estedio (Algerian vessel) 299, 300
Estella, J. E. (master) 157
USS *Etna* 104
Eunice (57-ton sloop) 215
Eunice (189-ton schooner) 127
Euphemia (90-ton schooner) 149
Euphemia (vessel) 82
Euphrates (ship) 57
Eustis, Secretary of War William 23, 24, 28, 30, 59, 72, 74, 78, 86; resigns 81
Evans, Doctor 84
Evans, J. (master) 262
Evans, John 87
Evans, Lieutenant 242
Evans, Mr. 169
Evans, Brigade Major Thomas 70
Evans, British Captain William 87
Eveleth, Ebenezer (master) 39
Evelyn, G. J. 87
Everard, British commander Thomas 141
Ewell, Captain D. 37
Ewing, Captain William 154
Ex Bashaw (vessel) 216
Expedition (125-ton schooner) 105
Expedition (American privateer) 86
Experience (brigantine) 174
Experience (vessel) 31
USS *Experiment* 295
Experiment (seized 13 May 1814) 212
Experiment (sloop; seized 8 August 1812) 47

Experiment (sloop; seized 24 June 1813) 129
Experiment (sloop; seized 21 January 1815) 292
Express (British packet) 115

Fabius (vessel) 60
Factor (ship) 60
USS *Fair American* (schooner) 68, 109, 115, 120, 144, 146, 151
Fair Trader (privateer) 34, 43
Fairbanks, Prescott 212
Fairfield, John (master) 48
Fairplay (sloop) 139
Fairtrader (privateer schooner) 38
Fairtrader (schooner; seized 6 December 1814) 38, 266
Fairy (vessel) 31
HMS *Falcon* 175
Falcon (letter of marque) 39
Falcon, Captain George 294
Falkner, Major 127
Falun (ship) 189
Fame (privateer) 36, 43, 69, 70, 260
Fame (sloop) 104, 212, 222
Fame (sloop; seized 31 May 1814) 214
Fanning, Captain Alexander 230
Fanning, Lieutenant 120
Fanny (brigantine) 205
Fanny (formerly *Shadow*) 44
Fanny (schooner) 43, 217
HMS *Fantine* 260
HMS *Fantome* 104, 135, 163, 169, 211, 217
Fanuir, Lt. 64
Farmer (sloop) 36
Farnum, Lt. 182
Farragut, Davy (later admiral) 203
Farrow, T. J. 104
Faulkner, Captain John 153
Faussett, Lieutenant Robert 256
Favorite (brigantine) 49
Favorite (schooner) 102
Favourite (67-ton sloop) 104
Favourite (158-ton brigantine) 242
HMS *Fawn* 87
Federal (115-ton brigantine) 63
Federal Republican (newspaper) 31, 41
Federalists 177
Feleira, Antonio Jose (master) 263
Feliciana Dragoons 272
Fellows, Captain 82
Fellows, Thomas 87
Felucca Bee (privateer) 31
Fenelon (schooner) 82
Fenton, Colonel James 198
Fenwick, George (governor of Saybrook colony) 86
Fenwick, Lt. Colonel John B. 59, 185
Ferdinand VII of Spain, King 14, 105, 241
Fernald, Captain W. 48
Fernandez, Eman 213
Fernandina (Amelia Island) 23, 29, 114

USS *Ferret* (schooner) 76, 192
Ferris, Master J. D. 104, 267, 268
Fidella (243-ton ship) 115
Field, Midshipman 246
HMS *Fierce* 87
Fife, Jim 190
Filmore, Millard (later president of the United States) 289
Financier (schooner) 171
HMS *Finch* (formerly USS *Eagle*) 123, 249
Finch, Captain 164
Finch, Lt. USN 76
Findlay, Colonel James 26, 31, 32, 35, 51, 52, 64
Finland (vessel) 115
Finley, C. (master) 126
Finnie, Captain 127
Finnis, British Lieutenant Robert 154
Finns Point 104
USS *Firebrand* 303
Firefly (privateer) 31
Firmina (ship) 263
First Bank of the United States 19
First Legion of the District of Columbia 65
Fischer, British Lt. Col. Victor 210, 229
Fish, Captain J. 200, 241
Fish, Colonel Nicholas 227
Fish Dam 168
Fish Pond Indians 193
Fisher, British colonel 229
Fisher, Mr. 152
Fisher family 152
Fisk, Lieutenant 185
Fitzgibbon, Lieutenant (later captain) James 128, 129
Fitzgibbon, Laura 128
Five Mile Meadows 178
Five Nations 196
USS *Flamneau* (formerly *Leader*) 266
Flash (vessel) 214
Fleming, Lieutenant-Colonel 183
Fletcher, Josiah 149, 150
Flight (schooner) 105
Flinn, sailing (master) 104
Flint Hill Camp 86
Flint River 187
Flirt (privateer) 41
Flor de Lisboa (brigantine) 123
Flor De Mar 148
Flor de Tejo (brigantine) 142
HMS *Florida* (formerly USS *Frolic*) 205
Flournoy, Captain Matthews 153
Flournoy, Brigadier General Thomas 22, 100, 103, 134, 135, 136, 141, 143, 144, 164, 180, 213, 229
Flower (26-ton schooner) 156
Floyd, Charles 294
Floyd, General Charles L. 294
Floyd, Colonel George R. C. 154
Floyd, Brigadier General John 22, 86, 151, 174, 175, 183, 184, 185, 191, 294
Floyd, Richard (later lieutenant Confederate States Navy) 294

Index

HMS *Fly* 148
Fly (British privateer) 139, 148
Fly (privateer) 47
Fly (privateer out of Maine 262
Fly (vessel) 72
Flying Fish (ship) 264
Foot, Captain 69, 70
Foot Guards (Connecticut militia) 28
Foote, Brigadier General Enoch 28, 87
Forbes, Sandy 169
Forrest, Thomas 87
Forster, Brigadier General (Pennsylvania) 254
Forsyth, Captain (later major) Benjamin 63, 69, 70, 94, 97, 98, 106, 117, 120, 137, 169, 171, 193
Forsyth, L. (master) 103
Fort, Captain Tomlinson 48, 61
Fort Allen 183
Fort Amanda, Ohio 22, 63, 64, 86, 94
Fort Andrew 15
Fort Apalachicola, Alabama 86, 175
Fort Apalachicola (Negro Fort), Florida 303
Fort Appollonia 72
Fort Armstrong, Alabama 86
Fort Armstrong, Illinois 303
Fort Armstrong, Wisconsin 245
Fort Astor (aka Astoria Post; later Fort George) 19
Fort Babcock 86
Fort Bainbridge 183
Fort Ball, Ohio 63, 86, 94, 135, 156
Fort Barbee, Ohio 63, 64, 67, 68, 86, 94
Fort Barrancas 229, 238, 260, 262
Fort Belle Fontaine (earlier Cantonment Belle Fontaine) 259
Fort Bender 183
Fort Benning (Georgia-Alabama) 86, 175
Fort Blount (aka Negro Fort), Florida 279, 303
Fort Bowyer (later Fort Morgan) 105, 204, 229, 238, 267, 293, 294
Fort Brown, New York 248, 249
Fort Brown, Ohio 22, 86, 94
Fort Burnt Corn *see* Fort Warren, Alabama
Fort Burrows, Maine 86, 152
Fort Butler, Illinois 221
Fort Carleton 32
Fort Carlotta (formerly Fort Charlotte) 105
Fort Carney 131
Fort Cassin 86
Fort Castine (Fort Madison) 242
Fort Chamby 24
Fort Charlotte (previously Fort Conde; later Fort Carlotta and Fort Mobile) 105, 131, 164
Fort Chauncey 85, 116
Fort Chilton 50

Fort Claiborne 174, 175, 180, 184, 192, 201
Fort Clark (at Sibley, Missouri) 15
Fort Clark, Troy 15
Fort Clark, Illinois 86
Fort Clemson, Missouri 14
Fort Clinton (Orange County) 183
Fort Clinton (West Point) 183
Fort Clinton, Central Park, New York 183, 235
Fort Clinton, Schuylerville, New York 183
Fort Colville 17
Fort Conde (later Fort Charlotte, Fort Carlotta and Fort Mobile) 105, 131, 145
Fort Constitution, New Hampshire 16, 81, 213
Fort Covington 86, 246, 252
Fort Crawford, Alabama 303
Fort Creve Coeur 303
Fort Daniel 57
Fort Dearborn (Chicago) Massacre 49, 50
Fort Decatur, Alabama 205
Fort Defiance, Georgia (formerly Fort Morris) 105
Fort Defiance, Maryland 86, 110
Fort Defiance, Ohio (Fort Winchester) 22, 64, 85, 111
Fort Delaware 104
Fort Deposit, Alabama 164, 180, 195, 201
Fort Deposit, Ohio 90
Fort Detroit 35, 36, 50, 52, 157
Fort Early 183
Fort Easley 131, 145, 148, 164
Fort Edgecomb 15
Fort Edwards, Illinois 245
Fort Erie, Canada 33, 56, 80, 117, 118, 186, 189, 218, 219, 224, 225, 229, 231, 238, 239, 254, 255, 257, 260
Fort Fenwick 86
Fort Feree 17, 67, 156
Fort Findlay, Ohio 22, 32, 67
Fort Fireman, New York 235
Fort Fish, New York 235
Fort Foot 86
Fort Gadsden 303
Fort Gaines, Georgia 183
Fort Gaines, New York 250
Fort Gaines, Pennsylvania 183
Fort George (Astoria Post), Oregon 303
Fort George, Canada 35, 70, 71, 72, 79, 92, 108, 114, 116, 117, 118, 124, 124, 125, 134, 136, 151, 152, 157, 159, 164, 178, 179, 183, 191, 206, 207, 216, 220, 221; abandoned by Americans 177
Fort George, Castine, Maine 242, 298
Fort George (Fort Michilimackinac; separate from Fort George at Brunswick; later Fort Holmes) 211, 226
Fort George, St. George, Maine 15, 18
Fort Glass 131, 150, 152
Fort Gratiot, Michigan 183, 221
Fort Gray 177

Fort Gray, Niagara Falls 86
Fort Greene, New York 235, 260
Fort Griswold 131
Fort Haldimand 27
Fort Hancock, Maine 15
Fort Handy, Illinois 303
Fort Harrison, Terre Haute, Indiana 18, 58, 76
Fort Hawkins, Georgia 42, 183
Fort Hawn 152
Fort Henry, Idaho 17
Fort Hickory 86
Fort Hollingsworth 86, 110
Fort Hope, Sandwich, Canada 46
Fort Hull 184, 191
Fort Huntington, Cleveland 63, 86, 94
Fort Independence, Illinois (Cap au Gris Fort) 242
Fort Jackson, Alabama 201, 206, 207, 221, 229, 302
Fort Jackson (Old Fort Jackson), Savannah, Georgia 17
Fort Jennings 22, 86, 94
Fort Johnson, Illinois 245
Fort Jonesboro, Alabama 279
Fort Kentucky, New York 85, 116
Fort Laight, New York 235
Fort La Motte 50
Fort LaMotte, Illinois 50, 886
Fort Lavier 152
Fort Lawrence 183
Fort Lee, Massachusetts 21
Fort Lernoult (later Fort Shelby) 164
Fort Leslie 170
Fort Lisa, Montana 22
Fort Lisa, Nebraska 22
Fort Lookout (aka Camp Lookout; later Fort Wood) 86
Fort Loramie 64
Fort Lyttleton 15
Fort MacDonough 15
Fort Madison, Iowa 15, 57, 132
Fort Madison, Maine (Fort Castine; later Fort Porter) 18, 183, 242
Fort Madison, Mississippi Valley, Alabama 131, 141, 145, 148, 150, 152, 153, 169, 173
Fort Madison, Missouri (aka Fort Matson) 59
Fort Malden (formerly Fort Amherstburg) 37, 38, 39, 41, 46, 157, 158
Fort Marion 15
Fort Marr 184
Fort Massac (earlier Fort Massiac and Fort de L'Ascension) 138, 259
Fort McArthur, Kenton, Ohio 22, 27, 31, 32, 67, 76, 85, 156
Fort McClary (formerly Fort Pepperell and Fort William) 15, 81
Fort McHenry 86, 105, 125, 146, 246, 247, 250, 251, 252, 254, 255, 278, 298
Fort Meigs 22, 38, 50, 63, 86, 92, 94, 98, 100, 103, 108, 109, 110, 111, 113, 114, 127, 128, 131, 133, 134, 135, 138, 139, 141, 142, 158, 159, 191
Fort Miami (Fort Miamis) 33, 34, 88, 100, 109, 110
Fort Michilimackinac (Mackinac; formerly Fort de Buade; known by British as Fort George) 30, 35, 37, 38, 41, 43, 211, 243, 257
Fort Mifflin 183
Fort Mims 131, 140, 141, 145, 147, 151, 152, 158, 160, 168, 169, 170, 171, 180, 201; massacre 149
Fort Mississauga 178, 179, 220
Fort Mitchell, Alabama 86, 103, 175, 184, 191, 302
Fort Mobile 105
Fort Montgomery, Alabama 177, 262
Fort Moreau 239
Fort Morris, Georgia (later Fort Defiance) 105
Fort Morrow at Waldo 22
Fort Mose (Old Fort Moosa) 24, 25, 29
Fort Moultrie 279
Fort Murray at Jeromesville 22
Fort Necessity at Williamstown 22
Fort Necessity, Ohio 32, 67
Fort Niagara 25, 56, 62, 64, 70, 73, 79, 116, 117, 158, 164, 177, 178, 179, 180, 181, 182, 183, 189, 190, 195, 198, 204, 206, 207, 220, 257
Fort Norfolk 127
Fort Okanogan 18, 19
Fort Ontario, Oswego, New York 209
Fort Osage (aka Fort Clark) 15
Fort Osage, Troy, Missouri 15
Fort Oswego 210, 211
Fort Payne, Alabama 164
Fort Peachtree 57
Fort Pentagoet 18
Fort Perry 86
Fort Petites Coquilles (in New Orleans; later Fort at the Rigolets) 279
Fort Phoenix, Massachusetts 215
Fort Pickering 21
Fort Pierce (Pierce's Stockade) 131, 145, 149, 150, 176
Fort Pike (later Madison Barracks) 86, 116
Fort Pike (Sackets Harbor) 299
Fort Portaga 22
Fort Preble (formerly Spring Point Battery) 15
Fort Presentation 63
Fort Raymond (Big Horn River) 15, 16
Fort Raymond on the Yellowstone River 17
Fort Riall *see* Fort Mississauga
Fort Richmond, New York 45
Fort Rigolets *see* Fort Petites Coquilles (New Orleans)

Fort Ross 19
Fort Russell (Camp Russell) 50, 76, 221
Fort St. Anthony (later Fort Snelling) 12
Fort St. Charles (Fort St. Carlos) 271
Fort St. George, Thomaston, Maine 242
Fort St. John, New Orleans 277
Fort St. Joseph, St. Joseph's Island, Canada (later Fort George) 35, 37, 38
Fort St. Michael 229, 260, 261, 262
Fort St. Philip 289, 290
Fort St. Stephens 131
Fort Ste. Joseph 183, 221
Fort San Carlos *see* Fort St. Charles
Fort San Nicholas 23
Fort Saybrook 86
Fort Scammel 15
Fort Schlosser 133, 223
Fort Scott, Georgia (initially Camp Crawford) 303
Fort Scott, New York 239, 250
Fort Selden 303
Fort Seneca, Ohio 63, 86, 94, 135, 141, 156, 188
Fort Severn 15, 99
Fort Sewall 183
Fort Shelby, Detroit (formerly Fort Lernoult) 164
Fort Shelby, Wisconsin (aka Fort Crawford; later Fort McKay) 184, 217, 218, 222
Fort Sherbrooke 221
Fort Sinquefield 131, 151, 152
Fort Spokane, Miles 17
Fort Spokane, Spokane 17
Fort Stark 85, 116
Fort Stephenson, Fremont 22, 127, 133, 139, 140, 141, 142, 144, 156, 221
Fort Stevens, New York 235
Fort Stirling, New York 235
Fort Stoddert, Alabama 100, 131, 136, 141, 150, 151, 152, 231
Fort Strong 183
Fort Strother 169, 170, 177, 184, 187, 190, 193, 195, 199, 207
Fort Sullivan, Easton, Maine 221
Fort Sullivan, New Hampshire 15, 213
Fort Swift, New York 235
Fort Talbot 196
Fort Three Forks 16, 17
Fort Tompkins, Buffalo, New York (aka Fort Adams) 86
Fort Tompkins, Plattsburgh 250
Fort Tompkins, Sackets Harbor, Jefferson County, New York 85, 108, 116, 119, 120, 186
Fort Tonyn 21
Fort Toulouse 201, 206
Fort Trumbull 131, 296
Fort Turman 18
Fort Union, Wilmington 104
Fort Vallonia 18

Fort Virginia, New York 86, 116
Fort Volunteer 86, 116, 119, 120
Fort Wallace (later Fort Champooick) 18
Fort Warburton, Virginia 138, 236
Fort Warren, Alabama 168
Fort Washington, Maryland (aka Fort Warburton) 232, 235, 236, 238
Fort Washington, New Hampshire 206, 213
Fort Wayne 48, 52, 61, 62, 63, 65, 68, 81
Fort Wellington, Preston, Canada 67, 94, 169, 206
Fort White 131
Fort William (formerly Fort Pepperell; later Fort McClary) 15
Fort Williams, Alabama 199, 200, 201, 205, 207
Fort Winchester (formerly Fort Defiance) 22, 63, 67, 68, 72, 76, 78, 85, 86, 94, 108, 113, 135, 139, 154
Fort Wooster 86
HMS *Forth* 235
Fortuna (vessel) 209
Fortune (317-ton schooner) 33
Fortune (schooner; seized 28 August 1812) 57
Fortune (schooner; seized 31 August 1813) 151
Forty Mile Creek 124, 125
Foster, Augustus (British foreign minister to U.S.) 16
Foster, Benjamin 169
Foster, Captain C. 197
Foster, E. (master) 176
Foster, Captain John 192, 229
Foster, Captain William 230
Four Brothers (schooner) 70, 73, 144
Four Friends 31, 215
Four Sons (schooner) 70
Fowler, Lt. Colonel Benjamin 250
Fowltown (Seminole village) 183
HMS *Fox* 136
Fox (armed boat) 137
Fox (British schooner) 41
Fox (British vessel) 247
Fox (privateer) 115
Fox (schooner) 102, 266, 298
Fox, James 190
Fox Indians 14, 217, 245
France: invades Russia 33; Napoleon escapes and returns 241
Francis (schooner) 205
Francis, Josiah 66
Francis and Eliza 269
Francis and Lucy (schooner) 181
Francisca De Paula (90-ton brigantine) 214
Franklin (80-ton sloop) 174
Franklin (privateer) 31
Franklin (schooner) 133
Franklin (vessel) 31
Franklin, Benjamin 16
Franklin, Jesse 303
Frazer, Sergeant (later colonel) 124

Frazier, Lieutenant Solomon 235, 246
Frederick Augustus (328-ton ship) 105
Frederick's Island 221
Fredericktown, Maryland 113
Fredericktown Blockhouse 22
Free Trader (privateer) 43
Freeman, Major 175, 181
Freeman, W. (master) 135
Freeport (*Free Port*) (sloop) 144
Freer, Military Secretary Noah 196
Fremont, Ohio 156
French Canadian Fencibles 165, 171
French Creek 168, 216
French Grand Army 74
French Mills 186, 189
Frenchtown (Monroe), Michigan 90
Frenchtown, Maryland 110
Frend, British major 137, 138
Friends (brigantine) 216
Friends (brigantine out of Bristol, England) 34
Friends (brigantine; seized August 1812) 43
Friends (snow) 112
Friends Adventure (British brigantine) 147
Friends and Mary (brigantine) 41
Friendship (74-ton sloop; seized 28 July 1813) 140
Friendship (97-ton schooner; seized 13 July 1813) 136
Friendship (114-ton schooner) 100
Friendship (schooner; seized 19 July 1812) 40
Friendship (schooner; seized 11 September 1812) 61
Friendship (schooner; seized 5 March 1813) 40
Friendship (schooner; seized 6 July 1813) 40
Friendship (schooner; seized 11 July 1813) 40
Friendship (schooner; seized 28 July 1813) 40
Friendship (ship) 181
Friendship (sloop) 134
Friendship (sloop; seized 11 July 1813) 135
Friendship (sloop; seized July 1814) 217
Frink, Ensign 228
Frisbec, S. (master) 168
Frisby's farm 240
Frith, Captain 45
HMS *Frolic* 73, 87, 175
USS *Frolic* 195, 199, 203, 205
Frolic (privateer) 34
Frontier Light Infantry 177
Fry, Captain 70
Fuller, Captain Charles 51
Fuller, W. O. (master) 169
Fulton (the first) 184
Fulton, Robert 184, 185
Funk, Lt. John Musser 75
Furber, Brigadier General Richard (New Hampshire militia) 33
Futzen, British Lieutenant W.P. 260
Fylinda (40-ton sloop) 257

Gadsden, General Christopher 57
Gadsden, Master Commandant Christopher, Jr. 57
Gaines, Lt. Colonel (later major general) Edmund Pendleton 35, 139, 172, 190, 206, 222, 225, 226, 229, 230, 250, 274, 279, 296
Gaines, Captain Francis A. 153
Gaines, Colonel George S. 147, 164
Galapagos 133
Gallagher, Lieutenant 290
USS *Gallatin* 36, 45, 48, 104
Gallatin, Albert (Secretary of the Treasury) 26, 100, 168, 184, 226
Gallinipper (American privateer) 112
Galloway (privateer) 41, 205
Galloway (ship) 255
Galloway, Archer 25, 26
Gamala La Delso (brigantine) 157
Gambia (brigantine) 89
Gambier, Lord 226
Gambit, Lieutenant 90
Gamble, Catherine Gratton 17
Gamble, Lieutenant John (USMC) 118, 137, 156, 159, 176, 204
Gamble, Colonel Robert 17
Gamble, Lieutenant Thomas (USS *Guerriere*) 246, 300
Gambles, British Captain Henry 43
Gananoqui, Canada 63
Gannett (35-ton schooner) 147
Gano, Brigadier General (later major general) John 187, 188, 191
Gansevoort, General Peter 21, 34
Gardiner (ship) 175
Gardiner (quartermaster) 188
Gardiner, B. (master) 110
Gardiner, David 123
Gardiner, John Lyon 123
Gardiner, Sarah Griswold 123
Gardner, A. (master) 175
HMS *Garland* 33, 80, 87
Garland (ship) 281
Garrard, Captain William 65, 66, 108
Garrett, Lieutenant Ashton 91
Garrique, French general 278, 280, 282, 286
Garrison, Captain A. 31
Gates, General Horatio 12
Gates, Mary Valance 12
Gates, Robert 12
Gattanewa 167
Gavet, Captain 55, 56
Geisinger, Midshipman 255
Gell, Captain 242
General Armstrong (privateer) 100, 101, 104, 133, 153, 247, 253, 255, 256
General Blake (British brigantine) 48
General Green (83-ton sloop) 100
USS *General Greene* (frigate) 154

General Hodgson (61-ton sloop) 115
USS *General Madison* 158
General Marion (schooner) 175
USS *General Pike* 139, 142, 144, 147, 151, 156, 158, 197, 225
General Prevost (brigantine) 82
General Putnam (privateer) 47, 247
General Smyth (British privateer) 49, 57, 69, 75
General Stark (privateer) 34
USS *General Tompkins* 158
General Wellesley (ship) 257
HMS *General Wolfe* 151
Genesee Packet (later *Conquest*) 63
Genesee River 255
Geoghan, Sailing Master 216
George (3-masted schooner) 264
George (149-ton brigantine) 36
George (172-ton brigantine; seized 22 February 1815) 36
George (211-ton brigantine; seized 17 July 1812) 39
George (brigantine; recaptured 20 July 1812) 39
George (brigantine; seized 8 July 1812) 39
George (brigantine; seized 22 July 1812) 36, 39
George (brigantine; seized 16 August 1812) 53
George (brigantine; seized 16 February 1814) 294
George (British brigantine) 158
George (schooner) 47
George (vessel) 89
George III, King 18, 29, 33, 275
George, 1st Lieutenant Edward 154
George, Captain J. 31
George Washington (3-ton schooner privateer) 31
George Washington (105-ton schooner) 112
Georgetown, Maryland 113
Georgetown Artillery 215
Georgetown Dragoons 215
Georgetown militia 234
Georgetown Riflemen 215
USS *Georgiana* 118, 129, 133, 136, 137, 139
Georgiana (ship) 57
Georgiana (vessel) 101
Ghent, Belgium 168, 216, 226, 227
Gibbs, P. (master) 100
Gibbs, British General Samuel 274, 275, 276, 277, 281, 282, 285, 286, 287, 288, 289
Gibbs, W. (master) 156
Gibraltar 193, 261
Gibson, Colonel John H. 273
Gift (41-ton schooner) 291
Gilbert, G. H. (master) 67
Gill, British Captain Charles 87, 104
Gilleland's Creek 211
Gilman, Governor John Taylor (New Hampshire) 115, 206, 213
Gilmer, Lt. George Rockingham (later governor of Georgia) 57
Girod, Nicholas (mayor of New Orleans) 265
Girty, James 50
Gittings, James 250
Glass, Zacharia 131
Gleaner (American privateer) 40
Gleaner (British provincial schooner; formerly American privateer *Gleaner*) 40
Gleaner (schooner; seized 3 December 1814) 157, 266
Gleason, Mr. 34
Glegg, British captain (later Lt. Col.) 50, 51, 52, 206
Glegg, Major 189
Glengarry Regiment (Glengarry Fencibles) 31, 67, 79, 107, 116, 117, 119, 179, 211
Glieg, British lieutenant 274
Globe (privateer) 40, 41, 42, 44, 49, 68, 169
Gloucester, Massachusetts 35
Glover, W. (master) 146
Godoy, Manuel de *see* De Godoy, Manuel
HMS *Golden Fleece* 260
Goldsborough, Mrs. 113
Good Hope (schooner) 256
Good Intent (brigantine) 151
Goodrich, Charles (master) 40, 42
Goose Creek 138
Gordon, A. 87
Gordon, British lieutenant 143, 295
Gordon, J. A. 87
Gordon, British Captain James 238, 242, 246
Gordon, Captain John 190
Gore, Lt. Governor Francis 19
HMS *Goree* 87
HMS *Gorgon* 268
Gorham, D. (master) 222, 238
Gorin, Captain James 154
Gossamer (ship) 40, 42
Gossard, T. (master) 40
Gosselin, British Major General Gerard 242
Gottenburg, Sweden 184
Goulbourn, Henry 226
Government House 73
Governor Gerry (privateer) 74, 75
Governor McKean (privateer) 43
Governor Plumer (schooner) 118
Governor Shelby (schooner) 222
Governor Tompkins (American privateer) 83, 84
USS *Governor Tompkins* (formerly *Charles and Ann*) 68, 77, 83, 84, 108, 118, 146, 152, 192, 196
Grace (brigantine) 45
Gracie, Archibald 29
Graham, Brigadier General Joseph 202
Graham, Captain Robinson 154

Index

Graham, Thomas 87
HMS *Grampus* 87
Grampus (privateer) 215
Gramsby, George British (master) 225
Grand Prairie Blockhouse 22
Grand Terre Island 254, 267
Grand Turk (privateer) 87, 112, 207, 208, 281, 294, 296, 297
Granger, British Lt. Colonel 182
Granger, Lt. Colonel 181
HMS *Granicus* 261, 266
Grant, Lt. Colonel Andrew 243
Grant (possibly Gavet), Captain J. 40
Grant, Captain J. 76
Grant, Captain Squire 153
Grassin, Captain 60
Gratiot, Captain Charles 82, 133, 221
Gratton, John 17
Gratton, Major John 17
Graves, Major Benjamin 90
Graves, Captain J. 31
Gray, British colonel 120
Gray, Captain D. 66
Gray, Nicholas 35
Gray, R. (master) 55
Grayson's Farm 172
Great Rat Island 90
Grecian (privateer) 210
Green, British captain 82, 294
Green, G. 87
Green, Captain Nathan 69, 70, 281, 296, 297
Green Camp 22
HMS *Green Linnet* 87
Green Wood Cemetery 102
Greene, General Nathaniel 57
Greenup, Governor Christopher 17
USS *Greenwich* 133, 136, 137, 176, 204
Greenwich (vessel) 101, 118
Greggs, mail-rider 121
Gregory, Lieutenant USN 216, 217
Gregory, William 87
Grenada (vessel) 41
Grenadier Island 159, 169, 216
Greyhound (schooner) 31
Griffith, British Rear Admiral Richard 242
Grimes, Colonel John R. 283
Griswold, Governor Roger 28, 131
Grotius (schooner) 34
Growler 211
Growler (American privateer) 134
USS *Growler* (schooner; later HMS *Hamilton*) 68, 77, 80, 118, 123, 146, 147, 151, 163, 175
Gruber, Reverend John 250
Guanajuato, Mexico 16
Gubbins, British major (later Lt. Colonel) 272, 284
HMS *Guerriere* 19, 29, 30, 36, 38, 44, 48, 53, 54, 55, 56, 85, 266
USS *Guerriere* 216, 299, 300, 301, 302

Guerriere (169-ton brigantine) 281
Guise, Lt. G. M. 87
Gunboat (No. 5) 267, 268
Gunboat (No. 8) 289
Gunboat (No. 23) 266, 267, 268
Gunboat (No. 149) 303
Gunboat (No. 154) 303
Gunboat (No. 156) 267
Gunboat (No. 163) 266, 267
Gunboat (No. 164) 157
Gunboat (No. 166) *see* USS *Alligator*
Gunboat (No. 169) 267
Gustava (seized 22 January 1814) 190
Gustava (vessel) 128
Guttle Hoffnung 34
Guy, Michael 60
Gypsey (letter of marque) 34
Gypsey (privateer) 39

Hackett, Captain 106, 153
Haddock (brigantine) 211
Hadji Ali (The Tiger) 300
Hague, J. (master) 57
Haig, Lt. George (U.S. Dragoons) 28
Haile, Brigadier General James 231
Hailey, Captain Joshua 99
Hale, Major General Samuel (New Hampshire militia) 33
Halifax (schooner) 44
Halifax (ship) 260
Hall, Major General Amos 72, 178, 180, 181, 182, 183, 185, 186, 188, 189, 190, 191, 192, 195, 206
Hall, Colonel 232
Hall, Judge Dominic A. 295, 296
Hall, Captain Elias 25
Hall, Hulda 228
Hall, Captain John 154
Hall, Major Nathaniel 230
Hall, Moses (master) 137
Hall, William 87
Hallem, British captain 273
Hallet, L. (master) 102
Halsey's Corner 241, 246
Hamblen, E. (master) 106
HMS *Hamilton* (formerly USS *Growler*) 151, 163
USS *Hamilton* (schooner) 68, 77, 146, 175
Hamilton, Canada 164, 171
Hamilton, Lieutenant A. 290
Hamilton, Alexander 13, 14
Hamilton, British colonel 189, 190, 269
Hamilton, Captain 109, 113
Hamilton, Colonel Everard 263
Hamilton, Secretary of the Navy Paul (former U.S. senator and governor of South Carolina) 25, 30, 42, 69, 84, 85, 87
Hamilton, Lieutenant Thomas 59, 132
Hamilton, Major (later colonel) William S. USA 103, 279
Hammida, Admiral Rais 299, 300

Hammond, Amelia O'Keefe 11
Hammond, Captain 168
Hammond, Captain Eli 168
Hammond, J. (master) 106
Hammond, Colonel Samuel 11
Hampton, Virginia 129, 130
Hampton, Captain 186
Hampton, Confederate General Wade 22, 99
Hampton, Major General Wade 22, 61, 85, 89, 99, 103, 139, 146, 148, 151, 152, 157, 159, 160, 165, 166, 169, 173, 186, 190
Hampton Roads 127
Hanchett, British Captain John M. (natural son of King George III) 127
Hancock (vessel) 242
Hancock, British major 203
Hancock, British private 42
Hand, J. P. (master) 100
Hanks, Lt. Porter 38, 51
Hannah (47-ton schooner) 144
Hannah (71-ton schooner) 135
Hanson, Alexander 31, 41
Happahs 166, 167
Happy (brigantine) 151
Harbison, Captain Samuel 154
Hardin, Major 67, 79
Hardy, Captain T. 37
Hardy, Commodore Sir Thomas 87, 115, 123, 130, 131, 221, 227, 228
Hare (brigantine) 43
Hare (British privateer) 187
Harlequin (privateer) 259
Harmar, General Josiah 61
Harmony 216
Harmony (brigantine; seized by the *Chasseur*) 102, 298
Harmony (brigantine; seized by the *Yankee*) 43
Harmony (schooner) 89
Harper, Brigadier General Robert Goodloe 257
Harpy (privateer) 242, 281
HMS *Harriet* 43
Harriet (brigantine) 121
Harriet (brigantine; seized 7 June 1813) 125
Harriet (schooner) 41, 56
Harriet (schooner; seized 28 June 1813) 131
Harriet (sloop; captured 13 July 1813) 136
Harriet and Matilda (brigantine) 73
Harris, Lt. Colonel John 190, 181
Harris, Lt. 79
Harris, Captain Samuel D. 213, 223
Harris, Brigadier General William 54
Harrisburg Volunteers 25
Harrison (privateer) 225
Harrison, John 169
Harrison, Jonas 179
Harrison, Major Reuben 282, 283
Harrison, Major General (later president) William Henry 16, 20, 21, 27, 50,

52, 56, 57, 58, 59, 61, 62, 63, 65, 67, 74, 75, 78, 80, 82, 83, 85, 87, 88, 89, 91, 92, 93, 94, 95, 96, 98, 99, 101, 102, 103, 108, 109, 110, 111, 112, 113, 114, 127, 128, 131, 132, 133, 134, 135, 138, 139, 141, 142, 143, 153, 154, 155, 156, 157, 158, 159, 160, 161, 162, 163, 164, 188, 191, 197, 255; forced from active service 165; succeeds Winchester as commander of Northwestern army 64
Hart, Reverend Ira 225
Hart, John (seaman) 97
Hart, Captain Nathaniel 89, 90
Hartford Convention 268
Harvey, Captain 55
Harvey, Col. John (later Sir John Harvey, Lt. Governor of Nova Scotia) 124, 125, 165, 181, 206, 211
Hassan (14-gun ship) 43
Hatchechubba 135
Hathaway, A. (master) 221
Hathway, W. (master) 106
Hatt, British captain (later major) 71, 80
Havre de Grace, Maryland 110, 112, 113
Hawk (privateer) 208
Hawke (privateer) 196
Hawkes, Captain Edward 87
Hawkins, British Lieutenant Abel 258
Hawkins, Colonel Benjamin (Indian agent) 24, 26, 66, 93, 121, 183, 207, 227, 279
Hawkins, Ensign 63
Hawkins, British Captain R. 87
Hawkins, Governor William 202
Haydon, Captain John 154
Hayes (Hays), British Captain John 290
Hayes, Colonel Richard 65
Hayne, Colonel Arthur 229, 272
Hays, John (master) 61
HMS *Hazard* 87
Hazard (American privateer) 31, 94, 96, 97
Hazard (brigantine) 49
Hazard (schooner) 31, 222
Hazelton, P. (master) 38
Head, Michael 87
Heald, Mrs. 50
Heald, Captain Nathan 49, 50
Heard, Captain Bailey 140, 180
Heard, British Captain John 38
Hearn, Andrew 190
Hearn, John (master) 177
Heath, W. (master) 39
Heaton (Hayden), Isaac 151, 152
Hebe (British vessel) 93
Hebe (privateer; formerly HMS *Laura*) 60, 98
Hector (11-gun vessel) 129, 133, 194
Hector (156-ton brigantine) 111

Hector (258-ton brigantine) 56
Hector (vessel) 101
Hedden, Captain Eleazor 154
Helen (237-ton schooner) 231
Helen (vessel) 78
Hempstead, Lieutenant 245
Henderson, Colonel James 277
Henderson Bay 119
Hendon, Lt. 175
Henley, Lieutenant John D. 126, 249, 272
Henley, Captain Robert USN 276
Henrietta (bark) 151
Henrietta (galiot) 216
Henrietta (ship) 56
Henrietta (vessel) 214
Henry (10-gun ship) 42
Henry (181-ton ship) 110
Henry (brigantine) 44
USS *Henry* (brigantine) 146
Henry (brigantine; seized March 1814) 196
Henry (British brigantine) 34, 48
Henry (schooner) 184
Henry (schooner; seized 20 June 1813) 127
Henry (ship) 48
Henry, Andrew 15, 16, 17, 19, 27
Henry, British captain 286
Henry, Major General William 153, 160
Henry Guilder (privateer) 41
Henry House (formerly Williamette Post) 22
HMS *Herald* 289
Herald (privateer) 181, 231
Herald (privateer out of New York) 181
Herbert, Captain Edward 36, 48, 104
Herbert, Captain J. C. 232
Herculean (brigantine) 214
Herkimer, New York 38
Herman (413-ton ship) 129
HMS *Hermes* (20-gun ship) 87, 252, 253
HMS *Hero* 39, 60
Hero (cutter) 41
Hero (privateer) 41
Hero (schooner) 126, 149, 174, 218
Hero (sloop) 187
Hero (sloop; seized November 1814) 260
HMS *Heron* 87
HMS *Herring* 87
Hesper (American brigantine) 40, 47
Hester (Negro woman) 150, 151
Hetty (151-ton brigantine) 123
Hewitt, British Lt. (Royal Marines) 211
Heydon's Hill 175
Hibernia (22-gun ship) 102
Hibernia (69-ton schooner) 236
Hickey, Frederick 87
Hickman, Captain 92
Hickman, General Richard, Lt. Governor of Kentucky 135

Index

Hickory Ground 106, 174, 205
Hidatsa Indians 13
Higgins, Colonel William 187
High Head Jim 135
Highflyer (American privateer) 40, 41, 55, 76, 94, 116
HMS *Highflyer* (formerly American privateer *Highflyer*) 94, 116, 157, 175
HMS *Highflyer* (tender) 136
Highland Hill (18-ton sloop) 239
Hilghman, Brigadier General Jacob 54
Hill, E. (master) 215
Hill, Lieutenant John USN 237
Hillibee Indians 193
Hillibee towns 121, 171, 172
Hillinghagee (Indian prophet) 207
Hillyar, British Captain (commodore) James 83, 134, 193, 194, 202, 203
Hindman, Major Jacob 117, 204, 218, 230
Hinds, Major Thomas 164, 269, 271, 272, 276, 278, 282, 291
Hinkston, Captain 77
Hinman, Brigadier General Ephraim 29
Hiram (brigantine) 264
Hiram (privateer) 75
Hiram (schooner; seized in July 1812) 39
Hiram (schooner; seized 12 September 1812) 61
Hislop, Lt. General Thomas (governor of Bombay) 84, 85, 87, 88
Hitch, Captain J. 33
Hite, Captain James 154
Hitler, Adolph 74
Hoadley (navigator) 218
Hoare, Ensign 213
Hobart, Lt. C. 87
Hockings, Robert 87
Hocquard, F. (master) 110
Hodge, W. 184
Hodgson, Captain Charles Bayne 104
Hoffman, Lieutenant B. V. 54
Hoffman, Midshipman 299
Hoisington, Job 182
Holder, Captain Richard C. 154
Holkar (American privateer) 81, 211
HMS *Holly* 87
Holmes, Captain (later major) Andrew 104, 224, 226, 255
Holmes, Captain (24th U.S. Infantry) 197
Holmes, Brigadier General David 87
Holmes, Captain Jeremiah 196, 227
Holmes, Doctor Thomas H. 150
Holmes, Thomas (master) 231
Holstein (113-ton schooner) 103
Holy Ground (Econochaca) 164, 180
Homer, John (master) 105
Homes, R. (master) 79

Honestus (ship) 56
Hooke, Mr. 242
Hoople's Creek 171
Hope (12-gun ship) 80
Hope (164-ton ship) 144
Hope (brigantine) 112
Hope (brigantine; seized 15 December 1814) 269
Hope (schooner; seized April 1814) 205, 209
Hope (ship) 216, 217
Hope (ship; seized 28 August 1813) 149
Hope (ship; seized 16 August 1814) 231
Hope for Peace (seized 18 July 1813) 138
Hopewell (ship) 42
Hopkins, C. (master) 57
Hopkins, Lt. Col. C. 186
Hopkins, Captain (privateer *Providence*) 59
Hopkins, Major 284
Hopkins, Brigadier General Reuben 24, 157, 181, 182
Hopkins, Brigadier General T. S. 140
Hopkins, Major General Samuel 52, 57, 65, 76, 78, 79
Hoppet (150-ton brigantine) 165
Horatio (brigantine) 241
Hornbeck, Captain John 153
USS *Hornet* 26, 27, 31, 76, 82, 85, 88, 93, 94, 97, 98, 102, 123, 177, 297, 298, 299
Hornet (privateer 3-gun schooner) 31
Hornet (sloop) 35
Horse Island 119
Horsely, Doctor 155
Horseshoe Bend (Cholocco Litabixee) 193, 199, 200, 201
Hough, Lt. 227
House, Lt. Col. James 185
House of Representatives 179
Houston, Ensign Sam 164, 195, 201
Hoven, John 150
Howard, Brigadier General (Governor Missouri Territory) Benjamin 85, 217, 244, 245
Howard, Captain (privateer *Orders in Council*) 86
Howe (brigantine) 59, 156
Howe, Brigadier General Hezekia 28, 87
Howell, Lieutenant 290
Howell, Midshipman 299
Hrenvort, Captain 47
Hubbard, Abner 32
Hubbard, Captain 27
Hubbard, Major General John 28
Hudson Bay Company 17, 18, 19
Hudson's Blockhouse 22
Huffman, Peter 58
Hull, Captain Abraham F. 47, 51, 224
Hull, Captain (Commodore) Isaac USN 30, 36, 39, 42, 52, 53, 54, 55, 75, 85, 123, 206, 266
Hull, Brigadier General William (Governor Michigan Territory) 22, 24, 26, 27, 30, 31, 32, 33, 34, 35, 36, 37, 38, 40, 41, 44, 45, 46, 48, 49, 50, 51, 52, 53, 86, 127, 152, 162, 163; court martial 185
Humbert, General Jean 285, 292
Humes, Captain James 26
Humphrey, Captain 64
Humphrey, Captain Enoch 279, 280, 282, 286
Hungerford, Captain 113
Hungerford, General John P. (Virginia) 226, 236, 239
USS *Hunter* 98
Hunter (33-ton sloop) 101
Hunter (American privateer) 75, 83
Hunter (British brigantine) 216
Hunter (cartel) 34
HMS *Hunter* (formerly *General Hunter*) 45, 68, 154, 155, 156, 175
Hunter (privateer) 83
Hunter, Lt. Charles Newton 60
Huntley, Brigadier General Elisha (New Hampshire militia) 33
Huntress (vessel) 173
Huntsville, Alabama 151, 163, 166, 168, 193
Hurd, Brigadier General Jabez 231
Huron Indians 200
Husaren (brigantine) 174
Hussar (schooner) 213
Hussey, C. B. (master) 175
Hutchinson, British Lt. T. H. 87
Hutchison, Captain William Jr. 153
Hutkee *see* Chief William McIntosh
Huzzar (schooner) 86
HMS *Hyperion* 87, 214
HMS *Icicle* 81

Ida (brigantine) 227
Ida (privateer) 204, 205
Illinois Territory organized 16
Illuminator (brigantine) 36
HMS *Inconstant* (36-gun) 87
USS *Independence* 301, 302
Independent Blues 26
HMS *Indian* (brigantine) 36, 37, 38, 39, 40, 87
Indian Head 246
Indian Lass (brigantine) 112, 207
Indiana Territory 16; admitted to Union 303
Industrious Bee 209
Industry (schooner) 148
Industry (schooner; seized 3 November 1813) 169
Industry (schooner; seized 10 September 1814) 247
Industry (sloop; captured 16 January 1815) 291
Industry of Lynn (privateer) 43
Ingersoll, Captain J. 41
Inman, Captain 73
Ino (privateer) 295

Invincible (privateer) 181
Invincible Napoleon (French privateer) 115, 231
Ionian Islands (Greece) 14
Irvine, Captain Armstrong 172
Irving, Colonel Washington 257
Irvine, Colonel William N. 185
Irwin, Captain 175
Irwin, John 264
Isaac Hull (schooner privateer) 58
Isaacs, Colonel Ralph 28, 34
Isabella (brigantine) 138, 188
Isham, Brigadier General Jirah 28, 87, 130, 228
Island Packet (vessel) 25
Isle aux Nois 211
Isnardon, P. T. (master) 174
Ives, James (master) 121
Ivinada, J. (master) 126
Izard, Captain (later major general) George 22, 85, 103, 157, 166, 190, 204, 209, 220, 228, 238, 239, 254, 255, 257, 259, 260

Jack, Captain 115
Jack, Captain (Fort Mims) 149
Jack's Favourite (privateer) 34, 81, 87
Jackson, Major General Andrew (later president) 12, 33, 53, 70, 82, 93, 96, 98, 105, 116, 148, 150, 151, 157, 160, 163, 164, 166, 168, 170, 171, 175, 177, 184, 188, 189, 190, 193, 195, 199, 200, 201, 202, 205, 206, 207, 208, 213, 221, 227, 229, 237, 253, 254, 259, 260, 261, 262, 264, 265, 267, 269, 271, 272, 273, 274, 276, 277, 278, 279, 280, 281, 282, 283, 284, 285, 286, 287, 288, 289, 291, 292, 293, 295, 296, 302, 303
Jackson, Craven 190
Jackson, Francis J. (British foreign minister to U. S.) 16
Jackson, Lieutenant 224
Jackson, Rachel 297
Jackson, Thomas 31
Jacobs, Captain 264
Jacobs, Captain Richard 38
Jacoby, Frederick 68
Jamaica (7-gun vessel) 55
Jamaica (merchant ship) 40
James (schooner) 245
James (ship) 102, 298
James, Abner 151
James, British Lt. Colonel 179
James, Mary 151
James, Robert (master) 255
James, Sergeant 137
James, Thomas 151
James, William (English author) 63
James and Charlotte (brigantine) 64
James family 151
James Madison (privateer) 58, 179

Jameson, J. (master) 164
Jamison, Colonel 146
Jane (65-ton sloop) 176
Jane (70-ton sloop) 225
Jane (brigantine) 209
Jane (brigantine; captured 9 November 1814) 262
Jane (schooner) 40
Jane (schooner; seized 7 February 1813) 95
Jane (schooner; seized 10 December 1813) 176
Jane (schooner; seized 12 November 1814) 262
Jane (ship) 57
Jane (ship; seized 2 January 1815) 281
Jane (sloop; seized 6 December 1813) 176
Jane, British captain 38
Jane, Henry 87
Jane Gordon (brigantine) 34
Janus (77-ton sloop) 215
Janus (sloop) 215
Jarrett (2-gun vessel) 43
Jarrett (British ship) 38
Jarrett, Captain Henry 27
HMS *Jaseur* 165, 174, 200, 210, 214
HMS *Jason* 58, 87
Jason (schooner) 174
HMS *Java* 76, 84, 85, 87, 93
USS *Java* (frigate) 83, 137, 174, 175, 302
Jeannie (British privateer) 48
Jefferson (98-ton schooner) 136
Jefferson (brigantine) 104, 186
Jefferson (privateer) 34
Jefferson (schooner) 136
USS *Jefferson* (second) 206
Jefferson, Martha 102
Jefferson, President Thomas 11, 12, 13, 14, 183, 296, 303
Jeffrey, W. (master) 127
Jenkes, Captain William C. 257
Jenkins, F. (master) 213
Jenkins, British Captain John 97
Jennett (brigantine) 105
Jennings, Captain Samuel 25
Jennings, Colonel William 63, 66
Jenny (ship) 43
Jerusalem (760-ton ship) 152
Jerusha (sloop) 136
Jesup, Major (later major general) Thomas Sidney 50, 52, 218, 220, 223, 224, 268
Jicarilla Apaches 16
Joanna (48-ton schooner) 123
John (10-ton brigantine) 41
John (16-gun privateer) 34, 43
John (130-ton brigantine) 104
John (brigantine) 50
John (brigantine; seized 30 April 1814) 209
John (British ship) 42
John (sloop) 212
John VI of Portugal, King (formerly Prince Regent) 14
USS *John Adams* 44, 142
John Adams (brigantine) 56, 136
John and Isabella 93
John and Mary (brigantine) 156, 167

Index

John and Miriam (schooner) 148
John Hill's Fort 50
HMS *John of Lancaster* 35
John Sherbrooke (British privateer) 102
Johnson (American soldier) 108, 112
Johnson, Captain (privateer *Jack's Favorite*) 34
Johnson, Mayor Edward 41
Johnson, Ensign 63
Johnson, Captain F. 31, 81
Johnson, Lieutenant F. 136
Johnson, G. (master) 63
Johnson, Colonel James 161, 162
Johnson, John 221
Johnson, Lt. (Michigan dragoons) 47
Johnson, Lieutenant USN 282
Johnson, Major (later colonel) Richard M. 60, 64, 67, 131, 133, 154, 155, 158, 159, 160, 161, 162
Johnson, Lieutenant Robert 247, 256
Johnson, Rossiter 130, 150
Johnson, Brigadier General Thomas 202
Johnson, William (sailing master) 267
Johnston, Captain D. 196
Johnston, E. (master) 148
Johnston, John Indian agent 58
Jonathan (vessel) 185
USS *Jones* 186
Jones (brigantine) 105, 206
Jones, Ambrose (master) 262
Jones, British Lt. Col 288
Jones, Lieutenant (later commodore) Catesby 266, 267, 268
Jones, Captain (Indian interpreter) 179
Jones, Captain Horatio 179
Jones, Captain Jacob 225
Jones, Lieutenant (later captain) Jacob 73, 74, 123, 185, 231
Jones, Captain L. (brother of secretary of the navy, William Jones) 100, 177, 206, 215, 231
Jones, Captain Mississippi volunteers 173
Jones, Mr. 150
Jones, Captain Thomas 156
Jones, British Major Timothy 250
Jones, Secretary of the Navy William 26, 74, 84, 98, 115, 122, 133, 138, 197, 236, 289
Jonquille (privateer) 181
Jordan, Captain 81
Jordan, J. (master) 144
Joren Francisco 294
Joseph (schooner) 174
Joseph (vessel) 61
Joseph and Mary (brigantine) 293
Josiah Francis (prophet) *see* Prophet Francis
Jourdan, Captain 140
Jourdan's Plantation 278

Joy, David (master) 105
Joy, P. (master) 85
Juana (sloop) 112
Jubilee (schooner) 68
Jubon, J. M. (master) 115
Judge Woodward's garden 50
Judith (vessel) 235
Jugeat, Captain 271
Julia (schooner) 44, 68
USS *Julia* (schooner; later HMS *Hamilton*) 42, 77, 118, 146, 147, 163, 175
Julian (80-ton schooner) 78
Julian (schooner; recaptured 17 November 1814) 263
Julian (schooner; seized 8 December 1813) 176
Julian (seized 6 August 1814) 226
Juliana Smith (37-ton schooner) 114
Juliet (92-ton schooner) 114
HMS *Juniper* 38
Juno (privateer) 75
HMS *Junon* 59, 87, 105, 115, 125, 126, 127, 140, 176, 195, 263, 275, 281
Junot, French General Andoche 14
Justice, Dick (Cherokee) 303
Justin, P. (master) 215

Katy (schooner) 156
Keane, British General John 263, 269, 270, 271, 272, 274, 275, 276, 277, 282, 285, 286, 287, 288, 293, 297
Kearny, Lt. Colonel (later general) Stephen Watts 23, 72, 220
Kelley, Captain Samuel 154
Kelso, Brigadier General John 185
Kembell, Isam 151
Kemp (privateer) 264
Kemper, Colonel Reuben 291
Kendall, Captain 73
Kennedy, Captain 148, 174
Kennedy, James L. 261
Kennedy, Joshua 145
Kennedy, Major 175
Kennedy mills 176
Kent Island 145
Kent Volunteers 194
Kenton, Brigadier General Simon 163
Kerr, British Captain A. R. (HMS *Acasta*) 87
Kerr, Captain (Royal militia) 193
Kerr, Doctor David 291
Kerr, Lieutenant 282
Ketchum, Lieutenant 116, 120
Kettle-bottoms 140
Key, Francis Scott 252
Kialigee Indians 193, 195
Kickapoo Indians 57, 163
Kilby, Joshua (master) 38
Kimbell, Isam 151
Kimbell, Ransom 151
Kimbell family 151
Kimbell-James Massacre 151
Kindelan, Spanish governor Sebastian 28, 29, 30
King, British Lieutenant 80
King, British major 286
King, Captain 69, 70, 80

King, General George Edward 161
King, Brigadier General John 163
King, Captain Norfolk 293
King, Norfolk 87
King, Thomas 139
King, William 87
King Charles IV of Spain 14, 105
King Charles XIII of Sweden 16
King Ferdinand VII of Spain 14, 241
HMS *King George* 43
King George (204-ton brigantine) 148
King George III 18, 29, 33, 275
King John VI of Portugal (formerly Prince Regent) 14
King Louis XVIII 205
King of Rome *see* Bonaparte, Napoleon II
Kingsbury, British lieutenant 246
Kingsbury, Colonel 111
Kingsley, Lt. Alpha 15
Kingsley, Zephaniah 48
Kingsley Plantation 48
Kingston, Canada 100, 158, 165, 169, 178, 186, 188, 189, 194, 199, 204, 205, 211, 231, 255
Kingston Packet 49
Kiowa Indians 16
Kirby, Colonel 80
Kitty 43
Knaggs, James 162
Kramer, Colonel 232, 234
Kuhn, Lieutenant Solomon 246

La Belleause (later Indian Creek), Illinois 221
L'Acadie (British post) 186
HMS *Lacedonian* 200
La Colle Creek 203
La Croll, Captain Hubert 22
La Colle Mill 203
Lacocke, General Abner 279
Lacoste, Major 288
Lacoste Plantation 273, 274
Lady Gore (vessel) 163
Lady Harriot (brigantine) 86
Lady Madison (privateer) 31
Lady Murray (British schooner) 126
USS *Lady of the Lake* 104, 108, 114, 117, 119, 126, 146, 151, 156, 158, 196, 212, 225
HMS *Lady Prevost* 53, 154, 175
Lady Prevost (brigantine) 266
Lady Sherbrook (brigantine) 43
HMS *Lady Warren* 43
Lady-Provost 43
Lafitte, Jean 104, 148, 244, 243, 254, 265, 267, 277
Lafitte, Pierre 104, 244
Laforey, Rear Admiral Sir F. 87
HMS *La Hogue* 31, 103, 105, 106, 110, 112, 114, 115, 116, 121, 131, 134, 135, 136, 137, 147, 148, 165, 208, 212, 215
L'Aimable (vessel) 209

Lake, British Captain Lake RN 42
Lake Borgne 267
Lake Champlain 245
Lake Fork Blockhouse 22
Lake Ontario 163, 210
Lambert, British Captain Henry 83, 84, 85
Lambert, British General Sir John 277, 281, 285, 286, 288, 289, 291, 296, 297
Lamont, British Lieutenant 80
Lamprey (brigantine) 35
Lancaster, British Lieutenant 221
Lancaster Phalanx 26
Landon, Captain 216
HMS *Landrail* 221, 237
Landrum's Fort 131
Lane, Joseph 159
Lane, Captain S. N. 145
Lang, John 73
Langdon, E. (master) 149
Langdon, Governor John 26
Langham, Captain Augustus L. 90, 91, 98, 99
La Plata 126
Lark (70-ton sloop) 106
Lark (schooner; captured 15 June 1813) 126
La Rochelle 203
La Ronde (Laronde), Colonel Piere Denis 291
La Ronde Plantation 273, 274
Larrabee, Lieutenant 203
Larwell, Lieutenant 185
Lassel, J. 178
La Teste, France 191, 198
Lathrop, Lieutenant 227
HMS *Latona* 68
La Tranche River 185, 197
Lauderdale, Colonel 170, 273
Laugharne, Captain T. L. P. 48, 49, 53
Laughlin, Captain Thomas 154
Laura (10-gun vessel) 53
Laura (12-gun vessel; later *Hebe*) 60
Laura Jane (78-ton schooner) 176
HMS *Laurestinus* 87, 129
Lavac, British lieutenant 288
Laval, Captain William 261, 262
Lavel, Lt. Colonel 232
Lavier's Fort 131
Lavina (ship) 138
USS *Lawrence* 127, 144, 154, 155, 166
Lawrence (privateer) 208, 262, 293
Lawrence, Lieutenant (later captain) James USN 31, 76, 82, 93, 94, 97, 98, 102, 105, 121, 122, 125, 146
Lawrence, Lt. Colonel 180
Lawrence, Major (later Lt. Col.) William 252, 293
Lawry (schooner) 100
Leader (vessel; renamed USS *Flambeau*) 266
Leander (privateer) 43
HMS *Leander* 12, 35, 216, 221, 222, 226, 227, 262, 270, 296

Lear, Tobias (American consul) 39
Leavenworth, Major (later Lt. Col.) Henry 220, 223, 224
Le Breton, British Lt. John 197
Le Chartrier, Captain P. 31, 96
Lee, General Henry "Lighthorse Harry" 31, 41
Leech (privateer) 47
Leftwich, Colonel Joel 94, 96
Legal Tender (brigantine) 264, 295
LeGate, Lieutenant Thomas C. 210
Leggett, Ensign 64
Lehigh Rifle Company 28
HMS *Leith Passket* 225
Leo (privateer) 261, 263, 264, 266
Leo (vessel) 205
Leonard, Captain James 246
Leonard, Captain Nathaniel 178, 179, 180, 183, 186
Leonidas (14-gun brigantine) 43
Leonidas (British vessel) 116
Leonidas (sloop) 134
HMS *Leopard* 12, 29, 301
HMS *Leopold* 14
Leslie, Alexander 170
Lester's guards 180
Letecau (Indian prophet) 121
Lethbridge, British colonel 67
Lettice (British brigantine) 225, 238
HMS *Levant* 294, 296
Levely, Captain 65
Levering Blockhouse 22
Le Vigoreux, British colonel 178
Levin, General 102
Lewes, Delaware 104
Lewes Battery 98
Lewis (privateer) 49
Lewis, Commander 299
Lewis, E. (master) 179
Lewis, Captain Henry R. 154
Lewis, Lt. Horatio G. 131, 142
Lewis, J. 134
Lewis, Commodore Jacob 175
Lewis, Jacob (master) 56
Lewis, Meriwether (Lewis and Clark Expedition) 13
Lewis, Major General Morgan 22, 72, 85, 103, 111, 118, 125, 128, 133, 148, 157, 171, 172, 245, 260
Lewis, Thomas 261
Lewis, Captain William 299
Lewis, Colonel William S. 50, 78, 87, 89, 90, 91, 92
Lewis' Blockhouse 22
Lewis Fort (Old Lewis Fort) 18
Lewiston, New York 72, 177, 178, 180, 181, 189, 190
Libby, Cyrus (master) 48
HMS *Liberty* 87
Liberty (privateer) 82, 86
Liberty, Mississippi 136
Lightfoot (Bright Horn) 79
HMS *Lightning* 87
Lincoln Militia 178
Lingan, General James M. 31, 41
HMS *Linnet* 249, 250

Lion (British privateer) 132
Lion (privateer) 33, 34, 43
Lion (schooner) 205
Lisa, Manuel 15, 22
Lisbon, Portugal 14
Littefutchee 166
Littefutchee Creek village 166
Little, Otis 242
Little, Colonel Peter 185
HMS *Little Belt* 19, 154, 155, 156
USS *Little Belt* 156, 166, 176, 184
Little Bill (schooner) 131
Little Fox (British brigantine) 199
Little James (brigantine) 93
Little Joe (schooner) 73
Little Ocfuske 121, 172
Little Sisters (schooner) 157
Little Warrior (Creek) 66, 93, 106
Lively (78-ton schooner) 37
Lively (88-ton sloop) 259
Lively (brigantine) 222
Lively (British privateer) 225, 226, 238, 239, 242, 247
Lively (schooner; seized 20 July 1813) 138
Lively (schooner; seized 24 July 1813) 139
Lively (sloop; captured 7 June 1814) 37
Lively (sloop; seized 26 October 1814) 37
Livermore, Samuel (chaplain) 122, 123
Liverpool Packet (British privateer) 60, 72, 73, 74, 78, 79, 81, 82, 83, 85, 100, 101, 103, 104, 105, 113, 131, 178, 179, 189, 190, 212, 214, 215, 225, 229, 231, 257, 266, 290
Liverpool Packet (owned by Americans; later *Young Teazer*) 78, 136
Liverpool Packet (ship) 131
Liverpool Trader 242
Livingston, Alexander 293
Livingston, Edward 265, 266, 293
Livingston, Mrs. Edward 265
Livingston, Philip (signer of Declaration of Independence) 37
Livingstone, Lt. Col. John W. 185
Lizard (privateer) 197
Lloyd, Commodore Robert 255, 256
Lloyd's Coffee House (London) 102
Lockyer, British Captain Nicholas 243, 253, 267, 268
Logan (31-ton sloop) 225
Logan, Captain George 15, 79
Logan, George 15
Logan, Captain John 78
Logan Act 15
HMS *Loire* 103, 165, 175, 176, 235, 256, 257
London, England 33
London, Captain 54, 88, 100
London Packet 93
London Statesman 27
London Times 55, 76, 216, 240

London Trader (merchant ship) 145
Long, Major (later brigadier general) Edward 213
Long, Lt. Colonel Kennedy 250
Long, Officer USN 62
Long Island 174
Long Rapids 171
Longwood (Longwoods), Canada 196
Longwood Road 161
Lord Bathurst (Henry, third earl) 255
Lord Hood (ship) 211
HMS *Lord Nelson* (later USS *Scourge*) 27, 39, 146
Lord Nelson (merchant ship) 95
Lord Nelson (schooner) 209
Lord Somers (transport) 208
Lord Wellington (brigantine) 279
L'Orient 217
Lorimer (Indian) 128
Lossing, Benson 204
Lotchway Indians (Seminoles) 64
Lott, Mr. 26
Lottery (letter of marque schooner) 95
Lottery (privateer; later *Canso*) 95
Louis XVIII, King 205
Louisa (202-ton schooner) 86
Louisa (brigantine; seized 26 March 1815) 298
Louisa (ship) 138
Louisa (sloop) 144
Louisa Ann (sloop) 41
Louise of Prussia, Queen 14
USS *Louisiana* 274, 275, 276, 277, 278, 285
Louisiana Blues 293
Louisiana Gazette 22
HMS *Loup Cervier* 131, 149, 167, 177
Loutre Island 14
Lovell, Z. (master) 212
Lovely Ann 194
Lovely Cornelia (American privateer) 31
Lovely Cornelia (privateer) 159
Lovely Lass (American privateer) 113
Lovett, John (attorney) 38
Lowe, Lt. (23rd U.S. Infantry Regiment) 179
Lowe, Moses (master) 213
Lowery, Colonel John 229
Lowery, John 169
Loyal Essex Rangers 255
Loyal Sam (10-gun ship) 66, 126
Lucia (sloop) 266
Luckett, Ensign 180
Luckett, Major 120
Luckyer, N. 87
Lucretia (galley) 78
Lucy (brigantine; seized 25 May 1813) 116
Lucy (privateer) 270
Lucy (schooner) 103
Lucy (schooner; captured September 1814) 242
Lucy and Alida (brigantine) 101, 153
USS *Ludlow* (gunboat) 241

Ludlow, Lieutenant Augustus C. 122, 146
Lumley, J. R. 87
Lumsden, Captain George 39
Lundy's Lane *see* Battle of Lundy's Lane
Lunenburg (British privateer) 247, 255, 256, 259, 260, 262, 292
Lurvey, Peter (master) 218
Lush, Lt. 70
Lusk, Brigadier General Levi 28, 87
Luskin, H. (master) 109
Lydia (74-ton schooner) 146
Lydia (89-ton schooner) 75
Lydia (schooner) 104
Lynn (privateer) 43
USS *Lynx* 301
Lynx (vessel; later *Musquetobite* in British service) 104
Lyon (cutter) 181
Lyon, Captain 74
Lyttleton, Royal Governor William Henry 15

Macarte House (New Orleans) 275
Macdonald, British Lt. A. 196
MacDonough (privateer) 260, 293, 294
Macdonough, Lt. (later Commodore) Thomas 123, 141, 206, 213, 248, 249, 262
HMS *Macedonian* 75, 76, 175
USS *Macedonian* 26, 74, 123, 142, 177, 299
Macedonian (privateer) 299
Mack, Captain Hubert Stephen 22
Mackenzie, Donald 57
MacKenzie's Post 57
HMS *Mackerel* 87
Mackinaw, Michigan 163, 225
Macnac, Sam 24
Macomb, Colonel (later general) Alexander 34, 35, 165, 171, 203, 238, 239, 245, 246, 248, 249
Macomb, Alexander Sr. 35
Macomb, Colonel R. 37
Macon's Bill Number Two 16, 18
MacRea, Lt. Colonel William 269, 272
Madeira, Portugal 169
Madis, M. 98
USS *Madison* 16, 69, 80, 106, 107, 108, 116, 117, 118, 142, 151, 178, 225
Madison (privateer) 37, 40, 44
Madison (schooner) 225
Madison, Dolley 234
Madison, Major George 90, 92
Madison, Secretary of State James (later president) 12, 13, 15, 17, 18, 19, 20, 21, 26, 27, 30, 33, 41, 52, 53, 58, 62, 70, 79, 86, 93, 95, 100, 105, 111, 112, 139, 140, 146, 153, 159, 165, 168, 175, 176, 185, 188, 189, 202, 214, 224, 226, 227, 231, 234, 236, 270, 294, 295, 300, 302

Madison, Lieutenant 91
Madison, Midshipman 50
Madison's Mob 41
Maffitt, Captain David 34, 45, 89, 136, 138, 147, 204, 214
Magdalena (62-ton schooner) 214
HMS *Magicienne* 89
HMS *Magnet* 87, 175, 210
Magnet (172-ton ship) 39
HMS *Magnificent* 42
Magruder, Colonel 232
HMS *Maidstone* 40, 42, 44, 47, 50, 61, 73, 74, 87, 95, 101, 104, 112, 115, 126, 127, 138, 164, 212, 256, 259, 262, 263, 298
Mainz, Germany 241
HMS *Majestic* 149, 152, 158, 165, 176, 213, 290
Makasukie tribe 65
Malaren (139-ton brigantine) 137
Malcolm (brigantine) 33
Malcolm, British Lt. Colonel (Royal Marines) 210, 211
Malcolm, Major 134
Malcolm, Richard 72
Malcom, British Admiral Sir Pulteney 276, 293
Malden, Canada 143, 156, 199
Mallory, Major (later colonel; Canadian volunteers) 176, 179, 181, 182, 224
Malone, Canada 194
Maloney, D. (master) 177
Malvina (British privateer) 106
Mammoth (privateer) 212
Mammouth (schooner) 212
Manary's Blockhouse 17
Manchester 178
Manchester (brigantine) 127, 177
Manhattan (sloop) 175
HMS *Manly* 136, 142, 149, 158, 208
Manly (4-gun ship) 217
Mann, Midshipman George 11
Manners, Captain 124
Manrique, Spanish governor 158, 180, 229
Mansfield, J. (master) 48
Mansfield's Blockhouse 22
Mantor, Jeremiah 204
Manuel (a Negro) 262
Maples, British captain 147
Maquatt (sloop) 141
Marant, Lieutenant 282
Marble, J. (master) 147
Marble Head, Ohio 65
Marcy, Lt. William (later 11th governor of New York) 74
Marengo (privateer) 43, 181
Margaret (10-gun brigantine; captured April 1814) 204
Margaret (brigantine; captured 28 February 1815) 295
Margaret (copper-bottomed vessel) 126
Margaret (schooner) 101
Margaret (seized March 1813) 99, 164
Margaret (vessel) 38
Margaret and Trevis 299
Margaretta (brigantine) 181

HMS *Maria* 87, 225
Maria (brigantine) 37
Maria (brigantine; seized 24 June 1813) 129
Maria (ketch) 37
Maria (schooner; captured January 1814) 184
Maria (schooner; captured 4 September 1814) 244
Maria (ship; seized 13 July 1813) 37
Maria (vessel) 225
Maria, J. D. (master) 149
Maria Frederica (brigantine) 37, 222
Maria Francisca (brigantine; captured 4 May 1814) 210
Maria Francisca (brigantine; seized 14 May 1813) 13
Maria Louisa, Queen 14, 105
Maria Windson (seized 29 March 1813) 103
Maria Windsor (vessel) 37
Maria Wirman (brigantine) 209
Marine Battery (Fort McHenry) 146
Marine Battery (New Orleans) 278, 280, 284, 286, 289
Marine Corps Barracks (Washington, D. C.) 235
Mariner (brigantine; seized 29 August 1813) 149
Mariner (schooner) 174
Mariner (ship) 40
Marines, U. S. 11, 19, 20, 23, 25, 29, 36, 42, 43, 47, 50, 54, 56, 61, 64, 68, 73, 103, 110, 114, 115, 127, 141, 142, 146, 147, 166, 167, 186, 194, 197, 204, 215, 217, 225, 226, 232, 234, 235, 236, 239, 243, 256, 267, 271, 273, 282, 284, 286, 297, 302, 303
HMS *Marlborough* (74-gun) 87, 104, 110, 115, 126, 127
Marlborough, Maryland 215
Marquis De Somerlous (ship) 36
Marquis of Cornwallis (brigantine) 102, 298
Mars (brigantine) 241
Mars (British letter of marque) 194
Mars (privateer) 41, 43, 192
Mars, Private Stephen 20
Marshall, Captain (Royal Navy) 43
Marshall, Captain William 106
Marsteller, Captain 232
Martha (schooner) 39
HMS *Martin* 21, 87, 115, 121, 123, 125, 126, 128, 140, 164, 174, 176, 213, 214, 217
Martin, J. (master) 215
Martin, Captain Jeremiah 153
Martin, British Captain John 137, 138
Martin, Brigadier General Walter 257
Marvin, Captain (cavalry) 180
HMS *Mary* 43, 216
Mary (8-ton brigantine) 121
Mary (14-gun ship) 43
Mary (43-ton sloop; seized 4 July 1813) 133

Index

Mary (50-ton sloop) 179
Mary (97-ton schooner; seized 23 March 1813) 36, 102
Mary (brigantine) 156, 241
Mary (brigantine; seized 17 July 1812) 36, 39
Mary (brigantine; seized by *Benjamin Franklin* in August 1812) 43
Mary (brigantine; seized by *Dolphin* in August 1812) 43
Mary (British brigantine) 35
Mary (British sloop; recaptured 27 July 1813) 140
Mary (British transport) 194
Mary (privateer out of Maine) 157
Mary (privateer schooner commissioned 27 August 1813) 148
Mary (schooner) 36, 146
Mary (schooner; renamed USS *Raven*) 94
Mary (schooner; seized 8 August 1812) 47
Mary (schooner; seized 23 March 1813) 36
Mary (schooner; seized 27 March 1813) 36, 39
Mary (schooner; seized 10 September 1813) 36
Mary (schooner; seized 13 September 1813) 156
Mary (schooner; seized 6 October 1814) 36, 39
Mary (schooner; seized October 1814) 257
Mary (ship; recaptured by British 1 June 1814) 214
Mary (ship; seized 23 July 1812) 40, 214
Mary (sloop; seized 4 July 1813) 133
Mary (sloop; seized 23 July 1813) 39
Mary (sloop; seized 27 July 1813) 36
Mary (sloop; seized 6 January 1814) 36, 39, 186
Mary (sloop; seized 1 June 1814) 36, 39
Mary and Ann (out of London) 55
Mary and Eliza (brigantine) 241
Mary and Joseph (ship) 216
Mary Ann (1-gun privateer schooner) 31, 113
Mary Ann (4-gun sloop) 72
Mary Ann (British ship) 40
Mary Ann (schooner; seized 23 July 1812) 36, 39
Mary Ann (schooner; seized 23 March 1813) 39
Mary Ann (schooner; seized July 1814) 217
Mary Ann (sloop) 43
Mary Ann (sloop; seized 22 December 1813) 36, 39
Mary Ann (vessel) 163
Mary Ann (vessel; seized 5 October 1813) 163
Mary Elizabeth (167-ton brigantine) 36, 39
Mashuda (Algerian vessel) 299, 300
Mason, Captain James 153
Masonic Redoubt 235

Massa, J. (master) 103
Massabeau, Captain P. 31
Massachusetts (286-ton ship) 156
Massey, Captain 145
Massias, Captain (later major) 29, 279
Massie, Major General Nathaniel 169
Massie, Captain Sylvanus 154
Matchadach Bay 221
Mathews, Brigadier General George (former governor of Georgia) 23, 24, 25, 57
Mathews, Sergeant 150
Mathias, Captain 259
Matilda (American privateer) 38, 132, 133, 147
Matilda (British privateer) 125, 126, 127, 135, 136, 142, 145, 146
Matterface, British Lieutenant William 256
Matthews, Brigadier General George (Georgia) 23
Matthews, Captain George 153
Matthews, J. (master) 102
Mattoax Creek 113
Maule, British major 141
Maumee River 138
Maurice, D. M. 87
Maury, Midshipman John M. 166
Maxcey, British Lieutenant 36
Maxwell, Captain 47
May (letter of marque) 44
May, Lt. Patrick 140
May Flower (sloop) 142
Maynard, Major 232
McAfee, Brigadier General Robert 163
McArthur, Colonel (later brigadier general) Duncan 26, 27, 35, 39, 42, 46, 50, 51, 52, 85, 103, 138, 143, 158, 163, 165, 257, 258, 260
McCabe, Ensign R. A. 46
McCall, Lt. Edward R. 152
McCarthy, David 65
McClary, Major Andrew 15
McClary, Adjutant General Daniel 115
McClary, Brigadier General Michael (New Hampshire militia) 33
McClellan, Lieutenant 273
McClintock, Midshipman H. 136
McCloskey, Captain Joseph 154
McClure, Brigadier General George 25, 159, 164, 176, 178, 179, 180, 181, 182, 186, 191, 192
McClure, Sergeant James USMC 103
McCobb, Colonel Denny 94
McComb, Colonel (later brigadier general) Alexander 117, 169, 171
McCoy, Ginsey 58
McCoy, Sergeant 65
McCulloch, William 87
McCullock, Captain William 46
McCullough, James (master) 82

McCune, Captain (Ohio militia) 138, 139
McDaniel, Jacob (master) 259
McDonald, British Lt. Colonel 50, 51, 52
McDonald, Captain R. 247
McDonald, Lt. Colonel William 250
McDonall, British Lt. Col. 225
McDonel, British Colonel 38, 71, 73
McDonnell, British Lt. Colonel (Red George) 74, 97, 165, 166
McDonough, Lieutenant Patrick 230
McDougal, British Col. 208, 211
McDougall, British captain 287
McDowell, Major Joseph 157
McEwen, British Captain 71
McFarland, Colonel 32
McFarland, Major Daniel 224
McFarlin, Captain 140
McFeeley, Lt. Colonel 79
McGary, Captain William R. 153
McGillivray, Sergeant 74
McGilton, Captain Thomas 154
McGlassin, Captain George 247
McGown's Pass 183
McGregor, British Lieut. 195
McGrew, Colonel William 159
McGrew, Major (later Lt. Colonel) William 140, 164
McGrew's Fort 131
McIntire, Captain 211
McIntosh, John H. 23
McIntosh, Major General Thomas 187
McIntosh, Captain William (of Savannah) 183, 201
McIntosh, William *see* Chief William McIntosh
McIntyre, British lieutenant 80
McKee, British major 204
McKee, Colonel John 147, 164
McKeever, Lieutenant (later commodore) Isaac 266, 267, 268
McKenzie, R. (master) 186
McKim, Isaac 37
McKnight, Lieutenant Stephen Decatur USN 118, 167, 202
McLean, Mr. 37
McLelland, A. (master) 148
McMahon, Joseph 65
McMahon, Lt. Colonel 181, 182
McMillan (M'Millan), Captain Alexander 210
McNac, Sam 180
McNeil, Colonel David B. 246
McNeil, Major (later brigadier general) John 220, 223, 224
McNitt, Captain 63
McNutt, James 31

McPherson, British captain 138
McPherson, Captain (artillery officer) 168, 203
McPherson, Lt. (USS *Hamilton*) 77
McQueen, Peter 111, 207
McWilliams, British Captain John 243
McWilliams, Captain John C. (Kentuckian) 154
Mead, Major General David 185, 188, 189
Medcalf, Samuel (master) 53
Medil Padria (70-ton brigantine) 163
HMS *Medway* 221
Meeks, Joe 18
Megowan, Captain Stewart W. 153
Meigs, Governor Return J. (Ohio) 26, 52, 56, 60, 63, 77, 88, 114, 155, 188, 227, 258
Meirers, George (master) 159
Melantho (ship) 40
Melvin, British captain 211
Menard, Pierre 17
HMS *Menelaus* 225, 235
Menifee, Captain Richard 153
Mentor (56-ton sloop) 136
Mentor (227-ton ship) 259
HMS *Mercury* 87
USS *Mercury* 135
Mercury (brigantine) 299
Meredith, Thomas 24
Meriwether, General David 303
Mermaid (ship) 209
Merrill, Sarah James 151
Merrimack (ship) 75
Merriman, Brigadier General James 28, 87
Merritt (British officer) 134
Merritt, British Captain William H. 176, 188, 195
Merritt's dragoons 71
Merriweather, Captain 175
Merryman, J. (master) 127
Mesier, Peter 227
Messa, Lt. 178
Messenger (schooner) 102
Metcalfe, Captain John 50
Metcalfe, Thomas P. 50
Meyers, Captain Henry 232
Mezado, P. J. (master) 142
Miamie (Miami, Miamis) Indians 48, 83, 163, 222
Miccasukie Indians 187
Micco, Hobothe 111
Michigan Legion 22, 46
Michigan Territory 11
Michilimackinac 221, 224
Midas (American privateer) 82, 205, 252
Middlebrook, R. (master) 242
Middlesex (ship) 60
Middleton, Captain 149
Middleton, W. (master) 60
Mifflin, Ohio 61
Miguel, P. (master) 147
Milan Decree 14, 16
Miles, Private Ambrose 14, 140
Miller, Captain Abram 153
Miller, Captain (privateer *Jack's Favorite*) 81

Miller, Brigadier General Daniel (Court County, New York) 25
Miller, Brigadier General Henry 113, 114
Miller, Captain J. 181
Miller, Brigadier General James (Ohio 2nd Brigade) 56
Miller, Lt. Colonel (later brigadier general) James (later governor of Arkansas) 34, 37, 38, 46, 47, 48, 52, 53, 64, 79, 220, 223, 230, 254, 274, 275
Miller, Major James 27
Miller, Colonel John 109
Miller, John (master) 231
Miller, Major 184
Miller, Captain R. 153, 217
Miller, Brigadier General Robert 123
Miller, Captain Samuel USMC 215, 216, 234, 235
Miller, Lt. Colonel Thomas 247
Miller's Blockhouse 22
Mills, Ensign 196
Mills, Colonel John 119, 120
Milne, British Rear Admiral David 242
Milnes (ship) 222
Milnes, British captain 138
Milton, Colonel Homer V. 205, 206
Milward, C. 87
Mims, David 150
Mims, Mr. 149, 150
Mim's Blockhouse 149
Mim's Ferry 259
HMS *Minerva* 87
Minerva (43-ton sloop) 145
Minerva (55-ton brigantine) 208
Minerva (256-ton brigantine) 35
Minerva (brigantine) 131
Minerva (brigantine; seized 30 June 1813) 35
Minerva (brigantine; seized 21 April 1814) 35
Minerva (schooner) 256
Minerva (schooner; captured 30 August 1813) 151
Minerva (schooner; captured 26 September 1814) 35
Minerva (schooner; seized 11 August 1814) 35
Minerva (ship) 60
Minerva (ship; seized 8 September 1812) 35
Minerva (sloop; seized 5 August 1813) 35
Minerva (sloop; seized 11 August 1814) 229
Minnetares 13
Minor, Lt. Colonel George 232, 235, 236
Missisquoi 164
Mississippi River 264
Missouri Fur Company 15, 16, 17, 19, 22
Missouri Territory 25, 27
Mitchell, Brigadier General (later major general) Andrew 259
Mitchell, Governor David B. (Georgia) 24, 25, 28, 29,

34, 36, 41, 42, 48, 62, 65, 81, 86, 144
Mitchell, Colonel George 257
Mitchell, Lt. Colonel James 204, 209, 210, 211
Mitchell, British Major Samuel 273
Mitchell, Captain William 26
Mitchener, Lt. G. 87
Mix, (sailing master) 77
Mobile, Alabama 158, 204, 238, 253
Mobile Point 229
Model (250-ton schooner) 213
HMS *Mohawk* 104, 126, 127, 129, 136
USS *Mohawk* (frigate) 74, 215, 225, 231, 255
HMS *Morne Fortunee* 87
Monahe (Indian prophet) 201
HMS *Monarch* 88
Money, British captain 284, 285
Monguagon, Michigan 47
Monk (ship) 56
Monk, Captain 33, 34
Monroe, James Secretary of State, Acting Secretary of War (later president) 12, 13, 19, 21, 76 81, 131, 204, 205, 234, 235, 236, 243, 247, 252, 254, 255, 259, 279, 294, 298; becomes acting secretary of state
Monsoon (ship) 56
HMS *Montague* 93
Montaigny, British captain 74
Montauk Point 26
Monte de los Cruces, Mexico 17
HMS *Montezuma* 110, 118, 133
USS *Montezuma* 101
Montezuma (ship) 101, 105
Montgomery (privateer) 81, 113
Montgomery, Alabama 259, 260
Montgomery, Captain John (artillery officer) 250
Montgomery, Lt. Colonel (later brigadier general) John (New Hampshire) 29
Montgomery, Major L. P. 201
Montgomery, Major Lemuel (39th Infantry) 201
Montgomery, Lt. (Mississippi volunteers) 173
Montgomery Court House 237
HMS *Montreal* 211
Montreal, Canada 139, 165, 166, 171, 176
Montressor, British Captain Henry 268
Moody, British colonel 120
Mooers, Major General Benjamin 24, 37, 61, 249, 274
Moon, Captain Richard 66, 169
Moore, Captain Abel 221
Moore, Major Thomas 26
Moore, William 221
Moore's Blockhouse 221
Moorsom, British captain 62
Moose Island *see* Eastport, Ohio
Moose Island (Massachusetts-Maine) 221
Moraviantown, Ontario 160, 162

Morgan, Brigadier General David Bannister 283, 284, 285
Morgan, Colonel Gideon 169, 172, 201
Morgan, John (master) 38
Morgan, Lewis (Quarter Master General) 34
Morgan, Colonel Ludowick 226
HMS *Morgiana* 48, 49, 87, 165, 213
Morgiana (British brigantine) 158
Morgiana (British packet) 95
Morgiana (privateer) 41, 192
Moriarity, T. (master) 36
Morning Star (schooner) 148
Morning Star (sloop) 126
Morning Starr (sloop) 215
Morrel, Doctor 290, 292
Morris, Captain 90
Morris, Captain Charles 243
Morris, Gouverneur 21
Morris, H. (British master's mate) 134
Morris, Captain John H. 153
Morris, Ensign Robert 72
Morrison, British Lt. Colonel Joseph W. 165, 169, 171, 206
Morrison, Major Robert 26
Morrison, Major Robertson 46
Morrison, William 15
Mortimer, Captain James M. 215
Moscow, Russia French army enters 58
HMS *Moselle* 87, 129, 175
Moss, Captain Thomas S. T. 153
Motte, Frances Motte Middleton 279
Motte, Jacob 279
Motte, Rebecca 279
Mott's Fort 131
Mouina (Island tribe) 167
Moultrie, General William 12
Mount St. Bernard 262
Mount Vernon (Alabama) 152, 176
Mount Vernon Blockhouse (Ohio) 22
Mountjoy, Lieutenant 138
Mountjoy, Colonel William 153
Mourice, Mr. 150
Mowbray, commander of HMS *Moselle* 87
Mudge, J. (master) 118
Muir, British Major Adam 46, 47, 64, 65, 98
Mulcaster, British captain 210, 211
Mullany, Major 72
Mullens, British Colonel Thomas 286, 287, 297
Munday's Point 226
Mundy, Lt. Harrison 17th U. S. Regiment 64
Murphy, Captain John of Baltimore 49, 215
HMS *Muros* 87
Murray, Commodore Alexander 295
Murray, Lieutenant Alexander 260

Murray, British Colonel John 141, 177, 179, 189
Murray, Lt. John 87
Murray, Captain Thomas 289
Murrell, Doctor 268
HMS *Musquetobite* 104
Myers, British Colonel Christopher 259

Nagle, Admiral Sir E. 87
Nancy (brigantine) 43, 253
Nancy (brigantine; captured 9 May 1814) 211
Nancy (brigantine; seized about 1–18 September 1814) 242
Nancy (privateer) 21
Nancy (schooner; seized 28 May 1813) 118
Nancy (schooner; seized 28 June 1813) 131
Nancy (ship) 53
Nancy (sloop; captured 28 July 1814) 225
Nancy Sanders (sloop) 178
Napoleon Bonaparte 12, 13, 14, 15, 17, 18, 20, 33, 62, 100, 105, 196, 209, 214, 241, 275, 297; abdicates 206; retreat from Russia 74
Napoleon II 19
Narborough Island (Galapagos) 125
HMS *Narcissus* 87, 89, 115, 125, 126, 127, 129, 166, 215, 221, 222, 259
Nash, Captain (privateer *General Stark*) 111
Nash, British Captain James 203
Nashville, Tennessee 116
Natchez, Mississippi 98
National Intelligencer 46, 213, 218
USS *Nautilus* 27, 32, 38, 39, 54, 74, 75
Nautilus (East India company ship) 300, 301
Nautilus (vessel) 293
Navarre, Colonel Francis 90
Navarre, Peter 109
Navy Point 119
HMS *Nayntine Fairy* 197
Neale, Lieutenant Benedict 301
Neale, Lt. 127
Ned (American privateer) 106, 152, 153
Neeley, Captain Samuel 62
Negro Fort *see* Fort Apalachiola
Neil, Captain 55
Nelles, British Captain 71
Nelly (schooner) 221
Nelson (British schooner) 197
Nelson (schooner) 43
Nelson (three decker ship) 145
Nelson, Admiral Lord 85
HMS *Nemesis* 136
USS *Neptune* 100
Neptune (8-gun ship) 269
Neptune (98-ton schooner) 103
Neptune (bark) 214
Neptune (brigantine) 34
Neptune (letter of marque) 137
Neptune (schooner) 153

Neptune (vessel) 214
Nerina (vessel) 45
Nevis, S. (master) 166
HMS *Netley* 87, 207
New Bern (Newbern) 135
New Dover Blockhouse 22
New Forge (schooner) 78
New Haven, Connecticut 142
New Haven Camp 22
New Liverpool (brigantine) 43
New London, Connecticut 26, 131, 177
New Orleans 253, 267, 270, 275; General Jackson arrives 264
New Orleans (frigate) 257
New Yaucas 193
USS *New York* 142
New York Evening Post 184, 185
New Zealander (ship) 101, 106, 137
Newark (Niagara Canada) 176, 177, 191
HMS *Newcastle* 227, 270, 296
Newcomb, F. 87
Newcomb, Lieutenant Henry S. 246
Newel, William (master) 298
Newell, Captain T. M. 31
Newford, P. (master) 56
Newfoundland Regiment (Fencibles) 31, 51, 80, 208
Newman, Colonel Daniel (Neil) USMC 42, 50, 56, 57, 64, 65, 95, 96
Newport, Rhode Island 174
Newyaucau (Creek village) 201
USS *Niagara* 127, 144, 154, 155, 157, 158, 159, 221
Niagara, New York 177, 186
Nichol, Lt. Col. Robert 52
Nicholas Island 217
Nicholas, Governor Wilson Cary (Virginia) 172
Nicholl, Captain (privateer *Scourge*) 138
Nicholls (Nichols), British Colonel Edward 229, 243, 262
Nicholn, Baron (Russian minister at Sweden) 20
Nichols, Captain Samuel 131, 200
Nichols, Captain William 53, 89, 145, 281
Nicholson, Captain Benjamin (14th Infantry) 108
Nicholson, Major 145
Nicholson, Captain William H. 108, 147
Nicholson Act 12
Nicoll, Brigadier General A. Y. 214
Nicoll, Brigadier General Matthias 28, 87
HMS *Niemen* (Nieman) 213, 214, 215, 222, 226, 236, 240, 245, 255, 257
Nimble (brigantine) 181
HMS *Nimrod* 126, 127, 136, 138, 140, 142, 157, 175, 212, 214, 215, 228, 244, 266
Nimrod (British cutter) 99
Nimrod (schooner) 39
Nitchie, John 227

Nitty Chaptoa (town) 172
Nixon, Lt. Colonel George Henry 176, 177
Noadie, British captain 247
Noah, M. M. 301
Noah Brown's shipyard 184
Nocton (British vessel) 76
Non-Intercourse Act 16, 18
Nonpareil (privateer) 37, 43
Nonsuch (privateer) 65
Nooaheevah, renamed Madison's Island (Nuka Hiva, Nukahiva) 137, 159, 165, 176, 166, 167, 204
Norderling, Mr. 300
Norfolk, Virginia 127
Norftsinger's Blockhouse 17
Norman, British Lieutenant Charles 256
Norris, Lieutenant 280, 282
North Point (Baltimore) 250
North Star (177-ton brigantine) 129
Northwest Fur Company 18, 19
Northwest Territory 23
Norton, British captain 196
Norton, Jacob 72
Norton, John 71
Norton Packet 82
Noyes, T. (master) 57
Nuera Constitucion (Spanish privateer) 139
Nuka Hiva (Nooaheevah, Nukahiva) *see* Nooaheevah
Nymph (vessel) 40
HMS *Nymphe* 40, 56, 57, 67, 76, 87, 105, 106, 113, 114, 131, 139, 147, 148, 215, 217, 220, 222, 247, 255
Nymphe (20-ton schooner; seized 11 June 1813) 125
Nymphe (48-ton schooner) 101
Nymphe (schooner; seized 14 March 1813) 101

Oak Bush 220
O'Bannon, Lt. Presley USMC 11
Ocean (brigantine) 83, 147
Ocean (British ship) 47
Ocfuske Indians 193
O'Connor, British Captain Richard James Lawrence 211
Ocracoke Inlet 136
O'Dell, Brigadier General Jacob 205
Odelltown, Canada 74, 78
Odenheimer, Lt. 202
Odiorne, Captain 34
Odom, Minnie 152
Ogden, Major General Aaron (former U.S. senator and governor of New Jersey) 85
Ogden, Lieutenant 282
Ogden, Brigadier General Mathias 85
Ogden, R. (master) 121
Ogdensburg 66, 97
Ogilive, Peter 72
O'Grady, H 87
USS *Ohio* 229
Ohio (brigantine) 136
O'Keefe, Amelia *see* Hammond, Amelia O'Keefe
Olaguebel, J.D. (master) 148

Index

Old Carpenter (schooner) 226
Old Chinnobe 166
Old Fields 236
Old Ironsides see USS *Constitution*
Old Sow 40
Old Stone Fort 21, 247
Old Towns (Alabama) 184, 192
Oliver, Captain (vessel *Osiris*) 174
Oliver, Seaman 169
Oliver, Captain William 108, 109, 110, 113
Oliver Spear 242
Olson, C. (master) 158
Omar (Algerian leader) 299
USS *Oneida* 27, 39, 42, 68, 77, 117, 142, 146, 151, 158, 225
Oneida Indians 213
Oneida Lake 213
O'Neil, Lt. John 113, 114
O'Neil, Mrs. 150
Onne, Josiah (master) 39
USS *Ontario* 109, 118, 149, 151, 299
Ontario (ship) 213
HMS *Opossum* 87
Oraeme, British Lt. P. 196
Orange (privateer) 156
Orange Boven (vessel) 214, 217
Orders in Council 16, 29, 32
Orders in Council (American privateer) 86
Ordronaux, Captain 258, 259
Orient (schooner) 215
Orient (vessel) 31
Orion (191 tons) 115
Orlando (privateer) 57
Orleans Battalion 278, 282
Orleans Rifles 286
Orleans Territory 18
Ormsby, British Major 80
Orne, Captain William B. 48, 54
Ornes, Frans 227
Oronoko (vessel) 29, 36
HMS *Orpheus* 40, 61, 87, 106, 114, 115, 123, 157, 205, 211
Orr, Major 89
Osage Indians 15, 18, 19
Osage Treaty 17
Osborn, Captain J. 47
Osborne (*Osbourne*; 10-gun) 43, 55
Osborne, Doctor 150
Osborne, Lt. 174
Osgood, Joseph (sailing master) 146
Osiris (sloop) 174
Oswego, New York 204, 210, 213, 217
Oswego Falls 211
Ottawa Indians 163
Overton, Colonel Walter H. 92
Overton, Major 289
Overturf, Captain Conrad 153
Owens, E. W. C. R. 87
Owl (privateer boat) 111

Pacha, Omar (dey of Algiers) 300
Pacific Fur Company 18
Packenham, British general 263

Packet (57-ton vessel) 105
Packet (ship; seized at an unspecific time during 1812) 105
Packet (sloop; seized 13 April 1813) see *Island Packet*
Packet (sloop; seized 18 June 1813) 127
HMS *Pactolus* 227
Pagia, Domingo (master) 134
Paine, Brigadier General Joel 56
Paine, Thomas 16
Pakenham, General Sir Edward Michel 255, 274, 275, 276, 277, 278, 279, 280, 281, 283, 286, 287, 288, 289, 291, 293
HMS *Pallas* 214, 215
Paragon (157-ton schooner) 147
Paragon (brigantine) 115
Paris (10-gun bark) 156, 166
Paris (vessel) 225
Paris, France 196, 203, 241
Park, British Lieutenant Thomas 256
Parker, B. (master) 242
Parker, British Admiral Christopher 240
Parker, Hyde 87
Parker, Isaac 28
Parker, J. (master) 242
Parker, Lieutenant USN 84, 268
Parker, Sir Peter 235, 238, 240
Parker, Brigadier General Thomas 103, 260
Parrot (privateer) 81
Parrott's Point 146
Parsons, Theophilus 28
Parsons, Doctor Usher 126, 155
Partridge (privateer) 69
Pasco, John 87
Patapsco (privateer) 31, 133, 215
Patch, T. (master) 106
Patrickson, British Lt. Col. Christopher Clarges 281
Patriot (49-ton sloop) 179
Patriot (140-ton schooner) 60
Patriot (schooner) 60
Patriot (sloop) 179
Patriots 25
Patriots' Army Captures Amelia Island 23
Patriot's War 23; conclusion of 113
Patterson, Captain 38
Patterson, Commodore Daniel Todd 244, 254, 266, 268, 272, 278, 279, 281, 282, 283, 284, 285, 286, 287, 289, 293
Patterson, Francis Engle 53
Patterson, Lieutenant James 168
Patterson, Mr. 215
Patterson, Lieutenant Robert (later general) 53
Patterson, Robert (master) 36
Patterson, Lt. W. L. 87
Patterson, Judge William 37
Patton's Fort 132, 135
Patty (75-ton schooner) 106
Patuxent River 214, 215

Paul, Lt. Colonel George 138
Paul Jones (privateer) 34, 43, 49, 88, 93, 116
Paulina (109-ton schooner) 106
Pawnee Indians 303
Paxton (American soldier) 108, 112
Payne (Indian village) 95, 96
Payne, Colonel Duval 61
Payne, General Eleazar 87
Payne, Colonel (later brigadier general) John 50, 88, 89
Payne, John Howard 31
Payne, Major 161
Payne, Captain William R. 154
Paynter, William (master) 222
HMS *Paz* 39, 81, 114, 156, 160, 164
Paz (British brigantine) 147
Peachland, John 164
HMS *Peacock* (formerly USS *Wasp*) 74, 82, 94, 97, 98, 102, 175
Peacock (schooner) 225
USS *Peacock* (sloop) 101, 157, 198, 208, 209, 214, 217, 225, 298, 299, 300, 301
Peake, British captain 97
Pearce, British lieutenant 240
Pearce, Colonel Cromwell (major general, Pennsylvania militia) 33, 108, 172
Pearce, Lt. USN 211
Pearl (sloop) 93
Pearley, Nathaniel (master) 247
Pearson, British Lt. Col. Thomas 67, 218, 219
Peggy (91-ton sloop) 169
HMS *Peggy and Jane* 225
Peire, Major Henry 269, 271, 282
Pelham (vessel) 209
HMS *Pelican* 88, 127, 133, 147
Pemaquid Point 152
Pendergast, R. (master) 96
Pendleton, P. (master) 105
Penelope (brigantine) 49
HMS *Penguin* 297, 298
Pennoyer, S. (master) 229
Penobscot, Maine 241
Pensacola, Florida 105, 176, 229, 253, 259, 262; General Jackson arrives 260
Peoria Indians 57
Percevil, Prime Minister 29
Percival (master) 133
Percy, British Captain William Henry 252
Pere, N. W. 87
Perez, Spanish Governor Don Gayetano (Coyeltano) 105
Perkins, Constantine 190
Perkins, Colonel Nicholas 187, 190
Perkins, Brigadier General Simon 52, 56, 60, 65, 75, 89, 93
Perry (privateer) 205, 247, 293
Perry, Alexander 96
Perry, Captain Christopher 154
Perry, H. (master) 225

Perry, J. (master) 136
Perry, Joseph (Mississippi volunteers) 150
Perry, Captain J. R. 205
Perry, Lt. (later commodore) Oliver Hazard 69, 86, 96, 99, 116, 118, 126, 127, 135, 144, 148, 154, 155, 156, 157, 158, 159, 165, 166, 207, 239, 240, 302; promoted to captain 174
Perry, Colonel Simeon 278, 282
Perrysburg, Ohio 38
Perseverance (188-ton vessel) 255
Perseverance (British sloop) 147
HMS *Persian* 131, 175
USS *Pert* (formerly *Collector*) 68, 77, 115, 120, 146
Peru 148
HMS *Peruvian* 53, 75, 87, 222, 238, 242
Peter, Major George 216, 232, 234, 236
Peter Waldo (brigantine) 43
Petit, Brigadier General Micahja 208
Pettaupaug Point 204
Petti, Lt. USN 114
Pettis, Brigadier General Micajah 24
Peyton, John H. 31
HMS *Pheasant* 270
Phebe (brigantine) 63
USS *Philadelphia* 11, 291, 299
Philadelphia Blues 38
Philadelphia Light Troop 238
Philibert (British officer) 284
Philips, John (master) 262
Phillips, Mrs. Sarah 152
Phillips, Captain Zacharia 140
Phippen, Joseph USN 297
HMS *Phoebe* 83, 134, 192, 193, 194, 202
Phoebe (schooner) 196
Phoenix (British vessel) 194
Piatt, Colonel William 273
Picarrere, Captain J. 104
Pickerel (*Pickrel*; schooner) 209
Pickering (merchant ship) 22, 35
Pickering, Senator Thomas 16, 41, 291
Pickering, Timothy 291
HMS *Picton* 138
HMS *Pictou* 194, 242, 247
Pierce, Captain 211
Pierna's canal 283
Pierre, Major 260
Pierre, Major (Pierre Chastang, a slave) 105
Piget, British captain 225
Pigot (volunteer) 196
Pigott, Hugh 87
Pig's Point 236
USS *Pike* 120, 121, 231
Pike (British privateer) 209
Pike (privateer) 209
Pike (vessel) 133
Pike, Lieutenant (later Brigadier General) Zebulon M. 12, 26, 79, 85, 103, 106, 107, 108, 109, 117
Pike's Cantonment 249
Pilgrim (22-ton schooner) 135

Pilgrim (boat) 109
Pilgrim (brigantine; seized 16 May 1813) 115
Pilkington, Deputy Adjutant General 221
Pillow, Colonel William 170
Pillsbury, Captain T. 75
Pilot (privateer schooner) 135
Pinckney, General Charles Coatesworth 279
Pinckney, Elizabeth Motte 279
Pinckney, Major General Thomas (governor of South Carolina) 23, 34, 42, 93, 103, 105, 115, 206, 207, 279, 294
Pinckney, Major William 232, 234
Pinckney, Mrs. William 113
Pinckney, William (minister to England) 12, 13, 19
Pink (schooner) 112
HMS *Pique* 208
Piscataqua Harbor 213
Pitchlyn, John 147
Pitt (brigantine) 67
Pittman, Colonel James J. 263
Place, John (seaman) 97
Plank, Jacob 230
HMS *Plantagenet* 138, 156, 175, 255
Planter (British vessel) 45
Planter (sloop; seized September 1814) 242
Platt, Isaac 246
USS *Plattsburgh* 269
Plattsburgh, New York 141, 166, 176, 194, 203, 204, 238, 244, 245
Plauche, Major Francis 271, 273, 282
Plough Boy (sloop) 120
Plumer, Governor William (New Hampshire) 26, 29, 106, 115
Plummer (American officer) 141
HMS *Plumper* 39, 59, 60, 87, 126, 175
Plumpley, J. (master) 176
Plutus (182-ton ship) 105
Plymouth, England 217
Poague, Colonel John 63, 153
HMS *Poictiers* 63, 74, 87, 94, 103, 104, 126, 127, 134, 138, 139, 149, 152, 164
Point Iroquois 165
Point Lookout 148, 227
Point Peter, Georgia 279
Point Peter Battery see Battery at Point Peter
Point Shares (brigantine) 86
Policy (vessel) 101, 118, 133
Polk, President James Knox 289
Polkinghorne, British Lt. 104
Pollard, M. (master) 60
Polly (85-ton schooner; seized 14 October 1812) 72
Polly (88-ton schooner; seized 10 December 1813) 176
Polly (92-ton sloop; seized 28 July 1813) 140
Polly (brigantine) 222
Polly (British sloop) 147

Polly (privateer) 37, 43, 159, 206; captured 48
Polly (sloop; captured 10 August 1814) 229
Polly (vessel) 242
HMS *Pomone* 290
Poole's Island 110
Poor Sailor (privateer) 31
Pope Pius VII 12
Popham, Captain Sir Home 42, 211, 213
Poplar's Island 110
USS *Porcupine* 158, 165
Porcupine (brigantine) 127
Porpois (32-ton schooner) 142
Port Dover, Canada 163
Port Huron 183
Port Ryerse, Canada 212
Port Talbot 231
Porter (privateer) see *David Porter* (privateer)
Porter, Captain David Dixon 25, 32, 36, 45, 48, 49, 53, 76, 82, 90, 93, 96, 101, 118, 126, 127, 128, 129, 133, 137, 139, 144, 148, 156, 159, 163, 165, 166, 167, 168, 176, 181, 182, 192, 193, 194, 202, 204, 216, 239, 240
Porter, Major 172, 173
Porter, Colonel (later general) Moses 117, 218, 220
Porter, General Peter B. 80, 135, 182, 204, 212, 221, 223, 230
Portland Packet (schooner; seized 5 October 1813) 163
Portland Packet (seized April 1813) 106
Portsea (brigantine) 264
Portugal: invaded by Spanish and French 14
Post Boy (schooner) 116
Potato Battery 112
Pothier, Toussaint 35
Pottawatomie Indians 14, 59, 92, 108, 163
Potter, Captain William 227, 228
Poultneyville, New York 212
Powell, Colonel 80
Powell, Captain James 152
Powell, Major 164
Powell, Sergeant 186
Powell's Ferry 179
Powell's Fort 131
Powers, British Major General Manley 245
Powers, British Lieutenant Thomas Barret 225
Prairie Du Chien, Wisconsin 217, 245
Pratt, British Lieutenant George 268
USS *Preble* (also known as *Commodore Preble*) 145, 241, 248, 249, 250
Preble, Commodore Edward 14, 248
Preble, Mr. (of Rhode Island) 99
USS *President* 19, 27, 31, 35, 44, 68, 88, 112, 138, 142, 156, 157, 176, 185, 193, 290, 291, 295, 301
President (British brigantine) 159
USS *President* (second) 80, 81

Presque Isle 217
Presstman, Lt. 68
Preston, Canada 169
Preston, Brigadier General Francis 31
Preston, Lt. Colonel James Patton (later governor of Virginia) 118, 172
Preston, Sarah Buchanan Campbell 31
Prevost, Sir General George (governor general) 22, 24, 35, 52, 53, 56, 71, 97, 98, 100, 108, 118, 119, 120, 138, 159, 163, 165, 178, 179, 183, 186, 188, 189, 192, 194, 195, 197, 198, 199, 200, 204, 205, 206, 207, 208, 210, 235, 239, 241, 244, 245, 246, 247, 248, 249, 250, 254
Prevoyante (schooner) 42
Price, British Captain David 260
Price, Lewis USMC 93, 96
Price, Midshipman W. 134
Prichard, John (master) 105
Prince (free black man) 61
Prince, Pyam 146
Prince Adolphus (ship) 43
Prince Christian of Denmark 16
Prince de Neuchatel (American privateer) 258, 259, 269, 270
Prince Karl August von Hardenberg 241
Prince Klemens von Metternich 241
Prince of Austria (brigantine) 49
Prince of Parma see Bonaparte, Napoleon II
Prince Regent (10-gun schooner) 181, 222
HMS *Prince Regent* 40, 77, 118, 151
HMS *Prince William* 227
HMS *Princess Amelia* 62
HMS *Princess Charlotte* (packet) 144, 145, 211
Princess Elizabeth 242
Princess Royal (ship) 42
Pring, British Captain Daniel 211, 249
Pringle, Mark 113
Priscilla (61-ton schooner) 135
Pritchard, John (master) 105, 148
Proctor, British Colonel (later major general) General Henry A. 37, 41, 47, 50, 53, 88, 90, 91, 92, 98, 104, 106, 108, 109, 110, 111, 114, 127, 128, 138, 139, 140, 142, 143, 144, 156, 157, 158, 159, 161, 162, 163, 178, 199
Procter, John (master) 255
HMS *Prometheus* 197
Prophet Francis 21, 151, 152
Prophet's Town 20, 21, 79
HMS *Protection* 87
Protectress (290-ton ship) 127
Providence (American privateer) 59
Providence (brigantine) 216
Providence (schooner) 139
Provincial Council of New Brunswick, Canada 221

Prudence (brigantine) 48
Prudence (schooner) 221
Prudentia (ship) 134
Prussia 241
Pryor, Captain 130
Purcell, Captain H. 47
Purdy, Colonel 166
Pursuit (16-gun British vessel) 45
Pushmataha Indians 180
Put-in-Bay 154, 187
Putnam, Major Perley 221
HMS *Pylades* 247, 253
Pythagoras (sloop) 48

Quarles, Captain R. 116, 184, 190
Quebec 195
Quebec (vessel) 93
Queen (16-gun ship) 101
Queen Charlotte (brigantine) 222
USS *Queen Charlotte* 187
HMS *Queen Charlotte* 52, 154, 155, 157, 175
Queen Louise of Prussia 14
Queen Maria Louisa 14, 105
Queenston, Canada 70, 147, 176, 220
Queenston Road 225
Quiz (214-ton schooner) 213

Race Horse (brigantine) 257
Race Horse (schooner) 44
Racer (later *Shelbourne* in British service) 104
Rachel (brigantine) 260
Rachel (letter of marque) 81, 82
Ragan, Lt. Colonel John 232, 234
Raines, John (master) 259
Raisin River Massacre see Battle of Raisin River
Ralph Nickerson (8-gun vessel) 79
Ramage, Sailing Master James 246
HMS *Rambler* 194
Rambouillet Decree 17, 18
HMS *Ramillies* 103, 114, 115, 123, 131, 175, 176, 221, 227
Ramsey, Lt. 65
Randall, Captain 127, 128
Randall, Colonel William 142, 227, 228
Randolph (32-ton sloop) 139
Randolph (schooner; seized 14 October 1813) 164
Randolph, Governor Edmund 21
Randolph, Midshipman 290
Randolph, Peyton 21
Randolph, Lt. Colonel (later colonel) Thomas Mann 102
Randon, John 149, 150
Randon, Lieutenant (John or Peter) 150
Randon, Peter 147, 150
Randon's Plantation 173
Ranger (85-ton schooner) 260
Ranger (British brigantine) 38, 43
Ranger (schooner) 222
USS *Ranger* (third) 225
Rankin's Fort 131, 152
Ransom, Captain 181
Rantin, Captain H. 38, 132

Rapid (brigantine privateer out of Maine) 43; captured 73
Rapid (privateer out of Charleston) 31, 69, 82
Rapid (privateer out of Boston) 34, 43
HMS *Rapide* 87
Rathbone, Lieutenant 72
HMS *Rattler* 87, 103, 104, 105, 112, 114, 116, 134, 136, 142
Rattler (brigantine privateer) 136
Rattlesnake (American privateer) 136, 138, 147, 204, 205, 214, 221
USS *Rattlesnake* (brigantine) 188, 194, 216
USS *Raven* (formerly schooner *Mary*) 151
Raven (schooner) 149
Ravenscroft, Captain Thomas 153
Rawle, British Lieutenant Richard 256
Rayen, Colonel 60
Rayo (brigantine) 42
Razor (privateer) 106
Read, Captain 1st Artillery 183
Read, Captain Henry 23
Read, James USN 55
Reading, Captain Joseph 153
Reagan, Rachael (massacre) 221
Reaper (privateer) 106
Reardon, W. (master) 60
Rebecca (64-ton schooner) 140
Rebecca (86-ton schooner) 131
Rebecca (schooner) 112, 144
Rebecca (schooner; seized 3 August 1813) 34
Rebecca (seized 10 August 1812) 48
Rebecca Sims (cartel) 139
Recovery (190-ton brigantine) 187
Recovery (brigantine) 216
HMS *Recruit* 87, 148, 214
Rector, Captain Stephen 218, 245
Red Bird (55-ton sloop) 115
Red House 80
Red Mill 169
Red Sticks see Creek Indians
Red Warrior's Bluff 106
Reed, Captain USN 240
Reed, Lt. George Washington 57
Reed, General Joseph 57
Reed, Lieutenant Joseph 79
Reed, Lt. Colonel Philip 240
Reed, Captain William 153
Reed, General William 53
Reese, Sergeant Major USMC 65
HMS *Regulator* 217
Regulator (privateer schooner) 48
Reid, J. (master) 211
Reid, Captain Samuel 247, 255, 256
HMS *Reindeer* 214, 217, 219
Reindeer (brigantine) 102
Reliance (56-ton sloop) 100
Renick, Colonel Henry 153
Rennie, British Colonel Robert 277, 286, 289

Reprisal (bark) 151
Reprisal (ship) 34
Republican (ship) 136
Resolution (brigantine) 21
Resolution (British brigantine) 94
Resolution (sloop) 156
Retaliation (British privateer) 101, 105, 106, 112, 133, 134, 135, 136, 189, 190, 215, 218, 221
Retrieve (British privateer) 125, 134, 135, 136, 144, 146, 165
Return (brigantine) 93
USS *Revenge* 96
Revenge (69-ton sloop) 81
Revenge (fourth; privateer) 133
Revenge (privateer 4-gun schooner) 31
Revenge (privateer schooner out of Baltimore or Norfolk) 217
Revenge (privateer sloop) 153
HMS *Revolution* 88
Reward (brigantine) 69
Reynolds, Governor John 245
Reynolds, British (Canadian) Major 90, 92
Reynolds, Squire 143
Rhea, Captain 61
Rhoda (129-ton schooner) 295
Riall, British Major General Phineas 178, 181, 182, 188, 189, 190, 194, 195, 198, 200, 204, 206, 207, 208, 209, 210, 218, 219, 220, 222, 223
Rice, T. (master) 148, 169
Richard (brigantine) 43, 212
Richard, A. (master) 40
Richard D. Staley (115-ton schooner) 156
Richards, Captain John 29
Richardson, Captain 127
Richmond (150-ton brigantine) 106, 108
Riddle, Lt. 106, 180, 189
Rider, D. (master) 140
Ridgely, Captain Charles G. 206, 225
Ridle, 2nd Lt. Robert B. USMC 20
HMS *Rifleman* 174, 214, 219, 225, 238, 247
Rigdon, Martin 150
Riggs, A. R. (master) 127
Riggs, Lieutenant 218
Riker, Major Tunis 157
Riley, Lewis 65
HMS *Ringdove* (*Ring Dove*) 36, 39, 40, 80, 140, 166
Rinker, Captain Abraham 28
Ripley, Lt. Colonel (later major general) Eleazar Wheelock 22, 23, 35, 108, 171, 190, 207, 218, 220, 223, 224, 225, 230, 231, 254, 274
Rising Sun (privateer) 40
Rising Sun (schooner) 102
Rising Sun (sloop) 103
Rising Sun (sloop; seized 1 December 1813) 175
Riva, J. (master) 157
Rivera, Sergeant Major Don Francisco 28

Index

Rivier's Fort *see* Lavier's Fort
Roach, Lt. Isaac (engineers) 68
Roahooga (aka Adams Island; Washington Islands) 165, 166
USS *Roanoke* (schooner) 192
Robb, Major Joseph 67
Robert (brigantine) 205
Robert Hartwell (schooner) 41
Robert Stewart (brigantine) 112
Roberts, British captain 284
Roberts, Captain, of Winchester 127
Roberts, British Captain Charles 35, 37, 38
Roberts, Colonel 170
Roberts, Mr. 279
Roberts, British Captain Samuel 268
Robertson, British Lt. Col. (King's Regiment) 208
Robertson, J. (master) 36
Robertson, General James 93, 241
Robertson, Captain Samuel 153
Robin (schooner) 153
Robinson, Brigadier General Asa 33
Robinson, J. (master) 40
Robinson, M. (master) 216
Robyns, Captain USMC 236
Rochelle, France 204
Rochester, New York 183
Rock Island, Illinois 218
Rock Island Arsenal Museum 245
Rock Island National Cemetery 245
Rockford, Ohio 60
Rockport, Massachusetts 21
Rodgers, Captain 186
Rodgers, Commodore John 11, 12, 19, 29, 31, 32, 35, 48, 68, 113, 138, 142, 148, 157, 176, 193, 239, 242, 243, 246, 302
Rodger's Bastion 246
Rodgerson, W. 147
Rodriguez Canal 272, 274, 276
HMS *Roebuck* 197
Roger (privateer) 31, 116, 184, 209
Rogers, Mrs. John 113
Rogers, William 82
Roger's Fort 132, 135
Rolette, Lieutenant (Canadian Provincial Marine) 35, 45
Rolla (10-gun British privateer) 87, 217, 221, 266
Rolla (privateer schooner) 82, 176, 177
Romanskoff, Count 20
Romayne, British captain 211
HMS *Romulus* 136, 166
Ronan, Ensign 50
Roosevelt, Theodore President 81
Roper, Captain (cavalry) 64
Ropes, Captain Joseph 60, 77, 80, 205
Rosa Spanish (schooner) 197
Rosabella (16-gun ship) 264
Roscio (brigantine) 119
Rose (8-gun vessel) 129

Rose (vessel) 101
Rose, General Abraham 37
Rose and Charlton 101
Rose in Bloom (58-ton sloop) 134
Ross, Acting Brigadier General 283
Ross, British Captain B. H. 87
Ross, Captain Charles 238
Ross, Colonel George 244, 269, 273
Ross, British General Robert 226, 231, 234, 235, 236, 237, 240, 246, 247, 250, 252, 254, 268, 275
Rossie (privateer) 37, 39, 40, 42, 43, 44, 48, 49, 56, 57, 60, 61, 62, 68, 69, 75, 77
HMS *Rota* 255, 256
Rotette, British lieutenant 74
HMS *Rover* 177
Rover (British privateer) 260, 262, 266, 291
Rover (vessel) 40
Rover (schooner out of Maine) 81
Rover (schooner; seized 6 November 1813) 169
Rowe, British captain 195
Rowland, Captain Thomas 36, 52, 211
Royal Bounty (British privateer) 43
HMS *Royal Charlotte* 50
HMS *Royal George* 40, 62, 68, 77, 118, 151, 158, 179
Royal Island (Bahamas) 253
Royal Newfoundland Regiment 91, 107, 116, 119
Royal Oak 254
HMS *Royal Regent* 108
HMS *Royalist* 153
Rubicon (schooner) 178
HMS *Ruby* 139
Ruddle, A. 87
Ruffner, Martin 61
Rush, Attorney General Richard 236
Russell (brigantine) 54
Russell, Colonel Gilbert C. 174, 176, 177, 180, 184, 190, 192
Russell, Jonathan 168, 184
Russell, Colonel William 76, 83
Russia 58, 241
Rutgers, Henry 227
Ruth (21-ton schooner) 262
Ryan, Isaac 190
Ryan, W. (master) 125
Ryerse, Captain Samuel 212

Sabine (letter of marque) 86
Sable Island 42
Sac Indians 218, 245
Sacajawea 13
Sackets Harbor 40, 53, 116, 119, 133, 138, 151, 157, 158, 164, 176, 178, 193, 208, 211, 213, 214, 220, 225, 231, 254, 255; fighting erupts between workers and soldiers 210
Sacs (Indians) 14, 39
Sag Harbor 37, 131
Sago, Jacob USN 55
Sailors' Battery 182

St. Andrews (barque) 43
St. Andrews (brigantine) 34, 40
St. Andrews (ship) 257
St. Anthony, Idaho 17
St. Anthony Falls 12, 19
St. Augustine 29
St. Cecilia (ship) 156
St. Clair (Sinclair), Captain Arthur 221, 224
St. David, Canada 220, 222
St. Geme, British major 282
St. George, Colonel 92
St. George Island 113
St. John (British post) 186
HMS *St. Lawrence* 259, 295
USS *St. Lawrence* 200, 221
St. Lawrence (vessel) 132
St. Lawrence River 169
St. Leonard's Creek 133, 214, 216, 217
St. Louis, Missouri 218
St. Louis cathedral 271
St. Martin's Planter (vessel) 93
St. Mary's, Georgia 34, 36
St. Mary's (Girty's Town), Ohio 59
St. Mary's blockhouse (Ohio) 110
St. Mary's River 227
St. Michael's, Maryland 146
St. Philip (British post) 186
St. Regis, Canada 75
St. Rose battery 262
Salem, Massachusetts 21, 111
Sally (33-ton schooner; seized 12 July 1813) 136
Sally (74-ton schooner) 115
Sally (148-ton brigantine) 106
Sally (194-ton ship) 106
Sally (brigantine) 47
Sally (schooner) 62
Sally (schooner; captured 17 October 1813) 165
Sally (schooner out of Cape Ann) 36, 157
Sally (schooner; seized 23 July 1814) 222
Sally (sloop; seized 21 May 1814) 213
Salmon River 189
Salt River Prairie 14
Salter, Midshipman William 246
Sam Nac 129
Samson (prison ship) 125
Samuel (schooner) 148
HMS *Samuel and Sarah* 35
Samuel Cummings (ship) 209
HMS *San Domingo* 63, 76, 81, 87, 104, 114, 115
San Domingo (ship) 158
San Gabriel (brigantine) 115
San Joaquin (190-ton brigantine) 200
San Jose Indiano (ship) 209
Sandbird (vessel) 247
Sanders, British Captain James 95
Sanderson, Captain (later general) George 52
Sands, Lieutenant 242
Sandwich, Canada 50, 158, 159, 163
Sandwich Islands (Hawaii) 215
Sandy Bay Militia *see* Sea Fencibles

Sandy Creek 213
Sanford, Colonel Elihu 28, 87
Santander, Spain 42
Santiago (267-ton brigantine) 131
HMS *Sapphire* 113
HMS *Sappho* 87
HMS *Saracen* 259
Sarah (brigantine) 96
Sarah (schooner; captured 26 September 1814) 256
Sarah (schooner; seized 22 April 1814) 208
Sarah (schooner; seized 28 September 1814) 256
Sarah Ann (American privateer) 66
USS *Saranac* 299, 300, 302
Saranac River 247, 248
Saratoga (American privateer) 61, 81, 82, 95, 158, 165
USS *Saratoga* (second) 206, 207, 241, 248, 249, 250
Sarnac River 239
HMS *Saturn* 203, 213, 221, 222, 235, 260, 262
Saucy Jack (privateer) 31, 43, 53, 58, 131, 138, 179, 209, 260
Saucy Jack (vessel) 259
Sauk Indians 15
Saulte Indians 38
Saulte Ste. Marie, Canada 222
Saunders, British Captain James 87, 135
Sawyer, British Vice Admiral Herbert 55
HMS *Sceptre* 136
Schutz, Lt. Colonel 232, 234
Schuyler, Margaret *see* Van Rensselaer, Margaret Schuyler
Schuyler, Colonel (later general) Philip P. 37, 111
Science (privateer) 48, 56
Scorpion (Commodore Barney's squadron) 236
HMS *Scorpion* 80
USS *Scorpion* 136, 154, 155, 156, 158, 159, 221, 225, 243, 246, 247
Scorpion (privateer) 47
Scott, Captain Abram M. 141
Scott, British Lieutenant (Royal Navy) 137, 138
Scott, Captain 148
Scott, General Charles (governor of Kentucky) 56, 57, 92
Scott, David 87
Scott, British Colonel Hercules 194, 229
Scott, J. E. (master) 151
Scott, Brigadier General John 22
Scott, Colonel John M. 50
Scott, Lt. Colonel William 185, 232, 236
Scott, Lt. Colonel (later major general) Winfield 22, 35, 68, 70, 71, 72, 85, 103, 117, 141, 142, 159, 164, 183, 190, 196, 204, 209, 218, 219, 220, 223, 224, 234, 245, 260, 274, 279, 292
USS *Scourge* (formerly HMS *Lord Nelson*) 27, 68, 146

Scourge (privateer) 136, 138, 205, 206, 207, 208, 209, 211
Sea Fencibles (Sandy Bay Militia) 140
Sea Flower (brigantine) 135
Sea Flower (schooner) 31
HMS *Sea Horse* (Seahorse) 87, 222, 266, 267
Searcher (British privateer) 34
Seaton (ship) 49
Seaton (vessel) 88
Sebring, 1st Lieutenant 158
Sebry, Captain 113
Secord, Captain James 128
Seeley, Lieut. 181
Selly, T. (master) 115
Semerimes (85-ton sloop) 104
Seminole Indians 64, 183, 186, 303
HMS *Seneca* 40, 151
Seneca Indians 134, 222
Senoya (mother of Chief William McIntosh) 183, 201
Sergeant, Mr. 227
USS *Seringapatam* 176, 204
Seringapatam (British vessel) 101, 137
Servant, Sergeant 130
Servos, Captain John D. 182
Seven Nations 179
HMS *Severn* 209, 227, 295
Sevier, Lt. Alexander USMC 73, 95, 96, 115
Sewall, Major General Henry 243
Sewall, Samuel 28, 183
Shackford, J. (master) 216
Shackleford, W. (master) 215
Shadock (schooner) 41
Shadow (American privateer; later British *Fanny*) 44, 56
Shaffer's Blockhouse 22
Shaler, Captain Nathaniel 83, 84, 115, 136
Shaler, Mr. William 300
Shamrock (British brigantine) 40
HMS *Shannon* 29, 35, 36, 38, 39, 67, 76, 113, 116, 121, 122, 146, 157, 168, 169, 171, 212, 213
Shannon (brigantine sometimes referred to as the *Andalusia*) 73, 158
Shannon (British privateer) 60, 177, 178, 215, 228, 229
Shannon, Lieutenant 197
Shark (British schooner) 126
Shark (privateer) 257
Sharp's Island 110
Shaw, Aeneas 188
Shaw, British Major General Aeneas 35
Shaw, Benjamin (master) 61
Shaw, Captain John 18
Shaw, Commodore John 99, 103, 105, 302
Shaw, Mr. 137
Shaw, Captain T. 48
Shawnee Indians 134, 180, 200
Shead, Sailing Master 141
Sheaffe, British Major General Roger Hale 19, 71, 72, 73, 79, 106, 108, 116, 133
"Shear Hulk *Etna*" 47

Index

HMS *Shelbourne* (formerly American privateer *Racer*) 148, 205
Shelby, Governor Isaac 52, 57, 59, 63, 65, 78, 92, 94, 111, 135, 153, 155, 156, 157, 158, 159, 160, 161, 162, 163, 164
Sheldon, Lieutenant 203, 204
Shepard, Colonel Timothy 28, 87
Shepherd, R. D. 283, 293
Sheppard, Richard S. (sailing master) 267
Sherbrooke, British Brigadier General John Cope 242
Sherwood, British captain 193
Shields, Mr. 268, 292
Shields (purser) 290
Ship Island 267, 268
Shipley, George 62
Shipp, Lieutenant Edmund 143
Shippensburg Troop of Light Horse 28
Shirley, P. (master) 169
Shiveley, Captain Philip 154
Shoemaker, Abram 227
Short, British Lt. Colonel 143
Shortland, British Major Thomas George 214, 298
Shubrick, Lt. John T. USN 37, 97, 209, 290, 301
Sibae (115-ton brigantine) 106
Sicard, Captain P. 31
Sicily 302
Sigourney, Midshipman 136
Silena (brigantine) 217
Silliman, Captain John H. 104
Silo (privateer) 226
Silver Keys (West Indies) 131
HMS *Simcoe* 40, 77, 151
Simonds, Colonel 111
Simon's Blockhouse 22
Simpson (soldier) 192
Simpson, British Lieutenant 29
Simpson, Captain James 153
Simpson, John 87
Simrall, Colonel James 62, 154, 158, 161
Sims, Lt. 70
Sincerity (Swedish vessel) 188
Sinclair, Captain USN 31, 151
Sinclair, R. (master) 144
Singleton, Captain Mason 153
Singleton, Thomas 135
Sir Alexander Ball (ship) 222
HMS *Sir Andrew Hammond* 101, 148, 156
USS *Sir Andrew Hammond* 176, 204, 216
Sir Edward Pellen 225
Sir Hugh Jones (ship) 209
Sir Isaac Brock (vessel) 103
Sir John Broke (or *Sir John Brook*; privateer) 264
Sir John Sherbrooke (British privateer) 78, 102, 103, 104, 105, 106, 115, 118, 121, 126, 263
HMS *Sir Sidney Smith* 169
Sir Simon Clark (vessel) 49
Siren (earlier *Syren*) 221, 222
Siro (American privateer; later British *Atlanta*) 66, 88
Sisemore's Ferry 169
Sitler, Adjutant 189
Six Nations 132, 179
Skekel, John 87
Skidmore, J. (master) 145
Skinner, H. (master) 124
Skinner, Mr. 215
Skull Lick 14
Skylark (schooner) 43
Slate, Oliver (master) 291
Slaughter, Colonel Gabriel (later governor of Kentucky) 282
Slaves 13
Slaygur, P. (master) 138
Sloan, Captain 35, 46
Smart, Captain R. 21
Smith, Caleb USN 55
Smith, British Lt. Colonel 141
Smith, Captain (*Betsey* lookout boat) 116
Smith, Governor George William (Virginia) 21
Smith, Gerard D. (Army officer) 220
Smith, Brigadier General Gerrit 29
Smith, Captain J. USN 31, 113
Smith, J. (master; British privateer *Matilda*) 136
Smith, J. Kilty 264, 265
Smith, James (Jim) 173, 174
Smith, Jim see Smith, James
Smith, Brigadier General John 189
Smith, John (master) 74
Smith, John 169
Smith, Governor John Cotton (Federalist, formerly Lt. Governor) 131, 142
Smith, Lieutenant (later rear admiral) Joseph 250
Smith, Judge (father of Colonel Melancton Smith) 248
Smith, Colonel Melancton 248
Smith, Doctor Neal 192
Smith, Presley C. 154
Smith, Robert (Secretary of State) 16
Smith, Brigadier General Samuel (Maryland) 105, 125, 229, 235, 247, 250, 252, 253, 257
Smith, Brigadier General Samuel (Pennsylvania) 54, 259
Smith, Samuel (half-breed) 150
Smith, Samuel D. 169
Smith, Lt. Colonel (later brigadier general) Thomas A. USA 23, 24, 25, 28, 29, 33, 34, 36, 41, 42, 47, 48, 56, 57, 62, 65, 73, 190
Smith, W. H. 87
Smith, Brigadier General Walter 234
Smith, General Walter 113, 236
Smith, Lt. Colonel William 65
Smith, Lt. William 87
Smoot, Captain (later major) Benjamin 140, 180
Smyth, Brigadier General Alexander 22, 34, 68, 71, 72, 75, 78, 79, 80, 81, 86
Smythe, Captain Richard 22
Snap Dragon (privateer) 151, 217
Snelling, Captain Josiah 46, 47
Snow, Captain Elisha 115, 133, 139, 140, 156, 209, 257
Snow, H. (master) 72, 151
Snow, J. (master) 146
Snow, John (master) 262
Snow, T. (master) 148
Snow Alexander (207-ton vessel) 247
Snow Wanderer (vessel) 232
Snowbird (privateer) 43
Snowchild (privateer) 33, 34
Snyder, Governor Simon (Pennsylvania) 23, 25, 26, 114, 193, 198, 255
Socca (Indian) 150
USS *Somers* 169, 229
Somerset (260-ton ship) 299
Somerville, Captain Philip 255
HMS *Sophia* 87, 243, 289
Sophia (sloop) 57
Sophia (vessel) 25
HMS *Sophie* 177
Sorel River 203
Sotto, Spanish colonel 262
South Carolina (brigantine) 77
HMS *Southampton* 79, 87, 175
Southcomb, Captain John 95
Southworth, C. Maaster 114
Souza, J. DeLonza Carvatho (master) 128
Sovereign (300-ton brigantine) 205
Spain 240, 303
USS *Spark* 299, 300
Sparrow (privateer) 175
Sparrow's Point Road 246
HMS *Spartan* 38, 39, 40, 44, 73, 74, 87, 105, 112, 115, 120, 123, 125, 126, 128
Specie (schooner) 105
Speculator (brigantine) 215, 257
Spedden, Lieutenant Robert 267, 268
HMS *Spellcer* 242
HMS *Spencer* 222, 226, 263, 264, 295
Spencer (schooner) 205
Spencer, Colonel Ambrose 224
Spencer, British Captain Robert Churchill 252
Spencer Creek 14
HMS *Spider* 87
Spilsbury, British Captain Francis Brockell 213
USS *Spitfire* 19, 20
HMS *Spitfire* (gunboat) 22, 137
Spitfire (vessel) 19
Spokane House 17
Spotts, Lieutenant 278, 280, 282, 286
Sprague's Blockhouse, Florence, Ohio 18
Springer, British captain 195
Springer, J. (master) 135
Sproul, Captain John 246
HMS *Spy* 57
Spy (privateer 4-gun schooner) 31
Squaw Island 69
Squid (schooner) 44
Stackpole, Captain Hassard 87, 95
Stacy, Captain S. 33
Stafford, Captain 174
Stafford, Captain W. S. 93, 98, 104
Stallings, Lt. 47
Stamper (brigantine) 140
Stanley, Major William 28, 87
Stansbury, Lieutenant Dixon 46
Stansbury, Brigadier General Tobias 232, 236
Stanton, Stephen (master) 293
Stanwood, Captain 75
USS *Star* 210
Star (British privateer) 148, 156, 290
Starbird, Benjamin 34
Stark, Captain Horatio 59
Starks Corner Blockhouse 22
Starr (409-ton vessel) 126
Start (brigantine) 38
HMS *Statira* 40, 47, 49, 53, 54, 56, 57, 87, 95, 104, 115, 120, 123, 125, 126, 128, 147, 148, 151, 157, 159, 177, 255
Stavers, British Captain William 137
Steadman, Edward 150
Steadman, Jesse 150
Steddiford, Brigadier General Gerard 24
Steel, Captain (cavalry) 175, 199
Steele, J. 87
Steele, Major General James 114
Steele, Brigadier General John 33
Steingal, General (Governor and Captain General of Finland) 20
Steinhaven, F. R. 125
Stephanie (schooner) 222
Stephen (brigantine) 174
Stephens, Captain William 154
Stephenson, Colonel Mills 142
Sterett, Major Charles 232
Sterett, Lt. Colonel (later major general) James (Maryland) 257
Sterling, E. (master) 214
Sterrett, Lt. Colonel Joseph 232, 233, 234, 236, 250
Stevens, Major General Ebenezer 235
Stevens, J. (master) 56
Stevens, R. (master) 177
Steward, Doctor Abram 218
Stewart, British Lt. Col. 196
Stewart, Captain 45
Stewart, Captain Charles USN 20, 26, 27, 95, 269, 275, 294, 295, 296
Stewart, Commander 24
Stewart, Brigadier General Daniel 81, 151
Stewart, Martha 81
Stewart, Robert Viscount Castlereagh, British prime minister 29, 168, 226, 241, 292
Stewart, Colonel William 185
Stiles, Captain 146
Stockholm (schooner) 58
Stoddard, Major Amos 109, 111
Stokes, Major General Montford 202
Stone, British Captain (Canadian militia) 63
Stone, Lt. Colonel Isaac W. 220
Stoney Creek 124, 212
Stonington, Connecticut 174, 225, 227
Storer, Brigadier General Clement (New Hampshire militia) 33, 206, 255
Storrs, Lt. Colonel Experience 248
Stover, J. L. 212
Stover, N. (master) 148
Stover, Robert (master) 153
Stovin, British major general 178, 179, 194, 195
Stowe, Jeremiah 141
Strang, Alexander (master) 266
Strang, J. (master) 217
Stratton, Captain Aaron 153
Stricker, Brigadier General John 41, 250, 251, 252, 257
Strong (privateer schooner) 215
Strong, Governor Caleb 28
Strong, Lieutenant 175
Strong, Governor Samuel 25, 274
Strong, Major General Samuel (Vermont) 249
Strout, J. (master) 113
Stuart, David 18
Stuart, James 87
Stuart, General Philip 216, 222
Stuart, Robert 85
Stull, Captain 236
Stump, Lt. Col. Frederick 190
Sturdivant, Ephraim 106
Sturdivant, Captain Joseph 36, 106, 135
HMS *Subtle* 81, 87, 175
HMS *Success* 129
Success (brigantine) 214
Success (schooner) 41
Suggett, Major James (chaplain) 160, 161
Sukey (44-ton schooner) 225
Sullivan, Colonel George (son of General John Sullivan) 213
Sultan (schooner) 192
Sumpter, Lieutenant 249
HMS *Superb* 103, 210, 212, 213, 222, 225
Superb (brigantine) 192
Superb (privateer) 157
USS *Superior* (66-gun frigate) 186, 210, 212, 213, 214, 225, 232, 256
HMS *Surinam* 81
HMS *Surprise* 89
Surprise (American privateer) 112, 222, 290

Index

USS *Surprise* (renamed USS *Eagle*) 247
HMS *Surveillante* 22, 26, 42, 68, 83
USS *Surveyor* (revenue cutter) 125
Susan (cartel) 34
Susan (sloop) 83
Susannah (89-ton sloop) 106
Susannah and Lucy (117-ton schooner) 113
Sutherland, British captain 72
Sutter, John A 19
HMS *Swaggerer* 87, 95
Swain, J. C. (master) 225
HMS *Swallow* 74
Swallow (schooner privateer) 58
Swallow (schooner) 168
Swan (vessel) 296
Swan, Major 118, 120
Swan, Captain Samuel 63
Swan, Captain Thomas 225
Swanton, Vermont 141
Swarthout, Brigadier General Robert 85, 148, 165, 171
Swasy, Samuel (master) 266
Sweden: declares war against Great Britain 17
Sweeney, British Lt. 103
Swenburg, C. (master) 128
Swift (63-ton schooner) 134
Swift (107-ton brigantine) 101
Swift (brigantine) 205
Swift (privateer) 75
Swift (schooner) 82
Swift, Asa 275
Swift, Major General John 186, 191, 206, 212, 221, 275
Swift, Brigadier General Joseph Gardner 206, 221, 227, 262
Swift, Colonel Philetus 126, 190
Swordfish (privateer) 82
HMS *Sybelle* 87
HMS *Sybille* 22
HMS *Sylph* 87, 103, 104, 128, 148, 156, 212, 242
USS *Sylph* 151, 158, 225, 226
Sylph (schooner) 205
Sylvester, Lieutenant 126
Symmes, Anna 56
Symmes, Judge 56
Symmetry (British vessel) 205
USS *Syren* 27, 222
Syren (privateer) 262, 263, 264

Table Rock 223
Tagus River 261
Talbot, British Colonel Thomas 212
Talladega, Alabama 187
Tallahatta (Barshi Creek) 160, 164
Tallapoosa River 188, 194, 201
Tallase Indians 135
Talleyrand, Charles Maurice de 241
Talluschatches (Tallaschatches; now Jacksonville, Alabama) 164
Talman, Lieutenant 120
Tamaba 176
Tangier Island 196
Tangier Sound 214
Tannehill, Major General Adamson 53
Taplin, Captain 178
Tarchachee 173
HMS *Tartarus* 87
Tasche, British captain 207
Tate, Captain John 33
Tate, Captain Samuel 154
Tatnall, British Lieutenant James Barnwell 268
Taul, Colonel Micahis 154
Taylor, Major General Augustine 87
Taylor, British Lt. Colonel 141
Taylor, Captain J. (privateer *Shadow*) 44
Taylor, General James 52
Taylor, General Robert Barraud 94, 130
Taylor, Lt. Colonel Samuel 236
Taylor, Lieutenant (later general and president of the U.S.) Zachary 18, 58, 59, 218, 242, 244, 245, 289, 303
Tchifonta (corvette) 289
Teazer (privateer) 31, 38, 43, 81, 126
Tecumseh 19, 21, 46, 47, 50, 51, 66, 88, 109, 110, 121, 127, 139, 142, 161, 162, 163, 164
HMS *Tededos* 147
Tedrick, John 62
Teebooa, Marquesas 165
Telemachus (brigantine) 156, 166
Ten Brothers (114-ton schooner) 186
Ten Islands 164, 169
HMS *Tenedos* 76, 87, 96, 113, 116, 129, 205, 216, 222, 232, 242, 247, 260
HMS *Tenerife* 261
HMS *Teneuos* 290
Tercilla (brigantine) 53
Terrible (American privateer) 89
Terrible (Spanish schooner) 104
Terrill, Captain 189
Terrill (Quarter Master) 175
HMS *Terror* (bomb ship) 227
Terry, Master's Mate James 137
Terry, Brigadier General Nathaniel 28, 87
HMS *Thais* 256
Thames (brigantine) 72
Thames (seized 30 May 1813) 121
Thames River 160, 192
Thelis, James 169
Theodore (237-ton brigantine) 262
Theodore (ship) 102
Thetis (British brigantine) 147
Thetis (vessel) 208
Thinks to Myself 259, 260
Thistle (100-ton schooner) 297
Thistle (privateer) 96
Thomas (2-gun brigantine) 145
Thomas (American privateer) 48, 157
Thomas (brigantine) 128
Thomas (schooner; seized 30 June 1813) 131
Thomas, Captain (Floyd's artillery) 175, 191
Thomas, Captain F. 31
Thomas, George (master) 125
Thomas, Brigadier General John 281
Thomas, N. (master) 57
Thomas, Brigadier General Philemon 282
Thomas and Sally (vessel) 128, 207
Thomas Pickering (privateer) 21
Thompson, Captain Alexander (privateer *Midas*) 82, 205
Thompson, Lieutenant Charles B. USN 276, 278
Thompson, Brigadier General David 29, 87
Thompson, Major David 161
Thompson, David (Canadian trader) 16
Thompson, J. 87
Thompson, James 221
Thompson's Creek 164
Thompson's Trading Post (aka Kullyspell House) 16
Thorn (brigantine) 76
Thorn (schooner; captured 8 November 1813) 169
Thorn (schooner; seized 13 July 1814) 221
Thorn, Captain Jonathan 19
Thornton, Captain (artillery officer) 211, 215, 232
Thornton, Lt. Francis USMC 19
Thornton, British Colonel William 234, 269, 270, 271, 272, 281, 282, 284, 285, 286, 289
Thornton, Doctor William 235
Thorold, Canada 128
Thrasher (American privateer) 89
Three Brothers (10-gun vessel) 53, 98
Three Brothers (94-ton schooner) 146
Three Brothers (brigantine) 138, 253
Three Brothers (schooner) 43
Three Friends (79-ton schooner) 83
Three Friends (aka sloop *Pictou*; seized 30 July 1814) 225
Three Friends (schooner; seized 12 November 1814) 262
Three Sisters (schooner) 70
Three Sisters (seized 1 September 1812) 58
Throckmorton, Captain Aris 153
HMS *Thunderer* 88
Tibberts, E. (master) 176
Tibbet's Point 137
Tickler (65-ton sloop) 215
Tickler (schooner) 257
USS *Ticonderoga* 123, 241, 248
USS *Tigress* 158, 159, 165, 221, 225, 243, 246, 247
Tilbury, Canada 195
Tilden, Captain 74
Tilghman, Lt. Colonel 232, 235
Tilsit Agreement 13, 14
Tipton, Colonel (later brigadier general) John 83
Todd, Ensign (later colonel) Charles S. 78, 158, 159
Todd, Captain David 153
Todd, Doctor 92
Todd, Leticia Shelby 159
Tohopeka (Creek village) 201
Tom (privateer) 41, 43, 44
Tom Bowline (store-ship) 291, 298
Tomahawk (schooner) 292
Tombigbee River 259
Tombigby (Indian village) 135
Tompkins, Governor Daniel D. (New York) 25, 30, 32, 35, 37, 40, 42, 44, 45, 60, 61, 62, 63, 69, 70, 72, 75, 85, 120, 131, 140, 157, 181, 182, 183, 185, 189, 192, 204, 205, 208, 229, 231, 245, 250, 257, 259, 260, 262, 274, 275, 298
Tonawanda, New York 177
Tonawanda Blockhouse 86, 177
Tonawanda Creek 179
HMS *Tonnant* 266, 293
Tonquin (vessel) 19
Tookabatcha, Alabama 106, 121
Tookabatcha Indians 106, 175
Toole, British captain 72
Topedo (schooner) 156
Tor Abbey (brigantine) 89
USS *Torch* 299, 300
Townsend (British packet) 44
Townsend, Lord James 29, 87
Townsend, Lt. Colonel John 229
Towson, Captain (later brigadier general) Nathan 68, 69, 220, 223, 229
Transport No. 50 (British) 37
Trant, (sailing master) 77
HMS *Traveler* 35
Traveller (94-ton sloop; seized 4 April 1813) 104
Traveller (brigantine) 222
Traveller (schooner; seized early July 1813) 34
Traveller (ship) 216
Traveller (sloop; seized 4 April 1813) 104
Travis, Captain Samuel 125
Treacher, British Lt. S. S. 87
Treadwell, Judge 141
Treaty of Fontainbleau 14
Treaty of Fort Armstrong 245
Treaty of Fort Jackson (Treaty of Conquest) 183, 227
Treaty of Fort Wayne 16
Treaty of Ghent 274, 294
Treaty of Greensville 222
Trenchard, Captain Edward 225
Trent (69-ton schooner) 176
Tres Hermanos (Portuguese brigantine) 261
Trianon Decree 18
Trident (brigantine) 211
Trimble, Colonel Allen (cavalry) 68
Trimble, Major David 109, 113
Trimble, Major William Allen 26, 230
Tripoli 291, 301, 302
USS *Trippe* (formerly merchant ship *Contractor*) 155, 178, 184
Trippe, Captain W. H. 196
HMS *Triton* 225
Triton (122-ton schooner) 137
Triton (brigantine) 40
Trotter, Colonel (later acting brigadier general) George 153, 162
Troubridge, Sir Thomas RN 277
USS *Troup* 21
Troup, Governor George (Georgia) 187, 263
Trucksville Post 22
True Blooded Yankee (privateer) 75, 99, 157
Tryon, Brigadier General Moses Jr. 28
Tuckabatchee, Alabama 175
Tuckahoe (vessel) 31
Tulip (brigantine) 82
Tulip (vessel) 33
Tumbez 128, 129
Tunis 291, 301, 302
Tupper, Brigadier General Edward 53, 64, 67, 68, 76, 77, 78, 79, 83, 85, 96
Turkey Town 169
Turner, Abner 131
Turner, Captain Daniel 225
Turner, Midshipman Henry E. 246
Turner's Fort 131
Tuscarora, New York 177, 178
Tuscarora Indians 179
Tustunnuggee *see* Chief William McIntosh
Tuttle, Lt. Colonel (regulars) 120
Twelve Mile Creek (Canada) 195
Twelve Mile Swamp (Florida) 61, 73
Twiggs, Captain David E. (later Confederate general) 22
Twiggs, Lieutenant USMC 290
Two Brothers (131-ton schooner) 103
Two Brothers (55-ton schooner) 134
Two Brothers (bark; seized 25 May 1814) 213
Two Brothers (brigantine) 41
Two Brothers (cartel) 44
Two Friends (38-ton schooner) 83
Two Friends (privateer 3-gun schooner) 31
Two Friends (schooner; seized 11 June 1814) 215
Tybee lighthouse 82
Tydeman, Captain 72
Tyger (brigantine) 222
Tyler, Captain 262
Tyler, John (president) 165
Tyndell, Sir John 287
Typee (Island tribe) 167, 168

Tyron, Brigadier General Moses Jr. 87
Tyson, Captain 46

Uchee Indians 191
Ufaula Indians 193
UK *see* England
Ulrick, Lieutenant George 266, 267, 268
Ultor (xebec, 3-masted vessel) 205, 217, 222
Ulysses (156-ton brigantine) 106
Ulysses (brigantine) 34
Ulysses (brigantine; seized 30 June 1813) 131
Ulysses (British brigantine) 116
Umfreville, British Captain John Brand 253
Unice (sloop) 134
Union (22-ton schooner; captured 30 July 1814) 225
Union (95-ton schooner) 104
Union (brigantine) 49
Union (privateer out of Maine) 290
Union (schooner) 34
Union (schooner; captured 14 October 1812) 72
Union (schooner; seized 1 April 1814) 205
Union (ship; seized 16 August 1812) 53
Union (ship; seized 26 June 1813) 131
Union Light Infantry Company 65
United States: declares war on England 30; divided into military districts 103
USS *United States* ("Old Wagon") 18, 26, 27, 31, 74, 75, 76, 88, 123, 142, 177, 291, 295, 302
United We Stand (privateer) 41
Unity (36-ton sloop) 225
Upham, Major (later major general) Timothy 81, 89, 172, 254, 255
Upper Creeks (Red Sticks) 184
Upsham, Lt. Colonel 172
Upton (ship) 216
Upton, British Captain C. 22, 87
Upton, C. 87
Upton, Captain (privateer *Montgomery*) 81
Upton, Captain Jeduthan 83
Upton, Captain John 24, 78
Upton, John (master) 24, 78
Upton, Lt. Col. (later major general New Hampshire militia) Timothy 33
Ute Indians 16

Vail, S. B. (master) 174
Valaria (96-ton sloop) 134
HMS *Valiant* 103, 104, 105, 123, 127, 128, 173, 177
Valleau, Lieutenant 72
Valparaiso 133, 159, 193, 202
Van Buren, Martin (judge advocate; later 8th U.S. president) 185
Van Courtlandt, General Pierre 157

Vandine, C. (master) 255
Van Horn (Van Horne), Captain 224
Van Horne, Major Thomas 26, 44, 46, 47
Van Ness, Major General John Peter 113, 215, 231
Van Rensselaer, Cornelia Patterson 37
Van Rensselaer, Margaret Schuyler 37
Van Rensselaer, Colonel Solomon (adjutant general of New York) 24, 69, 70, 72
Van Rensselaer, Stephen II 37
Van Rensselaer, General Stephen III 24, 37, 38, 48, 56, 59, 60, 62, 64, 65, 67, 69, 70, 71, 72, 75, 78, 79, 86
HMS *Variable* 87
Vaughan, G. (master) 131
Vaughan, Captain William 40, 42, 216, 217
Vaughn, Captain 247
Vaughn Cemetery 221
Veasey, Captain E. 86, 262, 293
HMS *Venerable* 42
Venus (14-gun ship) 49
Venus (72-ton schooner) 136
Venus (100-ton schooner) 174
Venus (208-ton ship; seized 23 September 1813) 157
Venus (brigantine) 151
Vestal (British ship) 254
Venus (recaptured 23 July 1812) 40
Venus (schooner) 43, 209
HMS *Vestal* 89
Vester (ship) 241
Vickers, Lt. 146
Victor (brigantine) 212
Victoria (schooner) 41
HMS *Victorious* 105, 118, 125, 126, 127, 129
Victory (45-ton schooner) 226
Victory (52-ton schooner) 186
Victory (brigantine) 102
Victory (British 10-gun ship) 197
Victory (privateer 1-gun schooner) 31
Victory (ship) 241
Victress (65-ton sloop) 228
Viena, F. D. (master) 123
USS *Vigilant* 147
Vigilant (cartel) 34
Vigilant (tender) 102
Villere, Celestin 270
Villere, Major Gabriel 270, 271, 272
Villere, Major General Jacques Philippe 244
Villere House 272, 274
Villere Plantation 268, 269, 271, 275, 281, 283, 289, 291
Vincent, British Major General John 108, 116, 117, 118, 124, 125, 133, 134, 177, 178, 181
Vinson, Major 248
USS *Viper* (formerly USS *Ferret*) 27, 47, 89, 175, 301
USS *Viper* (gunboat) 241
Viper (privateer) 47, 98

Vivid (100-ton brigantine) 106
USS *Vixen* 27, 57, 79, 139
Voador 215, 217
Volant (ship) 103
HMS *Volcano* 260
Voltigeurs (British light infantry unit) 24, 119
Volunteer (22-gun) 58
Von Steuben, Major General Baron 204
Voorhis, Doctor 50

Wabash River 17, 21, 61, 65
Wabisch (vessel) 43
Wadsworth, Colonel Decius 105, 216
Wadsworth, General Elijah 65, 75
Wadsworth, Henry 183
Wadsworth, General James 185
Wadsworth, Brigadier General William 25, 35, 56, 65, 71
Wagner, Jacob 31, 41
Wagner, Major 127
Waibisch (ship) 40
Waide, Captain 289
Waightstill, Colonel 151
Walbach, Adjutant General 172
Walden, G. (master) 104
Wales, British captain 208
Walker (Shawnee) 108
Walker, Alexander 271
Walker, British Major 84
Walker, Colonel George 157
Walker, Lt. 100
Walker, Tandy 169
Wallace, Captain 186
Waller, Henry 238
Walsh, Captain 289
Walton, N. (master) 125
Walworth, Chancellor R. H. 249
HMS *Wanderer* 87
Wanderer (vessel) 185
Wanton, Mr. 48
Warburton, British Colonel 161
Warburton Heights 138
Warden, Lt. Col. 181
Ward's place 180
Warhawks 20
Waring, Captain (19th Regiment) 113
Waring, Major 232
Warner, Asher 126
Warnock, Robert 62
Warren, British Admiral John Borlaise 86, 87, 94, 104, 113, 114, 123, 127, 130, 138, 197
Warren, Colonel Richard 168, 182
Warrington, Captain Lewis 208, 209, 291, 300, 301
Warrior (privateer) 269
Warsaw Forts 50
Warters, Midshipman 152
Wasa (Portuguese brigantine) 88
USS *Washington* 302
Washington (65-ton schooner) 124
Washington (privateer) 165
Washington, George 234
Washington Battery (New York) 235

Washington Navy Yard 237
Washington Troop of Horse 65
HMS *Wasp* 126, 127, 128, 156, 216, 231, 237, 240, 247, 257
Wasp (2-gun privateer) 142
Wasp (99-ton schooner) 135
USS *Wasp* (fifth) 209, 214, 215, 216, 217, 225, 226, 238, 241, 242, 253, 254, 255
USS *Wasp* (fourth) 123
Wasp (sloop) 135
USS *Wasp* (third) 27, 33, 73; lost 74
Wasp (privateer; third) 80, 81, 159, 175
Water Battery 246
Watervliet Arsenal 86
Waterwitch (privateer) 75
Watmaugh, Lieutenant (later colonel) 302
Watson (brigantine) 131, 152
Watson (brigantine; seized 22 June 1813) 127, 131
Watson, C. H. 87
Watson, General Nathaniel 72, 254, 255
Watson, James 40
Watson, Lieutenant 147
Watson, Major 174, 191
Watts, George (army officer) 220
Watts, Sailing Master George 68, 69
Wayne, General Anthony 27, 33, 64
Wayne Blockhouse 22
Weatherford, William *see* Chief Red Eagle
Weatherford's place 180
Weathers, Captain 144
Weazel (British privateer) 133, 134, 147, 151
Webb, Captain 36
Webber, A. (master) 171
Webber, S. (master) 57
Webster, Daniel 115
Webster, J. (master) 139
Webster, Captain John (privateer *Parrot*) 81
Webster, Captain John (privateer *Rover*) 81
Webster, Sailing Master John Adams 246
Weeks, B. (master) 156
Welborn, Major General James 103
Wellesley, Arthur (Duke of Wellington) 191, 206, 217, 226, 241, 254, 255, 275, 297
Wellington (brigantine) 222
Wellington (cutter) 86
Wellington, Duke of *see* Wellesley, Arthur
Wellington, British Lt. Col. James 246, 249
Wells, Captain Archelaus 180
Wells, British captain 40
Wells, Lieutenant USN 42
Wells, Colonel Samuel 61, 90, 91, 141
Wells, Captain William 48, 49, 50, 162
West, British Lieutenant 210
West, George (master) 104

West Florida 23; annexed by U.S. 25
West Indian (schooner) 176
West Point (Military Academy) 303
Westbrook (British soldier) 192
Westphall, British Lt. 110
Westropp, A. F. 87
Wharton, Commandant (Lt. Colonel) Franklin USMC 19, 47, 73
Wheeler, Joseph (West Point 1859; later Confederate general) 53
Whelan, British Captain 80
Whelan, James (master) 36
Wheldon, S. T. (master) 83
Whig (privateer) 257
Whistler, Ensign 47
Whitcomb, Major General Philemon (New Hampshire militia) 33
White House 233, 234, 235
White House (not presidential White House) 239
White Warrior *see* Chief William McIntosh
White, A. C. (master) 208
White, Major H. O. 289
White, Colonel Isaac 21
White, General James 169, 170, 171, 172, 173
White, Captain Maunsel 289, 293
White, Mr. (master) 122
White, Richard 212
White, Thomas 159
White, William Augustus USN 123
Whiteside, Captain William F. 221, 244, 245
Whiting (British schooner) 36
Whitley, Private 163
Whitsett, Captain William 154
Whittaker, Captain James S. 154
Wickes, Captain Simon 240
Wickliffe, Captain Martin H. 153
Widrig, Major General George 231
Wier, Captain Obadiah 118
Wierman, G. (master) 129
Wilcox, Lt. Colonel George 79
Wilcox, Colonel Joseph (Canadian Volunteers) 176, 224
Wilcox, Lieutenant 184, 192
Wiley Renard (privateer) 43, 45, 67
Wilkinson (naval officer) 65
Wilkinson, British major (brigade major) 288
Wilkinson, Major General James 12, 18, 21, 25, 44, 72, 85, 95, 98, 99, 103, 105, 115, 129, 133, 134, 139, 146, 147, 148, 151, 152, 157, 159, 164, 165, 166, 168, 169, 171, 173, 176, 183, 186, 189, 191, 194, 203, 204
Wilkinson, Lieutenant USN 29
Willcox (officer) *see* Wilcox, Joseph

Index

William (10-gun ship) 112
William (102-ton schooner) 101
William (bark) 36
William (brigantine) 258
William (brigantine; captured 11 October 1814) 36
William (brigantine; seized in August 1812) 43
William (brigantine; seized 16 August 1812) 36, 53
William (brigantine; seized 31 May 1813) 36, 121
William (brigantine; seized 14 June 1814) 215
William (brigantine; seized 3 June 1814) 214
William (British brigantine) 115, 116
William (schooner; captured 19 June 1814) 216
William (schooner; seized 12 March 1813) 36
William (schooner; seized 27 October 1813) 166
William (schooner; seized 19 June 1814) 215
William (schooner; seized unspecified time 1814) 36
William (ship) 216
William (sloop; seized 7 August 1813) 146
William (vessel) 44
William and Alfred (ship) 281
HMS *William and Ann* 225
William and Ann (77-ton sloop) 142
Williamette Post (later Henry House) 22
Williams, Captain Alexander John 230
Williams, 2nd Lieutenant Alexander O. 247, 256
Williams, British Lt. Col. 141
Williams, Captain (General Winchester's command) 88
Williams, Captain (privateer *Alfred*) 53
Williams, Brigadier General David Rodgerson (governor of South Carolina) 135
Williams, Captain John USMC 23, 25, 29, 61, 73
Williams, Colonel John USA 193
Williams, John (master) 101, 275
Williams, Joseph (seaman) 97
Williams, Major (son of General Otho Williams) 126, 232
Williams, General Robert (Virginia) 128
Williams, Colonel (later major general) William 28, 87, 154, 163
Williamsburg, New York 171
Williamsville, New York 189
Willich, F. G. 87
Willing Maid (brigantine) 222
Willooughby, Charles (master) 225
Will's Creek 166
USS *Wilmer* (gunboat) 241
Wilmer, Lieutenant 90, 118, 202
Wilson (marooned Englishman) 166
Wilson, A. (master) 41, 63
Wilson, Captain 115
Wilson, Captain Daniel 154
Wilson, Captain George 39
Wilson, John 87
Wilson, Matthew 184
Wilson, Mrs. 223, 224
Wilson, Captain Oliver 38, 72, 123, 124, 293
Wilson, Captain Samuel 154
Wilson, Captain T. 41
Wiltshire, John 99

Wimberly, Colonel Ezekiel 253
Winchester (ship) 205
Winchester, Brigadier General James 22, 59, 60, 62, 64, 66, 67, 76, 77, 78, 83, 85, 87, 88, 89, 90, 91, 92, 93, 109, 110, 190, 204
Winder, Governor Levin (Maryland) 218, 229
Winder, Colonel (later brigadier general) William Henry 65, 80, 85, 103, 118, 124, 125, 190, 205, 208, 212, 218, 226, 231, 232, 234, 235, 236, 237, 247, 292
Windsor Castle (10-gun vessel) 116, 209
Winnebago Indians 15, 38, 59
Winnerholt, A. (master) 131
Winter, J. H. (master) 165
Winyates, British captain 73, 74, 87
Wirt, Elizabeth Gamble 17
Wirt, William (attorney general of U.S.) 17
Wise, Francis 216
Wise, British Captain W. F. 261, 266
Withers (marksman) 286
Wolcott, Oliver 227
HMS *Wolfe* 118, 210
Wolstonecraft (Wolstoncraft), Captain John 289
Wolverine (British privateer) 156, 176, 186
Wood, British Captain 84
Wood, British Lt. Col. (85th Regiment) 234
Wood, Captain 110
Wood, Captain (later Colonel) Eleazer (Eleazar) 96, 229, 254
Wood, James (former governor of Virginia) 138

Wood, Colonel John 92
Wood, Major 140
Wood, Captain William 154
Wood River Massacre 221
Woodbine, British Captain George 298, 303
HMS *Woodbridge* 197
Woodbury, Levi (Secretary of the Navy) 302
Woodruff, Captain Joseph 28
Woods, John (soldier) executed 195
Woodward, C. 104
Wool, Captain (later major general) John Ellis 71, 72, 92, 245, 246
Woolfolk, Captain John 92
Woolridge, Thomas 87
Woolsey, Lieutenant Commander (later captain) Melancton 40, 57, 68, 77, 151, 212, 213, 214, 225
HMS *Woolwick* 131
Wooster, Captain Charles W. 81, 95
Wooster's Blockhouse 22
Workman's Blockhouse 22
Worrell (Worrall), Major General Isaac 25, 53, 279
Worth, 1st Lieutenant Frederick 247, 256
Worth, Lt. William Jenkins (later major general) 102, 172, 220, 247
Worthington, Governor Thomas (Ohio) 258
Wyandotte Indians 34, 134, 222
Wyer, William (master) 40
Wylie, Doctor Jacques 20

Yankee (American privateer) 35, 38, 43, 72, 73, 75, 115, 116, 121, 123, 127, 131, 133, 139, 140, 156, 209, 257

Yankee (fishing boat) 133
Yankee Lass (privateer) 75, 209
Yankee Porter (privateer) 75
Yates, R. R. B. 87
Yates, Captain Robert E. 154
Yeo, British Commodore James 87, 115, 118, 120, 124, 125, 126, 147, 149, 153, 158, 163, 189, 192, 197, 199, 206, 207, 209, 210, 211, 212, 213, 214
York (privateer) 208, 241, 298
York, Canada (Toronto) 107, 111, 195, 217
York, Oliver 228
York, S. (master) 81
York River 125
York Town (ship) 138
Yorke, Samuel 78
You, Dominique 277, 279, 280, 282
Young, Brigadier General Robert 113, 231, 232, 236, 238
Young, British Colonel Robert 189, 190, 198, 283
Young American (privateer) 41
Young Connecticut (American schooner) 26
Young Farmer (schooner) 41
Young Phoenix (ship) 114
Young Teazer (privateer; formerly *Liverpool Packet*) 78, 80, 115, 121, 136
Young Teazer's Ghost (privateer; formerly *Liverpool Packet*) 136
Youngstown, New York 178
Yusef, Sidi 301
Yusuf, Pasha 11

Zimmer, Frederick 61
Zodiac (ship) 57
Zone (vessel) 22
Zwaanendael Museum 104

www.ingramcontent.com/pod-product-compliance
Ingram Content Group UK Ltd.
Pitfield, Milton Keynes, MK11 3LW, UK
UKHW050703160426
5217IPUK00038B/2073